The HarperCollins
Dictionary of Biography

Other Helicon titles of interest

The Hutchinson Encyclopedia (tenth edition)

Hutchinson Gallup Info 94

The Hutchinson Guide to the World

The HarperCollins
Dictionary of
Biography

HarperCollins*Publishers*

PREFACE

In this second edition of *The Hutchinson Dictionary of Biography* there are over 8000 entries on the most important, topical or noteworthy people of our own times and previous eras. Some are major historical figures of universally recognized importance such as Alexander the Great, Julius Caesar, St Augustine. Others are individuals of achievement in their chosen field such as Marie Curie, Agatha Christie, Claude Debussy, Eleanor Roosevelt, while still others are people in the news today, such as Saddam Hussein, Spike Lee, Bill Clinton.

Also in this re-set and re-designed edition we have added over 500 new entries as well as updated many hundreds of others. Several special features have been introduced:

● over 350 quotes spread throughout the book

● forty pages of indexes organized by category so that, for instance, you can look up who are the composers, the astronomers, the actresses, the writers, the inventors and so on

● over 280 newly researched photographs.

We have avoided a purely mechanical alphabetization in cases where a different order corresponds more with human logic. For example, sovereigns with the same name are grouped according to country before number, so that George II of England is placed before George III of England, and not next to George II of Greece. Words beginning 'Mc' and Mac' are treated as if they begin 'Mac'; 'St' and 'Saint' are both treated as if they were spelt 'Saint'.

Foreign names and titles

Names of foreign sovereigns are usually shown in their English form, except where the foreign name is more familiar; thus, there is an entry for Charles V of Spain, but Juan Carlos (not John Charles). Entries for titled people are under the name by which they are best known to the general reader; thus, Anthony Eden, not Lord Avon.

Cross-references

These are shown by a symbol immediately preceding the reference.

Units

SI (metric) units are used throughout for scientific entries. Measurements of distances, temperatures, sizes, and so on, usually include an approximate imperial equivalent.

Chinese names

Pinyin, the preferred system for transcribing Chinese names of people, is generally used: thus, there is an entry at Mao Zedong, not Mao Tse-tung; an exception is made for a few names which are more familiar in their former (Wade-Giles) form, such as Sun Yat-sen and Chiang Kai-Shek. Where confusion is likely, Wade-Giles forms are given as a cross-reference.

Acknowledgements

California Institute of Technology
Columbia Records
The Conservative Party
Dominic
The Irish Embassy
The French Embassy
The Japanese Embassy
The Library of Congress
Terry Lott
The National Portrait Gallery
National Film Archive
Michael Nicholson
Phonogram
Poseidon Pictures
Sachem
Blair Seitz
Sony Classical
United States Information Service
Vintage Books
Josiah Wedgwood and Sons Ltd
The TUC

CONTRIBUTORS

Project Editor
Anne-Lucie Norton

Co-ordinating Editor
Frances Lass

Proofreaders
Sarah George
A Germing
Edith Harkness

Design
Behram Kapadia

Page Make-up
Roger Walker Graphics
and Typography

David Armstrong PhD
Christine Avery MA, PhD
John Ayto MA
Paul Bahn
David Black
Malcolm Bradbury BA, MA, PhD, Hon D Litt, FRSL
Brendan Bradley MA, MSc, PhD
Tia Cockerell LLB
Sue Cusworth
Nigel Davis MSc
Ian D Derbyshire MA, PhD
J Denis Derbyshire BCs, PhD, FBIM
Col Michael Dewar
Dougal Dixon BSc, MSc
Professor George du Boulay FRCR, FRCP, Hon FACR
Nigel Dudley
Suzanne Duke
Ingrid von Essen
Anna Farkas
Jane Farron BA
Kent Fedorowich BA, MA, PhD
Peter Fleming BA, PhD
Derek Gjertsen BA
Lawrence Garner BA
Joseph Harrison BA, PhD
Robert Halasz
Michael Hitchcock PhD
Stuart Holroyd
H G Jerrard PhD
Robin Kerrod FRAS
Charles Kidd
Stephen Kite B Arch, RIBA
Peter Lafferty
Chris Lawn BA, MA
Mike Lewis
Graham Ley BA, MPhil
Carol Lister BSc, PhD
Graham Littler BSc, MSc, FSS
Robin Maconie MA
Morven MacKillop
Tom McArthur PhD
Isabel Miller
Karin Mogg BSc, MSc, PhD
Bob Moore BA, PhD
David Munro BSc, PhD
Joanne O'Brien
Roger Owen MA, DPhil
Robert Paisley PhD
Michael Pudio MSc, PhD
Tim Pulleine
Ian Ridpath FRAS
Adrian Room MA
Julian Rowe PhD
Jack Schofield BA, MA
Mark Slade MA
Steve Smyth
Joe Staines
Glyn Stone
Callum Storrie
Stephen Webster BSc, MPhil
Liz Whitelegg BSc

Aalto /ˈɑːltəʊ/ Alvar 1898–1976. Finnish architect and designer. One of Finland's first Modernists, he had a unique architectural style, characterized by asymmetry, curved walls, and contrast of natural materials. He invented a new form of laminated bent-plywood furniture 1932 and won many design awards for household and industrial items.

Aalto's buildings include the Hall of Residence at the Massachusetts Institute of Technology, Cambridge, Massachusetts, 1947–49; Technical High School, Otaniemi, 1962–65; and Finlandia Hall, Helsinki, 1972.

It is the task of the architect to give life a gentler structure.

Alvar Aalto *Connoisseur* June 1987

Aaltonen /ˈɑːltənen/ Wäinö 1894–1966. Finnish sculptor best known for his monumental figures and busts portraying citizens of Finland, following the country's independence in 1917. He was one of the early 20th-century pioneers of direct carving and favoured granite as his medium.

The bronze monument to the athlete Nurmi (1925, Helsinki Stadium) and the bust of the composer Sibelius (1928) are examples of his work. He also developed a more sombre style of modern Classicism, well suited to his public commissions, such as the allegorical figures in the Finnish Parliament House (1930–32).

Aaron /ˈeərən/ c. 13th century BC. In the Old Testament, the elder brother of Moses and co-leader of the Hebrews in their march from Egypt to the Promised Land of Canaan. He made the Golden Calf for the Hebrews to worship when they despaired of Moses' return from Mount Sinai, but he was allowed to continue as high priest. All his descendants are hereditary high priests, called the *cohanim*, or cohens, and maintain a special place in worship and ceremony in the synagogue.

Aaron \ˈeərən\ Hank (Henry Louis) 1934– . US baseball player. He played for 23 years with the Milwaukee (later Atlanta) Braves (1954–74) and the Milwaukee Brewers (1975–76), hitting a major-league record of 755 home runs and 2,297 runs batted in. He was elected to the Baseball Hall of Fame 1982.

Aasen /ˈɔːsən/ Ivar Andreas 1813–1896. Norwegian philologist, poet, and playwright. Through a study of rural dialects he evolved by 1853 a native 'country language', which he called Landsmaal, to take the place of literary Dano-Norwegian.

Abbadid dynasty /ˈæbədɪd/ 11th century. Muslim dynasty based in Seville, Spain, which lasted from 1023 until 1091. The dynasty was founded by Abu-el-Kasim Muhammad Ibn Abbad, who led the townspeople against the Berbers when the Spanish caliphate fell. The dynasty continued under Motadid (1042–1069) and Motamid (1069–1091) when the city was taken by the →Almoravids.

Abbado /əˈbɑːdəʊ/ Claudio 1933– . Italian conductor, long associated with the La Scala opera house, Milan. Principal conductor of London Symphony Orchestra from 1979, he also worked with the European Community Youth Orchestra from 1977.

Abbas I /ˈæbəs/ *the Great* c. 1557–1629. Shah of Persia from 1588. He expanded Persian territory by conquest, defeating the Uzbeks near Herat 1597 and also the Turks. The port of Bandar-Abbas is named after him. At his death his empire reached from the river Tigris to the Indus. He was a patron of the arts.

Abbas II /ˈæbəs/ Hilmi 1874–1944. Last khedive (viceroy) of Egypt, 1892–1914. On the outbreak of war between Britain and Turkey in 1914, he sided with Turkey and was deposed following the establishment of a British protectorate over Egypt.

Abbasid dynasty /ˈæbəsɪd/ family of rulers of the Islamic empire, whose caliphs reigned in Baghdad 750–1258. They were descended from Abbas, the prophet Muhammad's uncle, and some of them, such as Harun al-Rashid and Mamun (reigned 813–33), were outstanding patrons of cultural development. Later their power dwindled, and in 1258 Baghdad was burned by the Tatars.

From then until 1517 the Abbasids retained limited power as caliphs of Egypt.

Abbott and Costello /ˈæbət, kɒˈsteləʊ/ stage names of William Abbott (1895–1974) and Louis Cristillo (1906–1959) US comedy duo. They moved to films from vaudeville, and most, including *Buck Privates* 1941 and *Lost in a Harem* 1944, were showcases for their routines. They also appeared on radio and television.

Abd Allah Sudanese dervish leader *Abdullah el Taaisha* 1846–1899. Successor to the Mahdi as Sudanese ruler from 1885, he was defeated by British forces under General →Kitchener at Omdurman 1898 and later killed in Kordofan.

Abd al-Malik /æbd æl'maːlɪk/ Ibn Marwan AD 647– . Caliph who reigned 685–705. Based in Damascus, he waged military campaigns to unite Muslim groups and battled against the Greeks. He instituted a purely Arab coinage and replaced Syriac, Coptic, and Greek with Arabic as the language for his lands. His reign was turbulent but succeeded in extending and strengthening the power of the Omayyad dynasty. He was also a patron of the arts.

Abd el-Kader /'æbd el 'kaːdə/ c. 1807–1873. Algerian nationalist. Emir (Islamic chieftain) of Mascara from 1832, he led a struggle against the French until his surrender in 1847.

Abd el-Krim /æbd el 'krɪm/ el-Khettabi 1881–1963. Moroccan chief known as the 'Wolf of the Riff'. With his brother Muhammad, he led the *Riff revolt* against the French and Spanish invaders, inflicting disastrous defeat on the Spanish at Anual in 1921, but surrendered to a large French army under Pétain in 1926. Banished to the island of Réunion, he was released in 1947 and died in voluntary exile in Cairo.

Abdul-Hamid II /æbdʊl 'hæmɪd/ 1842–1918. Last sultan of Turkey 1876–1909. In 1908 the Young Turks under Enver Pasha forced Abdul-Hamid to restore the constitution of 1876 and in 1909 insisted on his deposition. He died in confinement. For his part in the Armenian massacres suppressing the revolt of 1894–96 he was known as 'the Great Assassin'; his actions still motivate Armenian violence against the Turks.

Abdullah /æb'dʌlə/ ibn Hussein 1882–1951. King of Jordan from 1946. He worked with the British guerrilla leader T E →Lawrence in the Arab revolt of World War I. Abdullah became king of Trans-Jordan 1946; on the incorporation of Arab Palestine (after the 1948–49 Arab–Israeli War) he renamed the country the Hashemite Kingdom of Jordan. He was assassinated.

Abdullah /æb'dʌlə/ Sheik Muhammad 1905–1982. Indian politician, known as the 'Lion of Kashmir'. He headed the struggle for constitutional government against the Maharajah of Kashmir, and in 1948, following a coup, became prime minister. He agreed to the accession of the state to India, but was dismissed and imprisoned from 1953 (with brief intervals) until 1966, when he called for Kashmiri self-determination. He became chief minister of Jammu and Kashmir 1975, accepting the sovereignty of India.

Abdul Mejid I /'bdʊl 'hæmɪd/ 1823–1861. Sultan of Turkey from 1839. During his reign the Ottoman Empire was increasingly weakened by internal nationalist movements and the incursions of the great European powers.

Abel /'eɪbəl/ Frederick Augustus 1827–1902. British scientist and inventor who developed explosives. As a chemist to the War Department, he introduced a method of making gun-cotton and was joint inventor with James →Dewar of cordite. He also invented the Abel close-test instrument for determining the flash point (ignition temperature) of petroleum.

Abel /'eɪbəl/ John Jacob 1857–1938. US biochemist, discoverer of adrenaline. He studied the chemical composition of body tissues, and this led, in 1898, to the discovery of adrenaline, the first hormone to be identified, which Abel called epinephrine. He later became the first to isolate amino acids from blood.

Abel /'aːbəl/ Niels Henrik 1802–1829. Norwegian mathematician. He demonstrated that the general quintic equation

$$ax^5 + bx^4 + cx^3 + dx^2 + ex + f = 0$$

could not be solved algebraically. Subsequent work covered elliptic functions, integral equations, infinite series, and the binomial theorem.

He lived a life of poverty and ill health, dying of tuberculosis shortly before the arrival of an offer of a position at the University of Berlin.

Abelard /'æbəlaːd/ Peter 1079–1142. French scholastic philosopher who worked on logic and theology. His romantic liaison with his pupil →Héloïse caused a medieval scandal. Details of his controversial life are contained in the autobiographical *Historia Calamitatum Mearum/The History of My Misfortunes*.

Abelard, born near Nantes, became canon of Notre Dame in Paris and master of the cathedral school 1115. When his seduction of, and secret marriage to, Héloïse became known, she entered a convent and he was castrated at the instigation of her uncle, Canon Fulbert, and became a monk. Resuming teaching a year later, he was cited for heresy and became a hermit at Nogent, where he built the oratory of the Paraclete, and later abbot of a monastery in Brittany. He died at Châlon-sur-Saône on his way to defend himself against a new charge of heresy. Héloïse was buried beside him at the Paraclete 1164; their remains were taken to Père Lachaise cemetery, Paris, 1817.

He opposed realism in the debate over universals, and propounded 'conceptualism' whereby universal terms have only a mental existence. His love letters from Héloïse survive.

Abercrombie /'ebəkrʌmbi/ Leslie Patrick 1879–1957. Pioneer of British town planning. He is known for his work replanning British cities after damage in World War II (such as the Greater London Plan, 1944) and for the new town policy.

Abercromby /'æbəkrʌmbi/ Ralph 1734–1801. Scots soldier who in 1801 commanded an expedition to the Mediterranean, charged with the liquidation of the French forces left behind by Napoleon in Egypt. He fought a brilliant action against the French at Aboukir Bay in 1801, but was mortally wounded at the battle of Alexandria a few days later.

Aberdeen /ˌæbəˈdiːn/ George Hamilton Gordon, 4th Earl of Aberdeen 1784–1860. British Tory politician, prime minister 1852–55 when he resigned because of the criticism aroused by the miseries and mismanagement of the Crimean War.

Aberdeen began his career as a diplomat. In 1828 and again in 1841 he was foreign secretary under Wellington. In 1852 he became prime minister in a government of Peelites and Whigs (Liberals), but resigned 1855 because of the Crimean War losses. Although a Tory, he supported Catholic emancipation and followed Robert Peel in his conversion to free trade.

Abraham /ˈeɪbrəhæm/ c. 2300 BC. In the Old Testament, founder of the Jewish nation. In his early life he was called Abram. God promised him heirs and land for his people in Canaan (Israel), renamed him Abraham ('father of many nations'), and tested his faith by a command (later retracted) to sacrifice his son Isaac.

Abraham was born in Ur, in Sumeria, the son of Terah. With his father, wife Sarah, and nephew Lot, he migrated to Haran, N Mesopotamia, then to Canaan where he received God's promise of land. After visiting Egypt he separated from Lot at Bethel and settled in Hebron (now in Israel). He was still childless at the age of 76, subsequently had a son (Ishmael) with his wife's maidservant Hagar, and then, at the age of 100, a son Isaac with his wife Sarah. God's promise to Abraham that his descendants would be a nation and Canaan their land was fulfilled when the descendants of Abraham's grandson, Jacob, were led out of Egypt by Moses. Abraham was buried in Machpelah Cave, Hebron.

Abraham /ˈeɪbrəhæm/ Edward Penley 1913– . British biochemist who isolated the antibiotic *cephalosporin*, capable of destroying penicillin-resistant bacteria.

Abu Bakr /ˌæbuːˈbækə/ or *Abu-Bekr* 573–634. 'Father of the virgin', name used by Abd-el-Ka'aba from about 618 when the prophet Muhammad married his daughter Ayesha. He was a close adviser to Muhammad in the period 622–32. On the prophet's death, he became the first caliph, adding Mesopotamia to the Muslim world and instigating expansion into Iraq and Syria.

Traditionally he is supposed to have encouraged some of those who had known Muhammad to memorize his teachings; these words were later written down to form the Koran.

Abú Nuwás /ˈæbuː ˈnuːwæs/ Hasan ibn Háni 762–c. 815. Arab poet celebrated for the freedom, eroticism and ironic lightness of touch he brought to traditional forms.

A brook, a bottle, a bench, a way of waiting,
The body sweetens, the ghost stirs,
Golden four.

Abú Nuwás
from J Kritzeck
An Anthology of Islamic Literature

Achaemenid dynasty /əˈkiːmənɪd/ family ruling the Persian Empire 550–330 BC, and named after Achaemenes, ancestor of Cyrus the Great, founder of the empire. His successors included Cambyses, Darius I, Xerxes, and Darius III, who, as the last Achaemenid ruler, was killed after defeat in battle against Alexander the Great 330 BC.

Achard /ˈæxɑːt/ Franz Karl 1753–1821. German chemist who was largely responsible for developing the industrial process by which table sugar (sucrose) is extracted from beet. He improved the quality of available beet and erected the first factory for the extraction of sugar in Silesia (now in Poland) 1802.

Achebe /əˈtʃeɪbi/ Chinua 1930– . Nigerian novelist whose themes include the social and political impact of European colonialism on African people, and the problems of newly independent African nations. His novels include the widely acclaimed *Things Fall Apart* 1958 and *Anthills of the Savannah* 1987.

Acheson /ˈætʃɪsən/ Dean (Gooderham) 1893–1971. US politician. As undersecretary of state 1945–47 in ➔Truman's Democratic administration, he was associated with George C Marshall in preparing the Marshall Plan, and succeeded him as secretary of state 1949–53.

Great Britain has lost an Empire and has not yet found a role.

Dean Acheson
speech at the Military Academy,
West Point 5 Dec 1962

Acton /ˈæktən/ Eliza 1799–1859. English cookery writer and poet, whose *Modern Cookery for Private Families* 1845 influenced Mrs ➔Beeton.

Acton /ˈæktən/ John Emerich Edward Dalberg-Acton, 1st Baron Acton 1834–1902. British historian and Liberal politician. Elected to Parliament 1859, he was a friend and adviser of Prime Minister Gladstone. Appointed professor of modern history at Cambridge in 1895, he planned and edited the *Cambridge Modern History* but did not live to complete more than the first two volumes.

Acton *British historian and Liberal politician John Acton, 1st Baron Acton, in a portrait by F Sargent (c. 1890), National Portrait Gallery, London. As a leader of the liberal Roman Catholics in England, Acton strongly opposed the dogma of papal infallibility. He coined the maxim 'Power tends to corrupt and absolute power corrupts absolutely.'*

Adam /ˈædəm/ family of Scottish architects and designers. **William Adam** (1689–1748) was the leading Scottish architect of his day, and his son **Robert Adam** (1728–1792) is considered one of the greatest British architects of the late 18th century, who transformed the prevailing Palladian fashion in architecture to a Neo-Classical style. He designed interiors for many great country houses and earned a considerable reputation as a furniture designer. With his brother **James Adam** (1732–1794), also an architect, he speculatively developed the Adelphi near Charing Cross, London, largely rebuilt 1936.

Adam /æˈdɒŋ/ Adolphe Charles 1803–1856. French composer of light operas. Some 50 of his works were staged, including the classic ballet *Giselle*.

Adam de la Halle /æˈdɒm də lɑː ˈæl/ c. 1240–c. 1290. French poet and composer. His *Jeu de Robin et Marion*, written in Italy about 1282, is a theatrical work with dialogue and songs set to what were apparently popular tunes of the day. It is sometimes called the forerunner of comic opera.

Adams /ˈædəmz/ Ansel 1902–1984. US photographer known for his printed images of dramatic landscapes and organic forms of the American West. He was associated with the zone system of exposure estimation.

Adams /ˈædəmz/ Franklin Pierce, popularly known as *F P A* 1881–1960. US humorist and social critic. He gained fame as a columnist for the New York *Evening Mail, Tribune, World*, and *Post*. In addition to publishing books of light verse (*The Melancholy Lute* 1936) and collections of his syndicated newspaper columns (*The Diary of Our Own Samuel Pepys* 1935), he served as a panellist on the popular radio game show *Information Please*.

> *For us the British Parliament is as foreign as the French Parliament, the Japanese diet, or the American Senate.*
>
> **Gerry Adams** *Observer* Jan 1984

Adams /ˈædəmz/ Gerry (Gerard) 1948– . Northern Ireland politician, president of Provisional Sinn Féin (the political wing of the IRA) from 1978. He was elected member of Parliament for Belfast West 1983 but declined to take up his Westminster seat, stating that he did not believe in the British government. He has been criticized for failing to denounce IRA violence. He was interned in the 1970s because of his connections with the IRA, and later released.

Adams /ˈædəmz/ Henry Brooks 1838–1918. US historian and novelist, a grandson of President John Quincy Adams. He published the acclaimed nine-volume *A History of the United States During the Administrations of Jefferson and Madison* 1889–91, a study of the evolution of democracy in the USA.

His other works include *Mont-Saint-Michel and Chartres* 1904, and a classic autobiography *The Education of Henry Adams* 1907.

Adams /ˈædəmz/ John 1735–1826. 2nd president of the USA 1797–1801, and vice president 1789–97. He was a member of the Continental Congress 1774–78 and signed the Declaration of Independence. In 1779 he went to France and negotiated the treaties that ended the American Revolution. Although suspicious of the French Revolution, he resisted calls for war with France. He became the first US ambassador in London 1785.

Adams /ˈædəmz/ John Coolidge 1947– . US composer and conductor, director of the New Music Ensemble 1972–81, and artistic adviser to the San Francisco Symphony Orchestra from 1978. His works include *Electric Wake* 1968, *Heavy Metal* 1971, *Bridge of Dreams* 1982, and the operas *Nixon in China* 1988 and *The Death of Klinghoffer* 1990.

> *One friend in a lifetime is much; two are many; three are hardly possible.*
>
> **Henry Adams**
> *The Education of Henry Adams 1907*

Adams John Adams, 2nd president of the USA, was prominent in the Continental Congress and helped draft the Declaration of Independence. He was sent to France and Holland as Congressional commissioner, and was a signatory, along with Benjamin Franklin and John Jay, of the 1783 peace treaty of Versailles.

Adams /ˈædəmz/ John Couch 1819–1892. English astronomer who mathematically deduced the existence of the planet Neptune 1845 from the effects of its gravitational pull on the motion of Uranus, although it was not found until 1846 by J G →Galle. Adams also studied the Moon's motion, the Leonid meteors, and terrestrial magnetism.

Adams /ˈædəmz/ John Quincy 1767–1848. 6th president of the USA 1825–29. Eldest son of President John Adams, he was born in Quincy, Massachusetts, and became US minister in The Hague, Berlin, St Petersburg, and London. He negotiated the Treaty of Ghent to end the War of 1812 (fought between Britain and the USA) on generous terms for the USA. In 1817 he became →Monroe's secretary of state, formulated the Monroe Doctrine 1823 (stating that any further European colonial ambitions in the Western hemisphere would be threats to US peace and security, and that, in turn, the USA would not interfere in European affairs), and was elected president by the House of Representatives, despite receiving fewer votes than his main rival, Andrew →Jackson. As president, Adams was an advocate of strong federal government.

Adams /ˈædəmz/ Neil 1958– . English judo champion. He won two junior and five senior European titles 1974–85, eight senior national titles, and two Olympic silver medals 1980, 1984. In 1981 he was world champion in the 78 kg class.

Adams /ˈædəmz/ Richard 1920– . English novelist. A civil servant 1948–72, he wrote *Watership Down* 1972, a tale of a rabbit community, which is read by adults and children. Later novels include *Shardik* 1974, *The Plague Dogs* 1977, and *Girl on a Swing* 1980.

Adams /ˈædəmz/ Roger 1889–1971. US organic chemist, known for his painstaking analytical work to determine the composition of naturally occurring substances such as complex vegetable oils and plant alkaloids.

Adams /ˈædəmz/ Samuel 1722–1803. US politician, second cousin of President John Adams. He was the chief instigator of the Boston Tea Party (a protest 1773 against the British tea tax imposed by colonists in Massachusetts, before the American Revolution). He was also a signatory to the Declaration of Independence, served in the Continental Congress, and anticipated the French emperor Napoleon in calling the British a 'nation of shopkeepers'.

Adams /ˈædəmz/ William 1564–1620. English sailor and shipbuilder, the only foreigner ever to become a samurai. He piloted a Dutch vessel that reached Japan in 1600, and became adviser to the first →Tokugawa shogun, for whom he built two warships, the first Western-style ships in Japan. He is regarded by the Japanese as the symbolic founder of the Japanese navy.

Adams John Quincy Adams, 6th president of the USA. As Monroe's secretary of state he negotiated the treaty with Spain for the acquisition of Florida. After failing to win presidential re-election, Adams was elected Representative in Congress 1831 and was noted as a promoter of antislavery views; he was returned to each successive congress until his death.

Adamson /ˈædəmsən/ Joy 1910–1985. German-born naturalist whose work with wildlife in Kenya, including the lioness Elsa, is described in *Born Free* 1960 which was adapted as a film in 1975. She was murdered at her home in Kenya. She worked with her third husband, British game warden *George Adamson* (1906–1989), who was murdered by bandits.

Adamson /ˈædəmsən/ Robert R 1821–1848. Scottish photographer who, with David Octavius Hill, produced 2,500 calotypes (mostly portraits) in five years from 1843.

Addams /ˈædəmz/ Charles 1912–1988. US cartoonist, creator of the ghoulish family featured in the *New Yorker* magazine. A successful television comedy series was based on the cartoon in the 1960s.

Addams /ˈædəmz/ Jane 1860–1935. US sociologist and campaigner for women's rights. In 1889 she founded and led the social settlement of Hull House, Chicago, one of the earliest community centres. She was vice president of the National American Women Suffrage Alliance 1911–14, and in 1915 led the Women's Peace Party and the first Women's Peace Congress. She shared the Nobel Peace Prize 1931.

Her publications include *Newer Ideals of Peace* 1907 and *Twenty Years at Hull House* 1910.

Addington /ˈædɪŋtən/ Henry 1757–1844. British Tory politician and prime minister 1801–04, he was created Viscount Sidmouth 1805. As home secretary 1812–1822, he was responsible for much reprieve legislation, including the notorious Six Acts to curtail political radicalism.

Addison /ˈædɪsən/ Joseph 1672–1719. English writer. In 1704 he celebrated →Marlborough's victory at Blenheim in a poem, 'The Campaign', and subsequently held political appointments, including undersecretary of state and secretary to the Lord-Lieutenant of Ireland 1708. In 1709 he contributed to the *Tatler* magazine, begun by Richard →Steele, with whom he was cofounder 1711 of the *Spectator*.

Addison /ˈædɪsən/ Thomas 1793–1863. British physician who first recognized the condition known as Addison's disease in 1855, a rare deficiency or failure of the adrenal glands to produce corticosteroid hormones.

Adelaide /ˈædɪleɪd/ 1792–1849. Queen consort of →William IV of England. Daughter of the Duke of Saxe-Meiningen, she married William, then Duke of Clarence, in 1818. No children of the marriage survived infancy.

Adenauer /ˈædənaʊə/ Konrad 1876–1967. German Christian Democrat politician, chancellor of West Germany 1949–63. With the French president de Gaulle he achieved the postwar reconciliation of France and Germany and strongly supported all measures designed to strengthen the Western bloc in Europe.

Adenauer was mayor of his native city of Cologne from 1917 until his imprisonment by Hitler in 1933 for opposition to the Nazi regime. After the war he headed the Christian Democratic Union and became chancellor.

He was known as the 'Old Fox'. He supported the UK's entry into the Common Market (now the European Community).

Ader /æˈdeə/ Clément 1841–1925. French aviation pioneer and inventor. He demonstrated stereophonic sound transmission by telephone at the 1881 Paris Exhibition of Electricity. His steam-driven aeroplane, the *Eole*, made the first powered takeoff in history 1890, but it could not fly. In 1897, with his *Avion III*, he failed completely, despite false claims made later.

Adi Granth /ˈɑːdi ˈɡrɑːnθ/ or *Guru Granth Sahib* the holy book of Sikhism.

Adjani /ˌædʒɑːˈniː/ Isabelle 1955– . French actress of Algerian-German descent. She played the title role in Truffaut's *L'Histoire d'Adèle H*/*The Story of Adèle H* 1975 and has since appeared in international productions including *Le Locataire*/*The Tenant*, *Nosferatu Phantom der Nacht* 1979, and *Ishtar* 1987.

Adler /ˈɑːdlə/ Alfred 1870–1937. Austrian psychologist. Adler saw the 'will to power' as more influential in accounting for human behaviour than the sexual drive theory. A dispute over this theory led to the dissolution of his ten-year collaboration with →Freud.

Born in Vienna, he was a general practitioner and nerve specialist there 1897–1927, serving as an army doctor in World War I. He joined the circle of Freudian doctors in Vienna about 1900. The concepts of inferiority complex and overcompensation originated with Adler, for example in his books *Organic Inferiority and Psychic Compensation* 1907 and *Understanding Human Nature* 1927.

Whenever a child lies you will always find a severe parent. A lie would have no sense unless the truth were felt to be dangerous.

Alfred Adler *New York Times* 1949

Adler /ˈɑːdlə/ Larry 1914– . US musician, a virtuoso performer on the harmonica, who commissioned the English composer Vaughan Williams's *Romanza in D flat* 1951.

Adrian /ˈeɪdriən/ Edgar, 1st Baron Adrian 1889–1977. British physiologist who received the Nobel Prize for Medicine in 1932 for his work with Charles Sherrington in the field of nerve impulses and the function of the nerve cell.

Adrian IV /ˈeɪdriən/ (Nicholas Breakspear) *c.* 1100–1159. Pope 1154–59, the only British pope.

He secured the execution of →Arnold of Brescia; crowned Frederick I Barbarossa as German emperor; refused Henry II's request that Ireland should be granted to the English crown in absolute ownership; and was at the height of a quarrel with the emperor when he died.

Aehrenthal /'eərəntɑːl/ Count Aloys von 1854–1912. Foreign minister of Austria–Hungary during the Bosnian Crisis of 1908.

Aelfric /'ælfrɪk/ c. 955–1020. Anglo-Saxon writer and abbot, author of two collections of *Catholic Homilies* 990–92, sermons, and the *Lives of the Saints* 996–97, written in vernacular Old English prose.

Aeschines /'iːskɪniːz/ lived 4th century BC. Orator of ancient Athens, a rival of →Demosthenes.

Aeschylus /'iːskələs/ c. 525–c. 456 BC. Greek dramatist, widely regarded as the founder of Greek tragedy (with →Euripides and →Sophocles). By the introduction of a second actor he made true dialogue and dramatic action possible. Aeschylus wrote some 90 plays between 499 and 458 BC, of which seven survive. These are *The Suppliant Women* performed about 490 BC, *The Persians* 472 BC, *Seven against Thebes* 467 BC, *Prometheus Bound c.* 460 BC, and the *Oresteia* trilogy 458 BC.

Aeschylus was born at Eleusis, near Athens, of a noble family. He took part in the Persian Wars and fought at Marathon 490 BC. He twice visited the court of Hieron I, king of Syracuse, and died at Gela in Sicily.

Every ruler is harsh whose rule is new.

Aeschylus *Prometheus Bound c.* 460 BC.

Aesop /'iːsɒp/ traditional writer of Greek fables. According to the historian Herodotus, he lived in the reign of Amasis of Egypt (mid-6th century BC) and was a slave of Iadmon, a Thracian. The fables, for which no evidence of his authorship exists, are anecdotal stories using animal characters to illustrate moral or satirical points.

Don't count your chickens before they're hatched.

Aesop 'The Milkmaid and the Pail'

Afonso /æ'fɒnseʊ/ six kings of Portugal, including:

Afonso I 1094–1185. King of Portugal from 1112. He made Portugal independent from León.

Aga Khan IV /'ɑːgə 'kɑːn/ 1936– . Spiritual head (*imam*) of the *Ismaili* Muslim sect. He succeeded his grandfather 1957.

Agassiz /'ægəsi/ Jean Louis Rodolphe 1807–1873. Swiss-born US palaeontologist and geologist, one of the foremost scientists of the 19th century. He established his name through his work on the classification of the fossil fishes. Unlike Darwin, he did not believe that individual species themselves changed, but that new species were created from time to time.

Agassiz was the first to realize that an ice age had taken place in the northern hemisphere, when, in 1840, he observed ice scratches on rocks in Edinburgh. He is now criticized for holding racist views concerning the position of blacks in American society.

Agate /'eɪgət/ James Evershed 1877–1947. British essayist and theatre critic, author of *Ego*, a diary in nine volumes published 1935–49.

Agee /'eɪdʒiː/ James 1909–1955. US journalist, screenwriter, and author. He rose to national prominence as a result of his investigation of the plight of sharecroppers in the South during the Depression. In collaboration with photographer Walker Evans, he published the photo and text essay *Let Us Now Praise Famous Men* 1941. His screenwriting credits include *The African Queen* 1951 and *The Night of the Hunter* 1955. His novel *A Death in the Family* won a Pulitzer Prize 1958.

Agnew /'ægnjuː/ Spiro 1918– . US vice president 1969–73. A Republican, he was governor of Maryland 1966–69, and vice president under →Nixon. He took the lead in a campaign against the press and opponents of the Vietnam War. Although he was one of the few administration officials not to be implicated in the Watergate affair, he resigned 1973, shortly before pleading 'no contest' to a charge of income-tax evasion.

Agnon /'ægnɒn/ Shmuel Yosef 1888–1970. Israeli novelist. Born in Buczacz, Galicia (now part of W Ukraine), he made it the setting of his most celebrated work, *A Guest for the Night* 1945. He shared a Nobel prize 1966.

Agostini /ægɒ'stiːni/ Giacomo 1943– . Italian motorcyclist who won a record 122 grand prix and 15 world titles. His world titles were at 350cc and 500cc and he was five times a dual champion.

In addition he was ten times winner of the Isle of Man TT (Tourist Trophy) races; a figure bettered only by Mike →Hailwood and Joey Dunlop.

Agricola /ə'grɪkələ/ Gnaeus Julius AD 37–93. Roman general and politician. Born in Provence, he became Consul of the Roman Republic 77 AD, and then governor of Britain AD 78–85. He extended Roman rule to the Firth of Forth in Scotland and won the battle of Mons Graupius. His fleet sailed round the north of Scotland and proved Britain an island.

Agrippa /ə'grɪpə/ Marcus Vipsanius 63–12 BC. Roman general. He commanded the victorious fleet at the battle of Actium and married Julia, daughter of the emperor →Augustus.

Ahab /'eɪhæb/ c. 875–854 BC. King of Israel. His empire included the suzerainty of Moab, and Judah was his subordinate ally, but his kingdom was weakened by constant wars with Syria. By his marriage with Jezebel, princess of Sidon, Ahab introduced into Israel the worship of the Phoencian god Baal, thus provoking the hostility of Elijah and other prophets. Ahab died in battle against the Syrians at Ramoth Gilead.

Ahmad Shah Durrani /'aːmæd 'ʃaː/ 1724–1773. Founder and first ruler of Afghanistan. Elected shah in 1747, he had conquered the Punjab by 1751.

Aidan, St /'eɪdn/ c. 600–651. Irish monk who converted Northumbria to Christianity and founded Lindisfarne monastery on Holy Island off the NE coast of England. His feast day is 31 Aug.

Aidoo /'eɪduː/ Ama Ata 1940– . Ghanaian writer of plays (*Dilemma of a Ghost* 1965), novels (*Our Sister Killjoy* 1977), and short stories.

Aiken /'eɪkən/ Conrad (Potter) 1899–1973. US poet, novelist, and short-story writer whose *Selected Poems* 1929 won the Pulitzer prize. His works were influenced by early psychoanalytic theory and the use of the stream-of-consciousness technique.

Aiken /'eɪkən/ Howard 1900– . US mathematician and computer pioneer. In 1939, in conjunction with engineers from IBM, he started work on the design of an automatic calculator using standard business-machine components. In 1944 the team completed one of the first computers, the Automatic Sequence Controlled Calculator (known as the Mark 1), a programmable computer controlled by punched paper tape and using punched cards.

Ailey /'eɪli/ Alvin 1931–1989. US dancer, choreographer, and director whose Alvin Ailey City Center Dance Theater, formed 1958, was the first truly interracial dance company and opened dance to a wider audience. Ailey studied modern, ethnic, jazz, and academic dance, and his highly individual work celebrates rural and urban black America in pieces like *Blues Suite* 1958 and the company signature piece *Revelations* 1960.

Ainsworth /'eɪnzwɜːθ/ William Harrison 1805–1882. English historical novelist. He wrote more than 40 novels and helped popularize the legends of Dick →Turpin in *Rookwood* 1834 and Herne the Hunter in *Windsor Castle* 1843.

Airy /'eəri/ George Biddell 1801–1892. English astronomer. He installed a transit telescope at the Royal Observatory at Greenwich, England, and accurately measured Greenwich Mean Time by the stars as they crossed the meridian.

Airy was made director of the Cambridge University Observatory 1828, and became the seventh Astronomer Royal 1835. He began the distribution of Greenwich time signals by telegraph, and Greenwich Mean Time as measured by Airy's telescope was adopted as legal time in Britain 1880.

Akbar /'ækbɑː/ Jalal ud-Din Muhammad 1542–1605. Mogul emperor of N India from 1556, when he succeeded his father. He gradually established his rule throughout N India. He is considered the greatest of the Mogul emperors, and the firmness and wisdom of his rule won him the title 'Guardian of Mankind'; he was a patron of the arts.

A monarch should be ever intent on conquest, otherwise his neighbours rise in arms against him.

Jalal ud-Din Muhammad Akbar c. 1590

à Kempis Thomas; see →Thomas à Kempis, religious writer.

Akhmatova /æk'mætəvə/ Anna. Pen name of Anna Andreevna Gorenko 1889–1966. Russian poet. Among her works are the cycle *Requiem* 1963 (written in the 1930s), which deals with the Stalinist terror, and *Poem Without a Hero* 1962 (begun 1940).

In the 1920s she published several collections of poetry in the realist style of →Mandelshtam, but her lack of sympathy with the post-revolutionary regimes inhibited her writing, and her work was banned 1922–40 and again from 1946. From the mid-1950s her work was gradually rehabilitated in the USSR. In 1989 an Akhmatova Museum was opened in Leningrad (now St Petersburg).

Akihito /æki'hiːtəʊ/ 1933– . Emperor of Japan from 1989, succeeding his father Hirohito (Showa). His reign is called the Heisei ('achievement of universal peace') era.

Unlike previous crown princes, Akihito was educated alongside commoners at the elite Gakushuin school and in 1959 he married Michiko Shoda (1934–), the daughter of a flour-company president. Their three children, the Oxford university-educated Crown Prince Hiro, Prince Aya, and Princess Nori, were raised at Akihito's home instead of being reared by tutors and chamberlains in a separate imperial dormitory.

Akins /'eɪkɪnz/ Zoe 1886–1958. US writer. Born in Missouri, she wrote poems, literary criticism, and plays, including *The Greeks Had a Word for It* 1930.

Aksakov /æk'saːkɒv/ Sergei Timofeyevich 1791–1859. Russian writer, born at Ufa, in the Urals. Under the influence of →Gogol, he wrote autobiographical novels, including *Chronicles of a Russian Family* 1856 and *Years of Childhood* 1858.

Alain-Fournier /æ'læŋ 'fʊənieɪ/ pen name of Henri-Alban Fournier 1886–1914. French novelist. His haunting semi-autobiographical fantasy

Le Grand Meaulnes/The Lost Domain 1913 was a cult novel of the 1920s and 1930s. His life is intimately recorded in his correspondence with his brother-in-law Jacques Rivière. He was killed in action on the Meuse in World War I.

Alanbrooke Alan Francis Brooke, 1st Viscount Alanbrooke 1883–1963. British army officer, Chief of Staff in World War II and largely responsible for the strategy that led to the German defeat.

He was born in Ireland. He served in the artillery in World War I, and in World War II, as commander of the 2nd Corps 1939–40, did much to aid the extrication of the British Expeditionary Force from Dunkirk. He was commander in chief of the Home Forces 1940–41 and chief of the Imperial General Staff 1941–46. He became a field marshal in 1944, was created a baron 1945 and viscount 1946.

Alarcón /ˌælɑːˈkɒn/ Pedro Antonio de 1833–1891. Spanish journalist and writer. The acclaimed *Diario/Diary* was based upon his experiences as a soldier in Morocco. His *El Sombrero de tres picos/The Three-Cornered Hat* 1874 was the basis of Manuel de Falla's ballet.

Alaric /ˈælərɪk/ *c.* 370–410. King of the Visigoths. In 396 he invaded Greece and retired with much booty to Illyria. In 400 and 408 he invaded Italy, and in 410 captured and sacked Rome, but died the same year on his way to invade Sicily. The river Busento was diverted by his soldiers so that he could be buried in its course with his treasures; the labourers were killed to keep the secret.

Alban, St /ˈɔːlbən/ died AD 303. First Christian martyr in England. In 793 King Offa founded a monastery on the site of Alban's martyrdom, around which the city of St Albans grew up.

According to tradition, he was born at Verulamium, served in the Roman army, became a convert to Christianity after giving shelter to a priest, and, on openly professing his belief, was beheaded.

Albee /ˈælbiː/ Edward 1928– . US playwright. His internationally performed plays are associated with the Theatre of the Absurd and include *The Zoo Story* 1960, *The American Dream* 1961, *Who's Afraid of Virginia Woolf?* 1962 (his most successful play; also filmed with Elizabeth Taylor and Richard Burton as the quarrelling, alcoholic, academic couple 1966), and *Tiny Alice* 1965. *A Delicate Balance* 1966 and *Seascape* 1975 both won Pulitzer prizes.

Albéniz /ælˈbeɪnɪθ/ Isaac 1860–1909. Spanish composer and pianist, born in Catalonia. He composed the suite *Iberia* and other piano pieces, making use of traditional Spanish melodies.

Alberoni /ˌælbəˈrəʊni/ Giulio 1664–1752. Spanish-Italian priest and politician, born in Piacenza, Italy. Philip V made him prime minister of Spain in 1715. In 1717 he became a cardinal. He introduced many domestic reforms, but was forced to

Albert, Prince Consort *Portrait of Albert, Prince Consort, by Francis Xavier Winterhaler (1867), National Portrait Gallery, London. Although noted for the high moral standards he set for the royal household and aristocracy, Prince Albert often aroused ministerial and popular distrust because of his German origins.*

flee to Italy in 1719, when his foreign policies failed.

Albert /ˈælbət/ Prince Consort 1819–1861. Husband of British Queen ➔Victoria from 1840; a patron of the arts, science, and industry. Albert was the second son of the Duke of Saxe Coburg-Gotha and first cousin to Queen Victoria, whose chief adviser he became. He planned the Great Exhibition of 1851; the profit was used to buy the sites in London of all the South Kensington museums and colleges and the Royal Albert Hall, built 1871. He died of typhoid.

Albert also popularized the Christmas tree in England. He was regarded by the British people with groundless suspicion because of his German connections.

The *Albert Memorial* 1872, designed by Sir Gilbert Scott, in Kensington Gardens, London, typifies Victorian decorative art.

Albert I /ˈælbət/ 1875–1934. King of the Belgians from 1909, the younger son of Philip, Count of Flanders, and the nephew of Leopold II. In 1900 he married Duchess Elisabeth of Bavaria. In World War I he commanded the Allied army that retook the Belgian coast in 1918.

He re-entered Brussels in triumph on 22 Nov. He was killed while mountaineering in the Ardennes.

Alberti /æl'beəti/ Leon Battista 1404–1472. Italian Renaissance architect and theorist who recognized the principles of Classical architecture and their modification for Renaissance practice in *On Architecture* 1452.

Albertus Magnus, St /æl'bɜːtəs 'mægnəs/ 1206–1280. German scholar of Christian theology, philosophy (especially Aristotle), natural science, chemistry, and physics. He was known as 'doctor universalis' because of the breadth of his knowledge. Feast day 15 Nov.

He studied at Bologna and Padua, and entered the Dominican order 1223. He taught at Cologne and lectured from 1245 at Paris University. St Thomas Aquinas was his pupil there, and followed him to Cologne 1248. He became provincial of the Dominicans in Germany 1254, and was made bishop of Ratisbon 1260. Two years later he resigned and eventually retired to his convent at Cologne. He tried to reconcile Aristotelian thought with Christian teachings.

Albinoni /ælbɪ'nəʊni/ Tomaso 1671–1751. Italian Baroque composer and violinist, whose work was studied and adapted by →Bach. He composed over 40 operas.

The popular *Adagio* often described as being by Albinoni was actually composed by his biographer Remo Giazotto (1910–).

Alboin /'ælbɔɪn/ 6th century. King of the Lombards about 561–573. At that time the Lombards were settled north of the Alps. Early in his reign he attacked the Gepidae, a Germanic tribe occupying present-day Romania, killing their king and taking his daughter Rosamund to be his wife. About 568 he crossed the Alps to invade Italy, conquering the country as far S as Rome. He was murdered at the instigation of his wife, after he forced her to drink wine from a cup made from her father's skull.

Albone /'ɔːlbəʊn/ Dan 1860–1906. English inventor of one of the first commercially available farm tractors, the Ivel, in 1902. It was a three-wheeled vehicle with a midmounted twin-cylinder petrol engine which could plough an acre in 1.5 hours.

Albuquerque /'ælbəkɜːki/ Afonso de 1453–1515. Viceroy and founder of the Portuguese East Indies with strongholds in Ceylon, Goa, and Malacca 1508–15, when the king of Portugal replaced him by his worst enemy. He died at sea on the way home when his ship *Flor del Mar* was lost between Malaysia and India.

Alcaeus /æl'siːəs/ *c.* 611–*c.* 580 BC. Greek lyric poet. Born at Mytilene in Lesvos, he was a member of the aristocratic party and went into exile when the popular party triumphed. He wrote odes, and the Alcaic stanza is named after him.

Alcibiades /ˌælsɪ'baɪədiːz/ 450–404 BC. Athenian general. Handsome and dissolute, he became the archetype of capricious treachery for his military intrigues against his native state with Sparta and Persia; the Persians eventually had him assassinated. He was brought up by →Pericles and was a friend of →Socrates, whose reputation as a teacher suffered from the association.

Alcmaeonidae /ˌælkmi'ɒnɪdiː/ noble family of ancient Athens; its members included →Pericles and →Alcibiades.

Alcock /'ælkɒk/ John William 1892–1919. British aviator. On 14 June 1919, he and Arthur Whitten Brown (1886–1948) made the first nonstop transatlantic flight, from Newfoundland to Ireland.

Alcoforado /ˌælkəʊfə'rɑːdəʊ/ Marianna 1640–1723. Portuguese nun. The *Letters of a Portuguese Nun* 1699, supposedly written by her to a young French nobleman (who abandoned her when their relationship became known), is no longer accepted as authentic.

Alcott Louisa May 1832–1888. US author. Her children's classic *Little Women* 1869 drew on her own home circumstances, the heroine Jo being a partial self-portrait.

Good Wives 1869 was among its sequels.

Alcuin /'ælkwɪn/ (Flaccus Albinus Alcuinus) 735–804. English scholar. Born in York, he went to Rome 780, and in 782 took up residence at Charlemagne's court in Aachen. From 796 he was abbot of Tours. He disseminated Anglo-Saxon scholarship, organized education and learning in the Frankish empire, gave a strong impulse to the Carolingian Renaissance, and was a prominent member of Charlemagne's academy.

Aldhelm, St /'ɔːldhelm/ *c.* 640–709. English prelate and scholar. He was abbot of Malmesbury from 673 and bishop of Sherborne from 705. Of his poems and treatises in Latin, some survive, notably his *Riddles* in hexameters, but his English verse has been lost. He was also known as a skilled architect.

Aldington /'ɔːldɪŋtən/ Richard 1892–1962. British Imagist poet, novelist, and critic who was married to Hilda →Doolittle from 1913 to 1937. He wrote biographies of D H Lawrence and T E Lawrence. His novels include *Death of a Hero* 1929 and *All Men are Enemies* 1933.

Aldiss /'ɔːldɪs/ Brian 1925– . English science-fiction writer, anthologist, and critic. His novels include *Non-Stop* 1958, *The Malacia Tapestry* 1976, and the 'Helliconia' trilogy. *Trillion Year Spree* 1986 is a history of science fiction.

Aldrin /'ɔːldrɪn/ Edwin (Eugene 'Buzz') 1930– . US astronaut who landed on the Moon with Neil →Armstrong during the *Apollo 11* mission in July 1969, becoming the second person to set foot on the Moon.

Aleixandre /æleɪk'sɑːndreɪ/ Vicente 1898–1984. Spanish lyric poet, born in Seville. His verse, which influenced younger Spanish writers, had Republican sympathies, and his work was for a time banned by Franco's government. Nobel Prize for Literature 1977.

Alembert /ˌælɒm'beə/ Jean le Rond d' 1717–1783. French mathematician and encyclopedist. He was associated with Denis →Diderot in planning the great *Encyclopédie*.

Alençon /ˌælɒn'sɒn/ François, duke of, later duke of Anjou 1554–1584. Fourth son of Henry II of France and Catherine de' Medici. At one time he was considered as a suitor to Elizabeth I of England.

Alexander /ˌælɪg'zɑːndə/ Frederick Matthias 1869–1955. Australian founder and teacher of the *Alexander technique*, a psycho-physical relaxation method. At one time a professional reciter, he developed throat and voice trouble, and his experiments in curing himself led him to work out the system of mental and bodily control described in his book *Use of the Self* 1931.

Alexander /ˌælɪg'zɑːndə/ Harold Rupert Leofric George, 1st Earl Alexander of Tunis 1891–1969. British field marshal, a commander in World War II in Burma (now Myanmar), N Africa, and the Mediterranean. He was governor general of Canada 1946–52 and UK minister of defence 1952–54.

In World War II he was the last person to leave in the evacuation of Dunkirk. In Burma he fought a delaying action for five months against superior Japanese forces. In Aug 1942 he went to N Africa, and in 1943 became deputy to Eisenhower in charge of the Allied forces in Tunisia. After the Axis forces in N Africa surrendered, Alexander became supreme Allied commander in the Mediterranean, and in 1944, field marshal.

Alexander /ˌælɪg'zɑːndə/ Samuel 1859–1938. Australian philosopher who originated the theory of emergent evolution: that the space-time matrix evolved matter; matter evolved life; life evolved mind; and finally God emerged from mind. His books include *Space, Time and Deity* 1920.

He was professor at Manchester University, England, 1893–1924.

Alexander /ˌælɪg'ʒɑːndə/ eight popes, including:

Alexander III /ˌælɪg'zɑːndə/ (Orlando Barninelli) Pope 1159–81. His authority was opposed by Frederick I Barbarossa, but Alexander eventually compelled him to render homage 1178. He supported Henry II of England in his invasion of Ireland, but imposed penance on him after the murder of Thomas à →Becket.

Alexander VI (Rodrigo Borgia) 1431–1503. Pope 1492–1503. Of Spanish origin, he bribed his way to the papacy, where he furthered the advancement of his illegitimate children, who included Cesare and Lucrezia →Borgia. When →Savonarola preached against his corrupt practices Alexander had him executed.

Alexander was a great patron of the arts in Italy, as were his children. He is said to have died of a poison he had prepared for his cardinals.

Alexander I Alexander I, tsar of Russia from 1801, spent the first part of his reign fighting Napoleon. In 1815 he turned to religious mysticism, and ended his reign as a recluse.

Alexander three tsars of Russia:

Alexander I /ˌælɪg'zɑːndə/ 1777–1825. Tsar from 1801. Defeated by Napoleon at Austerlitz 1805, he made peace at Tilsit 1807, but economic crisis led to a break with Napoleon's continental system and the opening of Russian ports to British trade; this led to Napoleon's ill-fated invasion of Russia 1812. After the Congress of Vienna 1815, Alexander hoped through the Holy Alliance with Austria and Prussia to establish a new Christian order in Europe.

He gave a new constitution to Poland, presented to him at the Congress of Vienna.

Alexander II 1818–1881. Tsar from 1855. He embarked on reforms of the army, the government, and education, and is remembered as 'the Liberator' for his emancipation of the serfs 1861, but he lacked the personnel to implement his reforms. However, the revolutionary element remained unsatisfied, and Alexander became increasingly autocratic and reactionary. He was assassinated by an anarchistic terrorist group, the Nihilists.

Alexander III 1845–1894. Tsar from 1881, when he succeeded his father, Alexander II. He pursued a reactionary policy, promoting Russification and persecuting the Jews. He married Dagmar (1847–1928), daughter of Christian IX of Denmark and sister of Queen Alexandra of Britain, 1866.

Alexander /ˌælɪgˈzɑːndə/ three kings of Scotland:

Alexander I *c.* 1078–1124. King of Scotland from 1107, known as *the Fierce*. He ruled to the north of the rivers Forth and Clyde while his brother and successor David ruled to the south. He assisted Henry I of England in his campaign against Wales 1114, but defended the independence of the church in Scotland. Several monasteries, including the abbeys of Inchcolm and Scone, were established by him.

Alexander II 1198–1249. King of Scotland from 1214, when he succeeded his father William the Lion. Alexander supported the English barons in their struggle with King John after Magna Carta.

By the treaty of Newcastle 1244 he pledged allegiance to Henry III of England.

Alexander III 1241–1285. King of Scotland from 1249, son of Alexander II. In 1263, by military defeat of Norwegian forces, he extended his authority over the Western Isles, which had been dependent on Norway. He strengthened the power of the central Scottish government.

He died as the result of a fall from his horse, leaving his granddaughter Margaret, the Maid of Norway, to become queen of Scotland.

Alexander I Karageorgevich 1888–1934. Regent of Serbia 1912–21 and king of Yugoslavia 1921–34, as dictator from 1929. Second son of →Peter I, king of Serbia, he was declared regent for his father 1912 and on his father's death became king of the state of South Slavs – Yugoslavia – that had come into being 1918.

Rivalries with neighbouring powers and among the Croats, Serbs, and Slovenes within the country led Alexander to establish a personal dictatorship. He was assassinated on a state visit to France, and Mussolini's government was later declared to have instigated the crime.

Alexander Nevski, St /ˈnevski/ 1220–1263. Russian military leader, son of the grand duke of Novgorod. In 1240 he defeated the Swedes on the banks of the Neva (hence Nevski), and 1242 defeated the Teutonic Knights on the frozen Lake Peipus.

Alexander Obrenovich /oˈbrenevits/ 1876–1903. King of Serbia from 1889 while still a minor, on the abdication of his father, King Milan. He took power into his own hands 1893 and in 1900 married a widow, Draga Mashin. In 1903 Alexander and his queen were murdered, and →Peter I Karageorgevich was placed on the throne.

Alexander Severus /sɪˈvɪərəs/ AD 208–235. Roman emperor from 222, when he succeeded his cousin Heliogabalus. He was born in Palestine. His campaign against the Persians 232 achieved some success, but in 235, on his way to defend Gaul against German invaders, he was killed in a mutiny.

Alexander the Great /ˌælɪgˈzɑːndə/ 356–323 BC. King of Macedonia and conqueror of the large Persian empire. As commander of the vast Macedonian army he conquered Greece 336. He defeated the Persian king Darius in Asia Minor 333, then moved on to Egypt, where he founded Alexandria. He defeated the Persians again in Assyria 331, then advanced further east to reach the Indus. He conquered the Punjab before diminished troops forced his retreat.

The son of King Philip of Macedonia and Queen Olympias, Alexander was educated by the philosopher Aristotle. He first saw fighting 340, and at the battle of Chaeronea 338 contributed to the victory by a cavalry charge. At the age of 20, when his father was murdered, he assumed command of the throne and the army. He secured his northern frontier, suppressed an attempted rising in Greece by his capture of Thebes, and in 334 crossed the Dardanelles for the campaign against the vast Persian empire; at the river Granicus near the Dardanelles he won his first victory. In 333 he routed Darius at Issus, and then set out for Egypt, where he was greeted as Pharaoh. Meanwhile, Darius assembled half a million men for a final battle but at Arbela on the Tigris 331 Alexander, with 47,000 men, drove the Persians into retreat. After the victory he stayed a month in Babylon, then marched to Susa and Persepolis and in 330 to Ecbatana (now Hamadán, Iran). Soon after, he learned that Darius was dead. In Afghanistan he founded colonies at Herat and Kandahar, and in 328 reached the plains of Sogdiana, where he married Roxana, daughter of King Oxyartes. India now lay before him, and he pressed on to the Indus. Near the river Hydaspes (now Jhelum) he fought one of his fiercest battles against the rajah Porus. At the river Hyphasis (now Beas) his men refused to go farther, and reluctantly he turned back down the Indus and along the coast. They reached Susa 324, where Alexander made Darius's daughter his second wife. He died in Babylon of a malarial fever.

I will not steal a victory.

Alexander the Great
refusing to fall on the army of King Darius
before the Battle of Arbela, 331 BC,
quoted in Plutarch, *Lives*

Alexandra /ˌælɪgˈzɑːndrə/ 1936– . Princess of the UK. Daughter of the Duke of Kent and Princess Marina, she married Angus Ogilvy (1928–), younger son of the earl of Airlie. They have two children, James (1964–) and Marina (1966–).

Alexandra /ˌælɪgˈzɑːndrə/ 1844–1925. Queen consort of →Edward VII of the UK, whom she married 1863. She was the daughter of Christian IX of Denmark. An annual Alexandra Rose Day in aid of hospitals commemorates her charitable work.

Alexandra /ˌælɪg'zɑːndrə/ 1872–1918. Last tsarina of Russia 1894–1917. She was the former Princess Alix of Hessen and granddaughter of Britain's Queen Victoria. She married →Nicholas II and, from 1907, fell under the spell of →Rasputin, a 'holy man' brought to the palace to try to cure her son of haemophilia. She was shot with the rest of her family by the Bolsheviks in the Russian Revolution.

Alexeev /æ'leksief/ Vasiliy 1942– . Soviet weightlifter who broke 80 world records 1970–77, a record for any sport.

He was Olympic super-heavyweight champion twice, world champion seven times, and European champion on eight occasions. At one time the most decorated man in the USSR, he was regarded as the strongest man in the world. He carried the Soviet flag at the 1980 Moscow Olympics opening ceremony, but retired shortly afterwards.

Alexi II (Alexei Mikhailovich Ridiger) 1929– . Estonian priest, patriarch of the Russian Orthodox Church from 1990. He was made bishop of Tallinn 1961, archbishop 1964, metropolitan 1968, and metropolitan of Leningrad 1986. He is active in the World Council of Churches, and became chair of the Conference of European Churches 1987.

Alexius /ə'leksies/ five emperors of Byzantium, including:

Alexius I /ə'leksiəs kɒm'niːnəs/ (Comnenus) 1048–1118. Byzantine emperor 1081–1118. The Latin (W European) Crusaders helped him repel Norman and Turkish invasions, and he devoted great skill to buttressing the threatened empire. His daughter →Anna Comnena chronicled his reign.

Alexius III /ə'leksiəs/ (Angelos) died c. 1210. Byzantine emperor 1195–1203. He gained power by deposing and blinding his brother Isaac II, but Isaac's Venetian allies enabled him and his son Alexius IV to regain power as coemperors.

Alexius IV (Angelos) 1182–1204. Byzantine emperor from 1203, when, with the aid of the army of the Fourth Crusade, he deposed his uncle Alexius III. He soon lost the support of the Crusaders (by that time occupying Constantinople), and was overthrown and murdered by another Alexius, Alexius Mourtzouphlus (son-in-law of Alexius III) 1204, an act which the Crusaders used as a pretext to sack the city the same year.

Alfieri /ælfi'eəri/ Vittorio, Count Alfieri 1749–1803. Italian dramatist. The best of his 28 plays, most of them tragedies, are *Saul* 1782 and *Mirra* 1786.

Alfonsín Foulkes /ælfɒn'siːn 'fuːks/ Raúl Ricardo 1927– . Argentine politician, president 1983–89, leader of the moderate Radical Union Party (UCR). As president from the country's return to civilian government, he set up an investigation of the army's human-rights violations.

Economic problems caused him to seek help from the International Monetary Fund and introduce austerity measures.

Educated at a military academy and a university law school, Alfonsín joined the UCR at the age of 18 and eventually went on to lead it. He was active in local politics 1951–62, being imprisoned 1953 by the right-wing Perón regime, and was a member of the national congress 1963–66. With the return to civilian government 1983 and the legalization of political activity, Alfonsín and the UCR won convincing victories and he became president. He stepped down 1989 several months before the end of his term to allow his successor, the Perónist Carlos Menem, to institute emergency economic measures.

Alfonso kings of Portugal; see →Afonso.

Alfonso /æl'fɒnseʊ/ thirteen kings of León, Castile, and Spain, including:

Alfonso VII c. 1107–1157. King of León and Castile from 1126 who attempted to unite Spain. Although he protected the Moors, he was killed trying to check a Moorish rising.

Alfonso X *el Sabio* ('the Wise') 1221–1284. King of Castile from 1252. His reign was politically unsuccessful but he contributed to learning: he made Castilian the official language of the country and commissioned a history of Spain and an encyclopedia, as well as several translations from Arabic concerning, among other subjects, astronomy and games.

Alfonso XI *the Avenger* 1311–1350. King of Castile and León from 1312. He ruled cruelly, repressed a rebellion by his nobles, and defeated the last Moorish invasion 1340.

Alfonso XII 1857–1885. King of Spain from 1875, son of →Isabella II. He assumed the throne after a period of republican government following his mother's flight and effective abdication 1868. His rule was peaceful. He ended the civil war started by the Carlists and drafted a constitution, both 1876.

Alfonso XIII /æl'fɒnseʊ/ 1886–1941. King of Spain 1886–1931. He assumed power 1906 and married Princess Ena, granddaughter of Queen Victoria of the United Kingdom, in the same year. He abdicated 1931 soon after the fall of the Primo de Rivera dictatorship 1923–30 (which he supported), and Spain became a republic. His assassination was attempted several times.

Alfred /'ælfrɪd/ *the Great* c. 848–c. 900. King of Wessex from 871. He defended England against Danish invasion, founded the first English navy, and put into operation a legal code. He encouraged the translation of works from Latin (some he translated himself), and promoted the development of the Anglo-Saxon Chronicle.

Alfred was born at Wantage, Berkshire, the youngest son of Ethelwulf (died 858), king of the West Saxons. In 870 Alfred and his brother

Alfred Alfred the Great, king of Wessex from 871. He defended England against the Danes and captured London 886, bringing all the English not under Danish rule to accept him as king. He and other members of his family established fortified towns (burghs), many of which are still county towns.

Ethelred fought many battles against the Danes. He gained a victory over the Danes at Ashdown 871, and succeeded Ethelred as king April 871 after a series of defeats. Five years of uneasy peace followed while the Danes were occupied in other parts of England. In 876 the Danes attacked again, and in 878 Alfred was forced to retire to the stronghold of Athelney, from where he finally emerged to win the victory of Edington, Wiltshire. By the Peace of Wedmore 878 the Danish leader Guthrum (died 890) agreed to withdraw from Wessex and from Mercia west of Watling Street. A new landing in Kent encouraged a revolt of the East Anglian Danes, which was suppressed 884–86, and after the final foreign invasion was defeated 892–96, Alfred strengthened the navy to prevent fresh incursions.

Algardi /æl'gɑːdi/ Alessandro c. 1595–1654. Italian Baroque sculptor, active in Rome and at the papal court. His major work, on which he was intermittently occupied from 1634 to 1652, is the tomb of Pope Leo XI (Medici) in St Peter's, Rome.

Although Algardi's work is more restrained in expression than that of his contemporary and rival Bernini, it is Baroque in style, with figures often violently contorted and full of movement. His portrait busts include *St Philip Neri* 1640 (Sta Maria Vallicella, Rome).

Alger /ˈældʒə/ Horatio 1834–1899. US writer of children's books. He wrote over 100 didactic moral tales in which the heroes rise from poverty to riches through hard work, luck, and good deeds, including the series 'Ragged Dick' from 1867 and 'Tattered Tom' from 1871.

It is estimated that his books sold more than 20 million copies. In US usage a 'Horatio Alger tale' has now come to mean any rags-to-riches story, often an implausible one.

Alhazen /æl'hɑːzən/ Ibn al Haytham c. 965–1038. Arabian scientist, author of the *Kitab al Manazir*/*Book of Optics*, translated into Latin as *Perspectiva*. For centuries it remained the most comprehensive and authoritative treatment of optics in both East and West.

Ali /ɑːli/ c. 598–660. 4th caliph of Islam. He was born in Mecca, the son of Abu Talib, uncle to the prophet Muhammad, who gave him his daughter Fatima in marriage. On Muhammad's death 632, Ali had a claim to succeed him, but this was not conceded until 656. After a stormy reign, he was assassinated. Around Ali's name the controversy has raged between the Sunni and the Shi'ites, the former denying his right to the caliphate and the latter supporting it.

Ali /ɑːli/ (Ali Pasha) 1741–1822. Turkish politician, known as *Arslan* ('the Lion'). An Albanian, he was appointed pasha (governor) of the Janina region 1788 (now Ioánnina, Greece). His court was visited by the British poet Byron. He was assassinated.

Ali /ɑːliː/ Muhammad. Adopted name of Cassius Marcellus Clay, Jr, 1942– . US boxer. Olympic light-heavyweight champion 1960, he went on to become world professional heavyweight champion 1964, and was the only man to regain the title twice. He was known for his fast footwork and extrovert nature.

He had his title stripped from him 1967 for refusing to be drafted into the US Army. He regained his title 1974, lost it Feb 1978, and regained it seven months later.

Âli /ɑːli/ Mustafa 1541–1600. Historian and writer of the Ottoman Empire. Âli was responsible for much of the myth of the preceding reign of Suleyman (1520–1566) as a golden age.

Alia /ˈæliə/ Ramiz 1925– . Albanian communist politician, head of state 1982–92. He gradually relaxed the isolationist policies of his predecessor Enver Hoxha and following public unrest introduced political and economic reforms, including free elections 1991, when he was elected executive president.

Born in Shkodër in NW Albania, the son of poor Muslim peasants, Alia joined the National Liberation Army 1944, actively opposing Nazi control. After a period in charge of agitation and propaganda, Alia was inducted into the secretariat and politburo of the ruling Party of Labour of

Albania (PLA) 1960–61. On the death of Hoxha he became party leader, soon earning the description of the Albanian Gorbachev. In April 1991, he was elected executive president of the Republic of Albania, following the PLA's victory in multiparty elections. A month later, in conformity with the provisions of the new interim constitution, which debarred the Republic's president from holding party office, he resigned as PLA first secretary and from its politburo and central committee. Sali Berisha replaced Alia as president March 1992.

Ali Pasha /ɑːliˈpɑːʃə/ Mehmed Emin 1815–1871. Grand vizier (chief minister) of the Ottoman empire 1855–56, 1858–59, 1861, and 1867–71, noted for his attempts to westernize the Ottoman Empire.

After a career as ambassador to the UK, minister of foreign affairs 1846, delegate to the Congress of Vienna 1855 and of Paris 1856, he was grand vizier a total of five times. While promoting friendship with Britain and France, he defended the vizier's powers against those of the sultan.

Alken /ˈælkən/ Henry Thomas 1784–1851. British sporting artist. Fox-hunting and steeplechasing were the subjects that most frequently occupied him, but the whole range of field sports was covered in his *National Sports of Great Britain* 1821.

Allan /ˈælən/ David 1744–1796. Scottish historical painter, director of the Academy of Arts in Edinburgh from 1786. He is known for portraits and genre paintings such as *Scotch Wedding*.

Allan /ˈælən/ William 1782–1850. Scottish historical painter, born in Edinburgh, who spent several years in Russia and neighbouring countries, and returned to Edinburgh 1814. He was elected president of the Royal Scottish Academy 1838. His paintings include scenes from Walter Scott's Waverley novels.

Allbutt /ˈɔːlbʌt/ Thomas Clifford 1836–1925. British physician who invented a compact medical thermometer, proved that angina is caused by narrowing of the coronary artery, and studied hydrophobia and tetanus.

Allegri /əˈleɪɡriː/ Gregorio 1582–1652. Italian Baroque composer, born in Rome, who became a priest and entered the Sistine chapel choir 1629. His *Miserere* for nine voices was reserved for performance by the chapel choir until Mozart, at the age of 14, wrote out the music from memory.

Allen /ˈæln/ Ethan 1738–1789. US military leader who founded the 'Green Mountain Boys' 1770. At the outbreak of the American Revolution 1775 they joined with Benedict →Arnold and captured Fort Ticonderoga, the first victory for the American side. Captured by the British in the subsequent invasion of Canada, Allen continued his campaign for Vermont's independence after his

release in 1778. He died before it achieved statehood in 1791.

Born in Litchfield, Connecticut, USA, Allen also served in the French and Indian War (1755–60), part of the American Seven Years' War before taking up the campaign to protect Vermont from territorial claims by New Hampshire and New York.

Allen /ˈælən/ Hervey 1889–1949. US novelist, poet, and biographer, known for his historical novel *Anthony Adverse* 1933 set in the Napoleonic era. He also wrote a biography of Edgar Allen Poe, *Israfel* 1926.

Allen /ˈælən/ Woody. Adopted name of Allen Stewart Konigsberg 1935– . US film writer, director, and actor, known for his cynical, witty, often self-deprecating parody and offbeat humour. His film *Annie Hall* 1975 won him three Academy Awards.

His other films include *Sleeper* 1973, *Manhattan* 1979, and *Hannah and Her Sisters* 1986, all of which he directed, wrote, and appeared in. From the late 1970s, Allen mixed his output of comedies with straight dramas, such as *Interiors* 1978 and *Another Woman* 1988, but *Crimes and Misdemeanors* 1990 broke with tradition by combining humour and straight drama. In 1992 his acrimonious split from his lover Mia Farrow and subsequent revelations about his relationship with their adopted daughter Soon Yi, heightened public interest in his *Husbands and Wives* which addressed the subject of marriage and long-term relationships.

Allenby /ˈælənbi/ Henry Hynman, 1st Viscount Allenby 1861–1936. English field marshal. In World War I he served in France before taking command 1917–19 of the British forces in the Middle East. His defeat of the Turkish forces at Megiddo in Palestine in Sept 1918 was followed almost at once by the capitulation of Turkey. He was high commissioner in Egypt 1919–35.

Allende (Gossens) /aɪˈendi/ Salvador 1908–1973. Chilean left-wing politician. Elected president 1970 as the candidate of the Popular Front alliance, Allende never succeeded in keeping the electoral alliance together in government. His failure to solve the country's economic problems or to deal with political subversion allowed the army, backed by the CIA, to stage the 1973 coup which brought about the death of Allende and many of his supporters.

Allende became a Marxist activist in the 1930s and rose to prominence as a presidential candidate in 1952, 1958, and 1964. In each election he had the support of the socialist and communist movements but was defeated by the Christian Democrats and Nationalists. As president, his socialism and nationalization of US-owned copper mines led the CIA to regard him as a communist and to their involvement in the coup that replaced him by General Pinochet.

Allingham English detective novelist Margery Allingham, creator of the fictional detective Albert Campion. She wrote a string of elegant, witty, and often ingenuous novels, including Flowers for the Jungle *1936,* The China Governess *1963, and* The Mind Readers *1965.*

Allingham /ˈælɪŋəm/ Margery (Louise) 1904–1966. English detective novelist, creator of detective Albert Campion, as in *More Work for the Undertaker* 1949.

Allston /ˈɔːlstən/ Washington 1779–1843. US painter of sea- and landscapes, a pioneer of the Romantic movement in the USA. His handling of light and colour earned him the title 'the American Titian'. He also painted classical, religious, and historical subjects.

Allyson /ˈælɪsən/ June. Stage name of Ella Geisman 1917– . US film actress, popular in musicals and straight drama in the 1940s and 1950s. Her work includes *Music for Millions* 1945, *The Three Musketeers* 1948, and *The Glenn Miller Story* 1954.

Alma-Tadema /ˈælmə ˈtædɪmə/ Laurence 1836–1912. Dutch painter who settled in the UK 1870. He painted romantic, idealized scenes from Greek, Roman, and Egyptian life in a distinctive, detailed style.

Almeida /ælˈmeɪdə/ Francisco de *c.* 1450–1510. First viceroy of Portuguese India 1505–08.

He was killed in a skirmish with the Hottentots (present-day Khoikhoi) at Table Bay, S Africa.

Almohad /ˈælməhæd/ Berber dynasty 1130–1269 founded by the Berber prophet Muhammad ibn Tumart (*c.* 1080–1130). The Almohads ruled much of Morocco and Spain, which they took by defeating the Almoravids; they later took the area that today forms Algeria and Tunis. Their policy of religious 'purity' involved the forced conversion and massacre of the Jewish population of Spain. The Almohads were themselves defeated by the Christian kings of Spain 1212, and in Morocco 1269.

Almoravid /ælˈmɔːrəvɪd/ Berber dynasty 1056–1147 founded by the prophet Abdullah ibn Tashfin, ruling much of Morocco and Spain in the 11th–12th centuries. The Almoravids came from the Sahara and in the 11th century began laying the foundations of an empire covering the whole of Morocco and parts of Algeria; their capital was the newly founded Marrakesh. In 1086 they defeated Alfonso VI of Castile to gain much of Spain. They were later overthrown by the Almohads.

Alonso Alicia 1914– . Cuban ballerina and director. Purely classical in style, she was one of the most famous Giselles of the century, and in 1959 became prima ballerina and director of the Cuban National Ballet.

Aloysius, St /ˌæləʊˈɪsiəs/ 1568–1591. Italian Jesuit who died while nursing plague victims. He is the patron saint of youth. Feast day 21 June.

Alphege, St /ˈælfɪdʒ/ 954–1012. Anglo-Saxon priest, bishop of Winchester from 984, archbishop of Canterbury from 1006. When the Danes

Alma-Tadema Dutch-born English painter, Sir Laurence Alma-Tadema, who specialized in skilfully executed classical scenes. His knighthood 1899 and the award of the Order of Merit 1905 testify the extent to which he satisfied Victorian taste.

attacked Canterbury he tried to protect the city, was thrown into prison, and, refusing to deliver the treasures of his cathedral, was stoned and beheaded at Greenwich 19 April, his feast day.

Altdorfer /ˈæltdɔːfə/ Albrecht c. 1480–1538. German painter and printmaker, active in Regensburg, Bavaria. Altdorfer's work, inspired by the linear, Classical style of the Italian Renaissance, often depicts dramatic landscapes that are out of scale with the figures in the paintings. His use of light creates tension and effects of movement. Many of his works are of religious subjects.

With Albrecht Dürer and Lucas Cranach, Altdorfer is regarded as one of the leaders of the German Renaissance. *St George and the Dragon* 1510 (Alte Pinakothek, Munich) is an example of his landscape style; *The Battle of Issus* 1529 (also Munich) is a dramatic panorama.

Altgeld /ˈɔːltgeld/ John Peter 1847–1902. US political and social reformer. Born in Prussia, he was taken in infancy to the USA. During the Civil War he served in the Union army. He was a judge of the Supreme Court in Chicago 1886–91, and as governor of Illinois 1893–97 was a champion of the worker against the government-backed power of big business.

Althusser /ˌæltuˈseə/ Louis 1918–1990. French philosopher and Marxist, born in Algeria, who argued that the idea that economic systems determine family and political systems is too simple. He attempted to show how the ruling class ideology of a particular era is a crucial form of class control.

Althusser divides each mode of production into four key elements – the economic, political, ideological, and theoretical – all of which interact. His structuralist analysis of capitalism sees individuals and groups as agents or bearers of the structures of social relations, rather than as independent influences on history. His works include *For Marx* 1965, *Lenin and Philosophy* 1969, and *Essays in Self-Criticism* 1976.

He dismisses mainstream sociology as bourgeois and has influenced thinkers in fields as diverse as social anthropology, literature, and history.

Altman /ˈæltmən/ Robert 1925– . US maverick film director. His antiwar comedy *M.A.S.H.* 1970 was a critical and commercial success; subsequent films include *McCabe and Mrs Miller* 1971, *The Long Goodbye* 1973, *Nashville* 1975, *Popeye* 1980, and *The Player* 1992.

Alva /ˈælvə/ or *Alba* Ferdinand Alvarez de Toledo, duke of 1508–1582. Spanish politician and general. He successfully commanded the Spanish armies of the Holy Roman emperor Charles V and his son Philip II of Spain. In 1567 he was appointed governor of the Netherlands, where he set up a reign of terror to suppress Protestantism and the revolt of the Netherlands. In 1573 he was recalled at his own request. He later led a successful expedition against Portugal 1580–81.

Alvarado /ˌælvəˈrɑːdəʊ/ Pedro de c. 1485–1541. Spanish conquistador. In 1519 he accompanied Hernaándo Cortés in the conquest of Mexico. In 1523–24 he conquered Guatemala.

Alvarez /ˈælvarez/ Luis Walter 1911–1988. US physicist who led the research team that discovered the Xi-zero atomic particle 1959. He had worked on the US atom bomb project for two years, at Chicago and Los Alamos, New Mexico, during World War II. He was awarded a Nobel prize 1968.

Alvarez was professor of physics at the University of California from 1945 and an associate director of the Lawrence Livermore Radiation Laboratory 1954–59. In 1980 he was responsible for the theory that dinosaurs disappeared because a meteorite crashed into Earth 70 million years ago, producing a dust cloud that blocked out the Sun for several years, and causing dinosaurs and plants to die.

Alvárez Quintero /ˈælvˈarez kɪnˈteərəʊ/ Serafin 1871–1938 and Joaquin 1873–1945. Spanish dramatists. The brothers, born near Seville, always worked together and from 1897 produced some 200 plays, principally dealing with Andalusia. Among them are *Papá Juan: Centenario* 1909 and *Los Mosquitos* 1928.

Alwyn /ˈælwɪn/ William 1905–1985. British composer. Professor of composition at the Royal Academy of Music 1926–55, he wrote film music (*Desert Victory*, *The Way Ahead*) and composed symphonies and chamber music.

Amalia Anna 1739–1807. Duchess of Saxe-Weimar-Eisenach. As widow of Duke Ernest, she reigned 1758–75, when her son Karl August succeeded her with prudence and skill, making the court of Weimar a literary centre of Germany. She was a friend of the writers Wieland, Goethe, and Herder.

Amanullah Khan /ˌæməˈnʊlə ˈkɑːn/ 1892–1960. Emir (ruler) of Afghanistan 1919–29. Third son of Habibullah Khan, he seized the throne on his father's assassination and concluded a treaty with the British, but his policy of westernization led to rebellion 1928. Amanullah had to flee, abdicated 1929, and settled in Rome, Italy.

Amar Das /əˈmɑːdəs/ 1495–1574. Indian religious leader, third guru (teacher) of Sikhism 1552–74. He laid emphasis on equality and opposed the caste system. He initiated the custom of the *langar* (communal meal).

Amaya /əˈmaɪə/ Carmen 1913–1963. Spanish Romany dancer whose inspired and passionate style made her popular especially in Argentina. One of a family of dancers, she performed in public from the age of seven and toured the world in the following years.

Ambler /ˈæmblə/ Eric 1909– . English novelist. He used Balkan/Levant settings in the thrillers *The Mask of Dimitrios* 1939 and *Journey into Fear* 1940.

Amboise /dæm'bɔɪz/ Jacques d' 1934– . US dancer who created roles in many of George →Balanchine's greatest works as a principal dancer with New York City Ballet. He also appeared in films and TV productions, including *Seven Brides for Seven Brothers* 1954.

Ambrose, St /'æmbrəʊz/ c. 340–397. One of the early Christian leaders and theologians known as the Fathers of the Church. Feast day 7 Dec.

Born at Trèves, in S Gaul, the son of a Roman prefect, Ambrose became governor of N Italy. In 374 he was chosen bishop of Milan, although he was not yet a member of the church. He was then baptized and consecrated. He wrote many hymns, and devised the regulation of church music known as the *Ambrosian chant*, which is still used in.

Amenhotep III /a:mən'həʊtep/ King of Egypt (c. 1400 bc) who built great monuments at Thebes. His son Amenhotep IV changed his name to →Ikhnaton.

Amery /'eɪməri/ Leo(pold Stennett) 1873–1955. English Conservative politician, First Lord of the Admiralty 1922–24, secretary for the colonies 1924–29, secretary for the dominions 1925–29, and secretary of state for India and Burma (now Myanmar) 1940–45.

Ames /eɪmz/ Adelbert 1880–1955. US scientist who studied optics and the psychology of visual perception. He concluded that much of what a person sees depends on what he or she expects to see, based (consciously or unconsciously) on experience.

Amici Giovanni Batista 1786–1863. Italian botanist and microscopist who in the 1820s made a series of observations clarifying the process by which pollen fertilizes the ovule.

Amiel /'æmi'el/ Henri Frédéric 1821–1881. Swiss philosopher and writer who wrote *Journal Intime* 1882–84. Born in Geneva, he became professor of philosophy at the university there.

Truth is not only violated by falsehood; it may be outraged by silence.

Henri Frédéric Amiel, *Journal* 1856

Amies /'eɪmiz/ (Edwin) Hardy 1909– . English couturier, one of Queen Elizabeth II's dressmakers. Noted from 1934 for his tailored clothes for women, he also designed for men from 1959.

Amin (Dada) /æ'mi:n 'dɑːdɑː/ Idi 1926– . Ugandan politician, president 1971–79. He led the coup that deposed Milton Obote 1971, expelled the Asian community 1972, and exercised a reign of terror over his people. He fled to Libya when insurgent Ugandan and Tanzanian troops invaded the country 1979.

Amis /'eɪmɪs/ Kingsley 1922– . English novelist and poet. His works include *Lucky Jim* 1954, a comic portrayal of life in a provincial university, and *Take a Girl Like You* 1960. He won the UK's Booker Prize 1986 for *The Old Devils*. He is the father of Martin Amis.

It was no wonder that people were so horrible when they started life as children.

Kingsley Amis *Lucky Jim*

Amis /'eɪmɪs/ Martin 1949– . English novelist. His works are characterized by their savage wit and include *The Rachel Papers* 1974, *Money* 1984, *London Fields* 1989, and *Time's Arrow* 1991.

Ammanati Bartolomeo 1511–1592. Italian Mannerist sculptor and architect. His best known sculpture is the Fountain of Neptune in the Piazza della Signoria, Florence 1560–75. Ammanati rivalled Vasari as a Mannerist architect. He built the rusticated garden façade of the Palazzo Pitti 1560, Florence, and the graceful bridge of Sta Trinità, also in Florence, completed 1570 (destroyed 1944 but rebuilt).

Ampère /ɒm'peə/ André Marie 1775–1836. French physicist and mathematician who made many discoveries in electromagnetism and electrodynamics. He followed up the work of Hans →Oersted on the interaction between magnets and electric currents, developing a rule for determining the direction of the magnetic field associated with an electric current. The ampere is named after him.

Amundsen /'æməndsən/ Roald 1872–1928. Norwegian explorer who in 1903–06 became the first person to navigate the Northwest Passage. Beaten to the North Pole by US explorer Robert Peary 1910, he reached the South Pole ahead of Captain Scott 1911.

In 1918, Amundsen made an unsuccessful attempt to drift across the North Pole in the airship *Maud* and in 1925 tried unsuccessfully to fly from Spitsbergen, in the Arctic Ocean north of Norway, to the Pole by aeroplane. The following year he joined the Italian explorer Umberto Nobile (1885–1978) in the airship *Norge*, which circled the North Pole twice and landed in Alaska. Amundsen was killed in a plane crash over the Arctic Ocean while searching for Nobile and his airship *Italia*.

Ananda /ə'nændə/ 5th century bc. Favourite disciple of the Buddha. At his plea, a separate order was established for women. He played a major part in collecting the teachings of the Buddha after his death.

Anastasia /ænə'steɪzɪə/ 1901–1918. Russian Grand Duchess, youngest daughter of →Nicholas II. During the Russian Revolution she was presumed shot with her parents by the Bolsheviks after the Revolution of 1917, but it has been alleged that Anastasia escaped.

Those who claimed her identity included Anna Anderson (1902–1984). Alleged by some detractors to be a Pole, Franziska Schanzkowski, she was rescued from a Berlin canal 1920. The German Federal Supreme Court found no proof of her claim 1970.

Anaximander /ˌænæksɪˈmændə/ c. 610–c. 546 BC. Greek astronomer and philosopher. He claimed that the Earth was a cylinder three times wider than it is deep, motionless at the centre of the universe, and he is credited with drawing the first geographical map. He said that the celestial bodies were fire seen through holes in the hollow rims of wheels encircling the Earth. According to Anaximander, the first animals came into being from moisture and the first humans grew inside fish, emerging once fully developed.

Andersen /ˈændəsən/ Hans Christian 1805–1875. Danish writer of fairy tales, such as 'The Ugly Duckling', 'The Snow Queen', 'The Little Mermaid', and 'The Emperor's New Clothes'. A gothic inventiveness, strong sense of wonder, and a redemptive evocation of material and spiritual poverty have given these stories perennial and universal appeal; they have been translated into many languages. He also wrote adult novels and travel books.

Andersen was born the son of a shoemaker in Odense. His first children's stories were published 1835. Some are based on folklore; others are original. His other works include the novel *The Improvisatore* 1845, romances, and an autobiography *Mit Livs Eventyr* 1855 (translated 1954 as *The Tale of My Life*).

Anderson Carl David 1905–1991. US physicist who discovered the positive electron (positron) in 1932; he shared the Nobel Prize for Physics in 1936.

Carl Anderson was one of the pioneers in cosmic ray physics. He made two of the first discoveries in the field and launched what is now known as 'elementary particle physics'. The first discovery in 1932 was the positive electron or positron, a particle whose existence had been predicted by British theorist Paul Dirac. Anderson found that positrons were present in cosmic rays, energetic particles reaching Earth from outer space. For this discovery, Anderson shared the 1936 Nobel Prize for Physics with Victor Hess, the discoverer of cosmic rays. In 1937, Anderson discovered a new particle in cosmic rays, one with a mass between that of an electron and a proton. The new particle was first called a mesotron and then a meson muon. The discovery of the muon was a great step forward in physics; the muon was the first elementary particle to be discovered beyond the constituents of ordinary matter (proton, neutron, and electron). This could be said to be the birth of elementary particle physics.

Anderson /ˈændəsən/ Elizabeth Garrett 1836–1917. The first English woman to qualify in

Anderson English physician Elizabeth Garrett Anderson, the first woman to qualify in medicine in England. She established a dispensary for women in London 1866 where she instituted medical courses. Her efforts to obtain the admission of women into medicine were rewarded by the founding of the London School of Medicine for Women 1874.

medicine. Refused entry into medical school, Anderson studied privately and was licensed by the Society of Apothecaries in London 1865. She was physician to the Marylebone Dispensary for Women and Children (later renamed the Elizabeth Garrett Anderson Hospital), a London hospital now staffed by women and serving women patients.

Anderson /ˈændəsən/ Marian 1902–1993. US contralto whose voice was remarkable for its range and richness. She toured Europe 1930, but in 1939 she was barred from singing at Constitution Hall, Washington DC, because she was black. In 1955 she sang at the Metropolitan Opera, the first black singer to appear there. In 1958 she was appointed an alternate (deputizing) delegate to the United Nations.

Anderson /ˈændəsn̩/ Maxwell 1888–1959. US playwright, noted for *What Price Glory?* 1924, a realistic portrayal of the American soldier in action during World War I, co-written with Laurence Stallings. He won a Pulitzer Prize for his comedic prose satire *Both Your Houses* 1933. Most of his plays had moral and social problems as themes.

Anderson wrote numerous other plays, many in the form of verse tragedies, including *Elizabeth the Queen* 1930, *Winterset* 1935, and *Anne of the Thousand Days* 1948.

Anderson /ˈændəsən/ Sherwood 1876–1941. US writer, a member of the Chicago Group, who was encouraged by Theodore Dreiser and Carl Sandburg. He was best known for his sensitive, experimental, and poetic novels of the desperation of small-town Midwestern life, such as in his most noted work, *Winesburg, Ohio* 1919.

Andrássy /æn'dræsi/ Gyula, Count Andrássy 1823–1890. Hungarian revolutionary and states-man who supported the Dual Monarchy of Aus-tro-Hungary 1867 and was Hungary's first constitutional prime minister 1867–71. He became foreign minister of the Austro-Hungarian Empire 1871–79 and tried to halt Russian expansion into the Balkans.

André /ɑːndreɪ/ Carl 1935– . US sculptor, a Minimalist, who uses industrial materials to affirm basic formal and aesthetic principles. His *Equivalent VIII* 1976, an arrangement of bricks in Palladian proportion (Tate Gallery, London), was much criticized.

André /ændreɪ/ John 1751–1780. British army major in the American Revolution, with whom Benedict →Arnold plotted the surrender of West Point. André was caught by Washington's army, tried, and hanged as a spy.

Andrea del Sarto /ændreɪə del 'sɑːtəʊ/ (Andrea d'Agnola) 1486–1531. Italian Renaissance painter active in Florence, one of the finest portraitists and religious painters of his time. His style is serene and noble, characteristic of High Renaissance art.

He trained under Piero de Cosimo and others but was chiefly influenced by →Masaccio and →Michelangelo. In 1518 he went to work for Francis I in France and returned to Italy in 1519 with funds to enlarge the royal French art collection; he spent it on a house for himself and never went back. His pupils included Pontormo and Vasari. Del Sarto was the foremost painter in Florence after about 1510, along with Fra Bartolommeo, although he was gradually superseded by the emerging Mannerists during the 1520s. Apart from portraits, such as *A Young Man* (National Gallery, London), he painted many religious works, including the *Madonna of the Harpies* (Uffizi, Florence), an example of Classical beauty reminiscent of Raphael. He painted frescoes at Sta Annunziata and the Chiostro dello Scalzo, both in Florence.

Andreotti /ˌændri'ɒti/ Giulio 1919– . Italian Christian Democrat politician. He headed six post-war governments: 1972–73, 1976–79 (four successive terms), and 1989–92. In addition he was defence minister eight times, and foreign minister five times. He was a fervent European.

Andress /ændres/ Ursula 1936– . Swiss actress specializing in glamour leads. Her international career started with *Dr No* 1962. Other films include *She* 1965, *Casino Royale* 1967, *Red Sun* 1971, and *Clash of the Titans* 1981.

Andrew /ændruː/ (full name Andrew Albert Christian Edward) 1960– . Prince of the UK, Duke of York, second son of Queen Elizabeth II. He married Sarah Ferguson 1986; their first

daughter, Princess Beatrice, was born 1988, and their second daughter, Princess Eugenie, was born 1990. The couple separated 1992. Prince Andrew is a naval helicopter pilot.

Andrewes /ændruːz/ Lancelot 1555–1626. Church of England bishop. He helped prepare the text of the Authorized Version of the Bible, and was known for the intellectual and literary quality of his sermons.

He was also bishop of Chichester (1605), Ely (1609), and Winchester (1618).

Pilate asked, Quid est veritas? *And then some other matter took him in the head, and so up he rose and went his way before he had his answer.*

Lancelot Andrewes
Sermons: of the Resurrection

Andrews /ændruːz/ John 1813–1885. Irish chemist who conducted a series of experiments on the behaviour of carbon dioxide under varying temperature and pressure. In 1869 he introduced the idea of a critical temperature: 30.9°C in the case of carbon dioxide, beyond which no amount of pressure would liquefy the gas.

Andrews /ændruːz/ Julie. Stage name of Julia Elizabeth Wells 1935– . British-born US singer and actress. A child performer with her mother and stepfather in British music halls, she first appeared in the USA in the Broadway production *The Boy Friend* 1954. She was the original Eliza Doolittle in *My Fair Lady* 1956. In 1960 she appeared in Lerner and Loewe's *Camelot* on Broadway. Her films include *Mary Poppins* 1964, *The Americanization of Emily* 1963, *The Sound of Music* 1965, *'10'* 1980, and *Victor/Victoria* 1982.

Andrew, St /ændruː/ New Testament apostle. According to tradition, he went with John to Ephesus, preached in Scythia, and was martyred at Patras on an X-shaped cross (*St Andrew's cross*). He is the patron saint of Scotland. Feast day 30 Nov.

A native of Bethsaida, he was Simon Peter's brother. With Peter, James, and John, who worked with him as fishermen at Capernaum, he formed the inner circle of Jesus' 12 disciples.

Andreyev /æn'dreɪev/ Leonid Nicolaievich 1871–1919. Russian author. Many of his works show an obsession with death and madness, including the symbolic drama *Life of Man* 1907, the melodrama *He Who Gets Slapped* 1915, and the novels *Red Laugh* 1904 and *S.O.S.* 1919 published in Finland, where he fled after the Russian Revolution.

Andrić /ændritʃ/ Ivo 1892–1974. Yugoslav novelist and nationalist. He became a diplomat, and was ambassador to Berlin 1940. *Na Drini Ćuprija/The*

Bridge on the Drina 1945 is an epic history of a small Bosnian town. Nobel prize 1961.

He was a member of the Young Bosnia organization (another member of which shot the heir to the Austrian throne 1914), and spent World War I in an internment camp because of his political views.

Andropov /æn'drɒpɒf/ Yuri 1914–1984. Soviet communist politician, president of the USSR 1983–84. As chief of the KGB 1967–82, he established a reputation for efficiently suppressing dissent.

Andropov was politically active from the 1930s. His part in quelling the Hungarian national uprising 1956, when he was Soviet ambassador, brought him into the Communist Party secretariat 1962 as a specialist on East European affairs. He became a member of the Politburo 1973 and succeeded Brezhnev as party general secretary 1982. Elected president in 1983, he instituted economic reforms.

Angad /'æŋgæd/ 1504–1552. Indian religious leader, second guru (teacher) of Sikhism 1539–52, succeeding Nanak. He popularized the alphabet known as *Gurmukhi*, in which the Sikh scriptures are written.

Angelico /æn'dʒelɪkəʊ/ Fra (Guido di Pietro) *c.* 1400–1455. Italian painter of religious scenes, active in Florence. He was a monk and painted a series of frescoes at the monastery of San Marco, Florence, begun after 1436. He also produced several altarpieces in a simple style.

Fra Angelico joined the Dominican order about 1420. After his novitiate, he resumed a career as a painter of religious images and altarpieces, many of which have small predella scenes beneath them, depicting events in the life of a saint. The central images of the paintings are highly decorated with pastel colours and gold-leaf designs, while the predella scenes are often lively and relatively unsophisticated. There is a similar simplicity to his frescoes in the cells at San Marco, which are principally devotional works.

Fra Angelico's later fresco sequences, *Scenes from the Life of Christ* (Orvieto Cathedral) and *Scenes from the Lives of SS Stephen and Lawrence* 1440s (chapel of Nicholas V, Vatican Palace), are more elaborate.

Angell /'eɪndʒəl/ Norman 1874–1967. British writer on politics and economics. In 1910 he acquired an international reputation with his book *The Great Illusion*, which maintained that any war must prove ruinous to the victors as well as to the vanquished. Nobel Peace Prize 1933.

Angelou /'ændʒəluː/ Maya (born Marguerite Johnson) 1928– . US novelist, poet, playwright, and short-story writer. Her powerful autobiographical works, *I Know Why the Caged Bird Sings* 1970 and its three sequels, tell of the struggles towards physical and spiritual liberation of a black woman growing up in the South.

Anger /'æŋgə/ Kenneth 1929– . US avant-garde filmmaker, brought up in Hollywood. His films, which dispense with conventional narrative, often use homosexual iconography and a personal form of mysticism. They include *Fireworks* 1947, *Scorpio Rising* 1964, and *Lucifer Rising* 1973.

He wrote the exposé *Hollywood Babylon*, the original version of which was published in France in 1959.

Anglesey /'æŋgəlsi/ Henry William Paget 1768–1854. British cavalry leader during the Napoleonic wars. He was twice Lord Lieutenant of Ireland, and succeeded his father as earl of Uxbridge 1812. At the Battle of Waterloo he led a charge, losing.

Ångström /'ɒŋstrɜːm/ Anders Jonas 1814–1874. Swedish astrophysicist who worked in spectroscopy and solar physics. In 1861 Ångström identified the presence of hydrogen in the Sun. His major work *Recherches sur le spectre solaire* 1868, an atlas of solar spectra, presented the measurements of 1,000 spectral lines expressed in units of one-ten-millionth of a millimetre, the unit which later became the angstrom.

Anna Comnena /'ænə kɒm'niːnə/ 1083–after 1148. Byzantine historian, daughter of the emperor →Alexius I, who was the historian of her father's reign. After a number of abortive attempts to alter the imperial succession in favour of her husband, Nicephorus Bryennius (*c.*1062–1137), she retired to a convent to write her major work, the *Alexiad*. It describes the Byzantine view of public office, as well as the religious and intellectual life of the period.

Anne /æn/ 1665–1714. Queen of Great Britain and Ireland 1702–14. She was the second daughter of James, Duke of York, who became James II, and Anne Hyde. She succeeded William III 1702. Events of her reign include the War of the Spanish Succession, Marlborough's victories at Blenheim, Ramillies, Oudenarde, and Malplaquet, and the union of the English and Scottish parliaments 1707. Anne was succeeded by George I.

She received a Protestant upbringing, and in 1683 married Prince George of Denmark (1653–1708). Of their many children only one survived infancy, William, Duke of Gloucester (1689–1700). For the greater part of her life Anne was a close friend of Sarah Churchill (1650–1744), wife of John Churchill (1650–1722), afterwards Duke of Marlborough; the Churchills' influence helped lead her to desert her father for her brother-in-law, William of Orange, during the Revolution of 1688, and later to engage in Jacobite intrigues. Her replacement of the Tories by a Whig government 1703–04 was her own act, not due to Churchillian influence. Anne finally broke with the Marlboroughs 1710, when Mrs Masham succeeded the duchess as her favourite, and supported the Tory government of the same year.

Anne /ɑn/ (full name Anne Elizabeth Alice Louise) 1950– . Princess of the UK, second child of Queen Elizabeth II, declared Princess Royal 1987. She is an excellent horsewoman, winning a gold medal at the 1976 Olympics, and is actively involved in global charity work, especially for children. In 1973 she married Capt Mark Phillips (1949–); they separated 1989 and were divorced 1992.

Their son Peter (1977–) was the first direct descendant of the Queen not to bear a title. They also have a daughter, Zara (1981–).

When I appear in public people expect me to neigh, grind my teeth, paw the ground and swish my tail – none of which is easy.

Princess Anne Observer 1977

Anne of Austria /æn/ 1601–1666. Queen of France from 1615 and regent 1643–61. Daughter of Philip III of Spain, she married Louis XIII of France (whose chief minister, Cardinal Richelieu, worked against her). On her husband's death she became regent for their son, Louis XIV, until his majority.

She was much under the influence of Cardinal Mazarin, her chief minister, to whom she was supposed to be secretly married.

Anne of Cleves /æn/ 1515–1557. Fourth wife of →Henry VIII of England 1540. She was the daughter of the Duke of Cleves, and was recommended to Henry as a wife by Thomas →Cromwell, who wanted an alliance with German Protestantism against the Holy Roman Empire. Henry did not like her looks, had the marriage declared void after six months, pensioned her, and had Cromwell beheaded.

Anne of Denmark /æn/ 1574–1619. Queen consort of James VI of Scotland (later James I of Great Britain 1603). She was the daughter of Frederick II of Denmark and Norway, and married James 1589. Anne was suspected of Catholic leanings and was notably extravagant.

Annigoni /ænɪˈɡəʊni/ Pietro 1910–1988. Italian portrait painter whose style is influenced by Italian Renaissance portraiture. His sitters included John F Kennedy and Queen Elizabeth II, 1969 (National Portrait Gallery, London).

Anouilh /ænuːˈiː/ Jean 1910–1987. French dramatist. His plays, influenced by the Neo-Classical tradition, include *Antigone* 1942, *L'Invitation au château/Ring Round the Moon* 1947, *Colombe* 1950, and *Becket* 1959, about St Thomas à Becket and Henry II.

Anquetil /ˌɒŋkəˈtiːl/ Jacques 1934–1988. French cyclist, the first person to win the Tour de France five times (between 1957 and 1964), a record later equalled by Eddie →Merckx and Bernard →Hinault.

Anselm, St /ˈænselm/ *c.* 1033–1109. Medieval priest and philosopher. As abbot from 1078, he made the abbey of Bec in Normandy, France, a centre of scholarship in Europe. He was appointed archbishop of Canterbury by William II of England 1093, but was later forced into exile. He holds an important place in the development of Scolasticism.

As archbishop of Canterbury St Anselm was recalled from exile by Henry I, with whom he bitterly disagreed on the investiture of the clergy; a final agreement gave the king the right of temporal investiture and the clergy that of spiritual investiture.

In his *Proslogion* he developed the ontological proof of theism, which infers God's existence from our capacity to conceive of a perfect Being. His *Cur deus homo?/Why did God become Man?* treats the subject of the Atonement. Anselm was canonized 1494.

Ansermet /ɑːnseəme/ Ernest 1883–1969. Swiss conductor with Diaghilev's Russian Ballet 1914–23. In 1918 he founded the Swiss Romande Orchestra, conducting many first performances of works by →Stravinsky.

Anson /ˈænsən/ George, 1st Baron Anson 1697–1762. English admiral who sailed around the world 1740–44. In 1740 he commanded the squadron attacking the Spanish colonies and shipping in South America; he returned home by circumnavigating the world, with £500,000 of Spanish treasure. He carried out reforms at the Admiralty, which increased the efficiency of the British fleet and contributed to its success in the Seven Years' War (1756–63) against France.

Antheil /ˈɑːntaɪl/ George 1900–1959. US composer and pianist, the son of a Polish political exile. He is known for his *Ballet mécanique* 1926, scored for anvils, aeroplane propellers, electric bells, automobile horns, and pianos.

Anthony /ˈænθəni/ Susan B(rownell) 1820–1906. US pioneering campaigner for women's rights who also worked for the antislavery and temperance movements. Her causes included equality of pay for women teachers, married women's property rights, and women's suffrage. In 1869, with Elizabeth Cady →Stanton, she founded the National Woman Suffrage Association.

She edited and published a radical women's newspaper, *The Revolution* 1868–70, and worked on the *History of Woman Suffrage* 1881–86. She organized the International Council of Women and founded the International Woman Suffrage Alliance in Berlin 1904. Her profile appears on the 1979 US dollar coin.

Anthony, St /ˈæntəni/ *c.* 251–356. Also known as Anthony of Thebes. He was the founder of Christian monasticism. At the age of 20, he renounced all his possessions and began a hermetic life of study and prayer, later seeking further solitude in a cave in the desert.

Anson An engraving of the English admiral George Anson who circumnavigated the world and looted £500,000 of Spanish treasure.

Anthony was born in Egypt. In 305 he founded the first cenobitic order, a community of Christians following a rule of life under a superior. Late in his life he went to Alexandria and preached against Arianism. He lived to over 100, and a good deal is known about his life since a biography (by St Athanasius) has survived. Anthony's temptations in the desert were a popular subject in art; he is also often depicted with a pig and a bell.

Anthony of Padua, St /ˈæntəni/ 1195–1231. Portuguese Franciscan preacher who opposed the relaxations introduced into the order. Born in Lisbon, the son of a nobleman, he became an Augustinian monk, but in 1220 joined the Franciscans. Like St Francis, he is said to have preached to animals. He died in Padua, Italy and was canonized 1232.

Antigonus /ænˈtɪɡənəs/ 382–301 BC. A general of Alexander the Great, after whose death 323 Antigonus made himself master of Asia Minor. He was defeated and slain by →Seleucus I at the battle of Ipsus.

Antiochus /ænˈtaɪəkəs/ four kings of Commagene (69 BC–AD 72), affiliated to the Seleucid dynasty, including:

Antiochus IV Epiphanes 1st century AD. King of Commagene, son of Antiochus III. He was made king 38 by Caligula, who deposed him immediately. He was restored 41 by Claudius, and reigned as an ally of Rome against Parthia. He was deposed on suspicion of treason 72.

Antiochus /ænˈtaɪəkəs/ thirteen kings of Syria of the Seleucid dynasty, including:

Antiochus I /ænˈtaɪəkəs/ c. 324–c. 261 BC. King of Syria from 281 BC, son of Seleucus I, one of the generals of Alexander the Great. He earned the title of Antiochus Soter, or Saviour, by his defeat of the Gauls in Galatia 278.

Antiochus II c. 286–c. 246 BC. King of Syria 261–246 BC, son of Antiochus I. He was known as Antiochus Theos, the Divine. During his reign the eastern provinces broke away from the Graeco-Macedonian rule and set up native princes. He made peace with Egypt by marrying the daughter of Ptolemy Philadelphus, but was a tyrant among his own people.

Antiochus III the Great c. 241–187 BC. King of Syria from 223 BC, nephew of Antiochus II. He secured a loose suzerainty over Armenia and Parthia 209, overcame Bactria, received the homage of the Indian king of the Kabul valley, and returned by way of the Persian Gulf 204. He took possession of Palestine, entering Jerusalem 198. He crossed into NW Greece, but was decisively defeated by the Romans at Thermopylae 191 and at Magnesia 190. He had to abandon his domains in Anatolia, and was killed by the people of Elymais.

Antiochus IV c. 215–164 BC. King of Syria from 175 BC, known as Antiochus Epiphanes, the Illustrious; second son of Antiochus III. He occupied Jerusalem about 170, seizing much of the Temple treasure, and instituted worship of the Greek type in the Temple in an attempt to eradicate Judaism. This produced the revolt of the Hebrews under the Maccabees; Antiochus died before he could suppress it.

Antiochus VII Sidetes c. 159–129 BC. King of Syria from 138 BC. The last strong ruler of the Seleucid dynasty, he took Jerusalem 134, reducing the Maccabees to subjection, and fought successfully against the Parthians.

Antiochus XIII Asiaticus 1st century BC. King of Syria 69–65 BC, the last of the Seleucid dynasty. During his reign Syria was made a Roman province by Pompey the Great.

Antonello da Messina /ˌæntəˈneləʊ/ c. 1430–1479. Italian painter, born in Messina, Sicily, a pioneer of the technique of oil painting, which he is said to have introduced to Italy from N Europe. Flemish influence is reflected in his technique, his use of light, and sometimes in his imagery. Surviving works include bust-length portraits and sombre religious paintings.

He visited Venice in the 1470s where his work inspired, among other Venetian painters, the young Giovanni Bellini. *St Jerome in His Study* about 1460 (National Gallery, London) and *A Young Man* 1478 (Staatliche Museen, Berlin) are examples of his work.

Antonescu /ˌæntəˈnesku/ Ion 1882–1946. Romanian general and politician who headed a pro-German government during World War II and was executed for war crimes 1946.

Antoninus Pius /Æœnt´nin´s/ AD 86–161. Roman emperor who had been adopted 138 as Hadrian's heir, and succeeded him later that year. He enjoyed a prosperous reign, during which he built the Antonine Wall. His daughter married →Marcus Aurelius Antoninus.

Antonio /æn'təuniəu/ Stage name of Antonio Ruiz Soler 1922– . Spanish dancer, choreographer, and director, who toured the world with his partner Rosario. He established a National Ballet Company 1953, choreographing in a blend of classical ballet and Spanish dance, but is remembered primarily for his mesmerizing personality and dazzling technique as a soloist in pure Spanish dance.

Antonioni /æn,təuni'əuni/ Michelangelo 1912– . Italian film director, famous for his subtle presentations of neuroses and personal relationships among the leisured classes. His elliptical approach to narrative is best seen in *L'Avventura* 1959.

Beginning his career making documentaries, Antonioni directed his first feature film, *Cronaca di un Amore/Story of a Love Affair* 1950. His other films include *Blow Up* 1966, *Zabriskie Point* 1970, and *The Passenger* 1975.

Aouita /ɑːˈwiːtə/ Said 1960– . Moroccan runner. Outstanding at middle and long distances, he won the 1984 Olympic and 1987 World Championship 5,000-metres title, and has set many world records.

In 1985 he held world records at both 1,500 and 5,000 metres, the first person for 30 years to hold both. He has since broken the 2 miles, 3,000 metres, and 2,000 metres world records.

Aoun /ɑːˈuːn/ Michel 1935– . Lebanese soldier and Maronite Christian politician, president 1988–90. As commander of the Lebanese army, he was made president without Muslim support, his appointment precipitating a civil war between Christians and Muslims. His unwillingness to accept a 1989 Arab League-sponsored peace agreement increased his isolation until the following year when he surrendered to military pressure. He left the country 1991 and was pardoned by the new government the same year.

Aoun, born in Beirut, joined the Lebanese army and rose to become, in 1984, its youngest commander. When, in 1988, the Christian and Muslim communities failed to agree on a Maronite successor to the outgoing president Amin Gemayel (as required by the constitution), Gemayel unilaterally appointed Aoun. This precipitated the creation of a rival Muslim government, and, eventually, a civil war. Aoun, dedicated to freeing his country from Syrian domination, became isolated in the presidential palace and staunchly opposed the 1989 peace plan worked out by parliamentarians under the auspices of the Arab League. After defying the government led by Prime Minister Selim al-Hoss in the face of strong military opposition, in Oct 1990 Aoun sought political asylum in the French embassy, and in 1991 left Lebanon for exile in France. He obtained a pardon from the Lebanese government the same year.

Apelles 4th century BC. Greek painter, said to have been the greatest in antiquity. He was court painter to Philip of Macedonia and his son Alexander the Great. None of his work survives, only descriptions of his portraits and nude Venuses.

Apollinaire /əˌpɒlɪˈneə/ Guillaume. Pen name of Guillaume Apollinaire de Kostrowitsky 1880–1918. French poet of aristocratic Polish descent. He was a leader of the avant-garde in Parisian literary and artistic circles. His novel *Le Poète assassiné/The Poet Assassinated* 1916, followed by the experimental poems *Alcools/Alcohols* 1913 and *Calligrammes/Word Pictures* 1918, show him as a representative of the Cubist and Futurist movements.

Born in Rome and educated in Monaco, Apollinaire went to Paris in 1898. His work greatly influenced younger French writers, such as Louis →Aragon. He coined the word *surrealism* to describe his play *Les Mamelles de Tirésias/The Breasts of Tiresias* 1917.

Memories are hunting horns whose sound dies on the wind.

Guillaume Apollinaire *Cors de Chasse*

Apollonius of Perga /ˌæpəˈləuniəs/ c. 260–c. 190 BC. Greek mathematician, called 'the Great Geometer'. In his work *Conic Sections* he showed that a plane intersecting a cone will generate an ellipse, a parabola, or a hyperbola, depending on the angle of intersection. In astronomy, he used a system of circles called epicycles and deferents to explain the motion of the planets; this system, as refined by Ptolemy, was used until the Renaissance.

Apollonius of Rhodes /ˌæpəˈləuniəs/ c. 220–180 BC. Greek poet, author of the epic *Argonautica*, which tells the story of Jason and the Argonauts and their quest for the Golden Fleece.

Apollonius of Tyana early 1st century AD. Greek ascetic philosopher of the Neo-Pythagorean school. He travelled in Babylonia and India, where he acquired a wide knowledge of oriental religions and philosophies, and taught at Ephesus. He was said to have had miraculous powers but claimed only that he could see the future.

Appel /æpəl/ Karel 1921– . Dutch painter and sculptor, founder of **Cobra** 1948, a group of European abstract painters.

Appert /æˈpeə/ Nicolas 1750–1841. French pioneer of food preservation by canning. He devised a system of sealing food in glass bottles and subjecting it to heat. His book *L'Art de conserver les substances animales et végétales* appeared in 1810. Shortly after, others applied the same principles to iron or sheet steel containers plated with tin.

Appleton /ˈæpəltən/ Edward Victor 1892–1965. British physicist who worked at Cambridge under Ernest →Rutherford from 1920. He proved the existence of the Kennelly–Heaviside layer (now called the E layer) in the atmosphere, and the Appleton layer beyond it, and was involved in the initial work on the atom bomb. Nobel prize 1947.

Apuleius /ˌæpjuˈliːəs/ Lucius lived *c.* AD 160. Roman lawyer, philosopher, and author of *Metamorphoses*, or *The Golden Ass*.

Aquaviva /ˌækwəˈviːvə/ Claudius (Claudio) 1543–1615. Fifth general of the Roman Catholic monastic order of Jesuits. Born in Naples, of noble family, he entered the order in 1567 and became its head in 1581. Under his rule they greatly increased in numbers, and the revolt of the Spanish Jesuits was put down. He published a treatise on education.

Aquinas /əˈkwaɪnəs/ St Thomas *c.* 1226–1274. Neapolitan philosopher and theologian, the greatest figure of the school of Scholasticism. He was a Dominican monk, known as the 'Angelic Doctor'. In 1879 his works were recognized as the basis of Catholic theology. His *Summa contra Gentiles/Against the Errors of the Infidels* 1259–64 argues that reason and faith are compatible. He assimilated the philosophy of Aristotle into Christian doctrine.

His unfinished *Summa Theologica*, begun 1265, deals with the nature of God, morality, and the work of Jesus. His works embodied the world view taught in universities until the mid-17th century, and include scientific ideas derived from Aristotle.

Aquino /əˈkiˈnəʊ/ (Maria) Corazon (born Cojuangco) 1933– . President of the Philippines 1986–92. She was instrumental in the nonviolent overthrow of President Ferdinand Marcos 1986. As president, she sought to rule in a conciliatory manner, but encountered opposition from left (communist guerrillas) and right (army coup attempts), and her land reforms were seen as inadequate.

The daughter of a sugar baron, she studied in the USA and in 1956 married the politician Benigno Aquino (1933–1983). The chief political opponent of the right-wing president Marcos, he was assassinated by a military guard at Manila airport on his return from exile. Corazon Aquino was drafted by the opposition to contest the Feb 1986 presidential election and claimed victory over Marcos, accusing the government of ballot-rigging. She led a nonviolent 'people's power' campaign, which overthrew Marcos 25 Feb. A devout Roman Catholic, Aquino enjoyed strong church backing in her 1986 campaign. The USA

provided strong support as well and was instrumental in turning back a 1989 coup attempt. In 1991 she announced she would not enter the 1992 presidential elections.

Arafat /ˈærəfæt/ Yassir 1929– . Palestinian nationalist politician, cofounder of al-Fatah 1956 and president of the Palestine Liberation Organization (PLO) from 1969. His support for Saddam Hussein after Iraq's invasion of Kuwait 1990 weakened his international standing, but he has since been influential in Middle East peace talks.

In the 1970s Arafat's activities in pursuit of an independent homeland for Palestinians made him a prominent figure in world politics, but in the 1980s the growth of factions within the PLO effectively reduced his power. He was forced to evacuate Lebanon 1983, but remained leader of most of the PLO and in 1990 persuaded it to recognize formally the state of Israel. In 1992 he narrowly escaped injury when his aircraft was forced to land in a sand storm.

Arago /ˌærəˈgəʊ/ Dominique 1786–1853. French physicist and astronomer who made major contributions to the early study of electromagnetism. In 1820 he found that iron enclosed in a wire coil could be magnetized by the passage of an electric current. Later, in 1824, he was the first to observe the ability of a floating copper disc to deflect a magnetic needle, the phenomenon of magnetic rotation.

Aragon /ˌærəˈgɒn/ Louis 1897–1982. French poet and novelist. Beginning as a Dadaist, he became one of the leaders of Surrealism, published volumes of verse, and in 1930 joined the Communist party. Taken prisoner in World War II, he escaped to join the Resistance; his experiences are reflected in the poetry of *Le Crève-coeur* 1942 and *Les Yeux d'Elsa* 1944.

The function of genius is to furnish cretins with ideas twenty years later.

Louis Aragon
'Le Porte-Plume'
Traité du Style 1928

Aram /ˈærəm/ Eugene 1704–1759. British murderer, the subject of works by the novelist Bulwer Lytton, the poet Thomas Hood, and others.

He was a schoolmaster in Knaresborough, Yorkshire, and achieved some distinction as a philologist. In 1745 he was tried and acquitted on a charge concerned with the disappearance of a local shoemaker. Several years later he was arrested in Lynn, Norfolk, following the discovery of a skeleton in a cave at Knaresborough. He was tried at York, confessed to the murder after his conviction, and was hanged.

Archer English champion jockey Frederick Archer. The foremost jockey of his day, Archer's record of 246 winners in a single season remained until 1933.

Arany /ɒrɒni/ János 1817–1882. Hungarian writer. His comic epic *The Lost Constitution* 1846 was followed in 1847 by *Toldi*, a product of the popular nationalist school. In 1864 his epic masterpiece *The Death of King Buda* appeared. During his last years Arany produced the rest of the *Toldi* trilogy, and his most personal lyrics.

Arbenz Guzmán /ɑːbens gʊsˈmæn/ Jácobo 1913–1971. Guatemalan social democratic politician and president from 1951 until his overthrow 1954 by rebels operating with the help of the US Central Intelligence Agency.

Guzmán brought in policies to redistribute land, much of which was owned by overseas companies, to landless peasants; he also encouraged labour organization. His last years were spent in exile in Mexico, Uruguay, and Cuba.

Arbuckle /ɑːbʌkəl/ Fatty (Roscoe Conkling) 1887–1933. US silent-film comedian; also a writer and director. His successful career in such films as *The Butcher Boy* 1917 and *The Hayseed* 1919 ended in 1921 after a sex-party scandal in which a starlet died. Although acquitted, he was spurned by the public and his films were banned.

Arbuthnot /ɑːbʌθnət/ John 1667–1735. Scottish writer and physician, attendant on Queen Anne 1705–14. He was a friend of Alexander Pope, Thomas Gray, and Jonathan Swift and was the chief author of the satiric *Memoirs of Martinus Scriblerus*. He created the English national character of John Bull, a prosperous farmer, in his *History of John Bull* 1712, pamphlets advocating peace with France.

Arch /ɑːtʃ/ Joseph 1826–1919. English Radical member of Parliament and trade unionist, founder of the National Agricultural Union (the first of its

kind) 1872. He was born in Warwickshire, the son of an agricultural labourer. Entirely self-taught, he became a Methodist preacher, and was Liberal-Labour MP for NW Norfolk.

Joseph Arch started work at the age of nine, and travelled all over England for 40 years as an agricultural labourer. Appalled at the miserable conditions, he grew to hate the rural elite and became politically active, first as a trade unionist and later as an MP.

Archer /ɑːtʃə/ Frederick 1857–1886. English jockey. He rode 2,748 winners in 8,084 races 1870–86, including 21 classic winners.

He won the Derby five times, Oaks four times, St Leger six times, the Two Thousand Guineas four times, and the One Thousand Guineas twice. He rode 246 winners in the 1885 season, a record that stood until 1933 (see Gordon →Richards). Archer shot himself in a fit of depression.

Archer /ɑːtʃə/ Jeffrey 1940– . English writer and politician. A Conservative member of Parliament 1969–74, he lost a fortune in a disastrous investment, but recouped it as a best-selling novelist and dramatist. His books include *Not a Penny More, Not a Penny Less* 1975 and *First Among Equals* 1984. In 1985 he became deputy chair of the Conservative Party but resigned Nov 1986 after a scandal involving an alleged payment to a prostitute.

Archimedes /ˌɑːkɪˈmiːdiːz/ c. 287–212 BC. Greek mathematician who made major discoveries in geometry, hydrostatics, and mechanics. He formulated a law of fluid displacement (Archimedes' principle), and is credited with the invention of the Archimedes screw, a cylindrical device for raising water.

He was born at Syracuse in Sicily. It is alleged that Archimedes' principle was discovered when he stepped into the public bath and saw the water overflow. He was so delighted that he rushed home naked, crying 'Eureka! Eureka!' ('I have found it! I have found it!') He used his discovery to prove that the goldsmith of the king of Syracuse had adulterated a gold crown with silver. Archimedes designed engines of war for the defence of Syracuse, and was killed when the Romans besieged the town.

Give me where to stand and I will move the Earth.

Archimedes
quoted in Pappus *Collection c.* 300 AD

Archipenko /ˌɑːkɪˈpeŋkəʊ/ Alexander 1887–1964. Ukrainian-born abstract sculptor who lived in France from 1908 and in the USA from 1923. He pioneered Cubist works composed of angular forms and spaces and later experimented with clear plastic and sculptures incorporating lights.

Arden /ɑːdn/ John 1930– . English playwright. His early plays *Serjeant Musgrave's Dance* 1959 and *The Workhouse Donkey* 1963 show the influence of Brecht. Subsequent works, often written in collaboration with his wife, Margaretta D'Arcy, show increasing concern with the political situation in Northern Ireland and a dissatisfaction with the professional and subsidized theatre world.

Arendt /ɑːrənt/ Hannah 1906–1975. German-born US scholar and political scientist. With the rise of the Nazis, she moved to Paris and emigrated to the USA 1940. Her works include *The Origins of Modern Totalitarianism* 1951, *The Human Condition* 1958, *On Revolution* 1963, *Eichmann in Jerusalem* 1963, and *On Violence* 1972.

Aretino /ˌærəˈtiːnəʊ/ Pietro 1492–1556. Italian writer. He earned his living, both in Rome and Venice, by publishing satirical pamphlets while under the protection of a highly placed family. His *Letters* 1537–57 are a unique record of the cultural and political events of his time, and illustrate his vivacious, exuberant character. He also wrote poems and comedies.

Aretino began as a protégé of Pope Leo X, but left Rome after the publication of his lewd verses. He settled in Venice, and quickly became known as the 'Scourge of Princes' with his vicious satires on powerful contemporaries; he was also well paid for not taking up his pen.

Anger represents a certain power when a great mind, prevented from executing its own generous desires, is moved by it.

Pietro Aretino
letter to Girolamo Quirini Nov 1537

Arevalo Bermejo /əˈrevələʊ bɜːˈmeɪx/ Juan José 1904–1990. Guatemalan president 1945–51, elected to head a civilian government after a popular revolt ended a 14-year period of military rule. However, many of his liberal reforms were later undone by subsequent military rulers.

Argentina, La /aːxenˈtiːnə/ Stage name of Antonia Merce 1890–1936. Spanish dancer, choreographer, and director. She took her artistic name from the land of her birth. She toured the world and revolutionized the technique of castanet playing.

Argyll /ɑːˈgaɪl/ line of Scottish peers who trace their descent to the Campbells of Lochow. The earldom dates from 1457. They include:

Argyll /ɑːˈgaɪl/ Archibald Campbell, 5th Earl of Argyll 1530–1573. Adherent of the Scottish presbyterian John →Knox. A supporter of Mary Queen of Scots from 1561, he commanded her forces after her escape from Lochleven Castle 1568. He revised his position and became Lord High Chancellor of Scotland 1572.

Arias Sanchez /ɑːriəs ˈsæntʃes/ Oscar 1940– . Costa Rican politician, president 1986–90, secretary general of the left-wing National Liberation Party (PLN) from 1979. He advocated a neutralist policy and in 1987 was the leading promoter of the Central American Peace Plan. He lost the presidency to Rafael Angel Caldéron 1990. He was awarded the Nobel Peace Prize 1987.

Ariosto /ˌæriˈɒstəʊ/ Ludovico 1474–1533. Italian poet who wrote Latin poems and comedies on Classical lines, including the poem *Orlando Furioso* 1516, published 1532, an epic treatment of the *Roland* story, the perfect poetic expression of the Italian Renaissance.

Ariosto was born in Reggio, and joined the household of Cardinal Ippolito d'Este 1503. He was frequently engaged in ambassadorial missions and diplomacy for the Duke of Ferrara. In 1521 he became governor of a province in the Apennines, and after three years retired to Ferrara, where he died.

Aristarchus of Samos /ˌærɪˈstɑːkəs/ *c.* 280–264 BC. Greek astronomer. The first to argue that the Earth moves around the Sun, he was ridiculed for his beliefs. He was also the first astronomer to estimate the sizes of the Sun and Moon and their distances from the Earth.

His only surviving work is *Magnitudes and Distances of the Sun and Moon*, although Archimedes quotes from another tract that no longer exists. Aristarchus produced methods for finding the relative distances of the Sun and Moon that were geometrically correct but rendered useless by inaccuracies in observation.

Aristide /ˌærɪˈstiːd/ Jean-Bertrand 1953– . President of Haiti Dec 1990–Oct 1991. A left-wing Catholic priest opposed to the right-wing regime of the Duvalier family, he campaigned for the National Front for Change and Democracy, representing a loose coalition of peasants, trade unionists, and clerics, and won 70% of the vote. He was deposed by the military Sept 1991.

Aristides /ˌærɪˈstaɪdiːz/ *c.* 530–468 BC. Athenian politician. He was one of the ten Athenian generals at the battle of Marathon 490 BC and was elected chief archon, or magistrate. Later he came into conflict with the democratic leader Themistocles, and was exiled about 483 BC. He returned to fight against the Persians at Salamis 480 BC and in the following year commanded the Athenians at Plataea.

He was sent into political exile 482 BC because the citizens tired of hearing him praised as 'Aristides the Just', probably derived from his just assessment of the contribution to be paid by the Greek states who entered the Delian league against the Persians.

Aristippus /ˌærɪˈstɪpəs/ *c.* 435–356 BC. Greek philosopher, founder of the Cyrenaic or hedonist school. A pupil of Socrates, he developed the doctrine that pleasure is the highest good in life. He lived at the court of Dionysius of Syracuse and then with Laïs, a courtesan, in Corinth.

Arkwright *The English inventor Richard Arkwright, painted at the studio of Joseph Wright 1790. Arkwright designed a water-driven spinning frame and utilized water and steam to power his factories.*

Aristophanes /ærɪ'stɒfəniːz/ *c.* 448–380 BC. Greek comedic dramatist. Of his 11 extant plays (of a total of over 40), the early comedies are remarkable for the violent satire with which he ridiculed the democratic war leaders. He also satirized contemporary issues such as the new learning of Socrates in *The Clouds* 423 BC and the power of women in *Lysistrata* 411 BC. The chorus plays a prominent role, frequently giving the play its title, as in *The Wasps* 422 BC, *The Birds* 414 BC, and *The Frogs* 405 BC.

Aristotle /ˈærɪstɒtl/ 384–322 BC. Greek philosopher who advocated reason and moderation. He maintained that sense experience is our only source of knowledge, and that by reasoning we can discover the essences of things, that is, their distinguishing qualities. In his works on ethics and politics, he suggested that human happiness consists in living in conformity with nature. He derived his political theory from the recognition that mutual aid is natural to humankind, and refused to set up any one constitution as universally ideal. Of Aristotle's works some 22 treatises survive, dealing with logic, metaphysics, physics, astronomy, meteorology, biology, psychology, ethics, politics, and literary criticism.

Born in Stagira in Thrace, he studied in Athens, became tutor to →Alexander the Great, and in 335 BC opened a school in the Lyceum (grove sacred to Apollo) in Athens. It became known as the 'peripatetic school' because he walked up and down as he talked, and his works are a collection of his lecture notes. When Alexander died, Aristotle was forced to flee to Chalcis, where he died. Among his many contributions to political thought were the first systematic attempts to distinguish between different forms of government, ideas about the role of law in the state, and the conception of a science of politics.

In the Middle Ages, Aristotle's philosophy first became the foundation of Islamic philosophy, and was then incorporated into Christian theology; medieval scholars tended to accept his vast output without question. Aristotle held that all matter consisted of a single 'prime matter', which was always determined by some form. The simplest kinds of matter were the four elements – earth, water, air, and fire – which in varying proportions constituted all things. Aristotle saw nature as always striving to perfect itself, and first classified organisms into species and genera.

The principle of life he termed a soul, which he regarded as the form of the living creature, not as a substance separable from it. The intellect, he believed, can discover in sense impressions the universal, and since the soul thus transcends matter, it must be immortal. Art embodies nature, but in a more perfect fashion, its end being the purifying and ennobling of the affections. The essence of beauty is order and symmetry.

Man is by nature a political animal.

Aristotle *Politics*

Arius /ˈɛəriəs/ *c.* 256–336. Egyptian priest whose ideas gave rise to Arianism, a Christian belief which denied the complete divinity of Jesus.

He was born in Libya, and became a priest in Alexandria 311. In 318 he was excommunicated and fled to Palestine, but his theology spread to such an extent that the emperor Constantine called a council at Nicaea 325 to resolve the question. Arius and his adherents were condemned and banished.

Arkwright /ˈɑːkraɪt/ Richard 1732–1792. English inventor and manufacturing pioneer who developed a machine for spinning cotton (he called it a 'spinning frame') 1768. He set up a water-powered spinning factory 1771 and installed steam power in another factory 1790.

Arkwright was born in Preston and experimented in machine designing with a watchmaker, John Kay of Warrington (1704–1780), until, with Kay and John Smalley (died 1782), he set up the 'spinning frame'. Soon afterwards he moved to Nottingham to escape the fury of the spinners, who feared that their handicraft skills would become redundant. In 1771 he went into partnership with Jebediah Strutt (1726–1797), a Derby man who had improved the stocking frame, and Samuel Need (died 1781), and built a water-powered factory at Cromford in Derbyshire. Steam power was used in his Nottingham works from 1790. This was part of the first phase of the Industrial Revolution.

Arlen /ˈɑːlən/ Michael. Adopted name of Dikran Kuyumjian 1895–1956. Bulgarian novelist of Armenian descent who became a naturalized British subject 1922. His wrote *The Green Hat* 1924, the cynical story of a *femme fatale*.

Armani /ɑːˈmɑːni/ Giorgio 1935– . Italian fashion designer. He launched his first menswear collection 1974 and the following year started designing women's clothing. His work is known for understated styles, precise tailoring, and fine fabrics. He designs for young men and women under the Emporio label.

Arminius /ɑːˈmɪniəs/ 17 BC–21 AD. German chieftain. An ex-soldier of the Roman army, he annihilated a Roman force led by Varus in the Teutoburger Forest area AD 9, and saved Germany from becoming a Roman province. He thus ensured that the empire's frontier did not extend beyond the Rhine.

Arminius /ɑːˈmɪniəs/ Jacobus. Latinized name of Jakob Harmensen 1560–1609. Dutch Protestant priest who founded Arminianism, a school of Christian theology opposed to Calvin's doctrine of predestination. His views were developed by Simon Episcopius (1583–1643). Arminianism is the basis of Wesleyan Methodism.

He was born in S Holland, ordained in Amsterdam 1588, and from 1603 was professor of theology at Leyden. He asserted that forgiveness and eternal life are bestowed on all who repent of their sins and sincerely believe in Jesus Christ. He was drawn into many controversies, and his followers were expelled from the church and persecuted.

Armstrong /ˈɑːmstrɒŋ/ Edwin Howard 1890–1954. US radio engineer who developed a system known as superheterodyne tuning for reception over a very wide spectrum of radio frequencies and frequency modulation for static-free reception.

Armstrong /ˈɑːmstrɒŋ/ Henry. Born Henry Jackson, nicknamed 'Homicide Hank' 1912–1988. US boxer. He was the only man to hold world titles at three different weights simultaneously. Between May and Nov 1938 he held the feather-, welter-, and lightweight titles. He retired in 1945 and became a Baptist minister.

Armstrong /ˈɑːmstrɒŋ/ Louis ('Satchmo') 1901–1971. US jazz cornet and trumpet player and singer. His Chicago recordings in the 1920s with the Hot Five and Hot Seven brought him recognition for his warm and pure trumpet tone, his skill at improvisation, and his quirky, gravelly voice. From the 1930s he also appeared in films.

Armstrong was born in New Orleans. In 1923 he joined the Creole Jazz Band led by the cornet player Joe 'King' Oliver (1885–1938) in Chicago,

but soon broke away and fronted various bands of his own. In 1947 he formed the Louis Armstrong All-Stars. He firmly established the pre-eminence of the virtuoso jazz soloist. He is also credited with the invention of scat singing (vocalizing meaningless syllables chosen for their sound).

Armstrong /ˈɑːmstrɒŋ/ Neil Alden 1930– . US astronaut. In 1969, he became the first person to set foot on the Moon, and said, 'That's one small step for a man, one giant leap for mankind.' The Moon landing was part of the Apollo project.

Born in Ohio, he gained his pilot's licence at 16, and served as a naval pilot in Korea 1949–52 before joining NASA as a test pilot. He was selected to be an astronaut 1962 and landed on the Moon 20 July 1969.

Armstrong /ˈɑːmstrɒŋ/ Robert, Baron Armstrong of Ilminster 1927– . British civil servant, cabinet secretary in Margaret Thatcher's government. He achieved notoriety as a key witness in the *Spycatcher* trial in Australia 1987. Defending the British Government's attempts to prevent Peter Wright's book alleging 'dirty tricks' from being published, he admitted to having sometimes been 'economical with the truth'. He retired 1988 and was made a life peer.

After Oxford University he joined the civil service and rose rapidly to deputy-secretary rank. In 1970 he became Prime Minister Edward Heath's principal private secretary; Thatcher later made him cabinet secretary and head of the home civil service.

Armstrong /ˈɑːmstrɒŋ/ William George 1810–1900. English engineer who developed a revolutionary method of making gun barrels 1855, by building a breech-loading artillery piece with a steel and wrought-iron barrel (previous guns were muzzle-loaded and had cast-bronze barrels). By 1880 the 150 mm/16 in Armstrong gun was the standard for all British ordnance.

Arnauld /ɑːˈnəʊ/ French family closely associated with Jansenism, a Christian church movement that began in the 17th century. *Antoine Arnauld* (1560–1619) was a Parisian advocate, strongly critical of the Jesuits; along with the philosopher Pascal and others, he produced not only Jansenist pamphlets, but works on logic, grammar, and geometry. Many of his 20 children were associated with the abbey of Port Royal, a convent of Cistercian nuns near Versailles which became the centre of Jansenism. His youngest child, *Antoine* (1612–1694), the 'great Arnauld', was religious director there.

For years the elder Antoine had to live in hiding, and the last 16 years of his life were spent in Brussels. At Port Royal his second daughter, *Angélique* (1591–1661), became abbess at the age of 11 through her father's influence. Later she served as prioress under her sister **Agnes** (1593–1671); her niece, **la Mère Angélique** (1624–1684), succeeded to both positions.

Arne /ɑːn/ Thomas Augustus 1710–1778. English composer, whose musical drama *Alfred* 1740 includes the song 'Rule Britannia!'.

Arnim /ɑːnɪm/ Ludwig Achim von 1781–1831. German Romantic poet and novelist. Born in Berlin, he wrote short stories, a romance (*Gräfin Dolores/Countess Dolores* 1810), and plays, but left the historical novel *Die Kronenwächter* 1817 unfinished. With Clemens Brentano he collected the German folk songs in *Des Knaben Wunderhorn/The Boy's Magic Horn* 1805–08.

Arnold /ɑːnld/ Benedict 1741–1801. US soldier and military strategist who, during the American Revolution, won the turning point battle at Saratoga 1777 for the Americans. He is chiefly remembered as a traitor to the American side. A merchant in New Haven, Connecticut, he joined the colonial forces but in 1780 plotted to betray the strategic post at West Point to the British.

Arnold was bitter at having been passed over for promotion, and he contacted Henry Clinton to propose defection. Major André was sent by the British to discuss terms with him, but was caught and hanged as a spy. Arnold escaped to the British, who gave him an army command.

Arnold /ɑːnld/ Edwin 1832–1904. English scholar and poet. He wrote the *Light of Asia* 1879, a rendering of the life and teaching of the Buddha in blank verse. *The Light of the World* 1891 retells the life of Jesus.

Arnold /ɑːnld/ Malcolm (Henry) 1921– . English composer. His work is tonal and includes a large amount of orchestral, chamber, ballet, and vocal music. His operas include *The Dancing Master* 1951, and he has written music for more than 80 films, including *The Bridge on the River Kwai* 1957, for which he won an Academy Award.

Arnold /ɑːnld/ Matthew 1822–1888. English poet and critic. His poems, characterized by their elegiac mood and pastoral themes, include *The Forsaken Merman* 1849, *Thyrsis* 1867 (commemorating his friend Arthur Hugh Clough), *Dover Beach* 1867, and *The Scholar Gypsy* 1853. Arnold's critical works include *Essays in Criticism* 1865 and 1888, and *Culture and Anarchy* 1869, which attacks 19th-century philistinism.

The son of Thomas Arnold, he was educated at public schools and Oxford University. After a short spell as an assistant master at Rugby, Arnold became a school inspector 1851–86. He published two unsuccessful volumes of anonymous poetry, but two further publications under his own name 1853 and 1855 led to his appointment as professor of poetry at Oxford. Arnold first used the word 'philistine' in its present sense in his attack on the cultural values of the middle classes.

Arnold /ɑːnld/ Thomas 1795–1842. English schoolmaster, father of the poet and critic Matthew Arnold. He was headmaster of Rugby School 1828–42. His regime has been graphically described in Thomas Hughes's *Tom Brown's Schooldays* 1857. He emphasized training of character, and had a profound influence on public school education.

Arnold of Brescia /ɑːnld, 'breʃə/ 1100–1155. Italian Augustinian monk, who attacked the holding of property by the Catholic church; he was hanged and burned, and his ashes thrown into the Tiber river.

Arp /ɑːp/ Hans or Jean 1887–1966. French abstract painter and sculptor. He was one of the founders of the rebellious and disillusioned Dada movement about 1917, and later was associated with the Surrealists. His innovative wood sculptures use organic shapes in bright colours.

In his early experimental works, such as collages, he collaborated with his wife *Sophie Taeuber-Arp* (1889–1943).

Arrau /əˈraʊ/ Claudio 1903–1991. Chilean pianist. A concert performer from the age of five, he specialized in 19th-century music and was known for his thoughtful interpretation.

Arrhenius /əˈreɪnɪəs/ Svante August 1859–1927. Swedish scientist, the founder of physical chemistry. Born near Uppsala, he became a professor at Stockholm in 1895, and made a special study of electrolysis. He wrote *Worlds in the Making* and *Destinies of the Stars*, and in 1903 received the Nobel Prize for Chemistry. In 1905 he predicted global warming as a result of carbon dioxide emission from burning fossil fuels.

Artaud /ɑːˈtəʊ/ Antonin 1896–1948. French theatre director. Although his play, *Les Cenci/The Cenci* 1935, was a failure, his concept of the *Theatre of Cruelty*, intended to release feelings usually repressed in the unconscious, has been an important influence on modern dramatists such as Albert Camus and Jean Genet and on directors and producers. Declared insane 1936, Artaud was confined in an asylum.

Arthur /ɑːθə/ 6th century AD. Legendary British king and hero in stories of Camelot and the quest for the Holy Grail. Arthur is said to have been born in Tintagel, Cornwall, and buried in Glastonbury, Somerset. He may have been a Romano-Celtic leader against pagan Saxon invaders.

The legends of Arthur and the knights of the Round Table were developed in the 12th century by Geoffrey of Monmouth, Chrétien de Troyes, and the Norman writer Wace. Later writers on the theme include the anonymous author of *Sir Gawayne and the Greene Knight* 1346, Thomas Malory, Tennyson, T H White, and Mark Twain.

Arthur /ɑːθə/ Chester Alan 1830–1886. 21st president of the USA 1881–85, a Republican. In 1880 he was chosen as James →Garfield's vice president, and was his successor when Garfield was assassinated the following year.

He was born in Vermont, the son of a Baptist minister, and became a lawyer and Republican political appointee in New York.

Arthur During his term as the USA's 21st president, Chester Arthur became a determined enemy of the corrupt use of patronage to gain political support. Prior to his selection as Garfield's vice-presidential running mate, Arthur had headed an eminent law firm and was the leader of the Republican Party in New York State.

Arthur /ˈɑːθə/ Duke of Brittany 1187–1203. Grandson of Henry II of England and nephew of King →John, who is supposed to have had him murdered, 13 April 1203, as a rival for the crown.

Arthur /ˈɑːθə/ Prince of Wales 1486–1502. Eldest son of Henry VII of England. He married →Catherine of Aragon 1501, when he was 16 and she was 15, but died the next year.

Arundel /ˈærəndl/ Thomas Howard, 2nd Earl of Arundel 1586–1646. English politician and patron of the arts. The Arundel Marbles, part of his collection of Italian sculptures, were given to Oxford University in 1667 by his grandson.

Ascham /ˈæskəm/ Roger c. 1515–1568. English scholar and royal tutor, author of *The Scholemaster* 1570 on the art of education.

After writing a treatise on archery, King Henry VIII's favourite sport, Ascham was appointed tutor to Princess Elizabeth in 1548. He retained favour under Edward VI and Queen Mary (despite his Protestant views), and returned to Elizabeth's service as her secretary after she became queen.

Ashbee /ˈæʃbi/ Charles Robert 1863–1942. British designer, architect, and writer, one of the major figures of the Arts and Crafts movement. He founded a Guild and School of Handicraft in the East End of London in 1888, but later modified his views, accepting the importance of machinery and design for industry.

He based his ideas on the social function of art from the writings of William →Morris and John →Ruskin. His Guild and School of Handicraft (later moved to Chipping Campden, Gloucestershire) aimed to achieve high standards in craftwork and quality of life, which were both threatened by the onset of mass production. At its peak, the guild employed over 100 craftworkers.

Ashbery John 1927– . US poet and art critic. His collections of poetry – including *Self-Portrait in a Convex Mirror* 1975, which won a Pulitzer prize – are distinguished by their strong visual element and narrative power. Other volumes include *Some Trees* 1956, *As We Know* 1979, and *Shadow Train* 1981.

Ashcroft /ˈæʃkrɒft/ Peggy 1907–1991. English actress. Her Shakespearean roles included Desdemona in *Othello* (with Paul Robeson) and Juliet in *Romeo and Juliet* 1935 (with Laurence Olivier and John Gielgud), and she appeared in the British TV play *Caught on a Train* 1980 (BAFTA award), the series *The Jewel in the Crown* 1984, and the film *A Passage to India* 1985.

She was born in Croydon, Surrey, where a theatre is named after her.

Ashdown /ˈæʃdaʊn/ Paddy (Jeremy John Durham) 1941– . English politician, leader of the merged Social and Liberal Democrats from 1988. He served in the Royal Marines as a commando, leading a Special Boat Section in Borneo, and was a member of the Diplomatic Service 1971–76. He became a Liberal member of Parliament 1983. His constituency is Yeovil, Somerset.

Ashe /æʃ/ Arthur Robert, Jr 1943–1993. US tennis player and coach. He won the US national men's singles title at Forest Hills and the first US Open 1968. Known for his exceptionally strong serve, Ashe turned professional 1969. He won the Australian men's title 1970 and Wimbledon 1975. Cardiac problems ended his playing career 1979, but he continued his involvement with the sport as captain of the US Davis Cup team.

Ashford /ˈæʃfəd/ Daisy 1881–1972. English author of *The Young Visiters* 1919, a classic of unconscious humour written when she was nine.

Ashkenazy /ˌæʃkəˈnɑːzi/ Vladimir 1937– . Russian-born pianist and conductor. His keyboard technique differs slightly from standard Western technique. In 1962 he was joint winner of the Tchaikovsky Competition with John Ogdon. He excels in Rachmaninov, Prokofiev, and Liszt.

After studying in Moscow, he toured the USA in 1958. He settled in England in 1963 and moved to Iceland in 1968. He was musical director of the Royal Philharmonic, London, from 1987.

Asquith British Liberal politician Herbert Asquith, caricatured by 'Spy', the pseudonym of Leslie Ward (1851–1922). Asquith introduced old-age pensions, and became prime minister 1908.

Ashley /ˈæʃli/ Laura (born Mountney) 1925–1985. Welsh designer who established and gave her name to a Neo-Victorian country style in clothes and furnishings manufactured by her company from 1953. She founded an international chain of shops.

Ashmole /ˈæʃməʊl/ Elias 1617–1692. English antiquary, whose collection forms the basis of the Ashmolean Museum, Oxford, England.

He wrote books on alchemy and on antiquarian subjects, and amassed a fine library and a collection of curiosities, both of which he presented to Oxford University 1682. His collection was housed in the 'Old Ashmolean' (built 1679–83); the present Ashmolean Museum was erected 1897.

Ashton Frederick 1904–1988. British choreographer, director of the Royal Ballet, London, 1963–70. He studied with Marie Rambert before joining the Vic-Wells (now Royal) Ballet 1935 as chief choreographer. His long association with

Ninette de Valois and Margot Fonteyn, for whom he created many roles, gave the Royal Ballet a worldwide reputation.

His major works include *Façade* 1931 and *Les Rendezvous* 1933 for Rambert; *Cinderella* 1948, *Ondine* 1958, *La Fille mal gardée* 1960, *Marguerite and Armand* – for Margot Fonteyn and Rudolf Nureyev – 1963, and *A Month in the Country* 1976. He contributed much to the popularity of ballet in the mid-20th century.

Asimov /ˈæzɪmɒf/ Isaac 1920–1992. Russian-born US author and editor of science fiction and nonfiction.

He published more than 400 books including his science fiction *I, Robot* 1950 and the *Foundation* trilogy 1951–53, continued in *Foundation's Edge* 1983.

Asimov received a PhD in biochemistry from Columbia University 1948 and joined the faculty of the Boston University Medical School.

Asoka /əˈsəʊkə/ *c.* 273–238 BC. Indian emperor, and Buddhist convert from Hinduism. He issued edicts, carved on pillars and rock faces throughout his dominions, promoting wise government and the cultivation of moral virtues according to Buddhist teachings. Many still survive, and are among the oldest deciphered texts in India. In Patna there are the remains of a hall built by him.

Aspasiac. 440 BC. Greek courtesan, the mistress of the Athenian politician →Pericles. As a 'foreigner' from Miletus, she could not be recognized as his wife, but their son was later legitimized. The philosopher Socrates visited her salon, a meeting place for the celebrities of Athens. Her free thinking led to a charge of impiety, from which Pericles had to defend her.

Asplund /ˈæsplənd/ (Erik) Gunnar 1885–1940. Swedish architect. His early work, for example at the Stockholm South Cemetery 1914, was in the Neo-Classical tradition. Later buildings, such as the Stockholm City Library 1924–27 and Gothenburg City Hall 1934–37, developed a refined Modern-Classical style, culminating in the Stockholm South Cemetery Crematorium 1935–40.

His fusion of Classicism and Modernism holds great appeal for many Post-Modern architects and designers.

Asquith /ˈæskwɪθ/ Herbert Henry, 1st Earl of Oxford and Asquith 1852–1928. British Liberal politician, prime minister 1908–16. As chancellor of the Exchequer he introduced old-age pensions 1908. He limited the powers of the House of Lords and attempted to give Ireland Home Rule.

Asquith was born in Yorkshire. Elected a member of Parliament 1886, he was home secretary in Gladstone's 1892–95 government. He was chancellor of the Exchequer 1905–08 and succeeded Campbell-Bannerman as prime minister. Forcing through the radical budget of his chancellor →Lloyd George led him into two elections 1910, which resulted in the Parliament Act 1911, limiting the right of the Lords to veto legislation. His endeavours to pass the Home Rule for Ireland Bill led to the Curragh 'Mutiny' and incipient civil war. Unity was re-established by the outbreak of World War I 1914, and a coalition government was formed May 1915. However, his attitude of 'wait and see' was not adapted to all-out war, and in Dec 1916 he was replaced by Lloyd George. In 1918 the Liberal election defeat led to the eclipse of the party.

Assad /æsæd/ Hafez al 1930– . Syrian Ba'athist politician, president from 1971. He became prime minister after a bloodless military coup 1970, and the following year was the first president to be elected by popular vote. Having suppressed dissent, he was re-elected 1978 and 1985. He is a Shia (Alawite) Muslim.

He has ruthlessly suppressed domestic opposition, and was Iran's only major Arab ally in its war against Iraq. He steadfastly pursued military parity with Israel, and has made himself a key player in any settlement of the Lebanese civil war or Middle East conflict generally. His support for UN action against Iraq following its invasion of Kuwait 1990 raised his international standing.

Astaire /ə'steə/ Fred. Adopted name of Frederick Austerlitz 1899–1987. US dancer, actor, singer, and choreographer who starred in numerous films, including *Top Hat* 1935, *Easter Parade* 1948, and *Funny Face* 1957, many containing inventive sequences he designed and choreographed himself. He made ten classic films with the most popular of his dancing partners, Ginger Rogers. He later played straight dramatic roles in such films as *On the Beach* 1959.

Astaire was born in Omaha, Nebraska, and taken to New York in 1904. He danced in partnership with his sister *Adele Astaire* (1897–1981) from 1906 until her marriage in 1932, and they became public favourites on Broadway and in London. He entered films in 1933. Among his many other films are *Roberta* 1935 and *Follow the Fleet* 1936. Astaire was a virtuoso dancer and a perfectionist known for his elegant style.

Aston /æstən/ Francis William 1877–1945. English physicist who developed the mass spectrometer, which separates isotopes by projecting their ions (charged atoms) through a magnetic field. He received the Nobel Prize for Chemistry 1922.

Astor /æst/ John Jacob 1763–1848. Germanborn US merchant who founded the monopolistic American Fur Company 1808. His subsidiary enterprise, the Pacific Fur Company, was created 1881 following the US government's Louisiana Purchase 1803 facilitating trade with the West. He founded Astoria, now in Oregon, as his trading post at the mouth of the Columbia River.

Astor immigrated to the USA 1784 and worked in small shops before entering the fur trade. He made farsighted agreements with Canadian mer-

Astaire US dancer Fred Astaire and his partner, Ginger Rogers. The sophisticated, intimate style of dancing, its grace and technical excellence, and the integration of plot and music in the Rogers–Astaire films revolutionized the musical comedy. Astaire's later co-stars included Judy Garland, Leslie Caron, and Audrey Hepburn.

chants and traded with the British East India Company. He systematically invested his profits in New York City real estate. When he retired in 1834 he was the wealthiest man in the USA, owning most of the southern half of Manhattan, which his sons subsequently inherited and administered.

His estate endowed the Astor library, now a part of The New York Public Library.

Astor /æstə/ Mary. Stage name of Lucille Langhanke 1906–1987. US film actress, renowned for her poise, whose many films included *Don Juan* 1926, *Dodsworth* 1936, and *The Maltese Falcon* 1941. Her memoirs *My Story* 1959 were remarkable for their frankness.

Asturias /æ'stuəriəs/ Miguel Ángel 1899–1974. Guatemalan author and diplomat. He published poetry, Guatemalan legends, and novels, such as *El señor presidente/The President* 1946, *Men of Corn* 1949, and *Strong Wind* 1950, attacking Latin-American dictatorships and 'Yankee imperialism'. Nobel prize 1967.

Atahualpa /ætə'waːlpə/ c. 1502–1533. Last emperor of the Incas of Peru. He was taken prisoner 1532 when the Spaniards arrived, and agreed to pay a substantial ransom, but was accused of plotting against the conquistador Pizarro and sentenced to be burned. On his consenting to Christian baptism, the sentence was commuted to strangulation.

Atatürk /ˈætətɜːk/ Kemal. Name assumed 1934 by Mustafa Kemal Pasha 1881–1938. (Atatürk 'Father of the Turks') Turkish politician and general, first president of Turkey from 1923. After World War I he established a provisional rebel government and in 1921–22 the Turkish armies under his leadership expelled the Greeks who were occupying Turkey. He was the founder of the modern republic, which he ruled as virtual dictator, with a policy of consistent and radical westernization.

Kemal, born in Thessaloniki, was banished 1904 for joining a revolutionary society. Later he was pardoned and promoted in the army, and was largely responsible for the successful defence of the Dardanelles against the British 1915. In 1918, after Turkey had been defeated, he was sent into Anatolia to implement the demobilization of the Turkish forces in accordance with the armistice terms, but instead he established a provisional government opposed to that of Constantinople (under Allied control), and in 1921 led the Turkish armies against the Greeks, who had occupied a large part of Anatolia. He checked them at the Battle of the Sakaria, 23 Aug–13 Sept 1921, for which he was granted the title of Ghazi (the Victorious), and within a year had expelled the Greeks from Turkish soil. War with the British was averted by his diplomacy, and Turkey in Europe passed under Kemal's control. On 29 Oct 1923, Turkey was proclaimed a republic with Kemal as first president.

Atget /æˈdʒeɪ/ Eugène 1857–1927. French photographer. He took up photography at the age of 40, and for 30 years documented urban Paris, leaving some 10,000 photos.

Athanasius, St /ˌæθəˈneɪʃəs/ 298–373. Bishop of Alexandria, supporter of the doctrines of the Trinity and Incarnation. He was a disciple of St Anthony the hermit, and an opponent of Arianism in the great Arian controversy. Following the official condemnation of Arianism at the Council of Nicaea 325, Athanasius was appointed bishop of Alexandria 328. The Athanasian creed was not actually written by him, although it reflects his views.

Banished 335 by the emperor Constantine because of his intransigence towards the defeated Arians, he was recalled in 346 but suffered three more banishments before his final reinstatement about 366.

He became what we are that he might make us what he is.

St Athanasius on Jesus in *De Incarnatione*

Athelstan /ˈæθəlstən/ c. 895–939. King of the Mercians and West Saxons. Son of Edward the Elder and grandson of Alfred the Great, he was crowned king 925 at Kingston upon Thames. He subdued parts of Cornwall and Wales, and defeated the Welsh, Scots, and Danes at Brunanburh 937.

Attenborough /ˈætnbərə/ David 1926– . English traveller and zoologist, brother of the actor and director Richard Attenborough. He was director of programmes for BBC Television 1969–72, and writer and presenter of the television series *Life on Earth* 1979, *The Living Planet* 1983, and *The Trials of Life* 1990.

Attenborough /ˈætnbərə/ Richard 1923– . English actor, director, and producer. He began his acting career in war films and comedies. His films include *Brighton Rock* 1947 and *10 Rillington Place* 1970 (as actor), and *Oh! What a Lovely War* 1969, *Gandhi* (which won eight Academy Awards) 1982, *Cry Freedom* 1987, and *Chaplin* 1992 (as director).

Atterbury /ˈætəbəri/ Francis 1662–1732. English bishop and Jacobite politician. In 1687 he was appointed a royal chaplain by William III. Under Queen Anne he received rapid promotion, becoming bishop of Rochester 1713. His Jacobite sympathies prevented his further rise, and in 1722 he was sent to the Tower of London and subsequently banished. He was a friend of the writers Alexander Pope and Jonathan Swift.

Attila /əˈtɪlə/ c. 406–453. King of the Huns in an area from the Alps to the Caspian Sea from 434, known to later Christian history as the 'Scourge of God'. He twice attacked the Eastern Roman Empire to increase the quantity of tribute paid to him, 441–443 and 447–449, and then attacked the Western Roman Empire 450–452.

Attila first ruled jointly with his brother Bleda, whom he murdered in 444. In 450 Honoria, the sister of the western emperor Valentinian III, appealed to him to rescue her from an arranged marriage, and Attila used her appeal to attack the West. He was forced back from Orléans by Aetius and Theodoric, king of the Visigoths, and defeated by them on the Catalaunian Fields in 451. In 452 he led the Huns into Italy, and was induced to withdraw by Pope →Leo I.

He died on the night of his marriage to the German Ildico, either by poison, or, as Chaucer represents it in his *Pardoner's Tale*, from a nasal haemorrhage induced by drunkenness.

Attila lived in relative simplicity in his camp close to the Danube, which was described by the Greek historian Priscus after a diplomatic mission. But his advisers included a Greek, Orestes, and his control over a large territory required administrative abilities. His conscious aims were to prevent the Huns from serving in the imperial armies, and to use force to exact as much tribute or land from both parts of the empire as he could. His burial place was kept secret.

Attlee /ˈætli/ Clement (Richard), 1st Earl 1883–1967. British Labour politician. In the coalition government during World War II he was

Lord Privy Seal 1940–42, dominions secretary 1942–43, and Lord President of the Council 1943–45, as well as deputy prime minister from 1942. As prime minister 1945–51 he introduced a sweeping programme of nationalization and a whole new system of social services.

Attlee was educated at Oxford and practised as a barrister 1906–09. Social work in London's East End and cooperation in poor-law reform led him to become a socialist; he joined the Fabian Society and the Independent Labour Party 1908. He became lecturer in social science at the London School of Economics 1913. After service in World War I he was mayor of Stepney, E London, 1919–20; Labour member of Parliament for Limehouse 1922–50 and for W Walthamstow 1950–55. In the first and second Labour governments he was undersecretary for war 1924 and chancellor of the Duchy of Lancaster and postmaster general 1929–31. In 1935 he became leader of the opposition. In July 1945 he became prime minister after a Labour landslide in the general election. The government was returned to power with a much reduced majority 1950 and was defeated 1951. Created 1st Earl 1955 on his retirement as leader of the opposition.

Attwell /ˈætwel/ Mabel Lucie 1879–1964. British artist, illustrator of many books for children, including her own stories and verse.

Atwood /ˈætwʊd/ Margaret (Eleanor) 1939– . Canadian novelist, short-story writer, and poet. Her novels, which often treat feminist themes with wit and irony, include *The Edible Woman* 1969, *Life Before Man* 1979, *Bodily Harm* 1981, *The Handmaid's Tale* 1986, and *Cat's Eye* 1989.

Collections of poetry include *Power Politics* 1971, *You are Happy* 1974, and *Interlunar* 1984.

Auber /əʊˈbeə/ Daniel François Esprit 1782–1871. French operatic composer who studied under the Italian composer and teacher Cherubini. He wrote about 50 operas, including *La Muette de Portici/The Mute Girl of Portici* 1828 and the comic opera *Fra Diavolo* 1830.

Aubrey /ˈɔːbri/ John 1626–1697. English biographer and antiquary. His *Lives*, begun in 1667, contains gossip, anecdotes, and valuable insights into the celebrities of his time. Unpublished during his lifetime, a standard edition of the work appeared as Brief Lives 1898 in two volumes (edited by A Clark). Aubrey was the first to claim Stonehenge as a Druid temple.

Aubrey was born in Wiltshire. He studied law but became dependent on patrons, including the antiquary Ashmole and the philosopher Hobbes. *Miscellanies* 1696, a work on folklore and ghost stories, was the only one of his books to be published during his lifetime. His major work, *Brief Lives*, and his observations on the natural history of Surrey and Wiltshire were published posthumously. A one-volume edition of three of his works *Miscellanies, Remaines of Gentilisme and Judaisme*, and

Observations appeared 1972 under the title *Three Prose Works* (edited by J Buchanan-Brown).

Auchinleck /ˈɔːkɪnlek/ Sir Claude John Eyre 1884–1981. British commander in World War II. He won the First Battle of El Alamein 1942 in N Egypt. In 1943 he became commander in chief in India and founded the modern Indian and Pakistani armies. In 1946 he was promoted to field marshal; he retired 1947.

Auchinleck, nicknamed 'the Auk', succeeded Wavell as commander in chief Middle East July 1941, and in the summer of 1942 was forced back to the Egyptian frontier by the German field marshal Rommel, but his victory at the First Battle of El Alamein is regarded by some as more important to the outcome of World War II than the Second Battle. From India he gave background support to the Burma campaign.

Auckland /ˈɔːklənd/ George Eden, 1st Earl of Auckland 1784–1849. British Tory politician after whom Auckland, New Zealand, is named. He became a member of Parliament 1810, and 1835–41 was governor general of India.

Auden /ˈɔːdn/ W(ystan) H(ugh) 1907–1973. English-born US poet. He wrote some of his most original poetry, such as *Look, Stranger!* 1936, in the 1930s when he led the influential left-wing literary group that included Louis MacNeice, Stephen Spender, and Cecil Day Lewis. He moved to the USA 1939, became a US citizen 1946, and adopted a more conservative and Christian viewpoint, for example in *The Age of Anxiety* 1947.

Born in York, Auden was associate professor of English literature at the University of Michigan from 1939, and professor of poetry at Oxford 1956–61. He also wrote verse dramas with Christopher →Isherwood, such as *The Dog Beneath the Skin* and *The Ascent of F6* 1951, and opera librettos, notably for Stravinsky's *The Rake's Progress* 1951.

We must love one another or die.

W H Auden 'September 1, 1939'

Audubon /ˈɔːdəbɒn/ John James 1785–1851. US naturalist and artist. In 1827, after extensive travels and observations of birds, he published the first part of his *Birds of North America*, with a remarkable series of colour plates. Later he produced a similar work on North American quadrupeds.

He was born in Santo Domingo (now Haiti) and educated in Paris. The National Audubon Society (founded 1886) has branches throughout the USA and Canada for the study and protection of birds.

Auerbach /ˈaʊəbæk/ Frank Helmuth 1931– . British artist, whose portraits and landscapes blend figurative and abstract work.

Augier /əʊʒi'eɪ/ Émile 1820–1889. French dramatist. In collaboration with Jules Sandeau he wrote *Le Gendre de M Poirier* 1854, a realistic delineation of bourgeois society.

Augustin /əʊgʊ'stæn/ Eugène 1791–1861. French dramatist, the originator and exponent of 'well-made' plays, which achieved success but were subsequently forgotten. He wrote *Une Nuit de la Garde Nationale* 1815.

Augustine of Hippo, St /ɔː'gʌstɪn/ 354–430. One of the early Christian leaders and writers known as the Fathers of the Church. He was converted to Christianity by Ambrose in Milan and became bishop of Hippo (modern Annaba, Algeria) 396. Among Augustine's many writings are his *Confessions*, a spiritual autobiography, and *De Civitate Dei/The City of God*, vindicating the Christian church and divine providence in 22 books.

Born in Thagaste, Numidia (now Algeria), of Roman descent, he studied rhetoric in Carthage, where he became the father of an illegitimate son, Adeodatus. He lectured in Tagaste and Carthage and for ten years was attached to the Manichaeist belief. In 383 he went to Rome, and on moving to Milan came under the influence of Ambrose. After prolonged study of Neo-Platonism he was baptized by Ambrose together with his son. Resigning his chair in rhetoric, he returned to Africa – his mother, St Monica, dying in Ostia on the journey – and settled in Thagaste. In 391, while visiting Hippo, Augustine was ordained priest, and in 396 he was appointed bishop of Hippo. He died there in 430, as the city was under siege by the Vandals.

Augustine's written output was vast, with 113 books and treatises, over 200 letters, and more than 500 sermons surviving. Many of Augustine's books resulted from his participation in three great theological controversies: he refuted Manichaeism; attacked (and did much to eliminate) the exclusive N African Donatist sect at the conference of Carthage 411; and devoted the last 20 years of his life to refute →Pelagius, maintaining the doctrine of original sin and the necessity of divine grace.

Augustine, St /ɔː'gʌstɪn/ first archbishop of Canterbury, England. He was sent from Rome to convert England to Christianity by Pope Gregory I. He landed at Ebbsfleet in Kent 597, and soon after baptized Ethelbert, King of Kent, along with many of his subjects. He was consecrated bishop of the English at Arles in the same year, and appointed archbishop 601, establishing his see at Canterbury. Feast day 26 May.

Augustine was originally prior of the Benedictine monastery of St Andrew, Rome. In 603 he attempted unsuccessfully to unite the Roman and native Celtic churches at a conference on the Severn. He founded Christ Church, Canterbury, in 603, and the abbey of Saints Peter and Paul, now the site of Saint Augustine's Missionary College.

Augustus /ɔː'gʌstəs/ 63 BC–AD 14. Title of Octavian (Gaius Julius Caesar Octavianus), first of the Roman emperors. He joined forces with Mark Antony and Lepidus in the Second Triumvirate. Following Mark Antony's liaison with the Egyptian queen Cleopatra, Augustus defeated her troops at Actium 31 BC. As emperor (from 27 BC) he reformed the government of the empire, the army, and Rome's public services, and was a patron of the arts. The period of his rule is known as the Augustan Age.

He was the son of a senator who married a niece of Julius Caesar, and he became his great-uncle's adopted son and principal heir. Following Caesar's murder, Octavian formed with Mark Antony and Lepidus the Triumvirate that divided the Roman world between them and proceeded to eliminate the opposition. Antony's victory 42 BC over Brutus and Cassius had brought the republic to an end. Antony then became enamoured of Cleopatra and spent most of his time at Alexandria, while Octavian consolidated his hold on the western part of the Roman dominion. War was declared against Cleopatra, and the naval victory at Actium left Octavian in unchallenged supremacy, since Lepidus had been forced to retire. After his return to Rome 29 BC, Octavian was created *princeps senatus*, and in 27 BC he was given the title of Augustus ('venerable'). He then resigned his extraordinary powers and received from the Senate, in return, the proconsular command, which gave him control of the army, and the tribunician power, whereby he could initiate or veto legislation. In his programme of reforms Augustus received the support of three loyal and capable helpers, Agrippa, Maecenas, and his wife, Livia, while Virgil and Horace acted as the poets laureate of the new regime. A firm frontier for the empire was established: to the north, the friendly Batavians held the Rhine delta, and then the line followed the course of the Rhine and Danube; to the east, the Parthians were friendly, and the Euphrates gave the next line; to the south, the African colonies were protected by the desert; to the west were Spain and Gaul. The provinces were governed either by imperial legates responsible to the *princeps* or by proconsuls appointed by the Senate. The army was made a profession, with fixed pay and length of service, and a permanent fleet was established. Finally, Rome itself received an adequate water supply, a fire brigade, a police force, and a large number of public buildings. The years after 12 BC were marked by private and public calamities: the marriage of Augustus' daughter Julia to his stepson Tiberius proved disastrous; a serious revolt occurred in Pannonia AD 6; and in Germany three legions under Varus were annihilated in the Teutoburg Forest AD 9. Augustus died a broken man, but his work remained secure.

Aung San /aʊŋ 'sæn/ 1916–1947. Burmese politician. He was a founder and leader of the Anti-

Fascist People's Freedom League, which led Burma's fight for independence from Great Britain. During World War II he collaborated first with Japan and then with the UK. In 1947 he became head of Burma's provisional government but was assassinated the same year by political opponents; Burma (now Myanmar) became independent 1948.

Imprisoned for his nationalist activities while a student in Rangoon, Aung escaped to Japan 1940. He returned to lead the Burma Independence Army, which assisted the Japanese invasion 1942, and became defence minister in the puppet government set up. Before long, however, he secretly contacted the Resistance movement, and from March 1945 openly cooperated with the British in the expulsion of the Japanese. He was assassinated by political opponents July 1947. He was the father of Suu Kyi.

Aurangzeb /ˈɔːrəŋzeb/ or *Aurungzebe* 1618–1707. Mogul emperor of N India from 1658. Third son of Shah Jahan, he made himself master of the court by a palace revolution. His reign was the most brilliant period of the Mogul dynasty, but his despotic tendencies and Muslim fanaticism aroused much opposition. His latter years were spent in war with the princes of Rajputana and Maratha.

Aurelian /ɔːˈriːliən/ (Lucius Domitius Aurelianus) *c.* AD 214–275. Roman emperor from 270. A successful soldier, he was chosen emperor by his troops on the death of Claudius II. He defeated the Goths and Vandals, defeated and captured →Zenobia of Palmyra, and was planning a campaign against Parthia when he was murdered. The *Aurelian Wall*, a fortification surrounding Rome, was built by Aurelian 271. It was made of concrete, and substantial ruins exist. The *Aurelian Way* ran from Rome through Pisa and Genoa to Antipolis (Antibes) in Gaul.

Aurelius Antoninus /ɔːˈriːliəs/ Marcus. Roman emperor; see →Marcus Aurelius Antoninus.

Auric /ˈɔːriːk/ Georges 1899–1983. French composer. He was one of the musical group called *Les Six*. Auric composed a comic opera, several ballets, and incidental music to films of Jean Cocteau.

Auriol /ˌɔːriˈəʊl/ Vincent 1884–1966. French Socialist politician. He was president of the two Constituent Assemblies of 1946 and first president of the Fourth Republic 1947–54.

Austen /ˈɔːstɪn/ Jane 1775–1817. English novelist who described her raw material as 'three or four families in a Country Village'. *Sense and Sensibility* was published 1811, *Pride and Prejudice* 1813, *Mansfield Park* 1814, *Emma* 1816, *Northanger Abbey* and *Persuasion* 1818, all anonymously. She observed speech and manners with wit and precision, revealing her characters' absurdities in relation to high standards of integrity and appropriateness.

She was born at Steventon, Hampshire, where her father was rector, and began writing early; the burlesque *Love and Freindship* (sic), published 1922, was written 1790. In 1801 the family moved to Bath and after the death of her father in 1805, to Southampton, finally settling in Chawton, Hampshire, with her brother Edward. Between 1795 and 1798 she worked on three novels. The first to be published (like its successors, anonymously) was *Sense and Sensibility* (drafted in letter form 1797–98). *Pride and Prejudice* (written 1796–97) followed, but *Northanger Abbey*, a skit on the contemporary Gothic novel (written 1798, sold to a London publisher 1803, and bought back 1816), did not appear until 1818. The fragmentary *Watsons* and *Lady Susan*, written about 1803–05, remained unfinished. The success of her published works, however, stimulated Jane Austen to write in rapid succession *Mansfield Park*, *Emma*, *Persuasion*, and the final fragment *Sanditon* written 1817. She died in Winchester, and is buried in the cathedral.

Auster /ˈɔːstə/ Paul 1947– . US novelist. His experimental use of detective-story techniques to explore modern urban identity is exemplified in his *New York Trilogy: City of Glass* 1985, *Ghosts* 1986, and *The Locked Room* 1986.

Austin /ˈɔːstɪn/ Alfred 1835–1913. British poet. He published the satirical poem *The Season* 1861, which was followed by plays and volumes of poetry little read today; from 1896 he was poet laureate.

Austin /ˈɔːstɪn/ Herbert, 1st Baron 1866–1941. English industrialist who began manufacturing cars 1905 in Northfield, Birmingham, notably the Austin Seven 1921.

Austin /ˈstɪn/ J(ohn) L(angshaw) 1911–1960. British philosopher. Influential in his later work on the philosophy of language, Austin was a pioneer in the investigation of the way words are used in everyday speech. His lectures *Sense and Sensibilia* and *How to do Things with Words* were published posthumously in 1962.

Austin /ˈɒstɪn/ Stephen Fuller 1793–1836. American pioneer and political leader. A settler in Texas 1821, he was a supporter of the colony's autonomy and was imprisoned 1833–35 for his opposition to Mexican rule. Released during the Texas revolution, he campaigned for US support. After the end of the war 1836, he was appointed secretary of state of the independent Republic of Texas but died shortly afterwards.

Born in Austinville, Virginia, USA, Austin grew up in Missouri and followed his father to Texas 1821 where he accepted Mexican citizenship and political privileges in spite of his support of the colony's independence.

The state capital of Austin was named in his honour.

Avebury /ˈeɪvbəri/ John Lubbock, 1st Baron Avebury 1834–1913. British banker. A Liberal (from 1886 Liberal Unionist) member of Parliament 1870–1900, he was responsible for the Bank Holidays Act 1871 introducing statutory public holidays.

Avedon /ˈeɪvdən/ Richard 1923– . US photographer. A fashion photographer with *Harper's Bazaar* magazine in New York from the mid-1940s, he moved to *Vogue* 1965. He later became the highest-paid fashion and advertising photographer in the world. Using large-format cameras, his work consists of intensely realistic images, chiefly portraits.

Averroës /ˌævəˈrəʊiːz/ (Arabic **Ibn Rushd**) 1126–1198. Arabian philosopher who argued for the eternity of matter and against the immortality of the individual soul. His philosophical writings, including commentaries on Aristotle and on Plato's *Republic*, became known to the West through Latin translations. He influenced Christian and Jewish writers into the Renaissance, and reconciled Islamic and Greek thought in that philosophic truth comes through reason. St Thomas Aquinas opposed this position.

Averroës was born in Córdoba, Spain, trained in medicine, and became physician to the caliph as well as judge of Seville and Córdoba. He was accused of heresy by the Islamic authorities and banished 1195. Later he was recalled, and died in Marrakesh. 'Averroism' was taught at Paris and elsewhere in the 13th century by the 'Averroists', who defended a distinction between philosophical truth and revealed religion.

Avery /ˈeɪvəri/ Milton 1893–1965. US painter, whose early work was inspired by Henri →Matisse, with subjects portrayed in thin, flat, richly coloured strokes. His later work, although it remained figurative, shows the influence of Mark →Rothko and other experimental US artists.

Avery /ˈeɪvəri/ Tex (Frederick Bean) 1907–1980. US cartoon-film director who used violent, sometimes surreal humour. At Warner Bros he helped develop Bugs Bunny and Daffy Duck, before moving to MGM 1942 where he created, among others, Droopy the dog and Screwball Squirrel.

Avianus /ˌeɪviˈeɪnəs/ *c.* AD 400. Roman fable writer. Written in elegiac couplets, his fables number 42 in total, and are dedicated to Theodosius.

Avicenna /ˌævɪˈsenə/ (Arabic **Ibn Sina**) 979–1037. Arabian philosopher and physician. He was the most renowned philosopher of medieval Islam. His *Canon Medicinae* was a standard work for many centuries. His philosophical writings were influenced by al-Farabi, Aristotle, and the neo-Platonists, and in turn influenced the scholastics of the 13th century.

Avogadro /ˌævəˈɡɑːdrəʊ/ Amedeo Conte di Quaregna 1776–1856. Italian physicist who proposed Avogadro's hypothesis on gases 1811, stating that equal volumes of all gases, when at the same temperature and pressure, have the same number of molecules. His work enabled scientists to calculate Avogadro's number – the number of carbon atoms in 12 g of the carbon-12 isotope (6.022045×10^{23}) – and still has relevance for today's atomic studies.

Axelrod /ˈæksəlrɒd/ Julius 1912– . US neuropharmacologist who shared the 1970 Nobel Prize for Medicine with the biophysicists Bernard Katz and Ulf von Euler (1905–1983) for his work on neurotransmitters (the chemical messengers of the brain).

Axelrod wanted to know why the messengers, once transmitted, should stop operating. Through his studies he found a number of specific enzymes that rapidly degraded the neurotransmitters.

Ayckbourn /ˈeɪkbɔːn/ Alan 1939– . English playwright. His prolific output, characterized by comic dialogue and experiments in dramatic structure, includes the trilogy *The Norman Conquests* 1974, *A Woman in Mind* 1986, *Henceforward* 1987, and *Man of the Moment* 1988.

Ayer /eə/ A(lfred) J(ules) 1910–1989. English philosopher. He wrote *Language, Truth and Logic* 1936, an exposition of the theory of 'logical positivism', presenting a criterion by which meaningful statements (essentially truths of logic, as well as statements derived from experience) could be distinguished from meaningless metaphysical utterances (for example, claims that there is a God or that the world external to our own minds is illusory).

He was Wykeham professor of logic at Oxford 1959–78. Later works included *Probability and Evidence* 1972 and Philosophy in the Twentieth Century 1982.

Ayesha /ˈaɪʃə/ 611–678. Third and favourite wife of the prophet Muhammad, who married her when she was nine. Her father, Abu Bakr, became caliph on Muhammad's death 632. She bitterly opposed the later succession to the caliphate of Ali, who had once accused her of infidelity.

Ayrton /ˈeətn/ Michael 1921–1975. British painter, sculptor, illustrator, and writer. From 1961, he concentrated on the Daedalus myth, producing bronzes of Icarus and a fictional autobiography of Daedalus, *The Maze Maker*, 1967.

Aytoun /ˈeɪtn/ Robert 1570–1638. Scottish poet, employed and knighted by James I; he was noted for his love poems. Aytoun is the reputed author of the lines on which Robert Burns based 'Auld Lang Syne'.

Aytoun /ˈeɪtn/ W(illiam) E(dmonstoune) 1813–1865. Scottish poet, born in Edinburgh, chiefly remembered for his *Lays of the Scottish Cavaliers* 1848 and *Bon Gaultier Ballads* 1855, which he wrote in collaboration with the Scottish nationalist Theodore Martin (1816–1909).

Ayub Khan /ɑːˈjuːb/ Muhammad 1907–1974. Pakistani soldier and president from 1958 to

1969. He served in the Burma Campaign 1942–45, and was commander in chief of the Pakistan army 1951. In 1958 martial law was proclaimed in Pakistan and Ayub Khan assumed power after a bloodless army coup. He won the presidential elections 1960 and 1965, and established a stable economy and achieved limited land reforms. His militaristic form of government was unpopular, particularly with the Bengalis, and in 1968 student riots resulted from imprisonment of the opposition. He resigned 1969 after widespread opposition and civil disorder, notably in Kashmir.

Azaña /ə'θænjə/ Manuel 1880–1940. Spanish politician and first prime minister 1931–33 of the second Spanish republic. He was last president of the republic during the Civil War 1936–39, before the establishment of a dictatorship under Franco.

Azorín. Pen name of José Martínez Ruiz 1873–1967. Spanish writer. His works include volumes of critical essays and short stories, plays and novels, such as the autobiographical *La voluntad/The Choice* 1902 and *Antonio Azorín* 1903. He adopted the name of the hero of the latter as his pen name.

B

Baade /ˈbɑːdə/ Walter 1893–1960. German-born US astronomer who made observations that doubled the distance, scale, and age of the universe. Baade worked at Mount Wilson Observatory, USA, and discovered that stars are in two distinct populations according to their age, known as Population I (the younger) and Population II (the older). Later, he found that Cepheid variable stars of Population I are brighter than had been supposed, and that distances calculated from them were wrong. Baade's figures showed that the universe was twice as large as previously thought, and twice as old.

Bab, the /bɑːb/ name assumed by Mirza Ali Mohammad 1819–1850. Persian religious leader, born in Shiraz, founder of Babism, an offshoot of Islam. In 1844 he proclaimed that he was a gateway to the Hidden Imam, a new messenger of Allah who was to come. He gained a large following whose activities caused the Persian authorities to fear a rebellion, and who were therefore persecuted. The Bab was executed for heresy.

Babangida /bɑːˈbæŋɡɪdɑː/ Ibrahim 1941– . Nigerian politician and soldier, president from 1985. He became head of the Nigerian army in 1983 and in 1985 led a coup against President Buhari, assuming the presidency himself. He has promised a return to civilian rule.

Babangida was born in Minna, Niger state; he trained at military schools in Nigeria and the UK. He became an instructor in the Nigerian Defence Academy and by 1983 had reached the rank of major general. In 1983, after taking part in the overthrow of President Shehu Shagari, he was made army commander-in-chief. Responding to public pressure 1989, he allowed the formation of competing political parties and promised a return to a democratic civilian government in 1992. In an attempt to end corruption, he banned all persons ever having held elective office from being candidates in the new civilian government. Similarly, applications for recognition from former political parties were also rejected. In Jan 1992, responding to calls for a return to civilian rule, he announced dates for assembly and presidential elections later in the year. Alleging fraudulent electoral practices in the first primaries Sept 1992, Babangida subsequently delayed the date for a transition to civilian rule.

Babbage /ˈbæbɪdʒ/ Charles 1792–1871. English mathematician who devised a precursor of the computer. He designed an analytical engine, a general-purpose mechanical computing device for performing different calculations according to a program input on punched cards (an idea borrowed from the Jacquard loom). This device was never built, but it embodied many of the principles on which present digital computers are based.

As a young man, Babbage assisted John →Herschel with his astronomical calculations. He became involved with calculating machines when he worked on his difference engine for the British Admiralty, which was partly built in 1822.

His most important book was *On the Economy of Machinery and Manufactures* 1832, an analysis of industrial production systems and their economics. Altogether he wrote about 100 books. In 1991, the British Science Museum completed Babbage's second difference engine (to demonstrate that it would have been possible to complete it with the materials then available), which evaluates polynomials up to the seventh power, with 30-figure accuracy.

Babbage English mathematician Charles Babbage. His machines were a mechanical method for solving mathematical problems. More adequate means only became available a hundred years later with the digital computer.

Babbitt /ˈbæbɪt/ Milton 1916– . US composer. After studying with Roger →Sessions he developed a personal style of serialism influenced by jazz. He was a leading composer of electronic music using the 1960 RCA Mark II synthesizer, which he helped to design.

Babel /ˈbɑːbl/ Isaak Emmanuilovich 1894–1939/40. Russian writer. Born in Odessa, he was an ardent supporter of the Revolution and fought with Budyenny's cavalry in the Polish campaign of 1921–22, an experience which inspired *Konarmiya/Red Cavalry* 1926. His other works include *Odesskie rasskazy/Stories from Odessa* 1924, which portrays the life of the Odessa Jews.

Babeuf /bɑːˈbɜːf/ François-Noël 1760–1797. French revolutionary journalist, a pioneer of practical socialism. In 1794 he founded a newspaper in Paris, later known as the *Tribune of the People*, in which he demanded the equality of all people. He was guillotined for conspiring against the ruling Directory during the French Revolution.

Babington /ˈbæbɪŋtən/ Anthony 1561–1586. English traitor who hatched a plot to assassinate Elizabeth I and replace her with →Mary Queen of Scots; its discovery led to Mary's execution and his own.

Babrius lived *c.* 3rd century AD. Roman writer of fables, written in Greek. He probably lived in Syria, where his stories first gained popularity. In 1842 a manuscript of his fables was discovered in a convent on Mount Athos, Greece. There were 123 fables, arranged alphabetically, but stopping at the letter O.

Babur (Arabic 'lion') title given to →Zahir uddin Muhammad, founder of the Mogul Empire in N India.

Bacall /bəˈkɔːl/ Lauren. Stage name of Betty Joan Perske 1924– . Striking US actress who became an overnight star when cast by Howard Hawks opposite Humphrey Bogart in *To Have and Have Not* 1944. She and Bogart married in 1945, and starred together in *The Big Sleep* 1946 and several other films. She also appeared in *The Cobweb* 1955, *Harper* 1966, and *The Shootist* 1976.

Bach /bɑːx/ Carl Philip Emmanuel 1714–1788. German composer, third son of J S Bach. He introduced a new 'homophonic' style, light and easy to follow, which influenced Mozart, Haydn, and Beethoven.

In the service of Frederick the Great 1740–67, he left to become master of church music at Hamburg in 1768. He wrote over 200 pieces for keyboard instruments, and published a guide to playing the piano. Through his music and concert performances he helped to establish a leading solo role for the piano in Western music.

Bach /bɑːx/ Johann Christian 1735–1782. German composer, the 11th son of J S Bach, who became celebrated in Italy as a composer of operas. In 1762 he was invited to London, where he became music master to the royal family. He remained in England until his death, enjoying great popularity both as composer and performer.

Bach /bɑːx/ Johann Sebastian 1685–1750. German composer. He was a master of counterpoint, and his music epitomizes the Baroque polyphonic style. His orchestral music includes the six *Brandenburg Concertos*, other concertos for keyboard instrument and violin, and four orchestral suites. Bach's keyboard music, for clavier and organ, his fugues, and his choral music are of equal importance. He also wrote chamber music and songs.

Born at Eisenach, Bach came from a distinguished musical family. At 15 he became a chorister at Lüneburg, and at 19 he was organist at Arnstadt. His appointments included positions at the courts of Weimar and Anhalt-Köthen, and from 1723 until his death he was musical director at St Thomas's choir school in Leipzig. He married twice and had over 20 children (although several died in infancy). His second wife, Anna Magdalena Wülkens, was a soprano; she also worked for him when his sight failed in later years.

Bach's sacred music includes 200 church cantatas, the Easter and Christmas oratorios, the two great Passions, of St Matthew and St John, and the Mass in B minor. His keyboard music includes a collection of 48 preludes and fugues known as the *Well-Tempered Clavier*, the *Goldberg Variations*, and the *Italian Concerto*. Of his organ music the finest examples are the chorale preludes. Two works written in his later years illustrate the principles and potential of his polyphonic art – the *Musical Offering* and *The Art of Fugue*.

Bach /bɑːx/ Wilhelm Friedemann 1710–1784. German composer, who was also an organist, improviser, and master of counterpoint. He was the eldest son of J S Bach.

Bachelard /bæʃˈlɑː/ Gaston 1884–1962. French philosopher and scientist who argued for a creative interplay between reason and experience. He attacked both Cartesian and positivist positions, insisting that science was derived neither from first principles nor directly from experience.

Bacon /ˈbeɪkən/ Francis 1561–1626. English politician, philosopher, and essayist. He became Lord Chancellor 1618, and the same year confessed to bribe-taking, was fined £40,000 (which was later remitted by the king), and spent four days in the Tower of London. His works include *Essays* 1597, characterized by pith and brevity; *The Advancement of Learning* 1605, a seminal work discussing scientific method; the *Novum Organum* 1620, in which he redefined the task of natural science, seeing it as a means of empirical discovery and a method of increasing human power over nature; and *The New Atlantis* 1626, describing a utopian state in which scientific knowledge is systematically sought and exploited.

Bacon was born in London, studied law at Cambridge from 1573, was part of the embassy in France until 1579, and became a member of Parliament 1584. He was the nephew of Queen Elizabeth's adviser Lord →Burghley, but turned against him when he failed to provide Bacon with patronage. He helped secure the execution of the earl of Essex as a traitor 1601, after formerly being his follower. Bacon was accused of ingratitude, but he defended himself in *Apology* 1604. The satirist Pope called Bacon 'the wisest, brightest, and meanest of mankind'. Knighted on the accession of James I 1603, he became Baron Verulam 1618 and Viscount St Albans 1621. His writing helped to inspire the founding of the Royal Society. The *Baconian Theory*, originated by James Willmot in 1785, suggesting that the works of Shakespeare were written by Bacon, is not taken seriously by scholars.

Bacon /ˈbeɪkən/ Francis 1909–1992. British painter, born in Dublin. He moved to London in 1925 and taught himself to paint. He practised abstract art, then developed a distorted Expressionist style with tortured figures presented in loosely defined space. From 1945 he focused on studies of figures, as in his series of screaming popes based on the portrait of Innocent X by Velázquez.

Bacon began to paint about 1930 and held his first show in London in 1949. He destroyed much of his early work. *Three Studies for Figures at the Base of a Crucifixion* 1944 (Tate Gallery, London) is an early example of his mature style.

Bacon /ˈbeɪkn/ Nathaniel 1647–1676. American colonial leader and wealthy plantation owner. An advocate of social reform in Virginia and an opponent of Governor William →Berkeley, he gained wide public support and was proclaimed 'General of Virginia'. In 1676 he organized Bacon's Rebellion, forcing Berkeley to flee from the capital at Jamestown. Bacon's sudden death ended the uprising but Berkeley was removed from power for his brutal treatment of the rebels.

Born in Suffolk, England, Bacon emigrated to Virginia 1673 and soon began making demands that frontier settlements be protected against Indian attacks. He led colonist forces in raids against local Indian tribes 1675.

Bacon /ˈbeɪkən/ Roger 1214–1292. English philosopher, scientist, and a teacher at Oxford University. He was interested in alchemy, the biological and physical sciences, and magic. Many discoveries have been credited to him, including the magnifying lens. He foresaw the extensive use of gunpowder and mechanical cars, boats, and planes.

In 1266, at the invitation of his friend Pope Clement IV, he began his *Opus Majus/Great Work*, a compendium of all branches of knowledge. In 1268 he sent this with his *Opus Minus/Lesser Work* and other writings to the pope. In 1277 Bacon was condemned and imprisoned

Bacon *English philosopher, politician, and author Sir Francis Bacon. A pioneer of the empirical scientific method, it is said that he died as a result of one of his experiments. In an attempt to prove that cold temperatures preserve flesh, he collected snow to stuff a chicken. As a result he caught a chill and died soon after.*

by the church for 'certain novelties' (heresy) and not released until 1292.

Bacon was born in Somerset and educated at Oxford and Paris. He became a Franciscan monk and was in Paris until about 1251 lecturing on Aristotle. He wrote in Latin and his works include *On Mirrors*, *Metaphysical* and *On the Multiplication of Species*. He followed the maxim 'Cease to be ruled by dogmas and authorities; look at the world!'

Baden-Powell /ˈbeɪdn ˈpəʊəl/ Agnes 1854–1945. Sister of Robert Baden-Powell, she helped him found the Girl Guides.

Baden-Powell /ˈbeɪdn ˈpəʊəl/ Lady Olave 1889–1977. Wife of Robert Baden-Powell from 1912, she was the first and only World Chief Guide 1918–1977.

Baden-Powell /ˈbeɪdn ˈpəʊəl/ Robert Stephenson Smyth, 1st Baron Baden-Powell 1857–1941. British general, founder of the Scout Association. He fought in defence of Mafeking (now Mafikeng) during the Second South African War. After 1907 he devoted his time to developing the Scout movement, which rapidly spread throughout the world. He was created a peer in 1929.

Born in London, he was educated at Charterhouse. After failing to gain a place at Oxford University he joined the Indian Army, being commissioned in the Hussars in 1876; he became its youngest colonel by the age of 40. His defence of Mafikeng brought him worldwide fame. He was invalided home and was knighted in 1910 with the rank of lieutenant general.

Baden-Powell began the Scout movement in 1907 with a camp for 20 boys on Brownsea Island, Poole Harbour, Dorset. He published *Scouting for Boys* 1908 and about thirty other books. He was World Chief Scout from 1920 and received the Order of Merit 1937.

Bader /ˈbɑːdə/ Douglas 1910–1982. British fighter pilot. He lost both legs in a flying accident 1931, but had a distinguished flying career in World War II. He was knighted 1976 for his work with disabled people.

Badoglio /bɑːˈdəʊljəʊ/ Pietro 1871–1956. Italian soldier and Fascist politician. A veteran of campaigns against the peoples of Tripoli and Cyrenaica, in 1935 he became commander in chief in Ethiopia, adopting ruthless measures to break patriot resistance. He was created viceroy of Ethiopia and duke of Addis Ababa in 1936. He resigned during the disastrous campaign into Greece 1940 and succeeded Mussolini as prime minister of Italy from July 1943 to June 1944, negotiating the armistice with the Allies.

Baedeker /ˈbeɪdɪkə/ Karl 1801–1859. German editor and publisher of foreign travel guides; the first was for Coblenz 1829. These are now published from Hamburg (before World War II from Leipzig).

Baekeland /ˈbeɪklənd/ Leo Hendrik 1863–1944. Belgian-born US chemist. He invented Bakelite, the first commercial plastic, made from formaldehyde and phenol. He later made a photographic paper, Velox, which could be developed in artificial light.

Baer /beə/ Karl Ernst von 1792–1876. German zoologist who was the founder of comparative embryology. Born in Estonia, he held scientific posts in Königsberg, Germany, and St Petersburg, Russia.

Baez /baɪez/ Joan 1941– . US folk singer who achieved fame in the early 1960s with versions of traditional English and American folk songs such as 'Silver Dagger' and 'We Shall Overcome', the latter becoming the anthem of anti-Vietnam War protesters. She was a major influence in the popularization of folk music, helped Bob Dylan at the start of his career, and has also remained active as a pacifist and antiwar campaigner.

Baffin /ˈbæfɪn/ William 1584–1622. English explorer and navigator. In 1616, he and Robert Bylot explored Baffin Bay, NE Canada, and reached latitude 77° 45′ N, which for 236 years remained the 'furthest north'.

In 1612, Baffin was chief pilot of an expedition in search of the Northwest Passage, and in 1613–14 commanded a whaling fleet near Spitsbergen, Norway. He piloted the *Discovery* on an expedition to Hudson Bay lead by Bylot in 1615. After 1617, Baffin worked for the East India

Company and made surveys of the Red Sea and Persian Gulf. In 1622 he was killed in an Anglo-Persian attack on Hormuz.

Bagehot /ˈbædʒət/ Walter 1826–1877. British writer and economist, author of *The English Constitution* 1867, a classic analysis of the British political system. He was editor of *The Economist* magazine 1860–77.

One of the greatest pains to human nature is the pain of a new idea.
Walter Bagehot *Physics and Politics* 1869

Bagnold /ˈbægnəʊld/ Enid 1889–1981. British author of *National Velvet* 1935, a novel about horse racing that was also successful as a film (1944, starring Elizabeth Taylor).

Bagritsky /bəˈgrɪtski/ Eduard. Pen name of Eduard Dzyubin 1895–1934. Russian poet. One of the Constructivist group, he published the heroic poem *Lay About Opanas* 1926, and collections of verse called *The Victors* 1932 and *The Last Night* 1932.

Bahadur Shah II /bəˈhɑːdə ˈʃɑː/ 1775–1862. Last of the Mogul emperors of India. He reigned, though in name only, as king of Delhi 1837–57, when he was hailed by the mutineers of the Indian Mutiny as an independent emperor at Delhi. After the rebellion he was exiled to Burma (now Myanmar) with his family.

Baha'ullah /ˌbɑːhɑːˈʊlə/ title of Mirza Hosein Ali 1817–1892. Persian founder of the Baha'i religion. Baha'ullah, 'God's Glory', proclaimed himself as the prophet the →Bab had foretold.

Bailey /ˈbeɪli/ David 1938– . British fashion photographer, chiefly associated with *Vogue* magazine from the 1960s. He has published several books of his work, exhibited widely, and also made films.

Bailey /ˈbeɪli/ Donald Coleman 1901–1985. English engineer, inventor in World War II of the portable *Bailey bridge*, made of interlocking, interchangeable, adjustable, and easily transportable units.

Baillie /ˈbeɪli/ Isobel 1895–1983. British soprano. Born in Hawick, Scotland, she became celebrated for her work in oratorio. She was professor of singing at Cornell University in New York 1960–61.

Bailly /bɑːˈjiː/ Jean Sylvain 1736–1793. French astronomer who wrote about the satellites of Jupiter and the history of astronomy. Early in the French Revolution, was president of the National Assembly and mayor of Paris, but resigned in 1791; he was guillotined during the Reign of Terror.

Bainbridge /'beɪnbrɪdʒ/ Beryl 1934– . English novelist, originally an actress, whose works have the drama and economy of a stage play. They include *The Dressmaker* 1973, *The Bottle Factory Outing* 1974, *Injury Time* 1977, *Young Adolf* 1978, *The Winter Garden* 1980, the collected short stories in *Mum and Mr Armitage* 1985, and *The Birthday Boys* 1991.

Her book *An Awfully Big Adventure* 1990 was shortlisted for the Booker Prize.

Bainbridge /'beɪnbrɪdʒ/ Kenneth Tompkins 1904– . US physicist who was director of the first atomic bomb test at Alamogordo, New Mexico, in 1945.

Bainbridge worked at the Cavendish Laboratory, Cambridge, England, in the 1930s. He also carried out research in radar. From 1961 he was George Vasmer Everett Professor of Physics at Harvard University.

Baird /beəd/ John Logie 1888–1946. Scottish electrical engineer who pioneered television. In 1925 he gave the first public demonstration of television and in 1926 pioneered fibre optics, radar (in advance of Robert →Watson-Watt), and 'noctovision', a system for seeing at night by using infrared rays.

Born at Helensburgh, Scotland, Baird studied electrical engineering in Glasgow at what is now the University of Strathclyde, at the same time serving several practical apprenticeships. He was working on television possibly as early as 1912, and he took out his first provisional patent 1923. He also developed video recording on both wax records and magnetic steel discs (1926–27), colour TV (1925–28), 3-D colour TV (1925–46), and transatlantic TV (1928). In 1936 his mechanically scanned 240-line system competed with EMI- Marconi's 405-line, but the latter was preferred for the BBC service from 1937, partly because it used electronic scanning and partly because it handled live indoor scenes with smaller, more manoeuvrable cameras. In 1944 he developed facsimile television, the forerunner of Ceefax, and demonstrated the world's first all-electronic colour and 3-D colour receiver (500 lines).

Bairnsfather /'beənzfɑːðə/ Bruce 1888–1959. British artist, celebrated for his 'Old Bill' cartoons of World War I. In World War II he was official cartoonist to the US Army in Europe 1942–44.

Baker /'beɪkə/ Benjamin 1840–1907. English engineer who designed (with English engineer John Fowler (1817–1898)) London's first underground railway (the Metropolitan and District) in 1869, the Forth Bridge, Scotland, 1890, and the original Aswan Dam on the river Nile, Egypt.

Baker /'beɪkə/ Chet (Chesney) 1929–1988. US jazz trumpeter of the cool school, whose good looks, occasional vocal performances, and romantic interpretations of ballads helped make him a cult figure. He became known with the Gerry Mulligan Quartet in 1952 and formed his own quartet 1953. Recordings include 'My Funny Valentine' and 'The Thrill Is Gone'.

Baker /'beɪkə/ James (Addison), III 1930– . US Republican politician. Under President Reagan, he was White House chief of staff 1981–85 and Treasury secretary 1985–88. After managing George Bush's successful presidential campaign 1988, Baker was appointed secretary of state 1989 and played a prominent role in the 1990–91 Gulf crisis, and the subsequent search for a lasting Middle East peace settlement. In 1992 he left the State Department to head Bush's re-election campaign. After Democrat Bill Clinton's victory, he took over the post of White House Chief of Staff in the interim period leading up to the new president's inauguration Jan 1993.

A lawyer from Houston, Texas, Baker entered politics 1970 as one of the managers of his friend George Bush's unsuccessful campaign for the Senate. He served as undersecretary of commerce 1975–76 in the Ford administration and was deputy manager of the 1976 and 1980 Ford and Bush presidential campaigns. Baker joined the Reagan administration 1981. The most powerful member of the Bush team, he was described as an effective 'prime minister'.

He has been criticized for the unscrupulousness of the 1988 Bush campaign.

Baker /'beɪkə/ Janet 1933– . English mezzo-soprano who excels in lied, oratorio, and opera. Her performances include Dido in both *Dido and Aeneas* and *The Trojans*, and Marguerite in *Faust*. She retired from the stage in 1981 but continues to perform recitals, oratorio, and concerts.

Baker /'beɪkə/ Kenneth (Wilfrid) 1934– . British Conservative politician, home secretary 1990–92. He was environment secretary 1985–86, education secretary 1986–89, and chair of the Conservative Party 1989–90, retaining his cabinet seat, before becoming home secretary in John Major's government.

Undergoing national service in N Africa Baker was, for a time, a gunnery instructor to the Libyan army. He then read history at Oxford. He was elected to the House of Commons in 1968 (representing Mole Valley from 1983). Despite a reputation of being on the liberal wing of the Conservative Party, he became a minister of state in Thatcher's 1979 administration.

Baker /'beɪkə/ Samuel White 1821–1893. English explorer, in 1864 the first European to sight Lake Albert Nyanza (now Lake Mobutu Sese Seko) in central Africa, and discover that the river Nile flowed through it.

He founded an agricultural colony in Ceylon (now Sri Lanka), built a railway across the Dobruja, and in 1861 set out to discover the source of the Nile. His wife, Florence von Sass, accompanied him. From 1869 to 1873 he was governor general of the Nile equatorial regions.

Baker *Following her 1957 operatic debut in Smetana's The Secret at Glyndebourne, English mezzo-soprano Janet Baker enjoyed an extensive operatic career. Especially admired for her stylish performance of early Italian opera and the works of Benjamin Britten, she also excelled as an interpreter of Bach, Schubert, and Mahler.*

Bakewell /ˈbeɪkwel/ Robert 1725–1795. Pioneer improver of farm livestock. From his home in Leicestershire, England, he developed the Dishley or New Leicester breed of sheep and worked on raising the beef-producing qualities of Longhorn cattle.

Bakewell's work was in response to a general requirement for stock that would fatten to greater weights at an earlier age and at less cost. His method was to select animals that possessed at least some of the desired characteristics, and mate the offspring that inherited the same features with near relatives in order to fix the type. Known as 'breeding in and in', the technique was adopted widely. Bakewell's Longhorns found less favour because they were outshone by the rapidly emerging Shorthorns, but his New Leicesters proved popular as crosses to improve other native breeds of sheep.

Bakhuyzen /ˈbækhaʊzən/ Ludolf 1631–1708. Dutch painter of seascapes. *Stormy Sea* 1697 (Rijksmuseum, Amsterdam) is typically dramatic.

Bakke /ˈbækə/ Allan 1940– . US student who, in 1978, gave his name to a test case claiming 'reverse discrimination' when appealing against his exclusion from medical school, since less well-qualified blacks were to be admitted as part of a special programme for ethnic minorities. He won his case against quotas before the Supreme Court, although other affirmative action for minority groups was still endorsed.

Bakst /bækst/ Leon. Assumed name of Leon Rosenberg 1886–1924. Russian painter and theatrical designer. He used intense colours and fantastic images from Oriental and folk art, with an Art Nouveau tendency to graceful surface pattern. His designs for Diaghilev's touring *Ballets Russes* made a deep impression in Paris 1909–14.

To exploit and to govern mean the same thing... Exploitation and government are two inseparable expressions of what is called politics.

Mikhail Bakunin,
*The Knouto-Germanic Empire and the
Soviet Revolution*

Bakunin /bəˈkuːnɪn/ Mikhail 1814–1876. Russian anarchist, active in Europe. In 1848 he was expelled from France as a revolutionary agitator. In Switzerland in the 1860s he became recognized as the leader of the anarchist movement. In 1869 he joined the First International (a coordinating socialist body) but, after stormy conflicts with Karl Marx, was expelled 1872.

Born of a noble family, Bakunin served in the Imperial Guard but, disgusted with tsarist methods in Poland, resigned his commission and travelled abroad. For his share in a brief revolt at Dresden 1849 he was sentenced to death. The sentence was commuted to imprisonment, and he was handed over to the tsar's government and sent to Siberia 1855. In 1861 he managed to escape to Switzerland. He had a large following, mainly in the Latin American countries. He wrote books and pamphlets, including *God and the State*.

Balakirev /bəˈlɑːkɪref/ Mily Alexeyevich 1837–1910. Russian composer. He wrote orchestral works including the fantasy *Islamey* 1869/1902, piano music, songs, and a symphonic poem *Tamara*, all imbued with the Russian national character and spirit. He was leader of the group known as the Five and taught its members, Mussorgsky, Cui, Rimsky-Korsakov, and Borodin.

Balakirev was born at Nizhni Novgorod. At St Petersburg he worked with Mikhail →Glinka, established the Free School of Music 1862, which stressed the national element, and was director of the Imperial Chapel 1883–95.

Balanchine /ˈbælənˌtʃiːn/ George 1904–1983. Russian-born US choreographer. After leaving the USSR in 1924, he worked with →Diaghilev in France. Moving to the USA in 1933, he became a major influence on dance, starting the New York City Ballet in 1948. He was the most influential 20th-century choreographer of ballet in the USA. He developed an 'American Neo-Classic' dance style and made the New York City Ballet one of the world's great companies. He also pioneered choreography in Hollywood films.

His many works include *Apollon Musagète* 1928 and *The Prodigal Son* 1929 for Diaghilev, *Serenade* 1934; several works for music by →Stravinsky, such as *Agon* 1957 and *Duo Concertante* 1972; and Broadway musicals such as *On Your Toes* 1936 and *The Boys from Syracuse* 1938.

Balboa /bælˌbəʊə/ Vasco Núñez de 1475–1519. Spanish conquistador. He founded a settlement at Darien (now Panama) 1511 and crossed the Isthmus in search of gold, reaching the Pacific Ocean (which he called the South Sea) on 25 Sept 1513, after a 25-day expedition. He was made admiral of the Pacific and governor of Panama but was removed by Spanish court intrigue, imprisoned, and executed.

He was the first European to see the eastern side of the Pacific Ocean.

Balchin /ˈbɔːltʃɪn/ Nigel Marlin 1908–1970. British author. During World War II he was engaged on scientific work for the army and wrote *The Small Back Room* 1943, a novel dealing with the psychology of the 'back room boys' of wartime research.

Balcon /ˈbɔːlkən/ Michael 1896–1977. British film producer, responsible for the influential 'Ealing comedies' of the 1940s and early 1950s, such as *Kind Hearts and Coronets* 1949, *Whisky Galore!* 1949, and *The Lavender Hill Mob* 1951.

Baldung Grien /ˌbældʊŋˈgriːn/ Hans 1484/85–1545. German Renaissance painter, engraver, and designer, based in Strasbourg. He painted the theme *Death and the Maiden* in several versions.

Balfour Arthur Balfour, British statesman, formulator of the Balfour Declaration. An intellectual – he delivered the Gifford Lectures on Theism and Humanism 1915 – he was sometimes considered too detached to excel in politics.

Baldwin /ˈbɔːldwɪn/ James 1924–1987. US writer, born in New York City, who portrayed the condition of black Americans in contemporary society. His works include the novels *Go Tell It on the Mountain* 1953, *Another Country* 1962, and *Just Above My Head* 1979; the play *The Amen Corner* 1955; and the autobiographical essays *Notes of a Native Son* 1955 and *The Fire Next Time* 1963. He was active in the civil-rights movement.

Baldwin /ˈbɔːldwɪn/ Stanley, 1st Earl Baldwin of Bewdley 1867–1947. British Conservative politician, prime minister 1923–24, 1924–29, and 1935–37; he weathered the general strike 1926, secured complete adult suffrage 1928, and handled the abdication crisis of Edward VIII 1936, but failed to prepare Britain for World War II.

Born in Bewdley, Worcestershire, the son of an iron and steel magnate, in 1908 he was elected Unionist member of Parliament for Bewdley, and in 1916 he became parliamentary private secretary to Bonar Law. He was financial secretary to the Treasury 1917–21, and then appointed to the presidency of the Board of Trade. In 1919 he gave the Treasury £150,000 of War Loan for cancellation, representing about 20% of his fortune. He was a leader in the disruption of the Lloyd George coalition 1922, and, as chancellor under Bonar Law, achieved a settlement of war debts with the USA.

As prime minister 1923–24 and again 1924–29, Baldwin passed the Trades Disputes Act of 1927 after the general strike, granted widows' and orphans' pensions, and complete adult suffrage 1928. He joined the national government of Ramsay MacDonald 1931 as Lord President of the Council. He handled the abdication crisis during his third premiership 1935–37, but was later much criticized for his failures to resist popular desire for an accommodation with the dictators Hitler and Mussolini, and to rearm more effectively. Created 1st Earl Baldwin of Bewdley 1937.

Baldwin five kings of the Latin kingdom of Jerusalem, including:

Baldwin I /ˈbɔːldwɪn/ 1058–1118. King of Jerusalem from 1100. A French nobleman, he joined his brother →Godfrey de Bouillon on the First Crusade in 1096 and established the kingdom of Jerusalem in 1100. It was destroyed by Islamic conquest in 1187.

Baldwin II Baldwin du Bourg died 1131. King of the Latin kingdom of Jerusalem from 1118. During his reign Tyre became the seat of a Latin archbishop.

Balewa /bəˈleɪwə/ alternative title of Nigerian politician →Tafawa Balewa.

Balfe /bælf/ Michael William 1808–1870. Irish composer and singer. He was a violinist and baritone at Drury Lane, London, when only 16. In 1825 he went to Italy, where he sang in Palermo and at La Scala, and in 1846 he was appointed conductor at Her Majesty's Theatre, London. He composed operas, including *The Bohemian Girl* 1843.

Balfour /ˈbælfə/ Arthur James, 1st Earl of Balfour 1848–1930. British Conservative politician, prime minister 1902–05 and foreign secretary 1916–19, when he issued the Balfour Declaration 1917 and was involved in peace negotiations after World War I, signing the Treaty of Versailles.

Son of a Scottish landowner, Balfour was elected a Conservative member of Parliament in 1874. In Lord Salisbury's ministry he was secretary for Ireland 1887, and for his ruthless vigour was called 'Bloody Balfour' by Irish nationalists. In 1891 and again in 1895 he became First Lord of the Treasury and leader of the Commons, and in 1902 he succeeded Salisbury as prime minister. His cabinet was divided over Joseph Chamberlain's tariff-reform proposals, and in the 1905 elections suffered a crushing defeat.

Balfour retired from the party leadership in 1911. In 1915 he joined the Asquith coalition as First Lord of the Admiralty. As foreign secretary 1916–19 he issued the Balfour Declaration in favour of a national home in Palestine for the Jews. He was Lord President of the Council 1919–22 and 1925–29. Created 1st Earl of Balfour 1922. He also wrote books on philosophy.

Balfour Eve 1898–1990. English agriculturalist and pioneer of modern organic farming. She established the Haughley Experiment, a farm research project at New Bells Farm near Haughley, Suffolk, to demonstrate that a more sustainable agricultural alternative existed. The experiment ran for almost 30 years, comparing organic and chemical farming systems. The wide-ranging support it attracted led to the formation of the Soil Association 1946.

Baliol /ˈbeɪliəl/ John de *c.* 1250–1314. King of Scotland 1292–96. As an heir to the Scottish throne on the death of Margaret, the Maid of Norway, his cause was supported by the English king, Edward I, against 12 other claimants. Having paid homage to Edward, Baliol was proclaimed king but soon rebelled and gave up the kingdom when English forces attacked Scotland.

Ball /bɔːl/ John died 1381. English priest, one of the leaders of the Peasants' Revolt 1381, known as 'the mad priest of Kent'. A follower of John Wycliffe and a believer in social equality, he was imprisoned for disagreeing with the archbishop of Canterbury. During the revolt he was released from prison, and when in Blackheath, London, incited people against the ruling classes by preaching from the text 'When Adam delved and Eve span, who was then the gentleman?' When the revolt collapsed he escaped but was captured near Coventry and executed.

Ball /bɔːl/ Lucille 1911–1989. US comedy actress, famed as TV's Lucy. She began her film career as a bit player 1933, and appeared in dozens of movies over the next few years, including *Room Service* 1938 (with the Marx Brothers) and *Fancy Pants* 1950 (with Bob Hope). From 1951 to 1957 she starred with her husband, Cuban bandleader Desi Arnaz, in *I Love Lucy*, the first US television show filmed before an audience. It was followed by *The Lucy Show* 1962–68 and *Here's Lucy* 1968–74.

Ballance /ˈbæləns/ John 1839–1893. New Zealand Liberal politician, born in Northern Ireland; prime minister 1891–93. He emigrated to New Zealand, founded and edited the *Wanganui Herald*, and held many cabinet posts. He passed social legislation and opposed federation with Australia.

Ballantyne /ˈbæləntaɪn/ R(obert) M(ichael) 1825–1894. Scottish writer of children's books. Childhood visits to Canada and six years as a trapper for the Hudson's Bay Company provided material for his adventure stories, which include *The Young Fur Traders* 1856, *Coral Island* 1857, and *Martin Rattler* 1858.

Ballard /ˈbælɑːd/ J(ames) G(raham) 1930– . English novelist whose works include science fiction on the theme of disaster, such as *The Drowned World* 1962 and *High-Rise* 1975; the partly autobiographical *Empire of the Sun* 1984, dealing with his internment in China during World War II; and the autobiographical novel *The Kindness of Women* 1991.

Ballesteros /ˌbælɪˈstɪərɒs/ Seve(riano) 1957– . Spanish golfer who came to prominence 1976 and has won several leading tournaments in the USA, including the Masters Tournament 1980 and 1983. He has also won the British Open three times: in 1979, 1984, and 1988.

Born in Pedrena, N Spain, he is one of four golf-playing brothers. He has won more than 60 tournaments worldwide.

Balmer /ˈbælmə/ Johann Jakob 1825–1898. Swiss physicist and mathematician who developed a formula in 1884 that gave the wavelengths of the light emitted by the hydrogen atom (the hydrogen spectrum). This simple formula played a central role in the development of spectral and atomic theory.

Balzac /ˈbælˈzæk/ Honoré de 1799–1850. French novelist. His first success was *Les Chouans/The Chouans* and *La Physiologie du mariage/The Physiology of Marriage* 1829, inspired by Walter Scott. This was the beginning of the long series of novels *La Comédie humaine/The Human Comedy*. He also wrote the Rabelaisian *Contes drolatiques/Ribald Tales* 1833.

Born in Tours, Balzac studied law and worked as a notary's clerk in Paris before turning to literature. His first attempts included tragedies such as *Cromwell* and novels published pseudonymously with no great success. A venture in printing and publishing 1825–28 involved him in a lifelong web of debt. His patroness, Madame de Berny, figures in *Le Lys dans la vallée/The Lily in the Valley* 1836. Balzac intended his major work *La Comédie humaine/The Human Comedy* to comprise 143 volumes, depicting every aspect of society in 19th-century France, of which he completed 80. The series includes *Eugénie Grandet* 1833, *Le Père Goriot* 1834, and *Cousine Bette* 1846. Balzac corresponded constantly with the Polish countess Evelina Hanska after meeting her 1833, and they married four months before his death in Paris. He was buried in Père Lachaise cemetery.

Bancroft /bænkrɒft/ George 1800–1891. US diplomat and historian. A Democrat, he was secretary of the navy 1845 when he established the US Naval Academy at Annapolis, Maryland, and as acting secretary of war (May 1846) was instrumental in bringing about the occupation of California and the Mexican War. He wrote a *History of the United States* 1834–76.

Banda /bændə/ Hastings Kamuzu 1902– . Malawi politician, president from 1966. He led his country's independence movement and was prime minister of Nyasaland (the former name of Malawi) from 1963. He became Malawi's first president 1966 and 1971 was named president for life; his rule has been authoritarian. Despite civil unrest during 1992, he has resisted calls for free, multiparty elections.

Banda studied in the USA, and was a doctor in Britain until 1953.

Bandaranaike /ˌbændərəˈnaɪkə/ Sirimavo (born Ratwatte) 1916– . Sri Lankan politician, who succeeded her husband Solomon Bandaranaike to become the world's first female prime minister 1960–65 and 1970–77, but was expelled from parliament 1980 for abuse of her powers while in office. She was largely responsible for the new constitution 1972.

Bandaranaike /ˌbændərəˈnaɪkə/ Solomon West Ridgeway Dias 1899–1959. Sri Lankan nationalist politician. In 1952 he founded the Sri Lanka Freedom party and in 1956 became prime minister, pledged to a socialist programme and a neutral foreign policy. He failed to satisfy extremists and was assassinated by a Buddhist monk.

Bankhead /bæŋkhed/ Tallulah 1903–1968. US actress, renowned for her wit and flamboyant lifestyle. Her stage appearances include *Dark Victory* 1934, *The Little Foxes* 1939, and *The Skin of Our Teeth* 1942. Her films include Hitchcock's *Lifeboat* 1943.

Banks /bæŋks/ Jeff 1943– . British textile, fashion, and interior designer. He helped establish the Warehouse Utility chain 1974 and combines imaginative designs with inexpensive materials to provide stylish and affordable garments for the younger market.

Banks /bæŋks/ Joseph 1744–1820. British naturalist and explorer. He accompanied Capt James →Cook on his voyage round the world 1768–71 and brought back 3,600 plants, 1,400 of them never before classified. The *Banksia* genus of shrubs is named after him.

A founder and unofficial first director of the Botanical Gardens, Kew, Banks was president of the Royal Society from 1778 to 1819.

Banks /bæŋks/ Nathaniel Prentiss 1816–1894. US politician and American Civil War general. He was Speaker in the US House of Representatives 1853–57. At the outbreak of the war 1861, he was appointed major general in command of the Department of Annapolis. Defeated by Stonewall →Jackson in the Shenandoah Valley, he was sent to New Orleans 1863, taking command of the Department of the Gulf. He led the ill-fated Red River expedition 1864.

Born in Waltham, Massachusetts, USA, Banks was governor of Massachusetts 1857–60. He entered Congress after the end of the Civil War and served there until 1891.

Bannister /bænɪstə/ Roger Gilbert 1929– . English track and field athlete, the first person to run a mile in under four minutes. He achieved this feat at Oxford, England, on 6 May 1954 in a time of 3 min 59.4 sec.

Studying at Oxford to be a doctor at the time, Bannister broke the four-minute barrier on one more occasion: at the 1954 Commonwealth Games in Vancouver, Canada, when he was involved with John Landy (1930–) from Australia, in the 'Mile of the Century', so called because it was a clash between the only two people to have broken the four-minute barrier for the mile at that time.

Running has given me a glimpse of the greatest freedom a man can ever know, because it results in the simultaneous liberation of both body and mind.

Roger Bannister
First Four Minutes

Banting /bæntɪŋ/ Frederick Grant 1891–1941. Canadian physician who discovered a technique for isolating the hormone insulin 1921 when, experimentally, he and his colleague Charles →Best tied off the ducts of the pancreas to determine the function of the cells known as the islets of Langerhans. This allowed for the treatment of diabetes. Banting and John J R Macleod (1876–1935), his mentor, shared the 1923 Nobel Prize for Medicine, and Banting divided his prize with Best.

Bantock /bæntək/ Granville 1868–1946. English composer and conductor; professor of music at the University of Birmingham 1908–34. His works include the oratorio *Omar Khayyám*

Antony and Cleopatra 1966, was commissioned for the opening of the new Metropolitan Opera House at Lincoln Center, New York City. Barber's music is lyrical and fastidiously worked. His later works include *The Lovers* 1971.

As to what happens when I compose, I really haven't the faintest idea.

Samuel Barber

Bara *US silent-film actress Theda Bara who created and popularized the image of the 1920s 'vamp'. Her sensational success in more than 40 silent films was aided by massive publicity campaigns.*

1906–09, *Hebridean Symphony* 1915, and *Pagan Symphony* 1928.

Banu Musa three brothers, Muhammad (died 873), Ahmad, and al-Hasan, who lived in Baghdad during the reign of the Caliph al-Ma'mun (813–833). They compiled an important mathematical work on the measurement of plane and spherical figures, and one of the earliest works on mechanical engineering *Kitab al-hiyal/The Book of Ingenious Devices*.

Bara /ˈbɑːrə/ Theda. Stage name of Theodosia Goodman 1890–1955. US silent-film actress who became known as 'the vamp', and the first movie sex symbol, after appearing in *A Fool There Was* 1915, based on 'The Vampire', a poem by Rudyard Kipling.

Barbarossa /ˌbɑːbəˈrɒsə/ nickname 'red beard' given to the Holy Roman emperor →Frederick I, and also to two brothers, Horuk and Khair-ed-Din, who were Barbary pirates. Horuk was killed by the Spaniards 1518; Khair-ed-Din took Tunis 1534 and died in Constantinople 1546.

Barbellion /bɑːˈbeliən/ W N P. Pen name of Bruce Frederick Cummings 1889–1919. English diarist, author of *The Journal of a Disappointed Man* 1919, an account of his struggle with the illness multiple sclerosis.

Barber /ˈbɑːbə/ Samuel 1910–1981. US composer of a Neo-Classical, later somewhat dissonant style, whose works include *Adagio for Strings* 1936 and the opera *Vanessa* 1958, which won him one of his two Pulitzer prizes. Another Barber opera,

Barbie /ˈbɑːbi/ Klaus 1913–1991. German Nazi, a member of the SS from 1936. During World War II he was involved in the deportation of Jews from the occupied Netherlands 1940–42 and in tracking down Jews and Resistance workers in France 1942–45. He was arrested 1983 and convicted of crimes against humanity in France 1987.

His work as SS commander, based in Lyon, included the rounding-up of Jewish children from an orphanage at Izieu and the torture of the Resistance leader Jean Moulin. His ruthlessness during this time earned him the epithet 'Butcher of Lyon'. Having escaped capture 1945, Barbie was employed by the US intelligence services in Germany before moving to Bolivia 1951. Expelled from there in 1983, he was returned to France, where he was tried by a court in Lyon. He died in prison.

Barbirolli /ˌbɑːbɪˈrɒli/ John 1899–1970. English conductor. He made his name as a cellist, and in 1937 succeeded Toscanini as conductor of the New York Philharmonic Orchestra. He returned to England 1943, where he remained conductor of the Hallé Orchestra, Manchester, until his death.

Barbour /ˈbɑːbə/ John *c.* 1316–1395. Scottish poet whose chronicle poem *The Brus* is among the earliest Scottish poetry.

Barbour /ˈbɑːbə/ Philip Pendleton 1783–1841. US jurist and political leader. He served as Speaker of the House in the US House of Representatives 1821–23. A strong supporter of states' rights, he was appointed federal district judge by President →Jackson 1830. He served on the US Supreme Court 1836–41, consistently ruling in favour of the prerogative of the states over federal authority.

Born in Barboursville, Virginia, Barbour studied law and briefly practised in Kentucky before returning to Virginia and beginning a political career.

Bardeen /bɑːˈdiːn/ John 1908–1991. US physicist who won a Nobel prize 1956, with Walter Brattain and William Shockley, for the development of the transistor 1948. In 1972 he became the first double winner of a Nobel prize in the same subject (with Leon Cooper and John Schrieffer) for his work on superconductivity.

Bardot /bɑːˈdəʊ/ Brigitte 1934– . French film actress whose sensual appeal did much to popularize French cinema internationally. Her films include *Et Dieu créa la femme/And God Created Woman* 1950, *Viva Maria* 1965, and *Shalako* 1968.

Barenboim /ˈbærənbɔɪm/ Daniel 1942– . Israeli pianist and conductor, born in Argentina. Pianist/conductor with the English Chamber Orchestra from 1964, he became conductor of the New York Philharmonic Orchestra 1970 and musical director of the Orchestre de Paris 1975. Appointed artistic and musical director of the Opéra de la Bastille, Paris, July 1987, he was dismissed from his post July 1989, a few months before its opening, for reasons which he claimed were more political than artistic. His dismissal was the subject of a highly publicized and controversial dispute. He is a celebrated interpreter of Mozart and Beethoven.

Barents /ˈbærənts/ Willem *c.* 1550–1597. Dutch explorer and navigator. He made three expeditions to seek the Northeast Passage; he died on the last voyage. The Barents Sea, part of the Arctic Ocean N of Norway, is named after him.

Barham /ˈbɑːrəm/ Richard Harris 1788–1845. British writer and clergyman, author of verse tales of the supernatural, and *The Ingoldsby Legends*, published under his pen name Thomas Ingoldsby.

Baring-Gould /ˈbeərɪŋ ˈguːld/ Sabine 1834–1924. British writer, rector of Lew Trenchard in N Devon from 1881. He was a prolific writer of novels and books of travel, mythology, and folklore and wrote the words of the hymn 'Onward, Christian Soldiers'.

Barker /ˈbɑːkə/ Clive 1952– . British writer whose *Books of Blood* 1984–85 are in the sensationalist tradition of horror fiction.

Barker /ˈbɑːkə/ George 1913–1991. British poet, known for his vivid imagery, as in *Calamiterror* 1937, *The True Confessions of George Barker* 1950, *Collected Poems* 1930–50, and the posthumously published *Street Ballads* 1992.

Barker /ˈbɑːkə/ Herbert 1869–1950. British manipulative surgeon, whose work established the popular standing of orthopaedics (the study and treatment of disorders of the spine and joints), but who was never recognized by the world of orthodox medicine.

Barker Howard 1946– . English playwright whose plays, renowned for their uncompromising and poetically dense language, confront the issues of private ambition and the exploitation of power. Among his works are *Victory* 1982; *The Castle* 1985; *The Last Supper*, *The Possibilities*, and *The Bite of the Night*, all in 1988; and *Seven Lears* 1989.

In 1988 he formed The Wrestling School, a theatre company dedicated to the performance of his own work.

Barlach /ˈbɑːlæx/ Ernst 1870–1938. German Expressionist sculptor, painter, and poet. His simple, evocative figures carved in wood (for example, those in St Catherine's, Lübeck, 1930–32) often express melancholy.

Barlow /ˈbɑːləʊ/ Joel 1754–1812. US poet and diplomat. A member of the literary circle the 'Connecticut Wits,' he published an epic entitled *The Vision of Columbus* 1787. As US consul in Algiers 1795–97, he gained the release of American hostages taken by the Barbary pirates operating against US and European shipping. On diplomatic mission to France 1811 he died whilst accompanying Napoleon in his retreat from Russia 1812.

Born in Redding, Connecticut, USA, Barlow was educated at Yale University. Living as an expatriate in Europe, Barlow was deeply affected by the philosophical ideals of the Enlightenment and was granted citizenship in revolutionary France.

Barnabas, St /ˈbɑːnəbəs/ in the New Testament, a 'fellow labourer' with St Paul; he went with St Mark on a missionary journey to Cyprus, his birthplace. Feast day 11 June.

Barnard /ˈbɑːnɑːd/ Christiaan (Neethling) 1922– . South African surgeon who performed the first human heart transplant 1967 in Cape Town. The patient, 54-year-old Louis Washkansky, lived for 18 days.

Barnardo /bəˈnɑːdəʊ/ Thomas John 1845–1905. British philanthropist, who was known as Dr Barnardo, although not medically qualified. He opened the first of a series of homes for destitute children 1867 in Stepney, E London.

Barnes /bɑːnz/ Ernest William 1874–1953. British cleric. A lecturer in mathematics at Cambridge 1902–15, he was an ardent advocate of the influence of scientific thought on religion. In 1924 he became bishop of Birmingham; he published *The Rise of Christianity* 1947.

Barnes /bɑːnz/ Thomas 1785–1841. British journalist, forthright and influential editor of *The Times* from 1817, during whose editorship it became known as 'the Thunderer'.

Barnum /ˈbɑːnəm/ Phineas T(aylor) 1810–1891. US showman. In 1871, after an adventurous career, he established the 'Greatest Show on Earth', which included the midget 'Tom Thumb', a circus, a menagerie, and an exhibition of 'freaks', conveyed in 100 railway carriages. He coined the phrase 'there's a sucker born every minute'.

How were the receipts today in Madison Square Garden?

Phineas Taylor Barnum last words 1891

Barocci /bəˈrɒtʃi/ Federico *c.* 1535–1612. Italian artist, born and based in Urbino. He painted religious themes in a highly coloured, sensitive style that falls between Renaissance and Baroque. His *Madonna del Graffo* (National Gallery, London) shows the influence of Raphael (also from Urbino) and Correggio on his art.

Baroja /bæˈrəuxə/ Pio 1872–1956. Spanish novelist of Basque extraction whose works include a trilogy dealing with the Madrid underworld, *La lucha por la vida/The Struggle for Life* 1904–05, and the multivolume *Memorias de un hombre de acción/Memoirs of a Man of Action* 1913–28.

Barragán /ˌbærəˈgɑːn/ Luis 1902–1988. Mexican architect, known for his use of rough wooden beams, cobbles, lava, and adobe.

Barras /bæˈrɑː/ Paul François Jean Nicolas, Count 1755–1829. French revolutionary. He was elected to the National Convention 1792 and helped to overthrow Robespierre 1794. In 1795 he became a member of the ruling Directory. In 1796 he brought about the marriage of his former mistress, Joséphine de Beauharnais, with Napoleon and assumed dictatorial powers. After Napoleon's coup d'état 19 Nov 1799, Barras fell into disgrace.

Barrault /bæˈrəu/ Jean-Louis 1910– . French actor and director. His films include *La Symphonie fantastique* 1942, *Les Enfants du paradis* 1945, and *La Ronde* 1950.

He was producer and director to the Comédie Française 1940–46, and director of the Théâtre de France (formerly Odéon) from 1959 until his dismissal 1968 because of statements made during the occupation of the theatre by student rebels.

Barre /bɑː/ Raymond 1924– . French politician, member of the centre-right Union pour la Démocratie Française; prime minister 1976–81, when he also held the Finance Ministry portfolio and gained a reputation as a tough and determined budget-cutter.

Barre, born on the French dependency of Réunion, was a liberal economist at the Sorbonne and vice president of the European Commission 1967–72. He served as minister of foreign trade to President Giscard d'Estaing and became prime minister on the resignation of Chirac 1976. He built up a strong political base in the Lyon region during the early 1980s. Once considered a candidate for the presidency, in 1988 he effectively ruled himself out of contention.

Barrett Browning /ˈbraunɪŋ/ Elizabeth 1806–1861. English poet. In 1844 she published *Poems* (including 'The Cry of the Children'), which led to her friendship with and secret marriage to Robert Browning 1846. The *Sonnets from the Portuguese* 1847 were written during their courtship. Later works include *Casa Guidi Windows* 1851 and the poetic novel *Aurora Leigh* 1857.

Barrett Browning was born near Durham. As a child she fell from her pony and injured her spine and was subsequently treated by her father as a confirmed invalid. Freed from her father's oppres-

Barrett Browning Lyric poet Elizabeth Barrett Browning eloped with Robert Browning to Italy 1846. In later years she became involved in Italian politics, the abolition of slavery, and spiritualism.

sive influence, her health improved. She wrote strong verse about social injustice and oppression in Victorian England.

Barrie /ˈbæri/ J(ames) M(atthew) 1860–1937. Scottish playwright and novelist, author of *The Admirable Crichton* 1902 and the children's fantasy *Peter Pan* 1904.

He became known by his studies of Scottish rural life in plays such as *A Window in Thrums* 1889, which began the vogue of the Kailyard school. His reputation as a playwright was established with *The Professor's Love Story* 1894 and *The Little Minister* 1897. His later plays include *Quality Street* 1901 and *What Every Woman Knows* 1908.

Every time a child says 'I don't believe in fairies' there is a little fairy somewhere that falls down dead.

J M **Barrie** *Peter Pan* 1904

Barrios de Chamorro Violeta. President of Nicaragua from 1990; see ➔Chamorro.

Barrow /ˈbærəu/ Clyde 1900–1934. US criminal; see ➔Bonnie and Clyde.

Barrow /ˈbærəu/ Isaac 1630–1677. British mathematician, theologian, and classicist. His *Lectiones geometricae* 1670 contains the essence of the theory of calculus, which was later expanded by Isaac Newton and Gottfried Leibniz.

Barry English architect Sir Charles Barry designed the Traveller's Club and the Reform Club in London and the Manchester Athenaeum. His commission to design the new Houses of Parliament, after the 1839 fire, stipulated a Gothic style which went against the grain of his Italian Renaissance tastes and principles.

Barry /ˈbæri/ Charles 1795–1860. English architect of the Neo-Gothic Houses of Parliament at Westminster, London, 1840–60, in collaboration with Augustus ➔Pugin.

Barry /ˈbæri/ Comtesse du. See ➔du Barry, mistress of Louis XV of France.

Barrymore /ˈbærɪmɔː/ US family of actors, the children of British-born Maurice Barrymore and Georgie Drew, both stage personalities.

Lionel Barrymore (1878–1954) first appeared on the stage with his grandmother, Mrs John Drew, 1893. He played numerous film roles from 1909, including *A Free Soul* 1931 and *Grand Hotel* 1932, but was perhaps best known for his annual radio portrayal of Scrooge in Dickens's *A Christmas Carol*.

John Barrymore (1882–1942), a flamboyant actor who often appeared on stage and screen with his brother and sister. In his early years he was a Shakespearean actor. From 1923 he acted almost entirely in films, including *Dinner at Eight* 1933, and became a screen idol, nicknamed 'the Profile'.

Ethel Barrymore (1879–1959) played with the British actor Henry Irving in London 1898 and 1928 opened the Ethel Barrymore Theatre in New York; she also appeared in many films from 1914, including *None but the Lonely Heart* 1944.

Barstow /ˈbɑːstəʊ/ Stan 1928– . English novelist born in W Yorkshire. His novels describe northern working-class life and include *A Kind of Loving* 1960.

Bart /bɑːt/ Lionel 1930– . English composer, author of both words and music for many musicals including *Fings Ain't Wot They Us'd T'Be* 1959 and *Oliver!* 1960.

Barth /bɑːt/ Heinrich 1821–1865. German geographer and explorer who in explorations of N Africa between 1844 and 1855 established the exact course of the river Niger.

He studied the coast of N Africa from Tunis to Egypt 1844–45, travelled in the Middle East 1845–47, crossed the Sahara from Tripoli 1850, and then spent five years exploring the country between Lake Chad and Cameroon which he described in the five-volume *Travels and Discoveries in Central Africa* 1857–58.

Barth /bɑːt/ John 1930– . US novelist and short-story writer who was influential in the 'academic' experimental movement of the 1960s. His works are usually interwoven fictions based on language games, since he is concerned with the relationship of language and reality. They include the novels *The Sot-Weed Factor* 1960, *Giles Goat-Boy* 1966, *Letters* 1979, *Sabbatical: A Romance* 1982, and *The Tidewater Tales* 1987. He also wrote the novella *Chimera* 1972 and *Lost in the Funhouse* 1968, a collection of short stories.

Barth /bɑːt/ Karl 1886–1968. Swiss Protestant theologian. A socialist in his political views, he attacked the Nazis. His *Church Dogmatics* 1932–62 makes the resurrection of Jesus the focal point of Christianity.

Barthes /bɑːt/ Roland 1915–1980. French critic and theorist of semiology, the science of signs and symbols. One of the French 'new critics' and an exponent of structuralism, he attacked traditional literary criticism in his early works, including *Le Degré zéro de l'ecriture/Writing Degree Zero* 1953 and *Sur Racine/On Racine* 1963.

His structuralist approach involved exposing and analysing the system of signs, patterns, and laws that may be conveyed by a novel or play. He also wrote an autobiographical novel, *Roland Barthes sur Roland Barthes* 1975.

Bartholdi /bɑːˈtɒldi/ Frédéric Auguste 1834–1904. French sculptor. He designed the Statue of Liberty overlooking New York harbour, 1884.

Bartholomew, St /bɑːˈθɒləmjuː/ in the New Testament, one of the apostles. Some legends relate that after the Crucifixion he took Christianity to India; others that he was a missionary in Anatolia and Armenia, where he suffered martyrdom by being flayed alive. Feast day 24 Aug.

Bartók /ˈbɑːtɒk/ Béla 1881–1945. Hungarian composer who developed a personal musical language, combining folk elements with mathematical concepts of tone and rhythmic proportion. His large output includes six string quartets, concertos, an opera, and graded teaching pieces for piano.

A child prodigy, Bartók studied music at the

Budapest Conservatory, later working with Zoltan →Kodály in recording and transcribing local folk music for a government project. His ballet *The Miraculous Mandarin* 1919 was banned because of its subject matter (it was set in a brothel). Bartók died in the USA, having fled from Hungary 1940.

Bartolommeo /baːˌtɒləˈmeɪəu/ Fra, also called *Baccio della Porta* c. 1472–c. 1517. Italian religious painter of the High Renaissance, active in Florence. His painting of *The Last Judgment* 1499 (Museo di San Marco, Florence) influenced Raphael.

Barton /ˈbɑːtn/ Clara 1821–1912. US health worker, founder of the American Red Cross 1881 and its president until 1904. A volunteer nurse, she tended the casualties of the American Civil War 1861–65 and in 1864 General Benjamin Butler named her superintendent of nurses for his forces.

Born in Oxford, Massachusetts, USA, Barton was trained as a teacher before becoming involved in projects for the welfare of American soldiers. She was present at the Baltimore riot at the outbreak of the Civil War 1861 and also at the Battles of Antietam and Fredericksburg 1862.

Barton /ˈbɑːtn/ Edmund 1849–1920. Australian politician. He was leader of the federation movement from 1896 and first prime minister of Australia 1901–03.

Baruch /bəˈruːk/ Bernard (Mannes) 1870–1965. US financier. He was a friend of British prime minister Churchill and a self-appointed, unpaid adviser to US presidents Wilson, F D Roosevelt, and Truman. He strongly advocated international control of nuclear energy.

Baryshnikov /bəˈrɪʃnɪkɒf/ Mikhail 1948– . Latvian-born dancer, now based in the USA. He joined the Kirov Ballet 1967 and became one of their most brilliant soloists. After defecting from the Soviet Union 'on artistic, not political grounds' while on tour in Canada 1974, he danced with various companies, and later joined the American Ballet Theater (ABT) as principal dancer, partnering Gelsey Kirkland. He left to join the New York City Ballet 1978–80, but rejoined ABT as director 1980–90. From 1990 he has danced for various companies.

He has created many roles, for example in Twyla Tharp's *Push Comes to Shove* 1976 (music by Haydn/Lamb) and in Jerome Robbins's *Opus 19* 1979 (Prokofiev). He made his film debut in *The Turning Point* 1978 and has since acted in other films, including *White Nights* 1985. He made his dramatic stage debut in *Metamorphosis* 1989.

Barzun /ˈbɑːzʌn/ Jacques Martin 1907– . French-born US historian and educator whose speciality was 19th-century European intellectual life. His book *The Modern Researcher* 1970 is recognized as a classic study of historical method.

Among his many historical works is *Romanticism and the Modern Ego* 1943.

Barzun emigrated to the USA with his parents 1919. He was educated at Columbia University, earning a PhD in history 1932, and soon afterward joined the faculty there, becoming a member of the administration.

Bashkirtseff /ˈbæʃˈkɪəstsef/ Marie 1860–1884. Russian diarist and painter whose journals, written in French, were cited by Simone de Beauvoir as the archetypal example of 'self-centred female narcissism', but which also revealed the discovery by the female of her independent existence. She died of tuberculosis at 24.

Basie /ˈbeɪsi/ Count (William) 1904–1984. US jazz band leader, pianist, and organist who developed the big-band sound and a simplified, swinging style of music. He led impressive groups of musicians in a career spanning more than 50 years. Basie's compositions include 'One O'Clock Jump' and 'Jumpin at the Woodside'.

His solo piano technique was influenced by the style of Fats Waller. Some consider his the definitive dance band.

Basil II /ˈbæzl/ c. 958–1025. Byzantine emperor from 976. His achievement as emperor was to contain, and later decisively defeat, the Bulgarians, earning for himself the title 'Bulgar-Slayer' after a victory 1014. After the battle he blinded almost all 15,000 of the defeated, leaving only a few men with one eye to lead their fellows home. The Byzantine empire had reached its largest extent at the time of his death.

Basil, St /ˈbæzl/ c. 330–379. Cappadocian monk, known as 'the Great', founder of the Basilian monks. Elected bishop of Caesarea 370, Basil opposed the heresy of Arianism. He wrote many theological works and composed the 'Liturgy of St Basil', in use in the Eastern Orthodox Church. His feast day is 2 Jan.

Born in Caesarea, Anatolia, he studied in Constantinople and Athens, and visited the hermit saints of the Egyptian desert. He entered a monastery in Anatolia about 358, and developed a monastic rule based on community life, work, and prayer. These ideas form the basis of monasticism in the Greek Orthodox Church, and influenced the foundation of similar monasteries by St Benedict.

Teaching a Christian how he ought to live does not call so much for words as for daily example.

St Basil *Oration*

Baskerville /ˈbæskəvɪl/ John 1706–1775. English printer and typographer, who experimented in casting types from 1750 onwards. The Baskerville typeface is named after him.

Bates English actor Alan Bates studied at RADA and made his stage debut in You and Your Wife 1955 in Coventry. He made his film debut in The Entertainer 1960 and featured in some of the most popular British films of the decade. His television work includes An Englishman Abroad 1982, which won a BAFTA award.

He manufactured fine printing paper and inks, and in 1756 published a quarto edition of the Classical poet Virgil, which was followed by 54 highly crafted books.

Basov /ˈbɑːsɒf/ Nikolai Gennadievich 1912– . Soviet physicist who in 1953, with his compatriot Aleksandr Prokhorov, developed the microwave amplifier called a maser. They were both awarded the Nobel Prize for Physics 1964, which they shared with Charles Townes of the USA.

Bass /bæs/ George 1763–c. 1808. English naval surgeon who with Matthew →Flinders explored the coast of New South Wales and the strait that bears his name between Tasmania and Australia 1795–98.

Bastos /ˈbæstɒs/ Augusto Roa 1917– . Paraguayan writer of short stories and novels, including Son of Man 1960 about the Chaco War between Bolivia and Paraguay, in which he fought.

Bateman /ˈbeɪtmən/ H(enry) M(ayo) 1887–1970. Australian cartoonist who lived in England. His cartoons were based on themes of social embarrassment and confusion, in such series as The Man who ... (as in The Guardsman who Dropped his Rifle).

Bates /beɪts/ Alan 1934– . English actor, a versatile male lead in over 60 plays and films. His films include Zorba the Greek 1965, Far from the Madding Crowd 1967, Women in Love 1970, The Go-Between 1971, The Shout 1978, and Duet for One 1986.

Bates /beɪts/ H(enry) W(alter) 1825–1892. English naturalist and explorer, who spent 11 years collecting animals and plants in South America and identified 8,000 new species of insects. He made a special study of camouflage in animals, and his observation of insect imitation of species that are unpleasant to predators is known as 'Batesian mimicry'.

Bates /beɪts/ H(erbert) E(rnest) 1906–1974. English author. Of his many novels and short stories, The Jacaranda Tree 1949 and The Darling Buds of May 1958 demonstrate the fineness of his natural observation and compassionate portrayal of character. Fair Stood the Wind for France 1944 was based on his experience as a Squadron Leader in World War II.

Báthory /ˈbɑːtəri/ Stephen 1533–1586. King of Poland, elected by a diet convened 1575 and crowned 1576. Báthory succeeded in driving the Russian troops of Ivan the Terrible out of his country. His military successes brought potential conflicts with Sweden, but he died before these developed.

Batista /bəˈtiːstə/ Fulgencio 1901–1973. Cuban dictator 1933–44, when he stood down, and again 1952–59, after seizing power in a coup. His authoritarian methods enabled him to jail his opponents and amass a large personal fortune. He was overthrown by rebel forces led by Fidel →Castro 1959.

Batoni /bəˈtəʊni/ Pompeo 1708–1787. Italian painter celebrated for his detailed portraits of princes and gentlemen.

Batten /ˈbætn/ Jean 1909–1982. New Zealand aviator who made the first return solo flight by a woman Australia–Britain 1935, and established speed records.

Battenberg /ˈbætnbɜːg/ title (conferred 1851) of German noble family; its members included →Louis, Prince of Battenberg, and Louis Alexander, Prince of Battenberg, who anglicized his name to Mountbatten 1917.

Baudelaire /ˌbəʊdəˈleə/ Charles Pierre 1821–1867. French poet whose work combined rhythmical and musical perfection with a morbid romanticism and eroticism, finding beauty in decadence and evil. His first book of verse was Les Fleurs du mal/Flowers of Evil 1857.

But the real travellers are only those who leave
For the sake of leaving

Charles Baudelaire *The Voyage*

Baudouin /ˌbəʊduˈæn/ 1930– . King of the Belgians from 1951. In 1950 his father, →Leopold III, abdicated and Baudouin was known until his succession July 1951 as Le Prince Royal. In 1960 he married Fabiola de Mora y Aragón (1928–), member of a Spanish noble family.

Baum /bɔːm/ L(yman) Frank 1856–1919. US writer, author of the children's fantasy *The Wonderful Wizard of Oz* 1900 and its 13 sequels. The series was continued by another author after his death. The film *The Wizard of Oz* 1939 with Judy Garland became a US classic.

Bausch /bauʃ/ Pina 1940– . German avant-garde dance choreographer and director from 1974 of the Wuppertal Tanztheater. Her works incorporate dialogue, elements of psychoanalysis, comedy, and drama, and have been performed on floors covered with churned earth, rose petals, or water. She never accepts requests to restage her creations.

Bawa /bauə/ Geoffrey 1919– . Sri Lankan architect, formerly a barrister. His buildings are a contemporary interpretation of vernacular traditions, and include houses, hotels, and gardens. More recently he has designed public buildings such as the New Parliamentary Complex, Colombo 1982, and Ruhuru University, Matara 1984.

Bax /bæks/ Arnold Edward Trevor 1883–1953. English composer. His works, often based on Celtic legends, include seven symphonies and *The Garden of Fand* 1913–16 and *Tintagel* 1917–19 (both tone poems). He was Master of the King's Musick 1942–53.

Baxter /bækstə/ George 1804–1867. English engraver and printmaker; inventor 1834 of a special process for printing in oil colours, which he applied successfully in book illustrations.

Baxter /bækstə/ Richard 1615–1691. English cleric. During the English Civil War he was a chaplain in the Parliamentary army, and after the Restoration became a royal chaplain. Baxter was driven out of the church by the Act of Uniformity of 1662, which he saw as an unacceptable administrative and spiritual imposition. In 1685 he was imprisoned for nearly 18 months for alleged sedition.

Bayard /beɪɑːd/ Pierre du Terrail, Chevalier de 1473–1524. French soldier. He served under Charles VIII, Louis XII, and Francis I and was killed in action at the crossing of the Sesia in Italy. His heroic exploits in battle and in tournaments, and his chivalry and magnanimity, won him the accolade of 'knight without fear and without reproach'.

Bayes /beɪz/ Thomas 1702–1761. English mathematician whose investigations into probability led to what is now known as Bayes' theorem.

Bayle /beɪl/ Pierre 1647–1706. French critic and philosopher. He was suspended from the chair of philosophy at Rotterdam under suspicion of religious scepticism 1693. Three years later his *Dictionnaire historique et critique* appeared, which influenced among others the French *Encyclopédistes*.

Baxter English clergyman Richard Baxter. Originally chaplain to Cromwell's army, he was appointed Royal Chaplain by Charles II at the Restoration. He was driven out of the Church of England by the 1662 Act of Uniformity and later imprisoned by Judge Jeffreys.

Bayliss /beɪlɪs/ William Maddock 1860–1924. English physiologist who discovered the digestive hormone secretin with Ernest →Starling 1902. During World War I, Bayliss introduced the use of saline (salt water) injections to help the injured recover from shock.

Bazaine /bæˈzeɪn/ Achille François 1811–1888. Marshal of France. From being a private soldier 1831 he rose to command the French troops in Mexico 1862–67 and was made a marshal 1864. In the Franco-Prussian War Bazaine allowed himself to be taken in the fortress of Metz, surrendering 27 Oct 1870 with nearly 180,000 men. For this he was court-martialled 1873 and imprisoned; he escaped to Spain 1874.

Bazalgette /bæzldʒet/ Joseph 1819–1890. British civil engineer who, as chief engineer to the London Board of Works, designed London's sewer system, a total of 155 km/83 mi of sewers, covering an area of 256 sq km/100 sq mi. It was completed 1865. He also designed the Victoria Embankment 1864–70, which was built over the river Thames and combined a main sewer, a water frontage, an underground railway, and a road.

Beach Boys, the US pop group formed 1961. They began as exponents of vocal-harmony surf music with Chuck Berry guitar riffs (their hits include 'Surfin' USA' 1963 and 'Help Me, Rhonda' 1965) but the compositions, arrangements, and production by Brian Wilson (1942–) became highly complex under the influence of psychedelic rock, peaking with 'Good Vibrations' 1966. Wilson spent most of the next 20 years in retirement but returned with a solo album 1988.

Beaconsfield /ˈbikənzfiːld/ title taken by Benjamin →Disraeli, prime minister of Britain 1868 and 1874–80.

Beadle /ˈbiːdl/ George Wells 1903–1989. US biologist. Born in Wahoo, Nebraska, he was professor of biology at the California Institute of Technology 1946–61. In 1958 he shared a Nobel prize with Edward L Tatum for his work in biochemical genetics, forming the 'one-gene–one-enzyme' hypothesis (a single gene codes for a single kind of enzyme).

Beale /biːl/ Dorothea 1831–1906. British pioneer in women's education whose work helped to raise the standard of women's education and the status of women teachers.

She was headmistress of the Ladies' College at Cheltenham from 1858, and founder of St Hilda's Hall, Oxford, 1892.

Beard /bɪəd/ Charles Austin 1874–1948. US historian and a leader of the Progressive movement, active in promoting political and social reform. As a chief exponent of critical economic history, he published *An Economic Interpretation of the Constitution of the United States* 1913 and *The Economic Origins of Jeffersonian Democracy* 1915. With his wife, Mary, he wrote *A Basic History of the United States* 1944, long a standard textbook in the USA.

Born near Knightstown, Indiana, Beard earned a PhD from Columbia University 1904. He resigned from the Columbia faculty 1917 over issues of academic freedom. He helped found the New School for Social Research 1918.

Beardsley /ˈbɪədzli/ Aubrey (Vincent) 1872–1898. British illustrator. His meticulously executed black-and-white work displays the sinuous line and decorative mannerisms of Art Nouveau and was often charged with being grotesque and decadent.

He became known through the *Yellow Book* magazine and his drawings for Oscar Wilde's *Salome* 1894.

Beatles, the /ˈbiːtlz/ English pop group 1960–70. The members, all born in Liverpool, were John Lennon (1940–80, rhythm guitar, vocals), Paul McCartney (1942– , bass, vocals), George Harrison (1943– , lead guitar, vocals), and Ringo Starr (formerly Richard Starkey, 1940– , drums). Using songs written largely by Lennon and McCartney, the Beatles dominated rock music and pop culture in the 1960s.

The Beatles gained early experience in Liverpool and Hamburg, West Germany. They had a top-30 hit with their first record, 'Love Me Do' 1962, followed by 'Please Please Me' which reached number two. Every subsequent single and album released until 1967 reached number one in the UK charts. At the peak of Beatlemania they starred in two films, *A Hard Day's Night* 1964 and *Help!* 1965, and provided the voices for the animated film *Yellow Submarine* 1968. Their song

'Yesterday' 1965 was covered by 1,186 different performers in the first ten years. The album *Sgt Pepper's Lonely Hearts Club Band* 1967, recorded on two four-track machines, anticipated subsequent technological developments.

The Beatles were the first British group to challenge the US dominance of rock and roll, and continued to influence popular music beyond their break-up 1970. Of the 30 songs most frequently broadcast in the USA 1955–91, 13 were written by members of the Beatles. They pursued separate careers with varying success. George Harrison's biggest hit, 'My Sweet Lord' 1970, fell victim to a plagiarism suit. His album *Cloud Nine* 1987 was particularly well received, and in 1988 he became a member of the Traveling Wilburys, a group that also includes Bob Dylan. Ringo Starr has appeared in a number of films, and his album *Ringo* 1973 came close to being a Beatles reunion. See also John →Lennon and Paul →McCartney.

Beaton /ˈbiːtn/ Cecil 1904–1980. English portrait and fashion photographer, designer, illustrator, diarist, and conversationalist. He produced portrait studies and also designed scenery and costumes for ballets, and sets for plays and films.

Beaton /ˈbiːtn/ David 1494–1546. Scottish nationalist cardinal and politician, adviser to James V. Under Mary Queen of Scots, he was opposed to the alliance with England and persecuted reformers such as George Wishart, who was condemned to the stake; he was killed by Wishart's friends.

Beatrix /ˈbɪətrɪks/ 1936– . Queen of the Netherlands. The eldest daughter of Queen →Juliana, she succeeded to the throne on her mother's abdication 1980. In 1966 she married West German diplomat Claus von Amsberg (1926–), who was created Prince of the Netherlands. Her heir is Prince Willem Alexander (1967–).

Beattie /ˈbiːti/ John Hugh Marshall 1915–1990. British anthropologist whose work on cross-cultural analysis influenced researchers in other fields, particularly philosophy. His book *Other Cultures: Aims, Methods and Achievements in Social Anthropology* 1964 has been translated into many languages. Beattie was appointed University Lecturer in Social Anthropology at Oxford 1953 and took up the Chair in Cultural Anthropology and Sociology of Africa in Leiden 1971.

Beatty /ˈbiːti/ David, 1st Earl 1871–1936. British admiral in World War I. He commanded the cruiser squadron 1912–16 and bore the brunt of the Battle of Jutland.

In 1916 he became commander of the fleet, and in 1918 received the surrender of the German fleet.

Beatty /ˈbeɪti/ Warren. Stage name of Warren Beaty 1937– . US actor and director, popular for such films as *Splendour in the Grass* 1961, *Bonnie and Clyde* 1967, and *Heaven Can Wait* 1978.

His more recent productions include *Reds* 1981 (Academy Award for Best Producer), *Ishtar* 1987, and *Dick Tracy* 1990.

Beauclerk /ˈbəʊkleə/ family name of the dukes of St Albans, descended from King Charles II by his mistress Nell Gwyn.

Beaufort /ˈbəʊfət/ Francis 1774–1857. British admiral, hydrographer to the Royal Navy from 1829; the Beaufort scale and the Beaufort Sea in the Arctic Ocean are named after him.

Beaufort /ˈbəʊfət/ Henry 1375–1447. English priest, bishop of Lincoln from 1398, of Winchester from 1405. As chancellor of England, he supported his half-brother Henry IV, and made enormous personal loans to Henry V to finance war against France. As a guardian of Henry VI from 1421, he was in effective control of the country until 1426. In the same year he was created a cardinal. In 1431 he crowned Henry VI as king of France in Paris.

Beauharnais /ˌbəʊɑːˈneɪ/ Alexandre, Vicomte de 1760–1794. French liberal aristocrat and general who served in the American Revolution and became a member of the National Convention in the early days of the French Revolution. He was the first husband of Josephine (consort of Napoleon I). Their daughter Hortense (1783–1837) married Louis, a younger brother of Napoleon, and their son became →Napoleon III. Beauharnais was guillotined during the Terror for his alleged lack of zeal for the revolutionary cause and his lack of success as Commander of the Republican Army of the North.

Beaumarchais /ˌbəʊmɑːˈʃeɪ/ Pierre Augustin Caron de 1732–1799. French dramatist. His great comedies *Le Barbier de Seville/The Barber of Seville* 1775 and *Le Mariage de Figaro/The Marriage of Figaro* (1778, but prohibited until 1784) form the basis of operas by →Rossini and →Mozart.

Louis XVI entrusted Beaumarchais with secret missions, notably for the profitable shipment of arms to the American colonies during the War of Independence. Accused of treason 1792, he fled to Holland and England, but in 1799 he returned to Paris.

Beaumont /ˈbəʊmɒnt/ Francis 1584–1616. English dramatist and poet. From about 1608 he collaborated with John →Fletcher. Their joint plays include *Philaster* 1610, *The Maid's Tragedy* about 1611, and *A King and No King* about 1611. *The Woman Hater* about 1606 and *The Knight of the Burning Pestle* about 1607 are ascribed to Beaumont alone.

Beaumont /ˈbəʊmɒnt/ William 1785–1853. US surgeon who conducted pioneering experiments on the digestive system. In 1882 he saved the life of a Canadian trapper wounded in the side by a gun blast; the wound only partially healed and, through an opening in the stomach wall, Beaumont was able to observe the workings of the stomach. His *Experiments and Observations on the Gastric Juice and the Physiology of Digestion* was published 1833.

Beauregard /ˌbəʊrəˈgɑː/ Pierre Gustave Toutant 1818–1893. US military leader and Confederate general whose opening fire on Fort Sumter, South Carolina, started the American Civil War 1861. His military successes were clouded by his conflicts with Confederate President Jefferson Davis.

Beauvoir /bəʊˈvwɑː/ Simone de 1908–1986. French socialist, feminist, and writer who taught philosophy at the Sorbonne university in Paris 1931–43. Her book *Le Deuxième sexe/The Second Sex* 1949 became a seminal work for many feminists.

Her novel of postwar Paris, *Les Mandarins/The Mandarins* 1954, has characters resembling the writers Albert Camus, Arthur Koestler, and Jean-Paul →Sartre. She also published autobiographical volumes.

Beaverbrook /ˈbiːvəbrʊk/ (William) Max(well) Aitken, 1st Baron Beaverbrook 1879–1964. British financier, newspaper proprietor, and politician, born in Canada. He bought a majority interest in the *Daily Express* 1919, founded the *Sunday Express* 1921, and bought the London *Evening Standard* 1929. He served in Lloyd George's World War I cabinet and Churchill's World War II cabinet.

Between the wars he used his newspapers, in particular the *Daily Express*, to campaign for empire and free trade and against Prime Minister Baldwin.

Bebel /ˈbeɪbəl/ August 1840–1913. German socialist and founding member of the Verband deutsche Arbeitervereine (League of German Workers' Clubs), together with Wilhelm Liebknecht 1869. Also known as the Eisenach Party, he became its leading speaker in the Reichstag; it was based in Saxony and SW Germany before being incorporated into the SPD (Sozialdemokratische Partei Deutschlands/German Social Democratic Party) 1875.

Beccaria /ˌbekəˈriːə/ Cesare, Marese di Beccaria 1738–1794. Italian philanthropist, born in Milan. He opposed capital punishment and torture; advocated education as a crime preventative; influenced English philosopher Jeremy →Bentham; and coined the phrase 'the greatest happiness of the greatest number', the tenet of utilitarianism.

Bechet /ˈbeʃeɪ/ Sidney (Joseph) 1897–1959. US jazz musician, born in New Orleans. He played clarinet and was the first to forge an individual style on soprano saxophone. Bechet was based in Paris in the late 1920s and the 1950s, where he was recognized by classical musicians as a serious artist.

Beckenbauer Franz 1945– . German footballer who made a record 103 appearances for his country. He captained West Germany to the 1972 European Championship and the 1974 World Cup, and was twice European Footballer of the Year. After retiring as a player, he became West Germany's team manager, taking them to the runners-up spot in the 1986 World Cup and victory in the 1990 World Cup. He is the only person both to captain and manage a winning World Cup team.

Becker /bekə/ Boris 1967– . German tennis player. In 1985, at the age of 17, he became the youngest winner of a singles title at Wimbledon. He has won the title three times and helped West Germany to win the Davis Cup 1988 and 1989. He also won the US Open 1989.

Becker /bekə/ Lydia 1827–1890. English botanist and campaigner for women's rights. She established the Manchester Ladies Literary Society 1865 as a forum for women to study scientific subjects. In 1867 she cofounded and became secretary of the National Society for Women's Suffrage. In 1870 she founded a monthly newsletter, *The Women's Suffrage Journal.*

Becket /bekɪt/ St Thomas à 1118–1170. English priest and politician. He was chancellor to →Henry II 1155–62, when he was appointed archbishop of Canterbury. The interests of the church soon conflicted with those of the crown and Becket was assassinated; he was canonized 1172.

A friend of Henry II, Becket was a loyal chancellor, but on becoming archbishop of Canterbury transferred his allegiance to the church. In 1164 he opposed Henry's attempt to regulate the relations between church and state, and had to flee the country; he returned 1170, but the reconciliation soon broke down. Encouraged by a hasty outburst from the king, four knights murdered Becket before the altar of Canterbury cathedral. He was declared a saint, and his shrine became the busiest centre of pilgrimage in England until the Reformation.

Beckett /bekɪt/ Samuel 1906–1989. Irish novelist and dramatist who wrote in French and English. His *En attendant Godot/Waiting for Godot* 1952 is possibly the most universally known example of Theatre of the Absurd, in which life is taken to be meaningless. This genre is taken to further extremes in *Fin de Partie/Endgame* 1957 and *Happy Days* 1961. Nobel Prize for Literature 1969.

Beckford /bekfəd/ William 1760–1844. English author and eccentric. Forced out of England by scandals about his private life, he published *Vathek* 1787 in Paris, a fantastic Arabian Nights tale, and on returning to England 1796 rebuilt his home, Fonthill Abbey in Wiltshire, as a Gothic fantasy.

Beckmann /bekmən/ Max 1884–1950. German Expressionist painter who fled the Nazi regime for the USA 1933. After World War I his art was devoted to themes of cruelty in human society, portraying sadists and their victims with a harsh style of realism.

Beckmann was born in Leipzig. He fought in World War I and was discharged following a breakdown, reflected in the agony of his work; pictures include *Carnival* and *The Titanic*. He later painted enormous triptychs, full of symbolic detail. He died in New York.

Becquerel /ˌbekəˈrel/ Antoine Henri 1852–1908. French physicist who discovered penetrating radiation coming from uranium salts, the first indication of radioactivity, and shared a Nobel prize with Marie and Pierre →Curie 1903.

Beddoes /bedəuz/ Thomas Lovell 1803–1849. English poet and dramatist. His play *Death's Jest Book* was begun 1825, but it was not published until 1850, much revised.

Bede /biːd/ *c.* 673–735. English theologian and historian, known as *the Venerable Bede*, active in Durham and Northumbria. He wrote many scientific, theological, and historical works. His *Historia Ecclesiastica Gentis Anglorum/Ecclesiastical History of the English People* 731 is a seminal source for early English history.

Born at Monkwearmouth, Durham, he entered the local monastery at the age of seven, later transferring to Jarrow, where he became a priest in about 703. He devoted his life to writing and teaching; among his pupils was Egbert, archbishop of York.

Bedford /bedfəd/ John Robert Russell, 13th Duke of Bedford 1917– . English peer. Succeeding to the title 1953, he restored the family seat Woburn Abbey, Bedfordshire, now a tourist attraction.

Beebe /biːb/ Charles 1877–1962. US naturalist, explorer, and writer. He was curator of birds for the New York Zoological Society 1899–1952. He wrote the comprehensive *Monograph of the Pheasants* 1918–22. His interest in deep-sea exploration led to a collaboration with the engineer Otis Barton and the development of a spherical diving vessel, the bathysphere. On 24 August 1934 the two men made a record-breaking dive to 923 m/3028 ft. Beebe's expeditions are described in a series of memoirs.

Beecham /biːtʃəm/ Thomas 1879–1961. British conductor and impresario. He established the Royal Philharmonic Orchestra 1946 and fostered the works of composers such as Delius, Sibelius, and Richard Strauss.

Beecher /biːtʃə/ Harriet Unmarried name of Harriet Beecher →Stowe, author of *Uncle Tom's Cabin*.

Beecher /biːtʃə/ Henry Ward 1813–1887. US Congregational minister and militant opponent of slavery, son of the pulpit orator Lyman →Beecher and brother of the writer Harriet Beecher →Stowe.

Beecher /biːtʃə/ Lyman 1775–1863. US Congregational and Presbyterian minister, one of the most popular pulpit orators of his time. He was the father of Harriet Beecher →Stowe and Henry Ward Beecher.

As pastor from 1847 of Plymouth church, Brooklyn, New York, he was a leader in the movement for the abolition of slavery.

Beeching /biːtʃɪŋ/ Richard, Baron Beeching 1913–1985. British scientist and administrator. He was chair of the British Railways Board 1963–65, producing the controversial *Beeching Report* 1963, which advocated concentrating resources on intercity passenger traffic and freight, at the cost of closing many rural and branch lines.

Beerbohm /bɪəbəʊm/ Max 1872–1956. British caricaturist and author, the half-brother of actor and manager Herbert Beerbohm Tree. A perfectionist in style, he contributed to *The Yellow Book* 1894; wrote a novel of Oxford undergraduate life *Zuleika Dobson* 1911; and published volumes of caricature, including *Rossetti and His Circle* 1922. He succeeded George Bernard Shaw as critic to the *Saturday Review* 1898.

Beethoven /beɪthəʊvən/ Ludwig van 1770–1827. German composer and pianist whose mastery of musical expression in every genre made him the dominant influence on 19th-century music. Beethoven's repertoire includes concert overtures; the opera *Fidelio*; five piano concertos and two for violin (one unfinished); 32 piano sonatas, including the *Moonlight* and *Appassionata*; 17 string quartets; the *Mass in D* (*Missa solemnis*); and nine symphonies, as well as many youthful works. He usually played his own piano pieces and conducted his orchestral works until he was hampered by deafness 1801; nevertheless he continued to compose.

Born in Bonn, the son and grandson of musicians, Beethoven became deputy organist at the court of the Elector of Cologne at Bonn before he was 12; later he studied under →Haydn and possibly →Mozart, whose influence dominated his early work. From 1809, he received a small allowance from aristocratic patrons.

Beethoven's career spanned the transition from Classicism to Romanticism. Of his symphonies the best-known are the Third (*Eroica*, originally intended to be dedicated to Napoleon, with whom Beethoven became disillusioned), the Fifth, the Sixth (*Pastoral*), and Ninth (*Choral*), which includes the passage from Schiller's 'Ode to Joy' chosen as the national anthem of Europe.

Beeton, Mrs /biːtn/ (Isabella Mary Mayson) 1836–1865. British writer on cookery and domestic management. She produced *Beeton's Household Management* 1859, the first comprehensive work on domestic science.

Begin /beɪgɪn/ Menachem 1913–1992. Israeli politician. He was leader of the extremist Irgun Zvai Leumi organization in Palestine from 1942, and prime minister of Israel 1977–83, as head of the right-wing Likud party. In 1978 Begin shared a Nobel Peace Prize with President Sadat of Egypt for work on the Camp David Agreements for a Middle East peace settlement.

Begin was born in Brest-Litovsk, Poland, studied law in Warsaw, and fled to the USSR 1939. As leader of the Irgun group, he was responsible in 1946 for a bomb attack at the King David Hotel, Jerusalem, which killed over 100 people.

Behan /biːən/ Brendan 1923–1964. Irish dramatist. His early experience of prison and knowledge of the workings of the IRA (recounted in his autobiography *Borstal Boy* 1958) provided him with two recurrent themes in his plays. *The Quare Fellow* 1954 was followed by the tragicomedy *The Hostage* 1958, first written in Gaelic.

Behn /ben/ Aphra 1640–1689. English novelist and playwright, the first woman in England to earn her living as a writer. Her writings were criticized for their explicitness; they frequently present events from a woman's point of view. Her novel *Oroonoko* 1688 is an attack on slavery.

Between 1670 and 1687 fifteen of her plays were produced, including *The Rover*, which attacked forced and mercenary marriages. She had the patronage of James I and was employed as a government spy in Holland 1666.

Behn English dramatist and novelist Aphra Behn, the first professional female author in England, wrote many coarse but popular Restoration plays. She wrote 22 plays and 14 novels, including Oroonoko which, based on an enslaved black prince she had made the acquaintance of in Surinam, anticipated Rousseau's 'noble savage'.

Behrens /ˈbeərənz/ Peter 1868–1940. German architect. He pioneered the adaptation of architecture to industry, and designed the AEG turbine factory in Berlin 1909, a landmark in industrial design. He taught →Le Corbusier and Walter →Gropius.

Behring /ˈbeərɪŋ/ Emil von 1854–1917. German physician who discovered that the body produces antitoxins, substances able to counteract poisons released by bacteria. Using this knowledge, he developed new treatments for diseases such as diphtheria.

Educated in Berlin, Behring was Robert →Koch's assistant before becoming professor of hygiene at Halle and Marburg. He won the first Nobel Prize for Medicine, in 1901.

Beiderbecke /ˈbaɪdəbek/ Bix (Leon Bismarck) 1903–1931. US jazz cornetist, composer, and pianist. A romantic soloist with King Oliver, Louis Armstrong, and Paul Whiteman's orchestra, Beiderbecke was the first acknowledged white jazz innovator. He was inspired by the classical composers Debussy, Ravel, and Stravinsky.

His reputation grew after his early death with the publication of Dorothy Baker's novel *Young Man with a Horn* 1938.

Belasco /bəˈlæskəʊ/ David 1859–1931. US playwright and producer. His works include *Madame Butterfly* 1900 and *The Girl of the Golden West* 1905, both of which Puccini used as libretti for operas.

Belaúnde Terry /belɑːˈundeɪ ˈteri/ Fernando 1913– . President of Peru from 1963 to 1968 and from 1980 to 1985. He championed land reform and the construction of roads to open up the Amazon valley. He fled to the USA 1968 after being deposed by a military junta. After his return, his second term in office was marked by rampant inflation, enormous foreign debts, terrorism, mass killings, and human-rights violations by the armed forces.

Belgrano /belˈɡrɑːnəʊ/ Manuel 1770–1820. Argentine revolutionary. He was a member of the military group that led the 1810 revolt against Spain. Later, he commanded the revolutionary army until he was replaced by José de →San Martín 1814.

Belisarius /belɪˈsɑːriəs/ c. 505–565. Roman general under Emperor →Justinian I. He won major victories over the Persians in 530 and the Vandals in 533 when he sacked Carthage. Later he invaded Sicily and fought a series of campaigns against the Goths in Italy.

As a young man he was a member of Justinian's bodyguard before becoming commander of the eastern army. Although not always favoured by the Emperor, it was largely his military skill which preserved the Byzantine Empire from being overthrown.

Bell /bel/ Alexander Graham 1847–1922. Scottish-born US scientist and inventor of the telephone. He patented his invention 1876, and later experimented with a type of phonograph and, in aeronautics, invented the tricycle undercarriage.

Born in Edinburgh, he was educated at the universities of Edinburgh and London, and in 1870 went first to Canada and then to the USA, where he opened a school for teachers of the deaf in Boston 1872, and in 1873 became professor of vocal physiology at the university.

Mr Watson, come here; I want you.

Alexander Graham Bell
first complete sentence spoken over the
telephone March 1876

Bell /bel/ John 1928–1990. British physicist who in 1964 devised a test to verify a point in quantum theory: whether two particles that were once connected are always afterwards interconnected even if they become widely separated. As well as investigating fundamental problems in theoretical physics, Bell contributed to the design of particle accelerators.

One of the most profound thinkers in modern physics, Bell worked for 30 years at CERN, the European research laboratory near Geneva, Switzerland. He demonstrated how to measure the continued interconnection of particles that had once been closely connected, and put forward mathematical criteria that had to be obeyed if such a connection existed, as required by quantum theory. In the early 1980s, a French team tested Bell's criteria, and a connection between widely separated particles was detected.

Bell /bel/ Patrick c. 1800–1869. Scottish inventor of a reaping machine, developed around 1828. It was pushed by two horses and used a rotating cylinder of horizontal bars to bend the standing corn on to a reciprocating cutter that was driven off the machine's wheels (in much the same way as on a combine harvester).

Bellamy /ˈbelmi/ Edward 1850–1898. US author and social critic. In 1888, deeply concerned with the social problems of the day, he published *Looking Backward: 2000–1887*, a utopian novel. A huge bestseller, it inspired wide public support for Bellamy's political programme of state socialism. He published a second utopian novel, *Equality* 1897.

Born in Chicopee Falls, Massachusetts, USA, Bellamy wrote for the New York *Post* and the Springfield *Union*. He founded the Springfield *Daily News* 1880 and later the *New Nation* but eventually abandoned journalism to become a full-time author.

Bellarmine /ˈbelɑːmɪn/ Roberto Francesco Romolo 1542–1621. Italian Roman Catholic theologian and cardinal. He taught at the Jesuit College in

Rome, and became archbishop of Capua 1602. His *Disputationes de controversersiis fidei christianae* 1581–93 was a major defence of Catholicism in the 16th century. He was canonized 1930.

Bellay /be'leɪ/ Joaquim du *c.* 1522–1560. French poet and prose writer who published the great manifesto of the new school of French poetry, the Pléiade: *Défense et illustration de la langue française* 1549.

Bellingshausen /belɪŋzhaʊzən/ Fabian Gottlieb von 1779–1852. Russian Antarctic explorer, the first to sight and circumnavigate the Antarctic continent 1819–21, although he did not realize what it was.

Bellini /be'liːni/ family of Italian Renaissance painters. Jacopo and his sons Gentile and Giovanni were founders of the Venetian school in the fifteenth and early sixteenth centuries.

Jacopo (*c.* 1400–1470) has left little surviving work, but two of his sketchbooks (now in the British Museum and the Louvre) contain his ideas and designs.

Gentile (*c.* 1429–1507) assisted in the decoration of the Doge's Palace 1474 and worked in the court of Muhammad II at Constantinople (a portrait of the sultan is in the National Gallery, London). His also painted processional groups (Accademia, Venice).

Giovanni (*c.*1430–1516), Gentile's younger brother, studied under his father, and painted portraits and various religious subjects. Giovanni Bellini's early works show the influence of his brother-in-law, Mantegna. His style developed from the static manner of mid-15th century Venetian work towards a High Renaissance harmony and grandeur, as in the altarpiece 1505 in Sta Zaccaria, Venice. He introduced softness in tone, harmony in composition, and a use of luminous colour that influenced the next generation of painters (including his pupils Giorgione and Titian). He worked in oil rather than tempera, a technique adopted from Antonello da Messina.

Bellini /be'liːni/ Vincenzo 1801–1835. Italian opera composer whose lyrical, melodic treatments of classic themes include *La Sonnambula* 1831, *Norma* 1831, and *I Puritani* 1835.

Born in Catania, Sicily, Bellini was still a student at the Naples Conservatory when his first opera *Adelson et Salvina* 1825 was performed to great success. Subsequently he was guided by the tenor Giovanni Battista Rubini (1793–1854) to develop a new simplicity of melodic expression which proved irresistible to soloists and concert audiences. His genius for elegiac lyricism found ideal expression in Romantic evocations of classic themes, as in *La Sonnambula*, a great success in Britain, and *Norma*. In *I Puritani*, his last work, he discovered a new boldness and vigour of orchestral effect.

Belloc /belɒk/ (Joseph) Hilaire Pierre 1870–1953. English author, remembered primarily for his nonsense verse for children *The Bad Child's Book of Beasts* 1896 and *Cautionary Tales* 1907. Belloc also wrote travel and religious books (he was a devout Catholic). With G K →Chesterton, he advocated a return to the late medieval guild system of commercial association in place of capitalism or socialism.

Bellot /be'lɔu/ Joseph René 1826–1853. French Arctic explorer who reached the strait now named after him 1852, and lost his life while searching for English explorer John →Franklin.

Bellow /belə/ Saul 1915– . Canadian-born US novelist. Novels such as *Herzog* 1964, *Humboldt's Gift* 1975, and *The Dean's December* 1982 show his method of inhabiting the consciousness of a central character, frequently a Jewish-American intellectual, to portray an individual's frustration with the ongoing events of an indifferent society. His finely styled works and skilled characterizations won him the Nobel Prize for Literature 1976.

Bellow's sensitivity to mythic dimensions is evident in such novels as *Henderson the Rain King* 1959. His other works include *The Adventures of Augie March* 1953, *Him With His Foot in His Mouth* 1984, and *More Die of Heartbreak* 1987.

Belloc In addition to his extensive and versatile literary activities, English author Hilaire Belloc became a Liberal member of Parliament 1906–10. Best known for his nonsense verse, Belloc also wrote essays, innumerable travel books and historical studies, satirical novels, and serious political works, and is considered a master of the English prose style.

Bellows /ˈbeləʊz/ George Wesley 1882–1925. US painter known for the vigorous style of his portrayals of the drama of street life and sport. His most famous works, such as *Stag at Sharkey's* 1909, show the violence and excitement of illegal boxing matches. Taught by Robert →Henri, he became the youngest academician of his time.

Born in Columbus, Ohio, USA, Bellows painted in the realist style of the Ashcan school whose subjects centred on city life, the poor, and outcasts. He was involved in the progressive artists movement and helped create the Armory Show 1913 which marked the arrival of abstract art in the USA.

Belmondo /belˈmɒndəʊ/ Jean-Paul 1933– . French film actor who became a star in Jean-Luc Godard's *A bout de souffle/Breathless* 1959. His other films include *Cartouche* 1962, *That Man from Rio* 1964, *The Brain* 1968, *Borsalino* 1970 and *Stavisky* 1974.

Belmont /ˈbelmɒnt/ August 1816–1890. German-born US financier, who became the →Rothschilds' exclusive representative in the USA when he established a private bank in New York 1837. Belmont was a leading member of New York City society's most exclusive clique (the '400'), and was instrumental in financing the costs of the Mexican War (1846–48).

Belmont became a naturalized American citizen 1844. An active Democrat, he supported the presidential candidacy of Stephen Douglas 1860 but remained a strong Unionist after President Abraham Lincoln's election. He served as the Democratic National Chairman 1872.

Ben Ali /ben ˈæli/ Zine el Abidine 1936– . Tunisian politician, president from 1987. After training in France and the USA, he returned to Tunisia and became director-general of national security. He was made minister of the interior and then prime minister under the ageing president for life, Habib →Bourguiba, whom he deposed 1987 by a bloodless coup with the aid of ministerial colleagues. He ended the personality cult established by Bourguiba and moved toward a pluralist political system.

Ben Barka /ben ˈbɑːkə/ Mehdi 1920–1965. Moroccan politician. He became president of the National Consultative Assembly 1956 on the country's independence from France. He was assassinated by Moroccan agents with the aid of the French secret service.

Ben Barka had been tutor to King Hassan. As a major opposition leader after independence he was increasingly leftist in his views, and was twice sentenced to death in his absence during 1963 following allegations of his involvement in an attempt on the king's life and for backing Algeria in border disputes. Lured to Paris to discuss an anticolonial film, he was kidnapped and shot by Moroccan agents with the support of the French secret service because of his alleged involvement in an attempt on King Hassan's life and for sup-

porting Algeria in Algerian-Moroccan border disputes. The case led to de Gaulle's reorganization of the French secret service.

Ben Bella /ben ˈbelə/ Ahmed 1916– . Algerian politician. He was leader of the National Liberation Front (FLN) from 1952, the first prime minister of independent Algeria 1962–63, and its first president 1963–65. In 1965 Ben Bella was overthrown by Col Houari →Boumédienne and detained until 1979. In 1985 he founded a new party, Mouvement pour la Démocratie en Algérie, and returned to Algeria 1990 after nine years in exile.

Benbow /ˈbenbəʊ/ John 1653–1702. English admiral, hero of several battles with France. He ran away to sea as a boy, and from 1689 served in the navy. He fought at the battles of Beachy Head 1690 and La Hogue 1692, and died of wounds received in a fight with the French off Jamaica.

Benchley /ˈbentʃli/ Robert 1889–1945. US humorist, actor, and drama critic whose books include *Of All Things* 1921 and *Benchley Beside Himself* 1943. His film skit *How to Sleep* illustrates his ability to extract humour from everyday life.

Benda /bænˈdɑː/ Julien 1867–1956. French writer and philosopher. He was an outspoken opponent of the philosophy of →Bergson, and in 1927 published a manifesto on the necessity of devotion to the absolute truth, which he felt his contemporaries had betrayed, *La Trahison des clercs/The Treason of the Intellectuals*.

Benedict /ˈbenɪdɪkt/ 15 popes, including:

Benedict XV 1854–1922. Pope from 1914. During World War I he endeavoured to bring about a peace settlement, and it was during his papacy that British, French, and Dutch official relations were renewed with the Vatican.

Benedict, St /ˈbenɪdɪkt/ *c.* 480–*c.* 547. Founder of Christian monasticism in the West and of the Benedictine order. He founded the monastery of Monte Cassino, Italy. Here he wrote out his rule for monastic life, and was visited shortly before his death by the Ostrogothic king Totila, whom he converted to the Christian faith. His feast day is 11 July.

Beneš /ˈbeneʃ/ Eduard 1884–1948. Czechoslovak politician. He worked with Tomáš →Masaryk towards Czechoslovak nationalism from 1918 and was foreign minister and representative at the League of Nations. He was president of the republic from 1935 until forced to resign by the Germans; he headed a government in exile in London during World War II. He returned home as president 1945 but resigned again after the Communist coup 1948.

Benét /bəˈneɪ/ Stephen Vincent 1898–1943. US poet, novelist, and short-story writer who won a Pulitzer prize 1929 for his narrative poem of the Civil War, *John Brown's Body* 1928. One of his short stories, 'The Devil and Daniel Webster,' became a classic and was made into a play, an opera, and a film (*All That Money Can Buy*). He published more than 17 volumes of verse and prose.

Ben-Gurion /ben 'guəriən/ David. Adopted name of David Gruen 1886–1973. Israeli statesman and socialist politician, one of the founders of the state of Israel, the country's first prime minister 1948–53, and again 1955–63.

He was born in Poland, and went to Palestine 1906 to farm. He was a leader of the Zionist movement, and as defence minister he presided over the development of Israel's armed forces into one of the strongest armies in the Middle East.

Benjamin /bendʒəmɪn/ Arthur 1893–1960. Australian pianist and composer who taught composition at the Royal College of Music in London from 1925, where ➔Britten was one of his pupils. His works include *Jamaican Rumba*, inspired by a visit to the West Indies 1937.

Benjamin /bendʒəmɪn/ George (William John) 1960– . British composer, conductor and pianist. A pupil of Messiaen, his colourful and sonorous works include *Ringed by the Flat Horizon* 1980, *At First Light* 1982, *Antara* 1987, and *Cascade* 1990.

Benjamin /bendʒmɪn/ Judah Philip 1811–1884. US Confederate official. Holding office in the US Senate 1852–61, he was a proponent of secession of the South and resigned from office at the outbreak of the American Civil War. As one of the leaders of the Confederacy, he served as attorney general, secretary of war, and secretary of state.

Born in St Thomas, Virgin Islands, Benjamin was raised in South Carolina, USA, and educated at Yale University. He later joined the legal profession before serving in the state legislature. After the defeat of the Confederacy 1865, he escaped to England where he spent the rest of his life practising law.

Benn /ben/ Tony (Anthony Wedgwood) 1925– . British Labour politician, formerly the leading figure on the party's left wing. He was minister of technology 1966–70 and of industry 1974–75, but his campaign against entry to the European Community led to his transfer to the Department of Energy 1975–79. A skilled parliamentary orator, he unsuccessfully contested the Labour Party leadership 1988.

Son of Lord Stansgate, a Labour peer, Benn was elected MP for Bristol SE 1950–60, succeeded his father 1960, but never used his title and in 1963 was the first person to disclaim a title under the Peerage Act. He was again MP for Bristol SE 1963–83. In 1981 he challenged Denis Healey for the deputy leadership of the party and was so narrowly defeated that he established himself as the acknowledged leader of the left. His diaries cover in enormous detail the events of the period. In 1984 he became MP for Chesterfield.

Bennett /benɪt/ Alan 1934– . English playwright. His works (set in his native north of England) treat subjects such as class, senility, illness, and death with macabre comedy. They include TV films, for example *An Englishman Abroad* 1982; the cinema film *A Private Function* 1984; and plays such as *Forty Years On* 1968, *Getting On* 1971, *Kafka's Dick* 1986, and *The Madness of George III* 1991.

Bennett /benɪt/ (Enoch) Arnold 1867–1931. English novelist. He became a London journalist 1893 and editor of *Woman* 1896. His many novels include *Anna of the Five Towns* 1904, *The Old Wives' Tale* 1908, and the trilogy *Clayhanger*, *Hilda Lessways*, and *These Twain* 1910–16.

Bennett came from one of the 'five towns' of the Potteries in Staffordshire, the setting for his major works.

Bennett /benɪt/ Richard Rodney 1936– . English composer of jazz, film music, symphonies, and operas. His film scores for *Far from the Madding Crowd* 1967, *Nicholas and Alexandra* 1971, and *Murder on the Orient Express* 1974 all received Oscar nominations. His operas include *The Mines of Sulphur* 1963 and *Victory* 1970.

Benny /beni/ Jack. Stage name of Benjamin Kubelsky 1894–1974. US comedian notable for his perfect timing and lugubrious manner. Over the years, Benny appeared on the stage, in films, and on radio and television. His radio programme, from 1932, made him a national institution. Featuring his wife Mary Livingston, singer Dennis Day, announcer Don Wilson, and valet Eddie 'Rochester' Anderson, it was produced for television in the 1950s. His film appearances, mostly in the 1930s and 1940s, included a starring role in *To Be or Not to Be* 1942. He also played in *Charley's Aunt* 1941, *It's In the Bag* 1945, and *A Guide for the Married Man* 1967.

Benson /bensən/ E(dward) F(rederic) 1867–1940. English writer. He specialized in novels gently satirizing the foibles of upper-middle-class society, and wrote a series of books featuring the formidable female antagonists Mapp and Lucia, including *Queen Lucia* 1920. He was the son of Edward White Benson, archbishop of Canterbury 1883–96.

Benson /bensən/ Edward White 1829–1896. English cleric, first headmaster of Wellington College 1859–68, and, as archbishop of Canterbury from 1883, responsible for the 'Lincoln Judgment' on questions of ritual 1887.

Bentham /benθəm/ Jeremy 1748–1832. English philosopher, legal and social reformer, and founder of utilitarianism. The essence of his moral philosophy is found in the pronouncement of his *Principles of Morals and Legislation* (written 1780, published 1789): that the object of all legislation should be 'the greatest happiness for the greatest number'.

Bentham *English Utilitarian philosopher Jeremy Bentham. His failure to appreciate quality and poetry was criticized by John Stuart Mill, among others, but his radical social reformism greatly influenced subsequent practice.*

Bentham declared that the 'utility' of any law is to be measured by the extent to which it promotes the pleasure, good, and happiness of the people concerned. In 1776 he published *Fragments on Government*. He made suggestions for the reform of the poor law 1798, which formed the basis of the reforms enacted 1834, and in his *Catechism of Parliamentary Reform* 1817 he proposed annual elections, the secret ballot, and universal male suffrage. He was also a pioneer of prison reform.

In economics he was an apostle of *laissez-faire*, and in his *Defence of Usury* 1787 and *Manual of Political Economy* 1798 he contended that his principle of 'utility' was best served by allowing every man (sic) to pursue his own interests unhindered by restrictive legislation. He was made a citizen of the French Republic 1792.

Bentinck /'bentɪŋk/ Lord George 1802–48. English Tory politician, was private secretary to George Canning, 1822–25 then foreign secretary. He supported Whig causes but left the party in 1834 to a separate parliamentary group with Lord Stanley.

Bentley /'bentli/ Edmund Clerihew 1875–1956. English author. He invented the four-line humorous verse form known as the clerihew, used in *Biography for Beginners* 1905 and in *Baseless Biography* 1939. He was also the author of the classic detective story *Trent's Last Case* 1912.

Bentley /'bentli/ John Francis 1839–1902. English architect, a convert to Catholicism, who designed Westminster Cathedral, London (1895–1903). It is outwardly Byzantine but inwardly shaped by shadowy vaults of bare brickwork. The campanile is the tallest church tower in London.

Bentley /'bentli/ Richard 1662–1742. English classical scholar whose textual criticism includes *Dissertation upon the Epistles of Phalaris* 1699. He was Master of Trinity College, Cambridge University, from 1700.

Benton /'bentn/ Thomas Hart 1782–1858. US political leader. He was elected to the US Senate 1820, where he served for the next 30 years. He distinguished himself as an outspoken opponent of the Bank of the United States and the extension of slavery as well as a strong supporter of westward expansion.

Born in Hillsboro (now Hillsborough), North Carolina, USA, Benton moved to Tennessee and was admitted to the bar 1806. During the Anglo-American War 1812–14, he served as General Andrew →Jackson's aide-de-camp, eventually rising to the rank of colonel.

Moving to St Louis 1815, he opened a law practice and published the *Missouri Enquirer* 1818–20.

Benz /bents/ Karl Friedrich 1844–1929. German automobile engineer who produced the world's first petrol-driven motor vehicle. He built his first model engine 1878 and the petrol-driven car 1885.

Ben Zvi /ben 'zviː/ Izhak 1884–1963. Israeli politician, president 1952–63. He was born in Atpoltava, Russia, and became active in the Zionist movement in Ukraine. In 1907 he went to Palestine but was deported 1915 with →Ben-Gurion. They served in the Jewish Legion under Field Marshal Allenby, who commanded the British forces in the Middle East.

Bentinck *Lord George Bentinck, English Tory politician, supporter of emancipation. A keen sportsman, he reformed abuses in horse racing and field sports. He was greatly admired by Disraeli.*

Béranger /ˌbeɪrɒn'ʒeɪ/ Pierre Jean de 1780–1857. French poet who wrote light satirical lyrics dealing with love, wine, popular philosophy, and politics.

Berchtold /'beəxtəʊlt/ Count Leopold von 1863–1942. Prime minister and foreign minister of Austria–Hungary 1912–15 and a crucial figure in the events that led to World War I, because his indecisive stance caused tension with Serbia.

Berdyaev /bɪə'djaɪef/ Nikolai Alexandrovich 1874–1948. Russian philosopher who often challenged official Soviet viewpoints after the Revolution of 1917. Although appointed professor of philosophy in 1919 at Moscow University, he was exiled 1922 for defending Orthodox Christian religion. His books include *The Meaning of History* 1923 and *The Destiny of Man* 1935.

Bérégovoy Pierre 1925–1993. French socialist politician, prime minister from 1992–1993. A close ally of François →Mitterrand, he was named chief of staff 1981 after managing the successful presidential campaign. He was social affairs minister 1982–84 and finance minister 1984–86 and 1988–92. In April 1992 he replaced Edith Cresson as prime minister.

The son of a Ukrainian immigrant, he was largely self-educated and his working-class background contrasted sharply with that of the other Socialist Party leaders. As finance minister, he was widely respected by France's financial community. However, in 1993, allegations of personal financial irregularities, which he denied, followed by the Socialist government's overwhelming defeat in the March national assembly elections, which saw him turned out of office, apparently plunged him into a depression which led to his suicide in May.

Berengaria of Navarre /ˌberən'geərɪə/ 1165–1230. Queen of England. The only English queen never to set foot in England, she was the daughter of King Sancho VI of Navarre. She married Richard I of England in Cyprus 1191, and accompanied him on his crusade to the Holy Land.

Berenson /'berənsən/ Bernard 1865–1959. Lithuanian-born US art historian who was once revered as a leading scholar of Italian Renaissance art. He became wealthy through his advisory work for art galleries, although many of his attributions of anonymous Italian paintings were later questioned.

Berg /beəg/ Alban 1885–1935. Austrian composer. He studied under Arnold →Schoenberg and was associated with him as one of the leaders of the serial, or 12-tone, school of composition. His output includes orchestral, chamber, and vocal music as well as two operas, *Wozzeck* 1925, a grim story of working-class life, and the unfinished *Lulu* 1929–35. His music is emotionally expressive, and sometimes anguished, but can also be lyrical, as in the *Violin Concerto* 1935.

Berg /bɜːg/ Paul 1926– . US molecular biologist. In 1972, using gene-splicing techniques developed by others, Berg spliced and combined into a single hybrid DNA from an animal tumour virus (SV40) and DNA from a bacterial virus. Berg's work aroused fears in other workers and excited continuing controversy. For his work on recombinant DNA, he shared the 1980 Nobel Prize for Chemistry with Walter →Gilbert and Frederick →Sanger.

Bergius /'beəgɪəs/ Friedrich Karl Rudolph 1884–1949. German research chemist who invented processes for converting coal into oil and wood into sugar. He shared a Nobel prize 1931 with Carl Bosch for his part in inventing and developing high-pressure industrial methods.

Bergman /'beəgmən/ Ingmar 1918– . Swedish stage producer (from the 1930s) and film director (from the 1950s), regarded by many as one of the great masters of modern cinema. His work deals with complex moral, psychological, and metaphysical problems and is tinged with pessimism. His films include *Wild Strawberries* 1957, *The Seventh Seal* 1957, *Persona* 1966, *Autumn Sonata* 1978 and *Fanny and Alexander* 1982.

Bergman /'beəgmən/ Ingrid 1917–1982. Swedish actress whose films include *Intermezzo* 1939, *Casablanca*, *For Whom the Bell Tolls* both 1943, and *Gaslight* 1944, for which she won an Academy Award. By leaving her husband to have a child with director Roberto Rossellini, she broke an unofficial moral code of Hollywood star behaviour and was ostracized for many years. During her 'exile', she made films in Europe such as *Stromboli* 1949 (directed by Rossellini). Later films include *Anastasia* 1956, for which she won an Academy Award.

Keep it simple. Make a blank face and the music and the story will fill it in.

Ingrid Bergman
advice on film acting *Time* May 1983

Bergson /beək'sɒn/ Henri 1859–1941. French philosopher who believed that time, change, and development were the essence of reality. He thought that time was not a succession of distinct and separate instants but a continuous process in which one period merged imperceptibly into the next. Nobel Prize for Literature 1928.

Beria /'beərɪə/ Lavrenti 1899–1953. Soviet politician who in 1938 became minister of the interior and head of the Soviet police force that imprisoned, liquidated, and transported millions of Soviet citizens. On Stalin's death 1953, he attempted to seize power but was foiled and shot after a secret trial. Apologists for Stalin have blamed Beria for the atrocities committed by Soviet police during Stalin's dictatorship.

Bering /'beərɪŋ/ Vitus 1681–1741. Danish explorer, the first European to sight Alaska. He died on Bering Island in the Bering Sea, both named after him, as is the Bering Strait, which separates Asia (Russia) from North America (Alaska).

Berio /ˈbeəriəʊ/ Luciano 1925– . Italian composer. His style has been described as graceful serialism, and he has frequently experimented with electronic music and taped sound. His works include nine *Sequenzas/Sequences* 1957–75 for various solo instruments or voice, *Sinfonia* 1969 for voices and orchestra, *Points on the curve to find ...* 1974, and a number of dramatic works, including the opera *Un re in ascolto/A King Listens* 1984, loosely based on Shakespeare's *The Tempest*.

Beriosova /ˌberiˈɒsəvə/ Svetlana 1932– . British ballerina. Born in Lithuania and brought up partly in the USA, she danced with the Royal Ballet from 1952. Her style had a lyrical dignity and she excelled in *The Lady and the Fool*, *Ondine*, and *Giselle*.

Berkeley /ˈbɜːkli/ Busby. Stage name of William Berkeley Enos 1895–1976. US choreographer and film director who used ingenious and extravagant sets and teams of female dancers to create large-scale kaleidoscopic patterns through movement and costume when filmed from above, as in *Gold Diggers of 1933* and *Footlight Parade* 1933.

Berkeley /ˈbɑːkli/ George 1685–1753. Irish philosopher and cleric who believed that nothing exists apart from perception, and that the all-seeing mind of God makes possible the continued apparent existence of things. For Berkeley, everyday objects are collections of ideas or sensations, hence the dictum *esse est percipi* ('to exist is to be perceived'). He became bishop of Cloyne 1734.

I do know that I, who am a spirit or thinking substance, exist as certainly as I know my ideas exist.

George Berkeley
Three Dialogues between Hylas and Philonous 1713

Berkeley /ˈbɑːkli/ Lennox (Randal Francis) 1903–1989. English composer. His works for the voice include *The Hill of the Graces* 1975, verses from Spenser's *Fairie Queene* set for eight-part unaccompanied chorus; and his operas *Nelson* 1953 and *Ruth* 1956.

Berkeley /ˈbɜːkli, ˈbɑːkli/ Sir William 1606–1677. British colonial administrator in North America, governor of the colony of Virginia 1641–1677. Siding with the Royalists during the English Civil War, he was removed from the governorship by Oliver Cromwell 1652. He was reappointed 1660 by Charles II after the Restoration of the monarchy. However, growing opposition to him in the colony culminated in ➔Bacon's Rebellion 1676 and in 1677 Berkeley was removed from office for his brutal repression of that uprising.

Born in Bruton, England, Berkeley was educated at Oxford University. When first appointed as governor of Virginia, he proved himself to be an able administrator, but was drawn into English politics and neglected the affairs of his colony. He was knighted by Charles I in 1639.

Berlage /ˈbeəlɑːɡə/ Hendrikus 1856–1934. Dutch architect of the Amsterdam Stock Exchange 1897–1903. His individualist style marked a move away from 19th-century historicism and towards Dutch Expressionism.

Berlin /ˈbɜːlɪn/ Irving. Adopted name of Israel Baline 1888–1989. Russian-born US composer who wrote over 1,500 songs including such hits as 'Alexander's Ragtime Band' 1911, 'Always' 1925, 'God Bless America' 1939, and 'White Christmas' 1942, and the musicals *Top Hat* 1935, *Annie Get Your Gun* 1950, and *Call Me Madam* 1953. He also wrote film scores such as *Blue Skies* and *Easter Parade*.

The son of a poor Jewish cantor, Berlin learned music by ear. He was instrumental in the development of the popular song, taking it from jazz and ragtime to swing and romantic ballads.

Berlin /ˈbɜːlɪn/ Isaiah 1909– . Latvian-born British philosopher. He emigrated to England with his family 1920, and was professor of social and political theory at Oxford 1957–67. He wrote about Tolstoy's theory of irresistible historical forces and about Marxism; his books include *Historical Inevitability* 1954 and *Four Essays on Liberty* 1969.

Berlinguer /ˌbeəlɪŋˈɡweə/ Enrico 1922–1984. Italian Communist who freed the party from Soviet influence. Secretary general of the Italian Communist Party, by 1976 he was near to the premiership, but the murder of Aldo Moro, the prime minister, by Red Brigade guerrillas, prompted a move toward support for the socialists.

A leading spokesman for 'national communism', he sought to adapt Marxism to local requirements and to steer away from slavish obedience to Moscow. The rift between the Italian Communist Party and the Soviet Union widened during the late 1970s and early 1980s, when Berlinguer heavily criticized the Soviet Union's policies of intervention in Afghanistan and Poland.

Berlioz /ˈbeəliəʊz/ (Louis) Hector 1803–1869. French romantic composer, the founder of modern orchestration.

Much of his music was inspired by drama and literature and has a theatrical quality. He wrote symphonic works, such as *Symphonie fantastique* 1830–31 and *Roméo et Juliette* 1839; dramatic cantatas including *La Damnation de Faust* 1846 and *L'Enfance du Christ* 1854; sacred music; and three operas.

Berlioz studied music at the Paris Conservatoire. He won the Prix de Rome 1830, and spent two years in Italy. In 1833 he married Harriet Smithson, an Irish actress playing Shakespearean parts in Paris, but they separated 1842. After some years of poverty and public neglect, he went to Germany 1842 and conducted his own works. He subsequently visited Russia and England. In 1854 he married Marie Recio, a singer. His operas are *Benvenuto Cellini* 1838, *Les Troyens* 1856–58, and *Béatrice et Bénédict* 1862.

Time is a great teacher, but unfortunately it kills all its pupils.

Hector Berlioz
Almanach des lettres françaises

Bernadette, St /ˌbɜːnəˈdet/ 1844–1879. French saint, born in Lourdes in the French Pyrenees. In Feb 1858 she had a vision of the Virgin Mary in a grotto, and it became a centre of pilgrimage. Many sick people who were dipped in the water of a spring there were said to have been cured. Her feast day is 16 April.

The grotto of Massabielle was opened to the public by command of Napoleon III, and a church built on the rock above became a shrine. At the age of 20 Bernadette became a nun at Nevers, and nursed the wounded of the Franco-Prussian War.

Bernadotte /ˌbɜːnəˈdɒt/ Count Folke 1895–1948. Swedish diplomat and president of the Swedish Red Cross. In 1945 he conveyed Nazi commander Himmler's offer of capitulation to the British and US governments, and in 1948 was United Nations mediator in Palestine, where he was assassinated by Israeli Stern Gang guerrillas. He was a nephew of Gustaf VI of Sweden.

Bernadotte /ˌbɜːnəˈdɒt/ Jean-Baptiste Jules 1764–1844. Marshal in Napoleon's army who in 1818 became ➔Charles XIV of Sweden. Hence, Bernadotte is the family name of the present royal house of Sweden.

Bernanos /ˌbeənəˈnəʊs/ Georges 1888–1948. French author. He achieved fame in 1926 with *Sous le soleil de Satan/The Star of Satan*. His strongly Catholic viewpoint is also expressed in his *Journal d'un curé de campagne/The Diary of a Country Priest* 1936.

Bernard /beəˈnɑː/ Claude 1813–1878. French physiologist and founder of experimental medicine. Bernard first demonstrated that digestion is not restricted to the stomach, but takes place throughout the small intestine. He discovered the digestive input of the pancreas, several functions of the liver, and the vasomotor nerves which dilate and contract the blood vessels and thus regulate body temperature. This led him to the concept of the *milieu intérieur* ('internal environment') whose stability is essential to good health.

Bernard of Clairvaux, St /kleəˈvəʊ/ 1090–1153. Christian founder in 1115 of Clairvaux monastery in Champagne, France. He reinvigorated the Cistercian order, preached in support of the Second Crusade in 1146, and had the scholastic philosopher Abelard condemned for heresy. He is often depicted with a beehive. His feast day is 20 Aug.

Bernard of Menthon, St /mɒnˈtɒn/ or *Bernard of Montjoux* 923–1008. Christian priest, founder of the hospices for travellers on the Alpine passes that bear his name. The large, heavily built *St Bernard* dogs, formerly employed to find travellers lost in the snow, were also named after him. He is the patron saint of mountaineers. His feast day is 28 May.

Bernhard /ˈbeənɑːt/ Prince of the Netherlands 1911– . Formerly Prince Bernhard of Lippe-Biesterfeld, he married Princess ➔Juliana in 1937. When Germany invaded the Netherlands in 1940, he escaped to England and became liaison officer for the Dutch and British forces, playing a part in the organization of the Dutch Resistance.

In 1976 he was widely censured for his involvement in the purchase of Lockheed aircraft by the Netherlands.

Bernhardt /ˈbɜːnhɑːt/ Sarah. Stage name of Rosine Bernard 1845–1923. French actress who dominated the stage of her day, frequently performing at the Comédie-Française in Paris. She excelled in tragic roles, including Cordelia in Shakespeare's *King Lear*, the title role in Racine's *Phèdre*, and the male roles of Hamlet and of Napoleon's son in Edmond ➔Rostand's *L'Aiglon*.

Bernini /beəˈniːni/ Giovanni Lorenzo 1598–1680. Italian sculptor, architect, and painter, a leading figure in the development of the Baroque style. His work in Rome includes the colonnaded piazza in front of St Peter's Basilica (1656), fountains (as in the Piazza Navona), and papal monuments. His sculpture includes *The Ecstasy of St Theresa* 1645–52 (Sta Maria della Vittoria, Rome) and numerous portrait busts.

Bernini's sculptural style is full of movement and drama, as captured in billowing drapery and facial expressions. His subjects are religious and mythological. A fine example is the marble *Apollo and Daphne* for the Cardinal Borghese, 1622–25 (Borghese Palace, Rome), with the figures shown in full flight. Inside St Peter's, he created several marble monuments and the elaborate canopy over the high altar. He also produced many fine portrait busts, such as one of Louis XIV of France.

I have freed my soul.

St Bernard of Clairvaux

Bernoulli /bɜːˈnuːli/ Swiss family that produced many mathematicians and scientists in the 17th, 18th, and 19th centuries, in particular the brothers *Jakob* (1654–1705) and *Johann* (1667–1748).

Jakob and Johann were pioneers of →Leibniz's calculus. Jakob used calculus to study the forms of many curves arising in practical situations, and studied mathematical probability (*Ars conjectandi* 1713); **Bernoulli numbers** are named after him. Johann developed exponential calculus and contributed to many areas of applied mathematics, including the problem of a particle moving in a gravitational field. His son, **Daniel** (1700–1782) worked on calculus and probability, and in physics proposed **Bernoulli's principle**, which states that the pressure of a moving fluid decreases the faster it flows (which explains the origin of lift on the aerofoil of an aircraft's wing). This and other work on hydrodynamics was published in *Hydrodynamica* 1738.

Bernstein /ˈbɜːnstaɪn/ Edouard 1850–1932. German socialist thinker, journalist, and politician. He was elected to the Reichstag 1902. He was a proponent of reformist rather than revolutionary socialism, whereby a socialist society could be achieved within an existing parliamentary structure merely by workers' parties obtaining a majority.

Bernstein /ˈbɜːnstaɪn/ Leonard 1918–1990. US composer, conductor, and pianist, one of the most energetic and versatile of US musicians in the 20th century. His works, which established a vogue for realistic, contemporary themes, include symphonies such as *The Age of Anxiety* 1949, ballets such as *Fancy Free* 1944, and scores for musicals, including *Wonderful Town* 1953, *West Side Story* 1957, and *Mass* 1971 in memory of President J F Kennedy.

From 1958 to 1970 he was musical director of the New York Philharmonic. Among his other works are the symphony *Jeremiah* 1944, the ballet *Facsimile* 1946, the musicals *Candide* 1956 and the *Chichester Psalms* 1965.

Bernstein US composer, conductor, and pianist Leonard Bernstein juxtaposed a romantic intensity with jazz and Latin American elements in his large instrumental and choral works. He wrote works in widely different styles, from West Side Story *1957, a musical based on the Romeo and Juliet theme, to the* Chichester Psalms *1965.*

Berri /ˈberi/ Nabih 1939– . Lebanese politician and soldier, leader of Amal ('Hope'), the Syrian-backed Shi'ite nationalist movement. He became minister of justice in the government of President →Gemayel 1984. In 1988 Amal was disbanded after defeat by the Iranian-backed Hezbollah ('Children of God') during the Lebanese civil wars, and Berri joined the cabinet of Selim Hoss 1989. In Dec 1990 Berri was made minister of state in the newly formed Karami cabinet, and in 1992 retained the same post in the cabinet of Rashid al-Sohl.

Berry /ˈberi/ Chuck (Charles Edward) 1926– . US rock-and-roll singer, prolific songwriter, and guitarist. His characteristic guitar riffs became staples of rock music, and his humorous storytelling lyrics were also emulated. He had a string of hits in the 1950s and 1960s beginning with 'Maybellene' 1955.

Born in St Louis, Missouri, Berry began as a blues guitarist in local clubs. His other early tunes, among them 'Roll Over Beethoven' 1956, 'Rock 'n' Roll Music' 1957, 'Sweet Little Sixteen' 1958, and 'Johnny B Goode' 1958, are classics of the genre, and one of them was chosen as a sample of Earth music for the *Voyager* space probes. Berry's later career was marred by trouble with the law, and he often seemed to have lost respect for his own work. He was the subject of a film tribute, *Hail! Hail! Rock 'n' Roll* 1987.

Roll over, Beethoven, and tell Tchaikovsky the news.

    Chuck Berry 'Roll Over Beethoven' 1956

Berryman /ˈberimən/ John 1914–1972. US poet whose sombre, complex, and personal works include *Homage to Mistress Bradstreet* 1956, *77 Dream Songs* 1964 (Pulitzer Prize 1965), *His Toy, His Dream, His Rest* 1968, and *Delusions, etc.* 1972.

Berthelot /ˌbeətəˈləʊ/ Pierre Eugène Marcellin 1827–1907. French chemist and politician who carried out research into dyes and explosives proving that hydrocarbons and other organic compounds can be synthesized from inorganic materials.

Bertholet /ˌbeətəˈleɪ/ Claude Louis 1748–1822. French chemist who carried out research into dyes and bleaches (introducing the use of chlorine as a bleach) and determined the composition of ammonia. Modern chemical nomenclature is based on a system worked out by Bertholet and Antoine ➔Lavoisier.

Bertolucci /ˌbeətəʊˈluːtʃi/ Bernardo 1940– . Italian film director whose work combines political and historical perspectives with an elegant and lyrical visual appeal. His films include *The Spider's Stratagem* 1970, *Last Tango in Paris* 1972, *1900* 1976, *The Last Emperor* 1987, for which he received an Academy Award, and *The Sheltering Sky* 1990.

Bertrand de Born /beəˈtrɒn də ˈbɔːn/ *c.* 1140–*c.* 1215. Provençal troubadour. He was viscount of Hautefort in Périgord, accompanied Richard the Lionheart to Palestine, and died a monk.

Berwick /ˈberɪk/ James Fitzjames, Duke of Berwick 1670–1734. French marshal, illegitimate son of the Duke of York (afterwards James II of England) and Arabella Churchill (1648–1730), sister of the great duke of Marlborough, his enemy in battle. He was made duke of Berwick in 1687. After the revolution of 1688 he served under his father in Ireland, joined the French army, fought against William III and Marlborough, and in 1707 defeated the English at Almansa in Spain. He was killed at the siege of Philippsburg.

Berzelius /bəˈziːliəs/ Jöns Jakob 1779–1848. Swedish chemist who accurately determined more than 2,000 relative atomic and molecular masses. He devised (1813–14) the system of chemical symbols and formulae now in use and proposed oxygen as a reference standard for atomic masses. His discoveries include the elements cerium (1804), selenium (1817), and thorium (1828); he was the first to prepare silicon in its amorphous form and to isolate zirconium. The words *isomerism, allotropy,* and *protein* were coined by him.

Besant /ˈbesənt/ Annie 1847–1933. English socialist and feminist activist. Separated from her clerical husband in 1873 because of her freethinking views, she was associated with the radical atheist Charles Bradlaugh and the socialist Fabian Society. She and Bradlaugh published a treatise advocating birth control and were prosecuted; as a result she lost custody of her daughter. In 1889 she became a disciple of Madame ➔Blavatsky. She thereafter preached theosophy and went to India. As a supporter of Indian independence, she founded the Central Hindu College 1898 and the Indian Home Rule League 1916, and became president of the Indian National Congress in 1917. Her *Theosophy and the New Psychology* was published 1904. She was the sister-in-law of Walter Besant.

Besant /ˈbesənt/ Walter 1836–1901. English writer. He wrote novels in partnership with James Rice (1844–1882), and produced an attack on the social evils of the East End of London, *All Sorts and Conditions of Men* 1882, and an unfinished *Survey of London* 1902–12. He was the brother-in-law of Annie Besant.

Bessel /ˈbesl/ Friedrich Wilhelm 1784–1846. German astronomer and mathematician, the first person to find the approximate distance to a star by direct methods when he measured the parallax (annual displacement) of the star 61 Cygni in 1838. In mathematics, he introduced the series of functions now known as *Bessel functions*.

Bessemer /ˈbesɪmə/ Henry 1813–1898. British engineer and inventor who developed a method of converting molten pig iron into steel (the *Bessemer process*).

Bessmertnykh /bɪˈsmeətnɪx/ Aleksandr 1934– . Soviet politician, foreign minister Jan–Aug 1991. He began as a diplomat and worked mostly in the USA, at the United Nations headquarters in New York and the Soviet embassy in Washington DC. He succeeded Edvard Shevardnadze as foreign minister in Jan 1991, but was dismissed in August of the same year for exhibiting 'passivity' during the failed anti-Gorbachev coup.

Best /best/ Charles Herbert 1899–1978. Canadian physiologist, one of the team of Canadian scientists including Frederick ➔Banting whose research resulted in 1922 in the discovery of insulin as a treatment for diabetes.

A Banting–Best Department of Medical Research was founded in Toronto, and Best was its director 1941–67.

Best /best/ George 1946– . Irish footballer. He won two League championship medals and was a member of the Manchester United side that won the European Cup in 1968.

Born in Belfast, he joined Manchester United as a youth and made his debut at 17; seven months later he made his international debut for Northern Ireland. Trouble with managers, fellow players, and the media led to his early retirement.

Bethe /ˈbeɪtə/ Hans Albrecht 1906– . German-born US physicist who worked on the first atom bomb. He was awarded a Nobel prize 1967 for his discoveries concerning energy production in stars.

Bethe left Germany for England in 1933, and worked at Manchester and Bristol universities. In 1935 he moved to the USA where he became professor of theoretical physics at Cornell University; his research was interrupted by the war and by his appointment as head of the theoretical division of the Los Alamos atom bomb project. He has since become a leading peace campaigner, and opposed the US government's Strategic Defense Initiative (Star Wars) programme.

Bethmann Hollweg /ˈbeɪtmæn ˈhɒlveg/ Theobald von 1856–1921. German politician, imperial chancellor 1909–17, largely responsible for engineering popular support for World War I in Germany, but his power was overthrown by a military dictatorship under ➔Ludendorff and ➔Hindenburg.

Betjeman English poet John Betjeman's works celebrated the supposedly more settled times of prewar Britain. They were welcomed warmly by a public suffering the upheavals of two world wars and their aftermath. Betjeman's admiration for Edwardian and Victorian taste and architecture was voiced not only in his verse but also in the mass media. He was knighted in 1969.

Betjeman /ˈbetʃɪmən/ John 1906–1984. English poet and essayist, originator of a peculiarly English light verse, nostalgic, and delighting in Victorian and Edwardian architecture. His *Collected Poems* appeared in 1968 and a verse autobiography, *Summoned by Bells*, in 1960. He became poet laureate 1972.

Bettelheim /ˈbetlhaɪm/ Bruno 1903–1990. Austrian-born US child psychologist. At the University of Chicago he founded a treatment centre for emotionally disturbed children based on the principle of a supportive home environment. Among his most influential books are *Love is Not Enough* 1950, *Truants from Life* 1954, and *Children of the Dream* 1962.

Imprisoned in the Dachau and Buchenwald concentration camps 1933–35, he emigrated to the USA in 1939. His other books include *The Uses of Enchantment: The Meaning and Importance of Fairy Tales* 1976, and *A Good Enough Parent* 1987. He took his own life.

Betterton /ˈbetətən/ Thomas *c.* 1635–1710. British actor, member of the Duke of York's company after the Restoration. He was greatly admired in many Shakespearean parts, including Hamlet and Othello.

Betti /ˈbeti/ Ugo 1892–1953. Italian poet and dramatist. His plays include *Delitto all'isola delle capre/Crime on Goat Island* 1948 and *La Regina e gli insorte/The Queen and the Rebels* 1949.

Betty /ˈbeti/ William Henry West 1791–1874. British boy actor, called the 'Young Roscius' after

the greatest comic actor of ancient Rome. He was famous, particularly in Shakespearean roles, from the age of 11 to 17.

Beuys /bɔɪs/ Joseph 1921–1986. German sculptor and performance artist, one of the leaders of avant-garde art in Europe during the 1970s and 1980s. His sculpture makes use of unusual materials such as felt and fat.

He was strongly influenced by his wartime experiences.

Bevan /ˈbevən/ Aneurin (Nye) 1897–1960. British Labour politician. Son of a Welsh miner, and himself a miner at 13, he became member of Parliament for Ebbw Vale 1929–60. As minister of health 1945–51, he inaugurated the National Health Service (NHS); he was minister of labour Jan–April 1951, when he resigned (with Harold Wilson) on the introduction of NHS charges and led a Bevanite faction against the government. In 1956 he became chief Labour spokesperson on foreign affairs, and deputy leader of the Labour party 1959. He was an outstanding speaker.

Beveridge /ˈbevərɪdʒ/ William Henry, 1st Baron Beveridge 1879–1963. British economist. A civil servant, he acted as Lloyd George's lieutenant in the social legislation of the Liberal government before World War I. The *Beveridge Report* 1942 formed the basis of the welfare state in Britain.

Bevin /ˈbevɪn/ Ernest 1881–1951. British Labour politician. Chief creator of the Transport and General Workers' Union, he was its general secretary from 1921 to 1940, when he entered the war cabinet as minister of labour and national service. He organized the 'Bevin boys', chosen by ballot to work in the coal mines as war service, and was foreign secretary in the Labour government 1945–51.

Bewick /ˈbjuːɪk/ Thomas 1753–1828. English wood engraver, excelling in animal subjects. His illustrated *A General History of Quadrupeds* 1790 and *A History of British Birds* 1797–1804 display his skill.

Beza /beɪˈzɑː/ Théodore (properly *De Bèsze*) 1519–1605. French church reformer. He settled in Geneva, Switzerland, where he worked with the Protestant leader John Calvin and succeeded him as head of the reformed church there 1564. He wrote in defence of the burning of →Servetus (1554) and translated the New Testament into Latin.

Bhindranwale /ˈbɪndrəwɒlə/ Sant Jarnail Singh 1947–1984. Indian Sikh fundamentalist leader who campaigned for the creation of a separate state of Khalistan during the early 1980s, precipitating a bloody Hindu–Sikh conflict in the Punjab. Having taken refuge in the Golden Temple complex in Amritsar and built up an arms cache for guerrilla activities, Bhindranwale, along with around 500 followers, died at the hands of Indian security forces who stormed the temple in 'Operation Blue Star' June 1984.

Bhumibol Adulyadej /puːmɪpəʊn əˈdʊnlədeɪt/ 1927– . King of Thailand from 1946. Born in the USA and educated in Bangkok and Switzerland, he succeeded to the throne on the assassination of his brother. In 1973 he was active, with popular support, in overthrowing the military government of Marshal Thanom Kittikachorn and thus ended a sequence of army-dominated regimes in power from 1932.

Bhutto /ˈbuːtəʊ/ Benazir 1953– . Pakistani politician, leader of the Pakistan People's Party (PPP) from 1984 (in exile until 1986), and prime minister of Pakistan 1988–90, when the opposition manoeuvred her from office and charged her with corruption. In May 1991 new charges were brought against her. She was the first female leader of a Muslim state.

Benazir Bhutto was educated at Harvard and Oxford universities. She returned to Pakistan 1977 but was placed under house arrest after General →Zia ul-Haq seized power from her father, Prime Minister Zulfikar Ali Bhutto. On her release she moved to the UK and became, with her mother Nusrat (1934–), the joint leader in exile of the opposition PPP. When martial law had been lifted, she returned to Pakistan April 1986 to launch a campaign for open elections. In her first year in office she struck an uneasy balance with the military establishment and improved Pakistan's relations with India.

She led her country back into the Commonwealth 1989. In Aug 1990, she was removed from office by presidential decree, and a caretaker government installed. Charges of corruption and abuse of power were levelled against her and her husband Asif Ali Zardari (who was also accused of mass murder, kidnapping, and extortion), and her party was defeated in the subsequent general election. Bhutto and her husband claimed that the charges were fabrications, with the government's intention being to strike a deal whereby they would receive pardons on condition that they left the country and effectively abandoned politics. In May 1991 new charges (eight in all), alleging misuse of secret service funds, were brought against Benazir Bhutto. She denied all charges. Her husband, who was acquitted on 5 May 1991 of fraudulently obtaining a bank loan, was charged on 13 May with criminal conspiracy leading to the death of political opponents.

My politics are a commitment to freedom and the meaning of life.

Benazir Bhutto *Daughter of the East*

Bhutto /ˈbuːtəʊ/ Zulfikar Ali 1928–1979. Pakistani politician, president 1971–73; prime minister from 1973 until the 1977 military coup led by General →Zia ul-Haq. In 1978 Bhutto was sentenced to death for conspiring to murder a political opponent and was hanged the following year.

Biber /ˈbiːbə/ Heinrich von 1644–1704. Bohemian composer, kapellmeister at the archbishop of Salzburg's court. A virtuoso violinist, he composed a wide variety of musical pieces including the *Nightwatchman Serenade*.

Bichat /biːˈʃɑː/ Marie François Xavier 1771–1802. French physician and founder of histology, the study of tissues. He studied the organs of the body, their structure, and the ways in which they are affected by disease. This led to his discovery and naming of 'tissue', a basic biological and medical concept; he identified 21 types. He argued that disease does not affect the whole organ but only certain of its constituent tissues.

Bidault /biːˈdəʊ/ Georges 1899–1983. French politician, prime minister 1946, 1949–50. He was a leader of the French resistance during World War II and foreign minister and president in de Gaulle's provisional government. He left the Gaullists over Algerian independence and in 1962 he became head of the Organisation de l'Armée Secrète (OAS), formed 1961 by French settlers devoted to perpetuating their own rule in Algeria. He was charged with treason in 1963 and left the country, but was allowed to return in 1968.

Biddle /ˈbɪdl/ Nicholas 1786–1844. US financier and public figure. An expert in international commerce, he was appointed a director of the Bank of the United States by President James Monroe 1819 and became president of the bank 1822. An extreme fiscal conservative, Biddle became the focus of Andrew →Jackson's campaigns against the power of the bank in 1828 and 1832. After the withdrawal of the bank's federal charter 1836, he remained its president under a state charter.

Born in Philadelphia, Biddle was admitted to the Pennsylvania bar 1809 and elected to the state legislature 1814.

Bienville /biˈenvɪl/ Jean Baptiste Le Moyne, Sieur de 1680–1768. French colonial administrator, governor of the North American colony of Louisiana 1706–13, 1717–23, and 1733–43. During his first term he founded the settlement at Mobile in Alabama and in his second term, established the Louisiana colonial capital at New Orleans. During his final term Bienville was drawn into a costly and ultimately unsuccessful war with the Indians of the lower Mississippi Valley.

Born in Ville-Marie (now Montreal), Quebec, Canada, Bienville served in the French navy and in 1698 accompanied →Iberville on a mission to establish a French colony at the mouth of the Mississippi River.

Bierce /bɪəs/ Ambrose (Gwinett) 1842–c. 1914. US author. He established his reputation as a master of supernatural and psychological horror with *Tales of Soldiers and Civilians* 1891 and *Can Such Things Be?* 1893. He also wrote *The Devil's Dictionary* 1911 (first published as *The Cynic's Word Book* 1906), a collection of ironic definitions. He disappeared in Mexico 1913.

Bierstadt /ˈbɪəstæt/ Albert 1830–1902. German-born US landscape painter. His spectacular panoramas of the American wilderness fell out of favour after his death until interest in the Hudson River School rekindled late in the century. A classic work is *Thunderstorm in the Rocky Mountains* 1859 (Museum of Fine Arts, Boston).

Biffen /ˈbɪfɪn/ (William) John 1930– . British Conservative politician. In 1971 he was elected to Parliament for a Shropshire seat. Despite being to the left of Margaret Thatcher, he held key positions in government from 1979, including leader of the House of Commons from 1982, but was dropped after the general election of 1987.

Biko /ˈbiːkəʊ/ Steve (Stephen) 1946–1977. South African civil-rights leader. An active opponent of apartheid, he was arrested in Sept 1977; he died in detention six days later. Since his death in the custody of South African police, he has been a symbol of the anti-apartheid movement.

He founded the South African Students Organization (SASO) in 1968 and was cofounder in 1972 of the Black People's Convention, also called the Black Consciousness movement, a radical association of South African students that aimed to develop black pride. His death in the hands of the police caused much controversy.

Billy the Kid /ˈbɪli/ nickname of William H Bonney 1859–1881. US outlaw, a leader in the 1878 Lincoln County cattle war in New Mexico, who allegedly killed his first victim at 12 and was reputed to have killed 21 men by age 22, when he died.

Born in Brooklyn, New York, Bonney moved west with his family to Kansas and then New Mexico. He was sentenced to death for murdering a sheriff, but escaped (killing two guards), and was finally shot by Sheriff Pat Garrett while trying to avoid recapture.

Binet /ˈbiːneɪ/ Alfred 1857–1911. French psychologist who introduced the first intelligence tests 1905. They were standardized so that the last of a set of graded tests the child could successfully complete gave the level described as 'mental age'. If the test was passed by most children over 12, for instance, but failed by those younger, it was said to show a mental age of 12. Binet published these in collaboration with Theodore Simon.

Bingham /ˈbɪŋm/ George Caleb 1811–1879. US painter. The influence of the Hudson River School is evident in such frontier landscapes as *Fur Traders Descending the Missouri* 1845.

Born near Charlottesville, Virginia, USA, he grew up in Missouri and studied at the Pennsylvania Academy of the Fine Arts 1837. After painting in New York and Washington, he returned to Missouri.

Bingham /ˈbɪŋəm/ Hiram 1875–1919. US explorer and politician who from 1907 visited Latin America, discovering Machu Picchu, Vitcos, and other Inca settlements in Peru. He later entered politics, becoming a senator.

Binyon /ˈbɪnjən/ Laurence 1869–1943. British poet. His verse volumes include *Lyric Poems* 1894 and *London Visions*, but he is best remembered for his ode *For the Fallen* 1914.

Biot /biˈəʊ/ Jean 1774–1862. French physicist who studied the polarization of light. In 1804 he made a balloon ascent to a height of 5 km/3 mi, in an early investigation of the Earth's atmosphere.

Birch /bɜːtʃ/ John M 1918–1945. American Baptist missionary, commissioned by the US Air Force to carry out intelligence work behind the Chinese lines where he was killed by the communists; the US extreme right-wing *John Birch Society* 1958 is named after him.

Bird /bɜːd/ Isabella 1832–1904. British traveller and writer who wrote extensively of her journeys in the USA, Persia, Tibet, Kurdistan, China, Japan, and Korea.

Her published works include *The Englishwoman in America* 1856, *A Lady's Life in the Rocky Mountains* 1874, *Unbeaten Tracks in Japan* 1880, *Among the Tibetans* 1894, and *Pictures from China* 1900. Her last great journey was made 1901 when she travelled over 1,600 km/1,000 mi in Morocco.

Birdseye /ˈbɜːdzaɪ/ Clarence 1886–1956. US inventor who pioneered food refrigeration processes. While working as a fur trader in Labrador 1912–16 he was struck by the ease with which food could be preserved in an Arctic climate. Back in the USA he found that the same effect could be obtained by rapidly freezing prepared food between two refrigerated metal plates. To market his products he founded the General Sea Foods Co. 1924, which he sold to General Foods 1929.

Birendra Bir Bikram Shah Dev 1945– . King of Nepal from 1972, when he succeeded his father Mahendra; he was formally crowned 1975. King Birendra has overseen Nepal's return to multiparty politics and introduced a new constitution 1990.

Birkenhead /ˈbɜːkənhed/ Frederick Edwin Smith, 1st Earl of Birkenhead 1872–1930. British Conservative politician. A flamboyant character, known as 'FE', he joined with Edward Carson in organizing armed resistance in Ulster to Irish Home Rule. He was Lord Chancellor 1919–22 and a much criticized secretary for India 1924–28.

Biro /ˈbɪrəʊ/ Lazlo 1900–1985. Hungarian-born Argentine who invented a ballpoint pen 1944. His name became generic for ballpoint pens in the UK.

Birtwistle /ˈbɜːtwɪsl/ Harrison 1934– . English avant-garde composer. He has specialized in chamber music, for example, his chamber opera *Punch and Judy* 1967 and *Down by the Greenwood Side* 1969.

Birtwistle's early music was influenced by →Stravinsky and by the medieval and Renaissance masters, and for many years he worked alongside

Maxwell →Davies. Orchestral works include *The Triumph of Time* 1972 and *Silbury Air* 1977; he has also written operas including *The Mask of Orpheus* 1986 (with electronic music by Barry Anderson) and *Gawain* 1991 a reworking of the medieval English poem 'Sir Gawain and the Green Knight'. His *Chronometer* 1972 (assisted by Peter Zinovieff) is based on clock sounds.

Bishop Isabella. Married name of the travel writer Isabella →Bird.

Bishop /ˈbɪʃəp/ Ronald Eric 1903–1989. British aircraft designer. He joined the de Havilland Aircraft Company 1931 as an apprentice, and designed the Mosquito bomber, the Vampire fighter, and the Comet jet airliner.

Bishop /ˈbɪʃəp/ William Avery 1894–1956. Canadian air ace. He shot down over 70 enemy aircraft in World War I, and was awarded the Victoria Cross 1917.

Bismarck /ˈbɪzmɑːk/ Otto Eduard Leopold, Prince von 1815–1898. German politician, prime minister of Prussia 1862–90 and chancellor of the German Empire 1871–90. He pursued an aggressively expansionist policy, waging wars against Denmark 1863–64, Austria 1866, and France 1870–71, which brought about the unification of Germany.

Bismarck was ambitious to establish Prussia's leadership within Germany and eliminate the influence of Austria. He secured Austria's support for his successful war against Denmark then, in 1866, went to war against Austria and its allies (the Seven Weeks' War), his victory forcing Austria out of the German Bund and unifying the N German states into the North German Confederation under his own chancellorship 1867. He then defeated France, under Napoleon III, in the Franco-Prussian War 1870–71, proclaimed the German Empire 1871, and annexed Alsace-Lorraine. He tried to secure his work by the Triple Alliance 1881 with Austria and Italy but ran into difficulties at home with the Roman Catholic church and the socialist movement and was forced to resign by Wilhelm II 18 March 1890.

Not by speech-making and the decisions of majorities will the questions of the day be settled...but by iron and blood

Prince Otto von Bismarck Sept 1862

Bizet /ˈbiːzeɪ/ Georges (Alexandre César Léopold) 1838–1875. French composer of operas, among them *Les Pêcheurs de perles/The Pearl Fishers* 1863, and *La jolie Fille de Perth/The Fair Maid of Perth* 1866. He also wrote the concert overture *Patrie* and incidental music to Daudet's *L'Arlésienne*. His operatic masterpiece *Carmen* was produced a few months before his death 1875.

Bjelke-Petersen /ˈbjelkə ˈpɪtəsən/ Joh(annes) 1911– . Australian right-wing politician, leader of the Queensland National Party (QNP) and premier of Queensland 1968–87.

Bjelke-Petersen was born in New Zealand. His Queensland state chauvinism and extremely conservative policies, such as lack of support for Aboriginal land rights or for conservation issues and attacks on the trade-union movement, made him a controversial figure outside as well as within Queensland, and he was accused more than once of electoral gerrymandering. In 1987 he broke the coalition of the QNP with the Australian Liberal Party to run for prime minister, but his action, by splitting the opposition, merely strengthened the hand of the Labor prime minister Bob Hawke. Amid reports of corruption in his government, Bjelke-Petersen was forced to resign the premiership 1987.

Björnson /ˈbjɜːnsɒn/ Björnstjerne 1832–1910. Norwegian novelist, playwright, poet, and journalist. His plays include *The Newly Married Couple* 1865 and *Beyond Human Power* 1883, dealing with politics and sexual morality. Among his novels is *In God's Way* 1889. Nobel Prize for Literature 1903.

Black /blæk/ Conrad (Moffat) 1940– . Canadian newspaper publisher. Between 1985 and 1990 he gained control of the right-wing *Daily Telegraph, Sunday Telegraph,* and *Spectator* weekly magazine in the UK, and he owns a number of Canadian newspapers.

Black /blæk/ Davidson 1884–1934. Canadian anatomist. In 1927, when professor of anatomy at the Union Medical College, Peking (Beijing), he unearthed the remains of Peking man, an example of one of our human ancestors.

Black /blæk/ Hugo LaFayette 1886–1971. US jurist. He was elected to the US Senate 1926 and despite his earlier association with the Ku Klux Klan, distinguished himself as a progressive populist. He was appointed to the US Supreme Court by F D Roosevelt 1937, resigning shortly before his death.

Born in Harlan, Alabama, USA, Black was admitted to the bar 1906. He served as judge and prosecuting attorney in Birmingham, Alabama before entering the Senate.

Among his decisions concerning personal and civil rights were those rendered in *Board of Education* v *Barnette* 1943, *Korematsu* v *US* 1944, and *Gideon* v *Wainwright* 1963.

Black /blæk/ James 1924– . British physiologist, director of therapeutic research at Wellcome Laboratories (near London) from 1978. He was active in the development of beta-blockers (which reduce the rate of heartbeat) and anti-ulcer drugs. He shared the Nobel Prize for Medicine 1988 with US scientists Gertrude Elion (1918–) and George Hitchings (1905–).

Black /blæk/ Joseph 1728–1799. Scottish physicist and chemist who in 1754 discovered carbon dioxide (which he called 'fixed air'). By his investigations in 1761 of latent heat and specific heat, he laid the foundation for the work of his pupil James Watt.

Born in Bordeaux, France, Black qualified as a doctor in Edinburgh. In chemistry, he prepared the way for the scientists Henry Cavendish, Joseph Priestley, and Antoine Lavoisier.

Blackett /blækɪt/ Patrick Maynard Stuart, Baron Blackett 1897–1974. British physicist. He was awarded a Nobel prize 1948 for work in cosmic radiation and his perfection of the Wilson cloud chamber.

A first-rate laboratory is one in which mediocre scientists can produce outstanding work.

Patrick Maynard Stuart Blackett

Black Hawk /ˌblæk ˈhɔːk/ or *Black Sparrow Hawk*; (Sauk name *Makataimeshekiakiak*). 1767–1838. North American Sauk Indian leader. A principal opponent of the cession of Indian lands to the US government, he sided with the British during the Anglo-American War 1812–14 and joined his people in their removal to Iowa at the end of the war. In 1832 he led a large contingent back to Illinois to resettle the Sauk homeland. Defeated by Illinois militia in the bloody 'Black Hawk War', he was captured and permanently exiled to Iowa.

Blacking John 1928–1990. British anthropologist and ethnomusicologist who researched the relationship between music and body movement, and the patterns of social and musical organization. Blacking was from 1970 chair of social anthropology at Queen's University, Belfast, where he established a centre for ethnomusicology. His most widely read book is *How Musical is Man?* 1973.

Blackmore /blækmɔː/ R(ichard) D(oddridge) 1825–1900. English novelist, author of *Lorna Doone* 1869, a romance set on Exmoor, SW England, in the late 17th century.

Black Prince nickname of →Edward, Prince of Wales, eldest son of Edward III of England.

Blackstone /blækstəʊn/ William 1723–1780. English jurist who published his *Commentaries on the Laws of England* 1765–70. A barrister from 1746, he became professor of law at Oxford 1758, and a justice of the Court of Common Pleas 1770.

Blackwell /blækwel/ Elizabeth 1821–1910. English-born US physician, the first woman to qualify in medicine in the USA 1849, and the first woman to be recognized as a qualified physician in the UK 1869.

Elizabeth Blackwell was taken to the USA as a child. She studied at Geneva Medical School in New York State and then opened a private clinic in New York City. On her return to the UK 1869, she became the first woman to appear in the Medical Register. She was professor of gynaecology at the London School of Medicine for Women 1875–1907.

Her example inspired Elizabeth Garrett →Anderson and many other aspiring female doctors.

Blaine /bleɪn/ James Gillespie 1830–1893. US politician and diplomat. Elected to the US House of Representatives 1862, he became Speaker 1868. Unsuccessful in the Republican presidential nominations 1876 and 1880, he served briefly as President Garfield's secretary of state. Gaining the Republican presidential nomination 1884, he was defeated by Grover Cleveland. During the Harrison administration 1889–93, Blaine again served as secretary of state.

Born in West Brownsville, Pennsylvania, Blaine moved to Maine 1854 and served in the state legislature 1858–62.

Blake /bleɪk/ George 1922– . British double agent who worked for MI6 and also for the USSR. Blake was unmasked by a Polish defector 1960 and imprisoned, but escaped to the Eastern bloc 1966. He is said to have betrayed at least 42 British agents to the Soviet side.

Blake /bleɪk/ Quentin 1932– . English book illustrator whose animated pen-and-ink drawings for children's books are instantly recognizable. His own picture books include *The Marzipan Pig* 1986; he has illustrated more than 200 books.

Blake /bleɪk/ Robert 1599–1657. British admiral of the Parliamentary forces during the English Civil War. Appointed 'general-at-sea' 1649, he destroyed Prince Rupert's privateering fleet off Cartagena, Spain, in the following year. In 1652 he won several engagements against the Dutch navy. In 1654 he bombarded Tunis, the stronghold of the Barbary corsairs, and in 1657 captured the Spanish treasure fleet in Santa Cruz.

He represented his native Bridgwater, Somerset, in the Short Parliament of 1640, and distinguished himself in defending Bristol 1643 and Taunton 1644–45 in the Civil War. In the naval war with the Netherlands (1652–54) he was eventually defeated by →Tromp off Dungeness, but had his revenge 1653 when he defeated the Dutch admiral off Portsmouth and the northern Foreland.

Blake /bleɪk/ William 1757–1827. English poet, artist, engraver, and visionary. His lyrics, as in *Songs of Innocence* 1789 and *Songs of Experience* 1794 express spiritual wisdom in radiant imagery and symbolism. Prophetic books like *The Mar-*

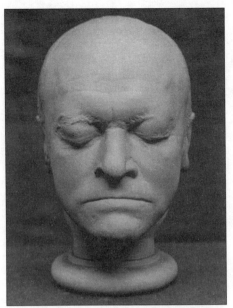

Blake *Plaster head of the English poet, artist, and mystic William Blake by James S Deville (1823). The author of mystical and metaphysical works and an illustrator of great visionary power, Blake was inspired throughout his life by a vivid faith in the unseen, and believed himself to be guided by visitations from the spiritual world.*

riage of Heaven and Hell 1790, *America* 1793, and *Milton* 1804 yield their meaning to careful study. He created a new composite art form in engraving and hand-colouring his own works.

Blake was born in Soho, London, and apprenticed to an engraver 1771–78. He illustrated the Bible, works by Dante and Shakespeare, and his own poems. His figures are heavily muscled, with elongated proportions. In his later years he attracted a group of followers, including Samuel Palmer, who called themselves the Ancients. Henry Fuseli was another admirer. Blake's poem *Jerusalem* 1820 was set to music by Charles Parry (1848–1918).

A Robin Red breast in a Cage
Puts all of Heaven in a Rage.

William Blake *Auguries of Innocence* 5

Blakey /ˈbleɪki/ Art. Muslim name Abdullah Ibn Buhaina 1919–1990. US jazz drummer and bandleader whose dynamic, innovative style made him one of the jazz greats. He contributed to the development of bebop in the 1940s and subsequently to hard bop, and formed the Jazz Messengers in the mid-1950s, continuing to lead the band for most of his life and discovering many talented musicians.

Blamey /ˈbleɪmi/ Thomas Albert 1884–1951. Australian field marshal. Born in New South Wales, he served at Gallipoli, Turkey, and on the Western Front in World War I. In World War II he was commander in chief, under MacArthur, of the Allied Land Forces in the SW Pacific 1942–45.

Blanc /blɒŋ/ Louis 1811–1882. French socialist and journalist. In 1839 he founded the *Revue du progrès*, in which he published his *Organisation du travail*, advocating the establishment of co-operative workshops and other socialist schemes. He was a member of the provisional government of 1848 and from its fall lived in the UK until 1871.

Blanchard /blɒnˈʃɑː/ Jean Pierre 1753–1809. French balloonist who made the first hot air balloon flight across the English Channel with John Jeffries 1785. He made the first balloon flight in the USA 1793.

Blanche of Castile /blɒnʃ kəˈstiːl/ 1188–1252. Queen of France, wife of →Louis VIII of France, and regent for her son Louis IX (St Louis of France) from the death of her husband 1226 until Louis IX's majority 1234, and again from 1247 while he was on a Crusade.

She quelled a series of revolts by the barons and in 1229 negotiated the Treaty of Paris, by which Toulouse came under control of the monarchy.

Blanco Serge 1958– . French rugby union player, renowned for his pace, skill, and ingenuity on the field. Blanco played a world-record 93 internationals before his retirement in 1991, scoring 38 tries of which 34 were from full back – another world record. He was instrumental in France's Grand Slam wins of 1981 and 1987.

Blanqui /blɒŋˈkiː/ Louis Auguste 1805–1881. French revolutionary politician. He formulated the theory of the 'dictatorship of the proletariat', used by Karl Marx, and spent a total of 33 years in prison for insurrection. Although in prison, he was elected president of the Commune of Paris 1871. His followers, the Blanquists, joined with the Marxists 1881.

He became a martyr figure for the French workers' movement.

Blashford-Snell /ˈblæʃfəd ˈsnel/ John 1936– . British explorer and soldier. His expeditions have included the first descent and exploration of the Blue Nile 1968; the journey N to S from Alaska to Cape Horn, crossing the Darien Gap between Panama and Colombia for the first time 1971–72; and the first complete navigation of the Zaïre River, Africa 1974–75.

From 1963 he organized adventure training at Sandhurst military academy. He was director of Operation Drake 1977–81 and Operation Raleigh 1978–82. His books include *A Taste for Adventure* 1978.

Blasis /blæ'si:/ Carlo 1797–1878. Italian ballet teacher of French extraction. He was successful as a dancer in Paris and in Milan, where he established a dancing school 1837. His celebrated treatise on the art of dancing, *Traité élémentaire, théoretique et pratique de l'art de la danse* 1820, forms the basis of Classical dance training.

Blavatsky /blə'vætski/ Helena Petrovna (born Hahn) 1831–1891. Russian spiritualist and mystic, cofounder of the Theosophical Society 1875, which has its headquarters near Madras, India. In Tibet she underwent spiritual training and later became a Buddhist. Her books include *Isis Unveiled* 1877 and *The Secret Doctrine* 1888. She was declared a fraud by the London Society for Psychical Research 1885.

Blériot /'bleriəʊ/ Louis 1872–1936. French aviator who, in a 24-horsepower monoplane of his own construction, made the first flight across the English Channel on 25 July 1909.

Blessington /'blesɪŋtən/ Marguerite, Countess of Blessington 1789–1849. Irish writer. A doyenne of literary society, she published *Conversations with Lord Byron* 1834, travel sketches, and novels.

Bligh /blaɪ/ William 1754–1817. English sailor who accompanied Capt James →Cook on his second voyage around the world 1772–74, and in 1787 commanded HMS *Bounty* on an expedition to the Pacific. On the return voyage the crew mutinied 1789, and Bligh was cast adrift in a boat with 18 men. He was appointed governor of New

Bligh English admiral William Bligh, who commanded HMS Bounty at the time of the mutiny on the ship, in a portrait dated 1794. An undoubtedly courageous and skilled navigator, Bligh does not seem to have been unduly tyrannical, but his abusive tongue and overbearing manner made him unpopular as a commander.

South Wales 1805, where his discipline again provoked a mutiny 1808 (the Rum Rebellion). He returned to Britain, and was made an admiral 1811.

Bligh went to Tahiti with the *Bounty* to collect breadfruit-tree specimens shortly before the mutiny, and gained the nickname 'Breadfruit Bligh'. In protest against harsh treatment, he and those of the crew who supported him were put in a small craft with no map and few provisions. They survived, after many weeks reaching Timor, near Java, having drifted 5,822 km/3,618 mi. Many of the crew members settled in the Pitcairn Islands.

Bliss /blɪs/ Arthur (Drummond) 1891–1975. English composer and conductor who became Master of the Queen's Musick 1953. Among his works are *A Colour Symphony* 1922, music for ballets *Checkmate* 1937, *Miracle in the Gorbals* 1944, and *Adam Zero* 1946; an opera *The Olympians* 1949; and dramatic film music, including *Things to Come* 1935. He conducted the first performance of Stravinsky's *Ragtime* for eleven instruments 1918.

Blitzstein /'blɪtssti:n/ Marc 1905–1964. US composer. Born in Philadelphia, he was a child prodigy as a pianist at the age of six. He served with the US Army 8th Air Force 1942–45, for which he wrote *The Airborne* 1946, a choral symphony. His operas include *The Cradle Will Rock* 1937.

Blixen /'blɪksən/ Karen, born Karen Dinesen 1885–1962. Danish writer. Her autobiography *Out of Africa* 1937 is based on her experience of running a coffee plantation in Kenya. She wrote fiction, mainly in English, under the pen name Isak Dinesen.

Bloch /blɒk/ Ernest 1880–1959. Swiss-born US composer. Among his works are the lyrical drama *Macbeth* 1910, *Schelomo* for cello and orchestra 1916, five string quartets, and *Suite Hébraique*, for viola and orchestra 1953. He often used themes based on Jewish liturgical music and folk song.

Bloch /blɒk/ Felix 1905–1983. Swiss-US physicist who invented the analytical technique of nuclear magnetic resonance (NMR) spectroscopy 1946. For this work he shared the Nobel Prize for Physics 1952 with US physicist Edward Purcell (1912–).

Bloch /blɒk/ Konrad 1912– . German-born US chemist whose research concerned cholesterol. Making use of the radioisotope carbon-14 (the radioactive form of carbon), Bloch was able to follow the complex steps by which the body chemically transforms acetic acid into cholesterol. For his work in this field Bloch shared the 1964 Nobel Prize for Medicine with Feodor Lynen (1911–1979).

Blok /blɒk/ Alexander Alexandrovich 1880– 1921. Russian poet who, as a follower of the French Symbolist movement, used words for their symbolic rather than actual meaning. He backed the 1917 Revolution, as in his poems *The Twelve* 1918, and *The Scythians* 1918, the latter appealing to the West to join in the revolution.

Blomberg /'blɒmbeək/ Werner von 1878–1946. German general and Nazi politician, minister of defence 1933–35, minister of war, and head of the *Wehrmacht* (army) 1935–38 under Hitler's chancellorship. He was discredited by his marriage to a prostitute and dismissed in Jan 1938, enabling Hitler to exercise more direct control over the armed forces. In spite of his removal from office, Blomberg was interrogated about war crimes by the Nuremberg tribunal. He died during the trial and was never in the dock.

Blomdahl /'blɒmdɑːl/ Karl-Birger 1916–1968. Swedish composer of ballets and symphonies in Expressionist style. His opera *Aniara* 1959 incorporates electronic music and is set in a spaceship.

Blondin /'blɒndɪn/ Charles. Assumed name of Jean François Gravelet 1824–1897. French tightrope walker who walked across a rope suspended above Niagara Falls, USA. He first crossed the falls 1859 at a height of 49 m/160 ft, and later repeated the feat blindfold and then pushing a wheelbarrow.

Blood /blʌd/ Thomas 1618–1680. Irish adventurer, known as Colonel Blood, who attempted to steal the crown jewels from the Tower of London, England, 1671.

Bloom /bluːm/ Claire 1931– . British film actress, who first made her reputation on the stage in Shakespearean roles. Her films include *Richard III* 1956 and *The Brothers Karamazov* 1958; television appearances include *Brideshead Revisited* 1980.

Bloomer /'bluːmə/ Amelia Jenks 1818–1894. US campaigner for women's rights. In 1849, when unwieldy crinolines were the fashion, she introduced a knee-length skirt combined with loose trousers gathered at the ankles, which became known as *bloomers* (also called 'rational dress'). She published the magazine *The Lily* 1849–54, which campaigned for women's rights and dress reform, and lectured with Susan B →Anthony in New York, USA.

Booth /buːθ/ Edwin Thomas 1833–1893. US actor. He was one of America's most acclaimed Shakespearean performers, famous for his portrayal of Hamlet. As lead actor, theatre manager, and producer, he successfully brought to the New York stage numerous Shakespearean tragedies. His career suffered in the wake of the public disgrace of his brother John Wilkes →Booth, who assassinated President Lincoln 1865.

Born near Bel Air, Maryland, USA, Booth was a member of a distinguished theatrical family. After the assassination scandal, Booth suffered a series of financial reverses and spent the rest of his life in performance tours of Europe, the British Isles, and the USA.

Blow /bləʊ/ John 1648–1708. British composer. He taught →Purcell, and wrote church music, for example the anthem 'I Was Glad when They Said unto Me' 1697. His masque *Venus and Adonis* 1685 is sometimes called the first English opera.

Bloy /blwɑː/ Léon-Marie 1846–1917. French author. He achieved a considerable reputation with his literary lampoons in the 1880s.

Blücher /'bluːkə/ Gebhard Leberecht von 1742–1819. Prussian general and field marshal, popularly known as 'Marshal Forward'. He took an active part in the patriotic movement, and in the War of German Liberation defeated the French as commander in chief at Leipzig 1813, crossed the Rhine to Paris 1814, and was made prince of Wahlstadt (Silesia).

In 1815 he was defeated by Napoleon at Ligny but came to the aid of British commander Wellington at Waterloo.

Blum /bluːm/ Léon 1872–1950. French politician. He was converted to socialism by the Dreyfus affair 1899 (see →Dreyfus) and in 1936 became the first socialist prime minister of France. He was again premier for a few weeks 1938. Imprisoned under the Vichy government 1942 as a danger to French security, he was released by the Allies 1945. He again became premier for a few weeks 1946.

A revolution is legality on holiday

Léon Blum

Blunden /'blʌndən/ Edmund 1896–1974. English poet. He served in World War I and published the prose work *Undertones of War* 1928. His poetry is mainly about rural life. Among his scholarly contributions was the discovery and publication of some poems by the 19th-century poet John →Clare.

Blunt /blʌnt/ Anthony 1907–1983. British art historian and double agent. As a Cambridge lecturer, he recruited for the Soviet secret service and, as a member of the British Secret Service 1940–45, passed information to the USSR. In 1951 he assisted the defection to the USSR of the British agents Guy →Burgess and Donald Maclean (1913–1983). He was the author of many respected works on French and Italian art. Unmasked 1964, he was given immunity after his confession.

He was director of the Courtauld Institute of Art 1947–74 and Surveyor of the Queen's Pictures 1945–1972. He was stripped of his knighthood 1979 when the affair became public.

Blunt /blʌnt/ Wilfrid Scawen 1840–1922. British poet. He married Lady Anne Noel, Byron's grand-daughter, and travelled with her in the Middle East, becoming a supporter of Arab nationalism. He also supported Irish Home Rule (he was imprisoned 1887–88), and wrote anti-imperialist books, poetry, and diaries.

Blyton One of Britain's most translated writers, children's author Enid Blyton published over 600 books, selling more than 200 million copies. She trained as a Froebel nursery teacher, then became a journalist, specializing in educational and children's publications, and began writing her popular children's stories in the 1930s.

Blyth /blaɪð/ 'Chay' (Charles) 1940– . British sailing adventurer who rowed across the Atlantic with Capt John Ridgeway 1966 and sailed solo around the world in a westerly direction during 1970–71. He sailed around the world with a crew in the opposite direction 1973–74, and in 1977 he made a record-breaking transatlantic crossing from Cape Verde to Antigua.

Blyton /'blaɪtn/ Enid 1897–1968. British writer of children's books. She created the character Noddy and the adventures of the 'Famous Five' and 'Secret Seven', but has been criticized by educationalists for social, racial, and sexual stereotyping.

She dealt with 17 different publishers, and on average wrote some 15 new books per year; she was able to complete a 50,000-word Famous Five adventure in a week.

Boadicea /ˌbəʊədɪ'siːə/ alternative spelling of British queen →Boudicca.

Boas /'bəʊæz/ Franz 1858–1942. German-born US anthropologist. Joining the faculty of Clark University 1888, Boas became one of America's first academic anthropologists; he stressed the need to study 'four fields' – ethnology, linguistics, physical anthropology, and archaeology – before generalizations might be made about any one culture or comparisons about any number of cultures.

He began his career in geography but switched to ethnology when he joined a German scientific expedition to the Arctic 1883. In 1886 he travelled to the Pacific Northwest to study the culture of the Kwakiutl Indian people, including their language. In 1896 he was appointed professor at Columbia University, where he trained the first generation of US anthropologists, such as Alfred Kroeber and Margaret Mead. From 1901 to 1905 he was also curator of the American Museum of Natural History in New York City. Boas spent much of his later career battling against unscientific theories of racial inequality.

Boateng /'bwaːteŋ/ Paul 1951– . British Labour politician and broadcaster. Elected member of Parliament for Brent South 1987, he was appointed to Labour's Treasury team in 1989, the first black appointee to a front-bench post. He has served on numerous committees on crime and race relations.

Boccaccio /bɒ'kaːtʃiəʊ/ Giovanni 1313–1375. Italian poet, chiefly known for the collection of tales called the *Decameron* 1348–53.

Son of a Florentine merchant, he lived in Naples 1328–41, where he fell in love with the unfaithful 'Fiammetta' who inspired his early poetry. Before returning to Florence 1341 he had written *Filostrato* and *Teseide* (used by Chaucer in his *Troilus and Criseyde* and *Knight's Tale*). He was much influenced by →Petrarch, whom he met 1350.

Boccherini /ˌbɒkə'riːni/ (Ridolfo) Luigi 1743–1805. Italian composer and cellist. He studied in Rome, made his mark in Paris 1768, and was court composer in Prussia and Spain. Boccherini composed some 350 instrumental works, an opera, and oratorios.

Boccioni /ˌbɒtʃi'əʊni/ Umberto 1882–1916. Italian painter and sculptor. One of the founders of the Futurist movement, he was a pioneer of abstract art.

Böcklin /'bɒklɪn/ Arnold 1827–1901. Swiss Romantic painter. His mainly imaginary landscapes have a dreamlike atmosphere: for example, *Island of the Dead* 1880 (Metropolitan Museum of Art, New York).

He was strongly attracted to Italy and lived for years in Rome. Many of his paintings are peopled with mythical beings, such as nymphs and naiads.

Bode /'bəʊdə/ Johann Elert 1747–1826. German astronomer, director of the Berlin observatory. He published the first atlas of all stars visible to the naked eye, *Uranographia* 1801, and devised Bode's Law.

Bodhidharma /ˌbəʊdɪ'dɜːmə/ 6th century AD. Indian Buddhist and teacher. He entered China from S India about 520, and was the founder of the Ch'an school (Zen is the Japanese derivation). Ch'an focuses on contemplation leading to intuitive meditation, a direct pointing to and stilling of the human mind. In the 20th century, the Japanese variation, Zen, has attracted many followers in the west.

Bodichon /ˈbəʊdɪʃɒn/ Barbara (born Leigh-Smith) 1827–1891. English feminist and campaigner for women's education and suffrage. She wrote *Women and Work* 1857, and was a founder of the magazine *The Englishwoman's Journal* 1858.

Born into a radical family that believed in female equality, she attended Bedford College, London. She was a founder of the college for women that became Girton College, Cambridge.

Bodin /bəʊˈdæn/ Jean 1530–1596. French political philosopher whose six-volume *De la République* 1576 is considered the first work on political economy.

An attorney in Paris, he published 1574 a tract explaining that prevalent high prices were due to the influx of precious metals from the New World. His theory of an ideal government emphasized obedience to a sovereign ruler.

Bodley /ˈbɒdli/ Thomas 1545–1613. English scholar and diplomat, after whom the Bodleian Library in Oxford is named. After retiring from Queen Elizabeth I's service 1597, he restored the university's library, which was opened as the Bodleian Library 1602.

The library had originally been founded in the 15th century by Humphrey, Duke of Gloucester (1391–1447).

Bodoni /bəˈdəʊni/ Giambattista 1740–1813. Italian printer who managed the printing press of the duke of Parma and produced high-quality editions of the classics. He designed several typefaces, including one bearing his name, which is in use today.

Boehme /ˈbɜːmə/ Jakob 1575–1624. German mystic, who had many followers in Germany, Holland, and England. He claimed divine revelation of the unity of everything and nothing, and found in God's eternal nature a principle to reconcile good and evil. He was the author of the treatise *Aurora* 1612.

Boethius /bəʊˈiːθɪəs/ Anicius Manilus Severinus AD 480–524. Roman philosopher. While imprisoned on suspicion of treason by the emperor →Theodoric the Great, he wrote treatises on music and mathematics and *De Consolatione Philosophiae/The Consolation of Philosophy*, a dialogue in prose. It was translated into European languages during the Middle Ages; English translations by Alfred the Great, Geoffrey Chaucer, and Queen Elizabeth I.

Bogarde /ˈbəʊɡɑːd/ Dirk. Stage name of Derek van den Bogaerde 1921– . English actor who appeared in comedies and adventure films such as *Doctor in the House* 1954 and *Campbell's Kingdom* 1957, before acquiring international recognition for complex roles in Joseph Losey's *The Servant* 1963 and *Accident* 1967, and Luchino Visconti's *Death in Venice* 1971.

He has also written autobiographical books and novels: *A Postillion Struck by Lightning* 1977,

Snakes and Ladders 1978, *Orderly Man* 1983, and *Backcloth* 1986.

Bogart /ˈbəʊɡɑːt/ Humphrey 1899–1957. US film actor who achieved fame as the gangster in *The Petrified Forest* 1936. He became an international cult figure as the tough, romantic 'loner' in such films as *The Maltese Falcon* 1941 and *Casablanca* 1943, a status resurrected in the 1960s and still celebrated today. He won an Academy Award for his role in *The African Queen* 1952.

He co-starred in *To Have and Have Not* 1944 and *The Big Sleep* 1946 with Lauren Bacall, who became his fourth wife.

Bogdanovich /bɒɡˈdænəvɪtʃ/ Peter 1939– . US film director, screenwriter, and producer, formerly a critic. *The Last Picture Show* 1971, a nostalgic look at a small Texas town in the 1950s, was followed by two films that attempted to capture the style of old Hollywood, *What's Up Doc?* 1972 and *Paper Moon* 1973.

Bohlen /ˈbəʊlən/ Charles 'Chip' 1904–1974. US diplomat. Educated at Harvard, he entered the foreign service 1929. Interpreter and adviser to presidents Roosevelt at Tehran and Yalta, and Truman at Potsdam, he served as ambassador to the USSR 1953–57.

Böhm /bɜːm/ Karl 1894–1981. Austrian conductor, known for his interpretation of Beethoven, and of the Mozart and Strauss operas.

Bohr /bɔː/ Aage 1922– . Danish physicist who produced a new model of the nucleus 1952, known as the collective model. For this work, he shared the 1975 Nobel Prize for Physics. He was the son of Niels Bohr.

Bohr /bɔː/ Niels Henrik David 1885–1962. Danish physicist. His theoretic work produced a new model of atomic structure, now called the Bohr model, and helped establish the validity of quantum theory.

After work with Ernest →Rutherford at Manchester, UK, he became professor at Copenhagen 1916, and founded there the Institute of Theoretical Physics of which he became director 1920. He was awarded the Nobel Prize for Physics 1922. Bohr fled from the Nazis in World War II and took part in work on the atomic bomb in the USA. In 1952, he helped to set up CERN, the European nuclear research organization in Geneva.

Boiardo /bɔɪˈɑːdəʊ/ Matteo Maria, Count 1434–1494. Italian poet, famed for his *Orlando innamorato/Roland in Love* 1486, a chivalrous epic glorifying military honour, patriotism, and religion. →Ariosto's *Orlando Furioso* 1516 was conceived as a sequel to this work.

Boileau /bwæˈləʊ/ Nicolas 1636–1711. French poet and critic. After a series of contemporary satires, his *Epîtres/Epistles* 1669–77 led to his joint appointment with Racine as royal historiographer 1677. Later works include *L'Art poétique/The Art of Poetry* 1674 and the mock-heroic *Le Lutrin/The Lectern* 1674–83.

Bolingbroke Portrait of English politician and political philosopher Henry St John Bolingbroke. A brilliant orator and writer, he was also a skilful if unscrupulous intriguer. His political writings concerning the role of the monarchy had profound influence on the development of political thought.

Bokassa /bʊˈkæsə/ Jean-Bédel 1921– . President of the Central African Republic 1966–79 and later self-proclaimed emperor 1977–79. Commander in chief from 1963, in Dec 1965 he led the military coup that gave him the presidency. On 4 Dec 1976 he proclaimed the Central African Empire and one year later crowned himself as emperor for life.

His regime was characterized by arbitrary state violence and cruelty. Overthrown in 1979, Bokassa was in exile until 1986. Upon his return he was sentenced to death, but this was commuted to life imprisonment 1988.

Bokassa, born at Bobangui, joined the French army 1939 and was awarded the Croix de Guerre for his service with the French colonial forces in Indochina. When the Central African Republic achieved independence 1960, he was invited to establish an army. After seizing power, he annulled the constitution and made himself president for life 1972, and marshal of the republic 1974. In 1976 he called in the former president Dacko, whom he had overthrown, as his adviser, and proclaimed the Central African Republic. In 1977 he made himself emperor for life. Backed by France, Dacko deposed him in a coup while Bokassa was visiting Libya.

Bol /bɒl/ Ferdinand 1610–1680. Dutch painter, a pupil and for many years an imitator of →Rembrandt. After the 1660s he developed a more independent style and prospered as a portraitist.

Boldrewood /ˈbəʊldəwʊd/ Rolf. Pen name of Thomas Alexander Browne 1826–1915. Australian writer. Born in London, he was taken to Australia as a child in 1830. He became a pioneer squatter, and a police magistrate in the goldfields. His books include *Robbery Under Arms* 1888.

Boleyn /bəˈlɪn/ Anne 1507–1536. Queen of England, the woman for whom Henry VIII broke with the pope and founded the Church of England. Second wife of Henry, she was married to him 1533 and gave birth to the future Queen Elizabeth I in the same year. Accused of adultery and incest with her half-brother (a charge invented by Thomas →Cromwell), she was beheaded.

Bolger /ˈbɒldʒə/ Jim (James) Brendan 1935– . New Zealand politician and prime minister from 1990. A successful sheep and cattle farmer, Bolger was elected to Parliament 1972. He held a variety of cabinet posts under Robert Muldoon's leadership 1977–84, and was an effective, if uncharismatic, leader of the opposition from March 1986, taking the National Party to electoral victory Oct 1990. His subsequent failure to honour election pledges, leading to cuts in welfare provision, led to a sharp fall in his popularity.

Bolingbroke /ˈbʊlɪŋbrʊk/ title of Henry of Bolingbroke, →Henry IV of England.

Bolingbroke /ˈbʊlɪŋbrʊk/ Henry St John, Viscount Bolingbroke 1678–1751. British Tory politician and political philosopher. He was foreign secretary 1710–14 and a Jacobite conspirator. His books, such as *Idea of a Patriot King* 1738 and *The Dissertation upon Parties* 1735, laid the foundations for 19th-century Toryism.

Secretary of war 1703–08, he became foreign secretary in Robert →Harley's ministry 1710, and in 1713 negotiated the Treaty of Utrecht. His plans to restore the 'Old Pretender' James Francis Edward Stuart were ruined by Queen Anne's death only five days after he had secured the dismissal of Harley 1714. He fled abroad, returning 1723, when he worked to overthrow Robert Walpole.

Bolívar /bɒˈliːvɑː/ Simón 1783–1830. South American nationalist, leader of revolutionary armies, known as *the Liberator*. He fought the Spanish colonial forces in several uprisings and eventually liberated his native Venezuela 1821, Colombia and Ecuador 1822, Peru 1824, and Bolivia (a new state named after him, formerly Upper Peru) 1825.

Born in Venezuela, he joined that country's revolution against Spain in 1810, and in the following year he declared Venezuela independent. His army was soon defeated by the Spanish, however, and he was forced to flee. Many battles and defeats followed, and it was not until 1819 that Bolívar won his first major victory, defeating the Spanish in Colombia and winning independence for that country. He went on to liberate Venezuela 1821 and (along with Antonio →Sucre) Ecuador 1822. These three countries were united into the republic of Gran Colombia with Bolívar as its president. In 1824 Bolívar helped bring about the defeat of Spanish forces in Peru, and the area known as Upper Peru was renamed 'Bolivia' in Bolívar's honour. Within the next few years, Venezuela and Ecuador seceded from the union, and in 1830 Bolívar resigned as president. He died the same year, despised by many for his dictatorial ways but since revered as South America's greatest liberator.

A people that loves freedom will in the end be free.

Simón Bolívar *Letter from Jamaica*

Bolkiah /ˈbolkiaː/ Hassanal 1946– . Sultan of Brunei from 1967, following the abdication of his father, Omar Ali Saifuddin (1916–1986). As absolute ruler, Bolkiah also assumed the posts of prime minister and defence minister on independence 1984.

As head of an oil- and gas-rich microstate, the sultan is reputedly the world's richest individual, with an estimated total wealth of $22 billion, which includes the Dorchester and Beverly Hills hotels in London and Los Angeles, and, at a cost of $40 million, the world's largest palace. He was educated at a British military academy.

Böll /bɜːl/ Heinrich 1917–1985. German novelist. A radical Catholic and anti-Nazi, he attacked Germany's political past and the materialism of its contemporary society. His many publications include poems, short stories, and novels which satirized West German society, for example *Billard um Halbzehn/Billiards at Half-Past Nine* 1959 and *Gruppenbild mit Dame/Group Portrait with Lady* 1971. Nobel Prize for Literature 1972.

Bolt /bəʊlt/ Robert (Oxton) 1924– . British dramatist, known for his historical plays, such as *A Man for All Seasons* 1960 (filmed 1967) about Thomas More, and for his screenplays, including *Lawrence of Arabia* 1962 and *Dr Zhivago* 1965.

Boltzmann /ˈbɒltsmæn/ Ludwig 1844–1906. Austrian physicist who studied the kinetic theory of gases, which explains the properties of gases by reference to the motion of their constituent atoms and molecules.

He derived a formula, the *Boltzmann distribution*, which gives the number of atoms or molecules with a given energy at a specific temperature. The constant in the formula is called the *Boltzmann constant*.

Bomberg /ˈbɒmbɜːɡ/ David 1890–1957. British painter who applied forms inspired by Cubism and Vorticism to traditional subjects in such early works as *The Mud Bath* 1914. Moving away from abstraction in the mid-1920s, his work became more representational and Expressionist.

Bomberg was apprenticed to a lithographer, then studied at the Slade School in London

1911–13 and was a founder member of the London Group. He began to gain recognition only towards the end of his life and is now seen as a major 20th-century painter.

Bonaparte /ˈbəʊnəpɑːt/ Corsican family of Italian origin that gave rise to the Napoleonic dynasty: see →Napoleon I, →Napoleon II, and →Napoleon III. Others were the brothers and sister of Napoleon I:

Joseph (1768–1844) whom Napoleon made king of Naples 1806 and Spain 1808;

Lucien (1775–1840) whose handling of the Council of Five Hundred on 10 Nov 1799 ensured Napoleon's future;

Louis (1778–1846) the father of Napoleon III, who was made king of Holland 1806–10;

Caroline (1782–1839) who married Joachim →Murat 1800;

Jerome (1784–1860) made king of Westphalia 1807.

Bonar Law British Conservative politician; see →Law, Andrew Bonar.

Bonaventura, St /ˌbɒnəvenˈtʊərə/ (John of Fidanza) 1221–1274. Italian Roman Catholic theologian. He entered the Franciscan order 1243, became professor of theology in Paris, and in 1256 general of his order. In 1273 he was created cardinal and bishop of Albano. Feast day 15 July.

Bond /bɒnd/ Alan 1938– . English-born Australian entrepreneur. He was chair of the Bond Corporation 1969–90 during the years when its aggressive takeover strategy gave the company interests in brewing, the media, mining, and retailing. In 1983 Bond led a syndicate that sponsored the winning yacht in the America's Cup race. The collapse of the Bond empire 1990 left thousands of investors impoverished and shook both Australian and international business confidence. Declared bankrupt April 1992 with debts of at least £110 million, Bond was jailed on criminal charges relating to the collapse of an Australian merchant bank.

By 1988 the Bond Corporation could boast assets of almost A$10 billion (£4 billion) and Bond himself, as Australia's fifth-richest man, had an estimated personal wealth of A$400 million. However, his compulsive takeover deals and excessive borrowing from banks eventually led to the corporation's bankruptcy, forcing his resignation Jan 1990 and leaving the company with debts of A$ 12 billion.

Bond /bɒnd/ Edward 1935– . English dramatist. His early work aroused controversy because of the savagery of some of his imagery, for example, the brutal stoning of a baby by bored youths in *Saved* 1965. Other works include *Early Morning* 1968, the last play to be banned in the UK by the Lord Chamberlain; *Lear* 1972, a reworking of Shakespeare's play; *Bingo* 1973, an account of Shakespeare's last days; and *The War Plays* 1985.

Bondfield /ˈbɒndfiːld/ Margaret Grace 1873–1953. British socialist who became a trade-union organizer to improve working conditions for women. She was a Labour member of Parliament 1923–24 and 1926–31, and was the first woman to enter the cabinet – as minister of labour 1929–31.

Bondi /ˈbɒndi/ Hermann 1919– . Viennese-born British cosmologist. In 1948 he joined with Fred →Hoyle and Thomas Gold (1920–) in developing the steady-state theory of cosmology, which suggested that matter is continuously created in the universe.

Bonham-Carter /ˈbɒnəm ˈkɑːtə/ Violet, Lady Asquith of Yarnbury 1887–1969. British peeress, president of the Liberal party 1945–47.

Bonheur /bɒˈnɜː/ Rosa (Marie Rosalie) 1822–1899. French animal painter. Her realistic animal portraits include *Horse Fair* 1853 (Metropolitan Museum of Art, New York).

She exhibited at the Paris Salon every year from 1841, and received international awards. In 1894 she became the first woman Officer of the Légion d'Honneur.

Bonhoeffer /ˈbɒnhɜːfə/ Dietrich 1906–1945. German Lutheran theologian and opponent of Nazism. Involved in a plot against Hitler, he was executed by the Nazis in Flossenburg concentration camp. His *Letters and Papers from Prison* 1953 became the textbook of modern radical theology, advocating the idea of a 'religionless' Christianity.

Boniface /ˈbɒnɪfeɪs/ name of nine popes, including:

Boniface VIII Benedict Caetani *c.* 1228–1303. Pope from 1294. He clashed unsuccessfully with Philip IV of France over his taxation of the clergy, and also with Henry III of England.

Boniface exempted the clergy from taxation by the secular government in a bull (edict) 1296, but was forced to give way when the clergy were excluded from certain lay privileges. His bull of 1302 Unam sanctam, asserting the complete temporal and spiritual power of the papacy, was equally ineffective.

Boniface, St /ˈbɒnɪfeɪs/ 680–754. English Benedictine monk, known as the 'Apostle of Germany'; originally named Wynfrith. After a missionary journey to Frisia 716, he was given the task of bringing Christianity to Germany 718 by Pope Gregory II, and was appointed archbishop of Mainz 746. He returned to Frisia 754 and was martyred near Dockum. His feast day is 5 June.

Bonington /ˈbɒnɪŋtən/ Chris(tian) 1934– . British mountaineer. He took part in the first ascent of Annapurna II 1960, Nuptse 1961, and the first British ascent of the north face of the Eiger 1962, climbed the central Tower of Paine in Patagonia 1963, and was the leader of an Everest expedition 1975 and again 1985, reaching the summit.

Bonington /ˈbɒnɪŋtən/ Richard Parkes 1801–1828. English painter of fresh, atmospheric seascapes and landscapes in oil and watercolour, mainly from an aerial perspective. He also painted historic genre works. He was much admired by Delacroix.

Initially taught watercolour painting by his father, Bonington entered the studio of Baron Gros in Paris 1821.

Bonnard /bɒˈnɑː/ Pierre 1867–1947. French Post-Impressionist painter. With other members of *les Nabis*, he explored the decorative arts (posters, stained glass, furniture). He painted domestic interiors and nudes.

Bonner /ˈbɒnə/ Yelena 1923– . Soviet human-rights campaigner. Disillusioned by the Soviet invasion of Czechoslovakia 1968, she resigned from the Communist Party after marrying her second husband, Andrei →Sakharov 1971, and became active in the dissident movement.

Bonney Charles 1813–1897. Australian politician and overlander, born in England. He is claimed to be Australia's first overlander, having taken 10,000 sheep south from the Murray River to the Goulburn River in 1837 and the next year helping to overland the first stock to Adelaide. He was later an administrator and member of the House of Assembly in South Australia.

Bonney William H; see →Billy the Kid.

Bonnie and Clyde /ˈbɒni, klaɪd/ Bonnie Parker (1911–1934) and Clyde Barrow (1900–1934). Infamous US criminals who carried out a series of small-scale robberies in Texas, Oklahoma, New Mexico, and Missouri between Aug 1932 and May 1934. They were eventually betrayed and then killed in a police ambush.

Much of their fame emanated from encounters with the police and their coverage by the press. Their story was filmed as *Bonnie and Clyde* 1967 by the US director Arthur Penn.

Bonnie Prince Charlie Scottish name for →Charles Edward Stuart, pretender to the throne.

Boole /buːl/ George 1815–1864. English mathematician whose work *The Mathematical Analysis of Logic* 1847 established the basis of modern mathematical logic, and whose *Boolean algebra* can be used in designing computers.

Boone /buːn/ Daniel 1734–1820. US pioneer who explored the Wilderness Road (East Virginia–Kentucky) 1775 and paved the way for the first westward migration of settlers.

Boorman /ˈbɔːmən/ John 1933– . English film director who, after working in television, directed successful films both in Hollywood (*Point Blank* 1967, *Deliverance* 1972) and in Britain (*Excalibur* 1981, *Hope and Glory* 1987).

He is the author of a telling book on film finance, *Money into Light* 1985.

Boot /buːt/ Jesse 1850–1931. British entrepreneur and founder of the Boots pharmacy chain. In 1863 Boot took over his father's small Nottingham shop trading in medicinal herbs. Recognizing that the future lay with patent medicines, he concentrated on selling cheaply, advertising widely, and offering a wide range of medicines. In 1892, Boot also began to manufacture drugs. He had 126 shops by 1900 and more than 1,000 by his death.

Booth /buːð/ Charles 1840–1916. English sociologist, author of the study *Life and Labour of the People in London* 1891–1903, and pioneer of an old-age pension scheme.

Booth /buːθ/ John Wilkes 1839–1865. US actor and fanatical Confederate sympathizer who assassinated President Abraham →Lincoln 14 April 1865; he escaped with a broken leg and was later shot in a barn in Virginia when he refused to surrender.

Booth /buːð/ William 1829–1912. British founder of the Salvation Army 1878, and its first 'general'.

Born in Nottingham, the son of a builder, he experienced religious conversion at the age of 15. In 1865 he founded the Christian Mission in Whitechapel, E London, which became the Salvation Army 1878. *In Darkest England, and the Way Out* 1890 contained proposals for the physical and spiritual redemption of the many down-and-outs. His wife Catherine (1829–1890, born Mumford), whom he married 1855, became a public preacher about 1860, initiating the ministry of women. Their eldest son, *William Bramwell Booth* (1856–1929), became chief of staff of the Salvation Army 1880 and was general from 1912 until his deposition 1929. *Evangeline Booth* (1865–1950), 7th child of General William Booth, was a prominent Salvation Army officer, and 1934–39 was general. She became a US citizen.

Catherine Bramwell Booth (1884–1987), a granddaughter of William Booth, was a commissioner in the Salvation Army.

Boothby /buːðbi/ Robert John Graham, Baron Boothby 1900–1986. Scottish politician. He became a Unionist member of Parliament 1924 and was parliamentary private secretary to Churchill 1926–29. He advocated Britain's entry into the European Community, and was a powerful speaker.

Boothe Claire; see →Luce, Claire Boothe.

Borah /bɔːrə/ William Edgar 1865–1940. US Republican politician. Born in Illinois, he was a senator for Idaho from 1906. An archisolationist, he was chiefly responsible for the USA's repudiation of the League of Nations following World War I.

Borchert Wolfgang 1921–1947. German playwright and prose writer. Borchert was sent home wounded during World War II while serving on the Russian front, where he had been sent for making anti-Nazi comments. *Draussen vor der Tür/The Outsider* 1947 is a surreal play about the chaotic conditions that a German soldier finds when he returns to Germany after walking home from the Russian front.

Border /bɔːdə/ Allan 1955– . Australian cricketer, captain of the Australian team from 1985. He has played in Australia New South Wales and Queensland, and in England for Gloucestershire and Essex. He holds the world record (1992) for appearances in test matches (125) and one-day internationals (223).

Bordet /bɒːdeɪ/ Jules 1870–1961. Belgian bacteriologist and immunologist who researched the role of blood serum in the human immune response. He was the first to isolate 1906 the whooping cough bacillus.

Borelli /bəˈreli/ Giovanni Alfonso 1608–1679. Italian scientist who explored the links between physics and medicine and showed how mechanical principles could be applied to animal physiology. This approach, known as iatrophysics, has proved basic to understanding how the mammalian body works.

Borg /bɒːg/ Björn 1956– . Swedish tennis player who won the men's singles title at Wimbledon five times 1976–80, a record since the abolition of the challenge system 1922. He also won six French Open singles titles 1974–75 and 1978–81 inclusive. In 1990 Borg announced plans to return to professional tennis, but he enjoyed little competitive success 1991–92.

Borges /bɔːxes/ Jorge Luis 1899–1986. Argentine poet and short-story writer, an exponent of magic realism. In 1961 he became director of the National Library, Buenos Aires, and was professor of English literature at the university there. He is known for his fantastic and paradoxical work *Ficciones/Fictions* 1944.

Borges explored metaphysical themes in early works such as *Ficciones* and *El Aleph/The Aleph, and other Stories* 1949. In a later collection of tales *El informe de Brodie/Dr Brodie's Report* 1972, he adopted a more realistic style, reminiscent of the work of the young Rudyard →Kipling, of whom he was a great admirer. *El libro de arena/The Book of Sand* 1975 marked a return to more fantastic themes.

Borgia /bɔːdʒə/ Cesare 1476–1507. Italian general, illegitimate son of Pope →Alexander VI. Made a cardinal at 17 by his father, he resigned to become captain-general of the papacy, campaigning successfully against the city republics of Italy. Ruthless and treacherous in war, he was an able ruler (the model for Machiavelli's *The Prince*), but his power crumbled on the death of his father. He was a patron of artists, including Leonardo da Vinci.

Borgia /ˈbɔːdʒə/ Lucrezia 1480–1519. Duchess of Ferrara from 1501. She was the illegitimate daughter of Pope →Alexander VI and sister of Cesare Borgia. She was married at 12 and again at 13 to further her father's ambitions, both marriages being annulled by him. At 18 she was married again, but her husband was murdered in 1500 on the order of her brother, with whom (as well as with her father) she was said to have committed incest. Her final marriage was to the duke of Este, the son and heir of the duke of Ferrara. She made the court a centre of culture and was a patron of authors and artists such as Ariosto and Titian.

Borglum /ˈbɔːɡləm/ Gutzon 1871–1941. US sculptor. He created a six-ton marble head of Lincoln in Washington, DC, and the series of giant heads of presidents Washington, Jefferson, Lincoln, and Theodore Roosevelt carved on Mount Rushmore, South Dakota (begun 1930).

Boris III /ˈbɒrɪs/ 1894–1943. Tsar of Bulgaria from 1918, when he succeeded his father, Ferdinand I. From 1934 he was virtual dictator until his sudden and mysterious death following a visit to Hitler. His son Simeon II was tsar until deposed 1946.

Boris Godunov /ˈbɒrɪs/ 1552–1605. See Boris →Godunov, tsar of Russia from 1598.

Borlaug /ˈbɔːlɔːɡ/ Norman Ernest 1914– . US microbiologist and agronomist. He developed high-yielding varieties of wheat and other grain crops to be grown in Third World countries, and was the first to use the term 'Green Revolution'. Nobel Prize for Peace 1970.

Bormann /ˈbɔːmæn/ Martin 1900–1945. German Nazi leader. He took part in the abortive Munich putsch (uprising) 1923 and rose to high positions in the Nazi (National Socialist) Party, becoming party chancellor May 1941.

Bormann was believed to have escaped the fall of Berlin May 1945 and was tried in his absence and sentenced to death at the Nuremberg trials 1945–46, but a skeleton uncovered by a mechanical excavator in Berlin 1972 was officially recognized as his by forensic experts 1973.

Born /bɔːn/ Max 1882–1970. German physicist who received a Nobel prize 1954 for fundamental work on the quantum theory. He left Germany for the UK during the Nazi era.

Borodin /ˈbɒrədɪn/ Alexander Porfir'yevich 1833–1887. Russian composer. Born in St Petersburg, the illegitimate son of a Russian prince, he became by profession an expert in medical chemistry, but in his spare time devoted himself to music. His principal work is the opera *Prince Igor*, left unfinished; it was completed by Rimsky-Korsakov and Glazunov and includes the Polovtsian Dances.

Borromeo, St /ˌbɒrəˈmeɪəʊ/ Carlo 1538–1584. Italian Roman Catholic saint and cardinal. He was instrumental in bringing the Council of Trent (1562–3) to a successful conclusion, and in drawing up the catechism that contained its findings. Feast day 4 Nov.

Born at Arona of a noble Italian family, Borromeo was created a cardinal and archbishop of Milan by his uncle Pope Pius IV 1560. He lived the life of an ascetic, and 1578 founded the community later called the Oblate Fathers of St Charles. He was canonized 1610.

Borromini /ˌbɒrəʊˈmiːni/ Francesco 1599–1667. Italian Baroque architect, one of the two most important (with →Bernini, his main rival) in 17th-century Rome. Whereas Bernini designed in a florid, expansive style, his pupil Borromini developed a highly idiosyncratic and austere use of the Classical language of architecture. His genius may be seen in the cathedrals of San Carlo 1641 and San Ivo 1660, and the oratorio of St Filippo Neri 1650.

Borrow /ˈbɒrəʊ/ George Henry 1803–1881. British author and traveller who travelled on foot through Europe and the East. His books, incorporating his knowledge of languages and Romany lore, include *Zincali* 1840, *The Bible in Spain* 1843, *Lavengro* 1851, *The Romany Rye* 1857, and *Wild Wales* 1862.

Boscawen /bɒsˈkəʊən/ Edward 1711–1761. English admiral who served against the French in the mid-18th-century wars, including the War of Austrian Succession and the Seven Years' War. He led expeditions to the East Indies 1748–50 and served as lord of the Admiralty from 1751, vice admiral from 1755, and admiral from 1758. To his men he was known as 'Old Dreadnought'.

Bosch /bɒʃ/ Carl 1874–1940. German metallurgist and chemist. He developed Fritz Haber's small-scale technique for the production of ammonia into an industrial high-pressure process that made use of water gas as a source of hydrogen. He shared the Nobel Prize for Chemistry 1931 with Friedrich Bergius.

Bosch /bɒʃ/ Hieronymus (Jerome) 1460–1516. Early Netherlandish painter. His fantastic visions of weird and hellish creatures, as shown in *The Garden of Earthly Delights* about 1505–10 (Prado, Madrid), show astonishing imagination and a complex imagery. His religious subjects focused not on the holy figures but on the mass of ordinary witnesses, placing the religious event in a contemporary Netherlandish context and creating cruel caricatures of human sinfulness.

Bosch is named after his birthplace, 'sHertogenbosch, in North Brabant, the Netherlands. His work foreshadowed Surrealism and was probably inspired by a local religious brotherhood. However, he was an orthodox Catholic and a prosperous painter, not a heretic, as was once believed. After his death, his work was collected by Philip II of Spain.

Bosch /bɒʃ/ Juan 1909– . President of the Dominican Republic 1963. His left-wing Partido Revolucionario Dominicano won a landslide victory in the 1962 elections. In office, he attempted agrarian reform and labour legislation. He was opposed by the USA, and overthrown by the army. His achievement was to establish a democratic political party after three decades of dictatorship.

Boscovich /bɒskəvɪtʃ/ Ruggiero 1711–1787. Italian scientist. An early supporter of Newton, he developed a theory, popular in the 19th century, of the atom as a single point with surrounding fields of repulsive and attractive forces.

Bose /bəʊs/ Jagadis Chunder 1858–1937. Indian physicist and plant physiologist. Born near Dakha, he was professor of physical science at Calcutta 1885–1915, and studied the growth and minute movements of plants, and their reaction to electrical stimuli. He founded the Bose Research Institute, Calcutta.

Bose /bəʊs/ Satyendra Nath 1894–1974. Indian physicist who formulated the Bose–Einstein law of quantum mechanics with →Einstein. He was professor of physics at the University of Calcutta 1945–58.

Bossuet /bɒsjuˈeɪ/ Jacques Bénigne 1627–1704. French Roman Catholic priest and theologian. Appointed to the Chapel Royal, Paris 1662, he became known for his funeral orations.

Bossuet was tutor to the young dauphin (crown prince). He became involved in a controversy between Louis XIV and the pope and did his best to effect a compromise. He wrote an *Exposition de la foi catholique* 1670 and *Histoire des variations des églises protestantes* 1688.

Life will not bear to be calmly considered. It appears insipid and ridiculous as a country dance.

James Boswell

Boswell /bɒzwəl/ James 1740–1795. Scottish biographer and diarist. He was a member of Samuel →Johnson's London Literary Club and the two men travelled to Scotland together 1773, as recorded in Boswell's *Journal of the Tour to the Hebrides* 1785. His classic English biography *Life of Samuel Johnson* was published 1791.

Born in Edinburgh, Boswell studied law but centred his ambitions on literature and politics. He first met Johnson 1763, before setting out on a European tour during which he met the French thinkers Rousseau and Voltaire, and the Corsican nationalist general Paoli (1726–1807), whom he commemorated in his popular *Account of Corsica* 1768. In 1766 he became a lawyer, and in 1772 renewed his acquaintance with Johnson in London. Boswell's long-lost personal papers were acquired for publication by Yale University 1949, and the *Journals* are of exceptional interest.

On his succession to his father's estate 1782, he made further attempts to enter Parliament, was called to the English Bar 1786, and was recorder of Carlisle 1788–90. In 1789 he settled in London, and in 1791 produced the classic English biography, the *Life of Samuel Johnson*.

Botero /bɒˈteərəʊ/ Fernando 1932– . Colombian painter. He studied in Spain and gained an international reputation for his paintings of fat, vulgar figures, often of women, parodies of conventional sensuality.

Botha /ˈbəʊtə/ Louis 1862–1919. South African soldier and politician, a commander in the Second South African War (Boer War). In 1907 Botha became premier of the Transvaal and in 1910 of the first Union South African government. On the outbreak of World War I 1914 he rallied South Africa to the Commonwealth, suppressed a Boer revolt, and conquered German South West Africa.

Botha was born in Natal. Elected a member of the Volksraad 1897, he supported the more moderate Joubert against Kruger. On the outbreak of the Second South African War he commanded the Boers besieging Ladysmith, and in 1900 succeeded Joubert in command of the Transvaal forces. When the Union of South Africa was formed 1910, Botha became prime minister, and at the Versailles peace conference 1919 he represented South Africa.

Botha /ˈbəʊtə/ P(ieter) W(illem) 1916– . South African politician, prime minister from 1978. Botha initiated a modification of apartheid, which later slowed in the face of Afrikaner (Boer) opposition. In 1984 he became the first executive state president. In 1989 he unwillingly resigned both party leadership and presidency after suffering a stroke, and was succeeded by F W de Klerk.

Botham /ˈbəʊθəm/ Ian (Terrence) 1955– . English cricketer whose Test record places him among the world's greatest all-rounders. He has played county cricket for Somerset, Worcestershire, and Durham, as well as playing in Australia. He played for England 1977–89 and returned to the England side 1991.

Botham made his Somerset debut 1974 and first played for England against Australia at Trent Bridge 1977; he took five wickets for 74 runs in Australia's first innings. In 1987 he moved from Somerset to Worcestershire and helped them to win the Refuge Assurance League in his first season.

Botham also played Football League soccer for Scunthorpe United 1979–84. He raised money for leukaemia research with much-publicized walks from John o'Groats to Land's End in the UK, and Hannibal-style across the Alps.

Bothe /ˈbəʊtə/ Walther 1891–1957. German physicist who showed 1929 that the cosmic rays bombarding the Earth are composed not of photons but of more massive particles. Nobel Prize for Physics 1954.

Bottomley British Conservative politician and health secretary Virginia Bottomley, one of two women MPs included in the cabinet formed by Prime Minister John Major April 1992. Bottomley served as minister of state for education and science 1985–86, minister of overseas development 1986–87, and secretary of state for foreign affairs 1987–88.

Bothwell /ˈbɒθwəl/ James Hepburn, 4th Earl of Bothwell *c.* 1536–1578. Scottish nobleman, third husband of →Mary Queen of Scots, 1567–70, alleged to have arranged the explosion that killed Darnley, her previous husband, 1567.

Tried and acquitted a few weeks after the assassination, he abducted Mary, and (having divorced his wife) married her 15 May. A revolt ensued, and Bothwell was forced to flee to Norway and on to Sweden. In 1570 Mary obtained a divorce on the ground that she had been ravished by Bothwell before marriage. Later, Bothwell was confined in a castle in Zeeland, the Netherlands, where he died insane.

Botta Mario 1943– . Swiss architect. Most of his work is in Ticino – the Italian canton of Switzerland. He is a key figure of the Ticinese school. His work shows a strong regionalist interpretation of modernism, close attention to topography, and a very formal geometry. These aspects are expressed in a striking series of single family houses including Riva San Vitale 1972–73 and Ligometto 1975–76.

Other works include a school at Morbio Inferiore 1972–77 and the Staatsbank, Fribour 1977–82.

Botticelli /ˌbɒtɪˈtʃeli/ Sandro 1445–1510. Florentine painter of religious and mythological subjects.

He was patronized by the ruling →Medici family, for whom he painted *Primavera* 1478 and *The Birth of Venus* about 1482–84 (both in the Uffizi, Florence). From the 1490s he was influenced by the religious fanatic →Savonarola and developed a harshly expressive and emotional style.

His real name was Filipepi, but his elder brother's nickname Botticelli 'little barrel' was passed on to him. His work for the Medicis was designed to cater to the educated classical tastes of the day. As well as his sentimental, beautiful young Madonnas, he produced a series of inventive compositions, including *tondi*, circular paintings. He broke with the Medicis after their execution of Savonarola.

Bottomley Virginia 1948– . British Conservative politician, health secretary from April 1992, member of Parliament for Surrey Southwest from 1984.

Before entering Parliament she was a magistrate and psychiatric social worker. As an MP she became parliamentary private secretary to Chris Patten, then to Geoffrey Howe, and was made a junior environment minister 1988. Her husband, Peter Bottomley (1943–) is Conservative MP for Eltham.

Boucher /buːˈʃeɪ/ François 1703–1770. French Rococo painter, court painter from 1765. He was much patronized for his light-hearted, decorative scenes: for example *Diana Bathing* 1742 (Louvre, Paris).

He also painted portraits and decorative chinoiserie for Parisian palaces. He became director of the Gobelins tapestry works, Paris, 1755.

Boucher de Crèvecoeur de Perthes /buːˈʃeɪ də krevˈkɜː də ˈpeət/ Jacques 1788–1868. French geologist whose discovery of Palaeolithic hand-axes 1837 challenged the acccepted view of human history dating only from 4004 BC, as proclaimed by the calculations of Bishop James Usher.

I am not fighting for my kingdom and wealth now. I am fighting as an ordinary person for my lost freedom, my bruised body, and my outraged daughters.

Boudicca address to her army before the Icenian revolt, AD 61, quoted by Tacitus

---

Boudicca /ˈbuːdɪkə/ Queen of the Iceni (native Britons), often referred to by the Latin form *Boadicea*. Her husband, King Prasutagus, had been a tributary of the Romans, but on his death AD 60 the territory of the Iceni was violently annexed. Boudicca was scourged and her daughters raped. Boudicca raised the whole of SE England in revolt, and before the main Roman armies could return from campaigning in Wales she burned Londinium (London), Verulamium (St Albans), and Camolodunum (Colchester). Later the Romans under governor Suetonius Paulinus defeated the British between London and Chester; they were virtually annihilated and Boudicca poisoned herself.

Boudin /buːˈdæŋ/ Eugène 1824–1898. French artist, a forerunner of the Impressionists, known for his fresh seaside scenes painted in the open air.

Bougainville /buːgənvɪl/ Louis Antoine de 1729–1811. French navigator. After service with the French in Canada during the Seven Years' War, he made the first French circumnavigation of the world 1766–69 and the first systematic observations of longitude.

Several Pacific islands are named after him, as is the climbing plant *bougainvillea*.

Bouguereau /ˌbuːgərəʊ/ Adolphe William 1825–1905. French academic painter of historical and mythological subjects. He was respected in his day but his style is now thought to be insipid.

Boulanger /ˌbuːlɒnˈʒeɪ/ George Ernest Jean Marie 1837–1891. French general. He became minister of war 1886, and his anti-German speeches nearly provoked war with Germany 1887. In 1889 he was suspected of aspiring to dictatorship by a coup d'état. Accused of treason, he fled into exile and committed suicide on the grave of his mistress.

Boulanger /ˌbuːlɒnˈʒeɪ/ Lili (Juliette Marie Olga) 1893–1918. French composer, the younger sister of Nadia Boulanger. At the age of 19, she won the Prix de Rome with the cantata *Faust et Hélène* for voices and orchestra.

Boulanger /ˌbuːlɒnˈʒeɪ/ Nadia (Juliette) 1887–1979. French music teacher and conductor. A pupil of Fauré, and admirer of Stravinsky, she included among her composition pupils at the American Conservatory in Fontainebleau (from 1921) Aaron Copland, Roy Harris, Walter Piston, and Philip Glass.

Boulestin /ˌbuːleˈstæŋ/ Marcel 1878–1943. French cookery writer and restaurateur. He spread the principles of simple but high-quality French cooking in Britain in the first half of the 20th century, with a succession of popular books such as *What Shall We Have Today?* 1931.

Boulez /ˈbuːlez/ Pierre 1925– . French composer and conductor. He studied with ➔Messiaen and promoted contemporary music with a series of innovative *Domaine Musical* concerts and recordings in the 1950s, as conductor of the BBC Symphony and New York Philharmonic orchestras during the 1970s, and as founder and director of IRCAM, a music research studio in Paris opened 1977.

His music, strictly serial and expressionistic in style, includes the cantatas *Le Visage nuptial*

1946–52 and *Le Marteau sans maître* 1955, both to texts by René Char; *Pli selon pli* 1962 for soprano and orchestra; and *Répons* 1981 for soloists, orchestra, tapes, and computer-generated sounds.

Boullée /buːleɪ/ Etienne-Louis 1729–1799. French Neo-Classical architect who, with Claude ➔Ledoux, influenced late 20th-century Rationalists such as the Italian Aldo Rossi. Boullée's abstract, geometric style is exemplified in his design for a spherical monument to the scientist Isaac Newton, 150 m/500 ft high. He built very little.

Boult /bəʊlt/ Adrian (Cedric) 1889–1983. British conductor of the BBC Symphony Orchestra 1930–50 and the London Philharmonic 1950–57. He promoted the work of Holst and Vaughan Williams, and was a celebrated interpreter of Elgar.

Boulting /ˈbəʊltɪŋ/ John 1913–1985 and Roy 1913– . British director–producer team that was successful in the years following World War II. Their films include *Brighton Rock* 1947, *Lucky Jim* 1957, and *I'm All Right Jack* 1959. They were twins.

Boulton /ˈbəʊltən/ Matthew 1728–1809. British factory owner who helped to finance James ➔Watt's development of the steam engine.

Boulton had an engineering works near Birmingham. He went into partnership with Watt 1775 to develop engines to power factory machines that had previously been driven by water.

Boumédienne /ˌbuːmeɪdˈjen/ Houari. Adopted name of Mohammed Boukharouba 1925–1978. Algerian politician who brought the nationalist leader Ben Bella to power by a revolt 1962, and superseded him as president in 1965 by a further coup.

Bourbon /ˈbʊəbən/ Charles, Duke of 1490–1527. Constable of France, honoured for his courage at the Battle of Marignano 1515. Later he served the Holy Roman Emperor Charles V, and helped to drive the French from Italy. In 1526 he was made duke of Milan, and in 1527 allowed his troops to sack Rome. He was killed by a shot the artist Cellini claimed to have fired.

Bourbon dynasty /ˈbʊəbən/ French royal house (succeeding that of ➔Valois) beginning with Henry IV, and ending with Louis XVI, with a brief revival under Louis XVIII, Charles X, and Louis Philippe. The Bourbons also ruled Spain almost uninterruptedly from Philip V to Alfonso XIII and were restored in 1975 (➔Juan Carlos); at one point they also ruled Naples and several Italian duchies. The Grand Duke of Luxembourg is also a Bourbon by male descent.

Bourdon /bʊəˈdɒŋ/ Eugène 1808–1884. French engineer and instrument maker who invented the pressure gauge that bears his name.

Bourgeois /ˈbʊəˈʒwɑː/ Léon Victor Auguste 1851–1925. French politician. Entering politics as a Radical, he was prime minister in 1895, and later served in many cabinets. He was one of the pioneer advocates of the League of Nations. He was awarded the Nobel Peace Prize 1920.

Bourguiba /bʊəˈɡiːbə/ Habib ben Ali 1903– . Tunisian politician, first president of Tunisia 1957–87. Educated at the University of Paris, he became a journalist and was frequently imprisoned by the French for his nationalist aims as leader of the Néo-Destour party. He became prime minister 1956, president (for life from 1974) and prime minister of the Tunisian republic 1957; he was overthrown in a bloodless coup 1987.

Bourke-White /bɜːk ˈwaɪt/ Margaret 1906–1971. US photographer. As an editor of *Fortune* magazine 1929–33, she travelled extensively in the USSR, publishing several collections of photographs. Later, with husband Erskine Caldwell, she also published photo collections of American and European subjects. She began working for *Life* magazine 1936, and covered combat in World War II and documented India's struggle for independence.

Bournonville /ˌbʊənɒŋˈviːl/ August 1805–1879. Danish dancer and choreographer. He worked with the Royal Danish Ballet for most of his life, giving Danish ballet a worldwide importance. His ballets, many of which have been revived in the last 50 years, include *La Sylphide* 1836 (music by Lövenskjöld) and *Napoli* 1842.

Bowen Irish novelist and short story writer Elizabeth Bowen, noted for her gift for delicate characterization and acute observation. Her first novel, The Hotel 1927, was the first of a string of gentle explorations of personal relationships. The Heat of the Day 1949, perhaps her most successful novel, embodies her experiences of wartime London.

Bouts /baʊts/ Dierick *c.* 1420–1475. Early Netherlandish painter. Born in Haarlem, he settled in Louvain, painting portraits and religious scenes influenced by Rogier van der Weyden. *The Last Supper* 1464–68 (St Pierre, Louvain) is one of his finest works.

Bovet /bəʊˈveɪ/ Daniel 1907–1992. Swiss physiologist. He pioneered research into antihistamine drugs used in the treatment of nettle rash and hay fever, and was awarded a Nobel Prize for Medicine 1957 for his production of a synthetic form of curare, used as a muscle relaxant in anaesthesia.

Bow /bəʊ/ Clara 1905–1965. US film actress known as a Jazz Baby and the 'It Girl' after her portrayal of a glamorous flapper in the silent film *It* 1927.

Bowditch /ˈbaʊdɪtʃ/ Nathaniel 1773–1838. US astronomer. He wrote *The New American Practical Navigator* 1802, having discovered many inaccuracies in the standard navigation guide of the day. His *Celestial Mechanics* 1829–39, was a translation of the first four volumes of French astronomer Pierre Laplace's *Traité de mécanique céleste* 1799–1825.

Born in Salem, Massachusetts, USA, Bowditch had little formal education but read widely as a merchant seaman during the years 1795–1803. In 1829 he became president of the American Academy of Arts and Sciences.

Bowdoin /ˈbʊdn/ James 1726–1790. American public official. A supporter of American independence, he was elected to the Massachusetts General Court 1753, chosen as a member of the Governor's Council 1757, and served on the Massachusetts Executive Council 1775–76. He was president of the state constitutional convention 1779–80 and governor 1785–87.

Born in Boston, Bowdoin was educated at Harvard University. He was the first president of the American Academy of Arts and Sciences.

Bowdoin College in Brunswick, Maine, is named in his honour.

Bowdler /ˈbaʊdlə/ Thomas 1754–1825. British editor whose prudishly expurgated versions of Shakespeare and other authors gave rise to the verb *bowdlerize*.

Bowen /ˈbəʊɪn/ Elizabeth 1899–1973. Irish novelist. She published her first volume of short stories, *Encounters* in 1923. Her novels include *The Death of the Heart* 1938, *The Heat of the Day* 1949, and *The Little Girls* 1964.

No, it is not only our fate but our business to lose innocence, and once we have lost that, it is futile to attempt a picnic in Eden.

Elizabeth Bowen 'Out of a Book'

Bowie /ˈbəʊi/ David. Stage name of David Jones 1947– . English pop singer, songwriter, and actor. He became a rock star with the release of the album *The Rise and Fall of Ziggy Stardust and the Spiders from Mars* 1972, and collaborated in the mid-1970s with the electronic virtuoso Brian Eno (1948–) and Iggy Pop. He has also acted in plays and films, including Nicolas Roeg's *The Man Who Fell to Earth* 1976.

Among his albums are *Aladdin Sane* 1973, *Station to Station* 1976, *Low*, *Heroes* both 1977, *Lodger* 1979, and *Let's Dance* 1983. In 1989 he formed and recorded with Tin Machine.

Bowie /ˈbəʊi/ James 'Jim' 1796–1836. US frontiersman and folk hero. A colonel in the Texan forces during the Mexican War, he is said to have invented the single-edge, guarded hunting and throwing knife known as a *Bowie knife*. He was killed in the battle of the Alamo.

Bowlby /ˈbəʊlbi/ John 1907–1990. English psychologist, honorary consultant to the Tavistock Clinic, London, and consultant in mental health for the World Health Organization 1972–90. In his book *Child Care and the Growth of Love*, published 1953, he argued that a home environment for children is preferable to an institution, and stressed the bond between mother and child.

Bowles /bəʊlz/ Paul 1910– . US novelist and composer. Born in New York City, he studied with Aaron Copland and Virgil Thomson, writing scores for ballets, films, and an opera, *The Wind Remains* 1943, as well as incidental music for plays. He settled in Morocco, the setting of his novels *The Sheltering Sky* 1949 and *Let It Come Down* 1952. His autobiography, *Without Stopping*, was published in 1972.

Boycott /ˈbɔɪkɒt/ Charles Cunningham 1832–1897. English land agent in County Mayo, Ireland, who strongly opposed the demands for agrarian reform by the Irish Land League 1879–81, with the result that the peasants refused to work for him; hence the word *boycott*.

Boycott /ˈbɔɪkɒt/ Geoffrey 1940– . English cricketer born in Yorkshire, England's most prolific run-maker with 8,114 runs in test cricket until overtaken by David Gower in 1992. He was banned as a test player in 1982 for taking part in matches against South Africa.

He played in 108 test matches and in 1981 overtook Gary Sobers' world record total of test runs. Twice, in 1971 and 1979, his average was over 100 runs in an English season. He was released by Yorkshire after a dispute in 1986.

Boyd-Orr /bɔɪd ˈɔː/ John 1880–1971. British nutritionist and health campaigner. He was awarded the Nobel Prize for Peace in 1949 in recognition of his work towards alleviating world hunger.

Boyer /ˈbwɑːjeɪ/ Charles 1899–1978. French film actor who made his name in Hollywood in the

Boyle Irish physicist and chemist Robert Boyle. He enunciated the law of the compressibility of gases 1662 (Boyle's law) and described the element and the make-up of all matter. His work led to the acceptance of chemistry as a separate branch of science.

1930s as the 'great lover' in such films as *The Garden of Allah* 1936 and *Maria Walewska* 1937.

Boyle /bɔɪl/ Charles, 4th Earl of Orrery 1676–1731. Irish soldier and diplomat. The *orrery*, a mechanical model of the solar system in which the planets move at the correct relative velocities, is named after him.

Boyle /bɔɪl/ Robert 1627–1691. Irish physicist and chemist who published the seminal *The Sceptical Chymist* 1661. He formulated *Boyle's law* 1662.

He was the first chemist to collect a sample of gas, was one of the founders of the Royal Society, and endowed the Boyle Lectures for the defence of Christianity.

Bo Zhu Yi /ˈbəʊ ˌdʒuː ˈjiː/ or *Po Chü-i* 772–846. Chinese poet. President from 841 of the imperial war department, he criticized government policy. He is said to have checked his work with an old peasant woman for clarity of expression.

Bracegirdle /ˈbreɪsɡɜːdl/ Anne *c.* 1663–1748. British actress, the mistress of →Congreve, and possibly his wife; she played Millamant in his *The Way of the World*.

Bracton /ˈbræktən/ Henry de, died 1268. English judge, writer on English law, and chancellor of Exeter cathedral from 1264. The account of the laws and customs of the English attributed to Henry de Bracton, *De Legibus et consuetudinibus Anglie/The Laws and Customs of England*, the first of its kind, was not in fact written by him.

Bradbury /ˈbrædbəri/ Malcolm 1932– . British novelist and critic, whose writings include comic and satiric portrayals of academic life. He became professor of American studies at the University of East Anglia 1970, and his major work is *The History Man* 1975, set in a provincial English university. Other works include *Rates of Exchange* 1983.

Bradbury /ˈbrædbəri/ Ray 1920– . US science-fiction writer, responsible for making the genre 'respectable' to a wider readership. His work shows nostalgia for small-town Midwestern life, and includes *The Martian Chronicles* 1950, *Fahrenheit 451* 1953, *R is for Rocket* 1962, and *Something Wicked This Way Comes* 1962.

Bradford /ˈbrædfd/ William 1590–1657. British colonial administrator in America, the first governor of Plymouth colony, Massachusetts, 1621–57. As one of the Pilgrim Fathers he sailed for America aboard the *Mayflower* 1620 and was among the signatories of the Mayflower Compact, the first written constitution in the New World. His memoirs, *History of Plimoth Plantation*, are an important source for the colony's early history.

Born in Yorkshire, England, Bradford joined the Puritan Separatists (later known as the Pilgrim Fathers or Pilgrims) at an early age and lived with them in exile in Leiden, Holland, 1609–20. In 1621 he was chosen as governor of Plymouth and served in that office almost continuously for the next 35 years.

Bradlaugh /ˈbrædlɔː/ Charles 1833–1891. British freethinker and radical politician. In 1880 he was elected Liberal member of Parliament for Northampton, but was not allowed to take his seat until 1886 because, as an atheist, he (unsuccessfully) claimed the right to affirm instead of taking the oath. He was associated with the feminist Annie Besant.

He served in the army, was a lawyer's clerk, became well known as a speaker and journalist under the name of Iconoclast, and from 1860 ran the *National Reformer*. He advocated the freedom of the press, contraception, and other social reforms.

Bradley /ˈbrædli/ Francis Herbert 1846–1924. British philosopher. In *Ethical Studies* 1876 and *Principles of Logic* 1883 he attacked the utilitarianism of J S Mill, and in *Appearance and Reality* 1893 and *Truth and Reality* 1914 he outlined his neo-Hegelian doctrine of the universe as a single ultimate reality.

Bradley /ˈbrædli/ James 1693–1762. English astronomer who in 1728 discovered the aberration of starlight. From the amount of aberration in star positions, he was able to calculate the speed of light. In 1748, he announced the discovery of nutation (variation in the Earth's axial tilt).

Bradley /ˈbrædli/ Omar Nelson 1893–1981. US general in World War II. In 1943 he commanded the 2nd US Corps in their victories in Tunisia and

Sicily, leading to the surrender of 250,000 Axis troops, and in 1944 led the US troops in the invasion of France. His command, as the 12th Army Group, grew to 1.3 million troops, the largest US force ever assembled.

He was Chief of Staff of the US Army 1948–49 and chair of the joint Chiefs of Staff 1949–53. He was appointed general of the army 1950.

Bradman /ˈbrædmən/ Don(ald George) 1908– . Australian test cricketer with the highest average in test history. From 52 test matches he averaged 99.94 runs per innings. He only needed four runs from his final test innings to average 100 but was dismissed second ball.

Bradman was born in Bowral, New South Wales, came to prominence at an early age, and made his test debut in 1928. He played for Australia for 20 years and was captain 1936–48.

He twice scored triple centuries against England and in 1930 scored 452 not out for New South Wales against Queensland, the highest first-class innings until 1959. In 1989 a Bradman Museum was opened in his home town.

Bradshaw /ˈbrædʃɔː/ George 1801–1853. British publisher who brought out the first railway timetable in 1839. Thereafter *Bradshaw's Railway Companion* appeared at regular intervals.

He was apprenticed to an engraver on leaving school, and set up his own printing and engraving business in the 1820s, beginning in 1827 with an engraved map of Lancashire.

Brady /ˈbreɪdi/ Mathew B *c.* 1823–1896. US photographer. Famed for his skill in photographic portraiture, he published *The Gallery of Illustrious Americans* 1850. With the outbreak of the US Civil War 1861, Brady and his staff became the foremost photographers of battle scenes and military life. Although his war photos were widely reproduced, Brady later suffered a series of financial reverses and died in poverty.

Born in Warren County, New York, Brady served as an apprentice to a portrait painter. Learning the rudiments of photography from Samuel →Morse, Brady established his own daguerreotype studio in New York 1844.

Braganza /brəˈgænsə/ the royal house of Portugal whose members reigned 1640–1910; another branch were emperors of Brazil 1822–89.

Bragg /bræg/ William Henry 1862–1942. British physicist. In 1915 he shared with his son *(William) Lawrence Bragg* (1890–1971) the Nobel Prize for Physics for their research work on X-rays and crystals.

Brahe /ˈbrɑːhə/ Tycho 1546–1601. Danish astronomer who made accurate observations of the planets from which the German astronomer and mathematician Johann →Kepler proved that planets orbit the Sun in ellipses. His discovery and report of the 1572 supernova brought him recognition, and his observations of the comet of 1577 proved that it moved on an orbit among the planets, thus disproving the Greek view that comets were in the Earth's atmosphere.

Brahe was a colourful figure who wore a false nose after his own was cut off in a duel, and who took an interest in alchemy. In 1576 Frederick II of Denmark gave him the island of Hven, where he set up an observatory. Brahe was the greatest observer in the days before telescopes, making the most accurate measurements of the positions of stars and planets. He moved to Prague as imperial mathematician in 1599, where he was joined by Kepler, who inherited his observations when he died.

Brahms /brɑːmz/ Johannes 1833–1897. German composer, pianist, and conductor. Considered one of the greatest composers of symphonic music and of songs, his works include four symphonies; lieder (songs); concertos for piano and for violin; chamber music; sonatas; and the choral *A German Requiem* 1868. He performed and conducted his own works.

In 1853 the violinist Joachim introduced him to Liszt and Schumann, who encouraged him. From 1868 Brahms made his home in Vienna. Although his music belongs to a reflective strain of Romanticism, similar to Wordsworth in poetry, Brahms saw himself as continuing the Classical tradition from the point to which Beethoven had brought it. To his contemporaries, he was a strict formalist, in opposition to the romantic sensuality of Wagner. His influence on Mahler and Schoenberg was profound.

Braine /breɪn/ John 1922–1986. English novelist. His novel *Room at the Top* 1957 created the character of Joe Lampton, one of the first of the northern working-class antiheroes.

Braithwaite /ˈbreɪθweɪt/ Eustace Adolph 1912– . Guyanese author. His experiences as a teacher in London prompted *To Sir With Love* 1959. His *Reluctant Neighbours* 1972 deals with black/white relations.

Braithwaite /ˈbreɪθweɪt/ Richard Bevan 1900– . British philosopher who experimented in the provision of a rational basis for religion and moral choice. Originally a physicist and mathematician, he was professor of moral philosophy at Cambridge 1953–67.

Bramah /ˈbrɑːmə/ Ernest. Pen name of Ernest Bramah Smith 1868–1948. British short story writer, creator of Kai Lung, and of Max Carrados, a blind detective.

Bramah /ˈbrɑːmə/ Joseph 1748–1814. British inventor of a flushing water closet 1778, an 'unpickable' lock 1784, and the hydraulic press 1795. The press made use of ➔Pascal's principle (that pressure in fluid contained in a vessel is evenly distributed) and employed water as the hydraulic fluid; it enabled the 19th-century bridge-builders to lift massive girders.

Branagh Hailed as a new Olivier, British actor and director Kenneth Branagh has played a wide range of Shakespearean and contemporary roles, including several for film and television. His film Dead Again 1991, which he both directed and starred in, was a major box office hit on both sides of the Atlantic.

Bramante /brəˈmænti/ Donato *c.* 1444–1514. Italian Renaissance architect and artist. Inspired by Classical designs, he was employed by Pope Julius II in rebuilding part of the Vatican and St Peter's in Rome.

Branagh /ˈbrænə/ Kenneth 1960– . British actor and director. He cofounded, with David Parfitt, the Renaissance Theatre Company 1987, was a notable Hamlet and Touchstone in 1988, and in 1989 directed and starred in a film of Shakespeare's *Henry V*.

Brancusi /brænˈkuːzi/ Constantin 1876–1957. Romanian sculptor, active in Paris from 1904, a pioneer of abstract forms and conceptual art. He developed increasingly simplified natural or organic forms, such as the sculpted head that gradually came to resemble an egg (*Sleeping Muse* 1910, Musée National d'Art Moderne, Paris).

In 1904 he walked from Romania to Paris, where he worked briefly in Rodin's studio. He began to explore direct carving in marble (producing many versions of Rodin's *The Kiss*), and was one of the first sculptors in the 20th century to carve directly from his material, working with granite, wood, and other materials. By the 1930s he had achieved monumental simplicity with structures of simple repeated forms (*Endless Column* and other works in Tirgu Jiu public park, Romania). Brancusi was revered by his contemporaries and remains a seminal figure in 20th-century sculpture.

Brand /brænd/ Dollar (Adolf Johannes) 1934– . Former name of the South African jazz musician Abdullah ➔Ibrahim.

Brandeis /ˈbrændaɪs/ Louis Dembitz 1856–1941. US jurist. As a crusader for progressive causes, he helped draft social-welfare and labour legislation. In 1916, with his appointment to the US Supreme Court by President Wilson, he became the first Jewish justice and maintained his support of individual rights in his opposition to the 1917 Espionage Act and in his dissenting opinion in the first wiretap case, *Olmstead* v *US* 1928.

Brando /ˈbrændəʊ/ Marlon 1924– . US actor whose casual style, mumbling speech, and use of Method acting earned him a place as a distinctive actor. He won best-actor Academy Awards for *On the Waterfront* 1954 and *The Godfather* 1972.

He made his Broadway debut in *I Remember Mama* 1944, appeared in *Candida* 1946, and achieved fame in *A Streetcar Named Desire* 1947. His films include *The Men* 1950, *A Streetcar Named Desire* 1951, *Julius Caesar* 1953, *The Wild One* 1954, *Mutiny on the Bounty* 1962, *Last Tango in Paris* 1973, *Apocalypse Now* 1979, and *The Freshman* 1990.

An actor is a guy who, if you aren't talking about him, isn't listening.

Marlon Brando *Observer* Jan 1956

Brandt /brænt/ Bill 1905–1983. British photographer who produced a large body of richly printed and romantic black-and-white studies of people, London life, and social behaviour.

Brandt /brænt/ Willy. Adopted name of Karl Herbert Frahm 1913–1992. German socialist politician, federal chancellor (premier) of West Germany 1969–74. He played a key role in the remoulding of the Social Democratic Party (SPD) as a moderate socialist force (leader 1964–87). As mayor of West Berlin 1957–66, Brandt became internationally known during the Berlin Wall crisis 1961. Nobel Peace Prize 1971.

Brandt, born in Lübeck, changed his name when he fled to Norway 1933 and became active in the anti-Nazi resistance. He returned 1945 and entered the Bundestag (federal parliament) 1949. In the 'grand coalition' 1966–69 he served as foreign minister and introduced *Ostpolitik*, a policy of reconciliation between East and West Europe, which was continued when he became federal chancellor 1969, and culminated in the 1972 signing of the Basic Treaty with East Germany. He chaired the Brandt Commission on Third World problems 1977–83 and was a member of the European Parliament 1979–83.

Brangwyn /ˈbræŋgwɪn/ Frank 1867–1956. British artist. Of Welsh extraction, he was born in Bruges, Belgium. He initially worked for William Morris as a textile designer. He produced furniture, pottery, carpets, schemes for interior decoration and architectural designs, as well as book illustrations, lithographs, and etchings.

Branson /ˈbrænsən/ Richard 1950– . British entrepreneur whose Virgin company developed quickly, diversifying from retailing records to the airline business.

He was born in Surrey, England, and the 1968 launch of *Student* magazine proved to be the first of his many successful business ventures.

Braque /brɑːk/ Georges 1882–1963. French painter who, with Picasso, founded the Cubist movement around 1907–10. They worked together at L'Estaque in the south of France and in Paris. Braque began to experiment in collages and invented a technique of gluing paper, wood, and other materials to canvas. His later work became more decorative.

Brassäi /ˌbræsɑːˈiː/ adopted name of Gyula Halesz 1899–1986. French photographer of Hungarian origin. From the early 1930s on he documented, mainly by flash, the nightlife of Paris, before turning to more abstract work.

Bratby /ˈbrætbi/ John 1928–1992. British artist, one of the leaders of the 'kitchen-sink' school of the 1950s because of a preoccupation in early work with working-class domestic interiors.

Brattain /ˈbrætn/ Walter Houser 1902–1987. US physicist. In 1956 he was awarded a Nobel prize jointly with William Shockley and John Bardeen for their work on the development of the transistor, which replaced the comparatively costly and clumsy vacuum tube in electronics.

Brauchitsch /ˈbraʊxɪtʃ/ Walther von 1881–1948. German field marshal. A staff officer in World War I, he became in 1938 commander in chief of the army and a member of Hitler's secret cabinet council. He was dismissed after his failure to invade Moscow 1941. Captured in 1945, he died before being tried in the Nuremberg trials.

Braun /braʊn/ Eva 1910–1945. German mistress of Adolf Hitler. Secretary to Hitler's photographer and personal friend, Heinrich Hoffmann, she became Hitler's mistress in the 1930s and married him in the air-raid shelter of the Chancellery in Berlin on 29 April 1945. The next day they committed suicide together.

Brautigan /ˈbrɔtɪgən/ Richard 1935–1984. US novelist, author of playful fictions set in California, such as *Trout Fishing in America* 1967, and Gothic works like *The Hawkline Monster* 1974.

Breakspear /ˈbreɪkspɪə/ Nicholas. Original name of →Adrian IV, the only English pope.

Bream /briːm/ Julian (Alexander) 1933– . British virtuoso of the guitar and lute. He has revived much Elizabethan lute music and encouraged composition by contemporaries for both instruments. Britten and Henze have written for him.

Breasted /ˈbrestd/ James Henry 1865–1935. US Orientalist. Well known as the author of textbooks and popular works on the history of the ancient Near East, Breasted founded the University of

Chicago Oriental Institute, funded by John D Rockefeller, as a centre of American archaeological research. He published *A History of Egypt* 1905, and directed the Chicago expedition to Egypt and Sudan 1905–07.

Born in Rockford, Illinois, USA, Breasted was first trained as a pharmacist but later pursued studies in Egyptology at Yale University and the University of Berlin, Germany. He entered the University of Chicago 1896.

Brecht /brext/ Bertolt 1898–1956. German dramatist and poet who aimed to destroy the 'suspension of disbelief' usual in the theatre and to express Marxist ideas. He adapted John Gay's *Beggar's Opera* as *Die Dreigroschenoper/The Threepenny Opera* 1928, set to music by Kurt Weill. Later plays include *Mutter Courage/Mother Courage* 1941, set during the Thirty Years' War, and *Der kaukasische Kreidekreis/The Caucasian Chalk Circle* 1949.

As an anti-Nazi, he left Germany in 1933 for Scandinavia and the US. He became an Austrian citizen after World War II; in 1949 he established the Berliner Ensemble theatre group in East Germany.

Unhappy the land that is in need of heroes.
Bertolt Brecht *Galileo* 1939

Breker /ˈbreɪkə/ Arno 1900–1991. German Neo-Classical sculptor who created several pieces on commission for the Nazi regime. After World War II much of his work was destroyed.

Brendel /ˈbrendl/ Alfred 1931– . Austrian pianist, known for his fastidious and searching interpretations of Beethoven, Schubert, and Liszt. He is the author of *Musical Thoughts and Afterthoughts* 1976 and *Music Sounded Out* 1990.

Brennan /ˈbrenən/ Christopher (John) 1870–1932. Australian Symbolist poet, influenced by Baudelaire and Mallarmé. Although one of Australia's greatest poets, he is virtually unknown outside his native country. His complex, idiosyncratic verse includes *Poems* 1914 and *A Chant of Doom and Other Verses* 1918.

Brennan /ˈbrenən/ Walter 1894–1974. US actor, often seen in Westerns as the hero's sidekick. His work includes *The Westerner* 1940, *Bad Day at Black Rock* 1955, and *Rio Bravo* 1959.

Brennan /ˈbrenən/ William Joseph, Jr 1906– . US jurist and associate justice of the US Supreme Court 1956–90. He wrote many important Supreme Court majority decisions that assured the freedoms set forth in the First Amendment and established the rights of minority groups. He is especially noted for writing the majority opinion in *Baker* v *Carr* 1962, in which state voting reapportionment ensured 'one person, one vote', and in *US* v *Eichman* 1990, which ruled that the law banning desecration of the flag was a violation of the right to free speech as provided for in the First Amendment.

Brenner /ˈbrenə/ Sidney 1927– . South African scientist, one of the pioneers of genetic engineering. Brenner discovered messenger RNA (a link between DNA and the ribosomes in which proteins are synthesized) 1960.

Brenner first studied medicine, but then moved into molecular biology at Oxford University. He worked for many years with Francis Crick, doing much research on nematode worms.

Brentano /brenˈtɑːnəʊ/ Franz 1838–1916. German-Austrian philosopher and psychologist whose *Psychology from the Empirical Standpoint* 1874 developed the concept of 'intentionality', the directing of the mind to an object; for example, in perception.

Brentano /brenˈtɑːnəʊ/ Klemens 1778–1842. German writer, leader of the Young Romantics. He published a seminal collection of folk-tales and songs with Ludwig von →Arnim (*Des Knaben Wunderhorn*) 1805–08, and popularized the legend of the Lorelei (a rock in the river Rhine). He also wrote mystic religious verse, as in *Romanzen vom Rosenkranz* 1852.

Brenton /ˈbrentən/ Howard 1942– . British dramatist, whose works include *The Romans in Britain* 1980, and a translation of Brecht's *The Life of Galileo*.

Breton /ˈbretɒn/ André 1896–1966. French author, among the leaders of the Dada art movement. *Les Champs magnétiques/Magnetic Fields* 1921, an experiment in automatic writing, was one of the products of the movement. He was also a founder of Surrealism, publishing *Le Manifeste de surréalisme/Surrealist Manifesto* 1924. Other works include *Nadja* 1928, the story of his love affair with a medium.

Breuer /ˈbrɔɪə/ Josef 1842–1925. Viennese physician, one of the pioneers of psychoanalysis. He applied it successfully to cases of hysteria, and collaborated with Freud in *Studien über Hysterie/Studies in Hysteria* 1895.

Breuer /ˈbrɔɪə/ Marcel 1902–1981. Hungarian-born architect and designer who studied and taught at the Bauhaus school in Germany. His tubular steel chair 1925 was the first of its kind. He moved to England, then to the USA, where he was in partnership with Walter Gropius 1937–40. His buildings show an affinity with natural materials; the best known is the Bijenkorf, Rotterdam, the Netherlands (with Elzas) 1953.

Breuil /brɔɪ/ Henri 1877–1961. French prehistorian, professor of historic ethnography and director of research at the Institute of Human Palaeontology, Paris, from 1910. He established the genuine antiquity of Palaeolithic cave art and stressed the anthropological approach to human prehistory.

Brewster /'bru:stə/ David 1781–1868. Scottish physicist who made discoveries about the diffraction and polarization of light, and invented the kaleidoscope.

Brezhnev /'breʒnef/ Leonid Ilyich 1906–1982. Soviet leader. A protégé of Stalin and Khrushchev, he came to power (after he and →Kosygin forced Khrushchev to resign) as general secretary of the Soviet Communist Party (CPSU) 1964–82 and was president 1977–82. Domestically he was conservative; abroad the USSR was established as a military and political superpower during the Brezhnev era, extending its influence in Africa and Asia.

Brezhnev, born in the Ukraine, joined the CPSU in the 1920s. In 1938 he was made head of propaganda by the new Ukrainian party chief Khrushchev and ascended in the local party hierarchy. After World War II he caught the attention of the CPSU leader Stalin, who inducted Brezhnev into the secretariat and Politburo 1952. Brezhnev was removed from these posts after Stalin's death 1953, but returned 1956 with Khrushchev's patronage. In 1960, as criticism of Khrushchev mounted, Brezhnev was moved to the ceremonial post of state president and began to criticize Khrushchev's policies.

Brezhnev stepped down as president 1963 and returned to the Politburo and secretariat. He was elected CPSU general secretary 1964, when Khrushchev was ousted, and gradually came to dominate the conservative and consensual coalition. In 1977 he regained the additional title of state president under the new constitution. He suffered an illness (thought to have been a stroke or heart attack) March–April 1976 that was believed to have affected his thought and speech so severely that he was not able to make decisions. These were made by his entourage, for example committing troops to Afghanistan to prop up the government. Within the USSR, economic difficulties mounted; the Brezhnev era was a period of caution and stagnation, although outwardly imperialist.

Brian /'braɪən/ Havergal 1876–1972. English composer of 32 symphonies in visionary Romantic style, including the *Gothic* 1919–27 for large choral and orchestral forces.

Brian /'braɪən/ known as *Brian Boru* ('Brian of the Tribute') 926–1014. High king of Ireland from 976, who took Munster, Leinster, and Connacht to become ruler of all Ireland. He defeated the Norse at Clontarf, thus ending Norse control of Dublin, although he was himself killed. He was the last high king with jurisdiction over most of Scotland. His exploits were celebrated in several chronicles.

Briand /bri'ɒn/ Aristide 1862–1932. French radical socialist politician. He was prime minister 1909–11, 1913, 1915–17, 1921–22, 1925–26 and 1929, and foreign minister 1925–32. In 1925 he concluded the Locarno Pact (settling Germany's western frontier) and in 1928 the Kellogg–Briand Pact renouncing war; in 1930 he outlined a scheme for a United States of Europe.

Bridge /brɪdʒ/ Frank 1879–1941. English composer, the teacher of Benjamin Britten. His works include the orchestral suite *The Sea* 1912, and *Oration* 1930 for cello and orchestra.

Bridges /'brɪdʒɪz/ Harry 1901–1990. Australian-born US labour leader. In 1931 he formed a trade union of clockworkers and in 1934, after police opened fire on a picket line and killed two strikers, he organized a successful general strike. He was head of the International Longshoremen's and Warehousemen's Union for many years.

Born in Melbourne, Australia, he ran away to sea and settled in San Francisco. Accusations by the Federal Bureau of Investigation that he had concealed membership in the Communist Party on his immigration papers were later proved false.

Bridges /'brɪdʒɪz/ Robert (Seymour) 1844–1930. British poet, poet laureate from 1913, author of *The Testament of Beauty* 1929, a long philosophical poem. In 1918 he edited and published posthumously the poems of Gerard Manley →Hopkins.

Bridget, St /'brɪdʒɪt/ 453–523. A patron saint of Ireland, also known as *St Brigit* or *St Bride*. She founded a church and monastery at Kildare, and is said to have been the daughter of a prince of Ulster. Feast day 1 Feb.

Bridgewater /'brɪdʒwɔːtə/ Francis Egerton, 3rd Duke of 1736–1803. Pioneer of British inland navigation. With James →Brindley as his engineer, he constructed 1762–72 the *Bridgewater canal* from Worsley to Manchester and on to the Mersey, a distance of 67.5 km/42 mi. Initially built to carry coal, the canal crosses the Irwell valley on an aqueduct.

Bridgman /'brɪdʒmən/ Percy Williams 1882–1961. US physicist. His research into machinery producing high pressure led in 1955 to the creation of synthetic diamonds by General Electric. He was awarded the Nobel Prize for Physics 1946.

Born in Cambridge, Massachusetts, he was educated at Harvard, where he was Hollis Professor of Mathematics and Natural Philosophy 1926–50 and Higgins university professor 1950–54.

Bridie /'braɪdi/ James. Pen name of Osborne Henry Mavor 1888–1951. Dramatist and professor of medicine, and a founder of the Glasgow Citizens' Theatre. His plays include *Tobias and the Angel* 1930 and *The Anatomist* 1931.

Brieux /bri'ɜː/ Eugène 1858–1932. French dramatist, an exponent of the naturalistic problem play attacking social evils. His most powerful plays are *Les trois filles de M Dupont* 1897; *Les Avar-*

Bright *John Bright, British Victorian politician and humanitarian campaigner against the Corn Laws and the Crimean War. A stirring orator, he said of the Crimean War: 'The angel of death has been abroad throughout the land; you may almost hear the beating of his wings'.*

iés/Damaged Goods 1901, long banned for its outspoken treatment of syphilis; and *Maternité* 1903.

Briggs /brɪgz/ Barry 1934– . New Zealand motorcyclist who won four individual world speedway titles 1957–66 and took part in a record 87 world championship races.

Brighouse /ˈbrɪghaʊs/ Harold 1882–1958. English playwright. Born and bred in Lancashire, in his most famous play, *Hobson's Choice* 1916, he dealt with a Salford bootmaker's courtship, using the local idiom.

Bright /braɪt/ John 1811–1889. British Liberal politician, a campaigner for free trade, peace, and social reform. A Quaker millowner, he was among the founders of the Anti-Corn Law League in 1839, and was largely instrumental in securing the passage of the Reform Bill of 1867.

After entering Parliament in 1843 Bright led the struggle there for free trade, together with Richard →Cobden, which achieved success in 1846. His *laissez-faire* principles also made him a prominent opponent of factory reform. His influence was constantly exerted on behalf of peace, as when he opposed the Crimean War, Palmerston's aggressive policy in China, Disraeli's anti-Russian policy, and the bombardment of Alexandria. During the American Civil War he was outspoken in support of the North. He sat in Gladstone's cabinets as president of the Board of Trade 1868–70 and chancellor of the Duchy of Lancaster 1873–74 and 1880–82, but broke with him over the Irish

Home Rule Bill. Bright owed much of his influence to his skill as a speaker.

> *England is the mother of Parliaments.*
> **John Bright**

Bright /braɪt/ Richard 1789–1858. British physician who described many conditions and linked oedema to kidney disease. *Bright's disease*, an inflammation of the kidneys, is named after him.

Brillat-Savarin /ˈbriːjɑː ˌsævˈræŋ/ Jean Anthelme 1755–1826. French gastronome, author of *La Physiologie du Goût/The Physiology of Taste* 1825, a compilation of observations on food and drink regarded as the first great classic of gastronomic literature. Most of his professional life was spent as a politician.

Brindley /ˈbrɪndli/ James 1716–1772. British canal builder, the first to employ tunnels and aqueducts extensively, in order to reduce the number of locks on a direct-route canal. His 580 km/360 mi of canals included the Bridgewater (Manchester–Liverpool) and Grand Union (Manchester–Potteries) canals.

Brinell /brɪˈnel/ Johann Auguste 1849–1925. Swedish engineer who devised the Brinell hardness test, for measuring the hardness of substances, in 1900.

Brisbane /ˈbrɪzbən/ Thomas Makdougall 1773–1860. Scottish soldier, colonial administrator, and astronomer. After serving in the Napoleonic Wars under Wellington, he was governor of New South Wales 1821–25. Brisbane in Queensland is named after him. He catalogued over 7,000 stars.

Brissot /briːˈsəʊ/ Jacques Pierre 1754–1793. French revolutionary leader, born in Chartres. He became a member of the legislative assembly and the National Convention, but his party of moderate republicans, the Girondins, or Brissotins, fell foul of Robespierre, and Brissot was guillotined.

Bristow /ˈbrɪstaʊ/ Eric 1957– . English darts player nicknamed 'the Crafty Cockney'. He has won all the game's major titles, including the world professional title a record five times between 1980 and 1986.

Britannicus /brɪˈtænɪkəs/ Tiberius Claudius *c.* AD 41–55. Roman prince, son of the Emperor Claudius and Messalina; so-called from his father's expedition to Britain. He was poisoned by Nero.

Brittain /ˈbrɪtn/ Vera 1894–1970. English socialist writer, a nurse to the troops overseas 1915–19, as told in her *Testament of Youth* 1933; *Testament of Friendship* 1950 commemorated Winifred →Holtby. She married political scientist Sir George Catlin (1896–1979); their daughter is the Liberal politician Shirley →Williams.

Brittain English writer Vera Brittain, best known for the works in which her experiences as a nurse in World War I were recorded. As well as writing a number of novels, Brittain made several lecture tours in the USA, promoting feminism and pacifism.

Brittan /ˈbrɪtn/ Leon 1939– . British Conservative politician and lawyer. Chief secretary to the Treasury 1981–83, home secretary 1983–85, secretary for trade and industry 1985–86 (resigned over his part in the Westland affair, the takeover of the British Westland helicopter company, about which there were allegations of malpractice), and senior European Commissioner from 1988.

Britten /ˈbrɪtn/ (Edward) Benjamin 1913–1976. English composer. He often wrote for the individual voice; for example, the role in the opera *Peter Grimes* 1945, based on verses by George Crabbe, was created for Peter ➔Pears. Among his many works are the *Young Person's Guide to the Orchestra* 1946; the chamber opera *The Rape of Lucretia* 1946; *Billy Budd* 1951; *A Midsummer Night's Dream* 1960; and *Death in Venice* 1973.

He studied at the Royal College of Music. From 1939 to 1942 he worked in the USA, then returned to England and devoted himself to composing at his home in Aldeburgh, Suffolk, where he established an annual music festival. His oratorio *War Requiem* 1962 was written for the rededication of Coventry Cathedral.

Broad /brɔːd/ Charles Dunbar 1887–1971. British philosopher. His books include *Perception, Physics and Reality* 1914, and *Lectures on Psychic Research* 1962, discussing scientific evidence for survival after death.

Born in London, he was educated at Trinity College, Cambridge, and was Knightbridge professor of moral philosophy at the university 1933–53.

Broch /brɒx/ Hermann 1886–1951. Austrian novelist, who used experimental techniques in *Die Schlafwandler/The Sleepwalkers* 1932, *Der Tod des Vergil/The Death of Virgil* 1945, and *Die Schuldlosen/The Guiltless*, a novel in 11 stories. He moved to the USA 1938 after being persecuted by the Nazis.

Brodsky /ˈbrɒdski/ Joseph 1940– . Russian poet who emigrated to the USA in 1972. His work, often dealing with themes of exile, is admired for its wit and economy of language, particularly in its use of understatement. Many of his poems, written in Russian, have been translated into English (*A Part of Speech* 1980). More recently he has also written in English. He was awarded the Nobel Prize for Literature in 1987 and became US poet laureate 1991.

Broglie /də ˈbrəʊli/ Louis de, 7th Duc de Broglie 1892–1987. French theoretical physicist. He established that all subatomic particles can be described either by particle equations or by wave equations, thus laying the foundations of wave mechanics. He was awarded the 1929 Nobel Prize for Physics.

Broglie /də ˈbrəʊli/ Maurice de, 6th Duc de Broglie 1875–1960. French physicist. He worked on X-rays and gamma rays, and helped to establish the Einsteinian description of light in terms of photons. He was the brother of Louis de Broglie.

Bromfield /ˈbrɒmfiːld/ Louis 1896–1956. US novelist. Among his books are *The Strange Case of Miss Annie Spragg* 1928, *The Rains Came* 1937, and *Mrs Parkington* 1943, dealing with the golden age of New York society.

Bronson /ˈbrɒnsn/ Charles. Stage name of Charles Bunchinsky 1921– . US film actor. His films are mainly violent thrillers such as *Death Wish* 1974. He was one of *The Magnificent Seven* 1960.

Brontë /ˈbrɒnti/ three English novelists, daughters of a Yorkshire parson. *Charlotte* (1816–1855), notably with *Jane Eyre* 1847 and *Villette* 1853, reshaped autobiographical material into vivid narrative. *Emily* (1818–1848) in *Wuthering Heights* 1847 expressed the intensity and nature mysticism which also pervades her poetry (*Poems* 1846). The more modest talent of *Anne* (1820–1849) produced *Agnes Grey* 1847 and *The Tenant of Wildfell Hall* 1848.

The Brontës were brought up by an aunt at Haworth rectory (now a museum) in Yorkshire. In 1846 the sisters published a volume of poems under the pen names Currer (Charlotte), Ellis (Emily) and Acton (Anne) Bell. In 1847 (using the same names), they published the novels *Jane Eyre*, *Wuthering Heights*, and *Agnes Grey*, Anne's much weaker work. During 1848–49 Emily, Anne, and their brother Patrick Branwell all died of tuberculosis, aided in Branwell's case by alcohol and opium addiction; he is remembered for his portrait of the sisters. Charlotte married her father's curate, A B Nicholls, in 1854, and died during pregnancy.

Bronzino /brɒnd'zi:nəʊ/ Agnolo 1503–1572. Italian painter active in Florence, court painter to Cosimo I, Duke of Tuscany. He painted in an elegant, Mannerist style and is best known for portraits and the allegory *Venus, Cupid, Folly and Time* about 1545 (National Gallery, London).

Brook /brʊk/ Peter 1925– . English director renowned for his experimental productions. His work with the Royal Shakespeare Company included a production of Shakespeare's *A Midsummer Night's Dream* 1970, set in a white gymnasium and combining elements of circus and commedia dell'arte. In the same year he established Le Centre International de Créations Théâtrales/The International Centre for Theatre Research in Paris. Brook's later productions transcend Western theatre conventions and include *The Conference of the Birds* 1973, based on a Persian story, and *The Mahabarata* 1985–8, a cycle of three plays based on the Hindu epic. His films include *Lord of the Flies* 1962 and *Meetings with Remarkable Men* 1979.

Brooke /brʊk/ James 1803–1868. British administrator who became rajah of Sarawak, on Borneo, 1841.

Born near Varanasi, he served in the army of the East India Company. In 1838 he headed a private expedition to Borneo, where he helped to suppress a revolt, and when the sultan gave him the title of rajah of Sarawak, Brooke became known as the 'the white rajah'. He was succeeded as rajah by his nephew, Sir Charles Johnson (1829–1917), whose son Sir Charles Vyner (1874–1963) in 1946 arranged for the transfer of Sarawak to the British crown.

Brooke /brʊk/ Peter Leonard 1934– . British Conservative politician, a member of Parliament from 1977. He was appointed chair of the Conservative Party by Margaret Thatcher 1987, and was Northern Ireland secretary 1989–April 1992. In Sept 1992 he was chosen to succeed David Mellor as National Heritage secretary.

Brooke was educated at Oxford and worked as a management consultant in New York and Brussels. The son of a former home secretary, Lord Brooke of Cumnor, he became an MP in 1977 and entered Thatcher's government in 1979. Following a number of junior appointments, he succeeded Norman Tebbit as chair of the Conservative Party 1987. After an undistinguished two years in that office, he succeeded Tom King as Northern Ireland secretary 1989. He aroused criticism (and praise) for observing that at some future time negotiations with the IRA might take place. In 1991 his efforts to institute all-party, and all-Ireland, talks on reconciliation eventually proved abortive but he continued to be held in high regard on both sides of the border.

Brooke /brʊk/ Rupert (Chawner) 1887–1915. English poet, symbol of the World War I 'lost generation'. His five war sonnets, the best known of which is 'The Patriot', were published posthumously. Other notable works include 'Grant chester' and 'The Great Lover'.

Born in Rugby, where he was educated, Brooke travelled abroad after a nervous breakdown 1911, but in 1913 won a fellowship at King's College, Cambridge. Later that year he toured America (*Letters from America* 1916), New Zealand, and the South Seas, and in 1914 became an officer in the Royal Naval Division. After fighting at Antwerp, he sailed for the Dardanelles, but died of blood-poisoning on the Greek island of Skyros, where he is buried.

---

*If I should die, think only this of me…
That there's some corner of a foreign field
That is forever England.*

Rupert Brooke 'The Soldier' 1915

Brookeborough /'brʊkbərə/ Basil Brooke, Viscount Brookeborough 1888–1973. Unionist politician of Northern Ireland. He entered Parliament in 1929, held ministerial posts 1933–45, and was prime minister of Northern Ireland 1943–63. He was a staunch advocate of strong links with Britain.

Brookner /brʊknə/ Anita 1928– . British novelist and art historian, whose novels include *Hotel du Lac* 1984, winner of the Booker prize, *A Misalliance* 1986, and *Latecomers* 1988.

Brooks /brʊks/ Louise 1906–1985. US actress, known for her roles in silent films such as *A Girl in Every Port* 1928, *Die Büchse der Pandora/Pandora's Box*, and *Das Tagebuch einer Verlorenen/Diary of a Lost Girl* both 1929 and both directed by G W →Pabst. At 25 she had appeared in 17 films. She retired from the screen 1938.

Brooks /brʊks/ Mel. Stage name of Melvin Kaminsky 1926– . US film director and comedian, known for madcap and slapstick verbal humour. He became well known with his record album *The 2,000-Year-Old Man* 1960. His films include *The Producers* 1968, *Blazing Saddles* 1974, *Young Frankenstein* 1975, *History of the World Part I* 1981, and *To Be or Not to Be* 1983.

Brooks /brʊks/ Van Wyck 1886–1963. US literary critic and biographer. His five-volume *Makers and Finders: A History of the Writer in America, 1800–1915* 1936–52 was an influential series of critical works on US literature. The first volume *The Flowering of New England* 1936 won a Pulitzer prize.

An earlier work, *America's Coming-of-Age* 1915, concerned the Puritan heritage and its effects on American literature. His other works include studies of Mark Twain, Henry James, and Ralph Waldo Emerson.

Brougham Scottish-born English politician, lawyer and reformer, Henry Brougham was often considered arrogant and eccentric. He campaigned vigorously for Benthamite legal reforms and co-founded London University. The carriage specially built for him became the prototype of the 'brougham'.

Broome /brʊm/ David 1940– . British show jumper. He won the 1970 world title on a horse named Beethoven. His sister Liz Edgar is also a top-class show jumper.

Brougham /brʊm/ Henry Peter, 1st Baron Brougham and Vaux 1778–1868. British Whig politician and lawyer. From 1811 he was chief adviser to the Princess of Wales (afterwards Queen Caroline), and in 1820 he defeated the attempt of George IV to divorce her. He was Lord Chancellor 1830–34, supporting the Reform Bill.

Born in Edinburgh, he was a founder of the *Edinburgh Review* 1802. He sat in Parliament 1810–12 and from 1816, and supported the causes of public education and law reform. He was one of the founders of University College, London, 1828. When the Whigs returned to power 1830, Brougham accepted the chancellorship and a peerage a few weeks later. His allegedly dictatorial and eccentric ways led to his exclusion from office when the Whigs next assumed power 1835. After 1837 he was active in the House of Lords.

Brouwer /braʊə/ Adriaen 1605–1638. Flemish painter who studied with Frans Hals. He excelled in scenes of peasant revelry.

Brown /braʊn/ (James) Gordon 1951– . British Labour politician. He entered Parliament in 1983, rising quickly to the opposition front bench, with a reputation as an outstanding debater.

Brown, the son of a Church of Scotland minister, won a first in history at Edinburgh University before he was 20. After four years as a college lecturer and three as a television journalist, he entered the House of Commons for Dunfermline East in 1983. He topped the Labour Party shadow-cabinet poll in 1989.

Brown /braʊn/ Capability (Lancelot) 1715–1783. English landscape gardener. He acquired his nickname because of his continual enthusiasm for the 'capabilities' of natural landscapes.

He advised on gardens of stately homes, including Blenheim, Oxfordshire; Stowe, Buckinghamshire; and Petworth, W Sussex, sometimes also contributing to the architectural designs.

Brown /braʊn/ Charles Brockden 1771–1810. US novelist and magazine editor. He introduced the American Indian into fiction and is called the 'father of the American novel' for his *Wieland* 1798, *Ormond* 1799, *Edgar Huntly* 1799, and *Arthur Mervyn* 1800. His works also pioneered the Gothic and fantastic traditions in US fiction.

Brown /braʊn/ Earle 1926– . US composer who pioneered graphic notation and mobile form during the 1950s, as in *Available Forms II* 1958 for ensemble and two conductors. He was an associate of John →Cage.

Brown /braʊn/ Ford Madox 1821–1893. British painter associated with the Pre- Raphaelite Brotherhood. His pictures include *The Last of England* 1855 (Birmingham Art Gallery) and *Work* 1852–65 (City Art Gallery, Manchester), packed with realistic detail and symbolic incident.

Brown /braʊn/ George, Baron George-Brown 1914–1985. British Labour politician. He entered Parliament in 1945, was briefly minister of works 1951, and contested the leadership of the party on the death of Gaitskell, but was defeated by Harold Wilson. He was secretary for economic affairs 1964–66 and foreign secretary 1966–68. He was created a life peer 1970.

Brown /braʊn/ James 1928– . US rhythm-and-blues and soul singer, a pioneer of funk. Staccato horn arrangements and shouted vocals characterize his hits, which include 'Please, Please, Please' 1956, 'Papa's Got a Brand New Bag' 1965, and 'Say It Loud, I'm Black and I'm Proud' 1968.

In 1988 he was arrested and charged with attempted assault for which he received a six-year prison sentence.

Brown /braʊn/ John 1800–1859. US slavery abolitionist. With 18 men, on the night of 16 Oct 1859, he seized the government arsenal at Harper's Ferry in W Virginia, apparently intending to distribute weapons to runaway slaves who would then defend the mountain stronghold, which Brown hoped would become a republic of former slaves. On 18 Oct the arsenal was stormed by US Marines under Col Robert E →Lee. Brown was tried and hanged on 2 Dec, becoming a martyr and the hero of the popular song 'John Brown's Body' about 1860.

Born in Connecticut, he settled as a farmer in Kansas in 1855. In 1856 he was responsible for the 'Pottawatomie massacre' when five proslavery farmers were killed. In 1858 he formed the plan for a refuge for runaway slaves in the mountains of Virginia.

Brown /braʊn/ John 1825–1883. Scottish servant and confidant of Queen Victoria from 1858.

Brown /braʊn/ Robert 1773–1858. Scottish botanist, a pioneer of plant classification and the first to describe and name the cell nucleus.

On an expedition to Australia in 1801 he collected 4,000 species of plant and later classified them using the 'natural' system of Bernard de Jussieu (1699–1777) rather than relying upon the system of Carolus →Linnaeus. The agitated movement of small particles suspended in water, now explained by kinetic theory, was described by Brown in 1827 and later became known as *Brownian movement*.

Browne /braʊn/ Hablot Knight 1815–1882. British illustrator, pseudonym Phiz, known for his illustrations of Charles Dickens's works.

Browne /braʊn/ Robert 1550–1633. English Puritan leader, founder of the Brownists. He founded communities in Norwich, East Anglia, and in the Netherlands which developed into present-day Congregationalism.

Browne, born in Stamford, Lincolnshire, preached in Norwich and then retired to Middelburg in the Netherlands, but returned after making his peace with the church and became master of Stamford Grammar School. In a work published in 1582 Browne advocated Congregationalist doctrine; he was imprisoned several times in 1581–82 for attacking Episcopalianism (church government by bishops). From 1591 he was a rector in Northamptonshire.

We all labour against our own cure; for death is the cure of all diseases.

Thomas Browne *Religio Medici* 1643

Browne /braʊn/ Thomas 1605–1682. English author and physician. Born in London, he travelled widely in Europe before settling in Norwich in 1637. His works display a richness of style as in *Religio Medici/The Religion of a Doctor* 1643, a justification of his profession; *Vulgar Errors* 1646, an examination of popular legend and superstition; *Urn Burial* and *The Garden of Cyrus* 1658; and *Christian Morals*, published posthumously in 1717.

Browning /braʊnɪŋ/ Robert 1812–1889. English poet, married to Elizabeth Barrett Browning. His work is characterized by the use of dramatic monologue and an interest in obscure literary and historical figures. It includes the play *Pippa Passes* 1841 and the poems 'The Pied Piper of Hamelin' 1842, 'My Last Duchess' 1842, 'Home Thoughts from Abroad' 1845, and 'Rabbi Ben Ezra' 1864.

Browning Robert Browning's works have influenced poets as disparate as Robert Frost and Ezra Pound. During Browning's lifetime, critical recognition came rapidly after 1864, and although his books never sold as well as his wife's or Tennyson's, he acquired a considerable and enthusiastic public.

Browning, born in Camberwell, London, wrote his first poem 'Pauline' 1833 under the influence of Shelley; it was followed by 'Paracelsus' 1835 and 'Sordello' 1840. From 1837 he achieved moderate success with his play *Strafford* and several other works. In the pamphlet series of *Bells and Pomegranates* 1841–46, which contained *Pippa Passes*, *Dramatic Lyrics* 1842 and *Dramatic Romances* 1845, he included the dramas *King Victor and King Charles*, *Return of the Druses*, and *Colombe's Birthday*.

In 1846 he met Elizabeth Barrett; they married the same year and went to Italy. There he wrote *Christmas Eve and Easter Day* 1850 and *Men and Women* 1855, the latter containing some of his finest love poems and dramatic monologues, which were followed by *Dramatis Personae* 1864 and *The Ring and the Book* 1868–69, based on an Italian murder story. After his wife's death in 1861 Browning settled in England and enjoyed an established reputation, although his later works, such as *Red-Cotton Night-Cap Country* 1873, *Dramatic Idylls* 1879–80, and *Asolando* 1889, prompted opposition by their rugged obscurity of style.

Grow old with me!
The best is yet to be.

Robert Browning *Rabbi ben Ezra*

Brubeck /bruːbek/ Dave (David Warren) 1920– . US jazz pianist, a student of the French composer Milhaud and Arnold Schoenberg, inventor of the 12-tone composition system. The Dave Brubeck Quartet (formed 1951) combined improvisation with classical discipline. Included in his large body of compositions is the internationally popular 'Take Five'.

Bruce /bruːs/ one of the chief Scottish noble houses. →Robert I (Robert the Bruce) and his son, David II, were both kings of Scotland descended from Robert de Bruis (died 1094), a Norman knight who arrived in England with William the Conqueror 1066.

Bruce /bruːs/ James 1730–1794. Scottish explorer, the first European to reach the source of the Blue Nile 1770, and to follow the river downstream to Cairo 1773.

Bruce Robert. King of Scotland; see →Robert I.

Bruce /bruːs/ Robert de, 5th Lord of Annandale 1210–1295. Scottish noble, one of the unsuccessful claimants to the throne at the death of Alexander II 1290. His grandson was →Robert I (the Bruce).

Bruce /bruːs/ Stanley Melbourne, 1st Viscount Bruce of Melbourne 1883–1967. Australian National Party politician, prime minister 1923–29. He was elected to parliament in 1918. As prime minister he introduced a number of social welfare measures.

Bruch /brʊx/ Max 1838–1920. German composer, professor at the Berlin Academy 1891. He wrote three operas including *Hermione* 1872. Among the most celebrated of his works are the *Kol Nidrei* for cello and orchestra, violin concertos, and many choral pieces.

Bruckner /'brʊknə/ (Joseph) Anton 1824–1896. Austrian Romantic composer. He was cathedral organist at Linz 1856–68, and from 1868 he was professor at the Vienna Conservatoire. His works include many choral pieces and 11 symphonies, the last unfinished. His compositions were influenced by Richard →Wagner and Beethoven.

Brueghel /'brɜːxəl/ family of Flemish painters. *Pieter Brueghel the Elder* (c. 1525–69) was one of the greatest artists of his time. He painted satirical and humorous pictures of peasant life, many of which include symbolic details illustrating folly and inhumanity, and a series of Months (five survive), including *Hunters in the Snow* (Kunsthistorisches Museum, Vienna).

The elder Pieter was nicknamed 'Peasant' Brueghel. Two of his sons were painters. *Pieter Brueghel the Younger* (1564–1638), called 'Hell' Brueghel, specialized in religious subjects, and another son, *Jan Brueghel* (1568–1625), called 'Velvet' Brueghel, painted flowers, landscapes, and seascapes.

Brulé /bruːle/ Étienne c. 1592–1632. French adventurer and explorer. He travelled with Samuel de →Champlain to the New World in 1608 and settled in Québec, where he lived with the Algonquin Indians. He explored the Great Lakes and travelled as far south as Chesapeake Bay. Returning north, he was killed by Huron Indians.

Brummell /'brʌməl/ Beau (George Bryan) 1778–1840. British dandy and leader of fashion. He introduced long trousers as conventional day and evening wear for men. A friend of the Prince of Wales, the future George IV, he later quarrelled with him. Gambling losses drove him in 1816 to exile in France, where he died in an asylum.

Brundtland Gro Harlem 1939– . Norwegian Labour politician. Environment minister 1974–76, she briefly took over as prime minister 1981, and was elected prime minister 1986 and again 1990. She chaired the World Commission on Environment and Development which produced the Brundtland Report, published as *Our Common Future* 1987. In 1992 she resigned as leader of the Norwegian Labour Party, a post she had held since 1981.

Brunel /bruːˈnel/ Isambard Kingdom 1806–1859. British engineer and inventor. In 1833 he became engineer to the Great Western Railway, which adopted the 2.1 m/7 ft gauge on his advice. He built the Clifton Suspension Bridge over the river Avon at Bristol and the Saltash Bridge over the river Tamar near Plymouth. His shipbuilding designs include the *Great Western* 1838, the first steamship to cross the Atlantic regularly; the *Great Britain* 1845, the first large iron ship to have a screw propeller; and the *Great Eastern* 1858, which laid the first transatlantic telegraph cable.

The son of Marc Brunel, he made major contributions in shipbuilding and bridge construction, and assisted his father in the Thames tunnel project. Brunel University in Uxbridge, London, is named after both father and son.

Brunel /bruːˈnel/ Marc Isambard 1769–1849. French-born British engineer and inventor, father of Isambard Kingdom Brunel. He constructed the Rotherhithe tunnel under the river Thames in London from Wapping to Rotherhithe 1825–43.

Brunel fled to the USA 1793 to escape the French Revolution. He became Chief Engineer in New York. In 1799 he moved to England to exploit a major new insight: pulley blocks were much needed by the navy. To manufacture them by hand required much labour and time; Brunel demonstrated that with specially designed machine tools 10 men could do the work of 100, more quickly, more cheaply, and yield a better product. Cheating partners and fire damage to his factory caused the business to fail and he was imprisoned for debt 1821. He spent the latter part of his life working on the Rotherhithe Tunnel.

Brunelleschi /ˌbruːnəˈleski/ Filippo 1377–1446. Italian Renaissance architect. One of the earliest and greatest Renaissance architects, he pioneered the scientific use of perspective. He was responsible for the construction of the dome of Florence

Cathedral (completed 1438), a feat deemed impossible by many of his contemporaries.

Bruning /ˈbruːnɪŋ/ Heinrich 1885–1970. German politician. Elected to the Reichstag (parliament) 1924, he led the Catholic Centre Party from 1929 and was federal chancellor 1930–32 when political and economic crisis forced his resignation.

Bruno Frank 1961– . English heavyweight boxer who challenged for the World Boxing Association (WBA) World Title against Tim Witherspoon in 1986 and for the Undisputed World Title against Mike Tyson in 1989. He retired 1989 but made a successful comeback 1992.

Bruno /ˈbruːnəʊ/ Giordano 1548–1600. Italian philosopher. He entered the Dominican order of monks 1563, but his sceptical attitude to Catholic doctrines forced him to flee Italy 1577. After visiting Geneva and Paris, he lived in England 1583–85, where he wrote some of his finest works. He was arrested by the Inquisition 1593 in Venice and burned at the stake for his adoption of Copernican astronomy and his heretical religious views.

Bruno, St /ˈbruːnəʊ/ 1030–1101. German founder of the monastic Catholic Carthusian order. He was born in Cologne, became a priest, and controlled the cathedral school of Rheims 1057–76. Withdrawing to the mountains near Grenoble after an ecclesiastical controversy, he founded the monastery at Chartreuse in 1084. Feast day 6 Oct.

Brussilov /ˈbruːˈsiːlɒf/ Aleksei Alekseevich 1853–1926. Russian general, military leader in World War I who achieved major successes against the Austro-Hungarian forces in 1916. Later he was commander of the Red Army 1920, which drove the Poles to within a few miles of Warsaw before being repulsed by them.

Brutus /ˈbruːtəs/ Marcus Junius c. 78–42 BC. Roman soldier, a supporter of →Pompey (against →Caesar) in the civil war. Pardoned by Caesar and raised to high office by him, he nevertheless plotted Caesar's assassination to restore the purity of the Republic. Brutus committed suicide when he was defeated (with →Cassius) by →Mark Antony, Caesar's lieutenant, at Philippi 42 BC.

Bryan /ˈbraɪən/ William Jennings 1860–1925. US politician who campaigned unsuccessfully for the presidency three times: as the Populist and Democratic nominee 1896, as an anti-imperialist Democrat 1900, and as a Democratic tariff reformer 1908. He served as President Wilson's secretary of state 1913–15. In the early 1920s he was a leading fundamentalist and opponent of Clarence Darrow in the Scopes monkey trial.

Bryant /ˈbraɪənt/ Arthur 1899–1985. British historian who produced studies of Restoration figures such as Pepys and Charles II, and a series covering the Napoleonic Wars including *The Age of Elegance* 1950.

Bryant /ˈbraɪənt/ David 1931– . English flat-green (lawn) bowls player. He has won every honour the game has offered, including four outdoor world titles (three singles and one triples) 1966–88 and three indoor titles 1979–81.

Bryant /ˈbraɪnt/ William Cullen 1794–1878. US poet and literary figure. His most famous poem, 'Thanatopsis', was published 1817. He was co-owner and co-editor of the *New York Evening Post* 1829–78 and was involved in Democratic party politics. However, his resolute opposition to slavery converted him to Republicanism at the inception of the party 1856.

Born in Cummington, Massachusetts, Bryant briefly attended Williams College and was trained as a lawyer but throughout his life maintained a deep interest in poetry.

Bryce /braɪs/ James, 1st Viscount Bryce 1838–1922. British Liberal politician, professor of civil law at Oxford University 1870–93. He entered Parliament 1880, holding office under Gladstone and Rosebery. He was author of *The American Commonwealth* 1888, ambassador to Washington 1907–13, and improved US–Canadian relations.

Brynner /ˈbrɪnə/ Yul 1915–1985. Actor, in the USA from 1940, who made a shaven head his trademark. He played the king in *The King and I* both on stage 1951 and on film 1956 (Academy Award), and was the leader of *The Magnificent Seven* 1960.

Although his origins were deliberately shrouded in mystery he is believed to have been born in Sakhalin, an island east of Siberia and north of Japan. He later acknowledged a gypsy background. He made his film debut in a B picture *Port of New York* 1949. His other films include *Taras Bulba* 1962, and *Westworld* 1973.

Bryusov /briˈuːsɒf/ Valery 1873–1924. Russian Symbolist poet, novelist and critic, author of *The Fiery Angel* 1908.

Brzezinski /brəˈʒɪnski/ Zbigniew 1928– . US Democrat politician, born in Poland; he taught at Harvard University, USA, and became a US citizen 1949. He was national security adviser to President Carter 1977–81 and chief architect of Carter's human-rights policy.

Buber /ˈbuːbə/ Martin 1878–1965. Austrian-born Israeli philosopher, a Zionist and advocate of the reappraisal of ancient Jewish thought in contemporary terms. His book *I and Thou* 1923 posited a direct dialogue between the individual and God; it had great impact on Christian and Jewish theology. When forced by the Nazis to abandon a professorship in comparative religion at Frankfurt, he went to Jerusalem and taught social philosophy at the Hebrew University 1937–51.

Bubka Sergey 1963– . Russian pole vaulter who achieved the world's first six-metre vault in 1985. World champion in 1983, he was unbeaten in a major event from 1981 to 1990. From 1984 he has broken the world record on 32 occasions.

Bucer /ˈbutsə/ Martin 1491–1551. German Protestant reformer, Regius professor of divinity at Cambridge University from 1549, who tried to reconcile the views of his fellow Protestants Luther and Zwingli with the significance of the eucharist.

Buchan /ˈbʌxən, ˈbʌkən/ John, Baron Tweedsmuir 1875–1940. Scottish politician and author. Called to the Bar 1901, he was Conservative member of Parliament for the Scottish universities 1927–35, and governor general of Canada 1934–40. His adventure stories, today criticized for their anti-semitism, include *The Thirty-Nine Steps* 1915, *Greenmantle* 1916, and *The Three Hostages* 1924.

Buchanan /bəˈkænən/ George 1506–1582. Scottish humanist. Forced to flee to France 1539 owing to some satirical verses on the Franciscans, he returned to Scotland about 1562 as tutor to Mary, Queen of Scots. He became principal of St Leonard's College, St Andrews 1566, and wrote *Rerum Scoticarum Historia/A History of Scotland* 1582, which was biased against →Mary, Queen of Scots.

Buchanan /bəˈkænən/ Jack 1891–1957. British musical-comedy actor. His songs such as 'Good-Night Vienna' epitomized the period between World Wars I and II.

Buchanan /bjuˈkæñn/ James 1791–1868. 15th president of the USA 1857–61, a Democrat. He was a member of the US House of Representatives 1821–31 and was US minister to Russia 1832–34 when he was elected to the Senate. Adhering to a policy of compromise on the issue of slavery, he left his Senate seat to serve as US secretary of state during the Mexican War (1846–48). Nominated by the Democrats and elected president 1856, he could do little to avert the secession of the South

over the issue of slavery, precipitating the outbreak of the Civil War 1861.

Born near Mercersburg, Pennsylvania, USA, Buchanan was trained as a lawyer and was admitted to the bar 1812. He served as a member of the state legislature 1813–16.

Buchman /ˈbʊkmən/ Frank N D 1878–1961. US Christian evangelist. In 1938 he launched in London the anticommunist campaign, the Moral Re-Armament movement.

Buchner /ˈbʊxnə/ Eduard 1860–1917. German chemist who researched the process of fermentation. In 1897 he observed that fermentation could be produced mechanically, by cell-free extracts. Buchner argued that it was not the whole yeast cell that produced fermentation, but only the presence of the enzyme he named zymase. Nobel prize 1907.

Buck /bʌk/ Pearl S(ydenstricker) 1892–1973. US novelist. Daughter of missionaries to China, she spent much of her life there and wrote novels about Chinese life, such as *East Wind–West Wind* 1930 and *The Good Earth* 1931, for which she received a Pulitzer prize 1932. She received the Nobel Prize for Literature 1938.

Buckingham /ˈbʌkɪŋəm/ George Villiers, 1st Duke of Buckingham 1592–1628. English courtier, adviser to James I and later Charles I. After Charles's accession, Buckingham attempted to form a Protestant coalition in Europe, which led to war with France, but he failed to relieve the Protestants (Huguenots) besieged in La Rochelle 1627. This added to his unpopularity with Parliament, and he was assassinated.

Introduced to the court of James I 1614, he soon became his favourite and was made Earl of Buckingham 1617 and a duke 1623. He failed to arrange the marriage of Prince Charles and the Infanta of Spain 1623, but on returning to England negotiated Charles's alliance with Henrietta Maria, sister of the French king. His policy on the French Protestants was attacked in Parliament, and when about to sail again for La Rochelle he was assassinated in Portsmouth.

Buckingham /ˈbʌkɪŋəm/ George Villiers, 2nd Duke of Buckingham 1628–1687. English politician, a member of the Cabal (group of king's counsellors) under Charles II. A dissolute son of the first duke, he was brought up with the royal children. His play *The Rehearsal* satirized the style of the poet Dryden, who portrayed him as Zimri in *Absalom and Achitophel*.

Buckley /ˈbʌkli/ William 1780–1856. Australian convict who escaped from Port Phillip and lived 1803–35 among the Aborigines before giving himself up, hence *Buckley's chance* meaning an 'outside chance'.

Buckley /ˈbʌkli/ William F(rank) 1925– . US conservative political writer, novelist, and founder-editor of the *National Review* 1955. In

Buchanan A great scholar, Buchanan had strong leanings towards Protestantism and was imprisoned by the Inquisition in Portugal. Despite this, he returned to Scotland to be tutor to the Catholic Mary, Queen of Scots.

such books as *Up from Liberalism* 1959, and in a weekly television debate *Firing Line*, he represented the 'intellectual' right-wing, antiliberal stance in US political thought.

Budaeus /bu:ˈdi:əs/ Latin form of the name of Guillaume Budé 1467–1540. French scholar. He persuaded Francis I to found the Collège de France, and also the library that formed the nucleus of the French national library, the Bibliothèque Nationale.

Buddha /ˈbʊdə/ 'enlightened one', title of Prince *Gautama Siddhārtha c.* 563–483 BC. Religious leader, founder of Buddhism, born at Lumbini in Nepal. At the age of 29 he left his wife and son and a life of luxury, to escape from the material burdens of existence. After six years of austerity he realized that asceticism, like overindulgence, was futile, and chose the middle way of meditation. He became enlightened under a bo, or bodhi, tree near Buddh Gaya in Bihar, India. He began teaching at Varanasi, and founded the Sangha, or order of monks. He spent the rest of his life travelling around N India, and died at Kusinagara in Uttar Pradesh.

The Buddha's teaching consisted of the Four Noble Truths: the fact of frustration or suffering; that suffering has a cause; that it can be ended; and that it can be ended by following the Noble Eightfold Path–right views, right intention, right speech, right action, right livelihood, right effort, right mindfulness, and right concentration – eventually arriving at nirvana, the extinction of all craving for things of the senses and release from the cycle of rebirth.

The life of a creature passes like the torrent in the mountain and the lightning in the sky.

Buddha attributed

Budge /bʌdʒ/ Donald 1915– . US tennis player. He was the first to perform the Grand Slam when he won the Wimbledon, French, US, and Australian championships all in 1938.

He won 14 Grand Slam events, including the Wimbledon singles twice.

Buffet /buːˈfeɪ/ Bernard 1928– . French figurative painter who created distinctive, thin, spiky forms with bold, dark outlines. He was a precocious talent in the late 1940s.

Buffon /buːˈfɒn/ George Louis Leclerc, Comte de 1707–1778. French naturalist and author of the 18th century's most significant work of natural history, the 44-volume *Histoire naturelle* (1749–67). In *The Epochs of Nature*, one of the volumes, he questioned biblical chronology for the first time, and raised the Earth's age from the traditional figure of 6,000 years to the seemingly colossal estimate of 75,000 years.

Bujones /buːˈhəʊnes/ Fernando 1955– . US ballet dancer who joined American Ballet Theater 1972. A virtuoso performer, he has danced leading roles both in the major classics and in contemporary ballets, including *Swan Lake*, *Bayadere*, and *Fancy Free*.

Bukharin /bʊˈxɑːrɪn/ Nikolai Ivanovich 1888–1938. Soviet politician and theorist. A moderate, he was the chief Bolshevik thinker after Lenin. Executed on Stalin's orders for treason 1938, he was posthumously rehabilitated 1988.

He wrote the major defence of war communism in his *Economics of the Transition Period* 1920. He drafted the Soviet constitution of 1936 but in 1938 was imprisoned and tried for treason in one of Stalin's 'show trials'. He pleaded guilty to treason, but defended his moderate policies and denied criminal charges. Nevertheless, he was executed, as were all other former members of Lenin's Politburo except Trotsky, who was murdered, and Stalin himself.

Bulfinch /ˈbʊlfɪntʃ/ Charles 1763–1844. US architect. He became one of New England's leading architects after his design for the Massachusetts State House was accepted 1787. He designed the Hollis Street Church, Harvard's University Hall, the Massachusetts General Hospital, and the Connecticut State House. In 1817 he was appointed architect of the US Capitol by President Monroe.

Born in Boston, Bulfinch was educated at Harvard and travelled widely in Europe. Involved in the municipal affairs of Boston, Bulfinch served on its board of selectmen 1791–1817.

Bulgakov /bʊlˈɡɑːkɒf/ Mikhail Afanasyevich 1891–1940. Russian novelist and playwright. His novel *The White Guard* 1924, dramatized as *The Days of the Turbins* 1926, deals with the Revolution and the civil war.

His satiric approach made him unpopular with the Stalin regime, and he was unpublished from the 1930s. *The Master and Margarita*, a fantasy about the devil in Moscow, was not published until 1967.

Bulganin /bʊlˈɡɑːnɪn/ Nikolai 1895–1975. Soviet politician and military leader. His career began in 1918 when he joined the Cheka, the Soviet secret police. He helped to organize Moscow's defence in World War II, became a marshal of the USSR 1947, and was minister of defence 1947–49 and 1953–55. On the fall of Malenkov he became prime minister (chair of Council of Ministers) 1955–58 until ousted by Khrushchev.

Bull /bʊl/ John *c.* 1562–1628. British composer, organist, and virginalist. Most of his output is for keyboard, and includes 'God Save the King'. He also wrote sacred vocal music.

Bull /bʊl/ Olaf 1883–1933. Norwegian lyric poet, son of humorist and fiction writer Jacob Breda Bull (1853–1930). He often celebrated his birthplace Christiania (now Oslo) in his poetry.

Bunsen Robert Wilhelm Bunsen, German chemist and physicist. As well as the Bunsen burner, he invented a grease-spot photometer (a means of comparing the intensities of two light sources), an electric cell and, with Gustav Kirchhoff, the method of spectrum analysis which facilitated the discovery of new elements.

Buller /ˈbʊlə/ Redvers Henry 1839–1908. British commander against the Boers in the South African War 1899–1902. He was defeated at Colenso and Spion Kop, but relieved Ladysmith; he was superseded by Lord Roberts.

Bülow /ˈbjuːləʊ/ Bernhard, Prince von 1849–1929. German diplomat and politician. He was chancellor of the German Empire 1900–09 under Kaiser Wilhelm II and, holding that self-interest was the only rule for any state, adopted attitudes to France and Russia that unintentionally reinforced the trend towards opposing European power groups: the Triple Entente (Britain, France, Russia) and Triple Alliance (Germany, Austria–Hungary, Italy).

Bülow /ˈbjuːləʊ/ Hans (Guido) Frieherr von 1830–1894. German conductor and pianist. He studied with Richard →Wagner and Franz →Liszt, and in 1857 married Cosima, daughter of Liszt. From 1864 he served Ludwig II of Bavaria, conducting first performances of Wagner's *Tristan und Isolde* and *Die Meistersinger*. His wife left him and married Wagner 1870.

Bulwer-Lytton /ˈbʊlwə ˈlɪtn/ Edward George Earle Lytton, 1st Baron Lytton 1803–1873. See →Lytton.

Bunche /bʌntʃ/ Ralph 1904–1971. US diplomat. Grandson of a slave, he was principal director of the UN Department of Trusteeship 1947–54, and UN undersecretary acting as mediator in Palestine 1948–49 and as special representative in the

Congo 1960. He taught at Harvard and Howard universities and was involved in the planning of the United Nations. In 1950 he was awarded the Nobel Prize for Peace, the first awarded to a black man.

Bundelas /bʊnˈdeɪləz/ Rajput clan prominent in the 14th century, which gave its name to the Bundelkhand in N central India. The clan had replaced the Chandelā dynasty in the 11th century and continued to resist the attacks of other Indian rulers until coming under British control after 1812.

Bunin /ˈbuːnɪn/ Ivan Alexeyevich 1870–1953. Russian writer, author of *Derevnya/The Village* 1910, which tells of the passing of peasant life; and *Gospodin iz San Frantsisko/The Gentleman from San Francisco* 1916 (about the death of a millionaire on Capri), for which he received a Nobel prize 1933. He was also a poet and translated Byron into Russian.

Bunsen /ˈbʊnzən/ Robert Wilhelm 1811–1899. German chemist credited with the invention of the *Bunsen burner*. His name is also given to the carbon–zinc electric cell, which he invented 1841 for use in arc lamps. In 1859 he discovered two new elements, caesium and rubidium.

Bunshaft /ˈbʌnʃaft/ Gordon 1909–1990. US architect whose Modernist buildings include the first to be completely enclosed in curtain walling (walls which hang from a rigid steel frame), the Lever Building 1952 in New York. He also designed the Heinz Company's UK headquarters 1965 at Hayes Park, London.

Buñuel /buːˈnjuel/ Luis 1900–1983. Spanish Surrealist film director. He collaborated with Salvador Dali on *Un Chien andalou/An Andalusian Dog* 1928 and *L'Age d'or/The Golden Age* 1930, and established his solo career with *Los olvidados/The Young and the Damned* 1950. His works are often anticlerical, with black humour and erotic imagery.

Later films include *Le Charme discret de la bourgeoisie/The Discreet Charm of the Bourgeoisie* 1972 and *Cet Obscur Objet du désir/That Obscure Object of Desire* 1977.

Bunyan /ˈbʌnjən/ John 1628–1688. English author. A Baptist, he was imprisoned in Bedford 1660–72 for unlicensed preaching. During a second jail sentence 1675 he started to write *The Pilgrim's Progress*, the first part of which was published 1678. Other works include *Grace Abounding* 1666, *The Life and Death of Mr Badman* 1680, and *The Holy War* 1682.

At 16, during the Civil War, he was conscripted into the Parliamentary army. Released 1646, he passed through a period of religious doubt before joining the Baptists 1653. In 1660 he was committed to Bedford county jail for preaching, where he remained for 12 years, refusing all offers of release conditional on his not preaching again. During his confinement he wrote *Grace Abounding* describing his early spiritual struggles. Set free

1672, he was elected pastor of the Bedford congregation, but in 1675 he was again arrested and imprisoned for six months in the jail on Bedford Bridge, where he began *The Pilgrim's Progress*. The book was an instant success, and a second part followed 1684.

Burbage /ˈbɜːbɪdʒ/ Richard *c.* 1567–1619. English actor, thought to have been →Shakespeare's original Hamlet, Othello, and Lear. He also appeared in first productions of works by Ben Jonson, Thomas Kyd, and John Webster. His father *James Burbage* (*c.* 1530–1597) built the first English playhouse, known as 'the Theatre'; his brother *Cuthbert Burbage* (*c.* 1566–1636) built the original Globe Theatre 1599 in London.

Burckhardt /ˈbʊəkhɑːt/ Jacob 1818–1897. Swiss art historian, professor of history at Basel University 1858–93. His *The Civilization of the Renaissance in Italy* 1860, intended as part of a study of world cultural history, influenced thought on the significance of this period.

Burckhardt /ˈbʊəkhɑːt/ Johann Ludwig 1784–1817. Swiss traveller whose knowledge of Arabic enabled him to travel throughout the Middle East, visiting Mecca disguised as a Muslim pilgrim 1814. In 1817 he discovered the ruins of Petra.

Burger /ˈbɜːgə/ Warren Earl 1907– . US jurist and chief justice of the United States 1969–86. His term in the US Supreme Court was marked by a conservative turn in civil-rights matters. His majority decision in the Watergate tapes case *US v Nixon* 1974 was instrumental in bringing about Nixon's resignation.

Bürger /ˈbjʊəgə/ Gottfried 1747–1794. German Romantic poet, remembered for his ballad 'Lenore' 1773.

Burges /ˈbɜːdʒɪz/ William 1827–1881. British Gothic revivalist architect. His chief works are Cork Cathedral 1862–76, additions to and remodelling of Cardiff Castle 1865, and Castle Coch near Cardiff 1875. His style is characterized by sumptuous interiors with carving, painting, and gilding.

Burgess /ˈbɜːdʒɪs/ Anthony. Pen name of Anthony John Burgess Wilson 1917– . British novelist, critic, and composer. His prolific work includes *A Clockwork Orange* 1962, set in a future London terrorized by teenage gangs, and the panoramic *Earthly Powers* 1980. His vision has been described as bleak and pessimistic, but his work is also comic and satiric, as in his novels featuring the poet Enderby.

Burgess /ˈbɜːdʒɪs/ Guy (Francis de Moncy) 1910–1963. British spy, a diplomat recruited by the USSR as an agent. He was linked with Kim →Philby, Donald Maclean (1913–1983), and Anthony →Blunt.

Burgh /də ˈbɜːg/ Hubert de died 1243. English justiciar and regent of England. He began his career in the administration of Richard I, and was promoted to the justiciarship by King John; he remained in that position under Henry III from 1216 until his dismissal. He was a supporter of King John against the barons, and ended French intervention in England by his defeat of the French fleet in the Strait of Dover 1217. He reorganized royal administration and the Common Law.

Burghley /ˈbɜːli/ William Cecil, Baron Burghley 1520–1598. English politician, chief adviser to Elizabeth I as secretary of state from 1558 and Lord High Treasurer from 1572. He was largely responsible for the religious settlement of 1559, and took a leading role in the events preceding the execution of Mary Queen of Scots 1587.

One of Edward VI's secretaries, he lost office under Queen Mary, but on Queen Elizabeth's succession became one of her most trusted ministers. He carefully avoided a premature breach with Spain in the difficult period leading up to the attack by the Spanish Armada 1588, did a great deal towards abolishing monopolies and opening up trade, and was created Baron Burghley 1571.

Burgoyne /bɜːˈgɔɪn/ John 1722–1792. British general and dramatist. He served in the American War of Independence and surrendered 1777 to the colonists at Saratoga, New York State, in one of the pivotal battles of the war. He wrote comedies, among them *The Maid of the Oaks* 1775 and *The Heiress* 1786. He figures in George Bernard Shaw's play *The Devil's Disciple* 1896.

Burke /bɜːk/ Edmund 1729–1797. British Whig politician and political theorist, born in Dublin, Ireland. In Parliament from 1765, he opposed the government's attempts to coerce the American colonists, for example in *Thoughts on the Present Discontents* 1770, and supported the emancipation of Ireland, but denounced the French Revolution, for example in *Reflections on the Revolution in France* 1790.

Burke wrote *A Philosophical Inquiry into the Origin of our Ideas on the Sublime and Beautiful* 1756, on aesthetics. He was paymaster of the forces in Rockingham's government 1782 and in the Fox–North coalition 1783, and after the collapse of the latter spent the rest of his career in opposition. He attacked Warren Hastings's misgovernment in India and promoted his impeachment. Burke defended his inconsistency in supporting the American but not the French Revolution in his *Appeal from the New to the Old Whigs* 1791 and *Letter to a Noble Lord* 1796, and attacked the suggestion of peace with France in *Letters on a Regicide Peace* 1795–97. He retired 1794. He was a skilled orator and is regarded by British Conservatives as the greatest of their political theorists.

Burke /bɜːk/ John 1787–1848. First publisher, in 1826, of *Burke's Peerage* (full title *Burke's Genealogical and Heraldic History of the Peerage, Baronetage, and Knightage of the United Kingdom*).

Burke /bɜːk/ Martha Jane *c.* 1852–1903. Real name of US heroine ➔Calamity Jane.

Burke /bɜːk/ Robert O'Hara 1820–1861. Australian explorer who made the first south-north crossing of Australia (from Victoria to the Gulf of Carpentaria), with William Wills (1834–1861). Both died on the return journey, and only one of their party survived. He was born in Galway, Ireland, and became a police inspector in the goldfields of Victoria.

Burke /bɜːk/ William 1792–1829. Irish murderer. He and his partner William Hare, living in Edinburgh, sold the body of an old man who had died from natural causes in their lodging house. After that, they increased their supplies by murdering at least 15 people. Burke was hanged on the evidence of Hare. Hare is said to have died a beggar in London in the 1860s.

Burlington /bɜːlɪŋtən/ Richard Boyle, 3rd Earl of Burlington 1694–1753. British architectural patron and architect; one of the premier exponents of the Palladian style in Britain. His buildings, such as Chiswick House, London, 1725–29, are characterized by absolute adherence to the Classical rules. His major protégé was William ➔Kent.

Burnaby /bɜːnəbi/ Frederick 1842–1885. English soldier, traveller, and founder of the weekly critical journal *Vanity Fair*. He travelled to Spain, Sudan, and Russian Asia during his leave from the Horse Guards. His books include *A Ride to Khiva* 1876 and *On Horseback through Asia Minor* 1877. Burnaby joined the British Nile expedition to relieve General Gordon, under siege in Khartoum, Sudan, and was killed in action at the battle of Abu Klea.

Burne-Jones /bɜːn ˈdʒəʊnz/ Edward Coley 1833–1898. English painter. In 1856 he was apprenticed to the Pre-Raphaelite painter Dante Gabriel ➔Rossetti, who remained a dominant influence. His paintings, inspired by legend and myth, were characterized by elongated forms as in King Cophetua and the Beggar Maid 1880–84 (Tate Gallery, London). He later moved towards Symbolism. He also designed tapestries and stained glass in association with William ➔Morris.

The best collection of his work is in the Birmingham City Art Gallery.

Burnell /bel bɜːˈnel/ (Susan) Jocelyn (Bell) 1943– . British astronomer. In 1967 she discovered the first pulsar (rapidly flashing star) with Antony ➔Hewish and colleagues at Cambridge University, England.

Burnes /bɜːnz/ Alexander 1805–1841. Scottish soldier, linguist, diplomat, and traveller in Central Asia. Following journeys to Rajputana and Lajhore he led an expedition across the Hindu Kush to Bokhara described in his *Travels into Bokhara* 1834. In 1836–37 he led a diplomatic mission to the Afghan leader Dost Mohammed,

described in his book *Kabul* 1842. He was killed in Kabul during a rising that sparked off the first Afghan War.

Burnet /bɜːnɪt/ Gilbert 1643–1715. English historian and bishop, author of *History of His Own Time* 1723–24. His Whig views having brought him into disfavour, he retired to the Netherlands on the accession of James II and became the confidential adviser of William of Orange, with whom he sailed to England 1688. He was appointed bishop of Salisbury 1689.

Burnet /bɜːnɪt/ Macfarlane 1899–1985. Australian physician, an authority on immunology and viral diseases. He was awarded the Order of Merit 1958 in recognition of his work on such diseases as influenza, poliomyelitis, and cholera, and shared the 1960 Nobel Prize for Medicine with Peter Medawar for his work on skin grafting.

Burnett /bəˈnet/ Frances (Eliza) Hodgson 1849–1924. English writer who emigrated with her family to the USA 1865. Her novels for children include the rags-to-riches tale *Little Lord Fauntleroy* 1886 and the sentimental *The Secret Garden* 1909.

Burney /bɜːni/ Frances (Fanny) 1752–1840. English novelist and diarist, daughter of musician Dr Charles Burney (1726–1814). She achieved success with *Evelina*, published anonymously 1778, became a member of Dr ➔Johnson's circle, received a post at court from Queen Charlotte, and in 1793 married the French émigré General d'Arblay. She published three further novels, *Cecilia* 1782, *Camilla* 1796, and *The Wanderer* 1814; her diaries and letters appeared 1842.

Burnham /bɜːnəm/ Forbes 1923–1985. Guyanese Marxist-Leninist politician. He was prime minister 1964–80, leading the country to independence 1966 and declaring it the world's first cooperative republic 1970. He was executive president 1980–85. Resistance to the US landing in Grenada 1983 was said to be due to his forewarning the Grenadans of the attack.

Burnham /bɜːnəm/ James 1905–1987. US philosopher who argued in *The Managerial Revolution* 1941 that world control is passing from politicians and capitalists to the new class of business executives, the managers.

Burns /bɜːnz/ John 1858–1943. British labour leader, sentenced to six weeks' imprisonment for his part in the Trafalgar Square demonstration on 'Bloody Sunday' 13 Nov 1887, and leader of the strike in 1889 securing the 'dockers' tanner' (wage of 6d per hour). An Independent Labour member of Parliament 1892–1918, he was the first working-class person to be a member of the cabinet, as president of the Local Government Board 1906–14.

Burns /bɜːnz/ Robert 1759–1796. Scottish poet who used the Scots dialect at a time when it was not considered suitably 'elevated' for literature. Burns's first volume, *Poems, Chiefly in the Scottish Dialect*, appeared 1786. In addition to his poetry, Burns wrote or adapted many songs, including 'Auld Lang Syne'.

Burns's fame rests equally on his poems (such as 'Holy Willie's Prayer', 'Tam o' Shanter', 'The Jolly Beggars', and 'To a Mouse') and his songs – sometimes wholly original, sometimes adaptations – of which he contributed some 300 to Johnson's *Scots Musical Museum* 1787–1803 and Thomson's *Scottish Airs with Poetry* 1793–1811.

Born at Alloway near Ayr, he became joint tenant with his brother of his late father's farm at Mossgiel in 1784, but it was unsuccessful. Following the publication of his first volume of poems in 1786 he farmed at Ellisland, near Dumfries. He became district excise officer on the failure of his farm in 1791. Burns Night is celebrated on 25 January.

Burns /bɜːnz/ Terence 1944– . British economist. A monetarist, he was director of the London Business School for Economic Forecasting 1976–79, and became chief economic adviser to the Thatcher government 1980.

Burnside /bɜːnsaɪd/ Ambrose Everett 1824–1881. US military leader and politician. He was appointed brigadier general in the Union army soon after the outbreak of the Civil War 1861. Named as George →McClellan's successor as commander of the Army of the Potomac, Burnside served briefly in that position before being transferred to the West. He was governor of Rhode Island 1866–69 and US Senator 1874–81.

Born in Liberty, Indiana, Burnside attended West Point military academy. Blamed for the Union defeat at Petersburg 1864, Burnside retired from active service. His distinctive side whiskers and moustache framing a clean-shaven chin became popularly known as 'burnsides', of which 'sideburns' is a modification.

Burr /bɜː/ Aaron 1756–1836. US politician, Republican vice president 1800–04, in which year he killed his political rival Alexander →Hamilton in a duel.

Burr was born in Newark, New Jersey of an eminent Puritan family. He was on George Washington's staff during the American Revolution but was critical of the general and was distrusted in turn. He tied with Thomas Jefferson in the presidential election of 1800, but Alexander Hamilton, Burr's longtime adversary, influenced the House of Representatives to vote Jefferson in, Burr becoming vice president. After killing Hamilton he fled to South Carolina, but returned briefly to Washington to complete his term of office.

In 1807 Burr was tried and acquitted of treason charges, which implicated him variously in a scheme to conquer Mexico, or part of Florida, or to rule over a seceded Louisiana. He spent some years in Europe, seeking British and French aid in overthrowing Jefferson, but reentered the USA

1812 under an assumed name. He died in poverty at the age of 80.

Burr /bɜː/ Raymond 1917– . Canadian actor who graduated from playing elegant villains to the heroes Perry Mason and Ironside in the long-running television series of the same names. He played the murderer in Alfred Hitchcock's *Rear Window* 1954.

Burra /bʌrə/ Edward 1905–1976. English painter devoted to themes of city life, its hustle, humour, and grimy squalor. *The Snack Bar* 1930 (Tate Gallery, London) and his watercolour scenes of Harlem, New York, 1933–34, are characteristic. Postwar works include religious paintings and landscapes.

Burroughs /bʌrəuz/ Edgar Rice 1875–1950. US novelist. He wrote *Tarzan of the Apes* 1914, the story of an aristocratic child lost in the jungle and reared by apes, and followed it with over 20 more books about the Tarzan character. He also wrote a series of novels about life on Mars.

Burroughs /bʌrəuz/ William S 1914– . US novelist. He 'dropped out' and, as part of the Beat Generation, wrote *Junkie* 1953, describing his addiction to heroin; *The Naked Lunch* 1959; *The Soft Machine* 1961; and *Dead Fingers Talk* 1963. His later novels include *Queer* and *Mind Wars*, both 1985.

Burroughs /bʌrəuz/ William Steward 1857–1898. US industrialist who invented the first hand-operated adding machine to give printed results.

Burt /bɜːt/ Cyril Lodowic 1883–1971. British psychologist. A specialist in child and mental development, he argued in *The Young Delinquent* 1925 the importance of social and environmental factors in delinquency. After his death it was claimed that he had falsified experimental results in an attempt to prove his theory that intelligence is largely inherited.

Burton /bɜːtn/ Richard Francis 1821–1890. British explorer and translator (he knew 35 oriental languages). He travelled mainly in the Middle East and NE Africa, often disguised as a Muslim; made two attempts to find the source of the Nile, 1855 and 1857–58 (on the second, with John →Speke, he reached Lake Tanganyika); and wrote many travel books. He translated oriental erotica and the *Arabian Nights* 1885–88.

After military service in India, Burton explored the Arabian peninsula and Somaliland. In 1853 he visited Mecca and Medina disguised as an Afghan pilgrim; he was then commissioned by the Foreign Office to explore the sources of the Nile. Later travels took him to North and South America. His translations include the *Kama Sutra of Vatsyayana* 1883 and *The Perfumed Garden* 1886. His wife, who had accompanied him on some journeys, burned his unpublished manuscripts and diaries after his death.

Burton /ˈbɜːtn/ Richard. Stage name of Richard Jenkins 1925–1984. Welsh actor of stage and screen. He had a rich, dramatic voice. Films in which he appeared with his wife, Elizabeth →Taylor, include *Cleopatra* 1962 and *Who's Afraid of Virginia Woolf?* 1966. Among his later films are *Equus* 1977 and *Nineteen Eighty-Four* 1984.

His films include *The Spy Who Came in from the Cold* 1966, and *Richard Wagner* 1982. His rendition of Dylan Thomas's *Under Milk Wood* for radio was another of his career highspots.

Burton /ˈbɜːtn/ Robert 1577–1640. English philosopher who wrote an analysis of depression, *Anatomy of Melancholy* 1621, a compendium of information on the medical and religious opinions of the time, much used by later authors.

Born in Leicester, he was educated at Oxford, and remained there for the rest of his life as a fellow of Christ Church College.

Busby /ˈbʌzbi/ Richard 1606–1695. English headmaster of Westminster school from 1640, renowned for his use of flogging. Among his pupils were Dryden, Locke, Atterbury, and Prior.

Bush /bʊʃ/ Alan (Dudley) 1900– . English composer. A student of John →Ireland, he later adopted a didactic simplicity in his compositions in line with his Marxist beliefs. He has written a large number of works for orchestra, voice, and chamber groups.

His operas include *Wat Tyler* 1952 and *Men of Blackmoor* 1956.

Bush /bʊʃ/ George 1924– . 41st president of the USA 1989–93, a Republican. He was director of the Central Intelligence Agency (CIA) 1976–81 and US vice president 1981–89. As president, his response to the Soviet leader Gorbachev's diplomatic initiatives were initially criticized as inadequate, but his sending of US troops to depose his former ally, General →Noriega of Panama, proved a popular move at home. Success in the 1991 Gulf War against Iraq further raised his standing. Domestic economic problems 1991–92 were followed by his defeat in the 1992 presidential elections by Democrat Bill Clinton.

Bush, son of a Connecticut senator, moved to Texas 1948 to build up an oil-drilling company. A congressman 1967–70, he was appointed US ambassador to the United Nations (1971–73) and Republican national chair (1973–74) by President Nixon, and special envoy to China 1974–75 under President Ford.

During Bush's time as head of the CIA, General Noriega of Panama was on its payroll, and Panama was later used as a channel for the secret supply of arms to Iran and the Nicaraguan Contra guerrillas. Evidence came to light 1987 linking Bush with the Irangate scandal. But Noriega became uncontrollable and, in Dec 1989, Bush sent an invasion force to Panama and set up a puppet government.

As president, Bush soon reneged on his election pledge of 'no new taxes', but not before he had introduced a cut in capital-gains tax which predominantly benefited the richest 3% of the population. In 1990, having proclaimed a 'new world order' as the Cold War was officially declared over and facing economic recession in the USA, he sent a large army to Saudi Arabia after Iraq's annexation of Kuwait, and ruled out negotiations. His response to Iraq's action contrasted sharply with his policy of support for Israel's refusal to honour various UN Security Council resolutions calling for its withdrawal from occupied territories, but the ousting of Iraqi forces from Kuwait was greeted as a great US victory. Despite this success, the signing of the long-awaited Strategic Arms Reduction Treaty July 1991, and Bush's unprecedented unilateral reduction in US nuclear weapons two months later, his popularity at home began to wane as criticism of his handling of domestic affairs mounted.

After his defeat at the polls Nov 1992 and prior to handing over to his successor Democrat Bill Clinton 20 Jan 1993, Bush helped to initiate two actions of global humanitarian concern: 'Operation Restore Hope' in Somalia, in which US Marines were drafted in as part of a multinational effort to deliver aid to famine-striken areas, and the signing of START II with Russia, which bound both countries to cut long-range nuclear weapons by two thirds by the year 2003. He also supported the more controversial bombing of strategic targets in Iraq after alleged infringements of the UN-imposed 'no-fly zone'.

Read my lips – no new taxes.

George Bush promise made during 1988
US presidential campaign.

Busoni /buːˈsəʊni/ Ferruccio (Dante Benvenuto) 1866–1924. Italian pianist, composer, and music critic. Much of his music was for the piano, but he also composed several operas including *Doktor Faust*, completed by a pupil after his death. An apostle of Futurism, he encouraged the French composer →Varèse.

Buss /bʌs/ Frances Mary 1827–1894. British pioneer in education for women. She first taught in a school run by her mother, and at 18 she founded her own school for girls in London, which became the North London Collegiate School in 1850. She founded the Camden School for Girls in 1871.

Her work helped to raise the status of women teachers and the academic standard of women's education in the UK. She is often associated with Dorothea →Beale, a fellow pioneer.

Bustamante /ˌbʌstəˈmænti/ (William) Alexander (born Clarke) 1884–1977. Jamaican socialist politician. As leader of the Labour Party, he was the first prime minister of independent Jamaica 1962–67.

Bute /bjuːt/ John Stuart, 3rd Earl of Bute 1713–1792. British Tory politician, prime minister 1762–63. On the accession of George III in 1760, he became the chief instrument in the king's policy for breaking the power of the Whigs and establishing the personal rule of the monarch through Parliament.

Bute succeeded his father 1723, and in 1737 was elected a representative peer for Scotland. His position as the king's favourite and supplanter of the popular prime minister Pitt the Elder made him hated in the country. He resigned 1763 after the Seven Years' War.

Buthelezi /ˌbuːtəˈleɪzi/ Chief Gatsha 1928– . Zulu leader and politician, chief minister of KwaZulu, a black 'homeland' in the Republic of South Africa from 1970. He is the founder (1975) and president of Inkatha, a paramilitary organization for attaining a nonracial democratic political system. He has been accused of complicity in the factional violence between Inkatha and African National Congress supporters that has continued to rack the townships despite his signing of a peace accord with ANC leader, Nelson Mandela, Sept 1991.

Buthelezi, great-grandson of King →Cetewayo, opposed KwaZulu becoming a Black National State, arguing instead for a confederation of black areas, with eventual majority rule over all South Africa under a one-party socialist system.

Butler /ˈbʌtlə/ Joseph 1692–1752. English priest and theologian who became dean of St Paul's in 1740 and bishop of Durham in 1750; his *Analogy of Religion* 1736 argued that it is no more rational to accept deism (arguing for God as the first cause) than revealed religion (not arrived at by reasoning).

Butler /ˈbʌtlə/ Josephine (born Gray) 1828–1906. English social reformer. She promoted women's education and the Married Women's Property Act, and campaigned against the Contagious Diseases Acts of 1862–70, which made women in garrison towns suspected of prostitution liable to compulsory examination for venereal disease. Refusal to undergo examination meant imprisonment. As a result of her campaigns the acts were repealed in 1883.

Butler /ˈbʌtlə/ Reg 1913–1981. English sculptor who taught architecture 1937–39 and then was a blacksmith for many years before becoming known for cast and forged iron works, abstract and figurative.

In 1953 he won the international competition for a monument to The Unknown Political Prisoner (a model is in the Tate Gallery, London).

Butler /ˈbʌtlə/ Richard Austen ('Rab'), Baron Butler 1902–1982. British Conservative politician. As minister of education 1941–45, he was responsible for the 1944 Education Act; he was chancellor of the Exchequer 1951–55, Lord Privy Seal 1955–59, and foreign minister 1963–64. As a can-

didate for the prime ministership, he was defeated by Harold Macmillan in 1957 (under whom he was home secretary 1957–62), and by Alec Douglas-Home in 1963.

Butler /ˈbʌtlə/ Samuel 1612–1680. English satirist. His poem *Hudibras*, published in three parts 1663, 1664, and 1678, became immediately popular for its biting satire against the Puritans.

Butler /ˈbʌtlə/ Samuel 1835–1902. English author who made his name 1872 with a satiric attack on contemporary utopianism, *Erewhon* (*nowhere* reversed), but is now remembered for his autobiographical *The Way of All Flesh* written 1872–85 and published 1903.

The Fair Haven 1873 examined the miraculous element in Christianity. *Life and Habit* 1877 and other works were devoted to a criticism of the theory of natural selection. In *The Authoress of the Odyssey* 1897 he maintained that Homer's *Odyssey* was the work of a woman.

It has been said that although God cannot alter the past, historians can.

Samuel Butler *Erewhon* 1872

Butlin /ˈbʌtlɪn/ Billy (William) 1899–1980. British holiday-camp entrepreneur. Born in South Africa, he went in early life to Canada, but later entered the fairground business in the UK. He originated a chain of camps (the first was at Skegness 1936) that provided accommodation, meals, and amusements at an inclusive price.

Butor /bjuːˈtɔː/ Michel 1926– . French writer, one of the *nouveau roman* novelists who made radical changes in the traditional form. His works include *Passage de Milan/Passage from Milan* 1954, *Dégrès/Degrees* 1960, and *L'Emploi du temps/Passing Time* 1963. *Mobile* 1962 is a volume of essays.

Butterfield /ˈbʌtəfiːld/ William 1814–1900. English Gothic Revival architect. His work is characterized by vigorous, aggressive forms and multicoloured striped and patterned brickwork, as in the church of All Saints, Margaret Street, London 1850–59, and Keble College, Oxford 1867–83.

His schools, parsonages, and cottages develop an appealing functional secular style that anticipates Philip →Webb and other Arts and Crafts architects. At Baldersby, Yorkshire, UK, he designed a whole village of church, rectory, almshouse, school, and cottages 1855–57.

Buxtehude /ˌbʊkstəˈhuːdə/ Diderik 1637–1707. Danish composer and organist at Lübeck, Germany, who influenced →Bach and →Handel. He is remembered for his organ works and cantatas, written for his evening concerts or *Abendmusiken*.

Byatt *English novelist and critic A S Byatt is one of the prominent literary figures writing in England today. Among her scholarly works is the first book-length study of Iris Murdoch,* Degrees of Freedom *1965.*

Byatt /ˈbaɪət/ A(ntonia) S(usan) 1936– . English novelist and critic. Her fifth novel, *Possession*, won the 1990 Booker Prize. *The Virgin in the Garden* 1978 is a confident, zestfully handled account of a varied group of characters putting on a school play during Coronation year, 1953. It has a sequel, *Still Life* 1985. Other works include *The Shadow of the Sun* 1964, *The Game* 1967, and, most recently, *Angels and Insects* 1992.

She was born in Sheffield and educated at a Quaker boarding school (with her sister, novelist Margaret Drabble) and at Newnham College, Cambridge. She taught before becoming a full-time writer.

Byng /bɪŋ/ George, Viscount Torrington 1663–1733. British admiral. He captured Gibraltar 1704, commanded the fleet that prevented an invasion of England by the 'Old Pretender' James Francis Edward Stuart 1708, and destroyed the Spanish fleet at Messina 1718. John →Byng was his fourth son.

Byng /bɪŋ/ John 1704–1757. British admiral. Byng failed in the attempt to relieve Fort St Philip when in 1756 the island of Minorca was invaded by France. He was court-martialled and shot. The French writer Voltaire ironically commented that it was done 'to encourage the others'.

Byng /bɪŋ/ Julian, 1st Viscount of Vimy 1862–1935. British general in World War I, commanding troops in Turkey and France, where, after a victory at Vimy Ridge, he took command of the Third Army.

On Nov 20–Dec 7 1917 he led the successful tank attack on Cambrai. He was governor general of Canada 1921–26, and was made a viscount 1926 and a field marshal 1932.

Byrd /bɜːd/ Richard Evelyn 1888–1957. US aviator and explorer. The first to fly over the North Pole (1926), he also flew over the South Pole (1929), and led five overland expeditions in Antarctica.

Byrd /bɜːd/ William 1543–1623. English composer. His church choral music (set to Latin words, as he was a firm Catholic), notably masses for three, four, and five voices, is among the greatest Renaissance music. He also composed secular vocal and instrumental music.

Probably born in Lincoln, he became organist at Lincoln cathedral in 1563. He shared with →Tallis the honorary post of organist in Queen Elizabeth's Chapel Royal, and in 1575 he and Tallis were granted a monopoly in the printing and selling of music.

Byron /ˈbaɪrən/ Augusta Ada 1815–1851. English mathematician, a pioneer in writing programs for Charles →Babbage's analytical engine. In 1983 a new, high-level computer language, ADA, was named after her. She was the daughter of the poet Lord Byron.

Byron /ˈbaɪrən/ George Gordon, 6th Baron Byron 1788–1824. English poet who became the symbol of Romanticism and political liberalism throughout Europe in the 19th century. His reputation was established with the first two cantos of *Childe Harold* 1812. Later works include *The Prisoner of Chillon* 1816, *Beppo* 1818, *Mazeppa* 1819, and, most notably, the satirical *Don Juan* 1819–24. He left England in 1816, spending most of his later life in Italy.

Born in London and educated at Harrow and Cambridge, Byron published his first volume *Hours of Idleness* 1807 and attacked its harsh critics in *English Bards and Scotch Reviewers* 1809. Overnight fame came with the first two cantos of *Childe Harold*, romantically describing his tours in Portugal, Spain, and the Balkans (third canto 1816, fourth 1818). In 1815 he married mathematician Anne Milbanke (1792–1860), with whom he had a daughter, Augusta Ada Byron, separating from her a year later amid much scandal. He then went to Europe, where he became friendly with Percy and Mary →Shelley. He engaged in Italian revolutionary politics and sailed for Greece in 1823 to further the Greek struggle for independence, but died of fever at Missolonghi. He is remembered for his lyrics, his colloquially easy *Letters*, and as the 'patron saint' of Romantic liberalism.

Byron Robert 1904–1941. English writer on travel and architecture, including *The Byzantine Achievement* 1929 and *The Road to Oxiana* 1937, an account of a journey from Iran to Afghanistan 1933–34.

Cabot /ˈkæbət/ Sebastian 1474–1557. Italian navigator and cartographer, the second son of Giovanni →Caboto. He explored the Brazilian coast and the Río de la Plata for the Holy Roman Emperor Charles V 1526–30.

He was also employed by Henry VIII, Edward VI, and Ferdinand of Spain. He planned a voyage to China by way of the North-East Passage, the sea route along the N Eurasian coast, encouraged the formation of the Company of Merchant Adventurers of London 1551, and in 1553 and 1556 directed the company's expeditions to Russia, where he opened British trade.

Caboto /kæˈbəutəu/ Giovanni or *John Cabot* 1450–1498. Italian navigator. Commissioned, with his three sons, by Henry VII of England to discover unknown lands, he arrived at Cape Breton Island on 24 June 1497, thus becoming the first European to reach the North American mainland (he thought he was in NE Asia). In 1498 he sailed again, touching Greenland, and probably died on the voyage.

Cabral /kəˈbrɑːl/ Pedro Alvarez 1460–1526. Portuguese explorer who made Brazil a Portuguese possession in 1500 and negotiated the first commercial treaty between Portugal and India.

Cabral set sail from Lisbon for the East Indies in March 1500, and accidentally reached Brazil by taking a course too far west. He claimed the country for Portugal 25 April, since Spain had not followed up Vicente Pinzón's (c. 1460–1523) landing there earlier in the year. Continuing around Africa, he lost 7 of his fleet of 13 ships (the explorer Bartolomeu →Diaz was one of those drowned), and landed in Mozambique. Proceeding to India, he negotiated the first Indo-Portuguese treaties for trade, and returned to Lisbon July 1501.

Cabrini /kəˈbriːni/ Frances or Francesca ('Mother Cabrini') 1850–1917. First Roman Catholic US citizen to become a saint. Born in Lombardy, Italy, she founded the Missionary Sisters of the Sacred Heart, and established many schools and hospitals in the care of her nuns. She was canonized 1946. Feast day 22 Dec.

Cacoyannis /ˌkækəʊˈjænɪs/ Michael 1922– . Greek film director and writer who directed *Zorba the Greek* 1965; other films include *Stella* 1955 and *Electra* 1961.

Cade /keɪd/ Jack died 1450. English rebel. He was a prosperous landowner, but led a revolt 1450 in Kent against the high taxes and court corruption of Henry VI and demanded the recall from Ireland of Richard, Duke of York. The rebels defeated the royal forces at Sevenoaks and occupied London. After being promised reforms and pardon they dispersed, but Cade was hunted down and killed.

Cadwalader /kædˈwɒlədə/ 7th century. Welsh hero. The son of Cadwallon, king of Gwynedd, N Wales, he defeated and killed Eadwine of Northumbria in 633. About a year later he was killed in battle.

Cadwallon 6th century. King of Gwynedd, N Wales, father of Cadwalader.

Caedmon /ˈkædmən/ 7th century. Earliest known English poet. According to the Northumbrian historian Bede, when Caedmon was a cowherd at the Christian monastery of Whitby, he was commanded to sing by a stranger in a dream, and on waking produced a hymn on the Creation. The poem is preserved in some manuscripts. Caedmon became a monk and may have composed other religious poems.

Light was first
Through the Lord's word
Named day...
Beauteous, bright creation.

        Caedmon *Creation. The First Day*

Caesar /ˈsiːzə/ powerful family of ancient Rome, which included Gaius Julius Caesar, whose grandnephew and adopted son →Augustus assumed the name of Caesar and passed it on to his adopted son →Tiberius. From then on, it was used by the successive emperors, becoming a title of the Roman rulers. The titles 'tsar' in Russia and 'kaiser' in Germany were both derived from the name Caesar.

Caesar /ˈsiːzə/ Gaius Julius c. 100–44 BC. Roman statesman and general. He formed with Pompey and Crassus the First Triumvirate 60 BC. He conquered Gaul 58–50 and invaded Britain 55 and 54. He fought against Pompey 49–48, defeating him at Pharsalus. After a period in Egypt, Caesar returned to Rome as dictator from 46. He was assassinated by conspirators on the Ides of March 44.

A patrician, Caesar allied himself with the popular party, and when elected to the office of aedile 65, nearly ruined himself with lavish amusements for the Roman populace. Although a free thinker, he was elected chief pontiff 63 and appointed governor of Spain 61. Returning to Rome 60, he formed with Pompey and Crassus the First Triumvirate. As governor of Gaul, he was engaged in its subjugation 58–50, defeating the Germans under Ariovistus and selling thousands of the Belgic tribes into slavery. In 55 he crossed into Britain, returning for a further campaigning visit 54. A revolt by the Gauls under Vercingetorix 52 was crushed 51.

His governorship of Spain was to end 49, and, Crassus being dead, Pompey became his rival. Declaring 'the die is cast', Caesar crossed the Rubicon (the small river separating Gaul from Italy) to meet the army raised against him by Pompey. In the ensuing civil war, he followed Pompey to Epirus 48, defeated him at Pharsalus, and chased him to Egypt, where he was murdered. Caesar stayed some months in Egypt, where Cleopatra, queen of Egypt, gave birth to his son, Caesarion.

Caesar executed a lightning campaign 47 against King Pharnaces II (ruled 63–47 BC) in Asia Minor, which he summarized: *Veni vidi vici* 'I came, I saw, I conquered'. With his final victory over the sons of Pompey at Munda in Spain 45, he established his position, having been awarded a ten-year dictatorship 46. On 15 March 44 he was stabbed to death at the foot of Pompey's statue (see →Brutus, →Cassius) in the Senate house. His commentaries on the campaigns and the civil war survive.

Caetano /kaɪˈtɑːnəʊ/ Marcello 1906–1980. Portuguese right-wing politician. Professor of administrative law at Lisbon from 1940, he succeeded the dictator Salazar as prime minister from 1968 until his exile after the military coup of 1974. He was granted political asylum in Brazil.

Cage /keɪdʒ/ John 1912–1992. US composer. A pupil of Arnold →Schoenberg, he maintained that all sounds should be available for musical purposes; for example, he used 24 radios, tuned to random stations, in *Imaginary Landscape No 4* 1951. He also worked to reduce the control of the composer over the music, introducing randomness (aleatory music) and inexactitude and allowing sounds to 'be themselves'. Cage's unconventional ideas have had a profound impact on 20th-century music.

Cage also studied with the experimental US composer Henry →Cowell, and joined others in reacting against the European music tradition in favour of a more realistic idiom open to non-Western attitudes. Working in films during the 1930s, Cage assembled and toured a percussion orchestra incorporating ethnic instruments and noise-makers, for which the *First Construction in Metal* 1930 was composed. He invented the prepared piano to tour as accompanist with the dancer Merce Cunningham, a lifelong collaborator. In a later work, *4 Minutes and 33 Seconds* 1952, the pianist sits at the piano reading a score for that length of time but does not play.

Cagliostro /kælˈjɒstrəʊ/ Alessandro di, Count Cagliostro. Assumed name of Giuseppe Balsamo 1743–1795. Italian adventurer, swindler, and specialist in the occult, born in Palermo. In Paris in 1785 he was involved in the *affair of the diamond necklace* – obtained by a band of swindlers supposedly on behalf of Marie Antoinette, dismantled and sold – and was imprisoned in the Bastille. Later arrested by the Inquisition in Rome, he died in the fortress of San Leone.

Cagney /ˈkægni/ James 1899–1986. US actor who moved to films from Broadway. Usually associated with gangster roles (*The Public Enemy* 1931), he was an actor of great versatility, playing Bottom in *A Midsummer Night's Dream* 1935 and singing and dancing in *Yankee Doodle Dandy* 1942.

Cain /keɪn/ James M(allahan) 1892–1977. US novelist. He was the author of *The Postman Always Rings Twice* 1934, *Mildred Pierce* 1941, and *Double Indemnity* 1943, which epitomized the 'hardboiled' fiction of the 1930s and 1940s.

Caine /keɪn/ Michael. Stage name of Maurice Micklewhite 1933– . English actor, an accomplished performer with an enduring Cockney streak. His films include *Alfie* 1966, *The Man Who Would Be King* 1975, *Educating Rita* 1983, and *Hannah and Her Sisters* 1986.

Calamity Jane /dʒeɪn/ nickname of Martha Jane Burke *c.* 1852–1903. US heroine of Deadwood, South Dakota. She worked as a teamster, transporting supplies to the mining camps, adopted male dress and, as an excellent shot, promised 'calamity' to any aggressor. Many fictional accounts of the Wild West featured her exploits.

Caldecott /ˈkɔːldɪkət/ Randolph 1846–1886. British artist and illustrator of books for children, including *John Gilpin* 1848.

Calder Alexander 1898–1976. US abstract sculptor, the inventor of *mobiles*, suspended shapes that move in the lightest current of air. In the 1920s he began making wire sculptures and *stabiles* (static mobiles), coloured abstract shapes attached by lines of wire. Huge versions adorn Lincoln Center in New York City and UNESCO in Paris.

Calderón de la Barca /ˌkældəˈrɒn deɪ lɑː ˈbɑːkə/ Pedro 1600–1681. Spanish dramatist and poet. After the death of Lope de Vega 1635, he was considered to be the leading Spanish dramatist. Most celebrated of the 118 plays is the philosophical *La vida es sueño/Life is a Dream* 1635.

Calderón was born in Madrid and 1613–19 studied law at Salamanca. In 1620 and 1622 he was successful in poetry contests in Madrid; while still writing dramas, he served in the army in Milan and the Netherlands (1625–35). By 1636 his first volume of plays was published and he had been made master of the revels at the court of Philip IV, receiving a knighthood in 1637. In 1640 he assisted in the suppression of the Catalan rebellion. After the death of his mistress he became a Franciscan in 1650, was ordained in 1651, and appointed as a prebendary of Toledo in 1653. As honorary chaplain to the king in 1663, he produced outdoor religious plays for the festival of the Holy Eucharist. He died in poverty.

His works include the tragedies *El pintor de su deshonra/The Painter of His Own Dishonour* 1645, *El alcalde de Zalamea/The Mayor of Zalamea* 1640, and *El médico de su honra/The Surgeon of His Honour* 1635; the historical *El príncipe constante/The Constant Prince* 1629; and the dashing intrigue *La dama duende/The Phantom Lady* 1629.

Caldwell /ˈkɔːldwel/ Erskine (Preston) 1903–1987. US novelist whose *Tobacco Road* 1932 and *God's Little Acre* 1933 are earthy and vivid presentations of poverty-stricken Southern sharecroppers.

Calhoun /kælˈhuːn/ John C(aldwell) 1782–1850. US politician; vice-president 1825–29 under John Quincy Adams and 1829–33 under Andrew Jackson. Throughout his vice-presidency, he was a defender of strong *states' rights* versus an overpowerful federal government and of the institution of slavery. He served in the US Senate 1841–43 and 1845–50, where he continued to espouse the right of states to legislate on slavery.

Caligula /kəˈlɪgjʊlə/ Gaius Caesar AD 12–41. Roman emperor, son of Germanicus and successor to Tiberius AD 37. Caligula was a cruel tyrant and was assassinated by an officer of his guard. Believed to have been mentally unstable, he is remembered for giving a consulship to his horse Incitatus.

Callaghan /ˈkæləhæn/ (Leonard) James, Baron Callaghan 1912– . British Labour politician. As chancellor of the Exchequer 1964–67, he introduced corporation and capital-gains taxes, and resigned following devaluation. He was home secretary 1967–70 and prime minister 1976–79 in a period of increasing economic stress.

As foreign secretary 1974, Callaghan renegotiated Britain's membership of the European Community. In 1976 he succeeded Harold Wilson as prime minister and in 1977 entered into a pact with the Liberals to maintain his government in office. Strikes in the so-called 'winter of discontent' 1978–79 led to the government losing a vote of no confidence in the Commons, forcing him to call an election, and his party was defeated at the polls May 1979.

This made Callaghan the first prime minister since Ramsay MacDonald 1924 to be forced into an election by the will of the Commons. In 1980 he resigned the party leadership under left-wing pressure, and in 1985 announced that he would not stand for Parliament in the next election. Created Baron Callaghan 1987 and a Knight Companion of the Garter in June of that year.

Callaghan /ˈkæləhæn/ Morley 1903–1990. Canadian novelist and short-story writer whose realistic novels include *Such is My Beloved* 1934, *More Joy in Heaven* 1937, and *Close to the Sun Again* 1977.

His other works include *They Shall Inherit the Earth* 1935, *The Loved and the Lost* 1951, *Stories* 1959, and *A Passion in Rome* 1961.

Callas /ˈkæləs/ Maria. Adopted name of Maria Kalogeropoulos 1923–1977. US lyric soprano, born in New York of Greek parents. With a voice of fine range and a gift for dramatic expression, she excelled in operas including *Norma*, *La Sonnambula*, *Madame Butterfly*, *Aïda*, *Lucia di Lammermoor*, and *Medea*.

She debuted in Verona, Italy, in 1947 and at New York's Metropolitan Opera in 1956. Although her technique was not considered perfect, she helped to popularize classical coloratura roles through her expressiveness and charisma.

Callicrates /kəˈlɪkrətiːz/ 5th century BC. Athenian architect (with Ictinus) of the Parthenon on the Acropolis.

Callimachus /kəˈlɪməkəs/ 310–240 BC. Greek poet and critic known for his epigrams. Born in Cyrene, he taught in Alexandria, Egypt, where he is reputed to have been head of the great library.

Tread where the traffic does not go.

Callimachus

Callot /kæˈləʊ/ Jacques 1592/93–1635. French engraver and painter. His series of etchings *Great Miseries of War* 1632–33, prompted by his own experience of the Thirty Years' War, are arrestingly composed and full of horrific detail.

Calmette /kælˈmet/ Albert 1863–1933. French bacteriologist. A student of Pasteur, he developed (with Camille Guérin, 1872–1961) the BCG vaccine against tuberculosis in 1921.

Calvert /ˈkælvət/ George, Baron Baltimore 1579–1632. English politician who founded the North American colony of Maryland 1632. As a supporter of colonization, he was granted land in Newfoundland 1628 but, finding the climate too harsh, obtained a royal charter for the more temperate Maryland 1632.

Born in Yorkshire, England, Calvert was educated at Oxford University. A confidant of King James I, Calvert served in Parliament and the Privy Council. He became secretary of state, but was forced to resign from that office 1625 because of his conversion to Roman Catholicism.

Camden *William Camden, early English antiquarian who toured England to research his* Britannia 1586, *written in Latin but translated into English 1610. He was headmaster of Westminster School and founded a Chair of Ancient History at Oxford.*

Calvin /ˈkælvɪn/ John (also known as *Cauvin* or *Chauvin*) 1509–1564. French-born Swiss Protestant church reformer and theologian. He was a leader of the Reformation in Geneva and set up a strict religious community there. His theological system is known as Calvinism, and his church government as Presbyterianism. Calvin wrote (in Latin) *Institutes of the Christian Religion* 1536 and commentaries on the New Testament and much of the Old Testament.

Calvin, born in Noyon, Picardie, studied theology and then law, and about 1533 became prominent in Paris as an evangelical preacher. In 1534 he was obliged to leave Paris and retired to Basel, where he studied Hebrew. In 1536 he accepted an invitation to go to Geneva, Switzerland, and assist in the Reformation, but was expelled 1538 because of public resentment against the numerous and too drastic changes he introduced. He returned to Geneva 1541 and, in the face of strong opposition, established a rigorous theocracy (government by priests). In 1553 he had the Spanish theologian Servetus burned for heresy. He supported the Huguenots in their struggle in France and the English Protestants persecuted by Queen Mary I.

Calvin /ˈkælvɪn/ Melvin 1911– . US chemist who, using radioactive carbon-14 as a tracer, determined the biochemical processes of photosynthesis, in which green plants use chlorophyll to convert carbon dioxide and water into sugar and oxygen. Nobel prize 1961.

Camargo /ˈkæmɑːˈɡəʊ/ Marie-Anne de Cupis 1710–1770. French ballerina, born in Brussels.

She became a ballet star in Paris in 1726 and was the first ballerina to attain the 'batterie' (movements involving beating the legs together) previously danced only by men. She shortened her skirt to expose the ankles and her brilliant footwork, gaining more liberty of movement.

Cambon /kæmˈbɒn/ Paul 1843–1924. French diplomat who was ambassador to London during the years leading to the outbreak of World War I, and a major figure in the creation of the Anglo-French entente during 1903–04.

Cambyses /kæmˈbaɪsiːz/ 6th century BC. Emperor of Persia 529–522 BC. Succeeding his father Cyrus, he assassinated his brother Smerdis and conquered Egypt in 525 BC. There he outraged many of the local religious customs and was said to have become insane. He died in Syria on his journey home, probably by suicide.

Camden /ˈkæmdən/ William 1551–1623. English antiquary. He published his topographical survey *Britannia* 1586, and was headmaster of Westminster School from 1593. The *Camden Society* (1838) commemorates his work.

The early bird catches the worm.

William Camden Remains

Cameron /ˈkæmərən/ Charles 1746–1812. Scottish architect. He trained under Isaac Ware in the Palladian tradition before being summoned to Russia in 1779. He created the palace complex at Tsarskoe Selo (now Pushkin), planned the town of Sofia, and from 1803, as chief architect of the Admiralty, executed many buildings, including the Naval Hospital and barracks at Kronstadt 1805.

Cameron /ˈkæmərən/ Julia Margaret 1815–1879. British photographer. She made lively, revealing portraits of the Victorian intelligentsia using a large camera, five-minute exposures, and wet plates. Her subjects included Charles Darwin and Alfred Tennyson.

Cameron /ˈkæmərən/ Simon 1799–1889. US political leader. He served two partial terms in the US Senate 1845–49 and 1857–60. A supporter of Abraham Lincoln at the 1860 Republican nominating convention, he was appointed secretary of war at the outbreak of the American Civil War 1861. A dismal failure in that position, Cameron was named minister to Russia 1862. After the end of the war 1865 he returned to the Senate 1867–77.

Born in Maytown, Pennsylvania, USA, Cameron was trained as a printer, became a newspaper editor in Harrisburg and then embarked on a political career. He acquired wealth through investments in transportation and industry.

Camoëns /ˈkæməʊenz/ or *Camões* Luís Vaz de 1524–1580. Portuguese poet and soldier. He went on various military expeditions, and was shipwrecked in 1558. His poem *Os Lusiades/The Lusiads* 1572 tells the story of the explorer Vasco da Gama and incorporates much Portuguese history; it has become the country's national epic. His posthumously published lyric poetry is also now valued.

Having wounded an equerry of the king in 1552, he was banished to India. He received a small pension, but died in poverty of plague.

Camp /kæmp/ Walter Chauncey 1859–1925. US football coach who was responsible for instituting some of the most basic rules of the game of American football, including team size, field dimensions, and the four-down system. He also initiated the tradition of selecting an annual all-American football team.

Born in New Britain, Connecticut, USA, Camp was educated at Yale University. In 1888, after a brief business career, he returned to Yale as athletic director, football coach, and member of the Intercollegiate Football Rules Committee.

Campbell /ˈkæmbəl/ Colin, 1st Baron Clyde 1792–1863. British field marshal. He commanded the Highland Brigade at Balaclava in the Crimean War and, as commander in chief during the Indian Mutiny, raised the siege of Lucknow and captured Cawnpore.

Campbell /ˈkæmbəl/ Donald Malcolm 1921–1967. British car and speedboat enthusiast, son of Malcolm Campbell, who simultaneously held the land-speed and water-speed records. In 1964 he set the world water-speed record of 444.57 kph/276.3 mph on Lake Dumbleyung, Australia, with the turbojet hydroplane *Bluebird*, and achieved the land-speed record of 648.7 kph/403.1 mph at Lake Eyre salt flats, Australia. He was killed in an attempt to raise his water-speed record on Coniston Water, England.

Campbell /ˈkæmbəl/ Gordon 1886–1953. British admiral in World War I. He commanded Q-ships, which were armed vessels that masqueraded as merchant ships to decoy German U-boats to destruction.

Campbell /ˈkæmbəl/ Malcolm 1885–1948. British racing driver who once held both land- and water-speed records. He set the land-speed record nine times, pushing it up to 484.8 kph/301.1 mph at Bonneville Flats, Utah, USA, in 1935, and broke the water-speed record three times, the best being 228.2 kph/141.74 mph on Coniston Water, England, in 1939. His car and boat were both called *Bluebird*.

His son Donald Campbell emulated his feats.

Campbell /ˈkæmbəl/ Mrs Patrick (born Beatrice Stella Tanner) 1865–1940. British actress whose roles included Paula in Pinero's *The Second Mrs Tanqueray* 1893 and Eliza in *Pygmalion*, written for her by G B Shaw, with whom she had an amusing correspondence.

Campbell /ˈkæmbəl/ Roy 1901–1957. South African poet, author of *The Flaming Terrapin* 1924. Born in Durban, he became a professional jouster and bullfighter in Spain and Provence, France. He fought for Franco in the Spanish Civil War and was with the Commonwealth forces in World War II.

Campbell /ˈkæmbəl/ Thomas 1777–1844. Scottish poet. After the successful publication of his *Pleasures of Hope* in 1799, he travelled in Europe, and there wrote his war poems 'Hohenlinden' and 'Ye Mariners of England'.

Campbell-Bannerman /ˈkæmbəl ˈbænəmən/ Henry 1836–1908. British Liberal politician, prime minister 1905–08. It was during his term of office that the South African colonies achieved self-government, and the Trades Disputes Act 1906 was passed.

Campbell-Bannerman, born in Glasgow, was chief secretary for Ireland 1884–85, war minister 1886 and again 1892–95, and leader of the Liberals in the House of Commons from 1899. In 1905 he became prime minister and led the Liberals to an overwhelming electoral victory 1906. He began the conflict between Commons and Lords that led to the Parliament Act of 1911. He resigned 1908.

Campbell Making her stage debut 1888, English actress Mrs Patrick Campbell quickly gained fame as a temperamental yet highly talented leading lady. Her early successes were in the plays of Pinero and Ibsen and she later became well known in the roles of Ophelia, Lady Teazle, Lady Macbeth, and Juliet.

Campese David 1962– . Australian rugby union player, one of the outstanding entertainers of the game. He holds the world record for the most tries scored in international rugby (46 international tries by 1 May 1992). Australia's most capped player, he was a key element in their 1991 World Cup victory.

Campese was a member of the 1984 Australian team, which won all four internationals in Britain. He plays for Randwick (New South Wales) and Milan (Italy).

Campi /ˈkæmpi/ family of Italian painters practising in Cremona, N Italy, in the 16th century, the best-known member being *Giulio Campi* (c. 1501–1572).

Campin /kɒmˈpiːn/ Robert, also known as the *Master of Flémalle* c. 1378–1444. Netherlandish painter of the early Renaissance, active in Tournai from 1406, one of the first northern masters to use oil. Several altarpieces are attributed to him. Rogier van der Weyden was his pupil.

His outstanding work is the *Mérode altarpiece*, about 1425 (Metropolitan Museum of Art, New York), which shows a distinctly naturalistic style, with a new subtlety in modelling and a grasp of pictorial space.

Campion /ˈkæmpiən/ Edmund 1540–1581. English Jesuit and Roman Catholic martyr. He became a Jesuit in Rome 1573 and in 1580 was sent to England as a missionary. He was betrayed as a spy 1581, imprisoned in the Tower of London, and hanged, drawn, and quartered as a traitor.

He took orders as a deacon in the English church, but fled to Douai, France, where he recanted Protestantism 1571.

Campion /ˈkæmpiən/ Thomas 1567–1620. English poet and musician. He was the author of the critical *Art of English Poesie* 1602 and four *Bookes of Ayres*, for which he composed both words and music.

Soul is the Man.

Thomas Campion
'Are You What Your Fair Looks Express?'

Camus /kæˈmjuː/ Albert 1913–1960. Algerian-born French writer. A journalist in France, he was active in the Resistance during World War II. His novels, which owe much to existentialism (a philosophy based on the concept of an absurd universe where humans have free will), include *L'Etranger/The Outsider* 1942, *La Peste/The Plague* 1948, and *L'Homme révolté/The Rebel* 1952. He was awarded the Nobel Prize for Literature 1957.

What is a rebel? A man who says no.

Albert Camus *The Rebel* 1952

Canaletto /ˌkænəˈletəʊ/ Antonio (Giovanni Antonio Canale) 1697–1768. Italian painter celebrated for his paintings of views (*vedute*) of Venice (his native city) and of the river Thames and London 1746–56.

Much of his work is very detailed and precise, with a warm light and a sparkling of tiny highlights on the green waters of canals and rivers. His later style became clumsier and more static.

Candela /kænˈdeɪlə/ Félix 1910– . Spanish-born Mexican architect, originator of the hypar (hyperbolic paraboloid) from 1951, in which doubly curved surfaces are built up on a framework of planks sprayed with cement. Professor at the National School of Architecture, University of Mexico, from 1953.

Canetti /kəˈneti/ Elias 1905– . Bulgarian-born writer. He was exiled from Austria as a Jew 1938 and settled in England 1939. His books, written in German, include *Die Blendung/Auto da Fé* 1935. He was awarded the Nobel Prize for Literature 1981.

He was concerned with crowd behaviour and the psychology of power, and wrote the anthropological study *Masse und Machte/Crowds and Power* 1960. His three volumes of memoirs are *Die gerettete Zunge: Geschichte einer Jugend/The Tongue Set Free: Remembrance of a European childhood* 1977, *Die Fackel im Ohr: Lebensgeschichte 1921–31/The Torch in My Ear* 1980, and *Das Augenspeil/The Play of the Eyes* 1985.

History portrays everything as if it could not have come otherwise. History is on the side of what happened.

Elias Canetti *The Human Province*

Canning /ˈkænɪŋ/ Charles John, 1st Earl 1812–1862. British administrator, first viceroy of India from 1858. As governor general of India from 1856, he suppressed the Indian Mutiny with a fair but firm hand which earned him the nickname 'Clemency Canning'. He was the son of George Canning.

Canning /ˈkænɪŋ/ George 1770–1827. British Tory politician, foreign secretary 1807–10 and 1822–27, and prime minister 1827 in coalition with the Whigs. He was largely responsible, during the Napoleonic Wars, for the seizure of the Danish fleet and British intervention in the Spanish peninsula.

Canning entered Parliament 1793. His verse, satires, and parodies for the *Anti-Jacobin* 1797–98 led to his advancement by Pitt the Younger. His disapproval of the Walcheren expedition 1809 involved him in a duel with the war minister, →Castlereagh, and led to Canning's resignation as foreign secretary. He was president of the Board of Control 1816–20. On Castlereagh's death 1822, he again became foreign secretary, supported the national movements in Greece and South America, and was made prime minister 1827. When Wellington, Peel, and other Tories refused to serve under him, he formed a coalition with the Whigs. He died in office.

Cannizzaro /ˌkæniˈzɑːrəʊ/ Stanislao 1826–1910. Italian chemist who revived interest in the work of Avogadro that had, in 1811, revealed the difference between atoms and molecules, and so established atomic and molecular weights as the basis of chemical calculations.

Cannizzaro also worked in aromatic organic chemistry. In 1853 he discovered reactions (named after him) that make benzyl alcohol and benzoic acid from benzaldehyde.

Cannon /ˈkænən/ Annie Jump 1863–1941. US astronomer who, from 1896, worked at Harvard College Observatory and carried out revolutionary work on the classification of stars by examining their spectra. Her system, still used today, has spectra arranged according to temperature and runs from O through B, A, F, G, K, and M. O-type stars are the hottest, with surface temperatures of over 25,000 K.

Cano /ˈkɑːnəʊ/ Alonso 1601–1667. Spanish sculptor, painter, and architect, an exponent of the Baroque style in Spain. He was active in Seville, Madrid, and Granada and designed the façade of Granada Cathedral 1667.

From 1637 he was employed by Philip IV to restore the royal collection at the Prado Museum in Madrid. Many of his religious paintings show the influence of the Venetian masters. He also created monumental carved screens, such as the reredos (altar screen) in Lebrija, near Seville, and graceful free-standing polychrome carved figures.

Cano /ˈkɑːnəʊ/ Juan Sebastian del c. 1476–1526. Spanish voyager. It is claimed that he was the first sea captain to sail around the world. He sailed with Magellan 1519 and, after the latter's death in the Philippines, brought the *Victoria* safely home to Spain.

Canova /kəˈnəʊvə/ Antonio 1757–1822. Italian Neo-Classical sculptor, based in Rome from 1781. He received commissions from popes, kings, and emperors for his highly finished marble portrait busts and groups. He made several portraits of Napoleon.

Canova was born near Treviso. His reclining marble *Pauline Borghese* 1805–07 (Borghese Gallery, Rome) is a fine example of cool, polished Classicism. He executed the tombs of popes Clement XIII, Pius VII, and Clement XIV. His marble sculptures include *Cupid and Psyche* (Louvre, Paris) and *The Three Graces*; the latter has been held in the Victoria and Albert Museum, London, since 1990 while efforts were made to raise £7.6 million necessary to keep it in the UK.

Cánovas del Castillo /ˈkænəvæs del kæˈstɪljəʊ/ Antonio 1828–1897. Spanish politician and chief architect of the political system known as the *turno*

politico through which his own Conservative party, and that of the Liberals under Práxedes Sagasta, alternated in power. Elections were rigged to ensure the appropriate majorities. Cánovas was assassinated 1897 by anarchists.

Cantor /ˈkæntɔː/ Georg 1845–1918. German mathematician who followed his work on number theory and trigonometry by considering the foundations of mathematics. He defined real numbers and produced a treatment of irrational numbers using a series of transfinite numbers. Cantor's set theory has been used in the development of topology and real function theory.

Canute /kəˈnjuːt/ c. 995–1035. King of England from 1016, Denmark from 1018, and Norway from 1028. Having invaded England 1013 with his father, Sweyn, king of Denmark, he was acclaimed king on his father's death 1014 by his Viking army. Canute defeated →Edmund II Ironside at Assandun, Essex, 1016, and became king of all England on Edmund's death. He succeeded his brother Harold as king of Denmark 1018, compelled King Malcolm to pay homage by invading Scotland about 1027, and conquered Norway 1028. He was succeeded by his illegitimate son Harold I.

The legend of Canute disenchanting his flattering courtiers by showing that the sea would not retreat at his command was first told by Henry of Huntingdon 1130.

Canute VI /kəˈnjuːt/ (*Cnut VI*) 1163–1202. King of Denmark from 1182, son and successor of Waldemar Knudsson. With his brother and successor, Waldemar II, he resisted Frederick I's northward expansion, and established Denmark as the dominant power in the Baltic.

Cao Chan /tsaʊ ˈtʃæn/ or *Ts'ao Chan* 1719–1763. Chinese novelist. His tragicomic love story *Hung Lou Meng/The Dream of the Red Chamber*, published 1792, involves the downfall of a Manchu family and is semiautobiographical.

Čapek /ˈtʃæpek/ Karel 1890–1938. Czech writer whose works often deal with social injustice in an imaginative, satirical way. *R.U.R.* 1921 is a play in which robots (a term he coined) rebel against their controllers; the novel *Válka s Mloky/War with the Newts* 1936 is a science-fiction classic.

Capet /kæˈpet/ Hugh 938–996. King of France from 987, when he claimed the throne on the death of Louis V. He founded the *Capetian dynasty*, of which various branches continued to reign until the French Revolution, for example, →Valois and →Bourbon.

Capone /kəˈpəʊn/ Al(phonse 'Scarface') 1898–1947. US gangster. During the Prohibition period, he built a formidable criminal organization in Chicago. He was brutal in his pursuit of dominance, killing seven members of a rival gang in the St Valentine's Day massacre. He was imprisoned 1931–39 for income-tax evasion, the only charge that could be sustained against him.

Capote /kəˈpəʊti/ Truman. Pen name of Truman Streckfus Persons 1924–1984. US novelist, journalist, and playwright. He wrote Breakfast at Tiffany's 1958; set a trend with the first 'nonfiction novel', In Cold Blood 1966, reconstructing a Kansas killing; and mingled recollection and fiction in Music for Chameleons 1980.

His other works range from musicals and screenplays to sketches and essays about travel, celebrities, and other topics. He was a prominent figure in the New York social and literary world in his later years.

Capra /ˈkæprə/ Frank 1897–1991. Italian-born US film director. His satirical, populist comedies, which often have the common man pitted against corrupt corporations, were hugely successful in the Depression years of the 1930s. He won Academy Awards for It Happened One Night 1934, Mr Deeds Goes to Town 1936, and You Can't Take It With You 1938. Among his other classic films are Mr Smith Goes to Washington 1939, and It's a Wonderful Life 1946.

Caprivi /kəˈpriːvi/ Georg Leo, Graf von 1831–1899. German soldier and politician. While chief of the admiralty (1883–88) he reorganized the German navy. He became imperial chancellor 1890–94 succeeding Bismarck and renewed the Triple Alliance but wavered between European allies and Russia. Although he strengthened the army, he alienated the conservatives.

Caracalla /ˌkærəˈkælə/ Marcus Aurelius Antoninus AD 186–217. Roman emperor. He succeeded

Caracalla A contemporary marble sculpture of Marcus Aurelius Antoninus Caracalla. Roman emperor from AD 211 until his assassination in 217, Caracalla was ruthless in achieving and retaining power. The extravagance of his reign was matched by the monuments he left behind, such as the Baths of Caracalla in Rome.

his father Septimus Severus AD 211, ruled with cruelty and extravagance, and was assassinated. He was nicknamed after the Celtic cloak (caracalla) that he wore.

With the support of the army he murdered his brother Geta and thousands of his followers to secure sole possession of the throne. During his reign, Roman citizenship was given to all subjects of the empire. He built on a grandiose scale (the Baths of Caracalla in Rome, however, were begun by Septimus AD 206–07 and completed by Caracalla's successors – Caracalla inaugurated them).

Caractacus /kəˈræktəkəs/ died c. AD 54. British chieftain who headed resistance to the Romans in SE England AD 43–51, but was defeated on the Welsh border. Shown in Claudius's triumphal procession, he was released in tribute to his courage and died in Rome.

Caradon /ˈkærədən/ Baron. Title of Hugh →Foot, British Labour politician.

Caravaggio /ˌkærəˈvædʒiəʊ/ Michelangelo Merisi da 1573–1610. Italian early Baroque painter, active in Rome 1592–1606, then in Naples, and finally in Malta. His life was as dramatic as his art (he had to leave Rome after killing a man). He created a forceful style, using contrasts of light and shade and focusing closely on the subject figures, sometimes using dramatic foreshortening.

He was born in Caravaggio, near Milan. His compositions were unusual, strong designs in the two-dimensional plane with little extraneous material. He painted from models, making portraits of real Roman people as saints and madonnas, which caused outrage. An example is The Conversion of St Paul (Sta Maria del Popolo, Rome).

He had a number of direct imitators (Caravaggisti), and several Dutch and Flemish artists who visited Rome, including Honthorst and Terbrugghen, were inspired by him.

Cardano /kɑːˈdɑːnəʊ/ Girolamo 1501–1576. Italian physician, mathematician, philosopher, astrologer, and gambler. He is remembered for his theory of chance, his use of algebra, and many medical publications, notably the first clinical description of typhus fever.

Cárdenas /ˈkɑːdɪnæs/ Lázaro 1895–1970. Mexican centre-left politician and general, president 1934–40. A civil servant in early life, Cárdenas took part in the revolutionary campaigns 1915–29 that followed the fall of President Díaz (1830–1915). As president of the republic, he attempted to achieve the goals of the revolution by building schools, distributing land to the peasants, and developing transport and industry. He was minister of defence 1943–45.

Cardiff /ˈkɑːdɪf/ Jack 1914– . English director of photography. He is considered one of cinema's finest colour-camera operators for his work on such films as A Matter of Life and Death 1946, The

Red Shoes 1948, and *The African Queen* 1951. He won an Academy Award for *Black Narcissus* 1947.

Cardin /kɑːdæn/ Pierre 1922– . French pioneering fashion designer whose clothes are bold and fantastic. He was the first women's designer to launch menswear (1960) and ready-to-wear collections (1963) and has given his name to a perfume.

Cardin moved to Paris 1944 and worked in the fashion houses of Madame Paquin, Elsa →Schiaparelli, and Christian →Dior. He began making theatrical costumes 1949, and launched his first couture collection 1957.

Cardozo /kɑːˈdəʊzəʊ/ Benjamin Nathan 1870–1938. US jurist and Supreme Court justice. He was appointed to the US Supreme Court by President Hoover 1932. During the F D Roosevelt administration, he upheld the constitutionality of New Deal programmes to counter the depression of 1929 conveyed in such famous cases as *Ashwander* v *Tennessee Valley Authority* 1936.

Born in New York, USA, Cardozo was educated at Columbia University and was admitted to the bar 1891. After a brief career as a corporate counsel, he was elected to the New York Supreme Court 1913 and was appointed associate justice of the court of appeals 1917, becoming its chief judge 1926.

Carducci /kɑːˈduːtʃi/ Giosuè 1835–1907. Italian poet. Born in Tuscany, he was appointed professor of Italian literature at Bologna 1860, and won distinction through his lecturing, critical work, and poetry. His revolutionary *Inno a Satana/Hymn to Satan* 1865 was followed by several other volumes of verse, in which his nationalist sympathies are apparent. Nobel prize 1906.

Cardwell /kɑːdwel/ Edward, Viscount Cardwell 1813–1886. British Liberal politician. He entered Parliament as a supporter of the Conservative prime minister Robert →Peel 1842, and was secretary for war under Gladstone 1868–74, when he carried out many reforms, including the abolition of the purchase of military commissions and promotions.

Carême /kəˈreɪm/ Antonin 1784–1833. French chef who is regarded as the founder of classic French haute cuisine. At various times he was chief cook to the Prince Regent in England and Tsar Alexander I in Russia.

Carew /kəˈruː/ Thomas *c.* 1595–*c.* 1640. English poet. He was a gentleman of the privy chamber to Charles I in 1628, and a lyricist as well as member of the school of Cavalier poets.

Carey George Leonard 1935– . 103rd archbishop of Canterbury from 1991. A product of a liberal evangelical background, he was appointed bishop of Bath and Wells 1987.

He is a supporter of the ordination of women, an issue that brought disagreement during his first meeting with Pope John Paul II in 1992.

Carey /keəri/ Henry 1690–1743. British poet and musician, remembered for the song 'Sally in Our Alley'. 'God Save the King' (both words and music) has also been attributed to him.

Carey /keəri/ Peter 1943– . Australian novelist. His works include *Bliss* 1981, *Illywhacker* (Australian slang for 'con man') 1985, and *Oscar and Lucinda* 1988, which won the Booker Prize. *The Tax Inspector* 1991 is set in modern-day Sydney, and depicts an eccentric Greek family under investigation for tax fraud.

Carissimi /kəˈrɪsɪmi/ Giacomo 1605–1674. Italian composer of church music. Chief choirmaster at Sant' Apollinaire, Rome, 1630–74, he pioneered the use of expressive solo aria as a commentary on the Latin biblical text. He wrote five oratorios, including Jephtha 1650.

Carl XVI Gustaf /kɑːl/ 1946– . King of Sweden from 1973. He succeeded his grandfather Gustaf VI, his father having been killed in an air crash 1947. Under the new Swedish constitution, which became effective on his grandfather's death, the monarchy was stripped of all power at his accession.

Carlos /kɑːlɒs/ four kings of Spain; see →Charles.

Carlos I /kɑːlɒs/ 1863–1908. King of Portugal, of the Braganza-Coburg line, from 1889 until he was assassinated in Lisbon with his elder son Luis. He was succeeded by his younger son Manuel.

Carlos /kɑːlɒs/ Don 1545–1568. Spanish prince. Son of Philip II, he was recognized as heir to the thrones of Castile and Aragon but became mentally unstable and had to be placed under restraint following a plot to assassinate his father. His story was the subject of plays by Friedrich von Schiller, Vittorio Alfieri, Thomas Otway, and others.

Carlson /kɑːlsən/ Chester 1906–1968. US scientist who invented xerography. A research worker with Bell Telephone, he lost his job 1930 during the Depression and set to work on his own to develop an efficient copying machine. By 1938 he had invented the Xerox photocopier.

Carlsson /kɑːlsən/ Ingvar (Gösta) 1934– . Swedish socialist politician, leader of the Social Democratic Party, deputy prime minister 1982–86 and prime minister 1986–91.

After studying in Sweden and the USA, Carlsson became president of the Swedish Social Democratic Youth League 1961. He was elected to the Riksdag (parliament) 1964 and became a minister 1969. With the return to power of the Social Democrats 1982, Carlsson became deputy to Prime Minister Palme and, on his assassination 1986, succeeded him. He lost his majority Sept 1991 and resigned.

Carlucci /kɑːˈluːtʃi/ Frank (Charles) 1930– . US politician. A former diplomat and deputy director of the CIA, he was national security adviser 1986–87 and defence secretary 1987–89 under Reagan, supporting Soviet–US arms reduction.

Educated at Princeton and Harvard, Carlucci, after fighting in the Korean War, was a career diplomat during the later 1950s and 1960s. He returned to the USA 1969 to work under presidents Nixon, Ford, and Carter, his posts including US ambassador to Portugal and deputy director of the CIA. An apolitical Atlanticist, Carlucci found himself out of step with the hawks in the Reagan administration, and left to work in industry after barely a year as deputy secretary of defence. In Dec 1986, after the Irangate scandal, he replaced John →Poindexter as national security adviser.

Carlyle /kɑːˈlaɪl/ Thomas 1795–1881. Scottish essayist and social historian. His works include *Sartor Resartus* 1833–34, describing his loss of Christian belief, *French Revolution* 1837, *Chartism* 1839, and *Past and Present* 1843. His prose style was idiosyncratic, encompassing grand, thunderous rhetoric and deliberate obscurity.

Carlyle was born at Ecclefechan in Dumfriesshire. Leaving Edinburgh University without a degree, he devoted several years to intensive study of German literature, translating Goethe and writing a life of Schiller. In 1821 he passed through the spiritual crisis described in *Sartor Resartus*. He married Jane Baillie Welsh (1801–1866) in 1826 and they moved to her farm at Craigenputtock, where *Sartor Resartus* was written. His reputation was established with *French Revolution*. The series of lectures he gave 1837–40

Carlyle Photograph of Scottish historian and essayist Thomas Carlyle by Julia Cameron (1867). Carlyle's works greatly influenced contemporary religious and political thought, and established him as one of the great sages of his era.

included *On Heroes, Hero-Worship and The Heroic in History* (published 1841). He also wrote several pamphlets, including *Chartism*, attacking the doctrine of laissez-faire; the notable *Letters and Speeches of Cromwell* 1845; and the miniature life of his friend, John Sterling 1851. He was also a friend of J S →Mill and Ralph Waldo →Emerson. Carlyle began his *History of Frederick the Great* 1858–65, and after the death of his wife 1866 edited her letters 1883 and prepared his *Reminiscences* 1881, which shed an unfavourable light on his character and his neglect of her, for which he could not forgive himself. His house in Cheyne Row, Chelsea, London, where they lived from 1834, is a museum.

The history of the world is but the biography of great men.

Thomas Carlyle *Heroes and Hero-Worship*

Carmichael /kɑːˈmaɪkəl/ Hoagy (Hoagland Howard) 1899–1981. US composer, pianist, singer, and actor. His songs include 'Stardust' 1927, 'Rockin' Chair' 1930, 'Lazy River' 1931, and 'In the Cool, Cool, Cool of the Evening' 1951 (Academy Award).

Carnap /ˈkɑːnæp/ Rudolf 1891–1970. German philosopher, in the USA from 1935, an exponent of logical empiricism (based on the belief that all knowledge is ultimately derived from sense experience). He was a member of the Vienna Circle, who adopted Ernst →Mach as their guide. His books include *The Logical Syntax of Language* 1934 and *Meaning and Necessity* 1956. He was professor of philosophy at the University of California 1954–62.

Carné /kɑːˈneɪ/ Marcel 1909– . French director known for the romantic fatalism of such films as *Drôle de Drame* 1936, *Hôtel du Nord* 1938, *Le Quai des brumes/Port of Shadows* 1938, and *Le Jour se lève/Daybreak* 1939. His masterpiece, *Les Enfants du paradis/The Children of Paradise* 1943–45, was made with his longtime collaborator, the poet and screenwriter Jacques Prévert (1900–1977).

Carnegie /kɑːˈneɪgɪ/ family name of the earls of Northesk and Southesk and of the duke of Fife, who is descended from Queen Victoria.

Carnegie /kɑːˈneɪgɪ/ Andrew 1835–1919. US industrialist and philanthropist, born in Scotland, who developed the Pittsburgh iron and steel industries, making the USA the world's leading producer. He endowed public libraries, education, and various research trusts.

Born in Dunfermline, Scotland, he was taken by his parents to the USA 1848 and at 14 became a telegraph boy in Pittsburgh. Subsequently he became a railway employee, rose to be superintendent, introduced sleeping-cars, and invested successfully in oil. He developed the Pittsburgh iron and steel industries, and built up a vast empire that he disposed of to the United States Steel Trust 1901. Then he moved to Skibo castle in Sutherland, Scotland, and used his wealth to endow libraries and universities, the Carnegie Endowment for International Peace, and other good causes. On his death the Carnegie Trusts continued his benevolent activities. *Carnegie Hall* in New York, opened 1891 as the Music Hall, was renamed 1898 because of his large contribution to its construction.

Carnegie /kɑːˈnegi/ Dale 1888–1955. US author and teacher who wrote the best-selling self-help book *How to Win Friends and Influence People* 1937.

Carnot /ˈkɑːnəʊ/ Lazare Nicolas Marguerite 1753–1823. French general and politician. A member of the National Convention in the French Revolution, he organized the armies of the republic. He was war minister 1800–01 and minister of the interior 1815 under Napoleon. His work on fortification, *De la Défense de places fortes* 1810, became a military textbook. Minister of the interior during the →Hundred Days, he was proscribed at the restoration of the monarchy and retired to Germany.

Carnot joined the army as an engineer, and his transformation of French military technique in the revolutionary period earned him the title of 'Organizer of Victory'. After the coup d'état of 1797 he went abroad, but returned 1799 when Napoleon seized power. In 1814, as governor of Antwerp, he put up a brilliant defence.

Carnot /ˈkɑːnəʊ/ Marie François Sadi 1837–1894. French president from 1887, grandson of Lazare Carnot. He successfully countered the Boulangist anti-German movement (see →Boulanger) and in 1892 the scandals arising out of French financial activities in Panama. He was assassinated by an Italian anarchist in Lyon.

Carnot /ˈkɑːnəʊ/ (Nicolas Leonard) Sadi 1796–1832. French scientist and military engineer who founded the science of thermodynamics. His pioneering work was *Réflexions sur la puissance motrice du feu/On the Motive Power of Fire*.

Caro /ˈkɑːrəʊ/ Anthony 1924– . British sculptor who has made bold, large abstracts using ready-made angular metal shapes, often without bases. His works include *Fathom* (outside the Economist Building, London).

Carol /ˈkærəl/ two kings of Romania:

Carol I 1839–1914. First king of Romania 1881–1914. A prince of the house of Hohenzollern-Sigmaringen, he was invited to become prince of Romania, then part of the Ottoman Empire, 1866. In 1877, in alliance with Russia, he declared war on Turkey, and the Congress of Berlin 1878 recognized Romanian independence.

He promoted economic development and industrial reforms but failed to address rural prob-

Carnegie The US industrialist Andrew Carnegie. On his retirement, he devoted his life to the philanthropic distribution of his vast fortune.

lems. This led to a peasant rebellion 1907 which he brutally crushed. At the beginning of World War I, King Carol declared Romania's neutrality but his successor (his nephew King Ferdinand I) declared for the Allies.

Carol II 1893–1953. King of Romania 1930–40. Son of King Ferdinand, he married Princess Helen of Greece and they had a son, Michael. In 1925 he renounced the succession because of his affair with Elena Lupescu and went into exile in Paris. Michael succeeded to the throne 1927, but in 1930 Carol returned to Romania and was proclaimed king. In 1938 he introduced a new constitution under which he practically became an absolute ruler. He was forced to abdicate by the pro-Nazi Iron Guard Sept 1940, went to Mexico, and married his mistress 1947.

Caroline of Anspach /ˈkærəlaɪn, ˈænspæx/ 1683–1737. Queen of George II of Great Britain and Ireland. The daughter of the Margrave of Brandenburg-Anspach, she married George, Electoral Prince of Hanover, 1705, and followed him to England 1714 when his father became King George I. She was the patron of many leading writers and politicians such as Alexander Pope, John Gay, and the Earl of Chesterfield. She supported Sir Robert Walpole and kept him in power and acted as regent during her husband's four absences.

Carpenter *Photograph of Edward Carpenter by Alvin Langdon Coburn (1907). English social reformer, and writer, Carpenter left the Anglican church and visited the USA where he met Walt Whitman, Ralph Waldo Emerson, and others. In England he became interested in the socialist and crafts movements, and became a sandal-maker and market-gardener.*

Caroline of Brunswick /ˈkærəlaɪn, ˈbrʌnzwɪk/ 1768–1821. Queen of George IV of Great Britain, who unsuccessfully attempted to divorce her on his accession to the throne 1820.

Second daughter of Karl Wilhelm, Duke of Brunswick, and Augusta, sister of George III, she married her first cousin, the Prince of Wales, 1795, but after the birth of Princess ➔Charlotte Augusta a separation was arranged. When her husband ascended the throne 1820 she was offered an annuity of £50,000 provided she agreed to renounce the title of queen and to continue to live abroad. She returned forthwith to London, where she assumed royal state. In July 1820 the government brought in a bill to dissolve the marriage, but Lord ➔Brougham's brilliant defence led to the bill's abandonment. On 19 July 1821 Caroline was prevented by royal order from entering Westminster Abbey for the coronation. She died 7 Aug, and her funeral was the occasion of popular riots.

Carolingian dynasty /kærəˈlɪndʒɪən/ Frankish dynasty descending from ➔Pepin the Short (died 768) and named after his son Charlemagne; its last ruler was Louis V of France (reigned 966–87), who was followed by Hugh ➔Capet, first ruler of the Capetian dynasty.

Carothers /kəˈrʌðəz/ Wallace 1896–1937. US chemist who carried out research into polymeriza-

tion. By 1930 he had discovered that some polymers were fibre-forming, and in 1937 he produced nylon.

Carpaccio /kɑːˈpætʃiəʊ/ Vittorio 1450/60–1525/26. Italian painter known for scenes of his native Venice. His series *The Legend of St Ursula* 1490–98 (Accademia, Venice) is full of detail of contemporary Venetian life. His other great series is the lives of saints George and Jerome 1502–07 (S Giorgio degli Schiavoni, Venice).

Carpeaux /kɑːˈpəʊ/ Jean-Baptiste 1827–1875. French sculptor whose lively naturalistic subjects include *La Danse* 1865–69 for the Opéra, Paris.

Another example is the *Neapolitan Fisherboy* 1858 (Louvre, Paris). The Romantic charm of his work belies his admiration of Michelangelo. He studied in Italy 1856–62 and won the Prix de Rome scholarship 1854.

Carpenter /ˈkɑːpəntə/ Edward 1844–1929. English socialist and writer. Inspired by reading ➔Thoreau, he resigned his post as tutor at Cambridge University 1874 to write poems and books, such as *The Simplification of Life* 1884, *Civilization: Its Cause and Cure* 1889, and *Love's Coming of Age* 1896, a plea for toleration of homosexuality.

Carpenter /ˈkɑːpəntə/ John 1948– . US director of horror and science-fiction films, notable for such films as *Dark Star* 1974 and *Assault on Precinct 13* 1976.

He continued with such films as *Halloween* 1978, *The Thing* 1982, *Christine* 1983 (adapted from a Stephen King story about a vindictive car), the underrated, gentle *Starman* 1984, *They Live* 1988, and *The Fog* 1980. He composes his own film scores, which have often added to the atmosphere of menace that haunt his more scary movies.

Carpini /kɑːˈpiːni/ Johannes de Plano 1182–1252. Italian Franciscan friar and traveller. Sent by Pope Innocent IV on a mission to the Great Khan, he visited Mongolia 1245–47 and wrote a history of the Mongols in Latin.

Carracci /kəˈrɑːtʃi/ Italian family of painters in Bologna, whose forte was murals and ceilings. The foremost of them, *Annibale Carracci* (1560–1609), decorated the Farnese Palace, Rome, with a series of mythological paintings united by simulated architectural ornamental surrounds (completed 1604).

Ludovico Carracci (1555–1619), with his cousin *Agostino Carracci* (1557–1602), founded Bologna's Academy of Art. Agostino collaborated with his brother Annibale on the Farnese Palace decorative scheme, which paved the way for a host of elaborate murals in Rome's palaces and churches, ever-more inventive illusions of pictorial depth and architectural ornament. Annibale also painted early landscapes such as *Flight into Egypt* 1603 (Doria Gallery, Rome).

Carradine /ˈkærədiːn/ John (Richmond Reed) 1906–1988. US film actor who often played sinister roles. He appeared in many major Hollywood films, such as *Stagecoach* 1939 and *The Grapes of Wrath* 1940, but was later seen mostly in horror B-movies, including *House of Frankenstein* 1944.

Carrel /kəˈrel/ Alexis 1873–1944. US surgeon born in France, whose experiments paved the way for organ transplantation. Working at the Rockefeller Institute, New York City, he devised a way of joining blood vessels end to end (anastomosing). This was a key move in the development of transplant surgery, as was his work on keeping organs viable outside the body, for which he was awarded the Nobel Prize for Medicine 1912.

Carreras /kəˈreərəs/ José 1947– . Spanish tenor whose roles include Handel's *Samson* and whose recordings include *West Side Story* 1984. In 1987, he became seriously ill with leukaemia, but resumed his career in 1988. Together with Placido Domingo and Luciano Pavarotti, he achieved worldwide fame in a recording of operatic hits released to coincide with the World Cup soccer series in Rome 1990.

Carrington /ˈkærɪŋtən/ Peter Alexander Rupert, 6th Baron Carrington 1919– . British Conservative politician. He was defence secretary 1970–74, and led the opposition in the House of Lords 1964–70 and 1974–79. While foreign secretary 1979–82, he negotiated independence for Zimbabwe, but resigned after failing to anticipate the Falklands crisis. He was secretary general of NATO 1984–88. He chaired EC-sponsored peace talks on Yugoslavia 1991.

Carroll /ˈkærəl/ Charles 1737–1832. American public official who, as a member of the Continental Congress, was one of the signatories of the Declaration of Independence 1776. He was one of the North American colony of Maryland's first US senators 1789–92.

Born in Annapolis, Maryland, Carroll was educated in France and England, returning to administer Carrollton, the family estate in Maryland. Because of his Catholic faith, he was not allowed to enter political life but was a strong supporter of the cause of American independence. In 1776 he accompanied Benjamin Franklin on a diplomatic mission to Canada before signing the Declaration of Independence in the same year.

Carroll /ˈkærəl/ Lewis. Pen name of Charles Lutwidge Dodgson 1832–1898. English author of children's classics *Alice's Adventures in Wonderland* 1865 and its sequel *Through the Looking-Glass* 1872. Among later works was the mock-heroic nonsense poem *The Hunting of the Snark* 1876. An Oxford don, he also published mathematical works.

Dodgson, born in Daresbury, Cheshire, was a mathematics lecturer at Oxford 1855–81. There he first told the fantasy stories to Alice Liddell and her sisters, daughters of the dean of Christ Church. He was a prolific letter writer and inventor of games and puzzles, and was one of the pioneers of portrait photography.

Carson /ˈkɑːsən/ Edward Henry, Baron Carson 1854–1935. Irish politician and lawyer who played a decisive part in the trial of the writer Oscar Wilde. In the years before World War I he led the movement in Ulster to resist Irish Home Rule by force of arms if need be.

Carson was a highly respected barrister both in England and Ireland. He acted as counsel for the Marquess of Queensbury in the trial that ruined Wilde's career. On the outbreak of war he campaigned in Ulster in support of the government, and took office under both Asquith and Lloyd George (attorney general 1915, First Lord of the Admiralty 1916, member of the war cabinet 1917–18). He was a Lord of Appeal in Ordinary 1921–29.

Carson /ˈkɑːsən/ Kit (Christopher) 1809–68. US frontier settler, guide, and Indian agent, who later fought for the Federal side in the Civil War. Carson City, Nevada, was named after him.

Carson /ˈkɑːsən/ Rachel 1907–1964. US naturalist. An aquatic biologist with the US Fish and Wildlife Service 1936–49, she then became its editor-in-chief until 1952. In 1951 she published *The Sea Around Us* and in 1963 *Silent Spring*, attacking the indiscriminate use of pesticides.

Carson /ˈkɑːsən/ Willie (William) 1942– . Scottish jockey who has ridden three Epsom Derby winners as well as the winners of most major races worldwide.

The top flat-race jockey on five occasions, he has ridden over 3,000 winners in Britain. For many years he has ridden for the royal trainer, Major Dick Hern.

Carter /ˈkɑːtə/ Angela 1940–1992. English writer of the magic realist school. Her novels include *The Magic Toyshop* 1967 (filmed by David Wheatley 1987) and *Nights at the Circus* 1984. She co-wrote the script for the film *The Company of Wolves* 1984, based on one of her stories. Her last novel was *Wise Children* 1991.

Carter /ˈkɑːtə/ Elliott (Cook) 1908– . US composer. His early work shows the influence of Igor →Stravinsky, but after 1950 his music became increasingly intricate and densely written in a manner resembling Charles →Ives. He invented 'metrical modulation', which allows different instruments or groups to stay in touch while playing at different speeds. He wrote four string quartets, the *Symphony for Three Orchestras* 1967, and the song cycle *A Mirror on Which to Dwell* 1975.

Carter /ˈkɑːtə/ Jimmy (James Earl) 1924– . 39th president of the USA 1977–81, a Democrat. In 1976 he narrowly wrested the presidency from Gerald Ford. Features of his presidency were the return of the Panama Canal Zone to Panama, the Camp David Agreements for peace in the Middle

East, and the Iranian seizure of US embassy hostages. He was defeated by Ronald Reagan 1980.

We should live our lives as though Christ were coming this afternoon.

Jimmy Carter speech to Bible class in Plains, Georgia, March 1976

Cartier /ˌkɑːtiˈeɪ/ Georges Étienne 1814–1873. French-Canadian politician. He fought against the British in the rebellion 1837, was elected to the Canadian parliament 1848, and was joint prime minister with John A Macdonald 1858–62. He brought Québec into the Canadian federation 1867.

Cartier /ˌkɑːtiˈeɪ/ Jacques 1491–1557. French navigator who was the first European to sail up the St Lawrence River 1534. He named the site of Montréal.

Cartier-Bresson /ˌkɑːtiˈeɪ brɛˈsɒn/ Henri 1908– . French photographer, considered one of the greatest photographic artists. His documentary work was shot in black and white, using a small-format camera. His work is remarkable for its tightly structured composition and his ability to capture the decisive moment.

Cartland /ˈkɑːtlənd/ Barbara 1904– . English romantic novelist. She published her first book, *Jigsaw* 1921 and since then has produced a prolific stream of stories of chastely romantic love, usually in idealized or exotic settings, for a mainly female audience (such as *Love Climbs In* 1978 and *Moments of Love* 1981).

Cartwright /ˈkɑːtraɪt/ Edmund 1743–1823. British inventor. He patented the power loom 1785, built a weaving mill 1787, and patented a wool-combing machine 1789.

He was born in Nottinghamshire, studied at Oxford University, and became a country rector (and also a farmer). He went bankrupt 1793, but was awarded £10,000 by the government 1809.

Caruso /kəˈruːsəʊ/ Enrico 1873–1921. Italian operatic tenor. In 1902 he starred, with Nellie Melba, in Puccini's *La Bohème*. He was one of the first opera singers to profit from gramophone recordings.

Carvel /ˈkɑːvəl/ Robert 1919–1990. British journalist. He was political editor of the *Evening Standard* for 25 years, retiring 1985. His columns did much to inform and entertain the ordinary reader who looked for a lighter, but still serious window on politics. He was widely respected in political and journalistic circles.

Carver /ˈkɑːvə/ George Washington 1864–1943. US agricultural chemist. Born a slave in Missouri, he was kidnapped and raised by his former owner, Moses Carver. He devoted his life to improving the economy of the US South and the condition of blacks. He advocated the diversification of crops, promoted peanut production, and was a pioneer in the field of plastics.

Carver /ˈkɑːvə/ Raymond 1939–1988. US short-story writer and poet, author of vivid tales of contemporary US life, a collection of which were published in *Cathedral* 1983. *Fires* 1985 includes his essays and poems.

Cary /ˈkeəri/ (Arthur) Joyce (Lunel) 1888–1957. British novelist. He used his experiences gained in Nigeria in the Colonial Service (which he entered 1918) as a backdrop to such novels as *Mister Johnson* 1939. Other books include *The Horse's Mouth* 1944.

Casals /kəˈsɑːlz/ Pablo 1876–1973. Catalan cellist, composer, and conductor. As a cellist, he was celebrated for his interpretations of J S Bach's unaccompanied suites. He left Spain 1939 to live in Prades, in the French Pyrenees, where he founded an annual music festival. In 1956 he moved to Puerto Rico, where he launched the Casals Festival 1957, and toured extensively in the USA. He wrote instrumental and choral works, including the Christmas oratorio *The Manger*.

Casals was born in Tarragona. In 1919 he founded the Barcelona orchestra, which he conducted until leaving Spain at the outbreak of the Spanish Civil War in 1936. He was an outspoken critic of fascism, and a tireless crusader for peace.

Casanova de Seingalt /ˌkæsəˈnəʊvə də ˈsæŋˈɡælt/ Giovanni Jacopo 1725–1798. Italian adventurer, spy, violinist, librarian, and, according to his *Memoirs*, one of the world's great lovers. From 1774 he was a spy in the Venetian police service. In 1782 a libel got him into trouble, and after more wanderings he was appointed 1785 librarian to Count Waldstein at his castle of Dûx in Bohemia. Here Casanova wrote his *Memoirs* (published 1826–38, although the complete text did not appear until 1960–61).

Casement /ˈkeɪsmənt/ Roger David 1864–1916. Irish nationalist. While in the British consular service, he exposed the ruthless exploitation of the people of the Belgian Congo and Peru, for which he was knighted 1911 (degraded 1916). He was hanged for treason by the British for his involvement in the Irish nationalist cause.

In 1914 Casement went to Germany and attempted to induce Irish prisoners of war to form an Irish brigade to take part in a republican insurrection. He returned to Ireland in a submarine 1916 (actually to postpone, not start, the Easter Rising), was arrested, tried for treason, and hanged.

Cash /kæʃ/ Johnny 1932– . US country singer, songwriter, and guitarist. His early hits, recorded for Sun Records in Memphis, Tennessee, include the million-selling 'I Walk the Line' 1956. Many of his songs have become classics.

Cash's gruff delivery and storytelling ability distinguish his work. He is widely respected beyond the country-music field for his concern for the underprivileged, expressed in albums like *Bitter Tears* 1964 about American Indians and *Live At Folsom Prison* 1968. He is known as the 'Man in Black' because of his penchant for dressing entirely in that colour.

Caslavska /tʃɑːslæfskə/ Vera 1943– . Czechoslovak gymnast, the first of the great present-day stylists. She won a record 21 world, Olympic, and European gold medals 1959–68; she also won eight silver and three bronze medals.

Cass /kæs/ Lewis 1782–1866. US political leader and diplomat. He was appointed secretary of war 1831 by President Jackson, and served as US minister to France 1836–42. He was the unsuccessful Democratic presidential candidate in 1848, returning to the Senate 1849–57. In the Buchanan administration 1856–60, he served as secretary of state 1857–60.

Born in Exeter, New Hampshire, Cass studied law in Ohio and was admitted to the bar 1802. During the Anglo-American War 1812–14, he rose to the rank of brigadier general and was appointed governor of the Michigan Territory 1813.

Cassatt /kəˈsæt/ Mary 1845–1926. US Impressionist painter and printmaker. In 1868 she settled in Paris. Her popular, colourful pictures of mothers and children show the then-new influence of Japanese prints, for example *The Bath* 1892 (Art Institute, Chicago).

Cassavetes /ˌkæsəˈveɪtiːz/ John 1929–1989. US director and actor whose experimental, apparently improvised films include *Shadows* 1960 and *The Killing of a Chinese Bookie* 1980. He acted in *The Dirty Dozen* 1967 and *Rosemary's Baby* 1968.

Cassini /kæˈsiːni/ Giovanni Domenico 1625–1712. Italian-French astronomer who discovered four moons of Saturn and the gap in the rings of Saturn now called the *Cassini division*.

Born in Italy, he became director of the Paris Observatory 1671. His son, grandson, and great-grandson in turn became directors of the Paris Observatory.

Cassius /ˈkæsiəs/ Gaius died 42 BC. Roman soldier, one of the conspirators who killed Julius →Caesar 44 BC. He fought at Carrhae 53, and with the republicans against Caesar at Pharsalus 48, was pardoned and appointed praetor, but became a leader in the conspiracy of 44, and after Caesar's death joined Brutus. He committed suicide after his defeat at Philippi 42.

Cassivelaunus /ˌkæsɪvəˈlaʊnəs/ chieftain of the British tribe, the Catuvellauni, who led the British resistance to the Romans under Caesar 54 BC.

Casson /ˈkæsən/ Hugh 1910– . British architect, professor at the Royal College of Art 1953–75, and president of the Royal Academy 1976–84. His books include *Victorian Architecture*

1948. He was director of architecture for the Festival of Britain 1948–51.

The British love permanence more than they love beauty.

Hugh Casson *The Observer* 1964

Castagno /kæˈstænjəʊ/ Andrea del c. 1421–1457. Italian Renaissance painter, active in Florence. In his frescoes in Sta Apollonia, Florence, he adapted the pictorial space to the architectural framework and followed →Masaccio's lead in perspective.

Castagno's work is sculptural and strongly expressive, anticipating the Florentine late 15th-century style, as in his *David*, about 1450–57 (National Gallery, Washington, DC).

Castello Branco /kəʃˈtelu ˈbræŋkuː/ Camillo Ferreira Botelho, Visconde de Corrêa Botelho 1825–1890. Portuguese novelist. His work fluctuates between mysticism and bohemianism, and includes *Amor de perdição/Love of Perdition* 1862, written during his imprisonment for adultery, and *Novelas do Minho* 1875, stories of the rural north.

Born illegitimately and then orphaned, he led a dramatic life.

Other works include *Onde está a felicidade?/Where is Happiness?* 1856 and *A brazileira de Prazins/The Brazilian Girl from Prazins* 1882. He was made a viscount 1885, and committed suicide when overtaken by blindness.

Castiglione /ˌkæsˌtiːliˈəʊni/ Baldassare, Count Castiglione 1478–1529. Italian author and diplomat who described the perfect Renaissance gentleman in *Il Cortegiano/The Courtier* 1528.

Born near Mantua, Castiglione served the Duke of Milan, and in 1506 was engaged by the Duke of Albino on a mission to Henry VII of England. While in Spain 1524 he was made bishop of Avila.

Castilla /kæˈstiːljə/ Ramón 1797–1867. President of Peru 1841–51 and 1855–62. He dominated Peruvian politics for over two decades, bringing political stability. Income from guano exports was used to reduce the national debt and improve transport and educational facilities. He abolished black slavery and the head tax on Indians.

Castle /ˈkɑːsəl/ Barbara, Baroness Castle (born Betts) 1911– . British Labour politician, a cabinet minister in the Labour governments of the 1960s and 1970s. She led the Labour group in the European Parliament 1979–89.

Castle was minister of overseas development 1964–65, transport 1965–68, employment 1968–70 (when her White Paper 'In Place of Strife', on trade-union reform, was abandoned because it suggested state intervention in industrial relations), and social services 1974–76, when she was dropped from the cabinet by Prime Minister James Callaghan. She criticized him in her *Diaries* 1980.

Castlemaine /ˈkɑːsəlmeɪn/ Lady (born Barbara Villiers) 1641–1709. Mistress of Charles II of England and mother of his son, the Duke of Grafton (1663–1690).

She was the wife from 1659 of Roger Palmer (1634–1705), created Earl of Castlemaine 1661. She became chief mistress of Charles 1660–70, when she was created Duchess of Cleveland. Among her descendants through the Duke of Grafton is Diana, Princess of Wales.

Castlereagh /ˈkɑːsəlreɪ/ Robert Stewart, Viscount Castlereagh 1769–1822. British Tory politician. As chief secretary for Ireland 1797–1801, he suppressed the rebellion of 1798 and helped the younger Pitt secure the union of England, Scotland, and Ireland 1801. As foreign secretary 1812–22, he coordinated European opposition to Napoleon and represented Britain at the Congress of Vienna 1814–15.

Castlereagh sat in the Irish House of Commons from 1790. When his father, an Ulster landowner, was made an earl 1796, he took the courtesy title of Viscount Castlereagh. In Parliament he was secretary for war and the colonies 1805–06 and 1807–09, when he had to resign after a duel with foreign secretary George →Canning. Castlereagh was foreign secretary from 1812, when he devoted himself to the overthrow of Napoleon and subsequently to the Congress of Vienna and the congress system. Abroad his policy favoured the development of material liberalism, but at home he repressed the Reform movement, and popular opinion held him responsible for the Peterloo massacre of peaceful demonstrators 1819. In 1821 he succeeded his father as Marquess of Londonderry.

Castro /ˈkæstrəʊ/ Cipriano 1858–1924. Venezuelan dictator 1899–1908, known as 'the Lion of the Andes'. When he refused to pay off foreign debts 1902, British, German, and Italian ships blockaded the country. He presided over a corrupt government. There were frequent rebellions during his rule, and opponents of his regime were exiled or murdered.

Castro (Ruz) /ˈkæstrəʊ ˈruːs/ Fidel 1927– . Cuban communist politician, prime minister 1959–76 and president from 1976. He led two unsuccessful coups against the right-wing Batista regime and led the revolution that overthrew the dictator 1959. He raised the standard of living for most Cubans but dealt harshly with dissenters.

Of wealthy parentage, Castro was educated at Jesuit schools and, after studying law at the University of Havana, gained a reputation through his work for poor clients. He opposed the Batista dictatorship, and took part, with his brother Raúl, in an unsuccessful attack on the army barracks at Santiago de Cuba 1953. After some time in exile in the USA and Mexico, Castro attempted a secret landing in Cuba 1956 in which all but 11 of his supporters were killed. He eventually gathered an army of over 5,000 which overthrew Batista on 1 Jan 1959 and he became prime minister a few months later. Raúl Castro was appointed minister of armed forces.

Castro's administration introduced a centrally planned economy based on the production for export of sugar, tobacco, and nickel. He nationalized the property of wealthy Cubans, Americans, and other foreigners 1960, resulting in the severance of relations by the USA, an economic embargo, and US attempts to subvert Cuba's government. This enmity came to a head in the Cuban missile crisis 1962 (when Soviet rockets were installed on Cuba and US president Kennedy compelled Soviet leader Khrushchev to remove them). Aid for development was provided by the USSR, which replaced the USA as Cuba's main trading partner, and Castro espoused Marxism-Leninism until, in 1974, he rejected Marx's formula 'from each according to his ability and to each according to his need' and decreed that each Cuban should 'receive according to his work'. He also improved education, housing, and health care for the majority of Cubans but lost the support of the middle class, hundreds of thousands of whom fled the country. Since 1990, events in E Europe and the disintegration of the USSR have left Castro increasingly isolated.

Cather /ˈkæðə/ Willa (Sibert) 1876–1947. US novelist and short-story writer. Born in Virginia, she moved to Nebraska as a child. Her novels frequently explore life in the pioneer West, both in her own time and in past eras; for example, *O Pioneers!* 1913 and *My Antonia* 1918, and *A Lost Lady* 1923. *Death Comes for the Archbishop* 1927 is a celebration of the spiritual pioneering of the Catholic church in New Mexico. She also wrote poetry and essays on fiction.

Catherine I /ˈkæθrɪn/ 1684–1727. Empress of Russia from 1725. A Lithuanian peasant, born Martha Skavronsky, she married a Swedish dragoon and eventually became the mistress of Peter the Great. In 1703 she was rechristened Katarina Alexeievna. The tsar divorced his wife 1711 and married Catherine 1712. She accompanied him on his campaigns, and showed tact and shrewdness. In 1724 she was proclaimed empress, and after Peter's death 1725 she ruled capably with the help of her ministers. She allied Russia with Austria and Spain in an anti-English bloc.

Catherine II *the Great* 1729–1796. Empress of Russia from 1762, and daughter of the German prince of Anhalt-Zerbst. In 1745, she married the Russian grand duke Peter. Catherine was able to dominate him; six months after he became Tsar Peter III 1762, he was murdered in a coup and Catherine ruled alone. During her reign Russia extended its boundaries to include territory from wars with the Turks 1768–74, 1787–92, and from the partitions of Poland 1772, 1793, and 1795, as well as establishing hegemony over the Black Sea.

Catherine's private life was notorious throughout Europe, but except for Grigory →Potemkin she did not permit her lovers to influence her policy.

She admired and aided the French Encyclopédistes, including d'Alembert, and corresponded with the radical writer Voltaire.

I shall be an autocrat: that's my trade. And the good Lord will forgive me: that's his.

Catherine II (attributed)

Catherine de' Medici /deɪ ˈmedɪtʃi/ 1519–1589. French queen consort of Henry II, whom she married 1533; daughter of Lorenzo de' Medici, Duke of Urbino; and mother of Francis II, Charles IX, and Henry III. At first outshone by Henry's mistress Diane de Poitiers (1490–1566), she became regent 1560–63 for Charles IX and remained in power until his death 1574.

During the religious wars of 1562–69, she first supported the Protestant Huguenots against the Roman Catholic *Guises* to ensure her own position as ruler; she later opposed them, and has been traditionally implicated in the Massacre of St Bartholomew 1572.

Catherine of Alexandria, St Christian martyr. According to legend she disputed with 50 scholars, refusing to give up her faith and marry Emperor Maxentius. Her emblem is a wheel, on which her persecutors tried to kill her (the wheel broke and she was beheaded). Feast day 25 Nov.

Catherine of Aragon /ˈærəgən/ 1485–1536. First queen of Henry VIII of England, 1509–33, and mother of Mary I. Catherine had married Henry's elder brother Prince Arthur 1501 and on his death 1502 was betrothed to Henry, marrying him on his accession. She failed to produce a male heir and Henry divorced her without papal approval, thus beginning the English Reformation.

Of their six children, only Mary lived. Wanting a male heir, Henry sought an annulment 1526 when Catherine was too old to bear children. When the pope demanded that the case be referred to him, Henry married Anne Boleyn, afterwards receiving the desired decree of nullity from Cranmer, the archbishop of Canterbury, in 1533. The Reformation in England followed, and Catherine went into retirement until her death.

Catherine of Braganza /brəˈgænzə/ 1638–1705. Queen of Charles II of England 1662–85. Her childlessness and practice of her Catholic faith were unpopular, but Charles resisted pressure for divorce. She returned to Lisbon 1692 after his death.

The daughter of John IV of Portugal (1603–1656), she brought the Portuguese possessions of Bombay and Tangier as her dowry and introduced tea drinking and citrus fruits to England.

Catherine of Genoa, St /ˈdʒenəʊə/ 1447–1510. Italian mystic who devoted herself to the sick and to meditation. Feast day 15 Sept.

Catherine of Aragon Miniature of Catherine of Aragon attributed to Lucas Hornebolte (c. 1525), National Portrait Gallery, London. Following Archbishop Cranmer's annulment of her marriage to Henry VIII, Catherine refused to accept the Act of Succession which declared her daughter Princess Mary illegitimate, and lived in seclusion and religious devotion until her death.

Catherine of Siena /siˈenə/ 1347–1380. Italian mystic, born in Siena. She persuaded Pope Gregory XI to return to Rome from Avignon 1376. In 1375 she is said to have received on her body the stigmata, the impression of Jesus' wounds. Her *Dialogue* is a classic mystical work. Feast day 29 April.

Catherine of Valois /vælˈwɑː/ 1401–1437. Queen of Henry V of England, whom she married 1420; the mother of Henry VI. After the death of Henry V, she secretly married Owen Tudor (*c.* 1400–1461) about 1425, and their son Edmund Tudor became the father of Henry VII.

Catherwood /ˈkæθəwʊd/ Frederick 1799–1854. British topographical artist and archaeological illustrator who accompanied John Lloyd →Stephens in his exploration of Central America 1839–40 and the Yucatán 1841–42. His engravings, published 1844, were the first accurate representation of Mayan civilization in the West.

Catiline /ˈkætɪlaɪn/ (Lucius Sergius Catilina) *c.* 108–62 BC. Roman politician. Twice failing to be elected to the consulship in 64/63 BC, he planned a military coup, but →Cicero exposed his conspiracy. He died at the head of the insurgents.

Catlin /ˈkætlɪn/ George 1796–1872. US painter and explorer. From the 1830s he made a series of visits to the Great Plains, painting landscapes and scenes of American Indian life.

He produced an exhibition of over 500 paintings with which he toured America and Europe. His style is factual, with close attention to detail. Many of his pictures are in the Smithsonian Institution, Washington DC.

Cato /ˈkeɪtəʊ/ Marcus Porcius 234–149 BC. Roman politician. Appointed censor (senior magistrate) in 184 BC, he excluded from the Senate those who did not meet his high standards. He was so impressed by the power of Carthage, on a visit 157, that he ended every speech by saying: 'Carthage must be destroyed.' His farming manual is the earliest surviving work in Latin prose.

Catullus /kəˈtʌləs/ Gaius Valerius c. 84–54 BC. Roman lyric poet, born in Verona of a well-to-do family. He moved in the literary and political society of Rome and wrote lyrics describing his unhappy love affair with Clodia, probably the wife of the consul Metellus, calling her Lesbia. His longer poems include two wedding songs. Many of his poems are short verses to his friends.

Cauchy /ˈkəʊʃi/ Augustin Louis 1789–1857. French mathematician who employed rigorous methods of analysis. His prolific output included work on complex functions, determinants, and probability, and on the convergence of infinite series. In calculus, he refined the concepts of the limit and the definite integral.

In 1843 he published a defence of academic freedom of thought that was instrumental in the abolition of the oath of allegiance soon after the fall of Louis Philippe in 1848.

Causley /ˈkɔːzli/ Charles (Stanley) 1917– . English poet. He published his first volume *Hands to Dance* in 1951. Later volumes include *Johnny Alleluia* 1961, *Underneath the Water* 1968, and *Figgie Hobbin* 1970. His work is characterized by simple diction and rhythms, reflecting the ballad tradition, and religious imagery.

Cauthen /ˈkɔːθən/ Steve 1960– . US jockey. He rode Affirmed to the US Triple Crown 1978 at the age of 18 and won 487 races 1977. He twice won the Epsom Derby, on Slip Anchor 1985 and on Reference Point 1987, and was UK champion jockey 1984, 1985, and 1987.

Cavaco Silva /kəˈvækəʊ ˈsɪlvə/ Anibal 1939– . Portuguese politician, finance minister 1980–81, and prime minister and Social Democratic Party (PSD) leader from 1985. Under his leadership Portugal joined the European Community 1985 and the Western European Union 1988.

Cavaco Silva studied economics in Britain and the USA, and was a university teacher and research director in the Bank of Portugal. In 1978, with the return of constitutional government, he entered politics. His first government fell in 1987, but an election later that year gave him Portugal's first absolute majority since democracy was restored. He was re-elected in the 1991 elections.

Cavafy /kəˈvɑːfi/ Constantinos. Pen name of Konstantínos Pétrou 1863–1933. Greek poet. An Alexandrian, he shed light on Greek history, recreating the classical period with zest. He published only one book of poetry and remained almost unknown until translations of his works appeared 1952.

Cavalli /kəˈvæli/ (Pietro) Francesco 1602–1676. Italian composer, organist at St Mark's, Venice, and the first to make opera a popular entertainment with such works as *Xerxes* 1654, later performed in honour of Louis XIV's wedding in Paris. 27 of his operas survive.

Cave /keɪv/ Edward 1691–1754. British printer and founder, under the pseudonym Sylvanus Urban, of *The Gentleman's Magazine* 1731–1914, the first periodical to be called a magazine. Samuel →Johnson was a contributor 1738–44.

Cavell /ˈkævəl/ Edith Louisa 1865–1915. British matron of a Red Cross hospital in Brussels, Belgium, in World War I, who helped Allied soldiers escape to the Dutch frontier. She was court-martialled by the Germans and condemned to death.

Cavendish /ˈlævəndɪʃ/ family name of dukes of Devonshire; the family seat is at Chatsworth, Derbyshire, England.

Cavendish /ˈkævəndɪʃ/ Frederick Charles, Lord Cavendish 1836–1882. British administrator, second son of the 7th Duke of Devonshire. He was appointed chief secretary to the lord lieutenant of Ireland in 1882. On the evening of his arrival in Dublin he was murdered in Phoenix Park with Thomas Burke, the permanent Irish undersecretary, by members of the Irish Invincibles, a group of Irish Fenian extremists founded 1881.

Cavendish /ˈkævəndɪʃ/ Henry 1731–1810. English physicist. He discovered hydrogen (which he called 'inflammable air') 1766, and determined the compositions of water and of nitric acid.

The Cavendish experiment (measurement of the gravitational attraction between lead and gold spheres) enabled him, using Newton's law of universal gravitation, to calculate the mass and density of the Earth.

A grandson of the 2nd duke of Devonshire, he devoted his life to scientific pursuits, living in rigorous seclusion in Clapham Common, London.

Cavendish Spencer; see →Hartington, Spencer Compton Cavendish, British politician.

Cavendish /ˈkævəndɪʃ/ Thomas 1555–1592. English navigator, and commander of the third circumnavigation of the world. He sailed in July 1586, touched Brazil, sailed down the coast to Patagonia, passed through the Straits of Magellan, and returned to Britain via the Philippines, the Cape of Good Hope, and St Helena, reaching Plymouth after two years and 50 days.

Cavour /kəˈvʊə/ Camillo Benso di, Count 1810–1861. Italian nationalist politician. He was the editor of *Il Risorgimento* from 1847. As prime minister of Piedmont 1852–59 and 1860–61, he enlisted the support of Britain and France for the concept of a united Italy achieved 1861; after expelling the Austrians 1859, he assisted Garibaldi in liberating southern Italy 1860.

Cavour was born in Turin, served in the army

in early life and entered politics in 1847. From 1848 he sat in the Piedmontese parliament and held cabinet posts 1850–52. As prime minister, he sought to secure French and British sympathy for the cause of Italian unity by sending Piedmontese troops to fight in the Crimean War. In 1858 he had a secret meeting with Napoleon III at Plombières, where they planned the war of 1859 against Austria, which resulted in the union of Lombardy with Piedmont. Then the central Italian states joined the kingdom of Italy, although Savoy and Nice were to be ceded to France. With Cavour's approval Garibaldi overthrew the Neapolitan monarchy, but Cavour occupied part of the Papal States which, with Naples and Sicily, were annexed to Italy, to prevent Garibaldi from marching on Rome.

Caxton /ˈkækstən/ William c. 1422–1491. The first English printer. He learned the art of printing in Cologne, Germany, 1471 and set up a press in Belgium where he produced the first book printed in English, his own version of a French romance, *Recuyell of the Historyes of Troye* 1474. Returning to England 1476, he established himself in London, where he produced the first book printed in England, *Dictes or Sayengis of the Philosophres* 1477.

Caxton, born in Kent, was apprenticed to a London cloth dealer 1438, and set up his own business in Bruges 1441–70; he became governor of the English merchants there, negotiating on their behalf with the dukes of Burgundy. In 1471 he went to Cologne, where he learned the art of printing, and then set up his own press in Bruges in partnership with Colard Mansion, a calligrapher. The books from Caxton's press in Westminster included editions of the poets Chaucer, John Gower, and John Lydgate (c. 1370–1449). He translated many texts from French and Latin and revised some English ones, such as Malory's *Morte d'Arthur*. Altogether he printed about 100 books.

And certaynly our langage now used varyeth ferre from that which was used and spoken when I was borne.

William Caxton 1490

Cayley /ˈkeɪli/ Arthur 1821–1895. British mathematician who developed matrix algebra, used by Werner →Heisenberg in his elucidation of quantum mechanics.

Cayley /ˈkeɪli/ George 1773–1857. British aviation pioneer, inventor of the first piloted glider in 1853, and the caterpillar tractor.

Ceausescu /tʃaʊˈʃesku/ Nicolae 1918–1989. Romanian politician, leader of the Romanian Communist Party (RCP), in power 1965–89. He pursued a policy line independent of and critical of the USSR. He appointed family members, including his wife *Elena Ceausescu*, to senior state and party posts, and governed in an increasingly repressive manner, zealously implementing schemes that impoverished the nation. The Ceausescus were overthrown in a bloody revolutionary coup Dec 1989 and executed.

Ceausescu joined the underground RCP in 1933 and was imprisoned for antifascist activities 1936–38 and 1940–44. After World War II he was elected to the Grand National Assembly and was soon given ministerial posts. He was inducted into the party secretariat and Politburo in 1954–55. In 1965 Ceausescu became leader of the RCP and from 1967 chair of the state council. He was elected president in 1974. As revolutionary changes rocked E Europe 1989, protests in Romania escalated until the Ceausescu regime was toppled. After his execution, the full extent of his repressive rule and personal extravagance became public.

Cecil /ˈsesəl/ Henry Richard Amherst 1943–   . Scottish-born racehorse trainer with stables at Warren Place, Newmarket. He was the first trainer to win over £1 million in a season (1985). He trained Slip Anchor and Reference Point to Epsom Derby wins.

Cecil /ˈsɪsəl/ Robert, 1st Earl of Salisbury 1563–1612. Secretary of state to Elizabeth I of England, succeeding his father, Lord Burghley; he was afterwards chief minister to James I (James VI of Scotland) whose accession to the English throne he secured. He discovered the Gunpowder Plot, the conspiracy to blow up the King and Parliament 1605. James I created him Earl of Salisbury 1605.

Cecil While in the service of Elizabeth I, English secretary of state Robert Cecil, 1st Earl of Salisbury, secured the succession of Scotland's James VI as James I of England. He continued as James's chief minister until his death

Cecilia, St /sə'siːliə/ Christian patron saint of music, martyred in Rome in the 2nd or 3rd century, who is said to have sung hymns while undergoing torture. Feast day 22 Nov.

Cela /ˈθela/ Camilo José 1916–   . Spanish novelist. Among his novels, characterized by their violence and brutal realism, are *La familia de Pascual Duarte*/*The Family of Pascal Duarte* 1942, and *La colmena*/*The Hive* 1951. He was awarded the Nobel Prize for Literature 1989.

Céline /se'liːn/ Louis Ferdinand. Pen name of Louis Destouches 1884–1961. French novelist whose writings (the first of which was *Voyage au bout de la nuit*/*Journey to the End of the Night* 1932) aroused controversy over their cynicism and misanthropy.

Cellini /tʃe'liːni/ Benvenuto 1500–1571. Italian sculptor and goldsmith working in the Mannerist style; author of an arrogant autobiography (begun 1558). Among his works are a graceful bronze *Perseus* 1545–54 (Loggia dei Lanzi, Florence) and a gold salt cellar made for Francis I of France 1540–43 (Kunsthistorisches Museum, Vienna), topped by nude reclining figures.

Cellini was born in Florence and apprenticed to a goldsmith. In 1519 he went to Rome, later worked for the papal mint, and was once imprisoned on a charge of having embezzled pontifical jewels. He worked for a time in France at the court of Francis I, but finally returned to Florence in 1545.

The difference between a painting and a sculpture is the difference between a shadow and the thing that casts it.

Benvenuto Cellini
letter to Benedetto Varchi 1547

Cerf /sɜːf/ Bennett Alfred 1898–1971. US editor and publisher. In 1925 co-purchased the rights to the Modern Library series, and subsequently founded Random House 1927. The company grew to be one of the world's largest publishing houses.

Born in New York, Cerf was educated at Columbia University and briefly worked as a reporter for the *New York Herald Tribune*. He published several collections of humour and appeared as a regular panellist on the popular television show 'What's My Line?'

Cervantes /sɜːˈvæntiːz/ Saavedra, Miguel de 1547–1616. Spanish novelist, playwright, and poet whose masterpiece *Don Quixote* (in full *El ingenioso hidalgo Don Quixote de la Mancha*) was published 1605. In 1613, his *Novelas ejemplares*/*Exemplary Novels* appeared, followed by *Viaje del Parnaso*/*The Voyage to Parnassus* 1614. A spurious second part of *Don Quixote*

prompted Cervantes to bring out his own second part 1615, often considered superior to the first in construction and characterization.

Born at Alcalá de Henares, he entered the army in Italy, and was wounded in the battle of Lepanto 1571. While on his way back to Spain 1575, he was captured by Barbary pirates and taken to Algiers, where he became a slave until ransomed 1580.

Returning to Spain, he wrote several plays, and in 1585 his pastoral romance *Galatea* was printed. He was employed in Seville 1587 provisioning the Armada. While working as a tax collector, he was imprisoned more than once for deficiencies in his accounts. He sank into poverty, and little is known of him until 1605 when he published *Don Quixote*. The novel was an immediate success and was soon translated into English and French.

Cesalpino, Andrea 1519–1603. Italian botanist who showed that plants could be and should be classified by their anatomy and structure. In *De plantis* 1583 Cesalpino offered the first remotely modern classification of plants. Before this plants were classed by their location – for example marsh plants, moorland plants, and even foreign plants.

César /se'zaː/ adopted name of César Baldaccini 1921–   . French sculptor who uses iron and scrap metal and, in the 1960s, crushed car bodies. His subjects are imaginary insects and animals.

Cetewayo /ketʃ'waɪəʊ/ (Cetshwayo) *c.* 1826–1884. King of Zululand, South Africa, 1873–83, whose rule was threatened by British annexation of the Transvaal 1877. Although he defeated the British at Isandhlwana 1879, he was later that year defeated by them at Ulundi. Restored to his throne 1883, he was then expelled by his subjects.

Cézanne /seɪ'zæn/ Paul 1839–1906. French Post-Impressionist painter, a leading figure in the development of modern art. He broke away from the Impressionists' spontaneous vision to develop a style that captured not only light and life, but the structure of natural forms in landscapes, still lifes, portraits, and his series of bathers.

He was born in Aix-en-Provence, where he studied, and was a friend of the novelist Émile Zola. In 1872 Cézanne met Pissarro and lived near him in Pontoise, outside Paris, but soon abandoned Impressionism. His series of paintings of Mont Sainte-Victoire in Provence from the 1880s into the 1900s show an increasing fragmentation of the painting's surface and a movement towards abstraction, with layers of colour and square brushstrokes achieving monumental solidity. He was greatly revered by early abstract painters, notably Picasso and Braque.

Chabrier /ˈʃæbrieɪ/ (Alexis) Emmanuel 1841–1894. French composer who wrote *España* 1883, an orchestral rhapsody, and the light opera *Le Roi* *malgré lui/King Against His Will* 1887. His orchestration inspired Debussy and Ravel.

Chabrol /ʃæˈbrɒl/ Claude 1930– . French film director. Originally a critic, he was one of the New Wave directors. His works of murder and suspense, which owe much to Hitchcock, include *Les Cousins/The Cousins* 1959, *Les Biches/The Girlfriends* 1968, *Le Boucher/The Butcher* 1970, and *Cop au Vin* 1984.

Chadli /ʃædˈliː/ Benjedid 1929– . Algerian socialist politician, president 1979–92. An army colonel, he supported Boumédienne in the overthrow of Ben Bella 1965, and succeeded Boumédienne 1979, pursuing more moderate policies. Chadli resigned Jan 1992 following a victory for Islamic fundamentalists in the first round of assembly elections.

Chadwick /ˈtʃædwɪk/ Edwin 1800–1890. English social reformer, author of the Poor Law Report 1834. He played a prominent part in the campaign which resulted in the Public Health Act 1848. He was commissioner of the first Board of Health 1848–54.

A self-educated protégé of Jeremy →Bentham and advocate of utilitarianism, he used his influence to implement measures to eradicate cholera, improve sanitation in urban areas, and clear slums in British cities.

Chadwick /ˈtʃædwɪk/ James 1891–1974. British physicist. In 1932 he discovered the particle in the nucleus of an atom that became known as the neutron because it has no electric charge. He received the Nobel Prize for Physics 1935.

Chadwick studied at Cambridge under Ernest →Rutherford. He was Lyon Jones professor of physics at Liverpool 1935–48, and master of Gonville and Caius College, Cambridge 1948–59. In 1940 he was one of the British scientists reporting on the atom bomb.

Chadwick /ˈtʃædwɪk/ Lynn 1914– . British abstract sculptor known for mobiles (influenced by Alexander →Calder) in the 1940s and for welded ironwork from the 1950s.

Chagall /ʃæˈɡæl/ Marc 1887–1985. Russian-born French painter and designer; much of his highly coloured, fantastic imagery was inspired by the village life of his boyhood and by Jewish and Russian folk tradition. He also designed stained glass, mosaics (for Israel's Knesset in the 1960s), the ceiling of the Paris Opera House 1964, tapestries, and stage sets. He was an original figure, often seen as a precursor of Surrealism, as in *The Dream* (Metropolitan Museum of Art, New York).

Chagall lived mainly in France from 1922. His stained glass can be found in, notably, a chapel in Vence, the south of France, 1950s, and a synagogue near Jerusalem 1961. He also produced illustrated books.

Chaillu /ʃaɪˈuː/ Paul Belloni du 1835–1903. French-born US explorer. In 1855 he began a four-year journey of exploration in West Africa. His *Explorations and Adventures in Equatorial Africa* 1861 describes his discovery of gorillas in Gabon.

Chain /tʃeɪn/ Ernst Boris 1906–1979. German-born British biochemist who worked on the development of penicillin. Chain fled to Britain from the Nazis 1933. After the discovery of penicillin by Alexander Fleming, Chain worked to isolate and purify it. For this work, he shared the 1945 Nobel Prize for Medicine with Fleming and Howard Florey. Chain also discovered penicillinase, an enzyme that destroys penicillin.

Chaka /ʃɑːɡə/ alternative spelling of →Shaka, Zulu chief.

Chaliapin /ʃæliˈæpɪn/ Fyodor Ivanovich 1873–1938. Russian bass singer, born in Kazan. His greatest role was that of Boris Godunov in Mussorgsky's opera of the same name. Chaliapin left the USSR 1921 to live and sing in the world's capitals.

Chalmers /tʃɑːməz/ Thomas 1780–1847. Scottish theologian. At the Disruption of the Church of Scotland 1843, Chalmers withdrew from the church along with a large number of other priests, and became principal of the Free Church college, thus founding the Free Church of Scotland.

As minister of Tron Church, Glasgow, from 1815, Chalmers became renowned for his eloquence and for his proposals for social reform. In 1823 he became professor of moral philosophy at St Andrews, and in 1828 of theology at Edinburgh.

Chamberlain /ˈtʃeɪmbəlɪn/ (Arthur) Neville 1869– 1940. British Conservative politician, son of Joseph Chamberlain. He was prime minister 1937–40; his policy of appeasement towards the fascist dictators Mussolini and Hitler (with whom he concluded the Munich Agreement 1938) failed to prevent the outbreak of World War II. He resigned 1940 following the defeat of the British forces in Norway.

Younger son of Joseph Chamberlain and half-brother of Austen Chamberlain, he was born in Birmingham, of which he was lord mayor 1915. He was minister of health 1923 and 1924–29 and worked at slum clearance. In 1931 he was chancellor of the Exchequer in the national government, and in 1937 succeeded Baldwin as prime minister. Trying to close the old Anglo-Irish feud, he agreed to return to Eire those ports that had been occupied by the navy. He also attempted to appease the demands of the European dictators, particularly Mussolini. In 1938 he went to Munich and negotiated with Hitler the settlement of the Czechoslovak question. He was ecstatically received on his return, and claimed that the Munich Agreement brought 'peace in our time'. Within a year, however, Britain was at war with Germany.

Chamberlain British politician (Joseph) Chamberlain was regarded as a radical. His scheme of preferential tariffs favouring colonies and protecting native manufacturers was adopted in part 1919, and wholly 1932.

Chamberlain /ˈtʃeɪmbəlɪn/ (Joseph) Austen 1863–1937. British Conservative politician, elder son of Joseph Chamberlain; as foreign secretary 1924–29 he negotiated the Pact of Locarno (settling the question of French security and guaranteeing Germany's existing frontiers with France and Belgium), for which he won the Nobel Peace Prize 1925, and signed the Kellogg–Briand pact to outlaw war 1928.

He was elected to Parliament 1892 as a Liberal-Unionist, and after holding several minor posts was chancellor of the Exchequer 1903–06. During World War I he was secretary of state for India 1915–17 and member of the war cabinet 1918. He was chancellor of the Exchequer 1919–21 and Lord Privy Seal 1921–22, but failed to secure the leadership of the party 1922, as many Conservatives resented the part he had taken in the Irish settlement of 1921. He was foreign secretary in the Baldwin government 1924–29, and negotiated and signed the Locarno Pact 1925 to fix the boundaries of Germany, and the Kellogg–Briand pact 1928 to ban war and provide for peaceful settlement of disputes.

Chamberlain /ˈtʃeɪmbəlɪn/ Joseph 1836–1914. British politician, reformist mayor of and member of Parliament for Birmingham; in 1886, he resigned from the cabinet over Gladstone's policy of home rule for Ireland, and led the revolt of the Liberal-Unionists.

By 1874 Chamberlain had made a sufficient fortune in the Birmingham screw-manufacturing business to devote himself entirely to politics. He adopted radical views, and took an active part in local affairs. Three times mayor of Birmingham, he carried through many schemes of municipal development. In 1876 he was elected to Parliament and joined the republican group led by Charles Dilke, the extreme left wing of the Liberal Party. In 1880 he entered Gladstone's cabinet as president of the Board of Trade. The climax of his radical period was reached with the unauthorized programme, advocating, among other things, free education, graduated taxation, and smallholdings of 'three acres and a cow'.

As colonial secretary in Salisbury's Conservative government, Chamberlain was responsible for relations with the Boer republics up to the outbreak of war 1899. In 1903 he resigned to campaign for imperial preference or tariff reform as a means of consolidating the empire. From 1906 he was incapacitated by a stroke. Chamberlain was one of the most colourful figures of British politics, and his monocle and orchid made him a favourite subject for political cartoonists.

Chamberlain /ˈtʃeɪmbəlɪn/ Owen 1920– . US physicist whose graduate studies were interrupted by wartime work on the Manhattan Project at Los Alamos. After World War II, working with Italian physicist Emilio Segrè, he discovered the existence of the antiproton. Both men were awarded the Nobel Prize for Physics 1959.

Chamberlain /ˈtʃeɪmbəlɪn/ Wilt (Wilton Norman) 1936– . US basketball player who set a record by averaging 50.4 points a game during the 1962 season, and was the only man to score 100 points in a game.

He was known as 'Wilt the Stilt' because of his height 2.16 m/7 ft 1 in.

Chambers /ˈtʃeɪmbəz/ William 1726–1796. British architect and popularizer of Chinese influence (for example, the pagoda in Kew Gardens, London) and designer of Somerset House, London.

Chamisso /ʃæˈmɪsəʊ/ Adelbert von. Pen name of Louis-Charles-Adélaide Chamisso de Boncourt 1781–1831. German writer of the story 'Peter Schlemihl', about a man who sold his shadow. He was born into a French family who left France because of the French Revolution; subsequently he went as a botanist on Otto von Kotzebue's trip around the world 1815–18, recounted in *Reise um de Welt* 1821. His verse includes the cycle of lyrics *Frauenliebe und Frauenleben* 1831, set to music by Schumann.

Chamorro /ʃəˈmɒrəʊ/ Violeta Barrios de *c.* 1939– . President of Nicaragua from 1990. With strong US support, she was elected to be the candidate for the National Opposition Union (UNO) 1989, winning the presidency from David Ortega Saavedra Feb 1990 and thus ending the period of Sandinista rule.

Chamorro's political career began 1978 with the assassination by the right-wing dictatorship of her husband, Pedro Joaquín Chamorro. Violeta became candidate for UNO, a 14-party coalition, Sept 1989. In the 1990 elections, UNO won 51 of the 92 seats in the National Assembly. The Sandinista Liberation Front (FSLN), however, remained the largest party, and together with reactionary elements within Chamorro's own coalition, obstructed the implementation of her policies. Her early presidency was marked by rising unemployment, strikes, and continuing skirmishes between Contra rebels and Sandinista militants in the mountains (despite official disbanding of the Contras June 1990).

Champaigne /ʃæm'peɪn/ Philippe de 1602–1674. French artist, the leading portrait painter of the court of Louis XIII. Of Flemish origin, he went to Paris 1621 and gained the patronage of Cardinal Richelieu. His style is elegant, cool, and restrained.

Champlain /ʃæm'pleɪn/ Samuel de 1567–1635. French pioneer, soldier, and explorer in Canada. Having served in the army of Henry IV and on an expedition to the West Indies, he began his exploration of Canada 1603. In a third expedition 1608 he founded and named Québec, and was appointed lieutenant governor of French Canada 1612.

Champollion /ʃɒmpɒl'jɒn/ Jean François, le Jeune 1790–1832. French Egyptologist who in 1822 deciphered Egyptian hieroglyphics with the aid of the Rosetta Stone.

Chandler /tʃɑːndlə/ Happy (Albert Benjamin) 1898–1991. US politician and sports administra-

Chambers British architect William Chambers was a founder of the Royal Academy and did much to raise the status of the architectural profession. His book Designs of Chinese Buildings 1717 and his pagoda in Kew Gardens were inspired by a voyage made to China in his youth.

tor. He was governor of Kentucky 1934–39 and 1955–59. After his first term as governor he resigned to enter the US Senate. In 1945 Chandler was appointed baseball commissioner but resigned 1951, mainly because of personality conflicts with several team owners.

Born in Corydon, Kentucky, USA, Chandler studied law at the University of Kentucky and was admitted to the bar 1924 before serving in the state legislature.

Chandler /tʃɑːndlə/ Raymond 1888–1959. US crime writer who created the hard-boiled private eye Philip Marlowe in books that include *The Big Sleep* 1939, *Farewell, My Lovely* 1940, and *The Long Goodbye* 1954.

Born in Chicago, he was educated at Dulwich College public school in London, England. He also wrote numerous screenplays, notably *Double Indemnity* 1944 and *Strangers on a Train* 1951.

Down these mean streets a man must go who is not himself mean, who is neither tarnished nor afraid.

Raymond Chandler *The Simple Art of Murder*

Chandrasekhar /tʃændrə'seɪkə/ Subrahmanyan 1910– . Indian-born US astrophysicist who made pioneering studies of the structure and evolution of stars. The *Chandrasekhar limit* of 1.4 Suns is the maximum mass of a white dwarf before it turns into a neutron star. Born in Lahore, he studied in Madras, India, and Cambridge, England, before emigrating to the USA. Nobel Prize for Physics 1983.

Chanel /ʃæ'nel/ Coco (Gabrielle) 1883–1971. French fashion designer, creator of the 'little black dress', informal cardigan suit, costume jewellery, and perfumes.

Chaney /tʃeɪni/ Lon (Alonso) 1883–1930. US star of silent films, often in grotesque or monstrous roles such as *The Phantom of the Opera* 1925. A master of make-up, he was nicknamed 'the Man of a Thousand Faces'. He sometimes used extremely painful devices for added effect, as in the title role in *The Hunchback of Notre Dame* 1923, when he carried over 30 kg/70 lb of costume in the form of a heavy hump and harness.

Chaney /tʃeɪni/ Lon, Jr (Creighton) 1906–1973. US actor, son of Lon Chaney, who gave an acclaimed performance as Lennie in *Of Mice and Men* 1940. He went on to star in many 1940s horror films, including the title role in *The Wolf Man* 1941. His other work includes *My Favorite Brunette* 1947 and *The Haunted Palace* 1963.

Chang Ch'ien /dʒæŋ 'tʃen/ lived 2nd century BC. Chinese explorer who pioneered the Silk Road, an overland route of about 6,400 km/4,000 mi by which silk was brought from China to Europe in return for trade goods.

Channing /ˈtʃænɪŋ/ William Ellery 1780–1842. US minister and theologian. He became a leader of the Unitarian movement 1819, opposing the strict Calvinism of the New England Congregationalist churches. He was an instrumental figure in the establishment of the American Unitarian Association. In his later years, Channing devoted his energies to abolitionism in its campaign to end the institution of slavery.

Born in Newport, Rhode Island, Channing was educated at Harvard University. He was appointed minister of the Federal Street Congregationalist Church in Boston 1803.

Chantrey /ˈtʃɑːntri/ Francis Legatt 1781–1841. British sculptor, known for portrait busts and monuments. His unaffected studies of children were much loved in his day, notably *Sleeping Children* 1817 (Lichfield cathedral).

Chaplin /ˈtʃæplɪn/ Charlie (Charles Spencer) 1889–1977. English film actor and director. He made his reputation as a tramp with a smudge moustache, bowler hat, and twirling cane in silent comedies from the mid-1910s, including *The Rink* 1916, *The Kid* 1920, and *The Gold Rush* 1925. His work often contrasts buffoonery with pathos, and his later films combine dialogue with mime and music, as in *The Great Dictator* 1940 and *Limelight* 1952. He was one of cinema's most popular and greatest stars.

Chaplin was born in south London and first appeared on the stage at the age of five. He joined Mack Sennett's Keystone Company in Los Angeles 1913. Along with Mary Pickford, Douglas Fairbanks, and D W →Griffith, Chaplin formed United Artists 1919 as an independent company to distribute their films. His other films include *City Lights* 1931, *Modern Times* 1936, and *Monsieur Verdoux* (in which he spoke for the first time) 1947. *Limelight* 1952 was awarded an Oscar for Chaplin's musical theme. When accused of communist sympathies during the McCarthy witchhunt, he left the USA 1952 and moved to Switzerland. He received special Oscars 1928 and 1972.

All I need to make a comedy is a park, a policeman and a pretty girl.

Charlie Chaplin *My Autobiography*

Chapman /ˈtʃæpmən/ Frederick Spencer 1907–1971. British explorer, mountaineer, and writer who explored Greenland, the Himalayas, and Malaysia. He accompanied Gino Watkins on the British Arctic Air Routes Expedition 1930–31, recalled in *Northern Lights* 1932, and in 1935 he joined a climbing expedition to the Himalayas. For two years he participated in a government mission to Tibet described in *Lhasa, the Holy City* 1938, before setting out to climb the 7,315 m/24,000 ft peak Chomollari.

Chapman /ˈtʃæpmən/ George 1559–1634. English poet and dramatist. His translations of the Greek epics of Homer (completed 1616) were celebrated; his plays include the comedy *Eastward Ho!* (with Jonson and Marston) 1605 and the tragedy *Bussy d'Amboise* 1607.

Chapman /ˈtʃæpmən/ John ('Johnny Appleseed') 1774–1845. US pioneer and folk hero, credited with establishing orchards throughout the Midwest by planting seeds as he travelled. Famous as the subject of local legends and folk tales, Chapman was described as a religious visionary with boundless generosity.

Born in Leominster, Massachusetts, Chapman roamed westward from Pennsylvania in the years after 1800, planting apple seeds in Ohio and Indiana. However, few specific details about his later life can be verified.

Charcot /ʃɑːˈkəʊ/ Jean-Martin 1825–1893. French neurologist who studied hysteria, sclerosis, locomotor ataxia, and senile diseases. Among his pupils was Sigmund →Freud.

Charcot worked at a hospital in Paris, where he studied the way certain mental illnesses cause physical changes in the brain. He exhibited hysterical women at weekly public lectures, which became highly fashionable events.

Chardin /ʃɑːˈdæn/ Jean-Baptiste-Siméon 1699–1779. French painter of naturalistic still lifes and quiet domestic scenes that recall the Dutch tradition. His work is a complete contrast to that of his contemporaries, the Rococo painters. He developed his own technique using successive layers of paint to achieve depth of tone and is generally considered one of the finest exponents of the genre.

Chardonnet /ʃɑːdɒˈneɪ/ Hilaire Bernigaud 1839–1924. French chemist who developed artificial silk 1883, the first artificial fibre.

Charlemagne /ˈʃɑːləmeɪn/ Charles I *the Great* 742–814. King of the Franks from 768 and Holy Roman emperor from 800. By inheritance (his father was →Pepin the Short) and extensive campaigns of conquest, he united most of W Europe by 804, when after 30 years of war the Saxons came under his control. He reformed the legal, judicial, and military systems; established schools; and promoted Christianity, commerce, agriculture, arts, and literature. In his capital, Aachen, scholars gathered from all over Europe.

Pepin had been mayor of the palace in Merovingian Neustria until he was crowned king by Pope Stephen II (died 757) in 754, and his sons Carl (Charlemagne) and Carloman were crowned as joint heirs. When Pepin died 768, Charlemagne inherited the N Frankish kingdom, and when Carloman died 771, he also took possession of his domains.

He was engaged in his first Saxon campaign when the Pope's call for help against the Lombards reached him; he crossed the Alps, captured

Pavia, and took the title of king of the Lombards. The pacification and christianizing of the Saxon peoples occupied the greater part of Charlemagne's reign. From 792 N Saxony was subdued, and in 804 the whole region came under his rule.

In 777 the emir of Zaragoza asked for Charlemagne's help against the emir of Córdoba. Charlemagne crossed the Pyrenees 778 and reached the Ebro but had to turn back from Zaragoza. The rearguard action of Roncesvalles, in which →Roland, warden of the Breton March, and other Frankish nobles were ambushed and killed by Basques, was later glorified in the *Chanson de Roland*. In 801 the district between the Pyrenees and the Llobregat was organized as the Spanish March. The independent duchy of Bavaria was incorporated in the kingdom 788, and the Avar people who dominated Russia north of the Black Sea and the lands occupied by the Bulgarians and Slavs, were subdued 791–96 and accepted Christianity. Charlemagne's last campaign was against a Danish attack on his northern frontier 810.

The supremacy of the Frankish king in Europe found outward expression in the bestowal of the imperial title: in Rome, during Mass on Christmas Day 800, Pope Leo III crowned Charlemagne emperor. He enjoyed diplomatic relations with Byzantium, Baghdad, Mercia, Northumbria, and other regions. Jury courts were introduced, the laws of the Franks revised, and other peoples' laws written down. A new coinage was introduced, weights and measures were reformed, and communications were improved. Charlemagne also took a lively interest in theology, organized the church in his dominions, and furthered missionary enterprises and monastic reform.

The *Carolingian Renaissance* of learning began when he persuaded the Northumbrian scholar Alcuin to enter his service 781. Charlemagne gathered a kind of academy around him. Although he never learned to read, he collected the old heroic sagas, began a Frankish grammar, and promoted religious instruction in the vernacular. He died 28 Jan 814 in Aachen, where he was buried. Soon a cycle of heroic legends and romances developed around him, including epics by Ariosto, Boiardo, and Tasso.

Charles /tʃɑːlz/ (Mary) Eugenia 1919– . Dominican politician, prime minister from 1980; cofounder and first leader of the centrist Dominica Freedom Party (DFP). Two years after Dominica's independence the DFP won the 1980 general election and she became the Caribbean's first female prime minister.

Charles qualified as a barrister in England and returned to practise in the Windward and Leeward Islands in the West Indies.

Charles /ʃɑːl/ Jacques Alexandre César 1746–1823. French physicist who studied gases and made the first ascent in a hydrogen-filled balloon 1783. His work on the expansion of gases led to the formulation of Charles's law, which states that the volume of a given mass of gas at constant pressure is directly proportional to its absolute temperature (in kelvin).

Charles /tʃɑːlz/ Ray 1930– . US singer, songwriter, and pianist whose first hits were 'I've Got A Woman' 1955, 'What'd I Say' 1959, and 'Georgia on My Mind' 1960. He has recorded gospel, blues, rock, soul, country, and rhythm and blues.

Charles /tʃɑːlz/ two kings of Britain:

Charles I 1600–1649. King of Great Britain and Ireland from 1625, son of James I of England (James VI of Scotland). He accepted the petition of right 1628 but then dissolved Parliament and ruled without a parliament 1629–40. His advisers were →Strafford and →Laud, who persecuted the Puritans and provoked the Scots to revolt. The Short Parliament, summoned 1640, refused funds, and the Long Parliament later that year rebelled.

Charles declared war on Parliament 1642 but surrendered 1646 and was beheaded 1649. He was the father of Charles II.

Charles was born at Dunfermline, and became heir to the throne on the death of his brother Henry 1612. He married Henrietta Maria, daughter of Henry IV of France. When he succeeded his father, friction with Parliament began at once. The parliaments of 1625 and 1626 were dissolved, and that of 1628 refused supplies until Charles had accepted the Petition of Right. In 1629 it attacked Charles's illegal taxation and support of the Arminians (see Jacobus →Arminius) in the church, whereupon he dissolved Parliament and imprisoned its leaders.

For 11 years he ruled without a parliament, the Eleven Years' Tyranny, raising money by expedients, such as ship money, that alienated the nation, while the Star Chamber suppressed opposition by persecuting the Puritans. When Charles attempted 1637 to force a prayer book on the English model on Presbyterian Scotland he found himself confronted with a nation in arms. The Short Parliament, which met April 1640, refused to grant money until grievances were redressed, and was speedily dissolved. The Scots then advanced into England and forced their own terms on Charles. The Long Parliament met 3 Nov 1640 and declared extraparliamentary taxation illegal, abolished the Star Chamber and other prerogative courts, and voted that Parliament could not be dissolved without its own consent. Laud and other ministers were imprisoned, and Strafford condemned to death. After the failure of his attempt to arrest the parliamentary leaders 4 Jan 1642, Charles, confident that he had substantial support among those who felt that Parliament was becoming too radical and zealous, withdrew from London, and on 22 Aug declared war on Parliament by raising his standard at Nottingham.

Charles's defeat at Naseby June 1645 ended all hopes of victory; in May 1646 he surrendered at

Newark to the Scots, who handed him over to Parliament Jan 1647. In June the army seized him and carried him off to Hampton Court. While the army leaders strove to find a settlement, Charles secretly intrigued for a Scottish invasion. In Nov he escaped, but was recaptured and held at Carisbrooke Castle; a Scottish invasion followed 1648, and was shattered by →Cromwell at Preston. In Jan 1649 the House of Commons set up a high court of justice, which tried Charles and condemned him to death. He was beheaded 30 Jan before the Banqueting House in Whitehall.

Charles II 1630–1685. King of Great Britain and Ireland from 1660, when Parliament accepted the restoration of the monarchy after the collapse of Cromwell's Commonwealth; son of Charles I. His chief minister Clarendon, who arranged his marriage 1662 with Catherine of Braganza, was replaced 1667 with the Cabal of advisers. His plans to restore Catholicism in Britain led to war with the Netherlands 1672–74 in support of Louis XIV of France and a break with Parliament, which he dissolved 1681. He was succeeded by James II.

Charles was born in St James's Palace, London; during the Civil War he lived with his father at Oxford 1642–45, and after the victory of Cromwell's Parliamentary forces withdrew to France. Accepting the Covenanters' offer to make him king, he landed in Scotland 1650, and was crowned at Scone 1 Jan 1651. An attempt to invade England was ended 3 Sept by Cromwell's victory at Worcester. Charles escaped, and for nine years he wandered through France, Germany, Flanders, Spain, and Holland until the opening of negotiations by George Monk (1608–1670) 1660. In April Charles issued the Declaration of Breda, promising a general

Charles II The eldest son of Charles I, Charles II, proclaimed king in 1660 was a popular King and a patron of the arts and sciences.

amnesty and freedom of conscience. Parliament accepted the Declaration and he was proclaimed king 8 May 1660, landed at Dover on 26 May, and entered London three days later.

Charles wanted to make himself absolute, and favoured Catholicism for his subjects as most consistent with absolute monarchy. The disasters of the Dutch war furnished an excuse for banishing Clarendon 1667, and he was replaced by the Cabal of Clifford and Arlington, both secret Catholics, and →Buckingham, Ashley (Lord →Shaftesbury), and →Lauderdale, who had links with the Dissenters. In 1670 Charles signed the Secret Treaty of Dover, the full details of which were known only to Clifford and Arlington, whereby he promised Louis XIV of France he would declare himself a Catholic, re-establish Catholicism in England, and support Louis's projected war against the Dutch; in return Louis was to finance Charles and in the event of resistance to supply him with troops. War with the Netherlands followed 1672, and at the same time Charles issued the Declaration of Indulgence, suspending all penal laws against Catholics and Dissenters.

In 1673, Parliament forced Charles to withdraw the Indulgence and accept a Test Act excluding all Catholics from office, and in 1674 to end the Dutch war. The Test Act broke up the Cabal, while Shaftesbury, who had learned the truth about the treaty, assumed the leadership of the opposition. →Danby, the new chief minister, built up a court party in the Commons by bribery, while subsidies from Louis relieved Charles from dependence on Parliament. In 1678 Titus →Oates's announcement of a 'popish plot' released a general panic, which Shaftesbury exploited to introduce his Exclusion Bill, excluding James, Duke of York, from the succession as a Catholic; instead he hoped to substitute Charles's illegitimate son →Monmouth.

In 1681 Parliament was summoned at Oxford, which had been the Royalist headquarters during the Civil War. The Whigs attended armed, but when Shaftesbury rejected a last compromise, Charles dissolved Parliament and the Whigs fled in terror. Charles now ruled without a parliament, financed by Louis XIV. When the Whigs plotted a revolt, their leaders were executed, while Shaftesbury and Monmouth fled to the Netherlands.

Charles was a patron of the arts and science. His mistresses included Lady →Castlemaine, Nell →Gwyn, Lady →Portsmouth, and Lucy →Walter.

This is very true: for my words are my own, and my actions are my ministers.

Charles II in reply to Lord Rochester's observation that the king 'never said a foolish thing, nor ever did a wise one'

Charles (full name Charles Philip Arthur George) 1948– . Prince of the UK, heir to the

British throne, and Prince of Wales since 1958 (invested 1969). He is the first-born child of Queen Elizabeth II and the Duke of Edinburgh. He studied at Trinity College, Cambridge, 1967–70, before serving in the Royal Air Force and Royal Navy. He is the first royal heir since 1659 to have an English wife, Lady Diana Spencer, daughter of the 8th Earl Spencer. They have two sons and heirs, William (1982–   ) and Henry (1984–   ).

Prince Charles's concern for social and environmental issues has led to many self-help projects for the young and underprivileged, and he is a leading critic of unsympathetic features of contemporary architecture.

Charles /tʃɑːlz/ ten kings of France, including:

Charles I king of France, better known as the Holy Roman emperor →Charlemagne.

Charles II *the Bald* king of France, see →Charles II, Holy Roman emperor.

Charles III *the Simple* 879–929. King of France 893–922, son of Louis the Stammerer. He was crowned at Reims. In 911 he ceded what later became the duchy of Normandy to the Norman chief Rollo.

Charles IV *the Fair* 1294–1328. King of France from 1322, when he succeeded Philip V as the last of the direct Capetian line.

Charles V *the Wise* 1337–1380. King of France from 1364. He was regent during the captivity of his father, John II, in England 1356–60, and became king on John's death. He reconquered nearly all France from England 1369–80.

Charles VI *the Mad* or *the Well-Beloved* 1368–1422. King of France from 1380, succeeding his father Charles V; he was under the regency of his uncles until 1388. He became mentally unstable 1392, and civil war broke out between the dukes of Orléans and Burgundy. Henry V of England invaded France 1415, conquering Normandy, and in 1420 forced Charles to sign the Treaty of Troyes, recognizing Henry as his successor.

Charles VII 1403–1461. King of France from 1429. Son of Charles VI, he was excluded from the succession by the Treaty of Troyes, but recognized by the south of France. In 1429 Joan of Arc raised the siege of Orléans and had him crowned at Reims. He organized France's first standing army and by 1453 had expelled the English from all of France except Calais.

Charles VIII 1470–1498. King of France from 1483, when he succeeded his father, Louis XI. In 1494 he unsuccessfully tried to claim the Neapolitan crown, and when he entered Naples 1495 was forced to withdraw by a coalition of Milan, Venice, Spain, and the Holy Roman Empire. He defeated them at Fornovo, but lost Naples. He died while preparing a second expedition.

Charles IX 1550–1574. King of France from 1560. Second son of Henry II and Catherine de' Medici, he succeeded his brother Francis II at the age of ten but remained under the domination of his mother's regency for ten years while France was torn by religious wars. In 1570 he fell under the influence of the Huguenot leader Gaspard de Coligny (1517–1572); alarmed by this, Catherine instigated his order for the Massacre of St Bartholomew, which led to a new religious war.

Charles X 1757–1836. King of France from 1824. Grandson of Louis XV and brother of Louis XVI and Louis XVIII, he was known as the comte d'Artois before his accession. He fled to England at the beginning of the French Revolution, and when he came to the throne on the death of Louis XVIII, he attempted to reverse the achievements of the Revolution. A revolt ensued 1830, and he again fled to England.

Charles /tʃɑːlz/ seven rulers of the Holy Roman Empire, including:

Charles I Holy Roman emperor, better known as →Charlemagne.

Charles II *the Bald* 823–877. Holy Roman emperor from 875 and (as Charles II) king of France from 843. Younger son of Louis I (the Pious), he warred against his eldest brother, Emperor Lothair I. The Treaty of Verdun 843 made him king of the West Frankish Kingdom (now France and the Spanish Marches).

Charles III *the Fat* 839–888. Holy Roman emperor 881–87; he became king of the West Franks 885, thus uniting for the last time the whole of Charlemagne's dominions, but was deposed.

Charles IV 1316–1378. Holy Roman emperor from 1355 and king of Bohemia from 1346. Son of John of Luxembourg, king of Bohemia, he was elected king of Germany 1346 and ruled all Germany from 1347. He was the founder of the first German university in Prague 1348.

Charles V 1500–1558. Holy Roman emperor 1519–56. Son of Philip of Burgundy and Joanna of Castile, he inherited vast possessions, which led to rivalry from Francis I of France, whose alliance with the Ottoman Empire brought Vienna under siege 1529 and 1532. Charles was also in conflict with the Protestants in Germany until the Treaty of Passau 1552, which allowed the Lutherans religious liberty.

Charles was born in Ghent and received the Netherlands from his father 1506; Spain, Naples, Sicily, Sardinia, and the Spanish dominions in N Africa and the Americas on the death of his maternal grandfather, Ferdinand V of Castile (1452–1516); and from his paternal grandfather, Maximilian I, the Habsburg dominions 1519, when he was elected emperor. He was crowned in Aachen 1520. From 1517 the empire was split by the rise of Lutheranism, Charles making unsuccessful attempts to reach a settlement at Augsburg 1530, and being forced by the Treaty of Passau to yield most of the Protestant demands. Worn out, he abdicated in favour of his son Philip II in the Netherlands 1555 and Spain 1556. He yielded the imperial crown to his brother Ferdinand I, and retired to the monastery of Yuste, Spain.

Charles VI 1685–1740. Holy Roman emperor from 1711, father of →Maria Theresa, whose succession to his Austrian dominions he tried to ensure, and himself claimant to the Spanish throne 1700, thus causing the War of the Spanish Succession.

Charles VII 1697–1745. Holy Roman emperor from 1742, opponent of →Maria Theresa's claim to the Austrian dominions of Charles VI.

Charles /tʃɑːlz/ (Karl Franz Josef) 1887–1922. Emperor of Austria and king of Hungary from 1916, the last of the Habsburg emperors. He succeeded his great-uncle Franz Josef 1916 but was forced to withdraw to Switzerland 1918, although he refused to abdicate. In 1921 he attempted unsuccessfully to regain the crown of Hungary and was deported to Madeira, where he died.

Charles /tʃɑːlz/ (Spanish *Carlos*) four kings of Spain, including:

Charles I 1500–1558. See →Charles V, Holy Roman emperor.

Charles II 1661–1700. King of Spain from 1665. The second son of Philip IV, he was the last of the Spanish Habsburg kings. Mentally handicapped from birth, he bequeathed his dominions to Philip of Anjou, grandson of Louis XIV, which led to the War of the Spanish Succession.

Charles III 1716–1788. King of Spain from 1759. Son of Philip V, he became duke of Parma 1732 and conquered Naples and Sicily 1734. On the death of his half-brother Ferdinand VI (1713–1759), he became king of Spain, handing over Naples and Sicily to his son Ferdinand (1751–1825). During his reign, Spain was twice at war with Britain: during the Seven Years' War, when he sided with France and lost Florida; and when he backed the colonists in the American Revolution and regained it. At home he carried out a programme of reforms and expelled the Jesuits.

Charles IV 1748–1819. King of Spain from 1788, when he succeeded his father, Charles III; he left the government in the hands of his wife and her lover, the minister Manuel de Godoy (1767–1851). In 1808 Charles was induced to abdicate by Napoleon's machinations in favour of his son Ferdinand VII (1784–1833), who was subsequently deposed by Napoleon's brother Joseph. Charles was awarded a pension by Napoleon and died in Rome.

Charles /tʃɑːlz/ (Swedish *Carl*) fifteen kings of Sweden (the first six were local chieftains), including:

Charles VIII 1408–1470. King of Sweden from 1448. He was elected regent of Sweden 1438, when Sweden broke away from Denmark and Norway. He stepped down 1441 when Christopher III of Bavaria (1418–1448) was elected king, but after his death became king. He was twice expelled by the Danes and twice restored.

Charles IX 1550–1611. King of Sweden from 1604, the youngest son of Gustavus Vasa. In 1568 he and his brother John led the rebellion against Eric XIV (1533–1577); John became king as John III and attempted to Catholicize Sweden, and Charles led the opposition. John's son Sigismund, king of Poland and a Catholic, succeeded to the Swedish throne 1592, and Charles led the Protestants. He was made regent 1595 and deposed Sigismund 1599. Charles was elected king of Sweden 1604 and was involved in unsuccessful wars with Russia, Poland, and Denmark. He was the father of Gustavus Adolphus.

Charles X 1622–1660. King of Sweden from 1654, when he succeeded his cousin Christina. He waged war with Poland and Denmark and in 1657 invaded Denmark by leading his army over the frozen sea.

Charles XI 1655–1697. King of Sweden from 1660, when he succeeded his father Charles X. His mother acted as regent until 1672 when Charles took over the government. He was a remarkable general and reformed the administration.

Charles XII 1682–1718. King of Sweden from 1697, when he succeeded his father, Charles XI. From 1700 he was involved in wars with Denmark, Poland, and Russia.

He won a succession of victories until, in 1709 while invading Russia, he was defeated at Poltava in the Ukraine, and forced to take refuge in Turkey until 1714. He was killed while besieging Fredrikshall, Norway, although it was not known whether he was murdered by his own side or by the enemy.

Charles XIII 1748–1818. King of Sweden from 1809, when he was elected; he became the first king of Sweden and Norway 1814.

Charles XIV (Jean Baptiste Jules →Bernadotte) 1763–1844. King of Sweden and Norway from 1818. A former marshal in the French army, in 1810 he was elected crown prince of Sweden under the name of Charles John (Carl Johan). Loyal to his adopted country, he brought Sweden into the alliance against Napoleon 1813, as a reward for which Sweden received Norway. He was the founder of the present dynasty.

Charles XV 1826–1872. King of Sweden and Norway from 1859, when he succeeded his father Oscar I. A popular and liberal monarch, his main achievement was the reform of the constitution.

Charles Albert /tsɑːlz 'ælbət/ 1798–1849. King of Sardinia from 1831. He showed liberal sympathies in early life, and after his accession introduced some reforms. On the outbreak of the 1848 revolution he granted a constitution and declared war on Austria. His troops were defeated at Custozza and Novara. In 1849 he abdicated in favour of his son Victor Emmanuel and retired to a monastery, where he died.

Charles Augustus /tʃɑːlz ɔːˈɡʌstəs/ 1757–1828. Grand Duke of Saxe-Weimar in Germany. He succeeded his father in infancy, fought against the French in 1792–94 and 1806, and was the patron and friend of the writer Goethe.

Charles Edward Stuart /tʃɑːlz 'edwəd 'stjuːət/ the *Young Pretender* or *Bonnie Prince Charlie* 1720–1788. British prince, grandson of James II and son of James, the Old Pretender. In the Jacobite rebellion 1745 Charles won the support of the Scottish Highlanders; his army invaded England to claim the throne but was beaten back by the duke of →Cumberland and routed at Culloden 1746. Charles went into exile.

He was born in Rome, and created Prince of Wales at birth. In July 1745 he sailed for Scotland, and landed in Inverness-shire with seven companions. On 19 Aug he raised his father's standard, and within a week had rallied an army of 2,000 Highlanders. He entered Edinburgh almost without resistance, won an easy victory at Prestonpans, invaded England, and by 4 Dec had reached Derby, where his officers insisted on a retreat. The army returned to Scotland and won a victory at Falkirk, but was forced to retire to the Highlands before Cumberland's advance. On 16 April at Culloden Charles's army was routed by Cumberland, and he fled. For five months he wandered through the Highlands with a price of £30,000 on his head before escaping to France. He visited England secretly in 1750, and may have made other visits. In later life he degenerated into a friendless drunkard. He settled in Italy 1766.

Charles Martel /tʃɑːlz mɑːˈtel/ c. 688–741. Frankish ruler (Mayor of the Palace) of the E Frankish kingdom from 717 and the whole kingdom from 731. His victory against the Moors at Moussais-la-Bataille near Tours 732 earned him his nickname of Martel, 'the Hammer', because he halted the Islamic advance by the Moors into Europe.

An illegitimate son of Pepin of Heristal (Pepin II, Mayor of the Palace c. 640–714), he was a grandfather of Charlemagne.

Charles the Bold /tʃɑːlz/ Duke of Burgundy 1433–1477. Son of Philip the Good, he inherited Burgundy and the Low Countries from him 1465. He waged wars attempting to free the duchy from dependence on France and restore it as a kingdom. He was killed in battle.

Charles' ambition was to create a kingdom stretching from the mouth of the Rhine to the mouth of the Rhône. He formed the League of the Public Weal against Louis XI of France, invaded France 1471, and conquered the country as far as Rouen. The Holy Roman emperor, the Swiss, and Lorraine united against him; he captured Nancy, but was defeated at Granson and again at Morat 1476. Nancy was lost, and he was killed while attempting to recapture it. His possessions in the Netherlands passed to the Habsburgs by the marriage of his daughter Mary to Maximilian I of Austria.

Charlotte Augusta /ʃɑːlət ɔːˈɡʌstə/ Princess 1796–1817. Only child of George IV and Caroline of Brunswick, and heir to the British throne. In 1816 she married Prince Leopold of Saxe-Coburg (later Leopold I of the Belgians), but died in childbirth 18 months later.

Charlotte Sophia /ʃɑːlət səˈfaɪə/ 1744–1818. British queen consort. The daughter of the German duke of Mecklenburg-Strelitz, she married George III of Great Britain and Ireland 1761, and they had nine sons and six daughters.

Charlton /tʃɑːltən/ Bobby (Robert) 1937– . English footballer, younger brother of Jack Charlton, who scored a record 49 goals in 106 appearances for England. An elegant midfield player who specialized in fierce long-range shots, he spent most of his playing career with Manchester United and played in the England team that won the World Cup 1966.

On retiring Charlton had an unsuccessful spell as manager of Preston North End. He later became a director of Manchester United.

Charlotte Augusta Charlotte Augusta, English princess and only child and heir of George IV. Her death in 1817 led to the expedient marriages of her uncles and consequently to the birth of the future Queen Victoria.

Charlton /ˈtʃɑːltən/ Jack 1935– . English foot-baller, older brother of Robert (Bobby) and nephew of Jackie Milburn. He spent all his play-ing career with Leeds United and played more than 750 games for them.

He and his brother both appeared in the Eng-land team that won the World Cup 1966. After retiring, Charlton managed Middlesbrough to the 2nd division title. Appointed manager of the Republic of Ireland national squad in 1986, he took the team to the 1988 European Champi-onship finals, after which he was made an 'hon-orary Irishman'. He led Ireland to the World Cup finals for the first time in 1990.

Charpentier /ʃɑːˈpɒntie/ Gustave 1860–1956. French composer who wrote an opera about Paris working-class life, *Louise* 1900.

Charpentier /ʃɑːˈpɒntie/ Marc-Antoine 1645–1704. French composer. He wrote sacred music including a number of masses; other works include instrumental theatre music and the opera *Médée* 1693.

Charrière /ʃæriˈeə/ Isabelle van Zuylen de 1740–1805. Dutch aristocrat who settled in Colombier, Switzerland, in 1761. Her works include plays, tracts, and novels, among them *Cal-iste* 1786. She had many early feminist ideas.

Charteris /ˈtʃɑːtərɪs/ Leslie 1907– . British nov-elist, a US citizen from 1946. His varied career in many exotic occupations gave authentic back-ground to some 40 novels about Simon Templar, the 'Saint', a gentleman adventurer on the wrong side of the law. The novels have been adapted for films, radio, and television. The first was *The Saint Meets the Tiger* 1928.

Chase /tʃeɪs/ Salmon Portland 1808–1873. US public official and chief justice of the USA. He held a US Senate seat 1849–55 and 1860; helped found the Republican Party 1854–56; was elected governor of Ohio 1855; became Abraham Lin-coln's secretary of the treasury 1861; and was appointed chief justice of the US Supreme Court 1864. He presided over the impeachment trial of President Andrew →Johnson 1868.

Born in Cornish, New Hampshire, USA, Chase was educated at Dartmouth. He studied law and was admitted to the bar 1829. Moving to Cincin-nati, Ohio, he became an abolitionist, often taking the cases of runaway slaves in the campaign to end the institution of slavery.

Chase /tʃeɪs/ James Hadley. Pen name of René Raymond 1906–1985. British author of the hard-boiled thriller *No Orchids for Miss Blandish* 1939 and other popular novels.

Chateaubriand /ʃætəʊbriˈɒn/ François René, vicomte de 1768–1848. French author. In exile from the French Revolution 1794–99, he wrote *Atala* 1801 (after his encounters with North American Indians) and the autobiographical *René*, which formed part of *Le Génie du Christian-isme/The Genius of Christianity* 1802. He later wrote *Mémoires d'outre tombe/Memoirs from Beyond the Tomb* 1849–50.

He visited the USA 1791 and, on his return to France, fought for the royalist side which was defeated at Thionville 1792. He lived in exile in England until 1800. When he returned to France, he held diplomatic appointments under Louis XVIII.

Châtelet /ʃɑːtəˈleɪ/ Emilie de Breteuil, Marquise du 1706–1749. French scientific writer and trans-lator into French of Isaac Newton's *Principia*.

Her marriage to the Marquis du Châtelet in 1725 gave her the leisure to study physics and mathematics. She met Voltaire in 1733, and set-tled with him at her husband's estate at Cirey, in the Duchy of Lorraine. Her study of Newton, with whom she collaborated on various scientific works, influenced Voltaire's work. She indepen-dently produced the first (and only) French trans-lation of Newton's *Principia Mathematica* (published posthumously in 1759).

Chatterji /ˈtʃætədʒiː/ Bankim Chandra 1838–1894. Indian novelist. Born in Bengal, where he established his reputation with his first book, *Durges-Nandini* 1864, he became a favourite of the nationalists. His book *Ananda Math* 1882 contains the Indian national song 'Bande-Mataram'.

Chatterton /ˈtʃætətən/ Thomas 1752–1770. Eng-lish poet whose medieval-style poems and brief life were to inspire English Romanticism. Born in Bristol, he studied ancient documents he found in the Church of St Mary Redcliffe and composed poems he ascribed to a 15th-century monk, 'Thomas Rowley', which were accepted as gen-uine. He committed suicide in London, after becoming destitute.

He sent examples to Horace Walpole who was advised that they were forgeries. He then began contributing to periodicals in many styles, includ-ing Junius.

Chatwin /ˈtʃætwɪn/ Bruce 1940–1989. English writer. His works include *The Songlines* 1987, written after living with Aborigines; the novel *Utz* 1988, about a manic porcelain collector in Prague; and travel pieces and journalism collected in *What Am I Doing Here* 1989.

Chaucer /ˈtʃɔːsə/ Geoffrey c. 1340–1400. English poet. *The Canterbury Tales*, a collection of stories told by a group of pilgrims on their way to Can-terbury, reveals his knowledge of human nature and his stylistic variety, from urbane and ironic to simple and bawdy. Early allegorical poems, including *The Book of the Duchess*, were influenced by French poems like *Roman de la Rose*. His *Troilus and Criseyde* is a substantial narrative poem about the tragic betrayal of an idealized courtly love.

Chaucer was born in London. Taken prisoner in the French wars, he had to be ransomed by

Chaucer *Posthumous portrait of English poet Geoffrey Chaucer by an unknown artist, National Portrait Gallery, London. Chaucer's work has been admired from his own time to the present day. It confirmed the domination of southern English as the language of literature throughout England.*

Edward III 1360. He married Philippa Roet 1366, becoming in later life the brother-in-law of →John of Gaunt. He achieved various appointments and was sent on missions to Italy (where he may have met →Boccaccio and →Petrarch), France, and Flanders. His early work showed formal French influence, as in his adaptation of the French allegorical poem on courtly love, *Romance of the Rose*; more mature works reflected the influence of Italian realism, as in his long narrative poem *Troilus and Criseyde*, adapted from Boccaccio. In *The Canterbury Tales* he showed his own genius for metre and characterization. He was the most influential English poet of the Middle Ages.

Chávez /tʃɑːves/ Carlos 1899–1978. Mexican composer. A student of the piano and of the complex rhythms of his country's folk music, he founded the Mexico Symphony Orchestra. He composed a number of ballets, seven symphonies, and concertos for both violin and piano.

Chavez /tʃɑːvez/ Cesar Estrada 1927– . US labour organizer who founded the National Farm Workers Association 1962 and, with the support of the AFL-CIO and other major unions, embarked on a successful campaign to unionize California grape workers. He led boycotts of citrus fruits, lettuce, and grapes in the early 1970s, but disagreement and exploitation of migrant farm labourers continued despite his successes.

Chayefsky /tʃeɪˈefski/ (Sidney) Paddy 1923–1981. US writer. He established his reputation with the television plays *Marty* 1955 (for which he won an Oscar when he turned it into a film) and *Bachelor Party* 1957. He also won Oscars for *The Hospital* 1971 and *Network* 1976.

Cheever /tʃiːvə/ John 1912–1982. US writer whose stories and novels focus on the ironies of upper-middle-class life in suburban America. His short stories were frequently published in *The New Yorker*. His first novel was *The Wapshot Chronicle* 1957, for which he won the National Book Award. Others include *Falconer* 1977.

Chekhov /tʃekɒf/ Anton (Pavlovich) 1860–1904. Russian dramatist and writer of short stories. His plays concentrate on the creation of atmosphere and delineation of internal development, rather than external action. His first play, *Ivanov* 1887, was a failure, as was *The Seagull* 1896 until revived by Stanislavsky 1898 at the Moscow Art Theatre, for which Chekhov went on to write his finest plays: *Uncle Vanya* 1899, *The Three Sisters* 1901, and *The Cherry Orchard* 1904.

Chekhov was born in Taganrog, S Russia. He qualified as a doctor 1884, but devoted himself to writing short stories rather than practising medicine. The collection *Particoloured Stories* 1886 consolidated his reputation and gave him leisure to develop his style, as seen in 'My Life' 1895, 'The Lady with the Dog' 1898, and 'In the Ravine' 1900.

He began to write short stories and comic sketches as a medical student.

Chénier /ʃemiˈeɪ/ André de 1762–1794. French poet, born in Constantinople. His lyrical poetry was later to inspire the Romantic movement, but he was known in his own time for his uncompromising support of the constitutional royalists after the Revolution. In 1793 he went into hiding, but finally he was arrested and, on 25 July 1794, guillotined. While in prison he wrote *Jeune Captive/Captive Girl* and the political *Iambes*, published after his death.

Little griefs make us tender; great ones make us hard.

André de Chénier

Cherenkov /tʃɪˈreŋkɒf/ Pavel 1904– . Soviet physicist. In 1934 he discovered *Cherenkov radiation*; this occurs as a bluish light when charged atomic particles pass through water or other media at a speed in excess of that of light. He shared a Nobel prize 1958 with his colleagues Ilya →Frank and Igor Tamm for work resulting in a cosmic-ray counter.

Cherenkov discovered that this effect was independent of any medium and depended for its production on the passage of high velocity electrons.

Chesterton English journalist, novelist and broadcaster G K Chesterton. He is probably best known as the creator of the detective-priest Father Ignatius Brown who first appeared in The Innocence of Father Brown *1911.*

Chernenko /tʃɜːˈneŋkəʊ/ Konstantin 1911–1985. Soviet politician, leader of the Soviet Communist Party (CPSU) and president 1984–85. He was a protégé of Brezhnev and from 1978 a member of the Politburo.

Chernenko, born in central Siberia, joined the Komsomol (Communist Youth League) 1929 and the CPSU 1931. The future CPSU leader Brezhnev brought him to Moscow to work in the central apparatus 1956 and later sought to establish Chernenko as his successor, but he was passed over in favour of the KGB chief Andropov. When Andropov died Feb 1984 Chernenko was selected as the CPSU's stopgap leader by cautious party colleagues and was also elected president. From July 1984 he gradually retired from public life because of failing health.

Cherubini /ˌkerʊˈbiːni/ Luigi (Carlo Zanobi Salvadore Maria) 1760–1842. Italian composer. His first opera *Quinto Fabio* 1779 was produced at Alessandria. In 1784 he went to London and became composer to King George III, but from 1788 he lived in Paris, where he produced a number of dramatic works including *Médée* 1797, *Les Deux Journées* 1800, and the ballet *Anacréon* 1803. After 1809 he devoted himself largely to church music.

Cherwell /ˈtʃɑːwəl/ Frederick Alexander Lindemann 1886–1957. British physicist. He was director of the Physical Laboratory of the RAF at Farnborough in World War I, and personal adviser to →Churchill on scientific and statistical matters during World War II. Cherwell served as

director of the Clarendon Laboratory, Oxford, 1919–56, and, though his own scientific output was slight, oversaw its transformation into a major research institute.

Cheshire /ˈtʃeʃə/ (Geoffrey) Leonard 1917–1992. British pilot. Commissioned into the Royal Air Force on the outbreak of the World War II, he won the Victoria Cross, Distinguished Service Order (with 2 bars), and Distinguished Flying Cross. A devout Roman Catholic, he founded the first Cheshire Foundation Home for the Incurably Sick 1948. In 1959 he married Susan Ryder (1923–) who established a foundation for the sick and disabled of all ages and became a life peeress 1978.

Chesterfield /ˈtʃestəfiːld/ Philip Dormer Stanhope, 4th Earl of Chesterfield 1694–1773. English politician and writer, author of *Letters to his Son* 1774. A member of the literary circle of Swift, Pope, and Bolingbroke, he incurred the wrath of Dr Samuel →Johnson by failing to carry out an offer of patronage.

He was ambassador to Holland 1728–32 and 1744. In Ireland, he established schools, helped to reconcile Protestants and Catholics, and encouraged manufacturing. An opponent of Walpole, he was a Whig member of Parliament 1715–26, Lord Lieutenant of Ireland 1745–46, and secretary of state 1746–48.

Chesterton /ˈtʃestətən/ G(ilbert) K(eith) 1874–1936. English novelist, essayist, and satirical poet, author of a series of novels featuring as detective a naive priest, Father Brown. Other novels include *The Napoleon of Notting Hill* 1904 and *The Man Who Knew Too Much* 1922.

Born in London, he studied art but quickly turned to journalism. Like Hilaire Belloc, he was initially a socialist sympathizer.

One bears great things from the valley, only small things from the peak.

G K Chesterton *The Hammer of God*

Chevalier /ʃəˈvælieɪ/ Maurice 1888–1972. French singer and actor. He began as dancing partner to the revue artiste →Mistinguett at the Folies-Bergère music hall in Paris, and made numerous films including *Innocents of Paris* 1929, which revived his song 'Louise', *The Merry Widow* 1934, and *Gigi* 1958.

Chevreul /ʃəˈvrɜːl/ Michel-Eugène 1786–1889. French chemist who studied the composition of fats and identified a number of fatty acids, including 'margaric acid', which became the basis of margarine.

Chiang Ching /dʒiˈæŋ ˈtʃɪŋ/ alternative transliteration of →Jiang Qing, Chinese actress, third wife of Mao Zedong.

Chiang Ching-kuo /tʃiˈæŋ ˌtʃɪŋ ˈkwəʊ/ 1910–1988. Taiwanese politician, son of Chiang Kai-shek, prime minister 1971–78, president 1978–88.

Chiang Kai-shek /tʃæŋ kaɪ ˈʃek/ (Pinyin *Jiang Jie Shi*) 1887–1975. Chinese nationalist Guomindang (Kuomintang) general and politician, president of China 1928–31 and 1943–49, and of Taiwan from 1949, where he set up a US-supported right-wing government on his expulsion from the mainland by the Communist forces. He was a commander in the civil war that lasted from the end of imperial rule 1911 to the Second Sino-Japanese War and beyond, having split with the Communist leader Mao Zedong 1927.

Chiang took part in the revolution of 1911 that overthrew the Qing dynasty of the Manchus, and on the death of the nationalist Guomindang leader Sun Yat-sen was made commander in chief of the nationalist armies in S China 1925. Collaboration with the Communists, broken 1927, was resumed after the Xian incident 1936 when China needed to pool military strength, and Chiang nominally headed the struggle against the Japanese invaders of World War II, receiving the Japanese surrender 1945. The following year, civil war between the nationalists and Communists erupted, and in Dec 1949 Chiang and his followers took refuge on the island of Taiwan, maintaining a large army in the hope of reclaiming the mainland. His authoritarian regime enjoyed US support until his death. His son, Chiang Ching-kuo (1910–1988), then became president.

We shall not talk lightly about sacrifice until we are driven to the last extremity which makes sacrifice inevitable.

Chiang Kai-shek
speech to Fifth Congress of the Guomindang

Chichester /ˈtʃɪtʃɪstə/ Francis 1901–1972. English sailor and navigator. In 1931 he made the first east–west crossing of the Tasman Sea in *Gipsy Moth*, and in 1966–67 circumnavigated the world in his yacht *Gipsy Moth IV*.

Chifley /ˈtʃɪfli/ Ben (Joseph Benedict) 1885–1951. Australian Labor prime minister 1945–49. He united the party in fulfilling a welfare and nationalization programme 1945–49 (although he failed in an attempt to nationalize the banks 1947) and initiated an immigration programme and the Snowy Mountains hydroelectric project.

Chifley was minister of postwar reconstruction 1942–45 under John Curtin, when he succeeded him as prime minister. He crushed a coal miners' strike 1949 by using troops as mine labour. He was leader of the Opposition from 1949 until his death.

Child /tʃaɪld/ Lydia Maria 1802–1880. US writer, social critic, and feminist, author of the popular women's guides *The Frugal Housewife* 1829 and *The Mother's Book* 1831. With her husband, David Child, she worked for the abolition of slavery, advocating educational support for black Americans. The Childs edited the weekly *National Anti-Slavery Standard* 1840–44.

Born in Medford, Massachusetts, USA, Child received little formal education but read widely and published several historical novels about life in colonial New England.

Childe /tʃaɪld/ Vere Gordon 1892–1957. Australian archaeologist who was an authority on early European and Middle Eastern societies. He pioneered current methods of analytical archaeology. His books include *The Dawn of European Civilization* 1925 and *What Happened in History* 1942. He was professor of prehistoric archaeology at Edinburgh University 1927–46, and director of the London Institute of Archaeology 1946–57.

Childers /ˈtʃɪldəz/ (Robert) Erskine 1870–1922. Irish Sinn Féin politician, author of the spy novel *The Riddle of the Sands* 1903. He was executed as a Republican terrorist.

Before turning to Irish politics, Childers was a clerk in the House of Commons in London. In 1921 he was elected to the Irish Parliament as a supporter of the Sinn Féin leader de Valera, and took up arms against the Irish Free State 1922. Shortly afterwards he was captured, court-martialled, and shot by the Irish Free State government of William T Cosgrave.

Chippendale /ˈtʃɪpəndeɪl/ Thomas *c.* 1718–1779. English furniture designer. He set up his workshop in St Martin's Lane, London 1753. His book *The Gentleman and Cabinet Maker's Director* 1754, was a significant contribution to furniture design. He favoured Louis XVI, Chinese, Gothic, and Neo-Classical styles, and worked mainly in mahogany.

Chirac /ʃɪəræk/ Jacques 1932– . French conservative politician, prime minister 1974–76 and 1986–88. He established the neo-Gaullist Rassemblement pour la République (RPR) 1976, and became mayor of Paris 1977.

Chirac held ministerial posts during the Pompidou presidency and gained the nickname 'the Bulldozer'. In 1974 he became prime minister to President Giscard d'Estaing, but the relationship was uneasy. Chirac contested the 1981 presidential election and emerged as the National Assembly leader for the parties of the right during the socialist administration of 1981–86. Following the rightist coalition's victory 1986, Chirac was appointed prime minister by President Mitterrand in a 'cohabitation' experiment. The term was marked by economic decline, nationality reforms, and student unrest.

Student demonstrations in autumn 1986 forced him to scrap plans for educational reform. He stood in the May 1988 presidential elections and was defeated by Mitterrand, who replaced him with the moderate socialist Michel Rocard.

Chirico /ˈkɪərɪkəʊ/ Giorgio de 1888–1978. Italian painter born in Greece, whose style presaged Surrealism in its use of enigmatic imagery and dreamlike settings, for example, *Nostalgia of the Infinite* 1911, Museum of Modern Art, New York.

In 1917, with Carlo Carrà (1881–1966), he founded Metaphysical painting, which aimed to convey a sense of mystery and hallucination. This was achieved by distorted perspective, dramatic lighting, and the use of dummies and statues in place of human figures.

Chisholm /ˈtʃɪzəm/ Jesse *c*. 1806–*c*. 1868. US pioneer who gained a reputation as a resourceful guide, trader, and military scout during the early 19th century. He established one of the main paths of the yearly Texas cattle drive, known among cowboys as the 'Chisholm Trail.' Ranging over the southern part of the Great Plains, he customarily followed a route from the Mexican border to Kansas, ending at the market town of Abilene.

Chissano /ʃɪˈsɑːnəʊ/ Joaquim 1939– . Mozambique nationalist politician, president from 1986; foreign minister 1975–86. In Oct 1992 Chissano signed a peace accord with the leader of the rebel Mozambique National Resistance (MNR) party, bringing to an end 16 years of civil war.

He was secretary to Samora →Machel, who led the National Front for the Liberation of Mozambique (Frelimo) during the campaign for independence in the early 1960s. When Mozambique achieved internal self-government 1974, Chissano was appointed prime minister.

Chladni /ˈklædni/ Ernst Florens Friedrich 1756–1827. German physicist, a pioneer in the field of acoustics. He developed an experimental technique whereby sand is vibrated on a metal plate, and settles into regular and symmetric patterns (*Chladni's figures*) indicating the nodes of the vibration's wave pattern.

Chodowiecki /ˌkɒdəvˈjetski/ Daniel Nicolas 1726–1801. German painter and engraver. His works include engravings of scenes from the Seven Years' War and the life of Christ, and the portrait *The Parting of Jean Calas From his family* 1767 (Berlin-Dahlem Museum).

Choiseul /ʃwæˈzɜːl/ Étienne François, duc de Choiseul 1719–1785. French politician. Originally a protégé of Madame de Pompadour, the mistress of Louis XV, he became minister for foreign affairs 1758, and held this and other offices until 1770. He banished the Jesuits, and was a supporter of the Enlightenment philosophers Diderot and Voltaire.

Chomsky /ˈtʃɒmski/ Noam 1928– . US professor of linguistics. He proposed a theory of transformational generative grammar, which attracted widespread interest because of the claims it made about the relationship between language and the mind and the universality of an underlying language structure. He has been a leading critic of the imperialist tendencies of the US government.

Chomsky distinguished between knowledge and behaviour and maintained that the focus of scientific enquiry should be on knowledge. In order to define and describe linguistic knowledge, he posited a set of abstract principles of grammar that appear to be universal and may have a biological basis.

Choong /ʃʊŋ/ Eddy (Ewe Beng) 1930– . Malaysian badminton player. Standing only 157 cm/5 ft 2 in tall, he was a dynamic player and won most major honours during his career 1950–1957, including All-England singles title four times 1953–1957.

Choonhavan /ʃuːnˈhævən/ Chatichai 1922– . Thai conservative politician, prime minister of Thailand 1988–91. He promoted a peace settlement in neighbouring Cambodia as part of a vision of transforming Indochina into a thriving open-trade zone. Despite economic success, he was ousted in a bloodless military coup 1991.

A field marshal's son, Choonhavan fought in World War II and the Korean War, rising to major-general. After a career as a diplomat and entrepreneur, he moved into politics and became leader of the conservative Chat Thai party and, in 1988, prime minister. He was overthrown Feb 1991 and was allowed, the following month, to leave the country for Switzerland.

Chopin /ˈʃɒpæn/ Frédéric (François) 1810–1849. Polish composer and pianist. He made his debut as a pianist at the age of eight. As a performer, Chopin revolutionized the technique of pianoforte-playing, turning the hands outwards and favouring a light, responsive touch. His compositions for piano, which include two concertos and other works with orchestra, are characterized by great volatility of mood, and rhythmic fluidity.

From 1831 he lived in Paris, where he became known in the fashionable salons, although he rarely performed in public. In 1836 the composer Liszt introduced him to Madame Dudevant (George →Sand), with whom he had a close relationship 1838–46. During this time she nursed him in Majorca for tuberculosis, while he composed intensively and for a time regained his health. His music was made the basis of the ballet *Les Sylphides* by Fokine 1909 and orchestrated by Alexander Gretchaninov (1864–1956), a pupil of Rimsky-Korsakov.

Chopin /ˈʃəʊpæn/ Kate 1851–1904. US novelist and short-story writer. Her novel *The Awakening* 1899, the story of a married New Orleans woman's awakening to her sexuality, is now regarded as a classic of feminist sensibility.

Chou En-lai /ˈtʃəʊ en ˈlaɪ/ alternative transcription of →Zhou Enlai.

Chrétien de Troyes /ˌkreti'æn də ˈtrwɑː/ lived second half of the 12th century. French poet, born in Champagne. His epics, which introduced the concept of the Holy Grail, include *Lancelot, ou le* *chevalier de la charrette*; *Perceval, ou le conte du Graal*, written for Philip, Count of Flanders; *Erec*; *Yvain, ou le chevalier au Lion*; and other Arthurian romances.

Christ /kraɪs/ (Greek *khristos* 'anointed one') the Messiah (saviour or deliverer) as prophesied in the Hebrew Bible, or Old Testament. Jews from the time of the Old Testament exile in Babylon have looked forward to the coming of the Messiah. Christians believe that the Messiah came in the person of →Jesus, and hence called him the Christ.

Christian /ˈkrɪstjən/ ten kings of Denmark and Norway, including:

Christian I /ˈkrɪstjən/ 1426–1481. King of Denmark from 1448, and founder of the Oldenburg dynasty. In 1450 he established the union of Denmark and Norway that lasted until 1814.

Christian III 1503–1559. King of Denmark and Norway from 1535. During his reign the Reformation was introduced.

Christian IV 1577–1648. King of Denmark and Norway from 1588. He sided with the Protestants in the Thirty Years' War (1618–48), and founded Christiania (now Oslo, capital of Norway). He was succeeded by Frederick II 1648.

Christian VIII 1786–1848. King of Denmark 1839–48. He was unpopular because of his opposition to reform. His attempt to encourage the Danish language and culture in Schleswig and Holstein led to an insurrection there shortly after his death. He was succeeded by Frederick VII.

Christian IX 1818–1906. King of Denmark from 1863. His daughter Alexandra married Edward VII of the UK and another, Dagmar, married Tsar Alexander III of Russia; his second son, George, became king of Greece. In 1864 he lost the duchies of Schleswig and Holstein after a war with Austria and Prussia.

Christian X 1870–1947. King of Denmark and Iceland from 1912, when he succeeded his father Frederick VIII. He married Alexandrine, Duchess of Mecklenburg-Schwerin, and was popular for his democratic attitude. During World War II he was held prisoner by the Germans in Copenhagen. He was succeeded by Frederick IX.

Christie /ˈkrɪsti/ Agatha (born Miller) 1890–1976. English detective novelist who created the characters Hercule Poirot and Miss Jane Marple. She wrote more than 70 novels, including *The Murder of Roger Ackroyd* 1926 and *Ten Little Indians* 1939. Her play *The Mousetrap*, which opened in London 1952, is the longest continuous running show in the world.

She was born in Torquay, married Col Archibald Christie 1914, and served during World War I as a nurse. Her first crime novel, *The Mysterious Affair at Styles* 1920, introduced Hercule Poirot. She often broke 'purist' rules, as in *The Murder of Roger Ackroyd* in which the narrator is

Christie *Dame Agatha Christie, pre-eminent among the detective novelists who formed the 'classical' school of the 1920s and 1930s. She wrote some 75 novels and many plays.*

the murderer. She caused a nationwide sensation 1926 by disappearing for ten days when her husband fell in love with another woman.

Christie /ˈkrɪsti/ Julie 1940– . English film actress who became a star following her award-winning performance in *Darling* 1965. She also appeared in *Doctor Zhivago* 1965, *The Go-Between* and *McCabe and Mrs Miller*, both 1971, *Don't Look Now* 1973, and *Heat and Dust* 1982.

Christie Linford 1960– . Jamaican-born English sprinter who, at the 1992 Barcelona Olympics, won a gold medal in the 100 metres race. In 1986, Christie won the European 100-metres championship and finished second to Ben Johnson in the Commonwealth Games. At the 1988 Seoul Olympics, he won silver medals in the 100 metres and 4 × 100 metres relay. In 1990 he won gold medals in the Commonwealth Games for the 100 metres and 4 × 100 metres relay.

Christina /krɪsˈtiːnə/ 1626–1689. Queen of Sweden 1632–54. Succeeding her father Gustavus Adolphus at the age of six, she assumed power 1644, but disagreed with the former regent →Oxenstjerna. Refusing to marry, she eventually nominated her cousin Charles Gustavus (Charles X) as her successor. As a secret convert to Roman Catholicism, which was then illegal in Sweden, she had to abdicate 1654, and went to live in Rome, twice returning to Sweden unsuccessfully to claim the throne.

Christine de Pisan /ˈkrɪstiːn də ˈpiːzɒn/ 1364–1430. French poet and historian. Her works include love lyrics, philosophical poems, a poem in praise of Joan of Arc, a history of Charles V, and various defences of women, including *La Cité des dames*/*The City of Ladies* 1405.

Born in Venice, she was brought to France as a child when her father entered the service of Charles V. In 1389, after the death of her husband, the Picardian nobleman Etienne Castel, she began writing to support herself and her family.

Just as women's bodies are softer than men's, so their understanding is sharper.
Christine de Pisan *The City of Ladies* 1405

Christo /ˈkrɪstəʊ/ adopted name of Christo Javacheff 1935– . US sculptor, born in Bulgaria, active in Paris in the 1950s and in New York from 1964. He is known for his wrapped works: structures, such as bridges and buildings, and even areas of coastline are temporarily wrapped in synthetic fabric tied down with rope. The *Running Fence* 1976 across California was another temporary work. In 1991 he simultaneously exhibited a work in both Japan and the USA.

Christoff /ˈkrɪstɒf/ Boris 1918– . Bulgarian bass who made his operatic debut 1946. His roles included Boris Godunov, Ivan the Terrible, and Mephistopheles.

Christophe /kriːˈstɒf/ Henri 1767–1820. West Indian slave, one of the leaders of the revolt against the French 1791, who was proclaimed king of Haiti 1811. His government distributed plantations to military leaders. He shot himself when his troops deserted him because of his alleged cruelty.

Christopher, St /ˈkrɪstəfə/ patron saint of travellers. His feast day, 25 July, was dropped from the Roman Catholic liturgical calendar 1969.

Traditionally he was a martyr in Syria in the 3rd century, and legend describes his carrying the child Jesus over the stream; despite his great strength, he found the burden increasingly heavy, and was told that the child was Jesus Christ bearing the sins of all the world.

Chrysler /ˈkraɪslə/ Walter Percy 1875–1940. US industrialist. After World War I, he became president of the independent Maxwell Motor Company and went on to found the Chrysler Corporation 1925. By 1928 he had acquired Dodge and Plymouth, making Chrysler Corporation one of the largest US motor-vehicle manufacturers.

Born in Wamego, Kansas, USA, Chrysler worked first as a railroad machinist, rising through the ranks to become manager of the American Locomotive Company in Pittsburgh 1912. Shifting to the car industry, he was hired by General Motors and was appointed president of the Buick division 1916.

Chukovsky /tʃuˈkɒfski/ Kornei Ivanovitch 1882–1969. Russian critic and poet. The leading authority on the 19th-century Russian poet Nekrasov, he was also an expert on the Russian language, as in, for example, *Zhivoi kak zhizn*/*Alive as Life* 1963. He was also beloved as 'Grandpa' Kornei Chukovsky for his nonsense poems, which owe much to English nursery rhymes and nonsense verse.

Chun Doo-hwan /tʃʌn ˌduːˈhwɑːn/ 1931– . South Korean military ruler who seized power 1979, president 1981–88 as head of the newly formed Democratic Justice Party.

Chun, trained in Korea and the USA, served as an army commander from 1967 and was in charge of military intelligence 1979 when President Park was assassinated by the chief of the Korean Central Intelligence Agency (KCIA). General Chun took charge of the KCIA and, in a coup, assumed control of the army and the South Korean government. In 1981 Chun was appointed president, and oversaw a period of rapid economic growth, governing in an authoritarian manner. In 1988 he retired to a Buddhist retreat.

Church /tʃɜːtʃ/ Frederic Edwin 1826–1900. US painter, a student of Thomas Cole and follower of the Hudson River school's style of grand landscape. During the 1850s he visited South America and the Arctic.

Churchill /tʃɜːtʃɪl/ Caryl 1938– . English playwright. Her predominantly radical and feminist works include *Top Girls* 1982, a study of the hazards encountered by 'career' women throughout history; *Serious Money* 1987, which satirized the world of London's brash young financial brokers; and *Mad Forest* 1990, set in Romania during the overthrow of the Ceausescu regime.

Churchill /tʃɜːtʃɪl/ Charles 1731–1764. British satirical poet. At one time a priest in the Church of England, he wrote coarse personal satires dealing with political issues. His poems include *The Rosciad* 1761, a satire on the London stage; *The Prophecy of Famine* 1763, the first of his political satires; *Epistle to Hogarth* 1763, which he wrote after a quarrel with the artist, William Hogarth.

Churchill /tʃɜːtʃɪl/ Randolph (Henry Spencer) 1849–1895. British Conservative politician, chancellor of the Exchequer and leader of the House of Commons 1886; father of Winston Churchill.

Born at Blenheim Palace, son of the 7th duke of Marlborough, he entered Parliament 1874. In 1880 he formed a Conservative group known as the Fourth Party with Drummond Wolff (1830–1908), J E Gorst, and Arthur Balfour, and in 1885 his policy of Tory democracy was widely accepted by the party. In 1886 he became chancellor of the Exchequer, but resigned within six months because he did not agree with the demands made on the Treasury by the War Office and the Admiralty. In 1874 he married Jennie Jerome (1854–1921), daughter of a wealthy New Yorker.

Churchill /ˈtʃɜːtʃɪl/ Winston (Leonard Spencer) 1874–1965. British Conservative politician, prime minister 1940–45 and 1951–55. In Parliament from 1900, as a Liberal until 1923, he held a number of ministerial offices, including First Lord of the Admiralty 1911–15 and chancellor of the Exchequer 1924–29. Absent from the cabinet in the 1930s, he returned Sept 1939 to lead a coalition government 1940–45, negotiating with Allied leaders in World War II to achieve the unconditional surrender of Germany 1945; he led a Conservative government 1951–55. He received the Nobel Prize for Literature 1953.

He was born at Blenheim Palace, the elder son of Lord Randolph Churchill. During the Boer War he was a war correspondent and made a dramatic escape from imprisonment in Pretoria. In 1900 he was elected Conservative member of Parliament for Oldham, but he disagreed with Chamberlain's tariff-reform policy and joined the Liberals. Asquith made him president of the Board of Trade 1908, where he introduced legislation for the establishment of labour exchanges. He became home secretary 1910.

In 1911 Asquith appointed him First Lord of the Admiralty. In 1915–16 he served in the trenches in France, but then resumed his parliamentary duties and was minister of munitions under Lloyd George 1917, when he was concerned with the development of the tank. After the armistice he was secretary for war 1918–21 and then as colonial secretary played a leading part in the establishment of the Irish Free State. During the postwar years he was active in support of the Whites (anti-Bolsheviks) in Russia.

In 1922–24 Churchill was out of Parliament. He left the Liberals 1923, and was returned for Epping as a Conservative 1924. Baldwin made him chancellor of the Exchequer, and he brought about Britain's return to the gold standard and was prominent in the defeat of the General Strike 1926. In 1929–39 he was out of office as he disagreed with the Conservatives on India, rearmament, and Chamberlain's policy of appeasement.

On the first day of World War II he went back to his old post at the Admiralty. In May 1940 he was called to the premiership as head of an all-party administration and made a much quoted 'blood, tears, toil, and sweat' speech to the House of Commons. He had a close relationship with US president Roosevelt, and Aug 1941 concluded the Atlantic Charter with him, largely a propaganda exercise to demonstrate public solidarity between the Allies. He travelled to Washington, Casablanca, Cairo, Moscow, and Tehran, meeting the other leaders of the Allied war effort. He met Stalin and Roosevelt in the Crimea Feb 1945 and agreed on the final plans for victory. On 8 May he announced the unconditional surrender of Germany.

The coalition was dissolved 23 May 1945, and Churchill formed a caretaker government drawn mainly from the Conservatives. Defeated in the general election July, he became leader of the opposition until the election Oct 1951, in which he again became prime minister. In April 1955 he resigned. His home from 1922, Chartwell in Kent, is a museum.

His books include a six-volume history of World War II (1948–54) and a four-volume *History of the English-Speaking Peoples* (1956–58).

Never in the field of human conflict was so much owed by so many to so few.

Winston Churchill
speech of 20 Aug 1940

Ciano /ˈtʃɑːnəʊ/ Galeazzo 1903–1944. Italian Fascist politician. Son-in-law of the dictator Mussolini, he was foreign minister and member of the Fascist Supreme Council 1936–43. He voted against Mussolini at the meeting of the Grand Council July 1943 that overthrew the dictator, but was later tried for treason and shot by the Fascists.

Cicero /ˈsɪsərəʊ/ Marcus Tullius 106–43 BC. Roman orator, writer, and politician. His speeches and philosophical and rhetorical works are models of Latin prose, and his letters provide a picture of contemporary Roman life. As consul 63 BC he exposed the Roman politician Catiline's conspiracy in four major orations.

Born in Arpinium, Cicero became an advocate in Rome, spent three years in Greece studying oratory, and after the dictator Sulla's death distinguished himself in Rome on the side of the popular party. When the First Triumvirate was formed 59 BC, Cicero was exiled and devoted himself to literature. He sided with Pompey during the civil war (49–48) but was pardoned by Julius Caesar and returned to Rome. After Caesar's assassination 44 BC he supported Octavian (the future emperor Augustus) and violently attacked Antony in speeches known as the *Philippics*. On the reconciliation of Antony and Octavian he was executed by Antony's agents.

Cid, El /sɪd/ Rodrigo Díaz de Bivar 1040–1099. Spanish soldier, nicknamed *El Cid* ('the lord') by the Moors. Born in Castile of a noble family, he fought against the king of Navarre and won his nickname *el Campeador* ('the Champion') by killing the Navarrese champion in single combat. Essentially a mercenary, fighting both with and against the Moors, he died while defending Valencia against them, and in subsequent romances became Spain's national hero.

Much of the Cid's present-day reputation is the result of the exploitation of the legendary character as a model Christian military hero by the Nationalists during the Civil War, with Franco presented as a modern equivalent in his reconquest of Spain.

Cierva /θiˈeəvə/ Juan de la 1895–1936. Spanish engineer. In trying to produce an aircraft that would not stall and could fly slowly, he invented the autogiro, the forerunner of the helicopter but differing from it in having unpowered rotors that revolve freely.

Cimabue /ˌtʃiːməˈbuːeɪ/ Giovanni (Cenni de Peppi) c. 1240–1302. Italian painter, active in Florence, traditionally styled the 'father of Italian painting'. His paintings retain the golden background of Byzantine art but the figures have a new naturalism. Among the works attributed to him are *Madonna and Child* (Uffizi, Florence), a huge Gothic image of the Virgin that nevertheless has a novel softness and solidity that points forwards to Giotto.

Cimarosa /ˌtʃiː məˈrəuzə/ Domenico 1749–1801. Italian composer of operas including *Il Matrimonio segreto/The Secret Marriage* 1792.

Cimino /tʃɪˈmiːnəu/ Michael 1943– . US film director whose reputation was made by *The Deer Hunter* 1978, a moral epic set against the Vietnam War (five Academy Awards). A later film, the Western *Heaven's Gate* 1980, lost its backers, United Artists, some $30 million, and subsequently became a byword for commercial disaster in the industry.

A film lives, becomes alive, because of its shadows, its spaces.

Michael Cimino in *Variety* July 1980

Clair /kleə/ René. Adopted name of René-Lucien Chomette 1898–1981. French filmmaker, originally a poet, novelist, and journalist. His *Sous les toits de Paris/Under the Roofs of Paris* 1930 was one of the first sound films. His other films include *Entr'acte* 1924, *Le Million*, and *A nous la Liberté* both 1931.

Clapperton /ˈklæpətən/ Hugh 1788–1827. English explorer who crossed the Sahara from Tripoli with Dixon Denham (1785–1828) and reached Lake Chad, of whose existence they had been unaware, 1823. With his servant Richard Lander (1804–1834), he attempted to reach the river Niger, but died at Sokoto. Lander eventually reached the mouth of the Niger 1830.

Clapton /ˈklæptən/ Eric 1945– . English blues and rock guitarist, singer, and composer, member of the Yardbirds 1963–65 and Cream 1966–68. Originally a blues purist, then one of the pioneers of heavy rock with Cream, he recorded with bands such as Blind Faith 1969, Derek and the Dominos (anonymously, on *Layla and Other Assorted Love Songs* 1970), and Delaney and Bonnie 1970–72. In his solo career he adopted a more laid-back style as on *461 Ocean Boulevard* 1974, *Journeyman* 1989, and the acoustic *Unplugged* 1992.

Clare /kleə/ John 1793–1864. English poet. His work includes *Poems Descriptive of Rural Life and Scenery* 1820, *The Village Minstrel* 1821, and *The Shepherd's Calendar* 1827. Clare's work was largely rediscovered in the 20th century.

Born at Helpstone, near Peterborough, the son of a farm labourer, Clare spent most of his life in poverty. He was given an annuity from the Duke of Exeter and other patrons, but had to turn to work on the land. He spent his last 20 years in Northampton asylum. His early life is described in his autobiography, first published 1931.

Clarendon /ˈklærəndən/ Edward Hyde, 1st Earl of Clarendon 1609–1674. English politician and historian, chief adviser to Charles II 1651–67. A member of Parliament 1640, he joined the Royalist side 1641. The *Clarendon Code* 1661–65, a series of acts passed by the government, was directed at Nonconformists (or Dissenters) and were designed to secure the supremacy of the Church of England.

In the Short and Long Parliaments Clarendon attacked Charles I's unconstitutional actions and supported the impeachment of Charles's minister Strafford. In 1641 he broke with the revolutionary party and became one of the royal advisers. When civil war began he followed Charles to Oxford, and was knighted and made chancellor of the Exchequer. On the king's defeat 1646 he followed Prince Charles to Jersey, where he began his *History of the Rebellion*, published 1702–04, which provides memorable portraits of his contemporaries.

In 1651 he became chief adviser to the exiled Charles II. At the Restoration he was created earl of Clarendon, while his influence was further increased by the marriage of his daughter Anne to James, Duke of York. His moderation earned the hatred of the extremists, however, and he lost Charles's support by openly expressing disapproval of the king's private life. After the disasters of the Dutch war 1667, he went into exile.

Clarendon /ˈklærəndən/ George William Frederick Villiers, 4th Earl of Clarendon 1800–1870. British Liberal diplomat, lord lieutenant of Ireland 1847–52, foreign secretary 1853–58, 1865–66, and 1868–70.

He was posted to Ireland at the time of the potato famine. His diplomatic skill was shown at the Congress of Paris 1856 and in the settlement of the dispute between Britain and the USA over the *Alabama* cruiser.

Clare, St /kleə/ c. 1194–1253. Christian saint. Born in Assisi, Italy, at 18 she became a follower of St Francis, who founded for her the convent of San Damiano. Here she gathered the first members of the *Order of Poor Clares*. In 1958 she was proclaimed the patron saint of television by Pius XII, since in 1252 she saw from her convent sickbed the Christmas services being held in the Basilica of St Francis in Assisi. Feast day 12 Aug.

Clark /klɑːk/ George Rogers 1752–1818. American military leader and explorer. He was made commander of the Virginia frontier militia at the outbreak of the American Revolution 1775. During 1778–79 he led an attack on the Indian allies of the British to the west of the Ohio River and founded a settlement at the site of Louisville, Kentucky.

Born near Charlottesville, Virginia, Clark spent his early adult years surveying and exploring Kentucky. After the war he remained in the Northwest Territory as Indian commissioner, leading an attack on the Wabash 1786. After leaving office, he accepted commissions from the French and Spanish colonial authorities.

Clark /klɑːk/ Jim (James) 1936–1968. Scottish-born motor-racing driver who was twice world champion 1963 and 1965. He spent all his Formula One career with Lotus.

His partnership with Lotus boss Colin Chapman was one of the closest in the sport. He won 25 Formula One Grand Prix races, a record at the time, before losing his life at Hockenheim, West Germany April 1968 during a Formula Two race.

Clark /klɑːk/ Joe (Joseph) Charles 1939– . Canadian Progressive Conservative politician who became party leader 1976, and May 1979 defeated Pierre →Trudeau at the polls to become the youngest prime minister in Canada's history. Following the rejection of his government's budget, he was defeated in a second election Feb 1980. He became secretary of state for external affairs (foreign minister) 1984 in the →Mulroney government.

Clark /klɑːk/ Kenneth, Lord Clark 1903–1983. British art historian, director of the National Gallery, London, 1934–45. His books include *Leonardo da Vinci* 1939 and *The Nude* 1956.

He popularized the history of art through his television series *Civilization*, broadcast in the UK 1969.

Clark /klɑːk/ Mark (Wayne) 1896–1984. US general in World War II. In 1942 he became Chief of Staff for ground forces, and deputy to General Eisenhower. He led a successful secret mission by submarine to get information in North Africa to prepare for the Allied invasion, and commanded the 5th Army in the invasion of Italy.

Clark, born in New York, fought in France in World War I and between the wars held various military appointments in the USA. He was commander in chief of the United Nations forces in the Korean War 1952–53.

Clark /klɑːk/ Michael 1962– . Scottish avant-garde dancer whose bare-bottomed costumes and zany stage props have earned him as much celebrity as his innovative dance technique. A graduate of the Royal Ballet school, he formed his own company, the Michael Clark Dance Company, in the mid-1980s and became a leading figure in the British avant-garde dance scene. In 1991 he played Caliban in Peter Greenaway's film *Prospero's Books*. He premiered his *Mmm … Modern Masterpiece* 1992.

Clarke /klɑːk/ Arthur C(harles) 1917– . English science-fiction and nonfiction writer, who originated the plan for a system of communications satellites in geostationary orbit 1945. His works include *Childhood's End* 1953 and *2001: A Space Odyssey* 1968 (which was made into a film by Stanley Kubrick), and *2010: Odyssey Two* 1982.

Any sufficiently advanced technology is indistinguishable from magic.

Arthur C Clarke
The Lost Worlds of 2001

Clarke /klɑːk/ Jeremiah 1659–1707. English composer. Organist at St Paul's, he composed 'The Prince of Denmark's March', a harpsichord piece that was arranged by Henry →Wood as a 'Trumpet Voluntary' and wrongly attributed to Purcell.

Clarke /klɑːk/ Kenneth (Harry) 1940– . British Conservative politician, member of Parliament from 1970, a cabinet minister from 1985, education secretary 1990–92, and home secretary from 1992.

Clarke was politically active as a law student at Cambridge. He was elected to Parliament for Rushcliff, Nottinghamshire 1970. From 1965–66, Clarke was secretary for the Birmingham Bow Group. He became a minister of state 1982, paymaster general 1985, with special responsibility for employment, and chancellor of the Duchy of Lancaster 1987. In 1988 he was made minister of health, in 1990 education secretary, and in 1992, following the April general election, home secretary.

Clarke /klɑːk/ Marcus Andrew Hislop 1846–1881. Australian writer. Born in London, he went to Australia when he was 18 and worked as a journalist in Victoria. He wrote *For the Term of his Natural Life* 1874, a novel dealing with life in the early Australian prison settlements.

Clarke /klɑːk/ Ron(ald William) 1937– . Australian middle- and long-distance runner. A prolific record breaker, he broke 17 world records ranging from 2 miles to the one-hour run.

The first man to break 13 minutes for the 3 miles 1966, he was also the first to better 28 minutes for the 10,000 metres. Despite his record-breaking achievements, he never won a gold medal at a major championship.

Clarkson /klɑːksən/ Thomas 1760–1846. British philanthropist. From 1785 he devoted himself to a campaign against slavery. He was one of the founders of the Anti-Slavery Society 1823 and was largely responsible for the abolition of slavery in British colonies 1833.

Claude /kləʊd/ Georges 1870–1960. French industrial chemist, responsible for inventing neon signs. He discovered 1896 that acetylene, normally explosive, could be safely transported when dissolved in acetone. He later demonstrated that neon gas could be used to provide a bright red light in signs. These were displayed publicly for the first time at the Paris Motor Show 1910. As an old man, Claude spent the period 1945–49 in prison as a collaborator.

Claudel /kləʊ'del/ Paul 1868–1955. French poet and dramatist. A fervent Catholic, he was influenced by the Symbolists and achieved an effect of mystic allegory in such plays as *L'Annonce faite à Marie/Tidings Brought to Mary* 1912 and *Le Soulier de satin/The Satin Slipper* 1929, set in 16th-century Spain. His verse includes *Cinq grandes odes/Five Great Odes* 1910.

Claude Lorrain /kləʊd lɒ'ræn/ (Claude Gelée) 1600–1682. French landscape painter, active in Rome from 1627. His distinctive, luminous, Classical style had great impact on late 17th- and 18th-century taste. His subjects are mostly mythological and historical, with insignificant figures lost in great expanses of poetic scenery, as in *The Enchanted Castle* 1664 (National Gallery, London).

Born in Lorraine, he established himself in Rome, where his many patrons included Pope Urban VIII. His *Liber Veritatis*, which contains some 200 drawings after his finished works, was made to prevent forgeries of his work by contemporaries.

Claudian /klɔːdiən/ (Claudius Claudianus) *c.* 370–404. Last of the great Latin poets of the Roman Empire, probably born in Alexandria, Egypt. He wrote official panegyrics, epigrams, and the epic *The Rape of Proserpine*.

Claudius /klɔːdiəs/ Tiberius Claudius Nero 10 BC–AD 54. Nephew of ➔Tiberius, made Roman emperor by his troops AD 41, after the murder of his nephew Caligula. Claudius was a scholar, historian, and able administrator. During his reign the Roman Empire was considerably extended, and in 43 he took part in the invasion of Britain.

Lame and suffering from a speech impediment, he was frequently the object of ridicule. He was dominated by his third wife, ➔Messalina, whom he ultimately had executed, and is thought to have been poisoned by his fourth wife, Agrippina the Younger. His life is described by the novelist Robert Graves in his books *I Claudius* 1934 and *Claudius the God* 1934.

Each man is the smith of his own fortune.
Claudius

Clausewitz /klaʊzəvɪts/ Karl von 1780–1831. Prussian officer and writer on war, born near Magdeburg. His book *Vom Kriege/On War* 1833, translated into English 1873, gave a new philosophical foundation to the art of war and put forward a concept of strategy that was influential until World War I.

Clausius /klaʊziəs/ Rudolf Julius Emanuel 1822–1888. German physicist, one of the founders of the science of thermodynamics. In 1850 he enunciated its second law: heat cannot pass from a colder to a hotter body.

Claverhouse /kleɪvəhaʊs/ John Graham, Viscount Dundee 1649–1689. Scottish soldier. Appointed by Charles II to suppress the Covenanters from 1677, he was routed at Drumclog 1679, but three weeks later won the battle of Bothwell Bridge, by which the rebellion was crushed. Until 1688 he was engaged in continued persecution and became known as 'Bloody Clavers', regarded by the Scottish people as a figure of evil. His army then joined the first Jacobite rebellion and defeated the loyalist forces in the pass of Killiecrankie, where he was mortally wounded.

Clay Cassius Marcellus, Jr, original name of boxer Muhammad ➔Ali.

Clay /kleɪ/ Frederic 1838–1889. British composer, born in Paris. Clay wrote light operas and the cantata *Lalla Rookh* 1877, based on a poem by Thomas Moore.

Clay /kleɪ/ Henry 1777–1852. US politician. He stood unsuccessfully three times for the presidency: as a Democratic-Republican 1824, as a National Republican 1832, and as a Whig 1844. He supported the war of 1812 against Britain, and tried to hold the Union together on the slavery issue by the Missouri Compromise of 1820, and again in the compromise of 1850. He was secretary of state 1825–29, and is also remembered for his 'American system', which favoured the national bank, internal improvements to facilitate commercial and industrial development, and the raising of protective tariffs.

Clay /kleɪ/ Lucius DuBignon 1897–1978. US commander in chief of the US occupation forces in Germany 1947–49. He broke the Soviet blockade of Berlin 1948 after 327 days, with an airlift – a term he brought into general use – which involved bringing all supplies into West Berlin by air.

Clayton /kleɪtn/ Jack 1921– . English film director, originally a producer. His first feature, *Room at the Top* 1958, heralded a new maturity in British cinema. Other works include *The Innocents* 1961, *The Great Gatsby* 1974, and *The Lonely Passion of Judith Hearne* 1987.

Cleese /kliːz/ John 1939– . English actor and comedian who has written for and appeared in both television programmes and films. On British television, he is particularly associated with the comedy series *Monty Python's Flying Circus* and *Fawlty Towers*. His films include *Monty Python and the Holy Grail* 1974, *The Life of Brian* 1979, and *A Fish Called Wanda* 1988.

Cleland /ˈkleələnd/ John 1709–1789. English author. He wrote *Fanny Hill, the Memoirs of a Woman of Pleasure* 1748–49 to try to extricate himself from the grip of his London creditors. The book was considered immoral.

Cleland was called before the Privy Council, but was granted a pension to prevent further misdemeanours.

Clemenceau /ˌklemɒnˈsəʊ/ Georges 1841–1929. French politician and journalist (prominent in the defence of Alfred →Dreyfus). He was prime minister 1906–09 and 1917–20. After World War I he presided over the peace conference in Paris that drew up the Treaty of Versailles, but failed to secure for France the Rhine as a frontier.

Clemenceau was mayor of Montmartre, Paris, in the war of 1870, and 1871 was elected a member of the National Assembly at Bordeaux. He was elected a deputy 1876 after the formation of the Third Republic. An extreme radical, he soon earned the nickname of 'the Tiger' on account of his ferocious attacks on politicians whom he disliked. He lost his seat 1893 and spent the next ten years in journalism. In 1902 he was elected senator for the Var, and was soon one of the most powerful politicians in France. When he became prime minister for the second time 1917, he made the decisive appointment of Marshal →Foch as supreme commander.

Clemens /ˈklemənz/ Samuel Langhorne. Real name of the US writer Mark →Twain.

Clement VII /ˈklemənt/ 1478–1534. Pope 1523–34. He refused to allow the divorce of Henry VIII of England and Catherine of Aragon. Illegitimate son of a brother of Lorenzo de' Medici, the ruler of Florence, he commissioned monuments for the Medici chapel in Florence from the Renaissance artist Michelangelo.

Clemente /kləˈmenti/ Roberto (Walker) 1934–1972. Puerto Rican-born US baseball player who played for the Pittsburgh Pirates 1955–72. He had a career batting average of .317, was the 11th player in history to reach 3,000 hits, and was an outstanding right fielder. He died in a plane crash while flying to aid Nicaraguan earthquake victims.

Born in Carolina, Puerto Rico, he led the league in hitting four times, hit 240 career home runs, and was the National League's Most Valuable Player 1966.

He was elected to the Baseball Hall of Fame 1973.

Clementi /kleˈmenti/ Muzio 1752–1832. Italian pianist and composer. He settled in London 1782 as a teacher and then as proprietor of a successful piano and music business. He was the founder of the new technique of piano playing, and his series of studies, *Gradus ad Parnassum* 1817, is still in use.

Clement of Alexandria /ˈklemənt/ c. AD 150–c. 215. Greek theologian who applied Greek philo-sophical ideas to Christian doctrine. He was the teacher of the theologian Origen.

Clements /ˈklemənts/ John 1910–1988. British actor and director whose productions included revivals of Restoration comedies and the plays of George Bernard Shaw.

Cleon Athenian demagogue and military leader in the Peloponnesian War 431–404 BC. After the death of Pericles, to whom he was opposed, he won power as representative of the commercial classes and was for some years the foremost man in Athens. He advocated a vigorous war policy in opposition to the moderates who favoured an early peace. He was killed fighting the Spartans at Amphipolis.

Cleopatra /ˌkliːəˈpætrə/ c. 68–30 BC. Queen of Egypt 51–48 and 47–30 BC. When the Roman general Julius Caesar arrived in Egypt, he restored her to the throne from which she had been ousted. Cleopatra and Caesar became lovers and she went with him to Rome. After Caesar's assassination 44 BC she returned to Alexandria and resumed her position as queen of Egypt. In 41 BC she was joined there by Mark Antony, one of Rome's rulers. In 31 BC Rome declared war on Egypt and scored a decisive victory in the naval Battle of Actium off the W coast of Greece. Cleopatra fled with her 60 ships to Egypt; Antony abandoned the struggle and followed her. Both he and Cleopatra committed suicide.

Cleopatra was Macedonian, and the last ruler of the Macedonian dynasty, which ruled Egypt from 323 until annexation by Rome 31. She succeeded her father Ptolemy XII jointly with her brother Ptolemy XIII, and they ruled together from 51 to 49 BC, when she was expelled by him. Her reinstatement in 48 BC by Caesar caused a war between Caesar and her brother, who was defeated and killed. The younger brother, Ptolemy XIV, was elevated to the throne and married to her, in the tradition of the pharaohs, although she actually lived with Caesar and they had a son, Ptolemy XV, known as Caesarion (he was later killed by Octavian).

After Caesar's death, Cleopatra and Mark Antony had three sons, and he divorced in 32 BC his wife Octavia. She was the sister of Octavian, the ruler of Rome, who then declared war on Egypt. Shakespeare's play *Antony and Cleopatra* recounts that Cleopatra killed herself with an asp (poisonous snake) after Antony's suicide.

Cleve /ˈkleɪvə/ Per Teodor 1840–1905. Swedish chemist and geologist who discovered the elements holmium and hulium 1879. He also demonstrated that the substance didymium, previously supposed to be an element, was in fact two elements, now known as neodymium and praseodymium. Towards the end of his life he developed a method for identifying the age of glacial and post-glacial deposits from the diatom fossils found in them.

Cleveland The 22nd and 24th president of the USA, Grover Cleveland, a Democrat. He had previously served as mayor of Buffalo, New York and as governor of New York.

Cleveland /ˈkliːvlənd/ (Stephen) Grover 1837–1908. 22nd and 24th president of the USA, 1885–89 and 1893–97; the first Democratic president elected after the Civil War, and the only president to hold office for two nonconsecutive terms. He attempted to check corruption in public life, and in 1895 initiated arbitration proceedings that eventually settled a territorial dispute with Britain concerning the Venezuelan boundary.

An unswerving conservative, Cleveland refused to involve the government in economic affairs. Within a year of his taking office for the second time, 4 million were unemployed and the USA was virtually bankrupt.

Cliff /klɪf/ Clarice 1899–1972. English pottery designer. Her Bizarre ware, characterized by brightly coloured floral and geometric decoration on often geometrically shaped china, became increasingly popular in the 1930s.

Born in the Potteries, she started as a factory apprentice at the age of 13, trained at evening classes and worked for many years at the Wilkinson factory. In 1963 she became art director of the factory, which was part of the Royal Staffordshire Pottery in Burslem.

Clift /klɪft/ (Edward) Montgomery 1920–1966. US film and theatre actor. A star of the late 1940s and 1950s in films such as *Red River* 1948, *A Place in the Sun* 1951, and *From Here to Eternity* 1953, he was disfigured in a car accident in 1957 but continued to make films. He played the title role in *Freud* 1962.

Clinton /ˈklɪntən/ Bill (William Jefferson) 1946– . 42nd president of the USA from 1993. A Democrat, he served as governor of Arkansas 1979–81 and 1983–93, establishing a liberal and progressive reputation. He won a successful 1992 presidential campaign, against the incumbent George Bush, by centring on domestic issues and economic recovery. He became the first Democrat in the White House for 12 years.

Born in the railway town of Hope, Arkansas, Clinton graduated from Georgetown University 1968, won a Rhodes scholarship to Oxford University 1968–70, and graduated from Yale University Law School 1973. He was elected attorney general for Arkansas in 1975. He secured the presidential election, with running mate Al →Gore, despite a series of allegations during the campaign, including those of draft-dodging and an extramarital affair.

Clinton /ˈklɪntən/ De Witt 1769–1828. American political leader. After serving in the US Senate 1802–03, he was elected mayor of New York City 1803–15 and governor of New York from 1817. A strong promoter of the Erie Canal, he was instrumental in the initiation of that project, completed 1825.

Born in Little Britain, New York, Clinton was educated at Columbia University, studied law, and became the personal assistant of his uncle George Clinton, governor of New York. He served in the state legislature 1797–1802 serving simultaneously as lieutenant governor.

Clive /klaɪv/ Robert, Baron Clive of Plassey 1725–1774. British soldier and administrator who established British rule in India by victories over the French 1751 and over the nawab of Bengal 1757. On his return to Britain his wealth led to allegations that he had abused his power. Although acquitted, he committed suicide.

Close /kləʊs/ Glenn 1948– . US actress who received Academy Award nominations for her roles as the embittered 'other woman' in *Fatal Attraction* 1987 and as the scheming antiheroine of *Dangerous Liaisons* 1988. She played Gertrude in Franco Zeffirelli's film of *Hamlet* 1990 and appeared as an opera star in *Meeting Venus* 1991.

She was born in Connecticut, made her New York stage debut on graduating from college, and went on to perform in musicals as well as dramatic productions. Her first film was *The World According to Garp* 1982; other screen appearances include *The Big Chill* 1983 and *Jagged Edge* 1985. More recently on Broadway she has had roles in Tom Stoppard's *The Real Thing* and Michael Frayn's *Benefactors*.

Clouet /kluːeɪ/ François *c.* 1515–1572. French portrait painter who succeeded his father Jean Clouet as court painter. He worked in the Italian style of Mannerism. His half-nude portrait of Diane de Poitiers, *The Lady in Her Bath* (National Gallery, Washington), is also thought to be a likeness of Marie Touchet, mistress of Charles IX.

Clinton Bill Clinton who defeated George Bush in the US presidential election of November 1992 to become the first Democratic president for twelve years. He had been governor of Arkansas since 1983.

Clouet /kluːeɪ/ Jean (known as *Janet*) 1486–1541. French artist, court painter to Francis I. His portraits and drawings, often compared to Holbein's, show an outstanding naturalism.

Clough /klʌf/ Arthur Hugh 1819–1861. English poet. Many of his lyrics are marked by a melancholy scepticism that reflects his struggle with his religious doubt.

Thou shalt not kill; but need'st not strive Officiously to keep alive.

Arthur Hugh Clough *The Last Decalogue* 1861

Clovis /kləʊvɪs/ 465–511. Merovingian king of the Franks from 481. He succeeded his father Childeric as king of the Salian (northern) Franks; defeated the Gallo-Romans (Romanized Gauls) near Soissons 486, ending their rule in France; and defeated the Alemanni, a confederation of Germanic tribes, near Cologne 496. He embraced Christianity and subsequently proved a powerful defender of orthodoxy against the Arian Visigoths, whom he defeated at Poitiers 507. He made Paris his capital.

Clunies-Ross /kluːniz ˈrɒs/ family that established a benevolently paternal rule in the Cocos Islands. John Clunies-Ross, a Scottish seaman, settled on Home Island in 1827. The family's rule ended in 1978 with the purchase of the Cocos by the Australian government.

Cnut alternative spelling of →Canute.

Coates /kəʊts/ Eric 1886–1957. English composer. He is remembered for the orchestral suites *London* 1933, including the 'Knightsbridge' march; 'By the Sleepy Lagoon' 1939; 'The Dam Busters March' 1942; and the songs 'Bird Songs at Eventide' and 'The Green Hills of Somerset'.

Coates /kəʊts/ Nigel 1949– . British architect. While teaching at the Architectural Association in London in the early 1980s, Coates and a group of students founded NATO (*N*arrative *A*rchitecture *T*oday) and produced an influential series of manifestos and drawings on the theme of the imaginative regeneration of derelict areas of London.

Drawing parallels with the ideas of the Situationists in the 1960s and of punk in the 1970s, Coates promoted an eclectic and narrative form of architecture that went against the contemporary grain.

Cobb /kɒb/ Ty(rus Raymond), nicknamed 'the Georgia Peach' 1886–1961. US baseball player, one of the greatest batters and base runners of all time. He played for Detroit and Philadelphia 1905–28, and won the American League batting average championship 12 times. He holds the record for runs scored (2,254) and batting average (.367). He had 4,191 hits in his career – a record that stood for almost 60 years.

Cobbett /kɒbɪt/ William 1763–1835. British Radical politician and journalist, who published the weekly *Political Register* 1802–35. He spent much time in North America. His crusading essays on the conditions of the rural poor were collected as *Rural Rides* 1830.

Born in Surrey, the self-taught son of a farmer, Cobbett enlisted in the army 1784 and served in Canada. He subsequently lived in the USA as a teacher of English, and became a vigorous pamphleteer, at this time supporting the Tories. In 1800 he returned to England. With increasing knowledge of the sufferings of the farm labourers, he became a Radical and leader of the working-class movement. He was imprisoned 1809–11 for criticizing the flogging of British troops by German mercenaries. He visited the USA again 1817–19. He became a strong advocate of parliamentary reform, and represented Oldham in the Reformed Parliament after 1832.

Cobden /kɒbdən/ Richard 1804–1865. British Liberal politician and economist, co-founder with John Bright of the Anti-Corn Law League 1839. A member of Parliament from 1841, he opposed class and religious privileges and believed in disarmament and free trade.

A typical early Victorian radical, he believed in the abolition of privileges, a minimum of government interference, and the securing of international peace through free trade and by disarmament and arbitration. He opposed trade unionism and most of the factory legislation of his time, because he regarded them as opposed to liberty of contract. His opposition to the Crimean War made him unpopular. He was largely responsible for the commercial treaty with France in 1860.

Cobden British Liberal politician Richard Cobden in 1869. The fourth of eleven children, Cobden's early struggles as a cloth merchant shaped his thinking on free trade and the increase of British commerce.

Born in Sussex, the son of a farmer, Cobden became a calico manufacturer in Manchester. With other businessmen he founded the Anti-Corn Law League and began his lifelong association with John Bright, until 1845 devoting himself to the repeal of the Corn Laws.

Cobden-Sanderson /ˈkɒbdən ˈsɑːndəsən/ Thomas James 1840–1922. British bookbinder and painter. Influenced by the designer William →Morris and the Pre-Raphaelite painter →Burne-Jones, he opened his own workshop in Maiden Lane, London, 1884; he founded the Doves Press 1900–16.

Coburn /ˈkəʊbɜːn/ James 1928– . US film actor, popular in the 1960s and 1970s. His films include *The Magnificent Seven* 1960, *Pat Garrett and Billy the Kid* 1973, and *Cross of Iron* 1977.

Cochise /kəʊˈtʃiːs/ c. 1812–1874. American Apache Indian leader who campaigned relentlessly against white settlement of his territory. Unjustly arrested by US authorities 1850, he escaped from custody and took American hostages, whom he later executed. Joining forces with the Mimbreño Apache, he successfully fought off a large force of California settlers 1862. Finally apprehended by General George Crook 1871, Cochise made peace with the US government the following year.

Born in Arizona, Cochise was as a member of the Chiricahua band of Apache. He gained a large number of followers in his long and bitter dispute with the US government and conducted repeated raids on American posts.

Cochran /ˈkɒkrən/ C(harles) B(lake) 1872–1951. British impresario who promoted entertainment ranging from wrestling and roller-skating to Diaghilev's *Ballets Russes.*

> *I am interested in everything so long as it is well done. I would rather see a good juggler than a bad Hamlet.*
>
> **C B Cochran** *Secrets of a Showman*

Cockcroft /ˈkɒkrɒft/ John Douglas 1897–1967. British physicist. In 1932 he and the Irish physicist Ernest Walton succeeded in splitting the nucleus of an atom for the first time. In 1951 they were jointly awarded a Nobel prize.

Born in Todmorden, W Yorkshire, Cockcroft held an engineering appointment with Metropolitan-Vickers, and took up research work under Ernest →Rutherford at the Cavendish Laboratory, Cambridge. He succeeded Edward →Appleton as Jacksonian professor of natural philosophy, Cambridge (1939–46), and worked on the atom bomb during World War II. He was director at Harwell atomic research establishment 1946–58.

Cockerell /ˈkɒkərəl/ Charles 1788–1863. English architect who built mainly in a Neo-Classical style derived from antiquity and from the work of Christopher Wren. His buildings include the Ashmolean Museum and Taylorian Institute in Oxford 1841–45.

Cockerell /ˈkɒkərəl/ Christopher 1910– . British engineer who invented the hovercraft 1959.

From an interest in radio, he switched to electronics, working with the Marconi Company from 1935 to 1950. In 1953 he began work on the hovercraft, carrying out his early experiments on Oulton Broad, Norfolk.

Cocteau /ˈkɒktəʊ/ Jean 1889–1963. French poet, dramatist, and film director. A leading figure in European Modernism, he worked with Picasso, Diaghilev, and Stravinsky. He produced many volumes of poetry, ballets such as *Le Boeuf sur le toit/The Ox on the Roof* 1920, plays, for example, *Orphée/Orpheus* 1926, and a mature novel of bourgeois French life, *Les Enfants terribles/Children of the Game* 1929, which he made into a film 1950.

> *Victor Hugo … a madman who thought he was Victor Hugo.*
>
> **Jean Cocteau** *Opium*

Cody /ˈkəʊdi/ (William Frederick) 'Buffalo Bill' 1846–1917. US scout and performer. From 1883 he toured the USA and Europe with a Wild West show which featured the re-creation of Indian attacks and, for a time, the cast included Chief

→Sitting Bull as well as Annie →Oakley. His nickname derives from a time when he had a contract to supply buffalo carcasses to railway labourers (over 4,000 in 18 months).

Cody /ˈkəʊdi/ Samuel Franklin 1862–1913. US aviation pioneer. He made his first powered flight on 16 Oct 1908 at Farnborough, England, in a machine of his own design. He was killed in a flying accident.

Born in Texas, USA, he took British nationality in 1909. He spent his early days with a cowboy stage and circus act, and made kites capable of lifting people.

Coe /kəʊ/ Sebastian 1956– . English middle-distance runner, Olympic 1,500-metres champion 1980 and 1984. He became Britain's most prolific world-record breaker with eight outdoor world records and three indoor world records 1979–81. After his retirement from running in 1990 he pursued a political career with the Conservative party, and in 1992 was elected member of Parliament for Falmouth and Camborne in Cornwall.

Coetzee /kuːtˈsɪə/ J(ohn) M 1940– . South African author whose novel *In the Heart of the Country* 1975 dealt with the rape of a white woman by a black man. In 1983 he won Britain's prestigious Booker Prize for *The Life and Times of Michael K*.

Other works include *Waiting for the Barbarians* 1982 and *Foe* 1987.

Cohan /ˈkəʊhæn/ George M(ichael) 1878–1942. US composer. His Broadway hit musical *Little Johnny Jones* 1904 included his songs 'Give My Regards to Broadway' and 'Yankee Doodle Boy'. 'You're a Grand Old Flag' 1906 further associated him with popular patriotism, as did his World War I song 'Over There' 1917.

Born to a theatrical family in Providence, Rhode Island, USA, Cohan spent his youth touring, writing songs, and appearing in musical comedies. A film version of his life, *Yankee Doodle Dandy*, appeared 1942.

He was honoured by Congress 1940.

Cohan /ˈkəʊhæn/ Robert Paul 1925– . US choreographer and founder of the London Contemporary Dance Theatre 1969–87; now artistic director of the Contemporary Dance Theatre. He was a student of Martha →Graham and co-director of her company 1966–69. His works include *Waterless Method of Swimming Instruction* 1974 and *Mass for Man* 1985.

Coke /kəʊk/ Edward 1552–1634. Lord Chief Justice of England 1613–17. He was a defender of common law against royal prerogative; against Charles I he drew up the Petition of Right 1628, which defines and protects Parliament's liberties.

Coke was called to the Bar in 1578, and in 1592 became speaker of the House of Commons and solicitor-general. As attorney-general from 1594 he conducted the prosecution of Elizabeth I's former favourites Essex and Raleigh, and of the Gunpowder Plot conspirators. In 1606 he became Chief Justice of the Common Pleas, and began his struggle, as champion of the common law, against James I's attempts to exalt the royal prerogative. An attempt to silence him by promoting him to the dignity of Lord Chief Justice proved unsuccessful, and from 1620 he led the parliamentary opposition and the attack on Charles I's adviser Buckingham. Coke's *Institutes* are a legal classic, and he ranks as the supreme common lawyer.

For a man's house is his castle.
Edward Coke *Third Institute*

Coke /kəʊk/ Thomas William 1754–1842. English pioneer and promoter of the improvements associated with the Agricultural Revolution. His innovations included regular manuring of the soil, the cultivation of fodder crops in association with corn, and the drilling of wheat and turnips.

He also developed a fine flock of Southdown sheep at Holkham, Norfolk, which were superior to the native Norfolks, and encouraged his farm tenants to do likewise. These ideas attracted attention at the annual sheep shearings, an early form of agricultural show, which Coke held on his home farm from 1776. By the end of the century these had become major events, with many visitors coming to see and discuss new stock, crops, and equipment.

Colbert /ˈkɒlbeə/ Claudette. Stage name of Claudette Lily Cauchoin 1905– . French-born film actress who lived in Hollywood from childhood. She was ideally cast in sophisticated, romantic roles, but had a natural instinct for comedy and appeared in several of Hollywood's finest, including *It Happened One Night* 1934 and *The Palm Beach Story* 1942.

Colbert /ˈkɒlbeə/ Jean-Baptiste 1619–1683. French politician, chief minister to Louis XIV, and controller-general (finance minister) from 1665. He reformed the Treasury, promoted French industry and commerce by protectionist measures, and tried to make France a naval power equal to England or the Netherlands, while favouring a peaceful foreign policy.

Colbert, born in Reims, entered the service of Cardinal Mazarin and succeeded him as chief minister to Louis XIV. In 1661 he set to work to reform the Treasury. The national debt was largely repaid, and the system of tax collection was drastically reformed. Industry was brought under state control, shipbuilding was encouraged by bounties, companies were established to trade with India and America, and colonies were founded in Louisiana, Guiana, and Madagascar. In his later years Colbert was supplanted in Louis's favour by the war minister Louvois (1641–1691), who supported a policy of conquests.

Cole /kəʊl/ Thomas 1801–1848. US painter, founder of the Hudson River school of landscape artists.

Cole wrote *An Essay on American Scenery* in 1835. Apart from panoramic views such as *The Oxbow* 1836 (Metropolitan Museum of Art, New York), he painted a dramatic historical series, *The Course of Empire* 1836 (New York Historical Society), influenced by the European artists Claude, Turner, and John Martin.

Coleman /ˈkəʊlmən/ Ornette 1930– . US alto saxophonist and jazz composer. In the late 1950s he rejected the established structural principles of jazz for free avant-garde improvisation. He has worked with small and large groups, ethnic musicians of different traditions, and symphony orchestras.

Colenso /kəˈlenzəʊ/ John William 1814–1883. Bishop of Natal, South Africa, from 1853. He was the first to write down the Zulu language. He championed the Zulu way of life (including polygamy) in relation to Christianity, and applied Christian morality to race relations in South Africa.

Coleridge /ˈkəʊlərɪdʒ/ Samuel Taylor 1772–1834. English poet, one of the founders of the Romantic movement. A friend of Southey and Wordsworth, he collaborated with the latter on *Lyrical Ballads* 1798. His poems include 'The Rime of the Ancient Mariner', 'Christabel', and 'Kubla Khan'; critical works include *Biographia Literaria* 1817.

While at Cambridge University, Coleridge was driven by debt to enlist in the Dragoons, and then in 1795, as part of an abortive plan to found a communist colony in the USA with Robert Southey, married Sarah Fricker, from whom he afterwards separated. He became addicted to opium and from 1816 lived in Highgate, London, under medical care. As a philosopher, he argued inferentially that even in registering sense-perceptions the mind was performing acts of creative imagination, rather than being a passive arena in which ideas interact mechanistically.

A brilliant talker and lecturer, he was expected to produce some great work of philosophy or criticism. His *Biographia Literaria*, much of it based on German ideas, is full of insight but its formlessness and the limited extent of his poetic output indicates a partial failure of promise.

No man was ever yet a great poet, without being at the same time a profound philosopher.

Samuel Taylor Coleridge
Biographia Literaria 1817

Coleridge /ˈkəʊlərɪdʒ/ Sara 1802–1852. English woman of letters, editor of the work of her father Samuel Taylor Coleridge. She was also a writer and translator.

Coleridge-Taylor /ˈkəʊlərɪdʒ ˈteɪlə/ Samuel 1875–1912. English composer who wrote the cantata *Hiawatha's Wedding Feast* 1898, a setting in three parts of Longfellow's poem. The son of a West African doctor and an English mother, he was a student and champion of traditional black music.

Colet /ˈkɒlɪt/ John c. 1467–1519. English humanist, influenced by the Italian reformer Savonarola and the Dutch scholar Erasmus. He reacted against the scholastic tradition in his interpretation of the Bible, and founded modern biblical exegesis. In 1505 he became dean of St Paul's Cathedral, London.

Colette /kɒˈlet/ Sidonie-Gabrielle 1873–1954. French writer. At 20 she married Henri Gauthier-Villars, a journalist known as 'Willy', under whose name and direction her four 'Claudine' novels, based on her own early life, were written. Divorced 1906, she worked as a striptease and mime artist for a while, but continued to write. Works from this later period include *Chéri* 1920, *La Fin de Chéri/The End of Chéri* 1926, and *Gigi* 1944.

Colfax /ˈkəʊlfæks/ Schuyler 1823–1885. US political leader. He was elected to the US House of Representatives 1854 and served as Speaker of the House 1863–69. A radical Republican, Colfax was elected vice president for President Grant's first term 1869–73. He was not renominated because of charges of corruption and financial improprieties.

Born in New York, USA, Colfax moved with his family to Indiana 1836 and, although having the benefit of little formal education, worked in a succession of jobs, including county auditor, newspaper reporter, and legal assistant before becoming active in Indiana state politics.

Coligny /ˌkɒlɪnˈjiː/ Gaspard de 1517–1572. French admiral and soldier, and prominent Huguenot. About 1557 he joined the Protestant party, helping to lead the Huguenot forces during the Wars of Religion. After the Treaty of St Germain 1570, he became a favourite of the young king Charles IX, but was killed on the first night of the massacre of St Bartholomew.

Collier /ˈkɒliə/ Jeremy 1650–1726. British Anglican cleric, a Nonjuror (refusing to take the oaths of allegiance to William and Mary), who was outlawed 1696 for granting absolution on the scaffold to two men who had tried to assassinate William III. His *Short View of the Immorality and Profaneness of the English Stage* 1698 was aimed at the dramatists William Congreve and John Vanbrugh.

Collier /ˈkɒliə/ Lesley 1947– . British ballerina, a principal dancer of the Royal Ballet from 1972. She created roles in Kenneth MacMillan's *Anastasia* 1971 and *Four Seasons* 1975, Hans van Manen's *Four Schumann Pieces* 1975, Frederick

Ashton's *Rhapsody*, and Glen Tetley's *Dance of Albiar* both 1980.

Collingwood /ˈkɒlɪŋwʊd/ Cuthbert, Baron Collingwood 1748–1810. British admiral who served with Horatio Nelson in the West Indies against France and blockaded French ports 1803–05; after Nelson's death he took command at the Battle of Trafalgar.

Collingwood /ˈkɒlɪŋwʊd/ Robin George 1889–1943. English philosopher who believed that any philosophical theory or position could be properly understood only within its own historical context and not from the point of view of the present. His aesthetic theory is outlined in *Principles of Art* 1938.

Perfect freedom is reserved for the man who lives by his own work, and in that work does what he wants to do.

R G Collingwood *Speculum Mentis*

Collins /ˈkɒlɪnz/ Michael 1890–1922. Irish nationalist. He was a Sinn Féin leader, a founder and director of intelligence of the Irish Republican Army 1919, minister for finance in the provisional government of the Irish Free State 1922, commander of the Free State forces in the civil war, and for ten days head of state before being killed.

Born in County Cork, Collins became an active member of the Irish Republican Brotherhood, and in 1916 fought in the Easter Rising. In 1918 he was elected a Sinn Féin member to the Dáil, and became a minister in the Republican Provisional government. In 1921 he and Arthur Griffith (1872–1922) were mainly responsible for the treaty that established the Irish Free State. During the ensuing civil war, Collins took command and crushed the opposition in Dublin and the large towns within a few weeks. When Griffith died on 12 Aug Collins became head of the state and the army, but he was ambushed near Cork by fellow Irishmen on 22 Aug and killed.

Collins /ˈkɒlɪnz/ Phil(lip David Charles) 1951– . English pop singer, drummer, and actor. A member of the group Genesis from 1970, he has also pursued a successful middle-of-the-road solo career since 1981, with hits (often new versions of old songs) including 'In the Air Tonight' 1981 and 'Groovy Kind of Love' 1988.

Collins /ˈkɒlɪnz/ (William) Wilkie 1824–1889. English author of mystery and suspense novels. He wrote *The Woman in White* 1860 (with its fat villain Count Fosco), often called the first English detective novel, and *The Moonstone* 1868 (with Sergeant Cuff, one of the first detectives in English literature).

Collins /ˈkɒlɪnz/ William 1721–1759. British poet. His *Persian Eclogues* 1742 were followed in 1746 by his series 'Odes', including the poem 'To Evening'.

Collodi /kɒˈləʊdi/ Carlo. Pen name of Carlo Lorenzini 1826–1890. Italian journalist and writer who in 1881–83 wrote *Le avventure di Pinocchio/The Adventure of Pinocchio*, a children's story of a wooden puppet that became a human boy.

Collor de Mello Fernando 1949– . Brazilian politician, president 1990–92. He founded the centre-right National Reconstruction Party (PRN) 1989 and won that year's presidential election by promising to root out government corruption and entrenched privileges. However, rumours of his misconduct lead his constitutional removal from office by a vote of impeachment 1992, leading to his clonstitutional removal from office by a vote of impeachment in congress Sept. He resigned in Dec at the start of his trial, and was subsequently banned from public office for eight years.

Colman /ˈkəʊlmən/ Ronald 1891–1958. English actor, in Hollywood from 1920, who played suave roles in *Beau Geste* 1924, *The Prisoner of Zenda* 1937, *Lost Horizon* 1937, and *A Double Life* 1947, for which he received an Academy Award.

Colombo /kəˈlɒmbəʊ/ Matteo Realdo *c.* 1516–1559. Italian anatomist who discovered pulmonary circulation, the process of blood circulating from the heart to the lungs and back.

This showed that →Galen's teachings were wrong, and was of help to William →Harvey in his work on the heart and circulation. Colombo was a pupil of Andreas →Vesalius and became his successor at the University of Padua.

Colonna /kɒˈlɒnə/ Vittoria *c.* 1492–1547. Italian poet. Many of her Petrarchan sonnets idealize her husband, who was killed at the battle of Paria 1525. She was a friend of Michelangelo, who addressed sonnets to her.

Colt /kəʊlt/ Samuel 1814–1862. US gunsmith who invented the revolver 1835 that bears his name.

He built up an immense arms-manufacturing business in Hartford, Connecticut, his birthplace, and subsequently in England.

Coltrane /kɒlˈtreɪn/ John (William) 1926–1967. US jazz saxophonist who first came to prominence 1955 with the Miles →Davis quintet, later playing with Thelonious Monk 1957. He was a powerful and individual artist, whose performances featured much experimentation. His 1960s quartet was highly regarded for its innovations in melody and harmony.

Like Charlie Parker, Coltrane marked a watershed in jazz and has been deified by his fans. The free-jazz movement of the 1960s owed much to his extended exploratory solos, for example on *Giant Steps* 1959, the year he traded tenor saxophone for soprano. A highly original musician, he has been much imitated, but the deeply emotional tone of his playing, for example on *A Love Supreme* 1964, is impossible to copy.

Colum /ˈkʊləm/ Padraic 1881–1972. Irish poet and playwright. He was associated with the foundation of the Abbey Theatre, Dublin, where his plays *Land* 1905 and *Thomas Muskerry* 1910 were performed. His *Collected Poems* 1932 show his gift for lyrical expression.

Columba, St /kəˈlʌmbə/ 521–597. Irish Christian abbot, missionary to Scotland. He was born in County Donegal of royal descent, and founded monasteries and churches in Ireland. In 563 he sailed with 12 companions to Iona, and built a monastery there that was to play a leading part in the conversion of Britain. Feast day 9 June.

From his base on Iona St Columba made missionary journeys to the mainland. Legend has it that he drove a monster from the river Ness, and he crowned Aidan, an Irish king of Argyll.

Columban, St /kəˈlʌmbən/ 543–615. Irish Christian abbot. He was born in Leinster, studied at Bangor, and about 585 went to the Vosges, France, with 12 other monks and founded the monastery of Luxeuil. Later, he preached in Switzerland, then went to Italy, where he built the abbey of Bobbio in the Apennines. Feast day 23 Nov.

Columbus /kəˈlʌmbəs/ Christopher (Spanish *Cristóbal Colón*) 1451–1506. Italian navigator and explorer who made four voyages to the New World: 1492 to San Salvador Island, Cuba, and Haiti; 1493–96 to Guadaloupe, Montserrat, Antigua, Puerto Rico, and Jamaica; 1498 to Trinidad and the mainland of South America; 1502–04 to Honduras and Nicaragua.

Believing that Asia could be reached by sailing westwards, he eventually won the support of King Ferdinand and Queen Isabella of Spain and set off on his first voyage from Palos 3 Aug 1492 with three small ships, the *Niña*, the *Pinta*, and his flagship the *Santa Maria*. Land was sighted 12 Oct, probably Watling Island (now San Salvador Island), and within a few weeks he reached Cuba and Haiti, returning to Spain March 1493.

Born in Genoa, Columbus went to sea at an early age, and settled in Portugal 1478. After his third voyage 1498, he became involved in quarrels among the colonists sent to Haiti, and in 1500 the governor sent him back to Spain in chains. Released and compensated by the king, he made his last voyage 1502–04, during which he hoped to find a strait leading to India. He died in poverty in Valladolid and is buried in Seville cathedral.

In 1968 the site of the wreck of the *Santa Maria*, sunk off Hispaniola 25 Dec 1492, was located.

Comaneci /kɒməˈnetʃ/ Nadia 1961– . Romanian gymnast. She won three gold medals at the 1976 Olympics at the age of 14, and was the first gymnast to record a perfect score of 10 in international competition. Upon retirement she became a coach of the Romanian team, but defected to Canada 1989.

Compton-Burnett English novelist Ivy Compton-Burnett, whose works examine the complexities of family strife, published her first novel Dolores 1911. Noted for her skilful dialogue, of which her novels largely consist, her books are eminently suitable for radio and many have been adapted for broadcasting.

Comines /kɒˈmiːn/ Philippe de c. 1445–1511. French diplomat in the service of Charles the Bold, Louis XI, and Charles VIII; author of *Mémoires* 1489–98.

Commodus /ˈkɒmədəs/ Lucius Aelius Aurelius AD 161–192. Roman emperor from 180, son of Marcus Aurelius Antoninus. He was a tyrant, spending lavishly on gladiatorial combats, confiscating the property of the wealthy, persecuting the Senate, and renaming Rome 'Colonia Commodia'. There were many attempts against his life, and he was finally strangled at the instigation of his mistress and advisers, who had discovered themselves on the emperor's death list.

Compton /ˈkɒmptən/ Arthur Holly 1892–1962. US physicist known for his work on X-rays. Working at Chicago 1923 he found that X-rays scattered by such light elements as carbon increased their wavelengths. Compton concluded from this unexpected result that the X-rays were displaying both wavelike and particlelike properties, since named the *Compton effect*. He shared a Nobel prize 1927 with Scottish physicist Charles Wilson (1869–1959).

Compton-Burnett /ˈkʌmptən ˈbɜːnɪt/ Ivy 1892–1969. English novelist. She used dialogue to show reactions of small groups of characters dominated by the tyranny of family relationships. Her novels, set at the turn of the century, include *Pastors and*

Masters 1925, *More Women Than Men* 1933, and *Mother and Son* 1955.

Comte /kɒmt/ Auguste 1798–1857. French philosopher regarded as the founder of sociology, a term he coined 1830. He sought to establish sociology as an intellectual discipline, using a scientific approach ('positivism') as the basis of a new science of social order and social development.

Comte, born in Montpellier, was expelled from the Paris Ecole Polytechnique for leading a student revolt 1816. In 1818 he became secretary to the socialist Saint-Simon and was much influenced by him. He began lecturing on the 'Positive Philosophy' 1826, but almost immediately succumbed to a nervous disorder and once tried to commit suicide in the river Seine. On his recovery he resumed his lectures and mathematical teaching.

In his six-volume *Cours de philosophie positive* 1830–42 he argued that human thought and social development evolve through three stages: the theological, the metaphysical, and the positive or scientific. Although he originally sought to proclaim society's evolution to a new golden age of science, industry, and rational morality, his radical ideas were increasingly tempered by the political and social upheavals of his time. His influence, however, continued in Europe and the USA until the early 20th century.

Conchobar /kɒnuə/ in Celtic mythology, king of Ulster whose intended bride, Deirdre, eloped with Noísi. She died of sorrow when Conchobar killed her husband and his brothers.

Condé /kɒn'deɪ/ Louis de Bourbon, Prince of Condé 1530–1569. Prominent French Huguenot leader, founder of the house of Condé and uncle of Henry IV of France. He fought in the wars between Henry II and the Holy Roman emperor Charles V, including the defence of Metz.

Condé /kɒn'deɪ/ Louis II 1621–1686. Prince of Condé called the **Great Condé**. French commander who won brilliant victories during the Thirty Years' War at Rocroi 1643 and Lens 1648, but rebelled 1651 and entered the Spanish service. Pardoned 1660, he commanded Louis XIV's armies against the Spanish and the Dutch.

Conder /kɒndə/ Charles 1868–1909. Australian artist, born in London, who painted in watercolour and oil. In 1888 Conder joined Tom →Roberts in Melbourne forming the Australian Impressionist group which became known as the Heidelberg School. Although his early work, such as *The Departure of the SS Orient–Circular Quay* 1888 (Art Gallery of New South Wales, Sydney), is distinctly Impressionist in style, he later became known for his delicate watercolours painted on silk and for lithograph sets, such as *Carnival* 1905 (painted following his return to Europe 1890).

Condillac /kɒndiːæk/ Étienne Bonnot de 1715–1780. French philosopher. He mainly followed

English philosopher John →Locke, but his *Traité de sensations* 1754 claims that all mental activity stems from the transformation of sensations. He was a collaborator on the French *Encyclopédie*. Born in Grenoble of noble parentage, he entered the church and was appointed tutor to Louis XV's grandson, the duke of Parma.

We cannot recollect the ignorance in which we were born.

Étienne Bonnot de Condillac
Traité de sensations 1754

Condorcet /ˌkɒndɔːˈseɪ/ Marie Jean Antoine Nicolas Caritat, Marquis de Condorcet 1743–1794. French philosopher, mathematician, and politician, associated with the *Encyclopédistes*. One of the Girondins, he opposed the execution of Louis XVI, and was imprisoned and poisoned himself. While in prison, he wrote *Esquisse d'un tableau des progrès de l'esprit humain/Historical Survey of the Progress of Human Understanding* 1795, which envisaged inevitable future progress, though not the perfectibility of human nature.

All errors in government and in society are based on philosophical errors which, in turn, are derived from errors in natural science.

Marquis de Condorcet *Report and Project of a Decree on the General Organization of Public Instruction*

Condorcet Marquis de Condorcet, French 18th-century mathematician and 'philosophe', advocate of reason, pacifism, and the equality of the sexes. A moderate during the Revolution, he committed suicide when imprisoned by the extremists.

Confucius /kən'fju:ʃəs/ (Latinized form of *Kong Zi*, 'Kong the master') 551–479 BC. Chinese sage whose name is given to Confucianism. He devoted his life to relieving suffering among the poor through governmental and administrative reform. His emphasis on tradition and ethics attracted a growing number of pupils during his lifetime. *The Analects of Confucius*, a compilation of his teachings, was published after his death. Within 300 years of the death of Confucius his teaching was adopted by the Chinese state.

Confucius was born in Lu, in what is now the province of Shangdong, and his early years were spent in poverty. Married at 19, he worked as a minor official, then as a teacher. In 517 there was an uprising in Lu, and Confucius spent the next year or two in the adjoining state of Ch'i. As a teacher he was able to place many of his pupils in government posts but a powerful position eluded him. Only in his fifties was he given an office, but he soon resigned because of the lack of power it conveyed. Then for 14 years he wandered from state to state looking for a ruler who could give him a post where he could put his reforms into practice. At the age of 67 he returned to Lu and devoted himself to teaching. At his death five years later he was buried with great pomp, and his grave outside Qufu has remained a centre of pilgrimage.

Study the past, if you would divine the future.

Confucius

Congreve /'kɒŋgri:v/ William 1670–1729. English dramatist and poet. His first success was the comedy *The Old Bachelor* 1693, followed by *The Double Dealer* 1694, *Love for Love* 1695, the tragedy *The Mourning Bride* 1697, and *The Way of the World* 1700. His plays, which satirize the social affectations of the time, are characterized by elegant wit and wordplay.

Conkling /'kɒŋklɪŋ/ Roscoe 1829–1888. US political leader, one of the founders of the Republican Party 1854. He served in the US House of Representatives 1859–63 and 1865–67, and in the US Senate 1867–81. A radical Republican, Conkling was an active prosecutor in President A ➔Johnson's impeachment trial.

Born in Albany, New York, USA, the son of a judge, Conkling was admitted to the bar 1850 and soon appointed district attorney. He served as mayor of Utica 1858. As an opponent of President Garfield, Conkling declined an appointment to the US Supreme Court 1882 and returned to private law practice.

Connell /'kɒnl/ James 1850–1929. Irish socialist who wrote the British Labour Party anthem 'The Red Flag' during the 1889 London strike.

Connery /'kɒnəri/ Sean 1930– . Scottish film actor, the first and best interpreter of James Bond in several films based on the novels of Ian Fleming. His films include *Dr No* 1962, *From Russia with Love* 1963, *Marnie* 1964, *Goldfinger* 1964, *Diamonds Are Forever* 1971, *A Bridge Too Far* 1977, *The Name of the Rose* 1986, and *The Untouchables* 1987 (Academy Award).

Connolly /'kɒnəli/ Cyril 1903–1974. English critic and author. As founder and editor of the literary magazine *Horizon* 1930–50, he had considerable critical influence. His works include *The Rock Pool* 1935, a novel of artists on the Riviera, and *The Unquiet Grave* 1944, a series of reflections published under the pseudonym of Palinurus.

Imprisoned in every fat man a thin one is wildly signalling to be let out.

Cyril Connolly 1937

Connolly /'kɒnəli/ Maureen 1934–1969. US lawn-tennis player, nicknamed 'Little Mo' because she was just 157 cm/5 ft 2 in tall. In 1953 she became the first woman to complete the Grand Slam by winning all four major tournaments.

All her singles titles (won at nine major championships) and her Grand Slam titles were won between 1951 and 1954. She also represented the USA in the Wightman Cup. Her career ended 1954 after a riding accident.

Connors /'kɒnəz/ Jimmy 1952– . US tennis player who won the Wimbledon title 1974 and 1982, and subsequently won ten Grand Slam events. He was one of the first players to popularize the two-handed backhand.

Conrad /'kɒnræd/ Joseph. Pen name of Teodor Jozef Conrad Korzeniowski 1857–1924. English novelist, born in the Ukraine of Polish parents. He joined the French merchant navy at the age of 17 and first learned English at 21. His greatest works include the novels *Lord Jim* 1900, *Nostromo* 1904, *The Secret Agent* 1907, and *Under Western Eyes* 1911, and the short stories 'Heart of Darkness' 1902 and 'The Shadow Line' 1917. These combine a vivid sensuous evocation of various lands and seas with a rigorous, humane scrutiny of moral dilemmas, pitfalls, and desperation.

Conrad is regarded as one of the greatest of modern novelists. His prose style, varying from eloquently sensuous to bare and astringent, keeps the reader in constant touch with a mature, truth-seeking, creative mind.

The terrorist and the policeman come from the same basket.

Joseph Conrad *The Secret Agent*

Conrad /ˈkɒnræd/ several kings of the Germans and Holy Roman emperors, including:

Conrad III 1093–1152. Holy Roman emperor from 1138, the first king of the →Hohenstaufen dynasty. Throughout his reign there was a fierce struggle between his followers, the *Ghibellines*, and the *Guelphs*, the followers of Henry the Proud, duke of Saxony and Bavaria (1108–1139), and later of his son Henry the Lion (1129–1195).

Conrad IV 1228–1254. Elected king of the Germans 1237. Son of the Holy Roman emperor Frederick II, he had to defend his right of succession against Henry Raspe of Thuringia (died 1247) and William of Holland (1227–56).

Conrad V (Conradin) 1252–1268. Son of Conrad IV, recognized as king of the Germans, Sicily, and Jerusalem by German supporters of the →Hohenstaufens 1254. He led Ghibelline forces against Charles of Anjou at the battle of Tagliacozzo, N Italy 1266, and was captured and executed.

Conran /ˈkɒnrən/ Terence 1931– . British designer and retailer of furnishings, fashion, and household goods. He was founder of the Storehouse group of companies, including Habitat and Conran Design, with retail outlets in the UK, the USA, and elsewhere.

In 1964 he started the Habitat company, then developed Mothercare. The Storehouse group gained control of British Home Stores 1986.

Constable /ˈkʌnstəbəl/ John 1776–1837. English landscape painter. He painted scenes of his native Suffolk, including *The Haywain* 1821 (National Gallery, London), as well as castles, cathedrals, landscapes, and coastal scenes in other parts of Britain. Constable inherited the Dutch tradition of sombre realism, in particular the style of Jacob →Ruisdael, but he aimed to capture the momentary changes of nature as well as to create monumental images of British scenery, such as *The White Horse* 1819 (Frick Collection, New York) and *Flatford Mill* 1825.

Constable's paintings are remarkable for their atmospheric effects and were admired by many French painters including Eugene Delacroix. His many sketches are often considered among his best work.

Constable first worked in his father's mills in East Bergholt, Suffolk, but in 1795 was sent to study art in London. He was finally elected to the Royal Academy in 1829. His many imitators included his son *Lionel*.

In Nov 1990 *The Lock* 1824 was sold at Sotheby's, London, to a private collector for the record price of £10.78 million.

Constant de Rebecque /kɒnˈstɒn də rəˈbek/ (Henri) Benjamin 1767–1830. French writer and politician. An advocate of the Revolution, he opposed Napoleon and in 1803 went into exile. Returning to Paris after the fall of Napoleon in 1814 he proposed a constitutional monarchy. He

published the autobiographical novel *Adolphe* 1816, which reflects his affair with Madame de →Staël, and later wrote the monumental study *De la Religion* 1825–31.

Constantine II /ˈkɒnstəntaɪn/ 1940– . King of the Hellenes (Greece). In 1964 he succeeded his father Paul I, went into exile 1967, and was formally deposed 1973.

Constantine the Great /ˈkɒnstəntaɪn/ c. AD 280–337. First Christian emperor of Rome and founder of Constantinople. He defeated Maxentius, joint emperor of Rome AD 312, and in 313 formally recognized Christianity. As sole emperor of the west of the empire, he defeated Licinius, emperor of the east, to become ruler of the Roman world 324. He presided over the church's first council at Nicaea 325. In 330 Constantine moved his capital to Byzantium, renaming it Constantinople.

Constantine was born at Naissus (Niš, Yugoslavia), the son of Constantius. He was already well known as a soldier when his father died in York in 306 and he was acclaimed by the troops there as joint emperor in his father's place. A few years later Maxentius, the joint emperor in Rome (whose sister had married Constantine), challenged his authority and mobilized his armies to invade Gaul. Constantine won a crushing victory outside Rome in 312. During this campaign he was said to have seen a vision of the cross of Jesus superimposed upon the sun, accompanied by the words: 'In this sign thou shalt conquer'. By the Edict of Milan 313 he formally recognized Christianity as one of the religions legally permitted within the Roman Empire and in 314 he summoned the bishops of the Western world to the Council of Arles. However, there has never been agreement on whether Constantine adopted Christianity for reasons of faith or as an act of imperial absolutism to further his power. Sole emperor of the West from 312, by defeating Licinius, the emperor in the East, Constantine became sole Roman emperor 324. He increased the autocratic power of the emperor, issued legislation to tie the farmers and workers to their crafts in a sort of caste system, and enlisted the support of the Christian church. He summoned, and presided over, the first general council of the church in Nicaea 325. Constantine moved his capital to Byzantium on the Bosporus 330 and renamed it Constantinople (now Istanbul).

In this sign shalt thou conquer.
Constantine the Great's vision 312

Conti /ˈkɒnti/ Tom 1945– . British stage and film actor specializing in character roles. His films include *The Duellists* 1977, *Merry Christmas Mr Lawrence* 1982, *Reuben, Reuben* 1983, *Beyond Therapy* 1987, and *Shirley Valentine* 1989.

Cook /kʊk/ James 1728–1779. British naval explorer. After surveying the St Lawrence 1759, he made three voyages: 1768–71 to Tahiti, New Zealand, and Australia; 1772–75 to the South Pacific; and 1776–79 to the South and North Pacific, attempting to find the Northwest Passage and charting the Siberian coast. He was killed in Hawaii.

In 1768 Cook was given command of an expedition to the South Pacific to witness Venus eclipsing the Sun. He sailed in the *Endeavour* with Joseph →Banks and other scientists, reaching Tahiti in April 1769. He then sailed around New Zealand and made a detailed survey of the east coast of Australia, naming New South Wales and Botany Bay. He returned to England 12 June 1771.

Now a commander, Cook set out 1772 with the *Resolution* and *Adventure* to search for the Southern Continent. The location of Easter Island was determined, and the Marquesas and Tonga Islands plotted. He also went to New Caledonia and Norfolk Island. Cook returned 25 July 1775, having sailed 60,000 mi in three years.

On 25 June 1776, he began his third and last voyage with the *Resolution* and *Discovery*. On the way to New Zealand, he visited several of the Cook or Hervey Islands and revisited the Hawaiian or Sandwich Islands. The ships sighted the North American coast at latitude 45° N and sailed north hoping to discover the Northwest Passage. He made a continuous survey as far as the Bering Strait, where the way was blocked by ice. Cook then surveyed the opposite coast of the strait (Siberia), and returned to Hawaii early 1779, where he was killed in a scuffle with islanders.

Cook /kʊk/ Peter 1937– . English comic actor and writer. With his partner Dudley Moore, he appeared in revue (*Beyond the Fringe* 1959–64) and opened London's first satirical nightclub, the Establishment, in 1960. His films include *The Wrong Box* 1966, *Bedazzled* 1968, *The Bed Sitting Room* 1969, a parody of *The Hound of the Baskervilles* 1977, and *Supergirl* 1984.

Cook /kʊk/ Robin Finlayson 1946– . English Labour politician. A member of the moderate-left Tribune Group, he entered Parliament 1974 and became a leading member of Labour's shadow cabinet, specializing in health matters. When John Smith assumed the party leadership July 1992, Cook remained in the shadow cabinet as spokesman for trade and industry.

The son of a headmaster, he graduated in English literature at Edinburgh University and worked for the Workers' Educational Association (WEA) before entering politics. He favours the introduction of proportional representation.

Cook /kʊk/ Thomas 1808–1892. Pioneer British travel agent and founder of Thomas Cook & Son. He introduced traveller's cheques (then called 'circular notes') in the early 1870s.

Cooke /kʊk/ Alistair 1908– . British-born US journalist. He was *Guardian* correspondent in the USA 1948–72, and broadcasts a weekly *Letter from America* on BBC radio.

Cooke Sam 1931–1964. US soul singer and songwriter who began his career as a gospel singer and turned to pop music 1956. His hits include 'You Send Me' 1957 and 'Wonderful World' 1960 (re-released 1986).

Coolidge /ˈkuːlɪdʒ/ (John) Calvin 1872–1933. 30th president of the USA 1923–29, a Republican. As governor of Massachusetts 1919, he was responsible for crushing a Boston police strike. As Warren →Harding's vice president 1921–23, he succeeded to the presidency on Harding's death (2 Aug 1923). He won the 1924 presidential election, and his period of office was marked by great economic prosperity.

The business of America is business.

Calvin Coolidge speech 17 Jan 1925

Cooney /ˈkuːni/ Ray(mond) 1932– . British actor, director, and playwright, known for his farces *Two into One* 1981 and *Run for Your Wife* 1983.

Cooper /ˈkuːpə/ Gary 1901–1962. US film actor. He epitomized the lean, true-hearted Yankee, slow of speech but capable of outdoing the 'bad guys' in *Lives of a Bengal Lancer* 1935, *Mr Deeds Goes to Town* (Academy Award for best picture 1936), *Sergeant York* 1940 (Academy Award for best actor 1941), and *High Noon* (Academy Award for best actor 1952).

Cooper /ˈkuːpə/ Henry 1934– . English heavyweight boxer, the only man to win three Lonsdale Belts outright, 1961, 1965, and 1970. He held the British heavyweight title 1959–71 and lost it to Joe Bugner. He fought for the world heavyweight title but lost in the sixth round to Muhammad Ali 1966.

Cooper /ˈkuːpə/ James Fenimore 1789–1851. US writer of 50 novels, becoming popular with *The Spy* 1821. He wrote volumes of *Leatherstocking Tales* about the frontier hero Leatherstocking and American Indians before and after the American Revolution, including *The Last of the Mohicans* 1826.

Cooper was born in New Jersey, grew up on the family frontier settlement of Cooperstown, New York State, and voyaged as an apprentice sailor to Europe. After success as a writer, he lived in Paris for seven years before returning to Cooperstown.

Cooper /ˈkuːpə/ Leon 1930– . US physicist who in 1955 began work on the puzzling phenomenon of superconductivity. He proposed that at low temperatures electrons would be bound in pairs (since known as *Cooper pairs*) and in this state electrical resistance to their flow through solids

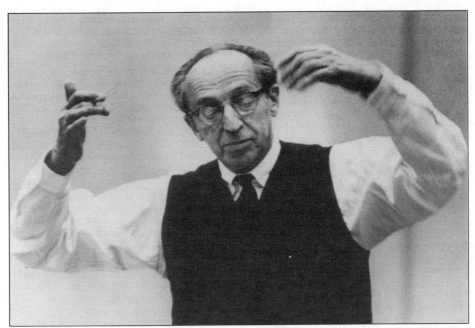

Copland *US composer Aaron Copland. The many styles and forms in which he worked brought him wide recognition, including a Pulitzer Prize for music 1945 and an Academy Award for his film score for* The Heiress *1949*

would disappear. He shared the 1972 Nobel Prize for Physics with John →Bardeen and John Schrieffer (1931–   ).

Cooper /ˈkuːpə/ Samuel 1609–1672. English miniaturist. His subjects included Milton, members of Charles II's court, the diarist Samuel Pepys's wife, and Oliver Cromwell.

Cooper /ˈkuːpə/ Susie. Married name Susan Vera Barker 1902–   . English pottery designer. Her style has varied from colourful Art Deco to softer, pastel decoration on more classical shapes. She started her own company 1929, which later became part of the Wedgwood factory, where she was senior designer from 1966.

Coote /kuːt/ Eyre 1726–1783. Irish general in British India. His victory 1760 at Wandiwash, followed by the capture of Pondicherry, ended French hopes of supremacy. He returned to India as commander in chief 1779, and several times defeated →Hyder Ali, sultan of Mysore.

Coper /ˈkəupə/ Hans 1920–1981. German potter, originally an engineer. His work resembles Cycladic Greek pots in its monumental quality.

Copernicus /kəˈpɜːnɪkəs/ Nicolaus 1473–1543. Polish astronomer who believed that the Sun, not the Earth, is at the centre of the Solar System, thus defying the Christian church doctrine of the time. For 30 years he worked on the hypothesis that the rotation and the orbital motion of the Earth were responsible for the apparent movement of the heavenly bodies. His great work *De Revolutionibus Orbium Coelestium/About the Revolutions of the Heavenly Spheres* was not published until the year of his death.

Born at Torun on the Vistula, then under the Polish king, Copernicus studied at Kraków and in Italy, and lectured on astronomy in Rome. On his return to Pomerania 1505 he became physician to his uncle, the bishop of Ermland, and was made canon at Frauenburg, although he did not take holy orders. Living there until his death, he interspersed astronomical work with the duties of various civil offices.

Finally we shall place the Sun himself at the centre of the Universe.

Nicolaus Copernicus
De Revolutionibus Orbium Coelestium 1543

Copland /ˈkəuplənd/ Aaron 1900–1990. US composer. His early works, such as his piano concerto 1926, were in the jazz idiom but he gradually developed a gentler style with a regional flavour drawn from American folk music. Among his works are the ballets *Billy the Kid* 1939, *Rodeo* 1942, *Appalachian Spring* 1944 (based on a poem by Hart Crane), and *Inscape for Orchestra* 1967.

Born in New York, Copland studied in France with Nadia Boulanger, and taught from 1940 at the Berkshire Music Center. He took avant-garde European styles and gave them a distinctive American accent. His eight film scores, including *The Heiress* 1949, set new standards for Hollywood.

Copley /ˈkɒpli/ John Singleton 1738–1815. American painter. He was the leading portraitist of the colonial period, but from 1775 he lived mainly in London, where he painted lively historical scenes such as *The Death of Major Pierson* 1783 (Tate Gallery, London).

Copley was born in Boston, Massachusetts. Some of his history paintings are unusual in that they portray dramatic events of his time, such as *Brook Watson and the Shark* 1778 (National Gallery, Washington DC).

Coppola /ˈkɒpələ/ Francis Ford 1939– . US film director and screenwriter. He directed *The Godfather* 1972, which became one of the biggest money-making films of all time, and its sequels *The Godfather Part II* 1974, which garnered seven Academy Awards, and *The Godfather Part III* 1990. His other films include *Apocalypse Now* 1979, *One From the Heart* 1982, *Rumblefish* 1983, *The Outsiders* 1983, and *Tucker: The Man and His Dream* 1988.

After working on horror B-films, his first successes were *Finian's Rainbow* 1968 and *Patton* 1969, for which his screenplay won an Academy Award. Among his other films are *The Conversation* 1972, *The Cotton Club* 1984, and *Gardens of Stone* 1987.

Coralli /ˌkɒrəˈliː/ Jean 1779–1854. French dancer and choreographer who made his debut as a dancer 1802. He choreographed *Le Diable boîteux* 1836 for the Austrian ballerina Fanny Elssler, *Giselle* 1841, and *La Péri* 1843 for the Italian ballerina Grisi.

Coram /ˈkɔːrəm/ Thomas 1668–1751. English philanthropist who established the Foundling Hospital for orphaned and abandoned children in Holborn, London, 1741. The site, now Coram Fields, is still a children's foundation.

Corbett /ˈkɔːbɪt/ Gentleman Jim (James John) 1866–1933. US boxer who gained the heavyweight title in his 1892 New Orleans fight with reigning champion John L Sullivan. It was the first title bout to be fought with gloves and according to the Marquess of Queensberry rules. Corbett held the title until his defeat 1897 by Robert Fitzsimmons.

Born in San Francisco, USA, Corbett became a professional boxer 1886 after a brief career as a bank clerk. He eventually gained a national reputation for his elegant manner and his dangerous right hook (a punch that he popularized).

Corbière /ˌkɔːbiˈeə/ Tristan 1845–1875. French poet. His volume of poems *Les Amours jaunes/Yellow Loves* 1873 went unrecognized until Paul Verlaine called attention to it 1884. Many of his poems, such as *La Rhapsodie foraine/Wandering Rhapsody*, deal with life in his native Brittany.

Corbusier, Le see →Le Corbusier, architect.

Corday /ˈkɔːdeɪ/ Charlotte 1768–1793. French Girondin (right-wing republican during the French Revolution). After the overthrow of the Girondins by the more extreme Jacobins May 1793, she stabbed to death the Jacobin leader, Jean Paul Marat, with a bread knife as he sat in his bath in July of the same year. She was guillotined.

Corelli /kəˈreli/ Arcangelo 1653–1713. Italian composer and violinist. He was one of the first virtuoso violinists and his music, marked by graceful melody, includes a set of *concerti grossi* and five sets of chamber sonatas.

Born near Milan, he studied in Bologna and in about 1685 settled in Rome, under the patronage of Cardinal Pietro Ottoboni, where he published his first violin sonatas.

Corelli /kəˈreli/ Marie. Pseudonym of Mary Mackay 1855–1924. English romantic novelist. Trained for a musical career, she turned instead to writing (she was said to be Queen Victoria's favourite novelist) and published *The Romance of Two Worlds* 1886. Her works were later ridiculed for their pretentious style.

Cori /ˈkɔːri/ Carl 1896–1984 and Gerty 1896–1957. Husband-and-wife team of US biochemists, both born in Prague, who, together with Argentine physiologist Bernardo Houssay (1887–1971), received a Nobel prize 1947 for their discovery of how glycogen (animal starch) – a derivative of glucose – is broken down and resynthesized in the body, for use as a store and source of energy.

Corinna /kəˈrɪnə/ lived 6th century BC. Greek lyric poet, said to have instructed Pindar. Only fragments of her poetry survive.

Corman /ˈkɔːmən/ Roger 1926– . US film director and prolific producer. He made a stylish series of Edgar Allan Poe films starring Vincent Price, beginning with *The House of Usher* 1960.

Corneille /kɔːˈneɪ/ Pierre 1606–1684. French dramatist. His many tragedies, such as *Oedipe* 1659, glorify the strength of will governed by reason, and established the French classical dramatic tradition for the next two centuries. His first play, *Mélite*, was performed 1629, followed by others that gained him a brief period of favour with Cardinal Richelieu. *Le Cid* 1636 was attacked by the Academicians, although it received public acclaim. Later plays were based on Aristotle's unities.

Although Corneille enjoyed public popularity, periodic disfavour with Richelieu marred his career, and it was not until 1639 that Corneille (again in favour) produced plays such as *Horace* 1639, *Polyeucte* 1643, *Le Menteur* 1643, and *Rodogune* 1645, leading to his election to the Académie 1647. His later plays were approved by Louis XIV.

Cornell /kɔːˈnel/ Katherine 1898–1974. US actress. Her first major success came with an appearance on Broadway in *Nice People* 1921. This debut was followed by a long string of New York stage successes, several of which were directed by her husband, Guthrie McClintic. From

1930 she began to produce her own plays; the most famous of them, *The Barretts of Wimpole Street* 1931, was later taken on tour and produced for television 1956.

Born in Berlin of American parents, Cornell was attracted to the stage at an early age, appearing with the Washington Square Players 1916.

Cornforth /ˈkɔːnfɔːθ/ John Warcup 1917– . Australian chemist. Using radioisotopes as markers, he found out how cholesterol is manufactured in the living cell and how enzymes synthesize chemicals that are mirror images of each other (optical isomers). He shared a Nobel prize 1975 with Swiss chemist Vladimir Prelog (1906–).

For him [the scientist], truth is so seldom the sudden light that shows new order and beauty; more often, truth is the uncharted rock that sinks his ship in the dark.

John Cornforth
Nobel prize address 1975

Cornwallis /kɔːnˈwɒlɪs/ Charles, 1st Marquess 1738–1805. British general in the American Revolution until 1781, when his defeat at Yorktown led to final surrender and ended the war. He then served twice as governor general of India and once as viceroy of Ireland.

Coronado /ˌkɒrəˈnɑːdəʊ/ Francisco de *c.* 1500–1554. Spanish explorer who sailed to the New World 1535 in search of gold. In 1540 he set out with several hundred men from the Gulf of California on an exploration of what are today the Southern states. Although he failed to discover any gold, his expedition came across the impressive Grand Canyon of the Colorado and introduced the use of the horse to the indigenous Indians.

Corot /ˈkɒrəʊ/ Jean-Baptiste-Camille 1796–1875. French painter, creator of a distinctive landscape style with cool colours and soft focus. His early work, including Italian scenes in the 1820s, influenced the Barbizon school of painters. Like them, Corot worked outdoors, but he also continued a conventional academic tradition with more romanticized paintings.

Born in Paris, Corot lived in Rome 1825–28, where he learnt the tradition of classical landscape painting, centred around a historical or mythological incident.

Correggio /kɒˈredʒiəʊ/ Antonio Allegri da *c.* 1494–1534. Italian painter of the High Renaissance whose style followed the Classical grandeur of Leonardo and Titian but anticipated the Baroque in its emphasis on movement, softer forms, and contrasts of light and shade.

Based in Parma, he painted splendid illusionistic visions in the cathedral there, including *The Ascenscion of the Virgin*. His religious paintings, including the night scene *Adoration of the Shepherds* about 1527–30 (Gemäldegalerie, Dresden), and mythological scenes, such as *The Loves of Jupiter* (Wallace Collection, London), were much admired in the 18th century.

Cort /kɔːt/ Henry 1740–1800. British iron manufacturer. For the manufacture of wrought iron, he invented the puddling process and developed the rolling mill, both of which were significant in the Industrial Revolution.

Cortázar /kɔːˈtɑːzə/ Julio 1914–1984. Argentine writer whose novels include *The Winners* 1960, *Hopscotch* 1963, and *Sixty-two: A Model Kit* 1968. One of his several volumes of short stories includes 'Blow-up', adapted for a film by the Italian director Michelangelo Antonioni.

Cortés /ˈkɔːtez/ Hernán (Ferdinand) 1485–1547. Spanish conquistador. He conquered the Aztec empire 1519–21, and secured Mexico for Spain.

Cortés went to the West Indies as a young man and in 1518 was given command of an expedition to Mexico. Landing with only 600 men, he was at first received as a god by the Aztec emperor →Montezuma II but was expelled from Tenochtitlán (Mexico City) when he was found not to be 'divine'. With the aid of Indian allies he recaptured the city 1521, and overthrew the Aztec empire. His conquests eventually included most of Mexico and N Central America.

I and my companions suffer from a disease of the heart that can be cured only with gold.

Hernán Cortés
message sent to Montezuma 1519

Cortona /kɔːˈtəʊnə/ Pietro da. Italian Baroque painter; see →Pietro da Cortona.

Corvo /ˈkɔːvəʊ/ Baron 1860–1913. Assumed name of British writer Frederick →Rolfe.

Cosby /ˈkɒzbi/ Bill (William Henry) 1937– . US comedian and actor. His portrayal of the dashing, handsome secret agent in the television series *I Spy* 1965–68 won him three Emmy awards and revolutionized the way in which blacks were presented on screen. His sardonic humour, based on wry observations of domestic life and parenthood, found its widest audience in *The Cosby Show* 1984–92, which consistently topped the national ratings and provided new role models for young African Americans. It also made him one of the richest performers in showbusiness.

Among his other TV series are *The Bill Cosby Show* 1969–77 and *Fat Albert and the Cosby Kids* 1972–84. He hosted the game show *You Bet Your Life* from 1992.

Cosgrave /ˈkɒzɡreɪv/ Liam 1920– . Irish Fine Gael politician, prime minister of the Republic of Ireland 1973–77. As party leader 1965–77, he headed a Fine Gael–Labour coalition government from 1973. Relations between the Irish and UK governments improved under his premiership.

Cosgrave /ˈkɒzɡreɪv/ William Thomas 1880–1965. Irish politician. He took part in the Easter Rising 1916 and sat in the Sinn Féin cabinet of 1919–21. Head of the Free State government 1922–33, he founded and led the Fine Gael opposition 1933–44. His eldest son is Liam Cosgrave.

Costello /kɒˈstɛləʊ/ Elvis. Stage name of Declan McManus 1954– . English rock singer, songwriter, and guitarist whose intricate yet impassioned lyrics have made him one of Britain's foremost songwriters. The great stylistic range of his work was evident from his 1977 debut *My Aim Is True*.

Costello emerged as part of the New Wave, too literate for punk but just as angry, and dominated the UK rock scene into the early 1980s. From his second album (*This Year's Model* 1978) to *Goodbye Cruel World* 1984 worked exclusively with his backing group, the Attractions; the group last appeared on *Blood and Chocolate* 1986. Other musicians were used on, for example, *King of America* 1986 and *Mighty Like a Rose* 1991. His hits range from the political rocker 'Oliver's Army' 1979 to the country weepy 'Good Year for the Roses' 1981 and the punning pop of 'Everyday I Write the Book' 1983.

Coster /ˈkɒstə/ Laurens Janszoon 1370–1440. Dutch printer. According to some sources, he invented movable type, but after his death an apprentice ran off to Mainz with the blocks and, taking Johann →Gutenberg into his confidence, began a printing business with him.

Costner Kevin 1955– . US film actor. He first achieved top-ranking success with his role as law-enforcer Elliot Ness, in the film version of the 1960s television series *The Untouchables* 1987. Increasingly identified with the embodiment of idealism and high principle, Costner went on to direct and star in *Dances With Wolves* 1990, a Western sympathetic to the native American Indian, which won several Academy Awards. Subsequent films include *Robin Hood – Prince of Thieves* 1991, *JFK* 1991, and *The Bodyguard* 1992.

Cosway /ˈkɒzweɪ/ Richard 1742–1821. British artist. Elected to the Royal Academy 1771, he was an accomplished miniaturist and painted members of the Prince Regent's court.

Cotman /ˈkɒtmən/ John Sell 1782–1842. British landscape painter, with John Crome a founder of the *Norwich school*, a group of realistic landscape painters influenced by Dutch examples. His early watercolours were bold designs in simple flat washes of colour, for example *Greta Bridge, Yorkshire* 1805 (British Museum, London).

Cotten /ˈkɒtn/ Joseph 1905– . US actor, intelligent and low-keyed, who was brought into films by Orson Welles. Cotten gave outstanding performances in *Citizen Kane* 1941, *The Magnificent Ambersons* 1942, and *The Third Man* 1949.

Cotton /ˈkɒtn/ John 1585–1652. English-born American religious leader. In England, his extreme Puritan views led to charges of heterodoxy being filed against him 1633. In the same year, he immigrated to the Massachusetts Bay Colony, where he was named teacher of Boston's First Congregational Church. A powerful force in the colony, he published widely circulated sermons and theological works.

Born in Derby, England, and educated at Cambridge University, Cotton was named vicar in Boston, Lincolnshire 1612 before the persecution of Puritans under Charles I forced him to leave the country.

Cotton /ˈkɒtn/ Robert Bruce 1571–1631. English antiquary. At his home in Westminster he built up a fine collection of manuscripts and coins, many of which had come from the despoiled monasteries. His son *Thomas Cotton* (1594–1662) added to the library. The collection is now in the British Museum.

Coué /ˈkuːeɪ/ Emile 1857–1926. French psychological healer, the pioneer of autosuggestion. He coined the slogan 'Every day, and in every way, I am becoming better and better'. Couéism reached the height of its popularity in the 1920s.

Coulomb /ˈkuːlɒm/ Charles Auguste de 1736–1806. French scientist, inventor of the torsion balance for measuring the force of electric and magnetic attraction. The coulomb was named after him.

Couperin /ˈkuːpəræn/ François *le Grand* 1668–1733. French composer. He held various court appointments under Louis XIV and wrote vocal, chamber, and harpsichord music.

Courbet /ˈkuəbeɪ/ Gustave 1819–1877. French artist, a portrait, genre, and landscape painter. Reacting against academic trends, both Classicist and Romantic, he sought to establish a new realism based on contemporary life. His *Burial at Ornans* 1850 (Louvre, Paris), showing ordinary working people gathered round a village grave, shocked the public and the critics with its 'vulgarity'.

His spirit of realism was to be continued by Edouard Manet. In 1871 Courbet was active in the Paris Commune (the provisional national government formed while Paris was besieged by Germans) and was later imprisoned for six months for his part in it.

I deny that art can be taught.

Gustave Courbet
letter to prospective students 1861

Courrèges /koˈreɪʒ/ André 1923– . French fashion designer who is credited with inventing the miniskirt 1964. His 'space-age' designs – square-shaped short skirts and trousers – were copied worldwide in the 1960s.

Courrèges worked for Cristobal Balenciaga 1950–61, and founded his own label 1961. From 1966 he produced both couture and ready-to-wear lines of well-tailored designs, often in pastel shades.

Court /kɔːt/ Margaret (born Smith) 1942– . Australian tennis player. The most prolific winner in the women's game, she won a record 64 Grand Slam titles, including 25 at singles.

Court was the first from her country to win the ladies title at Wimbledon 1963, and the second woman after Maureen Connolly to complete the Grand Slam 1970.

Courtauld /ˈkɔːtəʊld/ Samuel 1793–1881. British industrialist who developed the production of viscose rayon and other synthetic fibres from 1904. He founded the firm of Courtaulds 1816 in Bocking, Essex, and at first specialized in silk and crepe manufacture.

His great-nephew, *Samuel Courtauld* (1876–1947), was chair of the firm from 1921, and in 1931 gave his house and art collection to the University of London as the Courtauld Institute.

Courtneidge /ˈkɔːtnɪdʒ/ Cicely 1893–1980. British comic actress and singer who appeared both on stage and in films. She married comedian Jack Hulbert (1892–1978), with whom she formed a successful variety partnership.

Cousin /kuːˈzæn/ Victor 1792–1867. French philosopher who helped to introduce German philosophical ideas into France. In 1840 he was minister of public instruction and reorganized the system of elementary education.

We must have art for art's sake ... the beautiful cannot be the way to what is useful, or to what is good, or to what is holy; it leads only to itself.

Victor Cousin *Du vrai, du beau, et du bien*

Cousteau /kuːˈstəʊ/ Jacques Yves 1910– . French oceanographer, known for his researches in command of the *Calypso* from 1951, his film and television documentaries, and his many books; he pioneered the invention of the aqualung 1943 and techniques in underwater filming.

Coutts /kuːts/ Thomas 1735–1822. British banker. He established with his brother the firm of Coutts & Co (one of London's oldest banking houses, founded 1692 in the Strand), becoming sole head on the latter's death 1778. Since the reign of George III an account has been maintained there by every succeeding sovereign.

Other customers have included the politicians the Earl of Chatham, William Pitt, Charles Fox, and the Duke of Wellington, and the biographer, James Boswell.

Coverdale /ˈkʌvədeɪl/ Miles 1488–1569. English Protestant priest whose translation of the Bible 1535 was the first to be printed in English. His translation of the psalms is that retained in the Book of Common Prayer.

Coverdale, born in Yorkshire, became a Catholic priest, but turned to Protestantism and 1528 went to the continent to avoid persecution. In 1539 he edited the Great Bible which was ordered to be placed in churches. After some years in Germany, he returned to England 1548, and in 1551 was made bishop of Exeter. During the reign of Mary I he left the country.

I believe a composer must forge his own forms out of the many influences that play upon him and never close his ears to any part of the world of sound ...

Henry Cowell

Coward /ˈkaʊəd/ Noël 1899–1973. English playwright, actor, producer, director, and composer, who epitomized the witty and sophisticated man of the theatre. From his first success with *The Young Idea* 1923, he wrote and appeared in plays and comedies on both sides of the Atlantic such as *Hay Fever* 1925, *Private Lives* 1930 with Gertrude Lawrence, *Design for Living* 1933, and *Blithe Spirit* 1941.

Coward also wrote for and acted in films, including the patriotic *In Which We Serve* 1942 and the sentimental *Brief Encounter* 1945. After World War II he became a nightclub and cabaret entertainer, performing songs like 'Mad Dogs and Englishmen'.

Cowell /ˈkaʊəl/ Henry 1897–1965. US composer and writer. He experimented with new ways of playing the piano, strumming the strings in *Aeolian Harp* 1923 and introducing clusters, using a ruler on the keys in *The Banshee* 1925.

Cowell also wrote chamber and orchestral music and was active as a critic and publisher of 20th-century music.

Cowley /ˈkaʊlɪ/ Abraham 1618–1667. English poet. He introduced the Pindaric ode (based on the work of the Greek poet Pindar) to English poetry, and published metaphysical verse with elaborate imagery, as well as essays.

Cowper /ˈkuːpə/ William 1731–1800. English poet. He trained as a lawyer, but suffered a mental breakdown 1763 and entered an asylum, where he underwent an evangelical conversion. He later wrote hymns (including 'God Moves in a Mysterious Way'). His verse includes the six books of *The Task* 1785.

Cowper English poet William Cowper. Despite being plagued by melancholia, he wrote the long poem The Task, *the amusing narrative* John Gilpin, *and such hymns as 'God moves in a mysterious way.'. His letters to friends are graceful and personal models of letter-writing.*

Cox /kɒks/ David 1783–1859. British artist. He studied under John ➔Varley and made a living as a drawing master. His watercolour landscapes, many of scenes in N Wales, have attractive cloud effects, and are characterized by broad colour washes on rough, tinted paper.

Cox /kɒks/ Jacob Dolson 1828–1900. Canadian-born US educator and public figure. After service in the US Congress 1876–79, Cox was president of the University of Cincinnati 1885–89. He was elected governor of Ohio 1866 and served as secretary of the interior under President Grant.

Born in Montreal, Canada, Cox was raised in New York, USA, and educated at Oberlin College. Serving briefly as superintendent of schools in Warren, Ohio, he studied law and was elected to the state legislature 1859. During the American Civil War 1861–65, Cox was appointed brigadier general of volunteers and saw action in West Virginia and at Antietam.

Coysevox /kwæz'vɒks/ Antoine 1640–1720. French Baroque sculptor. He was employed at the palace of Versailles, contributing a stucco relief of a triumphant Louis XIV to the Salon de la Guerre.

He also produced portrait busts, for example a terracotta of the artist Le Brun 1676 (Wallace Collection, London), and more sombre monuments, such as the *Tomb of Cardinal Mazarin* 1689–93 (Louvre, Paris).

Cozens /kʌzənz/ John Robert 1752–1797. British landscape painter, a watercolourist, whose Romantic views of Europe, painted on tours in the 1770s and 1780s, influenced both Thomas Girtin and J M W Turner.

His father, *Alexander Cozens* (c. 1717–1786), also a landscape painter, taught drawing at Eton public school and produced books on landscape drawing.

Crabbe /kræb/ George 1754–1832. English poet. Originally a doctor, he became a cleric 1781, and wrote grimly realistic verse on the poor of his own time: *The Village* 1783, *The Parish Register* 1807, *The Borough* 1810 (which includes the story used in Benjamin Britten's opera *Peter Grimes*), and *Tales of the Hall* 1819.

Crabtree William 1905–1991. English architect who designed the Peter Jones department store in Sloane Square, London, 1935–39. It is regarded as one of the finest Modern movement buildings in England. It was a technically innovative building with its early application of the curtain wall, which flows in a gentle curve from the King's Road into the square.

Craig /kreɪg/ Edward Gordon 1872–1966. British director and stage designer. His innovations and theories on stage design and lighting effects, expounded in *On the Art of the Theatre* 1911, had a profound influence on stage production in Europe and the USA.

Craig /kreɪg/ James 1871–1940. Ulster Unionist politician, the first prime minister of Northern Ireland 1921–40. Craig became a member of Parliament 1906, and was a highly effective organizer of Unionist resistance to Home Rule. As prime minister he carried out systematic discrimination against the Catholic minority, abolishing proportional representation 1929 and redrawing constituency boundaries to ensure Protestant majorities.

Craik /kreɪk/ Dinah Maria (born Mulock) 1826–1887. British novelist, author of *John Halifax, Gentleman* 1857, the story of the social betterment of a poor orphan through his own efforts.

Cranach /krɑːnæx/ Lucas 1472–1553. German painter, etcher, and woodcut artist, a leading light in the German Renaissance. He painted many full-length nudes and precise and polished portraits, such as *Martin Luther* 1521 (Uffizi, Florence).

Born at Kronach in Bavaria, he settled at Wittenberg 1504 to work for the elector of Saxony. He is associated with the artists Albrecht Dürer and Albrecht Altdorfer and was a close friend of the Christian reformer Martin Luther, whose portrait he painted several times. His religious paintings feature splendid landscapes. His second son, *Lucas Cranach the Younger* (1515–1586), had a similar style and succeeded his father as director of the Cranach workshop.

Crane /kreɪn/ (Harold) Hart 1899–1932. US poet. His long mystical poem *The Bridge* 1930 uses the Brooklyn Bridge as a symbol. In his work he attempted to link humanity's present with its past, in an epic continuum. He drowned after jumping overboard from a steamer bringing him back to the USA after a visit to Mexico.

Crane /kreɪn/ Stephen 1871–1900. US writer who introduced grim realism into the US novel. His book *The Red Badge of Courage* 1895 deals vividly with the US Civil War.

Crane /kreɪn/ Walter 1845–1915. British artist, designer, and book illustrator. He was influenced by William Morris and became an active socialist in the 1880s.

While apprenticed to W J Linton, a wood engraver, he came under the influence of the Pre-Raphaelites. His book illustrations, both for children's and for adult books, included an edition of Spenser's *Faerie Queene* 1894–96.

Cranko /ˈkræŋkəʊ/ John 1927–1973. British choreographer, born in South Africa. He joined Sadler's Wells, London, 1946, and excelled in the creation of comedy characters, as in the *Tritsch-Tratsch Polka* 1946 and *Pineapple Poll* 1951.

Cranmer /ˈkrænmə/ Thomas 1489–1556. English cleric, archbishop of Canterbury from 1533. A Protestant convert, he helped to shape the doctrines of the Church of England under Edward VI. He was responsible for the issue of the Prayer Books of 1549 and 1552, and supported the succession of Lady Jane Grey 1553.

Condemned for heresy under the Catholic Mary Tudor, he at first recanted, but when his life was not spared, resumed his position and was burned at the stake, first holding to the fire the hand which had signed his recantation.

Cranmer suggested 1529 that the question of Henry VIII's marriage to Catherine of Aragon should be referred to the universities of Europe rather than to the pope, and in 1533 he declared it null and void.

This was the hand that wrote it, therefore it shall suffer punishment.

Thomas Cranmer
at the stake 21 March 1556

Crashaw /ˈkræʃɔː/ Richard 1613–1649. English religious poet of the metaphysical school. He published a book of Latin sacred epigrams 1634, then went to Paris, where he joined the Roman Catholic Church; his collection of poems *Steps to the Temple* appeared 1646.

Crassus /ˈkræsəs/ Marcus Licinius c. 108–53 BC. Roman general who crushed the Spartacus uprising 71 BC. In 60 BC he joined with Caesar and Pompey in the First Triumvirate and obtained command in the east 55 BC. Invading Mesopotamia, he was defeated by the Parthians at the battle of Carrhae, captured, and put to death.

Crawford /ˈkrɔːfəd/ Joan. Stage name of Lucille Le Seur 1908–1977. US film actress who became a star with her performance as a flapper (liberated young woman) in *Our Dancing Daughters* 1928. Later she appeared as a sultry, often suffering, mature woman. Her films include *Mildred Pierce* 1945 (for which she won an Academy Award), *Password* 1947, and *Whatever Happened to Baby Jane?* 1962.

Crawford /ˈkrɔːfəd/ Osbert Guy Stanhope 1886–1957. British archaeologist, who introduced aerial survey as a means of finding and interpreting remains, an idea conceived during World War I.

Craxi /ˈkræksi/ Bettino 1934– . Italian socialist politician, leader of the Italian Socialist Party (PSI) from 1976, prime minister 1983–87.

Craxi, born in Milan, became a member of the Chamber of Deputies 1968 and general secretary of the PSI 1976. In 1983 he became Italy's first socialist prime minister, successfully leading a broad coalition until 1987.

Crazy Horse /ˈkreɪzi hɔːs/ 1849–1877. Sioux Indian chief, one of the Indian leaders at the massacre of Little Bighorn 1876 when a US detachment of troops under General →Custer was defeated. Crazy Horse surrendered the following year to General Crook and was confined to Fort Robinson; he was killed when trying to escape.

Cranmer Thomas Cranmer, the archbishop of Canterbury who declared the marriage between Henry VIII and Catherine of Aragon null and void. He played a large part in the creation of the liturgy of the Church of England and drew up the Thirty-nine Articles of faith, to which Anglican clergy are still required to subscribe.

Creed /kriːd/ Frederick George 1871–1957. Canadian inventor who developed the teleprinter. He perfected the Creed telegraphy system (teleprinter), first used in Fleet Street, the headquarters of the British press, 1912 and subsequently, usually under the name Telex, in offices throughout the world.

Creevey /kriːvi/ Thomas 1768–1838. British Whig politician and diarist whose lively letters and journals give information on early 19th-century society and politics. He was a member of Parliament and opposed the slave trade.

Cresson /kreˈsɒn/ Edith 1934– . French politician and founder member of the Socialist Party, prime minister 1991–92. Cresson held successive ministerial portfolios in François Mitterrand's government 1981–86 and 1988–90. Her government was troubled by a struggling economy, a series of strikes, and unrest in many of the country's poor suburban areas, which eventually forced her resignation.

A long-time supporter of François Mitterrand, and an outspoken defender of French trade rights, she became minister of agriculture 1981, minister of tourism 1983, minister of trade 1984, and minister of European affairs 1988, resigning from the last-named post 1990 on the grounds that France was 'in danger of being undermined by a lack of industrial mobilization'. She replaced Michel Rocard as prime minister May 1991. Increasingly unpopular with the public, Cresson was replaced as prime minister April 1992 by Pierre Bérégovoy, the former finance minister.

Crichton /kraɪtn/ James c. 1560–1582. Scottish scholar, known as 'the Admirable Crichton' because of his extraordinary gifts as a poet, scholar, and linguist. He was also an athlete and fencer. According to one account he was killed at Mantua in a street brawl by his pupil, a son of the Duke of Mantua, who resented Crichton's popularity.

Crick /krɪk/ Francis 1916– . British molecular biologist. From 1949 he researched the molecular structure of DNA, and the means whereby characteristics are transmitted from one generation to another. For this work he was awarded a Nobel prize (with Maurice →Wilkins and James →Watson) 1962.

Crippen /krɪpən/ Hawley Harvey 1861–1910. US murderer of his wife, variety artist Belle Elmore. He buried her remains in the cellar of his London home and tried to escape to the USA with his mistress Ethel le Neve (dressed as a boy). He was arrested on board ship following a radio message, the first criminal captured 'by radio', and was hanged.

Cripps /krɪps/ (Richard) Stafford 1889–1952. British Labour politician, expelled from the Labour Party 1939–45 for supporting a 'Popular Front' against Chamberlain's appeasement policy. He was ambassador to Moscow 1940–42, minister of aircraft production 1942–45, and chancellor of the Exchequer 1947–50.

Crispi /krɪspi/ Francesco 1819–1907. Italian prime minister 1887–91 and 1893–96. He advocated the Triple Alliance of Italy with Germany and Austria, but was deposed 1896.

Crivelli /krɪˈveli/ Carlo 1435/40–1495/1500. Italian painter in the early Renaissance style, active in Venice. He painted extremely detailed, decorated religious works, sometimes festooned with garlands of fruit. His figure style is strongly Italian, reflecting the influence of Mantegna.

Croce /krəʊtʃi/ Benedetto 1866–1952. Italian philosopher, historian, and literary critic; an opponent of fascism. His *Filosofia dello spirito/Philosophy of the Spirit* 1902–17 was a landmark in idealism. Like Hegel, he held that ideas do not represent reality but *are* reality; but unlike Hegel, he rejected every kind of transcendence.

Crockett /krɒkɪt/ Davy 1786–1836. US folk hero, born in Tennessee, a Democratic Congressman 1827–31 and 1833–35. A series of books, of which he may have been part-author, made him into a mythical hero of the frontier, but their Whig associations cost him his office. He died in the battle of the Alamo during the War of Texan Independence.

He clashed with Andrew →Jackson, claiming Jackson had betrayed his frontier constituency, and left for Texas in bitterness.

Crockford /krɒkfəd/ William 1775–1844. British gambler, founder in 1827 of Crockford's Club in St James's Street, which became the fashionable place for London society to gamble.

Croesus /kriːsəs/ 6th century BC. Last king of Lydia, famed for his wealth. His court included →Solon, who warned him that no man could be called happy until his life had ended happily. When Croesus was overthrown by Cyrus the Great 546 BC and condemned to be burned to death, he called out Solon's name. Cyrus, having learned the reason, spared his life.

Croker /krəʊkə/ Richard 1841–1922. US politician, 'boss' of Tammany Hall, the Democratic Party political machine in New York 1886–1902.

Crome /krəʊm/ John 1768–1821. British landscape painter, founder of the *Norwich school* with John Sell Cotman 1803. His works include *The Poringland Oak* 1818 (Tate Gallery, London), showing Dutch influence.

Crompton /krɒmptən/ Richmal. Pen name of R C Lamburn 1890–1969. British writer. She is remembered for her stories about the mischievous schoolboy 'William'.

Crompton /krɒmptən/ Samuel 1753–1827. British inventor at the time of the Industrial Revolution. He invented the 'spinning mule' 1779, combining the ideas of Richard →Arkwright and James →Hargreaves. Though widely adopted, his invention brought him little financial return.

Cromwell /krɒmwel/ Oliver 1599–1658. English general and politician, Puritan leader of the Parliamentary side in the Civil War (1642–51). He raised cavalry forces (later called *Ironsides*) which aided the victories at Edgehill 1642 and Marston Moor 1644, and organized the New Model Army, which he led (with General Fairfax) to victory at Naseby 1645. He declared Britain a republic ('the Commonwealth') 1649, following the execution of Charles I. As Lord Protector (ruler) from 1653, Cromwell established religious toleration and raised Britain's prestige in Europe on the basis of an alliance with France against Spain.

Cromwell was born at Huntingdon, NW of Cambridge, son of a small landowner. He entered Parliament 1629 and became active in events leading to the Civil War. Failing to secure a constitutional settlement with Charles I 1646–48, he defeated the 1648 Scottish invasion at Preston. A special commission, of which Cromwell was a member, tried the king and condemned him to death, and a republic, known as 'the Commonwealth', was set up.

The Levellers demanded radical reforms, but he executed their leaders in 1649. He used terror to crush Irish clan resistance 1649–50, and defeated the Scots (who had acknowledged Charles II) at Dunbar 1650 and Worcester 1651. In 1653, having forcibly expelled the corrupt 'Rump' Parliament, he summoned a convention ('Barebone's Parliament'), soon dissolved as too radical, and under a constitution (Instrument of Government) drawn up by the army leaders, became Protector (king in all but name). The parliament of l654–55 was dissolved as uncooperative, and after a period of military dictatorship, his last parliament offered him the crown; he refused because he feared the army's republicanism.

A few honest men are better than numbers.

Oliver Cromwell
letter Sept 1643

Cromwell /krɒmwel/ Richard 1626–1712. Son of Oliver Cromwell, he succeeded his father as Lord Protector but resigned May 1659, having been forced to abdicate by the army. He lived in exile after the Restoration until 1680, when he returned.

Cromwell /krɒmwel/ Thomas, Earl of Essex *c.* 1485–1540. English politician who drafted the legislation making the Church of England independent of Rome. Originally in Lord Chancellor Wolsey's service, he became secretary to Henry VIII 1534 and the real director of government policy; he was executed for treason.

Cromwell had Henry divorced from Catherine of Aragon by a series of acts that proclaimed him head of the church. From 1536 to 1540 Cromwell suppressed the monasteries, ruthlessly crushed all opposition, and favoured Protestantism, which denied the divine right of the pope. His mistake in arranging Henry's marriage to Anne of Cleves (to cement an alliance with the German Protestant princes against France and the Holy Roman Empire) led to his being accused of treason and beheaded.

Cronkite /krɒŋkaɪt/ Walter 1916– . US broadcast journalist who was anchorperson of the national evening news programme for CBS, a US television network, from 1962 to 1981.

Crookes /krʊks/ William 1832–1919. English scientist whose many chemical and physical discoveries included the metallic element thallium 1861, the radiometer 1875, and the Crookes high-vacuum tube used in X-ray techniques.

Crosby /krɒzbi/ Bing (Harry Lillis) 1904–1977. US film actor and singer who achieved world success with his distinctive style of crooning in such songs as 'Pennies from Heaven' 1936 (featured in a film of the same name) and 'White Christmas' 1942. He won an acting Oscar for *Going My Way* 1944, and made a series of 'road' film comedies with Dorothy Lamour and Bob →Hope, the last being *Road to Hong Kong* 1962.

Crossley Paul 1944– . British pianist, joint artistic director of the London Sinfonietta from 1988. A specialist in the works of such composers as Maurice Ravel, Olivier →Messiaen, and Michael Tippett, he studied with Messiaen and Yvonne Loriod, leading to success at the Messiaen Piano Competition in Royan 1968.

Crossley British pianist Paul Crossley studied in Paris and is an expert interpreter of the French school. He is a champion of new music, and Michael Tippett's Third Piano Sonata is dedicated to him.

Crossman /ˈkrɒsmən/ Richard (Howard Stafford) 1907–1974. British Labour politician. He was minister of housing and local government 1964–66 and of health and social security 1968–70. His posthumous *Crossman Papers* 1975 revealed confidential cabinet discussion.

Crowley /ˈkrəʊli/ Aleister (Edward Alexander) 1875–1947. British occultist, a member of the theosophical Order of the Golden Dawn; he claimed to practise black magic, and his books include the novel *Diary of a Drug Fiend* 1923. He designed a tarot pack that bears his name.

Crowley /ˈkrəʊli/ John 1942– . US writer of science fiction and fantasy, notably *Little, Big* 1980 and *Aegypt* 1987, which contain esoteric knowledge and theoretical puzzles.

Cruden /ˈkruːdn/ Alexander 1701–1770. Scottish compiler of a biblical *Concordance* 1737.

Cruft /krʌft/ Charles 1852–1938. British dog expert. He organized his first dog show 1886, and from that year annual shows bearing his name were held in Islington, London. In 1948 the show's venue moved to Olympia and in 1979 to Earl's Court.

Cruikshank /ˈkrʊkʃæŋk/ George 1792–1878. British painter and illustrator, remembered for his political cartoons and illustrations for Charles Dickens's *Oliver Twist* and Daniel Defoe's *Robinson Crusoe*.

Cruyff Johan 1947– . Dutch footballer, an outstanding European player in the 1970s.

He was capped 48 times by his country, scoring 33 goals. He spent most of his career playing with Ajax and Barcelona and was named European Footballer of the Year on three occasions. As a coach he took both clubs to domestic and European honours.

Cruyff was a slightly built player who had razor-sharp reactions, excellent control, speed, acceleration, and the ability to change direction instantly.

Cubitt /ˈkjuːbɪt/ Thomas 1788–1855. English builder and property developer. One of the earliest speculators, Cubitt rebuilt much of Belgravia, London, an area of Brighton, and the east front of Buckingham Palace.

Cugnot /ˈkuːnjəʊ/ Nicolas-Joseph 1728–1804. French engineer who produced the first high-pressure steam engine. While serving in the French army, he was asked to design a steam-operated gun carriage. After several years, he produced a three-wheeled, high-pressure carriage capable of carrying 1,800 litres/400 gallons of water and four passengers at a speed of 5 kph/3 mph. Although he worked further on the carriage, the political upheavals of the French revolutionary era obstructed progress and his invention was ignored.

Cui /kwiː/ César Antonovich 1853–1918. Russian composer of operas and chamber music. A professional soldier, he joined →Balakirev's Group of Five and promoted a Russian national style.

Cukor /ˈkjuːkɔː/ George 1899–1983. US film director. He moved to the cinema from the theatre, and was praised for his skilled handling of such stars as Greta →Garbo (in *Camille* 1937) and Katharine Hepburn (in *The Philadelphia Story* 1940). He won an Academy Award for the direction of *My Fair Lady* 1964.

Culshaw /ˈkʌlʃɔː/ John 1924–1980. British record producer who developed recording techniques. Managing classical recordings for the Decca record company in the 1950s and 1960s, he introduced echo chambers and the speeding and slowing of tapes to achieve effects not possible in live performance. He produced the first complete recordings of Wagner's *Ring* cycle.

Cumberland /ˈkʌmbələnd/ Ernest Augustus, Duke of Cumberland 1771–1851. King of Hanover from 1837, the fifth son of George III of Britain. A high Tory and an opponent of all reforms, he attempted to suppress the constitution but met with open resistance that had to be put down by force.

Cumberland /ˈkʌmbələnd/ William Augustus, Duke of Cumberland 1721–1765. British general who ended the Jacobite rising in Scotland with the Battle of Culloden 1746; his brutal repression of the Highlanders earned him the nickname of 'Butcher'.

Third son of George II, he was created Duke of Cumberland 1726. He fought in the War of the Austrian Succession at Dettingen 1743 and Fontenoy 1745. In the Seven Years' War he surrendered with his army at Kloster-Zeven 1757.

I am now in a country so much our enemy that there is hardly any intelligence to be got, and whenever we do procure any it is the business of the country to have it contradicted.

Duke of Cumberland letter from Scotland 1746

Cummings /ˈkʌmɪŋz/ e(dward) e(stlin) 1894–1962. US poet whose published collections of poetry include *Tulips and Chimneys* 1923. His poems were initially notorious for their idiosyncratic punctuation and typography (he always wrote his name in lower-case letters, for example), but their lyric power has gradually been recognized.

Cunha /ˈkuːnjə/ Euclydes da 1866–1909. Brazilian writer. His novel *Os Sertões/Rebellion in the Backlands* 1902 describes the Brazilian *sertão* (backlands), and how a small group of rebels resisted government troops.

Cunningham /ˈkʌnɪŋəm/ Andrew Browne, 1st Viscount Cunningham of Hyndhope 1883–1963.

British admiral in World War II, commander in chief in the Mediterranean 1939–42, maintaining British control; as commander in chief of the Allied Naval Forces in the Mediterranean Feb–Oct 1943 he received the surrender of the Italian fleet.

Cunningham /ˈkʌnɪŋəm/ John 1885–1962. British admiral in World War II. He was commander in chief in the Mediterranean 1943–46, First Sea Lord 1946–48, and became admiral of the fleet in 1948.

In 1940 he assisted in the evacuation of Norway and, as Fourth Sea Lord in charge of supplies and transport 1941–43, prepared the way for the N African invasion in 1942.

Cunningham /ˈkʌnɪŋhæm/ Merce 1919– . US dancer and choreographer. Influenced by Martha →Graham, with whose company he was soloist from 1939–45, he formed his own avant-garde dance company and school in New York in 1953. His works include *The Seasons* 1947, *Antic Meet* 1958, *Squaregame* 1976, and *Arcade* 1985.

Cunninghame-Graham /ˈkʌnɪŋəm ˈgreɪəm/ Robert Bontine 1852–1936. Scottish writer, politician, and adventurer. He was the author of essays and short stories such as *Success* 1902, *Faith* 1909, *Hope* 1910, and *Charity* 1912. He wrote many travel books based on his experiences as a rancher in Texas and Argentina 1869–83, and as a traveller in Spain and Morocco 1893–98. He became the first president of the Scottish Labour Party in 1888 and the first president of the Scottish National Party in 1928.

Cuno /ˈkuːnəʊ/ Wilhelm 1876–1933. German industrialist and politician who was briefly chancellor of the Weimar Republic 1923.

Curie /ˈkjʊəri/ Marie (born Sklodovska) 1867–1934. Polish scientist. In 1898 she reported the possible existence of a new, powerfully radioactive element in pitchblende ores. Her husband, Pierre (1859–1906) abandoned his own researches to assist her, and in the same year they announced the existence of polonium and radium. They isolated the pure elements 1902. Both scientists refused to take out a patent on their discovery and were jointly awarded the Davy Medal 1903 and the Nobel Prize for Physics 1903, with Antoine →Becquerel. Marie Curie wrote a *Treatise on Radioactivity* 1910, and was awarded the Nobel Prize for Chemistry 1911.

Born in Warsaw, Marie Curie studied in Paris from 1891. Her decision to investigate the nature of uranium rays was influenced by the publication of Antoine Becquerel's experiments. She took no precautions against radioactivity and died a victim of radiation poisoning. Her notebooks, even today, are too contaminated to handle.

In 1904 Pierre was appointed to a chair in physics at the Sorbonne, and on his death in a street accident was succeeded by his wife.

Curley /ˈkɜːli/ James Michael 1874–1958. US Democrat politician. He was a member of the US House of Representatives 1912–14, several times mayor of Boston between 1914 and 1934, when he was elected governor. He lost a bid for the US Senate 1936 and did not hold political office again until elected to the House 1942. His fourth and last mayoral term began 1946, during which time he spent six months in federal prison on a mail-fraud conviction.

Born in Boston, Curley became active in the local Democratic party soon after leaving school. He served in the state legislature 1902–03, on the Boston Board of Aldermen 1904–09, and on the Boston City Council 1910–11. The flamboyant Curley's political career inspired Edwin O'Connor's *The Last Hurrah* 1956.

Curnonsky /kjʊəˈnɒnski/ pseudonym of Maurice Edmond Sailland 1872–1956. French gastronome and cookery writer, who was a pioneer in the cataloguing of French regional cuisine.

Curtin /ˈkɜːtɪn/ John 1885–1945. Australian Labor politician, prime minister and minister of defence 1941–45. He was elected leader of the Labor Party 1935. As prime minister, he organized the mobilization of Australia's resources to meet the danger of Japanese invasion during World War II.

Curtis /ˈkɜːtɪs/ Tony. Stage name of Bernard Schwartz 1925– . US film actor whose best work was characterized by a jumpy energy, as the press agent in *Sweet Smell of Success* 1957 and as a musician on-the-run in *Some Like It Hot* 1959 with Marilyn Monroe and Jack Lemmon.

He also starred in *The Vikings* 1958 and *The Boston Strangler* 1968.

Curtiss /ˈkɜːtɪs/ Glenn Hammond 1878–1930. US aeronautical inventor, pioneer aviator, and aircraft designer. In 1908 he made the first public flights in the USA, including the 1-mile flight. He belonged to Alexander Graham Bell's Aerial Experiment Association 1907–1909 and established the first flying school 1909. In 1910 Curtiss staged his sensational flight down the Hudson River from Albany to New York City.

In 1916 he founded the Curtiss Aeroplane and Motor Corp, based on his invention of ailerons, which he designed for the first seaplanes 1911. He designed and constructed many planes for the Allied nations during World War I.

Curtiz /ˈkɜːtɪz/ Michael. Adopted name of Mihaly Kertész 1888–1962. Hungarian-born film director who worked in Austria, Germany, and France before moving to the USA in 1926, where he made several films with Errol Flynn, directed *Mildred Pierce* 1945, which revitalized Joan Crawford's career, and *Casablanca* 1942 (Academy Award).

His wide range of films include *Doctor X* 1932, *The Adventures of Robin Hood* 1938, and *White Christmas* 1954.

Curwen /ˈkɜːwɪn/ John 1816–1880. English musician. In about 1840 he established the *tonic sol-fa* system of music notation (originated in the 11th century by Guido d'Arezzo) in which the notes of a scale are named by syllables (doh, ray, me, fah, soh, lah, te) with the key indicated, to simplify singing by sight.

Curzon /ˈkɜːzən/ George Nathaniel, 1st Marquess Curzon of Kedleston 1859–1925. British Conservative politician, viceroy of India 1899–1905. During World War I, he was a member of the cabinet 1916–19. As foreign secretary 1919–24, he set up a British protectorate over Persia.

Curzon /ˈkɜːzən/ Robert, Lord Zouche 1810–1873. English diplomat and traveller, author of *Monasteries in the Levant* 1849.

Cusack /ˈkjuːsæk/ Cyril 1910–   . Irish actor who joined the Abbey Theatre, Dublin, 1932 and appeared in many of its productions, including Synge's *The Playboy of the Western World*. In Paris he won an award for his solo performance in Beckett's *Krapp's Last Tape*.

In the UK he has played many roles as a member of the Royal Shakespeare Company and the National Theatre Company.

Cushing /ˈkʊʃɪŋ/ Harvey Williams 1869–1939. US neurologist who pioneered neurosurgery. He developed a range of techniques for the surgical treatment of brain tumours, and also studied the link between the pituitary gland and conditions such as dwarfism.

Cushing /ˈkʊʃɪŋ/ Peter 1913–   . British actor who specialized in horror roles in films made at Hammer studios 1957–73, including *Dracula* 1958, *The Mummy* 1959, and *Frankenstein Must Be Destroyed* 1969. Other films include *Doctor Who and the Daleks* 1966, *Star Wars* 1977, and *Top Secret* 1984.

Custer /ˈkʌstə/ George A(rmstrong) 1839–1876. US Civil War general, the Union's youngest brigadier general as a result of a brilliant war record. Reduced in rank in the regular army at the end of the Civil War, he campaigned against the Sioux from 1874, and was killed with a detachment of his troops by the forces of Sioux chief Sitting Bull in the Battle of Little Bighorn, Montana: also called *Custer's last stand*, 25 June 1876.

Cuthbert, St /ˈkʌθbət/ died 687. Christian saint. A shepherd in Northumbria, England, he entered the monastery of Melrose, Scotland, after receiving a vision. He travelled widely as a missionary and because of his alleged miracles was known as the 'wonderworker of Britain'.

He became prior of Lindisfarne 664, and retired 676 to Farne Island. In 684 he became bishop of Hexham and later of Lindisfarne. Feast day 20 March.

Cuvier /ˈkjuːvieɪ/ Georges, Baron Cuvier 1769–1832. French comparative anatomist. In 1799 he showed that some species have become extinct by reconstructing extinct giant animals that he believed were destroyed in a series of giant deluges. These ideas are expressed in *Recherches sur les ossiments fossiles de quadrupèdes* 1812 and *Discours sur les révolutions de la surface du globe* 1825.

In 1798 Cuvier produced *Tableau élémentaire de l'histoire naturelle des animaux*, in which his scheme of classification is outlined. He was professor of natural history in the Collège de France from 1799 and at the Jardin des Plantes from 1802; at the Restoration in 1815 he was elected chancellor of the University of Paris. Cuvier was the first to relate the structure of fossil animals to that of their living relatives. His great work *Le Règne animal/The Animal Kingdom* 1817 is a systematic survey.

Cuyp /kaɪp/ Aelbert 1620–1691. Dutch painter of countryside scenes, seascapes, and portraits.

His idyllically peaceful landscapes are bathed in golden light; for example, *A Herdsman with Cows by a River* (about 1650, National Gallery, London). His father, **Jacob Gerritsz Cuyp** (1594–1652), was also a landscape and portrait painter.

Cymbeline or **Cunobelin** 1st century AD. King of the Catuvellauni AD 5–40, who fought unsuccessfully against the Roman invasion of Britain. His capital was at Colchester.

Cynewulf /ˈkɪnɪwʊlf/ early 8th century. Anglo-Saxon poet. He is thought to have been a Northumbrian monk and is the undoubted author of 'Juliana' and part of the 'Christ' in the Exeter Book (a collection of poems now in Exeter Cathedral), and of the 'Fates of the Apostles' and 'Elene' in the Vercelli Book (a collection of Old English manuscripts housed in Vercelli, Italy), in all of which he inserted his name by using runic acrostics.

Cyprian, St /ˈsɪprɪən/ c. 210–258. Christian martyr, one of the earliest Christian writers, and bishop of Carthage about 249. He wrote a treatise on the unity of the church. Feast day 16 Sept.

He cannot have God for his father who has not had the church for his mother.

St Cyprian
On the Unity of the Catholic Church

Cyrano de Bergerac /ˈsɪrənəʊ də ˈbɜːʒəræk/ Savinien 1619–1655. French writer. He joined a corps of guards at 19 and performed heroic feats which brought him fame. He is the hero of a classic play by Edmond →Rostand, in which his excessively long nose is used as a counterpoint to his chivalrous character.

Cyril and Methodius, Sts /ˈsɪrəl, mɪˈθəʊdɪəs/ two brothers, both Christian saints: Cyril 826–869 and Methodius 815–885. Born in Thessalonica, they were sent as missionaries to what is today Moravia. They invented a Slavonic alphabet, and translated the Bible and the liturgy from Greek to Slavonic. The language (known as *Old Church Slavonic*) remained in use in churches and for literature among Bulgars, Serbs, and Russians up to the 17th century. The *cyrillic alphabet* is named after Cyril and may also have been invented by him. Feast day 14 Feb.

Cyril of Alexandria, St /sɪrəl/ 376–444. Bishop of Alexandria from 412, persecutor of Jews and other non-Christians, and suspected of ordering the murder of Hypatia (*c.* 370–*c.* 415), a philosopher whose influence was increasing at the expense of his. He was violently opposed to Nestorianism (the Christian doctrine held by Syrian ecclesiastic Nestorius who asserted that Jesus had two natures, human and divine, and that Mary was the mother of the man Jesus only).

Cyrus the Great /saɪrəs/ died 529 BC. Founder of the Persian Empire. As king of Persia, he was originally subject to the Medes, a people of NW Iran, whose empire he overthrew 550 BC. He captured Croesus 546 BC, and conquered all Asia Minor, adding Babylonia (including Syria and Palestine) to his empire 539 BC, allowing exiled Jews to return to Jersualem. He died fighting in Afghanistan.

Czerny /tʃeəni/ Carl 1791–1857. Austrian composer and pianist. He wrote an enormous quantity of religious and concert music, but is chiefly remembered for his books of graded studies and technical exercises used in piano teaching.

D

the same point simultaneously). In 1838 he invented the daguerreotype, a single image process superseded ten years later by →Talbot's negative/positive process.

Dahl /dɑːl/ Johann Christian 1788–1857. Norwegian landscape painter in the Romantic style. He trained in Copenhagen but was active chiefly in Dresden from 1818. He was the first great painter of the Norwegian landscape, in a style that recalls the Dutch artist Jacob van →Ruisdael.

Dahl /dɑːl/ Roald 1916–1990. British writer, celebrated for short stories with a twist, for example, *Tales of the Unexpected* 1979, and for children's books, including *Charlie and the Chocolate Factory* 1964. He also wrote the screenplay for the James Bond film *You Only Live Twice* 1967.

His autobiography *Going Solo* 1986 recounted his experiences as a fighter pilot in the RAF.

Do you know what breakfast cereal is made of? It's made of all those little curly wooden shavings you find in pencil sharpeners!

Roald Dahl
Charlie and the Chocolate Factory 1964

Dadd English painter Richard Dadd, known for his fantastically detailed fairy paintings executed during his 20-year incarceration in an asylum. Prior to his mental breakdown and murder of his father, Dadd had studied at the Royal Academy, travelled extensively, and had been considered a promising young artist.

Dadd /dæd/ Richard 1817–1887. British painter. In 1843 he murdered his father and was committed to an asylum, but continued to paint minutely detailed pictures of fantasies and fairy tales, such as *The Fairy Feller's Master-Stroke* 1855–64 (Tate Gallery, London).

Dafydd ap Gwilym /dævɪð æp ˈgwɪlɪm/ *c.* 1340–*c.* 1400. Welsh poet. His work is notable for its complex but graceful style, its concern with nature and love rather than with heroic martial deeds, and for its references to Classical and Italian poetry.

Daglish /dæglɪʃ/ Eric Fitch 1892–1966. British artist and author. He wrote a number of natural history books, and illustrated both these and classics by Izaak Walton, Henry Thoreau, Gilbert White, and W H Hudson with exquisite wood engravings.

Daguerre /dæˈgeə/ Louis Jacques Mande 1789–1851. French pioneer of photography. Together with Joseph Niépce, he is credited with the invention of photography (though others were reaching

Dahrendorf /dɑːrəndɔːf/ Ralf (Gustav) 1929– . German sociologist, director of the London School of Economics 1974–84. His works include *Life Chances* 1980, which sees the aim of society as the improvement of the range of opportunities open to the individual.

Daimler /deɪmlə/ Gottlieb 1834–1900. German engineer who pioneered the modern car. In 1886 he produced his first motor vehicle and a motorbicycle. He later joined forces with Karl →Benz and was one of the pioneers of the high-speed four-stroke petrol engine.

Daimler, born in Württemberg, had engineering experience at the Whitworth works, Manchester, England, before joining N A Otto of Cologne in the production of an internal-combustion gas engine 1872.

Daladier /ˌdælædˈjeɪ/ Edouard 1884–1970. French Radical politician. As prime minister April 1938–March 1940, he signed the Munich Agreement 1938 (by which the Sudeten districts of Czechoslovakia were ceded to Germany) and declared war on Germany 1939. He resigned 1940 because of his unpopularity for failing to assist Finland against Russia. He was arrested on the fall of France 1940 and was a prisoner in Germany 1943–45. Following the end of World War II he was re-elected to the Chamber of Deputies 1946–58.

Dalai Lama /ˈdælaɪ ˈlɑːmə/ 14th incarnation 1935– . Spiritual and temporal head of the Tibetan state until 1959, when he went into exile in protest against Chinese annexation and oppression. His people have continued to demand his return.

Tibetan Buddhists believe that each Dalai Lama is a reincarnation of his predecessor and also of Avalokiteśvara.

Enthroned 1940, the Dalai Lama temporarily fled 1950–51 when the Chinese overran Tibet, and in March 1959 – when a local uprising against Chinese rule was suppressed – made a dramatic escape from Lhasa to India. He then settled at Dharmsala in the Punjab. The Chinese offered to lift the ban on his living in Tibet, providing he would refrain from calling for Tibet's independence. His deputy, the Panchen Lama, has cooperated with the Chinese but failed to protect the monks. The Dalai Lama was awarded the Nobel Prize for Peace 1989 in recognition of his commitment to the nonviolent liberation of his homeland.

Dalcroze Emile Jaques see →Jaques-Dalcroze, Emile.

Dale /deɪl/ Henry Hallett 1875–1968. British physiologist, who in 1936 shared the Nobel Prize for Physiology and Medicine with Otto →Loewi for work on the chemical transmission of nervous effects.

d'Alembert see →Alembert, French mathematician.

Dalen /ˈdɑːleɪn/ Nils 1869–1937. Swedish industrial engineer who invented the light-controlled valve. This allowed lighthouses to operate automatically and won him the 1912 Nobel Prize for Physics.

Daley /ˈdeɪli/ Richard Joseph 1902–1976. US politician and controversial mayor of Chicago 1955–76. He built a formidable political machine and ensured a Democratic presidential victory 1960 when J F Kennedy was elected. He hosted the turbulent national Democratic convention 1968.

Born in Chicago, Daley became involved in local Democratic politics at an early age. He attended law school at DePaul University, gaining admission to the bar 1933. He served in the Illinois legislature 1936–46. He was Cook County clerk 1935–55 before being elected mayor of Chicago, remaining in office until his death.

Dalgarno /ˈdælɡɑːnəʊ/ George 1626–1687. Scottish schoolteacher and the inventor of the first sign-language alphabet 1680.

Dalglish /ˈdælɡliːʃ/ Kenny (Kenneth) 1951– . Scottish footballer, the first man to play 200 League games in England and Scotland, and score 100 goals in each country.

Born in Glasgow, he made over 200 appearances for Glasgow Celtic before joining Liverpool 1977. He played for Scotland 102 times, winning all national honours. He was manager of Liverpool Football Club 1985–91.

Dalhousie /dælˈhaʊzi/ James Andrew Broun Ramsay, 1st Marquess and 10th Earl of Dalhousie 1812–1860. British administrator, governor general of India 1848–56. In the second Sikh War he annexed the Punjab 1849, and, after the second Burmese War, Lower Burma 1853. He reformed the Indian army and civil service and furthered social and economic progress.

Dali /ˈdɑːli/ Salvador 1904–1989. Spanish painter. In 1928 he collaborated with Luis Buñuel on the film *Un chien andalou*. In 1929 he joined the Surrealists and became notorious for his flamboyant eccentricity. Influenced by the psychoanalytic theories of Freud, he developed a repertoire of dramatic images, such as the distorted human body, limp watches, and burning giraffes in such pictures as *The Persistence of Memory* 1931 (Museum of Modern Art, New York). They are painted with a meticulous, polished clarity. He also used religious themes and painted many portraits of his wife Gala.

Dali, born near Barcelona, initially came under the influence of the Italian Futurists. He is credited as co-creator of *Un chien andalou*, but his role is thought to have been subordinate; he abandoned film after collaborating on the script for Buñuel's *L'Age d'or* 1930. He designed ballet costumes, scenery, jewellery, and furniture.

The books *Secret Life of Salvador Dali* 1942 and *Diary of a Genius* 1966 are autobiographical. He was buried beneath a crystal dome in the museum of his work at Figueras on the Costa Brava, Spain.

There is only one difference between a madman and me. I am not mad.

Salvador Dali *The American* July 1956

Dallapiccola /ˌdæləˈpɪkələ/ Luigi 1904–1975. Italian composer. In his early years he was a Neo-Classicist in the manner of Stravinsky, but he soon turned to Serialism, which he adapted to his own style. His works include the operas *Il prigioniero/The Prisoner* 1949 and *Ulisse/Ulysses* 1968, as well as many vocal and instrumental compositions.

Dalton /ˈdɔːltən/ Hugh, Baron Dalton 1887–1962. British Labour politician and economist. Chancellor of the Exchequer from 1945, he oversaw nationalization of the Bank of England, but resigned 1947 after making a disclosure to a lobby correspondent before a budget speech.

Dalton /dɔːltən/ John 1766–1844. British chemist who proposed the theory of atoms, which he considered to be the smallest parts of matter. He produced the first list of relative atomic masses in *Absorption of Gases* 1805 and put forward the law of partial pressures of gases (Dalton's law).

From experiments with gases he noted that the proportions of two components combining to form another gas were always constant.

From this he suggested that if substances combine in simple numerical ratios then the macroscopic weight proportions represent the relative atomic masses of those substances. He also propounded the law of partial pressures, stating that for a mixture of gases the total pressure is the sum of the pressures that would be developed by each individual gas if it were the only one present.

Daly /deɪli/ Augustin 1838–1899. US theatre manager. He began as a drama critic and playwright before building his own theatre in New York 1879 and another, Daly's, in Leicester Square, London 1893.

Dalziel /dælziel/ family of British wood engravers. *George* (1815–1902), *Edward* (1817–1905), *John* (1822–1860), and *Thomas Bolton* (1823–1906) were all sons of Alexander Dalziel of Wooler, Northumberland. George went to London in 1835 and was joined by his brothers. They produced illustrations for the classics and magazines.

Dam /dæm/ (Henrik) Carl (Peter) 1895–1976. Danish biochemist who discovered vitamin K. For his success in this field he shared the 1943 Nobel Prize for Medicine with US biochemist Edward Doisy (1893–1986).

In 1928 Dam began a series of experiments to see if chickens could live on a cholesterol-free diet. The birds, it turned out, were able to metabolize their own supply. Yet they continued to die from spontaneous haemorrhages. Dam concluded that their diet lacked an unknown essential ingredient to control coagulation, which he eventually found in abundance in green leaves. Dam named the new compound vitamin K.

Damien, Father /dæmiˈæn/ name adopted by Belgian missionary Joseph de →Veuster.

Damocles /dæməkliːz/ lived 4th century BC. In Classical legend, a courtier of the elder Dionysius, ruler of Syracuse, Sicily. Having extolled the happiness of his sovereign, Damocles was invited by him to a feast, during which he saw above his head a sword suspended by a single hair. He recognized this as a symbol of the insecurity of the great.

Dampier /dæmpiə/ William 1652–1715. English explorer and hydrographic surveyor who circumnavigated the world three times.

He was born in Somerset, and went to sea in 1668. He led a life of buccaneering adventure, circumnavigated the globe, and published his *New Voyage Round the World* in 1697. In 1699 he was sent by the government on a voyage to Australia and New Guinea, and again circled the world. He accomplished a third circumnavigation 1703–07, and on his final voyage 1708–11 rescued Alexander →Selkirk (on whose life Daniel Defoe's *Robinson Crusoe* is based) from Juan Fernandez in the S Pacific.

Dana /deɪnə/ Charles Anderson 1819–1897. US journalist who covered the European revolutions of 1848 and earned a reputation as one of America's most able foreign correspondents. During the US Civil War he served as assistant secretary of war 1863–65 and in 1868 purchased the *New York Sun*, with which he pioneered the daily tabloid format.

Dana was manager of Brook Farm, an experimental community in West Roxbury, Massachusetts, 1841–47. He was later managing editor of the *New York Tribune* under Horace Greeley.

Dana Richard Henry 1815–1882. US author and lawyer who went to sea and worked for his passage around Cape Horn to California and back, then wrote an account of the journey *Two Years before the Mast* 1840. He also published *The Seaman's Friend* 1841, a guide to maritime law.

Danby /dænbi/ Thomas Osborne, Earl of Danby 1631–1712. British Tory politician. He entered Parliament 1665, acted as Charles II's chief minister 1673–78 and was created earl of Danby 1674, but was imprisoned in the Tower of London 1678–84. In 1688 he signed the invitation to William of Orange to take the throne. Danby was again chief minister 1690–95, and in 1694 was created Duke of Leeds.

Dance /dɑːns/ Charles 1946– . English film and television actor who became known when he played the sympathetic Guy Perron in *The Jewel in the Crown* 1984. He has also appeared in *Plenty* 1986, *Good Morning Babylon*, *The Golden Child* 1987, and *White Mischief* 1988.

Dandolo /dændələu/ Venetian family that produced four doges (rulers), of whom the most outstanding, *Enrico* (c. 1120–1205), became doge in 1193. He greatly increased the dominions of the Venetian republic and accompanied the crusading army that took Constantinople in 1203.

Daniel /dæniəl/ 6th century BC. Jewish folk hero and prophet at the court of Nebuchadnezzar; also the name of a book of the Old Testament, probably compiled in the 2nd century BC. It includes stories about Daniel and his companions Shadrach, Meshach, and Abednego, set during the Babylonian captivity of the Jews.

One of the best-known stories is that of Daniel in the den of lions, where he was thrown for refusing to compromise his beliefs, and was preserved by divine intervention. The book also contains a prophetic section dealing with the rise and fall of a number of empires.

Daniel /dæniəl/ Glyn 1914–1986. British archaeologist. Prominent in the development of the subject, he was Disney professor of archaeology,

Cambridge, 1974–81. His books include *Megaliths in History* 1973 and *A Short History of Archaeology* 1981.

Daniel /dænɪəl/ Samuel 1562–1619. English poet, author of the sonnet collection *Delia* 1592. From 1603 he was master of the revels at court, for which he wrote masques.

Custom that is before all law, Nature that is above all art.

Samuel Daniel *A Defence of Rhyme* 1603

Daniell /dænɪəl/ John Frederic 1790–1845. British chemist and meteorologist who invented a primary electrical cell 1836. The **Daniell cell** consists of a central zinc cathode dipping into a porous pot containing zinc sulphate solution. The porous pot is, in turn, immersed in a solution of copper sulphate contained in a copper can, which acts as the cell's anode. The use of a porous barrier prevents polarization (the covering of the anode with small bubbles of hydrogen gas) and allows the cell to generate a continuous current of electricity.

Daninos /ˌdænɪˈnəʊ/ Pierre 1913–   . French author. Originally a journalist, he was liaison agent with the British Army at Dunkirk in 1940, and created in *Les Carnets du Major Thompson/The Notebooks of Major Thompson* 1954, a humorous Englishman who caught the French imagination.

Dankworth John 1927–   . British jazz musician, composer, and bandleader, a leading figure in the development of British jazz from about 1950. His film scores include *Saturday Night and Sunday Morning* 1960 and *The Servant* 1963.

D'Annunzio Gabriele 1863–1938. Italian poet, novelist, and playwright. Marking a departure from 19th-century Italian literary traditions, his use of language and style of writing earned him much criticism in his own time.

His first volume of poetry, *Primo vere/In Early Spring* 1879, was followed by further collections of verse, short stories, novels, and plays (he wrote the play *La Gioconda* for the actress Eleonora Duse 1898). After serving in World War I, he led an expedition of volunteers in 1919 to capture Fiume, which he held until 1921. He became a national hero, and was created Prince of Montenevoso 1924. Influenced by Nietzsche's writings, he later became an ardent exponent of Fascism.

Dante Alighieri /dænti ælɪˈgjeəri/ 1265–1321. Italian poet. His masterpiece *La divina commedia/The Divine Comedy* 1307–21 is an epic account in three parts of his journey through Hell, Purgatory, and Paradise, during which he is guided part of the way by the poet Virgil; on a metaphorical level the journey is also one of Dante's own spiritual development. Other works include the philosophical prose treatise *Convivio/The Banquet* 1306–08, the first major work of its kind to be written in Italian rather than Latin; *Monarchia/On World Government* 1310–13, expounding his political theories; *De vulgari eloquentia/Concerning the Vulgar Tongue* 1304–06, an original Latin work on Italian, its dialects, and kindred languages; and *Canzoniere/Lyrics*, containing his scattered lyrics.

Dante was born in Florence, where in 1274 he first met and fell in love with Beatrice Portinari (described in *La vita nuova/New Life* 1283–92). His love for her survived her marriage to another and her death 1290 at the age of 24. He married Gemma Donati 1291.

In 1289 Dante fought in the battle of Campaldino, won by Florence against Arezzo, and from 1295 took an active part in Florentine politics. In 1300 he was one of the six Priors of the Republic, favouring the moderate 'White' Guelph party rather than the extreme papal 'Black' Ghibelline faction; when the Ghibellines seized power 1302, he was convicted in his absence of misapplication of public money, and sentenced first to a fine and then to death. He escaped from Florence and spent the remainder of his life in exile, in central and N Italy.

Danton /dɒnˈtɒn/ Georges Jacques 1759–1794. French revolutionary. Originally a lawyer, during the early years of the Revolution he was one of the most influential people in Paris. He organized the uprising 10 Aug 1792 that overthrew Louis XVI and the monarchy, roused the country to expel the Prussian invaders, and in April 1793 formed the revolutionary tribunal and the **Committee of Public Safety**, of which he was the leader until July of that year. Thereafter he lost power to the Jacobins, and, when he attempted to recover it, was arrested and guillotined.

Da Ponte Lorenzo (Conegliano Emmanuele) 1749–1838. librettist renowned for his collaboration with Mozart in *The Marriage of Figaro* 1786, *Don Giovanni* 1787, and *Così fan tutte* 1790. His adaptations of contemporary plays are deepened by a rich life experience and understanding of human nature.

Born in Ceneda (now Vittorio Veneto), he studied to take holy orders, proving a skilful versifier in both Italian and Latin.

Appointed as a professor in literature at Treviso Seminary 1773, his radical views and immoral behaviour led to his banishment from Venice 1779. Travelling to Vienna, he was appointed as librettist to the New Italian Theatre 1781 on the recommendation of Salieri. His first major success was in adapting Beaumarchais' comedy for Mozart's *The Marriage of Figaro*. *Don Giovanni* and *Così fan tutte* followed, together with libretti for other composers. In 1805 he emigrated to the USA, eventually becoming a teacher of Italian language and literature .

d'Arblay, Madame /dɑːbleɪ/ married name of British writer Fanny →Burney.

Darby /dɑːbi/ Abraham 1677–1717. English iron manufacturer who developed a process for smelting iron ore using coke instead of the more expensive charcoal.

He employed the cheaper iron to cast strong thin pots for domestic use as well as the huge cylinders required by the new steam pumping-engines. In 1779 his grandson (also Abraham) constructed the world's first iron bridge, over the river Severn at Coalbrookdale.

Dare /deə/ Virginia 1587–?. First English child born in America. She was the granddaughter of John White, the governor of Roanoke colony (now in North Carolina). White returned to England soon after her birth, leaving Dare in Roanoke with the rest of her settler family. English communication with Roanoke was cut off for nearly four years during the war with Spain 1585–88. In 1591 the crew of an English ship found the colony deserted.

The enigmatic inscription 'Croatan' carved in a tree led to speculation that the settlers, fearful of hostile Indians, had perhaps taken refuge with the friendly Croatan.

Darío Rubén. Pen name of Félix Rubén García Sarmiento 1867–1916. Nicaraguan poet. His first major work *Azul/Azure* 1888, a collection of prose and verse influenced by French Symbolism, created a sensation. He went on to establish *modernismo*, the Spanish-American modernist literary movement, distinguished by an idiosyncratic and deliberately frivolous style that broke away from the prevailing Spanish provincialism and adapted French poetic models. His vitality and eclecticism influenced every poet writing in Spanish after him, both in the New World and in Spain.

Darius I /dəˈraɪəs/ *the Great* c. 558–486 BC. King of Persia 521–486 BC. A member of a younger branch of the Achaemenid dynasty, he won the throne from the usurper Gaumata (died 522 BC) and reorganized the government. In 512 BC he marched against the Scythians, a people north of the Black Sea, and subjugated Thrace and Macedonia.

An expedition in 492 BC to crush a rebellion in Greece failed, and the army sent into Attica 490 BC was defeated at the battle of Marathon. Darius had an account of his reign inscribed on the mountain at Behistun, Persia.

Darlan /dɑːˈlɒn/ Jean François 1881–1942. French admiral and politician. He entered the navy 1899, and was appointed admiral and commander in chief 1939. He commanded the French navy 1939–40, took part in the evacuation of Dunkirk, and entered the Pétain cabinet as naval minister. In 1941 he was appointed vice premier, and became strongly anti-British and pro-German, but in 1942 he was dropped from the cabinet by

Laval and sent to N Africa, where he was assassinated.

Darling /dɑːlɪŋ/ Grace 1815–1842. British heroine. She was the daughter of a lighthouse keeper on the Farne Islands, off Northumberland. On 7 Sept 1838 the *Forfarshire* was wrecked, and Grace Darling and her father rowed through a storm to the wreck, saving nine lives. She was awarded a medal for her bravery.

Darnley /dɑːnli/ Henry Stewart or Stuart, Lord Darnley 1545–1567. British aristocrat, second husband of Mary Queen of Scots from 1565, and father of James I of England (James VI of Scotland). On the advice of her secretary, David →Rizzio, Mary refused Darnley the crown matrimonial; in revenge, Darnley led a band of nobles who murdered Rizzio in Mary's presence. Darnley was assassinated 1567.

He was born in England, the son of the 4th Earl of Lennox (1516–1571) and Lady Margaret Douglas (1515–1578), through whom he inherited a claim to the English throne. Mary was his first cousin. Mary and Darnley were reconciled after the murder of Rizzio 1566, but soon Darnley alienated all parties and a plot to kill him was formed by →Bothwell. Mary's part in it remains a subject of controversy.

Darrow /dærəʊ/ Clarence (Seward) 1857–1938. US lawyer, born in Ohio, a champion of liberal causes and defender of the underdog. He defended many trade-union leaders, including Eugene →Debs 1894. He was counsel for the defence in the Nathan Leopold and Richard Loeb murder trial in Chicago 1924, and in the Scopes monkey trial. Darrow matched wits in the trial with prosecution attorney William Jennings →Bryan. He was an opponent of capital punishment.

Dart /dɑːt/ Raymond 1893–1988. Australian-born South African palaeontologist and anthropologist who in 1924 discovered the first fossil remains of the Australopithecenes, early hominids, near Taungs in Botswana. He named them *Australopithecus africanus*, and spent many years trying to prove to sceptics that they were early humans, since their cranial and dental characteristics were not apelike in any way. In the 1950s and 1960s, the →Leakey family found more fossils of this type and of related types in the Olduvai Gorge of E Africa, establishing that Australopithecines were hominids, walked erect, made tools, and lived as early as 5.5 million years ago. After further discoveries in the 1980s, they are today classified as *Homo sapiens australopithecus*, and Dart's assertions have been validated.

Darwin /dɑːwɪn/ Charles Robert 1809–1882. English scientist who developed the modern theory of evolution and proposed, with Alfred Russel Wallace, the principle of natural selection. After research in South America and the Galápagos Islands as naturalist on HMS *Beagle* 1831–36, Darwin published *On the Origin of Species by*

Means of Natural Selection or the Preservation of Favoured Races in the Struggle for Life 1859. This explained the evolutionary process through the principles of natural and sexual selection. It aroused bitter controversy because it disagreed with the literal interpretation of the Book of Genesis in the Bible.

Darwin also made important discoveries in many other areas, including the fertilization mechanisms of plants, the classification of barnacles, and the formation of coral reefs. Born at Shrewsbury, the grandson of Erasmus Darwin, he studied medicine at Edinburgh and theology at Cambridge. By 1844 he had enlarged his sketch of ideas to an essay of his conclusions, but then left his theory for eight years while he studied barnacles. In 1858 he was forced into action by the receipt of a memoir from A R →Wallace, embodying the same theory. *On the Origin of Species* refuted earlier evolutionary theories, such as those of →Lamarck. Darwin himself played little part in the debates, but his *Descent of Man* 1871 added fuel to the theological discussion in which T H →Huxley and Haeckel took leading parts. Darwin then devoted himself chiefly to botanical studies until his death. Darwinism alone is not enough to explain the evolution of sterile worker bees, or altruism. Neo-Darwinism, the current theory of evolution, is a synthesis of Darwin and genetics based on the work of →Mendel.

What can be more curious than that the hand of a man, formed for grasping, that of a mole for digging, [...] and the wing of a bat, should all be constructed on the same pattern, and should include the same bones, in the same relative positions?

Charles Darwin
On the Origin of the Species

Darwin /ˈdɑːwɪn/ Erasmus 1731–1802. British poet, physician, and naturalist; he was the grandfather of Charles Darwin. He wrote *The Botanic Garden* 1792, which included a versification of the Linnaean system entitled 'The Loves of the Plants', and *Zoonomia* 1794–96, which anticipated aspects of evolutionary theory, but tended to →Lamarck's interpretation.

Daudet /dəʊdeɪ/ Alphonse 1840–1897. French novelist. He wrote about his native Provence in *Lettres de mon moulin/Letters from My Mill* 1866, and created the character Tartarin, a hero epitomizing southern temperament, in *Tartarin de Tarascon* 1872 and two sequels.

Other works include the play *L'Arlésienne/The Woman from Arles* 1872, for which Bizet composed the music; and *Souvenirs d'un homme de lettres/Recollections of a Literary Man* 1889.

Daudet French 19th-century novelist Alphonse Daudet, who wrote in a naturalistic style and frequently drew upon autobiographical material. He is best known for the charm of his reflective Lettres de mon moulin/ Letters from My Mill *1866*.

Daudet /dəʊdeɪ/ Léon 1867–1942. French writer and journalist, who founded the militant right-wing royalist periodical *Action Française* 1899 after the Dreyfus case. During World War II he was a collaborator with the Germans. He was the son of Alphonse Daudet.

Daumier /dəʊmiˈeɪ/ Honoré 1808–1879. French artist. His sharply dramatic and satirical cartoons dissected Parisian society. He produced over 4,000 lithographs and, mainly after 1860, powerful satirical oil paintings that were little appreciated in his lifetime.

Daumier drew for *La Caricature, Charivari*, and other periodicals. He created several fictitious stereotypes of contemporary figures and was once imprisoned for an attack on Louis Philippe. His paintings show a fluent technique and a mainly monochrome palette. He also produced sculptures of his caricatures, such as the bronze statuette of *Ratapoil* about 1850 (Louvre, Paris).

Davenant /ˈdævənənt/ William 1606–1668. English poet and dramatist, poet laureate from 1638. His *Siege of Rhodes* 1656 is sometimes considered the first English opera. He lost his nose after an attack of syphilis in 1630.

David /ˈdeɪvɪd/ c. 1060–970 BC. Second king of Israel. According to the Old Testament he played the harp for King Saul to banish Saul's melancholy; he later slew the Philistine giant Goliath with a sling and stone. After Saul's death David was anointed king at Hebron, took Jerusalem, and made it his capital.

David was celebrated as a secular poet and probably wrote some of the psalms attributed to him. He was the youngest son of Jesse of Bethlehem. While still a shepherd boy he was anointed by Samuel, a judge who ruled Israel before Saul. Saul's son Jonathan became David's friend, but Saul, jealous of David's prowess, schemed to murder him. David married Michal, Saul's daughter, but after further attempts on his life went into exile until Saul and Jonathan fell in battle with the Philistines at Gilboa. Once David was king, Absalom, his favourite son, led a rebellion but was defeated and killed.

David sent Uriah (a soldier in his army) to his death in the front line of battle in order that he might marry his widow, Bathsheba. Their son Solomon became the third king.

In both Jewish and Christian belief, the messiah would be a descendant of David; Christians hold this prophecy to have been fulfilled by Jesus.

David /ˈdeɪvɪd/ Elizabeth 1914–1992. British cookery writer. Her *Mediterranean Food* 1950 and *French Country Cooking* 1951 helped to spark an interest in foreign cuisine in Britain, and also inspired a growing school of informed, highly literate writing on food and wine.

David /dæˈviːd/ Félicien César 1810–1876. French composer. His symphonic fantasy *Desert* 1844 was inspired by travels in Palestine. He was one of the first Western composers to introduce oriental scales and melodies into his music.

David /dæˈviːd/ Gerard *c.* 1450–1523. Netherlandish painter active chiefly in Bruges from about 1484. His style follows that of van der Weyden, but he was also influenced by the taste in Antwerp for Italianate ornament. *The Marriage at Cana* about 1503 (Louvre, Paris) is an example of his work.

David /dæˈviːd/ Jacques Louis 1748–1825. French painter in the Neo-Classical style. He was an active supporter of and unofficial painter to the republic during the French Revolution, for which he was imprisoned 1794–95. In his *Death of Marat* 1793, he turned political murder into a Classical tragedy. Later he devoted himself to the empire in paintings such as the enormous, pompous *Coronation of Napoleon* 1805–07 (Louvre, Paris).

David won the Prix de Rome 1774 and studied in Rome 1776–80. Back in Paris, his strongly Classical themes and polished style soon earned success; a picture from this period is *The Oath of the Horatii* 1784 (Louvre, Paris). During the Revolution he was elected to the Convention and became a member of the Committee of Public Safety, and narrowly escaped the guillotine. He was later appointed court painter to the emperor Napoleon, of whom he created images such as the horseback figure of *Napoleon Crossing the Alps* 1800 (Louvre, Paris). After Napoleon's fall, David was banished by the Bourbons and settled in Brussels.

David /ˈdeɪvɪd/ two kings of Scotland:

David I 1084–1153. King of Scotland from 1124. The youngest son of Malcolm III Canmore and St →Margaret, he was brought up in the English court of Henry I, and in 1113 married →Matilda, widow of the 1st earl of Northampton. He invaded England 1138 in support of Queen Matilda, but was defeated at Northallerton in the Battle of the Standard, and again 1141.

David II 1324–1371. King of Scotland from 1329, son of →Robert I (the Bruce). David was married at the age of four to Joanna, daughter of Edward II of England. In 1346 David invaded England, was captured at the battle of Neville's Cross, and imprisoned for 11 years.

After the defeat of the Scots by Edward III at Halidon Hill 1333, the young David and Joanna were sent to France for safety. They returned 1341. On Joanna's death 1362 David married Margaret Logie, but divorced her 1370.

David, St /ˈdeɪvɪd/ or *Dewi* 5th–6th century. Patron saint of Wales, Christian abbot and bishop. According to legend he was the son of a prince of Dyfed and uncle of King Arthur; he was responsible for the adoption of the leek as the national emblem of Wales, but his own emblem is a dove. Feast day 1 March.

Tradition has it that David made a pilgrimage to Jerusalem, where he was consecrated bishop. He founded 12 monasteries in Wales, including one at Menevia (now St Davids), which he made his bishop's seat; he presided over a synod at Brefi and condemned the ideas of the British theologian Pelagius.

Davidson /ˈdeɪvɪdsən/ John 1857–1909. Scottish poet whose modern, realistic idiom, as in 'Thirty Bob a Week', influenced T S →Eliot.

Davies /ˈdeɪvɪs/ Henry Walford 1869–1941. English composer and broadcaster. From 1934 he was Master of the King's Musick, and he contributed to the musical education of Britain through his radio talks.

His compositions include the cantata *Everyman* 1904, the 'Solemn Melody' 1908 for organ and strings, chamber music, and part songs.

Davies Jonathan 1962– . Welsh rugby league player. He was capped 27 times between 1985 and 1988 for the Wales rugby union team. In 1988 he changed codes, joining Widnes for a fee of £225,000, and became a member of the Great Britain XIII.

Davies /ˈdeɪvɪs/ Peter Maxwell 1934– . English composer and conductor. His music combines medieval and serial codes of practice with a heightened Expressionism as in his opera *Taverner* 1962–68.

Davies /ˈdeɪvɪs/ Robertson 1913– . Canadian novelist. He published the first novel of his Deptford trilogy *Fifth Business* 1970, a panoramic work blending philosophy, humour, the occult, and ordinary life. Other works include *A Mixture of Frailties* 1958, *The Rebel Angels* 1981, and *What's Bred in the Bone* 1986.

Davies /deɪvɪs/ W(illiam) H(enry) 1871–1940. Welsh poet, born in Monmouth. He went to the USA where he lived the life of a vagrant and lost his right foot stealing a ride under a freight car. His first volume of poems was *Soul's Destroyer* 1906. He published his *Autobiography of a Super-Tramp* 1908.

da Vinci see →Leonardo da Vinci, Italian Renaissance artist.

Davis /deɪvɪs/ Angela 1944– . US left-wing activist for black rights, prominent in the student movement of the 1960s. In 1970 she went into hiding after being accused of supplying guns used in the murder of a judge who had been seized as a hostage in an attempt to secure the release of three black convicts. She was captured, tried, and acquitted. At the University of California she studied under Herbert →Marcuse, and was assistant professor of philosophy at UCLA 1969–70. In 1980 she was the Communist vice-presidential candidate.

Davis /deɪvɪs/ Bette 1908–1989. US actress. She entered films in 1930, and established a reputation as a forceful dramatic actress with *Of Human Bondage* 1934. Later films included *Dangerous* 1935 and *Jezebel* 1938, both winning her Academy Awards, *All About Eve* which won the 1950 Academy Award for best picture, and *Whatever Happened to Baby Jane?* 1962. She continued to make films throughout the 1980s such as *How Green Was My Valley* for television, and *The Whales of August* 1987, in which she co-starred with Lillian Gish.

Davis /deɪvɪs/ Colin 1927– . English conductor. He was musical director at Sadler's Wells 1961–65, chief conductor of the BBC Symphony Orchestra 1967–71, musical director of the Royal Opera 1971–86, and chief conductor of the Bavarian Radio Symphony Orchestra 1983.

Davis /deɪvɪs/ Jefferson 1808–1889. US politician, president of the short-lived Confederate States of America 1861–65. He was a leader of the Southern Democrats in the US Senate from 1857, and a defender of 'humane' slavery; in 1860 he issued a declaration in favour of secession from the USA. During the Civil War he assumed strong political leadership, but often disagreed with military policy. He was imprisoned for two years after the war, one of the few cases of judicial retribution against Confederate leaders.

Born in Kentucky, he graduated from West Point military academy and served in the US army before becoming a cotton planter in Mississippi. He sat in the US Senate 1847–51, was secretary of war 1853–57, and returned to the Senate 1857. His fiery temper and self-righteousness hindered effort to achieve broad unity among the Southern states. His call for conscription in the South raised protests that he was a military dictator, violating the very ideals of freedom for which the Confederacy was fighting.

Davis /deɪvɪs/ Joe 1901–1978. British billiards and snooker player. He was world snooker champion a record 15 times 1927–46 and responsible for much of the popularity of the game. His brother Fred (1913–) was also a billiards and snooker world champion.

Davis /deɪvɪs/ John 1550–1605. English navigator and explorer. He sailed in search of the Northwest Passage through the Canadian Arctic to the Pacific Ocean 1585, and in 1587 sailed to Baffin Bay through the straits named after him. He was the first European to see the Falkland Islands 1592.

Davis /deɪvɪs/ Miles (Dewey, Jr) 1926–1991. US jazz trumpeter, composer, and bandleader. He recorded bebop with Charlie Parker 1945, pioneered cool jazz in the 1950s and jazz-rock fusion beginning in the late 1960s. His significant albums include *Birth of the Cool* 1957 (recorded 1949 and 1950), *Sketches of Spain* 1959, and *Bitches' Brew* 1970.

Often criticized for his frequent changes of style and for drawing on rock music for material and inspiration, Davis was nevertheless one of the most popular and influential figures in jazz. His quintet in 1956 featured the saxophone player John Coltrane, who recorded with Davis until 1961, for example *Kind of Blue* 1959. In 1968 Davis introduced electric instruments, later adding electronic devices to his trumpet and more percussion to his band. Many of his recordings were made in collaboration with the composer and arranger Gil Evans (1912–1988).

Davis /deɪvɪs/ Sammy, Jr 1925–1990. US actor, singer, and tap dancer. He starred in the Broadway show *Mr Wonderful* 1956, and appeared in the film version of the opera *Porgy and Bess* 1959 and in films with Frank Sinatra in the 1960s.

Davis /deɪvɪs/ Steve 1957– . English snooker player who has won every major honour in the game since turning professional 1978. He has been world champion six times.

Davis won his first major title 1980 when he won the Coral UK Championship. He has also won world titles at Pairs and with the England team. His earnings regularly top £1 million through on- and off-the-table prize money and endorsements.

Davis /deɪvɪs/ Stuart 1894–1964. US abstract painter. He used hard-edged geometric shapes in primary colours and experimented with collage. Much of his work shows the influence of jazz tempos. In the 1920s he produced paintings of commercial packaging, such as *Lucky Strike* 1921 (Museum of Modern Art, New York), that foreshadow Pop art.

Davison /ˈdeɪvɪsən/ Emily 1872–1913. English militant suffragette who died after throwing herself under the king's horse at the Derby at Epsom (she was trampled by the horse). She joined the Women's Social and Political Union in 1906 and served several prison sentences for militant action such as stone throwing, setting fire to pillar boxes, and bombing Lloyd George's country house.

Her coffin was carried through London draped in the colours of the suffragette movement, purple, white, and green. It was escorted by 2,000 uniformed suffragettes. She was a teacher with degrees from Oxford and London universities.

Davisson /ˈdeɪvɪsən/ Clinton Joseph 1881–1958. US physicist. With Lester Germer (1896–1971), he discovered that electrons can undergo diffraction, so proving Louis de Broglie's theory that electrons, and therefore all matter, can show wavelike structure. George →Thomson carried through the same research independently, and in 1937 the two men shared the Nobel Prize for Physics.

Davitt /ˈdævɪt/ Michael 1846–1906. Irish nationalist. He joined the Fenians (forerunners of the Irish Republican Army) 1865, and was imprisoned for treason 1870–77. After his release, he and the politician Charles Parnell founded the Land League 1879. Davitt was jailed several times for land-reform agitation. He was a member of Parliament 1895–99, advocating the reconciliation of extreme and constitutional nationalism.

Davy /ˈdeɪvi/ Humphry 1778–1829. English chemist. He discovered, by electrolysis, the metallic elements sodium and potassium in 1807, and calcium, boron, magnesium, strontium, and barium in 1808. In addition, he established that chlorine is an element and proposed that hydrogen is present in all acids. He invented the 'safety lamp' for use in mines where methane was present, enabling miners to work in previously unsafe conditions.

In 1802 he became professor at the Royal Institution, London. He was elected president of the Royal Society in 1820.

Dawes /dɔːz/ Charles Gates 1865–1951. US Republican politician. In 1923 he was appointed by the Allied Reparations Commission president of the committee that produced the *Dawes Plan*, a $200 million loan that enabled Germany to pay enormous war debts after World War I. It reduced tensions temporarily in Europe but was superseded by the Young Plan (which reduced the total reparations bill) 1929. Dawes was elected US vice president (under Calvin Coolidge) 1924, received the Nobel Peace Prize 1925, and was ambassador to Britain 1929–32.

Dawkins /ˈdɔːkɪnz/ Richard 1941– . British zoologist whose book *The Selfish Gene* 1976 popularized the theories of sociobiology (social behaviour in humans and animals in the context of

evolution). A second book, *The Blind Watchmaker* 1986, explains the modern theory of evolution.

Dawson /ˈdɔːsən/ Peter 1882–1961. Australian baritone, remembered for his singing of marching songs and ballads.

Day /deɪ/ Clarence Shepard, Jr 1874–1935. US cartoonist and author. His autobiographical memoir *Life with Father* 1935 became a national bestseller, a long-running Broadway play from 1939, and a popular feature film 1947. Day's sequels to that work, *Life with Mother* 1937 and *Father and I* 1940, were published after his death.

Day /deɪ/ Doris. Stage name of Doris von Kappelhoff 1924– . US film actress and singing star of the 1950s and early 1960s, mostly in musicals and, later, coy sex comedies. Her films include *Tea for Two* 1950, *Calamity Jane* 1953, *Love Me or Leave Me* 1955, and Hitchcock's *The Man Who Knew Too Much* 1956. With *Pillow Talk* 1959, *Lover Come Back* 1962, and other 1960s light sex comedies, she played a self-confident but coy woman who manipulated some of the biggest male stars to capitulate.

Day /deɪ/ Robin 1923– . British broadcasting journalist. A barrister, he pioneered the probing political interview, notably when he questioned Harold Macmillan on the composition of his cabinet in 1958.

Dayan /daɪˈæn/ Moshe 1915–1981. Israeli general and politician. As minister of defence 1967 and 1969–74, he was largely responsible for the victory over neighbouring Arab states in the 1967 Six-Day War, but he was criticized for Israel's alleged unpreparedness in the 1973 October War and resigned along with Prime Minister Golda Meir. Foreign minister from 1977, Dayan resigned 1979 in protest over the refusal of the Begin government to negotiate with the Palestinians.

Day Lewis /deɪ ˈluːɪs/ Cecil 1904–1972. Irish poet, British poet laureate 1968–1972. With W H Auden and Stephen Spender, he was one of the influential left-wing poets of the 1930s. He also wrote detective novels under the pseudonym *Nicholas Blake*.

Born at Ballintubber, Ireland, he was educated at Oxford and then taught at Cheltenham College 1930–35. His work, which includes *From Feathers to Iron* 1931 and *Overtures to Death* 1938, is marked by accomplished lyrics and sustained narrative power. Professor of poetry at Oxford 1951–56, he published critical works and translations from Latin of Virgil's *Georgics* and the *Aeneid*.

In 1968 he succeeded John Masefield as poet laureate. His autobiography, *The Buried Day* 1960, was followed by a biography written by his eldest son Sean 1980.

Dazai /ˈdɑːzaɪ/ Osamu. Pen name of Shuji Tsushima 1909–1948. Japanese novelist. The title of his novel *The Setting Sun* 1947 became identified in Japan with the dead of World War II.

Day Lewis Irish-born British poet Cecil Day Lewis first attracted critical attention with his Transition Poem *1929. He was one of the circle of left-wing poets centred on W H Auden in the 1930s. He later turned to traditional lyric forms, and frequently gave readings of his own and other poetry.*

Deakin /ˈdiːkɪn/ Alfred 1856–1919. Australian politician, prime minister 1903–04, 1905–08, and 1909–10. In his second administration, he enacted legislation on defence and pensions.

Dean /diːn/ Basil 1888–1978. British founder and director-general of Entertainments National Service Association (ENSA) 1939, which provided entertainment for the Allied forces in Worl War II.

Dean /diːn/ Dizzy (Jay Hanna) 1911–1974. US baseball player. He joined the St Louis Cardinals 1930 and made his major-league pitching debut 1932. Winning 30 games and leading the Cardinals to a World Series win, he was voted the National League's most valuable player 1934. Following an injury in the 1937 All-Star Game, his pitching suffered. He was traded to the Chicago Cubs, for whom he pitched until his retirement 1941.

Born in Lucas, Arkansas, Dean worked as a farmhand until he was old enough to join the army, where his pitching skills were recognized. The offbeat brashness and good-natured arrogance that won him the nickname 'Dizzy' are as legendary as his explosive fast-ball pitch.

Dean was elected to the Baseball Hall of Fame 1953.

Dean /diːn/ James (Byron) 1931–1955. US actor. Killed in a car accident after the public showing of his first film, *East of Eden* 1955, he posthumously became a cult hero with *Rebel Without a Cause* 1955 and *Giant* 1956.

Deane /diːn/ Silas 1737–1789. American public leader and diplomat. He served in the Continental Congress 1774–76 and was dispatched to Paris to gain support from the French government during the American Revolution (1775–83), recruiting French soldier Marie Lafayette, amongst others, for the Continental army. Falsely accused of financial improprieties, Deane was discharged from his post; he was exonerated posthumously by Congress 1842.

Born in Groton, Connecticut, USA, Deane was educated at Yale University and admitted to the bar 1761. A supporter of American independence, he served in the colonial legislature 1772, on the Connecticut Committee of Correspondence 1773.

de Bono /də ˈbəʊnəʊ/ Edward 1933– . British medical doctor and psychologist whose concept of lateral thinking, first expounded in *The Use of Lateral Thinking* 1967, involves thinking round a problem rather than tackling it head-on.

Debray /dəˈbreɪ/ Régis 1941– . French Marxist theorist. He was associated with Che ➔Guevara in the revolutionary movement in Latin America in the 1960s. In 1967 he was sentenced to 30 years' imprisonment in Bolivia but was released after three years. His writings on Latin American politics include *Strategy for Revolution* 1970. He became a specialist adviser to President Mitterrand of France on Latin American affairs.

Dean US film star and cult hero James Dean who personified the restless American youth of the 1950s. In just over a year, with only three films to his name, Dean became a screen icon. His posthumous growth in popularity reached legendary proportions, rivalling that of Rudolf Valentino's.

Debrett /dəˈbret/ John 1753–1822. English publisher of a directory of the peerage 1802, baronetage 1808, and knightage 1866–73/4; the books are still published under his name.

de Broglie see →Broglie, de.

Debs /debz/ Eugene Victor 1855–1926. US labour leader and socialist who organized the Social Democratic Party 1897. He was the founder and first president of the American Railway Union 1893, and was imprisoned for six months in 1894 for defying a federal injunction to end the Pullman strike in Chicago. He was socialist candidate for the presidency in every election from 1900 to 1920, except that of 1916.

Debs was born in Terre Haute, Indiana. He opposed US intervention in World War I and was imprisoned 1918–21 for allegedly advocating resistance to conscription, but was pardoned by President Harding 1921. In 1920 he polled nearly 1 million votes, the highest socialist vote ever in US presidential elections, despite having to conduct the campaign from a federal penitentiary in Atlanta, Georgia.

Debussy /dəˈbuːsi/ (Achille-) Claude 1862–1918. French composer. He broke with the dominant tradition of German Romanticism and introduced new qualities of melody and harmony based on the whole-tone scale, evoking oriental music. His work includes *Prélude à l'après-midi d'un faune* 1894 and the opera *Pelléas et Mélisande* 1902.

Among his other works are numerous piano pieces, songs, orchestral pieces such as *La Mer* 1903–05, and the ballet *Jeux* 1910–13. Debussy also wrote with humour about the music of his day, using the fictional character Monsieur Croche 'antidilettante' (professional debunker).

Music is the arithmetic of sounds as optics is the geometry of light.

Claude Debussy

Debye /dəˈbaɪ/ Peter 1884–1966. Dutch physicist. A pioneer of X-ray powder crystallography, he also worked on polar molecules, dipole moments, and molecular structure. In 1940, he went to the USA where he was professor of chemistry at Cornell University 1940–52. He was awarded the 1936 Nobel Prize for Chemistry.

Decatur /dɪˈkeɪtə/ Stephen 1779–1820. US naval hero who, during the war with Tripoli 1801–05, succeeded in burning the *Philadelphia*, which the enemy had captured. During the War of 1812 with Britain, he surrendered only after a desperate resistance 1814. In 1815, he was active against Algerian pirates. Decatur coined the phrase 'our country, right or wrong'. He was killed in a duel.

Decius /diːsɪəs/ Gaius Messius Quintus Traianus 201–251. Roman emperor from 249. He fought a number of campaigns against the Goths but was finally beaten and killed by them near Abritum. He ruthlessly persecuted the Christians.

Dedekind /ˈdeɪdəkɪnd/ Richard 1831–1916. German mathematician, who made contributions to number theory. In 1872 he introduced the *Dedekind cut* (which divides a line of infinite length representing all real numbers) to categorize irrational numbers as fractions and thus increase their usefulness.

Dee /diː/ John 1527–1608. English alchemist, astrologer, and mathematician who claimed to have transmuted metals into gold, although he died in poverty. He long enjoyed the favour of Elizabeth I, and was employed as a secret diplomatic agent.

de Falla Manuel. Spanish composer; see →Falla, Manuel de.

Defoe /dɪˈfəʊ/ Daniel 1660–1731. English writer. His *Robinson Crusoe* 1719, though purporting to be a factual account of shipwreck and solitary survival, was influential in the development of the novel. The fictional *Moll Flanders* 1722 and the partly factual *A Journal of the Plague Year* 1724 are still read for their concrete realism. A prolific journalist and pamphleteer, he was imprisoned 1702–04 for the ironic *The Shortest Way with Dissenters* 1702.

Born in Cripplegate, London, Defoe was educated for the Nonconformist ministry, but became a hosier. He took part in Monmouth's rebellion, and joined William of Orange 1688. He was bankrupted three times as a result of various business ventures, once for the then enormous amount of £17,000. After his business had failed, he held a civil-service post 1695–99. He wrote numerous pamphlets, and first achieved fame with the satire *The True-Born Englishman* 1701, followed in 1702 by the ironic *The Shortest Way with Dissenters*, for which he was fined, imprisoned, and pilloried. In Newgate he wrote his 'Hymn to the Pillory' and started a paper, *The Review* 1704–13. Released 1704, he travelled in Scotland 1706–07, working to promote the Union, and published *A History of the Union* 1709. During the next ten years he was almost constantly employed as a political controversialist and pamphleteer. His version of the contemporary short story 'True Relation of the Apparition of one Mrs Veal' 1706 had revealed a gift for realistic narrative, and *Robinson Crusoe*, based on the story of Alexander Selkirk, appeared 1719. It was followed, among others, by the pirate story *Captain Singleton* 1720, and the picaresque *Colonel Jack* 1722 and *Roxana* 1724.

Since Defoe's death, an increasing number of works have been attributed to him, bringing the total from 128 in 1790 to 561 in 1960.

De Forest /də ˈfɒrɪst/ Lee 1873–1961. US physicist and inventor who perfected the triode valve and contributed to the development of radio, radar, and television.

Ambrose →Fleming invented the diode valve

1904. De Forest saw that if a third electrode were added, the triode valve would serve as an amplifier and radio communications would become a practical possibility. He patented his discovery 1906.

Degas /ˈdeɪgɑː/ (Hilaire Germain) Edgar 1834–1917. French Impressionist painter and sculptor. He devoted himself to lively, informal studies, often using pastels, of ballet, horse racing, and young women working. From the 1890s he turned increasingly to sculpture, modelling figures in wax in a fluent, naturalistic style.

Degas studied under a pupil of Ingres and worked in Italy in the 1850s, painting Classical themes. In 1861 he met Manet, and they developed Impressionism. Degas's characteristic style soon emerged, showing the influence of Japanese prints and of photography in inventive compositions and unusual viewpoints. An example of his sculpture is *The Little Dancer* 1881 (Tate Gallery, London).

De Gasperi /ˈgæspəri/ Alcide de 1881–1954. Italian politician. A founder of the Christian Democrat Party, he was prime minister 1945–53 and worked for European unification.

de Gaulle /də ˈgəʊl/ Charles André Joseph Marie 1890–1970. French general and first president of the Fifth Republic 1959–69. He organized the Free French troops fighting the Nazis 1940–44, was head of the provisional French government 1944–46, and leader of his own Gaullist party. In 1958 the national assembly asked him to form a government during France's economic recovery and to solve the crisis in Algeria. He became president at the end of 1958, having changed the constitution to provide for a presidential system, and served until 1969.

Born in Lille, he graduated from Saint-Cyr 1911 and was severely wounded and captured by the Germans 1916. In June 1940 he refused to accept the new prime minister Pétain's truce with the Germans and became leader of the Free French in England. In 1944 he entered Paris in triumph and was briefly head of the provisional government before resigning over the new constitution of the Fourth Republic 1946. In 1947 he founded the *Rassemblement du Peuple Français*, a nonparty constitutional reform movement, then withdrew from politics 1953. When national bankruptcy and civil war in Algeria loomed 1958, de Gaulle was called to form a government.

As prime minister he promulgated a constitution subordinating the legislature to the presidency and took office as president Dec 1958. Economic recovery followed, as well as Algerian independence after a bloody war. A nationalist, he opposed 'Anglo-Saxon' influence in Europe.

Re-elected president 1965, he pursued a foreign policy that opposed British entry to the EEC, withdrew French forces from NATO 1966, and pursued the development of a French nuclear deterrent. He violently quelled student demon-

De Havilland US film actress Olivia De Havilland won critical and public acclaim for the role of Melanie in Gone with the Wind 1939. In a celebrated court case against Warner Bros, De Havilland won her fight for better roles and in the process, broke the power of the studio over its stars. From that point, players' contracts were limited to a seven-year period.

strations May 1968 when they were joined by workers. The Gaullist party, reorganized as Union des Democrats pour la Cinquième République, won an overwhelming majority in the elections of the same year. In 1969 he resigned after the defeat of the government in a referendum on constitutional reform. He retired to the village of Colombey-les-Deux- Eglises in NE France.

De Havilland /də ˈhævɪlənd/ Geoffrey 1882–1965. British aircraft designer who designed and whose company produced the Moth biplane, the Mosquito fighter-bomber of World War II, and the postwar Comet, the world's first jet-driven airliner to enter commercial service.

De Havilland /də ˈhævɪlənd/ Olivia 1916– . US actress, a star in Hollywood from the age of 19, when she appeared in *A Midsummer Night's Dream* 1935. She later successfully played more challenging dramatic roles in *Gone With the Wind* 1939, *To Each His Own* (Academy Award) and *Dark Mirror* 1946, and *The Snake Pit* 1948. She won her second Academy Award for *The Heiress* 1949, and played in *Lady in a Cage* and *Hush, Hush, Sweet Charlotte*, both 1964.

Deighton /ˈdeɪtn/ Len 1929– . British author of spy fiction, including *The Ipcress File* 1963 and the trilogy *Berlin Game, Mexico Set,* and *London Match* 1983–85, featuring the spy Bernard Samson. Samson was also the main character in Deighton's second trilogy *Spy Hook* 1989, *Spy Line* 1989, and *Spy Sinker* 1990.

Dekker /ˈdekə/ Thomas c. 1572–c. 1632. English dramatist and pamphleteer who wrote mainly in collaboration with others. His play *The Shoemaker's Holiday* 1600 was followed by collaborations with Thomas Middleton, John Webster, Philip Massinger, and others. His pamphlets include *The Gull's Hornbook* 1609, a lively satire on the fashions of the day.

Dekker's plays include *The Honest Whore* 1604–05 and *The Roaring Girl* 1611 (both with Middleton), *Famous History of Sir Thomas Wyat* 1607 (with Webster), *Virgin Martyr* 1622 (with Massinger), and *The Witch of Edmonton* 1621 (with John Ford and William Rowley).

de Klerk /də ˈkleək/ F(rederik) W(illem) 1936– . South African National Party politician, president from 1989. Trained as a lawyer, he entered the South African parliament 1972. He served in the cabinets of B J Vorster and P W Botha 1978–89, and replaced Botha as National Party leader Feb 1989 and as state president Aug 1989. Projecting himself as a pragmatic conservative who sought gradual reform of the apartheid system, he won the Sept 1989 elections for his party, but with a reduced majority. In Feb 1990 he ended the ban on the African National Congress opposition movement and released its effective leader, Nelson Mandela. In Feb 1991 de Klerk promised the end of all apartheid legislation and a new multiracial constitution, and by June of the same year had repealed all racially discriminating laws. In March 1992 a nationwide, whites-only referendum gave de Klerk a clear mandate to proceed with plans for major constitutional reform to end white minority rule.

de Kooning /də ˈkuːnɪŋ/ Willem 1904– . Dutch-born US painter who immigrated to the USA 1926 and worked as a commercial artist. After World War II he became, together with Jackson Pollock, one of the leaders of the Abstract Expressionist movement. His *Women* series, exhibited 1953, was criticized for its grotesque figurative style.

Delacroix /ˌdeləˈkrwɑː/ Eugène 1798–1863. French Romantic painter. His prolific output included religious and historical subjects and portraits of friends, among them the musicians Paganini and Chopin. Against French academic tradition, he evolved a highly coloured, fluid style, as in *The Death of Sardanapalus* 1827 (Louvre, Paris).

The *Massacre at Chios* 1824 (Louvre, Paris) shows Greeks enslaved by wild Turkish horsemen, a contemporary atrocity (his use of a contemporary theme recalls Géricault's example). His style was influenced by the English landscape painter Constable. Delacroix also produced illustrations for Shakespeare, Dante, and Byron. His *Journal* is a fascinating record of his times.

Delafield /ˈdeləfiːld/ E M. Pen name of Edmée Elizabeth Monica de la Pasture 1890–1931. British writer, remembered for her amusing *Diary of a Provincial Lady* 1931, skilfully exploiting the foibles of middle-class life.

de la Mare /delə ˈmeə/ Walter 1873–1956. English poet, known for his verse for children, such as *Songs of Childhood* 1902, and the novels *The Three Royal Monkeys* 1910 for children and, for adults, *The Memoirs of a Midget* 1921.

His first book, *Songs of Childhood*, appeared under the pseudonym Walter Ramal. Later works include poetry for adults (*The Listeners* 1912 and *Collected Poems* 1942), anthologies (*Come Hither* 1923 and *Behold this Dreamer* 1939), and short stories.

Delane /dəˈleɪn/ John Thadeus 1817–1879. British journalist. As editor of *The Times* 1841–77, he gave the newspaper international standing. He pioneered the first newspaper war reports.

de la Ramée /də lɑː ˈrɑːmeɪ/ Louise British novelist who wrote under the name of →Ouida.

de la Roche /ˌdeləˈrɒʃ/ Mazo 1885–1961. Canadian novelist, author of the 'Whiteoaks' family saga.

Delaroche /ˌdeləˈrɒʃ/ Paul 1797–1856. French historical artist. His melodramatic, often sentimental, historical paintings achieved great contemporary popularity; an example is *Lady Jane Grey* 1833 (National Gallery, London).

Delaunay /dəˌləʊˈneɪ/ Robert 1885–1941. French painter, a pioneer in abstract art. With his wife Sonia Delaunay-Terk, he invented Orphism, an early variation on Cubism, focusing on the effects of pure colour.

In 1912 he painted several series, notably *Circular Forms* (almost purely abstract) and *Windows* (inspired by Parisian cityscapes).

Delaunay-Terk /dəˌləʊneɪˈteək/ Sonia 1885–1979. French painter and textile designer born in Russia, active in Paris from 1905. With her husband Robert Delaunay, she was a pioneer of abstract art.

De Laurentiis /deɪ lɔːˈrentɪs/ Dino 1919– . Italian producer. His early films, including Fellini's *La strada*/*The Street* 1954, brought more acclaim than later epics such as *Waterloo* 1970. He then produced a series of Hollywood films: *Death Wish* 1974, *King Kong* (remake) 1976, and *Dune* 1984.

de la Warr /ˈdeləweə/ Thomas West, Baron de la Warr 1577–1618. US colonial administrator, known as Delaware. Appointed governor of Virginia 1609, he arrived 1610 just in time to prevent the desertion of the Jamestown colonists, and by 1611 had revitalized the settlement. He fell ill, returned to England, and died during his return voyage to the colony 1618. Both the river and state are named after him.

Delbruck /ˈdelbrʊk/ Max 1906–1981. German-born US biologist who pioneered techniques in molecular biology, studying genetic changes occurring when viruses invade bacteria. He was awarded the Nobel Prize for Medicine 1969 which he shared with Salvador Luria (1912–1951) and Alfred Hershey (1908–   ).

Delcassé /ˌdelkæˈseɪ/ Théophile 1852–1923. French politician. He became foreign minister 1898, but had to resign 1905 because of German hostility; he held that post again 1914–15. To a large extent he was responsible for the Entente Cordiale 1904 with Britain, recognizing British interests in Egypt and French interests in Morocco.

de Lesseps /də leˈseps/ Ferdinand, Vicomte. French engineer; see de →Lesseps.

Delibes /dəˈliːb/ (Clément Philibert) Léo 1836–1891. French composer. His lightweight, perfectly judged works include the ballet *Coppélia* 1870, *Sylvia* 1876, and the opera *Lakmé* 1883.

Delius /ˈdiːliəs/ Frederick (Theodore Albert) 1862–1934. English composer. His works include the opera *A Village Romeo and Juliet* 1901; the choral pieces *Appalachia* 1903, *Sea Drift* 1904, *A Mass of Life* 1905; orchestral works such as *In a Summer Garden* 1908, *A Song of the High Hills* 1911; chamber music; and songs.

Born in Bradford, he tried orange-growing in Florida, before studying music in Leipzig 1888, where he met Grieg. From 1890 Delius lived mainly in France and in 1903 married the artist Jelka Rosen. Although blind and paralysed for the last ten years of his life, he continued to compose.

Dell /del/ Ethel M(ary) 1881–1939. British writer of romantic fiction. Her commercially successful novels usually included a hero who was ugly: *Way of an Eagle* 1912, *The Keeper of the Door* 1915, and *Storm Drift* 1930.

della Robbia Italian family of artists; see →Robbia, della.

Deller /ˈdelə/ Alfred 1912–1979. English singer who popularized the countertenor voice. He founded the Deller Consort 1950, a group that performed 16th- to 18th-century music.

Delon /dəˈlɒn/ Alain 1935–   . French actor who appeared in the films *Purple Noon* 1960, *Rocco e i suoi fratelli/Rocco and His Brothers* 1960, *Il gattopardo/The Leopard* 1963, *Texas Across the River* 1966, *Scorpio* 1972, and *Swann in Love* 1984.

Delors /dəˈlɔː/ Jacques 1925–   . French socialist politician, finance minister 1981–84. As president of the European Commission from 1984 he has overseen significant budgetary reform and the move towards a free European Community market in 1992, with increased powers residing in Brussels.

Delors, the son of a Paris banker, worked as social-affairs adviser to Prime Minister Jacques Chaban-Delmas 1969–72 before joining the Socialist Party 1973. He served as minister of economy and finance (and, later, budget) in the administration of President Mitterrand 1981–84, overseeing an austerity programme ('*rigueur*') from June 1982. Having been passed over for the post of prime minister, Delors left to become president of the European Commission. He accepted the extension of his term for another two years June 1992 despite problems over the ratification of the Maastricht Treaty. During bilateral US/EC talks in Brussels Oct 1992 aimed at concluding the Uruguay round of General Agreement on Tariffs and Trade (GATT) talks, he was criticized for putting his country's and his own interests before those of the world economy at large.

del Sarto /del ˈsɑːtəʊ/ Andrea 1486–1531. Italian Renaissance painter; see →Andrea del Sarto.

de Maiziere /dəˌmezˈjeə/ Lothar 1940–   . German politician, leader 1989–90 of the conservative Christian Democratic Union in East Germany. He became premier after East Germany's first democratic election April 1990 and negotiated the country's reunion with West Germany. In Dec 1990 he resigned from Chancellor Kohl's cabinet and as deputy leader of the CDU, following allegations that he had been an informer to the Stasi (East German secret police). In Sept 1991, he resigned as deputy chairman of the CDU and from the legislature, effectively leaving active politics.

His departure followed criticisms that he had not done enough to promote reform in the East. Shortly after his resignation, the press published allegations that, for at least a year, the western CDU had been actively working to discredit de Maiziere. Known as the 'CDU affair', the scandal threatened to embroil Chancellor Kohl.

Demetrius /dɪˈmitriəs/ Donskoi ('of the Don') 1350–1389. Grand prince of Moscow from 1363. In 1380 he achieved the first Russian victory over the Tatars on the plain of Kulikovo, next to the river Don (hence his nickname).

De Mille /də ˈmɪl/ Agnes 1905–1989. US dancer and choreographer. One of the most significant contributors to the American Ballet Theater with dramatic ballets like *Fall River Legend* 1948, she also led the change on Broadway to new-style musicals with her choreography of *Oklahoma!* 1943, *Carousel* 1945, and others.

De Mille studied ballet with Marie Rambert in the UK, dancing in ballets and musicals in Europe before making her debut as a choreographer in the USA.

De Mille /də ˈmɪl/ Cecil B(lount) 1881–1959. US film director and producer. He entered films 1913 with Jesse L Lasky (with whom he later established Paramount Pictures), and was one of the founders of Hollywood. He specialized in biblical epics, such as *The Sign of the Cross* 1932 and *The Ten Commandments* 1923; remade 1956. He also made the 1952 Academy-Award-winning *The Greatest Show on Earth*.

Demirel /ˌdemɪˈrel/ Suleyman 1924– . Turkish politician. Leader from 1964 of the Justice Party, he was prime minister 1965–71, 1975–77, and 1979–80. He favoured links with the West, full membership in the European Community, and foreign investment in Turkish industry.

De Mita /deˈmiːtə/ Luigi Ciriaco 1928– . Italian conservative politician, leader of the Christian Democratic Party (DC) from 1982, prime minister 1988–90. He entered the Chamber of Deputies 1963 and held a number of ministerial posts in the 1970s before becoming DC secretary general.

Democritus /dɪˈmɒkrɪtəs/ c. 460–361 BC. Greek philosopher and speculative scientist who made a significant contribution to metaphysics with his atomic theory of the universe: all things originate from a vortex of atoms and differ according to the shape and arrangement of their atoms.

His concepts come to us through Aristotle's work in this area. His discussion of the constant motion of atoms to explain the origins of the universe was the most scientific theory proposed in his time.

de Morgan William Frend 1839–1917. English pottery designer. He set up his own factory 1888 in Fulham, London, producing tiles and pottery painted with flora and fauna in a style typical of the Arts and Crafts movement.

Inspired by William →Morris and Edward →Burne-Jones, he started designing tiles and glass for Morris's Merton Abbey factory. His work was influenced by Persian and Italian styles – he spent many months in Italy in later years – and he also developed lustre techniques (a way of covering pottery with an iridescent metallic surface).

Demosthenes /dɪˈmɒsθəniːz/ c. 384–322 BC. Athenian orator and politician. From 351 BC he led the party that advocated resistance to the growing power of →Philip of Macedon and in his *Philippics* incited the Athenians to war. This policy resulted in the defeat of Chaeronea 338, and the establishment of Macedonian supremacy. After the death of Alexander he organized a revolt; when it failed, he took poison to avoid capture by the Macedonians.

Dempsey /ˈdempsi/ Jack (William Harrison) 1895–1983. US heavyweight boxing champion, nicknamed 'the Manassa Mauler'. He beat Jess Willard 1919 to win the title and held it until 1926, when he lost it to Gene Tunney. He engaged in the 'Battle of the Long Count' with Tunney 1927.

Honey, I just forgot to duck.

> **Jack Dempsey** to his wife after losing
> world heavyweight title Sept 1926

Dench /dentʃ/ Judi (Judith Olivia) 1934– . English actress who made her professional debut as Ophelia in *Hamlet* 1957 with the Old Vic Company. Her Shakespearean roles include Viola in *Twelfth Night* 1969, Lady Macbeth 1976, and Cleopatra 1987. She is also a versatile comedy actress and has directed *Much Ado about Nothing* 1988 and John Osborne's *Look Back in Anger* 1989 for the Renaissance Theatre Company.

Her films include *Wetherby* 1985, *A Room with a View* 1986, and *A Handful of Dust* 1988.

Deneuve /dəˈnɜːv/ Catherine 1943– . French actress acclaimed for her poise and her performance in Roman Polanski's film *Repulsion* 1965. She also appeared in *Les Parapluies de Cherbourg/Umbrellas of Cherbourg* 1964 (with her sister Françoise Dorléac (1942–1967)), *Belle de jour* 1967, *Hustle* 1975, *Le Dernier métro/The Last Metro* 1980 and *The Hunger* 1983.

Deng Xiaoping /dʌŋ ʃaʊˈpɪŋ/ or *Teng Hsiao-ping* 1904– . Chinese political leader. A member of the Chinese Communist Party (CCP) from the 1920s, he took part in the Long March 1934–36. He was in the Politburo from 1955 until ousted in the Cultural Revolution 1966–69. Reinstated in the 1970s, he gradually took power and introduced a radical economic modernization programme. He retired from the Politburo 1987 and from his last official position (as chair of State Military Commission) March 1990, but remained influential behind the scenes.

Deng, born in Sichuan province into a middle-class landlord family, joined the CCP as a student in Paris, where he adopted the name Xiaoping ('Little Peace') 1925, and studied in Moscow 1926. After the Long March, he served as a political commissar to the People's Liberation Army during the civil war of 1937–49. He entered the CCP Politburo 1955 and headed the secretariat during the early 1960s, working closely with President Liu Shaoqi. During the Cultural Revolution Deng was dismissed as a 'capitalist roader' and sent to work in a tractor factory in Nanchang for 're-education'.

Deng was rehabilitated by his patron Zhou Enlai 1973 and served as acting prime minister after Zhou's heart attack 1974. On Zhou's death Jan 1976 he was forced into hiding but returned to office as vice premier July 1977. By Dec 1978, although nominally a CCP vice chair, state vice premier, and Chief of Staff to the PLA, Deng was the controlling force in China. His policy of 'socialism with Chinese characteristics', misinterpreted in the West as a drift to capitalism, had success in rural areas. He helped to oust →Hua Guofeng in favour of his protégés →Hu Yaobang (later in turn ousted) and →Zhao Ziyang.

When Deng officially retired from his party and army posts, he claimed to have renounced political involvement. His reputation, both at home and in the West, was tarnished by his sanctioning of the army's massacre of more than 2,000 prodemocracy demonstrators in Tiananmen Square, Beijing, in June 1989.

Denikin /dɪˈniːkɪn/ Anton Ivanovich 1872–1947. Russian general. He distinguished himself in the Russo-Japanese War 1904–05 and World War I. After the outbreak of the Bolshevik Revolution 1917 he organized a volunteer army of 60,000 Whites (loyalists) but was routed 1919 and escaped to France. He wrote a history of the Revolution and the Civil War.

De Niro /də ˈnɪərəʊ/ Robert 1943– . US actor. He won Oscars for his performances in *The Godfather Part II* 1974 and *Raging Bull* 1979, for which role he put on weight in the interests of authenticity as the boxer gone to seed, Jake LaMotta. His other films include *Mean Streets* 1973, *Taxi Driver* 1976, *The Deer Hunter* 1978, *The Untouchables* 1987, *Midnight Run* 1988, and *Cape Fear* 1992. He showed his versatility in *The King of Comedy* 1982 and other Martin Scorsese vehicles.

Denis, St /ˈdenɪs/ 3rd century AD. First bishop of Paris and one of the patron saints of France who was martyred by the Romans. Feast day 9 Oct.

St Denis is often confused with Dionysius the Areopagite, as well as with the original martyr of the 1st century AD. According to legend, he was sent as a missionary to Gaul in 250, and was beheaded several years later at what is today Montmartre in Paris, during the reign of Emperor Valerian. He is often represented as carrying his head in his hands.

Denktaş /ˈdeŋktæʃ/ Rauf R 1924– . Turkish-Cypriot nationalist politician. In 1975 the Turkish Federated State of Cyprus (TFSC) was formed in the northern third of the island, with Denktaş as its head, and in 1983 he became president of the breakaway Turkish Republic of Northern Cyprus (TRNC).

Denktaş held law-officer posts under the British crown before independence in 1960. Relations between the Greek and Turkish communities progressively deteriorated, leading to the formation of the TFSC. In 1983 the TRNC, with Denktaş as its president, was formally constituted, but recognized internationally only by Turkey.

The accession of the independent politician Georgios Vassilou to the Cyprus presidency offered hopes of reconciliation, but meetings between him and Denktaş during 1989, under UN auspices, failed to produce an agreement. The talks resumed 1992.

Denning /ˈdenɪŋ/ Alfred Thompson, Baron Denning of Whitchurch 1899– . British judge, Master of the Rolls 1962–82. In 1963 he conducted the inquiry into the →Profumo scandal. A vigorous and highly innovative civil lawyer, he was controversial in his defence of the rights of the individual against the state, the unions, and big business.

De Palma /dəˈpɑːlmə/ Brian 1941– . US film director, especially of thrillers. His technical mastery and enthusiasm for spilling blood are shown in films such as *Sisters* 1973, *Carrie* 1976, and *The Untouchables* 1987.

Depardieu /dəˈpɑːdjɜː/ Gérard 1948– . French actor renowned for his imposing physique and screen presence. His films include *Deux hommes dans la ville* 1973, *Le camion* 1977, *Mon oncle d'Amérique* 1980, *The Moon in the Gutter* 1983, *Jean de Florette* 1985, and *Cyrano de Bergerac* 1990. His English-speaking films include the US romantic comedy *Green Card* 1990 and *1492 – Conquest of Paradise* 1992.

De Quincey /də ˈkwɪnsi/ Thomas 1785–1859. English author whose works include *Confessions of an English Opium-Eater* 1821 and the essays 'On the Knocking at the Gate in Macbeth' 1823 and 'On Murder Considered as One of the Fine Arts' 1827. He was a friend of the poets Wordsworth and Coleridge.

Born in Manchester, De Quincey ran away from school there to wander and study in Wales. He then went to London, where he lived in extreme poverty but with the constant companionship of the young orphan Ann, of whom he writes in the *Confessions*. In 1803 he was reconciled to his guardians and was sent to university at Oxford, where his opium habit began. In 1809 he settled with the Wordsworths and Coleridge in the Lake District. He moved to Edinburgh 1828, where he eventually died. De Quincey's work had a powerful influence on Charles →Baudelaire and Edgar Allan →Poe among others.

De Quincey English author Thomas De Quincey wrote voluminously, but published little, and most of his literary output consisted of magazine articles. Confessions of an English Opium-Eater, *his most famous work, appeared as a serial in* The London Magazine.

Derain /dəˈræn/ André 1880–1954. French painter. He experimented with the strong, almost primary colours associated with Fauvism but later developed a more sombre landscape style. His work includes costumes and scenery for Diaghilev's Ballets Russes.

Derby /ˈdɑːbi/ Edward (George Geoffrey Smith) Stanley, 14th Earl of Derby 1799–1869. British politician, prime minister 1852, 1858–59, and 1866–68. Originally a Whig, he became secretary for the colonies 1830, and introduced the bill for the abolition of slavery. He joined the Tories 1834, and the split in the Tory Party over Robert Peel's free-trade policy gave Derby the leadership for 20 years.

Derby /ˈdɑːbi/ Edward George Villiers Stanley, 17th Earl of Derby 1865–1948. British Conservative politician, member of Parliament from 1892. He was secretary of war 1916–18 and 1922–24, and ambassador to France 1918–20.

De Roburt /dəˈrɒbət/ Hammer 1923–1992. President of Nauru 1968–76, 1978–83, 1987–89. During the country's occupation 1942–45, he was deported to Japan. He became head chief of Nauru 1956 and was elected the country's first president 1968. He secured only a narrow majority in the 1987 elections and in 1989 was ousted on a no-confidence motion.

Desai /deˈsaɪ/ Morarji 1896– . Indian politician. An early follower of Mahatma Gandhi, he was prime minister 1977–79, as leader of the Janata party, after toppling Indira Gandhi. Party infighting led to his resignation of both the premiership and the party leadership.

De Savary /də ˈsævəri/ Peter 1944– . British entrepreneur. He acquired Land's End, Cornwall, England, 1987 and built a theme park there. He revived Falmouth dock and the port of Hayle in N Cornwall.

A yachting enthusiast, he sponsored the Blue Arrow America's Cup challenge team.

Descartes /deɪˈkɑːt/ René 1596–1650. French philosopher and mathematician. He believed that commonly accepted knowledge was doubtful because of the subjective nature of the senses, and attempted to rebuild human knowledge using as his foundation *cogito ergo sum* ('I think, therefore I am'). He also believed that the entire material universe could be explained in terms of mathematical physics, and founded coordinate geometry as a way of defining and manipulating geometrical shapes by means of algebraic expressions. Cartesian coordinates, the means by which points are represented in this system, are named after him. Descartes also established the science of optics, and helped to shape contemporary theories of astronomy and animal behaviour.

Born near Tours, Descartes served in the army of Prince Maurice of Orange, and in 1619, while travelling through Europe, decided to apply the methods of mathematics to metaphysics and sci-

ence. He settled in the Netherlands 1628, where he was more likely to be free from interference by the ecclesiastical authorities. In 1649 he visited the court of Queen Christina of Sweden, and shortly thereafter he died in Stockholm.

His works include *Discourse on Method* 1637, *Meditations on the First Philosophy* 1641, and *Principles of Philosophy* 1644, and numerous books on physiology, optics, and geometry.

The greatest spirits are capable of the greatest vices as well as of the greatest virtues.

René Descartes *Discourse on Method* 1637

Deschamps /deɪˈʃɒm/ Eustache 1346–1406. French poet, born in Champagne. He was the author of more than 1,000 ballades, and the *Miroir de mariage/The Mirror of Marriage*, an attack on women.

De Sica /deɪ ˈsiːkə/ Vittorio 1902–1974. Italian director and actor. He won his first Oscar in *Bicycle Thieves* 1948, a film of subtle realism. Later films included *Umberto D* 1952, *Two Women* 1960, and *The Garden of the Finzi-Continis* 1971. His considerable acting credits include *Madame de ...* 1953 and *The Millionaires* 1960.

Desmoulins /ˌdeɪmuːˈlæn/ Camille 1760–1794. French revolutionary who summoned the mob to arms on 12 July 1789, so precipitating the revolt that culminated in the storming of the Bastille. A prominent left-wing Jacobin, he was elected to the National Convention 1792. His *Histoire des Brissotins* was largely responsible for the overthrow of the right-wing Girondins, but shortly after he was sent to the guillotine as too moderate.

A dead king is not a man less.

Camille Desmoulins
voting for the death of Louis XVI

---

de Soto /də ˈsəʊtəʊ/ Hernando c. 1496–1542. Spanish explorer who sailed with d'Avila (c. 1400–1531) to Darien, Central America, 1519, explored the Yucatán Peninsula 1528, and travelled with Francisco Pizarro in Peru 1530–35. In 1538 he was made governor of Cuba and Florida. In his expedition of 1539, he explored Florida, Georgia, and the Mississippi River.

Desprez /deɪˈpreɪ/ Josquin. Franco-Flemish composer; see →Josquin Desprez.

Dessalines /ˌdesæˈliːn/ Jean Jacques c. 1758–1806. Emperor of Haiti 1804–06. Born in Guinea, he was taken to Haiti as a slave, where in 1802 he succeeded →Toussaint L'Ouverture as leader of the black revolt against the French. After defeating the French, he proclaimed Haiti's independence and made himself emperor. He was killed when trying to suppress an uprising provoked by his cruelty.

Dessau /desaʊ/ Paul 1894–1979. German composer. His work includes incidental music to Bertolt Brecht's theatre pieces; an opera, *Der Verurteilung des Lukullus* 1949, also to a libretto by Brecht; and numerous choral works and songs.

He studied in Berlin, becoming a theatre conductor until moving to Paris 1933, where he studied Schoenberg's serial method with René Leibowitz. He collaborated with Brecht from 1942, when they met as political exiles in the USA, returning with him to East Berlin 1948.

de Tocqueville Alexis. French politician; see →Tocqueville, Alexis de.

Dev Kapil 1959– . Indian cricketer who is one of the world's outstanding all-rounders. At the age of 20 he became the youngest player to complete the 'double' of 1,000 runs and 100 wickets in test cricket. In 1992 he followed Richard Hadlee as the second bowler to reach 400 wickets in test matches.

de Valera /də vəˈleərə/ Eámon 1882–1975. Irish nationalist politician, prime minister of the Irish Free State/Eire/Republic of Ireland 1932–48, 1951–54, and 1957–59, and president 1959–73. Repeatedly imprisoned, he participated in the Easter Rising 1916 and was leader of the nationalist Sinn Féin party 1917–26, when he formed the republican Fianna Fáil party; he directed negotiations with Britain 1921 but refused to accept the partition of Ireland until 1937.

De Valera was born in New York, the son of a Spanish father and an Irish mother, and sent to Ireland as a child, where he became a teacher of mathematics. He was sentenced to death for his part in the Easter Rising, but the sentence was commuted, and he was released under an amnesty 1917. In the same year he was elected member of Parliament for E Clare, and president of Sinn Féin. He was rearrested May 1918, but escaped to the USA 1919. He returned to Ireland 1920 and directed the struggle against the British government from a hiding place in Dublin. He authorized the negotiations of 1921, but refused to accept the ensuing treaty which divided Ireland into the Free State and the North.

Civil war followed. De Valera was arrested by the Free State government 1923, and spent a year in prison. In 1926 he formed a new party, Fianna Fáil, which secured a majority in 1932. De Valera became prime minister and foreign minister of the Free State, and at once abolished the oath of allegiance and suspended payment of the annuities due under the Land Purchase Acts. In 1938 he negotiated an agreement with Britain, under which all outstanding points were settled. Throughout World War II he maintained a strict neutrality, rejecting an offer by Winston Churchill

1940 to recognize the principle of a united Ireland in return for Eire's entry into the war. He resigned after his defeat at the 1948 elections but was again prime minister in the 1950s, and then president of the republic.

de Valois /də ˈvælwɑː/ Ninette. Stage name of Edris Stannus 1898– . Irish dancer, choreographer, and teacher. A pioneer of British national ballet, she worked with Sergei Diaghilev in Paris before opening a dance academy in London 1926. Collaborating with Lilian Baylis at the Old Vic, she founded the Vic-Wells Ballet 1931, which later became the Royal Ballet and Royal Ballet School. Among her works are *Job* 1931 and *Checkmate* 1937.

Devlin Patrick, Baron of West Wick 1905–1992. British judge, a distinguished jurist and commentator on the English legal system. He was justice of the High Court in the Queen's Bench Division 1948–60, Lord Justice of Appeal 1960–61, and Lord of Appeal in Ordinary 1961–64.

Devonshire /devənʃə/ William Cavendish, 7th Duke of Devonshire 1808–1891. British aristocrat whose development of Eastbourne, Sussex, England, was an early example of town planning.

Devonshire, 8th Duke of see →Hartington, Spencer Compton Cavendish, British politician.

De Vries /friːs/ Hugo 1848–1935. Dutch botanist who conducted important research on osmosis in plant cells and was a pioneer in the study of plant evolution. His work led to the rediscovery of →Mendel's laws and the discovery of spontaneously occurring mutations.

Dewar /djuːə/ James 1842–1923. Scottish chemist and physicist who invented the vacuum flask (Thermos) 1872 during his research into the properties of matter at extremely low temperatures.

de Wet /də ˈvet/ Christiaan Rudolf 1854–1922. Boer general and politician. He served in the South African Wars 1880 and 1899. When World War I began, he headed a pro-German rising of 12,000 Afrikaners but was defeated, convicted of treason, and imprisoned. He was sentenced to six years' imprisonment for his part in the uprising, but was released 1915.

Dewey /djuːi/ George 1837–1917. US naval officer. He was appointed chief of the Bureau of Equipment 1889 and of the Board of Inspection and Survey 1895. As commodore, Dewey was dispatched to the Pacific 1896. He destroyed the Spanish fleet in Manila harbour at the outbreak of the Spanish-American War 1898. Dewey was promoted to the rank of admiral of the navy (the highest naval rank ever awarded) 1899. He retired from active service 1900.

Born in Montpelier, Vermont, and educated at the US Naval Academy, Dewey saw action on the Mississippi River and in the blockade of Southern ports during the American Civil War 1861–65.

Diana, Princess of Wales Portrait of Diana, Princess of Wales, by Bryan Organ (1981) National Portrait Gallery, London. A popular royal figure both at home and abroad, the Princess is noted for her charitable work and concern with AIDS patients, and children. Her separation from Prince Charles, heir to the British throne, became the source of extensive, relentless, and damaging media coverage.

Dewey /ˈdjuːi/ John 1859–1952. US philosopher who believed that the exigencies of a democratic and industrial society demanded new educational techniques. He expounded his ideas in numerous writings, including *School and Society* 1899, and founded a progressive school in Chicago. A pragmatist thinker, influenced by William James, Dewey maintained that there is only the reality of experience and made 'inquiry' the essence of logic.

Dewey /ˈdjuːi/ Melvil 1851–1931. US librarian. In 1876, he devised the Dewey decimal system of classification for accessing, storing, and retrieving books, widely used in libraries. The system uses the numbers 000 to 999 to designate the major fields of knowledge, then breaks these down into more specific subjects by the use of decimals.

Dewey /ˈdjuːi/ Thomas Edmund 1902–1971. US public official. He was Manhattan district attorney 1937–38 and served as governor of New York 1942–54. Dewey was twice the Republican presidential candidate, losing to F D Roosevelt 1944 and to Truman 1948, the latter race being one of the greatest electoral upsets in US history.

Born in Owosso, Michigan, USA, Dewey received a law degree from Columbia University 1925. He was appointed chief assistant to the US attorney in the Southern District of New York 1931. He gained a reputation as a crime fighter while serving as special investigator of organized crime 1935–37.

de Wint /də ˈwɪnt/ Peter 1784–1849. English landscape painter, of Dutch descent. He was a notable watercolourist.

Diaghilev /diˈægələf/ Sergei Pavlovich 1872–1929. Russian ballet impresario who in 1909 founded the Ballets Russes/Russian Ballet (headquarters in Monaco), which he directed for 20 years. Through this company he brought Russian ballet to the West, introducing and encouraging a dazzling array of dancers, choreographers, and composers, such as Anna Pavlova, Vaslav Nijinsky, Mikhail Fokine, Léonide Massine, George Balanchine, Igor Stravinsky, and Sergey Prokofiev.

Diana /daɪˈænə/ Princess of Wales 1961– . The daughter of the 8th Earl Spencer, she married Prince Charles in St Paul's Cathedral, London 1981, the first English bride of a royal heir since 1659. She is descended from the only sovereigns from whom Prince Charles is not descended, Charles II and James II.

If men had to have babies they would only ever have one each.

Diana, Princess of Wales *Observer* 1984

Diaz /ˈdiːæʃ/ Bartolomeu *c.* 1450–1500. Portuguese explorer, the first European to reach the Cape of Good Hope 1488, and to establish a route around Africa. He drowned during an expedition with Pedro →Cabral.

Díaz Porfirio 1830–1915. Dictator of Mexico 1877–80 and 1884–1911. After losing the 1876 election, he overthrew the government and seized power. He was supported by conservative landowners and foreign capitalists, who invested in railways and mines. He centralized the state at the expense of the peasants and Indians, and dismantled all local and regional leadership. He faced mounting and revolutionary opposition in his final years and was forced into exile 1911.

Diaz de Solís /ˈdiːæs deɪ ˈsəʊlɪs/ Juan 1471–*c.* 1516. Spanish explorer in South America who reached the estuary of the Río de la Plata, and was killed and reputedly eaten by cannibals.

Dick /dɪk/ Philip K(endred) 1928–1982. US science-fiction writer whose works often deal with religion and the subjectivity of reality; his novels include *The Man in the High Castle* 1962 and *Do Androids Dream of Electric Sheep?* 1968.

Dickens /ˈdɪkɪnz/ Charles 1812–1870. English novelist, popular for his memorable characters and his portrayal of the social evils of Victorian

England. In 1836 he published the first number of the *Pickwick Papers*, followed by *Oliver Twist* 1838, the first of his 'reforming' novels; *Nicholas Nickleby* 1839; *Barnaby Rudge* 1840; *The Old Curiosity Shop* 1841; and *David Copperfield* 1849. Among his later books are *A Tale of Two Cities* 1859 and *Great Expectations* 1861.

Born in Portsea, Hampshire, the son of a clerk, Dickens received little formal education, although a short period spent working in a blacking factory in S London, while his father was imprisoned for debt in the Marshalsea prison during 1824, was followed by three years in a private school. In 1827 he became a lawyer's clerk, and then after four years a reporter for the *Morning Chronicle*, to which he contributed the *Sketches by Boz*. In 1836 he married Catherine Hogarth, three days after the publication of the first number of the *Pickwick Papers*. Originally intended merely as an accompaniment to a series of sporting illustrations, the adventures of Pickwick outgrew their setting and established Dickens's reputation.

In 1842 he visited the USA, where his attack on the pirating of English books by American publishers chilled his welcome; his experiences are reflected in *American Notes* and *Martin Chuzzlewit* 1843. In 1843 he published the first of his Christmas books, *A Christmas Carol*, followed 1844 by *The Chimes*, written in Genoa during his first long sojourn abroad, and in 1845 by the even more successful *Cricket on the Hearth*. A venture as editor of the Liberal *Daily News* 1846 was short-lived, and *Dombey and Son* 1848 was largely written abroad. *David Copperfield*, his most popular novel, appeared 1849 and contains many autobiographical incidents and characters.

Returning to journalism, Dickens inaugurated the weekly magazine *Household Words* 1850, reorganizing it 1859 as *All the Year Round*; many of his later stories were published serially in these periodicals.

In 1857 Dickens met the actress Ellen Ternan and in 1858 agreed with his wife on a separation; his sister-in-law remained with him to care for his children. In 1858 he began giving public readings from his novels, which proved such a success that he was invited to make a second US tour 1867. Among his later novels are *Bleak House* 1853, *Hard Times* 1854, *Little Dorrit* 1857, and *Our Mutual Friend* 1864. *Edwin Drood*, a mystery story influenced by the style of his friend Wilkie →Collins, was left incomplete on his death.

Dickens /ˈdɪkɪnz/ Monica (Enid) 1915–1992. British writer. Her first books were humorous accounts of her experiences in various jobs, beginning as a cook (*One Pair of Hands* 1939); she went on to become a novelist. She is a great-great-granddaughter of Charles Dickens.

Dickinson /ˈdɪkɪnsən/ Emily 1830–1886. US poet. Born in Amherst, Massachusetts, she lived in near seclusion there from 1862. Very few of her many short, mystical poems were published during her lifetime, and her work became well known only in the 20th century.

Dick-Read /dɪk ˈriːd/ Grantly 1890–1959. British gynaecologist. In private practice in London 1923–48, he developed the concept of natural childbirth: that by the elimination of fear and tension, labour pain could be minimized and anaesthetics, which can be hazardous to both mother and child, rendered unnecessary.

Diderot /ˈdiːdərəʊ/ Denis 1713–1784. French philosopher. He is closely associated with the Enlightenment, the European intellectual movement for social and scientific progress, and was editor of the enormously influential *Encyclopédie* 1751–80.

An expanded and politicized version of the English encyclopedia 1728 of Ephraim Chambers (*c.* 1680–1740), this work exerted an enormous influence on contemporary social thinking with its materialism and anticlericalism. Its compilers were known as *Encyclopédistes*.

Diderot's materialism, most articulately expressed in *D'Alembert's Dream*, published after Diderot's death, sees the natural world as nothing more than matter and motion. His account of the origin and development of life is purely mechanical.

Didion Joan 1934– . US novelist and journalist. Her sharp, culturally evocative writing includes the novel *A Book of Common Prayer* 1970 and the essays of *The White Album* 1979.

Diefenbaker /ˈdiːfənˌbeɪkə/ John George 1895–1979. Canadian Progressive Conservative politician, prime minister 1957–63; he was defeated after criticism of the proposed manufacture of nuclear weapons in Canada.

Diefenbaker was born in Ontario, and moved to Saskatchewan. A brilliant defence counsel, he became known as the 'prairie lawyer'. He became leader of his party 1956 and prime minister 1957. In 1958 he achieved the greatest landslide in Canadian history. A 'radical' Tory, he was also a strong supporter of Commonwealth unity. He resigned the party leadership 1967, repudiating a 'two nations' policy for Canada. He was known as 'the Chief'.

Diels /diːls/ Otto 1876–1954. German chemist. In 1950 he and his former assistant, Kurt Alder (1902–1958), were jointly awarded the Nobel Prize for Chemistry for their research into the synthesis of organic chemical compounds.

Diemen /ˈdiːmən/ Anthony van 1593–1645. Dutch admiral. In 1636 he was appointed governor general of Dutch settlements in the E Indies, and wrested Ceylon and Malacca from the Portuguese. In 1636 and 1642 he supervised expeditions to Australia, on the second of which the navigator Abel Tasman discovered land not charted by Europeans and named it *Van Diemen's Land*, now Tasmania.

Dietrich German-born US film actress and cabaret performer Marlene Dietrich whose enigmatic, sexually alluring mystique, became legendary. During World War II Dietrich entertained US troops and made fundraising appearances and propaganda broadcasts in German, for which she was awarded the US Medal of Freedom.

Diesel /ˈdiːzəl/ Rudolf 1858–1913. German engineer who patented the diesel engine. He began his career as a refrigerator engineer and, like many engineers of the period, sought to develop a more efficient power source than the conventional steam engine. Able to operate with greater efficiency and economy, the diesel engine soon found a ready market.

Dietrich /ˈdiːtrɪk/ Marlene (Maria Magdalene) 1904–1992. German-born US actress and singer who appeared with Emil Jannings in both the German and American versions of the film *The Blue Angel* 1930, directed by Josef von Sternberg. She stayed in Hollywood, becoming a US citizen 1937. Her husky, sultry singing voice added to her appeal. Her other films include *Blonde Venus* 1932, *Destry Rides Again* 1939, and *Just a Gigolo* 1978.

She also starred in *Judgment at Nuremberg* 1961 and was the subject of Maximilian Schell's documentary *Marlene* 1983.

The average man is more interested in a woman who is interested in him than he is in a woman – any woman – with beautiful legs.

Marlene Dietrich

Dilke /dɪlk/ Charles Wentworth 1843–1911. British Liberal politician, member of Parliament 1868–86 and 1892–1911. A Radical, he supported a minimum wage and legalization of trade unions.

Dillinger /ˈdɪlɪndʒə/ John 1903–1934. US bank robber and murderer. In 1923 he was convicted of armed robbery and spent the next ten years in state prison. Released in 1933, he led a gang on a robbery spree throughout the Midwest, staging daring raids on police stations to obtain guns. Named 'Public Enemy Number One' by the Federal Bureau of Investigation (FBI), Dillinger led the authorities on a long chase. He was finally betrayed by his mistress, the mysterious 'Lady in Red,' and was killed by FBI agents in Chicago as he left a cinema.

Dilthey /ˈdɪltaɪ/ Wilhelm 1833–1911. German philosopher, a major figure in the interpretive tradition of hermeneutics. He argued that the 'human sciences' (*Geisteswissenschaften*) could not employ the same methods as the natural sciences but must use the procedure of 'understanding' (*Verstehen*) to grasp the inner life of an alien culture or past historical period. Thus Dilthey extended the significance of hermeneutics far beyond the interpretation of texts to the whole of human history and culture.

DiMaggio Joe 1914– . US baseball player with the New York Yankees 1936–51. In 1941 he set a record by getting hits in 56 consecutive games. He was an outstanding fielder, played centre field, hit 361 home runs, and had a career average of .325. DiMaggio was married to the actress Marilyn Monroe. He was elected to the Baseball Hall of Fame in 1955.

Dimbleby /ˈdɪmbəlbi/ Richard 1913–1965. British broadcaster. He joined the BBC in 1936 and became the foremost commentator on royal and state events and current affairs on radio and television. He is commemorated by the *Dimbleby Lectures*.

Dimitrov /ˌdɪmɪˈtrɒf/ Georgi 1882–1949. Bulgarian communist, prime minister from 1946. He was elected a deputy in 1913 and from 1919 was a member of the executive of the Comintern, an international communist organization. In 1933 he was arrested in Berlin and tried with others in Leipzig for allegedly setting fire to the parliament building. Acquitted, he went to the USSR, where he became general secretary of the Comintern until its dissolution in 1943.

Dine /daɪn/ Jim 1935– . US Pop artist. He experimented with combinations of paintings and objects, such as a sink attached to a canvas.

Dine was a pioneer of happenings (art as live performance) in the 1950s and of environment art (three-dimensional works that attempt active interaction with the spectator, sometimes using sound or movement).

and two subordinate emperors, and in 303 initiated severe persecution of Christians.

Diogenes /daɪˈɒdʒəniːz/ *c.* 412–323 BC. Ascetic Greek philosopher of the Cynic school. He believed in freedom and self-sufficiency for the individual, and that the virtuous life was the simple life; he did not believe in social mores. His writings do not survive.

He was born at Sinope, captured by pirates, and sold as a slave to a Corinthian named Xeniades, who appointed Diogenes tutor to his two sons. He spent the rest of his life in Corinth. He is said to have carried a lamp during the daytime, looking for one honest man. The story of his having lived in a barrel arose when Seneca said that was where a man so crabbed ought to have lived.

Dion Cassius /daɪən ˈkæsiəs/ AD 150–235. Roman historian. He wrote, in Greek, a Roman history in 80 books (of which 26 survive), covering the period from the founding of the city to AD 229, including the only surviving account of the invasion of Britain by Claudius 43 BC.

Diophantus /ˌdaɪəʊˈfæntəs/ lived *c.* 250. Greek mathematician in Alexandria whose *Arithmetica* is one of the first known works on problem solving by algebra, in which both words and symbols were used.

Dior /diːˈɔː/ Christian 1905–1957. French couturier. He established his own Paris salon 1947 and made an impact with the 'New Look' – long, cinch-waisted, and full-skirted – after wartime austerity.

Diouf /diˈuːf/ Abdou 1935– . Senegalese left-wing politician, president from 1980. He became prime minister 1970 under President Leopold Senghor and, on his retirement, succeeded him, being re- elected in 1983 and 1988. His presidency has been characterized by authoritarianism.

Born in Louga in NW Senegal, Diouf studied at Paris University and was a civil servant before entering politics. He was chair of the Organization of African Unity 1985–86.

Dirac /dɪˈræk/ Paul Adrien Maurice 1902–1984. British physicist who worked out a version of quantum mechanics consistent with special relativity. The existence of the positron (positive electron) was one of its predictions. He shared the Nobel Prize for Physics 1933 with Austrian physicist Erwin Schrödinger (1887–1961).

Dirichlet /ˌdɪrɪˈkleɪ/ Peter Gustav Lejeune 1805–1859. German mathematician. His most important work was on the convergence of the Fourier series, which led him to the modern notion of a generalized function as represented in the form $f(x)$. He also made major contributions to number theory, producing *Dirichlet's theorem*: in every arithmetical sequence a, $a + d$, $a + 2d$, and so on, where a and d are relatively prime (that is, have no common divisors other than 1), there is an infinite number of prime numbers.

Dilke English politician Charles Dilke's progress to high office in Gladstone's government was reversed when he was cited as co-respondent in a divorce case. He subsequently organized members of the early Labour Party and wrote brilliantly on the subject of politics.

Dinesen /ˈdɪnɪsən/ Isak 1885–1962. Pen name of Danish writer Karen →Blixen, born Karen Christentze Dinesen.

Dingaan 1795–1962 Zulu chief who obtained the throne in 1828 by murdering his predecessor, Shaka, and became notorious for his cruelty. In warfare with the Boer immigrants into Natal he was defeated on 16 Dec 1838 - 'Dingaan's Day'. He escaped to Swaziland, where he was deposed by his brother Mpande and subsequently assassinated.

Ding Ling /ˈdɪŋ ˈlɪŋ/ 1904–1986. Chinese novelist. Her works include *Wei Hu* 1930 and *The Sun Shines over the Sanggan River* 1951.

She was imprisoned by the Guomindang (Chiang Kai-shek's nationalists) in the 1930s, wrongly labelled as rightist and expelled from the Communist Party 1957, imprisoned in the 1960s and intellectually ostracized for not keeping to Maoist literary rules; she was rehabilitated 1979. Her husband was the writer Hu Yapin, executed by Chiang Kai-shek's police 1931.

Dinkins /ˈdɪŋkɪnz/ David 1927– . Mayor of New York City from Jan 1990, a Democrat. He won a reputation as a moderate and consensual community politician and was Manhattan borough president before succeeding Edward I Koch to become New York's first black mayor.

Diocletian /ˌdaɪəˈkliːʃən/ Gaius Valerius Diocletianus AD 245–313. Roman emperor 284–305, when he abdicated in favour of Galerius. He reorganized and subdivided the empire, with two joint

Disch /dɪʃ/ Thomas M(ichael) 1940– . US writer and poet, author of such science-fiction novels as *Camp Concentration* 1968 and *334* 1972.

Disney /dɪzni/ Walt(er Elias) 1901–1966. US filmmaker and animator, a pioneer of family entertainment. He established his own studio in Hollywood 1923, and his first Mickey Mouse cartoons (*Plane Crazy*, which was silent, and *Steamboat Willie*, which had sound) appeared 1928. In addition to short cartoons, the studio made feature-length animated films, including *Snow White and the Seven Dwarfs* 1938, *Pinocchio* 1940, and *Dumbo* 1941. Disney's cartoon figures, for example Donald Duck, also appeared in comic books worldwide. In 1955, Disney opened the first theme park, Disneyland, in California.

Using the new medium of sound film, Disney developed the 'Silly Symphony', a type of cartoon based on the close association of music with visual images. He produced these in colour from 1932, culminating in the feature-length *Fantasia* 1940. The Disney studio also made nature-study films such as *The Living Desert* 1953, which have been criticized for their fictionalization of nature: wild animals were placed in unnatural situations to create 'drama'. Feature films with human casts were made from 1946, such as *The Swiss Family Robinson* 1960 and *Mary Poppins* 1964. Disney also produced the first television series in colour 1961.

I love Mickey Mouse more than any woman I've ever known.

Walt Disney

Disraeli /dɪz'reɪli/ Benjamin, Earl of Beaconsfield 1804–1881. British Conservative politician and novelist. Elected to Parliament 1837, he was chancellor of the Exchequer under Lord →Derby 1852, 1858–59, and 1866–68, and prime minister 1868 and 1874–80. His imperialist policies brought India directly under the crown, and he was personally responsible for purchasing control of the Suez Canal. The central Conservative Party organization is his creation. His popular, political novels reflect an interest in social reform and include *Coningsby* 1844 and *Sybil* 1845.

After a period in a solicitor's office, Disraeli wrote the novels *Vivian Grey* 1826, *Contarini Fleming* 1832, and others, and the pamphlet *Vindication of the English Constitution* 1835. Entering Parliament in 1837 after four unsuccessful attempts, he was laughed at as a dandy, but when his maiden speech was shouted down, he said: 'The time will come when you will hear me.'

Excluded from Peel's government of 1841–46, Disraeli formed his Young England group to keep a critical eye on Peel's Conservatism. Its ideas were expounded in the novel trilogy *Coningsby*, *Sybil*, and *Tancred* 1847. When Peel decided in 1846 to repeal the Corn Laws, Disraeli opposed the measure in a series of witty and effective speeches; Peel's government fell soon after, and Disraeli gradually came to be recognized as the leader of the Conservative Party in the Commons.

During the next 20 years the Conservatives formed short-lived minority governments in 1852, 1858–59, and 1866–68, with Lord Derby as prime minister and Disraeli as chancellor of the Exchequer and leader of the Commons. In 1852 Disraeli first proposed discrimination in income tax between earned and unearned income, but without success. The 1858–59 government legalized the admission of Jews to Parliament, and transferred the government of India from the East India Company to the crown. In 1866 the Conservatives took office after defeating a Liberal Reform Bill, and then attempted to secure the credit of widening the franchise by the Reform Bill of 1867. On Lord Derby's retirement in 1868 Disraeli became prime minister, but a few months later he was defeated by Gladstone in a general election. During the six years of opposition that followed he published another novel, *Lothair* 1870, and established Conservative Central Office, the prototype of modern party organizations.

In 1874 Disraeli took office for the second time, with a majority of 100. Some useful reform measures were carried, such as the Artisans' Dwelling Act, which empowered local authorities to undertake slum clearance, but the outstanding feature of the government's policy was its imperialism. It was Disraeli's personal initiative that purchased from the Khedive of Egypt a controlling interest in the Suez Canal, conferred on the Queen the title of Empress of India, and sent the Prince of Wales on the first royal tour of that country. He accepted an earldom 1876. The Bulgarian revolt of 1876 and the subsequent Russo-Turkish War of 1877–78 provoked one of many political duels between Disraeli and Gladstone, the Liberal leader, and was concluded by the Congress of Berlin 1878, where Disraeli was the principal British delegate and brought home 'peace with honour' and Cyprus. The government was defeated in 1880, and a year later Disraeli died.

D'Israeli /dɪz'reɪli/ Isaac 1766–1848. British scholar, father of Benjamin Disraeli and author of *Curiosities of Literature* 1791–93 and 1823.

Dix /dɪks/ Dorothea Lynde 1802–1887. US educator and medical reformer. From 1841 she devoted herself to a campaign for the rights of the mentally ill, helping to improve conditions and treatment in public institutions for the insane in the USA, Canada, and Japan. During the American Civil War 1861–65, she served as superintendent of nurses.

Born in Hampden, Maine, and raised in Boston, Dix began her career as a teacher at a girls' school in Worcester, Massachusetts, and opened her own school in Boston 1821. Forced by ill health to retire in 1835, she travelled in Europe and published several books.

Djilas /dʒiːləs/ Milovan 1911– . Yugoslav political writer and dissident. A former close wartime colleague of Marshal Tito, in 1953 he was dismissed from high office and subsequently imprisoned because of his advocacy of greater political pluralism. He was released 1966 and formally rehabilitated 1989.

Djilas was born in Montenegro and was a partisan during World War II. He rose to a senior position in Yugoslavia's postwar communist government before being ousted 1953. His writings, including the books *The New Class* 1957 and *The Undivided Society* 1969, were banned until May 1989.

The Party line is that there is no Party line.

Milovan Djilas
F Maclean *Disputed Barricade*

Dobell /dəʊ'bel/ William 1899–1970. Australian portraitist and genre painter, born in New South Wales. He studied art in the UK and the Netherlands 1929–39. His portrait of *Joshua Smith* 1943 (Sir Edward Hayward, Adelaide) provoked a court case (Dobell was accused of caricaturing his subject).

Döblin /dɜbliːn/ Alfred 1878–1957. German novelist. His *Berlin- Alexanderplatz* 1929 owes much to James Joyce in its minutely detailed depiction of the inner lives of a city's inhabitants, and is considered by many to be the finest 20th-century German novel. Other works include *November 1918: Eine deutsche Revolution/A German Revolution* 1939–50 (published in four parts) about the formation of the Weimar Republic.

Born in Stettin (modern Szczecin, Poland) to a Yiddish-speaking family, he grew up in Berlin where he practised as a doctor until 1933 when his books were banned and he was exiled; he moved first to France and from 1941 lived in the USA.

Dobrynin /də'briːnɪn/ Anataloy Fedorovich 1919– . Soviet diplomat, ambassador to the USA 1962–86, emerging during the 1970s as a warm supporter of détente.

Dobrynin joined the Soviet diplomatic service in 1941. He served as counsellor at the Soviet embassy in Washington DC 1952–55, assistant to the minister for foreign affairs 1955–57, under-secretary at the United Nations 1957–59, and head of the USSR's American department 1959–61, before being appointed Soviet ambassador to Washington in 1962. He remained at this post for 25 years. Brought back to Moscow by the new Soviet leader Mikhail Gorbachev, he was appointed to the Communist Party's Secretariat as head of the International Department, before retiring in 1988.

Dobzhansky /dɒb'ʒɑːnski/ Theodosius 1900–1975. US geneticist of Ukrainian origin. A pioneer of modern genetics and evolutionary theory, he showed that genetic variability between individuals of the same species is very high and that this diversity is vital to the process of evolution. His book *Genetics and the Origin of Species* was published in 1937.

Doc Pomus /pəʊməs/ (Jerome Solon Felder) 1925–1991. US pop-music songwriter who worked primarily in partnership with Mort Shuman (1936–). The team had its greatest successes in the early 1960s with hits for the Drifters ('Save the Last Dance for Me' 1960) and Elvis Presley ('Little Sister' and 'His Latest Flame' 1961). Fluent in a number of styles, they were innovators in none.

Pomus, born in New York, began as a blues singer in the style of Big Joe Turner, and made some recordings for Chess and other labels in he early 1950s. Through Turner, Pomus came in contact with Atlantic Records, who gave his composition 'Lonely Avenue' to Ray Charles in 1956. Soon afterwards he teamed up with Shuman. Their songs usually had a blues element but the lyrics were conventional and sentimental, and much of their material was written for prefabricated pop stars like Fabian ('I'm a Man' 1959). 'Teenager in Love' for Dion and the Belmonts 1959 capitalized successfully on the formula of Frankie Lymon's 1956 hit 'Why Do Fools Fall in Love'. Between 1960 and 1963 Pomus and Shuman were on contract to Atlantic's publishing arm. This was the age of the Brill Building, the New York Tin Pan Alley hit factory, where songwriters were employed by music-publishing firms to turn out songs custom-tailored to particular acts. (Another such team, Leiber and Stoller, wrote for some of the same artists, including the Drifters, and they cowrote 'She's Not You' 1962 for Presley with Pomus.) After an accident 1965, the team split up.

Doctorow /dɒktərəʊ/ E(dgar) L(awrence) 1931– . US novelist. Politically acute, artistically experimental, he is the author of the bestseller *Ragtime* 1975, set in the Jazz Age, *World's Fair* 1985, about a Jewish New York boyhood, and *Billy Bathgate* 1989.

Dodds /dɒdz/ Charles 1899–1973. English biochemist who was largely responsible for the discovery of stilboestrol, a powerful synthetic hormone used in treating prostate conditions and also for fattening cattle.

Dodds Johnny 1892–1940. US jazz clarinetist, generally ranked among the top New Orleans jazz clarinetists. He played with Louis Armstrong, Jelly Roll Morton, and the New Orleans Wanderers, as well as his own trio and orchestra, and was acclaimed for his warmth of tone and improvisation.

Dodgson /dɒdsən/ Charles Lutwidge. Real name of writer Lewis →Carroll.

Doe /dəʊ/ Samuel Kenyon 1950–1990. Liberian politician and soldier, head of state 1980–90. He seized power in a coup. Having successfully put down an uprising April 1990, Doe was deposed and killed by rebel forces Sept 1990.

Doe joined the army in 1969 and rose to the rank of master sergeant ten years later. He led a coup in which President Tolbert was killed 1980. Doe replaced him as head of state, then had 13 cabinet members shot in front of reporters. In 1981 he made himself general and army commander in chief. In 1985 he was narrowly elected president, as leader of the newly formed National Democratic Party of Liberia. His human-rights record was poor.

Dōgen /dəʊgen/ 1200–1253. Japanese Buddhist monk, pupil of Eisai; founder of the Sōtō school of Zen. He did not reject study, but stressed the importance of *zazen*, seated meditation, for its own sake.

Dohnányi /dəʊˈnɑːnji/ Ernst von (Ernö) 1877–1960. Hungarian pianist, conductor, and composer, whose influence is maintained through the examinations repertoire. His compositions include *Variations on a Nursery Song* 1914 and *Second Symphony for Orchestra* 1948.

Born in Bratislava, he studied in Budapest, then established his name as a concert pianist in the UK and the USA. He became conductor of the Budapest Philharmonic 1919, musical director of Hungarian Broadcasting 1931, and director of the Budapest conservatory 1934. Rumoured to have been friendly with the Nazis during the 1930s and 1940s, he left Hungary 1948 and subsequently settled in the USA.

Doi /dɔɪ/ Takako 1929– . Japanese socialist politician, leader of the Japan Socialist Party (JSP) from 1986 and responsible for much of its recent revival. She is the country's first female major party leader.

Doi was a law lecturer before being elected to the House of Representatives in 1969. She assumed leadership of the JSP at a low point in the party's fortunes and proceeded to moderate and modernize its image. With the help of 'housewife volunteers' she established herself as a charismatic political leader, and at a time when the ruling Liberal Democrats were beset by scandals, the JSP vote increased to make Doi the leader of an effective opposition.

Doisy /dɔɪzi/ Edward 1893–1986. US biochemist. In 1939 he succeeded in synthesizing vitamin K, a compound earlier discovered by Carl →Dam, with whom he shared the 1943 Nobel Prize for Medicine.

Dolci /dɒltʃi/ Carlo 1616–1686. Italian painter of the late Baroque period, active in Florence. He created intensely emotional versions of religious subjects, such as *The Last Communion of St Jerome*.

Dolci was the foremost painter in Florence in his time and continued to be much admired in the 18th century. He was also a portraitist, and was sent to Austria in 1675 to paint the Medici wife of the emperor Leopold I.

Dolin /dɒlɪn/ Anton. Stage name of Patrick Healey-Kay 1904–1983. British dancer and choreographer, a pioneer of UK ballet. After studying under Vaslav Nijinsky, he was a leading member of Sergei Diaghilev's company 1924–29. He formed the Markova–Dolin Ballet with Alicia Markova 1935–38, and was a guest soloist with the American Ballet Theater 1940–46.

Doll /dɒl/ William Richard 1912– . British physician who, working with Professor Bradford Hill (1897–) provided the first statistical proof of the link between smoking and lung cancer in 1950. In a later study of the smoking habits of doctors, they were able to show that stopping smoking immediately reduces the risk of cancer.

Dollfuss /dɒlfuːs/ Engelbert 1892–1934. Austrian Christian Socialist politician. He was appointed chancellor in 1932, and in 1933 suppressed parliament and ruled by decree. In Feb 1934 he crushed a protest by the socialist workers by force, and in May Austria was declared a 'corporative' state. The Nazis attempted a coup d'état on 25 July; the Chancellery was seized and Dollfuss murdered.

Dolmetsch /dɒlmetʃ/ Arnold 1858–1940. French-born musician and instrument-maker who settled in England in 1914 and became a leading figure in the revival of early music.

Domagk /dəʊmæk/ Gerhard 1895–1964. German pathologist, discoverer of antibacterial sulphonamide drugs. He found in 1932 that a coal-tar dye called Prontosil red contains chemicals with powerful antibacterial properties. Sulphanilamide became the first of the sulphonamide drugs, used before antibiotics were discovered to treat a wide range of conditions, including pneumonia and septic wounds. Domagk was awarded the 1939 Nobel Prize for Physiology and Medicine.

Domenichino /dəˌmenɪˈkiːnəʊ/ real name Domenico Zampieri 1582–1641. Italian Baroque painter and architect, active in Bologna, Naples, and Rome. He began as an assistant to the →Carracci family of painters and continued the early Baroque style in, for example, frescoes 1624–28 in the choir of S Andrea della Valle, Rome.

This style was superseded by High Baroque, and Domenichino retreated to Naples. He is considered a pioneer of landscape painting in the Baroque period.

Domenico Veneziano /dəˈmenɪkəʊ vɪˌnetsiˈɑːnəʊ/ c. 1400–1461. Italian painter, active in Florence. His few surviving frescoes and altarpieces show a remarkably delicate use of colour and light (which recurs in the work of Piero della Francesca, who worked with him).

He worked in Sta Egidio, Florence, on frescoes now lost. Remaining works include the *Carnesecchi Madonna and Two Saints* and the St Lucy altarpiece, now divided between Florence (Uffizi), Berlin, Cambridge (Fitzwilliam), and Washington, DC (National Gallery).

Domingo /dəˈmɪŋgəʊ/ Placido 1937– . Spanish tenor who excels in romantic operatic roles. He made his debut 1960 as Alfredo in Verdi's *La Traviata*, then spent four years with the Israel National Opera. He sang at the New York City Opera 1965 and has since performed diverse roles in opera houses worldwide. In 1986 he starred in the film version of *Otello*.

Dominic, St /ˈdɒmɪnɪk/ 1170–1221. Founder of the Roman Catholic Dominican order of preaching friars. Feast day 7 Aug.

Born in Old Castile, Dominic was sent by Pope Innocent III in 1205 to preach to the heretic Albigensian sect in Provence. In 1208 the Pope instigated the Albigensian crusade to suppress the heretics by force, and this was supported by Dominic. In 1215 the Dominican order was given premises at Toulouse; during the following years Dominic established friaries at Bologna and elsewhere in Italy, and by the time of his death the order was established all over W Europe.

Domino /ˈdɒmɪnəʊ/ 'Fats' (Antoine) 1928– . US rock-and-roll pianist, singer, and songwriter, exponent of the New Orleans style. His hits include 'Ain't That a Shame' 1955 and 'Blueberry Hill' 1956.

Domitian /dəˈmɪʃən/ Titus Flavius Domitianus AD 51–96. Roman emperor from AD 81. He finalized the conquest of Britain (see →Agricola), strengthened the Rhine–Danube frontier, and suppressed immorality as well as freedom of thought in philosophy (see →Epictetus) and religion (Christians were persecuted). His reign of terror led to his assassination.

Donald /ˈdɒnld/ Ian 1910–1987. English obstetrician who introduced ultrasound (very high-frequency sound wave) scanning. He pioneered its use in obstetrics as a means of scanning the growing fetus without exposure to the danger of X-rays. Donald's experience of using radar in World War II suggested to him the use of ultrasound for medical purposes.

Donaldson /ˈdɒnldsən/ Stephen 1947– . US fantasy writer, author of two Thomas Covenant trilogies 1978–83.

Donat /ˈdəʊnət/ Robert 1905–1958. English actor of Anglo-Polish parentage. He started out in the theatre and made one film in Hollywood (*The Count of Monte Cristo* 1934). His other films include Alfred Hitchcock's *The Thirty-Nine Steps*

Domingo Spanish opera singer Placido Domingo, one of today's most popular tenors. He was brought up in Mexico and made his operatic debut there 1961. Besides numerous recordings, he has made film versions of operas and has also sung some popular music.

1935, *Goodbye, Mr Chips* 1939 for which he won an Academy Award, and *The Winslow Boy* 1948.

Donatello /ˌdɒnəˈteləʊ/ (Donato di Niccolo) 1386–1466. Italian sculptor of the early Renaissance, born in Florence. He was instrumental in reviving the Classical style, as in his graceful bronze statue of the youthful *David* (Bargello, Florence) and his equestrian statue of the general *Gattamelata* 1443 (Padua). The course of Florentine art in the 15th century was strongly influenced by his style.

Donatello introduced true perspective in his relief sculptures, such as the panel of *St George Slaying the Dragon* about 1415–17 (Or San Michele, Florence). During a stay in Rome 1430–32 he absorbed Classical influences, and *David* is said to be the first free-standing nude since antiquity. In his later work, such as his wood-carving of the aged *Mary Magdalene* about 1456 (Baptistry, Florence), he sought dramatic expression through a distorted, emaciated figure style.

Donellan /ˈdɒnələn/ Declan 1953– . British theatre director, cofounder of the **Cheek by Jowl** theatre company 1981, and associate director of the National Theatre from 1989. His irreverent and audacious productions include many classics, such as Racine's *Andromaque* 1985, Corneille's *Le Cid* 1987, and Ibsen's *Peer Gynt* 1990.

Donen /dəʊnən/ Stanley 1924–   . US film director, formerly a dancer, who co-directed two of Gene Kelly's best musicals, *On the Town* 1949 and *Singin' in the Rain* 1952. His other films include *Charade* 1963 and *Two for the Road* 1968.

Dönitz /dɜːnɪts/ Karl 1891–1980. German admiral, originator of the wolf-pack submarine technique, which sank 15 million tonnes of Allied shipping in World War II. He succeeded Hitler in 1945, capitulated, and was imprisoned 1946–56.

Donizetti /ˌdɒnɪdˈzeti/ Gaetano 1797–1848. Italian composer who created more than 60 operas, including *Lucrezia Borgia* 1833, *Lucia di Lammermoor* 1835, *La Fille du régiment* 1840, *La Favorite* 1840, and *Don Pasquale* 1843. They show the influence of Rossini and Bellini, and are characterized by a flow of expressive melodies.

Donne /dʌn/ John 1571–1631. English metaphysical poet. His work consists of love poems, religious poems, verse satires, and sermons, most of which were first published after his death. His religious poems show the same passion and ingenuity as his love poetry. A Roman Catholic in his youth, he converted to the Church of England and finally became dean of St Paul's Cathedral, where he is buried.

Donne was brought up in the Roman Catholic faith and matriculated early at Oxford to avoid taking the oath of supremacy. Before becoming a law student 1592 he travelled in Europe. During his four years at the law courts he was notorious for his wit and reckless living. In 1596 he sailed as a volunteer in an expedition against Spain with the Earl of Essex and Walter Raleigh, and on his return became private secretary to Sir Thomas Egerton, Keeper of the Seal. This appointment was ended by his secret marriage to Ann More (died 1617), niece of Egerton's wife, and they endured many years of poverty. The more passionate and tender of his love poems were probably written to her.

From 1621 to his death Donne was dean of St Paul's. His sermons rank him with the century's greatest orators, and his fervent poems of love and hate, violent, tender, or abusive, give him a unique position among English poets. His verse was not published in collected form until after his death, and was long out of favour, but he is now recognized as one of the greatest English poets.

Donoghue /dɒnəhjuː/ Steve (Stephen) 1884–1945. British jockey. Between 1915 and 1925 he won the Epsom Derby six times, equalling the record of Jem Robinson (since beaten by Lester Piggott). Donoghue is the only jockey to have won the race in three successive years.

Donovan /dɒnəvən/ William Joseph 1883–1959. US military leader and public official. Donovan served as US district attorney 1922–24 and as assistant to the US attorney general 1925–29. He was national security adviser to Presidents Hoover and F D Roosevelt and founded the Office of Strategic Services (OSS) 1942. As OSS director 1942–45, Donovan coordinated US intelligence during World War II.

Born in Buffalo, New York, USA, Donovan was educated at Columbia University and was admitted to the bar 1907. He was decorated for bravery during World War I, gaining the nickname 'Wild Bill.' When the OSS became the CIA 1947, President Truman passed over Donovan as its first director. President Eisenhower appointed Donovan ambassador to Thailand 1953–54, calling him America's 'last hero.'

Dooley /duːli/ Thomas Anthony 1927–1961. US medical missionary. He founded Medico, an international welfare organization, 1957, after tending refugees in Vietnam who were streaming south after the partition of the country 1954. As well as Medico, he established medical clinics in Cambodia, Laos, and Vietnam.

Born in St Louis, USA, Dooley attended Notre Dame University, joined the navy, and received an MD degree from St Louis University 1953. His assignment in Vietnam aroused his compassion and he devoted the rest of his life to medical work in SE Asia.

Doolittle /duːlɪtl/ Hilda. Pen name *HD* 1886–1961. US poet who went to Europe 1911, and was associated with Ezra Pound and the British writer Richard →Aldington (to whom she was married 1913–37) in founding the Imagist school of poetry, advocating simplicity, precision, and brevity. Her work includes the *Sea Garden* 1916 and *Helen in Egypt* 1916.

Doolittle /duːlɪtl/ James Harold 1896–   . US aviation pioneer known for his participation in the development of new aircraft designs and more efficient aircraft fuel. During World War II he saw active service and in 1942 led a daring bombing raid over Tokyo. He later participated in the invasion of North Africa and the intensive bombing of Germany.

Born in Alameda, California, USA, Doolittle attended the University of California and served as an army flying instructor during World War I. Later, in the Army Air Corps, he became an aviation specialist, earning an engineering degree from the Massachusetts Institute of Technology (MIT).

Doone /duːn/ English family of freebooters who, according to legend, lived on Exmoor, Devon, until they were exterminated in the 17th century. They feature in R D →Blackmore's novel *Lorna Doone* 1869.

Doors, the US psychedelic rock group formed 1965 in Los Angeles by Jim Morrison (1943–1971, vocals), Ray Manzarek (1935–   , keyboards), Robby Krieger (1946–   , guitar), and John Densmore (1944–   , drums). Their first hit was 'Light My Fire' from their debut album *The Doors* 1967. They were noted for Morrison's poetic lyrics and flamboyant performance.

Morrison's extended, melodramatic recitations set against repetitive guitar and organ patterns gave the Doors a sinister, sexual edge that set them apart. However, his rather clumsy movements and pretentious lyrics, together with his alcohol problem and rapidly deteriorating looks, often marred performances, and the standard of their albums was uneven, with *Morrison Hotel* 1970 the best of the later output.

Doppler /ˈdɒplə/ Christian Johann 1803–1853. Austrian physicist. He became professor of experimental physics at Vienna. He described the *Doppler effect*.

Dorati /dɔːˈrɑːti/ Antál 1906–1988. US conductor, born in Hungary. He toured with ballet companies 1933–45 and went on to conduct orchestras in the USA and Europe in a career spanning more than half a century. Dorati gave many first performances of Bartók's music and recorded all Haydn's symphonies with the Philharmonia Hungarica.

Doré /ˈdɔːreɪ/ Gustave 1832–1883. French artist, chiefly known as a prolific illustrator, and also active as a painter, etcher, and sculptor. He produced closely worked engravings of scenes from, for example, Rabelais, Dante, Cervantes, the Bible, Milton, and Edgar Allan Poe.

Doré was born in Strasbourg. His views of Victorian London 1869–71, concentrating on desperate poverty and overcrowding in the swollen city, were admired by van Gogh.

Dornier /ˈdɔːniˈeɪ/ Claude 1884–1969. German pioneer aircraft designer who invented the seaplane and during World War II designed the 'flying pencil' bomber.

Born in Bavaria, he founded the Dornier Metallbau works at Friedrichshafen, Lake Constance, in 1922.

d'Orsay /ˈdɔːseɪ/ Alfred Guillaume Gabriel, Count d'Orsay 1801–1857. French dandy. For 20 years he resided with the Irish writer Lady →Blessington in London at Gore House, where he became known as an arbiter of taste.

Dorset /ˈdɔːsɪt/ 1st Earl of Dorset. Title of English poet Thomas →Sackville.

Dorsey /ˈdɔːsi/ Jimmy 1904–1957 and Tommy 1905–1956. US bandleaders, musicians, and composers during the swing era. They worked together in the Dorsey Brothers Orchestra 1934–35 and 1953–56, but led separate bands in the intervening period. The Jimmy Dorsey band was primarily a dance band; the Tommy Dorsey band was more jazz-oriented and featured the singer Frank Sinatra 1940–42. Both Dorsey bands featured in a number of films in the 1940s, and the brothers appeared together in *The Fabulous Dorseys* 1947.

Dos Passos /dəʊs ˈpæsəʊs/ John 1896–1970. US author. He made his reputation with the war novels *One Man's Initiation* 1919 and *Three Soldiers* 1921. His major work is the trilogy *U.S.A.*

1930–36, which gives a panoramic view of US life through the device of placing fictitious characters against the setting of real newspaper headlines and contemporary events.

Dos Santos /dɒs ˈsæntɒs/ José Eduardo 1942–   . Angolan left-wing politician, president from 1979, a member of the People's Movement for the Liberation of Angola (MPLA). By 1989, he had negotiated the withdrawal of South African and Cuban forces, and in 1991 a peace agreement to end the civil war. An upsurge of civil strife followed a victory for Dos Santos and the MPLA in Sept 1992 elections.

Dos Santos joined the MPLA in 1961 and went into exile the same year during the struggle for independence and the civil war between nationalist movements – the MPLA and the National Union for the Total Independence of Angola (UNITA) – backed by foreign powers. He returned to Angola 1970 and rejoined the war, which continued after independence 1975. He held key positions under President Agostinho Neto, and succeeded him on his death. Despite the uncertainty of the cease-fire between MPLA and UNITA 1989, Dos Santos confirmed his pledge of substantial political reform, and concluded a peace agreement 1991. In Sept 1992 his victory in multiparty elections was disputed by rebel leader Jonas Savimbi; fighting between government and UNITA supporters ensued.

Dostoevsky /ˌdɒstɔɪˈefski/ Fyodor Mihailovich 1821–1881. Russian novelist. Remarkable for their profound psychological insight, Dostoevsky's novels have greatly influenced Russian writers, and since the beginning of the 20th century have been increasingly influential abroad. In 1849 he was sentenced to four years' hard labour in Siberia, followed by army service, for printing socialist propaganda. *The House of the Dead* 1861 recalls his prison experiences, followed by his major works *Crime and Punishment* 1866, *The Idiot* 1868–69, and *The Brothers Karamazov* 1880.

Born in Moscow, the son of a physician, Dostoevsky was for a short time an army officer. His first novel, *Poor Folk*, appeared in 1846. In 1849, during a period of intense tsarist censorship, he was arrested as a member of a free-thinking literary circle and sentenced to death. After a last-minute reprieve he was sent to the penal settlement at Omsk for four years, where the terrible conditions increased his epileptic tendency. Finally pardoned in 1859, he published the humorous *Village of Stepanchikovo, The House of the Dead,* and *The Insulted and the Injured* 1862. Meanwhile he had launched two unsuccessful liberal periodicals, in the second of which his *Letters from the Underworld* 1864 appeared. Compelled to work by pressure of debt, he quickly produced *Crime and Punishment* 1866 and *The Gambler* 1867, before fleeing the country to escape from his creditors. He then wrote *The Idiot* (in which the hero is an epileptic like himself), *The Eternal Husband* 1870, and *The Possessed* 1871–72.

Returning to Russia in 1871, he again entered journalism and issued the personal miscellany *Journal of an Author*, in which he discussed contemporary problems. In 1875 he published *A Raw Youth*, but the great work of his last years is *The Brothers Karamazov*.

Dou /dau/ Gerard 1613–1675. Dutch genre painter, a pupil of Rembrandt. He is known for small domestic interiors, minutely observed. He was born in Leiden, where he founded a painters' guild with Jan Steen. He had many pupils, including Gabriel Metsu.

Doubleday /dʌbldeɪ/ Abner 1819–1893. American Civil War military leader and reputed inventor of baseball. He served as major general in the Shenandoah Valley campaign and at the Battles of Bull Run and Antietam 1862, and Gettysburg 1863. He retired from active service 1873. In an investigation into the origins of baseball 1907, testimony was given that Doubleday invented the game 1839 in Cooperstown, New York, a claim refuted by sports historians ever since.

Born in Ballston Spa, New York, Doubleday graduated from West Point military academy 1842 and saw action in the Mexican War 1846–48 and was present at Fort Sumter 1861 at the outbreak of the Civil War.

Doughty /dauti/ Charles Montagu 1843–1926. English travel writer, author of *Travels in Arabia Deserta* 1888, written after two years in the Middle East searching for Biblical relics. He was a role model for T E →Lawrence ('Lawrence of Arabia').

Douglas /dʌɡləs/ Alfred (Bruce) 1870–1945. British poet who became closely associated in London with the Irish writer Oscar →Wilde. Douglas's father, the 9th Marquess of Queensberry, strongly disapproved of the relationship and called Wilde a 'posing Somdomite' (sic). Wilde's action for libel ultimately resulted in his own imprisonment.

Douglas /dʌɡləs/ Gavin (or Gawain) 1475–1522. Scottish poet whose translation into Scots of Virgil's *Aeneid* 1515 was the first translation from the classics into a vernacular of the British Isles.

Douglas /dʌɡləs/ Kirk. Stage name of Issur Danielovitch Demsky 1916– . US film actor. Usually cast as a dynamic and intelligent hero, as in *Spartacus* 1960, he was a major star of the 1950s and 1960s in such films as *Ace in the Hole* 1951, *The Bad and the Beautiful* 1953, *Lust for Life* 1956, *The Vikings* 1958, *Seven Days in May* 1964, and *The War Wagon* 1967. He continues to act and produce, along with his son Michael Douglas.

Douglas /dʌɡləs/ Major (Clifford Hugh) 1879–1952. English social reformer, founder of the economic theory of *social credit*, which held

that interest should be abolished, and credit should become a state monopoly. During a depression, the state should provide purchasing power by subsidizing manufacture and paying dividends to individuals; as long as there was spare capacity in the economy, this credit would not cause inflation.

Douglas Michael 1944– . US film actor and producer. One of the biggest box-office draws of the late 1980s and 1990s, Douglas won an Academy Award for his portrayal of a ruthless corporate raider in *Wall Street* 1987. His acting range includes both romantic and heroic leads in films such as *Romancing the Stone* 1984 and *Jewel of the Nile* 1985, both of which he produced. Among his other films are *Fatal Attraction* 1987 and *Basic Instinct* 1991.

Douglas first achieved recognition in the television series *The Streets of San Francisco* 1972–76, and as co-producer of *One Flew Over the Cuckoo's Nest* 1975 which won an Academy Award for best picture. He is the son of actor Kirk →Douglas.

Douglas /dʌɡləs/ Norman 1868–1952. British diplomat and travel writer (*Siren Land* 1911 and *Old Calabria* 1915, dealing with Italy); his novel *South Wind* 1917 is set in his adopted island of Capri.

You can tell the ideals of a nation by its advertisements.

Norman Douglas, *South Wind* 1917

Douglas /dʌɡləs/ Stephen Arnold 1813–1861. US politician. He served in the US House of Representatives 1843–47 and US senator for Illinois 1847–61. An active Democrat, he urged a compromise on slavery, and debated Abraham Lincoln during the 1858 Senate race winning that election. After losing the 1860 presidential race to Lincoln, Douglas pledged his loyal support to the latter's administration 1861–65.

Born in Brandon, Vermont, Douglas moved west, settling in Illinois, where he studied law and was admitted to the bar 1834. He served in the Illinois state legislature 1836 and as a judge of the state supreme court 1841. He acquired the nickname 'Little Giant' for his support of westward expansion.

Douglas-Hamilton /dʌɡləs 'hæməltən/ family name of dukes of Hamilton, seated at Lennoxlove, East Lothian, Scotland.

Douglas-Home Alec. British politician; see →Home.

Douglas-Home /dʌɡləs 'hjuːm/ William 1912–1992. Scottish playwright. His plays include *The Chiltern Hundreds* 1947, *The Secretary Bird* 1968, and *Lloyd George Knew My Father* 1972. He is the younger brother of Alec Douglas-Home (see →Home).

Dowding British air chief marshal Hugh Dowding. As commander-in-chief of – Fighter Command 1936–40, he organized the defence of Britain.

Douglas of Kirtleside /kɜːtlsaɪd/ William Sholto Douglas, 1st Baron Douglas of Kirtleside 1893–1969. British air marshal. During World War II he was air officer commander in chief of Fighter Command 1940–42, Middle East Command 1943–44, and Coastal Command 1944–45.

Douglass /dʌɡləs/ Frederick 1817–1895. US antislavery campaigner active during the American Civil War 1861–65. He issued a call to blacks to take up arms against the South and helped organize two black regiments. After the Civil War, he held several US government posts, including minister to Haiti 1889–91. He published appeals for full civil rights for blacks and also campaigned for women's suffrage.

Born a slave in Maryland, Douglass escaped 1838 and fled to Britain to avoid re-enslavement. He returned to the US after he had secured sufficient funds to purchase his freedom. He campaigned relentlessly against slavery, especially through his speeches and his newspaper the *North Star*. His autobiographical *Narrative of the Life of Frederick Douglass* 1845 aroused support for the abolition of slavery.

Doulton /dəʊltən/ Henry 1820–1897. English ceramicist. He developed special wares for the chemical, electrical, and building industries, and established the world's first stoneware-drainpipe factory 1846. From 1870 he created art pottery and domestic tablewares in Lambeth, S London, and Burslem, near Stoke-on-Trent.

Doumer /duːmeə/ Paul 1857–1932. French politician. He was elected president of the Chamber in 1905, president of the Senate in 1927, and president of the republic in 1931. He was assassinated by Gorgulov, a White Russian emigré.

Doumergue /duːmeəg/ Gaston 1863–1937. French prime minister Dec 1913–June 1914 (during the time leading up to World War I); president 1924–31; and premier again Feb–Nov 1934 at head of 'national union' government.

Dowding /daʊdɪŋ/ Hugh Caswall Tremenheere, 1st Baron Dowding 1882–1970. British air chief marshal. He was chief of Fighter Command at the outbreak of World War II in 1939, a post he held through the Battle of Britain 10 July-12 Oct 1940.

Dowell /daʊəl/ Anthony 1943– . British ballet dancer in the Classical style. He was principal dancer with the Royal Ballet 1966–86, and director 1986–89.

Dowell joined the Royal Ballet in 1961. The choreographer Frederick Ashton chose him to create the role of Oberon in *The Dream* 1964 opposite Antoinette Sibley, the start of an outstanding partnership.

Dowland /daʊlənd/ John 1563–1626. English composer. He is remembered for his songs to lute accompaniment as well as music for lute alone, such as *Lachrymae* 1605.

Dowson /daʊsən/ Ernest 1867–1900. British poet, one of the 'decadent' poets of the 1890s. He wrote the lyric with the refrain 'I have been faithful to thee, Cynara! in my fashion'.

Doxiadis /ˌdɒksiˈɑːdiːs/ Constantinos 1913–1975. Greek architect and town planner; designer of Islamabad, the capital of Pakistan.

Doyle /dɔɪl/ Arthur Conan 1859–1930. British writer, creator of the detective Sherlock Holmes and his assistant Dr Watson, who first appeared in *A Study in Scarlet* 1887 and featured in a number of subsequent stories, including *The Hound of the Baskervilles* 1902. Conan Doyle also wrote historical romances (*Micah Clarke* 1889 and *The White Company* 1891) and the scientific romance *The Lost World* 1912.

Born in Edinburgh, Conan Doyle qualified as a doctor, and during the second South African War (or Boer War) was senior physician of a field hospital. His Sherlock Holmes character featured in several books, including *The Sign of Four* 1889 and *The Valley of Fear* 1915, as well as in volumes of short stories, first published in the *Strand Magazine*. In his later years Conan Doyle became a spiritualist.

Doyle /dɔɪl/ Richard 1824–1883. British caricaturist and book illustrator. In 1849 he designed the original cover for the humorous magazine *Punch*.

D'Oyly Carte /dɔɪli ˈkaːt/ Richard 1844–1901. British producer of the Gilbert and Sullivan operas at the Savoy Theatre, London, which he built. The old D'Oyly Carte Opera Company founded 1876 was disbanded 1982, but a new one opened its first season 1988. Since 1991 the company has moved to the Alexandra Theatre in Birmingham.

Drabble /dræbəl/ Margaret 1939– . British writer. Her novels include *The Millstone* 1966 (filmed as *The Touch of Love*), *The Middle Ground* 1980, *The Radiant Way* 1987, and *A Natural Curiosity* 1989. She edited the 1985 edition of the *Oxford Companion to English Literature*.

Draco /dreɪkəʊ/ 7th century BC. Athenian politician, the first to codify the laws of the Athenian city-state. These were notorious for their severity; hence *draconian*, meaning particularly harsh.

Drake /dreɪk/ Francis *c.* 1545–1596. English buccaneer and explorer. Having enriched himself as a pirate against Spanish interests in the Caribbean 1567–72, he was sponsored by Elizabeth I for an expedition to the Pacific, sailing round the world 1577–80 in the *Golden Hind*, robbing Spanish ships as he went. This was the second circumnavigation of the globe (the first was by the Portuguese explorer Ferdinand Magellan). Drake also helped to defeat the Spanish Armada 1588 as a vice admiral in the *Revenge*.

Drake was born in Devon and apprenticed to the master of a coasting vessel, who left him the ship at his death. He accompanied his relative, the navigator John Hawkins, 1567 and 1572 to plunder the Caribbean, and returned to England 1573 with considerable booty. After serving in Ireland as a volunteer, he suggested to Queen Elizabeth I an expedition to the Pacific, and Dec 1577 he sailed in the *Pelican* with four other ships and 166 men towards South America. In Aug 1578 the fleet passed through the Straits of Magellan and was then blown south to Cape Horn. The ships became separated and returned to England, all but the *Pelican*, now renamed the *Golden Hind*. Drake sailed north along the coast of Chile and Peru, robbing Spanish ships as far north as California, and then, in 1579, headed southwest across the Pacific. He rounded the South African Cape June 1580, and reached England Sept 1580. Thus the second voyage around the world, and the first made by an English person, was completed in a little under three years. When the Spanish ambassador demanded Drake's punishment, the Queen knighted him on the deck of the *Golden Hind* at Deptford, London.

In 1581 Drake was chosen mayor of Plymouth, in which capacity he brought fresh water into the city by constructing leats from Dartmoor. In 1584–85 he represented the town of Bosinney in Parliament. In a raid on Cadiz 1587 he burned 10,000 tons of shipping, 'singed the King of Spain's beard', and delayed the invasion of England by the Spanish Armada for a year. He was stationed off the French island of Ushant 1588 to intercept the Armada, but was driven back to England by unfavourable winds. During the fight in the Channel he served as a vice admiral in the *Revenge*. Drake sailed on his last expedition to the West Indies with Hawkins 1595, capturing Nombre de Dios on the N coast of Panama but failing to seize Panama City. In Jan 1596 he died of dysentery off the town of Puerto Bello (now Portobello), Panama.

Drayton /dreɪtn/ Michael 1563–1631. English poet. His volume of poems *The Harmony of the Church* 1591 was destroyed by order of the archbishop of Canterbury. His greatest poetical work was the topographical survey of England, *Poly-Olbion* 1612–22, in 30 books.

Drees /dreɪs/ Willem 1886–1988. Dutch socialist politician, prime minister 1948–58. Chair of the Socialist Democratic Workers' Party from 1911 until the German invasion of 1940, he returned to politics in 1947, after being active in the resistance movement.

In 1947, as the responsible minister, he introduced a state pension scheme.

Dreiser /draɪsə/ Theodore 1871–1945. US writer who wrote the naturalist novels *Sister Carrie* 1900 and *An American Tragedy* 1925, based on the real-life crime of a young man, who in his drive to 'make good', drowns a shop assistant he has made pregnant. It was filmed as *A Place in the Sun* 1951.

Born in Terre Haute, Indiana, Dreiser was a journalist 1889–90 in Chicago and was editor of several magazines. His other novels include *The Financier* 1912, *The Titan* 1914, and *The Genius* 1915. *An American Tragedy* finally won him great popularity after years of publishing works that had been largely ignored. His other works range from autobiographical pieces to poems and short stories. Although his work is criticized for being technically unpolished, it is praised for its powerful realism and sincerity. In the 1930s he devoted much of his energy to the radical reform movement.

Dreyer /draɪə/ Carl Theodor 1889–1968. Danish film director. His wide range of films include the austere silent classic *La Passion de Jeanne d'Arc/The Passion of Joan of Arc* 1928 and the Expressionist horror film *Vampyr* 1932, after the failure of which Dreyer made no full-length films until *Vredens Dag/Day of Wrath* 1943. His two late masterpieces are *Ordet/The Word* 1955 and *Gertrud* 1964.

Dreyfus /dreɪfəs/ Alfred 1859–1935. French army officer, victim of miscarriage of justice, anti-Semitism, and cover-up. Employed in the War Ministry, in 1894 he was accused of betraying military secrets to Germany, court-martialled, and sent to the penal colony on Devil's Island, French Guiana. When his innocence was discovered 1896 the military establishment tried to conceal it, and the implications of the Dreyfus affair were passionately discussed in the press until he was exonerated in 1906.

Dreyfus was born in Mulhouse, E France, of a Jewish family. He had been a prisoner in the French Guiana penal colony for two years when it emerged that the real criminal was a Major Esterhazy; the high command nevertheless attempted to suppress the facts and used forged documents to strengthen their case. After a violent controversy, in which the future prime minister Georges →Clemenceau and the novelist Emile →Zola championed Dreyfus, he was brought back for a retrial 1899, found guilty with extenuating circumstances, and received a pardon. In 1906 the court of appeal declared him innocent, and he was reinstated in his military rank.

Drinkwater /ˈdrɪŋkˌwɔːtə/ John 1882–1937. British poet and playwright. He was a prolific writer of lyrical and reflective verse, and also wrote many historical plays, including *Abraham Lincoln* 1918.

Drummond /ˈdrʌmənd/ William 1585–1649. Scottish poet, laird of his native Hawthornden, hence known as Drummond of Hawthornden. He was one of the first Scottish poets to use southern English.

Drummond de Andrade Carlos 1902–1987. Brazilian writer, generally considered the greatest modern Brazilian poet, and a prominent member of the Modernist school. His verse, often seemingly casual, continually confounds the reader's expectations of the 'poetical'.

Dryden /ˈdraɪdn/ John 1631–1700. English poet and dramatist, noted for his satirical verse and for his use of the heroic couplet. His poetry includes the verse satire *Absalom and Achitophel* 1681, *Annus Mirabilis* 1667, and 'St Cecilia's Day' 1687. Plays include the comedy *Marriage à la Mode* 1672 and *All for Love* 1678, a reworking of Shakespeare's *Antony and Cleopatra*.

On occasion, Dryden trimmed his politics and his religion to the prevailing wind, and, as a Roman Catholic convert under James II, lost the post of poet laureate (to which he had been appointed 1668) at the Revolution of 1688. Critical works include *Essay on Dramatic Poesy* 1668. Later ventures to support himself include a translation of Virgil 1697.

Errors, like straws, upon the surface flow/
He who would search for pearls must dive
below.

John Dryden *All for Love* Prologue

Drysdale /ˈdraɪzdeɪl/ George Russell 1912–1969. Australian artist, born in England. His drawings and paintings often depict the Australian outback, its drought, desolation, and poverty, and Aboriginal life.

Duarte /duːˈɑːteɪ/ José Napoleon 1925–1990. El Salvadorean politician, president 1980–82 and 1984–88. He was mayor of San Salvador 1964–70, and was elected president 1972, but exiled by the army 1982. On becoming president again 1984, he sought a negotiated settlement with the left-wing guerrillas 1986, but resigned on health grounds.

Drinkwater John Drinkwater, English poet, playwright and critic. As an actor and manager of the Birmingham Repertory Theatre, he produced poetic dramas before achieving greater success with the prose play Abraham Lincoln 1918.

du Barry /djuː ˈbæri/ Marie Jeanne Bécu, Comtesse 1743–1793. Mistress of →Louis XV of France from 1768. At his death 1774 she was banished to a convent, and during the Revolution fled to London. Returning to Paris 1793, she was guillotined.

Dubček /ˈdʊbtʃek/ Alexander 1921–1992. Czechoslovak politician, chair of the federal assembly 1989–92. He was a member of the Slovak resistance movement during World War II, and became first secretary of the Communist Party 1967–69. He launched a liberalization campaign (called the Prague Spring) that was opposed by the USSR and led to the Soviet invasion of Czechoslovakia 1968. He was arrested by Soviet troops and expelled from the party 1970. In 1989 he gave speeches at prodemocracy rallies, and after the fall of the hardline regime, he was elected speaker of the National Assembly in Prague, a position to which he was re-elected 1990. He was fatally injured in a car crash Nov 1992.

Du Bois /djuːˈbwɑː/ W(illiam) E(dward) B(urghardt) 1868–1963. US educator and social critic. Du Bois was one of the early leaders of the National Association for the Advancement of Colored People (NAACP) and the editor of its journal *Crisis* 1909–32. As a staunch advocate of black American rights, he came into conflict with Booker T →Washington opposing the latter's policy of compromise on the issue of slavery.

Born in Great Barrington, Massachusetts, Du Bois earned a PhD from Harvard 1895 and was appointed to the faculty of Atlanta University. In 1962 he established his home in Accra, Ghana.

Dubos /duːˈbəʊs/ René Jules 1901–1981. French-US microbiologist who studied soil microorganisms and became interested in their antibacterial properties.

The antibacterials he discovered had limited therapeutic use since they were toxic. However, he opened up a new field of research that eventually led to the discovery of such major drugs as penicillin and streptomycin.

Dubuffet /ˌduːbʊ'feɪ/ Jean 1901–1985. French artist. He originated *l'art brut*, 'raw or brutal art', in the 1940s. He used a variety of materials in his paintings and sculptures (plaster, steel wool, straw, and so on) and was inspired by graffiti and children's drawings.

L'art brut emerged 1945 with an exhibition of Dubuffet's own work and of paintings by psychiatric patients and naive or untrained artists. His own paintings and sculptural works have a similar quality, primitive and expressive.

Duccio di Buoninsegna /ˈduːtʃəʊ diː ˌbwɒnɪn'semjə/ *c.* 1255–1319. Italian painter, a major figure in the Sienese school. His greatest work is his altarpiece for Siena Cathedral, the *Maestà* 1308–11; the figure of the Virgin is Byzantine in style, with much gold detail, but Duccio also created a graceful linear harmony in drapery hems, for example, and this proved a lasting characteristic of Sienese style.

Duce /ˈduːtʃeɪ/ (Italian 'leader') title bestowed on the fascist dictator Benito →Mussolini by his followers and later adopted as his official title.

Duchamp /djuːˈʃɒ/ Marcel 1887–1968. US artist, born in France. He achieved notoriety with his *Nude Descending a Staircase* 1912 (Philadelphia Museum of Art), influenced by Cubism and Futurism. An active exponent of Dada, he invented 'ready- mades', everyday items like a bicycle wheel on a kitchen stool, which he displayed as works of art.

A major early work that focuses on mechanical objects endowed with mysterious significance is *La Mariée mise à nu par ses célibataires, même/ The Bride Stripped Bare by Her Bachelors, Even* 1915–23 (Philadelphia Museum of Art). Duchamp continued to experiment with collage, mechanical imagery, and abstract sculpture throughout his career. He lived mostly in New York and became a US citizen 1954.

Dudintsev /duːˈdɪntsef/ Vladimir Dmitriyevich 1918– . Soviet novelist, author of the remarkably frank *Not by Bread Alone* 1956, a depiction of Soviet bureaucracy and inefficiency.

Dufay /duːˈfaɪ/ Guillaume 1400–1474. Flemish composer. He is recognized as the foremost composer of his time, of both secular songs and sacred music (including 84 songs and eight masses). His work marks a transition between the music of the Middle Ages and that of the Renaissance and is characterized by expressive melodies and rich harmonies.

Du Fu another name for the Chinese poet →Tu Fu.

Dufy /duːˈfi/ Raoul 1877–1953. French painter and designer. He originated a fluent, brightly coloured style in watercolour and oils, painting scenes of gaiety and leisure, such as horse racing, yachting, and life on the beach. He also designed tapestries, textiles, and ceramics.

Duiker /ˈdaɪkə/ Johannes 1890–1935. Dutch architect of the 1920s and 1930s avant-garde period. His works demonstrate great structural vigour, and include the Zonnestraal sanatorium 1926, and the Open Air School 1932 and the Cineac News Cinema 1933, both in Amsterdam.

Dukakis /duːˈkɑːkɪs/ Michael 1933– . US Democrat politician, governor of Massachusetts 1974–78 and 1982–90, presiding over a high-tech economic boom, the 'Massachusetts miracle'. He was a presidential candidate 1988.

Dukakis was born in Boston, Massachusetts, the son of Greek immigrants. After studying law at Harvard and serving in Korea (1955–57), he concentrated on a political career in his home state. Elected as a Democrat to the Massachusetts legislature 1962, he became state governor 1974. After an unsuccessful first term, marred by his unwillingness to compromise, he was defeated 1978. He returned as governor 1982, committed to working in a more consensual manner, was re-elected 1986, and captured the Democratic Party's presidential nomination 1988. After a poor campaign, the diligent but uncharismatic Dukakis was defeated by the incumbent vice president George Bush. His standing in Massachusetts dropped and he announced that he would not seek a new term.

Dukas /duːˈkɑːs/ Paul (Abraham) 1865–1935. French composer. His orchestral scherzo *L'Apprenti sorcier/The Sorcerer's Apprentice* 1897 is full of the colour and energy that characterizes much of his work.

He was professor of composition at the Paris Conservatoire and composed the opera *Ariane et Barbe-Bleue/Ariane and Bluebeard* 1907, and the ballet *La Péri* 1912.

Dulles /ˈdʌlɪs/ Alan 1893–1969. US lawyer, director of the Central Intelligence Agency (CIA) 1953–61. He was the brother of John Foster Dulles.

He helped found the CIA 1950 but was embroiled in the Bay of Pigs controversy (an unsuccessful invasion attempt by US-sponsored Cuban exiles 1961), among others, which forced his resignation.

Dulles /ˈdʌlɪs/ John Foster 1888–1959. US politician. Senior US adviser at the founding of the United Nations, he was largely responsible for drafting the Japanese peace treaty of 1951. As secretary of state 1952–59, he secured US intervention in support of South Vietnam following the expulsion of the French 1954 and was critical of Britain during the Suez Crisis 1956.

Dulong /djuːˈlɒŋ/ Pierre 1785–1838. French chemist and physicist. In 1819 he discovered, along with the physicist Alexis Petit, the law that, for many elements solid at room temperature, the product of relative atomic mass and specific heat capacity is approximately constant. He had earlier, in 1811, and at the cost of an eye, discovered the explosive nitrogen trichloride.

Dumas /djuːmɑː/ Alexandre 1802–1870. French author, known as Dumas *père* (the father). He is remembered for his romances, the reworked output of a 'fiction-factory' of collaborators. They include *Les trois mousquetaires/The Three Musketeers* 1844 and its sequels. Dumas *fils* was his son.

His play *Henri III et sa cour/Henry III and His Court* 1829 established French romantic historical drama.

All for one and one for all.

Alexandre Dumas (père)
The Three Musketeers 1844

Dumas /djuːmɑː/ Alexandre 1824–1895. French author, known as Dumas *fils* (the son of Dumas *père*) and remembered for the play *La Dame aux camélias/The Lady of the Camellias* 1852, based on his own novel and the source of Verdi's opera *La Traviata*.

Du Maurier /duː ˈmɒrieɪ/ Daphne 1907–1989. British novelist whose romantic fiction includes *Jamaica Inn* 1936, *Rebecca* 1938, and *My Cousin Rachel* 1951. *Jamaica Inn*, *Rebecca*, and her short story 'The Birds' were made into films by the English director Alfred Hitchcock.

She was the granddaughter of British cartoonist and novelist George Du Maurier (1834–1896).

Du Maurier /duː ˈmɒrieɪ/ George (Louis Palmella Busson) 1834–1896. French-born British author of the novel *Trilby* 1894, the story of a natural singer able to perform only under the hypnosis of Svengali, her tutor.

Dumont d'Urville /djuːˈmɒn duəˈviːl/ Jean 1780–1842. French explorer in Australasia and the Pacific. In 1838–40 he sailed round Cape Horn on a voyage to study terrestial magnetism and reached Adélie Land in Antarctica.

Dumouriez /djuːˌmuəriˈeɪ/ Charles François du Périer 1739–1823. French general during the Revolution. In 1792 he was appointed foreign minister, supported the declaration of war against Austria, and after the fall of the monarchy was given command of the army defending Paris. After intriguing with the royalists he had to flee for his life, and from 1804 he lived in England.

Dunant /djuːˈnɒn/ Jean Henri 1828–1910. Swiss philanthropist; the originator of the international relief agency, the Red Cross. At the Battle of Solferino 1859 he helped tend the wounded, and in *Un Souvenir de Solferino* 1862 he proposed the

Dumas In 1844 over 40 works were published under Alexander Dumas père's name, including The Three Musketeers. Providing plots and hints and writing purple passages himself, he employed a changing band of literary assistants to maintain this 'fiction-factory' output.

establishment of an international body for the aid of the wounded – an idea that was realized in the Geneva Convention 1864. He shared the 1901 Nobel Peace Prize.

Dunaway /dʌnəweɪ/ Faye 1941– . US actress whose first starring role was in *Bonnie and Clyde* 1967. Her subsequent films, including *Network* 1976 (for which she won an Academy Award) and *Mommie Dearest* 1981, received a varying critical reception. She also starred in Roman Polanski's *Chinatown* 1974 and *The Handmaid's Tale* 1990.

Dunbar /dʌnˈbɑː/ William c. 1460–c. 1520. Scottish poet at the court of James IV. His poems include a political allegory, 'The Thrissil and the Rois' 1503, and the lament with the refrain 'Timor mortis conturbat me' about 1508.

Duncan /dʌŋkən/ Isadora 1878–1927. US dancer and teacher. An influential pioneer of Modern dance, she adopted an expressive free form, dancing barefoot and wearing a loose tunic, inspired by the ideal of Hellenic beauty. She toured extensively, often returning to Russia after her initial success there 1905.

She died in an accident when her long scarf caught in the wheel of the car in which she was travelling.

People do not live nowadays – they get about ten per cent out of life.

Isadora Duncan
This Quarter Autumn 'Memoirs'

Duncan-Sandys /dʌŋkən 'sændz/ Duncan (Edwin). British politician; see →Sandys, Duncan Edwin.

Dundas /dʌn'dæs/ Henry, 1st Viscount Melville 1742–1811. British Tory politician. In 1791 he became home secretary and, with revolution raging in France, carried through the prosecution of the English and Scottish radicals. After holding other high cabinet posts, he was impeached 1806 for corruption and, although acquitted on the main charge, held no further office.

Dunham /dʌnəm/ Katherine 1912– . US dancer and choreographer. She was noted for a free, strongly emotional method, and employed her extensive knowledge of anthropology as a basis for her dance techniques and choreography. Her interests lay in ethnic dance. In 1940 Dunham established an all-black dance company, which toured extensively. She also choreographed for and appeared in Hollywood films.

Dunlop /dʌnlɒp/ John Boyd 1840–1921. Scottish inventor who founded the rubber company that bears his name. In 1887, to help his child win a tricycle race, he bound an inflated rubber hose to the wheels. The same year he developed commercially practical pneumatic tyres, first patented by Robert William Thomson (1822–1873) 1846 for bicycles and cars.

Dunne /dʌn/ Finley Peter 1867–1936. US humorist and social critic. His fictional character 'Mr Dooley', the Irish saloonkeeper and sage, gained a national readership. Written in dialect, Mr Dooley's humorous yet pointed reflections on US politics and society appeared 1892–1915. From 1900 the 'Mr Dooley columns' appeared in such national magazines as *Collier's* and *Metropolitan*.

Born in Chicago, Dunne wrote humour pieces for local newspapers before becoming editor-in-chief of the *Chicago Journal* 1897.

Dunne /dʌn/ Irene 1904–1990. US actress. From 1930 to 1952, she appeared in a wide variety of films, including musicals and comedies, but was perhaps most closely associated with the genre of romantic melodrama, for example, in the film *Back Street* 1932.

Dunsany /dʌn'semi/ Edward John Moreton Drax Plunkett, 18th Baron Dunsany 1878–1957. Irish writer, author of the 'Jorkens' stories, beginning with *The Travel Tales of Mr Joseph Jorkens*, which employed the convention of a narrator (Jorkens) sitting in a club or bar. He also wrote short ironic heroic fantasies, collected in *The Gods of Pegana* 1905 and other books. His first play, *The Glittering Gate*, was performed at the Abbey Theatre, Dublin 1909.

Duns Scotus /dʌnz 'skəʊtəs/ John c. 1265–c. 1308. Scottish monk, a leading figure in the theological and philosophical system of medieval Scholasticism. The church rejected his ideas, and the word *dunce* is derived from Dunses, a term of ridicule applied to his followers. In the medieval controversy over universals he advocated nominalism, maintaining that classes of things have no independent reality. He belonged to the Franciscan order, and was known as Doctor Subtilis.

On many points he turned against the orthodoxy of Thomas →Aquinas; for example, he rejected the idea of a necessary world, favouring a concept of God as absolute freedom capable of spontaneous activity.

Dunstable /dʌnstəbəl/ John c. 1385–1453. English composer who wrote songs and anthems, and is generally considered one of the founders of Renaissance music.

Dunstan, St /dʌnstən/ c. 924–988. English priest and politician, archbishop of Canterbury from 960. He was abbot of Glastonbury from 945, and made it a centre of learning. Feast day 19 May.

Duparc /duːˈpɑːk/ (Marie Eugène) Henri Fouques 1848–1933. French composer. He studied under César →Franck. His songs, though only 15 in number, are memorable for their craft and for their place in the history of French songwriting.

Du Pré /duːˈpreɪ/ Jacqueline 1945–1987. English cellist. She was celebrated for her proficient technique and powerful interpretations of the Classical cello repertory, particularly of Edward →Elgar. She had an international concert career while still in her teens and made many recordings.

Jacqueline Du Pré married the Israeli pianist and conductor Daniel →Barenboim 1967 and worked with him in concerts, as a duo, and in a conductor-soloist relationship until her playing career was ended by multiple sclerosis. Although confined to a wheelchair for the last 14 years of her life, she continued to work as a teacher and to campaign on behalf of other sufferers of the disease.

Durand /dəˈrænd/ Asher Brown 1796–1886. US painter and engraver. His paintings expressed communion with nature, as in *Kindred Spirits* 1849, a tribute to Thomas Cole, William Cullen Bryant, and the Catskill mountains. The founding of the Hudson River School of landscape art is ascribed to Cole and Durand.

Born in Jefferson Village, New Jersey, Durand began as an engraver of portraits, landscapes, and banknotes but, influenced by Cole, turned to painting. Having studied in Europe 1840–41, he returned as a master of landscapes. Durand was president of the National Academy of Design 1840–61.

Duras /djuˈrɑː/ Marguerite 1914– . French author. Her work includes short stories (*Des Journées entières dans les arbres* 1954, stage adaption *Days in the Trees* 1965), plays (*La Musica* 1967), and film scripts (*Hiroshima mon amour* 1960). She also wrote novels including *Le Vice-Consul* 1966, evoking an existentialist world from the setting of Calcutta, and *Emily L.* 1989. *La Vie* *materielle* 1987 appeared in England as *Practicalities* 1990. Her autobiographical novel, *La Douleur* 1986, is set in Paris in 1945.

Dürer /djʊərə/ Albrecht 1471–1528. German artist, the leading figure of the northern Renaissance. He was born in Nuremberg and travelled widely in Europe. Highly skilled in drawing and a keen student of nature, he perfected the technique of woodcut and engraving, producing woodcut series such as the *Apocalypse* 1498 and copperplate engravings such as *The Knight, Death, and the Devil* 1513, and *Melancholia* 1514; he may also have invented etching. His paintings include altarpieces and meticulously observed portraits, including many self-portraits.

He was apprenticed first to his father, a goldsmith, then in 1486 to Michael Wolgemut, a painter, woodcut artist, and master of a large workshop in Nuremberg. From 1490 he travelled widely, studying Netherlandish and Italian art, then visited Colmar, Basel, and Strasbourg and returned to Nuremberg 1495. Other notable journeys were to Venice 1505–07, where he met the painter Giovanni Bellini, and to Antwerp 1520, where he was made court painter to Charles V of Spain and the Netherlands (recorded in detail in his diary).

If a man devotes himself to art, much evil is avoided that happens otherwise if one is idle.

Albrecht Dürer
Outline of a General Treatise on Painting c. 1510

Durham /dʌrəm/ John George Lambton, 1st Earl of Durham 1792–1840. British politician. Appointed Lord Privy Seal 1830, he drew up the first Reform Bill 1832, and as governor general of Canada briefly in 1837 drafted the Durham Report which led to the union of Upper and Lower Canada.

Durkheim /dɜːkhaɪm/ Emile 1858–1917. French sociologist, one of the founders of modern sociology, who also influenced social anthropology. He worked to establish sociology as a respectable and scientific discipline, capable of diagnosing social ills and recommending possible cures.

He was the first lecturer in social science at Bordeaux University 1887–1902, professor of education at the Sorbonne in Paris from 1902 and the first professor of sociology there 1913. He examined the bases of social order and the effects of industrialization on traditional social and moral order.

His four key works are *De la division du travail social/The Division of Labour in Society* 1893, comparing social order in small-scale societies with that in industrial ones; *Les Régles de la méthode/The Rules of Sociological Method* 1895, outlining his own brand of functionalism and proclaiming positivism as the way forward for sociology as a science; *Suicide* 1897, showing social causes of this apparently individual act; and *Les Formes élémentaires de la vie religieuse/The Elementary Forms of Religion* 1912, a study of the beliefs of Australian Aborigines, showing the place of religion in social solidarity.

Durrell /dʌrəl/ Gerald (Malcolm) 1925– . British naturalist, director of Jersey Zoological Park. He is the author of travel and natural history books, and the humorous memoir *My Family and Other Animals* 1956. He is the brother of Lawrence Durrell.

Shyness has laws: you can only give yourself, tragically, to those who least understand.

Lawrence Durrell *Justine* 1957

Durrell /dʌrəl/ Lawrence (George) 1912–1990. British novelist and poet. Born in India, he joined the foreign service and lived mainly in the E Mediterranean, the setting of his novels, including the Alexandria Quartet: *Justine, Balthazar, Mountolive,* and *Clea* 1957–60; he also wrote travel books. He was the brother of the naturalist Gerald Durrell.

Dürrenmatt Friedrich 1921–1991. Swiss dramatist, author of grotesquely farcical tragicomedies, for example *The Visit* 1956 and *The Physicists* 1962.

Duse /duːzeɪ/ Eleonora 1859–1924. Italian actress. She was the mistress of the poet Gabriele →D'Annunzio from 1897, as recorded in his novel *Il fuoco/The Flame of Life.*

Dutilleux /duːtɪˈjɜː/ Henri 1916– . French composer of instrumental music in elegant Neo-Romantic style. His works include *Métaboles* 1962–65 for orchestra and *Ainsi la nuit* 1975–76 for string quartet.

Duval /djuːˈvæl/ Claude 1643–1670. English criminal. He was born in Normandy and turned highwayman after coming to England at the Restoration. He was known for his gallantry. Duval was hanged at Tyburn, London.

Duvalier /djuːˈvælieɪ/ François 1907–1971. Right-wing president of Haiti 1957–71. Known as *Papa Doc,* he ruled as a dictator, organizing the Tontons Macoutes ('bogeymen') as a private security force to intimidate and assassinate opponents of his regime. He rigged the 1961 elections in order to have his term of office extended until 1967, and in 1964 declared himself president for life. He was excommunicated by the Vatican for harassing the church, and was succeeded on his death by his son Jean-Claude Duvalier.

Dylan US singer-songwriter and musician Bob Dylan's acoustic protest anthems of the 60s earned him the moniker 'the Voice of a Generation'. Since then his musical repertory has expanded to include rock, country and western, blues, and gospel. But his 1992 solo acoustic album Good as I Been to You, *of traditional folk and roots music, echoed the early Dylan sound.*

Duvalier /dju:ˈvælieɪ/ Jean-Claude 1951– . Right-wing president of Haiti 1971–86. Known as *Baby Doc*, he succeeded his father François Duvalier, becoming, at the age of 19, the youngest president in the world. He continued to receive support from the USA but was pressured into moderating some elements of his father's regime, yet still tolerated no opposition. In 1986, with Haiti's economy stagnating and with increasing civil disorder, Duvalier fled to France, taking much of the Haitian treasury with him.

Duve /dju:v/ Christian de 1917– . Belgian scientist, who shared the 1974 Nobel Prize for Medicine for his work on the structural and functional organization of the biological cell.

Duvivier /dju:ˈvɪvieɪ/ Julien 1896–1967. French film director whose work includes *La Belle Equipe* 1936, *Un Carnet de bal* 1937, and *La Fin du jour* 1938.

Duwez /duːˈvez/ Pol 1907– . US scientist, born in Belgium, who in 1959 developed metallic glasses (alloys rapidly cooled from the melt, which combine properties of glass and metal) with his team at the California Institute of Technology.

Dvořák /dvɔːˈʒɑːk/ Antonin (Leopold) 1841–1904. Czech composer. International recognition came with his series of *Slavonic Dances* 1877–86, and he was director of the National Conservatory, New York, 1892–95. Works such as his *New World Symphony* 1893 reflect his interest in American folk themes, including black and native American. He wrote nine symphonies; tone poems; operas, including *Rusalka* 1900; large-scale choral works; the *Carnival* 1891–92 and other overtures; violin and cello concertos; chamber music; piano pieces; and songs. His Romantic music extends the Classical tradition of Beethoven and Brahms and displays the influence of Czech folk music.

Dyck /daɪk/ Anthony Van 1599–1641. Flemish painter. Born in Antwerp, Van Dyck was an assistant to Rubens 1618–20, then briefly worked in England at the court of James I, and moved to Italy 1622. In 1626 he returned to Antwerp, where he continued to paint religious works and portraits. From 1632 he lived in England and produced numerous portraits of royalty and aristocrats, such as *Charles I on Horseback* about 1638 (National Gallery, London).

Dylan /ˈdɪlən/ Bob. Adopted name of Robert Allen Zimmerman 1941– . US singer and songwriter whose lyrics provided catchphrases for a generation and influenced innumerable songwriters. He began in the folk-music tradition. His early songs, as on his albums *Freewheelin'* 1963 and *The Times They Are A-Changin'* 1964, were associated with the US civil-rights movement and antiwar protest. From 1965 he worked in an individualistic rock style, as on the albums *Highway 61 Revisited* 1965 and *Blonde on Blonde* 1966.

Dylan's early songs range from the simple, catchy 'Blowin' in the Wind' 1962 to brooding indictments of social injustice like 'The Ballad of Hollis Brown' 1963. When he first used an electric rock band 1965, he was criticized by purists, but the albums that immediately followed are often cited as his best work, with songs of spite ('Like a Rolling Stone') and surrealistic imagery ('Visions of Johanna') delivered in his characteristic nasal whine. The film *Don't Look Back* 1967 documents the 1965 British tour.

Of Dylan's 1970s albums, *Blood on the Tracks* 1975 was the strongest. *Slow Train Coming* 1979 was his first album as a born-again Christian, a phase that lasted several years and alienated all but the die-hard fans. *Oh, Mercy* 1989 was seen as a partial return to form, but *Under the Red Sky* 1990 did not bear this out. However, *The Bootleg Years* 1991, a collection of 58 previously unreleased items from past years, reasserted his standing. In 1992 he released *Good as I Been to You*, which consisted of traditional tunes, and was his first completely solo acoustic album since *Another Side of Bob Dylan* 1964.

Eagling /ˈiːglɪŋ/ Wayne 1950– . Canadian dancer who joined the Royal Ballet in London 1969, becoming a soloist 1972 and a principal dancer 1975. He appeared in *Gloria* 1980 and other productions. In Sept 1991 he became artistic director of the Dutch National Ballet.

Eakins /ˈiːkɪnz/ Thomas 1844–1916. US painter. A trained observer of human anatomy and a devotee of photography, Eakins attempted to achieve a strong sense of visual realism. His work is characterized by strong contrasts between light and shade, as in *The Gross Clinic* 1875 (Jefferson Medical College, Philadelphia), a group portrait of a surgeon, his assistants, and students.

Born in Philadelphia, Eakins attended the Pennsylvania Academy of the Fine Arts and the Ecole des Beaux-Arts in Paris, later becoming an instructor at the Pennsylvania Academy. He studied with the French academic painter J-L Gérôme (1824–1904) in Paris in the 1860s and on a European tour drew inspiration from Rembrandt, Velázquez, and Ribera.

In the 1870s he began teaching at the Pennsylvania Academy but was dismissed for removing the loincloth from a nude model. In his later years he painted distinguished, powerful portraits.

The big artist ... keeps a sharp eye on Nature and steals her tools.

Thomas Eakins

Eames /iːmz/ Charles 1907–1978 and Ray 1916–1988. US designers, a husband-and-wife team who worked together in California 1941–78. They created some of the most highly acclaimed furniture designs of the 20th century: a moulded plywood chair 1945–46; the Lounge Chair, a black leather-upholstered chair 1956; and a fibreglass armchair 1950–53.

Eanes /eɪˈɑːneʃ/ António dos Santos Ramalho 1935– . Portuguese politician. He helped plan the 1974 coup that ended the Caetano regime, and as army chief of staff put down a left-wing revolt Nov 1975. He was president 1976–86.

Earhart /ˈeəhɑːt/ Amelia 1898–1937. US aviation pioneer and author, who in 1928 became the first woman to fly across the Atlantic. With copilot Frederick Noonan, she attempted a round-the-world flight 1937. Somewhere over the Pacific their plane disappeared.

Born in Atchison, Kansas, Earhart worked as an army nurse and social worker, before discovering that her true calling lay in aviation. In 1928 she became the first woman to fly across the Atlantic as a passenger and in 1932 completed a solo transatlantic flight. During a flight over the Pacific 1937, her plane disappeared without trace, although clues found 1989 on Nikumaroro island, SE of Kiribati's main island group, suggest that she and her copilot might have survived a crash only to die of thirst.

Early /ˈɜːli/ Jubal Anderson 1816–1894. American Confederate military leader. Although long a supporter of the Union, he joined the Confederate army at the outbreak of the American Civil War 1861. After the Battle of Bull Run 1862 he was made general in the Army of Northern Virginia, leading campaigns in the Shenandoah Valley 1862 and threatening Washington DC 1864.

Born in Franklin County, Virginia, Early graduated from West Point military academy 1837. After studying law, he was admitted to the bar 1840 and later served in the Virginia legislature. After a brief period of exile following the end of the Civil War, he resumed his Virginia law practice.

Earp /ɜːp/ Wyatt 1848–1929. US frontier law officer. With his brothers Virgil and Morgan, Doc Holliday, and the legendary Bat →Masterson he was involved in the famous gunfight at the OK Corral in Tombstone, Arizona, on 26 Oct 1881. Famous as a scout and buffalo hunter, he also gained a reputation as a gambler and brawler. After leaving Tombstone 1882, he travelled before settling in Los Angeles.

Born in Monmouth, Illinois, USA, Earp moved with his family to Iowa, finally settling in California 1864. He moved to Wichita, Kansas, 1874, where he was occasionally employed by the US marshal and was appointed assistant marshal in Dodge City, Kansas 1876.

Eastman /ˈiːstmən/ George 1854–1932. US entrepreneur and inventor who founded the Eastman Kodak photographic company 1892. From 1888 he marketed his patented daylight-loading flexible roll films (to replace the glass plates used previously) and portable cameras. By 1900 his company was selling a pocket camera for as little as one dollar.

Eastwood /iːstwʊd/ Clint 1930– . US film actor and director. As the 'Man with No Name' in *A Fistful of Dollars* 1964, he started the vogue for 'spaghetti Westerns'. Later Westerns include *The Good, the Bad, and the Ugly* 1966, *High Plains Drifter* 1973, *Outlaw Josey Wales* 1976, and *Unforgiven* 1992.

Eastwood starred in the TV series *Rawhide* and in the 'Dirty Harry' series of films, and directed *Bird* 1988. He was elected mayor of Carmel, California 1986.

Eban /ebæn/ Abba 1915– . Israeli diplomat and politician, ambassador in Washington 1950–59 and foreign minister 1966–74.

Eban was born in Cape Town, South Africa, and educated in England; he taught at Cambridge University before serving at Allied HQ during World War II. He subsequently settled in Israel.

Eccles /eklz/ John Carew 1903– . Australian physiologist who shared (with Alan Hodgkin and Andrew Huxley) the 1963 Nobel Prize for Medicine for work on conduction in the central nervous system. In some of his later works, he argued that the mind has an existence independent of the brain.

Echegaray /ˌetʃɪɡəˈraɪ/ José 1832–1916. Spanish dramatist. His dramas include *O locura o santidad/Madman or Saint* 1877, and *El gran Galeoto/The World and his Wife* 1881.

Eckert /ekət/ John Presper Jr 1919– . US mathematician who collaborated with John →Mauchly on the development of the early ENIAC (1946) and Univac 1 (1951) computers.

Eckhart /ekhɑːt/ Johannes, called Meister Eckhart *c.* 1260–1327. German theologian and leader of a popular mystical movement. In 1326 he was accused of heresy, and in 1329 a number of his doctrines were condemned by the pope as heretical. His theology stressed the absolute transcendence of God, and the internal spiritual development through which union with the divine could be attained.

Eco /ekəʊ/ Umberto 1932– . Italian writer, semiologist, and literary critic. His works include *The Role of the Reader* 1979, the 'philosophical thriller' *The Name of the Rose* 1983, and *Foucault's Pendulum* 1988.

Edberg /edbɜːg/ Stefan 1966– . Swedish tennis player, twice winner of Wimbledon 1988 and 1990. He won the junior Grand Slam 1983 and his first Grand Slam title, the Australian Open, 1985, repeated 1987. Other Grand Slam singles titles include the US Open 1991 and 1992. At Wimbledon in 1987 he became the first male player in 40 years to win a match without conceding a game.

Eddery /edəri/ Pat(rick) 1952– . Irish-born flat-racing jockey who has won the jockey's championship eight times, including four in succession.

He has won all the major races, including the Epsom Derby twice. He won the Prix de L'Arc de Triomphe four times, including three in succession 1985–87.

Eddington /edɪŋtən/ Arthur Stanley 1882–1944. British astrophysicist, who studied the motions, equilibrium, luminosity, and atomic structure of the stars, and became a leading exponent of Einstein's relativity theory. In 1919 his observation of stars during an eclipse confirmed Einstein's prediction that light is bent when passing near the Sun. His book *The Nature of the Physical World* 1928 is a popularization of science. In *The Expanding Universe* 1933 he expressed the theory that in the spherical universe the outer galaxies or spiral nebulae are receding from one another.

We used to think that if we knew one, we knew two, because one and one are two. We are finding that we must learn a great deal more about 'and'.

Arthur Stanley Eddington

Eddy /edi/ Mary Baker 1821–1910. US founder of the Christian Science movement.

She was born in New Hampshire and brought up as a Congregationalist. Her pamphlet *Science of Man* 1869 was followed by *Science and Health with Key to the Scriptures* 1875, which systematically set forth the basis of Christian Science. She founded the Christian Science Association 1876. In 1879 the Church of Christ, Scientist, was established, and although living in retirement after 1892 she continued to direct the activities of the movement until her death.

Her faith in divine healing was confirmed by her recovery from injuries caused by a fall, and she based a religious sect on this belief.

Edelman /edlmən/ Gerald Maurice 1929– . US biochemist who worked out the sequence of 1330 amino acids that makes up human immunoglobulin, a task completed 1969. For this work he shared the Nobel Prize for Medicine 1972 with Rodney Porter.

Eden /iːdn/ Anthony, 1st Earl of Avon 1897–1977. British Conservative politician, foreign secretary 1935–38, 1940–45, and 1951–55; prime minister 1955–57, when he resigned after the failure of the Anglo-French military intervention in the Suez Crisis.

Upset by his prime minister's rejection of a peace plan secretly proposed by Roosevelt Jan 1938, Eden resigned as foreign secretary Feb 1938 in protest against Chamberlain's decision to open conversations with the Fascist dictator Mussolini. He was foreign secretary again in the wartime coalition, formed Dec 1940, and in the Conservative government, elected 1951. With the Soviets, he negotiated an interim peace in Vietnam 1954. In April 1955 he succeeded Churchill as prime minister. His use of force in the Suez Crisis led to his resignation Jan 1957, but he continued to maintain that his action was justified.

We are not at war with Egypt. We are in an armed conflict.

Anthony Eden November 1956

Edgar /edgə/ known as the *Atheling* ('of royal blood') *c.* 1050–*c.* 1130. English prince, born in Hungary. Grandson of Edmund Ironside, he was supplanted as heir to Edward the Confessor by William the Conqueror. He led two rebellions against William 1068 and 1069, but made peace 1074.

Edgar the Peaceful /edgə/ 944–975. King of all England from 959. He was the younger son of Edmund I, and strove successfully to unite English and Danes as fellow subjects.

Edgeworth /edʒwɜːθ/ Maria 1767–1849. Irish novelist. Her first novel, *Castle Rackrent* 1800, dealt with Anglo-Irish country society and was followed by the similar *The Absentee* 1812 and *Ormond* 1817.

Edinburgh, Duke of title of Prince →Philip of the UK.

Edison /edɪsən/ Thomas Alva 1847–1931. US scientist and inventor, with over 1,000 patents. In Menlo Park, New Jersey, 1876–87, he produced his most important inventions, including the electric light bulb 1879. He constructed a system of electric power distribution for consumers, the telephone transmitter, and the phonograph.

Edison's first invention was an automatic repeater for telegraphic messages. Later came the carbon transmitter (used as a microphone in the production of the Bell telephone), the electric filament lamp, a new type of storage battery, and the kinetoscopic camera, an early cine camera. He also anticipated the Fleming thermionic valve. He supported direct current (DC) transmission, but alternating current (AC) was eventually found to be more efficient and economical.

Edmund II Ironside /aɪənsaɪd/ *c.* 989–1016. King of England 1016, the son of Ethelred II the Unready. He led the resistance to →Canute's invasion 1015, and on Ethelred's death 1016 was chosen king by the citizens of London, whereas the Witan (the king's council) elected Canute. In the struggle for the throne, Edmund was defeated by Canute at Assandun (Ashington), Essex, and they divided the kingdom between them; when Edmund died the same year, Canute ruled the whole kingdom.

Edmund, St /edmənd/ *c.* 840–870. King of East Anglia from 855. In 870 he was defeated and captured by the Danes at Hoxne, Suffolk, and martyred on refusing to renounce Christianity. He was canonized and his shrine at Bury St Edmunds became a place of pilgrimage.

Edric the Forester /edrɪtʃ/ or *Edric the Wild* 11th century. English chieftain on the Welsh border who revolted against William the Conqueror 1067, around what is today Herefordshire, burning Shrewsbury. He was subsequently reconciled with William, and fought with him against the Scots 1072. Later writings describe him as a legendary figure.

Edson /edsən/ J(ohn) T(homas) 1928– . English writer of Western novels. His books, numbering 129 by 1990 and with 25 million copies sold, have such titles as *The Fastest Gun in Texas* and feature a recurring hero, Rapido Clint.

Edward /edwəd/ (full name Edward Antony Richard Louis) 1964– . Prince of the UK, third son of Queen Elizabeth II. He is seventh in line to the throne after Charles, Charles's two sons, Andrew, and Andrew's two daughters.

Edward /edwəd/ the *Black Prince* 1330–1376. Prince of Wales, eldest son of Edward III of England. The epithet (probably posthumous) may refer to his black armour. During the Hundred Years' War he fought at the Battle of Crécy 1346 and captured the French king at Poitiers 1356. He ruled Aquitaine 1360–71; during the revolt that eventually ousted him, he caused the massacre of Limoges 1370.

In 1367 he invaded Castile and restored to the throne the deposed king, Pedro the Cruel (1334–69).

Edward /edwəd/ eight kings of England or the UK:

Edward I 1239–1307. King of England from 1272, son of Henry III. Edward led the royal forces against Simon de Montfort in the Barons' War 1264–67, and was on a crusade when he succeeded to the throne. He established English rule over all Wales 1282–84, and secured recognition of his overlordship from the Scottish king, although the Scots (under Wallace and Bruce) fiercely resisted actual conquest. In his reign Parliament took its approximate modern form with the Model Parliament 1295. He was succeeded by his son Edward II.

Edward II 1284–1327. King of England from 1307. Son of Edward I and born at Caernarvon Castle, he was created the first Prince of Wales 1301. His invasion of Scotland 1314 to suppress revolt resulted in defeat at Bannockburn. He was deposed 1327 by his wife Isabella (1292–1358), daughter of Philip IV of France, and her lover Roger de →Mortimer, and murdered in Berkeley Castle, Gloucestershire. He was succeeded by his son Edward III.

Incompetent and frivolous, and entirely under the influence of his favourites, Edward I struggled throughout his reign with discontented barons.

Edward VI Prince Edward, the only son of Henry VIII, became King Edward VI at the age of ten. He died of tuberculosis before reaching adulthood.

Edward III 1312–1377. King of England from 1327, son of Edward II. He assumed the government 1330 from his mother, through whom in 1337 he laid claim to the French throne and thus began the Hundred Years' War. He was succeeded by Richard II.

Edward began his reign by attempting to force his rule on Scotland, winning a victory at Halidon Hill 1333. During the first stage of the Hundred Years' War, English victories included the Battle of Crécy 1346 and the capture of Calais 1347. In 1360 Edward surrendered his claim to the French throne, but the war resumed 1369. During his last years his son John of Gaunt acted as head of government.

Edward IV 1442–1483. King of England 1461–70 and from 1471. He was the son of Richard, Duke of York, and succeeded Henry VI in the Wars of the Roses, temporarily losing the throne to Henry when Edward fell out with his adviser →Warwick, but regaining it at the Battle of Barnet 1471. He was succeeded by his son Edward V.

Edward was known as Earl of March until his accession. After his father's death he occupied London 1461, and was proclaimed king in place of Henry VI by a council of peers. His position was secured by the defeat of the Lancastrians at Towton 1461 and by the capture of Henry. He quarrelled, however, with Warwick, his strongest supporter, who in 1470–71 temporarily restored Henry, until Edward recovered the throne by his victories at Barnet and Tewkesbury.

Edward V 1470–1483. King of England 1483. Son of Edward IV, he was deposed three months after his accession in favour of his uncle (→Richard III), and is traditionally believed to have been murdered (with his brother) in the Tower of London on Richard's orders.

Edward VI 1537–1553. King of England from 1547, son of Henry VIII and Jane Seymour. The government was entrusted to his uncle the Duke of Somerset (who fell from power 1549), and then to the Earl of Warwick, later created Duke of Northumberland. He was succeeded by his sister, Mary I.

Jane Seymour was Henry VIII's third wife, and Edward was his only son. Edward became a staunch Protestant and during his reign the Reformation progressed. He died from tuberculosis.

Edward VII 1841–1910. King of Great Britain and Ireland from 1901. As Prince of Wales he was a prominent social figure, but his mother Queen Victoria considered him too frivolous to take part in political life. In 1860 he made the first tour of Canada and the USA ever undertaken by a British prince.

Edward was born at Buckingham Palace, the eldest son of Queen Victoria and Prince Albert. After his father's death 1861 he undertook many public duties, took a close interest in politics, and was on friendly terms with the party leaders. In 1863 he married Princess →Alexandra of Denmark, and they had six children. He toured India 1875–76. He succeeded to the throne 1901 and was crowned 1902. Although he overrated his political influence, he contributed to the Entente Cordiale 1904 with France and the Anglo-Russian agreement 1907.

Edward VIII 1894–1972. King of Great Britain and Northern Ireland Jan–Dec 1936, when he renounced the throne to marry Wallis Warfield →Simpson. He was created Duke of Windsor and was governor of the Bahamas 1940–45, subsequently settling in France.

Eldest son of George V, he received the title of Prince of Wales 1910 and succeeded to the throne 20 Jan 1936. In Nov 1936 a constitutional crisis arose when Edward wished to marry Mrs Simpson; it was felt that, as a divorcee, she would be unacceptable as queen. On 11 Dec Edward abdicated and left for France, where the couple were married 1937. He was succeeded by his brother, George VI.

I have found it impossible to carry the heavy burden of responsibility and to discharge my duties as king as I would wish to do, without the help and support of the woman I love.

King Edward VIII
abdication speech on radio Dec 1936

Edwards /edwədz/ Blake. Adopted name of William Blake McEdwards 1922– . US film director and writer, formerly an actor. Specializing in comedies, he directed the series of *Pink Panther* films 1963–78, starring Peter Sellers. His other work includes *Breakfast at Tiffany's* 1961 and *Blind Date* 1986.

Edwards /edwədz/ Gareth 1947– . Welsh rugby union player. He was appointed captain of his country when only 20 years old.

He appeared in seven championship winning teams, five Triple Crown winning teams, and two Grand Slam winning teams. In 53 international matches he scored a record 20 tries. He toured with the British Lions three times.

Edwards /edwədz/ George 1908– . British civil and military aircraft designer, associated with the Viking, Viscount, Valiant V- bomber, VC-10, and Concorde.

Edwards Jonathan 1703–1758. US theologian who took a Calvinist view of predestination and initiated a religious revival, the 'Great Awakening.' His *The Freedom of the Will* 1754 (defending determinism, the denial of human freedom of action) received renewed attention in the 20th century.

Edward the Confessor /edwəd/ c. 1003–1066. King of England from 1042, the son of Ethelred II. He lived in Normandy until shortly before his accession. During his reign power was held by Earl →Godwin and his son →Harold, while the king devoted himself to religion, including the rebuilding of Westminster Abbey (consecrated 1065), where he is buried. His childlessness led ultimately to the Norman Conquest 1066. He was canonized 1161.

Edward the Elder c. 870–924. King of the West Saxons. He succeeded his father →Alfred the Great 899. He reconquered SE England and the Midlands from the Danes, uniting Wessex and Mercia with the help of his sister, Athelflad. By the time Edward died, his kingdom was the most powerful in the British Isles. He was succeeded by his son →Athelstan.

Edward the Martyr c. 963–978. King of England from 975. Son of King Edgar, he was murdered at Corfe Castle, Dorset, probably at his stepmother Aelfthryth's instigation (she wished to secure the crown for her son, Ethelred). He was canonized 1001.

Edwin /edwɪn/ c. 585–633. King of Northumbria from 617. He captured and fortified Edinburgh, which was named after him, and was killed in battle with Penda of Mercia 632.

Egbert /egbɜːt/ died 839. King of the West Saxons from 802, the son of Ealhmund, an underking of Kent. By 829 he had united England for the first time under one king.

Egerton /edʒətən/ family name of dukes of Sutherland, seated at Mertoun, Roxburghshire, Scotland.

Egmont /egmɒnt/ Lamoral, Graaf von 1522–1568. Flemish nobleman, born in Hainault. As a servant of the Spanish crown, he defeated the French at St Quentin 1557 and Gravelines 1558, and became stadholder (chief magistrate) of Flanders and Artois. From 1561 he opposed Philip II's religious policy in the Netherlands of persecuting Protestants, but in 1567 the duke of Alva was sent to crush the resistance, and Egmont was beheaded.

Ehrenburg /erənbɜːg/ Ilya Grigorievich 1891–1967. Soviet writer, born in Kiev, Ukraine. His controversial work *The Thaw* 1954 depicts artistic circles in the USSR and contributed to the growing literary freedom of the 1950s.

Ehrlich /eəlɪk/ Paul 1854–1915. German bacteriologist and immunologist who produced the first cure for syphilis. He developed the arsenic compounds, in particular Salvarsan, that were used in the treatment of syphilis prior to the discovery of antibiotics. He shared the 1908 Nobel Prize for Medicine with Ilya →Mechnikov for his work on immunity.

Success in research needs four Gs: Glück, Geduld, Geschick und Geld. Luck, patience, skill, and money.

Paul Ehrlich

Eichendorff /aɪkəndɔːf/ Joseph Freiherr von 1788–1857. German Romantic poet and novelist, born in Upper Silesia. His work was set to music by Schumann, Mendelssohn, and Wolf. He held various judicial posts.

Eichmann /aɪkmən/ (Karl) Adolf 1906–1962. Austrian Nazi. As an SS official during Hitler's regime (1933–1945), he was responsible for atrocities against Jews and others, including the implementation of genocide. He managed to escape at the fall of Germany 1945, but was discovered in Argentina 1960, abducted by Israeli agents, tried in Israel 1961 for war crimes, and executed.

Eiffel /aɪfəl/ (Alexandre) Gustave 1832–1923. French engineer who constructed the *Eiffel Tower* for the 1889 Paris Exhibition. The tower, made of iron, is 320 m/1,050 ft high, and stands in the Champ de Mars, Paris.

Eiffel set up his own business in Paris and quickly established his reputation with the construction of a series of ambitious railway bridges, of which the 160 m/525 ft span across the Douro at Oporto, Portugal, was the longest. In 1881 he provided the iron skeleton for the Statue of Liberty.

Eiffel Chiefly known for his construction of the high tower in Paris named after him, Gustave Eiffel also designed many notable bridges and viaducts and conducted pioneer researches in aerodynamics and the use of wind tunnels

Eigen Manfred 1927– . German chemist who worked on extremely rapid chemical reactions (those taking less than 1 millisecond). From 1954 he developed a technique by which very short bursts of energy could be applied to solutions, disrupting their equilibrium and enabling him to investigate momentary reactions such as the formation and dissociation of water.

For this work he shared the Nobel Prize in Chemistry 1967 with English chemists George Porter and Ronald Norrish (1897–1978).

Eijkman /aɪkmən/ Christiaan 1858–1930. Dutch bacteriologist. He pioneered the recognition of vitamins as essential to health and identified vitamin B1 deficiency as the cause of the disease beriberi. He shared the 1929 Nobel Prize for Medicine with Frederick Hopkins.

Einstein /aɪnstaɪn/ Albert 1879–1955. German-born US physicist who formulated the theories of relativity, and worked on radiation physics and thermodynamics. In 1905 he published the special theory of relativity, and in 1915 issued his general theory of relativity. He received the Nobel Prize for Physics 1921. His latest conception of the basic laws governing the universe was outlined in his unified field theory, made public 1953.

Born at Ulm, in Württemberg, West Germany, he lived with his parents in Munich and then in Italy. After teaching at the polytechnic school at Zürich, he became a Swiss citizen and was appointed an inspector of patents in Berne. In his spare time, he took his PhD at Zürich. In 1909 he became a lecturer in theoretical physics at the university. After holding a similar post at Prague 1911, he returned to teach at Zürich 1912, and in 1913 took up a specially created post as director of the Kaiser Wilhelm Institute for Physics, Berlin. After being deprived of his position at Berlin by the Nazis, he emigrated to the USA 1933, and became professor of mathematics and a permanent member of the Institute for Advanced Study at Princeton, New Jersey. During World War II he worked for the US Navy Ordnance Bureau.

Einthoven /aɪnthəʊvən/ Willem 1860–1927. Dutch physiologist and inventor of the electrocardiograph. He demonstrated that certain disorders of the heart alter its electrical activity in characteristic ways. He was awarded the 1924 Nobel Prize for Medicine.

Eisai /eɪsaɪ/ 1141–1215. Japanese Buddhist monk who introduced Zen and tea from China to Japan and founded the Rinzai school of Zen, emphasizing rigorous monastic discipline and sudden enlightenment by meditation.

Eisenhower /aɪzənˌhaʊə/ Dwight David ('Ike') 1890–1969. 34th president of the USA 1953–60, a Republican. A general in World War II, he commanded the Allied forces in Italy 1943, then the Allied invasion of Europe, and from Oct 1944 all the Allied armies in the West. As president he promoted business interests at home and conducted the Cold War abroad. His vice president was Richard Nixon.

Eisenhower was born in Texas. A graduate of West Point military academy in 1915, he served in a variety of staff and command posts before World War II. He became commander in chief of the US and British forces for the invasion of North Africa Nov 1942; commanded the Allied invasion of Sicily July 1943; and announced the surrender of Italy 8 Sept 1943. In Dec he became commander of the Allied Expeditionary Force. He served as president of Columbia University and chair of the joint Chiefs of Staff between 1949 and 1950. He resigned from the army 1952 to campaign for the presidency; he was elected, and re-elected by a wide margin in 1956. A popular politician, Eisenhower held office during a period of domestic and international tension, with the growing civil rights movement at home and the Cold War dominating international politics, although the USA was experiencing an era of postwar prosperity and growth.

Eisenstein /aɪzənstaɪn/ Sergei Mikhailovich 1898–1948. Soviet film director who pioneered film theory and introduced the use of montage (the juxtaposition of shots to create a particular effect) as a means of propaganda, as in *The Battleship Potemkin* 1925.

The Soviet dictator Stalin banned the second part of Eisenstein's unfinished three-film masterpiece *Ivan the Terrible* 1944–46. His other films include *Strike* 1925, *October* 1928, *Que Viva Mexico!* 1931–32, and *Alexander Nevsky* 1938.

Eldem /el'dem/ Sedad Hakki 1908– . Turkish architect whose work is inspired by the spatial harmony and regular rhythms of the traditional Turkish house. These qualities are reinterpreted in modern forms with great sensitivity to context, as in the Social Security Agency Complex, Zeyrek, Istanbul (1962–64), and the Ataturk Library, Istanbul (1973).

Elder /eldə/ Mark 1947– . English conductor, music director of the English National Opera from 1979 and of Rochester Philharmonic Orchestra, USA, from 1989.

Elder worked at Glyndebourne from 1970, conducted with the Australian Opera from 1972, and joined the English National Opera 1974. Following his appointment as principal conductor of ENO 1979, he showed a lively command of 19th- and 20th- century music.

Eldon /eldən/ John Scott, 1st Earl of Eldon 1751–1838. English politician, born in Newcastle. He became a member of Parliament 1782, solicitor-general 1788, attorney-general 1793, and Lord Chancellor 1801–05 and 1807–27. During his period the rules of the Lord Chancellor's court governing the use of the injunction and precedent in equity finally became fixed.

Eleanor of Aquitaine /elɪnər əv ækwɪ'teɪn/ *c.* 1122–1204. Queen of France 1137–51 as wife of Louis VII, and of England from 1154 as wife of Henry II. Henry imprisoned her 1174–89 for supporting their sons, the future Richard I and King John, in revolt against him.

She was the daughter of William X, Duke of Aquitaine, and was married 1137–52 to Louis VII of France, but the marriage was annulled. The same year she married Henry of Anjou, who became king of England 1154.

Eleanor of Castile /elɪnər əv kæs'tiːl/ *c.* 1245–1290. Queen of Edward I of England, the daughter of Ferdinand III of Castile. She married Prince Edward 1254, and accompanied him on his crusade 1270. She died at Harby, Nottinghamshire, and Edward erected stone crosses in towns where her body rested on the funeral journey to London. Several *Eleanor Crosses* are still standing, for example at Northampton.

Elgar /elgɑː/ Edward (William) 1857–1934. English composer. His *Enigma Variations* appeared 1899, and although his celebrated choral work, the oratorio setting of John Henry Newman's *The Dream of Gerontius*, was initially a failure, it was well received at Düsseldorf in 1902. Many of his earlier works were then performed, including the *Pomp and Circumstance* marches.

Among his later works are oratorios, two symphonies, a violin concerto, a cello concerto, chamber music, songs, and the tone-poem *Falstaff* 1913.

Elijah /ɪ'laɪdʒə/ *c.* mid-9th century BC. In the Old Testament, a Hebrew prophet during the reigns of the Israelite kings Ahab and Ahaziah. He came from Gilead. He defeated the prophets of Baal, and was said to have been carried up to heaven in a fiery chariot in a whirlwind. In Jewish belief, Elijah will return to Earth to herald the coming of the Messiah.

Eliot /eliət/ Charles William 1834–1926. US educator credited with establishing the standards of modern American higher education. He was appointed professor at the Massachusetts Institute of Technology (MIT) 1865 and was named president of Harvard University 1869. Under Eliot's administration, the college and its graduate and professional schools were reorganized and the curriculum and admission requirements standardized. He retired 1909.

Born in Boston and educated at Harvard, Eliot specialized in mathematics and chemistry and later took up the cause of educational reform.

Eliot /eliət/ George. Pen name of Mary Ann Evans 1819–1880. English novelist whose works include the pastoral *Adam Bede* 1859, *The Mill on the Floss* 1860, with its autobiographical elements, *Silas Marner* 1861, which contains elements of the folktale, and *Daniel Deronda* 1876. *Middlemarch*, published serially in 1871–2, is considered her greatest novel for its confident handling of numerous characters and central social and moral issues. Her work is pervaded by a penetrating and compassionate intelligence.

Eliot English novelist Mary Ann Evans, who wrote under the name George Eliot. Her writing career was encouraged by literary journalist George Henry Lewes, with whom she lived from 1854 until his death 1878. She combined sympathetic analysis and detailed observation and moral judgement of her characters.

Born at Chilvers Coton, Warwickshire, George Eliot had a strict evangelical upbringing. In 1841 she was converted to free thought. As assistant editor of the *Westminster Review* under John Chapman 1851–53, she made the acquaintance of Thomas Carlyle, Harriet Martineau, Herbert Spencer, and the philosopher and critic George Henry Lewes (1817–1878). Lewes was married but separated from his wife, and from 1854 he and Eliot lived together in a relationship that she regarded as a true marriage and that continued until his death. In 1880 she married John Cross (1840–1924).

Nothing is so good as it seems beforehand.

George Eliot *Silas Marner* 1861

Eliot /elɪət/ John 1592–1632. English politician, born in Cornwall. He became a member of Parliament 1614, and with the Earl of Buckingham's patronage was made a vice-admiral 1619. In 1626 he was imprisoned in the Tower of London for demanding Buckingham's impeachment. In 1628 he was a formidable supporter of the petition of right opposing Charles I, and with other parliamentary leaders was again imprisoned in the Tower of London 1629, where he died.

Eliot /elɪət/ T(homas) S(tearns) 1888–1965. US poet, playwright, and critic who lived in London from 1915. His first volume of poetry, *Prufrock and Other Observations* 1917, introduced new verse forms and rhythms; further collections include *The Waste Land* 1922, *The Hollow Men* 1925, and *Old Possum's Book of Practical Cats* 1939. His plays include *Murder in the Cathedral* 1935 and *The Cocktail Party* 1949. His critical works include *The Sacred Wood* 1920. He was awarded the Nobel Prize for Literature 1948.

Eliot was born in St Louis, Missouri, and was educated at Harvard, the Sorbonne, and Oxford. He settled in London 1915 and became a British subject 1927. He was for a time a bank clerk, later lecturing and entering publishing at Faber & Faber. As editor of *The Criterion* 1922–39, he influenced the thought of his generation.

Prufrock and Other Observations expressed the disillusionment of the generation affected by World War I and caused a sensation with its experimental form and rhythms. His reputation was established by the desolate modernity of *The Waste Land*. *The Hollow Men* continued on the same note, but *Ash Wednesday* 1930 revealed the change in religious attitude that led him to become a Catholic. Among his other works are *Four Quartets* 1943, a religious sequence in which he seeks the eternal reality, and the poetic dramas *Murder in the Cathedral* (about Thomas à Becket); *The Cocktail Party*; *The Confidential Clerk* 1953; and *The Elder Statesman* 1958. His collection *Old Possum's Book of Practical Cats* was used for the pop-

ular British composer Andrew Lloyd Webber's musical *Cats* 1981. His critical works include *Notes toward the Definition of Culture* 1949.

Elisha /ɪˈlaɪʃə/ mid-9th century BC. In the Old Testament, a Hebrew prophet, successor to Elijah.

Elizabeth /ɪˈlɪzəbəθ/ the ***Queen Mother*** 1900– . Wife of King George VI of England. She was born Lady Elizabeth Angela Marguerite Bowes-Lyon, and on 26 April 1923 she married Albert, Duke of York, who became King George VI in 1936. Their children are Queen Elizabeth II and Princess Margaret.

She is the youngest daughter of the 14th Earl of Strathmore and Kinghorne (died 1944), through whom she is descended from Robert Bruce, king of Scotland. When her husband became King George VI she became Queen Consort, and was crowned with him 1937. She adopted the title Queen Elizabeth, the Queen Mother after his death.

Elizabeth /ɪˈlɪzəbəθ/ two queens of England or the UK:

Elizabeth I 1533–1603. Queen of England 1558–1603, the daughter of Henry VIII and Anne Boleyn. Through her Religious Settlement of 1559 she enforced the Protestant religion by law. She had →Mary, Queen of Scots, executed 1587. Her conflict with Roman Catholic Spain led to the defeat of the Spanish Armada 1588. The Elizabethan age was expansionist in commerce and geographical exploration, and arts and literature flourished. The rulers of many European states made unsuccessful bids to marry Elizabeth, and she used these bids to strengthen her power. She was succeeded by James I.

Elizabeth was born at Greenwich, London, 7 Sept 1533. She was well educated in several languages. During her Roman Catholic half-sister Mary's reign, Elizabeth's Protestant sympathies brought her under suspicion, and she lived in seclusion at Hatfield, Hertfordshire, until on Mary's death she became queen. Her first task was to bring about a broad religious settlement.

Many unsuccessful attempts were made by Parliament to persuade Elizabeth to marry or settle the succession. She found courtship a useful political weapon, and she maintained friendships with, among others, the courtiers →Leicester, Sir Walter →Raleigh, and →Essex. She was known as the Virgin Queen.

The arrival in England 1568 of Mary, Queen of Scots, and her imprisonment by Elizabeth caused a political crisis, and a rebellion of the feudal nobility of the north followed 1569. Friction between English and Spanish sailors hastened the breach with Spain. When the Dutch rebelled against Spanish tyranny Elizabeth secretly encouraged them; Philip II retaliated by aiding Catholic conspiracies against her. This undeclared war continued for many years, until the landing of an English army in the Netherlands 1585 and Mary's execution 1587, brought it into the open. Philip's Armada (the fleet sent to invade England 1588) met with total disaster.

The war with Spain continued with varying fortunes to the end of the reign, while events at home foreshadowed the conflicts of the 17th century. Among the Puritans discontent was developing with Elizabeth's religious settlement, and several were imprisoned or executed. Parliament showed a new independence, and in 1601 forced Elizabeth to retreat on the monopolies question. Yet her prestige remained unabated, as was shown by the failure of Essex's rebellion 1601.

Anger makes dull men witty, but it keeps them poor.

Queen Elizabeth I

Elizabeth II 1926– . Queen of Great Britain and Northern Ireland from 1952, the elder daughter of George VI. She married her third cousin, Philip, the Duke of Edinburgh, 1947. They have four children: Charles, Anne, Andrew, and Edward.

Princess Elizabeth Alexandra Mary was born in London 21 April 1926; she was educated privately, and assumed official duties at 16. During World War II she served in the Auxiliary Territorial Service, and by an amendment to the Regency Act she became a state counsellor on her 18th birthday. On the death of George VI in 1952 she succeeded to the throne while in Kenya with her husband and was crowned on 2 June 1953.

Elizabeth /ɪ'lɪzəbəθ/ 1709–1762. Empress of Russia from 1741, daughter of Peter the Great. She carried through a palace revolution and supplanted her cousin, the infant Ivan VI (1730–1764), on the throne. She continued the policy of westernization begun by Peter and allied herself with Austria against Prussia.

Ellington /elɪŋtən/ Duke (Edward Kennedy) 1899–1974. US pianist who had an outstanding career as a composer and arranger of jazz. He wrote numerous pieces for his own jazz orchestra, accentuating the strengths of individual virtuoso instrumentalists, and became one of the leading figures in jazz over a 55-year period. Some of his most popular compositions include 'Mood Indigo', 'Sophisticated Lady', 'Solitude', and 'Black and Tan Fantasy'. He was one of the founders of big band jazz.

Ellis /elɪs/ (Henry) Havelock 1859–1939. English psychologist and writer of many works on the psychology of sex, including *Studies in the Psychology of Sex* (seven volumes) 1898–1928.

Ellison /elɪsən/ Ralph 1914– . US novelist. His *Invisible Man* 1952 portrays with humour and energy the plight of a black man whom postwar American society cannot acknowledge; it is regarded as one of the most impressive novels published in the USA in the 1950s.

Ellsworth /elzwɜːθ/ Oliver 1745–1807. US jurist and chief justice of the US Supreme Court 1796–1800. As a Connecticut delegate to the Constitutional Convention 1777, he was instrumental in effecting the 'Connecticut Compromise,' which balanced large and small state interests. He was selected as US senator from Connecticut in 1787. Appointed chief justice by President Washington, his opinions shaped admiralty law and treaty law.

Born in Windsor, Connecticut, he attended Yale College and graduated from Princeton University 1766. After establishing himself as a lawyer he served concurrently in a number of political posts in Connecticut. He became a judge of the new state court of appeals in 1785, moving to the new state superior court as a judge in the same year.

Elsheimer /elshaɪmə/ Adam 1578–1610. German painter and etcher, active in Rome from 1600. His small paintings, nearly all on copper, depict landscapes darkened by storm or night, with figures picked out by beams of light, as in *The Rest on the Flight into Egypt* 1609 (Alte Pinakothek, Munich).

Elton /eltən/ Charles 1900–1991. British ecologist, a pioneer of the study of animal and plant forms in their natural environments, and of animal behaviour as part of the complex pattern of life. He defined the concept of food chains and was an early conservationist, instrumental in establishing (1949) the Nature Conservancy Council of which he was a member 1949–56, and much concerned with the impact of introduced species on natural systems.

His books include *Animal Ecology and Evolution* 1930 and *The Pattern of Animal Communities* 1966.

Eluard /ˌeɪluːˈɑː/ Paul. Pen name of Eugène Grindel 1895–1952. French poet, born in Paris. He expressed the suffering of poverty in his verse, and was a leader of the Surrealists. He fought in World War I, which inspired his *Poèmes pour la paix/Poems for Peace* 1918, and was a member of the Resistance in World War II. His books include *Poésie et vérité/Poetry and Truth* 1942 and *Au Rendezvous allemand/To the German Rendezvous* 1944.

Ely /iːli/ Richard Theodore 1854–1943. US economist and an early advocate of government economic intervention, central planning, and the organization of the labour force. He was appointed professor of political economy at Johns Hopkins University 1881 and in 1885 founded the American Economic Association. In 1892 he became chair of the department of economics at the University of Wisconsin before join the faculty of Northwestern University 1925.

Born in Ripley, New York, USA, Ely was educated at Columbia University and received his PhD from the University of Heidelberg 1879. He retired from teaching 1933.

Elyot /ˈeliət/ Thomas 1490–1546. English diplomat and scholar. In 1531 he published *The Governour*, the first treatise on education in English.

Elytis /eˈliːtɪs/ Odysseus. Pen name of Odysseus Alepoudelis 1911– . Greek poet, born in Crete. His verse celebrates the importance of the people's attempts to shape an individual existence in freedom. His major work *To Axion Esti/Worthy It Is* 1959 is a lyric cycle, parts of which have been set to music by Theodorakis. He was awarded the Nobel Prize for Literature in 1979.

Elzevir /ˈelzəvɪə/ Louis 1540–1617. Founder of the Dutch printing house Elzevir in the 17th century. Among the firm's publications were editions of Latin, Greek, and Hebrew works, as well as French and Italian classics.

Born at Louvain, Elzevir was obliged to leave Belgium in 1580 because of his Protestant and political views. He settled at Leyden as a bookseller and printer.

Emerson /ˈeməsən/ Ralph Waldo 1803–1882. US philosopher, essayist, and poet. He settled in Concord, Massachusetts, which he made a centre of the mystical and social doctrine of transcendentalism, and wrote *Nature* 1836, which states the movement's main principles emphasizing the value of self-reliance and the Godlike nature of human souls. His two volumes of *Essays* (1841, 1844) made his reputation: 'Self-Reliance' and 'Compensation' are among the best known.

Born in Boston, Massachusetts, and educated at Harvard, Emerson became a Unitarian minister. In 1832 he resigned and travelled to Europe, meeting the British writers Carlyle, Coleridge, and Wordsworth. On his return to Massachusetts in 1833 he settled in Concord. He made a second visit to England 1847 and incorporated his impressions in *English Traits* 1856. Much of his verse was published in the literary magazine *The Dial*. His poems include 'The Rhodora', 'Threnody', and 'Brahma'. His later works include *Representative Men* 1850 and *The Conduct of Life* 1870.

Emery /ˈeməri/ Walter Bryan 1903–1971. British archaeologist, who in 1929–34 in Nubia, N Africa, excavated the barrows at Ballana and Qustol, rich royal tombs of the mysterious X-group people (3rd to 6th centuries AD). He also surveyed the whole region 1963–64 before it was flooded as a result of the building of the Aswan High Dam.

Emin Pasha /eˈmiːn/ Mehmed. Adopted name of Eduard Schnitzer 1849–1892. German explorer, doctor, and linguist. Appointed by General Gordon as chief medical officer and then governor of the Equatorial province of S Sudan, he carried out extensive research in anthropology, botany, zoology, and meteorology.

Isolated by his remote location and cut off from the outside world by Arab slave traders, he was 'rescued' by an expedition led by H M Stanley in 1889. He travelled with Stanley as far as Zanzibar but returned to continue his work near Lake Victoria. Three years later he was killed by Arabs while leading an expedition to the W coast of Africa.

Emmet /ˈemɪt/ Robert 1778–1803. Irish nationalist leader. In 1803 he led an unsuccessful revolt in Dublin against British rule and was captured, tried, and hanged. His youth and courage made him an Irish hero.

Empedocles /emˈpedəkliːz/ *c.* 490–430 BC. Greek philosopher and scientist. He lived at Acragas (Agrigentum) in Sicily, and proposed that the universe is composed of four elements – fire, air, earth, and water – which through the action of love and discord are eternally constructed, destroyed, and constructed anew. According to tradition, he committed suicide by throwing himself into the crater of Mount Etna.

Empson /ˈempsən/ William 1906–1984. English poet and critic, born in Yorkshire. He was professor of English literature at Tokyo and Beijing (Peking), and from 1953 to 1971 at Sheffield University. His critical work examined the potential variety of meaning in poetry, as in *Seven Types of Ambiguity* 1930 and *The Structure of Complex Words* 1951. His *Collected Poems* were published 1955.

Ender /ˈendə/ Kornelia 1958– . German swimmer. She won a record-tying four gold medals at the 1976 Olympics at freestyle, butterfly, and relay; a total of eight Olympic medals 1972–76; and a record ten world championship medals 1973 and 1975.

Enders /ˈendəz/ John Franklin 1897–1985. US virologist. With Thomas Weller (1915–) and Frederick Robbins (1916–), he discovered the ability of the polio virus to grow in cultures of various tissues, which led to the perfection of an effective vaccine. The three were awarded the Nobel Prize for Medicine 1954. Enders also succeeded in isolating the measles virus.

Engel /ˈeŋəl/ Carl Ludwig 1778–1840. German architect, who from 1815 worked in Finland. His great Neo-Classical achievement is the Senate Square in Helsinki, which is defined by his Senate House 1818–22 and University Building 1828–32, and crowned by the domed Lutheran cathedral 1830–40.

Engels /ˈeŋəlz/ Friedrich 1820–1895. German social and political philosopher, a friend of, and collaborator with, Karl →Marx on *The Communist Manifesto* 1848 and other key works. His later interpretations of Marxism, and his own philosophical and historical studies such as *Origins of the Family, Private Property, and the State* 1884 (which linked patriarchy with the development of private property), developed such concepts as historical materialism. His use of positivism and Darwinian ideas gave Marxism a scientific and deterministic flavour which was to influence Soviet thinking.

In 1842 Engels's father sent him to work in the cotton factory owned by his family in Manchester, England, where he became involved with Chartism, a radical democratic movement. In 1844 his lifelong friendship with Karl Marx began, and together they worked out the materialist interpretation of history and in 1847–48 wrote the *Communist Manifesto*. Returning to Germany during the 1848–49 revolution, Engels worked with Marx on the *Neue Rheinische Zeitung/New Rhineland Newspaper* and fought on the barricades in Baden. After the defeat of the revolution he returned to Manchester, and for the rest of his life largely supported the Marx family.

Engels's first book was *The Condition of the Working Classes in England* 1845. He summed up the lessons of 1848 in *The Peasants' War in Germany* 1850 and *Revolution and Counter-Revolution in Germany* 1851. After Marx's death Engels was largely responsible for the wider dissemination of his ideas; he edited the second and third volumes of Marx's *Das Kapital* 1885 and 1894. Although Engels himself regarded his ideas as identical with those of Marx, discrepancies between their works are the basis of many Marxist debates.

Engels German socialist Friedrich Engels. The lifelong friend of Karl Marx, he dedicated himself to disseminating the central concepts of Marxism. Engels worked with Marx to produce The Communist Manifesto *1848 and continued to edit and translate the writings of Marx after his death.*

The State is not 'abolished', it withers away.

Friedrich Engels *Anti Dühring*

Engleheart /ˈeŋɡəlhɑːt/ George 1752–1829. English miniature painter. Born in Kew, London, he studied under Joshua Reynolds and in 40 years painted nearly 5,000 miniatures including copies of many of Reynolds's portraits.

Ennius /ˈeniəs/ Quintus 239–169 BC. Early Roman poet who wrote tragedies based on the Greek pattern. His epic poem *Annales* deals with Roman history.

Ensor /ˈensɔː/ James 1860–1949. Belgian painter and printmaker. His bold style used strong colours to explore themes of human cruelty and the macabre, as in the *Entry of Christ into Brussels* 1888 (Musée Royale des Beaux-Arts, Brussels) and anticipated Expressionism.

The Roman state survives by its ancient customs and its manhood.

Quintus Ennius *Annales*

Enver Pasha /ˈenvə ˈpɑːʃə/ 1881–1922. Turkish politician and soldier. He led the military revolt 1908 that resulted in the Young Turks' revolution (instrumental in achieving constitutional changes and the abdication of Sultan Abdul-Hamid 1909). He was killed fighting the Bolsheviks in Turkestan.

Eötvös /ˈɜːtvɜːʃ/ Roland von, Baron 1848–1919. Hungarian scientist, born in Budapest, who investigated problems of gravitation, and constructed the double-armed torsion balance for determining variations of gravity.

Epaminondas /eˌpæmɪˈnɒndæs/ *c.* 420–362 BC. Theban general and politician who won a decisive victory over the Spartans at Leuctra 371. He was killed at the moment of victory at Mantinea.

Epictetus /ˌepɪkˈtiːtəs/ *c.* AD 55–135. Greek Stoic philosopher who encouraged people to refrain from self-interest and to promote the common good of humanity. He believed that people were in the hands of an all-wise providence and that they should endeavour to do their duty in the position to which they were called.

Born at Hierapolis in Phrygia, he lived for many years in Rome as a slave but eventually secured his freedom. He was banished by the emperor ➔Domitian from Rome in AD 89.

Erasmus 16th-century carved oak sculpture of Erasmus, by an unknown artist. The humanistic scholar is portrayed here as a pilgrim. He holds a staff, which has a flask attached.

Epicurus /ˌepɪˈkʊərəs/ 341–270 BC. Greek philosopher, founder of Epicureanism, who taught at Athens from 306 BC.

Epstein /ˈepstaɪn/ Jacob 1880–1959. British sculptor, born in New York. He experimented with abstract forms, but is chiefly known for his controversial muscular nude figures such as *Genesis* 1931 (Whitworth Art Gallery, Manchester). He was better appreciated as a portraitist (bust of Einstein, 1933), and in later years executed several monumental figures, notably the expressive bronze of *St Michael and the Devil* 1959 (Coventry Cathedral).

In 1904 he moved to England, where most of his major work was done. An early example showing the strong influence of ancient sculptural styles is the angel over the tomb of Oscar Wilde 1912 (Père Lachaise cemetery, Paris), while *Rock Drill* 1913–14 (Tate Gallery, London) is Modernist and semi-abstract. Such figures outraged public sensibilities.

Equiano /ˌekwiˈɑːnəʊ/ Olaudah 1745–1797. African antislavery campaigner and writer. He travelled widely as a free man. His autobiography, *The Interesting Narrative of the Life of Olaudah Equiano, or Gustavus Vassa, the African* 1789, is one of the earliest significant works by an African written in English.

Equiano was born near the river Niger in what is now Nigeria, captured at the age of ten and sold to slavers, who transported him to the West Indies. He learned English and bought his freedom at the age of 21. He subsequently sailed to the Mediterranean and the Arctic, before being appointed commissary of stores for freed slaves returning to Sierra Leone. He was an active campaigner against slavery.

Erasmus /ɪˈræzməs/ Desiderius *c.* 1466–1536. Dutch scholar and leading humanist of the Renaissance era, who taught and studied all over Europe and was a prolific writer. His pioneer translation of the Greek New Testament 1516 exposed the Vulgate as a second-hand document. Although opposed to dogmatism and abuse of church power, he remained impartial during Martin →Luther's conflict with the pope.

Erasmus was born in Rotterdam, and as a youth he was a monk in an Augustinian monastery near Gouda. After becoming a priest, he went to study in Paris 1495. He paid the first of a number of visits to England 1499, where he met the physician Thomas Linacre, the politician Thomas More, and the Bible interpreter John Colet, and for a time was professor of divinity and Greek at Cambridge University. He edited the writings of St Jerome, and published *Colloquia* (dialogues on contemporary subjects) 1519. In 1521 he went to Basel, Switzerland, where he edited the writings of the early Christian leaders.

Eratosthenes /ˌerəˈtɒsθəniːz/ *c.* 276–194 BC. Greek geographer and mathematician whose map of the ancient world was the first to contain lines of latitude and longitude, and who calculated the Earth's circumference with an error of about 10%. His mathematical achievements include a method for duplicating the cube, and for finding prime numbers (Eratosthenes' sieve).

Erhard /ˈeəhɑːt/ Ludwig 1897–1977. West German Christian Democrat politician, chancellor of the Federal Republic 1963–66. The 'economic miracle' of West Germany's recovery after World War II is largely attributed to Erhard's policy of social free enterprise (German *Marktwirtschaft*), which he initiated during his period as federal economics minister (1949–63).

Ericsson /ˈerɪksən/ John 1803–1889. Swedish-born US engineer who took out a patent to produce screw-propeller powered paddle-wheel ships 1836. He built a number of such ships, including the *Monitor*, which was successfully deployed during the American Civil War.

Ericsson /ˈerɪksən/ Leif b. *c.* 970. Norse explorer and son of Eric the Red. He sailed westward from Greenland *c.* 1000 to find land first sighted by Norsemen 986. He visited Baffin Island then sailed along the Labrador coast to Newfoundland, which was named 'Vinland' (Wine Land) allegedly because grapes grew there.

The establishment of a base was confirmed 1961 when a Norwegian expedition, led by Helge Ingstad, discovered remains of a Viking settlement (dated *c.* 1000) near the fishing village of L'Anse-aux-Meadows at the northern tip of Newfoundland.

Eric the Red /erɪk/ c. 950–c. 1010. According to a 13th-century saga, he was the son of a Norwegian chieftain, and was banished from Iceland about 982 for murder. He then sailed westward and found land sighted earlier that century. In 986 he established a colony of c. 350 people on the South-west coast just north of modern Julianehåb.

Erigena /ɪˈrɪdʒɪnə/ Johannes Scotus 815–877. Medieval philosopher. He was probably Irish and, according to tradition, travelled in Greece and Italy. The French king Charles II (the Bald) invited him to France (before 847), where he became head of the court school. He is said to have visited Oxford, to have taught at Malmesbury, and to have been stabbed to death by his pupils. In his philosophy, he defied church orthodoxy in his writings on cosmology and predestination, and tried to combine Christianity with Neo-Platonism.

Erim /eˈriːm/ Kenan Tevfig 1929–1990. Turkish-born US historian and archaeologist. From 1961 he began to excavate the city of Aphrodisias in Turkey while teaching at New York University. In his efforts to conserve and protect the site, the excavation took 30 years to complete.

Ernst /eənst/ Max 1891–1976. German artist who worked in France 1922–38 and in the USA from 1941. He was an active Dadaist, experimenting with collage, photomontage, and surreal images, and helped found the Surrealist movement 1924. His paintings are highly diverse.

Ernst first exhibited in Berlin 1916. He produced a 'collage novel', *La Femme cent têtes* 1929, worked on films with Salvador Dali and Luis Buñuel, and designed sets and costumes for Sergei Diaghilev and the Ballets Russes. His pictures range from smooth Surrealist images to highly textured emotive abstracts, from 1925 making use of frottage (rubbing over textured materials).

Ershad /eəʃəd/ Hussain Mohammad 1930– . Military ruler of Bangladesh 1982–90. He became chief of staff of the Bangladeshi army 1979 and assumed power in a military coup 1982. As president from 1983, Ershad introduced a successful rural-oriented economic programme. He was re-elected 1986 and lifted martial law, but faced continuing political opposition, which forced him to resign Dec 1990. In 1991 he was formally charged with the illegal possession of arms, convicted, and sentenced to ten years' imprisonment. He received a further sentence of three years' imprisonment Feb 1992 after being convicted of corruption.

Erskine /ɜːskɪn/ Ralph 1914– . British architect who specialized in community architecture before it was named as such. A deep social consciousness and a concern to mould building form in response to climate determine his architecture. His Byker Estate in Newcastle-upon-Tyne (1969–80), where a great sheltering wall of dwellings embraces the development, involved a lengthy process of consultation with the residents. A later project is the 'Ark', an office building in Hammersmith, London (1989– 91). Its shiplike form shelters the internal activities from an adjoining motorway.

Erskine /ɜːskɪn/ Thomas, 1st Baron Erskine 1750–1823. British barrister and lord chancellor. He was called to the Bar in 1778 and defended a number of parliamentary reformers on charges of sedition. When the Whig Party returned to power 1806 he became lord chancellor and a baron. Among his speeches were those in defence of Lord George Gordon, Thomas Paine, and Queen Caroline.

Erté /eəˈteɪ/ adopted name of Romain de Tirtoff 1892–1990. Russian designer and illustrator, active in France and the USA. He designed sets and costumes for opera, theatre, and ballet, and his drawings were highly stylized and expressive, featuring elegant, curvilinear women.

Erté (the name was derived from the French pronunciation of his initials) went to Paris 1911 to work as a theatre and ballet set designer. From 1916 to 1926 he produced covers for US fashion magazine *Harper's Bazaar*, and went to Hollywood 1925 to work as a designer on several films. He continued to design sets and costumes in Europe and the USA for many decades. His illustrations were influenced by 16th- century Persian and Indian miniatures.

Esaki /ɪˈsɑːki/ Leo 1925– . Japanese physicist who in 1957 noticed that electrons could sometimes 'tunnel' through the barrier formed at the junctions of certain semiconductors. The effect is now widely used in the electronics industry. For this early discovery Esaki shared the 1973 Nobel Prize for Physics with British physicist Brian Josephson and Norwegian-born US physicist Ivar Giaever (1929–).

Esarhaddon /iːsɑːˈhædn/ King of Assyria from 680 BC, when he succeeded his father →Sennacherib. He conquered Egypt 674–71 BC.

Escher /eʃə/ M(aurits) C(ornelis) 1902–1972. Dutch graphic artist. His prints are often based on mathematical concepts and contain paradoxes and illusions. The lithograph *Ascending and Descending* 1960, with interlocking staircases creating a perspective puzzle, is a typical work.

Esenin /jeˈsenɪn/ or *Yesenin*, Sergey 1895–1925. Soviet poet, born in Konstantinovo (renamed Esenino in his honour). He went to Petrograd 1915, attached himself to the Symbolists, welcomed the Russian Revolution, revived peasant traditions and folklore, and initiated the Imaginist group of poets 1919. A selection of his poetry was translated in *Confessions of a Hooligan* 1973. He was married briefly to US dancer Isadora Duncan 1922–23.

Espronceda /esprɒnˈθeɪdə/ José de 1808–1842. Spanish poet. Originally one of the Queen's guards, he lost his commission because of his political activities, and was involved in the Republican uprisings of 1835 and 1836. His lyric poetry and lifestyle both owed much to Lord Byron.

Esquivel /ˌeskɪˈvel/ Adolfo 1932– . Argentinian sculptor and architect. As leader of the Servicio de Paz y Justicia (Peace and Justice Service), a Catholic-Protestant human-rights organization, he was awarded the 1980 Nobel Peace Prize.

Essex /ˈesɪks/ Robert Devereux, 2nd Earl of Essex 1566–1601. English soldier and politician. He became a favourite with Queen Elizabeth I from 1587, but was executed because of his policies in Ireland.

Essex fought in the Netherlands 1585–86 and distinguished himself at the Battle of Zutphen. In 1596 he jointly commanded a force that seized and sacked Cádiz. In 1599 he became Lieutenant of Ireland and led an army against Irish rebels under the Earl of Tyrone in Ulster, but was unsuccessful, made an unauthorized truce with Tyrone, and returned without permission to England. He was forbidden to return to court, and when he marched into the City of London at the head of a body of supporters, he was promptly arrested, tried for treason, and beheaded on Tower Green.

Essex /ˈesɪks/ Robert Devereux, 3rd Earl of Essex 1591–1646. English soldier. Eldest son of the 2nd earl, he commanded the Parliamentary army at the inconclusive English Civil War battle of Edgehill 1642. Following a disastrous campaign in Cornwall, he resigned his command 1645.

Esteve-Coll /əˈstevi ˈkɒl/ Elizabeth Anne Loosemore 1938– . British museum administrator. Keeper of the National Art Library at the Victoria and Albert Museum 1985–88, she became director of the museum itself in 1988. Her reorganization of it in 1989, when she split the administrative and research roles, led to widespread criticism and the resignation of several senior staff.

She spent ten years travelling round the world with her husband before taking a degree in art history and becoming a librarian.

Ethelbert c. 552–616. King of Kent 560–616. He was defeated by the West Saxons 568 but later became ruler of England S of the river Humber. Ethelbert received the Christian missionary Augustine 597 and later converted to become the first Christian ruler of Anglo-Saxon England. He issued the first written code of laws known in England.

He married a French princess, Bertha.

Ethelred II /ˈeθəlred/ *the Unready* c. 968–1016. King of England from 978. He tried to buy off the Danish raiders by paying Danegeld. In 1002, he ordered the massacre of the Danish settlers, provoking an invasion by Sweyn I of Denmark. War with Sweyn and Sweyn's son, Canute, occupied the rest of Ethelred's reign. He was nicknamed the 'Unready' because of his apparent lack of foresight.

The son of King Edgar, Ethelred became king after the murder of his half-brother, Edward the Martyr.

Etherege /ˈeθərɪdʒ/ George c. 1635–1691. English Restoration dramatist whose play *Love in a Tub* 1664 was the first attempt at the comedy of manners (a genre further developed by Congreve and Sheridan). Later plays include *She Would if She Could* 1668 and *The Man of Mode, or Sir Fopling Flutter* 1676.

Etty /ˈeti/ William 1787–1849. English painter who specialized in female nudes. He also painted mythological or historical subjects such as *Telemachus Rescuing Antiope* 1811. Many of his paintings are in the York City Art Gallery, England.

Euclid /ˈjuːklɪd/ c. 330–c. 260 BC. Greek mathematician, who lived in Alexandria and wrote the *Stoicheia/Elements* in 13 books, of which nine deal with plane and solid geometry and four with number theory. His great achievement lay in the systematic arrangement of previous discoveries, based on axioms, definitions, and theorems.

Euclid's geometry texts remained in common usage for over 2,000 years.

Eudoxus /juːˈdɒksəs/ of Cnidus c. 390–c. 340 BC. Greek mathematician and astronomer. He devised the first system to account for the motions of celestial bodies, believing them to be carried around the Earth on sets of spheres. Probably Eudoxus regarded these spheres as a mathematical device for ease of computation rather than as physically real, but the idea of celestial spheres was taken up by →Aristotle and became entrenched in astronomical thought until the time of Tycho →Brahe. Eudoxus also described the constellations in a work called *Phaenomena*, providing the basis of the constellation system still in use today.

Eugène /juːˈdʒiːn/ Prince of Savoy 1663–1736. Austrian general who had many victories against the Turkish invaders (whom he expelled from Hungary 1697 in the Battle of Zenta) and against France in the War of the Spanish Succession (battles of Blenheim, Oudenaarde, and Malplaquet).

The son of Prince Eugène Maurice of Savoy-Carignano, he was born in Paris. When Louis XIV refused him a commission he entered the Austrian army, and served against the Turks at the defence of Vienna 1683, and against the French on the Rhine and in Italy ten years later. In the War of the Spanish Succession 1701–14 he shared with the British commander Marlborough in his great victories against the French and won many successes as an independent commander in Italy. He again defeated the Turks 1716–18, and fought a last campaign against the French 1734–35.

Eugénie /ˈɜːʒeɪˈniː/ Marie Ignace Augustine de Montijo 1826–1920. Empress of France, daughter of the Spanish count of Montijo. In 1853 she married Louis Napoleon, who had become emperor as →Napoleon III. She encouraged court extravagance, Napoleon III's intervention in Mexico, and urged him to fight the Prussians. After his surrender to the Germans at Sedan, NE France, 1870 she fled to England.

Euler /ˈɔɪlə/ Leonhard 1707–1783. Swiss mathematician. He developed the theory of differential equations and the calculus of variations, and worked in astronomy and optics. He was a pupil of Johann →Bernoulli.

Euler became professor of physics at the University of St Petersburg in 1730. In 1741 he was invited to Berlin by Frederick the Great, where he spent 25 years before returning to Russia.

Euripides /jʊˈrɪpɪdiːz/ c. 484–407 BC. Greek dramatist whose plays deal with the emotions and reactions of ordinary people and social issues rather than with deities and the grandiose themes of his contemporaries. He wrote more than 80 plays, of which 18 survive, including *Alcestis* 438 BC, *Medea* 431 BC, *Andromache* 426 BC, *The Trojan Women* 415 BC, *Electra* 417 BC, *Iphigenia in Tauris* 413 BC, *Iphigenia in Aulis* 405 BC, and *Bacchae* 405 BC. His influence on later drama was probably greater than that of the other two accomplished tragedians, Aeschylus and Sophocles.

A realist, he was bitterly attacked for his unorthodox 'impiety' and sympathy for the despised: slaves, beggars, and women. He went into voluntary exile from Athens to Macedonia at the end of his life.

Eusebio /juːˈseɪbiəʊ/ adopted name of Eusebio Ferreira da Silva 1942– . Portuguese footballer, born in Lourenço Marques. He made his international debut 1961 and played for his country 77 times. He spent most of his league career with Benfica, but also played in the USA. He was European Footballer of the Year in 1965.

Eusebius /juːˈsiːbiəs/ c. 260–340. Bishop of Caesarea (modern Qisarya, Israel); author of a history of the Christian church to 324.

Eustachio /juːˈstɑːkiəʊ/ Bartolommeo 1520–1574. Italian anatomist, the discoverer of the Eustachian tube, leading from the middle ear to the pharynx, and of the Eustachian valve in the right auricles of the heart.

Eutyches /juːˈtaɪkiːz/ c. 384–456. Christian theologian. An archimandrite (monastic head) in Constantinople, he held that Jesus had only one nature, the human nature being subsumed in the divine (a belief which became known as Monophysitism). He was exiled after his ideas were condemned as heretical by the Council of Chalcedon (an ecumenical council of the early Christian church) 451.

Evans /ˈevənz/ Arthur John 1851–1941. English archaeologist. His excavation of Knossos on Crete resulted in the discovery of pre-Phoenician Minoan script and proved the existence of the legendary Minoan civilization.

Evans /ˈevənz/ Edith 1888–1976. English character actress who performed on the London stage and on Broadway. Her many imposing performances include the film role of Lady Bracknell in Oscar Wilde's comedy *The Importance of Being Earnest* 1952. Among her other films are *Tom Jones* 1963 and *Crooks and Coronets* 1969.

Evans /ˈevənz/ Walker 1903–1975. US photographer best known for his documentary photographs of people in the rural American South during the Great Depression. Many of his photographs appeared in James Agee's book *Let Us Now Praise Famous Men* 1941.

Evelyn /ˈiːvlɪn/ John 1620–1706. English diarist and author. He was a friend of Samuel Pepys, and like him remained in London during the Plague and the Great Fire. He wrote some 300 books, including his diary, first published 1818, which covers the period 1640–1706.

Born in Surrey, he enlisted for three years in the Royalist army 1624, but withdrew on finding his estate exposed to the enemy and lived mostly away from England until 1652. He declined all office under the Commonwealth, but after the Restoration enjoyed great favour, received court appointments, and was one of the founders of the Royal Society.

Evelyn English diarist and author John Evelyn in an engraving by Robert Nanteuil (1650). Writing on a wide range of topics, including numismatics, landscape gardening, education, and commerce, Evelyn is best known for his diary which contains vivid portraits of his contemporaries and is a valuable historical record.

Everett /ˈevərət/ Edward 1794–1865. US religious leader, educator, and public figure. He served in the US House of Representatives 1825–35, as governor of Massachusetts 1835–39, and as US minister to England 1841–45. He was president of Harvard University 1846–49. His four-month role as President Fillmore's secretary of state 1852–53 was followed by a short tenure in the US Senate 1853–54.

Born in Dorchester, Massachusetts, and educated at Harvard, Everett was named pastor of Boston's Brattle Street Church 1814. After gaining his PhD at Göttingen 1817 he taught at Harvard. After retiring from public office, he spent the rest of his life as a private citizen speaking out against slavery and in favour of the preservation of the Union.

Evert /ˈevət/ Chris(tine) 1954– . US tennis player. She won her first Wimbledon title 1974, and has since won 21 Grand Slam titles. She became the first woman tennis player to win $1 million in prize money. She has an outstanding two-handed backhand and is a great exponent of baseline technique. Evert retired from competitive tennis 1989.

From 1974 to 1989 she never failed to reach the quarter- finals at Wimbledon. She married British Davis Cup player John Lloyd 1979 but subsequently divorced him.

Eyck /aɪk/ Aldo van 1918– . Dutch architect with a strong commitment to social architecture. His works include an Orphans' Home 1957–60, and a refuge for single mothers, Mothers' House 1978; both are in Amsterdam.

Eyck Jan van c. 1390–1441. Flemish painter of the early northern Renaissance, one of the first to work in oils. His paintings are technically brilliant and sumptuously rich in detail and colour. In his *Arnolfini Wedding* 1434 (National Gallery, London) the bride and groom appear in a domestic interior crammed with disguised symbols, as a kind of pictorial marriage certificate.

Little is known of his brother *Hubert van Eyck* (died 1426), who is supposed to have begun the massive and complex altarpiece in St Bavo's cathedral, Ghent, *The Adoration of the Mystical Lamb*, completed by Jan 1432.

Jan van Eyck is known to have worked in The Hague 1422–24 for John of Bavaria, Count of Holland. He served as court painter to Philip the Good, Duke of Burgundy, from 1425, and worked in Bruges from 1430. Philip the Good valued him not only as a painter but also as a diplomatic representative, sending him to Spain and Portugal in 1427 and 1428, and he remained in the duke's employ after he settled in Bruges.

Oil painting allowed for subtler effects of tone and colour and greater command of detail than the egg-tempera technique then in common use, and van Eyck took full advantage of this.

Eyre /eə/ Edward John 1815–1901. English explorer who wrote *Expeditions into Central Australia* 1845. He was governor of Jamaica 1864–65. *Lake Eyre* in South Australia is named after him.

Eyre /eə/ Richard (Charles Hastings) 1943– . English stage and film director who succeeded Peter Hall as artistic director of the National Theatre, London, 1988. His stage productions include *Guys and Dolls* 1982, *Bartholomew Fair* 1988, and *Richard III* 1990, which he set in 1930s Britain. His films include *The Ploughman's Lunch* 1983 and *Laughterhouse* (US *Singleton's Pluck*) 1984.

Eysenck /ˈaɪsenk/ Hans Jurgen 1916– . English psychologist. His work concentrates on personality theory and testing by developing behaviour therapy. He is an outspoken critic of psychoanalysis as a therapeutic method.

Ezekiel /ɪˈziːkɪəl/ lived c. 600 BC. In the Old Testament, a Hebrew prophet. Carried into captivity in Babylon by →Nebuchadnezzar 597, he preached that Jerusalem's fall was due to the sins of Israel. The book of Ezekiel begins with a description of a vision of supernatural beings.

Fabergé /ˈfæbəʒeɪ/ Peter Carl 1846–1920. Russian goldsmith and jeweller. Among his masterpieces was a series of jewelled Easter eggs, the first of which was commissioned by Alexander III for the tsarina 1884.

His workshops in St Petersburg and Moscow were celebrated for the exquisite delicacy of their products, especially the use of gold in various shades. Fabergé died in exile in Switzerland.

Fabius /ˈfeɪbiəs/ Laurent 1946– . French politician, leader of the Socialist Party from 1992. As prime minister 1984–86, he introduced a liberal, free-market economic programme, but his career was damaged by the 1985 Greenpeace sabotage scandal.

Fabius became economic adviser to Socialist Party leader François Mitterrand in 1976, entered the National Assembly 1978, and was a member of the socialist government from 1981. In 1984, at a time of economic crisis, he was appointed prime minister. He resigned after his party's electoral defeat in March 1986, but remained influential as speaker of the National Assembly and as its president from 1988. In Jan 1992 he was elected first secretary (leader) of the Socialist Party, replacing Pierre Mauroy.

Fabre /ˈfɑːbrə/ Jean Henri Casimir 1823–1915. French entomologist, celebrated for his vivid and intimate descriptions and paintings of the life of wasps, bees, and other insects.

Fabricius /fəˈbrɪsiəs/ Geronimo 1537–1619. Italian anatomist and embryologist. He made a detailed study of the veins and discovered the valves that direct the blood flow towards the heart. He also studied the development of chick embryos.

Fabricius was a professor of surgery and anatomy at Padua, where his work greatly influenced and helped his pupil William →Harvey. Despite many errors, he raised anatomy and embryology to a higher scientific level.

Fabritius /fəˈbriːtsiəs/ Carel 1622–1654. Dutch painter, a pupil of Rembrandt. His own style, lighter and with more precise detail than his master's, is evident for example in *The Goldfinch* 1654 (Mauritshuis, The Hague). He painted religious scenes and portraits.

Fadden /ˈfædn/ Artie (Arthur) 1895–1973. Australian politician, leader of the Country Party 1941–58 and prime minister Aug–Oct 1941.

Fadiman /ˈfædɪmən/ Clifton Paul 1904– . US editor and media personality. Following his appointment as book reviewer for the *New Yorker* 1933, Fadiman became moderator of the national radio programme 'Information Please' 1938–1948. In 1944 he was appointed to the editorial board of the Book of the Month Club. From the 1950s, he published literary anthologies and continued to be a popular radio and television personality.

Born in Brooklyn, New York, USA, and educated at Columbia University, Fadiman began his career as a teacher at the New York Ethical Culture School. He became an editor for the US book publishing company Simon and Schuster 1927.

Fahd /fɑːd/ 1921– . King of Saudi Arabia from 1982, when he succeeded his half-brother Khalid. As head of government, he has been active in trying to bring about a solution to the Middle East conflicts.

Fahrenheit /ˈfɑːrənhaɪt/ Gabriel Daniel 1686–1736. German physicist who lived mainly in England and Holland. He devised the Fahrenheit temperature scale.

Fairbanks /ˈfeəbæŋks/ Douglas, Sr. Stage name of Douglas Elton Ulman 1883–1939. US actor. He played acrobatic swashbuckling heroes in silent films such as *The Mark of Zorro* 1920, *The Three Musketeers* 1921, *Robin Hood* 1922, *The Thief of Bagdad* 1924, and *Don Quixote* 1925. He was married to film star Mary Pickford ('America's Sweetheart') 1920–33. In 1919 founded United Artists with Charlie Chaplin and D W Griffith.

The man that's out to do something has to keep in high gear all the time.

Douglas Fairbanks Sr on success

Fairbanks /ˈfeəbæŋks/ Douglas, Jr 1909– . US actor who appeared in the same type of swashbuckling film roles as his father, Douglas Fairbanks; for example, in *Catherine the Great* 1934 and *The Prisoner of Zenda* 1937.

Fairfax /ˈfeəfæks/ Thomas, 3rd Baron Fairfax of Cameron 1612–1671. English general, commander in chief of the Parliamentary army in the English Civil War. With Oliver Cromwell he formed the New Model Army and defeated Charles I at

Naseby. He opposed the king's execution, resigned in protest 1650 against the invasion of Scotland, and participated in the restoration of Charles II after Cromwell's death.

Faisal /ˈfaɪsəl/ Ibn Abdul Aziz 1905–1975. King of Saudi Arabia from 1964. He was the younger brother of King Saud, on whose accession 1953 he was declared crown prince. He was prime minister from 1953–60 and from 1962–75. In 1964 he emerged victorious from a lengthy conflict with his brother and adopted a policy of steady modernization of his country. He was assassinated by his nephew.

Faisal I /ˈfaɪsəl/ 1885–1933. King of Iraq 1921–33. An Arab nationalist leader during World War I, he was instrumental in liberating the Near East from Ottoman control and was declared king of Syria in 1918 but deposed by the French in 1920. The British then installed him as king in Iraq, where he continued to foster pan-Arabism.

Falconet /ˌfælkɒˈneɪ/ Etienne-Maurice 1716–1791. French sculptor whose works range from formal Baroque to gentle Rococo in style. He directed sculpture at the Sèvres porcelain factory 1757–66. His bronze equestrian statue *Peter the Great* in Leningrad was commissioned 1766 by Catherine II.

Faldo /ˈfældəʊ/ Nick 1957– . English golfer who was the first Briton in 54 years to win three British Open titles, and the only person after Jack →Nicklaus to win two successive US Masters titles (1989 and 1990). He is one of only six golfers to win the Masters and British Open in the same year.

Since turning professional in 1976 he has won more than 25 tournaments worldwide, with career earnings in excess of £3 million.

Falkender /ˈfɔːlkəndə/ Marcia, Baroness Falkender (Marcia Williams) 1932– . British political secretary to Labour prime minister Harold Wilson from 1956. She was influential in the 'kitchen cabinet' of the 1964–70 government, as described in her book *Inside No 10* 1972.

Falkland /ˈfɔːklənd/ Lucius Cary, 2nd Viscount *c.* 1610–1643. English soldier and politician. He was elected to the Long Parliament 1640 and tried hard to secure a compromise peace between Royalists and Parliamentarians. He was killed at the Battle of Newbury in the Civil War.

Falla /ˈfæljə/ Manuel de 1876–1946. Spanish composer. His opera *La vida breve/Brief Life* 1905 (performed 1913) was followed by the ballets *El amor brujo/Love the Magician* 1915 and *El sombrero de tres picos/The Three-Cornered Hat* 1919, and his most ambitious concert work, *Noches en los jardines de España/Nights in the Gardens of Spain* 1916. The folk idiom of southern Spain is an integral part of his compositions. He also wrote songs and pieces for piano and guitar.

Born in Cádiz, he lived in France, where he was influenced by the Impressionist composers Claude Debussy and Maurice Ravel. In 1939 he moved to Argentina.

Fallopius /fəˈləʊpiəs/ Gabriel. Latinized name of Gabriello Fallopio 1523–1562. Italian anatomist who discovered the Fallopian tubes, which he described as 'trumpets of the uterus', and named the vagina. As well as the reproductive system, he studied the anatomy of the brain and eyes, and gave the first accurate description of the inner ear.

Fallopius studied at Padua under Andreas →Vesalius, and later taught there and at Ferrara and Pisa.

Fangio /ˈfændʒiəʊ/ Juan Manuel 1911– . Argentine racing-car driver who won the drivers' world championship a record five times 1951–57. For most of his career he drove a blue and yellow Maserati.

Fang Lizhi /ˈfæŋ ˌliːˈdʒɜː/ 1936– . Chinese political dissident and astrophysicist. He advocated human rights and Western-style pluralism and encouraged his students to campaign for democracy. In 1989, after the Tiananmen Square massacre, he sought refuge in the US embassy in Beijing and, over a year later, received official permission to leave China.

Fanon /ˈfænɒn/ Frantz 1925–1961. French political writer. His experiences in Algeria during the war for liberation in the 1950s led to the writing of *Les Damnés de la terre/The Wretched of the Earth* 1964, which calls for violent revolution by the peasants of the Third World.

For the black man there is only one destiny. And it is white.

Franz Fanon, *Black Skin White Masks*

Fantin-Latour /fɒnˈtæn læˈtʊə/ (Ignace) Henri (Joseph Théodore) 1836–1904. French painter excelling in delicate still lifes, flower paintings, and portraits. *Homage à Delacroix* 1864 (Musée d'Orsay, Paris) is a portrait group with many poets, authors, and painters, including Charles Baudelaire and James Whistler.

Faraday /ˈfærədeɪ/ Michael 1791–1867. English chemist and physicist. In 1821 he began experimenting with electromagnetism, and ten years later discovered the induction of electric currents and made the first dynamo. He subsequently found that a magnetic field will rotate the plane of polarization of light. Faraday also investigated electrolysis.

In 1812 he began researches into electricity, and made his first electrical cell. He became a laboratory assistant to Humphry Davy at the Royal Institution 1813, and in 1833 succeeded him as professor of chemistry. He delivered highly popular lectures at the Royal Institution, and published

Faraday English chemist and physicist Michael Faraday. He produced three important inventions – the dynamo, the transformer, and the electric motor – all in the year 1831, when he was 39 years old.

many treatises on scientific subjects. Deeply religious, he was a member of the Sandemanians (a small Congregationalist sect).

Fargo /ˈfɑːgəʊ/ William George 1818–1881. US long-distance transport pioneer. In 1844 he established with Henry Wells (1805–1878) and Daniel Dunning the first express company to carry freight west of Buffalo. Its success led to his appointment 1850 as secretary of the newly established American Express Company, of which he was president 1868–81. He also established *Wells, Fargo & Company* 1851, carrying goods express between New York and San Francisco via Panama.

Fargo, a city on the Red River in North Dakota, is named after him.

Farman /ˈfɑːmən/ Henry 1874–1958. Anglo-French aviation pioneer. He designed a biplane 1907–08 and in 1909 flew a record distance of 160 km/100 mi.

With his brother *Maurice Farman* (1878–1964), he founded an aircraft works at Billancourt, Brittany, supplying the army in France and other countries. The UK also made use of Farman's inventions, for example, air-screw reduction gears, in World War II.

Farmer /ˈfɑːmə/ Frances 1913–1970. US actress who starred in such films as *Come and Get It* 1936, *The Toast of New York* 1937, and *Son of Fury* 1942, before her career was ended by alcoholism and mental illness.

Farnaby Giles 1563–1640. English composer. He composed pieces for the virginal (an early key-

board instrument), psalms for Ravenscroft's Psalter 1621, and madrigals for voices.

Farnese /fɑːˈneɪseɪ/ an Italian family, originating in upper Lazio, who held the duchy of Parma 1545–1731. Among the family's most notable members were Alessandro Farnese (1468–1549), who became Pope Paul III in 1534 and granted his duchy to his illegitimate son Pier Luigi (1503–1547); Elizabeth (1692–1766), niece of the last Farnese duke, married Philip V of Spain and was a force in European politics of the time.

Farouk /fəˈruːk/ 1920–1965. King of Egypt 1936–52. He succeeded his father →Fuad I. In 1952 a coup headed by General Muhammed Neguib and Colonel Gamal Nasser compelled him to abdicate, and his son Fuad II was temporarily proclaimed in his place.

Farquhar /ˈfɑːkə/ George 1677–1707. Irish dramatist. His plays *The Recruiting Officer* 1706 and *The Beaux' Stratagem* 1707 are in the tradition of the Restoration comedy of manners, although less robust.

Farragut /ˈfærəgʌt/ David (Glasgow) 1801–1870. US admiral, born near Knoxville, Tennessee. During the US Civil War he took New Orleans 1862, after destroying the Confederate fleet, and in 1864 effectively put an end to blockade-running at Mobile. The ranks of vice admiral (1864) and admiral (1866) were created for him by Congress.

Farrell /ˈfærəl/ J(ames) G(ordon) 1935–1979. English historical novelist, born in Liverpool, author of *Troubles* 1970, set in Ireland, and *The Siege of Krishnapur* 1973.

Farrell /ˈfærəl/ James T(homas) 1904–1979. US novelist and short-story writer. His naturalistic *Studs Lonigan* trilogy 1932–35, comprising *Young Lonigan*, *The Young Manhood of Studs Lonigan*, and *Judgment Day*, describes the development of a young Catholic man in Chicago after World War I, and was written from his own experience. *The Face of Time* 1953 is one of his finest works.

Farrell Terry 1938– . British architect working in a Post-Modern idiom, largely for corporate clients seeking an alternative to the rigours of High Tech or Modernist office blocks. His Embankment Place scheme 1991 sits theatrically on top of Charing Cross station in Westminster, London, and has been likened to a giant jukebox.

Farrell's style is robust and eclectic, and he is not afraid to make jokes in architecture, such as the gaily painted giant egg cups that adorn the parapet of his TV AM building in London, built 1981–82.

Farr-Jones Nick (Nicholas) 1962– . Australian rugby union player. He is Australia's most capped scrum half and has captained his country on more than 30 occasions. He was captain of Australia's 1991 World Cup winning team, and plays for Sydney University and New South Wales.

Farrow /ˈfærəʊ/ Mia 1945– . US film and television actress. Popular since the late 1960s, she was associated with the director Woody Allen, both on and off screen 1982–92. She starred in his films *Zelig* 1983, *Hannah and Her Sisters* 1986, and *Crimes and Misdemeanors* 1990, as well as in Roman Polanski's *Rosemary's Baby* 1968.

Fassbinder /ˈfæsbɪndə/ Rainer Werner 1946–1982. West German film director who began as a fringe actor and founded his own 'anti-theatre' before moving into films. His works are mainly stylized indictments of contemporary German society. He made more than 40 films, including *Die bitteren Tränen der Petra von Kant/The Bitter Tears of Petra von Kant* 1972, *Angst essen Seele auf/Fear Eats the Soul* 1974, and *Die Ehe von Maria Braun/The Marriage of Maria Braun* 1979.

Fassett /ˈfæsɪt/ Kaffe 1940– . US knitwear and textile designer, in the UK from 1964. He co-owns a knitwear company and his textiles are in important art collections around the world.

Fassett took up knitting when encountering Shetland yarns on a trip to Scotland, and now designs and produces for Missoni, Bill Gibb, and others. His customers include the rich and famous.

Fathy /ˈfæθi/ Hassan 1900–1989. Egyptian architect. In his work at the village of New Gouma in Upper Egypt he demonstrated the value of indigenous building technology and natural materials in solving contemporary housing problems. This, together with his book *The Architecture of the Poor* 1973, influenced the growth of community architecture enabling people to work directly with architects in building their homes.

Compare the square to the vertical skyscraper – which is right for humanity and culture?

Hassan Fathy in *The Architect* Nov 1986

Fatimid /ˈfætɪmɪd/ dynasty of Muslim Shi'ite caliphs founded 909 by Obaidallah, who claimed to be a descendant of Fatima (the prophet Muhammad's daughter) and her husband Ali, in N Africa. In 969 the Fatimids conquered Egypt, and the dynasty continued until overthrown by Saladin 1171.

Faulkner /ˈfɔːknə/ Brian 1921–1977. Northern Ireland Unionist politician. He was the last prime minister of Northern Ireland 1971–72 before the Stormont Parliament was suspended.

Faulkner /ˈfɔːknə/ William 1897–1962. US novelist. He wrote in an experimental stream-of-consciousness style. His works include *The Sound and the Fury* 1929, dealing with a Southern family in decline; *As I Lay Dying* 1930; and *The Hamlet* 1940, *The Town* 1957, and *The Mansion* 1959, a trilogy covering the rise of the materialistic Snopes family. Nobel prize 1949.

Faulkner served in World War I and his first novel, *Soldier's Pay* 1929, is about a war veteran. After the war he returned to Oxford, Mississippi, on which he was to model the town of Jefferson in the county of Yoknapatawpha, the setting of his major novels. Other works include *Light in August* 1932, a study of segregation; *The Unvanquished* 1938, stories of the Civil War; and *The Wild Palms* 1939.

Fauré /ˈfɔːreɪ/ Gabriel (Urbain) 1845–1924. French composer of songs, chamber music, and a choral *Requiem* 1888. He was a pupil of Saint-Saëns, became professor of composition at the Paris Conservatoire 1896 and was director from 1905 to 1920.

Fawcett /ˈfɔːsɪt/ Millicent Garrett 1847–1929. English suffragette, younger sister of Elizabeth Garrett →Anderson. A non-militant, she rejected the violent acts of some of her contemporaries in the suffrage movement. She joined the first Women's Suffrage Committee 1867 and became president of the Women's Unionist Association 1889.

Fawcett /ˈfɔːsɪt/ Percy Harrison 1867–1925. British explorer. After several expeditions to delineate frontiers in South America during the rubber boom, he set off in 1925, with his eldest son John and a friend, into the Mato Grosso to find the legendary 'lost cities' of the ancient Indians, the 'cradle of Brazilian civilization'. They were never seen again.

Fawkes /ˈfɔːks/ Guy 1570–1606. English conspirator in the Gunpowder Plot to blow up King James I and the members of both Houses of Parliament. Fawkes, a Roman Catholic convert, was arrested in the cellar underneath the House 4 Nov 1605, tortured, and executed. The event is still commemorated in Britain and elsewhere every 5 Nov with bonfires, fireworks, and the burning of the 'guy', an effigy.

Fechner /ˈfexnə/ Gustav 1801–1887. German psychologist. He became professor of physics at Leipzig in 1834, but in 1839 turned to the study of psychophysics (the relationship between physiology and psychology). He devised *Fechner's law*, a method for the exact measurement of sensation.

Feininger /ˈfaɪnɪŋə/ Lyonel 1871–1956. US abstract artist, an early Cubist. He worked at the Bauhaus, a key centre of design in Germany 1919–33, and later helped to found the Bauhaus in Chicago.

Feininger was born in New York, the son of German immigrants. While in Germany, he formed the *Blaue Vier* (Blue Four) in 1924 with the painters Alexei von Jawlensky (1864–1941), Wassily Kandinsky, and Paul Klee. He returned to the USA after the rise of the Nazis.

Feldman /ˈfeldmən/ Morton 1926–1988. US composer. An associate of John →Cage and Earle →Brown in the 1950s, he composed large-scale set pieces using the orchestra mainly as a source of colour and texture.

Feller /felə/ Bob (Robert William Andrew) 1918– . US baseball pitcher. He made his major-league debut 1936 and went on to a brilliant pitching career that lasted for the next 20 years. He led the American League six times by winning 20 or more games in a season; he pitched 3 no-hitters and 12 one-hitters and posted 266 career wins. Feller was famed for his powerful fastball and pinpoint control.

Born in Van Meter, Iowa, USA, Feller was signed by the Cleveland Indians organization while he was still in high school.

He was elected to the Baseball Hall of Fame 1962.

Fellini /fe'liːni/ Federico 1920– . Italian film director and script writer whose films combine dream and fantasy sequences with satire and autobiographical details. His films include *I vitelloni/The Young and the Passionate* 1953, *La Strada/The Street* 1954, *La dolce vita* 1960, *Otto e mezzo/8¹/₂* 1963, *Giulietta degli spiriti/Juliet of the Spirits* 1965, *Satyricon* 1969, and *Amarcord* 1974.

Going to the cinema is like returning to the womb; you sit there, still and meditative in the darkness, waiting for life to appear on the screen.

Federico Fellini

Fender /fendə/ (Clarence) Leo 1909–1991. US inventor of the solid-body electric guitar, the Fender Broadcaster (renamed the Telecaster 1950), 1948, and the first electric bass guitar, the Fender Precision, 1951. The Fender Stratocaster guitar dates from 1954. In 1965 he sold the Fender name to CBS, which continues to make the instruments.

Fender began making amplifiers and Hawaiian-style guitars in 1945, and built solid-body guitars for several country musicians. Although the guitarist and producer Les →Paul was also working independently on a solid-body electric guitar, Fender was the first to get his model on the market. The design was totally new, with a one-piece neck bolted onto a wooden body, and could easily be mass-produced.

Fénelon /ˌfenɪˈlɒŋ/ François de Salignac de la Mothe 1651–1715. French writer and ecclesiastic. He entered the priesthood 1675 and in 1689 was appointed tutor to the duke of Burgundy, grandson of Louis XIV. For him he wrote his *Fables* and *Dialogues des morts/Dialogues of the Dead* 1690, *Télémaque/Telemachus* 1699, and *Plans de gouvernement/Plans of Government*.

Télémaque, with its picture of an ideal commonwealth, had the effect of a political manifesto, and Louis banished Fénelon to Cambrai, where he had been consecrated archbishop 1695. Fénelon's mystical *Maximes des Saints/Sayings of the Saints* 1697 had also led to condemnation by Pope Innocent XII and a quarrel with the Jansenists, who believed that only those chosen by God beforehand received salvation.

Fenton /fentən/ Roger 1819–1869. English photographer. The world's first war photographer, he went to the Crimea 1855; he also founded the Royal Photographic Society in London 1853.

Ferber /fɜːbə/ Edna 1887–1968. US novelist and playwright. Her novel *Show Boat* 1926 was adapted as an operetta 1927 by Jerome Kern and Oscar Hammerstein II, and her plays, in which she collaborated with George S Kaufmann, include *The Royal Family* 1927, about the Barrymore theatrical family, *Dinner at Eight* 1932, and *Stage Door* 1936.

Ferdinand /fɜːdɪnænd/ 1861–1948. King of Bulgaria 1908–18. Son of Prince Augustus of Saxe-Coburg-Gotha, he was elected prince of Bulgaria 1887 and, in 1908, proclaimed Bulgaria's independence of Turkey and assumed the title of tsar. In 1915 he entered World War I as Germany's ally, and in 1918 abdicated.

Ferdinand /fɜːdɪnænd/ five kings of Castile, including

Ferdinand I /fɜːdɪnænd/ *the Great* c. 1016–1065. King of Castile from 1035. He began the reconquest of Spain from the Moors and united all NW Spain under his and his brothers' rule.

Let justice be done, though the world perish.

Ferdinand I the Great
quoted in M Manlius, *Loci Communes* 1563

Ferdinand V 1452–1516. King of Castile from 1474, *Ferdinand II* of Aragon from 1479, and *Ferdinand III* of Naples from 1504; first king of all Spain. In 1469 he married his cousin →Isabella I, who succeeded to the throne of Castile 1474; they were known as *the Catholic Monarchs* because after 700 years of rule by the Moors, they Catholicized Spain. When Ferdinand inherited the throne of Aragon 1479, the two great Spanish kingdoms were brought under a single government for the first time. They introduced the Inquisition 1480 to suppress heresy; expelled the Jews, forced the final surrender of the Moors at Granada, and financed Columbus's expedition to the Americas, 1492.

Ferdinand conquered Naples 1500–03 and Navarre 1512, completing the unification of Spain and making it one of the chief powers in Europe.

Ferdinand /fɜːdɪnænd/ three Holy Roman emperors:

Ferdinand I /fɜːdɪnænd/ 1503–1564. Holy Roman emperor who succeeded his brother Charles V 1558; king of Bohemia and Hungary from 1526, king of the Germans from 1531. He reformed the German monetary system and reorganized the judicial Aulic council (*Reichshofrat*). He was the son of Philip the Handsome and grandson of Maximilian I.

Ferdinand II 1578–1637. Holy Roman emperor from 1619, when he succeeded his uncle Matthias; king of Bohemia from 1617 and of Hungary from 1618. A zealous Catholic, he provoked the Bohemian revolt that led to the Thirty Years' War. He was a grandson of Ferdinand I.

Ferdinand III 1608–1657. Holy Roman emperor from 1637 when he succeeded his father Ferdinand II; king of Hungary from 1625. Although anxious to conclude the Thirty Years' War, he did not give religious liberty to Protestants.

Ferdinand /fɜːdɪnænd/ 1865–1927. King of Romania from 1914, when he succeeded his uncle Charles I. In 1916 he declared war on Austria. After the Allied victory in World War I, Ferdinand acquired Transylvania and Bukovina from Austria-Hungary, and Bessarabia from Russia. In 1922 he became king of this Greater Romania. His reign saw agrarian reform and the introduction of universal suffrage.

Ferguson /fɜːgəsən/ Harry 1884–1960. Irish engineer who pioneered the development of the tractor, joining forces with Henry Ford 1938 to manufacture it in the USA. He also experimented in automobile and aircraft development.

Fermat /feəˈmɑː/ Pierre de 1601–1665. French mathematician, who with Blaise Pascal founded the theory of probability and the modern theory of numbers and who made contributions to analytical geometry.

Fermat's last theorem states that equations of the form $xn + yn = zn$ where x, y, z, and n are all integers have no solutions if $n>2$. There is no general proof of this, although it has never yet been disproved, so it constitutes a conjecture rather than a theorem.

Fermi /fɜːmi/ Enrico 1901–1954. Italian-born US physicist who proved the existence of new radioactive elements produced by bombardment with neutrons, and discovered nuclear reactions produced by low-energy neutrons. His theoretical work included study of the weak nuclear force, one of the fundamental forces of nature, and (with Paul Dirac) of the quantum statistics of fermion particles. He was awarded a Nobel prize 1938.

Born in Rome, he was professor of theoretical physics there 1926–38. Upon receiving the Nobel prize he and his family emigrated to the US. He was professor at Columbia University, New York 1939–42 and from 1946 at the University of Chicago, where he had built the first US nuclear reactor 1942. This was the basis for studies leading to the atomic bomb and nuclear energy.

In 1954, the US Atomic Energy Commission made a special award to Fermi in recognition of his outstanding work in nuclear physics; these annual awards subsequently were known as Fermi awards.

Whatever Nature has in store for mankind, unpleasant as it may be, man must accept, for ignorance is never better than knowledge.

Enrico Fermi, *Atoms in the Family*

Fermor /fɜːmɔː/ Patrick (Michael) Leigh 1915– . English travel writer who joined the Irish Guards in 1939 after four years' travel in central Europe and the Balkans. His books include *The Traveller's Tree* 1950, *A Time to Keep Silence* 1953, *Mani* 1958, *Roumeli* 1966, *A Time of Gifts* 1977, and *Between the Woods and the Water* 1986.

Fernández /fəˈnændez/ Juan c. 1536–c. 1604. Spanish explorer and navigator. As a pilot on the Pacific coast of South America 1563, he reached the islands off the coast of Chile that now bear his name. Alexander →Selkirk was later marooned on one of these islands, and his life story formed the basis of Daniel Defoe's *Robinson Crusoe*.

Fernandez de Quirós /fəˈnændez də kɪˈrɒs/ Pedro 1565–1614. Spanish navigator, one of the first Europeans to search for the great southern continent that Ferdinand →Magellan believed lay to the south of the Magellan Strait. Despite a series of disastrous expeditions, he took part in the discovery of the Marquesas Islands and the main island of Espíritu Santo in the New Hebrides.

Fernel /feəˈnel/ Jean François 1497–1558. French physician who introduced the terms physiology and pathology into medicine.

Ferneyhough /fɜːnihʌf/ Brian 1943– . English composer. His uncompromising, detailed compositions include *Carceri d'Invenzione*, a cycle of seven works inspired by the engravings of Piranesi, *Time and Motion Studies* 1974–77, and string quartets.

Ferranti /fəˈrænti/ Sebastian de 1864–1930. British electrical engineer who established the principle of a national grid, and an electricity generating system based on alternating current (AC) (successfully arguing against →Edison's proposal). He brought electricity to much of central London. In 1881 he made and sold his first alternator.

Ferranti became chief engineer with the London Electric Supply Company 1887, and worked on the design of a large power station at Deptford.

However, legislation permitting low- powered stations to operate killed the scheme. He resigned in 1892, moved to Oldham in Lancashire, and in 1896 he opened a business to develop high-voltage systems for long-distance transmission.

Ferrar /ferə/ Nicolas 1592–1637. English mystic and founder in 1625 of the Anglican monastic community at Little Gidding, Cambridgeshire, in 1625, which devoted itself to work and prayer. It was broken up by the Puritans in 1647.

Ferrari /fə'rɑːri/ Enzo 1898–1988. Italian founder of the Ferrari car manufacturing company, which specializes in Grand Prix racing cars and high-quality sports cars. He was a racing driver for Alfa Romeo in the 1920s, went on to become one of their designers and in 1929 took over their racing division. In 1947 the first 'true' Ferrari was seen. The Ferrari car has won more world championship Grands Prix than any other car.

Ferraro /fə'rɑːrəʊ/ Geraldine 1935– . US Democrat politician, vice-presidential candidate in the 1984 election.

Ferraro, a lawyer, was elected to Congress in 1981 and was selected in 1984 by Walter Mondale to be the USA's first female vice-presidential candidate from one of the major parties. The Democrats were defeated by the incumbent president Reagan, and Ferraro, damaged by investigations of her husband's business affairs, retired temporarily from politics.

Ferrier /feriə/ Kathleen (Mary) 1912–1953. English contralto who sang in oratorio and opera. In Benjamin Britten's *The Rape of Lucretia* 1946 she created the role of Lucretia, and she gave a memorable performance in Gustav Mahler's *Das Lied von der Erde* at the Edinburgh Festival 1947.

Ferrier /feriə/ Susan Edmundstone 1782–1854. Scottish novelist, born in Edinburgh. Her anonymously published books include *Marriage* 1818, *Inheritance* 1824, and *Destiny* 1831, all of which give a lively picture of Scottish manners and society.

Ferry /feri/ Jules François Camille 1832–1893. French republican politician, mayor of Paris during the siege of 1870–71. As a member of the republican governments of 1879–85 (prime minister 1880–81 and 1883–85) he was responsible for the 1882 law making primary education free, compulsory, and secular. He directed French colonial expansion in Tunisia 1881 and Indochina (the acquisition of Tonkin in 1885).

Fessenden /fesəndən/ Reginald Aubrey 1866–1932. Canadian physicist who worked in the USA, first for Thomas Edison and then for George Westinghouse. Fessenden patented the modulation of radio waves (transmission of a signal using a carrier wave), an essential technique for voice transmission. At the time of his death, he held 500 patents.

Early radio communications relied on telegra-

Ferrier English contralto Kathleen Ferrier whose vocal range and richness, combined with her remarkable technical control, rapidly gained her an international reputation. The contralto parts of Benjamin Britten's Spring Symphony *and* Abraham and Isaac *were written for her, as was Arthur Bliss's* The Enchantress.

phy by using bursts of single-frequency signals in Morse code. In 1900 Fessenden devised a method of making audio-frequency speech (or music) signals modulate the amplitude of a transmitted radio-frequency carrier wave – the basis of AM radio broadcasting.

Feyerabend /faɪərɑːbənd/ Paul K 1924– . US philosopher of science, who rejected the attempt by certain philosophers (for instance →Popper) to find a methodology applicable to all scientific research. His works include *Against Method* 1975.

Although his work relies on historical evidence, Feyerabend argues that successive theories that apparently concern the same subject (for instance the motion of the planets) cannot in principle be subjected to any comparison that would aim at finding the truer explanation. According to this notion of incommensurability, there is no neutral or objective standpoint and therefore no rational way in which one theory can be chosen over another. Instead, scientific progress is claimed to be the result of a range of sociological factors working to promote politically convenient notions of how nature operates.

Feynman /faɪnmən/ Richard Phillips 1918–1988. US physicist whose work laid the foundations of quantum electrodynamics. As a member of the committee investigating the *Challenger* space-shuttle disaster 1986, he demonstrated the lethal faults in rubber seals on the shuttle's booster rocket. For his work on the theory of radiation he shared the Nobel Prize for Physics 1965 with Julian Schwinger and Sin-Itiro Tomonaga (1906–1979).

Feynman US physicist Richard Feynman, noted for the major theoretical advances he made in quantum electrodynamics. Feynman began working on the Manhattan Project while at Princeton University and then worked in Los Alamos 1943-46, on the development of the first atomic bomb.

Feynman was professor of physics at Caltech (California Institute of Technology) from 1950 until his death. In the course of his work he developed his remarkably simple and elegant system of Feynman diagrams to represent interactions between particles. He also contributed to many aspects of particle physics including the nature of the weak nuclear force, and quark theory. Towards the end of his life he became widely known for his revealing autobiographies *Surely You're Joking, Mr Feynman!* 1985 and *What Do You Care What Other People Think?* 1988.

Fibonacci /ˌfɪbəˈnɑːtʃi/ Leonardo, also known as *Leonardo of Pisa c.* 1175-c. 1250. Italian mathematician. He published *Liber abaci* in Pisa 1202, which was instrumental in the introduction of Arabic notation into Europe. From 1960, interest increased in *Fibonacci numbers*, in their simplest form a sequence in which each number is the sum of its two predecessors (1, 1, 2, 3, 5, 8, 13, ..). They have unusual characteristics with possible applications in botany, psychology, and astronomy (for example, a more exact correspondence than is given by →Bode's law to the distances between the planets and the Sun).

Fichte Johann Gottlieb 1762-1814. German philosopher who developed a comprehensive form of subjective idealism, expounded in *The Science of Knowledge* 1794. He was an admirer of Immanuel →Kant.

In 1792, Fichte published *Critique of Religious Revelation*, a critical study of Kant's doctrine of the 'thing-in-itself'. For Fichte, the absolute ego posits both the external world (the non-ego) and finite self. Morality consists in the striving of this finite self to rejoin the absolute. In 1799 he was accused of atheism, and was forced to resign his post as professor of philosophy at Jena. He moved to Berlin, where he devoted himself to public affairs and delivered lectures, including *Reden an die deutsche Nation/Addresses to the German People* 1807-08, which influenced contemporary liberal nationalism.

Fiedler /ˈfiːldə/ Arthur 1894-1979. US orchestra conductor. Concerned to promote the appreciation of music among the public, he founded the Boston Sinfonetta chamber-music group 1924. He reached an even wider audience with the Esplanade concerts along the Charles River from 1929. Fiedler's greatest fame was as founder and conductor of the Boston Pops Orchestra 1930, dedicated to popularizing light classical music through live and televised concert appearances.

Born in Boston and trained at the Academy of Music in Berlin, Fiedler joined the Boston Symphony Orchestra 1916.

Field /fiːld/ Sally 1946– . US film and television actress. She won an Academy Award for *Norma Rae* 1979 and again for *Places in the Heart* 1984. Her other films include *Hooper* 1978, *Absence of Malice* 1981, and *Murphy's Romance* 1985.

Fielding /ˈfiːldɪŋ/ Henry 1707-1754. English novelist. His greatest work, *The History of Tom Jones, a Foundling* 1749 (which he described as 'a comic epic in prose'), realized for the first time in English the novel's potential for memorable characterization, coherent plotting, and perceptive analysis. In youth a prolific playwright, he began writing novels with *An Apology for the Life of Mrs Shamela Andrews* 1741, a merciless parody of Samuel →Richardson's *Pamela.*

He was appointed Justice of the Peace for Middlesex and Westminster in 1748. In failing health, he went to recuperate in Lisbon in 1754, writing on the way *A Journal of a Voyage to Lisbon.*

Fields /fiːldz/ Gracie. Stage name of Grace Stansfield 1898-1979. English comedian and singer, much loved by the public. Her humorously sentimental films include *Sally in Our Alley* 1931 and *Sing as We Go* 1934.

Fields /fiːldz/ W C. Stage name of William Claude Dukenfield 1879-1946. US actor and screenwriter. His distinctive speech and professed attitudes such as hatred of children and dogs gained him enormous popularity in such films as *David Copperfield* 1935, *My Little Chickadee* (co-written with Mae West) and *The Bank Dick* both 1940, and *Never Give a Sucker an Even Break* 1941.

Originally a vaudeville performer, he incorporated his former stage routines, such as juggling and pool playing, into his films. He was also a popular radio performer.

Fiennes /faɪnz/ Ranulph Twisleton-Wykeham 1944– . British explorer who made the first surface journey around the world's polar circumference between 1979 and 1982. In 1993 he and Dr Mike Stroud made the longest unsupported polar journey and were the first to cross the Antarctic land mass on foot. The 95-day trek from the Filchner ice shelf to the Ross ice shelf covered 1350 miles (2170 km). Earlier expeditions included explorations of the White Nile 1969, Jostedalsbre Glacier, Norway, 1970, and the Headless Valley, Canada, 1971. Accounts of his adventures include *A Talent for Trouble* 1970, *Hell on Ice* 1979, and the autobiographical *Living Dangerously* 1987.

Filchner /ˈfɪlʃnə/ Wilhelm 1877–1957. German explorer who travelled extensively in Central Asia, but is remembered for his expedition into the Weddell Sea of Antarctica 1911, where his ship became ice-bound for a whole winter. He landed a party and built a hut on the floating ice shelf, which eventually broke up and floated northwards.

Filchner also conducted cartographic surveys and magnetic observations in Tibet 1926–28 and made a magnetic survey of Nepal 1939–40.

Filene /fɪˈliːn/Edward Albert 1860–1937. US businessman renowned for his innovative retailing methods. One of his most imaginative merchandising ideas was the 'bargain basement,' where prices were dramatically lowered on certain goods. Incorporating his father's dry goods store in Boston as William Filene's Sons 1891, Filene was committed to employee profit-sharing and for that reason was removed by his partners 1928.

Born in Salem, Massachusetts, USA, Filene was political progressive, active in public welfare programmes in Boston.

Fillmore /ˈfɪlmɔː/ Millard 1800–1874. 13th president of the USA 1850–53, a Whig. Born into a poor farming family in New Cayuga County, New York State, he was Zachary Taylor's vice-president from 1849, and succeeded him on Taylor's death, July 9, 1850. Fillmore supported a compromise on slavery 1850 to reconcile North and South.

This compromise pleased neither side, and it contained a harsh fugitive slave act requiring escaped slaves to be returned to their owners. He threatened to enforce this act with troops, if necessary, earning the wrath of the abolitionists. Fillmore failed to be nominated for another term.

Filson /ˈfɪlsən/ John *c.* 1747–1788. American explorer and land promoter. He published *Discovery, Settlement, and Present State of Kentucky* 1784, the first book to popularize the personality and legend of Daniel →Boone. He founded a colonial settlement at the present site of Cincinnati.

Filson moved west to Kentucky after the American Revolution War 1775–83. Investing heavily in land he hoped to attract a new wave of settlers

to the area. After establishing a fur-trading outpost at Louisville, Filson moved farther west into the Illinois and Ohio territories.

Finch /fɪntʃ/ Peter 1916–1977. Australian-born English cinema actor who began his career in Australia before moving to London in 1949 to start on an international career with such roles as those in *A Town Like Alice* 1956, *The Trials of Oscar Wilde* 1960, *Sunday, Bloody Sunday* 1971, and *Network* 1976, for which he won an Academy Award.

Finney /ˈfɪni/ Albert 1936– . English stage and film actor. He created the title roles in Keith Waterhouse's stage play *Billy Liar* 1960 and John Osborne's *Luther* 1961, and was artistic director of the Royal Court Theatre from 1972 to 1975. His films include *Saturday Night and Sunday Morning* 1960, *Tom Jones* 1963, *Murder on the Orient Express* 1974, and *The Dresser* 1984.

Finney /ˈfɪni/ Tom (Thomas) 1922– . English footballer, known as the 'Preston Plumber'. He played for England 76 times, and in every forward position. He was celebrated for his ball control and goal-scoring skills, and was the first person to win the Footballer of the Year award twice.

Finn MacCumhaill /fɪn məˈkuːl/ legendary Irish hero, identified with a general who organized an Irish regular army in the 3rd century. James Macpherson (1736–96) featured him (as Fingal) and his followers in the verse of his popular epics 1762–63, which were supposedly written by a 3rd-century bard, →Ossian. Although challenged by the critic Dr Johnson, the poems were influential in the Romantic movement.

Finsen /ˈfɪnsən/ Niels Ryberg 1860–1904. Danish physician, the first to use ultraviolet light treatment for skin diseases. Nobel Prize for Medicine 1903.

Firbank /ˈfɜːbæŋk/ Ronald 1886–1926. English novelist. His work, set in the Edwardian decadent period, has a malicious humour and includes *Caprice* 1916, *Valmouth* 1918, and the posthumous *Concerning the Eccentricities of Cardinal Pirelli* 1926.

Firdausi /fɪəˈdaʊsi/ Abdul Qasim Mansur *c.* 935–1020. Persian poet, whose epic *Shahnama/The Book of Kings* relates the history of Persia in 60,000 verses.

Firestone /ˈfaɪəstəʊn/ Harvey Samuel 1868–1938. US industrialist who established a tyre-manufacturing firm, the Firestone Tire and Rubber Co., in Akron, Ohio, in 1900. He pioneered the principle of the detachable rim and, from 1906, was the major supplier of tyres to the Ford Motor Co.

Born in Columbiana, Ohio, Firestone was educated at local schools. He entered the family buggy business and quickly recognized the advantages of rubber for wheel rims, originally founding a retail tyre outlet in Chicago 1896. A strong opponent of organized labour, he long resisted the unionization of his work force.

Firestone /faɪəstəʊn/ Shulamith 1945– . Canadian feminist writer and editor, whose book *The Dialectic of Sex: the Case for Feminist Revolution* 1970, which analysed the limited future of feminism under Marxist and Freudian theories, exerted considerable influence on feminist thought.

She was one of the early organizers of the women's liberation movement in the USA. Her other works include *Notes from the Second Year* 1970.

Fischer /fɪʃə/ Bobby (Robert James) 1943– . US chess champion. In 1958, after proving himself in international competition, he became the youngest grand master in history. He was the author of *Games of Chess* 1959, and was also celebrated for his unorthodox psychological tactics. He won the world title from Boris Spassky in Reykjavik, Iceland, 1972 but retired the same year without defending his title. He returned to competitive chess, 1992.

Born in Chicago, Fischer was raised in New York and began serious involvement with chess at an early age. By 1956 he had won the US junior chess title and, within two years, had also won the US Chess Federation championship for adults.

Fischer /fɪʃə/ Emil Hermann 1852–1919. German chemist who produced synthetic sugars and from these various enzymes. His descriptions of the chemistry of the carbohydrates and peptides laid the foundations for the science of biochemistry. Nobel prize 1902.

Fischer /fɪʃə/ Hans 1881–1945. German chemist awarded a Nobel prize 1930 for his discovery of haemoglobin in blood.

Fischer-Dieskau /fɪʃədiːskaʊ/ Dietrich 1925– . German baritone, renowned for his interpretation of Franz Schubert's *lieder* (songs).

Fish /fɪʃ/ Hamilton 1808–1893. US public figure and diplomat. He held office in the US Senate 1851–57, by which time he had become a member of the Republican party. As secretary of state under President Grant 1869–77, his office was marked by moderation in his pursuit of US claims against the UK in the *Alabama* case and in averting war with Spain over Cuba.

Born in New York, and educated at Columbia University, Fish was admitted to the bar 1830. Active in Whig politics, he served as governor of New York 1849–50.

Fisher /fɪʃə/ Andrew 1862–1928. Australian Labor politician. Born in Scotland, he went to Australia 1885, and entered the Australian parliament in 1901. He was prime minister 1908–09, 1910–13, and 1914–15, and Australian high commissioner to the UK 1916–21.

Fisher /fɪʃə/ Geoffrey, Baron Fisher of Lambeth 1887–1972. English priest, archbishop of Canterbury 1945–61. He was the first holder of this office to visit the pope since the 14th century.

Fisher /fɪʃə/ John Arbuthnot, First Baron Fisher 1841–1920. British admiral, First Sea Lord 1904–10, when he carried out many radical reforms and innovations, including the introduction of the dreadnought battleship.

He served in the Crimean War 1855 and the China War 1859–60. He held various commands before becoming First Sea Lord, and returned to the post 1914, but resigned the following year, disagreeing with Winston Churchill over sending more ships to the Dardanelles, Turkey, in World War I.

The essence of war is violence. Moderation in war is imbecility.

John Arbuthnot Fisher
quoted in R H Bacon, *Life of Lord Fisher*

Fisher /fɪʃə/ John, St *c.* 1469–1535. English bishop, created bishop of Rochester 1504. He was an enthusiastic supporter of the revival in the study of Greek, and a friend of the humanists Thomas More and Desiderius Erasmus. In 1535 he was tried on a charge of denying the royal supremacy of Henry VIII and beheaded.

Fisher /fɪʃə/ Ronald Aylmer 1890–1962. English statistician and geneticist. He modernized Charles Darwin's theory of evolution, thus securing the key biological concept of genetic change by natural selection. Fisher developed several new statistical techniques and, applying his methods to genetics, published *The Genetical Theory of Natural Selection* 1930.

This classic work established that the discoveries of the geneticist Gregor Mendel could be shown to support Darwin's theory of evolution.

Fitch /fɪtʃ/ John 1743–1798. US inventor and early experimenter with steam engines and steamships. In 1786 he designed the first steamboat to serve the Delaware River. His venture failed, so Robert →Fulton is erroneously credited with the invention of the steamship.

Fitzalan-Howard /fɪtsælən ˈhaʊəd/ family name of dukes of Norfolk; seated at Arundel Castle, Sussex, England.

Fitzgerald /fɪtsˈdʒerəld/ family name of the dukes of Leinster.

Fitzgerald /fɪtsˈdʒerəld/ Edward 1809–1883. English poet and translator. In 1859 he published his poetic version of the *Rubaiyat of Omar Khayyam*, which is generally considered more an original creation than a translation.

Fitzgerald /fɪtsˈdʒerəld/ Ella 1918– . US jazz singer, recognized as one of the finest, most lyrical voices in jazz, both in solo work and with big bands. She is celebrated for her smooth interpretations of Gershwin and Cole Porter songs.

Fitzgerald mastered the 'scat' technique and

was widely imitated in the 1950s and 1960s. She is among the best-selling recording artists in the history of jazz.

Fitzgerald /fɪtsˈdʒerəld/ F(rancis) Scott (Key) 1896–1940. US novelist and short-story writer. His early autobiographical novel *This Side of Paradise* 1920 made him known in the postwar society of the East Coast, and *The Great Gatsby* 1925 epitomizes the Jazz Age.

Fitzgerald was born in Minnesota. His first book, *This Side of Paradise*, reflected his experiences at Princeton University. In *The Great Gatsby* 1925 the narrator resembles his author, and Gatsby, the self-made millionaire, is lost in the soulless society he enters. Fitzgerald's wife Zelda Sayre (1900–1948), a schizophrenic, entered an asylum 1930, after which he declined into alcoholism. Her descent into mental illness forms the subject of *Tender is the Night* 1934. His other works include numerous short stories and the novels *The Beautiful and the Damned* 1922 and *The Last Tycoon*, which was unfinished at his death.

FitzGerald /fɪtsˈdʒerəld/ Garret 1926– . Irish politician. As *Taoiseach* (prime minister) 1981–82 and again 1982–86, he was noted for his attempts to solve the Northern Ireland dispute, ultimately by participating in the Anglo-Irish agreement 1985. He tried to remove some of the overtly Catholic features of the constitution to make the Republic more attractive to Northern Protestants. He retired as leader of the Fine Gael Party 1987.

Fitzgerald /fɪtsˈdʒerəld/ George 1851–1901. Irish physicist known for his work on electromagnetics. In 1895 he explained the anomalous results of the →Michelson-Morley experiment 1887 by supposing that bodies moving through the ether contracted as their velocity increased, an effect since known as the *Fitzgerald-Lorentz contraction*.

Fitzherbert /fɪtsˈhɜːbət/ Maria Anne 1756–1837. Wife of the Prince of Wales, later George IV. She became Mrs Fitzherbert by her second marriage 1778 and, after her husband's death 1781, entered London society. She secretly married the Prince of Wales 1785 and finally parted from him 1803.

Fitzroy /fɪtsrɔɪ/ family name of dukes of Grafton; descended from King Charles II by his mistress Barbara Villiers; seated at Euston Hall, Norfolk, England.

Fitzroy /fɪtsrɔɪ/ Robert 1805–1865. British vice-admiral and meteorologist. In 1828 he succeeded to the command of HMS *Beagle*, then engaged on a survey of the Patagonian coast of South America, and in 1831 was accompanied by the naturalist Charles Darwin on a five-year survey. In 1843–45 he was governor of New Zealand. In 1855 the Admiralty founded the *Meteorological Office*, which issued weather forecasts and charts, under his charge

Fitzsimmons /fɪtsˈsɪmənz/ Robert Prometheus 1862–1917. English prizefighter best known for his US fights. He won the middleweight title in New Orleans 1891. Although he weighed only 73 kg/160 lb, he also competed as a heavyweight and in 1897 won the title from James J ('Gentleman Jim') Corbett in Carson City, Nevada. He lost that title to James J Jeffries in New York 1899.

Born in England and raised in New Zealand, Fitzsimmons began boxing at an early age and continued to fight professionally until 1914.

Fixx /fɪks/ James 1932–1984. US popularizer of jogging for cardiovascular fitness with his book *The Complete Book of Running* 1978. He died of a heart attack while jogging.

Flagg /flæg/ James Montgomery 1877–1960. US illustrator. His World War I recruiting poster 'I Want You,' features a haggard image of Uncle Sam modelled on Flagg himself.

Flagler /flæglə/ Henry Morrison 1830–1913. US entrepreneur. He founded a salt factory in Saginaw, Michigan 1862, but when that failed moved to Cleveland and entered the oil-refining business with John D Rockefeller 1867. Flagler served as a director of Standard Oil 1870–1911 and invested in the Florida tourist industry. He established the Florida East Coast Railroad 1886 and built a string of luxury hotels.

Born in Hopewell, New York, Flagler left home at age 14, settling in Ohio, where he worked as a clerk and grain merchant before moving into industry.

Fitzherbert Maria Anne Fitzherbert secretly married George, Prince of Wales (later George IV). Contracted without the king's consent, the marriage was invalid under the Royal Marriage Act 1772 and the Act of Settlement 1701, since George was under age at the time and Mrs Fitzherbert was a Roman Catholic.

Flamsteed English astronomer John Flamsteed. After petitioning Charles II for a national observatory, he was made the first Astronomer Royal 1675 and founded the Royal Observatory at Greenwich, London.

Flagstad /ˈflægstæd/ Kirsten (Malfrid) 1895–1962. Norwegian soprano who specialized in Wagnerian opera.

Flaherty /ˈflɑːti/ Robert 1884–1951. US film director, the father of documentary filmmaking. He exerted great influence through his pioneer documentary of Inuit (Eskimo) life, *Nanook of the North* 1922, a critical and commercial success.

Later films include *Moana* 1926, a South Seas documentary; *Man of Aran* 1934, *Elephant Boy* 1936, *The Lands* 1942, and the Standard Oil-sponsored *Louisiana Story* 1948. Critics subsequently raised questions about the truthfulness of his documentary method.

Flaminius /fləˈmɪnɪəs/ Gaius died 217 BC. Roman consul and general. He constructed the Flaminian Way northward from Rome to Rimini 220 BC, and was killed at the battle of Lake Trasimene fighting →Hannibal.

Flamsteed /ˈflæmstiːd/ John 1646–1719. English astronomer, who began systematic observations of the positions of the stars, Moon, and planets at the Royal Observatory he founded at Greenwich, London, 1676. His observations were published 1725.

Flanagan /ˈflænəgən/ Bud. Stage name of Robert Winthrop 1896–1968. British comedian, leader of the 'Crazy Gang' from 1931 to 1962. He played in variety theatres all over the world and, with his partner Chesney Allen, popularized such songs as 'Underneath the Arches'.

Flaubert /ˈfləʊˈbeə/ Gustave 1821–1880. French novelist, author of *Madame Bovary* 1857, *Salammbô* 1862, *L'Education sentimentale/Senti-*

mental Education 1869, and *La Tentation de Saint Antoine/The Temptation of St Anthony* 1874. Flaubert also wrote the short stories *Trois contes/Three Tales* 1877. His dedication to art resulted in a meticulous prose style, realistic detail, and psychological depth, which is often revealed through interior monologue.

Poetry is as exact a science as geometry.

Gustave Flaubert

Flaxman /ˈflæksmən/ John 1755–1826. English Neo-Classical sculptor and illustrator. From 1775 he worked for the Wedgwood pottery as a designer. His public works include the monuments of Nelson 1808–10 in St Paul's Cathedral, London, and of Burns and Kemble in Westminster Abbey.

Flaxman was born in York and studied at the Royal Academy in London. From 1787 to 1794 he was in Rome directing the Wedgwood studio there. Apart from designs for Wedgwood ware, he modelled friezes on classical subjects and produced relief portraits. In 1810 he became the first professor of sculpture at the Royal Academy.

Flecker /ˈflekə/ James Elroy 1884–1915. British poet. During a career in the consular service, he wrote several volumes of verse, including *The Bridge of Fire* 1907, *The Golden Journey to Samarkand* 1913, and *The Old Ships* 1915.

Fleischer /ˈflaɪʃə/ Max 1889–1972. Austrian-born US cartoonist. With his younger brother, Dave (1894–1972), as director, Fleischer animated and produced cartoon films from 1917. His first major series was *Out of the Inkwell* 1918 starring Koko the Clown. He created the long-running characters Betty Boop and Popeye. His feature films include *Gulliver's Travels* 1939 and *Superman* 1941.

Fleming /ˈflemɪŋ/ Alexander 1881–1955. Scottish bacteriologist who discovered the first antibiotic drug, penicillin, in 1928. In 1922 he had discovered lysozyme, an antibacterial enzyme present in saliva, nasal secretions, and tears. While studying this, he found an unusual mould growing on a neglected culture dish, which he isolated and grew into a pure culture; this led to his discovery of penicillin. It came into use in 1941. In 1945 he won the Nobel Prize for Physiology and Medicine with Howard W Florey and Ernst B Chain, whose research had brought widespread realization of the value of penicillin.

Fleming /ˈflemɪŋ/ Ian 1908–1964. English author of suspense novels featuring the ruthless, laconic James Bond, British Secret Service agent No. 007. Most of the novels were made into successful films.

Fleming /ˈflemɪŋ/ John Ambrose 1849–1945. English electrical physicist and engineer who invented the thermionic valve 1904 and devised Fleming's rules (memory aids to recall the relative directions of the magnetic field, current, and motion in an electric generator or motor, using one's fingers).

Fleming /ˈflemɪŋ/ Peter 1907–1971. British journalist and travel writer, remembered for his journeys up the Amazon and across the Gobi Desert recounted in *Brazilian Adventure* 1933 and *News from Tartary* 1941.

Fletcher /ˈfletʃə/ Horace 1849–1919. Writer and lecturer on nutrition. In 1895 a life-insurance company refused to accept him as a risk because he was 23 kg/50 lb overweight and was frequently ill. He attributed his recovery to a change in eating habits, popularized as *Fletcherism*: eat only when hungry; eat whatever appeals; chew each mouthful until it swallows itself; eat only when relaxed. He made no money from his zealous instruction.

Fletcher /ˈfletʃə/ John 1579–1625. English dramatist. He collaborated with →Beaumont, producing, most notably, *Philaster* 1609 and *The Maid's Tragedy* 1610–11. He is alleged to have collaborated with Shakespeare on *The Two Noble Kinsmen* and *Henry VIII* in 1612.

Among plays credited to Fletcher alone are the pastoral drama *The Faithful Shepherdess* 1610 and the tragedy *Bonduca* about 1614.

Flinders /ˈflɪndəz/ Matthew 1774–1814. English navigator who explored the Australian coasts 1795–99 and 1801–03.

Named after him are *Flinders Island*, NE of Tasmania, Australia; the *Flinders Range* in S Australia; and *Flinders River* in Queensland, Australia.

A poor dried-up land afflicted only by fever and flies.

Matthew Flinders,
Terra Australis 1801–03, on Australia

Flint /flɪnt/ William Russell 1880–1970. Scottish artist, president of the Royal Society of Painters in Water Colours 1936–56.

Florey /ˈflɔːri/ Howard Walter, Baron Florey 1898–1968. Australian pathologist whose research into lysozyme, an antibacterial enzyme discovered by Alexander →Fleming, led him to study penicillin (another of Fleming's discoveries), which he and Ernst →Chain isolated and prepared for widespread use. With Fleming, they were awarded the Nobel Prize for Physiology or Medicine 1945.

Florio /ˈflɔːriəʊ/ Giovanni c. 1553–1625. English translator, born in London, the son of Italian refugees. He translated Michel →Montaigne's essays in 1603.

Flotow /ˈfləʊtəʊ/ Friedrich (Adolf Ferdinand), Freiherr von 1812–1883. German composer who wrote 18 operas, including *Martha* 1847.

Fludd /flʌd/ Robert 1574–1637. British physician who attempted to present a comprehensive account of the universe based on Hermetic principles, *The History of the Macrocosm and the Microcosm* 1617.

Flynn /flɪn/ Errol. Stage name of Leslie Thompson 1909–1959. Australian-born US film actor. He is renowned for his portrayal of swashbuckling heroes in such films as *Captain Blood* 1935, *Robin Hood* 1938, *The Charge of the Light Brigade* 1938, *The Private Lives of Elizabeth and Essex* 1939, *The Sea Hawk* 1940, and *The Master of Ballantrae* 1953.

In *The Sun Also Rises* 1957 he portrayed a middle-aged Hemingway roué, and in *Too Much Too Soon* 1958 he portrayed his friend, actor John Barrymore. Flynn wrote an autobiography, *My Wicked, Wicked Ways* 1959. He became a US citizen 1942.

Flynn /flɪn/ John 1880–1951. Australian missionary. Inspired by the use of aircraft to transport the wounded of World War I, he instituted in 1928 the *flying doctor* service in Australia, which can be summoned to the outback by radios in individual homesteads.

Fo /fəʊ/ Dario 1926– . Italian playwright. His plays are predominantly political satires combining black humour with slapstick. They include *Morte accidentale di un anarchico/Accidental Death of an Anarchist* 1970, and *Non si paga non si paga/Can't Pay? Won't Pay!* 1975/1981.

Foch /fɒʃ/ Ferdinand 1851–1929. Marshal of France during World War I. He was largely responsible for the Allied victory at the first battle of the Marne Sept 1914, and commanded on the NW front Oct 1914–Sept 1916. He was appointed commander in chief of the Allied armies in the spring of 1918, and launched the Allied counteroffensive in July that brought about the negotiation of an armistice to end the war.

Fokine /ˈfɔːkiːn/ Mikhail 1880–1942. Russian dancer and choreographer, born in St Petersburg. He was chief choreographer to the Ballets Russes 1909–14, and with →Diaghilev revitalized and reformed the art of ballet, promoting the idea of artistic unity among dramatic, musical, and stylistic elements. His creations for Diaghilev include *Les Sylphides* 1907, *Carnival* 1910, *The Firebird* 1910, *Le Spectre de la Rose* 1911, and *Petrushka* 1911.

Fonda /ˈfɒndə/ Henry 1905–1982. US actor whose engaging style made him ideal in the role of the American pioneer and honourable man. His many films include the Academy Award-winning *The Grapes of Wrath* 1940, *My Darling Clementine* 1946, and *On Golden Pond* 1981, for which he won the Academy Award for best actor. He was the father of actress Jane Fonda and actor and director Peter Fonda (1939–).

Fonda /fɒndə/ Jane 1937– . US actress. Her early films include *Cat Ballou* 1965, *Barefoot in the Park* 1967, *Barbarella* 1968, *They Shoot Horses, Don't They?* 1969, *Julia*, 1977, *The China Syndrome* 1979, *On Golden Pond* 1981, in which she appeared with her father, Henry Fonda, *Agnes of God* 1985, *Morning After* 1986, *Old Gringo* 1989, and *Stanley and Iris* 1990. She won Academy Awards for *Klute* 1971 and *Coming Home* 1979.

She is active in left-wing politics and in promoting physical fitness.

Fontana /fɒn'tɑːnə/ Domenico 1543–1607. Italian architect. He was employed by Pope Sixtus V to build the Lateran Palace, Rome 1586–88, the Vatican library 1587-90, and the completion of the dome of St Peter's in Rome 1588–90, as well as the royal palace in Naples 1600–02.

Fontana /fɒn'tɑːnə/ Lucio 1899–1968. Italian painter and sculptor. He developed a unique abstract style, presenting bare canvases with straight parallel slashes. His *White Manifesto* 1946 made a bid for the blending of scientific ideas with a new art.

Fontanne /fɒn'tæn/ Lynn 1887–1983. US actress, one-half of the husband-and-wife acting partnership known as the 'Lunts' with her husband Alfred →Lunt.

Fonteyn /fɒnteɪn/ Margot. Stage name of Margaret Hookham 1919–1991. English ballet dancer. She made her debut with the Vic-Wells Ballet in *Nutcracker* 1934 and first appeared as Giselle 1937, eventually becoming prima ballerina of the Royal Ballet, London. Renowned for her perfect physique, musicality, and interpretive powers, she created many roles in Frederick →Ashton's ballets and formed a legendary partnership with Rudolf →Nureyev. She did not retire from dancing until 1979.

Fonteyn danced Aurora in Sergueyev's production of *The Sleeping Beauty* 1939, and created leading roles in *The Haunted Ballroom* 1939, *Symphonic Variations* 1946, and *The Fairy Queen* 1946.

Foot /fʊt/ Dingle 1905–1978. British lawyer and Labour politician, solicitor-general 1964–67. He was the brother of Michael Foot.

Foot /fʊt/ Hugh, Baron Caradon 1907–1990. British Labour politician. As governor of Cyprus 1957–60, he guided the independence negotiations, and he represented the UK at the United Nations 1964–70. He was the son of Isaac Foot and brother of Michael Foot.

Foot /fʊt/ Isaac 1880–1960. British Liberal politician. A staunch Nonconformist, he was minister of mines 1931–32. He was the father of Dingle, Hugh, and Michael Foot.

Foot /fʊt/ Michael 1913– . British Labour politician and writer. A leader of the left-wing Tribune Group, he was secretary of state for employment 1974–76, Lord President of the Council and leader of the House 1976–79, and succeeded James Callaghan as Labour Party leader 1980–83.

Men of power have no time to read; yet men who do not read are unfit for power.

Michael Foot *Debts of Honour*

Forbes /fɔːbz/ Bryan (John Clarke) 1926– . British film producer, director, and screenwriter. After acting in such films as *An Inspector Calls* 1954, he made his directorial debut with *Whistle Down the Wind* 1961; among his other films are *The L-Shaped Room* 1962, *The Wrong Box* 1966, and *The Raging Moon* 1971.

Ford /fɔːd/ Ford Madox. Adopted name of Ford Hermann Hueffer 1873–1939. English author of more than 82 books, the best known of which is the novel *The Good Soldier* 1915. He founded and edited the *English Review* 1909, to which Thomas Hardy, D H Lawrence, and Joseph Conrad contributed. He also founded *The Transatlantic Review* 1924. He was a grandson of the painter Ford Madox Brown.

Ford /fɔːd/ Gerald R(udolph) 1913– . 38th president of the USA 1974–77, a Republican. He was elected to the House of Representatives 1949, was nominated to the vice-presidency by Richard Nixon 1973 following the resignation of Spiro →Agnew, and became president 1974, when Nixon was forced to resign following the Watergate scandal. He pardoned Nixon and gave amnesty to those who had resisted the draft for the Vietnam War.

Ford was born in Omaha, Nebraska, was an All-American football player in college, and graduated from Yale Law School. He was appointed vice president Dec 1973, at a time when Nixon's re-election campaign was already being investigated for 'dirty tricks', and became president the following Aug. Ford's visit to Vladivostok 1974 resulted in agreement with the USSR on strategic arms limitation. He was defeated by Carter in the 1976 election by a narrow margin.

Ford /fɔːd/ Glenn (Gwyllym Samuel Newton) 1916– . Canadian-born US actor, active in Hollywood from the 1940s to the 1960s. Usually cast as the tough but good-natured hero, he was equally at home in Westerns, thrillers, and comedies. His films include *Gilda* 1946, *The Big Heat* 1953, and *Dear Heart* 1965.

Ford /fɔːd/ Henry 1863–1947. US automobile manufacturer, who built his first car 1896 and founded the Ford Motor Company 1903. His Model T (1908–27) was the first car to be constructed solely by assembly-line methods and to be mass marketed; 15 million of these cars were made and sold.

He was a pacifist, and visited Europe 1915–16 in an attempt to end World War I. In 1936 he

Ford 38th US president Gerald Ford, the first man to be sworn into office without ever winning a presidential or vice-presidential election. His reputation for integrity and candour, built up over his 25 years in the House of Representatives, stood him in good stead during and after the Watergate scandal.

founded, with his son Edsel Ford (1893–1943), the philanthropic *Ford Foundation*.

Ford /fɔːd/ John 1586–*c.* 1640. English poet and dramatist. His play *'Tis Pity She's a Whore* (performed about 1626, printed 1633) is a study of incest between brother and sister.

Ford /fɔːd/ John. Adopted name of Sean O'Feeney 1895–1973. US film director. Active from the silent film era, he was one of the original creators of the 'Western', directing *The Iron Horse* 1924; *Stagecoach* 1939 became his masterpiece. He won Academy Awards for *The Informer* 1935, *The Grapes of Wrath* 1940, *How Green Was My Valley* 1941, and *The Quiet Man* 1952.

Other films include *Rio Grande* 1950, *Mr Roberts* 1955, *The Last Hurrah* 1958, and *The Man Who Shot Liberty Valance* 1962.

Foreman George 1948– . US heavyweight boxer who was the undisputed world heavyweight champion 1973–74. After 11 years out of the ring, he made an amazing comeback, fighting for the world in 1991 title at the age of 42, the oldest fighter for the heavyweight championship.

Forester /fɒrɪstə/ C(ecil) S(cott) 1899–1966. English novelist, born in Egypt. He wrote a series of historical novels set in the Napoleonic era that, beginning with *The Happy Return* 1937, cover the career – from midshipman to admiral –of Horatio Hornblower.

He also wrote *Payment Deferred* 1926, a subtle crime novel, and *The African Queen* 1938, later filmed with Humphrey Bogart.

Formby /fɔːmbi/ George 1904–1961. English comedian. He established a stage and screen rep-

utation as an apparently simple Lancashire working lad, and sang such songs as 'Mr Wu' and 'Cleaning Windows', accompanying himself on the ukulele. His father was a music-hall star of the same name.

Forrest /fɒrɪst/ John, 1st Baron Forrest 1847–1918. Australian explorer and politician. He crossed Western Australia W–E 1870, when he went along the southern coast route, and in 1874, when he crossed much further north, exploring the Musgrave Ranges. He was born in Western Australia, and was its first premier 1890–1901.

Forrest /fɒrəst/ Nathan Bedford 1821–1877. American Confederate military leader and founder of the Ku Klux Klan 1866, a secret and sinister society dedicated to white supremacy. At the outbreak of the American Civil War 1861, Forrest escaped from Union troops before the fall of Fort Donelson in Tennessee 1862. After the Battle of Shiloh 1862, he was promoted to the rank of brigadier general.

Born in Chapel Hill, Tennessee, Forrest had little formal schooling but accumulated enough wealth through slave dealing to buy land in Mississippi and establish a cotton plantation. He founded the Klan while working as a civilian railroad executive after the end of the Civil War.

Forrestal /fɒrɪstl/ James Vincent 1892–1949. US Democratic politician. As under secretary from 1940 and secretary of the navy from 1944, he organized its war effort, accompanying the US landings on the Japanese island Iwo Jima. He was the first secretary of the Department of Defense 1947–49, a post created to unify the three armed forces at the end of World War II.

Forssmann /fɔːsmæn/ Werner 1904–1979. German heart surgeon. In 1929 he originated, by experiment on himself, the technique of cardiac catheterization (passing a thin tube from an arm artery up into the heart itself for diagnostic purposes). He shared the 1956 Nobel Prize for Physiology or Medicine.

Forster /fɔːstə/ E(dward) M(organ) 1879–1970. English novelist, concerned with the interplay of personality and the conflict between convention and instinct. His novels include *A Room with a View* 1908, *Howards End* 1910, and *A Passage to India* 1924. He also wrote short stories, for example 'The Eternal Omnibus' 1914; criticism, including *Aspects of the Novel* 1927; and essays, including *Abinger Harvest* 1936.

Forster published his first novel, *Where Angels Fear to Tread*, 1905. He enhances the superficial situations of his plots with unexpected insights in *The Longest Journey* 1907, *A Room with a View*, and *Howards End*. His many years spent in India and as secretary to the Maharajah of Dewas in 1921 provided him with the material for *A Passage to India*, which explores the relationship between the English and the Indians. *Maurice*, published 1971, has a homosexual theme.

Forster /fɔːstə/ William Edward 1818–1886. British Liberal reformer. In Gladstone's government 1868–74 he was vice president of the council, and secured the passing of the Education Act 1870 and the Ballot Act 1872. He was chief secretary for Ireland 1880–82.

Forsyth /fɔːˈsaɪθ/ Frederick 1938– . English thriller writer. His books include *The Day of the Jackal* 1970, *The Dogs of War* 1974, and *The Fourth Protocol* 1984.

He was a Reuters correspondent and BBC radio and television reporter before making his name with *The Day of the Jackal*, dealing with an attempted assassination of President de Gaulle of France. Later novels were *The Odessa File* 1972, and *The Devil's Alternative* 1979.

Fortin /fɔːˈtæn/ Jean 1750–1831. French physicist and instrument-maker who invented a mercury barometer that bears his name.

It measures atmospheric pressure by means of a column of mercury, formed by filling a tube, closed at one end, with mercury and upending it in a reservoir of the metal. At the upper end of the tube this leaves a gap (known as a Torricellian vacuum), which changes size with variations in atmospheric pressure, expressed as the height of the column of mercury in millimetres. On this scale, normal atmospheric pressure is 760 mm of mercury.

Foss /fɒs/ Lukas 1922– . US composer and conductor. He wrote the cantata *The Prairie* 1942 and *Time Cycle* for soprano and orchestra 1960.

Born in Germany, he studied in Europe before settling in the USA in 1937. A student of →Hindemith, his vocal music is composed in Neo-Classical style; in the mid-1950s he began increasingly to employ improvisation. Foss has also written chamber and orchestral music in which the players reproduce tape-recorded effects.

Fosse /fɒs/ Bob (Robert) 1927–1987. US film director who entered films as a dancer and choreographer from Broadway, making his directorial debut with *Sweet Charity* 1968. He received an Academy Award for his second film as director, *Cabaret* 1972. Other films includes *All That Jazz* 1979 and several musical productions, including *Pippin* 1975.

Fossey /fɒsi/ Dian 1938–1985. US zoologist. From 1975, Fossey studied mountain gorillas in Rwanda. Living in close proximity to them, she discovered that they led peaceful family lives. She was murdered by poachers whose snares she had cut.

Foster /fɒstə/ Greg 1958– . US hurdler. He has won three consecutive World Championship gold medals, the only athlete to achieve this feat.

Foster /fɒstə/ Jodie. Stage name of Alicia Christian Foster 1962– . US film actress and director who began as a child in a great variety of roles. She starred in *Taxi Driver* and *Bugsy Malone* both

1976, when only 14. Subsequent films include *The Accused* 1988 and *The Silence of the Lambs* 1991, for both of which she won the Academy Award for best actress.

Foster /fɒstə/ Norman 1935– . English architect of the high-tech school. His buildings include the Willis Faber office, Ipswich, 1978, the Sainsbury Centre for Visual Arts at the University of East Anglia 1974 (opened 1978), the headquarters of the Hong Kong and Shanghai Bank, Hong Kong, 1986, and Stansted Airport, Essex, 1991.

Foster /fɒstə/ Stephen Collins 1826–1864. US songwriter. He wrote sentimental popular songs including 'My Old Kentucky Home' 1853 and 'Beautiful Dreamer' 1864, and rhythmic minstrel songs such as 'Oh! Susannna' 1848 and 'Camptown Races' 1850.

Foucault /fuːkəʊ/ Jean Bernard Léon 1819–1868. French physicist who used a pendulum to demonstrate the rotation of the Earth on its axis, and invented the gyroscope.

He investigated heat and light, discovered eddy currents induced in a copper disc moving in a magnetic field, invented a polarizer, and made improvements in the electric arc.

Foucault /fuːkəʊ/ Michel 1926–1984. French philosopher who rejected phenomenology and existentialism. He was concerned with how forms of knowledge and forms of human subjectivity are constructed by specific institutions and practices.

Foucault was deeply influenced by →Nietzsche, and developed an analysis of the operation of power in society using Nietzschean concepts.

Fouché /fuːʃeɪ/ Joseph, duke of Otranto 1759–1820. French politician. He was elected to the National Convention (the post-Revolutionary legislature), and organized the conspiracy that overthrew the Jacobin leader →Robespierre. Napoleon employed him as police minister.

Fouquet /fuːkeɪ/ Jean *c.* 1420–1481. French painter. He became court painter to Charles VIII in 1448 and to Louis XI in 1475. His *Melun diptych* about 1450 (Musées Royaux, Antwerp, and Staatliche Museen, Berlin) shows Italian Renaissance influence.

Fouquet /fuːkeɪ/ Nicolas 1615–1680. French politician, a rival to Louis XIV's minister →Colbert. Fouquet became *procureur général* of the Paris *parlement* 1650 and *surintendant des finances* 1651, responsible for raising funds for the long war against Spain, a post he held until arrested and imprisoned for embezzlement (at the instigation of Colbert, who succeeded him).

Fourier /fʊrieɪ/ François Charles Marie 1772–1837. French socialist. In *Le Nouveau monde industriel/The New Industrial World* 1829–30, he advocated that society should be organized in self-sufficient cooperative units of about 1,500 people, and marriage should be abandoned.

Fourier /fʊrieɪ/ Jean Baptiste Joseph 1768–1830. French applied mathematician whose formulation of heat flow 1807 contains the proposal that, with certain constraints, any mathematical function can be represented by trigonometrical series. This principle forms the basis of *Fourier analysis*, used today in many different fields of physics. His idea, not immediately well received, gained currency and is embodied in his *Théorie analytique de la chaleur/The Analytical Theory of Heat* 1822.

Fowler /faʊlə/ (Peter) Norman 1938– . British Conservative politician. He was a junior minister in the Heath government, transport secretary in the first Thatcher administration 1979, social services secretary 1981, and employment secretary 1987–89. In May 1992 he succeeded Chris Patten as Conservative Party chairman.

Fowler was chair of the Cambridge University Conservative Association in 1960. He worked as correspondent for *The Times* until 1970, when he became a member of Parliament.

Fowler /faʊlə/ Henry Watson 1858–1933 and his brother Francis George 1870–1918. English scholars and authors of a number of English dictionaries. *Modern English Usage* 1926, the work of Henry Fowler, has become a classic reference work for matters of style and disputed usage.

Fowler /faʊlə/ William 1911– . US astrophysicist. In 1983 he and Subrahmanyan Chandrasekhar were awarded the Nobel Prize for Physics for their work on the life cycle of stars and the origin of chemical elements.

Fowles /faʊlz/ John 1926– . English writer whose novels, often concerned with illusion and reality and with the creative process, include *The Collector* 1963, *The Magus* 1965, *The French Lieutenant's Woman* 1969, *Daniel Martin* 1977, *Mantissa* 1982, and *A Maggot* 1985.

Fox /fɒks/ Charles James 1749–1806. English Whig politician, son of the 1st Baron Holland. He entered Parliament 1769 as a supporter of the court, but went over to the opposition 1774. As secretary of state 1782, leader of the opposition to Pitt, and foreign secretary 1806, he welcomed the French Revolution and brought about the abolition of the slave trade.

In 1782 he became secretary of state in Rockingham's government, but resigned when Shelburne succeeded Rockingham. He allied with North 1783 to overthrow Shelburne, and formed a coalition ministry with himself as secretary of state. When the Lords threw out Fox's bill to reform the government of India, George III dismissed the ministry, and in their place installed Pitt. Fox now became leader of the opposition, although cooperating with Pitt in the impeachment of Warren Hastings, the governor general of India. The 'Old Whigs' deserted to the government 1792 over the French Revolution, leaving Fox and a small group of 'New Whigs' to oppose Pitt's war of intervention and his persecution of

Fox English Whig politician Charles Fox. Dedicated to the abolition of the crown's excessive powers, which he saw as the source of all the country's ills, Fox first entered the House of Commons at the age of 19 and served almost continuously until his death.

the reformers. On Pitt's death 1806 a ministry was formed with Fox as foreign secretary, which at Fox's insistence abolished the slave trade. He opened peace negotiations with France, but died before their completion.

How much the greatest event it is that ever happened in the world! and how much the best!

Charles James Fox on the fall of the Bastille

Fox /fɒks/ George 1624–1691. English founder of the Society of Friends. After developing his belief in a mystical 'inner light', he became a travelling preacher 1647, and in 1650 was imprisoned for blasphemy at Derby, where the name Quakers was first applied derogatorily to him and his followers, supposedly because he enjoined Judge Bennet to 'quake at the word of the Lord'.

He suffered further imprisonments, made a missionary journey to America in 1671–72, and wrote many evangelical and meditative works, including a *Journal*, published 1694.

Fox /fɒks/ James 1939– . English film actor, usually cast in upper-class, refined roles but celebrated for his portrayal of a psychotic gangster in Nicolas Roeg's *Performance* 1970, which was followed by an eight-year break from acting. Fox appeared in *The Servant* 1963 and *Isadora* 1968. He returned to acting in *No Longer Alone* 1978. His other films include *Runners* 1984, *A Passage to India* 1984, and *The Russia House* 1990.

Fox /fɒks/ Margaret 1833–1893. Canadian-born US spiritual medium. With her sister, Katherine, she became famous for her psychic ability. The girls gave public demonstrations of their powers, sparking widespread public interest in spiritualism as a modern religious movement. In 1888 Margaret publicly confessed that her 'psychic powers' were a hoax.

Brought up in New York State, USA, the sisters moved to New York City 1850 and claimed to be able to communicate with 'departed spirits' from an early age.

Foxe /fɒks/ John 1516–1587. English Protestant propagandist. He became a canon of Salisbury 1563. His *Book of Martyrs* 1563 luridly described persecutions under Queen Mary, reinforcing popular hatred of Roman Catholicism.

Fracastoro /ˌfrækəˈstɔːrəʊ/ Girolamo *c.* 1478–1553. Italian physician known for his two medical books. He was born and worked mainly in Verona. His first book, *Syphilis sive morbus gallicus/Syphilis or the French disease* 1530, was written in verse. It was one of the earliest texts on syphilis, a disease Fracastoro named. In his second work, *De contagione/On contagion* 1546, he wrote, far ahead of his time, about 'seeds of contagion'.

Fra Diavolo /frɑː diˈævələʊ/ Nickname of Michele Pezza 1771–1806. Italian brigand. A renegade monk, he led a gang in the mountains of Calabria, S Italy, for many years, and was eventually executed in Naples.

Fragonard /ˌfrægəʊˈnɑː/ Jean Honoré 1732–1806. French painter, the leading exponent of the Rococo style (along with his master Boucher). His light-hearted subjects include *The Swing* about 1766 (Wallace Collection, London).

Frame /freɪm/ Janet 1924– . New Zealand novelist. After being wrongly diagnosed as schizophrenic, she reflected her experiences 1945–54 in the novel *Faces in the Water* 1961 and the autobiographical *An Angel at My Table* 1984.

Frampton /ˈfræmptən/ George James 1860–1928. British sculptor. His work includes the statue of *Peter Pan* in Kensington Gardens and the Nurse Cavell memorial near St Martin's, London.

France /frɒns/ Anatole. Pen name of Jacques Anatole Thibault 1844–1924. French writer renowned for the wit, urbanity, and style of his works. His earliest novel was *Le Crime de Sylvestre Bonnard/The Crime of Sylvester Bonnard* 1881; later books include the autobiographical series beginning with *Le Livre de mon ami/My Friend's Book* 1885, the satiric *L'Île des pingouins/Penguin Island* 1908, and *Les Dieux ont soif/The Gods Are Athirst* 1912. He was awarded the Nobel Prize for Literature 1921.

France was born in Paris. He published a critical study of Alfred de Vigny 1868, which was followed by several volumes of poetry and short stories. He was elected to the French Academy 1896. His other books include *Thaïs* 1890 and *Crainquebille* 1905. He was a socialist and supporter of →Dreyfus.

They [the poor] have to labour in the face of the majestic equality of the law, which forbids the rich as well as the poor to sleep under bridges, to beg in the streets, and to steal bread.

Anatole France, *Le Lys rouge* 1894

Francesca /frænˈtʃeskə/ Piero della. See →Piero della Francesca, Italian painter.

Francis /frɑːnsɪs/ or *François* two kings of France:

Francis I /frɑːnsɪs/ 1494–1547. King of France from 1515. He succeeded his cousin Louis XII, and from 1519 European politics turned on the rivalry between him and the Holy Roman emperor Charles V, which led to war 1521–29, 1536–38, and 1542–44. In 1525 Francis was defeated and captured at Pavia and released only after signing a humiliating treaty. At home, he developed absolute monarchy.

Francis II /frɑːnsɪs/ 1544–1560. King of France from 1559 when he succeeded his father, Henry II. He married Mary Queen of Scots 1558. He was completely under the influence of his mother, →Catherine de' Medici.

Francis II /frɑːnsɪs/ 1768–1835. Holy Roman emperor 1792–1806. He became Francis I, Emperor of Austria 1804, and abandoned the title of Holy Roman emperor 1806. During his reign Austria was five times involved in war with France, 1792–97, 1798–1801, 1805, 1809, and 1813–14. He succeeded his father Leopold II.

Francis Ferdinand English form of →Franz Ferdinand, archduke of Austria.

Francis Joseph English form of →Franz Joseph, emperor of Austria-Hungary.

Francis of Assisi, St /əˈsiːzi/ 1182–1226. Italian founder of the Roman Catholic Franciscan order of friars 1209 and, with St Clare, of the Poor Clares 1212. In 1224 he is said to have undergone a mystical experience during which he received the *stigmata* (five wounds of Jesus). Many stories are told of his ability to charm wild animals, and he is the patron saint of ecologists. His feast day is 4 Oct.

The son of a wealthy merchant, Francis changed his life after two dreams he had during an illness following spells of military service when he was in his early twenties. He resolved to follow literally the behests of the New Testament and live a life of poverty and service while preaching a simple form of the Christian gospel. In 1219 he went to Egypt to convert the sultan, and lived for a month in his camp. Returning to Italy, he resigned his leadership of the friars.

Francis of Sales, St /sæl/ 1567–1622. French bishop and theologian. He became bishop of Geneva 1602, and in 1610 founded the order of the Visitation, an order of nuns. He is the patron saint of journalists and other writers. His feast day is 24 Jan.

Francis of Sales was born in Savoy. His writings include *Introduction à la vie dévote/Introduction to a Devout Life* 1609, written to reconcile the Christian life with living in the real world.

Franck /fræŋk/ César Auguste 1822–1890. Belgian composer. His music, mainly religious and Romantic in style, includes the Symphony in D minor 1866–68, *Symphonic Variations* 1885 for piano and orchestra, the *Violin Sonata* 1886, the oratorio *Les Béatitudes/The Beatitudes* 1879, and many organ pieces.

Franck /fræŋk/ James 1882–1964. US physicist. He was awarded a Nobel prize 1925 for his experiments of 1914 on the energy transferred by colliding electrons to mercury atoms, showing that the transfer was governed by the rules of quantum theory.

Born and educated in Germany, he emigrated to the USA after publicly protesting against Hitler's racial policies. Franck participated in the wartime atomic-bomb project at Los Alamos but organized the 'Franck petition' 1945, which argued that the bomb should not be used against Japanese cities. After World War II he turned his research to photosynthesis.

Franco /fræŋkəʊ/ Francisco (Paulino Hermenegildo Teódulo Bahamonde) 1892–1975. Spanish dictator from 1939. As a general, he led the insurgent Nationalists to victory in the Spanish Civil War 1936–39, supported by Fascist Italy and Nazi Germany, and established a dictatorship. In 1942 Franco reinstated the Cortes (Spanish parliament), which in 1947 passed an act by which he became head of state for life.

Franco was born in Galicia, NW Spain. He entered the army 1910, served in Morocco 1920–26, and was appointed Chief of Staff 1935, but demoted to governor of the Canary Islands 1936. Dismissed from this post by the Popular Front (Republican) government, he plotted an uprising with German and Italian assistance, and on the outbreak of the Civil War organized the invasion of Spain by N African troops and foreign legionaries. After the death of General Sanjurjo, he took command of the Nationalists, proclaiming himself *Caudillo* (leader) of Spain. The defeat of the Republic with the surrender of Madrid 1939 brought all Spain under his government. On the outbreak of World War II, in spite of Spain's official attitude of 'strictest neutrality', his pro-Axis sympathies led him to send aid, later withdrawn, to the German side.

At home, he curbed the growing power of the Falange Española (the fascist party), and in later years slightly liberalized his regime. In 1969 he nominated →Juan Carlos as his successor and future king of Spain. He relinquished the premiership 1973, but remained head of state until his death.

In war the heart must be sacrificed.
General Franco,
Diario de una Bandera

François /frɒn'swɑ/ French form of →Francis, two kings of France.

Francome /fræŋkəm/ John 1952– . British jockey. He holds the record for the most National Hunt winners (over hurdles or fences). Between 1970 and 1985 he rode 1,138 winners from 5,061 mounts – the second person (after Stan Mellor) to ride 1,000 winners. He took up training after retiring from riding.

Frank /fræŋk/ Anne 1929–1945. German diarist who fled to the Netherlands with her family 1933 to escape Nazi anti-Semitism (the Holocaust). During the German occupation of Amsterdam, they and two other families remained in a sealed-off room, protected by Dutch sympathizers 1942–44, when betrayal resulted in their deportation and Anne's death in Belsen concentration camp. Her diary of her time in hiding was published 1947.

Previously suppressed portions of her diary were published 1989. The house in which the family took refuge is preserved as a museum. Her diary has sold 20 million copies in more than 50 languages and has been made into a play and a film publicizing the fate of millions.

Frank /fræŋk/ Ilya 1908– . Russian physicist known for his work on radiation. In 1934 →Cherenkov had noted a peculiar blue radiation sometimes emitted as electrons passed through water. It was left to Frank and his colleague at Moscow University, Igor Tamm (1895–1971), to realize that this form of radiation was produced by charged particles travelling faster through the medium than the speed of light in the same medium. Frank shared the 1958 Nobel Prize for Physics with Cherenkov and Tamm.

Frankel /fræŋkəl/ Benjamin 1906–1973. English composer. He studied the piano in Germany and continued his studies in London while playing jazz violin in nightclubs. He wrote chamber music and numerous film scores.

Frankenthaler /fræŋkənθɔːlə/ Helen 1928– . US Abstract Expressionist painter, inventor of the colour-staining technique whereby the unprimed, absorbent canvas is stained or soaked with thinned-out paint, creating deep, soft veils of translucent colour.

Frankfurter /fræŋkfɜːtə/ Felix 1882–1965. Austrian-born US jurist and Supreme Court justice. As a supporter of liberal causes, Frankfurter was

Franklin US politician and scientist Benjamin Franklin. The inventor of the Franklin stove, bifocal spectacles and the lightning rod, Franklin was also a skilled diplomat and one of the signatories to the Treaty of Versailles 1783, by which US independence was secured.

one of the founders of the American Civil Liberties Union 1920. Appointed to the US Supreme Court 1939 by F D Roosevelt, he opposed the use of the judicial veto to advance political ends. He received the Presidential Medal of Freedom 1963.

Born in Vienna, Frankfurter emigrated with his family to the US 1894, attended the City College of New York, and received a law degree from Harvard 1906. After law school he served as assistant to the US attorney for the southern district of New York and joined the faculty of Harvard Law School 1914.

Franklin /ˈfræŋklɪn/ (Stella Maria Sarah) Miles 1879–1954. Australian novelist. Her first novel, *My Brilliant Career* 1901, autobiographical and feminist, drew on her experiences of rural Australian life. *My Career Goes Bung*, written as a sequel, was not published until 1946. A literary award bearing her name is made annually for novels.

Franklin /ˈfræŋklɪn/ Benjamin 1706–1790. US printer, publisher, author, scientist, and statesman. He proved that lightning is a form of electricity, distinguished between positive and negative electricity, and invented the lightning conductor. He was the first US ambassador to France 1776–85, and negotiated peace with Britain 1783. As a delegate to the Continental Congress from Pennsylvania 1785–88, he helped to draft the Declaration of Independence and the US Constitution.

Born in Boston, Franklin moved to Philadelphia as a young man and combined a successful printing business with scientific experiment and inventions; he authored and published the popular *Poor Richard's Almanac* 1733–58. A member of the Pennsylvania Assembly 1751–64, he was sent to Britain to lobby Parliament about tax grievances

and achieved the repeal of the Stamp Act; on his return to the USA he was prominent in the deliberations leading up to independence. As ambassador in Paris he enlisted French help for the American Revolution.

Franklin /ˈfræŋklɪn/ John 1786–1847. English naval explorer who took part in expeditions to Australia, the Arctic, and N Canada, and in 1845 commanded an expedition to look for the Northwest Passage from the Atlantic to the Pacific, during which he and his crew perished.

The 1845 expedition had virtually found the Passage when it became trapped in the ice. No trace of the team was discovered until 1859. In 1984, two of its members, buried on King Edward Island, were found to be perfectly preserved in the frozen ground of their graves.

Franklin /ˈfræŋklɪn/ Rosalind 1920–1958. English biophysicist whose research on X-ray diffraction of DNA crystals helped Francis Crick and James D Watson to deduce the chemical structure of DNA.

Franz Ferdinand /frænts ˈfɜːdɪnænd/ or Francis Ferdinand 1863–1914. Archduke of Austria. He became heir to his uncle, Emperor Franz Joseph, in 1884 but while visiting Sarajevo 28 June 1914, he and his wife were assassinated by a Serbian nationalist. Austria used the episode to make unreasonable demands on Serbia that ultimately precipitated World War I.

Franz Joseph /frænts ˈjəʊzef/ or Francis Joseph 1830–1916. Emperor of Austria-Hungary from 1848, when his uncle, Ferdinand I, abdicated. After the suppression of the 1848 revolution, Franz Joseph tried to establish an absolute monarchy but had to grant Austria a parliamentary constitution 1861 and Hungary equality with Austria 1867. He was defeated in the Italian War 1859 and the Prussian War 1866. In 1914 he made the assassination of his heir and nephew Franz Ferdinand the excuse for attacking Serbia, thus precipitating World War I.

Fraser /ˈfreɪzə/ (John) Malcolm 1930– . Australian Liberal politician, prime minister 1975–83; nicknamed 'the Prefect' because of a supposed disregard of subordinates.

Fraser was educated at Oxford University, and later became a millionaire sheep farmer. In March 1975 he replaced Snedden as Liberal Party leader. In Nov, following the Whitlam government's economic difficulties, he blocked finance bills in the Senate, became prime minister of a caretaker government and in the consequent general election won a large majority. He lost to Hawke in the 1983 election.

Fraser /ˈfreɪzə/ Antonia 1932– . English author of biographies, including *Mary Queen of Scots* 1969; historical works, such as *The Weaker Vessel* 1984; and a series of detective novels featuring investigator Jemima Shore.

She is married to the playwright Harold Pinter, and is the daughter of Lord Longford.

Fraser /freɪzə/ Dawn 1937– . Australian swimmer. The only person to win the same swimming event at three consecutive Olympic Games: 100 metres freestyle in 1956, 1960, and 1964. The holder of 27 world records, she was the first woman to break the one-minute barrier for the 100 metres.

Fraser /freɪzə/ Peter 1884–1950. New Zealand Labour politician, born in Scotland. He held various cabinet posts 1935–40, and was prime minister 1940–49.

Fraser /freɪzə/ Simon 1776–1862. Canadian explorer and surveyor for the Hudson Bay Company who crossed the Rockies and travelled most of the way down the river that bears his name 1805–07.

Fraunhofer /fraʊnhəʊfə/ Joseph von 1787–1826. German physicist who did important work in optics. The dark lines in the solar spectrum (*Fraunhofer lines*), which reveal the chemical composition of the Sun's atmosphere, were accurately mapped by him.

Fraze /əfreɪz/ Ermal Cleon 1913–1989. US inventor of the ring-pull on drink cans, after having had to resort to a car bumper to open a can while picnicking.

Frazer /freɪzə/ James George 1854–1941. Scottish anthropologist, author of *The Golden Bough* 1890, a pioneer study of the origins of religion and sociology on a comparative basis. It exerted considerable influence on writers such as T S Eliot and D H Lawrence, but by the standards of modern anthropology, many of its methods and findings are unsound.

Frederick V /fredrɪk/ known as *the Winter King* 1596–1632. Elector palatine of the Rhine 1610–23 and king of Bohemia 1619–20 (for one winter, hence the name), having been chosen by the Protestant Bohemians as ruler after the deposition of Catholic emperor ➔Ferdinand II. His selection was the cause of the Thirty Years' War. Frederick was defeated at the Battle of the White Mountain, near Prague, in Nov 1620, by the army of the Catholic League and fled to Holland.

He was the son-in-law of James I of England.

Frederick IX /fredrɪk/ 1899–1972. King of Denmark from 1947. He was succeeded by his daughter who became Queen ➔Margrethe II.

Frederick /fredrɪk/ two Holy Roman emperors:

Frederick I *Barbarossa* ('red-beard') c. 1123–1190. Holy Roman emperor from 1152. Originally duke of Swabia, he was elected emperor 1152, and was engaged in a struggle with Pope Alexander III 1159–77, which ended in his submission; the Lombard cities, headed by Milan, took advantage of this to establish their independence of imperial control. Frederick joined the Third Crusade, and was drowned while crossing a river in Anatolia.

Frederick II 1194–1250. Holy Roman emperor from 1212, called 'the Wonder of the World'. He led a crusade 1228–29 that recovered Jerusalem by treaty, without fighting. He quarrelled with the pope, who excommunicated him three times, and a feud began that lasted with intervals until the end of his reign. Frederick, who was a religious sceptic, is often considered the most cultured man of his age. He was the son of Henry VI.

Frederick /fredrɪk/ three kings of Prussia:

Frederick I /fredrɪk/ 1657–1713. King of Prussia from 1701. He became elector of Brandenburg 1688.

Frederick II *the Great* 1712–1786. King of Prussia from 1740, when he succeeded his father Frederick William I. In that year he started the War of the Austrian Succession by his attack on Austria. In the peace of 1745 he secured Silesia. The struggle was renewed in the Seven Years' War 1756–63. He acquired West Prussia in the first partition of Poland 1772 and left Prussia as Germany's foremost state. He was an efficient and just ruler in the spirit of the Enlightenment and a patron of the arts.

In his domestic policy he encouraged industry and agriculture, reformed the judicial system, fostered education, and established religious toleration. He corresponded with the French writer Voltaire, and was a talented musician.

He received a harsh military education from his father, and in 1730 was threatened with death for attempting to run away. In the Seven Years' War, in spite of assistance from Britain, Frederick had a hard task holding his own against the Austrians and their Russian allies; the skill with which he did so proved him to be one of the great soldiers of history.

In Aug 1991, fulfilling his expressed wish to be buried in a simple grave at his beloved Sans Souci Palace at Potsdam, his embalmed remains, along with those of his father, Frederick William I, were taken from the Hohenzollern family castle near Stuttgart and reburied at Sans Souci. (Hitler had previously removed the two bodies from Potsdam's garrison church, where they were first buried 1786, to a salt mine in Thuringia as Soviet troops approached Berlin 1945.) Chancellor Kohl attended the reburial as a 'private citizen', but the occasion was criticized for sending the wrong, militaristic, signals for a United Germany to its European neighbours.

My people and I have come to an agreement which satisfies us both. They are to say what they please, and I am to do what I please.

Frederick II *the Great* (attrib.)

Frederick III 1831–1888. King of Prussia and emperor of Germany 1888. The son of Wilhelm I, he married the eldest daughter (Victoria) of Queen Victoria of the UK 1858 and, as a liberal, frequently opposed Chancellor Bismarck. He died three months after his accession.

Frederick William /ˈfredrɪk ˈwɪljəm/ 1620–1688. Elector of Brandenburg from 1640, 'the Great Elector'. By successful wars against Sweden and Poland, he prepared the way for Prussian power in the 18th century.

Frederick William /ˈfredrɪk ˈwɪljəm/ 1882–1951. Last crown prince of Germany, eldest son of Wilhelm II. During World War I he commanded a group of armies on the western front. In 1918, he retired into private life.

Frederick William /ˈfredrɪk ˈwɪljəm/ four kings of Prussia:

Frederick William I /ˈfredrɪk ˈwɪljəm/ 1688–1740. King of Prussia from 1713, who developed Prussia's military might and commerce.

Frederick William II 1744–1797. King of Prussia from 1786. He was a nephew of Frederick II but had little of his relative's military skill. He was unsuccessful in waging war on the French 1792–95 and lost all Prussia west of the Rhine.

Frederick William III 1770–1840. King of Prussia from 1797. He was defeated by Napoleon 1806, but contributed to his final overthrow 1813–15 and profited by being allotted territory at the Congress of Vienna.

Frederick William IV 1795–1861. King of Prussia from 1840. He upheld the principle of the divine right of kings, but was forced to grant a constitution 1850 after the Prussian revolution 1848. He suffered two strokes 1857 and became mentally debilitated. His brother William (later emperor) took over his duties.

Frege /ˈfreɪgə/ Friedrich Ludwig Gottlob 1848–1925. German philosopher, the founder of modern mathematical logic. He created symbols for concepts like 'or' and 'if ... then', which are now in standard use in mathematics. His *Die Grundlagen der Arithmetik/The Foundations of Arithmetic* 1884 influenced Bertrand →Russell and →Wittgenstein. His major work is *Berggriftsschrift/Conceptual Notation* 1879.

The *Grundgesetze der Arithmetik/Basic Laws of Arithmetic* was published 1903. His work, neglected for a time, has attracted renewed attention in recent years in Britain.

Frémont /ˈfriːmɒnt/ John Charles 1813–1890. US explorer and politician who travelled extensively throughout the western USA. He surveyed much of the territory between the Mississippi River and the coast of California with the aim of establishing an overland route E–W across the continent. In 1842 he crossed the Rocky Mountains, climbing a peak that is named after him.

French /frentʃ/ Daniel Chester 1850–1931. US sculptor, whose most famous works include *The Minute Man* 1875 in Concord, Massachusetts, *John Harvard* 1884 at Harvard College, *Alma Mater* at Columbia University, and the imposing seated *Abraham Lincoln* 1922 in the Lincoln Memorial, Washington DC.

French /frentʃ/ John Denton Pinkstone, 1st Earl of Ypres 1852–1925. British field marshal. In the second South African War 1899–1902, he relieved Kimberley and took Bloemfontein; in World War I he was Commander in Chief of the British Expeditionary Force in France 1914–15; he resigned after being criticized as indecisive.

It is a solemn thought that at my signal all these fine young fellows go to their death.

Field Marshal John French quoted in Brett, *Journals and Letters of Reginald, Viscount Esher*

Freneau /frɪˈnəʊ/ Philip Morin 1752–1832. US poet whose *A Political Litany* 1775 was a mock prayer for deliverance from British tyranny.

Frere /frɪə/ John 1740–1807. English archaeologist, a pioneering discoverer of Old Stone Age (Palaeolithic) tools in association with large extinct animals at Hoxne, Suffolk, in 1790. He suggested (long before Charles Darwin) that they predated the conventional biblical timescale. Frere was high sheriff of Suffolk and member of Parliament for Norwich.

Frescobaldi /ˌfreskəˈbældi/ Girolamo 1583–1643. Italian composer of virtuoso pieces for the organ and harpsichord.

Fresnel /ˈfreɪnel/ Augustin 1788–1827. French physicist who refined the theory of polarized light. Fresnel realized in 1821 that light waves do not vibrate like sound waves longitudinally, in the direction of their motion, but transversely, at right angles to the direction of the propagated wave.

Freud /frɔɪd/ Anna 1895–1982. Austrian-born founder of child psychoanalysis in the UK. Her work was influenced by the theories of her father, Sigmund Freud. She held that understanding of the stages of psychological development was essential to the treatment of children, and that this knowledge could only be obtained through observation of the child.

Anna Freud and her father left Nazi-controlled Vienna in 1938 and settled in London. There she began working in a Hampstead nursery. In 1947 she founded the Hampstead Child Therapy Course and Clinic, which specialized in the treatment of children and the training of child therapists.

Freud /frɔɪd/ Clement 1924– . British journalist, television personality, and until 1987 Liberal

Member of Parliament; a grandson of Sigmund Freud.

If you resolve to give up smoking, drinking and loving, you don't actually live longer; it just seems longer.

Clement Freud in *Observer* Dec 1964

Freud /frɔɪd/ Lucian 1922– . German-born British painter, whose realistic portraits with the subject staring intently from an almost masklike face include *Francis Bacon* 1952 (Tate Gallery, London). He is a grandson of Sigmund Freud.

Freud /frɔɪd/ Sigmund 1865–1939. Austrian physician who pioneered the study of the unconscious mind. He developed the methods of free association and interpretation of dreams that are basic techniques of psychoanalysis, and formulated the concepts of the id, ego, and superego. His books include *Die Traumdeutung/The Interpretation of Dreams* 1900, *Totem and Taboo* 1913, and *Das Unbehagen in der Kultur/Civilization and its Discontents* 1930.

Freud studied medicine in Vienna and was a member of the research team that discovered the local anaesthetic effects of cocaine. From 1885 to 1886 he studied hypnosis in Paris under the French physiologist →Charcot and 1889 in Nancy under two of Charcot's opponents. From 1886 to 1938 he had a private practice in Vienna, and his theories and writings drew largely on case studies of his own patients, who were mainly upper-middle class, middle-aged women. He was also influenced by the research into hysteria of the Viennese physician →Breuer. In the early 1900s a group of psychoanalysts gathered around Freud. Some of these later broke away and formed their own schools: Alfred →Adler in 1911 and Carl →Jung in 1913. Following the Nazi occupation of Austria in 1938, Freud left for London, where he died.

The word 'psychoanalysis' was, like much of its terminology, coined by Freud, and many terms have passed into popular usage, not without distortion. The way that unconscious forces influence people's thoughts and actions was Freud's discovery, and his theory of the repression of infantile sexuality as the root of neuroses in the adult (as in the Oedipus complex) was controversial. Later he also stressed the significance of aggressive drives. His work has changed the way people think about human nature. His theories have brought about a more open approach to sexual matters; antisocial behaviour is now understood to result in many cases from unconscious forces, and these new concepts have led to wider expression of the human condition in art and literature. Nevertheless, Freud's theories have caused disagreement among psychologists and psychiatrists, and his methods of psychoanalysis cannot be applied in every case.

[Poets] are masters of us ordinary men, in knowledge of the mind, because they drink at streams which we have not yet made accessible to science.

Sigmund Freud

Freyberg /ˈfraɪbɜːg/ Bernard Cyril, Baron Freyberg 1889–1963. New Zealand soldier and administrator born in England. He fought in World War I, and during World War II he commanded the New Zealand expeditionary force. He was governor general of New Zealand 1946–52.

Friedan Betty 1921– . US liberal feminist. Her book *The Feminine Mystique* 1963 started the contemporary women's movement, both in the US and the UK. She was a founder of the National Organization for Women (NOW) 1966 (and its president 1966–70), the National Women's Political Caucus 1971, and the First Women's Bank 1973. Friedan also helped to organize the Women's Strike for Equality 1970 and called the First International Feminist Congress 1973.

Friedman /ˈfriːdmən/ Maurice 1903–1991. US physician who in the 1930s developed the 'rabbit test' to determine if a woman was pregnant. Following injection of a woman's urine into a female rabbit, changes would occur in the animal's ovaries if the woman was pregnant. However, such changes could only be detected on dissection of the rabbit.

Friedman /ˈfriːdmən/ Milton 1912– . US economist. The foremost exponent of monetarism, he argued that a country's economy, and hence inflation, can be controlled through its money supply, although most governments lack the 'political will' to control inflation by cutting government spending and thereby increasing unemployment. He was awarded the Nobel Prize for Economics 1976.

Governments never learn. Only people learn.

Milton Friedman 1980

Friedrich German form of →Frederick.

Friedrich /ˈfriːdrɪk/ Caspar David 1774–1840. German Romantic landscape painter, active mainly in Dresden. He imbued his subjects – mountain scenes and moonlit seas – with poetic melancholy and was later admired by Symbolist painters.

Frink /frɪŋk/ Elisabeth 1930–1993. British sculptor of rugged, naturalistic bronzes, mainly based on animal forms such as *Horseman* (opposite the Ritz Hotel, London), *In Memoriam* (heads), and *Running Man* 1980.

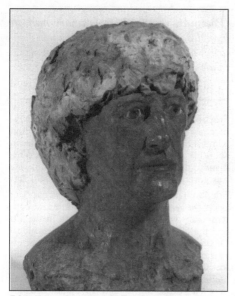

Frink Known for her bronze figures and larger-than-life sized heads, British sculptor Elisabeth Frink exhibited frequently from 1955 and received numerous public commissions. She is also a painter and graphic artist.

Frisch /frɪʃ/ Karl von 1886–1982. Austrian zoologist, founder with Konrad →Lorenz of ethology, the study of animal behaviour. He specialized in bees, discovering how they communicate the location of sources of nectar by movements called 'dances'. He was awarded the Nobel Prize for Medicine 1973 together with Lorenz and Nikolaas →Tinbergen.

Frisch /frɪʃ/ Max 1911– . Swiss dramatist. Inspired by →Brecht, his early plays such as *Als der Krieg zu Ende war/When the War Is Over* 1949 are more romantic in tone than his later symbolic dramas, such as *Andorra* 1962, dealing with questions of identity. He wrote *Biedermann und die Brandstifter/The Fire Raisers* 1958.

Frisch /frɪʃ/ Otto 1904–1979. Austrian physicist who coined the term 'nuclear fission'. A refugee from Nazi Germany, he worked from 1943 on the atom bomb at Los Alamos, New Mexico, and later at Cambridge, England. He was the nephew of Lise →Meitner.

Frisch /frɪʃ/ Ragnar 1895–1973. Norwegian economist, pioneer of econometrics (the application of mathematical and statistical methods in economics). He shared the first Nobel Prize for Economics in 1969 with Jan →Tinbergen.

Frith /frɪθ/ William Powell 1819–1909. British artist who painted large contemporary scenes with numerous figures and incidental detail. *Ramsgate Sands*, bought by Queen Victoria, is a fine example, as is *Derby Day* 1856–58 (both Tate Gallery, London).

Frobisher /ˈfrəʊbɪʃə/ Martin 1535–1594. English navigator. He made his first voyage to Guinea, West Africa, 1554. In 1576 he set out in search of the Northwest Passage, and visited Labrador, and Frobisher Bay, Baffin Island. Second and third expeditions sailed 1577 and 1578.

He was vice admiral in Drake's West Indian expedition 1585. In 1588, he was knighted for helping to defeat the Armada. He was mortally wounded 1594 fighting against the Spanish off the coast of France.

Froebel /ˈfrəʊbəl/ Friedrich August Wilhelm 1782–1852. German educationist. He evolved a new system of education using instructive play, described in *Education of Man* 1826 and other works. In 1836 he founded the first kindergarten (German 'garden for children') in Blankenburg, Germany. He was influenced by →Pestalozzi.

Fröhlich /ˈfrəʊlɪk/ Herbert 1905–1991. German-born English theoretical physicist who helped lay the foundations for modern theoretical physics in Britain. His main research interest was in solid state physics, but he also became familiar with quantum field theory – the application of quantum theory to particle interactions. In particular, he proposed a theory to explain superconductivity using the methods of quantum field theory. He also made important advances in the understanding of low-temperature superconductivity and biological systems.

Fröhlich studied in Munich under Arnold Sommerfeld, one of Germany's foremost theoretical physicists. The start of his academic career was spoiled by the Nazis, who engineered his dismissal from his teaching post in 1933. Fröhlich was one of many German scientists who left Germany at the time of World War II.

Fromm /frɒm/ Erich 1900–1980. German psychoanalyst who moved to the USA 1933 to escape the Nazis. His *The Fear of Freedom* 1941 and *The Sane Society* 1955 were source books for alternative lifestyles.

Fromm stressed the role of culture in the formation of personality, a view that distinguished him from traditional psychoanalysts. He also described the authoritarian personality, an important concept in the study of personality.

Frontenac et Palluau /ˌfrɒntəˈnæk eɪ ˌpæljuˈəʊ/ Louis de Buade, Comte de Frontenac et Palluau 1622–1698. French colonial governor. He began his military career 1635, and was appointed governor of the French possessions in North America 1672. Although efficient, he quarrelled with the local bishop and his followers and was recalled 1682. After the Iroquois, supported by the English, won several military victories, Frontenac was reinstated 1689. He defended Québec against the English 1690 and defeated the Iroquois 1696.

Frost /frɒst/ Robert (Lee) 1874–1963. US poet whose verse, in traditional form, is written with an individual voice and penetrating vision. His poems include 'Mending Wall' ('Something there is that does not love a wall'), 'The Road Not Taken', and 'Stopping by Woods on a Snowy Evening' and are collected in *A Boy's Will* 1913, *North of Boston* 1914, *New Hampshire* 1924, *Collected Poems* 1930, *A Further Range* 1936, and *A Witness Tree* 1942.

Born in San Francisco, Frost was raised in New England, where he attended Dartmouth College and Harvard University for brief periods. He was awarded four Pulitzer prizes (1924, 1931, 1937, 1943) and in 1961 read his 'The Gift Outright' at the inauguration of J F Kennedy.

Froude /fruːd/ James Anthony 1818–1894. English historian, whose *History of England from the Fall of Wolsey to the Defeat of the Spanish Armada* in twelve volumes 1856–70 was a classic Victorian work.

He was influenced by the Oxford Movement in the Church of England, in which his brother, *Richard Hurrell Froude* (1803–36), collaborated with Cardinal →Newman.

Fry /fraɪ/ Christopher 1907– . English dramatist. He was a leader of the revival of verse drama after World War II with *The Lady's Not for Burning* 1948, *Venus Observed* 1950, and *A Sleep of Prisoners* 1951.

He has also written screenplays and made successful translations of Anouilh and Giraudoux.

Fry /fraɪ/ Elizabeth (born Gurney) 1780–1845. English Quaker philanthropist. She formed an association for the improvement of conditions for female prisoners 1817, and worked with her brother, *Joseph Gurney* (1788–1847), on an 1819 report on prison reform.

Fry /fraɪ/ Roger Eliot 1866–1934. British artist and art critic, a champion of Post-Impressionism and an admirer of Cézanne. He founded the Omega Workshops to improve design and to encourage young artists.

Fuad /fuˈɑːd/ two kings of Egypt:

Fuad I /fuˈɑːd/ 1868–1936. King of Egypt from 1922. Son of the Khedive Ismail, he succeeded his elder brother Hussein Kiamil as sultan of Egypt 1917; when Egypt was declared independent 1922 he assumed the title of king.

Fuad II 1952– . King of Egypt 1952–53, between the abdication of his father →Farouk and the establishment of the republic. He was a grandson of Fuad I.

Fuchs /fʊks/ Klaus (Emil Julius) 1911–1988. German spy who worked on atom-bomb research in the USA in World War II, and subsequently in the UK. He was imprisoned 1950–59 for passing information to the USSR and resettled in eastern Germany.

Fuchs /fʊks/ Vivian 1908– . British explorer and geologist. Before World War II, he accompanied several Cambridge University expeditions to East Africa. From 1947 he worked in the Falkland

Fry A chief promoter of prison reform in Europe, English Quaker philanthropist Elizabeth Fry also founded charity organizations and hostels for the homeless. Appalled by the condition of women prisoners in Newgate Prison 1813, she devoted her life to prison reform and also worked hard to make improvements in the British hospital system and treatment of the insane.

Islands as director of the Scientific Bureau. In 1957–58, he led the overland Commonwealth Trans-Antarctic Expedition and published his autobiography *A Time to Speak* in 1991.

Fuentes /fuˈentes/ Carlos 1928– . Mexican novelist, lawyer, and diplomat whose first novel *La región más transparente*/*Where the Air Is Clear* 1958 encompasses the history of the country from the Aztecs to the present day.

More than other Mexican novelists he presents the frustrated social philosophy of the failed Mexican revolution. He received international attention for *The Death of Artemeo Cruz* 1962, *Terra nostra* 1975, and *El Gringo veijo*/*The Old Gringo* 1985. *The Campaign* 1991 is set during the revolutionary wars leading to independence in Latin America.

Führer /ˈfjʊərə/ or *Fuehrer* title adopted by Adolf →Hitler as leader of the Nazi Party.

Fujimori /fuːdʒɪˈmɔːri/ Alberto 1939– . President of Peru from July 1990. As leader of the newly formed Cambio 90 (Change 90) he campaigned on a reformist ticket and defeated his more experienced Democratic Front opponent. With no assembly majority, and faced with increasing opposition to his policies, he imposed military rule early in 1992.

Fulbright /ˈfʊlbraɪt/ (James) William 1905– . US Democratic politician. A US senator 1945–75, he was responsible for the *Fulbright Act* 1946, which provided grants for thousands of Americans to study abroad and for overseas students to study in the USA. Fulbright chaired the Senate

Foreign Relations Committee 1959–74, and was a strong internationalist and supporter of the United Nations.

He had studied at Oxford, UK, on a Rhodes scholarship.

Fuller /fʊlə/ (Richard) Buckminster 1895–1983. US architect, engineer, and futurist social philosopher who embarked on an unorthodox career in an attempt to maximize energy resources through improved technology. In 1947 he invented the lightweight geodesic dome, a half-sphere of triangular components independent of buttress or vault.

It combined the maximum strength with the minimum structure. Within 30 years over 50,000 had been built.

Fuller /fʊlə/ John Frederick Charles 1878–1966. British major general and military theorist who propounded the concept of armoured warfare which, when interpreted by the Germans, became *blitzkrieg* in 1940.

Fuller /fʊlə/ Margaret 1810–1850. US author and reformer. She was the editor of *The Dial*, the Transcendentalist magazine 1839–44, and noted for her public 'conversations' for the edification of the women of Boston during the same period. She became the literary critic for the *New York Tribune* 1844. Later, while on assignment in Italy, she joined Giuseppe Mazzini's doomed nationalist revolt 1848. Fuller was lost at sea while returning to the USA 1850.

Born in Cambridge, Massachusetts, and tutored by her father, Fuller began adult life as a teacher and writer.

Fuller /fʊlə/ Melville Weston 1833–1910. US jurist and chief justice of the US Supreme Court 1888–1910. Fuller endorsed court options that limited state and federal strengths to regulate private business. He sided with the majority of the Court in *Pollack* v *Farmers Loan and Trust Co* 1895, which held invalid a flat-rate US income tax leading to passage of the 16th Amendment to the Constitution in 1913, authorizing an income tax.

Born in Augusta, Maine, Fuller followed an early career in law and Democratic politics and then continued his activities in Chicago 1856. He was a supporter of Stephen Douglas in his 1858 election as US senator and in his bid for the presidency 1860. Fuller supported Grover Cleveland in the 1884 presidential who appointed him chief justice.

Fuller /fʊlə/ Peter 1947–1990. English art critic who from the mid-1970s attacked the complacency of the art establishment and emphasized tradition over fashion. From 1988 these views, and an increased interest in the spiritual power of art, were voiced in his own magazine *Modern Painters*.

Fuller Roy 1912– . English poet and novelist. His collections of poetry include *Poems* 1939, *Epitaphs and Occasions* 1951, *Brutus's Orchard* 1957, *Collected Poems* 1962, and *The Reign of Sparrows*

1980. Novels include *My Child, My Sister* 1965 and *The Carnal Island* 1970.

Fuller /fʊlə/ Thomas 1608–1661. English writer. He was chaplain to the Royalist army during the Civil War and, at the Restoration, became the king's chaplain. He wrote a *History of the Holy War* 1639, *Good Thoughts in Bad Times* 1645, its sequel *Good Thoughts in Worse Times* 1647, and the biographical *Worthies of England* 1662.

Fulton /fʊltən/ Robert 1745–1815. US gunsmith, artist, engineer, and inventor. He designed steamships based on those invented by James Rumsey 1787 and John →Fitch 1790. With French support he built the first submarine, the *Nautilus* 1801. Combining the British-built steam engine with his own design of riverboat, a sidewheeler, he built and registered the *North River Steam Boat* 1807 (now erroneously known as the *Clermont*).

Fulton had lived 20 years in Europe during 1786–1805, and was well known as a painter and as an engineer of naval technology and canals. He managed to acquire British steam engines to power his first vessels, although at the time the British were not selling to the newly independent US. The *North River Steam Boat* was commissioned by Robert →Livingston who had a licence to serve the Hudson by steamboat. This and other steamboats were established and maintained by Fulton, going from New York City to Albany. Fulton also designed and oversaw the building of the first steam-powered warship, the USS *Fulton*, for the new US Navy.

Funk /fʌŋk/ Casimir 1884–1967. US biochemist, born in Poland, who pioneered research into vitamins.

Funk proposed that certain diseases are caused by dietary deficiencies. In 1912 he demonstrated that rice extracts cure beriberi in pigeons. As the extract contains an amine, he mistakenly concluded that he had discovered a class of 'vital amines', a phrase soon reduced to 'vitamins'.

Furtwängler /fʊətveŋlə/ (Gustav Heinrich Ernst Martin) Wilhelm 1886–1954. German conductor; leader of the Berlin Philharmonic Orchestra 1922–54. His interpretations of the German Romantic composers, such as Wagner, were regarded as classically definitive. He remained in Germany during the Nazi regime.

Fuseli /fjuːzəli/ Henry 1741–1825. British Romantic artist born in Switzerland. He painted macabre and dreamlike images, such as *The Nightmare* 1781 (Detroit Institute of Arts). His subjects include scenes from Milton and Shakespeare.

Fyfe /faif/ David Maxwell, 1st Earl of Kilmuir. Scottish lawyer and Conservative politician; see →Kilmuir.

Fyffe /faif/ Will 1885–1947. Scottish music-hall comedian remembered for his vivid character sketches and for his song 'I Belong to Glasgow'

Gable /ˈgeɪbəl/ (William) Clark 1901–1960. US actor. A star for more than 30 years in 90 films, he played romantic roles such as Rhett Butler in *Gone With the Wind* 1939. His other films include *The Painted Desert* 1931 (his first), *It Happened One Night* 1934 (Academy Award), *Mutiny on the Bounty* 1935, and *The Misfits* 1960. He was nicknamed the 'King' of Hollywood.

Gabo /ˈgɑːbəʊ/ Naum. Adopted name of Naum Neemia Pevsner 1890–1977. US abstract sculptor, born in Russia. One of the leading exponents of the revolutionary art movement Constructivism, he left the USSR in 1922 for Germany and taught at the Bauhaus in Berlin (a key centre of modern design). He lived in Paris and England in the 1930s, then settled in the USA in 1946. He was one of the first artists to make kinetic (moving) sculpture and often used transparent coloured plastics.

Gabor /ˈgɑːbɔː/ Dennis 1900–1979. Hungarian-born British physicist. In 1947 he invented the holographic method of three-dimensional photography. He was awarded a Nobel prize 1971.

Gabrieli /ˌgæbriˈeli/ Giovanni *c.* 1555–1612. Italian composer and organist. Although he composed secular music and madrigals, he is best known for his motets, which are frequently dramatic and often use several choirs and groups of instruments. In 1585 he became organist at St Mark's, Venice.

Gadamer /ˈgɑːdəmə/ Hans-Georg 1900– . German hermeneutic philosopher. In *Truth and Method* 1960, he argued that 'understanding' is fundamental to human existence, and that all understanding takes place within a tradition. The relation between text and interpreter can be viewed as a dialogue, in which the interpreter must remain open to the truth of the text.

Gaddafi alternative form of →Khaddhafi, Libyan leader.

Gaddi /ˈgædi/ family of Italian painters in Florence: *Gaddo Gaddi* (*c.* 1250–1330); his son *Taddeo Gaddi* (*c.* 1300–1366), who was inspired by Giotto and painted the fresco cycle *Life of the Virgin* in Santa Croce, Florence; and grandson *Agnolo Gaddi* (active 1369–96), who also painted frescoes in Santa Croce, *The Story of the Cross* 1380s, and produced panel paintings in characteristic pale pastel colours.

Gaddis /ˈgædɪs/ William 1922– . US novelist. His work is experimental, and his best-known novel *The Recognitions* 1955 is about artistic counterfeiting. His other novels are *JR* 1976 and *Carpenter's Gothic* 1985.

Gadsden /ˈgædzdən/ James 1788–1858. US military leader and diplomat. In 1823 he was appointed by President Monroe to supervise the forced resettlement of the North American Seminole Indians to S Florida and participated in the ensuing Seminole Wars. He was appointed US minister to Mexico 1853 and negotiated the Gadsden Purchase, acquiring for the US from Mexico what is now New Mexico and Arizona.

Born in Charleston, South Carolina, USA, and educated at Yale University, Gadsden served in the Anglo-American War of 1812 as well as in the Seminole Wars. After several years as a railroad executive, Gadsden was named US minister to Mexico and agreed the sale of Mexican territory south of the Gila river, to be used as a route to California. The Gadsden Purchase was approved by the Senate 1854.

Gagarin /gəˈgɑːrɪn/ Yuri (Alexeyevich) 1934–1968. Soviet cosmonaut who in 1961 became the first human in space aboard the spacecraft *Vostok 1*.

Born in the Smolensk region, the son of a farmer, he qualified as a foundryman. He became a pilot 1957, and on 12 April 1961 completed one orbit of the Earth, taking 108 minutes from launch to landing. He died in a plane crash while training for the *Soyuz 3* mission.

Gaillard /ˈgeɪlɑːd/ Slim (Bulee) 1916–1991. US jazz singer, songwriter, actor, and musician. A light, humorous performer, he claimed to have invented his own language, Vout (nonsense syllables as in scat singing). His first hit was 'Flat Foot Floogie' 1938.

Gainsborough Thomas 1727–1788. English landscape and portrait painter. In 1760 he settled in Bath and painted society portraits. In 1774 he went to London and became one of the original members of the Royal Academy. He was one of the first British artists to follow the Dutch in painting realistic landscapes rather than imaginative Italianate scenery.

Born in Sudbury, Suffolk, Gainsborough began to paint while still at school. In London he learned etching and studied at the Academy of Arts, but remained largely self taught.

His portraits of Sir Charles Holte and the actor Garrick belong to this period. His sitters included the royal family, the Welsh actress Mrs Siddons, the lexicographer Dr Johnson, the politician Edmund Burke, and the dramatist Richard Sheridan.

Gaitskell /ˈgeɪtskəl/ Hugh (Todd Naylor) 1906–1963. British Labour politician. In 1950 he became minister of economic affairs, and then chancellor of the Exchequer until Oct 1951. In 1955 he defeated Aneurin Bevan for the succession to Attlee as party leader, and tried to reconcile internal differences on nationalization and disarmament. He was re-elected leader in 1960.

Galbraith /gælˈbreɪθ/ John Kenneth 1908– . Canadian-born US economist; he became a US citizen 1937. His major works include the *Affluent Society* 1958, in which he documents the tendency of the 'invisible hand' of free-market capitalism to create private splendour and public squalor, *Economics and the Public Purpose* 1974, and *The Culture of Containment* 1992.

Gale /geɪl/ George 1927–1990. British journalist and broadcaster. He worked for the *Manchester Guardian, Daily Mirror, Daily Express,* and, towards the end of his life, *Daily Mail.* His sometimes raw, iconoclastic views earned him a formidable reputation as a political journalist.

Galen /ˈgeɪlən/ c. 130–c. 200. Greek physician whose ideas dominated Western medicine for almost 1,500 years. Central to his thinking were the theories of humours and the threefold circulation of the blood. He remained the highest medical authority until Andreas Vesalius and William Harvey exposed the fundamental errors of his system.

Galen was born in Pergamum in Asia Minor. He attended the Roman emperor Marcus Aurelius. Although he made relatively few discoveries and relied heavily on the teachings of →Hippocrates, he wrote a large number of books, over 100 of which are known.

Galileo /ˌgælɪˈleɪəʊ/ properly Galileo Galilei 1564–1642. Italian mathematician, astronomer, and physicist. He developed the astronomical telescope and was the first to see sunspots, the four main satellites of Jupiter, mountains and craters on the Moon, and the appearance of Venus going through 'phases', thus proving it was orbiting the Sun. In mechanics, Galileo discovered that freely falling bodies, heavy or light, had the same, constant acceleration (although the story of his dropping cannonballs from the Leaning Tower of Pisa is questionable) and that a body moving on a perfectly smooth horizontal surface would neither speed up nor slow down.

He discovered in 1583 that each oscillation of a pendulum takes the same amount of time despite the difference in amplitude. He invented a hydrostatic balance, and discovered that the path of a projectile is a parabola.

Galileo was born in Pisa, and in 1589 became professor of mathematics at the university there; in 1592 he became a professor at Padua, and in 1610 was appointed chief mathematician to the Grand Duke of Tuscany. Galileo's observations and arguments were an unwelcome refutation of the ideas of →Aristotle taught at the (church-run) universities, largely because they made plausible for the first time the heliocentric (Sun-centred) theory of →Copernicus. Galileo's persuasive *Dialogues on the Two Chief Systems of the World* 1632 was banned by the church authorities in Rome; he was made to recant by the Inquisition and put under house arrest for his last years.

In questions of science the authority of a thousand is not worth the humble reasoning of a single individual.

Galileo

Gall /gɔːl/ c. 1840–1894. American Sioux Indian leader. He became a noted warrior of the Hunkpapa Sioux and a protégé of Chief Sitting Bull. Gall accompanied Sitting Bull to Montana 1876 and led the encirclement and annihilation of General →Custer's force at Little Bighorn.

Born along the Moreau river in the Dakota Territory, Gall participated in raids against the US Army along the Bozeman Trail and opposed the Treaty of Fort Laramie 1868, which established the reservation system in the N plains. After Custer's last stand 1876, he escaped to Canada with Sitting Bull and later settled on a reservation, becoming an Indian judge.

Gall /gæl/ Franz Joseph 1758–1828. Austrian anatomist, instigator of the discredited theory of phrenology.

Gallatin /ˈgælətɪn/ Albert 1761–1849. Swiss-born US political leader and diplomat. He served in the US House of Representatives 1795–1801 and was secretary of the treasury 1801–13 during the administrations of Jefferson and Madison. He negotiated the treaty ending the Anglo-American War of 1812–14 and served as US minister to France 1815–22 and to England 1826–27.

Gallatin served in the Pennsylvania state legislature 1790–94. A critic of the Federalists, he helped establish the fiscal power of the US House of Representatives. After the end of his political career, he devoted himself to banking and American Indian ethnology.

Gallé /gæl/ Emile 1846–1904. French Art Nouveau glassmaker. He produced glass in sinuous forms or rounded, solid-looking shapes almost as heavy as stone, typically decorated with flowers or leaves in colour on colour.

After training in Europe, he worked at his father's glass factory and eventually took it over. He was a founder of the Ecole de Nancy, a group of French Art Nouveau artists who drew inspiration from his 1890s work and adopted his style of decoration and techniques.

Galle /ˈgælə/ Johann Gottfried 1812–1910. German astronomer who located the planet Neptune 1846, close to the position predicted by French mathematician Urbain Leverrier.

Gallegos /gælˈjeɪgɒs/ Rómulo 1884–1969. Venezuelan politician and writer. He was Venezuela's first democratically elected president 1948 before being overthrown by a military coup the same year. He was also a professor of philosophy and literature. His novels include *La trepadora/The Climber* 1925 and *Doña Bárbara* 1929.

Gallico /ˈgælɪkəʊ/ Paul (William) 1897–1976. US author. Originally a sports columnist, he began writing fiction in 1936. His many books include *The Snow Goose* 1941.

Gallo /ˈgæləʊ/ Robert Charles 1937– . US scientist credited with identifying the virus responsible for AIDS. Gallo discovered the virus, now known as human immunodeficiency virus (HIV), in 1984; the French scientist Luc Montagnier (1932–) of the Pasteur Institute, Paris, discovered the virus, independently, in 1983. The sample in which Gallo discovered the virus was supplied by Montagnier, and it has been alleged that this may have been contaminated by specimens of the virus isolated by Montagnier a few months earlier.

Gallup /ˈgæləp/ George Horace 1901–1984. US journalist and statistician, who founded in 1935 the American Institute of Public Opinion and devised the Gallup Poll, in which public opinion is sampled by questioning a number of representative individuals.

Galois /gælˈwɑː/ Evariste 1811–1832. French mathematician who originated the theory of groups. His attempts to gain recognition for his work were largely thwarted by the French mathematical establishment, critical of his lack of formal qualifications. Galois was killed in a duel before he was 21. The night before, he had hurriedly written out his unpublished discoveries on group theory, the importance of which would come to be appreciated more and more as the 19th century progressed.

Galsworthy /ˈgɔːlzwɜːði/ John 1867–1933. English novelist and dramatist whose work examines the social issues of the Victorian period. He wrote *The Forsyte Saga* 1922 and its sequel *A Modern Comedy* 1929. His other novels include *The Country House* 1907 and *Fraternity* 1909; plays include *The Silver Box* 1906.

Galsworthy first achieved recognition with *The Man of Property* 1906, the first instalment of the *Forsyte* series, which includes *In Chancery* and *To Let*. Soames Forsyte, the central character, is the embodiment of Victorian values and feeling for property, and the wife whom he also 'owns' – Irene – was based on Galsworthy's wife. Later additions to the series are *A Modern Comedy* 1929,

Galsworthy John Galsworthy, English novelist and playwright. After a slow and diffident beginning he made his name with the novel sequence The Forsyte Saga *which sustained a moral critique of the upper middle class society from which he came. Social indignation also fuelled such successful plays as* The Silver Box.

which contained *The White Monkey*, *The Silver Spoon*, and *Swan Song*, and the short stories *On Forsyte Change* 1930. He was awared the Nobel Prize for Literature, 1932

Galt /gɔːlt/ John 1779–1839. Scottish novelist, author of *Annals of the Parish* 1821, in which he portrays the life of a Lowlands village, using the local dialect.

Born in Ayrshire, he moved to London in 1804 and lived in Canada 1826–29. He founded the Canadian town of Guelph, and Galt, on the Grand River, Ontario, was named after him.

Galtieri /ˌgæltiˈeəri/ Leopoldo 1926– . Argentine general, president 1981–82. A leading member from 1979 of the ruling right-wing military junta and commander of the army, Galtieri became president in 1981. Under his leadership the junta ordered the seizure 1982 of the Falkland Islands (Malvinas), a British colony in the SW Atlantic claimed by Argentina. After the surrender of his forces he resigned as army commander and was replaced as president. He and his fellow junta members were tried for abuse of human rights and court-martialled for their conduct of the war; he was sentenced to 12 years in prison in 1986.

Galton /ˈgɔːltən/ Francis 1822–1911. English scientist who studied the inheritance of physical and mental attributes in humans, with the aim of improving the human species. He discovered that no two sets of human fingerprints are the same, and is considered the founder of eugenics.

Galvani /gæl'vɑːni/ Luigi 1737–1798. Italian physiologist who discovered galvanic, or voltaic, electricity in 1762, when investigating the contractions produced in the muscles of dead frogs by contact with pairs of different metals. His work led quickly to Alessandro Volta's invention of the electrical cell, and later to an understanding of how nerves control muscles.

Galway /ɡɔːlweɪ/ James 1939– . Irish flautist, born in Belfast. He was a member of the Berlin Philharmonic Orchestra 1969–75, before taking up a solo career.

Gama /ɡɑːmə/ Vasco da *c.* 1469–1524. Portuguese navigator who commanded an expedition in 1497 to discover the route to India around the Cape of Good Hope in modern South Africa. On Christmas Day 1497 he reached land, which he named Natal. He then crossed the Indian Ocean, arriving at Calicut May 1498, and returning to Portugal Sept 1499.

Da Gama was born at Sines, and chosen by Portuguese King Manoel I for his 1497 expedition. In 1502 he founded a Portuguese colony at Mozambique. In the same year he attacked and plundered Calicut in revenge for the murder of some Portuguese sailors. After 20 years of retirement, he was dispatched to India again as Portuguese viceroy in 1524, but died two months after his arrival in Goa.

Gambetta /ɡæm'betə/ Léon Michel 1838–1882. French politician, organizer of resistance during the Franco-Prussian War, and founder in 1871 of the Third Republic. In 1881–82 he was prime minister for a few weeks.

Gambetta Léon Gambetta, French politician who took a leading role in proclaiming the Third Republic after the fall of Napoleon III in 1870.

Gamelin /ɡæmələn/ Maurice Gustave 1872–1958. French commander in chief of the Allied armies in France at the outset of World War II 1939. Replaced by Maxime Weygand after the German breakthrough at Sedan 1940, he was tried by the Vichy government as a scapegoat before the Riom 'war guilt' court 1942. He refused to defend himself and was detained in Germany until released by the Allies 1945.

Gamow /ɡeɪmaʊ/ George 1904–1968. Russian-born US cosmologist, nuclear physicist, and popularizer of science. His work in astrophysics included a study of the structure and evolution of stars and the creation of the elements. He also explained how the collision of nuclei in the solar interior could produce the nuclear reactions that power the Sun.

Gamow was also an early supporter of the Big Bang theory of the origin of the universe. He predicted that the electromagnetic radiation left over from the universe's formation, should, after having cooled down during the subsequent expansion of the universe, manifest itself as a microwave background radiation with a temperature of 10K (−263°C/−442°F). In 1965 the cosmic background radiation was discovered, which had a temperature of 3K (−270°C/−454°F), or 3°C above absolute zero.

Gamsakhurdia Zviad 1939– . Georgian politician, president 1990–92. He was an active anti-communist and became head of state after nationalist success in parliamentary elections. Directly elected to the post by a huge margin in May 1991, Gamsakhurdia's increasingly dictatorial style led to his forced removal and he fled to Armenia.

The son of the famous Georgian novelist Konstantin Gamsakhurdia, he became a linguist and university lecturer in American Studies. He founded the Initiative Group for the Defence of Human Rights in Georgia 1974.

Gance /ɡɒns/ Abel 1889–1981. French film director whose *Napoléon* 1927 was one of the most ambitious silent epic films. It features colour and triple-screen sequences, as well as multiple-exposure shots.

Gandhi /ɡændi/ Indira (born Nehru) 1917–1984. Indian politician, prime minister of India 1966–77 and 1980–84, and leader of the Congress Party 1966–77 and subsequently of the Congress (I) party. She was assassinated 1984 by members of her Sikh bodyguard, resentful of her use of troops to clear malcontents from the Sikh temple at Amritsar.

Her father, Jawaharlal Nehru, was India's first prime minister. She married Feroze Gandhi in 1942 (died 1960, not related to Mahatma Gandhi) and had two sons, Sanjay Gandhi (1946–1980), who died in an aeroplane crash, and Rajiv →Gandhi, who was assassinated 21 May 1991. In 1975 the validity of her re-election to parliament was questioned, and she declared a state of emergency. During this time her son Sanjay was implementing a social and economic programme (including an unpopular family-planning policy) which led to her defeat in 1977, although he masterminded her return to power in 1980.

Gandhi /ˈgændi/ Mohandas Karamchand, called *Mahatma* ('Great Soul') 1869–1948. Indian nationalist leader. A pacifist, he led the struggle for Indian independence from the UK by advocating nonviolent noncooperation (*satyagraha*, defence of and by truth) from 1915. He was imprisoned several times by the British authorities and was influential in the nationalist Congress Party and in the independence negotiations 1947. He was assassinated by a Hindu nationalist in the violence that followed the partition of British India into India and Pakistan.

Gandhi was born in Porbandar and studied law in London, later practising as a barrister. He settled in South Africa where until 1914 he led the Indian community in opposition to racial discrimination. Returning to India, he emerged as leader of the Indian National Congress. He organized hunger strikes and events of civil disobedience, and campaigned for social reform, including religious tolerance and an end to discrimination against the so-called untouchable caste. In 1947, after World War II, he played a significant role in negotiations for an autonomous Indian state.

An unjust law is itself a species of violence. Arrest for its breach is more so.

Mahatma K Gandhi
Non-Violence in Peace and War

Gandhi /ˈgændi/ Rajiv 1944–1991. Indian politician, prime minister from 1984 (following his mother Indira Gandhi's assassination) to Nov 1989. As prime minister, he faced growing discontent with his party's elitism and lack of concern for social issues. He was assassinated by a bomb at an election rally.

Elder son of Indira Gandhi and grandson of Nehru, Rajiv Gandhi was born into the Kashmiri Brahmin family that had governed India for all but four years since 1947. He initially displayed little interest in politics and became a pilot with Indian Airlines. But after the death in a plane crash of his brother *Sanjay* (1946–1980), he was elected to his brother's Amethi parliamentary seat 1981. In the Dec 1984 parliamentary elections he won a record majority. His reputation became tarnished by a scandal concerning alleged kickbacks to senior officials from an arms deal with the Swedish munitions firm Bofors and, following his party's defeat in the general election of Nov 1989, Gandhi was forced to resign as premier. He was killed in the middle of the 1991 election campaign at a rally near Madras, while attempting to regain office.

Garbo /ˈgɑːbəʊ/ Greta. Stage name of Greta Lovisa Gustafsson 1905–1990. Swedish-born US film actress. She went to the USA in 1925, and her captivating beauty and leading role in *The Torrent* 1926 made her one of Hollywood's first stars in silent films. Her later films include *Mata Hari* 1931, *Grand Hotel* 1932, *Queen Christina* 1933, *Anna Karenina* 1935, *Camille* 1936, and *Ninotchka* 1939. Her qualities of ethereality and romantic mystery on the screen intermingled with her seclusion in private life. She retired 1941.

García Lorca /gɑːˈθiːə ˈlɔːkə/ Federico. Spanish poet; see →Lorca, Federico García.

García Márquez /gɑːˈsiːə ˈmɑːkes/ Gabriel 1928– . Colombian novelist. His sweeping novel *Cien años de soledad/One Hundred Years of Solitude* 1967 (which tells the story of a family over a period of six generations) is an example of magic realism, a technique used to heighten the intensity of realistic portrayal of social and political issues by introducing grotesque or fanciful material. Nobel Prize for Literature 1982.

His other books include *El amor en los tiempos del cólera/Love in the Time of Cholera* 1985 and *The General in His Labyrinth* 1991, which describes the last four months of Simón Bolívar's life.

García Perez /gɑːˈsiːə ˈperes/ Alan 1949– . Peruvian politician, leader of the moderate, left-wing APRA party; president 1985–90. He inherited an ailing economy and was forced to trim his socialist programme.

He was born in Lima and educated in Peru, Guatemala, Spain, and France. He became APRA's secretary general 1982. In 1985 he succeeded Fernando →Belaúnde Terry as president, becoming the first civilian president democratically elected.

Garcilaso de la Vega /ˌgɑːθɪˈlɑːsəʊ/ 1503–1536. Spanish poet. A soldier, he was a member of Charles V's expedition in 1535 to Tunis; he was killed in battle at Nice. His verse, some of the greatest of the Spanish Renaissance, includes sonnets, songs, and elegies, often on the model of Petrarch.

Garcilaso de la Vega /ˌgɑːθɪˈlɑːsəʊ/ 1539–1616. Spanish writer, called *el Inca*. Son of a Spanish conquistador and an Inca princess, he wrote an account of the conquest of Florida and *Comentarios reales de los Incas* on the history of Peru.

Gardiner /ˈgɑːdnə/ Gerald Austin 1900–1990. British lawyer. As Lord Chancellor in the 1964–70 Labour governments, Gardiner introduced the office of ombudsman to Britain, and played a major role in the movement for abolition of capital punishment for murder (which became law in 1965).

Gardiner /ˈgɑːdnə/ Stephen *c.* 1493–1555. English priest and politician. After being secretary to Cardinal Wolsey, he became bishop of Winchester in 1531. An opponent of Protestantism, he was imprisoned under Edward VI, and as Lord Chancellor 1553–55 under Queen Mary he tried to restore Roman Catholicism.

Gardner /ˈgɑːdnə/ Ava 1922–1990. US film actress, a sensuous star in such films as *The Killers* 1946, *Pandora and the Flying Dutchman* 1951, and *The Barefoot Contessa* 1954, a tragically slanted Cinderella tale of a Romany girl who becomes an international celebrity. Her later roles include that of Lillie Langtry in *The Life and Times of Judge Roy Bean* 1972. She remained active in films until the 1980s, when she retired to London.

Gardner /ˈgɑːdnə/ Erle Stanley 1889–1970. US author of crime fiction. He created the character of the lawyer-detective Perry Mason, who was later featured in film and on television. Originally a lawyer, Gardner gave up his practice with the success of the first Perry Mason stories.

Gardner /ˈgɑːdnə/ Helen 1908– . British scholar. She edited the poetry and prose of Donne, and the *New Oxford Book of English Verse* 1972. She was Merton Professor of English Literature at Oxford 1966–75.

Gardner /ˈgɑːdnə/ Isabella Stewart 1840–1924. US art collector and founder of the Isabella Stewart Gardner Museum in Boston, USA. She was a patron of the Boston Symphony Orchestra (founded 1881). As an art collector, she specialized in the works of the Renaissance and of the Dutch masters. Her private art gallery in Boston was opened as a public museum 1903.

Born in New York and educated in Paris, France, she married prominent Boston manufacturer John Gardner 1860. She was participant in the intellectual life of the city but as a tireless world traveller, socialite, and local celebrity, she scandalized Bostonians with her lavish parties and public appearances.

Gardner /ˈgɑːdnə/ John 1917– . English composer. Professor at the Royal Academy of Music from 1956, he has produced a symphony 1951; the opera *The Moon and Sixpence* 1957, based on a Somerset Maugham novel; and other works, including film music.

Garfield /ˈgɑːfiːld/ James A(bram) 1831–1881. 20th president of the USA 1881, a Republican. A compromise candidate for the presidency, he held office for only four months before being assassinated in Washington DC railway station by a disappointed office-seeker. His short tenure was marked primarily by struggles within the Republican party over influence and cabinet posts.

He was born in a log cabin in Ohio, and served in the Civil War with the Union forces.

Garibaldi /ˌgærɪˈbɔːldi/ Giuseppe 1807–1882. Italian soldier who played a central role in the unification of Italy by conquering Sicily and Naples 1860. From 1834 a member of the nationalist Mazzini's Young Italy society, he was forced into exile until 1848 and again 1849–54. He fought against Austria 1848–49, 1859, and 1866, and led two unsuccessful expeditions to liberate Rome from papal rule in 1862 and 1867.

Born in Nice, he became a sailor and then joined the nationalist movement *Risorgimento*. Condemned to death for treason, he escaped to South America where he became a mercenary. He returned to Italy during the 1848 revolution, served with the Sardinian army against the Austrians, and commanded the army of the Roman republic in its defence of the city against the French. He subsequently lived in exile until 1854, when he settled on the island of Caprera. In 1860, at the head of his 1,000 redshirts, he won Sicily and Naples for the new kingdom of Italy. He served in the Austrian War of 1866 and fought for France in the Franco-Prussian War 1870–71.

I cannot offer you either wages or honours; I offer you hunger, thirst, forced marches, battles, and death. Anyone who loves his country, follow me.

Giuseppe Garibaldi

Garland /ˈgɑːlənd/ Judy. Stage name of Frances Gumm 1922–1969. US singer and actress whose performances are marked by a compelling intensity. Her films include *The Wizard of Oz* (which featured the tune that was to become her theme song, 'Over the Rainbow'), *Babes in Arms* 1939, *Strike Up the Band* 1940, *Meet Me in St Louis* 1944, *Easter Parade* 1948, *A Star is Born* 1954, and *Judgment at Nuremberg* 1961.

She began her acting career 1935 in the Andy Hardy series. She was the mother of actress and singer Liza Minnelli.

Garner /ˈgɑːnə/ Helen 1942– . Australian novelist, journalist, and short-story writer. She won the National Book Council's Award for her novel *Monkey Grip* 1977, which was filmed 1981. Her other books include *Honour and Other People's Children* 1980 and *The Children's Bach* 1984.

Garner /ˈgɑːnə/ John Nance 1868–1967. US political leader and vice president of the USA 1933–41. He served in the US House of Representatives 1903–33. A Democratic leader in the House, he was chosen as Speaker 1931. He later served as vice president during Franklin Roosevelt's first two terms. Opposing Roosevelt's reelection in 1940, Garner retired from public life.

Born in Red River County, Texas, USA, Garner briefly attended Vanderbilt University. After privately studying law in Clarksville, Texas, he was admitted to the bar 1890. He was appointed county judge 1895 before embarking on a career in Democratic party politics and serving in the state legislature 1898–1902.

Garret /ˈgəˈret/ Almeida 1799–1854. Portuguese poet, novelist, and dramatist. As a liberal, in 1823 he was forced into 14 years of exile. His works, which he saw as a singlehanded attempt to create a national literature, include the prose *Viagens na*

Minha Terra/Travels in My Homeland 1843–46 and the tragedy *Frei Luis de Sousa* 1843.

Garrick /ˈgærɪk/ David 1717–1779. British actor and theatre manager. He was a pupil of Samuel →Johnson. From 1747 he became joint licensee of the Drury Lane theatre with his own company, and instituted a number of significant theatrical conventions including concealed stage lighting and banishing spectators from the stage. He played Shakespearean characters such as Richard III, King Lear, Hamlet, and Benedick, and collaborated with George Colman (1732–1794) in writing the play *The Clandestine Marriage* 1766. He retired from the stage 1766, but continued as a manager.

Garrison William Lloyd 1805–1879. US editor and reformer who was an uncompromising opponent of slavery. He founded the abolitionist journal *The Liberator* 1831 and became a leader of the American Anti-Slavery Society. Although initially opposed to violence, he supported the Union cause in the Civil War. After the Emancipation Proclamation, he disbanded the Anti-Slavery Society and devoted his energies to prohibition, feminism, and Indian rights.

Garrod /ˈgærəd/ Archibald Edward 1857–1937. English physician who first recognized a class of metabolic diseases, while studying the rare disease alcaptonuria, in which the patient's urine turns black on contact with air. He calculated that the cause was a failure of the body's metabolism to break down certain amino acids into harmless substances like water and carbon dioxide.

Garshin /ˈgɑːʃɪn/ Vsevolod 1855–1888. Russian short-story writer. He served in the Russo-Turkish War and was invalided home 1878. His stories, fewer than 20, include allegories, fairy tales, and war stories, among them 'The Red Flower' 1883 and 'Four Days' 1877, set during the war.

Garvey /ˈgɑːvi/ Marcus (Moziah) 1887–1940. Jamaican political thinker and activist, an early advocate of black nationalism. He founded the UNIA (Universal Negro Improvement Association) in 1914, and moved to the USA in 1916, where he established branches in New York and other northern cities. Aiming to achieve human rights and dignity for black people through black pride and economic self-sufficiency, he was considered one of the first militant black nationalists. He led a Back to Africa movement for black Americans to establish a black-governed country in Africa. The Jamaican cult of Rastafarianism is based largely on his ideas.

Gascoigne /ˈgæskɔɪn/ Paul ('Gazza') 1967– . English footballer who played for Tottenham Hotspur from 1988 and for Lazio, Italy, from 1992. At the 1989 World Cup semifinal against West Germany, he committed a foul for which he was booked (cautioned by the referee), meaning that he would be unable to play in the final, should England win. His tearful response drew public

Garrick Considered by contemporaries to be the greatest of actors, David Garrick also wrote for the stage and managed the Drury Lane Theatre. He was in convivial contact with most of the celebrities of 18th-century London, including Dr Johnson, who had been his boyhood tutor in Lichfield.

sympathy, and he was subsequently lionized by the British press.

Gaskell /ˈgæskəl/ 'Mrs' (Elizabeth Cleghorn, born Stevenson) 1810–1865. British novelist. Her books include *Mary Barton* 1848, *Cranford* (set in the town in which she was brought up, Knutsford, Cheshire) 1853, *North and South* 1855, *Sylvia's Lovers* 1863–64, the unfinished *Wives and Daughters* 1866, and a life of her friend Charlotte →Brontë.

Gassendi /ˌgæsɒnˈdiː/ Pierre 1592–1655. French physicist and philosopher who played a crucial role in the revival of atomism (the theory that the world is made of small, indivisible particles), and the rejection of Aristotelianism so characteristic of the period. He was a propagandist and critic of other views rather than an original thinker.

Gates /ɡeɪts/ Horatio c. 1727–1806. British-born American military leader. George Washington appointed him brigadier general in the Continental army 1775 at the outbreak of the American Revolution. In command of the Northern Department, Gates won a tide-turning victory at the Battle of Saratoga 1777 after several American losses and retreats.

Born in England, Gates joined the British army, serving in Nova Scotia, Canada, and seeing action in the French and Indian War 1755–60. After returning to England, he emigrated to America 1772. Falling out of favour with Washington, he was dispatched to the South, where his defeat at the Battle of Camden in 1780 effectively ended his military career.

Gatling /ˈgætlɪŋ/ Richard Jordan 1818–1903. US inventor of a rapid-fire gun. Patented in 1862, the Gatling gun had ten barrels arranged as a cylinder rotated by a hand crank. Cartridges from an overhead hopper or drum dropped into the breech mechanism, which loaded, fired, and extracted them at a rate of 320 rounds per minute.

The Gatling gun was used in the Franco-Prussian War of 1870. By 1882 rates of fire of up to 1,200 rounds per minute were achieved, but the weapon was soon superseded by Hiram Maxim's machine gun in 1889.

Gaudí /gauˈdiː/ Antonio 1852–1926. Spanish architect distinguished for his flamboyant Art Nouveau style. Gaudí worked exclusively in Barcelona, designing both domestic and industrial buildings. He introduced colour, unusual materials, and audacious technical innovations. His spectacular Church of the Holy Family, Barcelona, begun 1883, is still under construction.

Gaudier-Brzeska /ˈgəudiei ˈbʒeskə/ Henri (Henri Gaudier) 1891–1915. French artist, active in London from 1911; he is regarded as one of the outstanding sculptors of his generation. He studied art in Bristol, Nuremberg, and Munich, and became a member of the English Vorticist movement, which sought to reflect the industrial age by a sense of motion and angularity. From 1913 his sculptures showed the influence of Constantin Brancusi and Jacob Epstein. He was killed in action during World War I.

Gauguin /ˈgəugæn/ Paul 1848–1903. French Post-Impressionist painter. Going beyond the Impressionists' notion of reality, he sought a more direct experience of life in the magical rites of the people and rich colours of the South Sea islands. He disliked theories and rules of painting, and his pictures are Expressionist compositions characterized by his use of pure, unmixed colours. Among his paintings is *Le Christe Jaune* 1889 (Albright-Knox Art Gallery, Buffalo, New York State, USA).

Born in Paris, Gauguin spent his childhood in Peru. After a few years as a stockbroker, he took up full-time painting in 1881, exhibited with the Impressionists, and spent two months with van →Gogh in Arles 1888. On his return to Brittany he concentrated on his new style, Synthetism, based on the use of powerful, expressive colours and boldly outlined areas of flat tone. Influenced by Symbolism, he chose subjects reflecting his interest in the beliefs of other cultures.

After a visit to Martinique 1887, he went to Pont Aven in Brittany, becoming the leading artist in the Synthetic movement, and abandoning conventional perspective. He lived in Tahiti 1891–93 and 1895–1901 and from 1901 in the Marquesas Islands.

Gaulle Charles de. French politician; see Charles →de Gaulle.

Gaultier Jean-Paul 1952– . French fashion designer who, after working for Pierre Cardin, launched his first collection in 1978, designing clothes that went against fashion trends, inspired by London's street style. Humorous and showy, his clothes are among the most influential in the French ready-to-wear market. He designed the costumes for Peter Greenaway's film *The Cook, the Thief, His Wife and Her Lover* 1989 and the singer Madonna's outfits for her world tour 1990.

Gauquelin /ˈgəukələn/ Michel 1928–1991. French neo-astrologist. Gauquelin trained as a psychologist and statistician, but became widely known for neo-astrology, or the scientific measurement of the correlations between the exact position of certain planets at birth and individual fame. His work attracted strong criticism as well as much interest. His book *Neo-Astrology: a Copernican Revolution* was published posthumously 1991.

Gauquelin studied the relationship between planet and personality, discovering the 'Mars effect' that sports personalities were more likely to be born with Mars in the crucial positions, actors with Jupiter, and scientists and doctors with Saturn. Gauquelin studied thousands of eminent people to obtain his data, using thousands of non-eminent people as a control group.

Gauss /gaus/ Karl Friedrich 1777–1855. German mathematician who worked on the theory of numbers, non-Euclidean geometry, and the mathematical development of electric and magnetic theory. A method of neutralizing a magnetic field, used to protect ships from magnetic mines, is called 'degaussing'.

Gautama /ˈgautəmə/ family name of the historical →Buddha.

Gautier /ˈgəutiei/ Théophile 1811–1872. French Romantic poet whose later works emphasized the perfection of form and the polished beauty of language and imagery (for example, *Emaux et camées/Enamels and Cameos* 1852). He was also a novelist (*Mlle de Maupin* 1835) and later turned to journalism.

Gavaskar /ˈgævəskɑː/ Sunil Manohar 1949– . Indian cricketer. Between 1971 and 1987 he scored a record 10,122 Test runs in a record 125 matches (including 106 consecutive Tests).

Gaviria (Trujillo) /gəˈvɪriə/ Cesar 1947– . Colombian Liberal Party politician, president from 1990; he was finance minister 1986–87 and minister of government 1987–89. He has supported the extradition of drug traffickers wanted in the USA and has sought more US aid in return for stepping up the drug war.

An economist, Gaviria began his career in local government at the age of 22 and became mayor of his home town Pereira at 27. He went on to the house of representatives and became a deputy minister at 31. As acting president in 1988, while

President Virgilio Barco was out of the country, Gaviria negotiated the freedom of a kidnapped presidential candidate. In 1989 he left the government to manage the campaign of another presidential candidate, who was, however, assassinated later the same year.

Gay /geɪ/ John 1685–1732. British poet and dramatist. He wrote *Trivia* 1716, a verse picture of 18th-century London. His *The Beggar's Opera* 1728, a 'Newgate pastoral' using traditional songs and telling of the love of Polly for highwayman Captain Macheath, was an extraordinarily popular success. Its satiric political touches led to the banning of *Polly*, a sequel.

He was a friend of the writers Alexander →Pope and John Arbuthnot.

An open foe may prove a curse,
But a pretended friend is worse.

John Gay
The Shepherd's Dog and the Wolf

Gaye /geɪ/ Marvin 1939–1984. US soul singer and songwriter whose hits, including 'Stubborn Kinda Fellow' 1962, 'I Heard It Through the Grapevine' 1968, and 'What's Goin' On' 1971, exemplified the Detroit Motown sound.

Gay-Lussac /geɪ luːˈsæk/ Joseph Louis 1778–1850. French physicist and chemist who investigated the physical properties of gases, and discovered new methods of producing sulphuric and oxalic acids. In 1802 he discovered the approximate rule for the expansion of gases now known as Charles's law.

Geber /ˈdʒiːbə/ Latinized form of *Jabir* ibn Hayyan *c.* 721–*c.* 776. Arabian alchemist. His influence lasted for more than 600 years, and in the late 1300s his name was adopted by a Spanish alchemist whose writings spread the knowledge and practice of alchemy throughout Europe.

The Spanish alchemist Geber probably discovered nitric and sulphuric acids, and he propounded a theory that all metals are composed of various mixtures of mercury and sulphur.

Geddes /ˈɡedɪs/ Patrick 1854–1932. Scottish town planner who established the importance of surveys, research work, and properly planned 'diagnoses before treatment'. His major work is *City Development* 1904. His protégé was Lewis →Mumford.

Gehrig /ˈɡerɪɡ/ Lou (Henry Louis) 1903–1941. US baseball player. Nicknamed 'The Iron Horse' for his incomparable stamina and strength, he was signed by the New York Yankees 1923. Voted the American League's most valuable player 1927, 1931, 1934, and 1936 he achieved a remarkable lifetime 493 home runs, a .340 lifetime batting average, and a record 2,130 consecutive games played.

Born in New York, USA, Gehrig attended Columbia University. He stayed with the Yankees' for 17 years as their first baseman and most consistent hitter. Diagnosed with a degenerative muscle disease (now known as 'Lou Gehrig's disease'), he retired from baseball 1939. A film biography, *Pride of the Yankees*, appeared 1942.

He was elected to the Baseball Hall of Fame 1939.

Gehry /ˈɡeəri/ Frank 1929– . US architect, based in Los Angeles. His architecture approaches abstract art in its use of collage and montage techniques.

His own experimental house in Santa Monica 1977, Edgemar Shopping Center and Museum, Santa Monica 1988, and the Vitra Furniture Museum, Weil am Rhein, Switzerland 1989 – his first building in Europe – demonstrate his vitality.

Geiger /ˈɡaɪɡə/ Hans 1882–1945. German physicist who produced the Geiger counter. After studying in Germany, he spent the period 1907–12 in Manchester, England, working with Ernest Rutherford on radioactivity. In 1908 they designed an instrument to detect and count alpha particles, positively charged ionizing particles produced by radioactive decay.

In 1928 Geiger and Walther Müller produced a more sensitive version of the counter, which could detect all kinds of ionizing radiation.

Geingob /ˈɡaɪŋɡəʊb/ Hage Gottfried 1941– . Namibian politician and prime minister. Geingob was appointed founding director of the United Nations Institute for Namibia in Lusaka, 1975. He became first prime minister of an independent Namibia March 1990.

He played a major role in the South West Africa's People's Organization (SWAPO), acting as a petitioner to the United Nations 1964–71, to obtain international recognition for SWAPO.

Geisel /ˈɡaɪzl/ Theodor Seuss; better known as *Dr Seuss*. 1904–1991. US author of children's books including *And to Think That I Saw It on Mulberry Street* 1937 and the classic *Horton Hatches the Egg* 1940. After winning Academy Awards for documentary films 1946 and 1947, he returned to writing children's books, including *Horton Hears a Who* 1954 and *The Cat in the Hat* 1957.

Born in Springfield, Massachusetts, USA, and educated at Dartmouth, Geisel began his career as a cartoonist and illustrator. He later wrote books for adults, including *Oh, the Places You'll Go!* 1989.

Geldof /ˈɡeldɒf/ Bob 1954– . Irish fundraiser and rock singer, leader of the group the Boomtown Rats 1975–86. In the mid-1980s he instigated the charity Band Aid, which raised large sums of money for famine relief, primarily for Ethiopia.

Geldof Irish rock musician and philanthropist Bob Geldof, celebrated for his fund-raising activities and his bluntly outspoken manner. Geldof worked as a pop journalist in Canada before becoming a professional musician. He was awarded a KBE 1986 and a variety of international honours for his role in pop charity events.

In partnership with fellow musician Midge Ure (1953–), Geldof gathered together many pop celebrities of the day to record Geldof's song 'Do They Know It's Christmas?' 1984, donating all proceeds to charity (it sold 7 million copies). He followed it up with two simultaneous celebrity concerts 1985 under the name Live Aid, one in London and one in Philadelphia, which were broadcast live worldwide. Apart from the money they raised for famine relief (about £60 million), his activities increased public awareness of global problems.

In 1992 his company Planet 24 began broadcasting a breakfast television programme called 'The Big Breakfast' on Channel 4.

But Prime Minister, I don't think that the possible death of 120 million people is a matter for charity. It is a matter of moral imperative.

Bob Geldof to Margaret Thatcher
on the threatened famine in Africa 1985

Gell-Mann /ˌgelˈmæn/ Murray 1929– . US physicist. In 1964 he formulated the theory of the quark as one of the fundamental constituents of matter. In 1969 he was awarded a Nobel prize for his work on elementary particles and their interaction.

He was R A Millikan professor of theoretical physics at the California Institute of Technology from 1967.

Gemayel /ˌgemaɪˈel/ Amin 1942– . Lebanese politician, a Maronite Christian; president 1982–88.

He succeeded his brother, president-elect *Bechir Gemayel* (1947–1982), on his assassination on 14 Sept 1982. The Lebanese parliament was unable to agree on a successor when his term expired, so separate governments were formed under rival Christian and Muslim leaders.

Genée /ʒəˈneɪ/ Adeline. Stage name of Anina Jensen 1878–1970. Danish-born British dancer, president of the Royal Academy of Dancing 1920–54.

Born in Aarhus, she settled in England 1897. Her work was commemorated by the *Adeline Genée Theatre* 1967–89, East Grinstead, Sussex.

Genet /ʒəˈneɪ/ Jean 1910–1986. French dramatist, novelist, and poet, an exponent of the Theatre of Cruelty. His turbulent life and early years spent in prison are reflected in his drama, characterized by ritual, role-play, and illusion, in which his characters come to act out their bizarre and violent fantasies. His plays include *Les Bonnes/The Maids* 1947, *Le Balcon/The Balcony* 1957, and two plays dealing with the Algerian situation: *Les Nègres/The Blacks* 1959 and *Les Paravents/The Screens* 1961.

God is white.

Jean Genet, *The Blacks*

Genghis Khan /ˈdʒeŋgɪs ˈkɑːn/ *c.* ?1167–1227. Mongol conqueror, ruler of all Mongol peoples from 1206. He began the conquest of N China 1213, overran the empire of the shah of Khiva 1219–25, and invaded N India, while his lieutenants advanced as far as the Crimea. When he died, his empire ranged from the Yellow Sea to the Black Sea; it continued to expand after his death to extend from Hungary to Korea. Genghis Khan controlled probably a larger area than any other individual in history. He was not only a great military leader, but the creator of a stable political system.

The ruins of his capital Karakorum are SW of Ulaanbaatar in Mongolia; his alleged remains are preserved at Ejin Horo, Inner Mongolia.

Temujin, as he was originally called, was the son of a chieftain. After a long struggle he established his supremacy over all the Mongols, when he assumed the title of Chingis or 'perfect warrior'.

Genscher /ˈgenʃə/ Hans-Dietrich 1927– . German politician, chair of the West German Free Democratic Party (FDP) 1974–85, foreign minister 1974–92. A skilled and pragmatic tactician, Genscher became the reunified Germany's most popular politician.

Born in Halle, East Germany, Genscher settled

in West Germany 1952. He served as interior minister 1969–74 and then as foreign minister, committed to Ostpolitik (the policy of reconciliation with the communist bloc) and European cooperation. As FDP leader, Genscher masterminded the party's switch of allegiance from the Social Democratic Party to the Christian Democratic Union, which resulted in the downfall of the Helmut →Schmidt government 1982.

Gentile /dʒen'tileɪ/ da Fabriano c. 1370–1427. Italian painter of frescoes and altarpieces in the International Gothic style. Gentile was active in Venice, Florence, Siena, Orvieto, and Rome and collaborated with the artists Pisanello and Jacopo Bellini. *The Adoration of the Magi* 1423 (Uffizi, Florence) is typically rich in detail and crammed with courtly figures.

Gentileschi /ˌdʒentɪ'leski/ Artemisia 1593–c. 1652. Italian painter, born in Rome. She trained under her father Orazio Gentileschi, but her work is more melodramatic than his. She settled in Naples from about 1630 and focused on macabre and grisly subjects, such as *Judith Decapitating Holofernes* (Museo di Capodimonte, Naples).

Gentileschi /ˌdʒentɪ'leski/ Orazio 1563–1637. Italian painter, born in Pisa. He was a follower and friend of Caravaggio, whose influence can be seen in the dramatic treatment of light and shade in *The Annunciation* 1623 (Galleria Sabauda, Turin). From 1626 he lived in London, painting for King Charles I.

He painted a series of ceilings for the Queen's House at Greenwich, now in Marlborough House, London.

Gentili /dʒen'tiːli/ Alberico 1552–1608. Italian jurist. He practised law in Italy but having adopted Protestantism was compelled to flee to England, where he lectured on Roman law in Oxford. His publications, such as *De Jure Belli libri tres/On the Law of War, Book Three* 1598, made him the first true international law writer and scholar.

Geoffrey of Monmouth /dʒefri, 'mɒnməθ/ c. 1100–1154. Welsh writer and chronicler. While a canon at Oxford, he wrote *Historia Regum Britanniae/History of the Kings of Britain c.* 1139, which included accounts of the semi-legendary kings Lear, Cymbeline, and Arthur, and *Vita Merlini*, a life of the legendary wizard. He was bishop-elect of St Asaph, N Wales, 1151 and ordained a priest 1152.

George /dʒɔːdʒ/ Henry 1839–1897. US economist, born in Philadelphia. His *Progress and Poverty* 1879 suggested a 'single tax' on land, to replace all other taxes on earnings and savings. He hoped such a land tax would abolish poverty, by ending speculation on land values. George's ideas have never been implemented thoroughly, although they have influenced taxation policy in many countries.

George /geɪ'ɔːgə/ Stefan 1868–1933. German poet. His early poetry was inspired by French

Symbolism, but his concept of himself as regenerating the German spirit first appears in *Des Teppich des Lebens/The Tapestry of Life* 1899, and later in *Der siebente Ring/The Seventh Ring* 1907.

Das neue Reich/The New Empire 1928 shows his realization that World War I had not had the right purifying effect on German culture. He rejected Nazi overtures and emigrated to Switzerland 1933.

George /dʒɔːdʒ/ six kings of Great Britain:

George I 1660–1727. King of Great Britain and Ireland from 1714. He was the son of the first elector of Hanover, Ernest Augustus (1629–1698), and his wife Sophia, and a great-grandson of James I. He succeeded to the electorate 1698, and became king on the death of Queen Anne. He attached himself to the Whigs, and spent most of his reign in Hanover, never having learned English.

He was heir through his father to the hereditary lay bishopric of Osnabrück and the duchy of Calenberg, which was one part of the Hanoverian possessions of the house of Brunswick. He acquired the other part by his marriage to *Sophia Dorothea of Zell* (1666–1726) in 1682. They were divorced 1694, and she remained in seclusion until her death. George's children were George II and *Sophia Dorothea* (1687–1757), who married Frederick William (later king of Prussia) 1706 and was the mother of Frederick the Great.

George II 1683–1760. King of Great Britain and Ireland from 1727, when he succeeded his father, George I. His victory at Dettingen 1743, in the War of the Austrian Succession, was the last battle commanded by a British king. He married Caroline of Anspach 1705. He was succeeded by his grandson George III.

George III 1738–1820. King of Great Britain and Ireland from 1760, when he succeeded his grandfather George II. His rule was marked by intransigence resulting in the loss of the American colonies, for which he shared the blame with his chief minister Lord North, and the emancipation of Catholics in England. Possibly suffering from porphyria, he had repeated attacks of insanity, permanent from 1811. He was succeeded by his son George IV.

He married Princess →Charlotte Sophia of Mecklenburg-Strelitz 1761.

George IV 1762–1830. King of Great Britain and Ireland from 1820, when he succeeded his father George III, for whom he had been regent during the king's period of insanity 1811–20. In 1785 he secretly married a Catholic widow, Maria →Fitzherbert, but in 1795 also married Princess →Caroline of Brunswick, in return for payment of his debts. His prestige was undermined by his treatment of Caroline (they separated 1796), his dissipation, and his extravagance. He was succeeded by his brother, the duke of Clarence, who became William IV.

George V 1865–1936. King of Great Britain from 1910, when he succeeded his father Edward VII. He was the second son, and became heir 1892 on the death of his elder brother Albert, Duke of Clarence. In 1893, he married Princess Victoria Mary of Teck (Queen Mary), formerly engaged to his brother. During World War I he made several visits to the front. In 1917, he abandoned all German titles for himself and his family. The name of the royal house was changed from Saxe-Coburg-Gotha (popularly known as Brunswick or Hanover) to Windsor.

His mother was Princess Alexandra of Denmark, sister of Empress Marie of Russia.

George VI 1895–1952. King of Great Britain from 1936, when he succeeded after the abdication of his brother Edward VIII, who had succeeded their father George V. Created Duke of York 1920, he married in 1923 Lady Elizabeth Bowes-Lyon (1900–   ), and their children are Elizabeth II and Princess Margaret. During World War II, he visited the Normandy and Italian battlefields.

We're not a family; we're a firm.

　　　　　　　　　　　　　　　　George VI

George /dʒɔːdʒ/ two kings of Greece:

George I 1845–1913.   King of Greece 1863–1913. The son of Christian IX of Denmark, he was nominated to the Greek throne and, in spite of early unpopularity, became a highly successful constitutional monarch. He was assassinated by a Greek, Schinas, at Salonika.

George II 1890–1947. King of Greece 1922–23 and 1935–47. He became king on the expulsion of his father Constantine I 1922 but was himself overthrown 1923. Restored by the military 1935, he set up a dictatorship under Joannis →Metaxas, and went into exile during the German occupation 1941–45.

George, St /dʒɔːdʒ/ patron saint of England. The story of St George rescuing a woman by slaying a dragon, evidently derived from the Perseus legend, first appears in the 6th century. The cult of St George was introduced into W Europe by the Crusaders. His feast day is 23 April.

He is said to have been martyred at Lydda in Palestine 303, probably under the Roman emperor Diocletian, but the other elements of his legend are of doubtful historical accuracy.

Gerald of Wales English name of →Giraldus Cambrensis, medieval Welsh bishop and historian.

Gerhard /dʒɛrɑːd/ Roberto 1896–1970. Spanish-born British composer. He studied with Enrique →Granados and Arnold →Schoenberg and settled in England 1939, where he composed 12-tone works in Spanish style. He composed the *Sym-*

phony No 1 1952–55, followed by three more symphonies and chamber music incorporating advanced techniques.

Gerhardie /dʒəˈhɑːdi/ William (born Gerhardi) 1895–1977. British novelist, born in Russia. His novels include *Futility: A Novel on Russian Themes* 1922 and *The Polyglots* 1925, both of which draw on his Russian upbringing.

Géricault /ʒɛrɪˈkəʊ/ Théodore (Jean Louis André) 1791–1824. French Romantic painter. *The Raft of the Medusa* 1819 (Louvre, Paris) was notorious for exposing a relatively recent scandal in which shipwrecked sailors had been cut adrift and left to drown. He painted *The Derby at Epsom* 1821 (Louvre, Paris) and pictures of cavalry. He also painted portraits.

Germain /ʒeəˈmæn/ Sophie 1776–1831. French mathematician, born in Paris. Although she was not allowed to study at the newly opened Ecole Polytechnique, she corresponded with the mathematicians →Lagrange and →Gauss. She is remembered for work she carried out in studying →Fermat's last theorem.

German /dʒɜː mən/ Edward 1862–1936. English composer. He is remembered for his operettas *Merrie England* 1902 and *Tom Jones* 1907, and he wrote many other instrumental, orchestral, and vocal works.

Germanicus Caesar /dʒɜːˈmænɪkəs ˈsiːzə/ 15 BC–AD 19. roman general. He was the adopted son of the emperor →Tiberius and married the emperor →Augustus' granddaughter Agrippina. Although he refused the suggestion of his troops that he claim the throne on the death of Augustus, his military victories in Germany made Tiberius jealous. Sent to the Middle East, he died near Antioch, possibly murdered at the instigation of Tiberius. He was the father of →Caligula and Agrippina, mother of →Nero.

Geronimo /dʒəˈrɒnɪməʊ/ 1829–1909. Chief of the Chiricahua Apache Indians and war leader. From 1875 to 1885, he fought US federal troops, as well as settlers encroaching on tribal reservations in the Southwest, especially in SE Arizona and New Mexico.

After surrendering to General George Crook March 1886, and agreeing to go to Florida where their families were being held, Geronimo and his followers escaped. Captured again Aug 1886, they were taken to Florida, then to Alabama. The climate proved unhealthy, and they were taken to Fort Sill, Oklahoma, where Geronimo became a farmer. He dictated *Geronimo's Story of His Life* 1906.

Gershwin /ˈgɜːʃwɪn/ George 1898–1937. US composer who wrote both 'serious' music, such as the tone poem *Rhapsody in Blue* 1924 and *An American in Paris* 1928, and popular musicals and songs, many with lyrics by his brother *Ira Gershwin* (1896–1983), including 'I Got Rhythm', ''S Wonderful', and 'Embraceable You'. His opera

Porgy and Bess 1935 was an ambitious work that incorporated jazz rhythms and popular song styles in an operatic format.

Gerson /ʒeə'sɒn/ Jean 1363–1429. French theologian. He was leader of the concilliar movement, which argued for the supremacy of church councils over popes, and denounced →Huss at the Council of Constance 1415. His theological works greatly influenced 15th-century thought.

Gertler /gɜːtlə/ Mark 1891–1939. English painter. He was a pacifist and a noncombatant during World War I; his *Merry-Go-Round* 1916 (Tate Gallery, London) is often seen as an expressive symbol of militarism. He suffered from depression and committed suicide.

Gesell /gə'zel/ Arnold Lucius 1880–1961. US psychologist and educator. He founded the Yale Clinic of Child Development which he directed 1911–48. Among the first to study the stages of normal development, he worked as a consultant to The Gesell Institute of Child Development, New Haven, Connecticut, which was founded 1950 to promote his educational ideas.

Born in Alma, Wisconsin, USA, Gesell received his PhD from Clark University 1906. Appointed to the Yale University faculty, he received a medical degree from Yale 1915 and became a professor of child hygiene, publishing both scholarly and popular works on child psychology.

Getty /geti/ J(ean) Paul 1892–1976. US oil billionaire, president of the Getty Oil Company from 1947, and founder of the Getty Museum (housing the world's highest-funded art gallery) in Malibu, California.

Geronimo Apache Indian chief Geronimo, shown here after his surrender 1886. He led his people against white settlers in Arizona for over ten years, but subsequently became a prosperous Christian farmer in Oklahoma and a national celebrity

CHIEF GERONIMO

Getty Tycoon and oil billionaire J Paul Getty devoted much of his personal fortune to art collecting. Getty acquired and controlled more than 100 companies and became one of the richest people in the world; in 1968 his personal wealth was estimated at over $1 billion.

In 1985 his son *John Paul Getty Jr* (1932–   ) established an endowment fund of £50 million for the National Gallery, London.

Getz Stan(ley) 1927–1991. US tenor saxophonist of the 1950s cool jazz school, closely identified with the Latin American bossa nova sound, which gave him a hit single, 'The Girl from Ipanema' 1964. He is regarded as one of the foremost tenor-sax players of his generation.

Getz became a professional musician at 15, working with the big-band leaders of the era: Jack Teagarden, Tommy Dorsey, Stan Kenton, Benny Goodman, Woody Herman. Technically brilliant but never showy, he was influenced by Lester Young, and became a cult hero in the cool-jazz movement with its tendency towards subtlety and restraint, as on the album *West Coast Jazz* 1955. In the early 1960s *Jazz Samba, Big Band Bossa Nova*, and other albums brought jazz to a wider public. Later he experimented with jazz-rock fusion. Getz returned to Latin American rhythms on his last LP, *Apasionado* 1990.

Ghali Boutros 1922–   . Egyptian diplomat and politician, deputy prime minister 1991–92. He worked towards peace in the Middle East in the foreign ministry posts he held 1977–91. He became secretary general of the United Nations Jan 1992.

A professor at Cairo University 1949–77, Ghali has expert knowledge of African affairs. In 1977 he accompanied President Sadat to Jerusalem on the diplomatic mission that led to the Camp David Agreements and was appointed minister of state for foreign affairs that year.

Ghazzali, al- /gæˈzɑːli/ 1058–1111. Muslim philosopher and Sufi (Muslim mystic). He was responsible for easing the conflict between the Sufi and the Ulema, a body of Muslim religious and legal scholars.

Initially, he believed that God's existence could be proved by reason, but later he became a wandering Sufi, seeking God through mystical experience; his book *The Alchemy of Happiness* was written on his travels.

Gheorghiu-Dej /giˌɔːˈdʒuːˈdeɪ/ Gheorge 1901–1965. Romanian communist politician. A member of the Romanian Communist Party from 1930, he played a leading part in establishing a communist regime 1945. He was prime minister 1952–55 and state president 1961–65. Although retaining the support of Moscow, he adopted an increasingly independent line during his final years.

Ghiberti /gɪˈbeəti/ Lorenzo 1378–1455. Italian sculptor and goldsmith. In 1401 he won the commission for a pair of gilded bronze doors for Florence's baptistry. He produced a second pair (1425–52), the *Gates of Paradise*, one of the masterpieces of the early Italian Renaissance. They show sophisticated composition and use of perspective.

He also wrote *Commentarii*/*Commentaries* about 1450, a mixture of art history, manual, and autobiography.

Ghirlandaio /ˌgɪəlænˈdaɪəʊ/ Domenico c. 1449–1494. Italian fresco painter, head of a large and prosperous workshop in Florence. His fresco cycle 1486–90 in Sta Maria Novella, Florence, includes portraits of many Florentines and much contemporary domestic detail. He also worked in Pisa, Rome, and San Gimignano, and painted portraits.

Giacometti /ˌdʒækəˈmeti/ Alberto 1901–1966. Swiss sculptor and painter who trained in Italy and Paris. In the 1930s, in his Surrealist period, he began to develop his characteristic spindly constructions. His mature style of emaciated single figures, based on wire frames, emerged in the 1940s.

Man Pointing 1947 is one of many examples in the Tate Gallery, London.

Giambologna /ˌdʒæmbəˈlɒnjə/ (Giovann i da Bologna or Jean de Boulogne) 1529–1608. Flemish-born sculptor active mainly in Florence and Bologna. In 1583 he completed his public commission for the Loggia dei Lanzi in Florence, *The Rape of the Sabine Women*, a dynamic group of muscular figures and a prime example of Mannerist sculpture.

He also produced the *Neptune Fountain* 1563–67 in Bologna and the equestrian statues of the Medici grand dukes Cosimo and Ferdinando. There are several versions of his figure of *Mercury* on tiptoe (the one in Bargello, Florence, for example). His workshop in Florence produced small replicas of his work in bronze.

Gibberd /ˈgɪbəd/ Frederick 1908–1984. British architect and town planner. His works include the new towns of Harlow, England, and Santa Teresa, Venezuela; the Catholic Cathedral, Liverpool; and the Central London mosque in Regent's Park.

Gibbon /ˈgɪbən/ Edward 1737–1794. British historian, author of *The History of the Decline and Fall of the Roman Empire* 1776–88.

The work is a continuous narrative from the 2nd century AD to the fall of Constantinople 1453. He began work on it while in Rome 1764. Although immediately successful, he was compelled to reply to attacks on his account of the early development of Christianity by a *Vindication* 1779.

From 1783 Gibbon lived in Lausanne, Switzerland, but he returned to England and died in London.

Gibbon /ˈgɪbən/ John Heysham 1903–1974. US surgeon who invented the heart–lung machine in 1953. It has become indispensable in heart surgery, maintaining the circulation while the heart is temporarily inactivated.

Gibbon /ˈgɪbən/ Lewis Grassic. Pen name of James Leslie Mitchell 1901–1935. Scottish novelist, author of the trilogy *A Scots Quair: Sunset Song, Cloud Howe*, and *Grey Granite* 1932–34, set in the Mearns, S of Aberdeen, where he was born and brought up. Under his real name he wrote *Stained Radiance* 1930 and *Spartacus* 1933.

Gibbons /ˈgɪbənz/ Grinling 1648–1721. British woodcarver, born in Rotterdam. He produced carved wooden panels (largely of birds, flowers, and fruit) for St Paul's Cathedral, London, and for many large houses including Petworth House, Sussex, and Hampton Court, Surrey. He became master carver to George I in 1741.

Features of his style include acanthus whorls in oak, and trophies of musical instruments.

Gibbons /ˈgɪbənz/ Orlando 1583–1625. English composer. A member of a family of musicians, he was appointed organist at Westminster Abbey, London, in 1623. His finest works are madrigals and motets.

Gibbons /ˈgɪbənz/ Stella (Dorothea) 1902–1989. English journalist. She is remembered for her *Cold Comfort Farm* 1932, a classic satire on the regional novel, in particular the works of Mary →Webb.

Gibbs /gɪbz/ James 1682–1754. Scottish Neo-Classical architect whose works include St Martin-in-the-Fields, London, 1722–26, Radcliffe Camera, Oxford, 1737–49, and Bank Hall, Warrington, Cheshire, 1750.

Gibbs /gɪbz/ Josiah Willard 1839–1903. US theoretical physicist and chemist who developed a mathematical approach to thermodynamics. His book *Vector Analysis* 1881 established vector methods in physics.

Gibson /ˈgɪbsən/ Althea 1927– . US tennis player, the first black American woman to compete at the US Championships at Forest Hills 1950 and at Wimbledon 1951. In 1957 she took both the women's singles and doubles titles at Wimbledon and the singles at Forest Hills. In 1958 she successfully defended all three titles.

Born in Silver, South Carolina, USA, and raised in New York, Gibson was hindered in her tennis career by racial discrimination and segregation. In 1943 she won the New York State Negro girls' singles title, and in 1948 the national Negro women's title. She later played professional golf.

Gibson /ˈgɪbsən/ Charles Dana 1867–1944. US illustrator. He portrayed an idealized type of American young woman, known as the 'Gibson Girl'.

Gibson was born in Roxbury, Massachusetts. He worked for *Life* magazine, eventually becoming its editor. He also illustrated books and later painted in oils.

Gibson /ˈgɪbsən/ Mel 1956– . Australian actor who became an international star following lead roles in *Mad Max* 1979 and *Mad Max II* 1982 which was released in the USA as *Road Warrior*. His other films include *The Year of Living Dangerously* 1982, *Mutiny on the Bounty* 1984 as Fletcher Christian, and the *Lethal Weapon* series, in which Danny Glover co- starred.

Gibson /ˈgɪbsən/ Mike (Cameron Michael Henderson) 1942– . Irish rugby player. He made a world record 81 international appearances between the years 1964 and 1979; 69 for Ireland and 12 for the British Lions on a record five tours. Of his 69 Ireland caps, 40 were played as centre, 25 at outside-half, and 4 on the wing.

Gibson /ˈgɪbsən/ William 1948– . US writer, whose debut novel *Neuromancer* 1984, with its computer-using 'cyberpunk' adventurers, won both the Hugo and Nebula awards for science fiction.

Gide /ʒiːd/ André 1869–1951. French novelist, born in Paris. His work is largely autobiographical and concerned with the dual themes of self-fulfilment and renunciation. It includes *L'Immoraliste/The Immoralist* 1902, *La Porte étroite/Strait Is the Gate* 1909, *Les Caves du Vatican/The Vatican Cellars* 1914, and *Les Faux-monnayeurs/The Counterfeiters* 1926; and an almost lifelong *Journal*. Nobel Prize for Literature 1947.

Gielgud /ˈgiːlgʊd/ John 1904– . English actor and director, renowned as one of the greatest Shakespearean actors of his time. He made his debut at the Old Vic 1921, and his numerous stage appearances ranged from roles in works by Chekhov and Sheridan to those of Alan Bennett, Harold Pinter, and David Storey. Gielgud's films include *Becket* 1964, *Oh! What a Lovely War* 1969, *Providence* 1977, and *Prospero's Books* 1991. He won an Academy Award for his role as a butler in *Arthur* 1981.

Gierek /ˈgɪərek/ Edward 1913– . Polish Communist politician. He entered the Politburo of the ruling Polish United Workers' Party (PUWP) in 1956 and was party leader 1970–80. His industrialization programme plunged the country heavily into debt and sparked a series of Solidarity-led strikes.

Gierek, a miner's son, lived in France and Belgium for much of the period between 1923 and 1948, becoming a member of the Belgian Resistance. He served as party boss in Silesia during the 1960s. After replacing Gomulka as PUWP leader in Dec 1970, he embarked on an ambitious programme of industrialization. A wave of strikes in Warsaw and Gdańsk, spearheaded by the Solidarity free trade-union movement, forced Gierek to resign in Sept 1980.

Giffard /ʒiˈfɑː/ Henri 1825–1882. French inventor of the first passenger-carrying powered and steerable airship, called a dirigible, built 1852. The hydrogen-filled airship was 43 m/144 ft long, had a 3-hp steam engine that drove a three-bladed propeller, and was steered using a saillike rudder. It flew at an average speed of 5 kph/3 mph.

Gigli /ˈdʒiːlji/ Beniamino 1890–1957. Italian lyric tenor. He made his operatic debut in 1914 and subsequently performed roles by Puccini, Gounod, and Massenet.

Gilbert /ˈgɪlbət/ Alfred 1854–1934. British sculptor, whose statue of *Eros* 1887–93 in Piccadilly Circus, London, was erected as a memorial to the 7th Earl of Shaftesbury.

Gilbert /ˈgɪlbət/ Cass 1859–1934. US architect, major developer of the skyscraper. His designed the Woolworth Building, New York, 1913, the highest building in America (868 ft/265 m) when built and famous for its use of Gothic decorative detail.

Gilbert /ˈgɪlbət/ Humphrey c. 1539–1583. English soldier and navigator who claimed Newfoundland (landing at St John's) for Elizabeth I in 1583. He died when his ship sank on the return voyage.

Gilbert /ˈgɪlbət/ W(illiam) S(chwenk) 1836–1911. British humorist and dramatist who collaborated with composer Arthur →Sullivan, providing the libretti for their series of light comic operas from 1871; they include *HMS Pinafore* 1878, *The Pirates of Penzance* 1879, and *The Mikado* 1885.

Born in London, he became a lawyer in 1863, but in 1869 published a collection of his humorous verse and drawings, *Bab Ballads*, which was followed by a second volume in 1873.

Gilbert /ˈgɪlbət/ Walter 1932– . US molecular biologist who studied genetic control, seeking the mechanisms that switch genes on and off. By 1966 he had established the existence of the *lac* repressor, the molecule that suppresses lactose production. Further work on the sequencing of DNA nucleotides won him a share of the 1980 Nobel Prize for Chemistry, with Frederick Sanger and Paul Berg.

Gilbert /ˈgɪlbət/ William 1544–1603. English scientist and physician to Elizabeth I and (briefly) James I. He studied magnetism and static electricity, deducing that the Earth's magnetic field behaves as if a bar magnet joined the North and South poles. His book on magnets, published 1600, is the first printed scientific book based wholly on experimentation and observation.

He erroneously thought that the planets were held in their orbits by magnetic forces.

Gilbert and George /ˈgɪlbət, dʒɔːdʒ/ Gilbert Proesch 1943– and George Passmore 1942– . English painters and performance artists. They became known in the 1960s for their presentation of themselves as works of art – living sculpture.

Giles /dʒaɪlz/ Carl Ronald 1916– . British cartoonist for the *Daily* and *Sunday Express* from 1943, noted for his creation of a family with a formidable 'Grandma'.

Gill /gɪl/ Eric 1882–1940. English sculptor and engraver. He designed the typefaces Perpetua 1925 and Gill Sans (without serifs) 1927, and created monumental stone sculptures with clean, simplified outlines, such as *Prospero and Ariel* 1929–31 (on Broadcasting House, London).

He studied lettering at the Central School of Art in London under Edward Johnston, and began his career carving inscriptions for tombstones. Gill was a leader in the revival of interest in the craft of lettering and book design.

Gillespie /gɪˈlespi/ Dizzy (John Birks) 1917–1993. US jazz trumpeter who, with Charlie →Parker, was the chief creator and exponent of the bebop style. He influenced many modern jazz trumpeters, including Miles Davis.

Although associated mainly with small combos, Gillespie formed his first big band 1945 and toured with a big band in the late 1980s, as well as in the intervening decades.

Gillette /dʒɪˈlet/ King Camp 1855–1932. US inventor of the Gillette safety razor.

Gillray /ˈgɪlreɪ/ James 1757–1815. English caricaturist. His 1,500 cartoons, 1779–1811, satirized the French, George III, politicians, and social follies of his day.

Gilman /ˈgɪlmən/ Charlotte Perkins 1860–1935. US feminist socialist poet, novelist, and historian, author of *Women and Economics* 1898, proposing the ending of the division between 'men's work' and 'women's work' by abolishing housework.

From 1909 to 1916 she wrote and published a magazine *The Forerunner* in which her feminist Utopian novel *Herland* 1915 was serialized.

Gilpin /ˈgɪlpɪn/ William 1724–1804. British artist. He is remembered for his essays on the 'picturesque', which set out precise rules for the production of this effect.

Ginner /ˈdʒɪnə/ Charles 1878–1952. British painter of street scenes and landscapes. He settled in London in 1910, and was one of the London

Group (set up in 1913 and including followers of Vorticism and the Camden Town Group) from 1914.

Ginsberg /ˈgɪnzbɜːg/ Allen 1926– . US poet. His 'Howl' 1956, an influential poem of the Beat Generation, criticizes the materialism of contemporary US society. In the 1960s Ginsberg travelled widely in Asia and was a key figure in introducing Eastern thought to students of that decade.

Giolitti /dʒəʊˈlɪti/ Giovanni 1842–1928. Italian liberal politician, born in Mondovi. He was prime minister 1892–93, 1903–05, 1906–09, 1911–14, and 1920–21. He opposed Italian intervention in World War I and pursued a policy of broad coalitions, which proved ineffective in controlling Fascism after 1921.

Giono /dʒiˈəʊnəʊ/ Jean 1895–1970. French novelist whose books are chiefly set in Provence. *Que ma joie demeure/Joy of Man's Desiring* 1935 is an attack on life in towns and a plea for a return to country life.

In 1956 he published a defence of Gaston Dominici, who allegedly murdered an English family on holiday, maintaining that the old farmer exemplified the misunderstandings between town and country people.

Giordano /dʒɔːˈdɑːnəʊ/ Luca 1632–1705. Italian Baroque painter, born in Naples, active in Florence in the 1680s. In 1692 he was summoned to Spain by Charles II and painted ceilings in the Escorial palace for the next ten years.

In Florence Giordano painted a ceiling in the Palazzo Riccardi-Medici 1682–83. He also produced altarpieces and frescoes for churches. His work shows a variety of influences, including Paolo →Veronese, and tends to be livelier than that of earlier Baroque ceiling painters.

Giorgione /dʒɔːˈdʒəʊni/ del Castelfranco *c.* 1475–1510. Italian Renaissance painter, active in Venice, probably trained by Giovanni Bellini. His work influenced Titian and other Venetian painters. His subjects are imbued with a sense of mystery and treated with a soft technique, reminiscent of Leonardo da Vinci's later works, as in *The Tempest* 1504 (Accademia, Venice).

Few details of his life are certain, but Giorgione created the Renaissance poetic landscape, with rich colours and a sense of intimacy; an example is the *Madonna and Child Enthroned with Two Saints*, an alterpiece for the church of Castelfranco.

Giotto /ˈdʒɒtəʊ/ di Bondone 1267–1337. Italian painter and architect. He broke away from the conventional Gothic style of the time, and introduced a naturalistic style, painting saints as real people. He painted cycles of frescoes in churches at Assisi, Florence, and Padua.

Giotto was born in Vespignano, N of Florence. The interior of the Arena Chapel, Padua, was covered by him in a fresco cycle (completed by 1306) illustrating the life of Mary and the life of Jesus. Giotto's figures occupy a definite pictorial space, and there is an unusual emotional intensity and dignity in the presentation of the story. In one of the frescoes he made the Star of Bethlehem appear as a comet; →Halley's comet had appeared 1303, just two years before.

From 1334 he was official architect to Florence and from 1335 overseer of works at the cathedral; he collaborated with Andrea →Pisano in decorating the cathedral façade with statues and designing the campanile, which was completed after his death.

Giraldus Cambrensis /dʒɪˈrældəs kæmˈbrensɪs/ (Welsh *Geralt Gymro* c. 1146–1220. Welsh historian, born in Pembrokeshire. He was elected bishop of St David's in 1198. He wrote a history of the conquest of Ireland by Henry II, and *Itinerarium Cambriae*/Journey through Wales 1191.

Girardon /ʒɪrɑːˈdɒn/ François 1628–1715. French academic sculptor. His *Apollo Tended by Nymphs*, commissioned 1666, is one of several marble groups sculpted for the gardens of Louis XIV's palace at Versailles.

Giraudoux /ʒɪrəʊˈduː/ (Hippolyte) Jean 1882–1944. French playwright and novelist who wrote the plays *Amphitryon 38* 1929 and *La Folle de Chaillot*/*The Madwoman of Chaillot* 1945, and the novel *Suzanne et la Pacifique*/*Suzanne and the Pacific* 1921.

His other plays include *La Guerre de Troie n'aura pas lieu*/*Tiger at the Gates* 1935.

Girtin /ˈɡɜːtɪn/ Thomas 1775–1802. English painter of watercolour landscapes, a friend of J M W Turner. His work is characterized by broad washes of strong colour and bold compositions, for example *The White House at Chelsea* 1800 Tate Gallery, London.

Giscard d'Estaing /ʒiːˈskɑː desˈtæŋ/ Valéry 1926– . French conservative politician, president 1974–81. He was finance minister to de Gaulle 1962–66 and Pompidou 1969–74. As leader of the Union pour la Démocratie Française, which he formed in 1978, Giscard sought to project himself as leader of a 'new centre'.

Giscard was active in the wartime Resistance. After a distinguished academic career, he worked in the Ministry of Finance and entered the National Assembly for Puy de Dôme in 1956 as an Independent Republican. After Pompidou's death he was narrowly elected president in 1974, in difficult economic circumstances; he was defeated by the socialist Mitterrand in 1981. He returned to the National Assembly in 1984. In 1989 he resigned from the National Assembly to play a leading role in the European Parliament.

Gish /ɡɪʃ/ Lillian. Stage name of Lillian de Guiche 1896–1993. US film and stage actress who worked with the director D W Griffith, playing virtuous heroines in *Way Down East* and *Orphans of the Storm* both 1920. Deceptively fragile, she made a notable Hester in Victor Sjöström's *The Scarlet Letter* (based on the novel by Nathaniel

Hawthorne). Her career continued well into the 1980s with movies such as *The Whales of August* 1987. She was the sister of the actress *Dorothy Gish* (1898–1968).

Gissing /ˈɡɪsɪŋ/ George (Robert) 1857–1903. English writer, dealing with social issues. Among his books are *New Grub Street* 1891 and the autobiographical *Private Papers of Henry Ryecroft* 1903.

Giulini /dʒuːˈliːni/ Carlo Maria 1914– . Italian conductor. Principal conductor at La Scala in Milan 1953–55, and musical director of the Los Angeles Philharmonic 1978–84, he is renowned as an interpreter of Verdi.

Giulio Romano /dʒuːliəʊ rəʊmɑːno/ c. 1499–1546. Italian painter and architect. An assistant to Raphael, he developed a Mannerist style, creating effects of exaggerated movement and using rich colours, for example the frescoes in the Palazzo del Tè (1526, Mantua).

Glackens /ˈɡlækənz/ William James 1870–1938. American painter. He was a member of the Ashcan school and one of 'The Eight,' a group of realists who exhibited at New York's Macbeth Gallery 1908. Glackens's painting eventually evolved into a realism that was strongly influenced by Impressionism. He painted subjects from everyday urban life, as well as those from fashionable society.

Born in Philadelphia, he studied at the Pennsylvania Academy of Fine Arts under Robert →Henri.

Gladstone /ˈɡlædstən/ William Ewart 1809–1898. British Liberal politician, repeatedly prime minister. He entered Parliament as a Tory in 1833 and held ministerial office, but left the party 1846 and after 1859 identified himself with the Liberals. He was chancellor of the Exchequer 1852–55 and 1859–66, and prime minister 1868–74, 1880–85, 1886, and 1892–94. He introduced elementary education 1870 and vote by secret ballot 1872 and many reforms in Ireland, although he failed in his efforts to get a Home Rule Bill passed.

Gladstone was born in Liverpool, the son of a rich merchant. In Peel's government he was president of the Board of Trade 1843–45, and colonial secretary 1845–46. He left the Tory Party with the Peelite group in 1846. He was chancellor of the Exchequer in Aberdeen's government 1852–55 and in the Liberal governments of Palmerston and Russell 1859–66. In his first term as prime minister he carried through a series of reforms, including the disestablishment of the Church of Ireland, the Irish Land Act, and the abolition of the purchase of army commissions and of religious tests in the universities.

Gladstone strongly resisted Disraeli's imperialist and pro-Turkish policy during the latter's government of 1874–80, not least because of Turkish pogroms against subject Christians, and by his Midlothian campaign of 1879 helped to overthrow Disraeli. Gladstone's second government

Gladstone *19th-century British Liberal prime minister William Gladstone. Queen Victoria disliked his pomposity, and many members of the upper classes feared him as the representative of a dangerous liberalism, but probably no other British minister has left behind so long and so successful a record of practical legislation.*

carried the second Irish Land Act and the Reform Act 1884 but was confronted with problems in Ireland, Egypt, and South Africa, and lost prestige through its failure to relieve General →Gordon. Returning to office in 1886, Gladstone introduced his first Home Rule Bill, which was defeated by the secession of the Liberal Unionists, and he thereupon resigned. After six years' opposition he formed his last government; his second Home Rule Bill was rejected by the Lords, and in 1894 he resigned. He led a final crusade against the massacre of Armenian Christians in 1896.

All the world over, I will back the masses against the classes.

William Ewart Gladstone

Glanville Ranalf died 1190. English justiciar from 1180 and legal writer. His *Treatise on the Laws and Customs of England* 1188 was written to instruct practising lawyers and judges and is now a historical source on medieval common law.

Glaser /ˈɡleɪzə/ Donald Arthur 1926– . US physicist who invented the bubble chamber in 1952, for which he received the Nobel Prize for Physics in 1960.

Glasgow /ˈɡlæzɡəʊ/ Ellen 1873–1945. US novelist. Her books, set mainly in her native Virginia, often deal with the survival of tough heroines in a world of adversity and include *Barren Ground* 1925, *The Sheltered Life* 1932, and *Vein of Iron* 1935.

Glashow /ˈɡlæʃəʊ/ Sheldon Lee 1932– . US particle physicist. In 1964 he proposed the existence of a fourth 'charmed' quark, and later argued that quarks must be coloured. Insights gained from these theoretical studies enabled Glashow to consider ways in which the weak nuclear force and the electromagnetic force (two of the fundamental forces of nature) could be unified as a single force now called the electroweak force. For this work he shared the Nobel Prize for Physics 1979 with Abdus Salam and Steven Weinberg.

Glass /ɡlɑːs/ Philip 1937– . US composer. As a student of Nadia →Boulanger, he was strongly influenced by Indian music; his work is characterized by repeated rhythmic figures that are continually expanded and modified. His compositions include the operas *Einstein on the Beach* 1975, *Akhnaten* 1984, and *The Making of the Representative for Planet 8* 1988.

Glasse /ɡlɑːs/ Hannah 1708–1770. British cookery writer whose *The Art of Cookery made Plain and Easy* 1747 is regarded as the first classic recipe book in Britain.

Glauber /ˈɡlaʊbə/ Johann 1604–1668. German chemist who discovered the salt known variously as 'Glauber's salt' and '*sal mirabile*'. He made his living selling patent medicines.

The salt, sodium sulphate decahydrate ($Na_2SO_4.10H_2O$), is produced by the action of sulphuric acid on common salt. It is now used as a laxative but was used by Glauber to treat almost any complaint.

Glendower /ɡlenˈdaʊə/ Owen *c.* 1359–*c.* 1416. (Welsh *Owain Glyndwr*) Welsh nationalist leader of a successful revolt against the English in N Wales, who defeated Henry IV in three campaigns 1400–02, although Wales was reconquered 1405–13. Glendower disappeared 1416 after some years of guerrilla warfare.

Glenn /ɡlen/ John (Herschel), Jr 1921– . US astronaut and politician. On 20 Feb 1962, he became the first American to orbit the Earth, doing so three times in the Mercury spacecraft *Friendship 7*, in a flight lasting 4 hr 55 min. After retiring from NASA, he was elected to the US Senate as a Democrat from Ohio 1974; re-elected 1980 and 1986. He unsuccessfully sought the Democratic presidential nomination 1984.

Glinka /ˈɡlɪŋkə/ Mikhail Ivanovich 1804–1857. Russian composer. He broke away from the prevailing Italian influence and turned to Russian folk music as the inspiration for his opera *A Life for the Tsar* (originally *Ivan Susanin*) 1836. His later

Glass *US composer Philip Glass revolutionized opera in the 1980s. His music appealed to a younger, wider audience and was performed both in opera houses and at pop concerts.*

works include another opera, *Ruslan and Lyudmila* 1842, and the orchestral *Kamarinskaya* 1848.

Gloucester /ˈglɒstə/ Richard Alexander Walter George, Duke of Gloucester 1944– . Prince of the UK. Grandson of →George V, he succeeded his father to the dukedom when his elder brother Prince William (1941–72) was killed in an air crash. In 1972 he married Birgitte van Deurs (1946–), daughter of a Danish lawyer. His heir is his son Alexander, Earl of Ulster (1974–).

Glubb /glʌb/ John Bagot 1897–1986. British soldier, founder of the Arab Legion (the Jordanian army), which he commanded 1939–56.

Gluck /glʊk/ Christoph Willibald von 1714–1787. German composer who settled in Vienna as kapellmeister to Maria Theresa in 1754. In 1762 his *Orfeo ed Euridice/Orpheus and Eurydice* revolutionized the 18th-century conception of opera by giving free scope to dramatic effect. *Orfeo* was followed by *Alceste/Alcestis* 1767 and *Paride ed Elena/Paris and Helen* 1770.

Born in Erasbach, Bavaria, he studied music at Prague, Vienna, and Milan, went to London in 1745 to compose operas for the Haymarket, but returned to Vienna in 1746 where he was knighted by the pope. In 1762 his *Iphigénie en Aulide/Iphigenia in Aulis* 1774, produced in Paris, brought to a head the fierce debate over the future of opera in which Gluck's French style had the support of Marie Antoinette while his Italian rival Nicolò Piccinni (1728–1800) had the support of Madame Du Barry. With *Armide* 1777 and *Iphigénie en Tauride/Iphigenia in Tauris* 1779 Gluck won a complete victory over Piccinni.

Gobbi /ˈgɒbi/ Tito 1913–1984. Italian baritone singer renowned for his opera characterizations of Figaro in *The Marriage of Figaro*, Scarpia in *Tosca*, and Iago in *Otello*.

Gobind Singh /ˈgəʊbɪnd ˈsɪŋ/ 1666–1708. Indian religious leader, the tenth and last guru (teacher) of Sikhism, 1675–1708, and founder of the Sikh brotherhood known as the Khalsa. On his death, the Sikh holy book, the *Guru Granth Sahib*, replaced the line of human gurus as the teacher and guide of the Sikh community.

During a period of Sikh persecution Gobind Singh asked those who were willing to die for their faith to join him, the first five willing to risk their lives were named the *pani pyares* 'the faithful ones' by him and proclaimed the first members of the Khalsa. He also introduced the names Singh (lion) for male Sikhs, and Kaur (princess) for female Sikhs.

Godard Jean-Luc 1930– . French film director, one of the leaders of New Wave cinema. His works are often characterized by experimental editing techniques and an unconventional dramatic form. His films include *A bout de souffle* 1959, *Vivre sa Vie* 1962, *Weekend* 1968, and *Je vous salue, Marie* 1985.

His other films include *Pierrot le fou* 1965.

Photography is truth. The cinema is truth 24 times per second.

Jean-Luc Godard
Le Petit Soldat

Goddard /ˈgɒdəd/ Paulette. Stage name of Marion Levy 1911–1990. US film actress. She starred with comedian Charlie Chaplin in *Modern Times* 1936 and *The Great Dictator* 1940, and her other films include the British-made version of Oscar Wilde's play *An Ideal Husband* 1948.

Goddard /ˈgɒdəd/ Robert Hutchings 1882–1945. US rocket pioneer. His first liquid-fuelled rocket was launched at Auburn, Massachusetts in 1926. By 1935 his rockets had gyroscopic control and carried cameras to record instrument readings. Two years later a Goddard rocket gained the world altitude record with an ascent of 3 km/1.9 mi.

Gödel /ˈgɜːdl/ Kurt 1906–1978. Austrian-born US mathematician and philosopher. He proved that a mathematical system always contains statements that can be neither proved nor disproved within the system; in other words, as a science, mathematics can never be totally consistent and totally complete. He worked on relativity, constructing a mathematical model of the universe that made travel back through time theoretically possible.

Goebbels *Josef Goebbels, German Nazi minister of propaganda under Hitler. Exempted from military service through a foot deformity, he attended eight universities before drifting into the Nazi party. There his ambition and ruthlessness and his skill in public relations made him second in power only to Hitler himself.*

Godfrey de Bouillon /ˈgɒdfri də ˈbuːjɒn/ *c.* 1060–1100. French crusader, second son of Count Eustace II of Boulogne. He and his brothers, →Baldwin I and Eustace, led 40,000 Germans in the First Crusade 1096. When Jerusalem was taken 1099, he was elected its ruler, but refused the title of king. After his death, Baldwin was elected king.

Godiva /gəˈdaɪvə/ Lady *c.* 1040–1080. Wife of Leofric, earl of Mercia (died 1057). Legend has it that her husband promised to reduce the heavy taxes on the people of Coventry if she rode naked through the streets at noon. The grateful citizens remained indoors as she did so, but 'Peeping Tom' bored a hole in his shutters and was struck blind.

Godkin Edwin Lawrence 1831–1902. Irish- born US editor and writer on political affairs who founded the liberal weekly magazine *The Nation* 1865.

Godunov /ˈgɒdənɒv/ Boris 1552–1605. Tsar of Russia from 1598, elected after the death of Fyodor I, son of Ivan the Terrible. He was assassinated by a pretender to the throne who professed to be Dmitri, a brother of Fyodor and the rightful heir. The legend that has grown up around this forms the basis of Pushkin's play *Boris Godunov* 1831 and Mussorgsky's opera of the same name 1874.

An apocryphal story of Boris killing the true Dmitri in order to gain the throne was fostered by Russian historians anxious to discredit Boris because he was not descended from the main ruling families.

Godunov's rule was marked by a strengthening of the Russian church. It was also the beginning of the Time of Troubles, a period of instability.

Godwin /ˈgɒdwɪn/ died 1053. Earl of Wessex from 1020. He secured the succession to the throne in 1042 of →Edward the Confessor, to whom he married his daughter Edith, and whose chief minister he became. King Harold II was his son.

Godwin /ˈgɒdwɪn/ William 1756–1836. English philosopher, novelist, and father of Mary Shelley. His *Enquiry concerning Political Justice* 1793 advocated an anarchic society based on a faith in people's essential rationality. At first a Nonconformist minister, he later became an atheist. His first wife was Mary →Wollstonecraft.

Goebbels /ˈgɜːbəlz/ (Paul) Josef 1897–1945. German Nazi leader. As minister of propaganda from 1933, he brought all cultural and educational activities under Nazi control and built up sympathetic movements abroad to carry on the 'war of nerves' against Hitler's intended victims. On the capture of Berlin by the Allies, he poisoned himself.

He was born in the Rhineland, became a journalist, joined the Nazi party in its early days, and was given control of its propaganda 1929.

Goehr /gɜː/ (Peter) Alexander 1932– . British composer, born in Berlin. A lyrical but often hard-edged serialist, he nevertheless usually remained within the forms of the symphony and traditional chamber works, and more recently turned to tonal and even Neo-Baroque models.

Goeppert-Mayer /ˈgəʊpətmaɪə/ Maria 1906–1972. German-born US physicist who studied the structure of the atomic nucleus. She shared the 1963 Nobel Prize for Physics with Eugene →Wigner and Hans Jensen (1907–1973).

Her explanation of the stability of particular atoms 1948 envisaged atomic nuclei as shell-like layers of protons and neutrons, with the most stable atoms having completely filled outermost shells.

Goering /ˈgɜːrɪŋ/ (German *Göring*) Hermann Wilhelm 1893–1946. Nazi leader, German field marshal from 1938. He was part of Hitler's inner circle, and with Hitler's rise to power in 1933, he established the Gestapo and concentration camps. Appointed successor to Hitler in 1939, he built a vast economic empire in occupied Europe, but later lost favour and was expelled from the party in 1945. Tried at Nuremberg for war crimes, he poisoned himself before he could be executed.

Goering was born in Bavaria. He was a renowned fighter pilot in World War I, and joined the Nazi party in 1922. He was elected to the

Reichstag in 1928 and became its president in 1932. As commissioner for aviation from 1933 he built up the Luftwaffe (airforce). In 1936 he took charge of the four-year plan for war preparations.

Goes /xuːs/ Hugo van der, died 1482. Flemish painter, chiefly active in Ghent. His *Portinari altarpiece* about 1475 (Uffizi, Florence) is a huge oil painting of the Nativity, full of symbolism and naturalistic detail, and the *Death of the Virgin* about 1480 (Musée Communale des Beaux Arts, Bruges) is remarkable for the varied expressions on the faces of the apostles.

Goethe /ˈgɜːtə/ Johann Wolfgang von 1749–1832. German poet, novelist, and dramatist, generally considered the founder of modern German literature, and leader of the Romantic *Sturm und Drang* movement. His works include the autobiographical *Die Leiden des Jungen Werthers/The Sorrows of the Young Werther* 1774 and *Faust* 1808, his masterpiece. A visit to Italy 1786–88 inspired the classical dramas *Iphigenie auf Tauris/Iphigenia in Tauris* 1787 and *Torquato Tasso* 1790.

Goethe was born in Frankfurt-am-Main, and studied law. Inspired by Shakespeare, to whose work he was introduced by →Herder, he wrote the play *Götz von Berlichingen* 1773. His autobiographical *The Sorrows of the Young Werther* 1774 and the poetic play *Faust* 1808, made him known throughout Europe. Other works include the *Wilhelm Meister* novels 1796–1829. Between 1775 and 1785 he served as prime minister at the court of Weimar.

He who seizes the right moment,
Is the right man.

Johann Wolfgang von Goethe *Faust* 1808

Goffman /ˈgɒfmən/ Erving 1922–1982. Canadian social scientist. He studied the ways people try to create, present, and defend a self-image within the social structures surrounding, controlling, and defining human interaction. He analysed human interaction and the ways people behave, such as in public places. His works include *The Presentation of Self in Everyday Life* 1956, *Gender Advertisements* 1979, and *Forms of Talk* 1981.

Gogh /gɒx/ Vincent van 1853–1890. Dutch Post-Impressionist painter. He tried various careers, including preaching, and began painting in the 1880s. He met Paul →Gauguin in Paris, and when he settled in Arles, Provence, 1888, Gauguin joined him there. After a quarrel van Gogh cut off part of his own earlobe, and in 1889 he entered an asylum; the following year he committed suicide. The Arles paintings vividly testify to his intense emotional involvement in his art; among them are *The Yellow Chair* and several *Sunflowers* 1888 (National Gallery, London).

Born in Zundert, van Gogh worked for a time as a schoolmaster in England before he took up painting. He studied under van Mauve at The Hague. One of the leaders of the Post-Impressionist painters, he executed still lifes and landscapes, including *A Cornfield with Cypresses* 1889 (National Gallery, London).

Van Gogh's painting *Irises* 1889 was sold for the record price of $53.9 million at Sotheby's, New York, on 11 Nov 1987.

Gogol /ˈgəʊgɒl/ Nicolai Vasilyevich 1809–1852. Russian writer. His first success was a collection of stories, *Evenings on a Farm near Dikanka* 1831–32, followed by *Mirgorod* 1835. Later works include *Arabesques* 1835, the comedy play *The Inspector General* 1836, and the picaresque novel *Dead Souls* 1842, which satirizes Russian provincial society.

Gogol was born near Poltava. He tried several careers before entering the St Petersburg civil service. From 1835 he travelled in Europe, and it was in Rome that he completed the earlier part of *Dead Souls* 1842. Other works include the short stories 'The Overcoat' and 'The Nose'.

Gambling is the great leveller. All men
are equal – at cards.

Nicolai Vasilyevich Gogol *Gamblers*

Goh Chok Tong /gəʊ ˌtʃɒkˈtɒŋ/ 1941– . Singapore politician, prime minister from 1990. A trained economist, Goh became a member of Parliament for the ruling People's Action Party 1976. Rising steadily through the party ranks, he was appointed deputy prime minister 1985, and subsequently chosen by the cabinet as Lee Kuan Yew's successor.

Gokhale /gəʊˈkɑːli/ Gopal Krishna 1866–1915. Indian political adviser and friend of Mohandas Gandhi, leader of the Moderate group in the Indian National Congress before World War I.

Goldberg /ˈgəʊldbɜːg/ Rube 1883–1970. US cartoonist whose most famous and widely read of his strips featured ridiculously complicated inventions. He produced several popular comic strips that were nationally syndicated from 1915. Goldberg also devoted time to political cartooning, winning a Pulitzer Prize 1948.

Born in San Francisco, USA, and trained in engineering at the University of California, he abandoned that profession and joined the staff of the *San Francisco Chronicle* 1904. He moved to New York City 1907.

Golding /ˈgəʊldɪŋ/ William 1911– . English novelist. His first book, *Lord of the Flies* 1954, was about savagery taking over among a group of English schoolboys marooned on a Pacific island. Later novels include *The Spire* 1964, *Rites of Passage* 1980 (Booker prize), and *The Paper Men* 1984. He was awarded the Nobel Prize for Literature in 1983.

Goldman /ˈgəʊldmən/ Emma 1869–1940. US political organizer, feminist and co-editor of the anarchist monthly *Mother Earth* 1906–17. In 1908 her citizenship was revoked and in 1919 she was deported to Russia. Breaking with the Bolsheviks 1921, she spent the rest of her life in exile. Her writings include *My Disillusionment in Russia* 1923 and *Living My Life* 1931.

Born in Lithuania and raised in Russia, Goldman emigrated to the USA 1885 and worked in a clothing factory in Rochester, New York. There she became attracted to radical socialism and moved to New York City 1889, where she became part of the anarchist movement. In 1893 she was jailed for inciting unemployed workers to riot; she was again imprisoned for opposing military conscription during World War I.

Goldoni /gɒlˈdəʊni/ Carlo 1707–1793. Italian dramatist, born in Venice. He wrote popular comedies for the Sant'Angelo theatre, including *La putta onorata/The Respectable Girl* 1749, *I pettegolezzi delle donne/Women's Gossip* 1750, and *La locandiera/Mine Hostess* 1753. In 1761 he moved to Paris, where he directed the Italian theatre and wrote more plays, including *L'Eventail/The Fan* 1763.

Goldsmith /ˈgəʊldsmɪθ/ James 1933– . Franco-British entrepreneur, one of the UK's wealthiest people. Early in his career he built up a grocery empire, Cavenham Foods; he went on to become the owner of several industrial, commercial (he was cofounder of Mothercare), and financial enterprises. His magazine *Now!*, launched 1979, closed two years later. He became a director of the *Daily Telegraph* 1990.

Goldsmith /ˈgəʊldsmɪθ/ Jerry (Jerrald) 1930– . US composer of film music who originally worked in radio and television. His prolific output includes *Planet of the Apes* 1968, *The Wind and the Lion* 1975, *The Omen* 1976 (Academy Award), and *Gremlins* 1984.

Goldsmith /ˈgəʊldsmɪθ/ Oliver 1728–1774. Irish writer whose works include the novel *The Vicar of Wakefield* 1766; the poem 'The Deserted Village' 1770; and the play *She Stoops to Conquer* 1773. In 1761 Goldsmith met Samuel Johnson, and became a member of his 'club'. *The Vicar of Wakefield* was sold (according to Johnson's account) to save him from imprisonment for debt.

Goldsmith was the son of a cleric. He was educated at Trinity College, Dublin, and Edinburgh, where he studied medicine 1752. After travelling extensively in Europe, he returned to England and became a hack writer, producing many works, including *History of England* 1764 and *Animated Nature* 1774. One of his early works was *The Citizen of the World* 1762, a series of letters by an imaginary Chinese traveller. In 1764 he published the poem 'The Traveller', and followed it with collected essays 1765.

Goldwater /ˈgəʊldwɔːtə/ Barry 1909– . US Republican politician; presidential candidate in the 1964 election, when he was overwhelmingly defeated by Lyndon →Johnson. As a US senator 1953–86, he voiced the views of his party's right-wing conservative faction. Many of Goldwater's conservative ideas were later adopted by the Republican right, especially the Reagan administration.

Goldwyn /ˈgəʊldwɪn/ Samuel. Adopted name of Samuel Goldfish 1882–1974. US film producer. Born in Poland, he emigrated to the USA 1896. He founded the Goldwyn Pictures Corporation 1917, which eventually merged into Metro-Goldwyn-Mayer (MGM) 1924, although he was not part of the deal. He remained a producer for many years, making classics such as *Wuthering Heights* 1939, *The Little Foxes* 1941, *The Best Years of Our Lives* 1946, and *Guys and Dolls* 1955.

He was famed for his illogical aphorisms known as 'goldwynisms', for example, 'Include me out'.

Goldwyn US film producer Sam Goldwyn became one of the most powerful figures in Hollywood during its golden age. Many stars, including Rudolf Valentino, Ronald Colman, Gary Cooper, Danny Kaye, and David Niven, began their screen careers in Goldwyn's studios.

An oral contract is not worth the paper it's written on.

Samuel Goldwyn

Golgi /ˈgɒldʒi/ Camillo 1843–1926. Italian cell biologist who with Santiago Ramón y Cajal produced the first detailed knowledge of the fine structure of the nervous system.

Golgi's use of silver salts in staining cells proved so effective in showing up the components and fine processes of nerve cells that even the synapses – tiny gaps between the cells – were visible. The *Golgi apparatus*, a series of flattened membranous cavities found in the cytoplasm of cells, was first described by him in 1898. Golgi and Ramón y Cajal shared the 1906 Nobel Prize for Physiology or Medicine.

Gollancz /gə'lænts/ Victor 1893–1967. British left-wing writer and publisher, founder in 1936 of the Left Book Club. His own firm published plays by R C Sherriff and novels by Daphne Du Maurier, Elizabeth Bowen, and Dorothy L Sayers, among others.

Gomez /gəʊmɪʃ/ Diego 1440–1482. Portuguese navigator who discovered the coast of Liberia during a voyage sponsored by →Henry the Navigator 1458–60.

Gómez /gəʊmes/ Juan Vicente 1864–1935. Venezuelan dictator 1908–35. The discovery of oil during his rule attracted US, British, and Dutch oil interests and made Venezuela one of the wealthiest countries in Latin America. Gómez amassed a considerable personal fortune and used his well-equipped army to dominate the civilian population.

Gompers /gɒmpəz/ Samuel 1850–1924. US labour leader. His early career in the Cigarmakers' Union led him to found and lead the American Federation of Labor 1882.

Gompers advocated nonpolitical activity within the existing capitalist system to secure improved wages and working conditions for members.

Gomułka /gə'mʊlkə/ Władysław 1905–1982. Polish Communist politician, party leader 1943–48 and 1956–70. He introduced moderate reforms, including private farming and tolerance for Roman Catholicism.

Gomułka, born in Krosno in SE Poland, was involved in underground resistance to the Germans during World War II, taking part in the defence of Warsaw. Leader of the Communist Party in Poland from 1943, he was ousted by the Moscow-backed Bolesław Bierut (1892–1956) in 1948, but was restored to the leadership in 1956, following riots in Poznań. Gomułka was forced to resign in Dec 1970 after sudden food- price rises induced a new wave of strikes and riots.

Goncharov /gɒntʃə'rɒf/ Ivan Alexandrovitch 1812–1891. Russian novelist. His first novel, *A Common Story* 1847, was followed in 1858 by his humorous masterpiece *Oblomov*, which satirized the indolent Russian landed gentry.

Goncourt, de /gɒnˈkʊə/ the brothers Edmond 1822–1896 and Jules 1830–1870. French writers. They collaborated in producing a compendium, *L'Art du XVIIIême siècle*/*18th-Century Art*

1859–75, historical studies, and a *Journal* published 1887–96 that depicts French literary life of their day. Edmond de Goncourt founded the Académie Goncourt, opened 1903, which awards an annual prize, the Prix Goncourt, to the author of the best French novel of the year.

Equivalent to the Commonwealth Booker Prize in prestige, it has a monetary value of only 50 francs.

González Márquez /gɒn'θɑːleθ 'mɑːkeθ/ Felipe 1942– . Spanish socialist politician, leader of the Socialist Workers' Party (PSOE), prime minister from 1982. Although re-elected in the 1989 election, his popularity suffered from economic upheaval and allegations of corruption.

After studying law in Spain and Belgium, in 1966 he opened the first labour-law office in his home city of Seville. In 1964 he had joined the PSOE, and he rose rapidly to the position of leader. In 1982 the PSOE won a sweeping electoral victory and González became prime minister. Under his administration left-wing members of the PSOE, disenchanted with Gonzá lez's policies, formed a new party called Social Democracy 1990.

Gooch /guːtʃ/ Graham Alan 1953– . English cricketer who plays for Essex and England. He made his first-class cricket debut in 1973, and was first capped for England two years later. Banned for three years for captaining a team for a tour of South Africa in 1982, he was later re-instated as England captain in 1989. He scored a world record 456 runs in a Test match against India in 1990.

He became the fourth person to average 100 runs per innings in an English season and has appeared in more than 90 Test matches.

Goodman /gʊdmən/ Benny (Benjamin David) 1909–1986. US clarinetist, nicknamed the 'King of Swing' for the new jazz idiom he introduced with arranger Fletcher Henderson (1897–1952). In 1934 he founded his own 12-piece band, which combined the expressive improvisatory style of black jazz with disciplined precision ensemble playing. He is associated with such numbers as 'Blue Skies' and 'Lets Dance'. He also recorded with a sextet 1939–41 that included the guitarist Charlie Christian (1916–1942).

In 1938 he embarked on a parallel classical career, recording the Mozart Clarinet Quintet with the Budapest String Quartet, and comissioning new works from Bartók (*Contrasts* 1939), Copland, Hindemith, and others. When swing lost popularity in the 1950s, Goodman took a series of smaller groups on world tours culminating in a US government-sponsored visit to Moscow in 1962.

Goodman /gʊdmən/ Paul 1911– . US writer and social critic whose many works (novels, plays, essays) express his anarchist, anti-authoritarian ideas. He studied young offenders in *Growing up Absurd* 1960.

Goodyear /ˈgʊdjɪə/ Charles 1800–1860. US inventor who developed rubber coating 1837 and vulcanized rubber 1839, a method of curing raw rubber to make it strong and elastic.

Gorbachev /ˌgɔːbəˈtʃɒf/ Mikhail Sergeyevich 1931– . Soviet president, in power 1985–91. He was a member of the Politburo from 1980. As general secretary of the Communist Party (CPSU) 1985–91, and president of the Supreme Soviet 1988–91, he introduced liberal reforms at home (*perestroika* and *glasnost*), proposed the introduction of multiparty democracy, and attempted to halt the arms race abroad. He became head of state 1989.

He was awarded the Nobel Peace Prize 1990 but his international reputation suffered in the light of harsh state repression of nationalist demonstrations in the Baltic states. Following an abortive coup attempt by hardliners Aug 1991, international acceptance of independence for the Baltic states, and accelerated moves towards independence in other republics, Gorbachev's power base as Soviet president was greatly weakened and in Dec 1991 he resigned.

Gorbachev, born in the N Caucasus, studied law at Moscow University and joined the CPSU 1952. In 1955–62 he worked for the Komsomol (Communist Youth League) before being appointed regional agriculture secretary. As Stavropol party leader from 1970 he impressed Andropov, and was brought into the CPSU secretariat 1978. Gorbachev was promoted into the Politburo and in 1983, when Andropov was general secretary, took broader charge of the Soviet economy. During the Chernenko administration 1984–85, he was chair of the Foreign Affairs Commission. On Chernenko's death 1985 he was appointed party leader. He initiated wide-ranging reforms and broad economic restructuring, and introduced campaigns against alcoholism, corruption, and inefficiency. In the 1988 presidential election by members of the Soviet parliament, he was the sole candidate. Gorbachev radically changed the style of Soviet leadership, encountering opposition to the pace of change in both conservative and radical camps, but he failed both to realize the depth of hostility this aroused against him in the CPSU and to distance himself from the party. In March 1990 he was elected to a five-year term as executive president with greater powers.

At home his plans for economic reform failed to avert a food crisis in the winter of 1990–91 and his desire to preserve a single, centrally controlled USSR met with resistance from Soviet republics seeking more independence. Early in 1991, Gorbachev shifted to the right in order to placate the conservative wing of the party and appointed some of the hardliners to positions of power. In late spring, he produced a plan for a new union treaty to satisfy the demands of reformers. This plan alarmed the hardliners, who, in late summer, temporarily removed him from office. He was saved from this attempted coup mainly by the efforts of Boris →Yeltsin and the ineptness of the plotters. Soon after his reinstatement, Gorbachev was obliged to relinquish his leadership of the party, renounce communism as a state doctrine, suspend all activities of the Communist Party (including its most powerful organs the Politburo and the Secretariat), and surrender many of his central powers to the states. During the following months he pressed for an agreement on his proposed union treaty in the hope of preventing a disintegration of the Soviet Union, but was unable to maintain control and on 25 Dec 1991 resigned as president, effectively yielding power to Boris Yeltsin.

Gordimer /ˈgɔːdɪmə/ Nadine 1923– . South African novelist, an opponent of apartheid. Her first novel, *The Lying Days*, appeared in 1953, her other works include *The Conservationist* 1974, the volume of short stories *A Soldier's Embrace* 1980, and *July's People* 1981. She was awarded the Nobel Prize for Literature in 1991.

Gordon /ˈgɔːdn/ Charles (George) 1833–1885. British general sent to Khartoum in the Sudan 1884 to rescue English garrisons that were under attack by the Mahdi, Muhammad Ahmed; he was himself besieged for ten months by the Mahdi's army. A relief expedition arrived 28 Jan 1885 to find that Khartoum had been captured and Gordon killed two days before.

Gordon served in the Crimean War and in China 1864, where he earned his nickname 'Chinese' Gordon in ending the Taiping Rebellion. In 1874 he was employed by the Khedive of Egypt to open the country and 1877–80 was British governor of the Sudan.

Gordon /ˈgɔːdn/ George 1751–1793. British organizer of the so-called *Gordon Riots* of 1778, a protest against removal of penalties imposed on Roman Catholics in the Catholic Relief Act of 1778; he was acquitted on a treason charge. Gordon and the 'No Popery' riots figure in Charles Dickens's novel *Barnaby Rudge*.

Gordon /ˈgɔːdn/ Richard. Pen name of Gordon Ostlere 1921– . British author of a series of lighthearted novels on the career of a young doctor, beginning with *Doctor in the House* 1952. Many of them were filmed.

Gordon-Lennox family name of dukes of Richmond; seated at Goodwood, Sussex; descended from King Charles II by his mistress Louise de Keroualle.

Gore /gɔː/ Al(bert) 1948– . US politician, vice president from 1993. A Democrat, he became a member of the House of Representatives 1977–79, and was elected senator for Tennessee 1985–92. Like his running mate, Bill →Clinton, he is on the conservative wing of the party, but holds liberal views on such matters as women's rights and abortion.

Born into a wealthy patrician family in Ten-

Gordon British army general Charles Gordon was governor of the Sudan 1877–80, and attempted to suppress the slave trade there. In 1860 he took part in the expedition that captured Peking and was personally responsible for the burning of the Summer Palace.

nessee, where his father was senator, Gore was a journalist, a real estate developer, and a farmer before going into politics. He is known to hold strong views on arms control, defence, and foreign policy, as well as environmental issues.

Goria /ɡɔːriə/ Giovanni 1943– . Italian Christian Democrat (DC) politician, prime minister 1987–88. He entered the Chamber of Deputies 1976 and held a number of posts, including treasury minister, until he was asked to form a coalition government in 1987.

Göring /ɡɜːrɪŋ/ Hermann. German spelling of →Goering, Nazi leader.

Gorky /ɡɔːki/ Arshile 1904–1948. Armenian-born US painter. He painted Cubist abstracts before developing a more surreal Abstract-Expressionist style, using organic shapes and bold paint strokes.

Among Gorky's major influences were Picasso, Kandinsky, Miró, and Cézanne. His works, such as *The Liver Is the Cock's Comb* 1944 Albright-Knox Art Gallery, Buffalo) are noted for their sense of fantasy. He lived in the USA from 1920.

Gorky /ɡɔːki/ Maxim. Pen name of Alexei Peshkov 1868–1936. Russian writer. Born in Nizhni Novgorod (named Gorky 1932–90 in his honour), he was exiled 1906–13 for his revolutionary principles. His works, which include the play *The Lower Depths* 1902 and the memoir *My Childhood* 1913–14, combine realism with optimistic faith in the potential of the industrial proletariat.

Gorst /ɡɔːst/ J(ohn) E(ldon) 1835–1916. English Conservative Party administrator. A supporter of Disraeli, Gorst was largely responsible for extending the Victorian Conservative Party electoral base

to include middle- and working-class support. Appointed Conservative Party agent in 1870, he established Conservative Central Office, and became secretary of the National Union in 1871. He was solicitor-general 1885–86.

Gort /ɡɔːt/ John Vereker, 1st Viscount Gort 1886–1946. British general who in World War II commanded the British Expeditionary Force 1939–40, conducting a fighting retreat from Dunkirk, France.

Gorton /ɡɔːtn/ John Grey 1911– . Australian Liberal politician. He was minister for education and science 1966–68, and prime minister 1968–71.

Goschen /ɡəʊʃən/ George Joachim, 1st Viscount Goschen 1831–1907. British Liberal politician. He held several cabinet posts under Gladstone 1868–74, but broke with him in 1886 over Irish Home Rule. In Salisbury's Unionist government of 1886–92 he was chancellor of the Exchequer, and 1895–1900 was First Lord of the Admiralty.

Gossaert /ɡɒsɑːt/ Jan, Flemish painter, known as →Mabuse.

Gosse /ɡɒs/ Edmund William 1849–1928. English author whose strict Victorian upbringing is reflected in his masterpiece of autobiographical work *Father and Son* (published anonymously in 1907). His father was a member of the Plymouth Brethren, a Christian fundamentalist sect.

Gough /ɡɒf/ Hubert 1870–1963. British general. He was initially blamed, as commander of the Fifth Army 1916–18, for the German breakthrough on the Somme, but his force was later admitted to have been too small for the length of the front.

Gosse English poet and critic Edmund Gosse, noted for his poems and sound literary criticisms, was librarian to the House of Lords 1904–14. He also wrote several biographical studies, was the first to introduce Scandinavian literature to the English-reading public, and did much to encourage young writers.

Gounod *French composer Charles Gounod whose lyric and dramatic gifts were displayed in such popular operatic adaptations of literature as Faust and Romeo and Juliet. His earliest recognition came for the Solemn Mass, first performed in London 1851. His pervasive religiosity, sometimes sinking to sentimentality, is most widely known through the 'Ave Maria'.*

Gould /guːld/ Bryan (Charles) 1939– . British Labour politician, member of the shadow cabinet from 1986 to 1992.

Born in New Zealand, he settled in Britain in 1964 as a civil servant and then a university lecturer. He joined the Labour Party, entering the House of Commons in 1974. He lost his seat in the 1979 general election but returned in 1983 as the member for Dagenham, having spent the intervening four years as a television journalist. His rise in the Labour Party was rapid and in 1986 he became a member of the shadow cabinet. His communication skills soon made him a nationally known figure. He was an unsuccessful candidate in the 1992 Labour Party leadership election and resigned from the shadow cabinet in Sept.

Gould /guːld/ Elliott. Stage name of Elliot Goldstein 1938– . US film actor. A successful child actor, his film debut *The Night They Raided Minsky's* 1968 led rapidly to starring roles in such films as *M.A.S.H.* 1970, *The Long Goodbye* 1972, and *Capricorn One* 1978.

Gould /guːld/ Jay 1836–1892. US financier, born in New York. He is said to have caused the financial panic on 'Black Friday', 24 Sept 1869, through his efforts to corner the gold market.

Gould was one of the 'Robber Barons' who built the transportation and communications structures of the USA while accumulating great wealth. His first major success came when he was made an associate of the Erie Railroad by Cor-

nelius →Vanderbilt. Following financial and political scandals, Gould was forced to relinquish control of the Erie Railroad, but he used the large fortune he had amassed to acquire control of western railroads, including the Union Pacific. He also controlled the Western Union Telegraph Company and elevated railways in New York City.

Gould /guːld/ Stephen Jay 1941– . US palaeontologist and author. In 1972 he proposed the theory of punctuated equilibrium, suggesting that the evolution of species did not occur at a steady rate but could suddenly accelerate, with rapid change occurring over a few hundred thousand years. His books include *Ever Since Darwin* 1977, *The Panda's Thumb* 1980, *The Flamingo's Smile* 1985, and *Wonderful Life* 1990.

Science is all those things which are confirmed to such a degree that it would be unreasonable to withhold one's provisional consent.

Stephen Jay Gould *Lecture on Evolution* 1984

Gounod Charles François 1818–1893. French composer. His operas include *Sappho* 1851, *Faust* 1859, *Philémon et Baucis* 1860, and *Roméo et Juliette* 1867. He also wrote sacred songs, masses, and an oratorio, *The Redemption* 1882. His music inspired many French composers of the late 19th century.

Gow /gaʊ/ Ian 1937–1990. British Conservative politician. After qualifying as a solicitor, he became member of Parliament for Eastbourne 1974. He became parliamentary private secretary to the then prime minister, Margaret Thatcher, 1979, and her close ally. He secured steady promotion but resigned his post as minister of state 1985 in protest at the signing of the Anglo-Irish Agreement. A strong critic of terrorist acts, he was killed by an IRA car bomb.

Gower /gaʊə/ David 1957– . English left-handed cricketer who played for Leicestershire 1975–89 and for Hampshire from 1990. In 1992, during the third Test against Pakistan, he became England's highest-scoring batsman in Test cricket, surpassing Geoffrey Boycott's record of 8,114 runs.

Gower /gaʊə/ John c. 1330–1408. English poet. He is remembered for his tales of love *Confessio Amantis* 1390, written in English, and other poems in French and Latin.

Gowon /gəʊˈɒn/ Yakubu 1934– . Nigerian politician, head of state 1966–75. Educated at Sandhurst military college in the UK, he became chief of staff, and in the military coup of 1966 seized power. After the Biafran civil war 1967–70, he reunited the country with his policy of 'no victor, no vanquished'. In 1975 he was overthrown by a military coup.

Goya /ˈgɔɪə/ Francisco José de Goya y Lucientes 1746–1828. Spanish painter and engraver. He painted portraits of four successive kings of Spain, and his etchings include *The Disasters of War*, depicting the French invasion of Spain 1810–14. Among his later works are the 'black paintings' (Prado, Madrid), with horrific images such as *Saturn Devouring One of His Sons c.*1822.

Goya was born in Aragon and was for a time a bullfighter, the subject of some of his etchings. After studying in Italy, he returned to Spain and was employed on a number of paintings for the royal tapestry factory. In 1789 he was court painter to Charles IV.

Goyen /ˈxɔɪən/ Jan van 1596–1656. Dutch landscape painter, active in Leiden, Haarlem, and from 1631 in The Hague. He was a pioneer of the realist style of landscape with →Ruisdael, and he sketched from nature and studied clouds and light effects.

Gozzoli /ˈgɒtsəli/ Benozzo *c.* 1421–1497. Florentine painter, a late exponent of the International Gothic style. He painted frescoes 1459 in the chapel of the Palazzo Medici-Riccardi, Florence: the walls are crammed with figures, many of them portraits of the Medici family.

Graaf /ɡrɑːf/ Regnier de 1641–1673. Dutch physician and anatomist who discovered the ovarian follicles, which were later named *Graafian follicles*. He named the ovaries and gave exact descriptions of the testicles. He was also the first to isolate and collect the secretions of the pancreas and gall bladder.

Grable /ˈgreɪbəl/ Betty (Elizabeth Ruth) 1916–1973. US actress, singer, and dancer, who starred in *Moon over Miami* 1941, *I Wake Up Screaming* 1941, and *How to Marry a Millionaire* 1953. As a publicity stunt, her legs were insured for a million dollars. Her popularity peaked during World War II when US soldiers voted her their number-one pin-up girl.

Gracchus /ˈgrækəs/ the brothers *Tiberius Sempronius* 163–133 BC and *Gaius Sempronius* 153–121 BC. Roman agrarian reformers. As tribune (magistrate) 133 BC, Tiberius tried to prevent the ruin of small farmers by making large slave-labour farms illegal but was murdered. Gaius, tribune 123–122 BC, revived his brother's legislation, and introduced other reforms, but was outlawed by the Senate and committed suicide.

Grace /greɪs/ W(illiam) G(ilbert) 1848–1915. English cricketer. By profession a doctor, he became the best batsman in England. He began playing first-class cricket at the age of 16, scored 152 runs in his first Test match, and scored the first triple century 1876. Throughout his career, which lasted nearly 45 years, he scored more than 54,000 runs.

He scored 2,739 runs in 1871, the first time any batsman had scored 2,000 runs in a season. An all-rounder, he took nearly 3,000 first-class wickets. Grace played in 22 Test matches.

Graf /grɑːf/ Steffi 1969– . German lawn-tennis player who brought Martina →Navratilova's long reign as the world's number-one female player to an end. Graf reached the semi-final of the US Open 1985 at the age of 16, and won five consecutive Grand Slam singles titles 1988–89.

Grafton /ˈgrɑːftən/ Augustus Henry, 3rd Duke of Grafton 1735–1811. British politician. Grandson of the first duke, who was the son of Charles II and Barbara Villiers (1641–1709), Duchess of Cleveland. He became First Lord of the Treasury in 1766 and an unsuccessful acting prime minister 1767–70.

Graham /ˈgreɪəm/ family name of dukes of Montrose.

Graham /ˈgreɪəm/ Billy (William Franklin) 1918– . US Protestant evangelist, known for the dramatic staging and charismatic eloquence of his preaching. Graham has preached to millions during worldwide crusades and on television, bringing many thousands to a 'decision for Christ'.

Graham /ˈgreɪəm/ Martha 1893–1991. US dancer, choreographer, teacher, and director. A leading exponent of modern dance in the USA, she developed a distinctive vocabulary of movement, the *Graham Technique*, now taught worldwide. Her pioneering technique, designed to express inner emotion and intention through dance forms, represented the first real alternative to classical ballet.

Graham founded her own dance school 1927 and started a company with students from the school 1929. She created over 170 works, including *Appalachian Spring* 1944 (score by Aaron Copland), *Clytemnestra* 1958, the first full-length modern dance work, and *Errand into the Maze*.

Graham /ˈgreɪəm/ Thomas 1805–1869. Scottish chemist who laid the foundations of physical chemistry (the branch of chemistry concerned with changes in energy during a chemical transformation) by his work on the diffusion of gases and liquids. *Graham's Law* 1829 states that the diffusion rate of a gas is inversely proportional to the square root of its density.

His work on colloids (which have larger particles than true solutions) was equally fundamental; he discovered the principle of dialysis, that colloids can be separated from solutions containing smaller molecules by the differing rates at which they pass through a semipermeable membrane (a process he termed 'osmosis'). The human kidney uses the principle of dialysis to extract nitrogenous waste.

Grahame /ˈgreɪəm/ Kenneth 1859–1932. Scottish author. The early volumes of sketches of childhood, *The Golden Age* 1895 and *Dream Days* 1898, were followed by his masterpiece *The Wind in the Willows* 1908, an animal fantasy created for his young son, which was dramatized by A A Milne as *Toad of Toad Hall* 1929.

Grainger /ˈɡreɪndʒə/ Percy Aldridge 1882–1961. Australian-born US composer and concert pianist. He is remembered for a number of songs and short instrumental pieces drawing on folk idioms, including *Country Gardens* 1925, and for his settings of folk songs, such as *Molly on the Shore* 1921.

He studied in Frankfurt, moved to London, then settled in the USA in 1914. Grainger shared his friend Ferruccio →Busoni's vision of a free music, devising a synthesizer and composing machine far ahead of its time.

Grange /ɡreɪndʒ/ Red (Harold Edward). Nickname 'the Galloping Ghost'. 1903–1991. US American football player. He joined the Chicago Bears professional football team 1925, becoming one of the first superstars of the newly founded National Football League. In both the 1923 and 1924 seasons he was chosen All-American halfback and won his nickname for his extraordinary open-field running ability.

Born in Forksville, Pennsylvania, USA and raised in Illinois, Grange attended the University of Illinois. He became a charter member of the Football Hall of Fame 1963.

Gramsci /ˈɡræmʃi/ Antonio 1891–1937. Italian Marxist who attempted to unify social theory and political practice. He helped to found the Italian Communist Party 1921 and was elected to parliament 1924, but was imprisoned by the Fascist leader Mussolini from 1926; his *Quaderni di carcere/Prison Notebooks* were published posthumously 1947.

Gramsci believed that politics and ideology were independent of the economic base, that no ruling class could dominate by economic factors alone, and that the working class could achieve liberation by political and intellectual struggle. His concept of *hegemony* argued that real class control in capitalist societies is ideological and cultural rather than physical, and that only the working class 'educated' by radical intellectuals could see through and overthrow such bourgeois propaganda.

His humane and gradualist approach to Marxism, specifically his emphasis on the need to overthrow bourgeois ideology, influenced European Marxists in their attempt to distance themselves from orthodox determinist Soviet communism.

Granados /ɡrəˈnɑːdɒs/ Enrique 1867–1916. Spanish composer and pianist. His piano-work *Goyescas* 1911, inspired by the art of →Goya, was converted to an opera in 1916.

Granby /ˈɡrænbi/ John Manners, Marquess of Granby 1721–1770. British soldier. His head appears on many inn-signs in England as a result of his popularity as a commander of the British forces fighting in Europe in the Seven Years' War.

Grandi /ˈɡrændi/ Dino 1895–1988. Italian politician who challenged Mussolini for leadership of the Italian Fascist Party in 1921 and was subsequently largely responsible for Mussolini's downfall in July 1943.

Granger /ˈɡreɪndʒə/ (James) Stewart 1913– . British film actor. After several leading roles in British romantic films during World War II, he moved to Hollywood in 1950 and subsequently appeared in such fanciful films as *Scaramouche* 1952, *The Prisoner of Zenda* 1952, and *The Wild Geese* 1978.

Grant /ɡrɑːnt/ Cary. Stage name of Archibald Leach 1904–1986. British-born actor who became a US citizen 1942. His witty, debonair personality made him a screen favourite for more than three decades. He was directed by Alfred →Hitchcock in *Suspicion* 1941, *Notorious* 1946, *To Catch a Thief* 1955, and *North by Northwest* 1959. He received a 1970 Academy Award for general excellence.

His other films include *She Done Him Wrong* 1933, *Bringing Up Baby* 1937, and *The Philadelphia Story* 1940.

Grant /ɡrɑːnt/ Duncan 1885–1978. British painter and designer, a member of the Bloomsbury group and a pioneer of abstract art in the UK. He lived with Vanessa Bell from about 1914 and worked with her on decorative projects. Later works, such as *Snow Scene* 1921, showed the influence of the Post-Impressionists.

Grant /ɡrɑːnt/ James Augustus 1827–1892. Scottish soldier and explorer who served in India and Abyssinia and, with Captain John Speke, explored the sources of the Nile 1860–63. Accounts of his travels include *A Walk across Africa* 1864 and *Botany of the Speke and Grant Expedition*.

Grant /ɡrɑːnt/ Ulysses S(impson) 1822–1885. American Civil War leader and 18th president of the USA 1869–77. He was a Union general in the American Civil War and commander in chief from 1864. As a Republican president, he carried through a liberal Reconstruction policy in the South, reformed the civil service, and ratified the Treaty of Washington with Great Britain 1871. He failed to suppress extensive political corruption within his own party and cabinet, which tarnished the reputation of his second term.

The son of an Ohio farmer, he had an unsuccessful career in the army 1839–54 and in business. On the outbreak of the Civil War received a commission on the Mississippi front. He took command there in 1862, and by his capture of Vicksburg in 1863 brought the whole Mississippi front under Northern control. He slowly wore down the Confederate general Lee's resistance, and in 1865 received his surrender at Appomattox. He was elected president 1868 and re-elected 1872.

Granville-Barker /ˈɡrænvɪl ˈbɑːkə/ Harley 1877–1946. British theatre director and author. He was director and manager with J E Vedrenne at the Royal Court Theatre, London, 1904–18, produc-

Grant *General Ulysses S Grant at City Point, near Hopewell, Virginia, June 1864. Respected as a war hero, Grant was nominated as the Republican Party's presidential candidate in 1868. He was elected and served two terms, marred by poor administration, financial scandals, and official corruption.*

ing plays by Shaw, Yeats, Ibsen, Galsworthy, and Masefield.

Grappelli /grə'peli/ Stephane 1908– . French jazz violinist who played in the Quintette de Hot Club de France 1934–39, in partnership with the guitarist Django →Reinhardt. Romantic improvisation is a hallmark of his style.

Grappelli spent World War II in the UK and returned several times to record there, including a number of jazz albums with the classical violinist Yehudi Menuhin in the 1970s. Of his other collaborations, an LP with the mandolinist David Grisman (1945–   ) reached the US pop chart 1981.

Grass /grɑːs/ Günter 1927–   . German writer. The grotesque humour and socialist feeling of his novels *Die Blechtrommel/The Tin Drum* 1959 and *Der Butt/The Flounder* 1977 are also characteristic of many of his poems.

Born in Danzig, he studied at the art academies of Düsseldorf and Berlin, worked as a writer and sculptor (first in Paris and later in Berlin), and in 1958 won the coveted 'Group 47' prize.

Grattan /'grætn/ Henry 1746–1820. Irish politician. He entered the Irish parliament in 1775, led the patriot opposition, and obtained free trade and legislative independence for Ireland 1782. He failed to prevent the Act of Union of Ireland and England in 1805, sat in the British Parliament from that year, and pressed for Catholic emancipation.

Graves /greɪvz/ Robert (Ranke) 1895–1985. English poet and author. He was severely wounded on the Somme in World War I, and his frank autobiography *Goodbye to All That* 1929 is one of the outstanding war books. Other works include the poems *Over the Brazier* 1916; two historical novels of imperial Rome, *I Claudius* and *Claudius the God*, both 1934; and books on myth – for example, *The White Goddess* 1948.

In love as in sport, the amateur status must be strictly maintained.

Robert Graves *Occupation: Writer*

Gray /greɪ/ Asa 1810–1888. US botanist and taxonomist who became America's leading expert in the field. His major publications include *Elements of Botany* 1836 and the definitive *Flora of North America* 1838, 1843. He based his revision of the Linnaean system of plant classification on fruit form rather than gross morphology.

Born in Saquoit, New York, USA, Gray graduated from medical school but chose botany rather than medicine as his career. A friend and supporter of Charles →Darwin, he was one of the founders of the American National Academy of Sciences.

His *Manual of Botany* 1850 remains the standard reference work on flora east of the Rockies.

Gray /greɪ/ Eileen 1879–1976. Irish-born architect and furniture designer. Her Art Deco furniture explored the use of tubular metal, glass, and new materials such as aluminium.

After training as a painter at the Slade School of Art, London, she worked for a Japanese lacquer painter in Paris. She set up her own workshop and gradually concentrated on the design of furniture, woven textiles, and interiors.

Gray /greɪ/ Thomas 1716–1771. English poet whose 'Elegy Written in a Country Churchyard' 1751 is one of the most quoted poems in English. Other poems include 'Ode on a Distant Prospect of Eton College', 'The Progress of Poesy', and 'The Bard'; these poems are now seen as the precursors of Romanticism.

A close friend of Horace →Walpole at Eton, Gray made a continental tour with him 1739–41, an account of which is given in his vivid letters. His first poem 'Ode on a Distant Prospect of Eton College' was published in 1747 and again in 1748 with 'Ode on the Spring' in Robert Dodsley's (1703–1764) *A Collection of Poems By Several Hands*.

Graziani /ˌgrætsi'ɑːni/ Rodolfo 1882–1955. Italian general. He was commander in chief of Italian forces in North Africa during World War II but was defeated by British forces 1940, and subsequently replaced. Later, as defence minister in the new Mussolini government, he failed to reorganize a republican Fascist army, was captured by the Allies 1945, tried by an Italian military court, and finally released 1950.

Graziano /ˌgrætsi'ɑːnəʊ/ Rocky (Thomas Rocco Barbella) 1922–1990. US middleweight boxing champion who fought in the 1940s and 1950s. Although he was not noted for his boxing skills or finesse, his colourful, brawling style made him popular. He compiled a record of 67 wins, 10 losses and 6 draws between 1942 and 1952. Three of his bouts, with Tony Zale 1946, 1947, and 1948, were considered classics.

Greco, El /ˈgrekəʊ/ (Doménikos Theotokopoulos) 1541–1614. Spanish painter called 'the Greek' because he was born in Crete. He studied in Italy, worked in Rome from about 1570, and by 1577 had settled in Toledo. He painted elegant portraits and intensely emotional religious scenes with increasingly distorted figures and flickering light; for example, *The Burial of Count Orgaz* 1586 (Toledo).

Greeley Horace 1811–1872. US editor, publisher, and politician. He founded the *New York Tribune* 1841 and, as a strong supporter of the Whig party, advocated many reform causes in his newspaper – among them, feminism and abolitionism. He was an advocate of American westward expansion, and is remembered for his advice 'Go west, young man'. One of the founders of the Republican party 1854, Greeley was the unsuccessful presidential candidate of the breakaway Liberal Republicans 1872.

Green /griːn/ Henry. Pen name of Henry Vincent Yorke 1905–1974. British novelist whose works (for example *Loving* 1945, and *Nothing* 1950) are characterized by an experimental colloquial prose style and extensive use of dialogue.

Green /griːn/ Lucinda (born Prior-Palmer) 1953– . British three-day eventer. She has won the Badminton Horse Trials a record six times 1973–84 and was world individual champion 1982.

Green /griːn/ Thomas Hill 1836–1882. English philosopher. He attempted to show the limitations of Herbert →Spencer and John Stuart →Mill, and advocated the study of the German philosophers Kant and Hegel. His chief works are *Prolegomena to Ethics* 1883 and *Principles of Political Obligation* 1895. He was professor of moral philosophy at Oxford from 1878.

Greenaway /ˈgriːnəweɪ/ Kate 1846–1901. English illustrator, known for her drawings of children. In 1877 she first exhibited at the Royal Academy, and began her collaboration with the colour-printer Edmund Evans, with whom she produced a number of children's books, including *Mother Goose*.

Greenaway /ˈgriːnəweɪ/ Peter 1942– . British director of highly stylized, cerebral but richly visual films. His feeling for perspective and lighting reveal his early training as a painter. His films, such as *A Zed & Two Noughts* 1985, are hallmarked by puzzle motifs and numerical games. Greenaway's other films include *The Draughtsman's Contract* 1982, *Belly of an Architect* 1986, *Drowning by Numbers* 1988, and *Prospero's Books* 1991.

Greene /griːn/ (Henry) Graham 1904–1991. English writer whose novels of guilt, despair, and penitence are set in a world of urban seediness or political corruption in many parts of the world. They include *Brighton Rock* 1938, *The Power and the Glory* 1940, *The Heart of the Matter* 1948, *The Third Man* 1950, *The Honorary Consul* 1973, and *Monsignor Quixote* 1982.

Greene /griːn/ Nathanael 1742–1786. American military leader. During the American Revolution 1775–83 he was commander of the Rhode Island regiments and later brigadier general in the Continental army, seeing action at the Battle of Long Island 1776 and Washington's New Jersey campaigns 1777. He commanded the successful American offensive in the South that ended the war.

Born in Warwick, Rhode Island, Greene was a member of a Quaker family but showed an exceptional interest in military affairs.

Greenspan /ˈgriːnspæn/ Alan 1926– . US economist who succeeded Paul →Volcker as chair of the Federal Reserve System 1987 and successfully pumped liquidity into the market to avert a sudden 'free fall' into recession after the Wall Street share crash of Oct 1987.

Greenstreet /ˈgriːnstriːt/ Sydney 1879–1954. British character actor. He made an impressive film debut in *The Maltese Falcon* 1941 and became one of the cinema's best-known villains. His other films include *Casablanca* 1943 and *The Mask of Dimitrios* 1944.

Greenwood /ˈgriːnwʊd/ Walter 1903–1974. English novelist of the Depression, born in Salford. His own lack of a job gave authenticity to *Love on the Dole* 1933, later dramatized and filmed.

Greer /grɪə/ Germaine 1939– . Australian feminist who became widely known on the publication of her book *The Female Eunuch* 1970. Later works include *The Obstacle Race* 1979, a study of contemporary women artists, and *Sex and Destiny: The Politics of Human Fertility* 1984. She is also a speaker and activist.

Gregg /greg/ Norman 1892–1966. Australian ophthalmic surgeon who discovered 1941 that German measles in a pregnant woman could cause physical defects in her child.

Gregory /gregəri/ Augustus Charles 1819–1905. English-born explorer and surveyor in Australia who in 1855–56 led an expedition of scientific exploration which crossed from Victoria River, on the NW coast of Australia, to Rockhampton on the NE coast, and located valuable pastures. In 1858 his expedition in search of →Leichhardt found traces of the lost explorer but failed to clear up the mystery of his disappearance.

Gregory /gregəri/ Isabella Augusta (born Persse) 1852–1932. Irish playwright, associated with W B Yeats in creating the Abbey Theatre, Dublin, 1904. Her plays include the comedy *Spreading the News* 1904 and the tragedy *Gaol Gate* 1906. Her journals 1916–30 were published 1946.

Gregory /gregəri/ name of 16 popes, including:

Gregory I St, *the Great* c. 540–604. Pope from 590 who asserted Rome's supremacy and exercised almost imperial powers. In 596 he sent St →Augustine to England. He introduced the choral *Gregorian chant* into the liturgy. Feast day 12 March.

Gregory VII or *Hildebrand* c. 1023–1085. Chief minister to several popes before his election to the papacy 1073. In 1077 he forced the Holy Roman emperor Henry IV to wait in the snow at Canossa for four days, dressed as a penitent, before receiving pardon. He was driven from Rome and died in exile. His feast day is 25 May.

He claimed power to depose kings, denied lay rights to make clerical appointments, and attempted to suppress simony (the buying and selling of church preferments) and to enforce clerical celibacy, making enemies of both rulers and the church.

Gregory XIII 1502–1585. Pope from 1572 who introduced the reformed *Gregorian calendar*, still in use, in which a century year is not a leap year unless it is divisible by 400.

Gregory of Tours, St /tʊə/ 538–594. French Christian bishop of Tours from 573, author of a *History of the Franks*. His feast day is 17 Nov.

Grenfell /grenfəl/ Julian 1888–1915. British poet, killed in World War I. His poem 'Into Battle' was first published in *The Times* 1915.

Grenville /grenvɪl/ George 1712–1770. British Whig politician, prime minister, and chancellor of the Exchequer, whose introduction of the Stamp Act 1765 to raise revenue from the colonies was one of the causes of the American Revolution. His government was also responsible for prosecuting the radical John →Wilkes.

Grenville took other measures to reduce the military and civil costs in North America, including the Sugar Act and the Quartering Act. His inept management of the Regency Act 1765 damaged his relationship with George III.

Grenville /grenvɪl/ Richard 1542–1591. English naval commander and adventurer who died heroically aboard his ship *The Revenge* when attacked by Spanish warships. Grenville fought in Hungary and Ireland 1566–69, and was knighted about 1577. In 1585 he commanded the expedition that founded Virginia, USA, for his cousin Walter →Raleigh. From 1586 to 1588 he organized the defence of England against the Spanish Armada.

In 1591 Grenville was second in command of a fleet under Lord Thomas Howard that sailed to seize Spanish treasure ships returning from South America, when his ship became isolated from the rest of the fleet off the Azores and was attacked by Spanish warships. After many hours of hand-to-hand combat, *The Revenge* succumbed; Grenville was captured and fatally wounded. He became a symbol of English nationalism and was commemorated in the poem 'The Revenge' 1880 by Alfred Tennyson.

Grenville /grenvɪl/ William Wyndham, Baron 1759–1834. British Whig politician, foreign secretary from 1791; he resigned along with Prime Minister Pitt the Younger 1801 over George III's refusal to assent to Catholic emancipation. He headed the 'All the Talents' coalition of 1806–07 that abolished the slave trade.

Grenville, son of George Grenville, entered the House of Commons 1782, held the secretaryship for Ireland, was home secretary 1791–94 and foreign secretary 1794–1801. He refused office in Pitt's government of 1804 because of the exclusion of Charles James →Fox.

Gresham /greʃəm/ Thomas c. 1519–1579. English merchant financier who founded and paid for the Royal Exchange and propounded *Gresham's Law*: 'bad money tends to drive out good money from circulation'.

Gresham Thomas Gresham, financial adviser and agent to Elizabeth I and founder of the Royal Exchange, revenues from which funded the establishment of Gresham College.

Gretzky Wayne 1961– . Canadian ice-hockey player, probably the best in the history of the National Hockey League (NHL). Gretzky played with the Edmonton Oilers 1979–88 and with the Los Angeles Kings from 1988. He took just 11 years to break the NHL scoring record of 1,850 goals (accumulated by Gordie Howe over 26 years) and won the Hart Memorial Trophy as the NHL's most valuable player of the season a record nine times (1980–87, 1989). By the start of the 1990–91 season he had scored 1,979 goals.

Greuze /grɜːz/ Jean Baptiste 1725–1805. French painter of sentimental narrative paintings, such as *The Bible Reading* 1755 (Louvre, Paris). His works were reproduced in engravings.

Greville /grevɪl/ Charles (Cavendish Fulke) 1794–1865. British diarist. He was Clerk of the Council in Ordinary 1821–59, an office which brought him into close contact with all the personalities of the court and of both political parties. They provided him with much of the material for his *Memoirs* 1817–60.

Greville /grevɪl/ Fulke, 1st Baron Brooke 1554–1628. English poet and courtier, friend and biographer of Philip Sidney. Greville's works, none of them published during his lifetime, include *Caelica*, a sequence of poems in different metres; *The Tragedy of Mustapha* and *The Tragedy of Alaham*, tragedies modelled on the Latin Seneca; and the *Life of Sir Philip Sidney* 1652. He has been commended for his plain style and tough political thought.

Grey /greɪ/ Beryl 1927– . British dancer. Prima ballerina with the Sadler's Wells Company

Grey Queen of England for ten days, Lady Jane Grey was known for her beauty, piety and intelligence. Tutored by John Aylmer (later bishop of London), she was proficient at languages and could read five, including Greek and Hebrew.

1942–57, she then danced internationally, and was artistic director of the London Festival Ballet 1968–79.

Her roles included the Black Queen in *Checkmate*, and Odette-Odile in *Swan Lake*.

Grey /greɪ/ Charles, 2nd Earl Grey 1764–1845. British Whig politician. He entered Parliament 1786, and in 1806 became First Lord of the Admiralty, and foreign secretary soon afterwards. As prime minister 1830–34, he carried the Great Reform Bill that reshaped the parliamentary representative system 1832 and the act abolishing slavery throughout the British Empire 1833.

Grey /greɪ/ Edward, 1st Viscount Grey of Fallodon 1862–1933. British Liberal politician, nephew of Charles Grey. As foreign secretary 1905–16 he negotiated an entente with Russia 1907, and backed France against Germany in the Agadir Incident of 1911. In 1914 he said: 'The lamps are going out all over Europe; we shall not see them lit again in our lifetime.'

Grey /greɪ/ George 1812–1898. British colonial administrator in Australia and New Zealand, born in Portugal. After several unsuccessful exploratory expeditions in Western Australia, he was appointed governor of South Australia 1840. Autocratic in attitude, he managed to bring the colony out of bankruptcy by 1844. He was lieutenant governor of New Zealand 1845–53, governor of Cape Colony, S Africa, 1854–61, and governor of New Zealand 1861–68. He then entered the New Zealand parliament and was premier 1877–79.

Grey /greɪ/ Henry, 3rd Earl Grey 1802–1894. British politician, son of Charles Grey. He served under his father as undersecretary for the colonies 1830–33, resigning because the cabinet would not back the immediate emancipation of slaves; he was secretary of war 1835–39 and colonial secretary 1846–52.

He was unique among politicians of the period in maintaining that the colonies should be governed for their own benefit, not that of Britain, and in his policy of granting self-government wherever possible. Yet he advocated convict transportation and was opposed to Gladstone's Home Rule policy.

Grey /greɪ/ Lady Jane 1537–1554. Queen of England for ten days, 9–19 July 1553, the great-granddaughter of Henry VII. She was married 1553 to Lord Guildford Dudley (died 1554), son of the Duke of →Northumberland. Edward VI was persuaded by Northumberland to set aside the claims to the throne of his sisters Mary and Elizabeth. When Edward died on 6 July 1553, Jane reluctantly accepted the crown and was subsequently proclaimed queen. Mary, although a Roman Catholic, had the support of the populace, and the Lord Mayor of London announced that she was queen 19 July. Lady Jane Grey was executed on Tower Green.

Grey /greɪ/ Zane 1875–1939. US author of Westerns, such as *Riders of the Purple Sage* 1912. He wrote more than 80 books and was primarily responsible for the creation of the Western as a literary genre.

Grieg /griːg/ Edvard Hagerup 1843–1907. Norwegian composer. Much of his music is small-scale, particularly his songs, dances, sonatas, and piano works. Among his orchestral works are the *Piano Concerto* 1869 and the incidental music for Ibsen's *Peer Gynt* 1876.

Grierson /ˈgrɪəsən/ John 1898–1972. Scottish film producer, director, and theoretician. He was a sociologist who pioneered the documentary film in Britain, viewing it as 'the creative treatment of actuality'. He directed *Drifters* 1929 and produced 1930–35 *Industrial Britain, Song of Ceylon,* and *Night Mail.* During World War II he created the National Film Board of Canada. Some of his writings were gathered in *Grierson on Documentary* 1946.

Griffith /ˈgrɪfɪθ/ D(avid) W(ark) 1875–1948. US film director, an influential figure in the development of cinema as an art. He made hundreds of 'one-reelers' 1908–13, in which he pioneered the techniques of masking, fade-out, flashback, crosscut, close-up, and long shot. After much experimentation with photography and new techniques he directed *The Birth of a Nation* 1915, about the aftermath of the Civil War, later criticized as degrading to blacks.

His other films include the epic *Intolerance* 1916, *Broken Blossoms* 1919, *Way Down East* 1920, *Orphans of the Storm* 1921, and *The Struggle* 1931. He was a cofounder of United Artists 1919. With the advent of sound, his silent films lost money, and he lived forgotten in Hollywood until his death.

Griffith-Joyner /ˌgrɪfɪθˈdʒɔɪnə/ (born Griffith) (Delorez) Florence 1959– . US track athlete who won three gold medals at the 1988 Seoul Olympics, the 100 and 200 metres and the sprint relay. Her time in the 200 metres was a world record 21.34 seconds.

Grignard /ɡriːnjɑː/ François Auguste-Victor 1871–1935. French chemist. In 1900 he discovered a series of organic compounds, the *Grignard reagents*, that found applications as some of the most versatile reagents in organic synthesis. Members of the class contain a hydrocarbon radical, magnesium, and a halogen such as chlorine. He shared the 1912 Nobel Prize for Chemistry.

Grillparzer /ˈgrɪlpɑːtsə/ Franz 1791–1872. Austrian poet and dramatist. His plays include the tragedy *Die Ahnfrau/ The Ancestress* 1817, the classical *Sappho* 1818, and the trilogy *Das goldene Vliess/ The Golden Fleece* 1821.

Born in Vienna, Grillparzer worked for the Austrian government service 1813–56. His historical tragedies *König Ottokars Glück und Ende/King Ottocar, His Rise and Fall* 1825 and *Ein treuer*

Diener seines Herrn/A True Servant of His Master 1826 both involved him with the censor. There followed his two greatest dramas, *Des Meeres und der Liebe Wellen/ The Waves of Sea and Love* 1831, returning to the Hellenic world, and *Der Traum, ein Leben/A Dream Is Life* 1834. He wrote a bitter cycle of poems *Tristia ex Ponto* 1835 after an unhappy love affair.

Grimaldi /grɪˈmɔːldi/ Joseph 1779–1837. British clown, born in London, the son of an Italian actor. He appeared on the stage at two years old. He gave his name 'Joey' to all later clowns, and excelled as 'Mother Goose' performed at Covent Garden 1806.

Grimm brothers /grɪm/ Jakob Ludwig Karl (1785–1863) and Wilhelm (1786–1859), philologists and collectors of German fairy tales such as Hansel and Gretel and Rumpelstiltskin. Joint compilers of an exhaustive dictionary of German, they saw the study of language and the collecting of folk tales as strands in a single enterprise.

Encouraged by a spirit of Romantic nationalism the brothers collected stories from friends, relatives, and villagers. *Kinder und Hausmärchen/Nursery and Household Tales* were published as successive volumes 1812, 1815, and 1822. Jakob was professor of philology at Göttingen and formulator of Grimm's law, a rule by which certain prehistoric sound changes have occurred in the consonants of Indo-European languages. His *Deutsche Grammatick/German Grammar* 1819 was the first historical treatment of the Germanic languages.

Grimmelshausen /ˈgrɪməlzˌhaʊzən/ Hans Jacob Christofel von 1625–1676. German picaresque novelist whose *Der Abenteuerliche Simplicissimus/ The Adventurous Simplicissimus* 1669 reflects his experiences in the Thirty Years' War.

Grimond /ˈgrɪmənd/ Jo(seph), Baron Grimond 1913– . British Liberal politician. As leader of the party 1956–67, he aimed at making it 'a new radical party to take the place of the Socialist Party as an alternative to Conservatism'.

Gris /griːs/ Juan 1887–1927. Spanish abstract painter, one of the earliest Cubists. He developed a distinctive geometrical style, often strongly coloured. He experimented with paper collage and made designs for Diaghilev's Ballet Russes 1922–23.

Grivas /ˈgriːvəs/ George 1898–1974. Greek Cypriot general who from 1955 led the underground group EOKA's attempts to secure the union (Greek *enosis*) of Cyprus with Greece.

Gromyko /grəˈmiːkəʊ/ Andrei 1909–1989. President of the USSR 1985–88. As ambassador to the USA from 1943, he took part in the Tehran, Yalta, and Potsdam conferences; as United Nations representative 1946–49, he exercised the Soviet veto 26 times. He was foreign minister 1957–85. It was Gromyko who formally nominated Mikhail Gorbachev as Communist Party leader 1985.

Gropius /ɡrəʊpiəs/ Walter Adolf 1883–1969. German architect who lived in the USA from 1937. He was an early exponent of the international modern style defined by glass curtain walls, cubic blocks, and unsupported corners – for example, the model factory and office building at the 1914 Cologne Werkbund exhibition. A founder-director of the Bauhaus school in Weimar 1919–28, he advocated teamwork in design and artistic standards in industrial production.

His other works include the Fagus Works (a shoe factory in Prussia) 1911 and the Harvard Graduate Center 1949–50.

The human mind is like an umbrella – it functions best when open.

Walter Gropius in the *Observer* 1965

Gross Michael 1964– . German swimmer who won gold medals at the 1984 and 1988 Olympics. He has also won gold medals at the World and European Championships.

Gross won a record six gold medals at the 1985 European Championships. He is known as 'the albatross' because of his exceptional arm span.

Grosseteste /ɡrəʊsteɪt/ Robert *c.* 1169–1253. English scholar and bishop. His prolific writings include scientific works, as well as translations of Aristotle, and commentaries on the Bible. He was a forerunner of the empirical school, being one of the earliest to suggest testing ancient Greek theories by practical experiment.

He was bishop of Lincoln from 1235 to his death, attempting to reform morals and clerical discipline, and engaging in controversy with Innocent IV over the pope's finances.

Grossmith /ɡrəʊsmɪθ/ George 1847–1912. British actor and singer. Turning from journalism to the stage, in 1877 he began a long association with the Gilbert and Sullivan operas, in which he created a number of parts. He collaborated with his brother *Weedon Grossmith* (1853–1919) on the comic novel *Diary of a Nobody* 1894.

Grosvenor family name of dukes of Westminster; seated at Eaton Hall, Cheshire, England.

Grosz /ɡrəʊs/ Georg 1893–1959. German Expressionist painter and illustrator, a founder of the Berlin group of the Dada movement 1918. Grosz excelled in savage satirical drawings criticizing the government and the military establishment. After numerous prosecutions he fled his native Berlin 1932 and became a naturalized American 1938.

Grosz /ɡrəʊs/ Károly 1930– . Hungarian Communist politician, prime minister 1987–88. As leader of the ruling Hungarian Socialist Workers' Party (HSWP) 1988–89, he sought to establish a flexible system of 'socialist pluralism'.

Grosz, a steelworker's son, was a printer and then a newspaper editor before moving to Budapest to serve as first deputy head and then head of the HSWP agitprop (agitation and propaganda) department 1968–79. He was Budapest party chief 1984–87 and briefly prime minister before succeeding János Kádár as HSWP leader in May 1988. In Oct 1989 the HSWP reconstituted itself as the Hungarian Socialist Party and Grosz was replaced as party leader by the social democrat Rezso Nyers.

Grotefend /ɡrəʊtəfent/ George Frederick 1775–1853. German scholar. Although a student of the classical rather than the oriental languages, he nevertheless solved the riddle of the wedgelike cuneiform script as used in ancient Persia: decipherment of Babylonian cuneiform followed from his work.

Grotius /ɡrəʊtiəs/ Hugo 1583–1645. Dutch jurist and politician, born in Delft. He became a lawyer, and later received political appointments. In 1618 he was arrested as a republican and sentenced to imprisonment for life. His wife contrived his escape 1620, and he settled in France, where he composed the *De Jure Belli et Pacis/On the Law of War and Peace* 1625, the foundation of international law. He was Swedish ambassador in Paris 1634–45.

Not to know something is a great part of wisdom.

Hugo Grotius *Docta Ignorantia*

Grünewald /ɡruːnəvælt/ (Mathias Gothardt/Neithardt) *c.* 1475–1528. German painter, active in Mainz, Frankfurt, and Halle. He was court painter, architect, and engineer to the archbishop of Mainz 1508–14. His few surviving paintings show an intense involvement with religious subjects.

The *Isenheim altarpiece*, 1515 (Colmar Museum, France), with its horribly tortured figure of Jesus, recalls medieval traditions.

Guardi /ɡwɑːdi/ Francesco 1712–1793. Italian painter. He produced souvenir views of his native Venice that were commercially less successful than Canaletto's but are now considered more atmospheric, with subtler use of reflected light.

Guare /ɡweə/ John 1938– . US playwright best known for his screenplay of Louis Malle's *Atlantic City* 1980. His stage plays include *House of Blue Leaves* 1971 and *Six Degrees of Separation* 1990.

Guareschi /ɡwəˈreski/ Giovanni 1909–1968. Italian author of short stories featuring the friendly feud between parish priest Don Camillo and the Communist village mayor.

Guarini /ɡwəˈriːni/ Giovanni 1924–1983. Italian architect whose intricate carved Baroque designs were produced without formal architectural training. Guarini was a secular priest of the Theatine Order, and many of his buildings are religious; for example, the Chapel of the Holy Shroud, Turin, 1667–90. His greatest similar work is the undulating Palazzo Carignano, Turin, 1679.

Guarneri /gwɑːrneəri/ family of stringed-instrument makers of Cremona, Italy. Giuseppe 'del Gesù' Guarneri (1698–1744) produced the finest models.

Guderian /gʊˈdeəriən/ Heinz 1888–1954. German general in World War II. He created the Panzer (German 'armour') divisions that formed the ground spearhead of Hitler's *Blitzkrieg* attack strategy, achieving a significant breakthrough at Sedan in Ardennes, France 1940, and leading the advance to Moscow 1941.

Guercino /gweəˈtʃiːnəʊ/ (Giovanni Francesco Barbieri) 1590–1666. Italian Baroque painter, active chiefly in Rome. In his ceiling painting of *Aurora* 1621–23 (Villa Ludovisi, Rome), the chariot-borne figure of dawn rides across the heavens, and the architectural framework is imitated in the painting, giving the illusion that the ceiling opens into the sky.

Guercino's use of dramatic lighting recalls →Caravaggio, but his brighter colours reflect a contrasting mood. His later works, produced when he had retired from Rome to Bologna, are closer in style to Guido →Reni.

Guérin /geəræn/ Camille 1872–1961. French bacteriologist who, with →Calmette, developed the *bacille* Calmette-Guérin (BCG) vaccine for tuberculosis.

Guesdes /ged/ Jules 1845–1922. French socialist leader from the 1880s who espoused Marxism and revolutionary change. His movement, the Partie Ouvrier Français (French Workers' Party), was eventually incorporated in the foundation of the SFIO (Section Française de l'International Ouvrière/French Section of International Labour) 1905.

Guest /gest/ Edgar Albert 1881–1959. US journalist and poet. From 1900 he wrote 'Breakfast Table Chat' for the *Detroit Free Press*. The column combined light verse and folksy wisdom and was later nationally syndicated. Guest's best-selling collections of verse include *A Heap o' Livin'* 1916 and *Harbor Lights of Home* 1928.

Born in Birmingham, England, Guest came to America 1891 with his parents, settling in Detroit, Michigan, leaving school at an early age. From 1938 to 1942 he was the host of a popular weekly radio programme.

Guevara /gɪˈvɑːrə/ 'Che' Ernesto 1928–1967. Latin American revolutionary. He was born in Argentina and trained there as a doctor, but left his homeland 1953 because of his opposition to the right-wing president Perón. In effecting the Cuban revolution of 1959, he was second only to

Castro and Castro's brother Raúl. In 1965 he went to the Congo to fight against white mercenaries, and then to Bolivia, where he was killed in an unsuccessful attempt to lead a peasant rising. He was an orthodox Marxist and renowned for his guerrilla techniques.

Guido /giːdəʊ/ Reni. Italian painter; see →Reni.

Guillaume /giːəʊm/ Charles 1861–1938. Swiss physicist who studied measurement and alloy development. He discovered a nickel–steel alloy, invar, which showed negligible expansion with rising temperatures. He was awarded the Nobel Prize for Physics 1920.

As the son of a clockmaker, Guillaume came early in life to appreciate the value of precision in measurement. He spent most of his life at the International Bureau of Weights and Measures in Sèvres, France, which established the standards for the metre, litre, and kilogram.

Guinness /gɪnɪs/ Alec 1914– . English actor of stage and screen. His films include *Kind Hearts and Coronets* 1949 (in which he played eight parts), *The Bridge on the River Kwai* 1957 (Academy Award), and *Star Wars* 1977.

Guinness joined the Old Vic 1936. A subtle actor, he played the enigmatic spymaster in TV adaptations of John Le Carré's *Tinker, Tailor, Soldier, Spy* 1979 and *Smiley's People* 1981.

An actor is totally vulnerable ... from head to toe, his total personality is exposed to critical judgement – his intellect, his bearing, his diction, his appearance. In short, his ego.

Alec Guinness
in *New York Times Magazine* May 1964

Guise /gwiːz/ Francis, 2nd Duke of Guise 1519–1563. French soldier and politician. He led the French victory over Germany at Metz 1552 and captured Calais from the English 1558. Along with his brother *Charles* (1527–1574), he was powerful in the government of France during the reign of Francis II. He was assassinated attempting to crush the Huguenots.

Guise /gwiːz/ Henri, 3rd Duke of Guise 1550–1588. French noble who persecuted the Huguenots and was partly responsible for the Massacre of St Bartholomew 1572. He was assassinated.

Guizot /giːˈzəʊ/ François Pierre Guillaume 1787–1874. French politician and historian, professor of modern history at the Sorbonne, Paris 1812–30. He wrote histories of French and European culture and became prime minister 1847. His resistance to all reforms led to the revolution of 1848.

Guizot French historian and statesman François Guizot who became Professor of Modern History at the Sorbonne 1812. A liberal in his earlier career, he moved to the right during his years in the Chamber and his repressive policies and denial of press freedom contributed to the revolution of 1848.

Gullit /ˈgʊlɪt/ Ruud 1962– . Dutch international footballer who was captain when the Netherlands captured the European Championship 1988. After playing in the Netherlands with Haarlem, Feyenoord, and PSV Eindhoven, he moved to AC Milan 1987 for a transfer fee of £5.5 million.

Gummer /ˈgʌmə/ John Selwyn 1939– . British Conservative politician, secretary of state for agriculture from 1989. He was minister of state for employment 1983–84, paymaster general 1984–85, minister for agriculture 1985–89, and chair of the party 1983–85.

Gunter /ˈgʌntə(r)/ Edmund 1581–1626. English mathematician who became professor of astronomy at Gresham College, London 1619. He is reputed to have invented a number of surveying instruments as well as the trigonometrical terms 'cosine' and 'cotangent'.

Gurdjieff /ˈgɜːdʒief/ George Ivanovitch 1877–1949. Russian occultist and mystic who influenced the modern human-potential movement. His famous text is *Meetings with Remarkable Men* (English translation 1963). The mystic →Ouspensky was a disciple who expanded his ideas.

After years of wandering in central Asia, in 1912 Gurdjieff founded in Moscow the Institute for the Harmonious Development of Man, based on a system of raising consciousness (involving learning, group movement, manual labour, dance, and a minimum of sleep) known as the Fourth Way. After the 1917 Revolution he established similar schools in parts of Europe.

Gustaf or Gustavus /ˈgʊstɑːf/ six kings of Sweden, including:

Gustaf V 1858–1950. King of Sweden from 1907, when he succeeded his father Oscar II. He married Princess Victoria, daughter of the Grand Duke of Baden 1881, thus uniting the reigning Bernadotte dynasty with the former royal house of Vasa.

Gustaf VI 1882–1973. King of Sweden from 1950, when he succeeded his father Gustaf V. He was an archaeologist and expert on Chinese art. He was succeeded by his grandson →Carl XVI Gustaf.

His first wife was Princess Margaret of Connacht (1882–1920), and in 1923 he married Lady Louise Mountbatten (1889–1965), sister of the Earl of Mountbatten of Burma.

Gustavus I king of Sweden, better known as →Gustavus Vasa.

Gustavus II king of Sweden, better known as →Gustavus Adolphus.

Gustavus Adolphus /gʊˈstɑːvəs əˈdɒlfəs/ (Gustavus II) 1594–1632. King of Sweden from 1611, when he succeeded his father Charles IX. He waged successful wars with Denmark, Russia, and Poland, and in the Thirty Years' War became a champion of the Protestant cause. Landing in Germany 1630, he defeated the German general Wallenstein at Lützen, SW of Leipzig 6 Nov 1632, but was killed in the battle. He was known as the 'Lion of the North'.

Gustavus Vasa /ˈvɑːsə/ (Gustavus I) 1496–1560. King of Sweden from 1523, when he was elected after leading the Swedish revolt against Danish rule. He united and pacified the country and established Lutheranism as the state religion.

Gutenberg /ˈguːtnbɜːg/ Johann *c.* 1400–1468. German printer, the inventor of printing from movable metal type, based on the Chinese woodblock-type method (although Laurens Janszoon →Coster has a rival claim).

Gutenberg began work on the process in the 1440s and in 1450 set up a printing business in Mainz with Johann Fust (*c.* 1400–1466) as a backer. By 1455 he had produced the first printed Bible (known as the Gutenberg Bible). Fust seized the press for nonpayment of the loan, but Gutenberg is believed to have gone on to print the Mazarin and Bamberg bibles.

Guthrie /ˈgʌθri/ Edwin R(ay) 1886–1959. US behaviourist who attempted to develop a theory of learning that was independent of the traditional principles of reward or reinforcement. His ideas served as a basis for later statistical models.

Guthrie /ˈgʌθri/ Tyrone 1900–1971. British theatre director, notable for his experimental approach. Administrator of the Old Vic and Sadler's Wells theatres 1939–45, he helped found the Ontario (Stratford) Shakespeare Festival 1953 and the Minneapolis theatre now named after him.

Gwyn English courtesan and actress Nell Gwyn. The liveliest and most popular of Charles II's mistresses, she was known as 'pretty, witty Nell'. She is said to have persuaded the king to found Chelsea Hospital for veteran soldiers.

Guthrie /gʌθri/ Woody (Woodrow Wilson) 1912–1967. US folk singer and songwriter whose left-wing protest songs, 'dustbowl ballads', and 'talking blues' influenced, among others, Bob Dylan; they include 'Deportees', 'Hard Travelin'', and 'This Land Is Your Land'.

Guys /gwiːs/ Constantin 1805–1892. French illustrator, remembered for his witty drawings of Paris life during the Second Empire. He was with the English poet →Byron at Missolonghi, Greeece, and made sketches of the Crimean War for the *Illustrated London News*.

Guzmán Blanco /guːsˈmæn ˈblæŋkəʊ/ Antonio 1829–1899. Venezuelan dictator and military leader (*caudillo*), who seized power 1870 and remained absolute ruler until 1889. He modernized Caracas to become the political capital; committed resources to education, communications, and agriculture; and encouraged foreign trade.

Gwyn /gwɪn/ Nell (Eleanor) 1651–1687. English comedy actress from 1665, formerly an orange-seller at Drury Lane Theatre, London. The poet Dryden wrote parts for her, and from 1669 she was the mistress of Charles II.

Gysi /giːzi/ Gregor 1948– . German politician, elected leader of the Communist Party Dec 1989 following the resignation of Egon →Krenz. A lawyer, Gysi had acted as defence counsel for dissidents during the 1960s.

Haakon /ˈhɔːkɒn/ seven kings of Norway, including:

Haakon I *the Good* c.– 915–961. King of Norway from about 935. The son of Harald Hárfagri ('Finehair') (c. 850–930), king of Norway, he was raised in England. He seized the Norwegian throne and tried unsuccessfully to introduce Christianity there. His capital was at Trondheim.

Haakon IV 1204–1263. King of Norway from 1217, the son of Haakon III. Under his rule, Norway flourished both militarily and culturally; he took control of the Faroe Islands, Greenland 1261, and Iceland 1262–64. His court was famed throughout N Europe.

Haakon VII 1872–1957. King of Norway from 1905. Born Prince Charles, the second son of Frederick VIII of Denmark, he was elected king of Norway on separation from Sweden, and in 1906 he took the name Haakon. In World War II he carried on the resistance from Britain during the Nazi occupation of his country. He returned 1945.

Haber /ˈhɑːbə/ Fritz 1868–1934. German chemist whose conversion of atmospheric nitrogen to ammonia opened the way for the synthetic fertilizer industry. His study of the combustion of hydrocarbons led to the commercial 'cracking' or fractional distillation of natural oil (petroleum) into its components (for example, diesel, petrol, and paraffin). In electrochemistry, he was the first to demonstrate that oxidation and reduction take place at the electrodes; from this he developed a general electrochemical theory.

In World War I he worked on poison gas and devised gas masks, hence there were protests against his Nobel prize 1918.

Habsburg or *Hapsburg* European royal family, former imperial house of Austria– Hungary. A Hapsburg, Rudolf I, became king of Germany 1273 and began the family's control of Austria and Styria. They acquired a series of lands and titles, including that of Holy Roman emperor which they held 1273–91, 1298–1308, 1438–1740, and 1745–1806. The Hapsburgs reached the zenith of their power under the emperor Charles V (1519–1556) who divided his lands, creating an Austrian Habsburg line (which ruled until 1918) and a Spanish line (which ruled to 1700).

The name comes from the family castle in Aargau, Switzerland.

Hackman /ˈhækmən/ Gene 1931– . US actor. He became a star as 'Popeye' Doyle in *The French Connection* 1971 and continued to play major combative roles in such films as *The Conversation* 1974, *The French Connection II* 1975, and *Mississippi Burning* 1988.

Hadlee /ˈhædli/ Richard John 1951– . New Zealand cricketer. In 1987 he surpassed Ian Botham's world record of 373 wickets in Test cricket and went on to set the record at 431 wickets. He played for Canterbury in New Zealand and Nottinghamshire in England, and retired from international cricket 1990.

Hadlee played first-class cricket in Australia for Tasmania. His father *Walter Arnold Hadlee* also played Test cricket for New Zealand, as did his brother *Dayle Robert Hadlee*.

Hadrian /ˈheɪdriən/ AD 76–138. Roman emperor from 117. Born in Spain, he was adopted by his relative, the emperor Trajan, whom he succeeded. He abandoned Trajan's conquests in Mesopotamia and adopted a defensive policy, which included the building of Hadrian's Wall in Britain.

Haeckel /ˈhekəl/ Ernst Heinrich 1834–1919. German scientist and philosopher. His theory of 'recapitulation', expressed as 'ontogeny repeats phylogeny' (or that embryonic stages represent past stages in the organism's evolution), has been superseded, but it stimulated research in embryology.

Born at Potsdam, he came professor of zoology at Jena 1865. He coined the term 'ecology', and is the author of bestselling general scientific works such as *The Riddles of the Universe*.

Hâfiz /ˈhɑːfɪz/ Shams al-Din Muhammad c. 1326–1390. Persian lyric poet who was born in Shiraz and taught in a Dervish college there. His *Diwan*, a collection of short odes, extols the pleasures of life and satirizes his fellow Dervishes.

There is an ambush everywhere from the army of accidents; therefore the rider of life runs with loosened reins.

Hâfiz *Diwan* 14th century

Hagen /ˈheɪgən/ Walter Charles 1892–1969. US golfer, a flamboyant character. He won 11 major championships 1914–29. An exponent of the match-play game, he won the US PGA Championship five times, four in succession.

Hagenbeck /ˈhɑːgənbek/ Carl 1844–1913. German zoo proprietor. In 1907 he founded Hagenbeck's Zoo, near his native Hamburg. He was a pioneer in the display of animals against a natural setting, rather than in restrictive cages.

Haggard /ˈhægəd/ H(enry) Rider 1856–1925. English novelist. He used his experience in the South African colonial service in his romantic adventure tales, including *King Solomon's Mines* 1885 and *She* 1887.

Hagler Marvin 1954– . US boxer who was the undisputed world middleweight champion from 1980 to 1987. He won 13 of his 15 World Title fights, losing only to Sugar Ray Leonard.

Hahn /hɑːn/ Kurt 1886–1974. German educationist. He was the founder of Salem School in Germany. After his expulsion by Hitler, he founded Gordonstoun School in Scotland and was its headmaster 1934–53. He cofounded the Atlantic College project 1960, and was associated with the Outward Bound Trust and the Duke of Edinburgh Award scheme.

Hahn /hɑːn/ Otto 1879–1968. German physical chemist who discovered nuclear fission. In 1938 with Fritz Strassmann (1902–1980), he discovered that uranium nuclei split when bombarded with neutrons, which led to the development of the atom bomb. He was awarded the Nobel Prize for Chemistry 1944.

He worked with Ernest Rutherford and William Ramsay, and became director of the Kaiser Wilhelm Institute for Chemistry 1928.

Haig /heɪg/ Alexander (Meigs) 1924– . US general and Republican politician. He became President Nixon's White House Chief of Staff at the height of the Watergate scandal, was NATO commander 1974–79, and secretary of state to President Reagan 1981–82.

Haig /heɪg/ Douglas, 1st Earl Haig 1861–1928. British army officer, commander in chief in World War I. His Somme offensive in France in the summer of 1916 made considerable advances only at enormous cost to human life, and his Passchendaele offensive in Belgium from July to Nov 1917 achieved little at a similar loss. He was created field marshal 1917 and, after retiring, became first president of the British Legion 1921.

A national hero at the time of his funeral, Haig's reputation began to fall after Lloyd George's memoirs depicted him as treating soldiers' lives with disdain, while remaining far from battle himself.

Haile Selassie /ˈhaɪli sɪˈlæsi/ Ras (Prince) Tafari ('the Lion of Judah') 1892–1975. Emperor of Ethiopia 1930–74. He pleaded unsuccessfully to the League of Nations against Italian conquest of his country 1935–36, and lived in the UK until his restoration 1941. He was deposed by a military

coup 1974 and died in captivity the following year. Followers of the Rastafarian religion believe that he was the Messiah, the incarnation of God (Jah).

Hailsham /ˈheɪlʃəm/ Quintin Hogg, Baron Hailsham of St Marylebone 1907– . British lawyer and Conservative politician. The 2nd Viscount Hailsham, he renounced the title in 1963 to re-enter the House of Commons, and was then able to contest the Conservative Party leadership elections, but took a life peerage 1970 on his appointment as Lord Chancellor 1970–74. He was Lord Chancellor again 1979–87.

The moment politics becomes dull democracy is in danger.

Lord Hailsham 1966

Hailwood /ˈheɪlwʊd/ Mike (Stanley Michael Bailey) 1940–1981. English motorcyclist. Between 1961 and 1967 he won nine world titles and a record 14 titles at the Isle of Man TT races between 1961 and 1979.

Haitink Bernard 1929– . Dutch conductor. He was chief conductor of the Concertgebouw Orchestra, Amsterdam, 1959–86; of the London Philharmonic Orchestra 1967–78; and of the Royal Opera House, Covent Garden, London, from 1983, becoming its music director 1986.

Hakluyt /ˈhækluːt/ Richard 1553–1616. English geographer whose chief work is *The Principal Navigations, Voyages and Discoveries of the English Nation* 1598–1600. He was assisted by Sir Walter Raleigh.

He lectured on cartography at Oxford, became geographical adviser to the East India Company, and was an original member of the Virginia Company.

The *Hakluyt Society*, established 1846, published later accounts of exploration.

Halas /ˈhæləs/ George Stanley 1895–1983. US athlete and sports promoter. He was founder of the Chicago Bears of the National Football League and was an active player until 1929. He acted as coach until retirement 1967, introducing the T-formation and giving special emphasis to the passing offence.

Born in Chicago, USA, and educated at the University of Illinois, Halas was an exceptional athlete and in 1919 briefly played professional baseball for the New York Yankees. From 1921 he devoted himself to professional American football.

He became a charter member of the Football Hall of Fame 1963.

Haldane /ˈhɔːldeɪn/ J(ohn) B(urdon) S(anderson) 1892–1964. English scientist and writer. A geneticist, Haldane was better known as a popular science writer of such books as *The Causes of Evolution* 1933 and *New Paths in Genetics* 1941.

Haldane /hɔːldeɪn/ Richard Burdon, Viscount Haldane 1856–1928. British Liberal politician. As secretary for war 1905–12, he sponsored the army reforms that established an expeditionary force, backed by a territorial army and under the unified control of an imperial general staff. He was Lord Chancellor 1912–15 and in the Labour government of 1924. His writings on German philosophy led to accusations of his having pro-German sympathies.

Hale /heɪl/ George Ellery 1868–1938. US astronomer who made pioneer studies of the Sun and founded three major observatories. In 1889 he invented the spectroheliograph, a device for photographing the Sun at particular wavelengths. In 1917 he established on Mount Wilson, California, a 2.5-m/100-in reflector, the world's largest telescope until superseded 1948 by the 5-m/200-in reflector on Mount Palomar, which Hale had planned just before he died.

In 1897 he founded the Yerkes Observatory in Wisconsin, with the largest refractor, 102 cm/40 in, ever built at that time.

Hale /heɪl/ Nathan 1755–1776. US nationalist hanged by the British as a spy in the American Revolution. Reputedly his final words were 'I only regret that I have but one life to lose for my country'.

Hale /heɪl/ Sarah Josepha Buell 1788–1879. US poet, author of 'Mary had a Little Lamb' 1830.

Hales /heɪlz/ Stephen 1677–1761. English priest and scientist who gave accurate accounts of water movement in plants. His work laid emphasis on measurement and experimentation.

Hales demonstrated that plants absorb air, and that some part of that air is involved in their nutrition. He also measured plant growth and water loss, relating this to the upward movement of water from plants to leaves (transpiration).

Halévy /ˌæleɪˈviː/ Ludovic 1834–1908. French novelist and librettist. He collaborated with Hector Crémieux in the libretto for Offenbach's *Orpheus in the Underworld*; and with Henri Meilhac on librettos for Offenbach's *La Belle Hélène* and *La Vie Parisienne*, as well as for Bizet's *Carmen*.

Haley /heɪli/ Bill 1927–1981. US pioneer of rock and roll who was originally a western-swing musician. His songs 'Rock Around the Clock' 1954 (recorded with his group the Comets and featured in the 1955 film *Blackboard Jungle*) and 'Shake, Rattle and Roll' 1955 became anthems of the early rock-and-roll era.

Halifax /hælɪfæks/ Charles Montagu, Earl of Halifax 1661–1715. British financier. Appointed commissioner of the Treasury 1692, he raised money for the French war by instituting the National Debt and in 1694 carried out William Paterson's plan for a national bank (the Bank of England) and became chancellor of the Exchequer.

Halifax /hælɪfæks/ Edward Frederick Lindley Wood, Earl of Halifax 1881–1959. British Conservative politician, viceroy of India 1926–31. As foreign secretary 1938–40 he was associated with Chamberlain's 'appeasement' policy. He received an earldom 1944 for services to the Allied cause while ambassador to the USA 1941–46.

Halifax /hælɪfæks/ George Savile, 1st Marquess of Halifax 1633–1695. English politician. He entered Parliament 1660, and was raised to the peerage by Charles II, by whom he was also later dismissed. He strove to steer a middle course between extremists, and became known as 'the Trimmer'. He played a prominent part in the revolution of 1688.

Hall /hɔːl/ (Marguerite) Radclyffe 1883–1943. English novelist. *The Well of Loneliness* 1928 brought her notoriety because of its lesbian theme. Its review in the *Sunday Express* newspaper stated: 'I had rather give a healthy boy or girl a phial of prussic acid than this novel'. Her other works include the novel *Adam's Bread* 1926 and four volumes of poetry.

Hall /hɔːl/ Charles 1863–1914. US chemist who developed a process for the commercial production of aluminium 1886.

He found that when aluminium was mixed with cryolite (sodium aluminium fluoride), its melting point was lowered and electrolysis became commercially viable. It had previously been as costly as gold.

Hall Peter (Reginald Frederick) 1930– . English theatre, opera, and film director. He was director of the Royal Shakespeare Theatre in Stratford-on-Avon 1960–68 and developed the Royal Shakespeare Company 1968–73 until appointed director of the National Theatre 1973–88, succeeding Laurence Olivier. He founded the Peter Hall Company 1988.

Hall's stage productions include *Waiting for Godot* 1955, *The Wars of the Roses* 1963, *The Homecoming* stage 1967 and film 1973, *The Oresteia* 1981, and *Orpheus Descending* 1988. He was appointed artistic director of opera at Glyndebourne 1984, with productions of *Carmen* 1985 and *Albert Herring* 1985–86.

Hallam /hæləm/ Henry 1777–1859. British historian. He was called to the Bar, but a private fortune enabled him to devote himself to historical study from 1812 and his *Constitutional History of England* 1827 established his reputation.

Haller /hælə/ Albrecht von 1708–1777. Swiss physician and scientist, founder of neurology. He studied the muscles and nerves, and concluded that nerves provide the stimulus that triggers muscle contraction. He also showed that it is the nerves, not muscle or skin, that receive sensation.

Halley /hæli/ Edmond 1656–1742. English scientist. In 1682 he observed the comet named after him, predicting that it would return 1759.

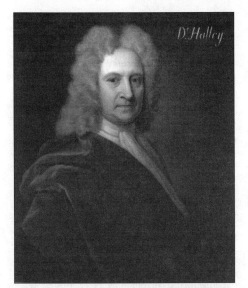

Halley Best known for his contributions to cometary astronomy, English scientist Edmond Halley also published studies on magnetic deviation, trade winds, and monsoons. At the age of 20, Halley went to St Helena to make the first catalogue of stars in the southern hemisphere.

Halley's other astronomical achievements include the discovery that stars have their own proper motion. He was a pioneer geophysicist and meteorologist and worked in many other fields including mathematics. He became the second Astronomer Royal 1720. He was a friend of Isaac →Newton, whose *Principia* he financed.

Hals /hæls/ Frans *c.* 1581–1666. Flemish-born painter of lively portraits, such as the *Laughing Cavalier* 1624 (Wallace Collection, London), and large groups of military companies, governors of charities, and others (many examples in the Frans Hals Museum, Haarlem, the Netherlands). In the 1620s he experimented with genre (domestic) scenes.

Halsey /ˈhɔːlsi/ William Frederick 1882–1959. US admiral, known as 'Bull'. He was the commander of the Third Fleet in the S Pacific from 1942 during World War II. The Japanese signed the surrender document ending World War II on his flagship, the battleship *Missouri.*

Halston /ˈhɔːlstən/ trade name of Roy Halston Frowick 1932–1990. US fashion designer who showed his first collection 1969 and created a vogue for easy-to-wear clothes that emphasized the body but left it free to move. In 1973 he diversified into loungewear, luggage, and cosmetics.

Hamaguchi /ˌhæməˈɡuːtʃi/ Hamaguchi Osachi, also known as *Hamaguchi Yuko* 1870–1931. Japanese politician and prime minister 1929–30. His policies created social unrest and alienated

military interests. His acceptance of the terms of the London Naval Agreement 1930 was also unpopular. Shot by an assassin Nov 1930, he died of his wounds nine months later.

Hamilcar Barca /hæˈmɪlkɑː ˈbɑːkə/ *c.* 270–228 BC. Carthaginian general, father of →Hannibal. From 247 to 241 BC he harassed the Romans in Italy and then led an expedition to Spain, where he died in battle.

Hamilton /ˈhæməltən/ family name of Dukes of Abercorn; seated at Barons Court, Co Tyrone; the 3rd duke was the great grandfather of Diana, Princess of Wales.

Hamilton /ˈhæməltən/ Alexander 1757–1804. US politician who influenced the adoption of a constitution with a strong central government and was the first secretary of the Treasury 1789–95. He led the Federalist Party, and incurred the bitter hatred of Aaron →Burr when he voted against Burr and in favour of Thomas Jefferson for the presidency 1801. Challenged to a duel by Burr, Hamilton was wounded and died the next day.

The interest of the State is in intimate connection with those of the rich individuals belonging to it.

Alexander Hamilton letter 1781

Hamilton /ˈhæməltən/ Edith 1867–1963. German-born US educator and classical scholar, best remembered as a collector and translator of ancient myths. Her anthologies *Mythology* 1942 and *The Great Age of Greek Literature* 1943 became standard textbooks. Also among her most important works are *The Greek Way* 1930 and *The Roman Way* 1932.

Born in Dresden, Germany, and raised in Fort Wayne, Indiana, USA, Hamilton was headmistress of the Bryn Mawr School in Baltimore 1896–1922, later devoting her energies to the study of Greek and Roman civilization.

Hamilton /ˈhæməltən/ Emma (born Amy Lyon) 1765–1815. English courtesan. In 1782 she became the mistress of Charles →Greville and in 1786 of his uncle Sir William Hamilton (1730–1803), the British envoy to the court of Naples, who married her 1791. After Admiral →Nelson's return from the Nile 1798 during the Napoleonic Wars, she became his mistress and their daughter, Horatia, was born 1801.

Hamilton /ˈhæməltən/ Iain Ellis 1922– . Scottish composer. Intensely emotional and harmonically rich, his works include striking viola and cello sonatas; the ballet *Clerk Saunders* 1951; the operas *Pharsalia* 1968 and *The Royal Hunt of the Sun* 1967–69, which renounced melody for inventive chordal formations; and symphonies.

Hamilton /ˈhæməltən/ Ian (Standish Monteith) 1853–1947. Scottish general. He was Chief of Staff and deputy to Lord Kitchener, commander in chief in the second South African War. In 1915 he directed the land operations in Gallipoli, Turkey.

Hamilton /ˈhæməltən/ James, 1st Duke of Hamilton 1606–1649. Scottish adviser to Charles I. He led an army against the Covenanters (supporters of the National Covenant 1638 to establish Presbyterianism) 1639 and subsequently took part in the negotiations between Charles and the Scots. In the second Civil War he led the Scottish invasion of England, but was captured at Preston and executed.

Hamilton /ˈhæməltən/ Richard 1922– . English artist, a pioneer of Pop art. His collage *Just What Is It That Makes Today's Homes So Different, So Appealing?* 1956 (Kunsthalle, Tübingen, Germany) is often cited as the first Pop art work.

Its 1950s interior, inhabited by the bodybuilder Charles Atlas and a pin-up, is typically humorous, concerned with popular culture and contemporary kitsch. His series *Swinging London 67* 1967 comments on the prosecution for drugs of his art dealer Robert Fraser and the singer Mick Jagger.

Hamilton /ˈhæməltən/ William 1730–1803. British diplomat, envoy to the court of Naples 1764–1800, whose collection of Greek vases was bought by the British Museum.

Hamilton /ˈhæməltən/ William D 1936– . New Zealand biologist. By developing the concept of inclusive fitness, he was able to solve the theoretical problem of explaining altruism in animal behaviour in terms of neo-Darwinism.

Hamilton /ˈhæməltən/ William Rowan 1805–1865. Irish mathematician whose formulation of Isaac Newton's dynamics proved adaptable to quantum theory, and whose 'quarternion' theory was a forerunner of the branch of mathematics known as vector analysis.

Hamlin /ˈhæmlɪn/ Hannibal 1809–1891. US political leader and vice-president 1861–65. Originally a Democrat, he served in the US House of Representatives 1843–47 and the US Senate 1848–61. Opposed to slavery, he joined the Republican Party 1856. He served as vice-president in Lincoln's first term. Returning to the Senate as a radical Republican 1868–80, he later served as US minister to Spain 1881–82.

Born in Paris Hill, Maine, USA, Hamlin worked at a succession of jobs before studying law and being admitted to the bar 1833. He served in the state legislature 1836–41 and was briefly governor of Maine 1857.

Hammarskjöld /ˈhæməʃʊld/ Dag 1905–1961. Swedish secretary general of the United Nations 1953–61. He opposed Britain over the Suez Crisis 1956. His attempts to solve the problem of the Congo (now Zaire), where he was killed in a plane crash, were criticized by the USSR. He was awarded the Nobel Peace Prize 1961.

The only kind of dignity which is genuine is that which is not diminished by the indifference of others.

Dag Hammarskjöld *Markings* 1964

Hammer /ˈhæmə/ Armand 1898–1990. US entrepreneur, one of the most remarkable business figures of the 20th century. A pioneer in trading with the USSR from 1921, he later acted as a political mediator. He was chair of the US oil company Occidental Petroleum until his death, and was also an expert on art.

Hammer visited the USSR 1921 and acquired the first private concession awarded by the Soviet government: an asbestos mine. He built up fortunes in several business areas, including the import-export business. He was renowned for his dynamism, his championing of East–West relations, and his many philanthropic and cultural activities.

Having received his medical degree from Columbia University, Hammer wanted to use his skills to aid victims of starvation and typhus in the Ural Mountains. While in the USSR, he developed the idea of importing food from the US grain surplus in exchange for luxury goods. Lenin approved, and Hammer established a large import-export business. During the next quarter of a century, he made a fortune in, among other things, livestock feed and cattle. In 1956, he and his wife each put $50,000 into a struggling oil company, Occidental Petroleum, which became one of America's largest.

Hammer /ˈhæmə/ (formerly *M C Hammer*) Stage name of Stanley Kirk Burrell 1963– . US rap vocalist and songwriter. His pop-oriented rap style and exuberant dancing gave him a wide appeal, especially in the video-based market, and his second LP, *Please Hammer Don't Hurt 'Em* 1990, sold 13 million copies in one year.

A born-again Christian who plugs Pepsi-Cola, Hammer is perceived as an all-round family entertainer, the first crossover rapper; his lyrics are intended to be inoffensive and he tours with an elaborate stage show.

Hammerstein Oscar, II 1895–1960. Lyricist and librettist who collaborated with Richard →Rodgers on some of the best-known American musicals, including *Oklahoma* 1943 (Pulitzer Prize), *Carousel* 1945, *South Pacific* 1949 (Pulitzer Prize), *The King and I* 1951, and *The Sound of Music* 1959.

Grandson of opera impresario Oscar Hammerstein, he earned his first successes with *Rose Marie* 1924, music by Rudolf Friml (1879–1972); *Desert Song* 1926, music by Sigmund Romberg (1887–1951); and *Show Boat* 1927, music by

Jerome Kern (1885–1945). *Show Boat* represented a major step forward in musical theatre in terms of integrated plot and character. After a moderate success at film scoring, he joined Rodgers and launched their 16-year monumentally successful collaboration.

Hammett /ˈhæmɪt/ (Samuel) Dashiell 1894–1961. US crime novelist. His works, *The Maltese Falcon* 1930, *The Glass Key* 1931, and the *The Thin Man* 1932, introduced the 'hard-boiled' detective character into fiction.

Hammett was a former Pinkerton detective agent. In 1951 he was imprisoned for contempt of court for refusing to testify during the McCarthy era of anticommunist witch hunts. He lived with the playwright Lillian →Hellman for the latter half of his life.

Hammond /ˈhæmənd/ Joan 1912– . Australian soprano, born in New Zealand. She is known in oratorio and opera, for example, *Madame Butterfly*, *Tosca*, and *Martha*.

Hamnett /ˈhæmnɪt/ Katharine 1948– . British fashion designer with her own business from 1979. An innovative designer, she is particularly popular in the UK and Italy. Her oversized T-shirts promoting peace and environmental campaigns attracted attention 1984. She produces well-cut, inexpensive designs for men and women, predominantly in natural fabrics.

Hampden /ˈhæmpdən/ John 1594–1643. English politician. His refusal in 1636 to pay ship money, a compulsory tax levied to support the navy, made him a national figure. In the Short and Long Parliaments he proved himself a skilful debater and parliamentary strategist. King Charles's attempt to arrest him and four other leading MPs made the Civil War inevitable. He raised his own regiment on the outbreak of hostilities, and on 18 June 1643 was mortally wounded at the skirmish of Chalgrove Field in Oxfordshire.

Hampton /ˈhæmptən/ Lionel 1909– . US jazz musician, a top band leader of the 1940s and 1950s. Originally a drummer, Hampton introduced the vibraphone, an electronically vibrated percussion instrument, to jazz music. With the Benny →Goodman band from 1936, he fronted his own big band 1941–65 and subsequently led small groups.

Hampton /ˈhæmptən/ Wade 1818–1902. US politician and Confederate military leader. During the American Civil War 1861–65, he was appointed brigadier general in the cavalry 1862 and commander of the entire Confederate cavalry corps 1864. After the end of the war 1865 he returned to South Carolina, serving as governor 1876–79 and US senator 1879–91.

Born in Charleston, South Carolina, Hampton was educated at Carolina College and later administered his family's plantation. At the outbreak of the Civil War, he raised and led a regiment of Confederate volunteers.

Hamsun /ˈhæmsuːm/ Knut 1859–1952. Norwegian novelist whose first novel *Sult/Hunger* 1890 was largely autobiographical. Other works include *Pan* 1894 and *The Growth of the Soil* 1917, which won him a Nobel prize 1920. His hatred of capitalism made him sympathize with Nazism, and he was fined in 1946 for collaboration.

Hanbury-Tenison /ˈhænbəri ˈtenɪsən/ (Airling) Robin 1936– . Irish adventurer, explorer, and writer who made the first land crossing of South America at its widest point 1958. He explored the southern Sahara intermittently during 1962–66, and in South America sailed in a small boat from the Orinoco River to Buenos Aires 1964–65. After expeditions to Ecuador, Brazil, and Venezuela, he rode across France 1984 and along the Great Wall of China 1986. In 1969 he became chair of Survival International, an organization campaigning for the rights of threatened tribal peoples.

Hancock /ˈhænkɒk/ John 1737–1793. US politician and a leader of the American Revolution. As president of the Continental Congress 1775–77, he was the first to sign the Declaration of Independence 1776. Because he signed it in a large, bold hand (in popular belief, so that it would be big enough for George III to see), his name became a colloquial term for a signature in the USA. He coveted command of the Continental Army, deeply resenting the selection of George →Washington. He was governor of Massachusetts 1780–85 and 1787–93.

Hancock /ˈhænkɒk/ Tony (Anthony John) 1924–1968. British lugubrious comedian on radio and television. *Hancock's Half Hour* from 1954 showed him famously at odds with everyday life.

Hand /hænd/ Learned Billings 1872–1961. US jurist. He became federal district judge under President Taft 1909 and was appointed to the Second Circuit Court of Appeals by President Coolidge 1924. He served as chief judge of that court 1939–1951, handing down opinions in landmark copyright, antitrust, and the constitutional First Amendment cases.

Born in Albany, New York, USA, and educated at Harvard University, Hand received his law degree 1896. Although never appointed to the US Supreme Court, Hand was considered a leading jurist of his day. A collection of his essays, *The Spirit of Liberty*, was published 1952.

Handel /ˈhændl/ Georg Friedrich 1685–1759. German composer who became a British subject 1726. His first opera, *Almira*, was performed in Hamburg 1705. In 1710 he was appointed Kapellmeister to the elector of Hanover (the future George I of England). In 1712 he settled in England, where he established his popularity with such works as the *Water Music* 1717 (written for George I). His great choral works include the *Messiah* 1742 and the later oratorios *Samson* 1743, *Belshazzar* 1745, *Judas Maccabaeus* 1747, and *Jephtha* 1752.

Handel Portrait by Thomas Hudson (1756), National Portrait Gallery, London. After settling in England, Handel composed 40 operas and received the patronage of George I and several other members of British royalty. When his patrons founded the Royal Academy of Music 1719 for the promotion of Italian opera, Handel was made its director.

Born in Halle, he abandoned the study of law 1703 to become a violinist at Keiser's Opera House in Hamburg. Visits to Italy (1706–10) inspired a number of operas and oratorios, and in 1711 his opera *Rinaldo* was performed in London. *Saul* and *Israel in Egypt* (both 1739) were unsuccessful, but his masterpiece the *Messiah* was acclaimed on its first performance in Dublin 1742. Other works include the pastoral *Acis and Galatea* 1718 and a set of variations for harpsichord that were later nicknamed 'The Harmonious Blacksmith'. In 1751 he became totally blind.

Handke /ˈhæntkə/ Peter 1942– . Austrian novelist and playwright whose first play *Insulting the Audience* 1966 was an example of 'anti-theatre writing'. His novels include *Die Hornissen/The Hornets* 1966 and *Die Angst des Tormanns beim Elfmeter/The Goalie's Anxiety at the Penalty Kick* 1970. He wrote and directed the film *Linkshandige Frau/The Left-handed Woman* 1977.

Handley /ˈhændli/ Tommy 1896–1949. English radio comedian. His popular programme *ITMA* (It's That Man Again) ran from 1939 until his death.

Hanley /ˈhænli/ Ellery 1965– . English rugby league player, a regular member of the Great Britain team since 1984 and the inspiration behind Wigan's domination of the sport in the 1980s. He joined Leeds 1991.

Hanley started his career in 1981 with Bradford Northern before his transfer to Wigan 1985 for a then world record £85,000. He has since won all the top honours of the game in Britain as well as earning a reputation in Australia, the world's top rugby league nation.

Hanna /ˈhænə/ Mark 1837–1904. US businessman and political leader. A Republican, he supported James Garfield in his presidential campaign 1880. He served in the US Senate 1896–1900 and as chairman of the Republican National Committee, Hanna engineered McKinley's victories in 1896 and 1900 becoming his closest adviser.

Born in New Lisbon, Ohio, USA, Hanna attended Case Western Reserve College before joining his father in business.

He later became one of Cleveland's civic leaders, founding the Union National Bank and buying the *Cleveland Herald*.

Hannibal /ˈhænɪbəl/ 247–182 BC. Carthaginian general from 221 BC, son of Hamilcar Barca. His siege of Saguntum (now Sagunto, near Valencia) precipitated the 2nd Punic War with Rome. Following a campaign in Italy (after crossing the Alps in 218 with 57 elephants), Hannibal was the victor at Trasimene in 217 and Cannae in 216, but he failed to take Rome. In 203 he returned to Carthage to meet a Roman invasion but was defeated at Zama in 202 and exiled in 196 at Rome's insistence.

Hanover /ˈhænəʊvə/ German royal dynasty that ruled Great Britain and Ireland 1714–1901. Under the Act of Settlement 1701, the succession passed to the ruling family of Hanover, Germany, on the death of Queen Anne. On the death of Queen Victoria, the crown passed to Edward VII of the house of Saxe-Coburg.

Hansom /ˈhænsəm/ Joseph Aloysius 1803–1882. British architect. His works include the Birmingham town hall 1831, but he is remembered as the designer of the **hansom cab** 1834, a two-wheel carriage with a seat for the driver on the outside.

Hanway /ˈhænweɪ/ Jonas 1712–1786. British traveller in Russia and Persia, and advocate of prison reform. He is believed to have been the first Englishman to carry an umbrella.

Hapsburg /ˈhæpsbɜːɡ/ English form of →Habsburg, former imperial house of Austria–Hungary.

Haq /hɑːk/ Fazlul 1873–1962. Leader of the Bengali Muslim peasantry. He was a member of the Viceroy's Defence Council, established 1941, and was Bengal's first Indian prime minister 1937–43.

Harald III Hardrada or Harald the Ruthless (Norwegian *Harald Hardråde*) 1015–1066. King of Norway 1045–66, ruling jointly with Magnus I 1045–47. He engaged in an unsuccessful attempt to conquer Denmark 1045–62; extended Norwegian rule in Orkney, Shetland, and the Hebrides; and tried to conquer England together with Tostig, Earl of Northumbria. They were defeated by King Harold of England at Stamford Bridge and both died in battle.

Harcourt /ˈhɑːkət/ William Vernon 1827–1904. British Liberal politician. Under Gladstone he was home secretary 1880–85 and chancellor of the Exchequer 1886 and 1892–95. He is remembered for his remark 1892: 'We are all Socialists now.'

Hardenberg /ˈhɑːdnbɜːg/ Karl August von 1750–1822. Prussian politician, foreign minister to King Frederick William III of Prussia during the Napoleonic Wars; he later became chancellor. His military and civic reforms were restrained by the reactionary tendencies of the king.

Hardicanute /ˌhɑːdɪkəˈnjuːt/ c. 1019–1042. King of England from 1040. Son of Canute, he was king of Denmark from 1028. In England he was considered a harsh ruler.

Hardie /ˈhɑːdi/ (James) Keir 1856–1915. Scottish socialist, member of Parliament 1892–95 and 1900–15. He worked in the mines as a boy and in 1886 became secretary of the Scottish Miners' Federation. In 1888 he was the first Labour candidate to stand for Parliament; he entered Parliament independently as a Labour member 1892 and was a chief founder of the Independent Labour Party 1893.

Hardie was born in Lanarkshire but represented the parliamentary constituencies of West Ham, London 1892–95 and Merthyr Tydfil, Wales, from 1900. A pacifist, he strongly opposed the Boer War, and his idealism in his work for socialism and the unemployed made him a popular hero.

Harding /ˈhɑːdɪŋ/ (Allan Francis) John, 1st Baron Harding of Petherton 1896–1989. British field marshal. He was Chief of Staff in Italy during World War II. As governor of Cyprus 1955–57, during the period of political agitation prior to independence 1960, he was responsible for the deportation of Makarios III from Cyprus 1955.

Harding /ˈhɑːdɪŋ/ Warren G(amaliel) 1865–1923. 29th president of the USA 1921–23, a Republican. Harding was born in Ohio, and entered the US Senate 1914. As president he concluded the peace treaties of 1921 with Germany, Austria, and Hungary, and in the same year called the Washington Naval Conference to resolve conflicting British, Japanese, and US ambitions in the Pacific. He opposed US membership of the League of Nations. There were charges of corruption among members of his cabinet (the Teapot Dome Scandal).

Hardouin-Mansart /ɑːˈdwæn mænˈsɑː/ Jules 1646–1708. French architect to Louis XIV from 1675. He designed the lavish Baroque extensions to the palace of Versailles (from 1678) and Grand Trianon. Other works include the Invalides Chapel (1680–91), the Place de Vendôme, and the Place des Victoires, all in Paris.

Hardy /ˈhɑːdi/ Oliver 1892–1957. US film comedian, member of the duo →Laurel and Hardy.

Hardy /ˈhɑːdi/ Thomas 1840–1928. English novelist and poet. His novels, set in rural 'Wessex' (his native West Country), portray intense human relationships played out in a harshly indifferent natural world. They include *Far From the Madding Crowd* 1874, *The Return of the Native* 1878, *The Mayor of Casterbridge* 1886, *The Woodlanders* 1887, *Tess of the d'Urbervilles* 1891, and *Jude the Obscure* 1895. His poetry includes the *Wessex Poems* 1898, the blank-verse epic of the Napoleonic Wars *The Dynasts* 1904–08, and several volumes of lyrics.

Born in Dorset, Hardy was trained as an architect. His first success was *Far From the Madding Crowd*. *Tess of the d'Urbervilles*, subtitled 'A Pure Woman', outraged public opinion by portraying as its heroine a woman who had been seduced. The even greater outcry that followed *Jude the Obscure* 1895 reinforced Hardy's decision to confine himself to verse.

My argument is that War makes rattling good history; but Peace is poor reading.

Thomas Hardy *The Dynasts*

Hardy /ˈhɑːdi/ Thomas Masterman 1769–1839. British sailor. At Trafalgar he was Nelson's flag captain in the *Victory*, attending him during his dying moments. He became First Sea Lord 1830.

Hare /heə/ David 1947– . British dramatist and director, whose plays include *Slag* 1970, *Teeth 'n' Smiles* 1975, *Pravda* 1985 (with Howard →Brenton), and *Wrecked Eggs* 1986.

Harewood /ˈhɑːwʊd/ George Henry Hubert Lascelles, 7th Earl of Harewood 1923– . Artistic director of the Edinburgh Festival 1961–65, director of the English National Opera 1972–85, and a governor of the BBC from 1985.

Hargobind /ˈhɑːgəbɪnd/ 1595–1644. Indian religious leader, sixth guru (teacher) of Sikhism 1606–44. He encouraged Sikhs to develop military skills in response to growing persecution. At the festival of Diwali, Sikhs celebrate his release from prison.

Hargraves /ˈhɑːgreɪvz/ Edward Hammond 1816–1891. Australian prospector, born in England. In 1851 he found gold in the Blue Mountains of New South Wales, thus beginning the first Australian gold rush.

Hargreaves /ˈhɑːgriːvz/ James died 1778. English inventor who co-invented a carding machine for combing wool 1760. About 1764 he invented his 'spinning jenny', which enabled a number of threads to be spun simultaneously by one person.

Harlow *US film actress Jean Harlow who established her screen image as the fast-talking, brazenly sensual platinum blonde at the age of 19. While under contract to MGM (from 1932) her image was further enhanced by her pairing with the studio's top male stars, including Clark Gable and Spencer Tracy.*

Harington /ˈhærɪŋtən/ John 1561–1612. English translator of Ariosto's *Orlando Furioso* and author of *The Metamorphosis of Ajax*, a ribald history of the privy ('jakes'). Elizabeth I of England referred to him as 'that saucy poet, my godson', and banished him from court on several occasions but also installed the water closet he invented.

Har Krishen /hɑː ˈkrɪʃən/ 1656–1664. Indian religious leader, eighth guru (teacher) of Sikhism 1661–64, who died at the age of eight.

Harlan /ˈhɑːlən/ John Marshall 1833–1911. US politician and jurist, associate justice of the US Supreme Court 1877–1911. Harlan supported the Union during the American Civil War 1861–65, serving as colonel in the 10th Kentucky Volunteer Infantry and elected Kentucky attorney general 1863. He was defeated as Republican candidate for governor of Kentucky 1871 and 1875.

Before embarking on his political career, Harlan practised law in Kentucky. He was appointed associate justice by President Hayes after service on a federal Reconstruction Commission in Louisiana 1877 and held the office until his death.

Harlan /ˈhɑːlən/ John Marshall 1899–1971. US jurist and Supreme Court associate justice 1954–71. Chief counsel for the New York Crime Commission 1951–53, Harlan was appointed by President Eisenhower to the US Supreme Court 1954. As associate justice, he was a conservative, especially in the areas of free speech and civil and criminal rights.

Born in Chicago, USA, and educated at Prince-

ton and Oxford universities, Harlan studied law at New York University and was admitted to the bar 1925. After service in the US attorney's office 1925–27 he joined the staff of the state attorney general 1928–30. Harlan later established a private practice before returning to public service 1951.

Harley /ˈhɑːli/ Robert, 1st Earl of Oxford 1661–1724. British Tory politician, chief minister to Queen Anne 1711–14, when he negotiated the Treaty of Utrecht 1713. Accused of treason as a Jacobite after the accession of George I, he was imprisoned 1714–17.

Harlow /ˈhɑːləʊ/ Jean. Stage name of Harlean Carpenter 1911–1937. US film actress, the first 'platinum blonde' and the wisecracking sex symbol of the 1930s. Her films include *Hell's Angels* 1930, *Red Dust* 1932, *Platinum Blonde* 1932, *Dinner at Eight* 1933, *China Seas* 1935, and *Saratoga* 1937, during the filming of which she died (her part was completed by a double – with rear and long shots).

Harold /ˈhærəld/ two kings of England:

Harold I died 1040. King of England from 1035. The illegitimate son of Canute, known as *Harefoot*, he claimed the throne 1035 when the legitimate heir Hardicanute was in Denmark. He was elected king 1037.

Harold II /ˈhærəld/ *c.* 1020–1066. King of England from Jan 1066. He succeeded his father Earl Godwin 1053 as earl of Wessex. In 1063 William of Normandy (➔William I) tricked him into swearing to support his claim to the English throne, and when the Witan (a council of high-ranking religious and secular men) elected Harold to succeed Edward the Confessor, William prepared to invade. Meanwhile, Harold's treacherous brother Tostig (died 1066) joined the king of Norway, Harald III Hardrada (1015–1066), in invading Northumbria. Harold routed and killed them at Stamford Bridge 25 Sept. Three days later William landed at Pevensey, Sussex, and Harold was killed at the Battle of Hastings 14 Oct 1066.

Har Rai /hɑː ˈraɪ/ 1630–1661. Indian religious leader, seventh guru (teacher) of Sikhism 1644–61.

Harriman /ˈhærɪmən/ (William) Averell 1891–1986. US diplomat, administrator of lend-lease (the ordering of defence articles for any country whose defence was deemed vital to the defence of the USA) in World War II, Democratic secretary of commerce in Truman's administration 1946–48, negotiator of the Nuclear Test Ban Treaty with the USSR 1963, and governor of New York 1955–58.

Harris /ˈhærɪs/ Arthur Travers 1892–1984. British marshal of the Royal Air Force in World War II. Known as 'Bomber Harris', he was commander in chief of Bomber Command 1942–45.

He was an autocratic and single-minded leader, and was criticized for his policy of civilian-bombing of selected cities in Germany; he authorized the fire-bombing raids on Dresden, in which more than 100,000 died.

Harris /hærɪs/ Frank 1856–1931. Irish journalist, later in the USA, who wrote colourful biographies of Oscar Wilde and George Bernard Shaw, and an autobiography, *My Life and Loves* 1926, originally banned in the UK and the USA for its sexual contents.

Harris /hærɪs/ Joel Chandler 1848–1908. US author, born in Georgia. He wrote tales narrated by the former slave 'Uncle Remus', based on black folklore, and involving the characters Br'er Rabbit and the Tar Baby.

Harris /hærɪs/ Louis 1921– . US pollster. He joined the Roper polling organization 1947 and became a partner in that firm 1954. Developing his own research techniques, he founded Louis Harris and Associates 1956. Hired by the 1960 Kennedy presidential campaign, Harris gained a national reputation and later served as a consultant to the CBS television network and as a political columnist.

Harris /hærɪs/ Paul P 1878–1947. US lawyer who founded the first *Rotary Club* in Chicago 1905.

Harris /hærɪs/ Richard 1932– . Irish film actor known for playing rebel characters in such films as *This Sporting Life* 1963. His other films include *Camelot* 1967, *A Man Called Horse* 1970, *Robin and Marian* 1976, *Tarzan the Ape Man* 1981, *The Field* 1990, and *Unforgiven* 1992.

Harris /hærɪs/ Roy 1898–1979. US composer, born in Oklahoma, who used American folk tunes. Among his works are the 10th symphony 1965 (known as 'Abraham Lincoln') and the orchestral *When Johnny Comes Marching Home* 1935.

Harrison /hærɪsən/ Benjamin 1833–1901. 23rd president of the USA 1889–93, a Republican. He called the first Pan-American Conference, which led to the establishment of the Pan American Union, to improve inter-American cooperation, and develop commercial ties. In 1948 this became the Organization of American States.

Born in North Bend, Ohio, Harrison graduated from Miami University in Oxford, Ohio, 1852 and practised law in Indianapolis, Indiana. Active in Republican politics before and after the Civil War, he returned from the war a brigadier general and by 1877 was the Republican leader of Indiana. He served in the US Senate 1881–87 before being nominated as the Republican presidential candidate in the election of 1888.

Harrison /hærɪsən/ Rex (Reginald Carey) 1908–1990. English film and theatre actor. He appeared in over 40 films and numerous plays, often portraying sophisticated and somewhat eccentric characters, such as the waspish Professor Higgins in *My Fair Lady* 1964, the musical version of Irish dramatist George Bernard Shaw's play *Pygmalion*. His other films include *Blithe*

Spirit 1945, *The Ghost and Mrs Muir* 1947, and *Dr Doolittle* 1967.

Harrison /hærɪsən/ Tony 1937– . British poet, translator, and dramatist who caused controversy with his poem *V* 1987, dealing with the desecration of his parents' grave by Liverpool football supporters, and the play *The Blasphemers' Banquet* 1989, which attacked (in the name of Molière, Voltaire, Byron, and Omar Khayyam) the death sentence on Salman Rushdie. He has also translated and adapted Molière.

Harrison /hærɪsən/ William Henry 1773–1841. 9th president of the US 1841. Elected 1840 as a Whig, he died one month after taking office. His political career was based largely on his reputation as an Indian fighter, and his campaign was constructed to give the impression that he was a man of the people with simple tastes and that the New Yorker, Martin →Van Buren, his opponent, was a 'foppish' sophisticate.

Born in Charles City County, Virginia, he joined the army 1791 at the age of 18. He resigned from the army 1798 and served as secretary of the Northwest Territory 1798–1800 and governor of the Indiana Territory 1801–12, where he drove off a minor Indian attack at Tippecanoe Creek, which was reported as a rout. Recalled to the army during the War of 1812, Harrison led his troops in the recapture of Detroit and was victorious at the Battle of the Thames River in Ontario, Canada. He served in the US House of Representatives 1816–19 and the Senate 1825–28. Benjamin →Harrison was his grandson.

Harrison 9th US president William Harrison was known more for his reputation as a war hero than for his skill as a Whig politician. He led a military campaign against the native American Indians, winning a renowned victory at Tippecanoe Creek 1811 and, as a general in the War of 1812, won several victories against the British.

Harrisson /ˈhærɪsən/ Tom 1911–1976. British anthropologist who set up Mass Observation with Charles Madge 1937, the earliest of the organizations for the analysis of public opinions and attitudes.

Hart /hɑːt/ Gary 1936– . US Democrat politician, senator for Colorado from 1974. In 1980 he contested the Democratic nomination for the presidency, and stepped down from his Senate seat 1986 to run, again unsuccessfully, in the 1988 presidential campaign.

Hart /hɑːt/ Moss 1904–1961. US playwright. He collaborated with such major figures as Irving Berlin, Cole Porter, Kurt Weill, and Ira Gershwin. Among Hart's most famous works are *The Man Who Came to Dinner* 1939 and the films *Gentlemen's Agreement* 1947 and *A Star is Born* 1954.

Born in New York City, USA, Hart had his first play produced in 1922. After working for an independent producer and at Catskill resorts in New York State, he gained Broadway success with *Once in a Lifetime*, 1930 co-written with George S Kaufman. Late in his career he became one of Broadway's most successful directors. His autobiography, *Act One*, appeared 1959.

Harte /hɑːt/ (Francis) Bret 1836–1902. US writer. He became a goldminer at 18 before founding the *Overland Monthly* 1868 in which he wrote short stories of the pioneer West, for example *The Luck of Roaring Camp* and poems such as *The Heathen Chinee*. From 1885 he settled in England after five years as US consul in Glasgow.

Hartington /ˈhɑːtɪŋtən/ Spencer Compton Cavendish 1833–1908. 8th Duke of Devonshire, Marquess of Hartington. British politician, first leader of the Liberal Unionists 1886–1903. As war minister he opposed devolution for Ireland in cabinet and later led the revolt of the Liberal Unionists that defeated Gladstone's Irish Home Rule bill 1886. Hartington refused the premiership three times, 1880, 1886, and 1887, and led the opposition to the Irish Home Rule bill in the House of Lords 1893.

Hartley /ˈhɑːtli/ L(eslie) P(oles) 1895–1972. English novelist, noted for his exploration of the sinister. His books include the trilogy *The Shrimp and the Anemone* 1944, *The Sixth Heaven* 1946, and *Eustace and Hilda* 1947, on the intertwined lives of a brother and sister. Later works include *The Boat* 1949, *The Go-Between* 1953 (also a film), and *The Hireling* 1957.

The past is a foreign country: they do things differently there.

L P Hartley
The Go-Between 1953

Hartly /ˈhɑːtli/ Marsden 1877–1943. US avant-garde painter. His works range from abstract,

brightly coloured representations of German soldiers and German military symbols, such as *Military* 1913, to New England landscapes, such as *Log Jam, Penobscot Bay* 1940–41.

Born in Lewiston, Maine, USA, he travelled in Europe to study art. He exhibited 1913 with the *Blaue Reiter* (Blue Rider) school and returned to the USA to exhibit with the Armory Show 1913. Typical of his later 'primitive' style is the painting *Fisherman's Last Supper* portraying the influence of the early German expressionists.

Harvey /ˈhɑːvi/ Laurence. Adopted name of Lauruska Mischa Skikne 1928–1973. British film actor of Lithuanian descent who worked both in England (*Room at the Top* 1958) and in Hollywood (*The Alamo* 1960, *The Manchurian Candidate* 1962).

Harvey /ˈhɑːvi/ William 1578–1657. English physician who discovered the circulation of blood. In 1628 he published his book *De Motu Cordis/ On the Motion of the Heart and the Blood in Animals*. He was court physician to James I and Charles I.

After studying at Padua, Italy, under →Fabricius, he set out to question →Galen's account of the action of the heart. Later, Harvey explored the development of chick and deer embryos.

Hašek /ˈhæʃek/ Jaroslav 1883–1923. Czech writer. His masterpiece is an anti-authoritarian comic satire on military life under Austro-Hungarian rule, *The Good Soldier Schweik* 1923. During World War I he deserted to Russia, and eventually joined the Bolsheviks.

Hassam /ˈhæsəm/ Childe 1859–1935. US Impressionist painter and printmaker. He studied in Paris 1886–89. He became one of the members of *The Ten*, a group of American Impressionists who exhibited together until World War I.

Hassan II /ˈhæsɑːn/ 1929– . King of Morocco from 1961. From 1976 he undertook the occupation of Western Sahara when it was ceded by Spain.

Hastings /ˈheɪstɪŋz/ Warren 1732–1818. British colonial administrator. A protégé of Lord Clive, who established British rule in India, Hastings carried out major reforms, and became governor of Bengal 1772 and governor general of India 1774. Impeached for corruption on his return to England 1785, he was acquitted 1795.

Hathaway /ˈhæθəweɪ/ Anne 1556–1623. Englishwoman, daughter of a yeoman farmer, who married William →Shakespeare 1582. She was born at Shottery, near Stratford, where her cottage can still be seen.

Hatshepsut /hætˈʃepsʊt/ c. 1540–c. 1481 BC. Queen of Egypt during the 18th dynasty. She was the daughter of Thothmes I, with whom she ruled until the accession to the throne of her husband and half-brother Thothmes II. Throughout his reign real power lay with Hatshepsut, and she continued to rule after his death, as regent for her nephew Thothmes III.

Her reign was a peaceful and prosperous time in a period when Egypt was developing its armies and expanding its territories. The ruins of her magnificent temple at Deir el-Bahri survive.

Hattersley /ˈhætəzli/ Roy 1932– . British Labour politician. On the right wing of the Labour Party, he was prices secretary 1976–79, and deputy leader of the party 1983–1992.

Hatton /ˈhætn/ Derek 1948– . British left-wing politician, former deputy leader of Liverpool Council. A leading member of the Militant Tendency, Hatton was removed from office and expelled from the Labour Party 1987.

He revealed in his autobiography 1988 how Militant acted as a subversive party-within-a-party. Subsequently he embarked on a career in advertising and public relations.

Haughey /ˈhɔːhi/ Charles 1925– . Irish Fianna Fáil politician of Ulster descent. Dismissed 1970 from Jack Lynch's cabinet for alleged complicity in IRA gun-running, he was afterwards acquitted. He was prime minister 1979–81, March–Nov 1982, and 1986–92, when he was replaced by Albert Reynolds.

Haussmann /əʊsˈmæn/ Georges Eugène, Baron Haussmann 1809–1891. French administrator who replanned medieval Paris 1853–70 to achieve the current city plan, with wide boulevards and parks. The cost of his scheme and his authoritarianism caused opposition, and he was made to resign.

Havel /ˈhævel/ Václav 1936– . Czech playwright and politician, president of Czechoslovakia 1989–92 and president of the Czech Republic from 1993. His plays include *The Garden Party* 1963 and *Largo Desolato* 1985, about a dissident intellectual. havel became widely known as a human-rights activist. He was imprisoned 1979–83 and again 1989 for support of Charter 77, a human-rights manifesto. As president of Czechoslovakia he sought to preserve a united republic, but resigned in recognition of the breakup of the federation 1992. in 1993 he became president of the newly independent Czech Republic.

Havers /ˈheɪvəz/ Robert Michael Oldfield, Baron Havers 1923–1992. British lawyer, Lord Chancellor 1987–88. After a successful legal career he became Conservative member of Parliament for Wimbledon 1970 and was solicitor general under Edward Heath and attorney general under Margaret Thatcher. He was made a life peer 1987 and served briefly, and unhappily, as Lord Chancellor before retiring 1988.

Hawke /ˈhɔːk/ Bob (Robert) 1929– . Australian Labor politician, prime minister 1983–91, on the right wing of the party. He was president of the Australian Council of Trade Unions 1970–80.

He announced his retirement from politics 1992.

Hawking /ˈhɔːkɪŋ/ Stephen 1942– . English physicist who has researched black holes and gravitational field theory. His books include *A Brief History of Time* 1988, in which he argues that our universe is only one small part of a 'super-universe' that has existed forever and that comprises an infinite number of universes like our own.

Professor of gravitational physics at Cambridge from 1977, he discovered that the strong gravitational field around a black hole can radiate particles of matter. Commenting on Einstein's remark, 'God does not play dice with the universe,' Hawking said: 'God not only plays dice, he throws them where they can't be seen.'

Confined to a wheelchair because of a muscular disease, he performs complex mathematical calculations entirely in his head.

Hawkins /ˈhɔːkɪnz/ Coleman (Randolph) 1904–1969. US virtuoso tenor saxophonist. He was, until 1934, a soloist in the swing band led by Fletcher Henderson (1898–1952), and was an influential figure in bringing the jazz saxophone to prominence as a solo instrument.

Hawkins /ˈhɔːkɪnz/ Jack 1910–1973. British film actor usually cast in authoritarian roles. His films include *The Cruel Sea* 1953, *The League of Gentlemen* 1959, *Zulu* 1963, and *Waterloo* 1970. After an operation for throat cancer that removed his vocal chords 1966 his voice had to be dubbed.

Hawkins /ˈhɔːkɪnz/ John 1532–1595. English navigator, born in Plymouth. Treasurer to the navy 1573–89, he was knighted for his services as a commander against the Spanish Armada 1588.

Hawkins /ˈhɔːkɪnz/ Richard c. 1562–1622. English navigator, son of John Hawkins. He held a command against the Spanish Armada 1588, was captured in an expedition against Spanish possessions 1593–94 and released 1602.

Hawks /ˈhɔːks/ Howard 1896–1977. US director, writer, and producer of a wide range of classic films, swift-moving and immensely accomplished, including *Scarface* 1932, *Bringing Up Baby* 1938, *The Big Sleep* 1946, and *Gentlemen Prefer Blondes* 1953.

Hawksmoor /ˈhɔːksmɔː/ Nicholas 1661–1736. English architect, assistant to Christopher →Wren in designing London churches and St Paul's Cathedral; joint architect with John →Vanbrugh of Castle Howard and Blenheim Palace. His genius is displayed in a quirky and uncompromising style incorporating elements from both Gothic and Classical sources.

The original west towers of Westminster Abbey, long attributed to Wren, were designed by Hawksmoor. After 1712 Hawksmoor completed six of the 50 new churches planned for London under the provisions made by the Fifty New Churches Act 1711.

Hayes Under the administration of Rutherford Hayes, 19th US president, the nation recovered commercial prosperity. Hayes, a compromise Republican candidate, opposed Democrat Samuel Tilden in the presidential election. Although Tilden led on the popular vote, some of the electoral votes were disputed, and Hayes won the presidency through the decision of an Electoral Commission.

Haworth /haʊəθ/ Norman 1883–1950. English organic chemist who was the first to synthesize a vitamin (ascorbic acid, vitamin C) 1933, for which he shared a Nobel prize 1937.

Hawthorne /hɔːθɔːn/ Nathaniel 1804–1864. US writer of *The Scarlet Letter* 1850, a powerful novel set in Puritan Boston. He wrote three other novels, including *The House of the Seven Gables* 1851, and many short stories, including *Tanglewood Tales* 1853, classic Greek legends retold for children.

Hay /heɪ/ Will 1888–1949. British comedy actor. Originally a music-hall comedian, he made many films from the 1930s in which he was usually cast as an incompetent in a position of authority, including *Good Morning Boys* 1937, *Oh Mr Porter* 1938, *Ask a Policeman* 1939, and *My Learned Friend* 1944.

Hayden /heɪdn/ Sterling. Stage name of John Hamilton 1916–1986. US film actor who played leading Hollywood roles in the 1940s and early 1950s. Although later seen in some impressive character roles, his career as a whole failed to do justice to his talent. His work includes *The Asphalt Jungle* 1950, *Johnny Guitar* 1954, *Dr Strangelove* 1964, and *The Godfather* 1972.

Hayden /heɪdn/ William (Bill) 1933– . Australian Labor politician. He was leader of the Australian Labor Party and of the opposition 1977–83, and minister of foreign affairs 1983. He became governor general 1989.

Haydn /haɪdn/ Franz Joseph 1732–1809. Austrian composer. A teacher of Mozart and Beethoven, he was a major exponent of the classical sonata form in his numerous chamber and orchestral works (he wrote more than 100 symphonies). He also composed choral music, including the oratorios *The Creation* 1798 and *The Seasons* 1801. He was the first great master of the string quartet.

Born in Lower Austria, he was Kapellmeister 1761–90 to Prince Esterházy. His work also includes operas, church music, and songs, and the 'Emperor's Hymn', adopted as the Austrian, and later the German, national anthem.

Melody is the main thing; harmony is useful only to charm the ear.

Franz Joseph Haydn

Haydon /heɪdn/ Benjamin Robert 1786–1846. British historical painter. His attempts at 'high art' include many gigantic canvasses such as *Christ's Entry into Jerusalem* 1820 (Philadelphia, USA). His genre pictures include *The Mock Election* and *Chairing the Member*. He published *Autobiography and Memoirs* 1853, a lively account of the contemporary art scene and his own tragicomic life.

Hayek /haɪek/ Friedrich August von 1899–1992. Austrian economist. Born in Vienna, he taught at the London School of Economics 1931–50. His *The Road to Serfdom* 1944 was a critical study of socialist trends in Britain. He won the 1974 Nobel Prize for Economics with Gunnar Myrdal.

Hayes /heɪz/ Rutherford Birchard 1822–1893. 19th president of the USA 1877–81, a Republican. Born in Ohio, he was a major general on the Union side in the Civil War. During his presidency federal troops were withdrawn from the Southern states and the Civil Service reformed.

Haywood /heɪwʊd/ William Dudley 1869–1928. US labour leader. One of the founders of the Industrial Workers of the World (IWW, 'Wobblies') 1905, Haywood was arrested for conspiracy to murder an antiunion politician. His acquittal in 1907 made him a labour hero. Arrested again for sedition during World War I, he spent his later years in exile in the Soviet Union.

Born in Salt Lake City, Utah, USA, Haywood worked in the mines, joining the Western Federation of Miners (WFM) 1896. By 1899 he had become a national leader of the WFM and, in his tireless tours of the country, won the nickname 'Big Bill'.

Hayworth /heɪwɜːθ/ Rita. Stage name of Margarita Carmen Cansino 1918–1987. US dancer and film actress who gave vivacious performances in 1940s musicals and steamy, erotic roles in *Gilda* 1946 and *Affair in Trinidad* 1952. She was known as Hollywood's 'Goddess' during the height of her career. She was married to Orson Welles 1943–48 and appeared in his films, including *The Lady from Shanghai* 1948. She was perfectly cast in *Pal Joey* 1957 and *Separate Tables* 1958.

Hazlitt /ˈhæzlɪt/ William 1778–1830. English essayist and critic whose work is characterized by invective, scathing irony, and a gift for epigram. His critical essays include *Characters of Shakespeare's Plays* 1817–18, *Lectures on the English Poets* 1818–19, *English Comic Writers* 1819, and *Dramatic Literature of the Age of Elizabeth* 1820. Other works are *Table Talk* 1821–22, *The Spirit of the Age* 1825, and *Liber Amoris* 1823.

Head /hed/ Bessie 1937– . South African writer living in exile in Botswana. Her novels include *When Rain Clouds Gather* 1969, *Maru* 1971, and *A Question of Power* 1973.

Head /hed/ Edith 1900–1981. US costume designer for Hollywood films who won eight Academy Awards for her designs, in such films as *The Heiress* 1949, *All About Eve* 1950, and *The Sting* 1973.

Heal /hiːl/ Ambrose 1872–1959. English cabinet-maker who took over the Heal's shop from his father and developed it into a large London store. He initially designed furniture in the Arts and Crafts style, often in oak, but in the 1930s he started using materials such as tubular steel.

Heal was a founder member of the Design and Industries Association, which aimed to improve the quality of mass-produced items.

Healey /ˈhiːli/ Denis (Winston) 1917– . British Labour politician. While minister of defence 1964–70 he was in charge of the reduction of British forces east of Suez. He was chancellor of the Exchequer 1974–79. In 1976 he contested the party leadership, losing to James Callaghan, and again in 1980, losing to Michael Foot, to whom he was deputy leader 1980–83. In 1987 he resigned from the shadow cabinet.

Heaney /ˈhiːni/ Seamus (Justin) 1939– . Irish poet, born in County Derry, who has written powerful verse about the political situation in Northern Ireland. Collections include *North* 1975, *Field Work* 1979, and *Station Island* 1984. In 1989, he was elected professor of poetry at Oxford University.

Hearn /hɜːn/ (Patrick) Lafcadio 1850–1904. Greek-born US writer and translator who lived in Japan from 1890 and became a Japanese citizen. His many books on Japanese life and customs introduced the country to many Western readers, for example, *Glimpses of Unfamiliar Japan* 1893 and *In Ghostly Japan* 1904.

A journalist, Hearn was sent to Japan to write an article for a US magazine and never left. His sympathetic understanding of the country and its culture made him accepted and appreciated by the Japanese, and his writings are still widely read. From 1896 he taught English literature at Tokyo University.

Hearns /hɜːnz/ Thomas 1958– . US boxer who in 1988 became the first man to win world titles at five different weight classes in five separate fights.

Hearst /hɜːst/ Patty (Patricia) 1955– . US socialite. A granddaughter of the newspaper tycoon William Randolph Hearst, she was kidnapped 1974 by an urban guerrilla group, the Symbionese Liberation Army. She joined her captors in a bank robbery, was sought, tried, convicted, and imprisoned 1976–79.

Hearst /hɜːst/ William Randolph 1863–1951. US newspaper publisher, celebrated for his introduction of banner headlines, lavish illustration, and the sensationalist approach known as 'yellow journalism'. A campaigner in numerous controversies, and a strong isolationist, he was said to be the model for Citizen Kane in the 1941 film of that name by Orson Welles.

Heath /hiːθ/ Edward (Richard George) 1916– . British Conservative politician, party leader 1965–75. As prime minister 1970–74 he took the UK into the European Community but was brought down by economic and industrial relations crises at home. He was replaced as party leader by Margaret Thatcher 1975, and became increasingly critical of her policies and her opposition to the UK's full participation in the EC. In 1990 he undertook a mission to Iraq in an attempt to secure the release of British hostages.

Hayworth With her flame-red hair, which became her trademark, US actress Rita Hayworth brought to her varied roles an erotic and alluring screen image. Frequently associated with tempestuous femme fatale roles, she was also the dancing star of 1940s musicals. She was seen to best advantage in the title role of the film Gilda 1946.

Heath entered Parliament 1950, was minister of Labour 1959–60, and as Lord Privy Seal 1960–63 conducted abortive negotiations for Common Market (European Community) membership. He succeeded Alec Home as Conservative leader 1965, the first elected leader of his party. Defeated in the general election 1966, he achieved a surprise victory 1970, but his confrontation with the striking miners as part of his campaign to control inflation led to Conservative defeats in the general elections of Feb 1974 and Oct 1974.

If politicians lived on praise and thanks, they'd be forced into some other line of business.

Edward Heath 1973

Heaviside /ˈhevɪsaɪd/ Oliver 1850–1925. British physicist. In 1902 he predicted the existence of an ionized layer of air in the upper atmosphere, which was known as the Kennelly-Heaviside layer but is now called the E layer of the ionosphere. Deflection from it makes possible the transmission of radio signals around the world, which would otherwise be lost in outer space.

His theoretical work had implications for radio transmission. His studies of electricity published in *Electrical Papers* 1892 had considerable impact on long-distance telephony.

Hecht /hekt/ Ben 1893–1964. US screenwriter and occasional film director, who was formerly a journalist. His play *The Front Page* 1928 was adapted several times for the cinema by other writers. His own screenplays included *Gunga Din* 1939, *Spellbound* 1945, and *Actors and Sin* 1952.

Hedin /heˈdiːn/ Sven Anders 1865–1952. Swedish archaeologist, geographer, and explorer in central Asia and China. Between 1891 and 1908 he explored routes across the Himalayas and produced the first maps of Tibet. During 1928–33 he travelled with a Sino–Swedish expedition which crossed the Gobi Desert. His publications include *My Life as Explorer* 1925 and *Across the Gobi Desert* 1928.

Heffer /ˈhefə/ Eric 1922–1991. English Labour politician, member of Parliament for Walton, Liverpool 1964–91. He held a ministerial post 1974–75, joined Michael Foot's shadow cabinet 1981, and was regularly elected to Labour's National Executive Committee, but found it difficult to follow the majority view.

Hefner /ˈhefnə/ Hugh (Marston) 1926– . US publisher, founder of *Playboy* magazine 1953. With its centrefolds of nude women, and columns of opinion, fashion, and advice on sex, *Playboy* helped reshape the social attitudes of the postwar generation. Its success declined in the 1980s owing to the rise of competing men's magazines and feminist protest.

Hegel /ˈheɪgəl/ Georg Wilhelm Friedrich 1770–1831. German philosopher who conceived of consciousness and the external object as forming a unity in which neither factor can exist independently, mind and nature being two abstractions of one indivisible whole. He believed development took place through dialectic: thesis and antithesis (contradiction) and synthesis, the resolution of contradiction. For Hegel, the task of philosophy was to comprehend the rationality of what already exists; leftist followers, including Karl Marx, used Hegel's dialectic to attempt to show the inevitability of radical change and to attack both religion and the social order of the European Industrial Revolution.

He wrote *The Phenomenology of Spirit* 1807, *Encyclopaedia of the Philosophical Sciences* 1817, and *Philosophy of Right* 1821.

He was professor of philosophy at Heidelberg 1817–18 and at Berlin 1818–31. As a rightist, Hegel championed religion, the Prussian state, and the existing order.

What experience and history teach is this – that people and governments never have learned anything from history, or acted on principles deduced from it.

G W F Hegel
Philosophy of History

Heidegger /ˈhaɪdegə/ Martin 1889–1976. German philosopher. In *Sein und Zeit/Being and Time* 1927 (translated 1962) he used the methods of Edmund →Husserl's phenomenology to explore the structures of human existence. His later writings meditated on the fate of a world dominated by science and technology.

He believed that Western philosophy had 'forgotten' the fundamental question of the 'meaning of Being'. Although one of his major concerns was the angst of human existence, he denied that he was an existentialist. His support for Nazism and his unwillingness or inability to defend his position damaged his reputation.

Heifetz /ˈhaɪfɪts/ Jascha 1901–1987. Russian-born US violinist, one of the great virtuosos of the 20th century. He first performed at the age of five, and before he was 17 had played in most European capitals, and in the USA, where he settled 1917. His style of playing was calm and objective.

Heine /ˈhaɪnə/ Heinrich 1797–1856. German Romantic poet and journalist who wrote *Reisebilder* 1826 and *Buch der Lieder/Book of Songs* 1827. From 1831 he lived mainly in Paris, working as a correspondent for German newspapers. Schubert and Schumann set many of his lyrics to music.

In 1835 he headed a list of writers forbidden to publish in Germany. He contracted a spinal disease 1845 that confined him to his bed from 1848 until his death.

Heinkel /ˈhaɪŋkəl/ Ernst 1888–1958. German aircraft designer who pioneered jet aircraft. He founded his firm 1922 and built the first jet aircraft 1939. During World War II his company was Germany's biggest producer of warplanes, mostly propeller-driven.

Heinlein /ˈhaɪnlaɪn/ Robert A(nson) 1907– . US science-fiction writer, associated with the pulp magazines of the 1940s, who wrote the militaristic novel *Starship Troopers* 1959 and the utopian cult novel *Stranger in a Strange Land* 1961. His work helped to increase the legitimacy of science fiction as a literary genre.

Heinz /haɪnz/ Henry John 1844–1919. US industrialist. Born in Pittsburgh, Heinz entered his family's brick business but became interested in the possibilities of wholesale food marketing, founding a firm for that purpose 1876. The firm, renamed the H J Heinz Co 1888, specialized in the manufacture of prepared foods and condiments. Heinz popularized the use of ketchup and made famous his company's slogan '57 Varieties'.

As president, Heinz oversaw every phase of production, from farming to advertising. Unlike some of his competitors, he was a strong supporter of the 1906 US Pure Food and Drug Act.

Heisenberg /ˈhaɪzənbɜːg/ Werner Carl 1901–1976. German physicist who developed quantum theory and formulated the uncertainty principle, which concerns matter, radiation, and their reactions, and places absolute limits on the achievable accuracy of measurement. He was awarded a Nobel prize 1932.

Hekmatyar /ˌhekmətˈjɑː/ Gulbuddin 1949– . Afghani Islamic fundamentalist guerrilla leader. He became a mujaheddin guerrilla in the 1980s, leading the fundamentalist faction of the Hizb-i Islami (Islamic Party), dedicated to the overthrow of the Soviet-backed communist regime in Kabul. He refused to countenance participation in any interim 'national unity' government that was to include Afghan communists. Hekmatyar resisted the takeover of Kabul by moderate mujaheddin forces April 1992 and refused to join the interim administration, continuing to bombard the city until being driven out. A renewed bombardment in Aug lead to his faction being barred from government posts.

Helena, St /ˈhelɪnə/ c. 248–328. Roman empress, mother of Constantine the Great, and a convert to Christianity. According to legend, she discovered the true cross of Jesus in Jerusalem. Her feast day is 18 Aug.

Heller /ˈhelə/ Joseph 1923– . US novelist. He drew on his experiences in the US air force in World War II to write *Catch-22* 1961, satirizing war and bureaucratic methods. A film based on the book appeared 1970.

After serving in the air force, he entered advertising. His other works include the novels *Something Happened* 1974 and *Good As Gold* 1979, and the plays *We Bombed In New Haven* 1968 and *Clevinger's Trial* 1974.

Hellman /ˈhelmən/ Lillian 1907–1984. US playwright whose work is concerned with contemporary political and social issues. *The Children's Hour* 1934, *The Little Foxes* 1939, and *Toys in the Attic* 1960 are all examples of the 'well-made play'.

She lived 31 years with the writer Dashiell Hammett, and in her will set up a fund to promote Marxist doctrine. Since her death there has been dispute over the accuracy of her memoirs, for example *Pentimento* 1973.

I cannot and will not cut my conscience to fit this year's fashions.

Lillian Hellman letter to the House Un-American Activities Committee May 1952

Helmholtz /ˈhelmhəʊlts/ Hermann Ludwig Ferdinand von 1821–1894. German physiologist, physicist, and inventor of the ophthalmoscope for examining the inside of the eye. He was the first to explain how the cochlea of the inner ear works, and the first to measure the speed of nerve impulses. In physics he formulated the law of conservation of energy, and worked in thermodynamics.

Helmont /ˈhelmɒnt/ Jean Baptiste van 1577–1644. Belgian doctor who was the first to realize that there are gases other than air, and claimed to have coined the word 'gas' (from Greek *cháos*).

Helms /helmz/ Richard 1913– . US director of the Central Intelligence Agency 1966–73, when he was dismissed by President Nixon. In 1977 he was convicted of lying before a congressional committee because his oath as chief of intelligence compelled him to keep secrets from the public. He was originally with the Office of Strategic Services, before it developed into the CIA 1947.

Héloïse /eləʊiːz/ 1101–1164. Abbess of Paraclete in Champagne, France, correspondent and lover of →Abelard. She became deeply interested in intellectual study in her youth and was impressed by the brilliance of Abelard, her teacher, whom she secretly married. After her affair with Abelard, and the birth of a son, Astrolabe, she became a nun 1129, and with Abelard's assistance, founded a nunnery at Paraclete. Her letters show her strong and pious character and her devotion to Abelard.

Helpmann /ˈhelpmən/ Robert 1909–1986. Australian dancer, choreographer, and actor. The leading male dancer with the Sadler's Wells Ballet, London 1933–50, he partnered Margot →Fonteyn in the 1940s.

His gift for mime and his dramatic sense is also apparent in his choreographic work, for example *Miracle in the Gorbals* 1944.

Helvetius /ˌelver'sjuːs/ Claude Adrien 1715–1771. French philosopher. In *De l'Esprit* 1758 he argued, following David →Hume, that self-interest, however disguised, is the mainspring of all human action and that since conceptions of good and evil vary according to period and locality there is no absolute good or evil. He also believed that intellectual differences are only a matter of education.

Helvetius's principle of artificial identity of interests (those manipulated by governments) influenced the utilitarian philosopher Jeremy Bentham. *De l'Esprit* was denounced and burned by the public hangman.

Hemingway /ˈhemɪŋweɪ/ Ernest 1898–1961. US writer. War, bullfighting, and fishing are used symbolically in his work to represent honour, dignity, and primitivism – prominent themes in his short stories and novels, which include *A Farewell to Arms* 1929, *For Whom the Bell Tolls* 1940, and *The Old Man and the Sea* 1952. His deceptively simple writing styles attracted many imitators. He received the Nobel Prize for Literature 1954.

He was born in Oak Park, Illinois, and in his youth developed a passion for hunting and adventure. He became a journalist and was wounded while serving on a volunteer ambulance crew in Italy in World War I. His style was influenced by Gertrude →Stein, who also introduced him to bullfighting, a theme in his first novel, *The Sun Also Rises* 1926, and the memoir *Death in the Afternoon* 1932. *A Farewell to Arms* deals with wartime experiences on the Italian front, and *For Whom the Bell Tolls* has a Spanish Civil War setting. He served as war correspondent both in that conflict and in Europe during World War II. After a full life, physical weakness, age, and depression contributed to his suicide.

Hendrix /ˈhendrɪks/ Jimi (James Marshall) 1942–1970. US rock guitarist, songwriter, and singer, legendary for his virtuoso experimental technique and flamboyance. *Are You Experienced?* 1967 was his first album. His performance at the 1969 Woodstock festival included a memorable version of 'The Star-Spangled Banner' and is recorded in the film *Woodstock*. He greatly expanded the vocabulary of the electric guitar and influenced both rock and jazz musicians.

Hendrix moved to the UK 1966 and formed a trio, the Jimi Hendrix Experience, which produced hit singles with their first recorded songs ('Hey Joe' and 'Purple Haze', both 1967), and attracted notice in the USA when Hendrix burned his guitar at the 1967 Monterey Pop Festival. The group disbanded early 1969 after three albums; Hendrix continued to record and occasionally perform until his death the following year.

Hench /hentʃ/ Philip Showalter 1896–1965. US physician who introduced cortisone treatment for rheumatoid arthritis for which he shared the 1950 Nobel Prize for Medicine with Edward →Kendall and Tadeus →Reichstein.

Henrietta Maria French-born queen consort of Charles I, Henrietta Maria, was much disliked in England because of her Roman Catholic entourage and her encouragement of Charles's belief in the divine right of kings.

Hench noticed that arthritic patients improved greatly during pregnancy or an attack of jaundice and concluded that a hormone secreted in increased quantity during both these conditions caused the improvement. This turned out to be cortisol, a steroid converted to cortisone in the liver.

Hendry Stephen 1970– . Scottish snooker player. He replaced Steve Davis as the top-ranking player during the 1989–90 season as well as becoming the youngest ever world champion.

Hendry was the youngest winner of a professional tournament when he claimed the 1986 Scottish professional title. He won his first ranking event in the 1987 Rothmans Grand Prix.

Hengist /ˈhengɪst/ 5th century AD. Legendary leader, with his brother Horsa, of the Jutes, who originated in Jutland and settled in Kent about 450, the first Anglo-Saxon settlers in Britain.

Heng Samrin /heŋ/ 1934– . Cambodian politician. A former Khmer Rouge commander 1976–78, who had become disillusioned with its brutal tactics, he led an unsuccessful coup against →Pol Pot 1978 and established the Kampuchean People's Revolutionary Party (KPRP) in Vietnam, before returning 1979 to head the new Vietnamese-backed government. He was replaced as prime minister by the reformist Hun Sen 1985.

Henie /ˈheni/ Sonja 1912–1969. Norwegian skater. Champion of her country at 11, she won ten world championships and three Olympic titles. She turned professional 1936 and went on to make numerous films in Hollywood.

Henlein /ˈhenlaɪn/ Konrad 1898–1945. Sudeten-German leader of the Sudeten Nazi Party in Czechoslovakia, and closely allied with Hitler's Nazis. He was partly responsible for the destabilization of the Czechoslovak state 1938, which led to the Munich Agreement and secession of the Sudetenland to Germany.

Henri /ˈhenri/ Robert. Adopted name of Robert Henry Cozad 1865–1929. US painter, a leading figure in the transition between 19th-century conventions and Modern art in America. He was a principal member of the realist *Ashcan School* which focused on city life, the poor, and the outcast.

Henrietta Maria /ˌhenriˈetə məˈriːə/ 1609–1669. Queen of England 1625–49. The daughter of Henry IV of France, she married Charles I of England 1625. By encouraging him to aid Roman Catholics and make himself an absolute ruler, she became highly unpopular and was exiled during the period 1644–60. She returned to England at the Restoration but retired to France 1665.

Henry /ˈhenri/ (Charles Albert David) known as *Harry* 1984–   . Prince of the UK; second child of the Prince and Princess of Wales.

Henry /ˈhenri/ Joseph 1797–1878. US physicist, inventor of the electromagnetic motor 1829 and of a telegraphic apparatus. He also discovered the principle of electromagnetic induction, roughly at the same time as Michael →Faraday, and the phenomenon of self-induction. A unit of inductance (henry) is named after him.

Henry /ˈhenri/ Patrick 1736–1799. US politician who in 1775 supported the arming of the Virginia militia against the British by a speech ending, 'Give me liberty or give me death!' He was governor of Virginia 1776–79 and 1784–86.

Henry /ˈhenri/ William 1774–1836. British chemist. In 1803 he formulated *Henry's law*, which states that when a gas is dissolved in a liquid at a given temperature, the mass that dissolves is in direct proportion to the pressure of the gas.

Henry /ˈhenri/ eight kings of England:

Henry I 1068–1135. King of England from 1100. Youngest son of William I, he succeeded his brother William II. He won the support of the Saxons by granting them a charter and marrying a Saxon princess. An able administrator, he established a professional bureaucracy and a system of travelling judges. He was succeeded by Stephen.

Henry II 1133–1189. King of England from 1154, when he succeeded →Stephen. He was the son of →Matilda and Geoffrey of Anjou (1113–1151). He curbed the power of the barons, but his attempt to bring the church courts under control had to be abandoned after the murder of Thomas à →Becket. During his reign the English conquest of Ireland began. He was succeeded by his son Richard I.

He was lord of Scotland, Ireland, and Wales, and count of Anjou, Brittany, Poitou, Normandy, Maine, Gascony, and Aquitaine. He was married to Eleanor of Aquitaine.

Henry III 1207–1272. King of England from 1216, when he succeeded John, but he did not rule until 1227. His financial commitments to the papacy and his foreign favourites led to de →Montfort's revolt 1264. Henry was defeated at Lewes, Sussex, and imprisoned. He was restored to the throne after the royalist victory at Evesham 1265. He was succeeded by his son Edward I.

The royal powers were exercised by a regency until 1232 and by two French nobles, Peter des Roches and Peter des Rivaux, until the barons forced their expulsion 1234, marking the start of Henry's personal rule. While he was in prison, de Montfort ruled in his name. On his release Henry was weak and senile and his eldest son, Edward, took charge of the government.

Henry IV (Bolingbroke) 1367–1413. King of England from 1399, the son of →John of Gaunt. In 1398 he was banished by →Richard II for political activity but returned 1399 to head a revolt and be accepted as king by Parliament. He was succeeded by his son Henry V.

He had difficulty in keeping the support of Parliament and the clergy, and had to deal with baronial unrest and →Glendower's rising in Wales. In order to win support he had to conciliate the church by a law for the burning of heretics, and to make many concessions to Parliament.

Henry III The son of King John, Henry III of England reissued the Magna Carta, with some omissions. Favouritism, inefficiency, and extortion marred his rule, but Westminster Abbey, built mainly during his reign, is its lasting monument.

Henry V 1387–1422. King of England from 1413, son of Henry IV. Invading Normandy 1415 (during the Hundred Years' War), he captured Harfleur and defeated the French at Agincourt. He invaded again 1417–19, capturing Rouen. His military victory forced the French into the Treaty of Troyes 1420, which gave Henry control of the French government. He married →Catherine of Valois 1420 and gained recognition as heir to the French throne by his father-in-law Charles VI, but died before him. He was succeeded by his son Henry VI.

Henry VI 1421–1471. King of England from 1422, son of Henry V. He assumed royal power 1442 and sided with the party opposed to the continuation of the Hundred Years' War with France. After his marriage 1445, he was dominated by his wife, →Margaret of Anjou. The unpopularity of the government, especially after the loss of the English conquests in France, encouraged Richard, Duke of →York, to claim the throne, and though York was killed 1460, his son Edward IV proclaimed himself king 1461. Henry was captured 1465, temporarily restored 1470, but again imprisoned 1471 and then murdered.

Henry VII 1457–1509. King of England from 1485, son of Edmund Tudor, Earl of Richmond (c. 1430–1456), and a descendant of →John of Gaunt. He spent his early life in Brittany until 1485, when he landed in Britain to lead the rebellion against Richard III which ended with Richard's defeat and death at Bosworth. By his marriage to Elizabeth of York 1486 he united the houses of York and Lancaster. Yorkist revolts continued until 1497, but Henry restored order after the Wars of the Roses by the Star Chamber and achieved independence from Parliament by amassing a private fortune through confiscations. He was succeeded by his son Henry VIII.

Henry VIII 1491–1547. King of England from 1509, when he succeeded his father Henry VII and married Catherine of Aragon, the widow of his brother. During the period 1513–29 Henry pursued an active foreign policy, largely under the guidance of his Lord Chancellor, Cardinal Wolsey who shared Henry's desire to make England a notable nation. Wolsey was replaced by Thomas More 1529 for failing to persuade the pope to grant Henry a divorce. After 1532 Henry broke with papal authority, proclaimed himself head of the church in England, dissolved the monasteries, and divorced Catherine. His subsequent wives were Anne Boleyn, Jane Seymour, Anne of Cleves, Catherine Howard, and Catherine Parr. He was succeeded by his son Edward VI.

He divorced Catherine 1533 because she was too old to give him an heir, and married Anne Boleyn, who was beheaded 1536, ostensibly for adultery. Henry's third wife, Jane Seymour, died 1537. He married Anne of Cleves 1540 in pursuance of Thomas Cromwell's policy of allying with the German Protestants, but rapidly abandoned this policy, divorced Anne, and beheaded Cromwell. His fifth wife, Catherine Howard, was beheaded 1542, and the following year he married Catherine Parr, who survived him. Henry never completely lost his popularity, but wars with France and Scotland towards the end of his reign sapped the economy, and in religion he not only executed Roman Catholics, including Thomas More, for refusing to acknowledge his supremacy in the church, but also Protestants who maintained his changes had not gone far enough.

Henry /ˈhenri/ four kings of France:

Henry I /ˈhenri, ɒnˈriː/ 1005–1060. King of France from 1031. He spent much of his reign in conflict with →William I the Conqueror, then duke of Normandy.

Henry II 1519–1559. King of France from 1547. He captured the fortresses of Metz and Verdun from the Holy Roman emperor Charles V and Calais from the English. He was killed in a tournament.

In 1526 he was sent with his brother to Spain as a hostage, being returned when there was peace 1530. He married Catherine de' Medici 1533, and from then on was dominated by her, Diane de Poitiers, and Duke Montmorency. Three of his sons, Francis II, Charles IX, and Henry III, became kings of France.

Henry III 1551–1589. King of France from 1574. He fought both the Huguenots (headed by his successor, Henry of Navarre) and the Catholic League (headed by the Duke of Guise). Guise expelled Henry from Paris 1588 but was assassinated. Henry allied with the Huguenots under Henry of Navarre to besiege the city, but was assassinated by a monk.

Henry IV 1553–1610. King of France from 1589. Son of Antoine de Bourbon and Jeanne, Queen of Navarre, he was brought up as a Protestant and from 1576 led the Huguenots. On his accession he settled the religious question by adopting Catholicism while tolerating Protestantism. He restored peace and strong government to France and brought back prosperity by measures for the promotion of industry and agriculture and the improvement of communications. He was assassinated by a Catholic extremist.

I want there to be no peasant in my kingdom so poor that he is unable to have a chicken in his pot every Sunday.

Henry IV quoted in H de Péréfixe
Histoire de Henry le Grand

Henry /ˈhenri/ seven Holy Roman emperors, including:

Henry I *the Fowler* c. 876–936. King of Germany from 919, and duke of Saxony from 912. He secured the frontiers of Saxony, ruled in harmony with its nobles, and extended German influence over the Danes, the Hungarians, and the Slavonic tribes. He was about to claim the imperial crown when he died.

Henry II *the Saint* 973–1024. King of Germany from 1002, Holy Roman emperor from 1014, when he recognized Benedict VIII as pope. He was canonized 1146.

Henry III *the Black* 1017–1056. King of Germany from 1028, Holy Roman emperor from 1039 (crowned 1046). He raised the empire to the height of its power, and extended its authority over Poland, Bohemia, and Hungary.

Henry IV 1050–1106. Holy Roman emperor from 1056, who was involved from 1075 in a struggle with the papacy (see ➔Gregory VII). Excommunicated twice (1076 and 1080), Henry deposed Gregory and set up the antipope Clement III (died 1191) by whom he was crowned Holy Roman emperor 1084.

Henry V 1081–1125. Holy Roman emperor from 1106. He continued the struggle with the church until the settlement of the investiture contest 1122.

Henry VI 1165–1197. Holy Roman emperor from 1190. As part of his plan for making the empire universal, he captured and imprisoned Richard I of England and compelled him to do homage.

Henry VII 1269–1313. Holy Roman emperor from 1308. He attempted unsuccessfully to revive the imperial supremacy in Italy.

Henry Frederick /ˈhenri ˈfredrɪk/ Prince of Wales 1594–1612. Eldest son of James I of England and Anne of Denmark; a keen patron of Italian art.

Henry, O /əʊˈhenri/ Pen name of William Sydney Porter 1862–1910. US short-story writer whose collections include *Cabbages and Kings* 1904 and *The Four Million* 1906. His stories are written in a colloquial style and employ skilled construction with surprise endings.

Henry of Blois died 1171. Brother of King Stephen of England, he was bishop of Winchester from 1129, and Pope Innocent II's legate to England from 1139. While remaining loyal to Henry II, he tried to effect a compromise between ➔Becket and the king.

Henryson /ˈhenrɪsən/ Robert 1430–1505. Scottish poet. His works include versions of Aesop and the *Testament of Cresseid*, a continuation of Chaucer.

Henry the Lion /ˈhenri/ 1129–1195. Duke of Bavaria 1156–80, duke of Saxony 1142–80, and duke of Lüneburg 1180–85. He was granted the Duchy of Bavaria by the Emperor Frederick Barbarossa. He founded Lübeck and Munich. In 1162 he married Matilda, daughter of Henry II of England. His refusal in 1176 to accompany Frederick Barbarossa to Italy led in 1180 to his being

deprived of the duchies of Bavaria and Saxony. Henry led several military expeditions to conquer territory in the East.

Henry the Navigator /ˈhenri/ 1394–1460. Portuguese prince, the fourth son of John I. He set up a school for navigators 1419 and under his patronage Portuguese sailors explored and colonized Madeira, the Cape Verde Islands, and the Azores; they sailed down the African coast almost to Sierra Leone.

Henson /ˈhensən/ Jim (James Maury) 1936–1990. US puppeteer who created the television Muppet characters, including Kermit the Frog, Miss Piggy, and Fozzie Bear. The Muppets became popular on the children's educational TV series *Sesame Street*, which first appeared in 1969 and soon became regular viewing in over 80 countries. In 1976 Henson created *The Muppet Show*, which ran for five years and became one of the world's most widely seen TV programmes, reaching 235 million viewers in 100 countries. Three Muppet movies followed. In 1989 the Muppets became part of the ➔Disney empire.

Henty /ˈhenti/ G(eorge) A(lfred) 1832–1902. British war correspondent, author of numerous historical novels for children, including *With the Allies to Peking* 1904.

Henze /ˈhentsə/ Hans Werner 1926–   . German composer whose large and varied output includes orchestral, vocal, and chamber music. He uses traditional symphony and concerto forms, and incorporates a wide range of styles including jazz. Operas include *Das Verratene Meer* (Berlin 1992) based on Yukio Mishima's *The Sailor Who Fell from Grace with the Sea*.

In 1953 he moved to Italy where his music became more expansive, as in the opera *The Bassarids* 1966.

Hepburn /ˈhepbɜːn/ Audrey (Audrey Hepburn-Rushton) 1929–1993. British actress of Anglo-Dutch descent who often played innocent, childlike characters. Slender and doe-eyed, she set a different style from the more ample women stars of the 1950s. After playing minor parts in British films in the early 1950s, she became a Hollywood star in such films as *Funny Face* 1957, *My Fair Lady* 1964, *Wait Until Dark* 1968, and *Robin and Marian* 1976.

Hepburn /ˈhepbɜːn/ Katharine 1909–   . US actress who made feisty self-assurance her trademark. She appeared in such films as *Morning Glory* 1933 (Academy Award), *Little Women* 1933, *Bringing Up Baby* 1938, *The Philadelphia Story* 1940, *Woman of the Year* 1942, *The African Queen* 1951, *Pat and Mike* 1952 (with her frequent partner Spencer Tracy), *Guess Who's Coming to Dinner* 1967 (Academy Award), *Lion in Winter* 1968 (Academy Award), and *On Golden Pond* 1981 (Academy Award). She also had a distinguished stage career.

Hepplewhite /ˈhepəlwaɪt/ George died 1786. English furniture maker. He developed a simple, elegant style, working mainly in mahogany or satinwood, adding delicately inlaid or painted decorations of feathers, shells, or ears of wheat. His book of designs, *The Cabinetmaker and Upholsterer's Guide* 1788, was published posthumously.

Hepworth /ˈhepwɜːθ/ Barbara 1903–1975. English sculptor. She developed a distinctive abstract style, creating hollowed forms of stone or wood with spaces bridged by wires or strings; many later works are in bronze.

She worked in concrete, bronze, wood, and aluminium, but her preferred medium was stone. She married first the sculptor John Skeaping and second the painter Ben →Nicholson. Under Nicholson's influence she became more interested in abstract form.

In 1939 she moved to St Ives, Cornwall (where her studio is now a museum). She was created a Dame of the British Empire 1965.

I rarely draw what I see. I draw what I feel in my body.

Barbara Hepworth

Heraclitus /ˌhɪərəˈklaɪtəs/ *c.* 544–483 BC. Greek philosopher who believed that the cosmos is in a ceaseless state of flux and motion, fire being the fundamental material that accounts for all change and motion in the world. Nothing in the world ever stays the same, hence the dictum, 'one cannot step in the same river twice'.

Heraclius /ˌhɪərəˈklaɪəs/ *c.* 575–641. Byzantine emperor from 610. His reign marked a turning point in the empire's fortunes. Of Armenian descent, he recaptured Armenia 622, and other provinces 622–28 from the Persians, but lost them to the Muslims 629–41.

Herapath /ˈherəpɑːθ/ John 1790–1868. English mathematician. His work on the behaviour of gases, though seriously flawed, was acknowledged by the physicist James Joule in his own more successful investigations.

Herbert /ˈhɜːbət/ Edward, 1st Baron Herbert of Cherbury 1583–1648. English philosopher, brother of George Herbert. His *De veritate* 1624, with its theory of natural religion, founded English deism.

Herbert /ˈhɜːbət/ Frank (Patrick) 1920–1986. US science-fiction writer, author of the *Dune* series from 1965 (filmed by David Lynch 1984), large-scale adventure stories containing serious ideas about ecology and religion.

Herbert /ˈhɜːbət/ George 1593–1633. English poet. His volume of religious poems, *The Temple*, appeared in 1633, shortly before his death. His poems depict his intense religious feelings in clear, simple language.

He became orator to Cambridge University 1619, and a prebendary in Huntingdonshire 1625. After ordination in 1630 he became vicar of Bemerton, Wiltshire, and died of consumption.

Be calm in arguing; for fierceness makes Error a fault and truth discourtesy.

George Herbert *The Church Porch*

Herbert /ˈhɜːbət/ Victor 1859–1924. Irish-born US conductor and composer. In 1893 he became conductor of the 22nd Regiment Band, also composing light operettas for the New York stage. He was conductor of the Pittsburgh Philharmonic 1898–1904, returning to New York to help found the American Society of Composers, Authors, and Publishers (ASCAP) 1914.

Born in Dublin, Republic of Ireland, and trained as a cellist at the Stuttgart Conservatory, Herbert began his professional musical career in Vienna, Austria. He emigrated to the USA in 1886 and played with the New York Metropolitan Opera and Philharmonic Orchestra.

Herbert /ˈhɜːbət/ Wally (Walter) 1934– . British surveyor and explorer. His first surface crossing by dog sledge of the Arctic Ocean 1968–69, from Alaska to Spitsbergen via the North Pole, was the longest sustained sledging journey (6,000 km/3,800 mi) in polar exploration.

Herbert of Lea /ˈhɜːbət, liː/ Sidney Herbert, 1st Baron Herbert of Lea 1810–1861. British politician. He was secretary for war in Aberdeen's Liberal-Peelite coalition of 1852–55, and during the Crimean War was responsible for sending Florence Nightingale to the front.

Herblock /ˈhɜːblɒk/ popular name of Herbert Lawrence Block 1909– . US cartoonist who gained a national reputation during the 1950s with his syndicated cartoons. He won Pulitzer Prizes 1942 and 1952 and published several collections of his work. He played a leading role in the public campaign against the communist witch-hunting tactics of Senator Joseph →McCarthy.

Born in Chicago, USA, Herblock joined the staff of the *Chicago Daily News* 1929 as an editorial cartoonist. After serving in the army during World War II, he joined the staff of the *Washington Post* 1946.

Herder /ˈheədə/ Johann Gottfried von 1744–1803. German poet, critic, and philosopher. Herder's critical writings indicated his intuitive rather than reasoning trend of thought. He collected folk songs of all nations 1778, and in the *Ideen zur Philosophie der Geschichte der Menschheit/Outlines of a Philosophy of the History of Man* 1784–91 he outlined the stages of human cultural development.

Born in East Prussia, Herder studied at Königsberg where he was influenced by Kant, became pastor at Riga, and in 1776 was called to Weimar as court preacher. He gave considerable impetus to the *Sturm und Drang* (storm and stress) Romantic movement in German literature.

Hereward /ˈherɪwəd/ *the Wake* 11th century. English leader of a revolt against the Normans 1070. His stronghold in the Isle of Ely was captured by William the Conqueror 1071. Hereward escaped, but his fate is unknown.

Hergé /eəˈʒeɪ/ Pen name of Georges Remi 1907–1983. Belgian artist, creator of the boy reporter Tintin, who first appeared in strip-cartoon form as *Tintin in the Land of the Soviets* 1929–30.

Herman Woody (Woodrow) 1913–1987. US bandleader and clarinetist. A child prodigy, he was leader of his own orchestra at 23, and after 1945 formed his famous Thundering Herd band. Soloists in this or later versions of the band included Lester →Young and Stan →Getz.

Herod /ˈherəd/ *the Great* 74–4 BC. King of the Roman province of Judaea, S Palestine, from 40 BC. With the aid of Mark Antony, he established his government in Jerusalem 37 BC. He rebuilt the Temple in Jerusalem, but his Hellenizing tendencies made him suspect to orthodox Jewry. His last years were a reign of terror, and in the New Testament Matthew alleges that he ordered the slaughter of all the infants in Bethlehem to ensure the death of Jesus, whom he foresaw as a rival. He was the father of Herod Antipas.

Herod Agrippa I /əˈɡrɪpə/ 10 BC–AD 44. Ruler of Palestine from AD 41. His real name was Marcus Julius Agrippa, erroneously called 'Herod' in the Bible. Grandson of Herod the Great, he was made tetrarch (governor) of Palestine by the Roman emperor Caligula and king by Emperor Claudius AD 41. He put the apostle James to death and imprisoned the apostle Peter. His son was Herod Agrippa II.

Herod Agrippa II /əˈɡrɪpə/ *c.* AD 40–93. King of Chalcis (now S Lebanon), son of Herod Agrippa I. He was appointed by the Roman emperor Claudius about AD 50, and in AD 60 tried the apostle Paul. He helped the Roman emperor Titus take Jerusalem AD 70, then went to Rome, where he died.

Herod Antipas /ˈæntɪpæs/ 21 BC–AD 39. Tetrarch (governor) of the Roman province of Galilee, N Palestine, 4 BC–AD 9, son of Herod the Great. He divorced his wife to marry his niece Herodias, who persuaded her daughter Salome to ask for John the Baptist's head when he reproved Herod's action. Jesus was brought before him on Pontius Pilate's discovery that he was a Galilean and hence of Herod's jurisdiction, but Herod returned him without giving any verdict. In AD 38 Herod Antipas went to Rome to try to persuade Emperor Caligula to give him the title of king, but was instead banished.

Herodotus /heˈrɒdətəs/ *c.* 484–424 BC. Greek historian. After four years in Athens, he travelled widely in Egypt, Asia, and eastern Europe, before settling at Thurii in S Italy 443 BC. He wrote a nine-book history of the Greek-Persian struggle that culminated in the defeat of the Persian invasion attempts 490 and 480 BC. Herodotus was the first historian to apply critical evaluation to his material.

Hero of Alexandria /ˈhɪərəʊ/ Greek mathematician and engineer, probably of the 1st century AD, who invented an automatic fountain and a kind of stationary steam-engine, described in his book *Pneumatica*.

Herophilus of Chalcedon /hɪˈrɒfɪləs/ *c.* 330–*c.* 260 BC. Greek physician, active in Alexandria. His handbooks on anatomy make pioneering use of dissection, which, according to several ancient sources, he carried out on live criminals condemned to death.

Herrera /eˈreərə/ Francisco de, *El Viejo* (the elder) 1576–1656. Spanish painter, active in Seville. He painted genre and religious scenes, with bold effects of light and shade.

Herrera /eˈreərə/ Francisco de, *El Mozo* (the younger) 1622–1685. Spanish still-life painter. He studied in Rome and worked in Seville and Madrid where he was court painter and architect. His paintings reflect Murillo's influence.

Herrick /ˈherɪk/ Robert 1591–1674. English poet and cleric, born in Cheapside, London. He published *Hesperides* 1648, a collection of sacred and pastoral poetry admired for its lyric quality, including 'Gather ye rosebuds' and 'Cherry ripe'.

To work a wonder, God would have her shown
At once, a bud, and yet a rose full-blown.

Robert Herrick
'The Virgin Mary'

Herriot /ˌeriˈəʊ/ Edouard 1872–1957. French Radical socialist politician. An opponent of Poincaré, who as prime minister carried out the French occupation of the Ruhr, Germany, he was briefly prime minister 1924–25, 1926, and 1932. As president of the chamber of deputies 1940, he opposed the policies of the right-wing Vichy government and was arrested and later taken to Germany; he was released 1945 by the Soviets.

Herriot /ˈheriət/ James. Pen name of James Alfred Wight 1916–   . English writer. A practising veterinary surgeon in Yorkshire from 1940, he wrote of his experiences in a series of books including *If Only They Could Talk* 1970, *All Creatures Great and Small* 1972, and *The Lord God Made Them All* 1981.

Herrmann /hɜːmən/ Bernard 1911–1975. American film composer whose long career began with *Citizen Kane* 1940 and included collaborations with Alfred Hitchcock (*North by Northwest* 1959 and *Psycho* 1960) and François Truffaut (*Fahrenheit 451* 1966). He wrote his best scores for thriller and mystery movies, and was a major influence in the establishment of a distinctively American musical imagery.

Born in New York, he studied composition at New York University and the Juilliard School. He joined CBS (Columbia Broadcasting System) 1933 as a composer and conductor of music for drama and documentary programmes and worked with Orson Welles on a number of radio projects before making his film debut. An eclectic stylist, he made his own orchestrations and sought out many new and exotic instruments for special effects and authentic colour.

Herschel /hɜːʃəl/ Caroline Lucretia 1750–1848. German-born English astronomer, sister of William →Herschel, and from 1772 his assistant in England. She discovered eight comets and was awarded the Royal Astronomical Society's gold medal for her work on her brother's catalogue of star clusters and nebulae.

Herschel /hɜːʃəl/ John Frederick William 1792–1871. English scientist and astronomer, son of William Herschel. He discovered thousands of close double stars, clusters, and nebulae, reported 1847. A friend of the photography pioneer Fox →Talbot, Herschel coined the terms 'photography', 'negative', and 'positive', discovered sodium thiosulphite as a fixer of silver halides, and invented the cyanotype process; his inventions also include astronomical instruments.

During the early days of photography he gave lectures on the subject and exhibited his own images.

Herschel /hɜːʃəl/ William 1738–1822. German-born English astronomer. He was a skilled telescope maker, and pioneered the study of binary stars and nebulae. He discovered the planet Uranus 1781 and infrared solar rays 1801. He catalogued over 800 double stars, and found over 2,500 nebulae, catalogued by his sister Caroline Herschel; this work was continued by his son John Herschel. By studying the distribution of stars, William established the basic form of our Galaxy, the Milky Way.

Born in Hanover, Germany, he went to England 1757 and became a professional musician and composer while instructing himself in mathematics and astronomy, and constructing his own reflecting telescopes. While searching for double stars, he found Uranus, and later several of its satellites. This brought him instant fame and, in 1782, the post of private astronomer to George III. He discovered the motion of double stars around one another, and recorded it in his *Motion of the Solar System in Space* 1783. In 1789 he built, at Slough, a 1.2 m/4 ft telescope of 12 m/40 ft

focal length (the largest in the world at the time), but he made most use of a more satisfactory 46 cm/18 in instrument.

Hertling /heətlɪŋ/ Count Georg von 1843–1919. German politician who was appointed imperial chancellor Nov 1917. He maintained a degree of support in the Reichstag (parliament) but was powerless to control the military leadership under →Ludendorff.

Hertz /heəts/ Heinrich 1857–1894. German physicist who studied electromagnetic waves, showing that their behaviour resembles that of light and heat waves.

He confirmed →Maxwell's theory of electromagnetic waves. The unit of frequency, the *hertz*, is named after him.

Hertzberger /hɜːtsbɜːgə/ Herman 1932– . Dutch architect working in the tradition of Brutalism but with the added element of user-friendliness. Notable examples of his work are the Central Beheer office building, Apeldoorn, 1973, and the Music Centre, Utrecht, 1978.

Hertzog /hɜːtsɒg/ James Barry Munnik 1866–1942. South African politician, prime minister 1924–39, founder of the Nationalist Party 1913 (the United South African National Party from 1933). He opposed South Africa's entry into both world wars.

Hertzog was born in Cape Colony of Boer descent. In 1914 he opposed South African participation in World War I. After the 1924 elections Hertzog became prime minister, and in 1933 the Nationalist Party and General Smuts's South African Party were merged as the United South African National Party. In Sept 1939 his motion against participation in World War II was rejected, and he resigned.

Herzl /heətsəl/ Theodor 1860–1904. Austrian founder of the *Zionist* movement. He was born in Budapest and became a successful playwright and journalist, mainly in Vienna. The →Dreyfus case convinced him that the only solution to the problem of anti-Semitism was the resettlement of the Jews in a state of their own. His book *Jewish State* 1896 launched political Zionism, campaigning for the establishment of a Jewish homeland, and he became the first president of the World Zionist Organization 1897.

Herzog /heətsɒg/ Werner 1942– . German maverick film director who often takes his camera to exotic and impractical locations. His highly original and visually splendid films include *Aguirre der Zorn Gottes/Aguirre Wrath of God* 1972, *Nosferatu Phantom der Nacht/Nosferatu Phantom of the Night* 1979, and *Fitzcarraldo* 1982.

I make films to rid myself of them, like ridding myself of a nightmare.

Werner Herzog

Heseltine /ˈhesəltaɪn/ Michael (Ray Dibdin) 1933– . English Conservative politician, member of Parliament from 1966 (for Henley from 1974), secretary of state for the environment 1990–92, and for trade and industry from 1992. Heseltine was minister of the environment 1979–83, when he succeeded John Nott as minister of defence Jan 1983 but resigned Jan 1986 over the Westland affair (the takeover of the British helicopter company, about which there were allegations of malpractice). He was then seen as a major rival to Margaret Thatcher. In Nov 1990, Heseltine's challenge to Thatcher's leadership of the Conservative Party brought about her resignation, though he lost the leadership election to John Major. In Oct 1992, adverse public reaction to his pit-closure programme forced the government to backtrack and review their policy.

The day before Heseltine announced his leadership challenge, Deputy Prime Minister Geoffrey Howe had attacked Thatcher's stance on Europe during his vitriolic resignation speech in the House of Commons. Heseltine supported closer ties with Europe and asserted that he had a better chance of leading the Conservative Party to victory at the next election. He also promised a review of the poll tax. On the first ballot of the leadership contest Thatcher narrowly failed to gain the 15% majority required for re-election and two days later announced her resignation as party leader. Foreign Secretary Douglas Hurd and chancellor of the Exchequer John Major then joined the contest against Heseltine. In the election 27 Nov 1990, with Major two votes short of an absolute majority, both Hurd and Heseltine conceded defeat. On 28 Nov Heseltine rejoined the cabinet as secretary of state for the environment. In April 1991 he announced a replacement for the unpopular poll tax. Following the general election April 1992, he was made secretary for trade and industry. His announcement of a drastic pit-closure programme Oct 1992 met with widespread opposition. Forced to bow to public pressure, he agreed, together with Prime Minister John Major, to instigate an inquiry into the country's future energy needs.

Heseltine /ˈhesəltaɪn/ Philip (Arnold). Real name of the English composer Peter →Warlock.

Hesiod /ˈhiːsiəd/ lived c. 700 BC. Greek poet. He is supposed to have lived a little later than Homer, and according to his own account he was born in Boeotia. He is the author of 'Works and Days', a poem that tells of the country life, and the *Theogony*, an account of the origin of the world and of the gods.

Hess /hes/ (Walter Richard) Rudolf 1894–1987. German Nazi leader. Imprisoned with Hitler 1923–25, he became his private secretary, taking down *Mein Kampf* from his dictation. In 1932 he was appointed deputy *Führer* to Hitler. On 10 May 1941 he landed by air in the UK with compromise peace proposals and was held a prisoner

Hess English pianist Myra Hess worked as a chamber musician, recitalist, and virtuoso, and achieved fame in the USA as well as in Britain. Her playing combined a brilliant technique with great warmth of feeling; her repertoire was wide and, in her early days, adventurous in the field of contemporary music.

of war until 1945, when he was tried at Nuremberg as a war criminal and sentenced to life imprisonment. He died in Spandau prison, Berlin.

He was effectively in charge of the Nazi party organization until his flight 1941. For the last years of his life he was the only prisoner left in Spandau.

Hess /hes/ Myra 1890–1965. British pianist. She is remembered for her morale-boosting National Gallery concerts in World War II, her transcription of the Bach chorale 'Jesu, Joy of Man's Desiring', and her interpretations of Beethoven.

Hess /hes/ Victor 1883–1964. Austrian physicist who emigrated to the USA shortly after sharing a Nobel prize in 1936 for the discovery of cosmic radiation.

Hesse /ˈhesə/ Hermann 1877–1962. German writer who became a Swiss citizen 1923. A conscientious objector in World War I and a pacifist opponent of Hitler, he published short stories, poetry, and novels, including *Peter Camenzind* 1904, *Siddhartha* 1922, and *Steppenwolf* 1927. Later works, such as *Das Glasperlenspiel/The Glass Bead Game* 1943, tend towards the mystical. He was awarded the Nobel Prize for Literature 1946.

Heston /ˈhestən/ Charlton. Stage name of Charles Carter 1924– . US film actor who often starred in biblical and historical epics (as Moses, for example, in *The Ten Commandments* 1956, and in the title role in *Ben-Hur* 1959).

Hevesy /ˈhevəʃi/ Georg von 1885–1966. Swedish chemist, discoverer of the element hafnium. He was the first to use a radioactive isotope (radioactive form of an element) to follow the steps of a biological process, for which he won the Nobel Prize for Chemistry 1943.

Hewish /ˈhjuːiʃ/ Antony 1924– . British radio astronomer who was awarded, with Martin →Ryle, the Nobel Prize for Physics 1974 for his work on pulsars, rapidly rotating neutron stars that emit pulses of energy.

Heydrich /ˈhaɪdrɪk/ Reinhard 1904–1942. German Nazi, head of the party's security service and Heinrich →Himmler's deputy. He was instrumental in organizing the final solution, the policy of genocide used against Jews and others. While deputy 'protector' of Bohemia and Moravia from 1941, he was ambushed and killed by three members of the Czechoslovak forces in Britain, who had landed by parachute. Reprisals followed, including several hundred executions and the massacre in Lidice.

Heyerdahl /ˈhaɪədɑːl/ Thor 1914– . Norwegian ethnologist. He sailed on the ancient-Peruvian-style raft *Kon-Tiki* from Peru to the Tuamotu Archipelago along the Humboldt Current 1947, and in 1969–70 used ancient-Egyptian-style papyrus reed boats to cross the Atlantic. His experimental approach to historical reconstruction is not regarded as having made any important scientific contribution.

His expeditions were intended to establish that ancient civilizations could have travelled the oceans in similar fashion, but his theories are largely discounted by anthropologists, who rely on linguistic, sociological, and archaeological information. His voyages are described in *Kon-Tiki*, translated into English 1950, and *The Ra Expeditions*, translated 1971. He also crossed the Persian Gulf 1977, written about in *The Tigris Expedition*, translated 1981.

Heywood /ˈheɪwʊd/ Thomas *c.* 1570–*c.* 1650. English actor and dramatist. He wrote or adapted over 220 plays, including the domestic tragedy *A Woman kilde with kindnesse* 1607.

Hiawatha /ˌhaɪəˈwɒθə/ 16th-century North American Indian teacher and Onondaga chieftain. He is said to have welded the Five Nations (later joined by a sixth) of the Iroquois into the league of the **Long House**, as the confederacy was known in what is now upper New York State. Hiawatha is the hero of Longfellow's epic poem *The Song of Hiawatha*.

Hick /hɪk/ Graeme 1966– . Rhodesian-born cricketer who became Zimbabwe's youngest professional cricketer at the age of 17. A prolific batsman, he joined Worcestershire, England, in 1984. He achieved the highest score in England in the 20th century in 1988 against Somerset with 405 not out. He made his Test debut for England in 1991 after a seven-year qualification period.

Hickey /ˈhɪki/ William 1749–1830. British writer, whose entertaining *Memoirs* were first published 1913–1925.

Hickok /ˈhɪkɒk/ 'Wild Bill' (James Butler) 1837–1876. US pioneer and law enforcer, a legendary figure in the West. In the Civil War he was a sharpshooter and scout for the Union army. He then served as marshal in Kansas, killing as many as 27 men. He established his reputation as a gunfighter when he killed a fellow scout, turned traitor. He was a prodigious gambler and was fatally shot from behind while playing poker in Deadwood, South Dakota.

Hidalgo y Costilla /iˈgælgəʊ iː kɒˈstiljə/ Miguel 1753–1811. Catholic priest, known as 'the Father of Mexican Independence'. A symbol of the opposition to Spain, he rang the church bell Sept 1810 to announce to his parishioners in Dolores that the revolution against the Spanish had begun. He was captured and shot the following year.

Higgins /ˈhɪgɪnz/ George V 1939– . US novelist who wrote many detective and underworld novels, often set in Boston, including *The Friends of Eddie Coyle* 1972 and *The Impostors* 1986.

Higgins Jack. Pseudonym of British novelist Harry →Patterson.

Highsmith Patricia 1921– . US crime novelist. Her first book, *Strangers on a Train* 1950, was filmed by Alfred Hitchcock. She excels in tension and psychological exploration of character.

She wrote a series dealing with the amoral Tom Ripley, including *The Talented Mr Ripley* 1956, *Ripley Under Ground* 1971, and *Ripley's Game* 1974.

Hilbert /ˈhɪlbət/ David 1862–1943. German mathematician who founded the formalist school with the publication of *Grundlagen der Geometrie/Foundations of Geometry* 1899, which was based on his idea of postulates. He attempted to put mathematics on a logical foundation through defining it in terms of a number of basic principles, which →Gödel later showed to be impossible; nonetheless, his attempt greatly influenced 20th-century mathematicians.

He who seeks for methods without having a definite problem in mind for the most part seeks in vain.

David Hilbert quoted in J R Oppenheimer *Physics in the Contemporary World*

Hildebrand /ˈhɪldəbrænd/ Benedictine monk who became Pope →Gregory VII.

Hildegard of Bingen /ˈhɪldəgɑːd, ˈbɪŋən/ 1098–1179. German scientific writer, abbess of the Benedictine convent of St Disibode, near the Rhine, from 1136. She wrote a mystical treatise, *Liber Scivias* 1141, and an encyclopedia of natural history, *Liber Simplicis Medicinae* 1150–60, giving both Latin and German names for the species described, as well as their medicinal uses; it is the earliest surviving scientific book by a woman.

Hill /hɪl/ Austin Bradford 1897–1991. English epidemiologist and statistician. He pioneered rigorous statistical study of patterns of disease and, together with William Richard Doll, was the first to demonstrate the connection between cigarette smoking and lung cancer.

Hill /hɪl/ David Octavius 1802–1870. Scottish photographer who, in collaboration with Robert →Adamson, made extensive use of the calotype process in their large collection of portraits taken in Edinburgh 1843–48.

Hill /hɪl/ Graham 1929–1975. English motor-racing driver. He won the Dutch Grand Prix in 1962, progressing to the world driver's title in 1962 and 1968. In 1972 he became the first world driver's champion to win the Le Mans Grand Prix d'Endurance (Le Mans 24–Hour Race). Hill started his Formula One career with Lotus 1958, went to BRM 1960–66, returned to Lotus 1967–69, moved to Brabham 1970–72, and formed his own team, Embassy Shadow, 1973–75. He was killed in an air crash.

Hill /hɪl/ Joe *c.* 1872–1915. Swedish-born US labour organizer. A member of the Industrial Workers of the World (IWW, 'Wobblies'), he was convicted of murder on circumstantial evidence in Salt Lake City, Utah, 1914. Despite calls by President Wilson and the Swedish government for a re-trial, Hill was executed 1915, becoming a martyr for the labour movement.

Born in Sweden, Hill emigrated to the USA 1901. His original name is given variously as Joel Emmanuel Haaglund (or Hagglund) or Joseph Hillstrom. He frequently contributed to the IWW's *Solidarity* and *Industrial Worker* and is remembered for his many popular pro-union songs.

Hill /hɪl/ Octavia 1838–1912. English campaigner for housing reform and public open spaces. She cofounded the National Trust 1894.

Hill /hɪl/ Rowland 1795–1879. British Post Office official who invented adhesive stamps and prompted the introduction of the penny prepaid post in 1840 (previously the addressee paid, according to distance, on receipt).

Hillary /hɪləri/ Edmund Percival 1919– . New Zealand mountaineer. In 1953, with Nepalese Sherpa mountaineer Tenzing Norgay, he reached the summit of Mount Everest, the first to climb the world's highest peak. As a member of the Commonwealth Transantarctic Expedition 1957–58, he was the first person since Scott to reach the South Pole overland, on 3 Jan 1958.

He was in the reconnaissance party to Everest in 1951. On the way to the South Pole he laid depots for Vivian →Fuchs's completion of the crossing of the continent.

Hill British reformer Rowland Hill who introduced the prepaid postal service – the penny post. Realizing that a low postage rate would provide greater income by increasing the volume of mail, Hill proposed a flat rate to cut administrative costs and developed a franking system to achieve his objective.

Hillel 1st century BC Hebrew scholar, lawyer, and teacher; member of the Pharisaic movement. His work was accepted by later rabbinic Judaism and is noted for its tolerance.

Hiller /hɪlə/ Wendy 1912– . British stage and film actress. Her many roles include Catherine Sloper in *The Heiress* 1947 and Eliza in the film version of Shaw's *Pygmalion* 1938.

Hilliard Nicholas *c.* 1547–1619. English miniaturist and goldsmith, court artist to Elizabeth I from about 1579. His sitters included the explorers Francis Drake and Walter Raleigh.

A fine collection of his delicate portraits, set in gold cases, including *Young Man Amid Roses* about 1590, is in the Victoria and Albert Museum, London.

Hilton /hɪltən/ Conrad Nicholson 1887–1979. US entrepreneur, founder of the Hilton Hotel Corporation 1946. During the 1930s he steadily expanded his chain of luxury hotels and resorts and reorganized it as the Hilton Hotel Corporation 1946. He based the firm's marketing appeal on its recognizable name and high-quality standardized service.

Born in San Antonio, New Mexico, USA, Hilton attended the New Mexico School of Mines and joined his father in various business ventures after graduation 1909. Originally successful in banking, he entered the hotel business after World War I, retiring 1966.

His autobiography, *Be My Guest*, was published 1957.

Hilton /ˈhɪltən/ James 1900–1954. English novelist. He settled in Hollywood as one of its most successful scriptwriters, for example, *Mrs Miniver*. His books include *Lost Horizon* 1933, envisaging Shangri-la, a remote district of Tibet where time stands still; *Goodbye, Mr Chips* 1934, a portrait of an old schoolmaster; and *Random Harvest* 1941.

Himes /haɪmz/ Chester 1909–1984. US novelist. After serving seven years in prison for armed robbery, he published his first novel *If He Hollers Let Him Go* 1945, a depiction of the drudgery and racism in a Californian shipyard.

Himmler /ˈhɪmlə/ Heinrich 1900–1945. German Nazi leader, head of the SS elite corps from 1929, the police and the Gestapo secret police from 1936, and supervisor of the extermination of the Jews in E Europe. During World War II he replaced Goering as Hitler's second-in-command. He was captured May 1945 and committed suicide.

Born in Munich, he joined the Nazi Party in 1925 and became chief of the Bavarian police 1933. His accumulation of offices meant he had command of all German police forces by 1936, which made him one of the most powerful people in Germany. In April 1945 he made a proposal to the Allies that Germany should surrender to the USA and Britain but not to the USSR, which was rejected.

Hinault /iˈnəʊ/ Bernard 1954– . French cyclist, one of three men to have won the Tour de France five times (1978–85); the others being Jacques →Anquetil and Eddie →Merckx.

Hindemith /ˈhɪndəmɪt/ Paul 1895–1963. German composer. His Neo-Classical, contrapuntal works include chamber ensemble and orchestral pieces, such as the *Symphonic Metamorphosis on Themes of Carl Maria von Weber* 1944, and the operas *Cardillac* 1926, revised 1952, and *Mathis der Maler/Mathis the Painter* 1938.

A fine viola player, he led the Frankfurt Opera Orchestra at 20, and taught at the Berlin Hochschule for music 1927–33. The modernity of his work, such as the *Philharmonic Concerto* 1932, led to a Nazi ban. In 1939 he went to the USA, where he taught at Yale University and in 1951 he became professor of musical theory at Zürich.

Hindenburg /ˈhɪndənbɜːg/ Paul Ludwig Hans von Beneckendorf und Hindenburg 1847–1934. German field marshal and right-wing politician. During World War I he was supreme commander and, with Ludendorff, practically directed Germany's policy until the end of the war. He was president of Germany 1925–33.

Born in Posen of a Prussian Junker (aristocratic landowner) family, he was commissioned 1866, served in the Austro-Prussian and Franco-German wars, and retired 1911. Given the command in East Prussia Aug 1914, he received the credit for the defeat of the Russians at Tannenberg and was promoted to supreme commander and field

marshal. Re-elected president 1932, he was compelled to invite Hitler to assume the chancellorship Jan 1933.

Hine /haɪn/ Lewis 1874–1940. US sociologist and photographer. His dramatic photographs of child labour conditions in US factories at the beginning of the 20th century led to changes in state and local labour laws.

Hines /haɪnz/ Duncan 1880–1959. US travel author and publisher. He published restaurant and hotel reviews such as *Adventures in Good Eating* 1936 and *Lodging for a Night* 1939. A pioneer travel critic, Hines helped raise the standard of travel accommodation in the USA.

He was born in Bowling Green, Kentucky, USA. His guides were based on notes compiled during his work as a travelling salesman.

He later licensed his name to a line of prepackaged cake mixes and founded his own publishing house for cookbooks and entertainment and travel guides.

Hinkler /ˈhɪŋklə/ Herbert John Louis 1892–1933. Australian pilot who in 1928 made the first solo flight from England to Australia. He was killed while making another attempt to fly to Australia.

Hinshelwood /ˈhɪnʃəlwʊd/ Cyril Norman 1897–1967. English chemist. He shared the 1956 Nobel Prize for Chemistry with Nikolai Semenov for his work on chemical chain reactions. He also studied the chemistry of bacterial growth.

Hipparchus /hɪˈpɑːkəs/ c. 555–514 BC. Greek tyrant. Son of →Pisistratus, he was associated with his elder brother Hippias as ruler of Athens 527–514 BC. His affection being spurned by Harmodius, he insulted her sister, and was assassinated by Harmodius and Aristogiton.

Hipparchus /hɪˈpɑːkəs/ c. 190–c. 120 BC. Greek astronomer who invented trigonometry, calculated the lengths of the solar year and the lunar month, discovered the precession of the equinoxes, made a catalogue of 800 fixed stars, and advanced Eratosthenes' method of determining the situation of places on the Earth's surface by lines of latitude and longitude.

Hippocrates /hɪˈpɒkrətiːz/ c. 460–c. 370 BC. Greek physician, often called the father of medicine. Important Hippocratic ideas include cleanliness (for patients and physicians), moderation in eating and drinking, letting nature take its course, and living where the air is good. He believed that health was the result of the 'humours' of the body being in balance; imbalance caused disease. These ideas were later adopted by →Galen.

He was born and practised on the island of Kos and died at Larissa. He is known to have discovered aspirin in willow bark. The *Corpus Hippocraticum*, a group of some 70 works, is attributed to him but was probably not written by him, although the works outline his approach to medicine. They include *Aphorisms* and the *Hippocratic*

Oath, which embodies the essence of medical ethics.

Hirohito /ˌhɪərəʊˈhiːtəʊ/ 1901–1989 . Emperor of Japan from 1926. He succeeded his father Yoshi-hito. After the defeat of Japan in World War II 1945, he was made constitutional monarch by the US-backed 1946 constitution. He is believed to have played a reluctant role in →Tojo's prewar expansion plans. Hirohito ruled postwar occupied Japan with dignity. His era is known as the Showa era. He was succeeded by his son →Akihito.

Hirohito was a scholar of botany and zoology and the author of books on marine biology.

We have resolved to endure the unendurable and suffer what is insufferable.

Emperor Hirohito on accepting the Allied terms of surrender, broadcasting to the nation Aug 1945

Hiroshige /ˌhɪəˈrəʊʃɪgeɪ/ Andō 1797–1858. Japanese artist whose landscape prints, often using snow or rain to create atmosphere, include *Tōkaidō gojūsan-tsugi/53 Stations on the Tokaido Highway* 1833. Whistler and van Gogh were among Western painters influenced by him.

Hiroshige was born in Edo (now Tokyo), and his last series was *Meisho Edo Hyakkei/100 Famous Views of Edo* 1856–58, uncompleted before his death. He is thought to have made over 5,000 different prints.

Hiss /hɪs/ Alger 1904– . US diplomat and liberal Democrat, a former State Department official, imprisoned 1950 for perjury. There are doubts about the justice of Hiss's conviction.

Hiss, president of the Carnegie Endowment for International Peace and one of President Roosevelt's advisers at the 1945 Yalta Conference, was accused 1948 by a former Soviet agent, Whittaker Chambers (1901–1961), of having passed information to the USSR during the period 1926–37. He was convicted of perjury for swearing before the House Un-American Activities Committee that he had not spied for the USSR (under the statute of limitations he could not be tried for the original crime). Richard →Nixon was a prominent member of the committee, which inspired the subsequent anticommunist witch-hunts of Senator Joseph →McCarthy.

Hitchcock /ˈhɪtʃkɒk/ Alfred 1899–1980. British film director who became a US citizen in 1955. A master of the suspense thriller, he was noted for his meticulously drawn storyboards that determined his camera angles and for his cameo 'walk-ons' in his own films. His *Blackmail* 1929 was the first successful British talking film; *The Thirty-Nine Steps* 1935 and *The Lady Vanishes* 1939 are British suspense classics. He went to Hollywood 1940, where he made *Rebecca* 1940, *Notorious*

Hitchcock Suspense, melodrama, and fleeting personal appearances are the hallmarks of Alfred Hitchcock's films. A meticulous director, and a supreme technician and visual artist, Hitchcock contributed significantly to the growth of cinema as an art form.

1946, *Strangers on a Train* 1951, *Rear Window* 1954, *Vertigo* 1958, *Psycho* 1960, and *The Birds* 1963. He also hosted two US television mystery series, *Alfred Hitchcock Presents* 1955–62 and *The Alfred Hitchcock Hour* 1963–65.

Hitchens /ˈhɪtʃɪnz/ Ivon 1893–1979. British painter. His semi-abstract landscapes were painted initially in natural tones, later in more vibrant colours. He also painted murals, for example, *Day's Rest, Day's Work* 1963 (Sussex University).

From the 1940s Hitchens lived in a forest near Midhurst in Sussex which provided the setting for many of his paintings.

Hitler /ˈhɪtlə/ Adolf 1889–1945. German Nazi dictator, born in Austria. He was *Führer* (leader) of the Nazi Party from 1921 and author of *Mein Kampf/My Struggle* 1925–27. As chancellor of Germany from 1933 and head of state from 1934, he created a dictatorship by playing party and state institutions against each other and continually creating new offices and appointments. His position was not seriously challenged until the 'Bomb Plot' 20 July 1944 to assassinate him. In foreign affairs, he reoccupied the Rhineland and formed an alliance with the Italian Fascist Mussolini 1936, annexed Austria 1938, and occupied the Sudetenland under the Munich Agreement. The rest of Czechoslovakia was annexed March 1939. The Hitler–Stalin pact was followed in Sept by the invasion of Poland and the declaration of war by Britain and France. He committed suicide as Berlin fell.

Hitler German Nazi leader Adolf Hitler. Only a small minority of Germans raised the slightest opposition to Hitler and there was only one serious conspiracy against him, in July 1944, when he narrowly escaped death from a bomb planted by a staff officer, Col Klaus von Stauffenberg.

Born at Braunau-am-Inn, the son of a customs official, he spent his early years in poverty in Vienna and Munich. After serving as a volunteer in the German army during World War I, he was employed as a spy by the military authorities in Munich and in 1919 joined, in this capacity, the German Workers' Party. By 1921 he had assumed its leadership, renamed it the National Socialist German Workers' Party (Nazi Party for short), and provided it with a programme that mixed nationalism with anti-Semitism. Having led an unsuccessful uprising in Munich 1923, he was sentenced to nine months' imprisonment during which he wrote his political testament, *Mein Kampf*. The party did not achieve national importance until the elections of 1930; by 1932, although Field Marshal Hindenburg defeated Hitler in the presidential elections, it formed the largest group in the Reichstag (parliament). As the result of an intrigue directed by Chancellor Franz von Papen, Hitler became chancellor in a Nazi–Nationalist coalition 30 Jan 1933. The opposition was rapidly suppressed, the Nationalists removed from the government, and the Nazis declared the only legal party. In 1934 Hitler succeeded Hindenburg as head of state. Meanwhile, the drive to war began; Germany left the League of Nations, conscription was reintroduced, and in 1936 the Rhineland was reoccupied. Hitler and Mussolini, who were already both involved in Spain, formed an alliance (the Axis) 1936, joined by Japan 1940. Hitler conducted the war in a ruthless but idiosyncratic way, took and ruled most of the neighbouring countries with repressive

occupation forces, and had millions of Slavs, Jews, Romanies, homosexuals, and political enemies killed in concentration camps and massacres. He narrowly escaped death 1944 from a bomb explosion at a staff meeting, prepared by high-ranking officers. On 29 April 1945, when Berlin was largely in Soviet hands, he married his mistress Eva Braun in his bunker under the chancellery building and on the following day committed suicide with her.

> *The broad mass of a nation ... will more easily fall victim to a big lie than a small one.*
>
> **Adolf Hitler** *Mein Kampf* 1927

Hoban /ˈhəʊbən/ James C 1762–1831. Irish-born architect who emigrated to the USA. He designed the White House, Washington DC; he also worked on the Capitol and other public buildings.

Hobbema /ˈhɒbɪmə/ Meindert 1638–1709. Dutch landscape painter, a pupil of Ruisdael. His early work is derivative, but later works are characteristically realistic and unsentimental.

He was popular with English collectors in the 18th and 19th centuries, and influenced English landscape painting.

Hobbes /hɒbz/ Thomas 1588–1679. English political philosopher and the first thinker since Aristotle to attempt to develop a comprehensive theory of nature, including human behaviour. In *The Leviathan* 1651, he advocates absolutist government as the only means of ensuring order and security; he saw this as deriving from the social contract (the concept that government authority derives originally from an agreement between ruler and ruled, in which the former agrees to provide order in return for obedience from the latter).

He was tutor to the exiled Prince Charles (later Charles II).

Hobbs /hɒbz/ Jack (John Berry) 1882–1963. English cricketer who represented his country 61 times. In all first class cricket he scored a world record 61,237 runs, including a record 197 centuries in a career that lasted nearly 30 years.

Hochhuth /ˈhɒxhuːt/ Rolf 1931– . Swiss dramatist whose controversial play *Soldaten/Soldiers* 1968 implied that the British politician Churchill was involved in a plot to assassinate the Polish general →Sikorski.

Ho Chi Minh /ˌhəʊ tʃiː ˈmɪn/ adopted name of Nguyen That Tan 1890–1969. North Vietnamese Communist politician, premier and president 1954–69. Having trained in Moscow shortly after the Russian Revolution, he headed the communist Vietminh from 1941 and fought against the French during the Indochina War 1946–54, becoming president and prime minister of the republic at the armistice. Aided by the Communist bloc, he did much to develop industrial potential. He relinquished the premiership 1955, but continued as president. In the years before his death, Ho successfully led his country's fight against US-aided South Vietnam in the Vietnam War 1954–75.

Hockney /hɒkni/ David 1937–   . English painter, printmaker, and designer, resident in California. He exhibited at the Young Contemporaries Show of 1961 and contributed to the Pop art movement. He developed an individual figurative style, as in his portrait *Mr and Mrs Clark and Percy* 1971, Tate Gallery, London, and has prolifically experimented with technique. His views of swimming pools reflect a preoccupation with surface pattern and effects of light. He has also produced drawings, etchings, photo collages, and sets for opera.

Hockney, born in Yorkshire, studied at Bradford School of Art and the Royal College of Art, London. He was the subject of Jack Hazan's semidocumentary 1974 film *A Bigger Splash*; it is also the title of one of his paintings (1967, Tate Gallery, London). He has designed sets for the opera at Glyndebourne, East Sussex; La Scala, Milan; and the Metropolitan Opera House, New York.

Hodgkin /hɒdʒkɪn/ Alan Lloyd 1914–   . British physiologist engaged in research with Andrew Huxley on the mechanism of conduction in peripheral nerves 1946–60. In 1963 they shared the Nobel Prize for Physiology and Medicine with John Eccles.

Hodgkin /hɒdʒkɪn/ Dorothy Crowfoot 1910–   . English biochemist who analysed the structure of penicillin, insulin, and vitamin B12. Hodgkin was the first to use a computer to analyse the molecular structure of complex chemicals, and this enabled her to produce three-dimensional models. She was awarded the Nobel Prize for Chemistry 1964.

Hodgkin /hɒdʒkɪn/ Thomas 1798–1856. British physician who first recognized *Hodgkin's disease*.

Hodler /hɒdlə/ Ferdinand 1853–1918. Swiss painter. His dramatic Art Nouveau paintings of allegorical, historical, and mythological subjects include large murals with dreamy Symbolist female figures, such as *Day* about 1900 (Kunsthaus, Zürich).

Hodza /hɒdʒə/ Milan 1878–1944. Czechoslovak politician, prime minister 1936–38. He and President Beneš were forced to agree to the secession of the Sudeten areas of Czechoslovakia to Germany before resigning 22 Sept 1938.

Hoess /hɜːs/ Rudolf 1900–1947. German commandant of Auschwitz concentration camp 1940–43. Under his control, more than 2.5 million people were exterminated. Arrested by Allied military police in 1946, he was handed over to the

Polish authorities, who tried and executed him in 1947.

Hoffa /hɒfə/ Jimmy (James Riddle) 1913–*c*. 1975. US labour leader, president of the International Brotherhood of Teamsters (transport workers) from 1957. He was jailed 1967–71 for attempted bribery of a federal court jury after he was charged with corruption. He was released by President Nixon with the stipulation that he did not engage in union activities, but was evidently attempting to reassert influence when he disappeared. He is generally believed to have been murdered.

Hoffman /hɒfmən/ Abbie (Abbot) 1936–1989. US left-wing political activist, founder of the Yippies (Youth International Party), a political offshoot of the hippies. He was a member of the Chicago Seven, a radical group tried for attempting to disrupt the 1968 Democratic Convention.

Hoffman was arrested 52 times and was a fugitive from justice 1973–80. He specialized in imaginative political gestures to gain media attention, for example throwing dollar bills to the floor of the New York Stock Exchange 1967. His books include *Revolution for the Hell of It* 1969. He campaigned against the Vietnam War and, later, for the environment. He committed suicide.

Hoffman /hɒfmən/ Dustin 1937–   . US actor, icon of the antiheroic 1960s. He won Academy Awards for his performances in *Kramer vs Kramer* 1979 and *Rain Man* 1988. His other films include *The Graduate* 1967, *Midnight Cowboy* 1969, *Little Big Man* 1970, *All the President's Men* 1976, *Tootsie* 1982, and *Hook* 1991. He appeared on Broadway in the 1984 revival of *Death of a Salesman*, which was also produced for television 1985.

Hoffmann /hɒfmən/   E(rnst)   T(heodor) A(madeus) 1776–1822. German composer and writer. He composed the opera *Undine* 1816 and many fairy stories, including *Nussknacker/Nutcracker* 1816. His stories inspired →Offenbach's *Tales of Hoffmann*.

Hoffmann /hɒfmən/ Josef 1870–1956. Austrian architect, one of the founders of the Wiener Werkstätte (a modern design cooperative of early 20th-century Vienna), and a pupil of Otto →Wagner.

Hofmann /haʊfmən/ August Wilhelm von 1818–1892. German chemist who studied the extraction and exploitation of coal tar derivatives. Hofmann taught chemistry in London from 1845 until his return to Berlin in 1865.

In 1881 he devised a process for the production of pure primary amines from amides.

Hofmann /haʊfmən/ Hans 1880–1966. German-born Abstract Expressionist painter, active in Paris and Munich from 1915 until 1932, when he moved to the USA. In addition to bold brushwork (he experimented with dribbling and dripping painting techniques in the 1940s), he used strong expressive colours. In the 1960s he moved towards a hard-edged abstract style.

Hogarth 18th-century English painter and engraver William Hogarth. He created a grand precursor to the comic strip in the form of his series of anecdotal paintings, of which Marriage à la Mode *and* A Rake's Progress *are examples. The popularity of pirated engravings from his paintings led to the Copyright Act 1735.*

Hofmeister /ˈhəʊfmeɪstə/ Wilhelm 1824–1877. German botanist. He studied plant development and determined how a plant embryo, lying within a seed, is itself formed out of a single fertilized egg (ovule).

Hofmeister also discovered that mosses and ferns display an alternation of generations, in which the plant has two forms, spore-forming and gamete-forming.

Hofstadter /ˈhɒfstætə/ Robert 1915–1990. US high-energy physicist who revealed the structure of the atomic nucleus. He demonstrated that the nucleus is composed of a high-energy core and a surrounding area of decreasing density. He shared the 1961 Nobel Prize for Physics with Rudolf Mössbauer.

Hofstadter helped to construct a new high-energy accelerator at Stanford University, California, with which he showed that the proton and the neutron have complex structures and cannot be considered elementary particles.

Hogan Ben 1912– . US golfer who won the Masters, the US Open, and the British Open in the same year, 1953. He was a member of four Ryder Cup teams, playing captain in 1947 and 1949.

Hogan Paul 1940– . Australian TV comic, film actor, and producer. The box-office hit *Crocodile Dundee* (considered the most profitable film in Australian history) 1986 and *Crocodile Dundee II* 1988 (of which he was co-writer, star, and producer) brought him international fame.

Hogarth /ˈhəʊgɑː θ/ William 1697–1764. English painter and engraver who produced portraits and moralizing genre scenes, such as the series *A Rake's Progress* 1735. His portraits are remarkably direct and full of character, for example *Heads of Six of Hogarth's Servants c.* 1750–55 (Tate Gallery, London).

Hogarth was born in London and apprenticed to an engraver. He published *A Harlot's Progress*, a series of six engravings, in 1732. Other series followed, including *Marriage à la Mode* 1745, *Industry and Idleness* 1749, and *The Four Stages of Cruelty* 1751. In his book *The Analysis of Beauty* 1753 he proposed a double curved line as a key to successful composition.

Hogg /hɒg/ James 1770–1835. Scottish novelist and poet, known as the 'Ettrick Shepherd'. Born in Ettrick Forest, Selkirkshire, he worked as a shepherd at Yarrow 1790–99. Until the age of 30, he was illiterate. His novel *Confessions of a Justified Sinner* 1824 is a masterly portrayal of personified evil.

Hogg /hɒg/ Quintin. British politician; see Lord →Hailsham.

Hohenlohe-Schillingsfürst /ˈhəʊənləʊə ˈʃɪlɪŋsfʊəst/ Prince Chlodwig von 1819–1901. German imperial chancellor from Oct 1894 until his replacement by Prince von Bülow Oct 1900.

Hohenstaufen /ˌhəʊənˈʃtaʊfən/ German family of princes, several members of which were Holy Roman emperors 1138–1208 and 1214–54. They were the first German emperors to make use of associations with Roman law and tradition to aggrandize their office, and included Conrad III; Frederick I (Barbarossa), the first to use the title Holy Roman emperor (previously the title Roman emperor was used); Henry VI; and Frederick II. The last of the line, Conradin, was executed 1268 with the approval of Pope Clement IV while attempting to gain his Sicilian inheritance.

Hohenzollern /ˌhəʊənˈzɒlən/ German family, originating in Württemberg, the main branch of which held the titles of elector of Brandenburg from 1415, king of Prussia from 1701, and German emperor from 1871. The last emperor, Wilhelm II, was dethroned 1918 after the disastrous course of World War I. Another branch of the family were kings of Romania 1881–1947.

Hokusai /ˌhəʊkʊˈsaɪ/ Katsushika 1760–1849. Japanese artist, the leading printmaker of his time. He published *Fugaku Sanjū-rokkei/36 Views of Mount Fuji* about 1823–29, but he produced outstanding pictures of almost every kind of subject – birds, flowers, courtesans, and scenes from legend and everyday life.

Hokusai was born in Edo (now Tokyo) and studied wood engraving and book illustration. He was interested in Western painting and perspective and introduced landscape as a woodblock-print genre. His *Manga*, a book crammed with inventive sketches, was published in 13 volumes from 1814.

Holbein /ˈhɒlbaɪn/ Hans, **the Elder** c. 1464–1524. German painter, active in Augsburg. His works include altarpieces, such as that of *St Sebastian* 1516 (Alte Pinakothek, Munich). He also painted portraits and designed stained glass.

Holbein /ˈhɒlbaɪn/ Hans, **the Younger** 1497/98–1543. German painter and woodcut artist; the son and pupil of Hans Holbein the Elder. Holbein was born in Augsburg. In 1515 he went to Basel, where he became friendly with Erasmus; he painted three portraits of him in 1523, which were strongly influenced by Quentin Massys. He travelled widely in Europe and was court painter to England's Henry VIII from 1536. He also painted portraits of Thomas More and Thomas Cromwell; a notable woodcut series is *Dance of Death* about 1525. He designed title pages for Luther's New Testament and More's *Utopia*.

Pronounced Renaissance influence emerged in the *Meyer Madonna* 1526, a fine altarpiece in Darmstadt. During his time at the English court, he also painted miniature portraits, inspiring Nicholas Hilliard.

Holborne /ˈhəʊlbɔːn/ Anthony 1584–1602. English composer. He wrote a book of *Pavans, Galliards, Almains and Other Short Aeirs* 1599.

Holden /ˈhəʊldən/ Edith 1871–1920. British artist and naturalist. Daughter of a Birmingham manufacturer, she made most of her observations near her native city, and her journal, illustrated with her own watercolours, was published in 1977 as *The Country Diary of an Edwardian Lady*.

Holden /ˈhəʊldən/ William. Stage name of William Franklin Beedle 1918–1981. US film actor, a star in the late 1940s and 1950s. He played leading roles in *Sunset Boulevard* 1950, *Stalag 17* 1953, *The Wild Bunch* 1969, and *Network* 1976.

Holford /ˈhɒlfəd/ William, Baron Holford 1907–1975. British architect, born in Johannesburg. A leading architect/planner of his generation, he was responsible for much redevelopment after World War II, including St Paul's Cathedral Precinct, London.

Holiday /ˈhɒlɪdeɪ/ Billie. Stage name of Eleanora Gough McKay 1915–1959. US jazz singer, also known as 'Lady Day'. She made her debut in Harlem clubs and became known for her emotionally charged delivery and idiosyncratic phrasing; she brought a blues feel to performances with swing bands. Songs she made her own include 'Stormy Weather', 'Strange Fruit' and 'I Cover the Waterfront'.

Holinshed /ˈhɒlɪnʃed/ Ralph c. 1520–c. 1580. English historian who published two volumes of the *Chronicles of England, Scotland and Ireland* 1578, on which Shakespeare based his history plays.

Holkeri /ˈhɒlkəri/ Harri 1937–   . Finnish politician, prime minister 1987–91. Joining the centrist National Coalition Party (KOK) at an early age, he eventually became its national secretary.

Holland /ˈhɒlənd/ Henry Richard Vassall Fox, 3rd Baron 1773–1840. British Whig politician. He was Lord Privy Seal 1806–07. His home, at Holland House, London, was for many years the centre of Whig political and literary society.

Holland /ˈhɒlənd/ John Philip 1840–1914. Irish engineer who developed some of the first submarines. He began work in Ireland in the late 1860s and emigrated to the USA 1873. His first successful boat was launched 1881 and, after several failures, he built the *Holland* 1893, which was bought by the US Navy two years later.

The first submarine, the *Fenian Ram* 1881, was built with financial support from the Irish Fenian society, who hoped to use it against England. Holland continued after 1895 to build submarines for various navies but died in poverty after his company became embroiled in litigation with backers.

Holland /ˈhɒlənd/ Sidney George 1893–1961. New Zealand politician, leader of the National Party 1940–57 and prime minister 1949–57.

Hollar /ˈhɒlə/ Wenceslaus 1607–1677. Bohemian engraver, active in England from 1637. He was the first landscape engraver to work in England and recorded views of London before the Great Fire of 1666.

Hollerith /ˈhɒlərɪθ/ Herman 1860–1929. US inventor of a mechanical tabulating machine, the first device for data processing. Hollerith's tabulator was widely publicized after being successfully used in the 1890 census. The firm he established, the Tabulating Machine Company, was later one of the founding companies of IBM.

After attending the Columbia University School of Mines, Hollerith worked on the 1880 US census and witnessed the huge task of processing so much information. In 1882 he became an instructor at the Massachusetts Institute of Technology, where he developed his machine for counting and collating census data.

Hollis /ˈhɒlɪs/ Roger 1905–1973. British civil servant, head of the secret intelligence service MI5 1956–65. He was alleged to have been a double agent together with Kim Philby, but this was denied by the KGB 1991.

Holloway /ˈhɒləweɪ/ Thomas 1800–1883. English manufacturer and philanthropist who made a fortune from patent medicines. He founded Royal Holloway College, London, opened 1886, as a college for women 'because they are the greatest sufferers'.

Holmes Oliver Wendell Holmes, US scientist and man of letters. His reflections in The Autocrat of the Breakfast - Table *and its sequels, many first published in* The Atlantic Monthly, *are learned, witty, and humane.*

Holly Buddy. Stage name of Charles Hardin Holley 1936–1959. US rock-and-roll singer, guitarist, and songwriter, born in Lubbock, Texas. Holly had a distinctive, hiccuping vocal style and was an early experimenter with recording techniques. Many of his hits with his band, the Crickets, such as 'That'll Be the Day' 1957, 'Peggy Sue' 1957, and 'Maybe Baby' 1958, have become classics. He died in a plane crash.

Holmes /həʊmz/ Oliver Wendell 1809–1894. US writer and physician. In 1857 he founded *The Atlantic Monthly* with J R Lowell, in which were published the essays and verse collected in 1858 as *The Autocrat of the Breakfast-Table*, a record of the imaginary conversation of boarding-house guests.

Holmes /həʊmz/ Oliver Wendell 1841–1935. US jurist and Supreme Court justice 1902–32, noted for the elegance of his written opinions. He was appointed to the US Supreme Court by President T Roosevelt, and during his office handed down landmark decisions in a number of antitrust, constitutional First Amendment, and labour law cases. He retired from the Court 1932.

Born in Boston, Massachusetts, USA, Holmes was the son of the writer and physician of the same name. He was educated at Harvard University. After service in the American Civil War 1861–65, he studied law and was admitted to the bar 1867. Holmes established a private practice in Boston and gained a reputation as an author and lecturer on legal subjects. He was appointed to the Massachusetts Supreme Court 1882.

Holmes à Court /həʊmz 'eɪkɔːt/ Robert 1937–1990. Australian entrepreneur. At the peak of his financial strength, before the stock-market crash 1987, he was the richest individual in Australia.

Holmes à Court owned 30% of Broken Hill Proprietary, Australia's biggest company; 10% of Texaco; and had substantial media, transport, and property interests. His personal fortune of about A$1.3 billion/£555 million halved in a matter of weeks after the stock-market crash. Having sold his master company, the Bell Group, to Alan Bond in 1988, he retired to being a private investor.

Holst /həʊlst/ Gustav(us Theodore von) 1874–1934. English composer. He wrote operas, including *Savitri* 1916 and *At the Boar's Head* 1925; ballets; choral works, including *Hymns from the Rig Veda* 1911 and *The Hymn of Jesus* 1920; orchestral suites, including *The Planets* 1918; and songs. He was a lifelong friend of Ralph →Vaughan Williams, with whom he shared an enthusiasm for English folk music. His musical style, although tonal and drawing on folk song, tends to be severe.

Holstein /həʊlstaɪn/ Friedrich von 1839–1909. German diplomat and foreign-affairs expert. He refused the post of foreign minister, but played a key role in German diplomacy from the 1880s until his death.

Holt /həʊlt/ Harold Edward 1908–1967. Australian Liberal politician, prime minister 1966–67. His brief prime ministership was dominated by the Vietnam War, to which he committed increased Australian troops.

He was minister of labour 1940–41 and 1949–58, and federal treasurer 1958–66, when he succeeded Menzies as prime minister. He was also minister for immigration 1949–56, during which time he made the first modifications to the White Australia Policy, relaxing some restrictions on Asian immigration.

Holtby /həʊltbi/ Winifred 1898–1935. English novelist, poet, and journalist. She was an ardent advocate of women's freedom and racial equality, and wrote the novel *South Riding* 1936, set in her native Yorkshire. Her other works include an analysis of women's position in contemporary society *Women and a Changing Civilization* 1934.

Holyoake /həʊliəʊk/ Keith Jacka 1904–1983. New Zealand National Party politician, prime minister 1957 (for two months) and 1960–72 during which time he was also foreign minister.

Home /hjuːm/ Alec Douglas-Home, Baron Home of the Hirsel 1903– . British Conservative politician. He was foreign secretary 1960–63, and succeeded Harold Macmillan as prime minister 1963. He renounced his peerage (as 14th Earl of Home) to fight (and lose) the general election 1963, and resigned as party leader 1965. He was again foreign secretary 1970–74, when he received a life peerage. The playwright William Douglas-Home was his brother.

Homer /həʊmər/ lived *c.* 8th century BC. Legendary Greek epic poet. According to tradition, he was a blind minstrel and the author of the *Iliad* and the *Odyssey*, which are probably based on much older stories, passed on orally, concerning war with Troy in the 12th century BC.

Homer /ˈhəʊmə/ Winslow 1836–1910. US painter and lithographer, known for his seascapes, both oils and watercolours, which date from the 1880s and 1890s.

Homer, born in Boston, made his reputation as a realist painter with *Prisoners from the Front* 1866 (Metropolitan Museum of Art, New York), recording miseries of the American Civil War. After a visit to Paris he turned to lighter subjects, studies of country life, which reflect early Impressionist influence.

As the generation of leaves, so is that of men.

Homer *Iliad*

Hondecoeter /ˈhɒndəkuːtə/ Melchior 1636–1695. Dutch artist who painted large pictures of birds (both domestic fowl and exotic species) in grandiose settings.

Hone William 1780–1842. British journalist and publisher. In 1817, he was unsuccessfully prosecuted for his *Political Litany*, in which he expounded the journalist's right to free expression.

Honecker /ˈhɒnekə/ Erich 1912– . German communist politician, in power 1973–89, elected chair of the council of state (head of state) 1976. He governed in an outwardly austere and efficient manner and, while favouring East–West détente, was a loyal ally of the USSR. In Oct 1989, following a wave of prodemocracy demonstrations, he was replaced as leader of the Socialist Unity Party (SED) and head of state by Egon →Krenz, and in Dec expelled from the Communist Party.

Honecker, the son of a miner, joined the German Communist Party 1929 and was imprisoned for antifascist activity 1935–45. He was elected to the East German parliament (Volkskammer) 1949 and became a member of the SED Politburo during the 1950s. A security specialist, during the 1960s he served as a secretary of the National Defence Council before being appointed first secretary of the SED 1971. After Walter Ulbricht's death 1973, Honecker became leader of East Germany.

In Oct 1989, following large-scale civil disturbances, Honecker was replaced by his protégé Egon Krenz. He was arrested Feb 1990 and charged with high treason, misuse of office, and corruption. In March 1991 he was transferred from a Soviet military hospital to Moscow, but the German government demanded his return to face manslaughter charges in connection with the killing of those illegally crossing the Berlin Wall 1961–89. In July 1992 he returned to Germany to stand trial.

There is no doubt that the first requirement for a composer is to be dead.

Arthur Honegger *Je suis compositeur?*

Honegger /ˈhɒnegə/ Arthur 1892–1955. Swiss composer, one of Les Six. His work was varied in form, for example, the opera *Antigone* 1927, the ballet *Skating Rink* 1922, the oratorio *Le Roi David/King David* 1921, programme music (*Pacific 231* 1923), and the *Symphonie liturgique/Liturgical Symphony* 1946.

Born at Le Havre, he was educated at Zürich and Paris.

Hōnen /ˈhəʊnen/ 1133–1212. Japanese Buddhist monk who founded the Pure Land school of Buddhism, which emphasizes faith in and love of Buddha, in particular Amitābha, the ideal 'Buddha of boundless light', who has vowed that all believers who call on his name will be reborn in his Pure Land, or Western Paradise.

Honthorst /ˈhɒnthɔːst/ Gerrit van 1590–1656. Dutch painter who used extremes of light and shade, influenced by Caravaggio; with Terbrugghen he formed the *Utrecht School*.

Around 1610–12 he was in Rome, studying Caravaggio. Later he visited England, painting *Charles I* 1628 (National Portrait Gallery, London) and became court painter in The Hague.

Hooch /ˈhəʊx/ Pieter de 1629–1684. Dutch painter, active in Delft and, later, Amsterdam. The harmonious domestic interiors and courtyards of his Delft period were influenced by Vermeer.

Hood /hʊd/ Samuel, 1st Viscount Hood 1724–1816. British admiral. A masterly tactician, he defeated the French at Dominica in the West Indies 1783, and in the Revolutionary Wars captured Toulon and Corsica.

Hooke /hʊk/ Robert 1635–1703. English scientist and inventor, originator of *Hooke's law* which states that the tension in a lightly stretched spring is proportional to its extension from its natural length, and considered the foremost mechanic of his time. His inventions included a telegraph system, the spirit level, marine barometer, and sea gauge. He coined the term 'cell' in biology.

Hooke was born at Freshwater on the Isle of Wight, the son of a priest. He studied elasticity, furthered the sciences of mechanics and microscopy, and helped improve such scientific instruments as watches, microscopes, telescopes, and barometers. He was elected to the Royal Society 1663, and became its curator for the rest of his life. He was professor of geometry at Gresham College, London, and designed several buildings, including the College of Physicians, London.

Hoover US Republican politician Herbert Hoover whose term as president coincided with the worldwide financial collapse 1929 and the ensuing Depression. Hoover, who believed in ultimate recovery through private enterprise, was criticized for the ineffectiveness of the measures he initiated.

Hooker /hʊkə/ Joseph Dalton 1817–1911. English botanist who travelled to the Antarctic and made many botanical discoveries. His works include *Flora Antarctica* 1844–47, *Genera Plantarum* 1862–83, and *Flora of British India* 1875–97.

In 1865 he succeeded his father, William Jackson Hooker (1785–1865), as director of the Royal Botanic Gardens, Kew, England.

Hooker /hʊkə/ Richard 1554–1600. English theologian, author of *The Laws of Ecclesiastical Polity* 1594, a defence of the episcopalian system of the Church of England.

Hooker /hʊkə/ Thomas 1586–1647. British colonial religious leader in America. A Puritan, he opposed the religious leadership of Cambridge colony, and led a group of his followers westward to the Connecticut Valley, founding Hartford 1636. He became the de facto leader of the colony and in 1639 helped to formulate Connecticut's first constitution, the Fundamental Orders.

Born in England and educated as a minister at Cambridge, Hooker served at parishes in England before fleeing to Holland in 1630 because of his Puritan beliefs. In 1633 he emigrated to the Massachusetts Bay Colony, settling in Cambridge.

Hooper /hu:pə/ John *c.* 1495–1555. English Protestant reformer and martyr. He adopted the views of →Zwingli and was appointed bishop of Gloucester 1550. He was burned to death for heresy.

Hoover /hu:və/ Herbert Clark 1874–1964. 31st president of the USA 1929–33, a Republican. He was secretary of commerce 1921–28. Hoover lost public confidence after the stock-market crash of 1929, when he opposed direct government aid for the unemployed in the Depression that followed.

As a mining engineer, Hoover travelled widely before World War I. After the war he organized relief work in occupied Europe; a talented administrator, he was subsequently associated with numerous international relief organizations, and became food administrator for the USA 1917–19. He defeated the Democratic candidate for the presidency, Al Smith (1873–1944) by a wide margin. The shantytowns or *Hoovervilles* of the homeless that sprang up around large cities were evidence of his failure to cope with the effects of the Depression. He was severely criticized for his adamant opposition to federal relief for the unemployed, even after the funds of states, cities, and charities were exhausted. In 1933 he was succeeded by F D Roosevelt.

Hoover /hu:və/ J(ohn) Edgar 1895–1972. US director of the Federal Bureau of Investigation (FBI) from 1924. He built up a powerful network for the detection of organized crime. His drive against alleged communist activities after World War II, and his opposition to the Kennedy administration and others brought much criticism over abuse of power.

Hoover /hu:və/ William Henry 1849–1932. US manufacturer who developed the vacuum cleaner. 'Hoover' soon became a generic name for vacuum cleaner.

Hope /həʊp/ Anthony. Pen name of Anthony Hope Hawkins 1863–1933. English novelist whose romance *The Prisoner of Zenda* 1894, and its sequel *Rupert of Hentzau* 1898, introduced the imaginary Balkan state of Ruritania.

Hope /həʊp/ Bob. Stage name of Leslie Townes Hope 1903– . British-born US comedian, best remembered for seven films he made with Bing →Crosby and Dorothy Lamour between 1940 and 1953, whose titles all began *The Road to* (*Singapore, Zanzibar, Morocco, Utopia, Rio, Bali*, and *Hong Kong*).

He was taken to the USA in 1907, and became a Broadway and radio star in the 1930s. He has received several special Academy Awards.

Hopkins /hɒpkɪnz/ Anthony 1937– . Welsh actor. Among his stage appearances are *Equus, Macbeth, Pravda*, and the title role in *King Lear*. His films include *The Lion in Winter* 1968, *A Bridge Too Far* 1977, *The Elephant Man* 1980, *84 Charing Cross Road* 1986, and *The Silence of the Lambs* (Academy Award) 1991.

Hopkins /hɒpkɪnz/ Frederick Gowland 1861–1947. English biochemist whose research into diets revealed the existence of trace substances, now known as vitamins. Hopkins shared the 1929 Nobel Prize for Physiology and Medicine with

Christiaan Eijkman, who had arrived at similar conclusions.

While studying diets, Hopkins noticed that, of two seemingly identical diets, only one was able to support life. He concluded that one must contain trace substances, or accessory food factors, lacking in the other. Among these were certain amino acids which the body cannot produce itself. The other factors were later named vitamins.

Hopkins /ˈhɒpkɪnz/ Gerard Manley 1844–1889. English poet and Jesuit priest. His work, marked by its religious themes and use of natural imagery, includes 'The Wreck of the Deutschland' 1876 and 'The Windhover' 1877. His employment of 'sprung rhythm' greatly influenced later 20th-century poetry. His poetry was written in secret, and published 30 years after his death by his friend Robert Bridges.

Hopkins converted to Roman Catholicism 1866 and in 1868 began training as a Jesuit. His poetry is profoundly religious and records his struggle to gain faith and peace, but also shows freshness of feeling and delight in nature.

Hopkins /ˈhɒpkɪnz/ Harry Lloyd 1890–1946. US government official. Originally a social worker, in 1935 he became head of the WPA (Works Progress Administration), which was concerned with Depression relief work. After a period as secretary of commerce 1938–40, he was appointed supervisor of the lend-lease programme 1941 (whereby the USA would order any defence article for countries whose defence was considered vital to the defence of the USA), and undertook missions to Britain and the USSR during World War II.

Hopkins /ˈhɒpkɪnz/ Mark 1802–1887. US educator and religious leader, president of the American Board of Commissioners for Foreign Missions 1857–87. He was also known as a popular lecturer and author on religious subjects.

Born in Stockbridge, Massachusetts, Hopkins was educated at Williams College and received an MD degree from Berkshire College 1829. In 1830 he was appointed professor of philosophy at Williams College and president 1836–72. Increasingly involved in religious affairs, Hopkins was ordained a Congregationalist minister 1836.

Hopper /ˈhɒpə/ Dennis 1936– . US film actor and director who caused a sensation with the anti-establishment *Easy Rider* 1969, the archetypal 'road' film, but whose *The Last Movie* 1971 was poorly received by the critics. He made a comeback in the 1980s. His work as an actor includes *Rebel Without a Cause* 1955, *The American Friend/Der amerikanische Freund* 1977, and *Blue Velvet* 1986.

Hopper /ˈhɒpə/ Edward 1882–1967. US painter and etcher. His views of New England and New York in the 1930s and 1940s captured the loneliness and superficial glamour of city life, as in *Nighthawks* 1942 (Art Institute, Chicago).

Hopper's teacher Robert →Henri, associated with the Ashcan School, was a formative influence.

If you could say it in words there would be no reason to paint it.

Edward Hopper

Hopper /ˈhɒpə/ Hedda 1890–1966. US actress and celebrity reporter. From 1915 she appeared in many silent films and after a brief retirement was hired as a radio gossip reporter in 1936. From 1938 Hopper wrote a syndicated newspaper column about the private lives of the Hollywood stars. She carried on a widely publicized feud with rival columnist Louella Parsons.

Hoppner /ˈhɒpnə/ John 1758–1810. English portrait painter, a follower of Joshua Reynolds and rival to Thomas Lawrence. He became portrait painter to the Prince of Wales (later George IV) in 1789 and a Royal Academician in 1795. Among his paintings are portraits of the royal princesses, William Pitt, Lord Grenville, Rodney, and Nelson.

Horace /ˈhɒrɪs/ 65–8 BC. Roman lyric poet and satirist. He became a leading poet under the patronage of Emperor Augustus. His works include *Satires* 35–30 BC; the four books of *Odes* about 25–24 BC; *Epistles*, a series of verse letters; and a critical work, *Ars poetica*. They are distinguished by their style, wit, and good sense.

Born at Venusia, S Italy, the son of a freedman, Horace fought under Brutus at Philippi, lost his estate, and was reduced to poverty. In about 38 Virgil introduced him to Maecenas, who gave him a farm in the Sabine hills and recommended him to the patronage of Augustus.

Hordern /ˈhɔːdən/ Michael 1911– . English character actor who appeared in stage roles such as Shakespeare's Lear and Prospero. His films include *The Man Who Never Was* 1956, *The Spy Who Came in From the Cold* 1965, *The Bed Sitting Room* 1969, and *Joseph Andrews* 1977.

Hore-Belisha /ˌhɔː bəˈliːʃə/ Leslie, Baron Hore-Belisha 1895–1957. British politician. A National Liberal, he was minister of transport 1934–37, introducing *Belisha beacons* to mark pedestrian crossings. As war minister from 1937, until removed by Chamberlain 1940 on grounds of temperament, he introduced peacetime conscription 1939.

Horn /hɔːn/ Philip de Montmorency, Count of Horn 1518–1568. Flemish politician. He held high offices under the Holy Roman emperor Charles V and his son Philip II. From 1563 he was one of the leaders of the opposition to the rule of Cardinal Granvella (1517–1586) and to the introduction of the Inquisition. In 1567 he was arrested, together with the Resistance leader Egmont, and both were beheaded in Brussels.

Horniman /ˈhɔːnɪmən/ Annie Elizabeth Frederika 1860–1937. English pioneer of repertory theatre who subsidized the Abbey Theatre, Dublin, and founded the Manchester company.

Hornsby /ˈhɔːnzbi/ Rajah (Rogers) 1896–1963. US baseball player. He won the National League batting title in six consecutive seasons 1920–25. His .424 batting average 1924 is the highest achieved in the National League and he was voted the National League's most valuable player 1925. His lifetime batting average of .358 is the second-highest in history.

Born in Winters, Texas, USA, Hornsby was signed by the St Louis Cardinals and broke into the major leagues 1915. In 1925 he was named the Cardinals' player-manager and, in the same year, he became the first player to win baseball's Triple Crown twice. Traded to the New York Giants 1927 he served variously as player/player-manager for the Boston Braves 1928, the Chicago Cubs 1929–32, the Cardinals 1933, and the St Louis Browns 1933–37.

Hornsby was elected to the Baseball Hall of Fame 1942.

Hornung /ˈhɔːnəŋ/ E(rnest) W(illiam) 1866–1921. English novelist who, at the prompting of Conan ➔Doyle, created 'A J Raffles', the gentleman-burglar, and his assistant Bunny Manders in *The Amateur Cracksman* 1899.

Horowitz /ˈhɒrəwɪts/ Vladimir 1904–1989. Russian-born US pianist. He made his debut in the USA 1928 with the New York Philharmonic Orchestra. Noted for his commanding virtuoso style, he was a leading interpreter of Liszt, Schumann, and Rachmaninov.

Horowitz toured worldwide until the early 1950s, when nervous disorders forced him to withdraw completely from the stage; he kept recording, however. After a triumphal return at Carnegie Hall 1965, in which it was clear that he had lost none of his ability, he toured briefly in the 1970s and 1980s.

Horrocks /ˈhɒrəks/ Brian Gwynne 1895–1985. British general. He served in World War I, and in World War II under Montgomery at Alamein and with the British Liberation Army in Europe.

Horsley /ˈhɔːzli/ John Calcott 1817–1903. English artist. A skilled painter of domestic scenes, he was also responsible for frescoes in the Houses of Parliament and is credited with designing the first Christmas card.

Horthy /ˈhɔːti də ˈnɒdʒbɑːnjə/ Nicholas Horthy de Nagybánya 1868–1957. Hungarian politician and admiral. Leader of the counterrevolutionary White government, he became regent 1920 on the overthrow of the communist Bela Kun regime by Romanian and Czechoslovak intervention. He represented the conservative and military class, and retained power until World War II, trying (although allied to Hitler) to retain independence of action. In 1944 he tried to negotiate a surrender to the USSR but Hungary was taken over by the Nazis and he was deported to Germany. He was released from German captivity the same year by the Western Allies and allowed to go to Portugal, where he died.

Hosea 8th century BC. Prophet in the Old Testament. His prophecy draws parallels between his own marriage and the relationship between God and Israel.

Hosking /ˈhɒskɪŋ/ Eric (John) 1909–1990. English wildlife photographer known for his documentation of British birds, especially owls. Beginning at the age of eight and still photographing in Africa at 80, he covered all aspects of birdlife and illustrated a large number of books, published between 1940 and 1990.

Hoskins /ˈhɒskɪnz/ Bob 1942– . British character actor who progressed to fame from a series of supporting roles. Films include *The Long Good Friday* 1980, *The Cotton Club* 1984, *Mona Lisa* 1985, *A Prayer for the Dying* 1987, and *Who Framed Roger Rabbit?* 1988.

Houdini /huːˈdiːni/ Harry. Stage name of Erich Weiss 1874–1926. US escapologist and conjurer. He was renowned for his escapes from ropes and handcuffs, from trunks under water, from straitjackets and prison cells.

He also campaigned against fraudulent mind-readers and mediums.

Houdon /uː ˈdɒŋ/ Jean-Antoine 1741–1828. French sculptor, a portraitist who made characterful studies of Voltaire and a Neo-Classical statue of George Washington, commissioned 1785.

His other subjects included the philosophers Diderot and Rousseau, the composer Gluck, the emperor Napoleon, and the American politician Benjamin Franklin. Houdon also produced popular mythological figures, such as *Diana* and *Minerva*.

Hounsfield /ˈhaʊnzfiːld/ Godrey (Newbold) 1919– . British engineer, a pioneer of tomography, the application of computer techniques to X-raying the human body. He shared the Nobel Prize for Physiology and Medicine 1979 with US physicist Allan Cormack (1924–).

Houphouët-Boigny /uːfˈweɪ bwɑːnˈjiː/ Félix 1905– . Ivory Coast right-wing politician. He held posts in French ministries, and became president of the Republic of the Ivory Coast on independence 1960, maintaining close links with France, which helped to boost an already thriving economy and encourage political stability. Pro-Western and opposed to communist intervention in Africa, Houphouët-Boigny has been strongly criticized for maintaining diplomatic relations with South Africa. He was re-elected for a seventh term 1990 in multiparty elections, amid allegations of ballot rigging and political pressure.

House /haʊs/ Edward Mandell 1858–1938. US politician and diplomat. He was instrumental in obtaining the presidential nomination for Woodrow Wilson 1912 and later served as Wilson's closest adviser. During World War I 1914–1918, House served as US liaison with Great Britain and was an important behind-the-scenes participant in the 1919 Versailles Peace Conference.

Born in Houston, Texas, USA, House attended Cornell University and, after working for many years on his family's holdings, became active in state Democratic politics. As personal adviser to a succession of Texas governors 1892–1904, he was awarded the honorary title of colonel.

Household /haʊshəʊld/ Geoffrey 1900–1988. British espionage and adventure novelist. His *Rogue Male* 1939 concerned an Englishman's attempt to kill Hitler, and the enemy hunt for him after his failure. Household served with British intelligence in World War II.

Houseman /haʊsmən/ John 1902–1988. US theatre, film, and television producer and actor, born in Romania. He co-founded the Mercury Theater with Orson Welles, and collaborated with Welles and Nicholas Ray as directors. He won an Academy Award for his acting debut in *The Paper Chase* 1973, and recreated his role in the subsequent TV series.

Housman /haʊsmən/ A(lfred) E(dward) 1859–1936. English poet and classical scholar. His *A Shropshire Lad* 1896, a series of deceptively simple, nostalgic, balladlike poems, was popular during World War I. This was followed by *Last Poems* 1922 and *More Poems* 1936.

Houston /hjuːstən/ Sam 1793–1863. US general who won independence for Texas from Mexico 1836 and was president of the Republic of Texas 1836–45. Houston, Texas, is named after him.

Houston was governor of the state of Tennessee and later US senator for and governor of the state of Texas. He took Indian citizenship when he married a Cherokee.

Hovell /həʊvəl/ William Hilton 1786–1875. English-born explorer in Australia who, with Hamilton →Hume, travelled overland from Gunning, SW of Sydney, to Port Phillip in 1824.

Howard /haʊəd/ Alan 1937– . British actor whose appearances with the Royal Shakespeare Company include *Henry V*, *Henry VI*, *Coriolanus*, and *Richard III*.

Howard /haʊəd/ Catherine *c*. 1520–1542. Queen consort of →Henry VIII of England from 1540. In 1541 the archbishop of Canterbury, Thomas Cranmer, accused her of being unchaste before marriage to Henry and she was beheaded 1542 after Cranmer made further charges of adultery.

Howard /haʊəd/ Charles, 2nd Baron Howard of Effingham and 1st Earl of Nottingham 1536–1624. English admiral, a cousin of Queen Elizabeth I. He commanded the fleet against the Spanish Armada while Lord High Admiral 1585–1618.

He cooperated with the Earl of Essex in the attack on Cadiz 1596.

Howard /haʊəd/ Constance 1919– . English embroiderer who helped to revive creative craftwork after World War II. Her work included framed pictures with fabrics outlined in bold black threads, wall hangings, and geometric studies in strong colour.

Howard /haʊəd/ Ebenezer 1850–1928. English town planner and founder of the ideal of the garden city, through his book *Tomorrow* 1898 (republished as *Garden Cities of Tomorrow* 1902).

Howard /haʊəd/ John 1726–1790. English philanthropist whose work to improve prison conditions is continued today by the *Howard League for Penal Reform*.

On his appointment as high sheriff for Bedfordshire 1773, he undertook a tour of English prisons which led to two acts of Parliament 1774, making jailers salaried officers and setting standards of cleanliness. After touring Europe 1775 he published his *State of the Prisons in England and Wales, with an account of some Foreign Prisons* 1777. He died of typhus fever while visiting Russian military hospitals at Kherson in the Crimea.

Howard /haʊəd/ Leslie. Stage name of Leslie Stainer 1893–1943. English actor whose films include *The Scarlet Pimpernel* 1935, *The Petrified Forest* 1936, *Pygmalion* 1938, and *Gone With the Wind* 1939.

Howard English actor Leslie Howard whose qualities of restraint and reserve won him the role of Ashley Wilkes in Gone with the Wind *1939. He accepted this part reluctantly and returned to England to make patriotic films such as* Pimpernel Smith *1941. He was shot down by the Germans in World War II on a mission between Lisbon and London.*

Howard /haʊəd/ Trevor (Wallace) 1916–1989. English actor whose films include *Brief Encounter* 1945, *Sons and Lovers* 1960, *Mutiny on the Bounty* 1962, *Ryan's Daughter* 1970, and *Conduct Unbecoming* 1975.

Howe /haʊ/ Elias 1819–1867. US inventor, in 1846, of a sewing machine using two threads, thus producing a lock stitch.

Howe /haʊ/ Geoffrey 1926– . British Conservative politician, member of Parliament for Surrey East. Under Edward Heath he was solicitor general 1970–72 and minister for trade 1972–74; as chancellor of the Exchequer 1979–83 under Margaret Thatcher, he put into practice the monetarist policy which reduced inflation at the cost of a rise in unemployment. In 1983 he became foreign secretary, and in 1989 deputy prime minister and leader of the House of Commons. On 1 Nov 1990 he resigned in protest at Thatcher's continued opposition to Britain's greater integration in Europe.

Many of the ideas proposed by Howe in the early 1960s were subsequently taken up by the Thatcher government.

Inflation is a great moral evil. Nations which lose confidence in their currency lose confidence in themselves.

Geoffrey Howe in *The Times* July 1982

Howe /haʊ/ Gordie 1926– . Canadian ice-hockey player who played for the Detroit Red Wings (National Hockey League) 1946–71 and then the New England Whalers (World Hockey Association). In the NHL, he scored more goals (801), assists (1,049), and points (1,850) than any other player in ice-hockey history until beaten by Wayne Gretsky. Howe played professional hockey until he was over 50.

Howe /haʊ/ James Wong. Adopted name of Wong Tung Jim 1899–1976. Chinese-born director of film photography, who lived in the USA from childhood. One of Hollywood's best camera operators, he is credited with introducing the use of hand-held cameras and deep focus. His work ranges from *The Alaskan* 1924 to *Funny Lady* 1975.

Howe /haʊ/ Julia Ward 1819–1910. US feminist and antislavery campaigner who wrote the 'Battle Hymn of the Republic' 1862, sung to the tune of 'John Brown's Body'.

Howe /haʊ/ Richard Earl 1726–1799. British admiral. He cooperated with his brother William against the colonists during the American Revolution and in the French Revolutionary Wars commanded the Channel fleets 1792–96.

Howe /haʊ/ Samuel Gridley 1801–1876. US educational reformer. A close associate of Horace ➔Mann and Dorothea ➔Dix, he campaigned for expanded public education and better mental health facilities. He served as chairman of the Massachusetts Board of State Charities 1865–74.

Born in Boston, Howe was educated at Brown University and received an MD degree from Harvard 1824. A Philhellene, he spent seven years in Greece during its War of Independence 1821–29. As director of a school for the blind in Boston 1831, he developed innovative educational techniques that were widely emulated.

Howe /haʊ/ William, 5th Viscount Howe 1729–1814. British general. During the War of American Independence he won the Battle of Bunker Hill 1775, and as commander in chief in America 1776–78 captured New York and defeated Washington at Brandywine and Germantown. He resigned in protest at lack of home government support.

Howells /haʊəlz/ William Dean 1837–1920. US novelist and editor. The 'dean' of US letters in the post-Civil War era, and editor of *The Atlantic Monthly*, he championed the realist movement in fiction and encouraged many younger authors. He wrote 35 novels, 35 plays, and many books of poetry, essays, and commentary.

His novels, filled with vivid social detail, include *A Modern Instance* 1882 and *The Rise of Silas Lapham* 1885, about the social fall and moral rise of a New England paint manufacturer, a central fable of the 'Gilded Age'.

Hoxha /hɒdʒə/ Enver 1908–1985. Albanian Communist politician, the country's leader from 1954. He founded the Albanian Communist Party 1941, and headed the liberation movement 1939–44. He was prime minister 1944–54, combining with foreign affairs 1946–53, and from 1954 was first secretary of the Albanian Party of Labour. In policy he was a Stalinist and independent of both Chinese and Soviet communism.

Hoyle /hɔɪl/ Fred(erick) 1915– . English astronomer and writer. In 1948 he joined with Hermann ➔Bondi and Thomas Gold (1920–) in developing the steady-state theory. In 1957, with Geoffrey and Margaret Burbidge (1925– and 1919–) and William ➔Fowler, he showed that chemical elements heavier than hydrogen and helium are built up by nuclear reactions inside stars. He has suggested that life originates in the gas clouds of space and is delivered to the Earth by passing comets. His science-fiction novels include *The Black Cloud* 1957.

His work on the evolution of stars was published in *Frontiers of Astronomy* 1955. He lectured in mathematics at Cambridge University 1945–58, when he became professor of astronomy. He was director of the Cambridge Institute of Theoretical Astronomy from 1967. He held numerous research and visiting posts at institutions in England and America, including Manchester University from 1972, and at University College, Cardiff from 1975.

Hrabal Bohumil 1914– . Czechoslovak writer, who began writing after 1962. His novels depict ordinary people caught up in events they do not control or comprehend, including *Ostŕe sledované vlaky/Closely Observed Trains* 1965, filmed 1967.

Hsuan Tung /ˈʃwæn ˈtʊŋ/ name adopted by Henry →P'u-i on becoming emperor of China 1908.

Hua Guofeng /hwɑ: ˌgwəʊˈfʌŋ/ or *Hua Kuofeng* 1920– . Chinese politician, leader of the Chinese Communist Party (CCP) 1976–81, premier 1976–80. He dominated Chinese politics 1976–77, seeking economic modernization without major structural reform. From 1978 he was gradually eclipsed by Deng Xiaoping. Hua was ousted from the Politburo Sept 1982 but remained a member of the CCP Central Committee.

Hua, born in Shanxi into a peasant family, fought under Zhu De, the Red Army leader, during the liberation war 1937–49. He entered the CCP Central Committee 1969 and the Politburo 1973. An orthodox, loyal Maoist, Hua was selected to succeed Zhou Enlai as prime minister Jan 1976 and became party leader on Mao Zedong's death Sept 1976. He was replaced as prime minister by Zhao Ziyang Sept 1980 and as CCP chair by Hu Yaobang June 1981.

Huáscar /ˈwɑːskə/ c. 1495–1532. King of the Incas. He shared the throne with his half-brother Atahualpa from 1525, but the latter overthrew and murdered him during the Spanish conquest.

Hubbard /ˈhʌbəd/ L(afayette) Ron(ald) 1911–1986. US science-fiction writer of the 1930s and 1940s, founder in 1954 of Scientology, an 'applied religious philosophy' based on dianetics, a form of psychotherapy.

Despite his later claims to be a war hero, he was in fact relieved of his command in the Navy for incompetence.

Hubble /ˈhʌbəl/ Edwin Powell 1889–1953. US astronomer who discovered the existence of other galaxies outside our own, and classified them according to their shape. His theory that the universe is expanding is now generally accepted.

At Mount Wilson observatory in 1923 he discovered Cepheid variable stars in the Andromeda galaxy, proving it to lie far beyond our own Galaxy. In 1925 he introduced the classification of galaxies as spirals, barred spirals, and ellipticals. In 1929 he announced *Hubble's law*, which states that the galaxies are moving apart at a rate that increases with their distance.

Huc /uːk/ Abbé 1813–1860. French missionary in China. In 1845 he travelled to the border of Tibet, where he stopped for eight months to study the Tibetan language and Buddhist literature before moving on to the city of Lhasa.

Hudson /ˈhʌdsən/ Henry c. 1565–c. 1611. English explorer. Under the auspices of the Muscovy Company 1607–08, he made two unsuccessful

Hudson US film actor Rock Hudson, whose height and manly good looks made him one of Hollywood's leading stars. A former lorry driver, Hudson had no acting experience when he was given his first chance in films; he later underwent intensive coaching and grooming, readied for a successful career by the mid-1950s.

attempts to find the Northeast Passage to China. In Sept 1609, commissioned by the Dutch East India Company, he reached New York Bay and sailed 240 km/150 mi up the river that now bears his name, establishing Dutch claims to the area. In 1610, he sailed from London in the *Discovery* and entered what is now the Hudson Strait. After an icebound winter, he was turned adrift by a mutinous crew in what is now Hudson Bay.

Hudson /ˈhʌdsən/ Rock. Stage name of Roy Scherer Jr 1925–1985. US film actor, a star from the mid-1950s to the mid-1960s, who appeared in several melodramas directed by Douglas Sirk and in three comedies co-starring Doris Day (including *Pillow Talk* 1959). He went on to have a successful TV career in the 1970s.

Hudson /ˈhʌdsən/ W(illiam) H(enry) 1841–1922. British author, born of US parents in Argentina. He was inspired by recollections of early days in Argentina to write the romances *The Purple Land* 1885 and *Green Mansions* 1904, and his autobiographical *Far Away and Long Ago* 1918. He wrote several books on birds, and on the English countryside, for example, *Nature in Down-Land* 1900 and *A Shepherd's Life* 1910.

Huggins /ˈhʌgɪnz/ William 1824–1910. British astronomer. He built a private observatory at Tulse Hill, London, in 1856, where he embarked on research in spectrum analysis that marked the beginning of astrophysics.

Hughes /hjuːz/ Charles Evans 1862–1948. US jurist and public official, appointed to the US Supreme Court by President Taft 1910. He resigned 1916 to accept the Republican nomination for president, losing narrowly to the incumbent Wilson. He served as secretary of state 1921–25 under President Harding. As Supreme Court chief justice 1930–41 in the Hoover administration, he presided over the constitutional tests of New Deal legislation.

Born in Glens Falls, New York, Hughes received his law degree from Columbia University 1884. After joining the Columbia law faculty 1891–93, he directed a state investigation of public utilities 1905 and served two terms as New York governor 1906–10. He retired from the US Supreme Court 1941.

Hughes /hjuːz/ David 1831–1900. British-born US inventor who patented an early form of telex in 1855, a type-printing instrument for use with the telegraph. He brought the instrument to Europe in 1857 where it became widely used.

Hughes /hjuːz/ Howard R 1905–1976. US tycoon. Inheriting wealth from his father, who had patented a successful oil-drilling bit, he created a legendary financial empire. A skilled pilot, he manufactured and designed aircraft. He formed a film company in Hollywood and made the classic film *Hell's Angels* 1930, about aviators of World War I; later successes included *Scarface* 1932 and *The Outlaw* 1944. From his middle years he was a recluse.

Hughes /hjuːz/ Langston 1902–1967. US poet and novelist. Known as 'the Poet Laureate of Harlem' he became one of the foremost black American literary figures, writing such collections of poems as *The Weary Blues* 1926. In addition to his poetry he wrote a series of novels, short stories, and essays. His autobiography *The Big Sea* appeared 1940.

Born in Joplin, Missouri, USA, and raised in Cleveland, Ohio, Hughes had a poem published while still in high school. After briefly attending Columbia University, he travelled widely and continued to write. He published *The Weary Blues* shortly after graduating from Lincoln University.

Hughes /hjuːz/ Richard (Arthur Warren) 1900–1976. English writer. His study of childhood, *A High Wind in Jamaica*, was published 1929, and the trilogy *The Human Predicament* 1961–73.

Hughes /hjuːz/ Ted 1930–   . English poet, poet laureate from 1984. His work includes *The Hawk in the Rain* 1957, *Lupercal* 1960, *Wodwo* 1967, and *River* 1983, and is characterized by its harsh portrayal of the crueller aspects of nature. In 1956 he married the poet Sylvia Plath.

Hughes /hjuːz/ Thomas 1822–1896. English writer, author of the children's book *Tom Brown's School Days* 1857, a story of Rugby school under

Humboldt Alexander Humboldt, German explorer of territories unknown to Europeans in South America and central Asia. Goethe described him as 'like a fountain with a vast number of outlets' and his scientific investigations, including plants, geology, the chemistry of the atmosphere, and physiology culminated in Cosmos: An Outline Description of the Physical World, published 1845–62.

Thomas →Arnold. It had a sequel, *Tom Brown at Oxford* 1861.

Hughes /hjuːz/ William Morris 1864–1952. Australian politician, prime minister 1915–23; originally Labor, he headed a national cabinet. After resigning as prime minister 1923, he held many other cabinet posts 1934–41.

Born in London, he emigrated to Australia 1884. He represented Australia in the peace conference after World War I at Versailles.

Hugo /hjuːgəʊ/ Victor (Marie) 1802–1885. French poet, novelist, and dramatist. The *Odes et poésies diverses* appeared 1822, and his verse play *Hernani* 1830 established him as the leader of French Romanticism. More volumes of verse followed between his series of dramatic novels, which included *The Hunchback of Notre Dame* 1831 and *Les Misérables* 1862.

Born at Besançon, Hugo was the son of one of Napoleon's generals. Originally a monarchist, his support of republican ideals in the 1840s led to his banishment 1851 for opposing Louis Napoleon's coup d'état. He lived in exile in Guernsey until the fall of the empire 1870, later becoming a senator under the Third Republic. He died a national hero and is buried in the Panthéon, Paris.

The word is the verb and the verb is God.

Victor Hugo *Contemplations* 1856

Hull /hʌl/ Cordell 1871–1955. US Democratic politician. As F D Roosevelt's secretary of state 1933–44, he opposed German and Japanese aggression. He was identified with the Good Neighbour Policy of nonintervention in Latin America. In his last months of office he paved the way for a system of collective security, for which he was called 'father' of the United Nations. He was awarded the Nobel Peace Prize 1945.

He was born in Tennessee. He was a member of Congress 1907–33.

Hulme /hjuːm/ Keri 1947– . New Zealand poet and novelist. She won the Commonwealth Booker Prize with her first novel *The Bone People* 1985. Other works include the novella *Lost Possessions* 1985, *The Windeater/Te Kaihau* 1986, a collection of short stories, and *Strands* 1990, a book of poetry.

Hulme /hjuːm/ T(homas) E(rnest) 1881–1917. British philosopher, critic, and poet, killed on active service in World War I. His *Speculations* 1924 influenced T S →Eliot and his few poems inspired the Imagist movement.

Humbert /hʌmbət/ anglicized form of →Umberto, two kings of Italy.

Humboldt /hʌmbəʊlt/ Friedrich Heinrich Alexander, Baron von 1769–1859. German botanist and geologist who, with the French botanist Aimé Bonpland (1773–1858), explored the regions of the Orinoco and the Amazon rivers in South America 1800–04, and gathered 60,000 plant specimens. On his return, Humboldt devoted 21 years to writing an account of his travels.

One of the first popularizers of science, he gave a series of lectures later published as *Cosmos* 1845–62, an account of the physical sciences.

Humboldt /hʌmbəʊlt/ Wilhelm von 1767–1835. German philologist whose stress on the identity of thought and language influenced Noam →Chomsky. He was the brother of Alexander Humboldt.

Hume /hjuːm/ Basil 1923– . English Roman Catholic cardinal from 1976. A Benedictine monk, he was abbot of Ampleforth in Yorkshire 1963–76, and in 1976 became archbishop of Westminster, the first monk to hold the office.

Hume /hjuːm/ David 1711–1776. Scottish philosopher. *A Treatise of Human Nature* 1739–40 is a central text of British empiricism. Hume denies the possibility of going beyond the subjective experiences of 'ideas' and 'impressions'. The effect of this position is to invalidate metaphysics.

His *History of Great Britain* 1754–62 was popular within his own lifetime but *A Treatise of Human Nature* was indifferently received. He shared many of the beliefs of the British empiricist school, including those of John →Locke. *Hume's law* in moral philosophy states that it is never possible to deduce evaluative conclusions from factual premises; this has come to be known as the 'is/ought problem'.

Hume Scottish empirical philosopher David Hume. On his deathbed he distressed Boswell by arguing against the immortality of the soul. His friend Adam Smith described him as the nearest possible realization of 'the idea of a perfectly wise and virtuous man'.

Beauty in things exists in the mind which contemplates them.

David Hume *Essays* 'Of Tragedy' 1742

Hume /hjuːm/ Fergus 1859–1932. British writer. Educated in New Zealand, he returned to England in 1888; his *Mystery of a Hansom Cab* 1887 was one of the first detective stories.

Hume /hjuːm/ Hamilton 1797–1873. Australian explorer. In 1824, with William Hovell, he led an expedition from Sydney to the Murray River and Port Phillip. The Melbourne–Sydney *Hume Highway* is named after him.

Hume /hjuːm/ John 1937– . Northern Ireland Catholic politician, leader of the Social Democrat Party (SDLP) from 1979. Hume was a founder member of the Credit Union Party, which later became the SDLP.

Hume /hjuːm/ Joseph 1777–1855. British Radical politician. Born in Montrose, Scotland, he went to India as an army surgeon 1797, made a fortune, and on his return bought a seat in Parliament. In 1818 he secured election as a Philosophic Radical and supported many progressive measures. His son *Allan Octavian Hume* (1829–1912) was largely responsible for the establishment of the Indian National Congress 1885.

Hume-Rothery /hjuːm ˈrɒðəri/ William 1899–1968. British metallurgist who studied the constitution of alloys. He was appointed to the first chair of metallurgy 1925.

Humperdinck /ˈhʊmpədɪŋk/ Engelbert 1854–1921. German composer. He studied music in Munich and in Italy and assisted Richard →Wagner at the Bayreuth Festival Theatre. He wrote the musical fairy operas *Hänsel und Gretel* 1893, and *Königskinder/King's Children* 1910.

Humphrey /ˈhʌmfri/ Hubert Horatio 1911–1978. US political leader, vice president 1965–69. He was elected to the US Senate 1948, serving for three terms, distinguishing himself an eloquent and effective promoter of key legislation. He was an unsuccessful presidential candidate 1960. Serving as vice president under L B Johnson, he made another unsuccessful run for the presidency 1968. He was re-elected to the Senate in 1970 and 1976.

Born in Wallace, South Dakota, USA, Humphrey was trained as a pharmacist. Settling in Minnesota, he became active in Democratic party politics and was elected mayor of Minneapolis 1945. He strongly supported the 1964 Civil Rights Act.

Humphries /ˈhʌmfriz/ (John) Barry 1934– . Australian actor and author who is best known for his satirical one-person shows and especially for the creation of the character of Mrs (later Dame) Edna Everage. His comic strip 'The Adventures of Barry Mackenzie', published in the British weekly *Private Eye* 1963–74, was the basis for two films, *The Adventures of Barry Mackenzie* 1972 and *Barry Mackenzie Holds His Own* 1974 (with Bruce Beresford), in which Humphries also acted.

Hun Sen /hʊn ˈsen/ 1950– . Cambodian political leader, prime minister from 1985. Originally a member of the Khmer Rouge army, he defected in 1977 to join Vietnam-based anti-Khmer Cambodian forces. His leadership has been characterized by the promotion of economic liberalization and a thawing in relations with exiled non-Khmer opposition forces as a prelude to a compromise political settlement. In Oct 1991, following a peace accord ending 13 years of civil war in Cambodia, Hun Sen agreed to rule the country in conjunction with the United Nations Transitional Authority in Cambodia (UNTAC) and representatives of the warring factions until UN-administered elections 1993.

Born into a poor peasant family in the eastern province of Kampang-Cham, Hun Sen joined the Khmer Rouge in 1970. He rose to become a regiment commander, but, disillusioned, defected to the anti-Khmer Cambodian forces in 1977. On his return to Cambodia, following the Vietnamese-backed communist takeover, he served as foreign minister 1979, and then as prime minister 1985.

Hunt /hʌnt/ (James Henry) Leigh 1784–1859. English poet and essayist. The appearance in his Liberal newspaper *The Examiner* of an unfavourable article that he had written about the Prince Regent caused him to be convicted for libel and imprisoned 1813. The friend and later enemy of Byron, he also knew Keats and Shelley.

Hurd A veteran of the diplomatic service, English Conservative politician and foreign secretary Douglas Hurd is regarded as a 'non-Thatcherite' moderate.

His verse is little appreciated today, but he influenced the Romantics, and his book on London *The Town* 1848 and his *Autobiography* 1850 survive. The character of Harold Skimpole in Dickens's *Bleak House* was allegedly based on him.

Hunt /hʌnt/ James Simon Wallis 1947– . English motor racing driver who won his first Formula One race at the 1975 Dutch Grand Prix. He went on to win the 1976 world champion driver's title. Hunt started his Formula One career with Hesketh 1973 and moved to Maclaren 1976–79, finishing in 1979 with Wolf. He has had ten Grand Prix wins.

Hunt /hʌnt/ John, Baron Hunt 1910– . British mountaineer, leader of the successful Everest expedition 1953 (with Edmund →Hillary and →Tenzing Norgay).

Hunt /hʌnt/ William Holman 1827–1910. English painter, one of the founders of the Pre-Raphaelite Brotherhood 1848. Obsessed with realistic detail, he travelled from 1854 onwards to Syria and Palestine to paint biblical subjects. His works include *The Awakening Conscience* 1853 (Tate Gallery, London) and *The Light of the World* 1854 (Keble College, Oxford).

Hunter /ˈhʌntə/ John 1728–1793. Scottish surgeon, pathologist, and comparative anatomist. His main contribution to medicine was his insistence on rigorous scientific method. He was also the first to understand the nature of digestion.

He experimented extensively on animals, and collected a large number of specimens and preparations (Hunterian Collections), which are now housed in the Royal College of Surgeons,

London. He trained under his elder brother *William Hunter* (1718–1783), anatomist and obstetrician, who became professor of anatomy in the Royal Academy 1768 and president of the Medical Society 1781. His collections are now in the Hunterian Museum of Glasgow University.

Hunyadi /hʊnjɒdi/ János Corvinus 1387–1456. Hungarian politician and general. Born in Transylvania, reputedly the son of the emperor →Sigismund, he won battles against the Turks from the 1440s. In 1456 he defeated them at Belgrade, but died shortly afterwards of the plague.

Huppert /uːˈpeə/ Isabelle 1955– . French actress with an international reputation for her versatility in such films as *La Dentellière/The Lacemaker* 1977, *Violette Nozière* 1978, and *Heaven's Gate* 1980.

Hurd /hɜːd/ Douglas (Richard) 1930– . English Conservative politician, home secretary 1986–89, appointed foreign secretary 1989 in the reshuffle that followed Nigel Lawson's resignation as chancellor of the Exchequer. In Nov 1990 he was an unsuccessful candidate in the Tory leadership contest following Margaret Thatcher's unexpected resignation. He retained his post as foreign secretary in Prime Minister John Major's new cabinet formed after the 1992 general election.

Hurd entered the House of Commons 1974, representing Witney in Oxfordshire from 1983. He was made a junior minister by Margaret Thatcher, and the sudden resignation of Leon Brittan projected him into the home secretary's post early in 1986.

Hurd was in the diplomatic service 1952–66, serving in Beijing and at the United Nations in New York and Rome. He then joined the Conservative research department and became a secretary to the party leader Edward Heath. As a hobby, he writes thrillers.

Hurok /hjʊərɒk/ Solomon 'Sol' 1888–1974. Russian-born US theatrical producer. From 1914 he produced musical and theatrical events and over the years arranged US appearances for the most prominent figures in European music and dance. His autobiographical *Impresario* and *S Hurok Presents* appeared 1946 and 1953 respectively.

Hurok emigrated to the USA 1906. As a lifelong devotee of music, he originally organized concerts for New York unions and social groups.

His Russian contacts proved especially valuable, and in later years he worked with the NBC television network producing television specials.

Hurston /hɜːstən/ Zora Neale 1901–1960. US novelist and short-story writer, associated with the Harlem Renaissance, which took Afro-American life and black culture as its subject matter. She collected traditional Afro-American folk tales in *Mules and Men* 1935; her novels include *Their Eyes Were Watching God* 1937.

Hurt /hɜːt/ William 1950– . US actor whose films include *Altered States* 1980, *The Big Chill*

1983, *Kiss of the Spider Woman* 1985, and *Broadcast News* 1987.

Husák /hʊsɑːk/ Gustáv 1913–1991. Leader of the Communist Party of Czechoslovakia (CCP) 1969–87 and president 1975–89. After the 1968 Prague Spring of liberalization, his task was to restore control, purge the CCP, and oversee the implementation of a new, federalist constitution. He was deposed in the popular uprising of Nov–Dec 1989 and expelled from the Communist Party Feb 1990.

Husák, a lawyer, was active in the Resistance movement during World War II, and afterwards in the Slovak Communist Party (SCP), and was imprisoned on political grounds 1951–60. Rehabilitated, he was appointed first secretary of the SCP 1968 and CCP leader 1969–87. As titular state president he pursued a policy of cautious reform. He stepped down as party leader 1987, and was replaced as state president by Václav →Havel Dec 1989 following the 'gentle revolution'.

Huskisson /hʌskɪsən/ William 1770–1830. British Conservative politician, financier, and advocate of free trade. He served as secretary to the Treasury 1807–09 and colonial agent for Ceylon (now Sri Lanka). He was active in the Corn Law debates and supported their relaxation in 1821.

He was the first person to be killed by a train when he was hit at the opening of the Liverpool and Manchester Railway.

Huskisson British politician William Huskisson who entered Parliament as a supporter of William Pitt and held a succession of ministerial posts. His career was cut short by fatal injuries sustained at the opening of the Liverpool and Manchester Railway 1830.

Huss /hʌs/ John (Czech *Jan*) *c.* 1373–1415. Bohemian Christian church reformer, rector of Prague University from 1402, who was excommunicated for attacks on ecclesiastical abuses. He was summoned before the Council of Constance 1414, defended the English reformer John Wycliffe, rejected the pope's authority, and was burned at the stake. His followers were called Hussites.

Hussein /hʊˈseɪn/ ibn Ali *c.* 1854–1931. Leader of the Arab revolt 1916–18 against the Turks. He proclaimed himself king of the Hejaz 1916, accepted the caliphate 1924, but was unable to retain it due to internal fighting. He was deposed 1924 by ibn Saud.

Hussein /hʊˈseɪn/ ibn Talal 1935–   . King of Jordan from 1952. Great-grandson of Hussein ibn Ali, he became king following the mental incapacitation of his father, Talal. By 1967 he had lost all his kingdom west of the river Jordan in the Arab-Israeli Wars, and in 1970 suppressed the Palestine Liberation Organization acting as a guerrilla force against his rule on the remaining East Bank territories. In recent years, he has become a moderating force in Middle Eastern politics. After Iraq's annexation of Kuwait 1990 he attempted to mediate between the opposing sides, at the risk of damaging his relations with both sides.

Hussein /hʊˈseɪn/ Saddam 1937–   . Iraqi politician, in power from 1968, president from 1979, progressively eliminating real or imagined opposition factions as he gained increasing dictatorial control. Ruthless in the pursuit of his objectives, he fought a bitter war against Iran 1980–88, with US economic aid, and dealt harshly with Kurdish rebels seeking independence, using chemical weapons against civilian populations. In 1990 he annexed Kuwait, to universal condemnation, before being driven out by a US-dominated coalition army Feb 1991. Iraq's defeat in the Gulf War undermined Saddam's position as the country's leader; when the Kurds rebelled again after the end of the war, he sent the remainder of his army to crush them, bringing international charges of genocide against him and causing hundreds of thousands of Kurds to flee their homes in northern Iraq. His continued bombardment of Shi'ites in southern Iraq caused the UN to impose a 'no-fly zone' in the area Aug 1992. Alleging infringements of the zone, US-led warplanes bombed strategic targets in Iraq Jan 1993, forcing Hussein to back down and comply with repeated UN requests for access to inspect his arms facilities.

Hussein joined the Arab Ba'ath Socialist Party as a young man and soon became involved in revolutionary activities. In 1959 he was sentenced to death and took refuge in Egypt, but a coup in 1963 made his return possible, although in the following year he was imprisoned for plotting to overthrow the regime he had helped to install. After his release he took a leading part in the 1968 revolution, removing the civilian government and

establishing a Revolutionary Command Council (RCC). At first discreetly, and then more openly, Hussein strengthened his position and in 1979 became RCC chair and state president. In 1977 Saddam Hussein al-Tikriti abolished the use of surnames in Iraq to conceal the fact that a large number of people in the government and ruling party all came from his home village of Tikrit and therefore bore the same surname. The 1990 Kuwait annexation followed a long-running border dispute and was prompted by the need for more oil resources after the expensive war against Iran. Saddam, who had enjoyed US support for being the enemy of Iran and had used poison gas against his own people in Kurdistan without any falling-off in trade with the West, suddenly found himself almost universally condemned. Iraqi assets were frozen and in the UN, Arab, communist, and capitalist nations east and west agreed on a trade embargo and aid to refugees, with the USA and the UK urging aggressive military action. Fears that Saddam might use chemical or even nuclear weapons were raised as predominantly US troops massed on the Saudi Arabian border. With the passing of the UN deadline of 15 Jan 1991 without any withdrawal from Kuwait, allied forces struck Baghdad in a series of air bombardments to which Saddam replied by firing Scud missiles on the Israeli cities of Tel Aviv and Haifa in an unsuccessful effort to bring Israel into the war and thus break up the Arab alliance with the West; he also failed to rally Arab support for a holy war or 'jihad' to eject the Western 'infidels'.

Husserl /ˈhʊsəl/ Edmund (Gustav Albrecht) 1859–1938. German philosopher, regarded as the founder of phenomenology, a philosophy concentrating on what is consciously experienced. His main works are *Logical Investigations* 1900, *Phenomenological Philosophy* 1913, and *The Crisis of the European Sciences* 1936.

He hoped phenomenology would become the science of all sciences. He influenced Martin →Heidegger and affected sociology through the work of Alfred Schütz (1899–1959).

Huston /ˈhjuːstən/ John 1906–1987. US film director, screenwriter, and actor. An impulsive and individualistic film maker, he often dealt with the themes of greed, treachery in human relationships, and the loner. His works as a director include *The Maltese Falcon* 1941 (his debut), *The Treasure of the Sierra Madre* 1948 (in which his father Walter Huston starred and for which both won Academy Awards), *The African Queen* 1951, and his last, *The Dead* 1987.

He was the son of the actor Walter Huston and the father of the actress Anjelica Huston. His other films include *Key Largo* 1948, *Moby Dick* 1956, *The Misfits* 1961, *Fat City* 1972, and *Prizzi's Honor* 1984.

Huston /ˈhjuːstən/ Walter 1884–1950. Canadian-born US actor. His career alternated between stage acting and appearances in feature films. He received critical acclaim for his Broadway performance in *Desire Under the Elms* 1924. In 1948 he won the Academy Award for the best supporting actor for his role in *The Treasure of the Sierra Madre*.

Born in Toronto, Canada, Huston trained and worked as an engineer before choosing theatrical career. He was the father of director John Huston who wrote and directed *The Treasure of the Sierra Madre*.

Hutchinson /ˈhʌtʃɪnsən/ Anne Marbury 1591–1643. American colonial religious leader. In 1634, she and her family followed John →Cotton to Massachusetts Bay Colony 1634. Preaching a unique theology which emphasized the role of faith, she gained a wide following. The colony's leaders, including Cotton, felt threatened by Hutchinson and in 1637 she was banished and excommunicated. Settling in Long Island, she and her family were killed by Indians.

Born in England, Hutchinson was noted for her intellect and forceful personality.

Hutton /ˈhʌtn/ Barbara 1912–1979. US heiress, granddaughter of F W →Woolworth, notorious in her day as the original 'poor little rich girl'. Her seven husbands included the actor Cary Grant.

Hutton /ˈhʌtn/ James 1726–1797. Scottish geologist, known as the 'founder of geology', who formulated the concept of uniformitarianism, the principle that processes that can be seen to occur on the Earth's surface today are the same as those that have occurred throughout geological time. In 1785 he developed a theory of the igneous origin of many rocks.

His *Theory of the Earth* 1788 proposed that the Earth was indefinitely old. Uniformitarianism suggests that past events could be explained in terms of processes that work today. For example, the kind of river current that produces a certain settling pattern in a bed of sand today must have been operating many millions of years ago, if that same pattern is visible in ancient sandstones.

Hutton /ˈhʌtn/ Len (Leonard) 1916–1990. English cricketer, born in Pudsey, West Yorkshire. He captained England in 23 Test matches 1952–56 and was England's first professional captain. In 1938 at the Oval he scored 364 against Australia, a world record Test score until beaten by Gary →Sobers 1958.

Huxley /ˈhʌksli/ Aldous (Leonard) 1894–1963. English writer of novels, essays, and verse. From the disillusionment and satirical eloquence of *Crome Yellow* 1921, *Antic Hay* 1923, and *Point Counter Point* 1928, Huxley developed towards the Utopianism exemplified by *Island* 1962. The science fiction novel *Brave New World* 1932 shows human beings mass-produced in laboratories and rendered incapable of freedom by indoctrination and drugs. He was the grandson of Thomas Henry Huxley and brother of Julian Huxley.

Huxley's later devotion to mysticism led to his experiments with the hallucinogenic drug mescalin, recorded in *The Doors of Perception* 1954. He also wrote the novel *Eyeless in Gaza* 1936, and two historical studies, *Grey Eminence* 1941 and *The Devils of Loudun* 1952.

Huxley /ˈhʌksli/ Andrew 1917– . English physiologist, awarded the Nobel Prize for Physiology or Medicine 1963 with Alan Hodgkin and John Eccles, for work on nerve impulses, discovering how ionic mechanisms are used in nerves to transmit impulses.

Huxley /ˈhʌksli/ Julian 1887–1975. English biologist, first director general of UNESCO, and a founder of the World Wildlife Fund (now the World Wide Fund for Nature).

Operationally, God is beginning to resemble not a ruler but the last fading smile of a cosmic Cheshire cat.

Julian Huxley *Religion without Revolution*

Huxley /ˈhʌksli/ Thomas Henry 1825–1895. English scientist and humanist. Following the publication of Charles Darwin's *On the Origin of Species* 1859, he became known as 'Darwin's bulldog', and for many years was a prominent champion of evolution. In 1869, he coined the word 'agnostic' to express his own religious attitude. His grandsons include Aldous, Andrew, and Julian Huxley.

He wrote *Man's Place in Nature* 1863, textbooks on physiology, and innumerable scientific papers. His later books, such as *Lay Sermons* 1870, *Science and Culture* 1881, and *Evolution and Ethics* 1893 were expositions of scientific humanism.

Hu Yaobang /ˈhuː jaʊˈbæŋ/ 1915–1989. Chinese politician, Communist Party (CCP) chair 1981–87. A protégé of the communist leader Deng Xiaoping, Hu presided over a radical overhaul of the party structure and personnel 1982–86. His death ignited the prodemocracy movement, which was eventually crushed in Tiananmen Square June 1989.

Hu, born into a peasant family in Hunan province, joined the Red Army at the age of 14 and was a political commissar during the 1934–36 Long March. In 1941 he served under Deng and later worked under him in provincial and central government. Hu was purged as a 'capitalist roader' during the 1966–69 Cultural Revolution and sent into the countryside for 're education'. He was rehabilitated 1975 but disgraced again when Deng fell from prominence 1976. In Dec 1978, with Deng established in power, Hu was inducted into the CCP Politburo and became head of the revived secretariat 1980 and CCP chair 1981. He attempted to quicken reaction against Mao. He was dismissed Jan 1987 for his relaxed handling of a wave of student unrest Dec 1986.

Huygens /haɪgənz/ Christiaan 1629–1695. Dutch mathematical physicist and astronomer who proposed the wave theory of light. He developed the pendulum clock, discovered polarization, and observed Saturn's rings.

Huysmans /wiːsˈmɒns/ J(oris) K(arl) 1848–1907. French novelist of Dutch ancestry. His novel *Marthe* 1876, the story of a courtesan, was followed by other realistic novels, including *A rebours/Against Nature* 1884, a novel of self-absorbed aestheticism that symbolized the 'decadent' movement.

Hyde /haɪd/ Douglas 1860–1949. Irish scholar and politician. Founder president of the Gaelic League 1893–1915, he was president of Eire 1938–45. He was the first person to write a book in modern Irish and to collect Irish folklore, as well as being the author of the first literary history of Ireland. His works include *Love Songs of Connacht* 1894.

From a Protestant family, he founded the Gaelic League to promote a cultural, rather than political, nationalism.

Hyder Ali /haɪdər ˈɑːli/ *c.* 1722–1782. Indian general, sultan of Mysore from 1759. In command of the army in Mysore from 1749, he became the ruler of the state 1759, and rivalled British power in the area until his triple defeat by Sir Eyre Coote 1781 during the Anglo-French wars. He was the father of Tippu Sultan.

Hyde-White /haɪd ˈwaɪt/ Wilfred 1903–1991. English actor, best known for character roles in British and occasionally US films, especially the role of Colonel Pickering in the screen version of *My Fair Lady* 1964. He tended to be cast as an eccentric or a pillar of the establishment, and sometimes as a mixture of the two.

Hypatia /haɪˈpeɪʃiə/ *c.* 370–*c.* 415. Greek philosopher, born in Alexandria. She studied Neo-Platonism in Athens, and succeeded her father Theon as professor of philosophy at Alexandria. She was murdered, it is thought by Christian fanatics.

Men will fight for a superstition quite as quickly as for a living truth – often more so.

Hypatia

I

Ibáñez /iːˈbɑːnjeθ/ Vicente Blasco 1867–1928. Spanish novelist and politician, born in Valencia. He was actively involved in revolutionary politics. His novels include *La barraca/The Cabin* 1898, the best of his regional works; *Sangre y arena/Blood and Sand* 1908, the story of a famous bullfighter; and *Los cuatro jinetes del Apocalipsis/The Four Horsemen of the Apocalypse* 1916, a product of the effects of World War I.

Ibarruri /iːˈbæruri/ Dolores, known as *La Pasionaria* (`the passion flower') 1895–1989. Spanish Basque politician, journalist, and orator; she was first elected to the Cortes in 1936. She helped to establish the Popular Front government and was a Loyalist leader in the Civil War. When Franco came to power in 1939 she left Spain for the USSR, where she was active in the Communist Party. She returned to Spain in 1977 after Franco's death and was re-elected to the Cortes (at the age of 81) in the first parliamentary elections for 40 years.

She joined the Spanish Socialist Party in 1917 and wrote for a workers' newspaper under the pen name La Pasionaria.

Iberville /iːˈbəvɪl, ˈaɪb-/ Pierre Le Moyne, Sieur d' 1661–1706. French colonial administrator and explorer in America. With his brother, the Sieur de →Bienville, he led an expedition from France and established a colony at the mouth of the Mississippi River in America. In 1699–1700 they established settlements at the later sites of Biloxi and New Orleans.

Born in Montreal, Canada, Iberville joined the French navy and saw action against the English in the struggle for Canada 1686– 97.

Ibn Battuta /ˈɪbən bəˈtuːtə/ 1304–1368. Arab traveller born in Tangiers. In 1325, he went on an extraordinary 120,675 km/75,000 mi journey via Mecca to Egypt, E Africa, India, and China, returning some 30 years later. During this journey he also visited Spain and crossed the Sahara to Timbuktu. The narrative of his travels, *The Adventures of Ibn Battuta*, was written with an assistant, Ibn Juzayy.

Ibn Saud /ˈɪbən ˈsaʊd/ 1880–1953. First king of Saudi Arabia from 1932. His father was the son of the sultan of Nejd, at whose capital, Riyadh, Ibn Saud was born. In 1891 a rival group seized Riyadh, and Ibn Saud went into exile with his father, who resigned his claim to the throne in his

son's favour. In 1902 Ibn Saud recaptured Riyadh and recovered the kingdom, and by 1921 he had brought all central Arabia under his rule. In 1924 he invaded the Hejaz, of which he was proclaimed king in 1926.

Nejd and the Hejaz were united 1932 in the kingdom of Saudi Arabia. Ibn Saud introduced programmes for modernization with revenue from oil, which was discovered 1936.

Ibn Sina /ˈɪbən ˈsiːnə/ Arabic name of →Avicenna, scholar, and translator.

Ibrahim /iːˈbrɑhɪm/ Abdullah 1934–1990. South African pianist and composer, formerly known as 'Dollar' Brand. He first performed in the USA in 1965 and has had a great influence on the fusion of African rhythms with American jazz. His compositions range from songs to large works for orchestra.

Ibsen /ˈɪbsən/ Henrik (Johan) 1828–1906. Norwegian playwright and poet, whose realistic and often controversial plays revolutionized European theatre. Driven into exile 1864-91 by opposition to the satirical *Love's Comedy* 1862, he wrote the verse dramas *Brand* 1866 and *Peer Gynt* 1867, followed by realistic plays dealing with social issues, including *Pillars of Society* 1877, *The Doll's House* 1879, *Ghosts* 1881, *An Enemy of the People* 1882, and *Hedda Gabler* 1891. By the time he returned to Norway, he was recognized as the country's greatest living writer.

His later plays, which are more symbolic, include *The Master Builder* 1892, *Little Eyolf* 1894, *John Gabriel Borkman* 1896, and *When We Dead Awaken* 1899.

The strongest man in the world is the man who stands most alone.

Henrik Ibsen
An Enemy of the People 1882

Ickes /ˈɪkəs/ Harold LeClair 1874–1952. US public official. A liberal Republican, he was appointed secretary of the interior by F D Roosevelt 1933. As director of the Public Works Administration (PWA, established 1935), he administered Roosevelt's New Deal development projects. He served briefly under President Truman, but resigned from the cabinet 1946.

Born in Blair County, Pennsylvania, USA, Ickes was educated at the University of Chicago and was admitted to the bar 1907. After resigning from his political post, Ickes wrote a newspaper column and published several autobiographical works. *The Secret Diary of Harold L Ickes* appeared 1953.

Iglesias /iːˈgleɪsiəs/ Pablo 1850–1925. Spanish politician, founder of the Spanish Socialist Party (Partido Socialista Obrero Español, PSOE) in 1879. In 1911 he became the first socialist deputy to be elected to the *Cortes* (Spanish parliament).

Ignatius Loyola, St /ɪgˈneɪʃəs lɔɪˈəʊlə/ 1491–1556. Spanish noble who founded the Jesuit order 1540, also called the Society of Jesus.

His deep interest in the religious life began in 1521, when reading the life of Jesus while recuperating from a war wound. He visited the Holy Land in 1523, studied in Spain and Paris, where he took vows with St Francis Xavier, and was ordained 1537. He then moved to Rome and with the approval of Pope Paul III began the Society of Jesus, sending missionaries to Brazil, India, and Japan, and founding Jesuit schools. Feast day 31 July.

Ignatius of Antioch, St /ɪgˈneɪʃəs ˈæntiok/ 1st–2nd century AD. Christian martyr. Traditionally a disciple of St John, he was bishop of Antioch, and was thrown to the wild beasts in Rome. He wrote seven epistles, important documents of the early Christian church. Feast day 1 Feb.

Ikhnaton /ɪkˈnɑːtən/ or *Akhenaton* 14th century BC. King of Egypt of the 18th dynasty (*c.* 1379–1362 BC), who may have ruled jointly for a time with his father Amenhotep III. He developed the cult of the Sun, Aton, rather than the rival cult of Ammon. Some historians believe that his attention to religious reforms rather than imperial defence led to the loss of most of Egypt's possessions in Asia.

Ikhnaton's favourite wife was Nefertiti, and two of their six daughters were married to his successors Smenkhare and Tutankaton (later known as Tutankhamen).

Iliescu /ˌiːliˈeskuː/ Ion 1930– . Romanian president from 1990. A former member of the Romanian Communist Party (PCR) and of Nicolae Ceauşescu's government, Iliescu swept into power on Ceauşescu's fall as head of the National Salvation Front.

Iliescu was elected a member of the PCR central committee 1968, becoming its propaganda secretary 1971. Conflict over the launching of a 'cultural revolution', and the growth of Ceauşescu's personality cult led to Iliescu's removal from national politics: he was sent to Timişoara as chief of party propaganda. At the outbreak of the 'Christmas revolution' 1989, Iliescu was one of the first leaders to emerge, becoming president of the Provisional Council of National Unity Feb 1990. He won an overwhelm-

ing victory in the presidential elections in May 1990, despite earlier controversy over his hard line.

Illich /ˈɪlɪtʃ/ Ivan 1926– . US radical philosopher and activist, born in Austria. His works, which include *Deschooling Society* 1971, *Towards a History of Need* 1978, and *Gender* 1983, are a critique of contemporary economic development, especially in the Third World.

Illich was born in Vienna and has lived in the USA and Latin America. He believes that modern technology and bureaucratic institutions are destroying peasant skills and self-sufficiency and creating a new form of dependency: on experts, professionals, and material goods. True liberation, he believes, can only be achieved by abolishing the institutions on which authority rests, such as schools and hospitals.

In a consumer society there are inevitably two kinds of slaves: the prisoners of addiction and the prisoners of envy.

Ivan Illich *Tools for Conviviality*

Imber /ˈɪmbə/ Naphtali Herz 1856–1909. Itinerant Hebrew poet. A Zionist and champion of the restoration of Hebrew as a modern spoken language, he wrote *Hatikva/The Hope* 1878, which became the Zionist anthem 1897 and the Israeli national anthem 1948. He wrote in Hebrew and Yiddish.

Born in Austria-Hungary, Imber travelled to Palestine and worked as secretary to the wife of British General Oliphant, then went to England and the USA.

Imhotep /ɪmˈhəʊtep/ *c.* 2800 BC. Egyptian physician and architect, adviser to King Zoser (3rd dynasty). He is thought to have designed the step pyramid at Sakkara, and his tomb (believed to be in the N Sakkara cemetery) became a centre of healing. He was deified as the son of Ptah and was identified with Aesculapius, the Greek god of medicine.

Indy /ænˈdiː/ (Paul Marie Théodore) Vincent d' 1851–1931. French composer. He studied under César →Franck, and was one of the founders of the *Schola Cantorum*. His works include operas (*Fervaal* 1897), symphonies, tone poems (*Istar* 1896), and chamber music.

Ingenhousz /ˈɪŋənhuːs/ Jan 1730–1799. Dutch physician and plant physiologist who established that in the light plants absorb carbon dioxide and give off oxygen.

Ingres /ˈæŋgrə/ Jean Auguste Dominique 1780–1867. French painter, a student of David and leading exponent of the Neo-Classical style. He studied and worked in Rome about 1807–20, where he began the *Odalisque* series of sensuous female nudes, then went to Florence, and returned to France 1824. His portraits painted in the 1840s–50s are meticulously detailed and highly polished.

Ingres's style developed in opposition to the Romanticism of Delacroix. Early works include portraits of Napoleon. Later he painted huge ceilings for the Louvre and for Autun Cathedral. His portraits include *Madame Moitessier* 1856 (National Gallery, London).

Inness /ɪnɪs/ George 1825–1894. US landscape painter influenced by the Hudson River school. His early works, such as *The Delaware Valley* 1865 (Metropolitan Museum of Art, New York), are on a grand scale and show a concern for natural effects of light. Later he moved towards Impressionism.

Innocent /ɪnəsənt/ thirteen popes including:

Innocent III 1161–1216. Pope from 1198 who asserted papal power over secular princes, in particular over the succession of Holy Roman Emperors. He also made King →John of England his vassal, compelling him to accept Stephen →Langton as archbishop of Canterbury. He promoted the fourth Crusade and crusades against the non-Christian Livonians and Letts, and the Albigensian heretics of S France.

Inoue /ɪnəʊeɪ/ Yasushi 1907–1991. Japanese writer (fiction, travel essays, art history) whose interest in China and central Asia is evident in many stories and historical novels. The novels feature isolated protagonists at dramatic moments of Asian history. Examples are *Tempyō no iraka* 1957/*The Roof Tile of Tempyo* 1976, *Koshi*, based on the life of Confucius, and *Shirobama*, describing a childhood in old Japan.

Ionesco /ˌiːəˈneskəʊ/ Eugène 1912– . Romanian-born French dramatist, a leading exponent of the Theatre of the Absurd. Most of his plays are in one act and concern the futility of language as a means of communication. These include *La Cantatrice chauve*/*The Bald Prima Donna* 1950 and *La Leçon*/*The Lesson* 1951. Later full-length plays include *Rhinocéros* 1958 and *Le Roi se meurt*/*Exit the King* 1961.

He has also written memoirs and a novel, *Le Solitaire*/*The Hermit* 1973.

Iqbāl /ɪkbɑːl/ Muhammad 1875–1938. Islamic poet and thinker. His literary works, in Urdu and Persian, were mostly verse in the classical style, suitable for public recitation. He sought through his writings to arouse Muslims to take their place in the modern world.

His most celebrated work, the Persian *Asrā-e khūdī*/*Secrets of the Self* 1915, put forward a theory of the self that was opposite to the traditional abnegation found in Islam. He was an influence on the movement that led to the creation of Pakistan.

Ireland /aɪələnd/ John (Nicholson) 1879–1962. English composer. His works include the mystic orchestral prelude *The Forgotten Rite* 1917 and the piano solo *Sarnia* 1941. Benjamin →Britten was his pupil.

Irene, St /aɪˈriːni/ *c.* 752–*c.* 803. Byzantine emperor 797–802. The wife of Leo IV (750–80), she became regent for their son Constantine (771–805) on Leo's death. In 797 she deposed her son, had his eyes put out, and assumed the full title of *basileus* ('emperor'), ruling in her own right until deposed and exiled to Lesvos by a revolt in 802. She was made a saint by the Greek Orthodox church for her attacks on iconoclasts.

Ireton /aɪətən/ Henry 1611–1651. English Civil War general. He joined the parliamentary forces and fought at Edgehill 1642, Gainsborough 1643, and Naseby 1645. After the Battle of Naseby, Ireton, who was opposed to both the extreme republicans and Levellers, strove for a compromise with Charles I, but then played a leading role in his trial and execution. He married his leader Cromwell's daughter in 1646. Lord Deputy in Ireland from 1650, he died after the capture of Limerick.

Irvine /ɜːvɪn/ Andrew Robertson 1951– . British rugby union player who held the world record for the most points scored in senior international rugby with 301 (273 for Scotland, 28 for the British Lions) between 1972 and 1982.

Irving /ɜːvɪŋ/ Henry. Stage name of John Brodribb 1838–1905. English actor. He established his reputation from 1871, chiefly at the Lyceum Theatre in London, where he became manager 1878. He staged a series of successful Shakespearean productions, including *Romeo and Juliet* 1882, with himself and Ellen →Terry playing the leading roles. He was the first actor to be knighted, in 1895.

Irving English actor-manager Henry Irving in the role of the Vicar of Wakefield. Irving dominated the London stage for the last 30 years of Victoria's reign.

Irving /'ɜːvɪŋ/ John 1942– . US novelist. His bizarre and funny novels include *The World According to Garp* 1978, a vivid comic tale about a novelist killed by a disappointed reader.

Irving /'ɜːvɪŋ/ Washington 1783–1859. US essayist and short-story writer. He published a mock-heroic *History of New York* in 1809, supposedly written by the Dutchman 'Diedrich Knickerbocker'. In 1815 he went to England where he published *The Sketch Book of Geoffrey Crayon, Gent.* 1820, which contained such stories as 'Rip van Winkle' and 'The Legend of Sleepy Hollow'.

Isaacs /'aɪzəks/ Alick 1921–1967. Scottish virologist who, with Jean Lindemann, in 1957 discovered interferon, a naturally occurring antiviral substance produced by cells infected with viruses. The full implications of this discovery are still being investigated.

Isaacs /'aɪzəks/ Rufus Daniel, 1st Marquess of Reading 1860–1935. British Liberal lawyer and politician. As Lord Chief Justice he tried the Irish nationalist Roger Casement in 1916. Viceroy of India 1921–26; foreign secretary 1931.

Isabella /ˌɪzə'belə/ two Spanish queens:

Isabella I /ˌɪzə'belə/ *the Catholic* 1451–1504. Queen of Castile from 1474, after the death of her brother Henry IV. By her marriage with Ferdinand of Aragon 1469, the crowns of two of the Christian states in the Moorish-held Spanish peninsula were united. In her reign, during 1492, the Moors were driven out of Spain. She introduced the Inquisition into Castile to suppress heresy, expelled the Jews, and gave financial encouragement to →Columbus. Her youngest daughter was Catherine of Aragon, first wife of Henry VIII of England. In 1992 the Catholic church proposes to beatify her, arousing the indignation of Jewish groups.

Whosoever hath a good presence and a good fashion, carries continual letters of recommendation.

Isabella I of Spain

Isabella II 1830–1904. Queen of Spain from 1833, when she succeeded her father Ferdinand VII (1784–1833). The Salic Law banning a female sovereign had been repealed by the Cortes (parliament), but her succession was disputed by her uncle Don Carlos de Bourbon (1788–1855). After seven years of civil war, the Carlists were defeated. She abdicated in favour of her son Alfonso XII in 1868.

Isabella of France /ˌɪzə'belə/ 1292–1358. Daughter of King Philip IV of France, wife of King Edward II of England; she intrigued with her lover, Roger Mortimer, to have the king deposed and murdered.

She was a strong-willed enemy of her husband's favourites, Piers Gaveston and the Despencers. She is known to history as the 'she-wolf of France'.

Isaiah /aɪ'zaɪə/ 8th century BC. In the Old Testament, the first major Hebrew prophet. The son of Amos, he was probably of high rank, and lived largely in Jerusalem.

Isaurian 8th-century Byzantine imperial dynasty, originating in Asia Minor.

Members of the family had been employed as military leaders by the Byzantines, and they gained great influence and prestige as a result. Leo III acceded in 717 as the first Isaurian emperor, and was followed by Constantine V (718–75), Leo IV (750–80), and Leo's widow Irene, who acted as regent for their son before deposing him 797 and assuming the title of emperor herself. She was deposed 802. The Isaurian rulers maintained the integrity of the empire's borders. With the exception of Irene, they attempted to suppress the use of religious icons.

Isherwood /'ɪʃəwʊd/ Christopher (William Bradshaw) 1904–1986. English novelist. He lived in Germany 1929–33 just before Hitler's rise to power, a period that inspired *Mr Norris Changes Trains* 1935 and *Goodbye to Berlin* 1939, creating the character of Sally Bowles (the basis of the musical *Cabaret* 1968). Returning to England, he collaborated with W H →Auden in three verse plays.

Ishiguro /ˌɪʃɪ'ɡʊrəʊ/ Kazuo 1954– . Japanese-born British novelist. His novel *An Artist of the Floating World* won the 1986 Whitbread Prize, and *The Remains of the Day* won the 1989 Booker Prize. His work is characterized by a sensitive style and subtle structure.

Ishiguro's first novel, *A Pale View of Hills*, takes place mainly in his native Nagasaki, dealing obliquely with the aftermath of the atom bomb. *An Artist of the Floating World* is set entirely in Japan but thematically linked to *The Remains of the Day*, which is about an English butler coming to realize the extent of his self-sacrifice and self-deception. All three have in common a melancholy reassessment of the past.

Isidore of Seville /'ɪzədɔː/ *c.* 560–636. Writer and missionary. His *Ethymologiae* was the model for later medieval encyclopedias and helped to preserve classical thought during the Middle Ages; his *Chronica Maiora* remains an important source for the history of Visigothic Spain. As bishop of Seville from 600, he strengthened the church in Spain and converted many Jews and Aryan Visigoths.

Ismail /ˌɪzmɑː'iːl/ 1830–1895. Khedive (governor) of Egypt 1866–79. A grandson of Mehemet Ali, he became viceroy of Egypt in 1863 and in 1866 received the title of khedive from the Ottoman sultan. He amassed huge foreign debts and in 1875 Britain, at Prime Minister Disraeli's suggestion, bought the khedive's Suez Canal shares for nearly £4 million, establishing Anglo-French control of Egypt's finances. In 1879 the UK and France persuaded the sultan to appoint Tewfik, his son, khedive in his place.

Ismail I /ˌɪzmɑːˈiːl/ 1486–1524. Shah of Persia from 1501, founder of the *Safavi dynasty*, who established the first national government since the Arab conquest and Shi'ite Islam as the national religion.

Isocrates /aɪˈsɒkrətiːz/ 436–338 BC. Athenian orator, a pupil of the philosopher Socrates. He was a professional speechwriter and teacher of rhetoric.

Isozaki /ˌɪsəʊˈzɑːki/ Arata 1931–   . Japanese architect. One of Kenzo →Tange's team 1954–63, his Post-Modernist works include Ochanomizu Square, Tokyo (retaining the existing facades), and buildings for the 1992 Barcelona Olympics.

Architecture is a machine for the production of meaning.

Arata Isozaki in *Contemporary Architects* 1980

Israels /ˈɪsrɑːelz/ Jozef 1824–1911. Dutch painter. In 1870 he settled in The Hague and became a leader of the *Hague school* of landscape painters, who shared some of their ideals with the Barbizon school in France. His sombre and sentimental scenes of peasant life recall the work of →Millet.

Issigonis /ˌɪsɪˈɡəʊnɪs/ Alec 1906–1988. British engineer who designed the Morris Minor 1948 and the Mini-Minor 1959 cars, thus creating economy motoring and adding the word 'mini' to the English language.

Itagaki /ˌiːtəˈɡɑːki/ Taisuke 1837–1919. Japanese military and political leader, the founder of Japan's first political party, the (Liberal) Jiyuto 1875–81. Involved in the overthrow of the Tokugawa shogunate and the Meiji restoration 1866–68 (see →Mutsuhito), Itagaki became a champion of democratic principles while continuing to serve in the government for short periods.

After ennoblement in 1887 he retained the leadership of the party and cooperated with Itō Hirobumi in the establishment of parliamentary government in the 1890s.

Itō /ˈiːtəʊ/ Hirobumi, Prince 1841–1909. Japanese politician, prime minister 1887, 1892–96, 1898, 1900–01. He was a key figure in the modernization of Japan and was involved in the Meiji restoration under →Mutsuhito 1866–68 and in government missions to the USA and Europe in the 1870s. As minister for home affairs, he helped draft the Meiji constitution of 1889.

Itō was a samurai from Chōshū, a feudal domain that rebelled against the shogunate in the 1850s–60s. In 1863 he became one of the first Japanese to study in England, and in 1871–73 he was a member of a diplomatic mission to Europe and the USA. Given responsibility for drafting the constitution, he went abroad again 1882–83 to study European models. He was appointed a government adviser 1885 and went on to become prime minister many times. While resident-general in Korea, he was assassinated by Korean nationalists, which led to Japan's annexation of that country. Politically Itō was a moderate, favouring negotiation and compromise.

Iturbide /ˌɪtʊəˈbiːdeɪ/ Agustín de 1783–1824. Mexican military leader (*caudillo*) who led the conservative faction in the nation's struggle for independence from Spain. In 1822 he crowned himself Emperor Agustín I. His extravagance and failure to restore order led all other parties to turn against him, and he reigned for less than a year.

Ivan /ˈaɪvən, ɪˈvɑːn/ six rulers of Russia, including:

Ivan III Ivan the Great 1440–1505. Grand duke of Muscovy from 1462, who revolted against Tatar overlordship by refusing tribute to Grand Khan Ahmed 1480. He claimed the title of tsar, and used the double-headed eagle as the Russian state emblem.

Ivan IV *the Terrible* 1530–1584. Grand duke of Muscovy from 1533; he assumed power 1544 and was crowned as first tsar of Russia 1547. He conquered Kazan 1552, Astrakhan 1556, and Siberia 1581. He reformed the legal code and local administration 1555 and established trade relations with England. In his last years he alternated between debauchery and religious austerities, executing thousands and, in rage, his own son.

Ivan attempted to centralize his rule in Muscovy. He campaigned against the Tatars of Kazan, Astrakhan, and elsewhere, but his policy of forming Russia into an empire led to the fruitless 24-year Livonian war. His regime was marked by brutality, evidenced by the destruction (sacking) of Novgorod.

Ives /aɪvz/ Charles (Edward) 1874–1954. US composer who experimented with atonality, quarter tones, clashing time signatures, and quotations from popular music of the time. He wrote five symphonies, including *Holidays Symphony* 1904–13, chamber music, including the *Concord Sonata*, and the orchestral *Three Places in New England* 1903–14 and *The Unanswered Question* 1908.

Ives /aɪvz/ Frederic Eugene 1856–1937. US inventor who developed the halftone process of printing photographs in 1878. The process uses a screen to break up light and dark areas into dots. By 1886 he had evolved the halftone process now generally in use. Among his many other inventions was a three-colour printing process (similar to the four-colour process).

Ivory /ˈaɪvəri/ James 1928–   . US film director best known for his collaboration with Indian producer Ismail →Merchant.

J

Jackson /dʒæksən/ Alexander Young 1882–1974. Canadian landscape painter, a leading member of the *Group of Seven*, who aimed to create a specifically Canadian school of landscape art.

Jackson /dʒæksən/ Andrew 1767–1845. 7th president of the USA 1829–37, a Democrat. A major general in the War of 1812, he defeated a British force at New Orleans in 1815 (after the official end of the war in 1814) and was involved in the war that led to the purchase of Florida in 1819. The political organization he built as president, with Martin Van Buren, was the basis for the modern Democratic Party.

Jackson was born in South Carolina and spent his early life in poverty. After an unsuccessful attempt in 1824, he was elected president in 1828. This was the first election in which electors were chosen directly by voters rather than state legislators. He demanded and received absolute loyalty from his cabinet members and made wide use of

Jackson Nicknamed 'Old Hickory' because of his popular image as the simple frontiersman, 7th US president Andrew Jackson was hailed as the friend of the people. Under his administration the spoils system (giving public offices as rewards for political support) was introduced, expansion into the West was encouraged, and the national debt was completely paid off.

his executive powers. In 1832 he vetoed the renewal of the US bank charter and was reelected, whereupon he continued his struggle against the power of finance.

Jackson /dʒæksən/ Glenda 1936– . English actress, Labour member of Parliament from 1992. She has made many stage appearances, including *Marat/Sade* 1966, and her films include the Oscar-winning *Women in Love* 1969, *Sunday Bloody Sunday* 1971, and *A Touch of Class* 1973. On television she played Queen Elizabeth I in *Elizabeth R* 1971.

In 1990 she was chosen by the Labour Party as a candidate for Parliament and was elected member for Hampstead and Highgate in N London in April 1992.

Jackson /dʒæksən/ Howell Edmunds 1832–1895. US jurist. Elected to the US Senate 1880, he was named federal district judge 1886 by Grover Cleveland and chief judge of the circuit court of appeals 1891 by Benjamin Harrison. In 1893 Jackson was appointed to the US Supreme Court, but illness prevented him from carrying out his duties.

Born in Paris, Tennessee, Jackson received his law degree from Cumberland University 1856. During the American Civil War 1861–65, he served as an official in Tennessee's Confederate government. Returning to private practise after the war, he was elected to the state legislature 1880.

Jackson /dʒæksən/ Jesse 1941– . US Democrat politician, a cleric and campaigner for minority rights. He contested his party's 1984 and 1988 presidential nominations in an effort to increase voter registration and to put black issues on the national agenda. He is an eloquent public speaker.

Born in North Carolina and educated in Chicago, Jackson emerged as a powerful Baptist preacher and black activist politician, working first with the civil-rights leader Martin Luther King, Jr, then on building the political machine that gave Chicago a black mayor 1983.

Jackson sought to construct what he called a *rainbow coalition* of ethnic-minority and socially deprived groups. He took the lead in successfully campaigning for US disinvestment in South Africa 1986.

Jackson /dʒæksən/ John Hughlings 1835–1911. English neurologist and neurophysiologist. As a result of his studies of epilepsy, Jackson demonstrated that specific areas of the cerebral cortex (outer mantle of the brain) control the functioning of particular organs and limbs.

He also demonstrated that →Helmholtz's ophthalmoscope is a crucial diagnostic tool for disorders of the nervous system.

Jackson /dʒæksən/ Lady. Title of British economist Barbara →Ward.

Jackson /dʒæksən/ Mahalia 1911–1972. US gospel singer. She made her first recording in 1934, and her version of the gospel song 'Move on Up a Little Higher' was a commercial success 1945. Jackson became a well-known radio and television performer in the 1950s and was invited to sing at the presidential inauguration of John F Kennedy.

Born in New Orleans and brought up in a religious home, Jackson began singing religious music in the choir of her local church. In 1927 she left home for Chicago and became a member of the Greater Salem Baptist Church choir, where she distinguished herself as an outstanding soloist.

Jackson /dʒæksən/ Michael 1958– . US rock singer and songwriter whose videos and live performances are meticulously choreographed. His first solo hit was 'Got to Be There' 1971; his worldwide popularity peaked with the albums *Thriller* 1982 and *Bad* 1987. The follow-up was *Dangerous* 1991.

He turned professional in 1969 as the youngest member of *the Jackson Five*, who had several hits on Motown Records, beginning with their first single, 'I Want You Back'. The group left Motown in 1975 and changed its name to *the Jacksons*. Michael was the lead singer, but soon surpassed his brothers in popularity as a solo performer. From *Off the Wall* 1979 to *Bad*, his albums were produced by Quincy Jones (1933–). *Thriller* sold 41 million copies, a world record, and yielded an unprecedented number of hit singles, among them 'Billie Jean' 1983.

Jackson /dʒæksən/ Stonewall (Thomas Jonathan) 1824–1863. US Confederate general in the American Civil War. He acquired his nickname and his reputation at the Battle of Bull Run, from the firmness with which his brigade resisted the Northern attack. In 1862 he organized the Shenandoah Valley campaign and assisted Robert E →Lee's invasion of Maryland. He helped to defeat General Joseph E Hooker's Union army at the battle of Chancellorsville, Virginia, but was fatally wounded by one of his own soldiers in the confusion of battle.

Jack the Ripper /dʒæk/ popular name for the unidentified mutilator and murderer of at least five women prostitutes in the Whitechapel area of London in 1888.

Jacob /dʒeɪkəb/ François 1920– . French biochemist who, with Jacques Monod, pioneered research into molecular genetics and showed how the production of proteins from DNA is controlled. He shared the Nobel Prize for Medicine in 1965.

Myths and science fulfil a similar function ... they both provide human beings with a representation of the world and of the forces that are supposed to govern it.

François Jacob
The Possible and the Actual 1982

Jacob /dʒeɪkəb/ Joseph 1854–1916. Australian-born US folklorist and collector of fairy tales. He published collections of vividly re-told fairy stories such as *English Fairy Tales* 1890, *Celtic Fairy Tales* 1892 and 1894, and *Indian Fairy Tales* 1892.

Jacobs /dʒeɪkəbz/ W(illiam) W(ymark) 1863–1943. British author who used his childhood knowledge of London's docklands in amusing short stories such as 'Many Cargoes' 1896. He excelled in the macabre, for example 'The Monkey's Paw' 1902.

Jacquard /dʒækɑːd/ Joseph Marie 1752–1834. French textile manufacturer who invented a punched-card system for programming designs on a carpet-making loom. In 1804 he constructed looms that used a series of punched cards to control the pattern of longitudinal warp threads depressed before each sideways passage of the shuttle. On later machines the punched cards were joined to form an endless loop that represented the 'program' for the repeating pattern of a carpet.

Jacquard-style punched cards were used in the early computers of the 1940s–1960s.

Jacuzzi /dʒəˈkuːzi/ Candido 1903–1986. Italian-born US engineer who invented the Jacuzzi, a pump that produces a whirlpool effect in a bathtub. The Jacuzzi was commercially launched as a health and recreational product in the mid-1950s.

Jagan /dʒeɪgən/ Cheddi (Berrat) 1918– . Guyanese left-wing politician. Educated in British Guyana and the USA, he led the People's Progressive Party (PPA) from 1950, and was the first prime minister of British Guyana 1961–64. As candidate for president 1992, he opposed privatization as leading to 'recolonization'. In Aug elections the PPA won a decisive victory, and Jagan as veteran leader replaced Desmond Hoyte.

Jagan /dʒeɪgən/ Janet 1920– . Guyanese left-wing politician, wife of Cheddi Jagan. She was general secretary of the People's Progressive Party 1950–70.

Jahangir /dʒəˈhɑːngɪə/ 'Conqueror of the World'. Adopted name of Salim 1569–1627. Mogul emperor of India 1605–27, succeeding his father →Akbar the Great. He designed the Shalimar Gardens in Kashmir and buildings and gardens in Lahore.

In 1622 he lost Kandahar province in Afghanistan to Persia. His rule was marked by the influence of his wife, Nur Jahan, and her conflict with Prince Khurran (later Shah Jahan). His addiction to alcohol and opium weakened his power.

Jakeš /jaːkeʃ/ Miloš 1922– . Czech communist politician, a member of the Politburo from 1981 and party leader 1987–89. A conservative, he supported the Soviet invasion of Czechoslovakia in 1968. He was forced to resign in Nov 1989 following a series of pro-democracy mass rallies.

Jakeš, an electrical engineer, joined the Communist Party of Czechoslovakia (CCP) in 1945 and studied in Moscow 1955–58. As head of the CCP's central control commission, he oversaw the purge of reformist personnel after the suppression of the 1968 Prague Spring. In Dec 1987 he replaced Gustáv Husák as CCP leader.

Although he enjoyed close relations with the Soviet leader Gorbachev, Jakeš was a cautious reformer who was unpopular with the people.

James /dʒeɪmz/ Henry 1843–1916. US novelist, who lived in Europe from 1875 and became a naturalized British subject 1915. His novels deal with the impact of sophisticated European culture on the innocent American. They include *The Portrait of a Lady* 1881, *Washington Square* 1881, *The Bostonians* 1886, *The Ambassadors* 1903, and *The Golden Bowl* 1904. He also wrote more than a hundred shorter works of fiction, notably the supernatural tale *The Turn of the Screw* 1898.

Other major works include *Roderick Hudson* 1876, *The American* 1877, *The Tragic Muse* 1890, *The Spoils of Poynton* 1897, *The Awkward Age* 1899, and *The Wings of the Dove* 1902.

It is art that makes life, makes interest, makes importance ... and I know of no substitute whatever for the force and beauty of its process.

Henry James letter to H G Wells July 1915

James /dʒeɪmz/ Jesse 1847–1882. US bank and train robber, born in Missouri and a leader, with his brother Frank (1843–1915), of the Quantrill raiders, a Confederate guerrilla band in the Civil War. Frank later led his own gang. Jesse was killed by Bob Ford, an accomplice; Frank remained unconvicted and became a farmer.

James /dʒeɪmz/ M(ontague) R(hodes) 1862–1936. British writer, theologian, linguist, and medievalist. He wrote *Ghost Stories of an Antiquary* 1904 and other supernatural tales.

James /dʒeɪmz/ P(hyllis) D(orothy) 1920– . British detective novelist, creator of the characters Superintendent Adam Dalgliesh and private investigator Cordelia Gray. She was a tax official,

James I The son of Mary, Queen of Scots, James I of England was already King of Scotland when he came to throne in England in 1603

hospital administrator, and civil servant before turning to writing. Her books include *Death of an Expert Witness* 1977, *The Skull Beneath the Skin* 1982, and *A Taste for Death* 1986. She was made a baroness in 1991.

James /dʒeɪmz/ William 1842–1910. US psychologist and philosopher, brother of the novelist Henry James. He turned from medicine to psychology and taught at Harvard 1872–1907. His books include *Principles of Psychology* 1890, *The Will to Believe* 1897, and *Varieties of Religious Experience* 1902, one of the most important works on the psychology of religion.

James I /dʒeɪmz/ *the Conqueror* 1208–1276. King of Aragon from 1213, when he succeeded his father. He conquered the Balearic Islands and took Valencia from the Moors, dividing it with Alfonso X of Castile by a treaty of 1244. Both these exploits are recorded in his autobiography *Libre dels feyts/Chronicle*. He largely established Aragon as the dominant power in the Mediterranean.

James /dʒeɪmz/ two kings of Britain:

James I 1566–1625. King of England from 1603 and Scotland (as *James VI*) from 1567. The son of Mary Queen of Scots and Lord Darnley, he succeeded on his mother's abdication from the Scottish throne, assumed power 1583, established a strong centralized authority, and in 1589 married Anne of Denmark (1574–1619). As successor to Elizabeth I in England, he alienated the Puritans by his High Church views and Parliament by his assertion of divine right, and was generally unpopular because of his favourites, such as →Buckingham, and his schemes for an alliance with Spain. He was succeeded by his son Charles I.

James II 1633–1701. King of England and Scotland (as *James VII*) from 1685, second son of Charles I. He succeeded Charles II. James married Anne Hyde 1659 (1637–1671, mother of Mary II and Anne) and →Mary of Modena 1673 (mother of James Edward Stuart). He became a Catholic 1671, which led first to attempts to exclude him from the succession, then to the rebellions of →Monmouth and →Argyll, and finally to the Whig and Tory leaders' invitation to William of Orange to take the throne in 1688. James fled to France, then led an uprising in Ireland 1689, but after defeat at the Battle of the Boyne 1690 remained in exile in France.

James /dʒeɪmz/ seven kings of Scotland:

James I 1394–1437. King of Scotland 1406–37, who assumed power 1424. He was a cultured and strong monarch whose improvements in the administration of justice brought him popularity among the common people. He was assassinated by a group of conspirators led by the Earl of Atholl.

James II 1430–1460. King of Scotland from 1437, who assumed power 1449. The only surviving son of James I, he was supported by most of the nobles and parliament. He sympathized with the Lancastrians during the Wars of the Roses, and attacked English possessions in S Scotland. He was killed while besieging Roxburgh Castle.

James III 1451–1488. King of Scotland from 1460, who assumed power 1469. His reign was marked by rebellions by the nobles, including his brother Alexander, Duke of Albany. He was murdered during a rebellion supported by his son, who then ascended the throne as James IV.

James IV 1473–1513. King of Scotland from 1488, who married Margaret (1489–1541, daughter of Henry VII) in 1503. He came to the throne after his followers murdered his father, James III, at Sauchieburn. His reign was internally peaceful, but he allied himself with France against England, invaded 1513 and was defeated and killed at the Battle of Flodden. James IV was a patron of poets and architects as well as a military leader.

James V 1512–1542. King of Scotland from 1513, who assumed power 1528. During the long period of his minority, he was caught in a struggle between pro-French and pro-English factions. When he assumed power, he allied himself with France and upheld Catholicism against the Protestants. Following an attack on Scottish territory by Henry VIII's forces, he was defeated near the border at Solway Moss 1542.

James VI of Scotland; see →James I of England.

James VII of Scotland; see →James II of England.

James Edward Stuart /dʒeɪmz/ 1688–1766. British prince, known as the *Old Pretender* (for the Jacobites, he was James III). Son of James II, he was born at St James's Palace and after the revolution of 1688 was taken to France. He landed in Scotland in 1715 to head a Jacobite rebellion but withdrew through lack of support. In his later years he settled in Rome.

Jameson /dʒemɪsən/ Leander Starr 1853–1917. British colonial administrator. In South Africa, early in 1896, he led the *Jameson Raid* from Mafeking into Transvaal to support the non-Boer colonists there, in an attempt to overthrow the government (for which he served some months in prison). Returning to South Africa, he succeeded Cecil →Rhodes as leader of the Progressive Party of Cape Colony, where he was prime minister 1904–08.

James, St /dʒeɪmz/ several Christian saints, incuding:

James, St *the Great* died AD 44. A New Testament apostle, originally a Galilean fisher, he was the son of Zebedee and brother of the apostle John. He was put to death by →Herod Agrippa I. James is the patron saint of Spain. Feast day 25 July.

James, St *the Just* 1st century AD. The New Testament brother of Jesus, to whom Jesus appeared after the Resurrection. Leader of the Christian church in Jerusalem, he was the author of the biblical Epistle of James.

James, St *the Little* 1st century AD. In the New Testament, a disciple of Christ, son of Alphaeus. Feast day 3 May.

Janáček /jænətʃek/ Leoš 1854–1928. Czech composer. He became director of the Conservatoire at Brno in 1919 and professor at the Prague Conservatoire in 1920. His music, highly original and influenced by Moravian folk music, includes arrangements of folk songs, operas (*Jenúfa* 1904, *The Cunning Little Vixen* 1924), and the choral *Glagolitic Mass* 1926.

Jannequin /ʒæn'kæn/ Clément *c.* 1472–*c.* 1560. French composer. He studied with →Josquin Desprez and is remembered for choral works that incorporate images from real life, such as birdsong and the cries of street vendors.

Jannings /jænɪŋs/ Emil. Stage name of Theodor Friedrich Emil Jarenz 1882–1950. German actor in films from 1914. In *Der Blaue Engel/The Blue Angel* 1930 he played a schoolteacher who becomes infatuated with Marlene Dietrich.

Jansen /dʒænsən/ Cornelius 1585–1638. Dutch Roman Catholic theologian, founder of Jansenism with his book *Augustinus* 1640, emphasizing the more predestinatory approach of Augustine's teaching as opposed to that of the Jesuits.

He became professor at Louvain, Belgium, in 1630, and bishop of Ypres, Belgium, in 1636.

Jansky /ˈdʒænski/ Karl Guthe 1905–1950. US radio engineer who discovered that the Milky Way galaxy emanates radio waves; he did not follow up his discovery, but it marked the birth of radioastronomy.

Jansky was born in Norman, Oklahoma. In 1928 he joined the Bell Telephone Laboratories, New Jersey, where he investigated causes of static that created interference on radio-telephone calls.

Jaques-Dalcroze /ˈʒæk dælˈkrəʊz/ Emile 1865–1950. Swiss composer and teacher. He is remembered for his system of physical training by rhythmical movement to music (eurhythmics), and founded the Institut Jaques-Dalcroze in Geneva, in 1915.

Järnefelt /ˈjeənəfelt/ (Edvard) Armas 1869–1958. Finnish composer who is chiefly known for his 'Praeludium' and the lyrical 'Berceuse' 1909 for small orchestra, from music for the drama *The Promised Land.*

Jarrett /ˈdʒærət/ Keith 1945– . US jazz pianist and composer, an eccentric innovator who performs both alone and with small groups. Jarrett was a member of the rock-influenced Charles Lloyd Quartet 1966–67, and played with Miles Davis 1970–71. *The Köln Concert* 1975 is a characteristic solo live recording.

Jarry /ˈʒæri/ Alfred 1873–1907. French satiric dramatist whose *Ubu Roi* 1896 foreshadowed the Theatre of the Absurd and the French Surrealist movement.

Jaruzelski /ˌjæruːˈzelski/ Wojciech 1923– . Polish general, communist leader from 1981, president 1985–90. He imposed martial law for the first year of his rule, suppressed the opposition, and banned trade-union activity, but later released many political prisoners. In 1989, elections in favour of the free trade union Solidarity forced Jaruzelski to speed up democratic reforms, overseeing a transition to a new form of 'socialist pluralist' democracy and stepping down as president 1990.

Jaruzelski, who served with the Soviet army 1939–43, was defence minister 1968–83 and entered the Politburo 1971. At the height of the crisis of 1980–81 he assumed power as prime minister and PUWP first secretary; in 1985 he resigned as prime minister to become president, but remained the dominant political figure in Poland. His attempts to solve Poland's economic problems were unsuccessful. He apologized for the 'pain and injustice' suffered by Poles during his term as head of state in his leaving speech of Dec 1990.

Jaspers /ˈjæspəz/ Karl 1883–1969. German philosopher whose works include *General Psychopathology* 1913 and *Philosophy* 1932. He studied medicine and psychology, and in 1921 became professor of philosophy at Heidelberg.

Jaurès /ʒəʊres/ Jean Léon 1859–1914. French socialist politician and advocate of international peace. He was a lecturer in philosophy at Toulouse until his election in 1885 as a deputy (member of parliament). In 1893 he joined the Socialist Party, established a united party, and in 1904 founded the newspaper *L'Humanité,* becoming its editor until his assassination.

Jay /dʒeɪ/ John 1745–1829. US diplomat and jurist, a member of the Continental Congress 1774–89 and its president 1779. With Benjamin Franklin and John Adams, he negotiated the Peace of Paris 1783, which concluded the American Revolution. President Washington named him first chief justice of the US 1789. He negotiated Jay's Treaty with England 1795, averting another war. He was governor of New York 1795–1801.

Born in New York City, Jay was admitted to the bar 1768. He became first chief justice of New York 1778. He was US minister to Spain 1779–82 and later served as foreign secretary for the Continental Congress 1783–89. A strong supporter of the federal constitution, he collaborated with Alexander Hamilton and James Madison on the *Federalist Papers* 1787–88, aiding ratification of the US constitution.

Jayawardene /ˌdʒaɪəˈwɑːdɪnə/ Junius Richard 1906– . Sri Lankan politician. Leader of the United Nationalist Party from 1973, he became prime minister 1977 and the country's first president 1978–88.

Jeans /dʒiːnz/ James Hopwood 1877–1946. British mathematician and scientist. In physics he worked on the kinetic theory of gases, and on forms of energy radiation; in astronomy, his work focused on giant and dwarf stars, the nature of spiral nebulae, and the origin of the cosmos. He did much to popularize astronomy.

Jefferies /ˈdʒefrɪz/ (John) Richard 1848–1887. British naturalist and writer, whose books on the countryside included *Gamekeeper at Home* 1878, *Wood Magic* 1881, and *Story of My Heart* 1883.

Jeffers /ˈdʒefəz/ (John) Robinson 1887–1962. US poet. He wrote free verse and demonstrated an antagonism to human society. His collected volumes include *Tamar and Other Poems* 1924, *The Double Axe* 1948, and *Hungerfield and Other Poems* 1954.

Jefferson /ˈdʒefəsən/ Thomas 1743–1826. 3rd president of the USA 1801–09, founder of the Democratic Republican Party. He published *A Summary View of the Rights of America* 1774 and as a member of the Continental Congresses of 1775–76 was largely responsible for the drafting of the Declaration of Independence. He was governor of Virginia 1779–81, ambassador to Paris 1785–89, secretary of state 1789–93, and vice president 1797–1801.

Jefferson was born in Virginia into a wealthy family. His interests included music, painting,

Jefferson 3rd US president and great liberal states-man, Thomas Jefferson. He was the first president to be inaugurated in Washington (a city which he helped to plan). Among the important events of his presidency were the Louisiana Purchase 1803 of the French terri-tories in the Mississippi Basin, and the abolition of the slave trade 1808.

architecture, and the natural sciences; he was very much a product of the 18th-century Enlightenment. His political philosophy of 'agrarian democracy' placed responsibility for upholding a virtuous American republic mainly upon a citizenry of independent yeoman farmers. Ironically, his two terms as president saw the adoption of some of the ideas of his political opponents, the Federalists.

No government ought to be without censors, and where the press is free, no one ever will.

Thomas Jefferson letter to George Washington
9 Sept 1792

Jeffrey /dʒefri/ Francis, Lord 1773–1850. Scottish lawyer and literary critic. Born in Edinburgh, he was a founder and editor of the *Edinburgh Review* 1802–29. In 1830 he was made Lord Advocate, and in 1834 a Scottish law lord. He was hostile to the Romantic poets, and wrote of Wordsworth's *Excursion*: 'This will never do.'

Jeffreys /dʒefrɪz/ Alec John 1950– . British geneticist who discovered the DNA probes necessary for accurate genetic fingerprinting so that a murderer or rapist could be identified by, for example, traces of blood, tissue, or semen.

Jeffreys /dʒefrɪz/ George, 1st Baron 1648–1689. Welsh judge, popularly known as the hanging

judge. He became Chief Justice of the King's Bench in 1683, and presided over many political trials, notably those of Philip Sidney, Titus Oates, and Richard Baxter, becoming notorious for his brutality.

Jeffreys was born in Denbighshire. In 1685 he was made a peer and Lord Chancellor and, after →Monmouth's rebellion, conducted the 'bloody assizes' during which 320 rebels were executed and hundreds more flogged, imprisoned, or transported. He was captured when attempting to flee the country after the revolution of 1688, and died in the Tower of London.

Jehosophat /dʒɪˈhɒsəfæt/ 4th king of Judah *c.* 873–849 BC; he allied himself with Ahab, king of Israel, in the war against Syria.

Jehu king of Israel *c.* 842–815 BC. He led a successful rebellion against the family of →Ahab and was responsible for the death of Jezebel.

Jekyll /dʒiːkl/ Gertrude 1843–1932. English landscape gardener and writer. She created over 200 gardens, many in collaboration with the architect Edwin →Lutyens. In her books, she advocated natural gardens of the cottage type, with plentiful herbaceous borders.

Originally a painter and embroiderer, she took up gardening at the age of 48 because of worsening eyesight. Her home at Munstead Wood, Surrey was designed for her by Lutyens.

Jellicoe /dʒelɪkəʊ/ John Rushworth, 1st Earl 1859–1935. British admiral who commanded the Grand Fleet 1914–16 during World War I; the only action he fought was the inconclusive battle of Jutland. He was First Sea Lord 1916–17, when he failed to push the introduction of the convoy system to combat U-boat attack. Created 1st Earl 1925.

Jencks /dʒeŋks/ Charles 1939– . US architectural theorist and furniture designer. He coined the term 'Post-Modern architecture' and wrote *The Language of Post-Modern Architecture* 1984.

Jenkins /dʒeŋkɪnz/ Roy (Harris), Lord Jenkins 1920– . British politician. He became a Labour minister 1964, was home secretary 1965–67 and 1974–76, and chancellor of the Exchequer 1967–70. He was president of the European Commission 1977–81. In 1981 he became one of the founders of the Social Democratic Party and was elected 1982, but lost his seat 1987. In the same year, he was elected chancellor of Oxford University and made a life peer.

Educated at Oxford University, Jenkins was a close friend of the future Labour leader Gaitskell. A Labour MP from 1948, he was minister of aviation 1964–65, then home secretary and chancellor of the Exchequer under Harold Wilson. In 1970 he became deputy leader of the Labour Party, but resigned 1972 because of disagreement with Wilson on the issue of UK entry to the European Community.

Jenner /ˈdʒenə/ Edward 1749–1823. English physician who pioneered vaccination. In Jenner's day, smallpox was a major killer. His discovery 1796 that inoculation with cowpox gives immunity to smallpox was a great medical breakthrough. He coined the word 'vaccination' from the Latin word for cowpox, *vaccina*.

Jenner observed that people who worked with cattle and contracted cowpox from them never subsequently caught smallpox. In 1798 he published his findings that a child inoculated with cowpox, then two months later with smallpox, did not get smallpox.

Jenner /ˈdʒenə/ Henry (Gwas Myhal) 1849–1934. English poet. He attempted to revive Cornish as a literary language, and in 1904 published a handbook of the Cornish language.

Jennings /ˈdʒenɪŋz/ Humphrey 1907–1950. British documentary filmmaker who introduced a poetic tone and subjectivity to factually based material. He was active in the General Post Office Film Unit from 1934 and his wartime films vividly portrayed London in the Blitz: *London Can Take It* 1940, *This Is England* 1941, and *Fires Were Started* 1943.

Jennings /ˈdʒenɪŋz/ Pat (Patrick) 1945– . Irish footballer. In his 21-year career he was an outstanding goalkeeper. He won a British record 119 international caps for Northern Ireland 1964–86 (now surpassed by Peter →Shilton), and played League football for Watford, Tottenham Hotspur, and Arsenal.

Jeremiah /ˌdʒerɪˈmaɪə/ 7th–6th century BC. Old Testament Hebrew prophet, whose ministry continued 626–586 BC. He was imprisoned during →Nebuchadnezzar's siege of Jerusalem on suspicion of intending to desert to the enemy. On the city's fall, he retired to Egypt.

Jeroboam 10th century BC. First king of Israel *c.* 922–901 BC after it split away from the kingdom of Judah.

Jerome /dʒəˈrəʊm/ Jerome K(lapka) 1859–1927. English journalist and writer. His works include the humorous essays *Idle Thoughts of an Idle Fellow* 1889, the novel *Three Men in a Boat* 1889, and the play *The Passing of the Third Floor Back* 1907.

Jerome, St /dʒəˈrəʊm/ *c.* 340–420. One of the early Christian leaders and scholars known as the Fathers of the Church. His Latin versions of the Old and New Testaments form the basis of the Roman Catholic Vulgate. He is usually depicted with a lion. Feast day 30 Sept.

Born in Strido, Italy, he was baptized in Rome in 360, and subsequently travelled in Gaul, Anatolia, and Syria. Summoned to Rome as adviser to Pope Damasus, he revised the Latin translation of the New Testament and the Latin psalter. On the death of Damasus in 384 he travelled to the east and settled in Bethlehem, where he translated the Old Testament from Hebrew into Latin.

Jervis /ˈdʒɜːvɪs/ John, Earl of St Vincent 1735–1823. English admiral who secured the blockage of Toulon, France, 1795 in the Revolutionary Wars, and the defeat of the Spanish fleet off Cape St Vincent 1797, in which Admiral →Nelson played a key part. Jervis was a rigid disciplinarian.

Jessop /ˈdʒesəp/ William 1745–1814. British canal engineer who built the first canal in England entirely dependent on reservoirs for its water supply (the Grantham Canal 1793–97), and designed (with Thomas →Telford) the 300 m/ 1,000 ft long Pontcysyllte aqueduct over the river Dee.

Jesus /ˈdʒiːzəs/ *c.* 4 BC–AD 29 or 30. Hebrew preacher on whose teachings Christianity was founded. According to the accounts of his life in the four Gospels, he was born in Bethlehem, Palestine, son of God and the Virgin Mary, and brought up by Mary and her husband Joseph as a carpenter in Nazareth. After adult baptism, he gathered 12 disciples, but his preaching antagonized the Roman authorities and he was executed by crucifixion. Three days later there came reports of his resurrection and, later, his ascension to heaven.

Through his legal father Joseph, Jesus belonged to the tribe of Judah and the family of David, the second king of Israel, a heritage needed by the Messiah for whom the Hebrew people were waiting. In AD 26/27 his cousin John the Baptist proclaimed the coming of the promised Messiah and baptized Jesus, who then made two missionary journeys through the district of Galilee. His teaching, summarized in the Sermon on the Mount, aroused both religious opposition from the Pharisees and secular opposition from the party supporting the Roman governor, →Herod Antipas. When Jesus returned to Jerusalem (probably in AD 29), a week before the Passover festival, he was greeted by the people as the Messiah, and the Hebrew authorities (aided by the apostle Judas) had him arrested and condemned to death, after a hurried trial by the Sanhedrin (supreme Jewish court). The Roman procurator, Pontius Pilate, confirmed the sentence, stressing the threat posed to imperial authority by Jesus' teaching.

Jevons /ˈdʒevənz/ William Stanley 1835–1882. British economist who introduced the concept of *marginal utility*: the increase in total utility (satisfaction or pleasure of consumption) relative to a unit increase of the goods consumed.

Jiang /dʒiˈæŋ/ Zemin 1926– . Chinese political leader. The son-in-law of →Li Xiannian, he joined the Chinese Communist Party's politburo in 1967 after serving in the Moscow embassy and as mayor of Shanghai. He succeeded →Zhao Ziyang as party leader after the Tiananmen Square massacre of 1989. A cautious proponent of economic reform coupled with unswerving adherence to the party's 'political line', he subsequently replaced →Deng Xiaoping as head of the influential central military commission.

Jiang Jie Shi /dʒizæŋ ˌdʒeɪ 'ʃiː/ alternate transcription of ➜Chiang Kai-shek.

Jiang Qing /dʒi'æŋ 'tʃɪŋ/ or *Chiang Ching* 1914–1991. Chinese communist politician, third wife of the party leader Mao Zedong. In 1960 she became minister for culture, and played a key role in the 1966–69 Cultural Revolution as the leading member of the Shanghai-based Gang of Four, who attempted to seize power 1976. Jiang was imprisoned 1981.

Jiang was a Shanghai actress when in 1937 she met Mao Zedong at the communist headquarters in Yan'an; she became his wife 1939. She emerged as a radical, egalitarian Maoist. Her influence waned during the early 1970s and her relationship with Mao became embittered. On Mao's death Sept 1976, the Gang of Four, with Jiang as a leading figure, sought to seize power by organizing military coups in Shanghai and Beijing. They were arrested for treason by Mao's successor Hua Guofeng and tried 1980–81. The Gang were blamed for the excesses of the Cultural Revolution, but Jiang asserted during her trial that she had only followed Mao's orders as an obedient wife. This was rejected, and Jiang received a death sentence Jan 1981, which was subsequently commuted to life imprisonment.

I was Chairman Mao's dog. If he said bite someone, I bit him.

Jiang Qing during her trial

Jiménez /xɪ'meɪneθ/ Juan Ramón 1881–1958. Spanish lyric poet. Born in Andalusia, he left Spain during the civil war to live in exile in Puerto Rico. Nobel prize 1956.

Jinnah /dʒɪnə/ Muhammad Ali 1876–1948. Indian politician, Pakistan's first governor general from 1947. He was president of the Muslim League 1916, 1934–48, and by 1940 was advocating the need for a separate state of Pakistan; at the 1946 conferences in London he insisted on the partition of British India into Hindu and Muslim states.

Jiricna /jɪrɪtʃnə/ Eva 1939– . Czech architect who has worked in the UK since 1968. Her striking fashion shops, bars, and cafés for Joseph Ettedgui (1900–) are built in a highly refined Modernist style.

Joachim /jəʊəkɪm/ Joseph 1831–1907. Austro-Hungarian violinist and composer. He studied under Mendelssohn and founded the Joachim Quartet (1869–1907). Joachim played and conducted the music of his friend ➜Brahms. His own compositions include pieces for violin and orchestra, chamber, and orchestral works.

Joachim of Fiore /dʒəʊəkɪm ɒ'fjɔːri/ c. 1132–1202. Italian mystic, born in Calabria. In his mystical writings he interpreted history as a sequence of three ages, that of the Father, Son, and Holy Spirit, the last of which, the age of perfect spirituality, was to begin in 1260. His messianic views were taken up enthusiastically by many followers.

Joannitius /ˌdʒəʊə'nɪtiəs/ Hunayn ibn Ishaq al Ibadi 809–873. Arabic translator, a Nestorian Christian, who translated Greek learning – including Ptolemy, Euclid, Hippocrates, Plato, and Aristotle – into Arabic or Syrian for the Abbasid court in Baghdad.

Everything that I have done that was good I did by command of my voices.

St Joan of Arc during her trial 1431

Joan of Arc, St /dʒəʊn, ɑːk/ 1412–1431. French military leader. In 1429 at Chinon, NW France, she persuaded Charles VII that she had a divine mission to expel the occupying English from N France during the Hundred Years' War and secure his coronation. She raised the siege of Orléans, defeated the English at Patay, north of Orléans, and Charles was crowned in Reims. However, she failed to take Paris and was captured May 1430 by the Burgundians, who sold her to the English. She was found guilty of witchcraft and heresy by a tribunal of French ecclesiastics who supported the English. She was burned to death at the stake in Rouen 30 May 1431. In 1920 she was canonized.

Job /dʒəʊb/ c. 5th century BC. In the Old Testament, Hebrew leader who in the *Book of Job* questioned God's infliction of suffering on the righteous while enduring great sufferings himself.

Although Job comes to no final conclusion, his book is one of the first attempts to explain the problem of human suffering in a world believed to be created and governed by a God who is all-powerful and all-good.

Jodl /jəʊdl/ Alfred 1892–1946. German general. In World War II he drew up the Nazi government's plan for the attack on Yugoslavia, Greece, and the USSR. In Jan 1945 he became Chief of Staff and headed the delegation that signed Germany's surrender in Reims 7 May 1945. He was tried for war crimes in Nuremberg 1945–46 and hanged.

Joffre /ʒɒfrə/ Joseph Jacques Césaire 1852–1931. Marshal of France during World War I. He was chief of general staff 1911. The German invasion of Belgium 1914 took him by surprise, but his stand at the Battle of the Marne resulted in his appointment as supreme commander of all the French armies 1915. His failure to make adequate preparations at Verdun 1916 and the military disasters on the Somme led to his replacement by Nivelle in Dec 1916.

King John Youngest son of Henry II of England, John's reign was marked by repressive policies and high taxation, which led to constant conflict with the barons. He died at Newark after eating peaches and beer and was buried in Worcester Cathedral.

John /dʒɒn/ Augustus (Edwin) 1878–1961. British painter of landscapes and portraits, including *The Smiling Woman* 1910 (Tate Gallery, London) of his second wife, Dorelia.

He led a bohemian and nomadic life and was the brother of the artist Gwen John.

John /dʒɒn/ Elton. Stage name of Reginald Kenneth Dwight 1947– . English pop singer, pianist, and composer, noted for his melodies and elaborate costumes and glasses. His best-known LP, *Goodbye Yellow Brick Road* 1973, includes the hit 'Bennie and the Jets'. His output is prolific and his hits continued intermittently into the 1990s; for example, 'Nikita' 1985.

From his second album, *Elton John* 1970, to *Blue Moves* 1976 he enjoyed his greatest popularity, especially in the USA, and worked exclusively with the lyricist Bernie Taupin (1950–).

John /dʒɒn/ Gwen 1876–1939. British painter who lived in France for most of her life. Many of her paintings depict Dominican nuns (she converted to Catholicism 1913); she also painted calm, muted interiors.

John /dʒɒn/ *Lackland* 1167–1216. King of England from 1199 and acting king from 1189 during his brother Richard I's (the Lion-Heart) absence on the third Crusade. He lost Normandy and almost all the other English possessions in France to Philip II of France by 1205. His repressive policies and excessive taxation brought him into conflict with his barons, and he was forced to seal the Magna Carta 1215. Later repudiation of it led to

the first Barons' War 1215–17, during which he died.

John's subsequent bad reputation was only partially deserved. It resulted from his intrigues against his brother Richard I, his complicity in the death of his nephew Prince Arthur of Brittany, a rival for the English throne, and the effectiveness of his ruthless taxation policy, as well as his provoking Pope Innocent III to excommunicate England 1208–13. John's attempt to limit the papacy's right of interference in episcopal elections, which traditionally were the preserve of English kings, was resented by monastic sources, and these provided much of the evidence upon which his reign was later judged.

John /dʒɒn/ two kings of France, including:

John II 1319–1364. King of France from 1350. He was defeated and captured by the Black Prince at Poitiers 1356 and imprisoned in England. Released 1360, he failed to raise the money for his ransom and returned to England 1364, where he died.

John /dʒɒn/ name of 23 popes, including:

John XXII 1249–1334. Pope 1316–34. He spent his papacy in Avignon, France, engaged in a long conflict with the Holy Roman emperor, Louis of Bavaria, and the Spiritual Franciscans, a monastic order who preached the absolute poverty of the clergy.

John XXIII Angelo Giuseppe Roncalli 1881–1963. Pope from 1958. He improved relations with the USSR in line with his encyclical *Pacem in Terris/Peace on Earth* 1963, established Roman Catholic hierarchies in newly emergent states, and summoned the Second Vatican Council, which reformed church liturgy and backed the ecumenical movement.

'John XXIII' Baldassare Costa died 1419. Antipope 1410–15. In an attempt to end the Great Schism he was elected pope by a council of cardinals in Bologna, but was deposed by the Council of Constance 1415, together with the popes of Avignon and Rome. His papacy is not recognized by the church.

John /dʒɒn/ three kings of Poland, including:

John III Sobieski 1624–1696. King of Poland from 1674. He became commander in chief of the army 1668 after victories over the Cossacks and Tatars. A victory over the Turks 1673 helped to get him elected to the Polish throne, and he saved Vienna from the besieging Turks 1683.

John /dʒɒn/ six kings of Portugal, including:

John I 1357–1433. King of Portugal from 1385. An illegitimate son of Pedro I, he was elected by the Cortes (parliament). His claim was supported by an English army against the rival king of Castile, thus establishing the Anglo-Portuguese Alliance 1386. He married Philippa of Lancaster, daughter of →John of Gaunt.

John IV 1603–1656. King of Portugal from 1640. Originally duke of Braganza, he was elected king when the Portuguese rebelled against Spanish rule. His reign was marked by a long war against Spain, which did not end until 1668.

John VI 1769–1826. King of Portugal and regent for his insane mother *Maria I* from 1799 until her death 1816. He fled to Brazil when the French invaded Portugal 1807 and did not return until 1822. On his return Brazil declared its independence, with John's elder son Pedro as emperor.

John Chrysostom, St /krɪsəstəm/ 345–407. Christian scholar, hermit, preacher, and Eastern Orthodox bishop of Constantinople 398–404. He was born in Antioch (now Antakya, Turkey). Feast day 13 Sept.

John of Austria /dʒɒn/ Don 1545–1578. Spanish soldier, the illegitimate son of the Holy Roman emperor Charles V. He defeated the Turks at the Battle of Lepanto 1571.

John captured Tunis 1573 but quickly lost it. He was appointed governor general of the Netherlands 1576 but discovered that real power lay in the hands of William of Orange. John withdrew 1577 and then attacked and defeated the patriot army at Gemblours 31 Jan 1578 with the support of reinforcements from Philip II of Spain. Lack of money stopped him from going any farther. He died of fever.

John of Damascus, St /dʒɒn/ *c.* 676–*c.* 754. Eastern Orthodox theologian and hymn writer, a defender of image worship against the iconoclasts (image-breakers). Contained in his *The Fountain of Knowledge* is *An Accurate Exposition of the Orthodox Faith*, an important chronicle of theology from the 4th–7th centuries. He was born in Damascus, Syria. Feast day 4 Dec.

John of Gaunt /dʒɒn/ 1340–1399. English politician, born in Ghent, fourth son of Edward III, Duke of Lancaster from 1362. He distinguished himself during the Hundred Years' War. During Edward's last years, and the years before Richard II attained the age of majority, he acted as head of government, and Parliament protested against his corrupt rule.

John of Salisbury /dʒɒn/ *c.* 1115–1180. English philosopher and historian. His *Policraticus* portrayed the church as the guarantee of liberty against the unjust claims of secular authority.

He studied in France 1130–1153, in Paris with →Abelard and at Chartres. He became secretary to Thomas à Becket and supported him against Henry II, and fled to France after Becket's murder, becoming bishop of Chartres 1176.

John of the Cross, St /dʒɒn/ 1542–1591. Spanish Roman Catholic Carmelite friar from 1564, who was imprisoned several times for attempting to impose the reforms laid down by St Teresa. His verse describes spiritual ecstasy. Feast day 24 Nov.

He was persecuted and sent to the monastery of Ubeda until his death. He was beatified 1674 and canonized 1726.

John Paul /dʒɒn pɔːl/ two popes:

John Paul I Albino Luciani 1912–1978. Pope 26 Aug–28 Sept 1978. His name was chosen as the combination of his two immediate predecessors.

John Paul II Karol Wojtyla 1920– . Pope from 1978, the first non-Italian to be elected since 1522. He was born near Kraków, Poland. He has upheld the tradition of papal infallibility, condemned artificial contraception, women priests, married priests, and modern dress for monks and nuns – views that have aroused criticism from liberalizing elements in the church.

In 1939, at the beginning of World War II, Wojtyla was conscripted for forced labour by the Germans, working in quarries and a chemical factory, but from 1942 studied for the priesthood illegally in Kraków. After the war he taught ethics and theology at the universities of Lublin and Kraków, becoming archbishop of Kraków 1964. In 1967 he was made a cardinal. He was shot and wounded by a Turk in an attempt on his life 1981. Although he has warned against the involvement of priests in political activity, he opposed the Gulf War 1991 and has condemned arms manufacturers as sinful.

Christ will never approve that man be considered ... merely as a means of production.

Pope John Paul II speech June 1979

Johns /dʒɒnz/ 'Captain' W(illiam) E(arl) 1893–1968. British author, from 1932, of popular novels of World War I flying ace 'Biggles', now sometimes criticized for chauvinism, racism, and sexism. Johns was a flying officer in the RAF (there is no rank of captain) until his retirement 1930.

Johns /dʒɒnz/ Jasper 1930– . US painter and printmaker who rejected the abstract in favour of such simple subjects as flags, maps, and numbers. He uses pigments mixed with wax (encaustic) to create a rich surface with unexpected delicacies of colour. He has also created collages and lithographs.

John, St /dʒɒn/ 1st century AD. New Testament apostle. Traditionally, he wrote the fourth Gospel and the Johannine Epistles (when he was bishop of Ephesus), and the Book of Revelation (while exiled to the Greek island of Patmos). His emblem is an eagle; his feast day 27 Dec.

St John is identified with the unnamed 'disciple whom Jesus loved'. Son of Zebedee, born in Judaea, he and his brother James were Galilean fishermen. Jesus entrusted his mother to John at the Crucifixion, where John is often shown dressed in red, with curly hair. Another of his symbols is a chalice with a little snake in it.

Johnson /dʒɒnsən/ Alvin Saunders 1874–1971. US social scientist and educator. He was a founder and an editor of the *New Republic* 1917. Joining with some of America's greatest scholars, Johnson was one of the founders of the New School for Social Research in New York City, serving as its director 1923–45. Johnson's memoir, *Progress: An Autobiography*, was published 1952.

Born near Homer, Nebraska, USA, Johnson was educated at the University of Nebraska, saw service in the Spanish-American War 1898, and received a PhD in economics from Columbia 1902, subsequently teaching at several universities.

Johnson /dʒɒnsən/ Amy 1903–1941. British aviator. She made a solo flight from England to Australia 1930, in 9½ days, and in 1932 made the fastest ever solo flight from England to Cape Town, South Africa. Her plane disappeared over the English Channel in World War II while she was serving with the Air Transport Auxiliary.

Johnson /dʒɒnsən/ Andrew 1808–1875. 17th president of the USA 1865–69, a Democrat. He was a congressman from Tennessee 1843–53, governor of Tennessee 1853–57, senator 1857–62, and vice president 1865. He succeeded to the presidency on Lincoln's assassination (15 April 1865). His conciliatory policy to the defeated South after the Civil War involved him in a feud with the Radical Republicans, culminating in his impeachment 1868 before the Senate, which failed to convict him by one vote.

Jackson was born in Raleigh, North Carolina.

Johnson Andrew Johnson, 17th US president, was faced with strong congressional opposition throughout his term in office. He sought to execute Lincoln's plan to readmit seceded states to the Union, but was blocked by a Radical Republican majority that insisted on keeping the states under military government for a period.

Among his achievements was the purchase of Alaska from Russia 1867. When he tried to dismiss Edwin Stanton, a cabinet secretary, his political opponents seized on the opportunity to charge him with 'high crimes and misdemeanours' and attempted to remove him from office; it was this battle that ended in his impeachment. Jackson's tenure as president was characterized by his frustration and political stalemate. He presided over the re-entry of the Southern states into the Union. He was returned to the Senate from Tennessee 1875, but died shortly afterwards.

Johnson /dʒɒnsən/ Ben 1961– . Canadian sprinter. In 1987, he broke the world record for the 100 metres, running it in 9.83 seconds. At the Olympic Games 1988, he again broke the record, but was disqualified and suspended for four years for using anabolic steroids to enhance his performance.

Johnson /dʒɒnsən/ Celia 1908–1982. British actress, perceived as quintessentially English, who starred with Trevor Howard in the romantic film *Brief Encounter* 1946.

Johnson Earvin ('Magic') 1959– . US basketball player. He played for the Los Angeles Lakers 1979–91 and 1992– , a team that won the National Basketball Association (NBA) championship 1980, 1982, 1985, 1987, and 1988. He played in the victorious 1992 US Olympic basketball team in Barcelona, Spain.

In 1991, he announced that he had contracted the HIV virus and would retire from basketball to devote his time to AIDS awareness and prevention programmes. However, later in 1992, Johnson announced that he would rejoin the Lakers.

Johnson /dʒɒnsən/ Eastman 1824–1906. US painter born in Germany, trained in Düsseldorf, The Hague, and Paris. Painting in the open air, he developed a fresh and luminous landscape style.

Johnson /dʒɒnsən/ Hiram Warren 1866–1945. US politician. He was the 'Bull Moose' party candidate for vice president in Theodore Roosevelt's unsuccessful bid to regain the presidency 1912. Elected to the US Senate 1917, Johnson served there until his death. He was an unyielding isolationist, opposing US involvement in World War I as well as membership in the League of Nations and World Court.

Born in Sacramento, California, USA, Johnson attended the University of California and was admitted to the bar 1888. In 1902 he established a law practice in San Francisco before entering politics and serving as governor of California 1911–17.

Johnson /dʒɒnsən/ Jack 1878–1968. US heavyweight boxer. He overcame severe racial prejudice to become the first black heavyweight champion of the world 1908 when he travelled to Australia to challenge Tommy Burns. The US authorities wanted Johnson 'dethroned' because of his colour but could not find suitable challengers until 1915, when he lost the title in a dubious fight decision to the giant Jess Willard.

Johnson /dʒɒnsən/ James Weldon 1871–1938. US writer, lawyer, diplomat, and social critic. He was a strong supporter of Theodore Roosevelt and served him and Taft as US consul in Venezuela and Nicaragua 1906–12. He was editor of *New York Age* 1912–22 and was active in the National Association for the Advancement of Colored People (NAACP). As poet and anthropologist, he became one of the chief figures of the Harlem Renaissance of the 1920s. His autobiography *Along This Way* was published 1933.

Born in Jacksonville, Florida, USA, and educated at Atlanta University, Johnson became the first black American admitted to the Florida bar 1897.

Johnson /dʒɒnsən/ Lyndon Baines 1908–1973. 36th president of the USA 1963–69, a Democrat. He was elected to Congress 1937–49 and the Senate 1949–60. Born in Texas, he brought critical Southern support as J F Kennedy's vice-presidential running mate 1960, and became president on Kennedy's assassination. After the Tonkin Gulf Incident, which escalated US involvement in the Vietnam War, support won by Johnson's Great Society legislation (civil rights, education, alleviation of poverty) dissipated, and he declined to run for re-election 1968.

Johnson /dʒɒnsən/ Pamela Hansford 1912–1981. British novelist, who in 1950 married C P →Snow; her novels include *Too Dear for my Possessing* 1940 and *The Honours Board* 1970.

Johnson /dʒɒnsən/ Philip (Cortelyou) 1906– . US architect who coined the term 'international

Johnson Lyndon B Johnson became the 36th president of the USA after Kennedy's assassination 1963. More than his predecessor, he was responsible for advances in black civil rights, but his term of office was troubled by the escalation of the Vietnam War.

style'. Originally designing in the style of →Mies van der Rohe, he later became an exponent of Post-Modernism. He designed the giant AT&T building in New York 1978, a pink skyscraper with a Chippendale-style cabinet top.

He was director of architecture and design at the Museum of Modern Art, New York 1932–54, where he built the annexe and sculpture court.

A man, Sir, should keep his friendship in constant repair.

Samuel Johnson

Johnson /dʒɒnsən/ Samuel, known as 'Dr Johnson', 1709–1784. English lexicographer, author, and critic, also a brilliant conversationalist and the dominant figure in 18th-century London literary society. His *Dictionary*, published 1755, remained authoritative for over a century, and is still remarkable for the vigour of its definitions. In 1764 he founded the Literary Club, whose members included the painter Joshua Reynolds, the political philosopher Edmund Burke, the playwright Oliver Goldsmith, the actor David Garrick, and James →Boswell, Johnson's biographer.

Born in Lichfield, Staffordshire, Johnson became first an usher and then a literary hack. In 1735 he married Elizabeth Porter and opened a private school. When this proved unsuccessful he went to London with his pupil David Garrick, becoming a regular contributor to the *Gentleman's Magazine* and publishing the poem *London* 1738. Other works include the satire imitating Juvenal, *Vanity of Human Wishes* 1749, the philosophical romance *Rasselas* 1759, an edition of Shakespeare 1765, and the classic *Lives of the Most Eminent English Poets* 1779–81. His first meeting with Boswell was 1763. A visit with Boswell to Scotland and the Hebrides 1773 was recorded in *Journey to the Western Isles of Scotland* 1775. He was buried in Westminster Abbey and his house, in Gough Square, London, is preserved as a museum; his wit and humanity are documented in Boswell's classic biography *Life of Samuel Johnson* 1791.

Johnson /dʒɒnsən/ Uwe 1934– . German novelist who left East Germany for West Berlin 1959, and wrote of the division of Germany in, for example, *Anniversaries* 1977.

Johnston /dʒɒnstən/ Joseph Eggleston 1807–1891. US military leader during the American Civil War 1861–65. Joining the Confederacy, he commanded the Army of Tennessee 1863. After the war, Johnston returned to private life, later serving in the US House of Representatives 1879–81 and as federal railroad commissioner 1887–91.

Born near Farmville, Virginia, Johnston graduated from West Point military academy 1829. As a military engineer, he served with distinction during the Mexican War 1846–48.

John the Baptist, St /dʒɒn/ *c.* 12 BC–*c.* AD 27. In the New Testament, an itinerant preacher. After preparation in the wilderness, he proclaimed the coming of the Messiah and baptized Jesus in the river Jordan. He was later executed by →Herod Antipas at the request of Salome, who demanded that his head be brought to her on a platter.

John was the son of Zacharias and Elizabeth (a cousin of Jesus' mother), and born in Nazareth, Galilee. He and Jesus are often shown together as children.

As an adult, he is depicted with a shaggy beard and robes.

Joinville /ʒwæn'viːl/ Jean, Sire de Joinville 1224–1317. French historian, born in Champagne. He accompanied Louis IX on the crusade of 1248–54, which he described in his *History of St Louis*.

Joliet /ʒɒl'jeɪ/ (or *Jolliet*) Louis 1645–1700. French-born Canadian explorer. He and Jesuit missionary Jacques →Marquette were the first to successfully chart the course of the Mississippi River down to its junction with the Arkansas River. They returned to Canada by way of the Illinois territory.

Born in Québec, Canada, Joliet was sent by the Canadian government on an extensive exploration of the Great Lakes 1669. After his expedition along the Mississippi, he later explored Labrador and the Hudson Bay.

The city of Joliet, Illinois, is named in his honor.

Joliot-Curie /ʒɒliəʊ 'kjʊəri/ Irène (born Curie) 1897–1956 and Frédéric (born Joliot) 1900–1958. French physicists who made the discovery of artificial radioactivity, for which they were jointly awarded the 1935 Nobel Prize for Chemistry.

Irène was the daughter of Marie and Pierre →Curie and began work at her mother's Radium Institute in 1921. In 1926 she married Frédéric, a pupil of her mother's, and they began a long and fruitful collaboration. In 1934 they found that certain elements exposed to radiation themselves become radioactive.

Jolson /'dʒəʊlsən/ Al. Stage name of Asa Yoelson 1886–1950. Russian-born US singer and entertainer. Popular in Broadway theatre and vaudeville, he was chosen to star in the first talking picture, *The Jazz Singer* 1927.

Jonah /'dʒəʊnə/ 7th century BC. Hebrew prophet whose name is given to a book in the Old Testament. According to this, he fled by ship to evade his mission to prophesy the destruction of Nineveh. The crew threw him overboard in a storm, as a bringer of ill fortune, and he spent three days and nights in the belly of a whale before coming to land.

Jonathan /'dʒɒnəθən/ Chief (Joseph) Leabua 1914–1987. Lesotho politician. A leader in the drive for independence, Jonathan became prime minister of Lesotho in 1965. His rule was ended by a coup in 1986.

As prime minister, Jonathan played a pragmatic role, allying himself in turn with the South African government and the Organization of African Unity.

Jones /dʒəʊnz/ Bobby (Robert Tyre) 1902–1971. US golfer. He was the game's greatest amateur player, who never turned professional but won 13 major amateur and professional tournaments, including the Grand Slam of the amateur and professional opens of both the USA and Britain 1930.

Born in Atlanta, Georgia, Jones finished playing competitive golf 1930 and concentrated on his law practice. He maintained his contacts with the sport and was largely responsible for inaugurating the US Masters.

Jones /dʒəʊnz/ Charles Martin (Chuck) 1912– . US film animator and cartoon director who worked at Warner Bros with characters such as Bugs Bunny, Daffy Duck, Wile E Coyote, and Elmer Fudd.

Jones /dʒəʊnz/ Gwyneth 1936– . Welsh soprano who has performed as Sieglinde in *Die Walküre* and Desdemona in *Otello*.

Jones /dʒəʊnz/ Henry Arthur 1851–1929. British playwright. Among some 60 of his melodramas, *Mrs Dane's Defence* 1900 is most notable as an early realist problem play.

Jones /dʒəʊnz/ Inigo 1573–*c.* 1652. English classical architect. Born in London, he studied in Italy and was influenced by the works of Palladio. He was employed by James I to design scenery for Ben Jonson's masques. He designed the Queen's House, Greenwich 1616–35 and his English Renaissance masterpiece, the Banquet House in Whitehall, London, 1619–22.

Jones /dʒəʊnz/ John Luther 'Casey' 1864–1900. US railroad engineer and folk hero. His death on the 'Cannonball Express ,' while on an overnight run 1900, is the subject of popular legend. Colliding with a stalled freight train, he ordered his fireman to jump to safety and rode the 'Cannonball' to his death. The folk song 'Casey Jones' is an account of the event.

Born in Cayce, Kentucky, USA, Jones gained his nickname from the name of his home town. He joined the railroad 1880,

Jones /dʒəʊnz/ John Paul 1747–1792. Scottish-born American naval officer in the War of Independence 1775. Heading a small French-sponsored squadron in the *Bonhomme Richard*, he captured the British warship *Serapis* in a bloody battle off Scarborough 1799.

Jones was born in Kirkcudbright, Scotland. He was originally a trader and slaver but became a privateer 1775, and then a commodore. After the War of Independence, he joined the Russian navy as a rear admiral 1788, fighting against Turkey, but lost the Empress Catherine's favour and died in France.

Jongkind /jɒŋkɪnt/ Johan Bartold 1819–1891. Dutch painter active mainly in France. His studies of the Normandy coast show a keen observation of the natural effects of light. He influenced the Impressionist painter →Monet.

Jonson /dʒɒnsən/ Ben(jamin) 1572–1637. English dramatist, poet, and critic. *Every Man in his Humour* 1598 established the English 'comedy of humours', in which each character embodies a 'humour', or vice, such as greed, lust, or avarice. This was followed by *Cynthia's Revels* 1600 and *Poetaster* 1601. His first extant tragedy is *Sejanus* 1603, with Burbage and Shakespeare as members of the original cast. The plays of his middle years include *Volpone, or The Fox* 1606, *The Alchemist* 1610, and *Bartholomew Fair* 1614.

Jonson was born in Westminster, London, and entered the theatre as actor and dramatist in 1597. In 1598 he narrowly escaped the gallows for killing a fellow player in a duel. He collaborated with Marston and Chapman in *Eastward Ho!* 1605, and shared their imprisonment when official exception was taken to the satirization of James I's Scottish policy.

Joplin /dʒɒplɪn/ Janis 1943–1970. US blues and rock singer, born in Texas. She was lead singer with the San Francisco group Big Brother and the Holding Company 1966–68. Her biggest hit, Kris Kristofferson's 'Me and Bobby McGee', was released on the posthumous *Pearl* LP 1971.

Joplin /dʒɒplɪn/ Scott 1868–1917. US ragtime pianist and composer, active in Chicago. His

Jones A drawing after Robert van Voerst of English architect Inigo Jones, National Portrait Gallery, London. Based on his studies in Italy, Inigo Jones's work revolutionized English architecture. His Banquet House in Whitehall, the first important building of the English Renaissance, caused great problems for its builders because of its unfamiliar design.

'Maple Leaf Rag' 1899 was the first instrumental sheet music to sell a million copies, and 'The Entertainer', as the theme tune of the film *The Sting* 1973, revived his popularity. He was an influence on Jelly Roll Morton and other early jazz musicians.

Jordaens /jɔːˈdɑːns/ Jacob 1593–1678. Flemish painter, born in Antwerp. His style follows Rubens, whom he assisted in various commissions. Much of his work is exuberant and on a large scale, including scenes of peasant life, altarpieces, portraits, and mythological subjects.

Jordan /dʒɔːdn/ Dorothea 1762–1816. British actress. She made her debut in 1777, and retired in 1815. She was a mistress of the Duke of Clarence (later William IV); they had ten children with the name FitzClarence.

Jordan /dʒɔːdn/ Michael 1963– . US basketball player. Playing for the Chicago Bulls from 1984, he led his team to consecutive National Basketball Association (NBA) championships 1991 and 1992. Jordan was the NBA's top points scorer (2,313) in his first year as a professional, and during the 1986–87 season, he scored over 3,000 points, only the second player in NBA history to do so.

In 1992 he became the world's highest paid sportsman, earning three times more in advertising endorsements than for playing basketball. He was a member of the victorious 1984 and 1992 US Olympic basketball teams.

Jörgensen /jɜːnsən/ Jörgen 1779–1845. Danish sailor who in 1809 seized control of Iceland, announcing it was under the protection of Britain. His brief reign of corruption ended later the same year when he was captured by a British naval ship. After long imprisonment, in about 1823 he was transported to Van Diemen's Land (Tasmania), where he was pardoned. He wrote a dictionary of Australian Aboriginal dialect.

Joseph /dʒəʊzəf/ Chief *c.* 1840–1904. American Indian chief of the Nez Percé people. After initially agreeing to leave tribal lands 1877, he later led his people in armed resistance. Defeated, Joseph ordered a mass retreat to Canada, but the Nez Percé were soon caught by General Nelson Miles. They were sent to the Colville Reservation, Washington 1885.

Born in the Wallowa Valley of Oregon, Joseph was the son of a Nez Percé leader who resisted territorial encroachment by the US government. At his father's death in 1873, Joseph assumed the title of chief and was originally an advocate of passive resistance.

Joseph /dʒəʊzɪf/ Keith (Sinjohn), Baron 1918– . British Conservative politician. A barrister, he entered Parliament 1956. He held ministerial posts 1962–64, 1970–74, 1979–81, and was secretary of state for education and science 1981–86. He was made a life peer 1987.

Joseph /dʒəʊzɪf/ Père. Religious name of Francis Le Clerc du Tremblay 1577–1638. French Catholic Capuchin monk. He was the influential secretary and agent to Louis XIII's chief minister Cardinal Richelieu, and nicknamed *L'Eminence Grise* ('the Grey Eminence') in reference to his grey habit.

Joseph /dʒəʊzɪf/ two Holy Roman emperors:

Joseph I 1678–1711. Holy Roman emperor from 1705 and king of Austria, of the house of Habsburg. He spent most of his reign involved in fighting the War of the Spanish Succession.

Joseph II 1741–1790. Holy Roman emperor from 1765, son of Francis I (1708–1765). The reforms he carried out after the death of his mother, →Maria Theresa, in 1780, provoked revolts from those who lost privileges.

Josephine /dʒəʊzɪfiːn/ Marie Josèphe Rose Tascher de la Pagerie 1763–1814. As wife of →Napoleon I Bonaparte, she was empress of France 1796–1809. Born on Martinique, she married in 1779 Alexandre de →Beauharnais, who played a part in the French Revolution, and in 1796 Napoleon, who divorced her in 1809 because she had not produced children.

Joseph of Arimathaea, St /ˌærɪməˈθiːə/ 1st century AD. In the New Testament, a wealthy Hebrew, member of the Sanhedrin (supreme court), and secret supporter of Jesus. On the evening of the Crucifixion he asked the Roman procurator Pilate for Jesus' body and buried it in his own tomb. Feast day 17 March.

According to tradition he brought the Holy Grail to England about AD 63 and built the first Christian church in Britain, at Glastonbury.

Josephs /dʒəʊzɪfs/ Wilfred 1927– . British composer. As well as film and television music, he has written nine symphonies, concertos, and chamber music. His works include the *Jewish Requiem* 1969 and the opera *Rebecca* 1983.

Josephson /dʒəʊzɪfsən/ Brian 1940– . British physicist, a leading authority on superconductivity. In 1973 he shared a Nobel prize for his theoretical predictions of the properties of a supercurrent through a tunnel barrier (the Josephson effect), which led to the development of the Josephson junction.

Josephus /dʒəʊˈsiːfəs/ Flavius AD 37–c. 100. Jewish historian and general, born in Jerusalem. He became a Pharisee and commanded the Jewish forces in Galilee in their revolt against Rome from AD 66 (which ended with the mass suicide at Masada). When captured, he gained the favour of the Roman emperor Vespasian and settled in Rome as a citizen. He wrote *Antiquities of the Jews*, an early history to AD 66; *The Jewish War*; and an autobiography.

Joshua /dʒɒʃuə/ 13th century BC. In the Old Testament, successor of Moses, who led the Jews in their return to and conquest of the land of Canaan. The city of Jericho was the first to fall – according to the Book of Joshua, the walls crumbled to the blast of his trumpets.

Josiah /dʒəʊˈsaɪə/ c. 647–609 BC. King of Judah. Grandson of Manasseh and son of Amon, he succeeded to the throne at the age of eight. The discovery of a Book of Instruction (probably Deuteronomy, a book of the Old Testament) during repairs of the Temple in 621 BC stimulated thorough reform, which included the removal of all sanctuaries except that of Jerusalem. He was killed in a clash at Megiddo with Pharaoh-nechoh, king of Egypt.

Josquin Desprez /ʒɒˈskæŋ deɪˈpreɪ/ or *des Prés* 1440–1521. Franco-Flemish composer. His music combines a technical mastery with the feeling for words that became a hallmark of Renaissance vocal music. His works, which include 18 masses, over 100 motets, and secular vocal works, are characterized by their vitality and depth of feeling.

Joubert /ʒuːˈbeə/ Petrus Jacobus 1831–1900. Boer general in South Africa. He opposed British annexation of the Transvaal 1877, proclaimed its independence 1880, led the Boer forces in the First South African War against the British 1880–81, defeated →Jameson 1896, and fought in the Second South African War.

Joule /dʒuːl/ James Prescott 1818–1889. English physicist whose work on the relations between electrical, mechanical, and chemical effects led to the discovery of the first law of thermodynamics.

Joule was born in Salford, Lancashire, into a wealthy brewery-owning family. He was educated mainly by private tutors, including the scientist John →Dalton, and dedicated his life to precise scientific research. Until neighbours protested, he kept a steam engine in his house in Manchester. He determined the mechanical equivalent of heat (Joule's equivalent), and the SI unit of energy, the joule, is named after him.

Jovian /dʒəʊviən/ 331–364. Roman emperor from 363. Captain of the imperial bodyguard, he was chosen as emperor by the troops after →Julian's death in battle with the Persians. He concluded an unpopular peace and restored Christianity as the state religion.

Jowett /dʒəʊɪt/ Benjamin 1817–1893. English scholar. He promoted university reform, including the abolition of the theological test for degrees, and translated Plato, Aristotle, and Thucydides.

Jowett was ordained in 1842. He became Regius professor of Greek at Oxford University 1855, and Master of Balliol College 1870.

Joyce /dʒɔɪs/ Eileen 1912–1991. Australian concert pianist whose playing combined subtlety with temperamental fire. Her immense repertoire included over 70 works for piano and orchestra. She made her UK debut in 1930 and retired in the early 1960s.

Joyce /dʒɔɪs/ James (Augustine Aloysius) 1882–1941. Irish writer, born in Dublin, who revolutionized the form of the English novel with his 'stream of consciousness' technique. His works include *Dubliners* 1914 (short stories), *Portrait of the Artist as a Young Man* 1916, *Ulysses* 1922, and *Finnegans Wake* 1939.

Ulysses, which records the events of a single Dublin day, experiments with language and combines direct narrative with the unspoken and unconscious reactions of the characters. Banned at first for obscenity in the USA and the UK, it enjoyed great impact. It was first published in Paris, where Joyce settled after World War I. *Finnegans Wake* continued Joyce's experiments with language, attempting a synthesis of all existence.

Joyce /dʒɔɪs/ William 1906–1946. Born in New York, son of a naturalized Irish-born American, he carried on fascist activity in the UK as a 'British subject'. During World War II he made propaganda broadcasts from Germany to the UK, his upper-class accent earning him the nickname *Lord Haw Haw*. He was hanged for treason.

Juan Carlos /hwæn ˈkɑːlɒs/ 1938– . King of Spain. The son of Don Juan, pretender to the Spanish throne, he married Princess Sofia in 1962, eldest daughter of King Paul of Greece. In 1969 he was nominated by ➔Franco to succeed on the restoration of the monarchy intended to follow Franco's death; his father was excluded because of his known liberal views. Juan Carlos became king in 1975.

Juárez /xwɑːreθ/ Benito 1806–1872. Mexican politician, president 1861–65 and 1867–72. In 1861 he suspended repayments of Mexico's foreign debts, which prompted a joint French, British, and Spanish expedition to exert pressure. French forces invaded and created an empire for ➔Maximilian, brother of the Austrian emperor. After their withdrawal in 1867, Maximilian was executed, and Juárez returned to the presidency.

Judah Ha-Nasi /ˌhɑːnɑːˈsiː/ 'the Prince' *c.* AD 135–*c.* 220. Jewish scholar who with a number of colleagues edited the collection of writings known as the *Mishna*, which formed the basis of the *Talmud*, the compilation of ancient Jewish law and tradition, in the 2nd century AD.

Judas Iscariot /dʒuːdəsɪˈskæriət/ 1st century AD. In the New Testament, the disciple who betrayed Jesus Christ. Judas was the treasurer of the group. At the last Passover supper, he arranged, for 30 pieces of silver, to point out Jesus to the chief priests so that they could arrest him. Afterwards Judas was overcome with remorse and committed suicide.

Jude, St /dʒuːd/ 1st century AD. Supposed half-brother of Jesus and writer of the Epistle of Jude in the New Testament; patron saint of lost causes. Feast day 28 Oct.

Judith of Bavaria /dʒuːdɪθ, bəˈveəriə/ 800–843. Empress of the French. The wife of Louis the Pious (➔Louis I of France) from 819, she exercised power over her husband to the benefit of their son Charles the Bold.

Judson /dʒʌdsən/ Edward Zane Carroll, better known by his pen name 'Ned Buntline' 1823–1886. US author. Specializing in short adventure stories, he developed a stereotyped frontier hero in the pages of his own periodicals *Ned Buntline's Magazine* and *Buntline's Own*. In his dime novels in the 1870s, he immortalized Buffalo Bill Cody.

Born in Stamford, New York, Judson served in the US Navy, and became an editor and writer in Cincinnati, eventually moving to New York. A violent racist, Judson was one of the founders of the antiforeign 'Know-Nothing' party in the 1850s.

Jugurtha /dʒuːˈgɜːθə/ died 104 BC. King of Numidia, N Africa, who, after a long resistance, was betrayed to the Romans in 107 BC, and put to death.

Julian /dʒuːliən/ *the Apostate c.* 331–363. Roman emperor. Born in Constantinople, the nephew of Constantine the Great, he was brought up as a Christian but early in life became a convert to paganism. Sent by Constantius to govern Gaul in 355, he was proclaimed emperor by his troops in 360, and in 361 was marching on Constantinople when Constantius' death allowed a peaceful succession. He revived pagan worship and refused to persecute heretics. He was killed in battle against the Persians.

Juliana /ˌdʒuːliˈɑːnə/ 1909– . Queen of the Netherlands 1948–80. The daughter of Queen Wilhelmina (1880–1962), she married Prince Bernhard of Lippe-Biesterfeld in 1937. She abdicated 1980 and was succeeded by her daughter ➔Beatrix.

Julian of Norwich /dʒuːliən, ˈnɒrɪtʃ/ *c.* 1342–1413. English mystic. She lived as a recluse, and recorded her visions in *The Revelation of Divine Love* 1403, which shows the influence of neo-Platonism.

Julius II /dʒuːliəs/ 1443–1513. Pope 1503–13. A politician who wanted to make the Papal States the leading power in Italy, he formed international alliances first against Venice and then against France. He began the building of St Peter's Church in Rome 1506 and was the patron of the artists Michelangelo and Raphael.

Jung /jʊŋ/ Carl Gustav 1875–1961. Swiss psychiatrist who collaborated with Sigmund ➔Freud until their disagreement in 1912 over the importance of sexuality in causing psychological problems. Jung studied religion and dream symbolism, saw the unconscious as a source of spiritual insight, and distinguished between introversion and extroversion. His books include *Modern Man in Search of a Soul* 1933.

Junkers /ˈjʊŋkəs/ Hugo 1859–1935. German aeroplane designer. In 1919 he founded in Dessau the aircraft works named after him. Junkers planes, including dive bombers, night fighters, and troop carriers, were used by the Germans in World War II.

Jurgens /ˈjʊəgəns/ Curt (Curd Jürgens) 1912–1982. German film and stage actor who was well established in his native country before moving into French and then Hollywood films in the 1960s. His films include *Operette/Operetta* 1940, *Et Dieu créa la Femme/And God Created Woman* 1956, *Lord Jim* 1965, and *The Spy Who Loved Me* 1977.

Justinian I /dʒʌˈstɪnɪən/ 483–565. Byzantine emperor from 527. He recovered N Africa from the Vandals, SE Spain from the Visigoths, and Italy from the Ostrogoths, largely owing to his great general Belisarius. He ordered the codification of Roman law, which has influenced European jurisprudence.

Justinian, born in Illyria, was associated with his uncle, Justin I, in the government from 518. He married the actress Theodora, and succeeded Justin in 527. Much of his reign was taken up by an indecisive struggle with the Persians. He built the church of Sta Sophia in Constantinople, and closed the university in Athens in 529.

Justin, St /dʒʌstɪn/ *c.* 100–*c.* 163. One of the early Christian leaders and writers known as the Fathers of the Church. Born in Palestine of a Greek family, he was converted to Christianity and wrote two *Apologies* in its defence. He spent the rest of his life as an itinerant missionary, and was martyred in Rome. Feast day 1 June.

Juvenal /ˈdʒuːvənl/ *c.* AD 60–140. Roman satirist and poet. His genius for satire brought him to the unfavourable notice of the emperor Domitian. Juvenal's 16 extant satires give an explicit and sometimes brutal picture of the decadent Roman society of his time.

This is the first of punishments, that no guilty man is acquitted if judged by himself.

Juvenal Satires

Kádár /ˈkɑːdɑː/ János 1912–1989. Hungarian Communist leader, in power 1956–88, after suppressing the national uprising. As Hungarian Socialist Workers' Party (HSWP) leader and prime minister 1956–58 and 1961–65, Kádár introduced a series of market-socialist economic reforms, while retaining cordial political relations with the USSR.

Kádár was a mechanic before joining the outlawed Communist Party and working as an underground resistance organizer in World War II. After the war he was elected to the National Assembly, served as minister for internal affairs 1948–50, and became a prominent member of the Hungarian Workers' Party (HSP). Imprisoned 1951–53 for deviation from Stalinism, Kádár was rehabilitated 1955, becoming party leader in Budapest, and in Nov 1956, at the height of the Hungarian national rising, he was appointed head of the new HSWP. With the help of Soviet troops, he suppressed the revolt. He was ousted as party general secretary May 1988, and forced into retirement May 1989.

Kafka /ˈkæfkə/ Franz 1883–1924. Czech novelist, born in Prague, who wrote in German. His three unfinished allegorical novels *Der Prozess/The Trial* 1925, *Der Schloss/The Castle* 1926, and *Amerika/America* 1927 were posthumously published despite his instructions that they should be destroyed. His short stories include 'Die Verwandlung/The Metamorphosis' 1915, in which a man turns into a huge insect. His vision of lonely individuals trapped in bureaucratic or legal labyrinths can be seen as a powerful metaphor for modern experience.

Kahlo /ˈkɑːləʊ/ Frida 1907–1954. Mexican painter who mingled folk art with Classical and Modern styles. She married the painter Diego →Rivera.

Kahn /kɑːn/ Louis 1901–1974. US architect, born in Estonia. A follower of Mies van de Rohe, he developed a classically romantic style, in which functional 'servant' areas, such as stairwells and air ducts, featured prominently, often as towerlike structures surrounding the main living and working, or 'served', areas. His projects are characterized by an imaginative use of concrete and brick and include the Salk Institute for Biological Studies, La Jolla, California, and the British Art Center at Yale University.

Kahn taught at the Yale School of Architecture from 1947 and also designed the Yale Art Gallery 1954, as well as the Richards Medical Research Building, University of Pennsylvania.

Kaifu /ˈkaɪfu/ Toshiki 1932– . Japanese conservative politician, prime minister 1989–91. A protégé of former premier Takeo Miki, he was selected as a compromise choice as Liberal Democratic Party (LDP) president and prime minister Aug 1989, following the resignation of Sosuke Uno. Kaifu resigned Nov 1991, having lost the support of important factional leaders in the LDP, and was replaced by Kiichi Miyazawa.

Kaifu entered politics 1961, was deputy chief secretary 1974–76 in the Miki cabinet, and was education minister under Nakasone. He is a member of the minor Komoto faction. In 1987 he received what he claimed were legitimate political donations amounting to £40,000 from a company later accused of bribing a number of LDP politicians. His popularity as prime minister was

Kaifu Japanese conservative politician Toshiki Kaifu was prime minister 1989-91. In 1991 he attempted to send Japanese troops to the Gulf War, the first time forces were to be sent overseas since 1945, but his plan was overruled by the government.

dented by the unconstitutional proposal, defeated in the Diet, to contribute Japanese forces to the UN coalition army in the Persian Gulf area after Iraq's annexation of Kuwait 1990. His lack of power led to his replacement as prime minister 1991.

Kaiser /ˈkaɪzə/ Georg 1878–1945. German playwright, the principal exponent of German Expressionism. His large output includes *Die Bürger von Calais/The Burghers of Calais* 1914 and *Gas* 1918–20.

Kaiser /ˈkaɪzə/ Henry J 1882–1967. US industrialist. He developed steel and motor industries, and his shipbuilding firms became known for the mass production of vessels, including the 'Liberty ships' – cheap, quickly produced transport ships – built for the UK in World War II.

Kaldor /ˈkældɔː/ Nicholas 1908–1986. British economist, born in Hungary, special adviser 1964–68 and 1974–76 to the UK government. He was a firm believer in long-term capital gains tax, selective employment tax, and a fierce critic of monetarism. He advised several Third World governments on economic and tax reform.

Kalf /kɑːlf/ Willem 1619–1693. Dutch painter, active in Amsterdam from 1653. He specialized in still lifes set off against a dark background. These feature arrangements of glassware, polished metalwork, decorated porcelain, and fine carpets, with the occasional half-peeled lemon (a Dutch still-life motif).

Kālidāsa /ˌkɑːlɪˈdɑːsə/ lived 5th century AD. Indian epic poet and dramatist. His works, in Sanskrit, include the classic drama *Sakuntala*, the love story of King Dushyanta and the nymph Sakuntala.

Kalinin /kəˈliːnɪn/ Mikhail Ivanovich 1875–1946. Soviet politician, founder of the newspaper *Pravda*. He was prominent in the 1917 October Revolution, and in 1919 became head of state (president of the Central Executive Committee of the Soviet government until 1937, then president of the Presidium of the Supreme Soviet until 1946).

Kaltenbrunner /ˈkæltənˌbrʊnə/ Ernst 1901–1946. Austrian Nazi leader. After the annexation of Austria 1938 he joined police chief Himmler's staff, and as head of the Security Police (SD) from 1943 was responsible for the murder of millions of Jews (the Holocaust) and Allied soldiers in World War II. After the war, he was tried at Nuremberg for war crimes and hanged.

Kamenev /ˈkæmənev/ Lev Borisovich 1883–1936. Russian leader of the Bolshevik movement after 1917 who, with Stalin and Zinoviev, formed a ruling triumvirate in the USSR after Lenin's death 1924. His alignment with the Trotskyists led to his dismissal from office and from the Communist Party by Stalin 1926. Arrested 1934 after Kirov's assassination, Kamenev was secretly tried

and sentenced, then retried, condemned, and shot 1936 for plotting to murder Stalin.

Kamerlingh-Onnes /ˈkɑːməlɪŋ ˈɒnəs/ Heike 1853–1926. Dutch physicist who worked mainly in the field of low-temperature physics. In 1911, he discovered the phenomenon of superconductivity (enhanced electrical conductivity at very low temperatures), for which he was awarded the 1913 Nobel Prize for Physics.

Kandinsky /kænˈdɪnski/ Wassily 1866–1944. Russian painter, a pioneer of abstract art. Born in Moscow, he travelled widely, settling in Munich 1896. Around 1910 he produced the first known examples of purely abstract work in 20th-century art. He was an originator of the *Blaue Reiter* movement 1911–12, a grouping of artists interested in the value of colours, in folk art, and in the necessity of painting 'the inner, spiritual side of nature'. From 1921 he taught at the Bauhaus school of design. He moved to Paris 1933, becoming a French citizen 1939.

Kandinsky originally experimented with Post-Impressionist styles and Fauvism. His highly coloured style had few imitators, but his theories on composition, published in *Concerning the Spiritual in Art* 1912, were taken up by the early abstract movement.

Kane /kɑːn/ Sheik Hamidou 1928– . Senegalese novelist, writing in French. His first novel, *L'Aventure ambiguë/Ambiguous Adventure* 1961, is an autobiographical account of a young African alienated from the simple faith of his childhood and initiated into an alien Islamic mysticism, before being immersed in materialist French culture.

Kant /kænt/ Immanuel 1724–1804. German philosopher who believed that knowledge is not merely an aggregate of sense impressions but is dependent on the conceptual apparatus of the human understanding, which is itself not derived from experience. In ethics, Kant argued that right action cannot be based on feelings or inclinations but conforms to a law given by reason, the *categorical imperative*.

Born in Königsberg (in what was then East Prussia), he attended the university there, and was appointed professor of logic and metaphysics 1770. His first book, *Gedanken von der wahren Schätzung der lebendigen Kräfte/Thoughts on the True Estimates of Living Forces*, appeared in 1747 and the *Theorie des Himmels/Theory of the Heavens* in 1755. In the latter he combined physics and theology in an argument for the existence of God. In *Kritik der reinen Vernunft/Critique of Pure Reason* 1781, he argued that God's existence could not be proved theoretically. Other works include *Prolegomena* 1783, *Metaphysik der Sitten/Metaphysic of Ethics* 1785, *Metaphysische Anfangsgründe der Naturwissenschaft/Metaphysic of Nature* 1786, *Kritik der praktischen Vernunft/Critique of Practical Reason* 1788, and *Kritik der Urteilskraft/Critique of*

Judgement 1790. In 1797 ill health led to his retirement.

Kantorovich /ˌkæntəˈrəʊvɪtʃ/ Leonid 1912–1986. Soviet mathematical economist whose theory that decentralization of decisions in a planned economy could only be made with a rational price system earned him a share (with Tjalling C Koopmans) of the 1975 Nobel Prize for Economics.

Kapitza /kəˈpɪtsə/ Peter 1894–1984. Soviet physicist who in 1978 shared a Nobel prize for his work on magnetism and low-temperature physics. He was assistant director of magnetic research at the Cavendish Laboratory, Cambridge, England, 1924–32, before returning to the USSR to work at the Russian Academy of Science.

The crocodile cannot turn its head. Like science, it must always go forward with all-devouring jaws.

Peter Kapitza

Kaplan /ˈkæplən/ Viktor 1876–1934. Austrian engineer who invented a water turbine with adjustable rotor blades. In the machine, patented 1920, the rotor was on a vertical shaft and could be adjusted to suit any rate of flow of water.

Horizontal Kaplan turbines are used at the installation on the estuary of the river Rance in France, the world's first tidal power station.

Karajan /ˈkærəjæn/ Herbert von 1908–1989. Austrian conductor. He was the principal conductor of the Berlin Philharmonic Orchestra 1955–89 and artistic director of the Vienna State Opera 1956–64. He was also the artistic director of the Salzburg Festival from 1956 to 1960. He was associated with the Classical and Romantic repertoire – Beethoven, Brahms, Mahler, and Richard Strauss.

Karamanlis /ˌkærəmænˈliːs/ Constantinos 1907– . Greek politician of the New Democracy Party. A lawyer and an anticommunist, he was prime minister Oct 1955–March 1958, May 1958–Sept 1961, and Nov 1961–June 1963 (when he went into self-imposed exile because of a military coup). He was recalled as prime minister on the fall of the regime of the 'colonels' in July 1974, and was president 1980–85.

Karg-Elert /ˈkɑːˌgelət/ Sigfrid 1877–1933. German composer. After studying at Leipzig he devoted himself to the European harmonium. His numerous concert pieces and graded studies exploit a range of impressionistic effects such as the 'endless chord' – music built on mysterious and unchanging harmonies.

Karloff /ˈkɑːlɒf/ Boris. Stage name of William Henry Pratt 1887–1969. English-born US actor best known for his work in the USA. He achieved Hollywood stardom with his role as the monster in the film *Frankenstein* 1931. Several popular sequels followed as well as starring appearances in other horror films including *Scarface* 1932, *The Lost Patrol* 1934, and *The Body Snatcher* 1945.

In 1941 Karloff gained acclaim on Broadway in *Arsenic and Old Lace*. He continued in television and films until *Targets* 1967, where he appeared as himself.

Karmal /ˈkɑːməl/ Babrak 1929– . Afghani communist politician, president 1979–86. In 1965 he formed what became the banned People's Democratic Party of Afghanistan (PDPA) 1977. As president, with Soviet backing, he sought to broaden the appeal of the PDPA but encountered wide resistance from the Mujaheddin Muslim guerrillas.

Karmal was imprisoned for anti-government activity in the early 1950s. He was a member of the government 1957–62 and of the national assembly 1965–72. In Dec 1979 he returned from brief exile in E Europe with Soviet support to overthrow President Hafizullah Amin and was installed as the new head of state. Karmal was persuaded to step down as president and PDPA leader May 1986 as the USSR began to search for a compromise settlement with opposition groupings and to withdraw troops. In July 1991, he returned to Afghanistan from exile in Moscow.

Karpov /kəˈspɑːrɒf/ Anatoly 1951– . Russian chess player. He succeeded Bobby Fischer of the USA as world champion 1975, and held the title until losing to Gary Kasparov 1985.

Kasparov /kəˈspɑːrɒf/ Gary 1963– . Russian chess player. When he beat his compatriot Anatoly Karpov to win the world title 1985, he was the youngest ever champion at 22 years 210 days.

Kassem /ˈkæsem/ Abdul Karim 1914–1963. Iraqi politician, prime minister from 1958; he adopted a pro-Soviet policy. Kassem pardoned the leaders of the pro-Egyptian party who tried to assassinate him 1959. He was executed after the 1963 coup.

Katō /ˈkɑːtəʊ/ Kiyomasa 1562–1611. Japanese warrior and politician who was instrumental in the unification of Japan and the banning of Christianity in the country. He led the invasion of Korea 1592, and helped Toyotomi Hideyoshi (1536–1598) and →Tokugawa Ieyasu in their efforts to unify Japan.

Katō /ˈkɑːtəʊ/ Taka-akira 1860–1926. Japanese politician, prime minister 1924–26. After a long political career with several terms as foreign minister, Katō led probably the most democratic and liberal regime of the Japanese Empire.

Katsura /ˈkætˌsuərə/ Tarō 1847–1913. Prince of Japan, army officer, politician, and prime minister (1901–06, 1908–11, 1912–13). He was responsible for the Anglo-Japanese treaty of 1902, the successful prosecution of the Russo-Japanese war 1904–05, and the annexation of Korea 1910.

Having assisted in the Meiji restoration (see →Mutsuhito) 1866–68, Katsura became increasingly involved in politics. His support for rearmament, distaste for political parties, and oligarchic rule created unrest; his third ministry Dec 1912–Jan 1913 lasted only seven weeks.

Katz /kæts/ Bernard 1911– . British biophysicist. He shared the 1970 Nobel Prize for Medicine with Ulf von Euler (1905–1983) and Julius Axelrod for work on the biochemistry of the transmission and control of signals in the nervous system, vital in the search for remedies for nervous and mental disorders.

Kauffer /ˈkɔːfə/ Edward McKnight 1890–1954. US poster artist. He lived in the UK 1914–41.

Kauffmann /ˈkaʊfmən/ Angelica 1741–1807. Swiss Neo-Classical painter who worked extensively in England. She was in great demand as a portraitist, but also painted mythological scenes for large country houses.

Born in Grisons, she lived in Italy until 1765 and in England 1765–81.

Kaufman /ˈkɔːfmən/ George S(imon) 1889–1961. US playwright. Author (often in collaboration with others) of many Broadway hits, including *Of Thee I Sing* 1932, a Pulitzer Prize-winning satire on US politics; *You Can't Take It with You* 1936; *The Man Who Came to Dinner* 1939; and *The Solid Gold Cadillac* 1952. Many of his plays became classic Hollywood films.

Kaunda /kɑːˈʊndə/ Kenneth (David) 1924– . Zambian politician, president 1964–91. Imprisoned in 1958–60 as founder of the Zambia African National Congress, he became in 1964 the first prime minister of Northern Rhodesia, then the first president of independent Zambia. In 1973 he introduced one-party rule. He supported the nationalist movement in Southern Rhodesia, now Zimbabwe, and survived a coup attempt 1980 thought to have been promoted by South Africa. He was elected chair of the Organization of African Unity 1987. In 1990 he was faced with wide anti-government demonstrations, leading to the acceptance of a multiparty political system. He lost the first multiparty election, in Nov 1991, to Frederick Chiluba.

The inability of those in power to still the voices of their own consciences is the great force leading to change.

Kenneth Kaunda in *Observer* July 1965

Kautsky /ˈkaʊtski/ Karl 1854–1938. German socialist theoretician who opposed the reformist ideas of Edouard →Bernstein from within the Social Democratic Party. In spite of his Marxist ideas he remained in the party when its left wing broke away to form the German Communist Party (KPD).

Kawabata /kaʊəˈbɑːtə/ Yasunari 1899–1972. Japanese novelist, translator of Lady →Murasaki, and author of *Snow Country* 1947 and *A Thousand Cranes* 1952. His novels are characterized by melancholy and loneliness. He was the first Japanese to win the Nobel Prize for Literature, in 1968.

Kay /keɪ/ John 1704–c. 1764. British inventor who developed the flying shuttle, a machine to speed up the work of hand-loom weaving. In 1733 he patented his invention but was ruined by the litigation necessary for its defence.

In 1753 his house in Bury was wrecked by a mob, who feared the use of machinery would cause unemployment. He is believed to have died in poverty in France.

Kaye /keɪ/ Danny. Stage name of David Daniel Kaminski 1913–1987. US actor, comedian, and singer. He appeared in many films, including *Wonder Man* 1944, *The Secret Life of Walter Mitty* 1946, and *Hans Christian Andersen* 1952.

He achieved success on Broadway in *Lady in the Dark* 1940 and *Let's Face It* 1941. He also starred on television, had his own show 1963–67, toured for UNICEF, and guest-conducted major symphony orchestras in later years.

Kazan /kəˈzæn/ Elia 1909– . US stage and film director, a founder of the Actors Studio 1947. Plays he directed include *The Skin of Our Teeth* 1942, *A Streetcar Named Desire* 1947, and *Cat on a Hot Tin Roof* 1955; films include *Gentlemen's Agreement* 1948, *East of Eden* 1954, and *The Visitors* 1972.

Kazantzakis /ˌkæzændˈzɑːkɪs/ Nikos 1885–1957. Greek writer whose works include the poem *I Odysseia/The Odyssey* 1938 (which continues Homer's *Odyssey*), and the novels *Zorba the Greek* 1946, *The Greek Passion*, and *The Last Temptation of Christ*, both 1951.

Kean /kiːn/ Edmund 1787–1833. British tragic actor, noted for his portrayal of villainy in the Shakespearean roles of Shylock, Richard III, and Iago.

Keane /kiːn/ Molly (Mary Nesta) 1905– . Irish novelist whose comic novels of Anglo-Irish life include *Good Behaviour* 1981, *Time After Time* 1983, and *Loving and Giving* 1988. She also writes under the name M J Farrell.

Kearny /ˈkɑːni/ Philip 1814–1862. US military leader. In 1859 he served in the army of Napoleon III in Italy and received the French Croix de Guerre for his actions. With the outbreak of the American Civil War 1861, Kearny returned to the USA and was named brigadier general of the New Jersey militia. He was killed in action near Chantilly, Virginia.

Born in New York, Kearny received a law degree from Columbia University 1833. Choosing a career in the military, he obtained a commission in the US Dragoons 1837. He was trained in cavalry techniques in France and saw action in the

Keaton *Nicknamed 'Great Stone Face' because of his distinctive deadpan expression, Buster Keaton was one of the silent screen's greatest comedians. The General 1927 (pictured), set in the American Civil War, is a fine example of both his acrobatic agility and comic timing.*

Mexican War 1846–48, where he lost an arm. He was the nephew of Stephen W →Kearny.

Kearny /ˈkɑːni/ Stephen Watts 1794–1848. US military leader. As brigadier general he was given command of the Army of the West 1846. During the Mexican War 1846–48, he was the military governor of New Mexico and joined in the conquest of California 1847 becoming military governor.

Born in Newark, New Jersey, Kearny attended Columbia University and saw action in the Anglo-American War of 1812. Later serving on the frontier, he was promoted In 1848 he served as governor general of occupied Veracruz and Mexico City. He died of a tropical fever acquired there.

Keating Paul 1954– . Australian politician, Labor Party (ALP) leader and prime minister from 1991. He was treasurer and deputy leader of the ALP 1983–91, and also held several posts in Labor's shadow ministry 1976–83.

Keating was active in ALP politics from the age of 15. As finance minister 1983–91 under Bob Hawke, Keating was unpopular with the public for his harsh economic policies. He successfully challenged Hawke for the ALP party leadership Dec 1991.

Keaton /ˈkiːtn/ Buster (Joseph Frank) 1896–1966. US comedian, actor, and film director. After being a star in vaudeville, he took up a career in 'Fatty' Arbuckle comedies, and became one of the great comedians of the silent film era, with an inimitable deadpan expression (the 'Great Stone Face') masking a sophisticated acting ability. His films include *One Week* 1920, *The Navigator* 1924, *The General* 1927, and *The Cameraman* 1928.

He rivalled Charlie Chaplin in popularity until studio problems ended his creative career. He then made only shorts and guest appearances, as in Chaplin's *Limelight* 1952 and *A Funny Thing Happened on the Way to the Forum* 1966.

Keats /kiːts/ John 1795–1821. English Romantic poet who produced work of the highest quality and promise before dying at the age of 25. *Poems* 1817, *Endymion* 1818, the great odes (particularly 'Ode to a Nightingale' and 'Ode on a Grecian Urn' 1819), and the narratives 'Lamia', 'Isabella', and 'The Eve of St Agnes' 1820, show his lyrical richness and talent for drawing on both classical mythology and medieval lore.

Born in London, Keats studied at Guy's Hospital 1815–17, but then abandoned medicine for poetry. *Endymion* was harshly reviewed by the Tory *Blackwood's Magazine* and *Quarterly Review*, largely because of Keats's friendship with the radical writer Leigh Hunt (1800–1865). In 1819 he fell in love with Fanny Brawne (1802–1865). Suffering from tuberculosis, he sailed to Italy 1820 in an attempt to regain his health, but died in Rome. Valuable insight into Keats's poetic development is provided by his *Letters*, published 1848.

Keble /ˈkiːbəl/ John 1792–1866. Anglican priest and religious poet. His sermon on the decline of religious faith in Britain, preached 1833, heralded the start of the Oxford Movement, a Catholic revival in the Church of England. Keble College, Oxford, was founded 1870 in his memory.

Keble was professor of poetry at Oxford 1831–41. He wrote four of the *Tracts for the Times* (theological treatises in support of the Oxford Movement), and from 1835 was vicar of Hursley in Hampshire.

Keeler /ˈkiːlə/ Christine 1942– . British prostitute of the 1960s. She became notorious in 1963 after revelations of affairs with both a Soviet attaché and the war minister John →Profumo, who resigned after admitting lying to the House of Commons about their relationship. Her patron, the osteopath Stephen Ward, convicted of living on immoral earnings, committed suicide and Keeler was subsequently imprisoned for related offences.

Kefauver /ˈkiːfɔːvə/ (Carey) Estes 1903–1963. US Democratic politician. He was elected to the US House of Representatives 1939 and served in the US Senate 1948 until his death. He was an unsuccessful candidate for the Democratic presidential nomination 1952 and 1956.

Born near Madisonville, Tennessee, USA, Kefauver was educated at the University of Tennessee and received a law degree from Yale University 1927 and established a private law practice in Chattanooga, Tennessee. As chairman of the Senate Judiciary Committee, he held widely publicized, televised hearings on organized crime 1950–51

Keillor /ˈkiːlə/ Garrison 1942– . US writer and humorist. His hometown Anoka, Minnesota, in the American Midwest, inspired his stories about Lake Wobegon, including *Lake Wobegon Days* 1985 and *Leaving Home* 1987, which often started as radio monologues about 'the town that time forgot, that the decades cannot improve'.

Keïta /ˈkeɪtɑː/ Salif 1949– . Malian singer and songwriter whose combination of traditional rhythms and vocals with electronic instruments made him popular in the West in the 1980s; in Mali he worked 1973–83 with the band Les Ambassadeurs and became a star throughout W Africa, moving to France 1984. His albums include *Soro* 1987 and *Amen* 1991.

Keitel /ˈkaɪtl/ Wilhelm 1882–1946. German field marshal in World War II, chief of the supreme command from 1938 and Hitler's chief military adviser. He signed Germany's unconditional surrender in Berlin 8 May 1945. Tried at Nuremberg for war crimes, he was hanged.

Kekulé von Stradonitz /ˈkekjʊleɪ/ Friedrich August 1829–1896. German chemist whose theory 1858 of molecular structure revolutionized organic chemistry. He proposed two resonant forms of the benzene ring.

Keller /ˈkelə/ Gottfried 1819–1890. Swiss poet and novelist whose books include *Der Grüne Heinrich/Green Henry* 1854–55. He also wrote short stories, of which the collection *Die Leute von Seldwyla/The People of Seldwyla* 1856–74 describes small-town life.

Keller /ˈkelə/ Helen Adams 1880–1968. US author and campaigner for the blind. She became blind and deaf after an illness when she was only 19 months old, but the teaching of Anne Sullivan, her lifelong companion, enabled her to learn the names of objects and eventually to speak. Keller graduated with honours from Radcliffe College in 1904; published several books, including *The Story of My Life* 1902; and toured the world, lecturing to raise money for the blind. She was born in Alabama.

Kellogg /ˈkelɒg/ Frank Billings 1856–1937. US political leader and diplomat. Elected to the US Senate 1916, he was appointed US ambassador to Great Britain by President Harding 1922 and secretary of state 1925. He formulated the Kellogg–Briand Pact 1927, the international antiwar resolution, for which he was awarded the Nobel Peace Prize 1929.

Born in Potsdam, New York, Kellogg studied law in Minnesota and was admitted to the bar 1877. He served as a prosecutor of federal antitrust cases before being elected to the US Senate. He later served as judge on the World Court 1930–35.

Kelly /ˈkeli/ Emmett 1898–1979. US clown and circus performer who created his 'Weary Willie' clown character while with the Hagenbeck-Wallace circus 1931. Joining the Ringling Brothers and Barnum and Bailey Circus 1942, he made 'Weary Willie' into one of the most famous clowns in the world.

Born in Sedan, Kansas, USA, Kelly had early aspirations to be a cartoonist. He moved to Kansas City 1917, where he created the hobo character 'Weary Willie' that was later to become the inspiration for his circus persona.

Kelly later became a familiar film and television personality.

Kelly /ˈkeli/ Gene (Eugene Curran) 1912– . US film actor, dancer, choreographer, and director. He was a major star of the 1940s and 1950s in a series of MGM musicals, including *On the Town* 1949, *An American in Paris* 1951, and *Singin' in the Rain* 1952.

Kelly /ˈkeli/ Grace (Patricia) 1928–1982. US film actress who retired from acting after marrying Prince Rainier III of Monaco 1956. She starred in *High Noon* 1952, *The Country Girl* 1954, for which she received an Academy Award, and *High Society* 1955. She also starred in three Hitchcock classics – *Dial M for Murder* 1954, *Rear Window* 1954, and *To Catch a Thief* 1955.

Kelly /ˈkeli/ Ned (Edward) 1855–1880. Australian bushranger. The son of an Irish convict, he wounded a police officer in 1878 while resisting the arrest of his brother Daniel for horse-stealing. The two brothers escaped and carried out bank robberies. Kelly wore a distinctive home-made armour. In 1880 he was captured and hanged.

Kelly /ˈkeli/ Petra 1947–1992. German politician and activist. She was a vigorous campaigner against nuclear power and other environmental issues and founded the German Green Party 1972. She was a member of parliament 1983–1990, but then fell out with her party over her assertive and domineering style of leadership. She died at the hands of her lover, the former general Gert Bastian.

Born in Germany, Kelly was brought up in the USA and was influenced by the civil rights movement there. She worked briefly in the office of Robert Kennedy, and returning to Germany, she joined the EEC as a civil servant 1972. Her goal, to see the ecological movement as a global organization, became increasingly frustrated by the provincialism of the German Green Party.

Kelvin /ˈkelvɪn/ William Thomson, 1st Baron Kelvin 1824–1907. Irish physicist who introduced the *kelvin scale*, the absolute scale of temperature. His work on the conservation of energy 1851 led to the second law of thermodynamics.

Popularly known for his contributions to telegraphy, he greatly improved transatlantic communications. Maritime endeavours led to a tide gauge and predictor, an improved compass, and simpler methods of fixing a ship's position at sea.

Kemal Atatürk Mustafa. Turkish politician; see →Atatürk.

Kemble /ˈkembəl/ (John) Philip 1757–1823. English actor and theatre manager. He excelled in tragedy, including the Shakespearean roles of Hamlet and Coriolanus. As manager of Drury Lane 1788–1803 and Covent Garden 1803–17 in London, he introduced many innovations in theatrical management, costume, and scenery.

He was the son of the strolling player Roger Kemble (1721–1802), whose children included the actors Charles Kemble and Mrs →Siddons.

Kemble /ˈkembəl/ Fanny (Frances Anne) 1809–1893. English actress, daughter of Charles Kemble (1773–1854). She first appeared as Shakespeare's Juliet in 1829. In 1834, on a US tour, she married a Southern plantation owner and remained in the USA until 1847. Her *Journal of a Residence on a Georgian Plantation* 1835 is a valuable document in the history of slavery.

Kempe /kemp/ Margery *c.* 1373–*c.* 1439. English Christian mystic. She converted to religious life after a period of mental derangement, and travelled widely as a pilgrim. Her *Boke of Margery Kempe* about 1420 describes her life and experiences, both religious and worldly. It has been called the first autobiography in English.

Kempe /ˈkempə/ Rudolf 1910–1976. German conductor. Renowned for the clarity and fidelity of his interpretations of the works of Richard Strauss and →Wagner's *Ring* cycle, he conducted Britain's Royal Philharmonic Orchestra 1961–75 and was musical director of the Munich Philharmonic from 1967.

Kempff /kempf/ Wilhelm (Walter Friedrich) 1895–1991. German pianist and composer who excelled at the 19th-century classical repertory of Beethoven, Brahms, Chopin, and Liszt. He resigned as director of the Stuttgart Conservatory when only 35 to concentrate on performing; he later played with Pablo Casals, Yehudi Menuhin, and Pierre Fournier.

Kempis Thomas à. Medieval German monk and religious writer; see →Thomas à Kempis.

Kendall /ˈkendl/ Edward 1886–1972. US biochemist. In 1914 he isolated the hormone thyroxine, the active compound of the thyroid gland. He went on to work on secretions from the adrenal gland, among which he discovered a compound E, which was in fact the steroid cortisone. For this Kendall shared the 1950 Nobel Prize for Medicine with Philip Hench (1896–1965) and Tadeus →Reichstein.

Kendrew /ˈkendruː/ John 1917– . British biochemist. Kendrew began, in 1946, the ambitious task of determining the three-dimensional structure of the major muscle protein myoglobin. This was completed in 1959 and won for Kendrew a share of the 1962 Nobel Prize for Chemistry with Max Perutz.

Keneally /kɪˈniːli/ Thomas (Michael) 1935– . Australian novelist who won the Booker Prize with *Schindler's Ark* 1982, a novel based on the true account of Polish Jews saved from the gas chambers in World War II by a German industrialist. Other works include *Woman of the Inner Sea* 1992.

Keneally has also written *The Chant of Jimmie Blacksmith* 1972, filmed in 1978 and based on the life of the Aboriginal bushranger Jimmy Governor, *Confederates* 1980, *A Family Madness* 1986, *The Playmaker* 1987, and *To Asmara* 1989.

Kennedy /ˈkenədi/ Anthony 1936– . US jurist, appointed associate justice of the US Supreme Court 1988. A conservative, he wrote the majority opinion in *Washington v Harper* 1990 that the administration of medication for mentally ill prisoners, without the prisoner's consent, is permissible.

Born in Sacramento, California, USA, he attended Stanford University (spending his fourth year at the London School of Economics) and the Harvard Law School.

Kennedy established a private law practice in California 1962–75. He taught constitutional law at McGeorge School of Law of the University of the Pacific 1965–88 and was appointed judge of the US Court of Appeals for the Seventh Circuit 1976. He was appointed to the Supreme Court by President Reagan.

Kennedy *35th president of the USA, John F Kennedy, the youngest person to hold the office. He was assassinated after less than three years in power.*

He supported the majority opinion in the 1989 case, *Texas* v *Johnson*, that ruled that the burning of the US flag in protest was protected by the First Amendment. In *Saffle* v *Parks* 1990 he wrote the opinion that a writ of habeas corpus may be obtained only according to the laws in force at the time of a prisoner's conviction.

Kennedy /ˈkenədi/ Edward (Moore) 'Ted' 1932– . US Democratic politician. He aided his brothers John and Robert Kennedy in the presidential campaign of 1960, and entered politics as a senator for Massachusetts 1962. He failed to gain the presidential nomination 1980, largely because of questions about his delay in reporting a car crash at Chappaquiddick Island, near Cape Cod, Massachusetts, in 1969, in which his passenger, Mary Jo Kopechne, was drowned.

Kennedy /ˈkenədi/ John F(itzgerald) 'Jack' 1917–1963. 35th president of the USA 1961–63, a Democrat; the first Roman Catholic and the youngest person to be elected president. In foreign policy he carried through the unsuccessful Bay of Pigs invasion of Cuba by US-sponsored Cuban exiles 1961, and in 1963 secured the withdrawal of Soviet missiles from the island. His programme for reforms at home, called the *New Frontier*, was posthumously executed by Lyndon Johnson. Kennedy was assassinated while on a state visit to Dallas, Texas, on 22 Nov 1963 by Lee Harvey Oswald (1939–1963), who was within a few days shot dead by Jack Ruby (1911–1967).

Son of successful financier Joseph Kennedy, John was born in Brookline, Massachusetts, educated at Harvard, and served in the navy in the Pacific during World War II. In 1946 he was elected to the House of Representatives and in 1952 to the Senate from Massachusetts. In 1953 he married socialite Jacqueline Lee Bouvier (1929–   ). In 1960 he defeated Richard →Nixon for the presidency, partly as a result of televised debates, and brought academics and intellectuals to Washington as advisers. The US involvement in the Vietnam War began during Kennedy's administration.

A number of conspiracy theories have been spun around the Kennedy assassination, which was investigated by a special commission headed by Chief Justice Earl →Warren. The commission determined that Oswald acted alone, although this is extremely unlikely. A later congressional committee re- examined the evidence and determined that Kennedy 'was probably assassinated as a result of a conspiracy'. Oswald was an ex-marine who had gone to live in the USSR 1959 and returned when he could not become a Soviet citizen. Ruby was a Dallas nightclub owner, associated with the underworld and the police.

Kennedy /ˈkenədi/ Joseph Patrick 1888–1969. US industrialist and diplomat; ambassador to the UK 1937–40. A self-made millionaire, he ventured into the film industry, then set up the Securities and Exchange Commission (SEC) for F D Roosevelt. He groomed each of his four sons – Joseph Patrick Kennedy Jr (1915–1944), John F →Kennedy, Robert →Kennedy, and Edward →Kennedy – for a career in politics. His eldest son, Joseph, was killed in action with the naval air force in World War II.

Kennedy /ˈkenədi/ Nigel 1956–   . British violinist, credited with expanding the audience for classical music. His 1986 recording of Vivaldi's *Four Seasons* sold more than 1 million copies.

Kennedy was educated at the Yehudi Menuhin School, Surrey, England, and the Juilliard School of Music, New York. He has allied Menuhin's ethic of openness and populism to modern marketing techniques. By cultivating a media image that challenges conventional standards of dress and decorum, he has succeeded in attracting young audiences to carefully understated performances of Bach, Max Bruch, and Alban Berg. His repertoire of recordings also includes jazz.

Do you realize the responsibility I carry? I'm the only person standing between Nixon and the White House.

John F Kennedy Oct 1960

Kennedy /ˈkenədi/ Robert (Francis) 1925–1968. US Democratic politician and lawyer. He was presidential campaign manager for his brother John F →Kennedy 1960, and as attorney general 1961–64 pursued a racket-busting policy and promoted the Civil Rights Act of 1964. He was also a key aide to his brother. When John Kennedy's successor, Lyndon Johnson, preferred Hubert H Humphrey for the 1964 vice-presidential nomination, Kennedy resigned and was elected senator for New York. In 1968 he campaigned for the Democratic Party's presidential nomination, but during a campaign stop in California was assassinated by Sirhan Bissara Sirhan (1944–), a Jordanian.

Kennedy /ˈkenədi/ William 1928– . US novelist, author of the *Albany Trilogy* consisting of *Legs* 1976, about the gangster 'Legs' Diamond; *Billy Phelan's Greatest Game* 1983, about a pool player; and *Ironweed* 1984, about a baseball player's return to the city of Albany, NY. He also wrote *Quinn's Book* 1988.

Kennelly /ˈkenəli/ Arthur Edwin 1861–1939. US engineer who gave his name to the Kennelly–Heaviside layer (now the E layer) of the ionosphere. He verified in 1902 the existence of an ionized layer in the upper atmosphere, predicted by Oliver →Heaviside.

Kenneth /ˈkenɪθ/ two kings of Scotland:

Kenneth I *MacAlpin* died 858. King of Scotland from *c.* 844. Traditionally, he is regarded as the founder of the Scottish kingdom (Alba) by virtue of his final defeat of the Picts about 844. He invaded Northumbria six times, and drove the Angles and the Britons over the river Tweed.

Kenneth II died 995. King of Scotland from 971, son of Malcolm I. He invaded Northumbria several times, and his chiefs were in constant conflict with Sigurd the Norwegian over the area of Scotland north of the river Spey. He is believed to have been murdered by his subjects.

Kent /kent/ Bruce 1929– . British peace campaigner who was general secretary for the Campaign for Nuclear Disarmament 1980–85. He has published numerous articles on disarmament, Christianity, and peace. He was a Catholic priest until 1987.

Kent /kent/ Edward George Nicholas Paul Patrick, 2nd Duke of Kent 1935– . British prince, grandson of George V. His father, *George* (1902–1942), was created Duke of Kent just before his marriage in 1934 to Princess Marina of Greece and Denmark (1906–1968). The second duke succeeded when his father (George Edward Alexander Edmund) was killed in an air crash on active service with the RAF.

He was educated at Eton public school and Sandhurst military academy, and then commissioned in the Royal Scots Greys. In 1961 he married Katharine Worsley (1933–) and his heir is *George* (1962–), Earl of St Andrews. His brother, *Prince Michael* (1942–), became an officer with the Hussars in 1962. His sister, *Princess Alexandra* (1936–), married in 1963 Angus Ogilvy (1928–), younger son of the 12th Earl of Airlie; they have two children, James (1964–) and Marina (1966–).

Kent and Strathearn /ˈstræθˈɜːn/ Edward, Duke of Kent and Strathearn 1767–1820. British general.

The fourth son of George III, he married Victoria Mary Louisa (1786–1861), widow of the Prince of Leiningen, in 1818, and had one child, the future Queen Victoria.

Kent /kent/ William 1686–1748. British architect, landscape gardener, and interior designer. In architecture he was foremost in introducing the Palladian style into Britain from Italy. Later, he was a foremost exponent of the 18th-century Gothic revival, and in Romantic landscape gardening.

Horace Walpole called him 'the father of modern gardening'.

Kentigern, St /ˈkentɪgən/ or *Mungo c.* 518–603. First bishop of Glasgow, born at Culross, Scotland. Anti-Christian factions forced him to flee to Wales, where he founded the monastery of St Asaph. In 573 he returned to Glasgow and founded the cathedral there. Feast day 14 Jan.

Kenton /ˈkentən/ Stan 1912–1979. US exponent of progressive jazz, who broke into West Coast jazz in 1941 with his 'wall of brass' sound. He helped introduce Afro-Cuban rhythms to US jazz, and combined jazz and classical music in compositions such as 'Artistry in Rhythm' 1943.

Kenyatta /kenˈjætə/ Jomo. Assumed name of Kamau Ngengi *c.* 1894–1978. Kenyan nationalist politician, prime minister from 1963, as well as the first president of Kenya from 1964 until his death. He led the Kenya African Union from 1947 (*KANU* from 1963) and was active in liberating Kenya from British rule.

A member of the Kikuyu ethnic group, Kenyatta was born near Fort Hall, son of a farmer. Brought up at a Church of Scotland mission, he joined the Kikuyu Central Association (KCA), devoted to recovery of Kikuyu lands from white settlers, and became its president. He spent some years in Britain, returning to Kenya in 1946. He became president of the Kenya African Union (successor to the banned KCA 1947). In 1953 he was sentenced to seven years' imprisonment for his management of the guerrilla organization Mau Mau, though some doubt has been cast on his complicity. Released to exile in N Kenya in 1958, he was allowed to return to Kikuyuland 1961 and in 1963 became prime minister (also president from 1964) of independent Kenya. His slogans were '*Uhuru na moja*' (Freedom and unity) and '*Harambee*' (Let's get going).

Kenyon /ˈkenjən/ Kathleen 1906–1978. British archaeologist whose all-female dig in Jericho uncovered remains of a New Stone Age (Neolithic) settlement dated to about 6800 BC.

Kenzo /ˈkenzəʊ/ trade name of Kenzo Takada 1940– . Japanese fashion designer, active in France from 1964. He opened his shop Jungle JAP 1970, and by 1972 he was well established, known initially for unconventional designs based on traditional Japanese clothing. He also produces innovative designs in knitted fabrics.

Kepler /keplə/ Johannes 1571–1630. German mathematician and astronomer. He formulated what are now called *Kepler's laws* of planetary motion: (1) the orbit of each planet is an ellipse with the Sun at one of the foci; (2) the radius vector of each planet sweeps out equal areas in equal times; (3) the squares of the periods of the planets are proportional to the cubes of their mean distances from the Sun.

Born in Württemberg, Kepler became assistant to Tycho →Brahe 1600, and succeeded him 1601 as imperial mathematician to the emperor Rudolph II. Kepler observed in 1604 a supernova, the first visible since the one discovered by Brahe 1572. His analysis of Brahe's observations of the planets, observations published by Kepler in his *Rudolphine Tables* 1627, led to the discovery of his three laws, the first two of which he published in *Astronomia Nova* 1609 and the third in *Harmonices Mundi* 1619. Kepler lived in turbulent times and was faced with many taxing domestic problems, not least of which was the unsuccessful prosecution in Wittenberg 1618 of his mother for witchcraft.

Kerekou /ˌkerəˈkuː/ Mathieu (Ahmed) 1933– . Benin socialist politician and soldier, president 1980–91. In 1972, when deputy head of the Dahomey army, he led a coup to oust the ruling president and establish his own military government. He embarked on a programme of 'scientific socialism', changing his country's name to Benin to mark this change of direction. In 1987 he resigned from the army and confirmed a civilian administration. He was re-elected president 1989, but lost to Nicéphore Soglo in the 1991 presidential elections.

Kerensky /kerənski/ Alexandr Feodorovich 1881–1970. Russian revolutionary politician, prime minister of the second provisional government before its collapse Nov 1917, during the Russian Revolution. He was overthrown by the Bolshevik revolution, since he insisted on staying in World War I and mismanaged internal economic affairs. He fled to France 1918 and to the USA 1940.

Kern /kɜːn/ Jerome (David) 1885–1945. US composer. Many of Kern's songs have become classics, notably 'Smoke Gets in Your Eyes' from his musical *Roberta* 1933. He wrote the operetta *Show Boat* 1927, which includes the song 'Ol' Man River'.

Kerouac /keruæk/ Jack 1923–1969. US novelist who named and epitomized the Beat Generation of the 1950s. His books, all autobiographical, include *On the Road* 1957, *Big Sur* 1963, and *Desolation Angel* 1965.

On the Road, written in three weeks in a formless, unpolished style, awoke the nation to the attitudes of a group of young people in pursuit of love, beauty, and new experiences, who were contemptuous of staid American values.

Kerr /kɜː/ Deborah 1921– . British actress who often played genteel, ladylike roles. Her performance in British films such as *Major Barbara* 1940 and *Black Narcissus* 1946 led to starring parts in Hollywood: *Quo Vadis* 1951, *From Here to Eternity* 1953, and *The King and I* 1956. She retired in 1969, but made a comeback with *The Assam Garden* 1985.

Kerr /kɜː/ John Robert 1914–1990. Australian lawyer who as governor general 1974–77 controversially dismissed the prime minister, Gough Whitlam, and his government 1975.

Kertész /kɜːtes/ André 1894–1986. Hungarian-born US photographer whose spontaneity had a great impact on photojournalism. A master of the 35-mm-format camera, he recorded his immediate environment (Paris, New York) with wit and style.

Kesselring /kesəlrɪŋ/ Albert 1885–1960. German field marshal in World War II, commander of the Luftwaffe (air force) 1939–40, during the invasions of Poland and the Low Countries and the early stages of the Battle of Britain. He later served under Field Marshal Rommel in N Africa, took command in Italy 1943, and was commander in chief on the western front March 1945. His death sentence for war crimes at the Nuremberg trials 1947 was commuted to life imprisonment, but he was released 1952.

Ketch /ketʃ/ Jack died 1686. English executioner who included →Monmouth in 1685 among his victims; his name was once a common nickname for an executioner.

Key /kiː/ Francis Scott 1779–1843. US lawyer and poet who wrote the song 'The Star-Spangled Banner' while Fort McHenry, Baltimore, was besieged by British troops in 1814; since 1931 it has been the national anthem of the USA.

Keynes /keɪnz/ John Maynard, 1st Baron Keynes 1883–1946. English economist, whose *The General Theory of Employment, Interest, and Money* 1936 proposed the prevention of financial crises and unemployment by adjusting demand through government control of credit and currency. He is responsible for that part of economics now known as *macroeconomics*.

Keynes led the British delegation at the Bretton Woods Conference 1944, which set up the International Monetary Fund. His theories were widely accepted in the aftermath of World War II, and he was one of the most influential economists of the 20th century. His ideas are today often contrasted with those of monetarism.

Keynes was Fellow of King's College, Cambridge. He worked at the Treasury during World War I, and took part in the peace conference as chief Treasury representative, but resigned in protest against the financial terms of the treaty. He justified his action in *The Economic Consequences of the Peace* 1919. His later economic works aroused much controversy.

Khachaturian /ˌkætʃə'tʊəriən/ Aram Il'yich 1903–1978. Armenian composer. His use of folk themes is shown in the ballets *Gayaneh* 1942, which includes the 'Sabre Dance', and *Spartacus* 1956.

Khaddhafi /kə'dæfi/ or *Gaddafi* or *Qaddafi*, Moamer al 1942– . Libyan revolutionary leader. Overthrowing King Idris 1969, he became virtual president of a republic, although he nominally gave up all except an ideological role 1974. He favours territorial expansion in N Africa reaching as far as Zaire, has supported rebels in Chad, and has proposed mergers with a number of countries. His theories, based on those of the Chinese communist leader Mao Zedong, are contained in a *Green Book*.

Khalaf /'kɑːlɑːf/ Salah, also known as *Abu Iyad* 1933–1991. Palestinian nationalist leader. He became a refugee in 1948 when Israel became independent, and was one of the four founder members – with Yassir Arafat – of the PLO in the 1960s. One of its most senior members, he was involved with the Black September group, and is believed to have orchestrated their campaign of terrorist attacks such as the 1972 killing of 11 Israeli atheletes at the Munich Olympics. He later argued for a diplomatic as well as a terrorist campaign. He was assassinated by an Arab dissident follower of Abu Nidal.

Khalifa Sudanese leader; see →Abd Allah.

Khama /'kɑːmə/ Seretse 1921–1980. Botswanan politician, prime minister of Bechuanaland 1965, and first president of Botswana from 1966 until his death.

Son of the Bamangwato chief *Sekoma II* (died 1925), Khama studied law in Britain and married an Englishwoman, Ruth Williams. This marriage was strongly condemned by his uncle Tshekedi Khama, who had been regent during his minority, as contrary to tribal custom, and Seretse Khama was banished 1950. He returned 1956 on his renunciation of any claim to the chieftaincy.

Khan /kɑːn/ Imran 1952– . Pakistani cricketer. He played county cricket for Worcestershire and Sussex in the UK, and made his Test debut for Pakistan 1971, subsequently playing for his country 85 times. He captained Pakistan to victory in the World Cup in 1992.

Khan /kɑːn/ Jahangir 1963– . Pakistani squash player who won the world open championship a record six times 1981–85 and 1988. He was ten times British Open champion 1982–91, and World Amateur champion 1979, 1983, and 1985.

After losing to Geoff Hunt (Australia) in the final of the 1981 British Open, he did not lose again until Nov 1986 when he lost to Ross Norman (New Zealand) in the World Open final.

Khan /kɑːn/ Liaquat Ali 1895–1951. Indian politician, deputy leader of the Muslim League 1941–47, first prime minister of Pakistan from 1947. He was assassinated by objectors to his peace policy with India.

Khan, Aga Islamic leader; see →Aga Khan IV

Khashoggi /kə'ʃɒgi/ Adnan 1935– . Saudi entrepreneur and arms dealer who built up a large property company, Triad, based in Switzerland, and through ownership of banks, hotels, and real estate became a millionaire. In 1975 he was accused by the USA of receiving bribes to secure military contracts in Arab countries, and in 1986 he was financially disadvantaged by the slump in oil prices and political problems in Sudan. In April 1989 he was arrested in connection with illegal property deals. He successfully weathered all three setbacks.

Khomeini /kɒ'meini/ Ayatollah Ruhollah 1900–1989. Iranian Shi'ite Muslim leader, born in Khomein, central Iran. Exiled for opposition to the Shah from 1964, he returned when the Shah left the country 1979, and established a fundamentalist Islamic republic. His rule was marked by a protracted war with Iraq, and suppression of opposition within Iran, executing thousands of opponents.

Khorana /kɔː'rɑːnə/ Har Gobind 1922– . Indian-born US biochemist who in 1976 led the team that first synthesized a biologically active gene. In 1968 he shared the Nobel Prize for Medicine for research on the interpretation of the genetic code and its function in protein synthesis.

Khrushchev /kruʃ'tʃɒf/ Nikita Sergeyevich 1894–1971. Soviet politician, secretary general of the Communist Party 1953–64, premier 1958–64. He emerged as leader from the power struggle following Stalin's death and was the first official to denounce Stalin, in 1956. His de-Stalinization programme gave rise to revolts in Poland and Hungary 1956. Because of problems with the economy and foreign affairs (a breach with China 1960; conflict with the USA in the Cuban missile crisis 1962), he was ousted by Leonid Brezhnev and Alexei Kosygin.

Born near Kursk, the son of a miner, Khrushchev fought in the post Revolutionary civil war 1917–20, and in World War II organized the guerrilla defence of his native Ukraine. He denounced Stalinism in a secret session of the party Feb 1956. Many victims of the purges of the 1930s were either released or posthumously rehabilitated, but when Hungary revolted in Oct against Soviet domination, there was immediate Soviet intervention. In 1958 Khrushchev succeeded Bulganin as chair of the council of ministers (prime minister). His policy of competition with capitalism was successful in the space programme, which launched the world's first satellite (*Sputnik*). Because of the Cuban crisis and the personal feud with Mao Zedong that led to the Sino-Soviet split, he was compelled to resign 1964, although by 1965 his reputation was to some extent officially restored. In April 1989 his Feb 1956 'secret speech' against Stalin was officially published for the first time.

Khufu /ˈkuːfuː/ c. 2600 BC. Egyptian king of Memphis, who built the largest of the pyramids, known to the Greeks as the pyramid of Cheops (the Greek form of Khufu).

Khwārizmī, al- /ˈkwɑːrɪzmi/ Muham mad ibn-Mūsā c. 780–c. 850. Persian mathematician from Khwarizm (now Khiva, Uzbekistan), who lived and worked in Baghdad. He wrote a book on algebra, from part of whose title (al-jabr) comes the word 'algebra', and a book in which he introduced to the West the Hindu-Arabic decimal number system. The word 'algorithm' is a corruption of his name.

He also compiled astronomical tables and was responsible for introducing the concept of zero into Arab mathematics.

Kidd /kɪd/ 'Captain' (William) c. 1645–1701. Scottish pirate. He spent his youth privateering for the British against the French off the North American coast, and in 1695 was given a royal commission to suppress piracy in the Indian Ocean. Instead, he joined a group of pirates in Madagascar. On his way to Boston, Massachusetts, he was arrested 1699, taken to England, and hanged.

His execution marked the end of some 200 years of semi-official condoning of piracy by the British government.

Kiefer /ˈkiːfə/ Anselm 1945– . German painter. He studied under Joseph →Beuys, and his works include monumental landscapes on varied surfaces, often with the paint built up into relief with other substances. Much of his highly Expressionist work deals with recent German history.

Kierkegaard /ˈkɪəkəgɑːd/ Søren (Aabye) 1813–1855. Danish philosopher considered to be the founder of existentialism (the branch of philosophy based on the concept of an absurd universe where humans have free will). Disagreeing with the German dialectical philosopher →Hegel, he argued that no system of thought could explain the unique experience of the individual. He defended Christianity, suggesting that God cannot be known through reason, but only through a 'leap of faith'. He believed that God and exceptional individuals were above moral laws.

Kierkegaard was born in Copenhagen, where he spent most of his life. The son of a Jewish merchant, he converted to Christianity in 1838, although he became hostile to the established church and his beliefs caused much controversy. He was a prolific author, but his chief works are *Enten-Eller/Either-Or* 1843, *Begrebet Angest/Concept of Dread* 1844, and *Efterskrift/Postscript* 1846, which summed up much of his earlier writings.

Killy /kɪˈliː/ Jean-Claude 1943– . French skier. He won all three gold medals (slalom, giant slalom, and downhill) at the 1968 Winter Olympics in Grenoble. The first World Cup winner 1967, he retained the title 1968 and also won three world titles.

Kilmer /ˈkɪlmə/ Joyce 1886–1918. US poet. His first collection of poems *Summer of Love* was published 1911. He later gained an international reputation with the title work of *Trees and Other Poems* 1914.

Born in New Brunswick, New Jersey, USA, Kilmer was educated at Rutgers and Columbia universities. Working briefly as a high school teacher, he moved to New York and worked in a variety of publishing jobs while pursuing his own literary career. At the outbreak of World War I, Kilmer joined the 165th Regiment and was killed in action in France.

Kilmuir /kɪlˈmjʊə/ David Patrick Maxwell Fyfe, 1st Earl of Kilmuir 1900–1967. British lawyer and Conservative politician. He was solicitor-general 1942–45 and attorney-general in 1945 during the Churchill governments. He was home secretary 1951–54 and lord chancellor 1954–62.

Kilvert /ˈkɪlvət/ Francis 1840–1879. British cleric who wrote a diary recording social life on the Welsh border 1870–79, published in 1938–39.

Kim Dae Jung /ˈkɪm ˌdeɪ ˈdʒʌŋ/ 1924– . South Korean social-democratic politician. As a committed opponent of the regime of General Park Chung Hee, he suffered imprisonment and exile. He was a presidential candidate in 1971 and 1987.

A Roman Catholic, born in the poor SW province of Cholla, Kim was imprisoned by communist troops during the Korean War. He rose to prominence as an opponent of Park and was only narrowly defeated when he challenged Park for the presidency in 1971. He was imprisoned 1976–78 and 1980–82 for alleged 'anti-government activities' and lived in the USA 1982–85. On his return to South Korea he spearheaded a fragmented opposition campaign for democratization, but, being one of several opposition candidates, was defeated by the government nominee, Roh Tae Woo, in the presidential election of Dec 1987.

A political firebrand, Kim enjoys strong support among blue-collar workers and fellow Chollans, but is feared and distrusted by the country's business and military elite.

Kim Il Sung /ˈkɪm ˌiːl ˈsʊŋ/ 1912– . North Korean Communist politician and marshal. He became prime minister 1948 and president 1972, retaining the presidency of the Communist Workers' party. He likes to be known as the 'Great Leader' and has campaigned constantly for the reunification of Korea. His son *Kim Jong Il* (1942–), known as the 'Dear Leader', has been named as his successor.

Kim Young Sam /ˈkɪm ˌjʌn ˈsæm/ 1927– . South Korean democratic politician. A member of the National Assembly from 1954 and president of the New Democratic Party (NDP) from 1974, he lost his seat and was later placed under house arrest because of his opposition to President Park Chung Hee. In 1983 he led a pro-democracy hunger strike but in 1987 failed to defeat Roh Tae-Woo in the presidential election. In 1990 he merged the NDP with the ruling party to form the new Democratic Liberal Party (DLP).

King /kɪŋ/ B B (Riley) 1925– . US blues guitarist, singer, and songwriter, one of the most influential electric-guitar players, who became an international star in the 1960s. His albums include *Blues Is King* 1967, *Lucille Talks Back* 1975, and *Blues 'n' Jazz* 1983.

King /kɪŋ/ Billie Jean (born Moffitt) 1943– . US tennis player. She won a record 20 Wimbledon titles 1961–79 and 39 Grand Slam titles. She won the Wimbledon singles title six times, the US Open singles title four times, the French Open once, and the Australian Open once.

Her first Wimbledon title was the doubles with Karen Hantze 1961, and her last, also doubles, with Martina Navratilova 1979. Her 39 Grand Slam wins at singles and doubles are third only to Navratilova and Margaret Court.

King /kɪŋ/ Martin Luther Jr 1929–1968. US civil-rights campaigner, black leader, and Baptist minister. He first came to national attention as leader of the Montgomery, Alabama, bus boycott 1955, and was one of the organizers of the massive (200,000 people) march on Washington DC 1963 to demand racial equality. An advocate of nonviolence, he was awarded the Nobel Peace Prize 1964. He was assassinated in Memphis, Tennessee, by James Earl Ray (1928–).

Born in Atlanta, Georgia, son of a Baptist minister, King founded the Southern Christian Leadership Conference 1957. A brilliant and moving speaker, he was the symbol of, and leading figure in, the campaign for integration and equal rights in the late 1950s and early 1960s. In the mid-1960s his moderate approach was criticized by black militants. He was the target of intensive investigation by the federal authorities, chiefly the FBI under J Edgar →Hoover. His personal life was scrutinized and criticized by those opposed to his policies. King's birthday (15 Jan) is observed on the third Monday in Jan as a public holiday in the USA.

James Earl Ray was convicted of the murder, but there is little evidence to suggest that he committed the crime. Various conspiracy theories concerning the FBI, the CIA, and the Mafia have been suggested.

King /kɪŋ/ Stephen 1946– . US writer of best-selling horror novels with small-town or rural settings. Many of his works have been filmed, including *Carrie* 1974, *The Shining* 1978, and *Christine* 1983.

King /kɪŋ/ William Lyon Mackenzie 1874–1950. Canadian Liberal prime minister 1921–26, 1926–30, and 1935–48. He maintained the unity of the English- and French-speaking populations, and was instrumental in establishing equal status for Canada with Britain.

Kingsley Charles Kingsley, English Victorian clergyman and writer, whose children's book The Water Babies *with its originality and moral conviction has survived better than the historical novels* Westward Ho! *and* Hereward the Wake. *His 'muscular Christianity' included a streak of anti-Catholic sentiment also evident in his literary battle with Cardinal Newman: Newman is considered to have won the argument.*

Kinglake /ˈkɪŋleɪk/ Alexander William 1809–1891. British historian of the Crimean War who also wrote a Middle East travel narrative *Eothen* 1844.

Kingsley /ˈkɪŋzli/ Ben (Krishna Banji) 1944– . British film actor who usually plays character parts. He played the title role of *Gandhi* 1982 and appeared in *Betrayal* 1982, *Testimony* 1987, and *Pascali's Island* 1988.

Kingsley /ˈkɪŋzli/ Charles 1819–1875. English author. A rector, he was known as the 'Chartist clergyman' because of such social novels as *Alton Locke* 1850. His historical novels include *Westward Ho!* 1855. He also wrote *The Water Babies* 1863.

Kingsley /ˈkɪŋzli/ Mary Henrietta 1862–1900. British ethnologist. She made extensive expeditions in W Africa, and published lively accounts of her findings, for example *Travels in West Africa* 1897. She died while nursing Boer prisoners during the South African War. She was the niece of the writer Charles Kingsley.

Kinnock /ˈkɪnək/ Neil 1942– . British Labour politician, party leader 1983–92. Born and educated in Wales, he was elected to represent a Welsh constituency in Parliament 1970 (Islwyn from 1983). He was further left than prime ministers Wilson and Callaghan, but as party leader (in succession to Michael Foot) adopted a moderate position, initiating a major policy review 1988–89. He resigned as party leader after Labour's defeat in the 1992 general election.

Kino /ˈkiːnəʊ/ Eusebio Francisco c. 1644–1711. Italian-born Jesuit missionary in America. In 1687 he began exploration of Pimería Alta, now modern Sonora, Mexico, and S Arizona. There he established the missions of Tumacacori and San Xavier del Bac near modern Tucson. Kino later explored the Colorado Valley and discovered the massive prehistoric Indian ruins of Casa Grande.

Born in Italy, Kino entered the Jesuit order 1665. After teaching at the University of Ingolstadt, he was sent as a missionary to New Spain 1678. He arrived in Mexico City 1681 and joined a short-lived colony in Baja California.

Kinsey /ˈkɪnzi/ Alfred 1894–1956. US researcher whose studies of male and female sexual behaviour 1948–53, based on questionnaires, were the first serious published research on this topic.

The Institute for Sex Research at Indiana University, founded 1947, continues the objective study of human sexual behaviour. Many misconceptions, social class differences, and wide variations in practice and expectations have been discovered as a result of Kinsey's work.

Kinski /ˈkɪnski/ Klaus 1926–1991. German actor of skeletal appearance who featured in Werner Herzog's films *Aguirre Wrath of God* 1972, *Nosferatu* 1978, and *Fitzcarraldo* 1982. His other films include *For a Few Dollars More* 1965, *Dr Zhivago* 1965, and *Venom* 1982. He is the father of the actress Nastassja Kinski (1961–).

Kipling /ˈkɪplɪŋ/ (Joseph) Rudyard 1865–1936. English writer, born in India. *Plain Tales from the Hills* 1888, about Anglo-Indian society, contains the earliest of his masterly short stories. His books for children, including *The Jungle Books* 1894–95, *Just So Stories* 1902, *Puck of Pook's Hill* 1906, and the novel *Kim* 1901, reveal his imaginative identification with the exotic. Poems such as 'Danny Deever', 'Gunga Din', and 'If–' express an empathy with common experience, which contributed to his great popularity, together with a vivid sense of 'Englishness' (sometimes denigrated as a kind of jingoist imperialism). His work is increasingly valued for its complex characterization and subtle moral viewpoints. Nobel prize 1907.

Born in Bombay, Kipling was educated at the United Services College at Westward Ho!, England, which provided the background for *Stalky and Co* 1899. He worked as a journalist in India 1882–89; during these years he wrote *Plain Tales from the Hills*, *Soldiers Three* 1890, *Wee Willie Winkie* 1890, and others. Returning to London he published *The Light that Failed* 1890 and *Barrack-Room Ballads* 1892. He lived largely in the USA 1892–96, where he produced the two *Jungle Books* and *Captains Courageous* 1897. Settling in Sussex, SE England, he published *Kim* (set in India), the *Just So Stories*, *Puck of Pook's Hill*, and *Rewards and Fairies* 1910.

Kirchhoff /ˈkɪəkhɒf/ Gustav Robert 1824–1887. German physicist who with Robert →Bunsen used the spectroscope to show that all elements, heated to incandescence, have their individual spectra.

Kirchner /ˈkɪəknə/ Ernst Ludwig 1880–1938. German Expressionist artist, a leading member of the group *die Brücke* (which strove for spiritual significance, using raw colours to express different emotions) in Dresden from 1905 and in Berlin from 1911. His Dresden work, which includes woodcuts, shows the influence of African art. In Berlin he turned to city scenes and portraits, using lurid colours and bold diagonal paint strokes recalling woodcut technique. He suffered a breakdown during World War I and settled in Switzerland, where he committed suicide.

Kirk /kɜːk/ Norman 1923–1974. New Zealand Labour politician, prime minister 1972–74. He entered parliament 1957 and led the Labour Party from 1964. During his office as prime minister he withdrew New Zealand troops from the Vietnam War and attempted to block French nuclear tests in the Pacific.

Kirkland /ˈkɜːklənd/ Gelsey 1952– . US ballerina of effortless technique and innate musicality. She joined the New York City Ballet 1968, where George Balanchine staged a new *Firebird* for her 1970 and Jerome Robbins chose her for his *Goldberg Variations* 1971 and other ballets. In 1974 Mikhail Baryshnikov sought her out and she joined American Ballet Theater, where they danced in partnership, for example in *Giselle*.

Kirkpatrick /kɜːkˈpætrɪk/ Jeane 1926– . US politician and professor of political science. She served as US ambassador to the United Nations 1981–85. Originally a Democrat, she often spoke out against Communism and left-wing causes. She joined the Republican Party 1985.

Kirov /ˈkɪərɒf/ Sergei Mironovich 1886–1934. Russian Bolshevik leader who joined the party 1904 and played a prominent part in the 1918–20 civil war. As one of →Stalin's closest associates, he became first secretary of the Leningrad Communist Party. His assassination, possibly engineered by Stalin, led to the political trials held during the next four years as part of the purge of suspected opponents.

Kishi /ˈkɪʃi/ Nobusuke 1896–1987. Japanese politician and prime minister 1957–60. A government minister during World War II and imprisoned 1945, he was never put on trial and returned to politics 1953. During his premiership, Japan began a substantial rearmament programme and signed a new treaty with the USA that gave greater equality in the relationship between the two states.

Kissinger /ˈkɪsɪndʒə/ Henry 1923– . German-born US diplomat. After a brilliant academic career at Harvard University, he was appointed national security adviser 1969 by President Nixon, and was secretary of state 1973–77. His missions to the USSR and China improved US relations with both countries, and he took part in negotiating US withdrawal from Vietnam 1973 and in Arab-Israeli peace negotiations 1973–75. Nobel Peace Prize 1973.

Born in Bavaria, Kissinger emigrated to the USA 1938. After work in Germany for army counterintelligence, he won a scholarship to Harvard, and subsequently became a government consultant. His secret trips to Beijing and Moscow led to Nixon's visits to both countries and a general détente. In 1973 he shared the Nobel Peace Prize with Le Duc Tho, the North Vietnamese Politburo member, for his part in the Vietnamese peace negotiations, and in 1976 he was involved in the negotiations in Africa arising from the Angola and Rhodesia crises. In 1983, President Reagan appointed him to head a bipartisan commission on Central America. He was widely regarded as the most powerful member of Nixon's administration.

Kitaj /kɪˈtaɪ/ Ron B 1932– . US painter and printmaker, active in Britain. His work is mainly figurative, and his distinctive decorative pale palette was in part inspired by studies of the Impressionist painter Degas.

Much of Kitaj's work is outside the predominant avant-garde trend and inspired by diverse historical styles. Some compositions are in triptych form.

Kitasato /ˌkiːtəˈsɑːtəʊ/ Shibasaburo 1852–1931. Japanese bacteriologist who discovered the plague bacillus while investigating an outbreak of plague in Hong Kong. Kitasato was the first to grow the tetanus bacillus in pure culture. He and the German bacteriologist Behring discovered that increasing nonlethal doses of tetanus toxin give immunity to the disease.

He founded the Tokyo Institute for Infectious Diseases 1914, and was a friend and one-time student of Robert →Koch.

Kitchener /ˈkɪtʃɪnə/ Horatio Herbert, Earl Kitchener of Khartoum 1850–1916. British soldier and administrator. He defeated the Sudanese dervishes at Omdurman 1898 and reoccupied Khartoum. In South Africa, he was Chief of Staff 1900–02 during the Boer War, and commanded the forces in India 1902–09. He was appointed war minister on the outbreak of World War I, and drowned when his ship was sunk on the way to Russia.

Kitchener was born in County Kerry, Ireland. He was commissioned 1871, and transferred to the Egyptian army 1882. Promoted to commander in chief 1892, he forced a French expedition to withdraw in the Fashoda Incident. During the South African War he acted as Lord Roberts's Chief of Staff. He conducted war by scorched-earth policy and created the earliest concentration camps for civilians. Subsequently he commanded the forces in India and acted as British agent in Egypt, and in 1914 received an earldom. As British secretary of state for war from 1914, he modernized the British forces.

Klammer /ˈklæmə/ Franz 1953– . Austrian skier who won a record 35 World Cup downhill races between 1974 and 1985. Olympic gold medallist 1976. He was the combined world champion 1974, and the World Cup downhill champion 1975–78 and 1983.

Klaproth /ˈklæprəʊt/ Martin Heinrich 1743–1817. German chemist who first identified the elements uranium, zirconium, cerium, and titanium.

At 16 he was apprenticed to an apothecary; he began research in 1780. The first professor of chemistry at the University of Berlin, he is sometimes called 'the father of analytical chemistry'.

Klee /kleɪ/ Paul 1879–1940. Swiss painter. He settled in Munich 1906, joined the Expressionist *Blaue Reiter* group 1912, and worked at the Bauhaus school of art and design 1920–31, returning to Switzerland 1933. His style in the 1920s and 1930s was dominated by humorous linear fantasies.

Klee travelled with the painter August Macke to Tunisia 1914, a trip that transformed his sense of colour. The Klee Foundation, Berne, has a large collection of his work.

His publications include *On Modern Art* 1948.

Klein /klaɪn/ Calvin (Richard) 1942– . US fashion designer whose collections are characterized by the smooth and understated. He set up his own business 1968 specializing in designing coats and suits, and expanded into sportswear in the mid-1970s. His designer jeans became a status symbol during the same period.

Klein /klaɪn/ Melanie 1882–1960. Austrian child psychoanalyst. She pioneered child psychoanalysis and play studies, and was influenced by Sigmund →Freud's theories. She published *The Psychoanalysis of Children* 1960.

Klein intended to follow a medical career. She gave this up when she married, but after the birth of her three children became interested in psychoanalysis. In 1919 she published her first paper on the psychoanalysis of young children. She moved to London 1926, where the major part of her work was done. In 1934 Klein extended her study to adult patients, and her conclusions, based on her observations of infant and childhood anxiety, were published in her book *Envy and Gratitude* 1957.

Klein /klaɪn/ Yves 1928–1962. French painter of bold abstracts and provocative experimental works, including imprints of nude bodies.

Kleist /klaɪst/ (Bernd) Heinrich (Wilhelm) von 1777–1811. German dramatist whose comedy *Der zerbrochene Krug*/*The Broken Pitcher* 1808 and drama *Prinz Friedrich von Homburg*/*The Prince of Homburg* 1811 achieved success only after his suicide.

Kleist entered the Prussian army at the age of 14, remaining for five years. His *Michael Kohlhaus* 1808 describes a righteous schoolmaster led to carry out robbery and murder for political ends.

Klemperer /'klempərə/ Otto 1885–1973. German conductor who is celebrated for his interpretation of contemporary and Classical music (especially →Beethoven and →Brahms). He conducted the Los Angeles Orchestra 1933–39 and the Philharmonia Orchestra, London, from 1959.

Kliegl /'kliːgəl/ John H 1869–1959 and Anton T 1872–1927. German-born US brothers who in 1911 invented the brilliant carbon-arc (*klieg*) lights used in television and films. They also created scenic effects for theatre and film.

Klimt /klɪmt/ Gustav 1862–1918. Austrian painter, influenced by Jugendstil ('youth style', a form of Art Nouveau); a founding member of the Vienna *Sezession* group 1897 (a group of artists 'seceding' from official academic institutions to form new schools of painting). His paintings have a jewelled effect similar to mosaics, for example *The Kiss* 1909 (Musée des Beaux-Arts, Strasbourg). His many portraits include *Judith I* 1901 (Österreichische Galerie, Vienna).

Kline /klaɪn/ Franz 1910–1962. US Abstract Expressionist painter. He created large, graphic compositions in monochrome using angular forms, like magnified calligraphic brushstrokes.

Klopstock /'klɒpʃtɒk/ Friedrich Gottlieb 1724–1803. German poet whose religious epic *Der Messias/The Messiah* 1748–73 and *Oden/Odes* 1771 anticipated Romanticism.

God and I both knew what it meant once; now God alone knows.

Friedrich Klopstock

Kneller /'nelə/ Godfrey 1646–1723. German-born portrait painter who lived in England from 1674. He was court painter to Charles II, James II, William III, and George I.

Among his paintings are the series *Hampton Court Beauties* (Hampton Court, Richmond, Surrey, a sequel to Lely's *Windsor Beauties*), and 48 portraits of the members of the Whig Kit Cat Club 1702–17 (National Portrait Gallery, London).

Knight /naɪt/ Laura 1877–1970. English painter. She focused on detailed, narrative scenes of Romany, fairground, and circus life, and ballet.

Knipper /'knɪpə/ Lev Konstantinovich 1898–1974. Soviet composer. His early work shows the influence of →Stravinsky, but after 1932 he wrote in a more popular idiom, as in the symphony *Poem of Komsomol Fighters* 1933–34 with its mass battle songs. He is known in the West for his song 'Cavalry of the Steppes'.

Knox /nɒks/ John *c.* 1505–1572. Scottish Protestant reformer, founder of the Church of Scotland. He spent several years in exile for his beliefs, including a period in Geneva where he met John →Calvin. He returned to Scotland 1559 to promote Presbyterianism. His books include *First Blast of the Trumpet Against the Monstrous Regiment of Women* 1558.

Originally a Roman Catholic priest, Knox is thought to have been converted by the reformer George Wishart. When Wishart was burned for heresy, Knox went into hiding, but later preached the reformed doctrines.

Captured by French troops in Scotland 1547, he was imprisoned in France, sentenced to the galleys, and released only by the intercession of the British government 1549. In England he assisted in compiling the Prayer Book, as a royal chaplain from 1551. On Mary's accession 1553 he fled the country and in 1557 was, in his absence, condemned to be burned. In 1559 he returned to Scotland. He was tried for treason but acquitted 1563. He wrote a *History of the Reformation in Scotland* 1586.

Knox /nɒks/ Ronald Arbuthnott 1888–1957. British Roman Catholic scholar, whose translation of the Bible (1945–49) was officially approved by the Roman Catholic Church.

Son of an Anglican bishop, he became chaplain to the University of Oxford following his ordination 1912, but resigned 1917 on his conversion, and was Catholic chaplain 1926–39.

Koch /kɒx/ Robert 1843–1910. German bacteriologist. Koch and his assistants devised the techniques to culture bacteria outside the body, and formulated the rules for showing whether or not a bacterium is the cause of a disease. Nobel Prize for Medicine 1905.

His techniques enabled him to identify the bacteria responsible for diseases like anthrax, cholera, and tuberculosis. This was a crucial first step to the later discovery of cures for these diseases. Koch was a great teacher, and many of his pupils, such as →Kitasato, →Ehrlich, and →Behring, became outstanding scientists.

Kodály /'kəʊdaɪ/ Zoltán 1882–1967. Hungarian composer. With Béla →Bartók, he recorded and transcribed Magyar folk music, the scales and rhythm of which he incorporated in a deliberately nationalist style. His works include the cantata *Psalmus Hungaricus* 1923, a comic opera *Háry János* 1925–27, and orchestral dances and variations.

Koestler /'kɜːstlə/ Arthur 1905–1983. Hungarian author. Imprisoned by the Nazis in France 1940, he escaped to England. His novel *Darkness at Noon* 1940, regarded as his masterpiece, is a fictional account of the Stalinist purges, and draws on his experiences as a prisoner under sentence of death during the Spanish Civil War. He also wrote extensively about creativity, parapsychology, politics, and culture. He endowed Britain's first chair of parapsychology at Edinburgh, established 1984.

Born in Budapest, and educated as an engineer in Vienna, he became a journalist in Palestine and the USSR. He joined the Communist party in

Berlin 1931, but left it 1938 (he recounts his disillusionment with communism in *The God That Failed* 1950). His account of being held by the Nazis is contained in *Scum of the Earth* 1941.

Koestler's other novels include *Thieves in the Night* 1946, *The Lotus and the Robot* 1960, and *The Call Girls* 1972. His nonfiction includes *The Yogi and the Commissar* 1945, *The Sleepwalkers* 1959, *The Act of Creation* 1964, *The Ghost in the Machine* 1967, *The Roots of Coincidence* 1972, *The Heel of Achilles* 1974, and *The Thirteenth Tribe* 1976. Autobiographical works include *Arrow in the Blue* 1952 and *The Invisible Writing* 1954. He was a member of the Voluntary Euthanasia Society, and committed suicide with his wife, after suffering for a long time from Parkinson's disease.

One may not regard the world as a sort of metaphysical brothel for emotions.

Arthur Koestler *Darkness at Noon* 1940

Kohl /kəʊl/ Helmut 1930– . German conservative politician, leader of the Christian Democratic Union (CDU) from 1976, West German chancellor (prime minister) 1982–90. He oversaw the reunification of East and West Germany 1989–90 and in 1990 won a resounding victory to become the first chancellor of reunited Germany. His miscalculation of the true costs of reunification and their subsequent effects on the German economy led to a dramatic fall in his popularity.

Kohl studied law and history before entering the chemical industry. Elected to the Rhineland-Palatinate *Land* (state) parliament 1959, he became state premier 1969. After the 1976 Bundestag (federal parliament) elections Kohl led the CDU in opposition. He became federal chancellor 1982, when the Free Democratic Party (FDP) withdrew support from the socialist Schmidt government, and was elected at the head of a new coalition that included the FDP. From 1984 Kohl was implicated in the Flick bribes scandal over the illegal business funding of political parties, but he was cleared of all charges 1986, and was re-elected chancellor Jan 1987.

Kokoschka Oskar 1886–1980. Austrian Expressionist painter and writer who lived in England from 1938. Initially influenced by the Vienna *Sezession* painters (seceding from official academic institutions), he developed a disturbingly expressive portrait style. His writings include several plays.

After World War I Kokoschka worked in Dresden, then in Prague, and fled from the Nazis to England, taking British citizenship 1947. To portraiture he added panoramic landscapes and townscapes in the 1920s and 1930s, and political allegories in the 1950s.

Kolchak /kɒlˈtʃæk/ Alexander Vasilievich 1875–1920. Russian admiral, commander of the White forces in Siberia after the Russian Revolution. He proclaimed himself Supreme Ruler of Russia 1918, but was later handed over to the Bolsheviks by his own men and shot.

Koller /kɒlə/ Carl 1857–1944. Austrian ophthalmologist who introduced local anaesthesia 1884, using cocaine.

When Sigmund →Freud discovered the painkilling properties of cocaine, Koller recognized its potential as a local anaesthetic. He carried out early experiments on animals and on himself, and the technique quickly became standard in ophthalmology, dentistry, and other areas in cases where general anaesthesia is unnecessary and exposes the patient to needless risk.

Kollontai /ˌkɒlənˈtaɪ/ Alexandra 1872–1952. Russian revolutionary, politician, and writer. In 1905 she published *On the Question of the Class Struggle*, and, as commissar for public welfare, was the only female member of the first Bolshevik government. She campaigned for domestic reforms such as acceptance of free love, simplification of divorce laws, and collective child care.

In 1896, while on a tour of a large textile factory with her husband, she saw the appalling conditions endured by factory workers in Russia. Thereafter she devoted herself to improving conditions for working women. She was harassed by the police for her views and went into exile in Germany 1914. On her return to the USSR 1917 she joined the Bolsheviks. She was sent abroad by Stalin, first as trade minister, then as ambassador to Sweden 1943.

She took part in the armistice negotiations ending the Soviet-Finnish War 1944. She toured the USA to argue against its involvement in World War I and organized the first all-Russian Congress of Working and Peasant Women 1918. She published *The Love of Worker Bees* 1923.

Kollwitz /kɒlvɪts/ Käthe 1867–1945. German sculptor and printmaker. Her early series of etchings depicting workers and their environment are realistic and harshly expressive. Later themes include war, death, and maternal love.

Kong Zi Pinyin form of →Confucius, Chinese philosopher.

Koniev /kɒnjef/ Ivan Stepanovich 1898–1973. Soviet marshal who in World War II liberated Ukraine from the invading German forces 1943 and advanced from the south on Berlin to link up with the British-US forces. He commanded all Warsaw Pact forces 1955–60.

Konoe /ˌkəʊnəʊˈjeɪ/ Fumimaro, Prince 1891–1946. Japanese politician and prime minister 1937–39 and 1940–41. Entering politics in the 1920s, Konoe was active in trying to curb the power of the army in government and preventing an escalation of the war with China. He helped to engineer the fall of the →Tojo government 1944 but committed suicide after being suspected of war crimes.

Korbut /ˈkɔːbʊt/ Olga 1955– . Soviet gymnast who attracted world attention at the 1972 Olympic Games with her lively floor routine, winning three gold medals for the team, beam, and floor exercises.

Korda /ˈkɔːdə/ Alexander 1893–1956. Hungarian-born British film producer and director, a dominant figure during the 1930s and 1940s. His films include *The Private Life of Henry VIII* 1933, *The Third Man* 1950, and *Richard III* 1956.

Kornberg /ˈkɔːnbɜːg/ Arthur 1918– . US biochemist. In 1956, Kornberg discovered the enzyme DNA-polymerase, which enabled molecules of DNA to be synthesized for the first time. For this work Kornberg shared the 1959 Nobel Prize for Medicine with Severo →Ochoa.

Korngold /ˈkɔːngəʊld/ Erich Wolfgang 1897–1957. Austrian-born composer. He began composing operas while still in his teens and is known for his violin concertos. In 1934 he moved to Hollywood to become a composer for Warner Brothers. His film scores combine a richly orchestrated and romantic style, reflecting the rapid changes of mood characteristic of screen action.

Kornilov /kɔːˈniːlɒv/ Lavr 1870–1918. Russian general, commander in chief of the army, who in Aug 1917 launched an attempted coup, backed by officers, against the revolutionary prime minister, →Kerensky. The coup failed, but brought down the provisional government, thus clearing the way for the Bolsheviks to seize power.

Korolev /kəˈrɒljef/ Sergei Pavlovich 1906–1966. Soviet designer of the first Soviet intercontinental missile, used to launch the first Sputnik satellite and the Vostok spacecraft, also designed by Korolev, in which Yuri Gagarin made the world's first space flight.

Kościuszko /kɒsˈtʃʊʃkəʊ/ Tadeusz 1746–1817. Polish general and nationalist who served with George Washington in the American Revolution (1776–83). He returned to Poland 1784, fought against the Russian invasion that ended in the partition of Poland, and withdrew to Saxony. He returned 1794 to lead the revolt against the occupation, but was defeated by combined Russian and Prussian forces and imprisoned until 1796.

Kosinski /kɒˈʃɪnski/ Jerzy 1933–1991. Polish-born US author, in the USA from 1957. His childhood experiences as a Jew in Poland during World War II are recounted in *The Painted Bird* 1965, a popular success. Later novels include *Being There* 1971, filmed 1979 with Peter Sellers, and *Pinball* 1982.

Kossuth /ˈkɒʃuːt/ Lajos 1802–1894. Hungarian nationalist and leader of the revolution of 1848. He proclaimed Hungary's independence of Habsburg rule, became governor of a Hungarian republic 1849, and, when it was defeated by Austria and Russia, fled first to Turkey and then to exile in Britain and Italy.

Kosygin /kɒˈsiːɡɪn/ Alexei Nikolaievich 1904–1980. Soviet politician, prime minister 1964–80. He was elected to the Supreme Soviet 1938, became a member of the Politburo 1946, deputy prime minister 1960, and succeeded Khrushchev as premier (while Brezhnev succeeded him as party secretary). In the late 1960s Kosygin's influence declined.

Koussevitsky /ˌkuːsəˈvɪtski/ Serge 1874–1951. Russian musician and conductor, well known for his work in the US. He established his own orchestra in Moscow 1909, introducing works of Sergey Prokofiev, Sergey Rachmaninoff, and Igor Stravinsky. Although named director of the State Symphony after the Bolshevik Revolution 1917 Koussevitsky left the USSR for the USA, becoming director of the Boston Symphony Orchestra 1924.

Born in Russia, Koussevitsky was trained at a conservatory in Moscow becoming a recognized virtuoso on the double bass. He first appeared as a conductor in Berlin 1908. In 1934 he founded the annual Tanglewood summer music festival in W Massachusetts.

Kovalevsky /ˌkɒvəˈlefski/ Sonja Vasilevna 1850–1891. Russian mathematician who received a doctorate from Göttingen University 1874 for her dissertation on partial differential equations. She was professor of mathematics at the University of Stockholm from 1884. In 1886 she won the Prix Bordin of the French Academy of Sciences for a paper on the rotation of a rigid body about a point, a problem the 18th-century mathematicians Euler and Lagrange had both failed to solve.

Krafft-Ebing /ˈkræft ˈeɪbɪŋ/ Baron Richard von 1840–1902. German pioneer psychiatrist and neurologist. He published *Psychopathia Sexualis* 1886.

Educated in Germany, Krafft-Ebing became professor of psychiatry at Strasbourg 1872. His special study was the little-understood relationship between minor paralysis and syphilis, a sexually transmitted disease. In 1897 he performed an experiment which conclusively showed that his paralysed patients must previously have been infected with syphilis. He also carried out a far-reaching study of sexual behaviour.

Kravchuk Leonid 1934– . Ukrainian politician, president from July 1990. Formerly a member of the Ukrainian Communist Party (UCP), he became its ideology chief in the 1980s. After the suspension of the UCP Aug 1991, Kravchuk became an advocate of independence and market-centred economic reform.

He was directly elected to the presidency in 1991 at the same time as a referendum voted overwhelmingly in favour of independence from the USSR.

Krebs /krebz/ Hans 1900–1981. German-born British biochemist who discovered the citric acid cycle, also known as the *Krebs cycle*, the final pathway by which food molecules are converted into energy in living tissues. For this work he shared with Fritz Lipmann the 1953 Nobel Prize for Medicine.

Kreisler /ˈkraɪslə/ Fritz 1875–1962. Austrian violinist and composer, renowned as an interpreter of Brahms and Beethoven. From 1911 he was one of the earliest recording artists of Classical music, including records of his own compositions.

Krenek Ernst 1900– . Austrian-born composer. His jazz opera *Jonny spielt auf/Johnny plays up* 1927 received international acclaim.

He moved to the USA 1939 and explored the implications of contemporary and Renaissance musical theories in a succession of works and theoretical writings.

Krenz /krents/ Egon 1937– . German communist politician. A member of the East German Socialist Unity Party (SED) from 1955, he joined its politburo 1983 and was a hardline protégé of Erich →Honecker, succeeding him as party leader and head of state 1989 after widespread prodemocracy demonstrations. Pledging a 'new course', Krenz opened the country's western border and promised more open elections, but his conversion to pluralism proved weak in the face of popular protest and he resigned Dec 1989 after only a few weeks as party general secretary and head of state.

Kreutzer /ˈkrɔɪtsə/ Rodolphe 1766–1831. French violinist and composer of German descent to whom Beethoven dedicated his violin sonata Opus 47, known as the *Kreutzer Sonata*.

Krier /ˈkriːə/ Leon 1946– . Luxembourg architect. He has built little but is a polemicist and makes vivid sketches for the reconstruction of the pre-industrial European city based on early 19th-century Neo-Classicism. Prince Charles commissioned him 1988 to design a model village adjoining Dorchester, Dorset. From 1968 to 1970 Krier assisted James →Stirling with significant projects such as the Derby Civic Centre 1970 competition.

Krishna Menon /ˈmenən/ Vengalil Krishnan 1897–1974. Indian politician who was a leading light in the Indian nationalist movement. He represented India at the United Nations 1952–62, and was defence minister 1957–62, when he was dismissed by Nehru following China's invasion of N India.

He was barrister of the Middle Temple in London, and Labour member of St Pancras Borough Council 1934–47. He was secretary of the India League in the UK from 1929, and in 1947 was appointed Indian high commissioner in London. He became a member of the Indian parliament 1953, and minister without portfolio 1956. He was dismissed by Nehru 1962 when China invaded India after Menon's assurances to the contrary.

Kristiansen /ˈkrɪstjənsən/ Ingrid 1956– . Norwegian athlete, an outstanding long-distance runner of 5,000 metres, 10,000 metres, marathon, and cross-country races. She has won all the world's leading marathons. In 1986 she knocked 45.68 seconds off the world 10,000 metres record. She was the world cross-country champion 1988 and won the London marathon 1984–85 and 1987–88.

Kroeber /ˈkrəʊbə/ Alfred Louis 1876–1960. US anthropologist. His extensive research into and analysis of the culture of California, Plains, Mexican, and South American Indians dramatically broadened the scope of anthropological studies. His textbook *Anthropology* 1923, 1948 remains a classic and influential work.

Born in Hoboken, New Jersey, USA, Kroeber was the first student of Franz →Boas to receive a PhD from Columbia University 1901. After establishing a department of anthropology at the University of California at Berkeley, he led archaeological expeditions to New Mexico beginning 1915.

In 1917 he became president of the American Anthropological Association, a group he helped found. At Berkeley, Kroeber served as professor 1919–46 and anthropology museum director 1925–46.

Kropotkin /krɒˈpɒtkɪn/ Peter Alexeivich, Prince Kropotkin 1842–1921. Russian anarchist. Imprisoned for revolutionary activities 1874, he escaped to the UK 1876 and later moved to Switzerland. Expelled from Switzerland 1881, he went to France, where he was imprisoned 1883–86. He lived in Britain until 1917, when he returned to Moscow. Among his works are *Memoirs of a Revolutionist* 1899, *Mutual Aid* 1902, and *Modern Science and Anarchism* 1903.

Kropotkin was a noted geologist and geographer. In 1879 he launched an anarchist journal, *Le Révolté*. Unsympathetic to the Bolsheviks, he retired from politics after the Russian Revolution.

The word state is identical with the word war.

Peter Kropotkin

Kruger /ˈkruːgə/ Stephanus Johannes Paulus 1825–1904. President of the Transvaal 1883–1900. He refused to remedy the grievances of the uitlanders (English and other non-Boer white residents) and so precipitated the Second South African War.

Krupp /krʊp/ German steelmaking armaments firm, founded 1811 by *Friedrich Krupp* (1787–1826) and developed by *Alfred Krupp* (1812–1887) by pioneering the Bessemer steelmaking process. The company developed the long-distance artillery used in World War I, and supported Hitler's regime in preparation for World War II, after which the head of the firm, *Alfred Krupp* (1907–1967), was imprisoned.

In 1850 the first Alfred Krupp, later known as the 'cannon king', moved into the armaments business. Further expansion took place under his son **Friedrich Alfred** (1854–1902) and his granddaughter **Bertha** (1886–1957). Krupp continued to flourish as two world wars demanded iron and steel. With Germany's defeat 1945, Alfred Krupp was convicted of war crimes, sentenced to 12 years in prison, and ordered to sell 75% of his holdings. When no buyers could be found, Krupp was given a generous amnesty 1951 and was soon back in business. The family interest ended shortly after his death when his heir, Arndt, renounced all interest in the business and Krupp became a public corporation.

Kryukov /kriˈuːkɒv/ Fyodor 1870–1920. Russian writer, alleged by Alexander ➔Solzhenitsyn to be the real author of *And Quiet Flows the Don* by Mikhail ➔Sholokhov.

Kubelik /ˈkuːbəlɪk/ Jan 1880–1940. Czech violinist and composer. He performed in Prague at the age of eight, and became one of the world's greatest virtuosos; he also wrote six violin concertos.

Kubelik /ˈkuːbəlɪk/ Rafael 1914–   . Czech conductor and composer, son of violinist Jan Kubelik. His works include symphonies and operas, such as *Veronika* 1947. He was musical director of the Royal Opera House, Covent Garden, London, 1955–58.

Kublai Khan /ˈkuːblaɪ ˈkɑːn/ 1216–1294. Mongol emperor of China from 1259. He completed his grandfather ➔Genghis Khan's conquest of N China from 1240, and on his brother Mungo's death 1259 established himself as emperor of China. He moved the capital to Beijing and founded the Yuan dynasty, successfully expanding his empire into Indochina, but was defeated in an attempt to conquer Japan 1281.

Kubrick /ˈkuːbrɪk/ Stanley 1928–   . US-born British film director, producer, and screenwriter. His films include *Paths of Glory* 1957, *Dr Strangelove* 1964, *2001: A Space Odyssey* 1968, *A Clockwork Orange* 1971, and *The Shining* 1979.

More than any of his American contemporaries, Kubrick achieved complete artistic control over his films, which have been eclectic in subject matter and ambitious in both scale and technique. His other films include *Lolita* 1962 and *Full Metal Jacket* 1987.

Kuhn /kuːn/ Richard 1900–1967. Austrian chemist. Working at Heidelberg University in the 1930s, Kuhn succeeded in determining the structures of vitamins A, B2, and B6. He was awarded the 1938 Nobel Prize for Chemistry, but was unable to receive it until after World War II.

Kuhn /kuːn/ Thomas S 1922–   . US historian and philosopher of science, who showed that social and cultural conditions affect the directions of science. *The Structure of Scientific Revolutions* 1962 argued that even scientific knowledge is rel-ative, dependent on the paradigm (theoretical framework) that dominates a scientific field at the time.

Such paradigms (for example, Darwinism and Newtonian theory) are so dominant that they are uncritically accepted as true, until a 'scientific revolution' creates a new orthodoxy. Kuhn's ideas have also influenced ideas in the social sciences.

Kuiper /ˈkaɪpə/ Gerard Peter 1905–1973. Dutch-born US astronomer who made extensive studies of the Solar System. His discoveries included the atmosphere of the planet Mars and that of Titan, the largest moon of the planet Saturn.

Kuiper was adviser to many NASA exploratory missions, and pioneered the use of telescopes on high-flying aircraft. The Kuiper Airborne Observatory, one such telescope, is named after him.

Kun /kuːn/ Béla 1885–1938. Hungarian politician who created a Soviet republic in Hungary March 1919, which was overthrown Aug 1919 by a Western blockade and Romanian military actions. The succeeding regime under Admiral Horthy effectively liquidated both socialism and liberalism in Hungary.

Kundera /ˈkʊndərə/ Milan 1929–   . Czech writer, born in Brno. His first novel, *The Joke* 1967, brought him into official disfavour in Prague, and, unable to publish further works, he moved to France. Other novels include *The Book of Laughter and Forgetting* 1979 and *The Unbearable Lightness of Being* 1984.

In the world of eternal return the weight of unbearable responsibility lies heavy on every move we make.

Milan Kundera
The Unbearable Lightness of Being 1984

Küng /kʊŋ/ Hans 1928–   . Swiss Roman Catholic theologian who was barred from teaching by the Vatican 1979 'in the name of the Church' because he had cast doubt on papal infallibility, and on whether Christ was the son of God.

Kuniyoshi /ˌkuːniˈjɒʃi/ Utagawa 1797–1861. Japanese printmaker. His series *108 Heroes of the Suikoden* depicts heroes of the Chinese classic novel *The Water Margin*. Kuniyoshi's dramatic, innovative style lent itself to warriors and fantasy, but his subjects also include landscapes and cats.

Kuropatkin /ˌkʊərəˈpætkɪn/ Alexei Nikolaievich 1848–1921. Russian general. He distinguished himself as chief of staff during the Russo-Turkish War 1877–78, was commander in chief in Manchuria 1903, and resigned after his defeat at Mukden 1905 in the Russo-Japanese War. During World War I he commanded the armies on the northern front until 1916.

Kurosawa /kʊərə'sɑːwə/ Akira 1929– . Japanese director whose film *Rashōmon* 1950 introduced Western audiences to Japanese cinema. Epics such as *Shichinin no samurai/Seven Samurai* 1954 combine spectacle with intimate human drama. The nostalgic and visionary *Yume/Dreams* 1990 has autobiographical elements.

Kurosawa's films with a contemporary setting include *Drunken Angel* 1948 and *Ikiru/Living* 1952, both using illness as metaphor. *Yōjimbō* 1961, *Kagemusha* 1981, and *Ran* 1985 (loosely based on Shakespeare's *King Lear*) are historical films with an increasingly bleak outlook.

Kuti /kuːti/ Fela Anikulapo 1938– . Nigerian singer, songwriter, and musician, a strong proponent of African nationalism and ethnic identity. He had his first local hit 1971 and soon became a W African star. His political protest songs (in English) caused the Nigerian army to attack his commune 1974 and again 1977. His albums include *Coffin for Head of State* 1978 and *Teacher Don't Teach Me Nonsense* 1987.

Kutuzov /kuː'tuːzɒf/ Mikhail Larionovich, Prince of Smolensk 1745–1813. Commander of the Russian forces in the Napoleonic Wars. He commanded an army corps at Austerlitz and the army in its reatreat 1812. After the burning of Moscow that year, he harried the French throughout their retreat and later took command of the united Prussian armies.

Kuznets /kʌznets/ Simon 1901–1985. Russian-born economist who emigrated to the USA 1922. He developed theories of national income and economic growth, used to forecast the future, in *Economic Growth of Nations* 1971. He won the Nobel Prize for Economics 1971.

Kuznetsov /,kuznit'sɒf/ Anatoli 1930–1979. Russian writer. His novels *Babi Yar* 1966, describing the wartime execution of Jews at Babi Yar, near Kiev, and *The Fire* 1969, about workers in a large metallurgical factory, were seen as anti-Soviet. He lived in Britain from 1969.

Kyprianou /,kıprıə'nuː/ Spyros 1932– . Cypriot politician, president 1977–88. Foreign minister 1961–72, he founded the federalist, centre-left Democratic Front (DIKO) 1976.

Educated in Cyprus and the UK, he was called to the English Bar 1954. He became secretary to Archbishop Makarios in London 1952 and returned with him to Cyprus 1959. On the death of Makarios 1977 he became acting president and was then elected. He was defeated in the 1988 presidential elections.

L

Labèque French piano duo, sisters Katia and Marielle Labèque made their concert debut 1961, going on to win a joint first prize at the Paris Conservatoire. Their repertory includes both classical and avant-garde.

Labèque Katia (1950–) and Marielle (1952–). French pianists whose careers began in 1961. As a duo their repertoire has encompassed works by classical composers (Bach, Mozart, Brahms) as well as modern pieces (Stravinsky, Messiaen, Boulez). They also play ragtime.

La Bruyère /ˌlæbruːˈjeə/ Jean de 1645–1696. French essayist. He was born in Paris, studied law, took a post in the revenue office, and in 1684 entered the service of the French commander the Prince of →Condé. His *Caractères* 1688, satirical portraits of his contemporaries, made him many enemies.

Laclos /læˈkləʊ/ Pierre Choderlos de 1741–1803. French author. An army officer, he wrote a single novel in letter form, *Les Liaisons dangereuses/Dangerous Liaisons* 1782, an analysis of moral corruption.

La Condamine /læ ˌkɒndəˈmiːn/ Charles Marie de 1701–1774. French soldier and geographer who was sent by the French Academy of Sciences to Peru 1735–43 to measure the length of an arc of the meridian. On his return journey he travelled the length of the Amazon, writing about the use of the nerve toxin curare, india rubber, and the advantages of inoculation.

Lacroix /læˈkrwɑː/ Christian 1951– . French fashion designer who opened his couture and ready-to-wear business in 1987, after working with Jean Patou 1981–87. He made headlines with his fantasy creations, including the short puffball skirt, rose prints, and low décolleté necklines.

Ladd /læd/ Alan 1913–1964. US actor whose first leading role, as the professional killer in *This Gun for Hire* 1942, made him a star. His career declined after the mid-1950s although his last role, in *The Carpetbaggers* 1964, is considered one of his best. His other films include *The Blue Dahlia* 1946 and *Shane* 1953.

Laënnec /leɪˈnek/ René Théophile Hyacinthe 1781–1826. French physician, inventor of the stethoscope 1814. He introduced the new diagnostic technique of auscultation (evaluating internal organs by listening with a stethoscope) in his book *Traité de l'auscultation médiaté* 1819, which quickly became a medical classic.

Lafarge /ləˈfɑːʒ/ John 1835–1910. US painter and ecclesiastical designer. He is credited with the revival of stained glass in America and also created woodcuts, watercolours, and murals. Lafarge visited Europe in 1856 and the Far East in 1886. In the 1870s he turned from landscape painting (inspired by the French painter Jean-Baptiste-Camille →Corot) to religious and still-life painting. Decorating the newly built Trinity Church in Boston, Massachusetts, he worked alongside the sculptor Augustus Saint-Gaudens.

Lafayette /ˌlæfeɪˈet/ Marie Joseph Gilbert de Motier, Marquis de Lafayette 1757–1834. French soldier and politician. He fought against Britain in the American Revolution 1777–79 and 1780–82. During the French Revolution he sat in the National Assembly as a constitutional royalist and in 1789 presented the Declaration of the Rights of Man. After the storming of the Bastille, he was given command of the National Guard. In 1792 he fled the country after attempting to restore the monarchy and was imprisoned by the Austrians until 1797. He supported Napoleon Bonaparte in 1815, sat in the chamber of deputies as a Liberal from 1818, and played a leading part in the revolution of 1830.

He was a popular hero in the USA, and the cities of Lafayette in Louisiana and Indiana are named after him, as was the Lafayette Escadrille – American aviators flying for France during World War I, before the USA entered 1917.

Lafayette /ˌlæfaɪˈet/ Marie-Madeleine, Comtesse de Lafayette 1634–1693. French author. Her *Mémoires* of the French court are keenly observed, and her *La Princesse de Clèves* 1678 is the first French psychological novel and *roman à clef* ('novel with a key'), in that real-life characters (including the writer François de →La Rochefoucauld, who was for many years her lover) are presented under fictitious names.

Lafitte /ləˈfiːt/ Jean *c.* 1780–*c.* 1825. Pirate in America. Suspected of complicity with the British, he was attacked by American forces soon after the outbreak of the Anglo-American War 1812. He proved his loyalty to General Andrew Jackson by his heroic participation in the Battle of New Orleans 1815.

Reportedly born in France, Lafitte settled in New Orleans, where he became a smuggler and privateer. Gathering a band of followers around him, he set up headquarters in nearby Barataria Bay and spent several years raiding Spanish shipping in the Gulf of Mexico. After the war with England 1814 Lafitte established headquarters in Galveston Bay.

La Follette /ləˈfɒlɪt/ Robert Marion 1855–1925. US political leader. A US senator 1906–25, he was a leader of the national progressive reform movement and unsuccessfully ran for president on the Progressive ticket 1924. His memoirs *Autobiography, A Personal Narrative of Political Experiences* appeared in 1913.

Born in Primrose, Wisconsin, USA, La Follette was educated at the state university and was admitted to the bar 1880. Entering politics, he served as district attorney 1880–94 and as a member of the US House of Representatives 1885–91. He was defeated for reelection to Congress 1890 and was elected Wisconsin governor 1900.

Better a living beggar than a dead emperor.

Jean de La Fontaine *La Matrone d'Ephèse*

La Fontaine /ˌlæ fɒnˈteɪn/ Jean de 1621–1695. French poet. He was born at Château-Thierry, and from 1656 lived largely in Paris, the friend of the playwrights Molière and Racine, and the poet Boileau. His works include *Fables* 1668–94 and *Contes* 1665–74, a series of witty and bawdy tales in verse.

Lafontaine /ˌlæ fɒnˈteɪn/ Oskar 1943– . German socialist politician, federal deputy chair of the Social Democrat Party (SPD) from 1987. Leader of the Saar regional branch of the SPD from 1977 and former mayor of Saarbrucken, he was nicknamed 'Red Oskar' because of his radical views on military and environmental issues. His attitude became more conservative once he had become minister-president of Saarland in 1985.

Laforgue /læˈfɔːg/ Jules 1860–1887. French poet who pioneered free verse and who inspired later French and English writers.

Lagerfeld /ˈlɑːgəfelt/ Karl (Otto) 1939– . German-born fashion designer, a leading figure on the fashion scene from the early 1970s. As design director at Chanel for both the couture and ready-to-wear collections from 1983, he updated the Chanel look. He showed his first collection under his own label 1984.

Lagerfeld joined Chloé in the early 1960s, where he became known for high-quality ready-to-wear clothing. As fashion consultant to Fendi from 1967, he made many innovative jackets and coats.

Lagerkvist /ˈlɑːgəkvɪst/ Pär 1891–1974. Swedish author of lyric poetry, dramas (including *The Hangman* 1935), and novels, such as *Barabbas* 1950. He was awarded the 1951 Nobel Prize for Literature.

Lagerlöf /ˈlɑːgəlɜːf/ Selma 1858–1940. Swedish novelist. Her first work was the romantic historical novel *Gösta Berling's Saga* 1891. The children's fantasy *Nils Holgerssons underbara resa/The Wonderful Voyage of Nils Holgersson* 1906–07 grew from her background as a schoolteacher. She was the first woman to receive a Nobel prize, in 1909.

Lagrange /læˈgrɒnʒ/ Joseph Louis 1736–1813. French mathematician. His *Mécanique analytique* 1788 applied mathematical analysis, using principles established by Newton, to such problems as the movements of planets when affected by each other's gravitational force. He presided over the commission that introduced the metric system in 1793.

La Guardia /lə ˈgwɑːdiə/ Fiorello (Henrico) 1882–1947. US Republican politician; congressman 1917, 1919, 1923–33; mayor of New York 1933–45. Elected against the opposition of the powerful Tammany Hall Democratic Party organization, he improved the administration, suppressed racketeering, and organized unemployment relief, slum-clearance schemes, and social services. Although nominally a Republican, he supported the Democratic president F D Roosevelt's New Deal 1933 to counter the depression of 1929. La Guardia Airport, in New York City, is named after him.

Laing /læŋ/ R(onald) D(avid) 1927–1989. Scottish psychoanalyst, originator of the 'social theory' of mental illness, for example that schizophrenia is promoted by family pressure for its members to conform to standards alien to themselves. His books include *The Divided Self* 1960 and *The Politics of the Family* 1971.

We are effectively destroying ourselves by violence masquerading as love.

R D Laing *The Politics of Experience*

Lake /leɪk/ Veronica. Stage name of Constance Frances Marie Ockelman 1919–1973. US film actress who was almost as celebrated for her much imitated 'peekaboo' hairstyle as for her acting. She co-starred with Alan Ladd in several films during the 1940s, including *This Gun for Hire* and *The Glass Key* both 1942, and *The Blue Dahlia* 1946. She also appeared in *Sullivan's Travels* 1942 and *I Married a Witch* 1942.

Lalande /læ'lɑːnd/ Michel de 1657–1726. French organist and composer of church music for the court at Versailles.

Lalique /læ'liːk/ René 1860–1945. French designer and manufacturer of Art Nouveau glass, jewellery, and house interiors. The Lalique factory continues in production at Wingen-sur-Moder, Alsace, under his son Marc and granddaughter Marie-Claude.

Lalo /lɑːləʊ/ (Victor Antoine) Edouard 1823–1892. French composer. His Spanish ancestry and violin training are evident in the *Symphonie Espagnole* 1873 for violin and orchestra, and *Concerto for cello and orchestra* 1877. He also wrote an opera, *Le Roi d'Ys* 1887.

Lam /læm/ Wilfredo 1902–1982. Cuban abstract painter. Influenced by Surrealism in the 1930s (he lived in Paris 1937–41), he created a semi-abstract style using mysterious and sometimes menacing images and symbols, mainly taken from Caribbean tradition. His *Jungle* series, for example, contains voodoo elements. He visited Haiti

Lamb Charles Lamb, the humane and humorous English essayist and critic. He was the friend of such contemporaries as the Romantics Wordsworth and Coleridge. His Tales from Shakespeare, in collaboration with his sister Mary, provide a simple and attractive means of access to the stories of Shakespeare's plays.

and Martinique in the 1940s, Paris 1952, and also made frequent visits to Italy.

Lamar /lə'mɑː/ Lucius Quintus Cincinnatus 1825–1893. US jurist and public official. He was a member of the US Senate 1877–85 and served as President Cleveland's secretary of the interior 1885–87. He sat on the US Supreme Court 1888–93.

Born in Elbert County, Georgia, and educated at Emory College, Lamar was admitted to the bar 1847. After teaching at the University of Mississippi, he was elected to the US House of Representatives, serving 1857–60. During the American Civil War 1861–65 he served briefly in the Confederate army and was named Confederate envoy to Russia. After the war Lamar returned to the University of Mississippi and sat in the US House of Representatives 1873–77.

Lamarck /læ'mɑːk/ Jean Baptiste de 1744–1829. French naturalist whose theory of evolution, known as **Lamarckism**, was based on the idea that acquired characteristics (changes acquired in an individual's lifetime) are inherited, and that organisms have an intrinsic urge to evolve into better-adapted forms. His works include *Philosophie Zoologique/Zoological Philosophy* 1809 and *Histoire naturelle des animaux sans vertèbres/Natural History of Invertebrate Animals* 1815–22.

Lamartine /læmɑː'tiːn/ Alphonse de 1790–1869. French poet. He wrote romantic poems, including *Méditations poétiques* 1820, followed by *Nouvelles méditations/New Meditations* 1823, and *Harmonies* 1830. His *Histoire des Girondins/History of the Girondins* 1847 helped to inspire the revolution of 1848.

He entered the Chamber of Deputies 1833.

The human species, according to the best theory I can form of it, is composed of two distinct races: the men who borrow, and the men who lend.

Charles Lamb *The Two Races of Men*

Lamb /læm/ Charles 1775–1834. English essayist and critic. He collaborated with his sister *Mary Lamb* (1764–1847) on *Tales from Shakespeare* 1807, and his *Specimens of English Dramatic Poets* 1808 helped to revive interest in Elizabethan plays. As 'Elia' he contributed essays to the *London Magazine* from 1820 (collected 1823 and 1833).

Born in London, Lamb was educated at Christ's Hospital. He was a contemporary of →Coleridge, with whom he published some poetry in 1796. He was a clerk at India House 1792–1825, when he retired to Enfield. His sister Mary stabbed their mother to death in a fit of insanity in 1796, and Charles cared for her between her periodic returns to an asylum.

Lamb /læm/ Willis 1913– . US physicist who revised the quantum theory of Paul →Dirac. The hydrogen atom was thought to exist in either of two distinct states carrying equal energies. More sophisticated measurements by Lamb in 1947 demonstrated that the two energy levels were not equal. This discrepancy, since known as the *Lamb shift* won him the 1955 Nobel Prize for Physics.

Lambert /læmbət/ John 1619–1683. English general, a cavalry commander in the Civil War under Cromwell (at the battles of Marston Moor, Preston, Dunbar, and Worcester). Lambert broke with Cromwell over the proposal to award him the royal title. After the Restoration he was imprisoned for life.

Lamburn /læmbɜːn/ Richmal Crompton. Full name of British writer Richmal →Crompton.

Lamming /læmɪŋ/ George 1927– . Barbadian novelist, author of the autobiographical *In the Castle of my Skin* 1953, describing his upbringing in the small village where he was born.

Lamont Norman 1942– . UK Conservative politician, chief secretary of the Treasury 1989–90, chancellor of the Exchequer from 1990. In Sept 1992, despite earlier assurances to the contrary, he was forced to suspend Britain's membership of the European Monetary System (EMS).

Born in the Shetland Islands and educated at Cambridge, Lamont was elected to Parliament 1972 as member for Kingston upon Thames. He masterminded John Major's leadership campaign. As chancellor of the Exchequer, he firmly backed Britain's membership of the ERM and, despite signs that the pound was in trouble, specifically ruled out devaluation 10 Sept 1992. A week later, in the face of mounting international pressure on the pound, he was forced to devalue and withdraw from the ERM, inciting fierce criticism and calls for his resignation. In Nov he produced a package of reforms aimed at stimulating economic growth, but his future as chancellor remained in doubt.

Lampedusa /ˌlæmpɪˈduːzə/ Giuseppe Tomasi di 1896–1957. Italian aristocrat, author of *The Leopard* 1958, a novel set in his native Sicily during the period following its annexation by Garibaldi in 1860. It chronicles the reactions of an aristocratic family to social and political upheavals.

Lancaster /ˈlæŋkəstə/ Burt (Burton Stephen) 1913– . US film actor, formerly an acrobat. A star from his first film, *The Killers* 1946, he proved himself adept both at action roles and more complex character parts as in such films as *From Here to Eternity* 1953, *The Rose Tattoo* 1955, *Elmer Gantry* 1960, and *The Leopard/Il Gattopardo* 1963.

Lancaster /ˈlæŋkəstə/ Osbert 1908–1986. English cartoonist and writer. In 1939 he began producing daily 'pocket cartoons' for the *Daily Express*, in which he satirized current social mores through such characters as Maudie Littlehampton. He was originally a book illustrator and muralist.

In the 1930s and 1940s he produced several tongue-in-cheek guides to architectural fashion (such as *Homes, Sweet Homes* 1939 and *Drayneflete Revisited* 1949), from which a number of descriptive terms, such as Pont Street Dutch and Stockbroker Tudor, have entered the language. He was knighted 1975.

Lancaster, House of English royal house, a branch of the Plantagenets.

It originated in 1267 when Edmund (died 1296), the younger son of Henry III, was granted the earldom of Lancaster. Converted to a duchy for Henry of Grosmont (died 1361), it passed to John of Gaunt in 1362 by his marriage to Blanche, Henry's daughter. John's son, Henry IV, established the royal dynasty of Lancaster in 1399, and he was followed by two more Lancastrian kings, Henry V and Henry VI.

Lancret /lɒŋˈkreɪ/ Nicolas 1690–1743. French painter. His graceful *fêtes galantes* (festive groups of courtly figures in fancy dress) followed a theme made popular by Watteau. He also illustrated amorous scenes from the *Fables* of La Fontaine.

Land /lænd/ Edwin Herbert 1909–1991. US inventor of the Polaroid Land camera 1947, which developed the film in one minute inside the camera and produced an 'instant' photograph.

Landau /lændaʊ/ Lev Davidovich 1908–1968. Russian theoretical physicist. He was awarded the 1962 Nobel Prize for Physics for his work on liquid helium.

Landis /lændɪs/ Kenesaw Mountain 1866–1944. US judge and baseball commissioner. He was judge in the fraud trial of the infamous 'Black Sox' who conspired with gamblers to deliberately lose the 1919 World Series. Appointed as the first commissioner of major-league baseball 1921 he established strict standards against players' involvement with betting.

Born in Millville, Ohio, Landis received his law degree 1891. He was appointed federal district judge in Chicago 1905 and presided in important antitrust and labour relations cases.

Landon /lændən/ Alf(red Mossman) 1887–1987. US public official. As a popular liberal Republican, Landon ran for president against the incumbent F D Roosevelt 1936 but was overwhelmingly defeated. He later accepted a presidential appointment as US delegate to the 1938 Pan-American Conference.

Born in West Middlesex, Pennsylvania, USA, Landon was raised in Kansas and received a law degree from the University of Kansas 1908. After a successful career in business, he entered politics and was elected governor of Kansas 1932. After World War II, Landon became a spokesman for the elimination of trade barriers and for international development.

Landor /ˈlændɔː/ Walter Savage 1775–1864. English poet and essayist. He lived much of his life abroad, dying in Florence, where he had fled after a libel suit in 1858. His works include the epic *Gebir* 1798 and *Imaginary Conversations of Literary Men and Statesmen* 1824–29.

Landowska /læn'dɒfskə/ Wanda 1877–1959. Polish harpsichordist and scholar. She founded a school near Paris for the study of early music, and was for many years one of the few artists regularly performing on the harpsichord. In 1941 she moved to the USA.

Landsbergis /lændzbɜːgɪs/ Vytautas 1932– . President of Lithuania 1990–1993. He became active in nationalist politics in the 1980s, founding and eventually chairing the anticommunist Sajudis independence movement 1988. When Sajudis swept to victory in the republic's elections March 1990, Landsbergis chaired the Supreme Council of Lithuania becoming, in effect, president. He immediately drafted the republic's declaration of independence from the USSR which, after initial Soviet resistance, was recognized Sept 1991.

Landseer /ˈlændsɪə/ Edwin Henry 1802–1873. English painter, sculptor, and engraver of animal studies. Much of his work reflects the Victorian taste for sentimental and moralistic pictures, for example *Dignity and Impudence* 1839 (Tate Gallery, London). The *Monarch of the Glen* (John Dewar and Sons Ltd) 1850, depicting a highland stag, was painted for the House of Lords. His sculptures include the lions at the base of Nelson's Column in Trafalgar Square, London, 1857–67.

Landsteiner /ˈlændstaɪnə/ Karl 1868–1943. Austrian-born immunologist who discovered the ABO blood group system 1900–02, and aided in the discovery of the Rhesus blood factors 1940. He also discovered the polio virus. He was awarded a Nobel prize in 1930.

Landsteiner worked at the Vienna Pathology Laboratory, and the Rockefeller Institute for Medical Research, New York, where he was involved in the discovery of the MN blood groups in 1927. In 1936 he wrote *The Specificity of Serological Reactions*, which helped establish the science of immunology. He also developed a test for syphilis.

Lane /leɪn/ Edward William 1801–1876. English traveller and translator, one of the earliest English travellers to Egypt to learn Arabic; his pseudo-scholarly writings, including *Manners and Customs of the Modern Egyptians* 1836 and an annotated translation of the *Arabian Nights* 1838–40, propagated a stereotyped image of the Arab world.

Lanfranc /ˈlænfræŋk/ *c*. 1010–1089. Italian archbishop of Canterbury from 1070; he rebuilt the cathedral, replaced English clergy by Normans, enforced clerical celibacy, and separated the ecclesiastical from the secular courts.

His skill in theological controversy did much to secure the church's adoption of the doctrine of transubstantiation. He came over to England with William the Conqueror, whose adviser he was.

Lanfranc was born in Pavia, Italy; he entered the monastery of Bec, Normandy, in 1042, where he opened a school; St Anselm, later his successor, was his pupil there.

Lang /læŋ/ Andrew 1844–1912. Scottish historian and folklore scholar. His writings include historical works; anthropological essays, such as *Myth, Ritual and Religion* 1887 and *The Making of Religion* 1898, which involved him in controversy with the anthropologist James G →Frazer; novels; and a series of children's books, beginning with *The Blue Fairy Tale Book* 1889.

Lang /læŋ/ Fritz 1890–1976. Austrian film director whose films are characterized by a strong sense of fatalism and alienation. His German films include *Metropolis* 1927, the sensational *M* 1931, in which Peter Lorre starred as a child-killer, and the series of Dr Mabuse films, after which he fled from the Nazis to Hollywood in 1936. His US films include *Fury* 1936, *You Only Live Once* 1937, *Scarlet Street* 1945, *Rancho Notorious* 1952, and *The Big Heat* 1953. He returned to Germany and directed a third picture in the Dr Mabuse series in 1960.

lang k d 1961– . Canadian singer whose mellifluous voice and androgynous image gained her a wide following beyond the country-music field where she first established herself. Albums include *Angel With a Lariat* 1987, *Shadowland* 1988, *Absolute Torch and Twang* 1989, and the mainstream *Ingénue* 1992.

Lang, born in Consort, Alberta, started out as a performance artist. As a vocalist, she has been particularly influenced by US country singer Patsy Cline, whose material she often covers; she calls her backing band the Reclines. She made her debut as an actress 1992 starring in the film *Salmonberries* by Percy Adlon.

Lange /læŋ/ David (Russell) 1942– . New Zealand Labour prime minister 1983–89. Lange, a barrister, was elected to the House of Representatives 1977. Labour had a decisive win in the 1984 general election on a non-nuclear military policy, which Lange immediately put into effect, despite criticism from the USA. He introduced a free-market economic policy and was re- elected 1987. He resigned Aug 1989 over a disagreement with his finance minister.

Lange /læŋ/ Dorothea 1895–1965. US photographer who was hired in 1935 by the federal Farm Security Administration to document the westward migration of farm families from the Dust Bowl of the S central USA. Her photographs, characterized by a gritty realism, were widely exhibited and subsequently published as *An American Exodus: A Record of Human Erosion* 1939.

Langer Bernhard 1957– . German golfer who came to prominence in 1981 when he became Europe's leading money winner and made his

Ryder Cup debut. In 1985 he won the US Masters.

Germany's first international golfing star, he may sadly be remembered for missing a putt on the final green that would have retained the 1991 Ryder Cup.

Langevin /lɒnʒ'væ̃/ Paul 1872–1946. French physicist who contributed to the studies of magnetism and X-ray emissions. During World War I he invented an apparatus for locating enemy submarines. The nuclear institute at Grenoble is named after him.

Langland /'læŋlənd/ William c. 1332–c. 1400. English poet. His alliterative *Vision Concerning Piers Plowman* appeared in three versions between about 1362 and 1398, but some critics believe he was only responsible for the first of these. The poem forms a series of allegorical visions, in which Piers develops from the typical poor peasant to a symbol of Jesus, and condemns the social and moral evils of 14th-century England.

In a somer season, when soft was the sonne.

William Langland
Vision Concerning Piers Plowman Prologue

Langley /'læŋli/ Samuel Pierpoint 1834–1906. US astronomer, scientist, and inventor of the bolometer. His steam-driven aeroplane flew for 90 seconds in 1896 – the first flight by an engine-equipped aircraft.

He was professor of physics and astronomy at the Western University of Pennsylvania 1866–87, and studied the infrared portions of the solar system.

Langmuir /'læŋmjʊə/ Irving 1881–1957. US scientist who invented the mercury vapour pump for producing a high vacuum, and the atomic hydrogen welding process; he was also a pioneer of the thermionic valve. In 1932 he was awarded a Nobel prize for his work on surface chemistry.

Langton /'læŋtən/ Stephen c. 1150–1228. English priest who was mainly responsible for drafting the charter of rights, the Magna Carta.

He studied in Paris, where he became chancellor of the university, and in 1206 was created a cardinal. When in 1207 Pope Innocent III secured Langton's election as archbishop of Canterbury, King John refused to recognize him, and he was not allowed to enter England until 1213. He supported the barons in their struggle against John and worked for revisions to both church and state policies.

Langtry /'læŋtri/ Lillie. Stage name of Emilie Charlotte le Breton 1853–1929. English actress, mistress of the future Edward VII. She was known as the 'Jersey Lily' from her birthplace in the

Channel Islands and considered to be one of the most beautiful women of her time.

She was the daughter of a rector, and married Edward Langtry (died 1897) in 1874. She first appeared professionally in London in 1881, and had her greatest success as Rosalind in Shakespeare's *As You Like It*. In 1899 she married Sir Hugo de Bathe.

Lanier /lə'nɪə/ Sidney 1842–1881. US flautist and poet. His *Poems* 1877 contain interesting metrical experiments, in accordance with the theories expounded in his *Science of English Verse* 1880, on the relation of verse to music.

Lansbury /'lænzbəri/ George 1859–1940. British Labour politician, leader in the Commons 1931–35. In 1921, while mayor of the London borough of Poplar, he went to prison with most of the council rather than modify their policy of more generous unemployment relief. He was a member of Parliament for Bow 1910–12, when he resigned to force a by-election on the issue of votes for women, which he lost. He was again member of Parliament for Bow 1922–40; he was leader of the parliamentary Labour party 1931–35, but resigned (as a pacifist) in opposition to the party's militant response to the Italian invasion of Abyssinia (present-day Ethiopia).

He was editor of the *Daily Herald* 1912, carried it on as a weekly through World War I, and again as a daily until 1922.

Langtry British actress Lillie Langtry, one of the celebrated beauties of her time. She made her first important stage appearance 1888 in London. In 1901 she opened the Imperial Theatre in London which she managed, although it never became successful. She later became well known as a racehorse owner.

Lansdowne /ˈlænzdaʊn/ Henry Charles, 5th Marquis of Lansdowne 1845–1927. British Liberal Unionist politician, governor-general of Canada 1883–88, viceroy of India 1888–93, war minister 1895–1900, and foreign secretary 1900–06. While at the Foreign Office he abandoned Britain's isolationist policy by forming an alliance with Japan and an entente cordiale with France. His letter of 1917 suggesting an offer of peace to Germany created a controversy.

Lao Zi /ˌlaʊˈdziː/ or Lao Tzu c. 604–531 BC. Chinese philosopher, commonly regarded as the founder of Taoism, with its emphasis on the Tao, the inevitable and harmonious way of the universe. Nothing certain is known of his life, and he is variously said to have lived in the 6th or the 4th century BC. The *Tao Tê Ching*, the Taoist scripture, is attributed to him but apparently dates from the 3rd century BC.

Laplace /læˈplæs/ Pierre Simon, Marquis de Laplace 1749–1827. French astronomer and mathematician. In 1796, he theorized that the solar system originated from a cloud of gas (the nebular hypothesis). He studied the motion of the Moon and planets, and published a five-volume survey of celestial mechanics, *Traité de méchanique céleste* 1799–1825. Among his mathematical achievements was the development of probability theory.

Lardner /ˈlɑːdnə/ Ring 1885–1933. US short-story writer. A sports reporter, he based his characters on the people he met professionally. His collected volumes of short stories include *You Know Me, Al* 1916, *Round Up* 1929, and *Ring Lardner's Best Short Stories* 1938, all written in colloquial language.

Largo Caballero /ˈlɑːgəʊ ˌkæbəˈjeərəʊ/ Francisco 1869–1946. Spanish socialist and leader of the Spanish Socialist Party (PSOE). He became prime minister of the Popular Front government elected in Feb 1936 and remained in office for the first ten months of the Civil War before being replaced in May 1937 by Juan Negrin (1887–1956).

Larionov /ˌlæriˈɒnəf/ Mikhail Fedorovich 1881–1964. Russian painter, active in Paris from 1919. With his wife Natalia Goncharova, he pioneered a semi-abstract style known as Rayonnism in which subjects appear to be deconstructed by rays of light from various sources. Larionov also produced stage sets for Diaghilev's *Ballets Russes* from 1915. In Paris he continued to work as a theatrical designer and book illustrator.

Larkin /ˈlɑːkɪn/ Philip 1922–1985. English poet. His perfectionist, pessimistic verse includes *The North Ship* 1945, *The Whitsun Weddings* 1964, and *High Windows* 1974. He edited *The Oxford Book of 20th-Century English Verse* 1973.

Born in Coventry, Larkin was educated at Oxford, and from 1955 was librarian at Hull University. He also wrote two novels.

La Rochefoucauld /læ ˌrɒʃfuːˈkəʊ/ François, duc de La Rochefoucauld 1613–1680. French writer. His *Réflexions, ou sentences et maximes morales/Reflections, or Moral Maxims* 1665 is a collection of brief, epigrammatic, and cynical observations on life and society, with the epigraph 'Our virtues are mostly our vices in disguise'. He was a lover of Mme de →Lafayette.

Born in Paris, he became a soldier, and took part in the *Fronde* revolts against the administration of the chief minister Mazarin during Louis XIV's minority. His later years were divided between the court and literary society.

One is never so happy or so unhappy as one thinks.

La Rochefoucauld *Maxims*

Larousse /læˈruːs/ Pierre 1817–1875. French grammarian and lexicographer. His encyclopedic dictionary, the *Grand dictionnaire universel du XIXème siècle/Great Universal 19th-Century Dictionary* 1865–76, continues to be published in revised form.

Larsson /ˈlɑːsən/ Carl 1853–1919. Swedish painter, engraver, and illustrator. His watercolours of domestic life, delicately coloured and full of detail, were painted for his book *Ett Hem/A Home* 1899.

Lartigue /lɑːˈtiːg/ Jacques-Henri 1894–1986. French photographer. He began taking photographs of his family at the age of seven, and went on to make autochrome colour prints of women. During his lifetime he took over 40,000 photographs, documenting everyday people and situations.

la Salle /lə ˈsæl/ René Robert Cavelier, Sieur de la Salle 1643–1687. French explorer. He made an epic voyage through North America, exploring the Mississippi River down to its mouth, and in 1682 founded Louisiana. When he returned with colonists, he failed to find the river mouth again, and was eventually murdered by his mutinous men.

Las Casas /læs ˈkɑːsəs/ Bartolomé de 1474–1566. Spanish missionary, historian, and colonial reformer, known as *the Apostle of the Indies*. He was one of the first Europeans to call for the abolition of Indian slavery in Latin America. He took part in the conquest of Cuba in 1513, but subsequently worked for American Indian freedom in the Spanish colonies. *Apologetica historia de las Indias* (first published 1875–76) is his account of Indian traditions and his witnessing of Spanish oppression of the Indians.

Las Casas sailed to Hispaniola in the West Indies in 1502 and was ordained priest there in 1512. From Cuba he returned to Spain in 1515 to plead for the Indian cause, winning the support of the Holy Roman emperor Charles V. In what is now Venezuela he unsuccessfully attempted to found a settlement of free Indians. In 1530, shortly before the conquest of Peru, he persuaded the Spanish government to forbid slavery there. In 1542 he became bishop of Chiapas in S Mexico. He returned finally to Spain in 1547.

Lasdun /ˈlæzdən/ Denys 1914– . British architect. He designed the Royal College of Surgeons in Regent's Park, London 1960–64, some of the buildings at the University of East Anglia, Norwich, and the National Theatre 1976–77 on London's South Bank. He was knighted 1976.

Laski /ˈlæski/ Harold 1893–1950. British political theorist. Professor of political science at the London School of Economics from 1926, he taught a modified Marxism and published *A Grammar of Politics* 1925 and *The American Presidency* 1940. He was chairman of the Labour Party 1945–46.

The meek do not inherit the Earth unless they are prepared to fight for their meekness.

Harold Laski (attrib.)

Lassalle /læˈsæl/ Ferdinand 1825–1864. German socialist. He was imprisoned for his part in the revolution of 1848, during which he met the philosopher Karl →Marx, and in 1863 founded the General Association of German Workers (later the Social-Democratic Party). His publications include *The Working Man's Programme* 1862 and *The Open Letter* 1863. He was killed in a duel arising from a love affair.

Lassus /ˈlæsəs/ Roland de. Also known as *Orlando di Lasso* c. 1532–1594. Franco-Flemish composer. His works include polyphonic sacred music, songs, and madrigals, including settings of poems by his friend →Ronsard.

Latimer /ˈlætɪmə/ Hugh 1490–1555. English Christian church reformer and bishop. After his conversion to Protestantism in 1524 he was imprisoned several times but was protected by Cardinal Wolsey and Henry VIII. After the accession of the Catholic Mary, he was burned for heresy.

Latimer was appointed bishop of Worcester in 1535, but resigned in 1539. Under Edward VI his sermons denouncing social injustice won him great influence, but he was arrested in 1553, once Mary was on the throne, and two years later he was burned at the stake in Oxford.

La Tour /læˈtuə/ Georges de 1593–1652. French painter active in Lorraine. He was patronized by the duke of Lorraine and perhaps also by Louis XIII. Many of his pictures are illuminated by a single source of light, with deep contrasts of light and shade. They range from religious paintings to domestic genre scenes.

La Trobe /lə ˈtrəub/ Charles Joseph 1801–1875. Australian administrator. He was superintendent of Port Phillip district 1839–51 and first lieutenant governor of Victoria 1851–54. The Latrobe River in Victoria is named after him.

Latsis /ˈlætsɪs/ John 1910– . Greek multimillionaire shipping tycoon who, in addition to a tanker and cargo fleet, has oil and construction interests. His donation of £2 million to the UK Conservative Party drew renewed attention to his support for the right-wing military junta that ruled Greece 1967–74.

Latynina /læˈtɪnɪnə/ Larissa Semyonovna 1935– . Soviet gymnast, winner of more Olympic medals than any person in any sport. She won 18 between 1956 and 1964, including nine gold medals. She won a total of 12 individual Olympic and world championship gold medals.

Laud /lɔːd/ William 1573–1645. English priest; archbishop of Canterbury from 1633. Laud's High Church policy, support for Charles I's unparliamentary rule, censorship of the press, and persecution of the Puritans all aroused bitter opposition, while his strict enforcement of the statutes against enclosures and of laws regulating wages and prices alienated the propertied classes. His attempt to impose the use of the Prayer Book on the Scots precipitated the English Civil War. Impeached by Parliament 1640, he was imprisoned in the Tower of London, summarily condemned to death, and beheaded.

Laud William Laud, Anglican cleric and archbishop of Canterbury under Charles I. A zealous opponent of Puritanism, he tried to suppress Presbyterianism in Scotland and Calvinism in England. He left his large collection of manuscripts and coins to the Bodleian Library, Oxford.

Laurel and Hardy US double act Laurel (left) and Hardy, one of the most successful comedy teams in cinema history. Together from 1926 to 1952, they made a huge number of short films as well as full-length feature films. Their career successfully spanned the eras of silent and talking pictures.

Lauda /ˈlaʊdə/ Niki 1949– . Austrian motor racing driver who won the world championship in 1975, 1977 and 1984. He was also runner-up in 1976 just six weeks after a serious accident at Nurburgring, Germany, which left him badly burned and permanently scarred.

Lauda was Formula Two champion in 1972, and drove for March, BRM, Ferrari, and Brabham before his retirement in 1978. He returned to the sport in 1984 and won his third world title in a McLaren before eventually retiring in 1985 to concentrate on his airline business, Lauda-Air.

Lauder /ˈlɔːdə/ Harry. Stage name of Hugh MacLennan 1870–1950. Scottish music-hall comedian and singer who began his career as an 'Irish' comedian.

Lauderdale /ˈlɔːdədeɪl/ John Maitland, Duke of Lauderdale 1616–1682. Scottish politician. Formerly a zealous Covenanter, he joined the Royalists 1647, and as high commissioner for Scotland 1667–1679 persecuted the Covenanters. He was created duke of Lauderdale 1672, and was a member of the Cabal ministry 1667–73.

Laue /ˈlaʊə/ Max Theodor Felix von 1879–1960. German physicist who was a pioneer in measuring the wavelength of X-rays by their diffraction through the closely spaced atoms in a crystal. His work led to the powerful technique (X-ray diffraction) now used to elucidate the structure of complex biological materials such as DNA. He was awarded a Nobel prize in 1914.

Laughton /ˈlɔːtn/ Charles 1899–1962. English actor who became a US citizen in 1950. Initially a classical stage actor, he joined the Old Vic 1933. His films were made in Hollywood and include such roles as the king in *The Private Life of Henry VIII* 1933 (Academy Award), Captain Bligh in *Mutiny on the Bounty* 1935, and Quasimodo in *The Hunchback of Notre Dame* 1939. In 1955 he directed *Night of the Hunter* and in 1961 appeared in *Judgment at Nuremberg*.

Method actors give you a photograph. Real actors give you an oil painting.

Charles Laughton in *Playboy* 1962

Laurel and Hardy /ˈlɒrəl, ˈhɑːdi/ Stan Laurel (stage name of Arthur Stanley Jefferson) (1890–1965) and Oliver Hardy (1892–1957). US film comedians who were one of the most successful comedy teams in film history (Stan was slim, Oliver rotund). Their partnership began in 1927, survived the transition from silent films to sound, and resulted in more than 200 short and feature-length films, which were revived as a worldwide cult in the 1970s. Among these are *Pack Up Your Troubles* 1932, *Our Relations* 1936, and *A Chump at Oxford* 1940.

Laurel, a British-born former music-hall comedian, conceived the gags and directed their feature films *Babes in Toyland* 1934, *Way Out West* 1937, and *Swiss Miss* 1938. In 1940 they formed a production company and made films until 1945.

Lauren /ˈlɔːrən/ Ralph 1939– . US fashion designer, producing menswear under the Polo label from 1968, women's wear from 1971, children's wear, and home furnishings from 1983. He also designed costumes for the films *The Great Gatsby* 1973 and *Annie Hall* 1977.

Laurence /ˈlɒrəns/ Margaret 1926–1987. Canadian writer whose novels include *A Jest of God* 1966 and *The Diviners* 1974. She also wrote short stories set in Africa, where she lived for a time.

Laurier /ˈlɒrieɪ/ Wilfrid 1841–1919. Canadian politician, leader of the Liberal Party 1887–1919 and prime minister 1896–1911. The first French-Canadian to hold the office, he encouraged immigration into Canada from Europe and the USA, established a separate Canadian navy, and sent troops to help Britain in the Boer War.

Laval /ləˈvæl/ Pierre 1883–1945. French right-wing politician. He was prime minister and foreign secretary 1931–32, and again 1935–36. In World War II he joined Pétain's Vichy government as vice-premier in June 1940; dismissed in Dec 1940, he was reinstated by Hitler's orders as head of the government and foreign minister in 1942. After the war he was executed.

Laval, born near Vichy, entered the chamber of deputies in 1914 as a socialist, but after World War I moved towards the right. His second period as prime minister was marked by the Hoare–Laval Pact for concessions to Italy in Abyssinia (now Ethiopia). His part in the deportation of French labour to Germany during World War II made him universally hated. When the Allies invaded, he fled the country but was arrested in Austria, tried for treason, and shot after trying to poison himself.

If peace is a chimera, I am happy to have caressed her.

Pierre Laval

La Vallière /læ ˌvæliˈeə/ Louise de la Baume le Blance, Duchesse de La Vallière 1644–1710. Mistress of the French king Louis XIV; she gave birth to four children 1661–74. She retired to a convent when superseded in his affections by the Marquise de Montespan.

Laver /ˈleɪvə/ Rod(ney George) 1938– . Australian lawn tennis player. He was one of the greatest left-handed players, and the only player to win the Grand Slam twice (1962 and 1969).

He won four Wimbledon singles titles, the Australian title three times, the US Open twice, and the French Open twice. He turned professional after winning Wimbledon in 1962 but returned when the championships were opened to professionals in 1968.

Lavery /ˈleɪvəri/ John 1856–1941. British portrait-painter of Edwardian society.

Lavoisier /læˈvwæzieɪ/ Antoine Laurent 1743–1794. French chemist. He proved that combustion needed only a part of the air, which he called oxygen, thereby destroying the theory of phlogiston (an imaginary 'fire element' released during combustion). With Pierre de Laplace, the astronomer and mathematician, he showed that water was a compound of oxygen and hydrogen. In this way he established the basic rules of chemical combination.

Lavrentiev /læˈvrentief/ Mikhail 1900– . Soviet scientist who developed the Akademgorodok ('Science City') in Novosibirsk, Russia from 1957.

Law /lɔː/ Andrew Bonar 1858–1923. British Conservative politician. Elected leader of the opposition 1911, he became colonial secretary in Asquith's coalition government 1915–16, chancellor of the Exchequer 1916–19, and Lord Privy Seal 1919–21 in Lloyd George's coalition. He formed a Conservative Cabinet 1922, but resigned on health grounds.

Born in New Brunswick, Canada, he made a fortune in Scotland as a banker and iron-merchant before entering Parliament 1900.

Law /lɔː/ William 1686–1761. English cleric. His Jacobite opinions caused him to lose his fellowship at Emmanuel College, Cambridge, in 1714. His work *A Serious Call to a Devout and Holy Life* 1728 influenced John Wesley, the founder of Methodism.

Lawes /lɔːz/ Henry 1596–1662. British composer whose works include music for Milton's masque *Comus* 1634. His brother **William Lawes** (1602–1645) was also a composer.

Lawes /lɔːz/ John Bennet 1814–1900. English agriculturist who patented the first artificial 'super-phosphate' fertilizer. In 1843 he established the Rothamsted Experimental Station (Hertfordshire) at his birthplace.

Lawler /ˈlɔːlə/ Ray(mond Evenor) 1921– . Australian playwright whose work includes *The Summer of the Seventeenth Doll* 1955, a play about sugar-cane cutters, in which he played the lead role in the first production in Melbourne.

Lawrence /ˈlɒrəns/ D(avid) H(erbert) 1885–1930. English writer whose work expresses his belief in emotion and the sexual impulse as creative and true to human nature. The son of a Nottinghamshire miner, Lawrence studied at University College, Nottingham, and became a teacher. His writing first received attention after the publication of the semi-autobiographical *Sons and Lovers* 1913, which includes a portrayal of his mother (died 1911). Other novels include, *The Rainbow* 1915, *Women in Love* 1921, and *Lady Chatterley's Lover* 1928. Lawrence also wrote short stories (for example 'The Woman Who Rode Away') and poetry.

In 1914 he married Frieda von Richthofen, ex-wife of his university professor, with whom he had run away in 1912. Frieda was the model for Ursula Brangwen in *The Rainbow*, which was suppressed for obscenity, and its sequel, *Women in Love*. Lawrence's travels in search of health (he suffered from tuberculosis, from which he eventually died near Nice) prompted books such as *Mornings in Mexico* 1927. *Lady Chatterley's Lover* was banned as obscene in the UK until 1960.

I like to write when I feel spiteful: it's like having a good sneeze.

D H Lawrence letter to Lady Cynthia Asquith
Nov 1913

Lawrence /ˈlɒrəns/ Ernest O(rlando) 1901–1958. US physicist. His invention of the cyclotron particle accelerator pioneered the production of artificial radioisotopes.

He was professor of physics at the University of California, Berkeley, from 1930 and director from 1936 of the Radiation Laboratory, which he built into a major research centre for nuclear physics. He was awarded a Nobel prize in 1939.

Lawrence /ˈlɒrəns/ Gertrude 1898–1952. English actress who began as a dancer in the 1920s and later took leading roles in musical comedies. Her greatest successes were in the play *Private Lives* 1930–31, written especially for her by Noël Coward, with whom she co-starred, and *The King and I* 1951.

Lawrence /ˈlɒrəns/ T(homas) E(dward), known as *Lawrence of Arabia* 1888–1935. British soldier and writer. Appointed to the military intelligence department in Cairo, Egypt, during World War I, he took part in negotiations for an Arab revolt against the Ottoman Turks, and in 1916 attached himself to the emir Faisal. He became a guerrilla leader of genius, combining raids on Turkish communications with the organization of a joint Arab revolt, described in *The Seven Pillars of Wisdom* 1926.

Lawrence /ˈlɒrəns/ Thomas 1769–1830. British painter, the leading portraitist of his day. He became painter to George III 1792 and president of the Royal Academy 1820.

In addition to British royalty, he painted a series of European sovereigns and dignitaries, including pope Pius VIII (Waterloo Chamber, Windsor Castle, Berkshire) commissioned after the Allied victory at Waterloo.

Lawrence, St /ˈlɒrəns/ Christian martyr. Probably born in Spain, he became a deacon of Rome under Pope Sixtus II and, when summoned to deliver the treasures of the church, displayed the beggars in his charge, for which he was broiled on a gridiron. Feast day 10 Aug.

Lawson /ˈlɔːsən/ Nigel 1932– . British Conservative politician. A former financial journalist, he was financial secretary to the Treasury 1979–81, secretary of state for energy 1981–83, and chancellor of the Exchequer from 1983. He resigned 1989 after criticism by government adviser Alan Walters over his policy of British membership of the European Monetary System.

Laxness /ˈlæksnes/ Halldor 1902– . Icelandic novelist who wrote about Icelandic life in the style of the early sagas. He was awarded a Nobel prize in 1955.

Layamon /ˈlaɪəmən/ lived about 1200. English poet, author of the *Brut*, a chronicle of about 30,000 alliterative lines on the history of Britain from the legendary Brutus onwards, which gives the earliest version of the Arthurian legend in English.

Layard /ˈleɪəd/ Austen Henry 1817–1894. British archaeologist. He travelled to the Middle East in 1839, conducted two expeditions to Nineveh and Babylon 1845–51, and sent to the UK the specimens forming the greater part of the Assyrian collection in the British Museum.

Lazarus /ˈlæzərəs/ Emma 1849–1887. US poet, author of the poem on the base of the Statue of Liberty that begins: 'Give me your tired, your poor/Your huddled masses yearning to breathe free.'

Leach /liːtʃ/ Bernard 1887–1979. British potter. His simple designs, inspired by a period of study in Japan, pioneered a revival of the art. He established the Leach Pottery at St Ives, Cornwall, in 1920.

Leacock /ˈliːkɒk/ Stephen Butler 1869–1944. Canadian humorist whose writings include *Literary Lapses* 1910, *Sunshine Sketches of a Little Town* 1912, and *Frenzied Fiction* 1918.

Born in Hampshire, England, Leacock lived in Canada from 1876 and was head of the department of economics at McGill University, Montreal, 1908–36. He published works on politics and economics, and studies of Mark Twain and Charles Dickens.

Leadbelly stage name of Huddie Ledbetter *c.* 1889–1949. US blues and folk singer, songwriter, and guitarist who was a source of inspiration for the urban folk movement of the 1950s. He was 'discovered' in prison by folklorists John Lomax (1875–1948) and Alan Lomax (1915–), who helped him begin a professional concert and recording career 1934. His songs include 'Rock Island Line' and 'Good Night, Irene'.

Leakey /ˈliːki/ Louis (Seymour Bazett) 1903–1972. British archaeologist, born in Kenya. In 1958, with his wife Mary Leakey, he discovered gigantic extinct-animal fossils in the Olduvai Gorge in Tanzania, as well as many remains of an early human type.

Leakey /ˈliːki/ Mary 1913– . British archaeologist. In 1948 she discovered, on Rusinga Island, Lake Victoria, E Africa, the prehistoric ape skull known as *Proconsul*, about 20 million years old; and human remains at Laetolil, to the south, about 3,750,000 years old.

Leakey /ˈliːki/ Richard 1944– . British archaeologist. In 1972 he discovered at Lake Turkana, Kenya, an apelike skull, estimated to be about 2.9 million years old; it had some human characteristics and a brain capacity of 800 cu cm. In 1984 his team found an almost complete skeleton of *Homo erectus* some 1.6 million years old. He is the son of Louis and Mary Leakey.

Lean /liːn/ David 1908–1991. British film director. His films, noted for their atmospheric quality, include early work codirected with playwright Noël ➔Coward. *Brief Encounter* 1946 established Lean as a leading talent. Among his later films are such accomplished epics as *The Bridge on the River Kwai* 1957 (Academy Award), *Lawrence of Arabia* 1962 (Academy Award), and *Dr Zhivago* 1965. The unfavourable reaction to *Ryan's Daughter* 1970 caused him to withdraw from filmmaking for over a decade, but *A Passage to India* 1984 represented a return to form.

Lear /lɪə/ Edward 1812–1888. English artist and humorist. His *Book of Nonsense* 1846 popularized the limerick (a five-line humorous verse). He first attracted attention by his paintings of birds, and later turned to landscapes. He travelled to Italy, Greece, Egypt, and India, publishing books on his travels with his own illustrations, and spent most of his later life in Italy.

And hand in hand, on the edge of the sand,
They danced by the light of the moon.

> Edward Lear 'The Owl and the Pussy-Cat'
> 1871

Leavis /ˈliːvɪs/ F(rank) R(aymond) 1895–1978. English literary critic. With his wife Q D Leavis (1906–81) he cofounded and edited the review *Scrutiny* 1932–53. He championed the work of D H Lawrence and James Joyce and in 1962 attacked C P Snow's theory of 'The Two Cultures' (the natural alienation of the arts and sciences in

intellectual life). His other works include *New Bearings in English Poetry* 1932 and *The Great Tradition* 1948. He was a lecturer at Cambridge University.

Leavitt /ˈlevɪt/ Henrietta Swan 1868–1921. US astronomer who in 1912 discovered the *period–luminosity law* that links the brightness of a Cepheid variable star to its period of variation. This law allows astronomers to use Cepheid variables as 'standard candles' for measuring distances in space.

Lebedev /ˈlebɪdjef/ Peter Nikolaievich 1866–1912. Russian physicist. He proved by experiment that light exerts a minute pressure upon a physical body, thereby confirming James Maxwell's theoretic prediction.

Leblanc /ləˈblɒn/ Nicolas 1742–1806. French chemist who in 1790 developed a process for making soda ash (sodium carbonate, Na_2CO_3) from common salt (sodium chloride, NaCl).

In the *Leblanc process*, salt was first converted into sodium sulphate by the action of sulphuric acid, which was then roasted with chalk or limestone (calcium carbonate) and coal to produce a mixture of sodium carbonate and sulphide. The carbonate was leached out with water and the solution crystallized. Leblanc devised this method of producing soda ash (for use in making glass, paper, soap, and various other chemicals) to win a prize offered in 1775 by the French Academy of Sciences, but the Revolutionary government granted him only a patent (1791), which they seized along with his factory three years later. A broken man, Leblanc committed suicide.

Lebrun /ləˈbrɜːn/ Albert 1871–1950. French politician. He became president of the senate in 1931 and in 1932 was chosen as president of the republic. In 1940 he handed his powers over to Marshal Pétain.

Le Brun /ləˈbrɜːŋ/ Charles 1619–1690. French artist, painter to Louis XIV from 1662. In 1663 he became director of the French Academy and of the Gobelins factory, which produced art, tapestries, and furnishings for the new palace of Versailles. In the 1640s he studied under the painter Poussin in Rome. Returning to Paris in 1646, he worked on large decorative schemes including the *Galerie des glaces* (Hall of Mirrors) at Versailles. He also painted portraits.

Le Carré /lə ˈkæreɪ/ John. Pen name of David John Cornwell 1931– . English writer of thrillers. His low-key realistic accounts of complex espionage include *The Spy Who Came in from the Cold* 1963, *Tinker Tailor Soldier Spy* 1974, *Smiley's People* 1980, and *The Russia House* 1989. He was a member of the Foreign Service 1960–64.

Leclair /ləˈkleə/ Jean-Marie 1697–1764. French violinist and composer. Originally a dancer and ballet-master, he composed ballet music, an opera, *Scilla et Glaucus*, and violin concertos.

Leclanché /ləˈklɒnʃeɪ/ Georges 1839–1882. French engineer. In 1866 he invented a primary electrical cell, the *Leclanché cell*, which is still the basis of most dry batteries. A Leclanché cell consists of a carbon rod (the anode) inserted into a mixture of powdered carbon and manganese dioxide contained in a porous pot, which sits in a glass jar containing an electrolyte (conducting medium) of ammonium chloride solution, into which a zinc cathode is inserted. The cell produces a continuous current, the carbon mixture acting as a depolarizer; that is, it prevents hydrogen bubbles from forming on the anode and increasing resistance. In a dry battery, the electrolyte is made in the form of a paste with starch.

Leconte de Lisle /ləˈkɒnt də ˈliːl/ Charles Marie René 1818–1894. French poet. He was born on the Indian Ocean Island of Réunion, settled in Paris in 1846, and headed the anti-Romantic group Les Parnassiens 1866–76. His work drew inspiration from the ancient world, as in *Poèmes antiques/Antique Poems* 1852, *Poèmes barbares/Barbaric Poems* 1862, and *Poèmes tragiques/Tragic Poems* 1884.

Le Corbusier /lə ˌkɔːˈbjuːzieɪ/ assumed name of Charles-Édouard Jeanneret 1887–1965. Swiss architect. His functionalist approach to town planning in industrial society was based on the interrelationship between machine forms and the techniques of modern architecture. His concept, *La Ville radieuse*, developed in Marseille, France (1945–50) and Chandigarh, India, placed buildings and open spaces with related functions in a circular formation, with buildings based on standard-sized units mathematically calculated according to the proportions of the human figure (see ➔Fibonacci).

Le Corbusier was originally a painter and engraver, but turned his attention to the problems of contemporary industrial society. His books *Vers une architecture* 1923 and *Le Modulor* 1948 have had worldwide significance for town planning and building design.

A house is a machine for living in.

Le Corbusier *Towards one Architecture* 1923

Lecouvreur /ləˌkuːˈvrɜː/ Adrienne 1692–1730. French actress. She performed at the Comédie Française national theatre, where she first appeared in 1717. Her many admirers included the philosopher Voltaire and the army officer Maurice de Saxe; a rival mistress of the latter, the Duchesse de Bouillon, is thought to have poisoned her.

Lederberg /ˈledəbɜːg/ Joshua 1925– . US geneticist who showed that bacteria can reproduce sexually, combining genetic material so that offspring possess characteristics of both parent organisms.

Lederberg is considered a pioneer of genetic engineering, a science that relies on the possibility of artificially shuffling genes from cell to cell. He realized that bacteriophages, viruses which invade bacteria, can transfer genes from one bacterium to another, a discovery that led to the deliberate insertion by scientists of foreign genes into bacterial cells. In 1958 he shared the Nobel Prize for Medicine with George ➔Beadle and Edward ➔Tatum.

Ledoux /ləˈduː/ Claude-Nicolas 1736–1806. French Neo-Classical architect, stylistically comparable to É L ➔Boullée in his use of austere, geometric forms, exemplified in his toll houses for Paris; for instance, the Barrière de la Villette in the Place de Stalingrad.

Ledru-Rollin /ləˈdruː rɒ'læŋ/ Alexandre Auguste 1807–1874. French politician and contributor to the radical and socialist journal *La Réforme*. He became minister for home affairs in the provisional government formed in 1848 after the overthrow of Louis Philippe and the creation of the Second Republic, but he opposed the elected president Louis Napoleon.

Le Duc Tho /leɪ ˌdʊk ˈtəʊ/ 1911–1990. North Vietnamese diplomat who was joint winner (with US Secretary of State Kissinger) of the 1973 Nobel Peace Prize for his part in the negotiations to end the Vietnam War. He indefinitely postponed receiving the award.

Ledyard /ˈledjəd/ John 1751–1789. American explorer and adventurer. As a British marine, he was sent to Long Island during the American Revolution 1775, but, refusing to fight against his own countrymen, he deserted in 1782. After an ill-fated journey through Siberia, he died in Cairo on his way to find the source of the Niger River.

Born in Groton, Connecticut, Ledyard briefly attended Dartmouth but left school for a life at sea.

Lee /liː/ Bruce. Stage name of Lee Yuen Kam 1941–1973. US 'Chinese Western' film actor, an expert in kung fu, who popularized the oriental martial arts in the West with pictures made in Hong Kong, such as *Fists of Fury* 1972 and *Enter the Dragon* 1973, his last film.

Lee /liː/ Christopher 1922– . English film actor whose gaunt figure was memorable in the title role of *Dracula* 1958 and its sequels. He has not lost his sinister image in subsequent Hollywood productions. His other films include *Hamlet* 1948, *The Mummy* 1959, *Julius Caesar* 1970, and *The Man with the Golden Gun* 1974.

Lee /liː/ Gyspy Rose 1914–1970. US entertainer. An 'elegant lady' in striptease routines, she was popular in literary circles. Also a published author, she wrote two mystery novels *The G-String Murders* 1941 and *Mother Finds a Body* 1942. Her autobiography *Gypsy: A Memoir* 1957 was adapted for stage 1959 and film 1962.

Lee US Confederate general Robert E Lee. Siding with the Southern states in the Civil War, he won a number of battles 1862–63 before surrendering 1865.

Born Rose Louise Hovick in Seattle, Washington, USA, she performed song and dance routines with her sister, actress June Havoc, from around the age of four. During her teenage years In New York, Lee learned the art of striptease.

Appearing on Broadway and television, she became a national celebrity.

Lee /liː/ Henry 1756–1818. American military and political leader. In the cavalry during the American Revolution 1775–83, he rose to the rank of major, winning the nickname 'Light-Horse Harry' for his lightning attacks. After the war, he entered politics and served in the Continental Congress 1785–88, as governor of Virginia 1792–95, and as a member of the US House of Representatives 1799–1801.

Born in Leesylvania, Virginia, Lee was educated at Princeton University. He was a close friend of George Washington and helped suppress the Whiskey Rebellion 1794. He was the father of Robert E →Lee.

Lee /liː/ Jennie, Baroness Lee 1904–1988. British socialist politician. She became a member of Parliament for the Independent Labour Party at the age of 24, and in 1934 married Aneurin →Bevan. On the left wing of the Labour Party, she was on its National Executive Committee 1958–70 and was minister of education 1967–70, during which time she was responsible for founding the Open University in 1969. She was made a baroness in 1970.

Lee /liː/ Laurie 1914– . English writer, born near Stroud, Gloucestershire. His works include the autobiographical novel *Cider with Rosie* 1959, a classic evocation of childhood; nature poetry such as *The Bloom of Candles* 1947; and travel writing including *A Rose for Winter* 1955.

Lee /liː/ Nathaniel 1653–1692. English dramatist. From 1675 on, he wrote a number of extravagant tragedies, such as *The Rival Queens* 1677.

Lee /liː/ Robert E(dward) 1807–1870. US Confederate general in the American Civil War, a military strategist. As military adviser to Jefferson →Davis, president of the Confederacy, and as commander of the army of N Virginia, he made several raids into Northern territory, but was defeated at Gettysburg and surrendered 1865 at Appomattox.

Lee, born in Virginia, was commissioned 1829 and served in the Mexican War. In 1859 he suppressed John →Brown's raid on Harper's Ferry. On the outbreak of the Civil War 1861 he joined the Confederate army of the Southern States, and in 1862 received the command of the army of N Virginia and won the Seven Days' Battle defending Richmond, Virginia, the Confederate capital, against General McClellan's Union forces. In 1863 Lee won victories at Fredericksburg and Chancellorsville, and in 1864 at Cold Harbor, but was besieged in Petersburg, June 1864–April 1865. He surrendered to General Grant 9 April 1865 at Appomattox courthouse.

It is well that war is so terrible, else we would grow too fond of it.

Robert E Lee to a fellow general during the battle of Fredericksburg

Lee /liː/ Spike (Shelton Jackson) 1957– . US film director, actor and writer. His work presents the bitter realities of contemporary Afro-American life in an aggressive, often controversial manner. His films, in which he sometimes appears, include *She's Gotta Have It* 1986, *Do The Right Thing* 1989, *Jungle Fever* 1991, and *Malcolm X* 1992.

Leech /liːtʃ/ John 1817–1864. British caricaturist. He illustrated many books, including Dickens's *A Christmas Carol*, and during 1841–64 contributed about 3,000 humorous drawings and political cartoons to *Punch* magazine. Born in London, he studied medicine before turning to art.

Lee Kuan Yew /liː ˌkwɑːn ˈjuː/ 1923– . Singapore politician, prime minister 1959–90. Lee founded the anticommunist Socialist People's Action Party 1954 and entered the Singapore legislative assembly 1955. He was elected the country's first prime minister 1959, and took Singapore out of the Malaysian federation 1965. He remained in power until his resignation 1990, and was succeeded by Goh Chok Tong.

Lee Teng-hui /ˈliː ˌtʌŋ ˈhuːi/ 1923– . Taiwanese right-wing politician, vice president 1984–88, president and Kuomintang (Guomindang) party leader from 1988. Lee, the country's first island-born leader, is viewed as a reforming technocrat.

Born in Tamsui, Taiwan, Lee taught for two decades as professor of economics at the National Taiwan University before becoming mayor of Taipei in 1979. A member of the Kuomintang party and a protégé of Chiang Ching-kuo, he became vice president of Taiwan in 1984 and succeeded to both the state presidency and Kuomintang leadership on Chiang's death in Jan 1988. He has significantly accelerated the pace of liberalization and Taiwanization in the political sphere.

Lee Tsung-Dao /tsʊŋ ˌdaʊˈliː/ 1926– . Chinese physicist whose research centred on the physics of weak nuclear forces. In 1956 Lee proposed that weak nuclear forces between elementary particles might disobey certain key assumptions for instance, the conservation of parity. He shared the 1957 Nobel Prize for Physics with his colleague Yang Chen Ning (1922–).

Leeuwenhoek /ˈleɪwənhuːk/ Anton van 1632–1723. Dutch pioneer of microscopic research. He ground his own lenses, some of which magnified up to 200 times. With these he was able to see individual red blood cells, sperm, and bacteria, achievements not repeated for more than a century.

Le Fanu /ˈlefənuː/ (Joseph) Sheridan 1814–1873. Irish writer, born in Dublin. He wrote mystery novels and short stories, such as *The House by the Churchyard* 1863, *Uncle Silas* 1864, and *In a Glass Darkly* 1872.

Lefebvre /ləˈfevrə/ Marcel 1905–1991. French Catholic priest in open conflict with the Roman Catholic Church. In 1976, he was suspended by Pope Paul VI for the unauthorized ordination of priests at his Swiss headquarters. He continued and in June 1988 he was excommunicated by Pope John Paul II, in the first formal schism within the church since 1870.

Ordained in 1929, Lefebvre was a missionary and an archbishop in W Africa until 1962. He opposed the liberalizing reforms of the Second Vatican Council 1962–65 and formed the 'Priestly Cofraternity of Pius X'.

Léger /leˈʒeɪ/ Fernand 1881–1955. French painter, associated with Cubism, pioneering abstract art. From around 1909 he evolved a characteristic style, composing abstract and semi-abstract works with cylindrical forms, reducing the human figure to constructions of pure shape. Mechanical forms are constant themes in his work, including his designs for the Swedish Ballet 1921–22, murals, and the abstract film *Ballet mécanique*/*Mechanical Ballet*.

Le Guin /ləˈgwɪn/ Ursula K(roeber) 1929– . US writer of science fiction and fantasy. Her novels include *The Left Hand of Darkness* 1969, which

questions sex roles; the *Earthsea* trilogy 1968–72; *The Dispossessed* 1974, which compares an anarchist and a capitalist society; *Orsinian Tales* 1976; and *Always Coming Home* 1985.

Lehár /leɪˈhɑː/ Franz 1870–1948. Hungarian composer. He wrote many operettas, among them *The Merry Widow* 1905, *The Count of Luxembourg* 1909, *Gypsy Love* 1910, and *The Land of Smiles* 1929. He also composed songs, marches, and a violin concerto.

Lehman /ˈliːmən/ Herbert Henry 1878–1963. US political leader. In 1932 he became governor of New York, and his subsequent support of F D Roosevelt's reform policies earned his own administration the name 'Little New Deal'. In 1942 Lehman was appointed director of the federal Office of Foreign Relief and Rehabilitation. He served in the US Senate 1949–57.

Born in New York and educated at Williams College, Lehman joined his family's banking business and served in the army during World War I. Later entering politics he was elected New York's lieutenant governor 1928.

Lehmann /ˈleɪmən/ Lotte 1888–1976. German soprano. She excelled in Wagnerian operas and was an outstanding Marschallin in Richard →Strauss's *Der Rosenkavalier*.

Lehmann /ˈleɪmən/ Rosamond (Nina) 1901–1990. English novelist whose books include *Dusty Answer* 1927, *The Weather in the Streets* 1936, *The Echoing Grove* 1953, and, following a long silence, *A Sea-Grape Tree* 1976. Once neglected as too romantic, her novels have regained popularity in the 1980s because of their sensitive portrayal of female adolescence.

Leibniz /ˈlaɪbnɪts/ Gottfried Wilhelm 1646–1716. German mathematician and philosopher. Independently of, but concurrently with, the British scientist Isaac Newton he developed the branch of mathematics known as calculus. In his metaphysical works, such as *The Monadology* 1714, he argued that everything consisted of innumerable units, *monads*, the individual properties of which determined each thing's past, present, and future. Monads, although independent of each other, interacted predictably; this meant that Christian faith and scientific reason need not be in conflict and that 'this is the best of all possible worlds'. His optimism is satirized in Voltaire's *Candide*.

Leicester /ˈlestə/ Robert Dudley, Earl of Leicester *c.* 1532–1588. English courtier. Son of the Duke of Northumberland, he was created Earl of Leicester 1564. Queen Elizabeth I gave him command of the army sent to the Netherlands 1585–87 and of the forces prepared to resist the threat of Spanish invasion of 1588. His lack of military success led to his recall, but he retained Elizabeth's favour until his death.

Leicester's good looks attracted Queen Elizabeth, who made him Master of the Horse 1558 and a privy councillor 1559. But his poor perfor-

Leicester The controversial favourite of Elizabeth I, Robert Dudley, Earl of Leicester. Their marriage was rumoured but never realized and Leicester secretly married Lady Sheffield. Despite Elizabeth's anger, they were reconciled and she continued to favour Leicester, placing him in positions of military power for which he was unsuited.

mance in the army ended any chance of marrying the queen. He was a staunch supporter of the Protestant cause.

Elizabeth might have married him if he had not been already married to Amy Robsart. When his wife died in 1560 after a fall downstairs, Leicester was suspected of murdering her. In 1576 he secretly married the widow of the Earl of Essex.

Leichhardt /ˈlaɪkhɑːt/ Friedrich 1813–1848. Prussian-born Australian explorer. In 1843, he walked 965 km/600 mi from Sydney to Moreton Bay, Queensland, and in 1844 walked from Brisbane to Arnhem Land; he disappeared during a further expedition from Queensland in 1848. Patrick White used the character of Leichhardt in *Voss* 1957.

Leif Ericsson Norse explorer; see ➔Ericsson, Leif.

Leigh /liː/ Mike 1943– . English playwright and filmmaker, noted for his sharp, carefully improvised social satires. He directs his own plays, which evolve through improvisation before they are scripted. His work for television includes *Nuts in May* 1976 and *Abigail's Party* 1977; his films include *High Hopes* 1989 and *Life Is Sweet* 1991.

Leigh /liː/ Vivien. Stage name of Vivien Mary Hartley 1913–1967. English actress who appeared on the stage in London and New York, and won Academy Awards for her performances as Scarlett

O'Hara in *Gone With the Wind* 1939 and as Blanche du Bois in *A Streetcar Named Desire* 1951.

She was born in India. Married to Laurence Olivier 1940–60, she starred with him in the play *Antony and Cleopatra* in 1951. Her films include *Lady Hamilton* 1941, *Anna Karenina* 1948, and *Ship of Fools* 1965.

Leigh-Mallory /liː ˈmæləri/ Trafford 1892–1944. British air chief marshal in World War II. He took part in the Battle of Britain and was Commander in Chief of Allied air forces during the invasion of France.

Leighton /ˈleɪtn/ Frederic, Baron Leighton 1830–1896. English painter and sculptor. He specialized in Classical Greek subjects such as *Captive Andromache* 1888 (Manchester City Art Gallery). He became president of the Royal Academy 1878 and was made a peer 1896. His house and studio near Holland Park, London, is now a museum.

Leisler Jacob 1640–1691. German-born colonial administrator in America. Taking advantage of the political instability caused by England's Glorious Revolution of 1688, he took command of New York in the name of William and Mary. Deposed in 1691 by troops dispatched from England, Leisler was tried and hanged for treason.

Born in Frankfurt, Germany, Leisler arrived in New Amsterdam (New York from 1664) as a mercenary for the Dutch West India Company 1660 becoming a successful merchant when the colony passed to English rule.

Leland /ˈliːlənd/ John 1506–1552. English antiquary whose manuscripts have proved a valuable source for scholars. He became chaplain and librarian to Henry VIII, and during 1534–43 toured England collecting material for a history of English antiquities. The *Itinerary* was published in 1710.

Lely /ˈliːli/ Peter. Adopted name of Pieter van der Faes 1618–1680. Dutch painter, active in England from 1641, who painted fashionable portraits in Baroque style. His subjects included Charles I, Cromwell, and Charles II. He painted a series of admirals, *Flagmen* (National Maritime Museum, Greenwich), and one of *The Windsor Beauties* (Hampton Court, Richmond), fashionable women of Charles II's court.

Lemaître /ləˈmeɪtrə/ Georges Edouard 1894–1966. Belgian cosmologist who in 1927 proposed the Big Bang theory of the origin of the universe. He predicted that the entire universe was expanding, which the US astronomer Edwin ➔Hubble confirmed. Lemaître suggested that the expansion had been started by an initial explosion, the Big Bang, a theory that is now generally accepted.

Lemmon /ˈlemən/ Jack (John Uhler III) 1925– . US character actor, often cast as the lead in comedy films, such as *Some Like It Hot* 1959 but equally skilled in serious roles, as in *The China Syndrome* 1979 and *Dad* 1990.

Lely Dutch portrait artist Peter Lely in a self-portrait painted about 1660. Lely was made principal painter to King Charles II in 1661.

LeMond /lə'mɒnd/ Greg 1961– . US racing cyclist, the first American to win the Tour de France 1986.

Although his career received a setback in 1987 through injury, he recovered sufficiently to regain his Tour de France title in 1989 by seven seconds, the smallest margin ever. He won it again in 1990. He also won the World Professional Road Race in 1983 and 1989.

Le Nain /lə 'næŋ/ family of French painters, the brothers Antoine (1588–1648), Louis (1593–1648), and Mathieu (1607–1677). They were born in Laon, settled in Paris, and were among the original members of the French Academy in 1648. Attribution of works among them is uncertain. They chiefly painted sombre and dignified scenes of peasant life.

Lenard /'leɪnɑːt/ Philipp Eduard Anton 1862–1947. German physicist who investigated the photoelectric effect (light causes metals to emit electrons) and cathode rays (the stream of electrodes emitted from the cathode in a vacuum tube). He was awarded a Nobel prize in 1905.

In later life he became obsessed with the idea of producing a purely 'Aryan' physics free from the influence of →Einstein and other Jewish physicists.

Lenclos /lɒŋ'kləu/ Ninon de 1615–1705. French courtesan. As the recognized leader of Parisian society, she was the mistress of many highly placed men, including General Condé and the writer La Rochefoucauld.

Lendl /'lendl/ Ivan 1960– . Czech-born American lawn tennis player. He has won eight Grand Slam singles titles, including the US and French titles three times each. He has won more than $15 million in prize money.

If I smile I have to think about smiling and that would break my concentration.

Ivan Lendl

Leng /leŋ/ Virginia 1955– . British three-day eventer (rider in horse trials), born in Malta. She has won world, European, and most major British championships.

She was a member of the British team at two world championships (1982 and 1986) and was the individual champion in 1986 on Priceless. She won the European individual title twice (1985 and 1989), the Badminton horse trials in the same years, and Burghley Horse Trials in 1983, 1984, and 1986.

Lenglen /'lɒŋglen/ Suzanne 1899–1938. French tennis player, Wimbledon singles and doubles champion 1919–23 and 1925, and Olympic champion 1921. She became professional in 1926. She also popularized sports clothes designed by Jean →Patou.

Lenin /'lenɪn/ Vladimir Ilyich. Adopted name of Vladimir Ilyich Ulyanov 1870–1924. Russian revolutionary, first leader of the USSR, and communist theoretician. Active in the 1905 Revolution, Lenin had to leave Russia when it failed, settling in Switzerland in 1914. He returned to Russia after the February revolution of 1917. He led the Bolshevik revolution in Nov 1917 and became leader of a Soviet government, concluded peace with Germany, and organized a successful resistance to White Russian (pro-tsarist) uprisings and foreign intervention 1918–20. His modification of traditional Marxist doctrine to fit conditions prevailing in Russia became known as *Marxism-Leninism*, the basis of communist ideology.

Lenin was born on 22 April, 1870 in Simbirsk (now renamed Ulyanovsk), on the river Volga, and became a lawyer in St Petersburg. His brother was executed in 1887 for attempting to assassinate Tsar Alexander III. A Marxist from 1889, Lenin was sent to Siberia for spreading revolutionary propaganda 1895–1900. He then edited the political paper *Iskra* ('The Spark') from abroad, and visited London several times. In *What Is to be Done?* 1902 he advocated that a professional core of Social Democratic Party activists should spearhead the revolution in Russia, a suggestion accepted by the majority (*bolsheviki*) at the London party congress 1903. From Switzerland he attacked socialist support for World War I as aiding an 'imperialist' struggle, and wrote *Imperialism* 1917.

After the renewed outbreak of revolution in Feb/March 1917, he returned to Russia in April and called for the transfer of power to the soviets (workers' councils). From the overthrow of the provisional government in Nov 1917 until his death, Lenin effectively controlled the Soviet Union, although an assassination attempt in 1918 injured his health. He founded the Third (Communist) International in 1919. With communism proving inadequate to put the country on its feet, he introduced the private-enterprise New Economic Policy 1921. His embalmed body is in a mausoleum in Red Square, Moscow. In 1898 he married *Nadezhda Konstantinova Krupskaya* (1869–1939), who shared his work and wrote *Memories of Lenin*.

Lennon John (Ono) 1940–1980. UK rock singer, songwriter, and guitarist, in the USA from 1971; a founder member of the Beatles. Both before the band's break-up 1969 and in his solo career, he collaborated intermittently with his wife **Yoko Ono** (1933–). 'Give Peace a Chance', a hit 1969, became an anthem of the peace movement. His solo work alternated between the confessional and the political, as on the album *Imagine* 1971. He was shot dead by a fan.

Lennon is regarded as having tempered with cynicism and acerbic wit the tendency to sentimentality of his Beatle cowriter Paul McCartney, but idealism was evident in Lennon's life outside the Beatles, with publicity stunts like the 1969 'bed-in for peace' (he and Ono stayed in bed in an Amsterdam hotel for a week, receiving the press). His first solo album, *John Lennon/Plastic Ono Band* 1970, contained deeply personal songs like 'Mother' and 'Working Class Hero'; subsequent work, though uneven, included big hits like 'Whatever Gets You Through the Night' 1974. He often worked with producer Phil →Spector. On *Rock 'n' Roll* 1975 Lennon covered nonoriginal songs that the Beatles had played in the early 1960s. *Double Fantasy* 1980, made in collaboration with Ono, reached number one in the album charts after his death.

At the height of Beatlemania, Lennon published two small books of his drawings and nonsense writings, *In His Own Write* 1964 and *A Spaniard in the Works* 1965.

Leno /ˈliːnəʊ/ Dan 1861–1904. British comedian. A former acrobat, he became the idol of the music halls, and was considered the greatest of pantomime 'dames'.

Le Nôtre /lə ˈnəʊtrə/ André 1613–1700. French landscape gardener, creator of the gardens at Versailles and Les Tuileries, Paris.

Lenthall /ˈlentɔːl/ William 1591–1662. English lawyer. Speaker of the House of Commons in the Long Parliament of 1640–60, he played an active part in the Restoration of Charles II.

Lenya /ˈleɪnjə/ Lotte. Adopted name of Karoline Blamauer 1905–1981. Austrian actress and singer. She was married five times, twice to the composer Kurt →Weill, first in 1926, with whom she emigrated to the USA 1935. She appeared in several of the Brecht–Weill operas, notably *Die Dreigroschenoper/The Threepenny Opera* 1928.

Leo III /ˈliːəʊ/ *the Isaurian* c. 680–740. Byzantine emperor and soldier. He seized the throne in 717, successfully defended Constantinople against the Saracens 717–18, and attempted to suppress the use of images in church worship.

Leo /ˈliːəʊ/ thirteen popes, including:

Leo I St *the Great* c. 390–461. Pope from 440 who helped to establish the Christian liturgy. Leo summoned the Chalcedon Council where his Dogmatical Letter was accepted as the voice of St Peter. Acting as ambassador for the emperor Valentinian III (425–455), Leo saved Rome from devastation by the Huns by buying off their king, Attila.

Leo III c. 750–816. Pope from 795. After the withdrawal of the Byzantine emperors, the popes had become the real rulers of Rome. Leo III was forced to flee because of a conspiracy in Rome and took refuge at the court of the Frankish king Charlemagne. He returned to Rome in 799 and crowned Charlemagne emperor on Christmas Day 800, establishing the secular sovereignty of the pope over Rome under the suzerainty of the emperor (who became the Holy Roman emperor).

Leo X Giovanni de' Medici 1475–1521. Pope from 1513. The son of Lorenzo the Magnificent of Florence, he was created a cardinal at 13. He bestowed on Henry VIII of England the title of Defender of the Faith. A patron of the arts, he sponsored the rebuilding of St Peter's Church, Rome. He raised funds for this by selling indulgences (remissions of punishment for sin), a sale that led the religious reformer Martin Luther to rebel against papal authority. Leo X condemned Luther in the bull *Exsurge domine* 1520 and excommunicated him in 1521.

Leo XIII Gioacchino Pecci 1810–1903. Pope from 1878. After a successful career as a papal diplomat, he established good relations between the papacy and European powers, the USA, and Japan. He remained intransigent in negotiations with the Italian government over the status of Rome, insisting that he keep control over part of it.

He was the first pope to emphasize the duty of the church in matters of social justice. His encyclical *Rerum novarum* 1891 pointed out the moral duties of employers towards workers.

Leonard /ˈlenəd/ Elmore (John, Jr) 1925– . US author of westerns and thrillers, marked by vivid dialogue, as in *City Primeval* 1980, *La Brava* 1983, *Stick* 1983, *Glitz* 1985, *Freaky Deaky* 1988, and *Get Shorty* 1990.

Leonard /ˈlenəd/ Sugar Ray 1956– . US boxer. In 1988 he became the first man to have won world titles at five officially recognized weights. In 1976 he was Olympic light-welterweight champion; he won his first professional title in 1979 when he beat Wilfred Benitez for the WBC welterweight title. He later won titles at junior middleweight (WBA version) 1981, middleweight (WBC) 1987, light-heavyweight (WBC) 1988, and super-middleweight (WBC) 1988. In 1989 he drew with Thomas Hearns.

The poet ranks far below the painter in the representation of visible things – and far below the musician in that of invisible things.

Leonardo da Vinci
Selection from the Notebooks

Leonardo da Vinci /ˌliːəˈnɑːdəʊ də ˈvɪntʃi/ 1452–1519. Italian painter, sculptor, architect, engineer, and scientist. One of the greatest figures of the Italian Renaissance, he was active in Florence, Milan, and, from 1516, France. As state engineer and court painter to the duke of Milan, he painted the *Last Supper* mural about 1495 (Sta Maria delle Grazie, Milan), and on his return to Florence painted the *Mona Lisa* (Louvre, Paris) about 1503–06. His notebooks and drawings show an immensely inventive and enquiring mind, studying aspects of the natural world from anatomy to aerodynamics.

Leonardo was born at Vinci in Tuscany and studied under →Verrocchio in Florence in the 1470s. His earliest dated work is a sketch of the Tuscan countryside 1473 (Uffizi, Florence); his early works include drawings, portraits, and religious scenes, such as the unfinished *Adoration of the Magi* (Uffizi). About 1482 he went to the court of Lodovico Sforza in Milan. In 1500 he returned to Florence (where he was architect and engineer to Cesare Borgia in 1502), and then to Milan in 1506. He went to France in 1516 and died at Château Cloux, near Amboise, on the Loire. Apart from portraits, religious themes, and historical paintings, Leonardo's greatest legacies were his notebooks and drawings. He influenced many of his contemporary artists, including Michelangelo, Raphael, Giorgione, and Bramante. He also revolutionized painting style. Instead of a white background, he used a dark one to allow the overlying colour a more three-dimensional existence. He invented 'aerial perspective' whereby the misty atmosphere (*sfumato*) blurs and changes the colours of the landscape as it dissolves into the distance. His principle of grouping figures within an imaginary pyramid, linked by their gestures and emotions, became a High Renaissance compositional rule. His two versions of the Madonna and child with St Anne, *Madonna on the Rocks* (Lou-

Leopold II *Leopold II, king of Belgium, amassed wealth from the rubber and ivory trade in the Congo from 1885. However, his mistreatment of the native peoples provoked international revulsion and he was obliged to relinquish his personal control of the territory.*

vre, Paris, and National Gallery, London) exemplify all these ideas. Other chief works include the *Mona Lisa* (wife of Zanoki del Giocondo, hence also known as *La Gioconda*) 1503, Louvre, Paris; and the *Battle of Anghiari* 1504–05, formerly in the Palazzo Vecchio, Florence.

Leoncavallo /ˌleɪɒnkəˈvæləʊ/ Ruggiero 1857–1919. Italian operatic composer, born in Naples. He played in restaurants, composing in his spare time, until the success of *Pagliacci* in 1892. His other operas include *La Bohème* 1897 (contemporary with Puccini's version) and *Zaza* 1900.

Leone /leɪˈəʊni/ Sergio 1928–1989. Italian film director, responsible for popularizing 'spaghetti' Westerns (Westerns made in Italy and Spain, usually with a US leading actor and a European supporting cast and crew) and making a world star of Clint Eastwood. His films include *Per un pugno di dollari/A Fistful of Dollars* 1964, *C'era una volta il West/Once Upon a Time in the West* 1968, and *C'era una volta il America/Once Upon a Time in America* 1984.

Leonidas /liːˈɒnɪdæs/ died 480 BC. King of Sparta. He was killed while defending the pass of Thermopylae with 300 Spartans, 700 Thespians, and 400 Thebans against a huge Persian army.

Leonov /ljeˈɔːnɔːf/ Aleksei Arkhipovich 1934– . Soviet cosmonaut. In 1965 he was the first person to walk in space, from the spacecraft *Voskhod 2*.

Leonov /lje'ɔnɔːf/ Leonid 1899– . Russian novelist and playwright, author of the novels *The Badgers* 1925 and *The Thief* 1927, and the drama *The Orchards of Polovchansk* 1938.

Leopardi /ˌleɪəʊ'pɑːdi/ Giacomo, Count Leopardi 1798–1837. Italian romantic poet. The first collection of his uniquely pessimistic poems, *I Versi/Verses*, appeared in 1824, and was followed by his philosophical *Operette morali/Minor Moral Works* 1827, in prose, and *I Canti/Lyrics* 1831.

Born at Recanati of a noble family, Leopardi wrote many of his finest poems, including his patriotic odes, before he was 21. Throughout his life he was tormented by ill health, by the consciousness of his deformity (he was hunchbacked), by loneliness and a succession of unhappy love affairs, and by his 'cosmic pessimism' and failure to find consolation in any philosophy.

Leopold /leɪəpəʊld/ three kings of the Belgians:

Leopold I 1790–1865. King of the Belgians from 1831, having been elected to the throne on the creation of an independent Belgium. Through his marriage, when prince of Saxe-Coburg, to Princess Charlotte Augusta, he was the uncle of Queen Victoria of Great Britain and had considerable influence over her.

Leopold II 1835–1909. King of the Belgians from 1865, son of Leopold I. He financed the US journalist Henry Stanley's explorations in Africa, which resulted in the foundation of the Congo Free State (now Zaire), from which he extracted a huge fortune by ruthless exploitation.

Leopold III 1901–1983. King of the Belgians 1934–51. He surrendered to the German army in World War II 1940. Postwar charges against his conduct led to a regency by his brother Charles and his eventual abdication 1951 in favour of his son Baudouin.

Leopold /liːəpəʊld/ two Holy Roman emperors:

Leopold I 1640–1705. Holy Roman emperor from 1658, in succession to his father Ferdinand III. He warred against Louis XIV of France and the Ottoman Empire.

Leopold II 1747–1792. Holy Roman emperor in succession to his brother Joseph II. He was the son of Empress Maria Theresa of Austria. His hostility to the French Revolution led to the outbreak of war a few weeks after his death.

Le Pen /lə 'pen/ Jean-Marie 1928– . French extreme right-wing politician. In 1972 he formed the French National Front, supporting immigrant repatriation and capital punishment; the party gained 14% of the national vote in the 1986 election. Le Pen was elected to the European Parliament in 1984.

Lermontov /leəməntɒf/ Mikhail Yurevich 1814–1841. Russian Romantic poet and novelist. In 1837 he was sent into active military service in the

Lesseps French engineer Ferdinand de Lesseps formed a plan for the Suez Canal when he was French consul in Egypt 1833 and oversaw its construction until its opening 1869. He was also president of the company that initially tried to construct the Panama Canal (1881–88) but the project foundered because of financial and political problems.

Caucasus for writing a revolutionary poem on the death of Pushkin, which criticized court values, and for participating in a duel. Among his works are the psychological novel *A Hero of Our Time* 1840 and a volume of poems *October* 1840.

Lerner /lɜːnə/ Alan Jay 1918–1986. US lyricist, collaborator with Frederick →Loewe on musicals including *Brigadoon* 1947, *Paint Your Wagon* 1951, *My Fair Lady* 1956, *Gigi* 1958, and *Camelot* 1960.

Le Sage /lə 'sɑːʒ/ Alain René 1668–1747. French novelist and dramatist. Born in Brittany, he abandoned law for literature. His novels include *Le Diable boîteux/The Devil upon Two Sticks* 1707 and his picaresque masterpiece *Gil Blas* 1715–35, which is much indebted to Spanish originals.

Lesseps /lesəps/ Ferdinand, Vicomte de Lesseps 1805–1894. French engineer, constructor of the Suez Canal 1859–69; he began the Panama Canal in 1879, but withdrew after failing to construct it without locks.

Lessing /lesɪŋ/ Doris (May) (née Taylor) 1919– . British novelist, born in Iran. Concerned with social and political themes, particularly the place of women in society, her work includes *The Grass is Singing* 1950, the five-novel series *Children of Violence* 1952–69, *The Golden Notebook* 1962, *The Good Terrorist* 1985, and *The Fifth Child* 1988. She has also written an 'inner space fiction' series *Canopus in Argus Archives* 1979–83, and under the pen name 'Jane Somers', *The Diary of a Good Neighbour* 1981.

Lessing /ˈlesɪŋ/ Gotthold Ephraim 1729–1781. German dramatist and critic. His plays include *Miss Sara Sampson* 1755, *Minna von Barnhelm* 1767, *Emilia Galotti* 1772, and the verse play *Nathan der Weise* 1779. His works of criticism *Laokoon* 1766 and *Hamburgische Dramaturgie* 1767–68 influenced German literature. He also produced many theological and philosophical writings.

Laokoon analysed the functions of poetry and the plastic arts; *Hamburgische Dramaturgie* reinterpreted Aristotle and attacked the restrictive form of French classical drama in favour of the freer approach of Shakespeare.

Lethaby /ˈleθəbi/ William Richard 1857–1931. English architect. An assistant to Norman Shaw, he embraced the principles of William Morris and Philip Webb in the Arts and Crafts movement, and was cofounder and first director of the Central School of Arts and Crafts from 1894. He wrote a collection of essays entitled *Form in Civilization* 1922.

Le Vau /ləˈvəʊ/ Louis 1612–1670. French architect who drafted the plan of Versailles, rebuilt the Louvre, and built Les Tuileries in Paris.

Leven /ˈliːvən/ Alexander Leslie, 1st Earl of Leven c. 1580–1661. Scottish general in the English Civil War. He led the Covenanters' army which invaded England in 1640, commanded the Scottish army sent to aid the English Puritans in 1643–46, and shared in the Parliamentarians' victory over the Royalists in the Battle of Marston Moor.

Lever /ˈliːvə/ Charles James 1806–1872. Irish novelist. He wrote novels of Irish and army life, such as *Harry Lorrequer* 1837, *Charles O'Malley* 1840, and *Tom Burke of Ours* 1844.

Leverrier /ləˌveriˈeɪ/ Urbain Jean Joseph 1811–1877. French astronomer who predicted the existence and position of the planet Neptune, discovered in 1846.

Lévesque /leˈvek/ René 1922–1987. French-Canadian politician. In 1968 he founded the Parti Québecois, with the aim of an independent Québec, but a referendum rejected the proposal in 1980. He was premier of Québec 1976–85.

Levi /ˈlevi/ Primo 1919–1987. Italian novelist. He joined the anti-Fascist resistance during World War II, was captured, and sent to the concentration camp at Auschwitz. He wrote of these experiences in *Se questo è un uomo/If This Is a Man* 1947.

Levi-Montalcini /ˈlevi ˌmɒntælˈtʃiːni/ Rita 1909– . Italian neurologist who discovered nerve-growth factor, a substance that controls how many cells make up the adult nervous system. She shared the 1986 Nobel Prize for Medicine with US biochemist Stanley Cohen (1922–).

Levi-Montalcini studied at Turin and worked there until the Fascist anti-Semitic laws forced her to go into hiding. She continued research into the nervous systems of chick embryos. After World War II she moved to the USA.

Levinson Barry 1932– . US film director and screenwriter. Working in Hollywood's mainstream, he has been responsible for some of the best adult comedy films of the 1980s and 1990s. Winning cult status for the offbeat realism of *Diner* 1982, Levinson went on to make such large-budget movies as *Good Morning Vietnam* 1987, *Tin Men* 1987, *Rain Man* 1988 (Academy Award), and *Bugsy* 1991.

Levinson began his career as a scriptwriter for television comedy programmes such as *The Carol Burnett Show*. Later, he turned to writing feature films such as *High Anxiety* 1977 (with Mel Brooks), *And Justice For All* 1979, and *Unfaithfully Yours* 1983.

Lévi-Strauss /ˈlevi ˈstraʊs/ Claude 1908–1990. French anthropologist who sought to find a universal structure governing all societies, as reflected in the way their myths are constructed. His works include *Tristes Tropiques* 1955 and *Mythologiques/Mythologies* 1964–71.

The world began without man, and it will complete itself without him.

Claude Lévi-Strauss *Tristes Tropiques* 1955

Lewes /ˈluːɪs/ George Henry 1817–1878. English philosopher and critic. Originally an actor he turned to literature and philosophy; his works include a *Biographical History of Philosophy* 1845–46, and *Life and Works of Goethe* 1855. He married 1840, but left his wife 1854 to live with the writer Mary Ann Evans (George →Eliot), whom he had met 1851.

Lewis /ˈluːɪs/ (William) Arthur 1915– . British economist born on St Lucia, West Indies. He specialized in the economic problems of developing countries and created a model relating the terms of trade between less developed and more developed nations to their respective levels of labour productivity in agriculture. He shared the Nobel Prize for Economics with an American, Theodore Schultz, 1979. He wrote many books, including the *Theory of Economic Growth* 1955.

Lewis /ˈluːɪs/ Carl (Frederick Carleton) 1961– . US track and field athlete who won eight gold medals and one silver in three successive Olympic Games. At the 1984 Olympic Games he equalled the performance of Jesse →Owens, winning gold medals in the 100 and 200 metres, 400-metre relay, and long jump.

In the 1988 Olympics, he repeated his golds in the 100 metres and long jump, and won a silver in the 200 metres. Although in the 1992 Olympics he failed to make the USA's 100-metre and 200-metre squads, he repeated his success in the long jump and anchored the USA's record-breaking 400-metre relay team.

Lewis Cecil Day. Irish poet; see →Day Lewis.

Lewis /luːɪs/ C(live) S(taples) 1898–1963. British academic and writer, born in Belfast. His books include the medieval study, *The Allegory of Love* 1936, and the space fiction, *Out of the Silent Planet* 1938. He was a committed Christian and wrote essays in popular theology such as *The Screwtape Letters* 1942 and *Mere Christianity* 1952; the autobiographical *Surprised by Joy* 1955; and a series of books of Christian allegory for children, set in the magic land of Narnia, including *The Lion, the Witch, and the Wardrobe* 1950.

Lewis /luːɪs/ (Harry) Sinclair 1885–1951. US novelist. He made a reputation with satirical novels: *Main Street* 1920, depicting American small-town life; *Babbitt* 1922, the story of a real-estate dealer of the Midwest caught in the conventions of his milieu; *Arrowsmith* 1925, a study of the pettiness in medical science; and *Elmer Gantry* 1927, a satiric portrayal of evangelical religion. *Dodsworth*, a gentler novel of a US industrialist, was published 1929. He was the first American to be awarded the Nobel Prize for Literature, in 1930.

Lewis /luːɪs/ Jerry. Stage name of Joseph Levitch 1926– . US comic actor and director. Formerly in partnership with Dean Martin (1946–56), their film debut was in *My Friend Irma* 1949. He was revered as a solo performer by French critics ('Le Roi du Crazy'), but films that he directed such as *The Nutty Professor* 1963 were less well received in the USA. He appeared with Robert De Niro in *The King of Comedy* 1982.

Lewis /luːɪs/ Jerry Lee 1935– . US rock-and-roll and country singer and pianist. His trademark was the 'pumping piano' style in hits such as 'Whole Lotta Shakin' Going On' and 'Great Balls of Fire' 1957; later recordings include 'What Made Milwaukee Famous' 1968.

Lewis /luːɪs/ John L(lewellyn) 1880–1969. US labour leader. President of the United Mine Workers (UMW) 1920–60, he was largely responsible for the adoption of national mining safety standards in the USA. His militancy and the miners' strikes during and after World War II, led to President Truman's nationalization of the mines in 1946.

Born in Lucas, Iowa, USA, Lewis worked in the coal mines from an early age. He became a regional officer of the United Mine Workers (UMW) and served as its liaison with the American Federation of Labor (AFL) 1911.

He helped found the AFL's offshoot, the Congress of Industrial Organizations 1935, that unionized workers in mass-production industries.

Lewis /luːɪs/ Matthew Gregory 1775–1818. British writer, known as 'Monk' Lewis from his gothic horror romance *The Monk* 1795.

Lewis /luːɪs/ Meriwether 1774–1809. US explorer. He was commissioned by president Thomas Jefferson to find a land route to the Pacific with William Clark (1770–1838). They followed the Missouri River to its source, crossed the Rocky Mountains (aided by an Indian woman, Sacajawea) and followed the Columbia River to the Pacific, then returned overland to St Louis 1804–06.

Lewis /luːɪs/ (Percy) Wyndham 1886–1957. English writer and artist who pioneered Vorticism, which with its feeling of movement sought to reflect the age of industry. He had a hard and aggressive style in both his writing and his painting. His literary works include the novels *Tarr* 1918 and *The Childermass* 1928, the essay *Time and Western Man* 1927, and autobiographies.

Born off Maine, on his father's yacht, he was educated at the Slade art school and in Paris. On returning to England he pioneered the new spirit of art that his friend the US poet Ezra Pound called Vorticism; he also edited *Blast*, a literary and artistic magazine proclaiming its principles. Of his paintings, his portraits are memorable, such as those of the writers Edith Sitwell and T S Eliot.

Lewton /luːtn/ Val. Stage name of Vladimir Ivan Leventon 1904–1951. Russian- born US film producer, responsible for a series of atmospheric B horror films made for RKO in the 1940s, including *Cat People* 1942 and *The Body Snatcher* 1946. He co-wrote several of his films under the adopted name of Carlos Keith.

Leyden /laɪdn/ Lucas van; see →Lucas van Leyden, Dutch painter.

Lhote /ləʊt/ André 1885–1962. French painter, art teacher, and critic. He opened the Académie Montparnasse 1922 and founded a South American branch of the school in Rio de Janeiro 1952. He also wrote treatises on landscape painting and figure painting. His own paintings are complicated compositions of geometrical forms painted in pure colours, for example *Rugby* (Musée d'Art Moderne, Paris).

Libby /lɪbi/ Willard Frank 1908–1980. US chemist whose development in 1947 of radiocarbon dating as a means of determining the age of organic or fossilized material won him a Nobel prize in 1960.

Liberator, the title given to Simón →Bolívar, South American revolutionary leader; also a title given to Daniel →O'Connell, Irish political leader; and to Bernardo →O'Higgins, Chilean revolutionary.

Liberty /lɪbəti/ Arthur Lasenby 1843–1917. English shopkeeper and founder of a shop of the same name in London, 1875. Originally importing oriental goods, it gradually started selling British Arts and Crafts and Art Nouveau furniture, tableware, and fabrics. Liberty was knighted 1913.

A draper's son, Liberty trained at Farmer & Rogers' Cloak and Shawl Emporium. Art Nouveau is sometimes still called *stile Liberty* in Italy.

Liebknecht German political activist Karl Liebknecht, co-founder of the radical group known as the Sparticists and leader of their uprising in Berlin 1919. He was closely associated with the political activist Rosa Luxemburg.

Lichfield /ˈlɪtʃfiːld/ Patrick Anson, 5th Earl of Lichfield 1939– . British portrait photographer.

Lichtenstein /ˈlɪktənstaɪn/ Roy 1923– . US Pop artist. He uses advertising imagery and comic-strip techniques, often focusing on popular ideals of romance and heroism, as in *Whaam!* 1963 (Tate Gallery, London). He has also produced sculptures in brass, plastic, and enamelled metal.

Liddell Hart /ˈlɪdl ˈhɑːt/ Basil 1895–1970. British military strategist. He was an exponent of mechanized warfare, and his ideas were adopted in Germany in 1935 in creating the 1st Panzer Division, combining motorized infantry and tanks. From 1937 he advised the UK War Office on army reorganization.

Fifty years were spent in the process of making Europe explosive. Five days were enough to detonate it.

Basil Liddell Hart *The Real War, 1914–1918*

Lie /liː/ Trygve (Halvdan) 1896–1968. Norwegian Labour politician and diplomat. He became secretary of the Labour Party in 1926. During the German occupation of Norway in World War II he was foreign minister in the exiled government 1941–46, when he helped retain the Norwegian fleet for the Allies. He became the first secretary general of the United Nations 1946–53, but resigned over Soviet opposition to his handling of the Korean War.

Liebig /ˈliːbɪɡ/ Justus, Baron von 1803–1873. German chemist, a major contributor to agricultural chemistry. He introduced the theory of radicals and discovered chloroform and chloral.

Liebknecht /ˈliːpknext/ Karl 1871–1919. German socialist, son of Wilhelm Liebknecht. A founder of the German Communist Party, originally known as the Spartacus League 1918, he was one of the few socialists who refused to support World War I. He led an unsuccessful revolt with Rosa Luxemburg in Berlin in 1919 and both were murdered by army officers.

Liebknecht /ˈliːpknext/ Wilhelm 1826–1900. German socialist. A friend of the communist theoretician Karl Marx, with whom he took part in the revolution of 1848, he was imprisoned for opposition to the Franco-Prussian War 1870–71. He was one of the founders of the Social Democratic Party 1875. He was the father of Karl Liebknecht.

Lifar /lɪˈfɑː/ Serge 1905–1986. Ukrainian dancer and choreographer. Born in Kiev, he studied under →Nijinsky, joined the Diaghilev company in 1923, and was *maître de ballet* at the Paris Opéra 1930–44 and 1947–59.

A great experimenter, he produced his first ballet without music, *Icare*, in 1935, and published the same year the controversial *Le Manifeste du choréographie*. He developed the role of the male dancer in his *Prometheus* 1929 and *Romeo and Juliet* (music by Prokofiev) 1955.

Ligachev /ˈlɪɡətʃef/ Egor (Kuzmich) 1920– . Soviet politician. He joined the Communist Party 1944, and became a member of the Politburo 1985. He was replaced as the party ideologist in 1988 by Vadim Medvedev.

Ligachev was regarded as the chief conservative ideologist, and the leader of conservative opposition to President →Gorbachev. In July 1990 he failed to secure election to the CPSU Politburo or Central Committee and also failed in his bid to become elected as party deputy general secretary.

Ligeti /ˈlɪɡəti/ György (Sándor) 1923– . Hungarian-born Austrian composer who developed a dense, highly chromatic, polyphonic style in which melody and rhythm are sometimes lost in shifting blocks of sound. He achieved international prominence with *Atmosphères* 1961 and *Requiem* 1965, which were used for Stanley Kubrick's film epic *2001: A Space Odyssey* 1968. Other works include an opera *Le Grand Macabre* 1978, and *Poème symphonique* 1962, for 100 metronomes (clockwork time-keeping devices).

Lighthill /ˈlaɪthɪl/ James 1924– . British mathematician who specialized in the application of mathematics to high-speed aerodynamics and jet propulsion.

Lilburne /ˈlɪlbɜːn/ John 1614–1657. English republican agitator. He was imprisoned 1638–40 for circulating Puritan pamphlets, fought in the

Parliamentary army in the Civil War, and by his advocacy of a democratic republic won the leadership of the Levellers, the democratic party in the English Revolution.

Lilienthal /ˈliːliəntɑːl/ Otto 1848–1896. German aviation pioneer who inspired the US aviators Orville and Wilbur Wright. He made and successfully flew many gliders before he was killed in a glider crash.

Lillee Dennis 1949– . Australian cricketer regarded as the best fast bowler of his generation. He made his Test debut in the 1970–71 season and subsequently played for his country 70 times. Lillee was the first Australian to take 300 wickets in Test cricket. He played Sheffield Shield cricket for Western Australia and at the end of his career made a comeback with Tasmania.

Liman von Sanders /ˈliːmæn fɒn ˈsɑːndəz/ Otto 1855–1929. German general assigned to the Turkish army to become inspector-general and a Turkish field marshal in Dec 1913. This link between the Turks and the Germans caused great suspicion on the part of the French and Russians.

Limbourg brothers Franco-Flemish painters, Pol, Herman, and Jan (Hennequin, Janneken), active in the late 14th and early 15th centuries, first in Paris, then at the ducal court of Burgundy. They produced richly detailed manuscript illuminations, including two Books of Hours.

Patronized by Jean de Berri, duke of Burgundy, from about 1404, they illustrated two Books of Hours that are masterpieces of the International Gothic style, the *Belles Heures* about 1408 (Metropolitan Museum of Art, New York), and *Les très riches Heures du Duc de Berri* about 1413–15 (Musée Condé, Chantilly). Their miniature paintings include a series of scenes representing the months, presenting an almost fairy-tale world of pinnacled castles with lords and ladies, full of detail and brilliant decorative effects. All three brothers were dead by 1416.

Linacre /ˈlɪnəkə/ Thomas c. 1460–1524. English humanist, physician to Henry VIII, from whom he obtained a charter in 1518 to found the Royal College of Physicians, of which he was first president.

Lin Biao /ˌlɪnˈbjaʊ/ 1907–1971. Chinese politician and general. He joined the Communists in 1927, became a commander of →Mao Zedong's Red Army, and led the Northeast People's Liberation Army in the civil war after 1945. He became defence minister in 1959, and as vice chair of the party in 1969 he was expected to be Mao's successor. But in 1972 the government announced that Lin had been killed in an aeroplane crash in Mongolia on 17 Sept 1971 while fleeing to the USSR following an abortive coup attempt.

Lincoln /ˈlɪŋkən/ Abraham 1809–1865. 16th president of the USA 1861–65, a Republican. In the American Civil War, his chief concern was the preservation of the Union from which the Con-

Lincoln President of the USA during the Civil War, Abraham Lincoln. His main aim was to preserve the union and prevent the secession of the Southern states.

federate (Southern) slave states had seceded on his election. In 1863 he announced the freedom of the slaves with the Emancipation Proclamation. He was re-elected in 1864 with victory for the North in sight, but was assassinated at the end of the war.

Lincoln was born in a log cabin in Kentucky. Self-educated, he practised law from 1837 in Springfield, Illinois. He was a member of the state legislature 1832–42, and was known as Honest Abe. He joined the new Republican Party in 1856, and was elected president in 1860 on a minority vote. His refusal to concede to Confederate demands for the evacuation of the federal garrison at Fort Sumter, Charleston, South Carolina, precipitated the first hostilities of the Civil War. In the Gettysburg Address 1863, he declared the aims of preserving a 'nation conceived in liberty, and dedicated to the proposition that all men are created equal'. Re-elected with a large majority in 1864 on a National Union ticket, he advocated a reconciliatory policy towards the South 'with malice towards none, with charity for all'. Five days after General Lee's surrender, Lincoln was shot in a theatre audience by an actor and Confederate sympathizer, John Wilkes Booth.

Lincoln /ˈlɪŋkən/ Benjamin 1733–1810. American military and political leader. As brigadier general in the Continental army during the American Revolution 1775–83, he aided the victory at Saratoga 1777 but was forced to surrender to the British at Charleston 1780. He was secretary of war for the Continental Congress 1781–83, and led the suppression of Shays' Rebellion 1787.

Born in Hingham, Massachusetts, Lincoln served in the legislature and provincial congress prior to the American Revolution.

Lindbergh Pioneer US aviator Charles Lindbergh. He was the first person to fly solo nonstop across the Atlantic, a journey of 5,808 km/3,610 mi which took 33¹/₂ hours in the monoplane the Spirit of St Louis. In 1932 he was again in the public eye when his infant son was kidnapped and murdered, a crime that horrified the American public.

Lind /lɪnd/ Jenny 1820–1887. Swedish soprano of remarkable range, nicknamed the 'Swedish nightingale'. She toured the USA 1850–52 under the management of P T →Barnum.

Lindbergh /ˈlɪndbɜːg/ Charles A(ugustus) 1902–1974. US aviator who made the first solo nonstop flight in 33.5 hours across the Atlantic (Roosevelt Field, Long Island, New York, to Le Bourget airport, Paris) 1927 in the *Spirit of St Louis*, a Ryan monoplane designed by him.

Under the rule of the dollar human life has fallen to its lowest value.

Charles Lindbergh

Lindsay /ˈlɪndzi/ (Nicholas) Vachel 1879–1931. US poet. He wandered the country, living by reciting his balladlike verse, collected in volumes including *General William Booth Enters into Heaven* 1913, *The Congo* 1914, and *Johnny Appleseed* 1928.

Lineker Gary 1960– . English footballer who scored over 250 goals in 550 games for Leicester, Everton, Barcelona, and Tottenham. With 48 goals in 75 internationals to the end of the 1991–92 English season, he needed just two goals to beat Bobby Charlton's record of 49 goals for England. Lineker was elected Footballer of the Year in 1986 and 1992, and was leading scorer at the 1986 World Cup finals.

Linlithgow /lɪnˈlɪθgəʊ/ John Adrian Louis Hope, 1st Marquess Linlithgow 1860–1908. British administrator, son of the 6th earl of Hopetoun, first governor general of Australia 1900–02.

Linnaeus /lɪˈniːəs/ Carolus 1707–1778. Swedish naturalist and physician. His botanical work *Systema naturae* 1735 contained his system for classifying plants into groups depending on shared characteristics (such as the number of stamens in flowers), providing a much-needed framework for identification. He also devised the concise and precise system for naming plants and animals, using one Latin (or Latinized) word to represent the genus and a second to distinguish the species.

For example, in the Latin name of the daisy, *Bellis perennis*, *Bellis* is the name of the genus to which the plant belongs, and *perennis* distinguishes the species from others of the same genus. By tradition the generic name always begins with a capital letter. The author who first described a particular species is often indicated after the name, for example, *Bellis perennis* Linnaeus, showing that the author was Linnaeus.

Lin Piao /lɪn piˈaʊ/ alternative transliteration of →Lin Biao.

Lipatti /lɪˈpæti/ Dinu 1917–1950. Romanian pianist who perfected a small repertoire, notably of the works of the Polish composer Frédéric Chopin. He died of leukaemia at 33.

Lipchitz /ˈlɪpʃɪts/ Jacques 1891–1973. Lithuanian-born sculptor, active in Paris from 1909; he emigrated to the USA in 1941. He was one of the first Cubist sculptors.

Li Peng /liː ˈpʌŋ/ 1928– . Chinese communist politician, a member of the Politburo from 1985, and head of government from 1987. During the pro-democracy demonstrations of 1989 he supported the massacre of students by Chinese troops and the subsequent execution of others. He sought improved relations with the USSR prior to its demise, and has favoured maintaining firm central and party control over the economy.

Li was born at Chengdu in Sichuan province, the son of the writer Li Shouxun (who took part in the Nanchang rising 1927 and was executed 1930), and was adopted by the communist leader Zhou Enlai. He studied at the communist headquarters in Yanan 1941–47 and trained as a hydroelectric engineer at the Moscow Power Institute from 1948. He was appointed minister of the electric power industry 1981, a vice premier 1983, and prime minister 1987. In 1989 he launched the crackdown on demonstrators in Beijing that led to the massacre in Tiananmen Square.

Lipmann /ˈlɪpmən/ Fritz 1899–1986. US biochemist. He investigated the means by which the cell acquires energy and highlighted the crucial role played by the energy-rich phosphate molecule, adenosine triphosphate (ATP). For this and further work on metabolism, Lipmann shared the 1953 Nobel Prize for Medicine with Hans Krebs.

Li Po /liːˈbəʊ/ 705–762. Chinese poet. He used traditional literary forms, but his exuberance, the boldness of his imagination, and the intensity of his feeling have won him recognition as perhaps the greatest of all Chinese poets. Although he was mostly concerned with higher themes, he is also remembered for his celebratory verses on drinking.

Lippershey /ˈlɪpəʃaɪ/ Hans c. 1570–1619. Dutch lens maker, credited with inventing the telescope in 1608.

Lippi /ˈlɪpi/ Filippino 1457–1504. Italian painter of the Florentine school, trained by Botticelli. He produced altarpieces and several fresco cycles, full of detail and drama, elegant and finely drawn. He was the son of Filippo Lippi.

His frescoes, typical of late 15th-century Florentine work, can be found in Sta Maria sopra Minerva, Rome, in Sta Maria Novella, Florence, and elsewhere.

Lippi /ˈlɪpi/ Fra Filippo 1406–1469. Italian painter whose works include frescoes depicting the lives of St Stephen and St John the Baptist in Prato Cathedral 1452–66. He also painted many altarpieces of Madonnas and groups of saints.

Lippi was born in Florence and patronized by the Medici family. The painter and biographer Giorgio →Vasari gave a colourful account of his life including how, as a monk, he was tried in the 1450s for abducting a nun (the mother of his son Filippino).

Lippmann /ˈlɪpmən/ Gabriel 1845–1921. French doctor who invented the direct colour process in photography. He was awarded the Nobel Prize for Physics in 1908.

Lippmann /ˈlɪpmən/ Walter 1889–1974. US liberal political commentator. From 1921 Lippmann was the chief editorial writer for the *New York World* and from 1931 wrote the daily column 'Today and Tomorrow', which was widely syndicated through the *New York Herald Tribune*. Among his books are *A Preface to Morals* 1929, *The Good Society* 1937, and *The Public Philosophy* 1955.

Born in New York and educated at Harvard, Lippmann was one of the founders of the *New Republic* 1914. After service in army intelligence during World War I, he became an adviser to President Wilson at the Versailles Peace Conference.

Lister /ˈlɪstə/ Joseph, 1st Baron Lister 1827–1912. English surgeon and founder of antiseptic surgery, influenced by Louis →Pasteur's work on bacteria. He introduced dressings soaked in carbolic acid and strict rules of hygiene to combat wound sepsis in hospitals.

The number of surgical operations greatly increased following the introduction of anaesthetics, and death rates were more than 40%. Under Lister's regime they fell dramatically.

Liszt /lɪst/ Franz 1811–1886. Hungarian pianist and composer. An outstanding virtuoso of the piano, he was an established concert artist by the age of 12. His expressive, romantic, and frequently chromatic works include piano music (*Transcendental Studies* 1851), symphonies, piano concertos, and organ music. Much of his music is programmatic; he also originated the symphonic poem. Liszt was taught by his father, then by Carl Czerny (1791–1857). He travelled widely in Europe, producing an opera *Don Sanche* in Paris at the age of 14. As musical director and conductor at Weimar 1848–59, he championed the music of Berlioz and Wagner.

Retiring to Rome, he turned again to his early love of religion, and in 1865 became a secular priest (adopting the title Abbé), but he continued to teach and give concert tours. Many of his compositions are lyrical, often technically difficult, piano works, including the *Liebesträume* and the *Hungarian Rhapsodies*, based on folk music. He also wrote an opera and a symphony; masses and oratorios; songs; and piano arrangements of works by Beethoven, Schubert, and Wagner among others. He died at Bayreuth in Germany.

To us musicians the work of Beethoven parallels the pillars of smoke and fire which led the Israelites through the desert.

Franz Liszt
letter to Wilhelm von Lenz 1852

Little Richard /ˈlɪtl ˈrɪtʃəd/ Stage name of Richard Penniman 1932– . US rock singer and pianist. He was one of the creators of rock and roll with his wildly uninhibited renditions of 'Tutti Frutti' 1956, 'Long Tall Sally' 1956, and 'Good Golly Miss Molly' 1957. His subsequent career in soul and rhythm and blues was interrupted by periods devoted to gospel music and religion.

Littlewood /ˈlɪtlwʊd/ Joan 1914– . English theatre director. She was responsible for many vigorous productions at the Theatre Royal, Stratford (London) 1953–75, such as *A Taste of Honey* 1959, *The Hostage* 1959–60, and *Oh, What a Lovely War* 1963.

Litvinov /lɪtˈviːnɒf/ Maxim 1876–1951. Soviet politician, commissioner for foreign affairs under Stalin from Jan 1931 until his removal from office in May 1939.

Litvinov believed in cooperation with the West and obtained US recognition of the USSR in 1934. In the League of Nations he advocated action against the Axis (the alliance of Nazi Germany and Fascist Italy); he was therefore dismissed just before the signing of the Hitler–Stalin nonaggression pact 1939. After the German invasion of the USSR, he was ambassador to the USA 1941–43.

Liu Shaoqi /ˈljuː ʃaʊˈtʃiː/ or *Liu Shao-chi* 1898–1969. Chinese communist politician, in effective control of government 1960–65. A labour organizer, he was a firm proponent of the Soviet style of government based around disciplined one-party control, the use of incentive gradings, and priority for industry over agriculture. This was opposed by Mao Zedong, but began to be implemented by Liu while he was state president 1960–65. Liu was brought down during the Cultural Revolution.

The son of a Hunan peasant farmer, Liu attended the same local school as Mao. As a member of the Chinese Communist Party (CCP), he was sent to Moscow to study communism, and returned to Shanghai in 1922. Mao yielded the title of president to him in 1960, and after the failure of the Great Leap Forward to create effective agricultural communes, Liu introduced a recovery programme. This was successful, but was seen as a return to capitalism. He was stripped of his post and expelled from the CCP in April 1969 and banished to Kaifeng in Henan province, where he died in Nov 1969 after being locked in a disused bank vault. He was rehabilitated posthumously ten years later.

Liverpool /ˈlɪvəpuːl/ Robert Banks Jenkinson, 2nd Earl Liverpool 1770–1825. British Tory politician. He entered Parliament 1790 and was foreign secretary 1801–03, home secretary 1804–06 and 1807–09, war minister 1809–12, and prime minister 1812–27. His government conducted the Napoleonic Wars to a successful conclusion, but its ruthless suppression of freedom of speech and of the press aroused such opposition that during 1815–20 revolution frequently seemed imminent.

Livia Drusilla /ˈlɪviə druːˈsɪlə/ 58 BC–AD 29. Roman empress, wife of →Augustus from 39 BC, she was the mother by her first husband of →Tiberius and engaged in intrigue to secure his succession to the imperial crown. She remained politically active to the end of her life.

Livingston /ˈlɪvɪŋstən/ Robert R 1746–1813. American public official and diplomat. As secretary for foreign affairs 1781, he directed negotiations for the Paris Peace Treaty 1783. In 1801 he was named minister to France by President Jefferson. With James Monroe, Livingston secured the purchase of the Louisiana Territory 1803, acquiring a large part of North America from the French.

Born in New York and educated at King's College (now Columbia University), Livingston was admitted to the bar 1770. After service in the Continental Congress 1775 he helped write the New York Constitution and served as state chancellor 1776–1801. He returned to the Continental Congress 1779.

Livingstone /ˈlɪvɪŋstən/ David 1813–1873. Scottish missionary explorer. In 1841 he went to Africa, reached Lake Ngami 1849, followed the Zambezi to its mouth, saw the Victoria Falls 1855, and went to East and Central Africa 1858–64, reaching Lakes Shirwa and Malawi. From 1866, he tried to find the source of the river Nile, and reached Ujiji in Tanganyika in Oct 1871. British explorer Henry Stanley joined Livingstone in Ujiji.

Livingstone not only mapped a great deal of the African continent but also helped to end the Arab slave trade. He died in Old Chitambo (now in Zambia) and was buried in Westminster Abbey, London.

Men are immortal until their work is done.

David Livingstone letter describing the death of Bishop Mackenzie, March 1862

Livingstone /ˈlɪvɪŋstən/ Ken(neth) 1945– . British left-wing Labour politician. He was leader of the Greater London Council (GLC) 1981–86 and a member of Parliament from 1987. He stood as a candidate for the Labour Party leadership elections 1992.

Livingstone joined the Labour Party in 1968, and was active in London politics from 1971. As leader of the GLC until its abolition in 1986, he displayed outside GLC headquarters current unemployment figures so that they were clearly visible to MPs in the Palace of Westminster across the river Thames. He was elected to Parliament representing the London constituency of Brent East in 1987.

Livy /ˈlɪvi/ Titus Livius 59 BC–AD 17. Roman historian, author of a *History of Rome* from the city's foundation to 9 BC, based partly on legend. It was composed of 142 books, of which 35 survive, covering the periods from the arrival of Aeneas in Italy to 293 BC and from 218 to 167 BC.

Li Xiannian /liː ʃiˌæn niˈæn/ 1905–1992. Chinese politician, member of the Chinese Communist Party (CCP) Politburo from 1956. He fell from favour during the 1966–69 Cultural Revolution, but was rehabilitated as finance minister in 1973, supporting cautious economic reform. He was state president 1983–88.

Li, born into a poor peasant family in Hubei province, joined the CCP in 1927 and served as a political commissar during the Long March of 1934–36. During the 1950s and early 1960s Li was vice premier to the State Council and minister for finance and was inducted into the CCP Politburo and secretariat in 1956 and 1958 respectively.

Llewellyn /əˈwelɪn/ Richard. Pen name of Richard Vivian Llewellyn Lloyd 1907–1983. Welsh writer. *How Green Was My Valley* 1939, a novel about a S Wales mining family, was made into a play and a film.

Llewelyn /:ʊ'welɪn, Welsh, ʃə'welɪn/ two kings of Wales:

Llewelyn I 1173–1240. King of Wales from 1194 who extended his rule to all Wales not in Norman hands, driving the English from N Wales 1212, and taking Shrewsbury 1215. During the early part of Henry III's reign, he was several times attacked by English armies. He was married to Joanna, illegitimate daughter of King John.

Llewelyn II c. 1225–1282. King of Wales from 1246, grandson of Llewelyn I. In 1277 Edward I of England compelled Llewelyn to acknowledge him as overlord and to surrender S Wales. His death while leading a national uprising ended Welsh independence.

Lloyd /lɔɪd/ Harold 1893–1971. US film comedian, noted for his 'trademark' of thick horn-rimmed glasses and straw hat, who invented the bumbling cliff-hanger and dangler. He appeared from 1913 in silent and talking films. His silent films include *Grandma's Boy* 1922, *Safety Last* 1923, and *The Freshman* 1925. His first talkie was *Movie Crazy* 1932. He produced films after 1938, including the reissued *Harold Lloyd's World of Comedy* 1962 and *Funny Side of Life* 1964.

Lloyd /lɔɪd/ John, known as *John Scolvus*, 'the skilful', lived 15th century. Welsh sailor who carried on an illegal trade with Greenland and is claimed to have reached North America, sailing as far south as Maryland, in 1477 (15 years before the voyage of Columbus).

Lloyd /lɔɪd/ Marie. Stage name of Matilda Alice Victoria Wood 1870–1922. English music-hall artist whose Cockney songs embodied the music-hall traditions of 1890s comedy.

Lloyd /lɔɪd/ Selwyn; see →Selwyn Lloyd, British Conservative politician.

Lloyd George /lɔɪd 'dʒɔːdʒ/ David 1863–1945. Welsh Liberal politician, prime minister of Britain 1916–22. A pioneer of social reform, as chancellor of the Exchequer 1908–15 he introduced old-age pensions 1908 and health and unemployment insurance 1911. High unemployment, intervention in the Russian Civil War, and use of the military police force, the Black and Tans, in Ireland eroded his support as prime minister, and the creation of the Irish Free State in 1921 and his pro-Greek policy against the Turks caused the collapse of his coalition government.

Lloyd George was born in Manchester, became a solicitor, and was member of Parliament for Caernarvon Boroughs from 1890. During the Boer War, he was prominent as a pro-Boer. His 1909 budget (with graduated direct taxes and taxing land values) provoked the Lords to reject it, and resulted in the Act of 1911 limiting their powers. He held ministerial posts during World War I until 1916 when there was an open breach between him and Prime Minister →Asquith, and he became prime minister of a coalition govern-

ment. Securing a unified Allied command, he enabled the Allies to withstand the last German offensive and achieve victory. After World War I he had a major role in the Versailles peace treaty.

In the 1918 elections, he achieved a huge majority over Labour and Asquith's followers. He had become largely distrusted within his own party by 1922, and never regained power.

Lloyd Webber /lɔɪd 'webə/ Andrew 1948– . English composer. His early musicals, with lyrics by Tim Rice, include *Joseph and the Amazing Technicolor Dreamcoat* 1968; *Jesus Christ Superstar* 1970; and *Evita* 1978, based on the life of the Argentine leader Eva Perón. He also wrote *Cats* 1981 and *The Phantom of the Opera* 1986.

Llull /lju:l/ Ramon 1232–1316. Catalan scholar and mystic. He began his career at the court of James I of Aragon (1212–1276) in Majorca. He produced treatises on theology, mysticism, and chivalry in Catalan, Latin, and Arabic. His *Ars magna* was a mechanical device, a kind of prototype computer, by which all problems could be solved by manipulating fundamental Aristotelian categories.

He also wrote the prose romance *Blanquerna*, in his native Catalan, the first novel written in a Romance language. In later life he became a Franciscan, and died a martyr at Bugia, Algeria.

Lobachevsky /ˌlɒbə'tʃefski/ Nikolai Ivanovich 1792–1856. Russian mathematician who concurrently with, but independently of, Karl →Gauss and the Hungarian János Bolyai (1802–1860), founded non-Euclidean geometry. Lobachevsky published the first account of the subject in 1829, but his work went unrecognized until Georg →Riemann's system was published.

Lobengula /ˌləʊbən'gjuːlə/ 1836–1894. King of Matabeleland (now part of Zimbabwe) 1870–93. He was overthrown in 1893 by a military expedition organized by Cecil →Rhodes's South African Company.

After accepting British protection from internal and external threats to his leadership in 1888, Lobengula came under increasing pressure from British mining interests to allow exploitation of goldfields near Bulawayo. This led to his overthrow by a British military expedition in 1893.

Lochner /lɒxnə/ Stephan died 1451. German painter, active in Cologne from 1442, a master of the International Gothic style. Most of his work is still in Cologne: for example, the *Virgin in the Rose Garden* (Wallraf-Richartz Museum) and *Adoration of the Magi* (Cologne Cathedral).

The finest eloquence is that which gets things done; the worst is that which delays them.

David Lloyd George speech at Paris Peace Conference Jan 1919

Locke English philosopher John Locke. He wrote Two Treatises on Government *and* Essay concerning Human Understanding.

Locke /lɒk/ John 1632–1704. English philosopher. His *Essay concerning Human Understanding* 1690 maintained that experience was the only source of knowledge (empiricism), and that 'we can have knowlege no farther than we have ideas' prompted by such experience. *Two Treatises on Government* 1690 helped to form contemporary ideas of liberal democracy.

Locke studied at Oxford, practised medicine, and in 1667 became secretary to the Earl of Shaftesbury. He consequently fell under suspicion as a Whig and in 1683 fled to Holland, where he lived until the 1688 revolution brought William of Orange to the English throne. In later life he published many works on philosophy, politics, theology, and economics; these include *Letters on Toleration* 1689–92 and *Some Thoughts concerning Education* 1693. His *Two Treatises on Government* supplied the classical statement of Whig theory and enjoyed great influence in America and France. It supposed that governments derive their authority from popular consent (regarded as a 'contract'), so that a government may be rightly overthrown if it infringes such fundamental rights of the people as religious freedom. He believed that at birth the mind was a blank, and that all ideas came from sense impressions.

Lockwood /lɒkwʊd/ Margaret. Stage name of Margaret Mary Lockwood 1919–1990. English actress. Between 1937 and 1949 she acted exclusively in the cinema, appearing in Alfred Hitchcock's *The Lady Vanishes* 1938 and in *The Wicked Lady* 1945. After 1955 she made only one film, *The Slipper and the Rose* 1976, although she periodically appeared on stage and on television until her retirement in 1980.

Lodge /lɒdʒ/ David (John) 1935– . English novelist, short-story writer, playwright, and critic. Much of his fiction concerns the role of Catholicism in mid-20th-century England, exploring the situation both through broad comedy and parody, as in *The British Museum is Falling Down* 1967, and realistically, as in *How Far Can You Go?* 1980. *Nice Work* 1988 was short-listed for the Booker Prize.

His other works include *Changing Places* 1975 and its sequel *Small World* 1984, both satirical 'campus' novels; the play, *The Writing Game* 1990; and *Paradise News* 1991.

Lodge /lɒdʒ/ Henry Cabot 1850–1924. US politician, Republican senator from 1893, and chairman of the Senate Foreign Relations Committee after World War I. He supported conservative economic legislation at home but expansionist policies abroad. Nevertheless, he influenced the USA to stay out of the League of Nations 1920 as a threat to US sovereignty.

Lodge /lɒdʒ/ Henry Cabot, II 1902–1985. US diplomat. He was Eisenhower's presidential campaign manager and the US representative at the United Nations 1953–60. Ambassador to South Vietnam 1963–64 and 1965–67, he replaced W A Harriman as President Nixon's negotiator in the Vietnam peace talks 1969. He was a grandson of Henry Cabot Lodge.

Lodge /lɒdʒ/ Oliver Joseph 1851–1940. British physicist. He developed a system of wireless communication in 1894, and his work was instrumental in the development of radio receivers. He became interested in psychic research after his son was killed in 1915.

Lodge /lɒdʒ/ Thomas *c.* 1558–1625. English author whose romance *Rosalynde* 1590 was the basis of Shakespeare's play *As You Like It*.

Loeb /lɜːb/ James 1867–1933. German banker, born in New York, who financed the **Loeb Classical Library** of Greek and Latin authors, which gives the original text with a parallel translation.

Loewe /ˈləʊi/ Frederick 1901–1988. US composer of musicals. In 1942 he joined forces with the lyricist Alan Jay Lerner (1918–1986), and their joint successes include *Brigadoon* 1947, *Paint Your Wagon* 1951, *My Fair Lady* 1956, *Gigi* 1958, and *Camelot* 1960.

Born in Berlin, the son of an operatic tenor, he studied under Busoni, and in 1924 went with his father to the USA.

Loewi /ˈlɜːvi/ Otto 1873–1961. German physiologist whose work on the nervous system established that a chemical substance is responsible for the stimulation of one nerve cell (neuron) by another.

The substance was shown by the physiologist Henry Dale to be acetylcholine, now known to be one of the most vital neurotransmitters. For this work Loewi and Dale were jointly awarded the 1936 Nobel Prize for Medicine.

Lofting /ˈlɒftɪŋ/ Hugh 1886–1947. English writer and illustrator of children's books, including the 'Dr Dolittle' series, in which the hero can talk to animals. Lofting was born in Maidenhead, Berkshire, was originally a civil engineer, and went to the USA in 1912.

Lombard /ˈlɒmbɑːd/ Carole. Stage name of Jane Alice Peters 1908–1942. US comedy film actress. A warm and witty actress, she starred in some of the best comedies of the 1930s: *Twentieth Century* 1934, *My Man Godfrey* 1936, and *To Be or Not to Be* 1942.

Lombardi /lɒmˈbɑːdi/ Vince(nt Thomas) 1913–1970. US football coach. As head coach of the Green Bay Packers 1959, he transformed a losing team into a major power, winning the first two Super Bowls 1967 and 1968. His last coaching position was with the Washington Redskins 1969–70.

Born in Brooklyn, New York, USA, Lombardi was educated at Fordham University. He was an assistant coach at Fordham 1947–48 and West Point 1949–54, after which he entered professional football as offensive coach with the New York Giants.

Lombroso /lɒmˈbrəʊsəʊ/ Cesare 1836–1909. Italian criminologist. His major work is *L'uomo delinquente/The Delinquent Man* 1889. He held the now discredited idea that there was a physically distinguishable 'criminal type'.

London /ˈlʌndən/ Jack (John Griffith) 1876–1916. US novelist, author of the adventure stories *The Call of the Wild* 1903, *The Sea Wolf* 1904, and *White Fang* 1906. By 1906 he was the most widely read writer in the US and had been translated into 68 languages.

Long /lɒŋ/ Huey 1893–1935. US Democratic politician, nicknamed 'the Kingfish', governor of Louisiana 1928–31, US senator for Louisiana 1930–35, legendary as a demagogue. He was popular with poor white voters for his programme of social and economic reform, which he called the 'Share Our Wealth' programme. It represented a significant challenge to F D Roosevelt's New Deal economic programme. Long's scheme called for massive redistribution of wealth through high inheritance taxes and confiscatory taxes on high incomes. His own extravagance, including the state capitol building at Baton Rouge built of bronze and marble, was widely criticized. He was assassinated.

Longfellow /ˈlɒŋfeləʊ/ Henry Wadsworth 1807–1882. US poet, remembered for ballads ('Excelsior', 'The Village Blacksmith', 'The Wreck of the Hesperus') and the mythic narrative epics *Evangeline* 1847, *The Song of →Hiawatha* 1855, and *The Courtship of Miles Standish* 1858.

Born in Portland, Maine, Longfellow graduated from Bowdoin College and taught modern languages there and at Harvard University 1835–54, after which he travelled widely. The most popular

Longfellow US poet Henry Wadsworth Longfellow. He was the most famous American poet of the 19th century and the first to be commemorated in Poets' Corner, Westminster Abbey, London. His best-known works are his long narrative poems such as The Song of Hiawatha.

US poet of the 19th century, Longfellow was also an adept translator. His other works include six sonnets on Dante, a translation of Dante's *Divine Comedy*, and *Tales of a Wayside Inn* 1863, which includes the popular poem 'Paul Revere's Ride.'

Let us, then, be up and doing, With a heart for any fate.

Henry Wadsworth Longfellow
'A Psalm of Life'

Longford /ˈlɒŋfəd/ Elizabeth, Countess of Longford (born Harman) 1906– . English historical writer whose books include *Victoria RI* 1964. She is married to Lord Longford; their eldest daughter is Lady Antonia →Fraser.

Longford /ˈlɒŋfəd/ Frank (Francis Aungier) Pakenham, 7th Earl of Longford 1905– . Anglo-Irish Labour politician. He was brought up a Protestant but is now a leading Catholic. He is an advocate of penal reform.

He worked in the Conservative Party Economic Research Department 1930–32, yet became a member of the Labour Party and held ministerial posts 1948–51 and 1964–68.

Longinus /lɒnˈdʒaɪnəs/ Cassius AD 213–273. Greek philosopher. He taught in Athens for many years. As adviser to →Zenobia of Palmyra, he instigated her revolt against Rome and was put to death when she was captured.

Longinus /lɒn'dʒaɪnəs/ Dionysius lived 1st century AD. Greek critic, author of the treatise *On the Sublime*, which influenced the English poets John Dryden and Alexander Pope.

Lonsdale /lɒnzdeɪl/ Hugh Cecil Lowther, 5th Earl of Lonsdale 1857–1944. British sporting enthusiast. *Lonsdale Belts* in boxing, first presented in 1909, are named after him. Any fighter who wins three British title fights in one weight division retains a Lonsdale Belt. A former president of the National Sporting Club, he presented his first belt to the club in 1909, and it was won by Freddie Welsh (lightweight) later that year.

Lonsdale was an expert huntsman, steeplechaser, boxer, and yachtsman. Notorious for extramarital affairs, he was ordered to leave Britain by Queen Victoria after a scandal with the actress Violet Cameron. As a result, he set off to the Arctic in 1888 for 15 months, travelling by boat and sleigh through N Canada to Alaska. The collection of Inuit artefacts he brought back is now in the Museum of Mankind, London.

Loos /ləʊs/ Adolf 1870–1933. Austrian architect and author of the article *Ornament and Crime* 1908, in which he rejected the ornamentation and curved lines of the Viennese *Jugendstil* movement. His buildings include private houses on Lake Geneva 1904 and the Steiner House in Vienna 1910.

Loos /luːz/ Anita 1888–1981. US writer, author of the humorous fictitious diary *Gentlemen Prefer Blondes* 1925. She became a screenwriter 1912 and worked on more than 60 films, including D W →Griffith's *Intolerance* 1916.

Lope de Vega (Carpio) Felix. Spanish poet and dramatist; see →Vega, Lope de.

Lopes /laʊpez/ Fernão *c.* 1380–1460. Portuguese historian, whose *Crónicas/Chronicles* (begun 1434) relate vividly the history of the Portuguese monarchy between 1357 and 1411.

López /ləʊpez/ Carlos Antonio 1790–1862. Paraguayan dictator (in succession to his uncle José Francia) from 1840. He achieved some economic improvement, and he was succeeded by his son Francisco López.

López /ləʊpez/ Francisco Solano 1827–1870. Paraguayan dictator in succession to his father Carlos López. He involved the country in a war with Brazil, Uruguay, and Argentina, during which approximately 80% of the population died.

Lopez /ləʊpez/ Nancy 1957– . US golfer who turned professional in 1977 and in 1979 became the first woman to win $200,000 in a season. She has won the US LPGA title three times and has won more than 35 tour events, and $3 million in prize money.

Lorca /lɔːkə/ Federico García 1898–1936. Spanish poet and playwright, born in Granada. His plays include *Bodas de sangre/Blood Wedding* 1933 and *La casa de Bernarda Alba/The House of Bernar-*da *Alba* 1936. His poems include *Lament*, written for the bullfighter Mejías. Lorca was shot by the Falangists during the Spanish Civil War.

Romancero gitano/Gipsy Ballad-book 1928 shows the influence of the Andalusian songs of the area. In 1929–30 Lorca visited New York, and his experiences are reflected in *Poeta en Nuevo York* 1940. Returning to Spain, he founded a touring theatrical company and began to write plays.

Loren /lɔːrən/ Sophia. Stage name of Sofia Scicolone 1934– . Italian film actress whose boldly sensual appeal was promoted by her husband, producer Carlo Ponti. Her work includes *Aida* 1953, *The Key* 1958, *La ciociara/Two Women* 1960, *Judith* 1965, and *Firepower* 1979.

Lorentz /lɔːrənts/ Hendrik Antoon 1853–1928. Dutch physicist, winner (with his pupil Pieter →Zeeman) of a Nobel prize in 1902 for his work on the Zeeman effect (when light from certain heated elements, such as sodium or lithium, is passed through a spectroscope in the presence of a strong magnetic field, the spectrum splits into a number of distinct lines).

Lorentz spent most of his career trying to develop and improve James →Maxwell's electromagnetic theory. He also attempted to account for the anomalies of the →Michelson–Morley experiment by proposing, independently of George Fitzgerald, that moving bodies contracted in their direction of motion. He took the matter further with his method of transforming space and time coordinates, later known as Lorentz transformations, which prepared the way for Albert Einstein's theory of relativity.

Lorenz /lɔːrənts/ Konrad 1903–1989. Austrian ethologist. Director of the Max Planck Institute for the Physiology of Behaviour in Bavaria 1955–73, he wrote the studies of ethology (animal behaviour) *King Solomon's Ring* 1952 and *On Aggression* 1966. In 1973 he shared the Nobel Prize for Medicine with Nikolaas Tinbergen and Karl von Frisch.

Lorenz sympathized with Nazi views on eugenics, and in 1938 applied to join the Nazi party.

It is a good morning exercise for a research scientist to discard a pet hypothesis every day before breakfast. It keeps him young.

Konrad Lorenz *On Aggression* 1966

Lorenz /lɔːrənts/ Ludwig Valentine 1829–1891. Danish mathematician and physicist. He developed mathematical formulae to describe phenomena such as the relation between the refraction of light and the density of a pure transparent substance, and the relation between a metal's electrical and thermal conductivity and temperature.

Lorenzetti /lɔːrən'zeti/ Ambrogio c. 1319–1347. Italian painter active in Siena and Florence. His allegorical frescoes *Good and Bad Government* 1337–39 (Town Hall, Siena) include a detailed panoramic landscape and a view of the city of Siena that shows an unusual mastery of spatial effects.

Lorenzetti /ˌlɔːrən'zeti/ Pietro c. 1306–1345. Italian painter of the Sienese school, active in Assisi. His frescoes in the Franciscan basilica, Assisi, reflect the Florentine painter ➔Giotto's concern with mass and weight. He was the brother of Ambrogio Lorenzetti.

Lorimer /lɒrɪmə/ Robert Stoddart 1864–1929. Scottish architect, the most prolific architect representative of the Scottish Arts and Crafts Movement. Lorimer drew particularly from Scottish vernacular buildings of the 16th and 17th centuries to create a series of mansions and houses, practically planned with picturesque, roughcast, turreted exteriors. Examples of his work include Ardkinglas House, Argyll, 1906, and Ruwallan House, Ayrshire, 1902.

Lorrain /lɒ'ræn/ Claude. French painter; see ➔Claude Lorrain.

Lorre /lɒri/ Peter. Stage name of Lazlo Löwenstein 1904–1964. Hungarian character actor with bulging eyes, high voice, and melancholy mien. He made several films in Germany before moving to Hollywood in 1935. He appeared in *M* 1931, *Mad Love* 1935, *The Maltese Falcon* 1941, *Casablanca* 1942, *Beat the Devil* 1953, and *The Raven* 1963. His last film was *Patsy* 1964.

Los Angeles /lɒs 'æŋheles/ Victoria de 1923– . Spanish soprano. She is renowned for her interpretations of Spanish songs and for the roles of Manon and Madame Butterfly in the Italian composer Giacomo Puccini's operas.

Losey /ləusi/ Joseph 1909–1984. US film director. Blacklisted as a former communist in the ➔McCarthy era, he settled in England, where his films included *The Servant* 1963 and *The Go-Between* 1971.

Lothair /ləu'θeə/ 825–869. King of Lotharingia from 855, when he inherited the region from his father, the Holy Roman emperor Lothair I.

Lothair /ləu'θeə/ two Holy Roman emperors:

Lothair I 795–855. Holy Roman emperor from 817 in association with his father Louis I. On Louis's death in 840, the empire was divided between Lothair and his brothers; Lothair took N Italy and the valleys of the rivers Rhône and Rhine.

Lothair II c. 1070–1137. Holy Roman emperor from 1133 and German king from 1125. His election as emperor, opposed by the ➔Hohenstaufen family of princes, was the start of the feud between the Guelph and Ghibelline factions, who supported the papal party and the Hohenstaufens' claim to the imperial throne respectively.

Lotto /lɒtəu/ Lorenzo c. 1480–1556. Italian painter, born in Venice, active in Bergamo, Treviso, Venice, Ancona, and Rome. His early works were influenced by Giovanni Bellini; his mature style belongs to the High Renaissance. He painted dignified portraits, altarpieces, and frescoes.

Louis, Prince of Battenberg /luːi/ 1854–1921. German-born British admiral who took British nationality in 1917 and translated his name to Mountbatten.

He was First Sea Lord 1912–14, but was forced to resign because of anti-German sentiment. In 1917 he was made marquess of Milford Haven. He was made admiral of the fleet in 1921.

Louis /luːis/ Joe. Assumed name of Joseph Louis Barrow 1914–1981. US boxer, nicknamed 'the Brown Bomber'. He was world heavyweight champion between 1937 and 1949 and made a record 25 successful defences (a record for any weight).

Louis was the longest reigning world heavyweight champion at 11 years and 252 days before announcing his retirement in 1949. He made a comeback and lost to Ezzard Charles in a world title fight in 1950.

Louis /luːis/ Morris 1912–1962. US abstract painter. From Abstract Expressionism he turned to the colour-staining technique developed by Helen ➔Frankenthaler, using thinned-out acrylic paints poured on rough canvas to create the illusion of vaporous layers of colour. The *Veil* paintings of the 1950s are examples.

Louis /luːi/ eighteen kings of France, including:

Louis I *the Pious* 788–840. Holy Roman emperor from 814, when he succeeded his father Charlemagne.

Louis II *the Stammerer* 846–879. King of France from 877, son of Charles II, the Bald. He was dominated by the clergy and nobility, who exacted many concessions from him.

Louis III 863–882. King of N France from 879, while his brother Carloman (866–884) ruled S France. He was the son of Louis II. Louis countered a revolt of the nobility at the beginning of his reign, and his resistance to the Normans made him a hero of epic poems.

Louis IV (d'Outremer) 921–954. King of France from 936. His reign was marked by the rebellion of nobles who refused to recognize his authority. As a result of his liberality they were able to build powerful feudal lordships.

He was raised in England after his father Charles III, the Simple, had been overthrown in 922 by Robert I. After the death of Raoul, Robert's brother-in-law and successor, Louis was chosen by the nobles to be king. He had difficulties with his vassal Hugh the Great, and skirmishes with the Hungarians, who had invaded S France.

Louis V 966–987. King of France from 986, last of the →Carolingian dynasty (descendants of Charlemagne).

Louis VI *the Fat* 1081–1137. King of France from 1108. He led his army against feudal brigands, the English (under Henry I), and the Holy Roman Empire, temporarily consolidating his realm and extending it into Flanders. He was a benefactor to the church, and his advisers included Abbot →Suger.

Louis VII *c.* 1120–1180. King of France from 1137, who led the Second Crusade.

Louis VIII 1187–1226. King of France from 1223, who was invited to become king of England in place of →John by the English barons, and unsuccessfully invaded England 1215–17.

Louis IX St 1214–1270. King of France from 1226, leader of the 7th and 8th Crusades. He was defeated in the former by the Muslims, spending four years in captivity. He died in Tunis. He was canonized in 1297.

Louis X *the Stubborn* 1289–1316. King of France who succeeded his father Philip IV in 1314. His reign saw widespread discontent among the nobles, which he countered by granting charters guaranteeing seignorial rights, although some historians claim that by using evasive tactics, he gave up nothing.

Louis XI 1423–1483. King of France from 1461. He broke the power of the nobility (headed by →Charles the Bold) by intrigue and military power.

Louis XII 1462–1515. King of France from 1499. He was duke of Orléans until he succeeded his cousin Charles VIII to the throne. His reign was devoted to Italian wars.

Louis XIII 1601–1643. King of France from 1610 (in succession to his father Henry IV), he assumed royal power in 1617. He was under the political control of Cardinal →Richelieu 1624–42.

Louis XIV *the Sun King* 1638–1715. King of France from 1643, when he succeeded his father Louis XIII; his mother was Anne of Austria. Until 1661 France was ruled by the chief minister, Jules Mazarin, but later Louis took absolute power, summed up in his saying *L'Etat c'est moi* ('I am the state'). Throughout his reign he was engaged in unsuccessful expansionist wars – 1667–68, 1672–78, 1688–97, and 1701–13 (the War of the Spanish Succession) – against various European alliances, always including Britain and the Netherlands. He was a patron of the arts.

The greatest of his ministers was Jean-Baptiste Colbert, whose work was undone by the king's military adventures. Louis attempted 1667–68 to annex the Spanish Netherlands, but was frustrated by an alliance of the Netherlands, Britain, and Sweden. Having detached Britain from the alliance, he invaded the Netherlands in 1672, but the Dutch stood firm (led by William of Orange;

see →William III of England) and despite European alliance formed against France, achieved territorial gains at the Peace of Nijmegen 1678.

When war was renewed 1688–97 between Louis and the Grand Alliance (including Britain), formed by William of Orange, the French were everywhere victorious on land, but the French fleet was almost destroyed at the Battle of La Hogue 1692. The acceptance by Louis of the Spanish throne in 1700 (for his grandson) precipitated the War of the Spanish Succession, and the Treaty of Utrecht 1713 ended French supremacy in Europe.

In 1660 Louis married the Infanta Maria Theresa of Spain, but he was greatly influenced by his mistresses, including Louise de La Vallière, Madame de Montespan, and Madame de Maintenon.

Louis XV 1710–1774. King of France from 1715, with the Duke of Orléans as regent until 1723. He was the great-grandson of Louis XIV. Indolent and frivolous, Louis left government in the hands of his ministers, the Duke of Bourbon and Cardinal Fleury (1653–1743). On the latter's death he attempted to rule alone but became entirely dominated by his mistresses, Madame de Pompadour and Madame Du Barry. His foreign policy led to French possessions in Canada and India being lost to England.

Louis XVI 1754–1793. King of France from 1774, grandson of Louis XV, and son of Louis the Dauphin. He was dominated by his queen, →Marie Antoinette, and French finances fell into such confusion that in 1789 the States General (parliament) had to be summoned, and the French Revolution began. Louis lost his personal popularity in June 1791 when he attempted to flee the country, and in Aug 1792 the Parisians stormed the Tuileries palace and took the royal family prisoner. Deposed in Sept 1792, Louis was tried in Dec, sentenced for treason in Jan 1793, and guillotined.

Louis XVII 1785–1795. Nominal king of France, the son of Louis XVI. During the French Revolution he was imprisoned with his parents in 1792 and probably died in prison.

Louis XVIII 1755–1824. King of France 1814–24, the younger brother of Louis XVI. He assumed the title of king in 1795, having fled into exile in 1791 during the French Revolution, but became king only on the fall of Napoleon I in April 1814. Expelled during Napoleon's brief return (the 'hundred days') in 1815, he resumed power after Napoleon's final defeat at Waterloo, pursuing a policy of calculated liberalism until ultra-royalist pressure became dominant after 1820.

Louis Philippe /luːi fiˈliːp/ 1773–1850. King of France 1830–48. Son of Louis Philippe Joseph, Duke of Orléans 1747–93; both were known as *Philippe Egalité* from their support of the 1792 Revolution. Louis Philippe fled into exile

1793–1814, but became king after the 1830 revolution with the backing of the rich bourgeoisie. Corruption discredited his regime, and after his overthrow, he escaped to the UK and died there.

Lovat /ˈlʌvət/ Simon Fraser, 12th Baron Lovat *c.* 1667–1747. Scottish Jacobite. Throughout a political career lasting 50 years he constantly intrigued with both Jacobites and Whigs, and was beheaded for supporting the 1745 rebellion.

Lovecraft /ˈlʌvkrɑːft/ H(oward) P(hillips) 1890–1937. US writer of horror fiction whose stories of hostile, supernatural forces have lent names and material to many other writers in the genre. Much of his work on this theme was collected in *The Outsider and Others* 1939.

Lovelace /ˈlʌvleɪs/ Richard 1618–1658. English poet. Imprisoned in 1642 for petitioning for the restoration of royal rule, he wrote 'To Althea from Prison', and in a second term in jail in 1648 revised his collection *Lucasta* 1649.

Lovell /ˈlʌvəl/ Bernard 1913–   . British radio astronomer, director (until 1981) of Jodrell Bank Experimental Station (now Nuffield Radio Astronomy Laboratories).

During World War II he worked at the Telecommunications Research Establishment (1939–45), and in 1951 became professor of radio astronomy at the University of Manchester. His books include *Radio Astronomy* 1951 and *The Exploration of Outer Space* 1961.

Low /ləʊ/ David 1891–1963. New Zealand-born British political cartoonist, creator (in newspapers such as the London *Evening Standard*) of Colonel Blimp, the TUC carthorse, and others.

Low /ləʊ/ Juliette Gordon 1860–1927. Founder of the Girl Scouts in the USA. She formed a troop of 16 'Girl Guides' in Savannah 1912, based on UK scouting organizations founded by Robert Baden-Powell. Establishing national headquarters in Washington DC 1913, she changed the name of the organization to the Girl Scouts of America (GSA).

Born in Savannah, Georgia, USA and educated in New York, Low moved temporarily to England. She served as president of the GSA 1915–20 and worked tirelessly to establish Girl Scout troops throughout the USA.

Lowe /ləʊ/ John 1947–   . English darts player. He has won most of the major titles including the world championships in 1979 and 1987. In 1986 he achieved the first televised nine-dart finish at the MFI Championship at Reading.

Lowell /ˈləʊəl/ Amy (Lawrence) 1874–1925. US poet who began her career by publishing the conventional *A Dome of Many-Colored Glass* 1912 but eventually succeeded Ezra Pound as leader of the Imagists, who adopted the principles of free verse, complex imagery, and poetic impersonality. Her works, in free verse, include *Sword Blades and Poppy Seed* 1916.

Lowell /ˈləʊəl/ Francis Cabot 1775–1817. US industrialist who imported the new technology of English textile mills to America. With the cutoff of international trade during the Anglo-American War of 1812, Lowell established the Boston Manufacturing Co, a mechanized textile mill at Waltham, Massachusetts.

Born in Newburyport, Massachusetts, USA, and educated at Harvard University, Lowell was a successful merchant. On a trip to England 1810–12 he was impressed by the country's mechanized mills and returned to the USA to build his own, similar mills.

After the war he campaigned for tariff protection for the US textile industry. In 1822 the mill town of Lowell, Massachusetts, was established and named after him.

Lowell /ˈləʊəl/ J(ames) R(ussell) 1819–1891. US poet whose works range from the didactic *The Vision of Sir Launfal* 1848 to such satirical poems as *The Biglow Papers* 1848.

As a critic, he developed a deep awareness of the US literary tradition. He was also a diplomat and served as minister to Spain 1877–80 and England 1880–85.

No man is born into the world whose work Is not born with him; there is always work, And tools to work withal, for those who will.

J R Lowell
'A Glance Behind the Curtain' 1843

Lowell /ˈləʊəl/ Percival 1855–1916. US astronomer who predicted the existence of a 'Planet X' beyond Neptune, and started the search that led to the discovery of Pluto in 1930. In 1894 he founded the Lowell Observatory at Flagstaff, Arizona, where he reported seeing 'canals' (now known to be optical artefacts) on the surface of Mars.

Lowell /ˈləʊəl/ Robert (Traill Spence, Jr) 1917–1977. US poet whose work stressed the importance of individualism, especially during times of war. His works include *Lord Weary's Castle* 1946 and *For the Union Dead* 1964.

Much of his poetry is confessional. During World War II he was imprisoned for five months for conscientious objection. Several of his poems, notably 'Memories of West Street and Lepke,' reflect on this experience. 'Skunk Hour,' included in *Life Studies* 1959, is another example of his autobiographical poetry.

Lowry /ˈlaʊri/ L(aurence) S(tephen) 1887–1976. English painter. Born in Manchester, he lived mainly in nearby Salford and painted northern industrial townscapes. His characteristic style of matchstick figures and almost monochrome palette emerged in the 1920s.

include *Trouble in Paradise* 1932, *Design for Living* 1933, *Ninotchka* 1939, and *To Be or Not to Be* 1942.

Starting as an actor in silent films in Berlin, he turned to writing and directing, including *Die Augen der Mummie Ma/The Eyes of the Mummy* 1918 and *Die Austernprinzessin/The Oyster Princess* 1919. In the USA he directed the silent films *The Marriage Circle* 1924 and *The Student Prince* 1927.

Lubovitch /luːˈbəvɪtʃ/ Lar 1945– . US modern-dance choreographer and director of the Lar Lubovitch Dance Company, founded 1976. He was the first to use Minimalist music, for which he created a new style of movement in works like *Marimba* 1977 and *North Star* 1978.

Lucan /luːkən/ (Marcus Annaeus Lucanus) AD 39–65. Latin poet, born in Córdoba, Spain, a nephew of the writer Seneca and favourite of Nero until the emperor became jealous of his verse. Lucan then joined a republican conspiracy and committed suicide on its failure. His epic *Pharsalia* deals with the civil wars of the Roman rulers Caesar and Pompey.

Lucan /luːkən/ John Bingham, 7th Earl of Lucan 1934– . British aristocrat and professional gambler. On 7 Nov 1974 his wife was attacked and their children's nanny murdered. No trace of Lucan has since been found, and there has been no solution to the murder.

Lucas /luːkəs/ George 1944– . US film director and producer whose imagination was fired by the comic books in his father's store. He wrote and directed (in collaboration with Steven Spielberg) *Star Wars* 1977, *The Empire Strikes Back* 1980, and *Return of the Jedi* 1983. His other films include *THX 1138* 1971, *American Graffiti* 1973, *Raiders of the Lost Ark* 1981, *Indiana Jones and the Temple of Doom* 1984, *Willow* 1988, and *Indiana Jones and the Last Crusade* 1989, most of which were box-office hits.

Lucas /luːkəs/ Robert 1937– . US economist, leader of the University of Chicago school of 'new classical' macroeconomics, which contends that wage and price adjustment is almost instantaneous and that the level of unemployment at any time must be the natural rate (it cannot be reduced by government action except in the short term and at the cost of increasing inflation).

Lucas van Leyden /luːkəs væn ˈlaɪdn/ 1494–1533. Dutch painter and engraver, active in Leiden and Antwerp. He was a pioneer of Netherlandish genre scenes, for example *The Chess Players* (Staatliche Museen, Berlin). His woodcuts and engravings were inspired by Albrecht Dürer, whom he met in Antwerp in 1521.

Luce /luːs/ Clare Boothe 1903–1987. US journalist, playwright, and politician. She was managing editor of *Vanity Fair* magazine 1933–34, and wrote several successful plays, including *The Women* 1936 and *Margin for Error* 1940, both of

Loy *US film actress Myrna Loy was known as the queen of sophisticated comedy in the late 1930s. Initially promoted in vamp and exotic roles, Loy's casting opposite William Powell in the first of the highly successful Thin Man movies, Manhattan Melodrama 1934, led to her typecasting as the epitome of the dream wife.*

Loy /lɔɪ/ Myrna. Stage name of Myrna Williams 1905– . US film actress who played Nora Charles in the *Thin Man* series (1943–47) costarring William Powell. Her other films include *The Mask of Fu Manchu* 1932 and *The Rains Came* 1939.

Loyola /lɔɪˈəʊlə/ founder of the Jesuits; see →Ignatius Loyola.

Lubbers /lʌbəs/ Rudolph Franz Marie (Ruud) 1939– . Dutch politician, prime minister of the Netherlands from 1982. Leader of the Christian Democratic Appeal (CDA), he is politically right of centre. He became minister for economic affairs 1973.

Lubetkin /luːˈbetkɪn/ Bertholdt 1901–1990. Russian-born architect who settled in the UK in 1930 and formed, with six young architects, a group called Tecton. His pioneering designs include a block of flats in Highgate, London (Highpoint I, 1933–35), and the curved lines of the Penguin Pool 1933 at London Zoo.

During the 1930s, Tecton was responsible for many of the public buildings erected in England in the architectural style then flourishing elsewhere in Europe, including the Gorilla House 1937 at the London Zoo and a health centre for the London borough of Finsbury 1938. The group was also a training ground for the avant-garde architects of the next generation, such as Denys Lasdun. Lubetkin retired in 1953.

Lubitsch /luːbɪtʃ/ Ernst 1892–1947. German film director known for his stylish comedies, who worked in the USA from 1921. His sound films which were made into films. She served as a Republican member of Congress 1943–47 and as ambassador to Italy 1953–57.

Luce /luːs/ Henry Robinson 1898–1967. US publisher, founder of Time Inc, which publishes the weekly news magazine *Time* 1923, the business magazine *Fortune* 1930, the pictorial magazine *Life* 1936, and the sports magazine *Sports Illustrated* 1954. He married Clare Boothe Luce in 1935.

Lucian /luːsiən/ *c.* 125–*c.* 190. Greek writer of satirical dialogues, in which he pours scorn on all religions. He was born at Samosata in Syria and for a time was an advocate at Antioch, but later travelled before settling in Athens about 165. He occupied an official post in Egypt, where he died.

All that belongs to mortals is mortal; all things pass us by, or if not, we pass them by.

Lucian *Greek Anthology*

Lucretia /luːˈkriːʃiə/ Roman woman, the wife of Collatinus, said to have committed suicide after being raped by Sextus, son of →Tarquinius Superbus, the king of Rome. According to tradition, this incident led to the dethronement of Tarquinius and the establishment of the Roman Republic in 509 BC.

Lucretius /luːˈkriːʃiəs/ (Titus Lucretius Carus) *c.* 99–55 BC. Roman poet and Epicurean philosopher whose *De Rerum natura*/ *On the Nature of The Universe* envisaged the whole universe as a combination of atoms, and had some concept of evolutionary theory.

According to Lucretius, animals were complex but initially quite fortuitous clusters of atoms, only certain combinations surviving to reproduce.

Lucullus /luːˈkʌləs/ Lucius Licinius 110–56 BC. Roman general and consul. He defeated →Mithridates VI Eupator of Pontus 81 BC and as commander against him 74–66 proved to be one of Rome's ablest generals and administrators, until superseded by Pompey who finally defeated Mithridates. Lucullus then retired from politics. His wealth enabled him to live a life of luxury, and Lucullan feasts became legendary.

Ludendorff /luːdndɔːf/ Erich von 1865–1937. German general, chief of staff to →Hindenburg in World War I, and responsible for the eastern-front victory at the Battle of Tannenberg in 1914. After Hindenburg's appointment as chief of general staff and Ludendorff's as quartermaster-general in 1916, he was also politically influential. He took part in the Nazi rising in Munich in 1923 and sat in the Reichstag (parliament) as a right-wing Nationalist.

Ludwig /lʊdvɪg/ Karl Friedrich Wilhelm 1816–1895. German physiologist who invented graphic methods of recording events within the body.

Ludwig demonstrated that the circulation of the blood is purely mechanical in nature and involves no occult vital forces. In the course of this work, he invented the kymograph, a rotating drum on which a stylus charts a continuous record of blood pressure and temperature. This was a forerunner of today's monitoring systems.

Ludwig /lʊdvɪg/ three kings of Bavaria, including:

Ludwig I 1786–1868. King of Bavaria 1825–48, succeeding his father Maximilian Joseph I. He made Munich an international cultural centre, but his association with the dancer Lola Montez, who dictated his policies for a year, led to his abdication in 1848.

Ludwig II 1845–1886. King of Bavaria from 1864, when he succeeded his father Maximilian II. He supported Austria during the Austro-Prussian War 1866, but brought Bavaria into the Franco-Prussian War as Prussia's ally and in 1871 offered the German crown to the king of Prussia. He was the composer Richard Wagner's patron and built the Bayreuth theatre for him. Declared insane 1886, he drowned himself soon after.

Ludwig III 1845–1921. King of Bavaria 1913–18, when he abdicated upon the formation of a republic.

Luening /luːnɪŋ/ Otto 1900– . US composer. He studied in Zurich, and privately with the Italian composer Feruccio Busoni. In 1949 he joined the staff at Columbia University, and in 1951 began a series of pioneering compositions for instruments and tape, some in partnership with Vladimir Ussachevsky (1911–) (*Incantation* 1952, *Poem in Cycles and* Bells 1954). In 1959 he became co-director, with Milton →Babbitt and Ussachevsky, of the Columbia-Princeton Electronic Music Center.

Lugard /luːˈgɑːd/ Frederick John Dealtry, 1st Baron Lugard 1858–1945. British colonial administrator. He served in the army 1878–89 and then worked for the British East Africa Company, for whom he took possession of Uganda in 1890. He was high commissioner for N Nigeria 1900–07, governor of Hong Kong 1907–12, and governor general of Nigeria 1914–19.

Lugosi /luːˈgəʊsi/ Bela. Stage name of Bela Ferenc Blasko 1882–1956. Hungarian-born US film actor. Acclaimed for his performance in *Dracula* on Broadway 1927, Lugosi began acting in feature films in 1930. His appearance in the film version of *Dracula* 1931 marked the start of Lugosi's long career in horror films – among them, *Murders in the Rue Morgue* 1932, *The Raven* 1935, and *The Wolf Man* 1941.

Lu Hsün /luː ˈʃuːn/ alternative transliteration of Chinese writer →Lu Xun.

Lukács Georg 1885–1971. Hungarian philosopher, one of the founders of 'Western' or 'Hegelian' Marxism, a philosophy opposed to the Marxism of the official communist movement.

In *History and Class Consciousness* 1923, he argued that the proletariat was the 'identical subject-object' of history. Under capitalism, social relations were 'reified' (turned into objective things), but the proletariat could grasp the social totality. Lukács himself repudiated the book and spent much of the rest of his life as an orthodox communist. He also made contributions to Marxist aesthetics and literary theory. He believed, as a cultural relativist, that the highest art was that which reflected the historical movement of the time: for the 20th century, this meant socialist realism. Lukács joined the Hungarian Communist Party in 1918 and was deputy minister of education during the short-lived Hungarian Soviet Republic, 1919.

Luke, St /luːk/ 1st century AD. Traditionally the compiler of the third Gospel and of the Acts of the Apostles in the New Testament. He is the patron saint of painters; his emblem is a winged ox, and his feast day 18 Oct.

Luke is supposed to have been a Greek physician born in Antioch (Antakiyah, Turkey) and to have accompanied Paul after the ascension of Jesus.

And it came to pass in those days, that there went out a decree from Caesar Augustus, that all the world should be taxed.

St Luke *Gospel* 2:1

Luks /lʌks/ George 1867–1933. US painter and graphic artist, a member of the Ashcan School; the style of the school was realist and subjects centred on city life, the poor, and the outcast.

Lully /luːˈliː/ Jean-Baptiste. Adopted name of Giovanni Battista Lulli 1632–1687. French composer of Italian origin who was court composer to Louis XIV. He composed music for the ballet, for Molière's plays, and established French opera with such works as *Alceste* 1674 and *Armide et Renaud* 1686. He was also a ballet dancer.

Lumet /luːˈmeɪ/ Sidney 1924– . US film director whose social conscience has sometimes prejudiced his invariably powerful films: *12 Angry Men* 1957, *Fail Safe* 1964, *Serpico* 1973, and *Dog Day Afternoon* 1975.

Lumière /ˌluːmiˈeə/ Auguste Marie 1862–1954 and Louis Jean 1864–1948. French brothers who pioneered cinematography. In 1895 they patented their cinematograph, a combined camera and projector operating at 16 frames per second, and opened the world's first cinema in Paris to show their films.

The Lumière's first films were short static shots of everyday events such as *La Sorties des Usines Lumière* 1895 about workers leaving a factory and *L'Arroseur Arrosé* 1895, the world's first fiction film. Production was abandoned in 1900.

Lumumba /lʊˈmʊmbə/ Patrice 1926–1961. Congolese politician, prime minister of Zaire 1960. Imprisoned by the Belgians, but released in time to attend the conference giving the Congo independence in 1960, he led the National Congolese Movement to victory in the subsequent general election. He was deposed in a coup d'état, and murdered some months later.

Lunardi /luːˈnɑːdi/ Vincenzo 1759–1806. Italian balloonist. He came to London as secretary to the Neapolitan ambassador, and made the first balloon flight in England from Moorfields in 1784.

Lunt /lʌnt/ Alfred 1893–1977. US actor. He went straight from school into the theatre, and in 1922 married the actress Lynn Fontanne with whom he subsequently co-starred in more than 30 plays. They formed a sophisticated comedy duo, and the New York Lunt-Fontanne theatre was named after them. Their shows included *Design for Living* by Noël Coward 1933, *There Shall Be No Night* 1940–41, and *The Visit* 1960.

Luo Guan Zhong /luːəʊ ˌgwænˈdzɒŋ/ or *Luo Kuan-chung* lived 14th-century. Chinese novelist who reworked popular tales into *The Romance of the Three Kingdoms* and *The Water Margin*.

Luo Kuan-chung alternative transliteration of Chinese writer →Luo Guan Zhong.

Lurçat /lʊəˈsɑː/ Jean 1892–1966. French artist inspired by the Cubists, who revived tapestry design, as in *Le Chant du Monde*.

Lurie /ˈlʊəri/ Alison 1926– . US novelist and critic. Her subtly written and satirical novels include *Imaginary Friends* 1967; *The War Between the Tates* 1974; *Foreign Affairs* 1985, a tale of transatlantic relations that won the Pulitzer Prize; and *The Truth About Lorin Jones* 1988.

Luther /ˈluːθə, German ˈlʊtə/ Martin 1483–1546. German Christian church reformer, a founder of Protestantism. While he was a priest at the University of Wittenberg, he wrote an attack on the sale of indulgences (remissions of punishment for sin) in 95 theses which he nailed to a church door in 1517, in defiance of papal condemnation. The Holy Roman emperor Charles V summoned him to the Diet (meeting of dignitaries of the Holy Roman Empire) of Worms in Germany, in 1521, where he refused to retract his objections. Originally intending reform, his protest led to schism, with the emergence, following the Augsburg Confession 1530 (a statement of the Protestant faith), of a new Protestant church. Luther is regarded as the instigator of the Protestant revolution, and Lutheranism is now the major religion of many N European countries, including Germany, Sweden, and Denmark.

Luther was born in Eisleben, the son of a miner; he studied at the University of Erfurt, spent three years as a monk in the Augustinian convent there, and in 1507 was ordained priest. Shortly afterwards he attracted attention as a teacher and preacher at the University of Wittenberg; and in 1517, after returning from a visit to Rome, he attained nationwide celebrity for his denunciation of the Dominican monk Johann Tetzel (1455–1519), one of those sent out by the Pope to sell indulgences as a means of raising funds for the rebuilding of St Peter's Basilica in Rome.

On 31 Oct 1517, Luther nailed on the church door in Wittenberg a statement of 95 theses concerning indulgences, and the following year he was summoned to Rome to defend his action. His reply was to attack the papal system even more strongly, and in 1520 he publicly burned in Wittenberg the papal bull (edict) that had been launched against him. On his way home from the imperial Diet of Worms he was taken into 'protective custody' by the elector of Saxony in the castle of Wartburg. Later he became estranged from the Dutch theologian Erasmus, who had formerly supported him in his attacks on papal authority, and engaged in violent controversies with political and religious opponents. After the Augsburg Confession 1530, Luther gradually retired from the Protestant leadership.

Luthuli /luːˈtuːli/ or **Lutuli** Albert 1899–1967. South African politician, president of the African National Congress 1952–67. Luthuli, a Zulu tribal chief, preached nonviolence and multiracialism.

Arrested in 1956, he was never actually tried for treason, although he suffered certain restrictions from 1959. He was under suspended sentence for burning his pass (an identity document required of non-white South Africans) when awarded the 1960 Nobel Peace Prize.

The laws of the land [South Africa] virtually criticize God for having created men of colour.

Albert Luthuli Nobel acceptance speech 1961

Lutosławski /ˌluːtəʊˈswæfski/ Witold 1913– . Polish composer and conductor, born in Warsaw. His early music, dissonant and powerful (*First Symphony* 1947), was criticized by the communist government, so he adopted a more popular style. With the lifting of artistic repression, he quickly adopted avant-garde techniques, including improvisatory and aleatoric forms. He has written chamber, vocal, and orchestral music, including three symphonies; *Livre pour orchestre* 1968 and *Mi-parti* 1976.

Lutyens /ˈlʌtjənz/ (Agnes) Elisabeth 1906–1983. English composer. Her works, using the 12-tone system, are expressive and tightly organized, and

Luxemburg Rosa Luxemburg, German political activist and co-founder of the radical Spartacists, a group that subsequently became the German Communist Party. An effective orator and writer, she wrote Sozialreform oder Revolution/Social Reform or Revolution *1889.*

include a substantial amount of chamber music, stage, and orchestral works. Her choral and vocal works include a setting of the Austrian philosopher Ludwig →Wittgenstein's *Tractatus* and a cantata *The Tears of Night*. She also composed much film and incidental music. Her autobiography *A Goldfish Bowl* was published 1973.

Lutyens /ˈlʌtjənz/ Edwin Landseer 1869–1944. English architect. His designs ranged from picturesque to Renaissance-style country houses and ultimately evolved into a Classical style as in the Cenotaph, London, and the Viceroy's House, New Delhi.

Luxemburg /ˈlʊksəmbʊəɡ/ Rosa 1870–1919. Polish-born German communist. She helped found the Polish Social Democratic Party in the 1890s (which later became the Polish Communist Party). She was a leader of the left wing of the German Social Democratic Party from 1898 and collaborator with Karl Liebknecht in founding the communist Spartacus League 1918. She was murdered with him by army officers during the Jan 1919 Berlin workers' revolt.

Lu Xun /ˈluː ˈʃuːn/ Pen name of Chon Shu-jêu 1881–1936. Chinese short-story writer. His three volumes of satirically realistic stories, *Call to Arms*, *Wandering*, and *Old Tales Retold*, reveal the influence of the Russian writer Nicolai Gogol.

Lyell Scottish geologist Charles Lyell, known as the father of modern geology. His Principles of Geology *1830-33 opposed the catastrophic theory of geologic changes and supported the uniformitarianism view that past events were occasioned by the same forces at work today.*

Lycurgus /laɪˈkɜːɡəs/ Spartan lawgiver. He is said to have been a member of the royal house of the ancient Greek city-state of Sparta, who, while acting as regent, gave the Spartans their constitution and system of education. Many scholars believe him to be purely mythical.

Lydgate /ˈlɪdɡeɪt/ John *c.* 1370–*c.* 1450. English poet. He was a Benedictine monk and later prior. His numerous works were often translations or adaptations, such as *Troy Book* and *Falls of Princes*.

Lydgate was probably born at Lydgate, Suffolk; he entered the Benedictine abbey of Bury St Edmunds, was ordained in 1397, and was prior of Hatfield Broadoak 1423–34. He was a friend of the poet Geoffrey Chaucer.

Lyell /ˈlaɪəl/ Charles 1797–1875. Scottish geologist. In his *Principles of Geology* 1830–33, he opposed the French anatomist Georges Cuvier's theory that the features of the Earth were formed by a series of catastrophes, and expounded the Scottish geologist James Hutton's view, known as uniformitarianism, that past events were brought about by the same processes that occur today – a view that influenced Charles Darwin's theory of evolution.

Lyell trained and practised as a lawyer, but retired from the law 1827 and devoted himself full time to geology and writing. He implied that the Earth was much older than the 6,000 years of prevalent contemporary theory, and provided the first detailed description of the Tertiary period, dividing it into the Eocene, Miocene, and older

and younger Pliocene periods. Although it was only in old age that he accepted that species had changed through evolution, he nevertheless provided Darwin with a geological framework within which evolutionary theories could be placed. Darwin simply applied Lyell's geological method – explaining the past through what is observable in the present – to biology.

Lyle Sandy 1958– . Scottish golfer who came to prominence in 1978 when he won the Rookie of the Year award. He won the British Open in 1985 and added the Masters and World Match-Play titles 1988. He was Europe's leading money winner in 1979, 1980, and 1985 and has played in five Ryder Cups.

Lyly /ˈlɪli/ John *c.* 1553–1606. English playwright and author of the romance *Euphues, or the Anatomy of Wit* 1578. Its elaborate stylistic devices gave rise to the word 'euphuism' for an affected rhetorical style.

Lynagh Michael 1963– . Australian rugby union player who holds the world record of 689 points (as at 1 May 1992) in internationals. He is Australia's most capped stand-off and, with Nicholas Farr-Jones, holds the world record of over 40 appearances as an international halfback partnership. A key member of Australia's 1991 World Cup winning team, he plays for Queensland University and Queensland.

Lynch /lɪntʃ/ 'Jack' (John) 1917– . Irish politician, prime minister 1966–73 and 1977–79. A Gaelic footballer and a barrister, in 1948 he entered the parliament of the republic as a Fianna Fáil member.

Lynn /lɪn/ Vera 1917– . British singer, known as the 'Forces' Sweetheart' of World War II. She became famous with such songs as 'We'll Meet Again', 'White Cliffs of Dover', and in 1952 'Auf Wiederseh'n, Sweetheart'.

Lyons /ˈlaɪənz/ Joseph 1848–1917. British entrepreneur, founder of the catering firm of J Lyons in 1894. He popularized teashops, and the 'Corner Houses' incorporating several restaurants of varying types were long a feature of London life.

A scientific hypothesis is elegant and exciting insofar as it contradicts common sense.

Charles Lyell attributed

Lyons /ˈlaɪənz/ Joseph Aloysius 1879–1939. Australian politician, founder of the United Australia Party 1931, prime minister 1931–39.

He was born in Tasmania and first elected to parliament in 1929. His wife *Enid Lyons* (1897–) was the first woman member of the House of Representatives and of the federal cabinet.

Lysander /laɪˈsændə/ died 395 BC. Spartan general, politician and admiral. He brought the Peloponnesian War between Athens and Sparta to a successful conclusion by capturing the Athenian fleet at Aegospotami 405 BC, and by starving Athens into surrender in the following year. He set up puppet governments in Athens and its former allies, and tried to secure for himself the Spartan kingship, but he was killed in battle with the Thebans.

Lysenko /lɪˈseŋkəʊ/ Trofim Denisovich 1898–1976. Soviet biologist who believed in the inheritance of acquired characteristics (changes acquired in an individual's lifetime) and used his position under Joseph Stalin officially to exclude Gregor →Mendel's theory of inheritance. He was removed from office after the fall of Khrushchev in 1964.

Lysippus /laɪˈsɪpəs/ 4th century BC. Greek sculptor. He made a series of portraits of Alexander the Great (Roman copies survive, including examples in the British Museum and the Louvre) and also sculpted the *Apoxyomenos*, an athlete (copy in the Vatican), and a colossal *Hercules* (lost).

Lyte /laɪt/ Henry Francis 1793–1847. British cleric, author of the hymns 'Abide with me' and 'Praise, my soul, the King of Heaven'.

Lytton /lɪtn/ Edward George Earle Bulwer-Lytton, 1st Baron Lytton of Knebworth 1803–1873. English writer. His novels successfully followed every turn of the public taste of his day and include the Byronic *Pelham* 1828, *The Last Days of Pompeii* 1834, and *Rienzi* 1835. His plays include *Richelieu* 1838.

Lytton /lɪtn/ Edward Robert Bulwer-Lytton, 1st Earl of Lytton 1831–1891. British diplomat, viceroy of India 1876–80, where he pursued a controversial 'forward' policy. Only son of the novelist, he was himself a poet under the pseudonym *Owen Meredith*, writing 'King Poppy' 1892 and other poems.

M

Maazel /mɑːˈzel/ Lorin (Varencove) 1930– . US conductor and violinist. He studied the violin and made his debut as a conductor at the age of nine. He was conductor of the Cleveland Orchestra 1972–82 and the first US director of the Vienna State Opera.

Mabuse /məˈbjuːz/ Jan. Adopted name of Jan Gossaert c. 1478–c. 1533. Flemish painter, active chiefly in Antwerp. His common name derives from his birthplace, Maubeuge. His visit to Italy 1508 with Philip of Burgundy started a new vogue in Flanders for Italianate ornament and Classical detail in painting, including sculptural nude figures.

His works include *The Adoration of the Magi* (National Gallery, London).

McAdam /məˈkædəm/ John Loudon 1756–1836. Scottish engineer, inventor of the macadam road surface. It originally consisted of broken granite bound together with slag or gravel, raised for drainage. Today, it is bound with tar or asphalt.

MacArthur /məˈkɑːθə/ Douglas 1880–1964. US general in World War II, commander of US forces

MacArthur US general Douglas MacArthur in 1945. He had been Allied supreme commander in the SW Pacific area since 1942 and helped plan the defeat of Japan in World War II.

in the Far East and, from March 1942, of the Allied forces in the SW Pacific. After the surrender of Japan he commanded the Allied occupation forces there. During 1950 he commanded the UN forces in Korea, but in April 1951, after expressing views contrary to US and UN policy, he was relieved of all his commands by President Truman.

The son of an army officer, born in Arkansas, MacArthur became Chief of Staff 1930–35. He defended the Philippines against the Japanese forces 1941–42 and escaped to Australia, where he based his headquarters. He was responsible for the reconquest of New Guinea 1942–45 and of the Philippines 1944–45, being appointed general of the army 1944. As commander of the UN forces in the Korean War, he invaded the North 1950 until beaten back by Chinese troops; his threats to bomb China were seen as liable to start World War III and he was removed from command, but received a hero's welcome on his return to the USA.

MacArthur /məˈkɑːθə/ John 1767–1834. Australian colonist, a pioneer of sheep breeding and vine growing. He quarrelled with successive governors of New South Wales, and, when arrested by William →Bligh, stirred up the Rum Rebellion 1808, in which Bligh was himself arrested and deposed.

Born in Devon, England, MacArthur went to Sydney 1790, and began experiments in sheep breeding 1794, subsequently importing from South Africa the merino strain. In later years he studied viticulture and planted vines from 1817, establishing the first commercial vineyard in Australia.

Macaulay /məˈkɔːli/ Rose 1881–1958. English novelist. The serious vein of her early novels changed to light satire in *Potterism* 1920 and *Keeping up Appearances* 1928. Her later books include *The Towers of Trebizond* 1956.

Macaulay /məˈkɔːli/ Thomas Babington, Baron Macaulay 1800–1859. English historian, essayist, poet, and politician, secretary of war 1839–41. His *History of England* in five volumes 1849–61 celebrates the Glorious Revolution of 1668 as the crowning achievement of the Whig party.

His works include an essay on Milton 1825 published in the *Edinburgh Review*; a volume of verse, *Lays of Ancient Rome* 1842; and the *History of England* covering the years up to 1702.

He entered Parliament as a liberal Whig 1830. In India 1834–38, he redrafted the Indian penal code. He sat again in Parliament 1839–47 and 1852–56, and in 1857 accepted a peerage.

McAuley Dave 1961– . Irish boxer who won the International Boxing Federation (IBF) flyweight championship in 1989, and has made more successful defences of a world title than any other boxer. McCauley won the British title in 1986.

Macbeth /mək'beθ/ died 1057. King of Scotland from 1040. The son of Findlaech, hereditary ruler of Moray, he was commander of the forces of Duncan I, King of Scotia, whom he killed in battle 1040. His reign was prosperous until Duncan's son Malcolm III led an invasion and killed him at Lumphanan.

McBride /mək'braɪd/ Willie John 1940– . Irish Rugby Union player. He was capped 63 times by Ireland, and won a record 17 British Lions caps. He played on five Lions tours, 1962, 1966, 1968, 1971, and in 1974 as captain when they returned from South Africa undefeated.

McCabe /mə'keɪb/ John 1939– . English pianist and composer whose works include three symphonies; orchestral works, including *The Chagall Windows*; and songs.

McCarran /mə'kærən/ Patrick 1876–1954. US Democrat politician. He became senator for Nevada 1932, and as an isolationist strongly opposed lend-lease during World War II (lend-lease was the authority of the president by act of Congress to supply defence equipment to any country whose defence was considered vital to the defence of the USA). He sponsored the Mc-Carran–Walter Immigration and Nationality Act of 1952, which severely restricted entry and immigration to the USA; the act was amended 1965.

McCarthy /mə'kɑːθi/ Eugene (Joseph) 1916– . US politician. He was elected to the US House of Representatives 1948 and to the US Senate 1958. An early opponent of the Vietnam War, he ran for president 1968. Although his upset victory in the New Hampshire primary forced incumbent L B Johnson out of the race, McCarthy lost the Democratic nomination to Hubert Humphrey.

Born in Watkins, Minnesota, USA, McCarthy received a master's degree in economics from the University of Minnesota and became active in the Democratic-Farmer-Labor party. After another unsuccessful bid for the presidency in 1972, he returned to private life, concentrating on writing and lecturing.

McCarthy /mə'kɒːθɪ/ Joe (Joseph Raymond) 1908–1957. US right-wing Republican politician. His unsubstantiated claim 1950 that the State Department and US army had been infiltrated by communists started a wave of anticommunist hysteria, wild accusations, and blacklists, which continued until he was discredited 1954. He was censured by the US senate for misconduct.

A lawyer, McCarthy became senator for his native Wisconsin 1946, and in Feb 1950 caused a sensation by claiming to hold a list of about 200 Communist Party members working in the State Department. This was in part inspired by the Alger →Hiss case. McCarthy continued a witch-hunting campaign against, among others, members of the →Truman administration. When he turned his attention to the army, and it was shown that he and his aides had been falsifying evidence, President →Eisenhower renounced him and his tactics. By this time, however, many people in public life and the arts had been unofficially blacklisted as suspected communists or fellow travellers (communist sympathizers). *McCarthyism* came to represent the practice of using innuendo and unsubstantiated accusations against political adversaries.

McCarthy /mə'kɑːθi/ Mary (Therese) 1912–1989. US novelist and critic. Much of her work looks probingly at US society, for example, the novel *The Groves of Academe* 1952, which describes the anti-Communist witch-hunts of the time (see Joe →McCarthy), and *The Group* 1963, which follows the post-college careers of eight women.

McCartney /mə'kɑːtni/ Paul 1942– . UK rock singer, songwriter, and bass guitarist; former member of the →Beatles, and leader of the pop group Wings 1971–81. His subsequent solo hits have included collaborations with Michael Jackson and Elvis Costello. Together with composer Carl Davis, McCartney wrote the *Liverpool Oratorio* 1991, his first work of classical music.

McCauley /mə'kɔːli/ Mary Ludwig Hays ('Molly Pitcher') 1754–1832. American war heroine. During the American Revolution, she accompanied her husband to the Battle of Monmouth 1778 and brought water in a pitcher to the artillerymen during the heat of the battle, thus gaining her nickname.

Born in Trenton, New Jersey, McCauley worked as a domestic servant and married a local man, John Hays.

When her husband became incapacitated during the battle, she took over one of the field pieces herself. In recognition of her valour whilst with the 7th Pennsylvania Regiment, the Pennsylvania General Assembly awarded her a lifetime annuity.

McClellan /mə'klelən/ George Brinton 1826–1885. US Civil War general, commander in chief of the Union forces 1861–62. He was dismissed by President Lincoln when he delayed five weeks in following up his victory over the Confederate General Lee at Antietam during the Civil War. He was the unsuccessful Democrat presidential candidate against Lincoln 1864.

McClintock /mə'klɪntɒk/ Barbara 1902–1992. US geneticist who discovered that some genes can change their position on a chromosome from generation to generation. This would explain how originally identical cells take on specialized functions as skin, muscle, bone, and nerve, and also how evolution could give rise to the multiplicity of species. He was awarded a Nobel prize 1983.

McClintock /məˈklɪntɒk/ Francis Leopold 1819–1907. Irish polar explorer and admiral. He discovered the fate of the John →Franklin expedition and further explored the Canadian Arctic.

McClure /məˈklʊə/ Robert John le Mesurier 1807–1873. Irish-born British admiral and explorer. While on an expedition 1850–54 searching for John →Franklin, he was the first to pass through the Northwest Passage.

McColgan Elizabeth 1964– . Scottish long-distance runner who became the 1992 world 10,000 metres champion. She won consecutive gold medals at the Commonwealth games in 1986 and 1990 at the same distance.

McCone /məˈkəʊn/ John Alex 1902–1991. US industrialist, head of the Central Intelligence Agency (CIA) in the 1960s. A devout Catholic and a fervent opponent of communism, he declined to use extreme measures to secure some of the political ends his political masters sought.

Early successes in the steel and construction industries made McCone a multimillionaire on the strength of winning several government contracts. He became chair of the US Atomic Energy Commission 1958, and was chosen by President Kennedy to succeed Allen Dulles as director of the CIA 1961. He was eventually removed from his post by President Johnson, and returned to his business career as a director of the International Telephone and Telegraph Corporation (ITT).

MacCormac /məˈkɔːmək/ Richard 1938– . British architect whose work shows a clear geometric basis. The residential building at Worcester College, Oxford, 1983 epitomizes his approach. The student rooms are intricately related in a complex geometric plan and stepped section.

He became president of the Royal Institute of British Architects 1991. His other works include Coffee Hall flat, Milton Keynes, 1974; housing, Duffryn, Wales, 1974; Fitzwilliam College, Cambridge, 1986.

McCormick /məˈkɔːmɪk/ Cyrus Hall 1809–1884. US inventor of the reaping machine 1831, which revolutionized 19th-century agriculture.

McCowen /məˈkaʊən/ Alec 1925– . British actor. His Shakespearean roles include Richard II and the Fool in *King Lear*; he is also known for his dramatic one-man shows.

McCrea /məˈkreɪ/ Joel 1905–1991. US film actor who rapidly graduated to romantic leads in the 1930s and played in several major 1940s productions, such as *Sullivan's Travels* 1941. In later decades he was associated almost exclusively with the Western genre, notably *Ride the High Country* 1962, now recognized as a classic Western film. McCrea's career stretched from 1928 to 1976.

He began as an extra, and by the time of *Dead End* 1937 and *Union Pacific* 1939, he was starring in major films. Alfred Hitchcock, who cast him in *Foreign Correspondent* 1940, described him as too 'easy-going', yet this aspect of his playing was both deceptive and the key to his skill, and contributed significantly to his success in the comedies of Preston Sturges, such as *The Palm Beach Story* 1944, which were the high point of his career.

MacCready /məˈkriːdi/ Paul 1925– . US designer of the *Gossamer Condor* aircraft, which made the first controlled flight by human power alone 1977. His *Solar Challenger* flew from Paris to London under solar power, and in 1985 he constructed a powered model of a giant pterosaur, an extinct flying animal.

McCullers /məˈkʌləz/ Carson (Smith) 1917–1967. US novelist. Most of her writing, including her novels *The Heart is a Lonely Hunter* 1940 and *Reflections in a Golden Eye* 1941, is set in the South, where she was born, and deals with spiritual isolation, containing elements of sometimes macabre violence.

McCullin Don(ald) 1935– . British war photographer. He began as a freelance photojournalist for Sunday newspapers and went on to cover hostilities in the Congo, Vietnam, Cambodia, Biafra, India, Pakistan, and Northern Ireland. He has published several books of his work and held many exhibitions.

MacDermot /mək'dɜːmət/ Galt 1928– . US composer. He wrote the rock musical *Hair* 1967, with lyrics by Gerome Ragni and James Rado. It challenged conventional attitudes about sex, drugs, and the war in Vietnam.

In the UK, the musical opened in London 1968, the day stage censorship ended.

McDiarmid /mək'dɜːmɪd/ Hugh. Pen name of Christopher Murray Grieve 1892–1978. Scottish nationalist and Marxist poet. His works include *A Drunk Man looks at the Thistle* 1926 and two *Hymns to Lenin* 1930, 1935.

Macdonald /məkˈdɒnld/ George 1824–1905. Scottish novelist and children's writer. *David Elginbrod* 1863 and *Robert Falconer* 1868 are characteristic novels but his children's stories, including *At the Back of the North Wind* 1871 and *The Princess and the Goblin* 1872, are today more often read. Mystical imagination pervades all his books and this inspired later writers including G K Chesterton, C S Lewis, and J R R Tolkien.

Macdonald /məkˈdɒnld/ Flora 1722–1790. Scottish heroine who rescued Prince Charles Edward Stuart, the Young Pretender, after his defeat at Culloden 1746. Disguising him as her maid, she escorted him from her home in the Hebrides to France. She was arrested, but released 1747.

MacDonald /məkˈdɒnld/ (James) Ramsay 1866–1937. British politician, first Labour prime minister Jan–Oct 1924 and 1929–31. Failing to deal with worsening economic conditions, he left the party to form a coalition government 1931, which was increasingly dominated by Conservatives, until he was replaced by Stanley Baldwin 1935.

MacDonald joined the Independent Labour Party 1894, and became first secretary of the new Labour Party 1900. In Parliament he led the party 1906–14 and 1922–31 and was prime minister of the first two Labour governments.

MacDonald was born in Scotland, the son of a labourer. He was elected to Parliament 1906, and led the party until 1914, when his opposition to World War I lost him the leadership. This he recovered 1922, and in Jan 1924 he formed a government dependent on the support of the Liberal Party. When this was withdrawn in Oct the same year, he was forced to resign. He returned to office 1929, again as leader of a minority government, which collapsed 1931 as a result of the economic crisis. MacDonald left the Labour Party to form a national government with backing from both Liberal and Conservative parties. He resigned the premiership 1935.

Macdonald /mək'dɒnld/ John   Alexander 1815–1891. Canadian Conservative politician, prime minister 1867–73 and 1878–91. He was born in Glasgow but taken to Ontario as a child. In 1857 he became prime minister of Upper Canada. He took the leading part in the movement for federation, and in 1867 became the first prime minister of Canada. He was defeated 1873 but returned to office 1878 and retained it until his death.

MacDowell /mək'daʊəl/   Edward   Alexander 1860–1908. US Romantic composer, influenced by →Liszt. His works include the *Indian Suite* 1896 and piano concertos and sonatas.

McDowell /məc'daʊəl/ Malcolm 1943–   . English actor who played the rebellious hero in Lindsay Anderson's film *If ...* 1969 and confirmed his acting abilities in Stanley Kubrick's *A Clockwork Orange* 1971.

McEnroe John Patrick 1959–   . US tennis player whose brash behaviour and fiery temper on court dominated the men's game in the early 1980s. He was three times winner of Wimbledon 1981 and 1983–84. He also won three successive US Open titles 1979–81 and again in 1984. A fine doubles player, McEnroe also won ten Grand Slam titles, seven in partnership with Peter Flemming.

McEvoy /mækɪvɔɪ/ Ambrose 1878–1927. English artist who painted delicate watercolour portraits of society women.

McEwan /mə'kjuːən/ Ian 1948–   . English novelist and short-story writer. His works often have sinister or macabre undertones and contain elements of violence and bizarre sexuality, as in the short stories in *First Love, Last Rites* 1975. His novels include *The Comfort of Strangers* 1981 and *The Child in Time* 1987. *Black Dogs* 1992 was short-listed for the Booker Prize.

McGinley /mə'gɪnli/ Phyllis 1905–1978. Canadian-born US writer of light verse. She was a contributor to *The New Yorker* magazine and published many collections of social satire. Her works include *One More Manhattan* 1937 and *The Love Letters of Phyllis McGinley* 1954.

McGonagall /mə'gɒnəgəl/ William 1830–1902. Scottish poet, noted for the unintentionally humorous effect of his extremely bad serious verse: for example, his poem on the Tay Bridge disaster of 1879.

McGovern /mə'gʌvn/ George (Stanley) 1922–   . US politician. A Democrat, he was elected to the US House of Representatives 1956, served as an adviser to the Kennedy administration, and was a US senator 1962–80. He won the presidential nomination 1968, but was soundly defeated by the incumbent Richard Nixon.

Born in Avon, South Dakota, USA, McGovern served as a combat pilot during World War II and received a PhD in history from Northwestern University 1953. He was defeated for re-election to the Senate 1980 and retired to a career of lecturing and writing.

McGraw /mə'grɔː/ John Joseph 1873–1934. US baseball manager. He became player-manager of the New York Giants 1902, and in this dual capacity led the team to two National League pennants and a World Series championship. After retiring as a player 1906, he managed the Giants to eight more pennants and two world championships.

Born in Truxton, New York, McGraw began his career 1891 as an infielder with the Baltimore Orioles, which joined the National League 1892, becoming the team's manager 1899.

He was elected to the Baseball Hall of Fame 1937.

McGuffey /mə'gʌfi/ William Holmes 1800–1873. US educator. He is best remembered for his series the *Eclectic Readers* which became standard reading textbooks throughout the USA in the 19th century. He was president of Cincinnati College 1836–39 and Ohio University 1839–45.

Born in Claysville, Pennsylvania, USA, and raised in Ohio, McGuffey attended Washington University and Jefferson College.

In 1825 he joined the faculty of Miami University, where he lectured on philosophy and became interested in the issue of public-school reform. He was professor at the University of Virginia 1845–73.

Mach /mɑːk, German mæx/ Ernst 1838–1916. Austrian philosopher and physicist. He was an empiricist, believing that science is a record of facts perceived by the senses, and that acceptance of a scientific law depends solely on its standing the practical test of use; he opposed concepts such as Newton's 'absolute motion'. He researched airflow, and Mach numbers are named after him (expressing the ratio of the speed of a body to the speed of sound in the undisturbed medium through which the body is travelling).

Machado /mətʃɑːdəʊ/ Antonio 1875–1939. Spanish poet and dramatist. Born in Seville, he was inspired by the Castilian countryside in his lyric verse, contained in *Campos de Castilla/Countryside of Castile* 1912.

Machado de Assis /məˈʃɑːdəʊ di əˈsiːs/ Joaquim Maria 1839–1908. Brazilian writer and poet, regarded as the greatest Brazilian novelist. His sceptical, ironic wit is well displayed in his 30 volumes of novels and short stories, including *Epitaph for a Small Winner* 1880 and *Dom Casmurro* 1900.

Machaut /mæˈʃəʊ/ Guillame de 1300–1377. French poet and composer. Born in Champagne, he was in the service of John of Bohemia for 30 years and, later, of King John the Good of France. He gave the forms of the *ballade* and *rondo* a new individuality and ensured their lasting popularity. His *Messe de Nostre Dame* about 1360, written for Reims Cathedral, is an early masterpiece of *ars nova*, 'new (musical) art', exploiting unusual rhythmic complexities.

Machel /mæˈʃel/ Samora 1933–1986. Mozambique nationalist leader, president 1975–86. Machel was active in the liberation front Frelimo from its conception 1962, fighting for independence from Portugal. He became Frelimo leader 1966, and Mozambique's first president from independence 1975 until his death in a plane crash near the South African border.

Machen /mækɪn/ Arthur (Llewellyn) 1863–1947. Welsh author whose stories of horror and the occult include *The Great God Pan* 1894 and *House of Souls* 1906. *The Hill of Dreams* 1907 is partly autobiographical.

Machiavelli /ˌmækɪəveli/ Niccolò 1469–1527. Italian politician and author whose name is synonymous with cunning and cynical statecraft. In his most celebrated political writings, *Il principe/The Prince* 1513 and *Discorsi/Discourses* 1531, he discussed ways in which rulers can advance the interests of their states (and themselves) through an often amoral and opportunistic manipulation of other people.

Machiavelli was born in Florence and was second chancellor to the republic 1498–1512. On the accession to power of the →Medici family 1512, he was arrested and imprisoned on a charge of conspiracy, but in 1513 was released to exile in the country. *The Prince*, based on his observations of Cesare →Borgia, is a guide for the future prince of a unified Italian state (which did not occur until the Risorgimento in the 19th century). In *L'Arte della guerra/The Art of War* 1520 Machiavelli outlined the provision of an army for the prince, and in *Historie fiorentine/History of Florence* he analysed the historical development of Florence until 1492. Among his later works are the comedies *Clizia* 1515 and *La Mandragola/The Mandrake* 1524.

McIndoe /mækɪndəʊ/ Archibald 1900–1960. New Zealand plastic surgeon. He became known in the UK during World War II for his remodelling of the faces of badly burned pilots.

MacInnes /məˈkɪnɪs/ Colin 1914–1976. English novelist, son of the novelist Angela Thirkell. His work is characterized by sharp depictions of London youth and subcultures of the 1950s, as in *City of Spades* 1957 and *Absolute Beginners* 1959.

Macintosh /mækɪntɒʃ/ Charles 1766–1843. Scottish manufacturing chemist who invented a waterproof fabric, lined with rubber, that was used for raincoats – hence **mackintosh**. Other waterproofing processes have now largely superseded this method.

Mack /mæk/ Connie. Adopted name of Cornelius McGillicuddy 1862–1956. US baseball manager. With the establishment of the American League 1901, he invested his own money in the Philadelphia Athletics ('A's') and became the team's first manager. In his record 50 years with the team 1901–51, he led them to nine American League pennants and five World Series championships.

Born in East Brookfield, Massachusetts, USA, Mack began his professional baseball career as a catcher 1883 and became player-manager of the Pittsburgh Pirates 1894.

He was elected to the Baseball Hall of Fame 1939.

McKay /məˈkaɪ/ Heather Pamela (born Blundell) 1941– . Australian squash player. She won the British Open title an unprecedented 16 years in succession 1962–1977.

She also won 14 consecutive Australian titles 1960–1973 and was twice World Open champion (inaugurated 1976). Between 1962 and 1980 she was unbeaten. She moved to Canada 1975 and became the country's outstanding racquetball player.

Mackay of Clashfern /məˈkaɪ, klæʃˈfɜːn/ Baron James Peter Hymers 1927– . Scottish lawyer and Conservative politician. He became Lord Chancellor 1987 and in 1989 announced a reform package to end legal restrictive practices.

He became a QC 1965 and 1979 was unexpectedly made Lord Advocate for Scotland and a life peer. His reform package included ending the barristers' monopoly of advocacy in the higher courts; promoting the combination of the work of barristers and solicitors in 'mixed' practices; and allowing building societies and banks to do property conveyancing, formerly limited to solicitors. The plans met with fierce opposition.

Macke /mækə/ August 1887–1914. German Expressionist painter, a founding member of the *Blaue Reiter* group in Munich. With Franz →Marc he developed a semi-abstract style comprising Cubist and Fauve characteristics. He was killed in World War I.

Macke visited Paris 1907. In 1909 he met Marc, and together they went to Paris 1912, where they encountered the abstract style of Robert Delaunay. In 1914 Macke visited Tunis with Paul →Klee, and was inspired to paint a series of brightly coloured watercolours largely composed of geometrical shapes but still representational.

McKellen /mə'kelən/ Ian Murray 1939– . English actor acclaimed as the leading Shakespearean player of his generation. His stage roles include Macbeth 1977, Max in Martin Sherman's *Bent* 1979, Platonov in Chekhov's *Wild Honey* 1986, Iago in *Othello* 1989, and Richard III 1990. His films include *Priest of Love* 1982 and *Plenty* 1985.

Mackendrick /mə'kendrɪk/ Alexander 1912– . US-born Scottish film director and teacher responsible for some of Ealing Studios' finest comedies, including *Whisky Galore!* 1949 and *The Man in the White Suit* 1951. After *Mandy* 1952 he left for Hollywood, where he made *Sweet Smell of Success* 1957.

Mackensen /'mækənzən/ August von 1849–1945. German field marshal. During World War I he achieved the breakthrough at Gorlice and the conquest of Serbia 1915, and in 1916 played a major role in the overthrow of Romania.

After the war Mackensen retained his popularity to become a folk hero of the German army.

Mackenzie /mə'kenzi/ Alexander c. 1755–1820. British explorer and fur trader. In 1789, he was the first European to see the river, now part of N Canada, named after him. In 1792–93 he crossed the Rocky Mountains to the Pacific coast of what is now British Columbia, making the first known crossing north of Mexico.

Mackenzie /mə'kenzi/ Compton 1883–1972. Scottish author. He published his first novel *The Passionate Elopement* 1911. Later works were *Carnival* 1912, *Sinister Street* 1913–14 (an autobiographical novel), and the comic *Whisky Galore* 1947. He published his autobiography in ten 'octaves' (volumes) 1963–71.

Mackenzie /mə'kenzi/ William Lyon 1795–1861. Canadian politician, born in Scotland. He emigrated to Canada 1820, and led the rebellion of 1837–38, an unsuccessful attempt to limit British rule and establish more democratic institutions in Canada. After its failure he lived in the USA until 1849, and in 1851–58 sat in the Canadian legislature as a Radical. He was grandfather of W L Mackenzie King, the Liberal prime minister.

McKern /mə'kɜːn/ (Reginald) Leo 1920– . Australian character actor, active in the UK. He is probably best known for his portrayal of the barrister Rumpole in the television series *Rumpole of the Bailey*. His films include *Moll Flanders* 1965, *A Man for All Seasons* 1966, and *Ryan's Daughter* 1971.

Mackerras /mə'kerəs/ Charles 1925– . Australian conductor who has helped to make the music of the Czech composer →Janáček better known. He was conductor of the English National Opera 1970–78.

McKinley *A champion of imperialism and high protective tariffs, 25th US president William McKinley derived a great deal of his political support from the business community. His name is identified with the high protective tariff carried by the McKinley Bill 1890, which he largely framed and passed; it was subsequently modified by the Democrats 1894.*

McKinley /mə'kɪnli/ William 1843–1901. 25th president of the USA 1897–1901, a Republican. His term as president was marked by the USA's adoption of an imperialist policy, as exemplified by the Spanish-American war 1898 and the annexation of the Philippines. He was first elected to congress 1876. He was assassinated.

Mackintosh /'mækɪntɒʃ/ Charles Rennie 1868–1928. Scottish architect, designer, and painter, whose chief work includes the Glasgow School of Art 1896, various Glasgow tea rooms 1897–about 1911, and Hill House, Helensburg, 1902–03. His early work is Art Nouveau; he subsequently developed a unique style, both rational and expressive.

Influenced by the Arts and Crafts Movement, he designed furniture and fittings, cutlery, and lighting to go with his interiors. Although initially influential, particularly on Austrian architects such as J M Olbrich and Josef Hoffman, Mackintosh was not successful in his lifetime and has only recently come to be regarded as a pioneeer of modern design.

Mackmurdo /mək'mɜːdəʊ/ Arthur H 1851–1942. English designer and architect. He founded the Century Guild 1882, a group of architects, artists, and designers inspired by William →Morris and John →Ruskin. His book and textile designs are forerunners of Art Nouveau.

MacLaine /məˈkleɪn/ Shirley. Stage name of Shirley MacLean Beatty 1934– . Versatile US actress whose films include Alfred Hitchcock's *The Trouble with Harry* 1955 (her debut), *The Apartment* 1960, and *Terms of Endearment* 1983, for which she won an Academy Award.

MacLaine trained as a dancer and has played in musicals, comedy, and dramatic roles. Her many offscreen interests (politics, writing) have limited her film appearances, which include *Some Came Running* 1958 and *The Turning Point* 1977. She is the sister of Warren Beatty.

Maclean /məˈkleɪn/ Alistair 1922–1987. Scottish adventure novelist whose first novel, *HMS Ulysses* 1955, was based on wartime experience. It was followed by *The Guns of Navarone* 1957 and other adventure novels. Many of his books were made into films.

Maclean /məˈkleɪn/ Donald 1913–1983. British spy who worked for the USSR while in the UK civil service. He defected to the USSR 1951 together with Guy →Burgess.

Maclean, brought up in a strict Presbyterian family, was educated at Cambridge, where he was recruited by the Soviet KGB. He worked for the UK Foreign Office in Washington 1944 and then Cairo 1948 before returning to London, becoming head of the American Department at the Foreign Office 1950.

Maclean /məˈkleɪn/ Fitzroy Hew 1911– . Scottish writer and diplomat whose travels in the USSR and Central Asia inspired his *Eastern Approaches* 1949 and *A Person from England* 1958. His other books include *To the Back of Beyond* 1974, *Holy Russia* 1979, and *Bonnie Prince Charlie* 1988.

During 1943–45 he commanded a unit giving aid to partisans in Yugoslavia.

McLean /məˈkleɪn/ John 1785–1861. US jurist. In 1829 he was appointed to the US Supreme Court by President Jackson. During his Court tenure, McLean was an outspoken advocate of the abolition of slavery, writing a passionate dissent in the Dred Scott Case 1857.

Born in Morris County, New Jersey, USA, and raised in Ohio, McLean studied law in Cincinnati and was admitted to the bar 1807. After editing a local newspaper, he served in the US Congress 1813–16 and as a judge on the Ohio Supreme Court 1816– 22.

Appointed postmaster general by President Monroe 1823, McLean reorganized the post office department, eliminating much corruption and waste.

MacLeish /məˈkliːʃ/ Archibald 1892–1982. US poet. He made his name with the long narrative poem 'Conquistador' 1932, which describes Cortés's march to the Aztec capital, but his later plays in verse, *Panic* 1935 and *Air Raid* 1938, deal with contemporary problems.

He was born in Illinois, was assistant secretary

of state 1944–45, and helped to draft the constitution of UNESCO. From 1949 to 1962 he was Boylston Professor of Rhetoric at Harvard, and his essays in *Poetry and Opinion* 1950 reflect his feeling that a poet should be 'committed', expressing his outlook in his verse.

A faith cannot be a faith against but for.
Archibald MacLeish *Survey Graphic* Feb 1941

MacLennan /məˈklenən/ Robert (Adam Ross) 1936– . Scottish centrist politician; member of Parliament for Caithness and Sutherland from 1966. He left the Labour Party for the Social Democrats (SDP) 1981, and was SDP leader 1988 during merger negotiations with the Liberals. He then became a member of the new Social and Liberal Democrats.

MacLennan was educated in Scotland, England, and the USA, and called to the English Bar 1962. When David Owen resigned the SDP leadership 1988, MacLennan took over until the merger with the Liberal Party had been completed. He took a leading part in the negotiations.

Macleod /məˈklaʊd/ Iain Norman 1913–1970. British Conservative politician. As colonial secretary 1959–61, he forwarded the independence of former British territories in Africa; he died in office as chancellor of the Exchequer.

Maclise /məˈkliːs/ Daniel 1806–1870. Irish painter, active in London from 1827. He drew caricatures of literary contemporaries, such as Dickens, and his historical paintings include *The Meeting of Wellington and Blücher after Waterloo* and *Death of Nelson*, both 1860s murals in the House of Lords, London.

McLuhan /məˈkluːən/ (Herbert) Marshall 1911–1980. Canadian theorist of communication, famed for his views on the effects of technology on modern society. He coined the phrase 'the medium is the message', meaning that the form rather than the content of information has become crucial. His works include *The Gutenberg Galaxy* 1962 (in which he coined the phrase 'the global village' for the worldwide electronic society then emerging), *Understanding Media* 1964, and *The Medium is the Massage* (sic) 1967.

Advertising is the greatest art form of the 20th century.
Marshall McLuhan 1976

MacMahon /məkˈmɑːn/ Marie Edmé Patrice Maurice, Comte de 1808–1893. Marshal of France. Captured at Sedan 1870 during the Franco-Prussian War, he suppressed the Paris Commune (the provisional national government while Paris was besieged by the Germans) after his release, and as president of the republic 1873–79 worked for a royalist restoration until forced to resign.

Macmillan /mək'mɪlən/ (Maurice) Harold, 1st Earl of Stockton 1894–1986. British Conservative politician, prime minister 1957–63; foreign secretary 1955 and chancellor of the Exchequer 1955–57. In 1963 he attempted to negotiate British entry into the European Economic Community, but was blocked by French president de Gaulle. Much of his career as prime minister was spent defending the retention of a UK nuclear weapon, and he was responsible for the purchase of US Polaris missiles 1962.

Macmillan was MP for Stockton 1924–29 and 1931–45, and for Bromley 1945–64. As minister of housing 1951–54 he achieved the construction of 300,000 new houses a year. He became prime minister on the resignation of Anthony →Eden after the Suez crisis, and led the Conservative Party to victory in the 1959 elections on the slogan 'You've never had it so good' (the phrase was borrowed from a US election campaign). Internationally, his realization of the 'wind of change' in Africa advanced the independence of former colonies. Macmillan's nickname Supermac was coined by the cartoonist Vicky.

McMillan /mək'mɪlən/ Edwin Mattison 1907– . US physicist. In 1940 he discovered neptunium, the first transuranic element, by bombarding uranium with neutrons. He shared a Nobel prize with Glenn →Seaborg 1951 for their discovery of transuranic elements. In 1943 he developed a method of overcoming the limitations of the cyclotron, the first accelerator, for which he shared, 20 years later, an Atoms for Peace award with I Veksler, director of the Soviet Joint Institute for Nuclear Research, who had come to the same discovery independently. McMillan was a professor at the University of California 1946–73.

MacMillan /mək'mɪlən/ Kenneth 1929–1992. Scottish choreographer. After studying at the Sadler's Wells Ballet School he was director of the Royal Ballet 1970–77 and then principal choreographer. His works include *Romeo and Juliet* for Margot Fonteyn and Rudolf Nureyev.

He is renowned for his work with the Canadian dancer Lynn Seymour, such as *Le Baiser de la fée* 1960 and *Anastasia* 1967–71. Other works include *Elite Syncopations* 1974, *Mayerling* 1978, *Orpheus* 1982, *Different Drummer* 1984, and *The Prince of the Pagodas* 1989 (originally choreographed by John Cranko 1957 to music by Benjamin Britten).

McMurtry /mək'mɜːtri/ Larry (Jeff) 1936– . US writer. Many of his works were made into films, including *Terms of Endearment* 1975, the film of which won the 1983 Academy Award for Best Picture. He also wrote the *The Desert Rose* 1983, *Texasville* 1987, and *Buffalo Girls* 1990.

Born in Wichita Falls, Texas, USA, McMurtry mostly wrote about the Southwest and about his home state of Texas in particular. Among his

many other titles are *Horseman, Pass By* 1961 (film *Hud* 1963), *Leaving Cheyenne* 1963 (film *Lovin' Molly* 1963), and *The Last Picture Show* 1966 (film 1971).

He also wrote *Somebody's Darling* 1978, *Cadillac Jack* 1982, and *Lonesome Dove* 1985 (Pulitzer Prize 1986; TV mini-series 1989).

MacNeice /mək'niːs/ Louis 1907–1963. British poet, born in Belfast. He made his debut with *Blind Fireworks* 1929 and developed a polished ease of expression, reflecting his classical training, as in *Autumn Journal* 1939. Unlike many of his contemporaries, he was politically uncommitted.

Later works include the play *The Dark Tower* 1947, written for radio, for which medium he also wrote features 1941–49; a verse translation of Goethe's *Faust*; and the radio play *The Administrator* 1961.

McPartland /mək'pɑːtlənd/ Jimmy (James Duigald) 1907–1991. US cornet player, one of the founders of the Chicago school of jazz in the 1920s. He was influenced by Louis Armstrong and Bix Beiderbecke, whom he replaced in a group called the Wolverines 1924. He also recorded with the guitarist Eddie Condon, and from the late 1940s often worked with his wife, the British pianist Marian McPartland (1920–).

McPhee /mək'fiː/ Colin 1900–1964. US composer whose studies of Balinese music 1934–36 produced two works, *Tabuh-tabuhan* for two pianos and orchestra 1936 and *Balinese Ceremonial Music* for two pianos 1940, which influenced John →Cage and later generations of US composers.

McPherson /mək'fɜːsn/ Aimee Semple 1890–1944. Canadian-born US religious leader. As a popular preacher, 'Sister Aimee' reached millions through radio broadcasts of her weekly sermons, in which she emphasized the power of faith. She established the Church of the Four-Square Gospel in Los Angeles 1918.

Born in Ingersoll, Ontario, USA, McPherson worked as a missionary to China before becoming an itinerant evangelist in the USA, gaining a large following through her revival tours. She committed suicide 1944.

Her brief but suspicious 1926 'disappearance' tarnished her reputation.

Macpherson /mək'fɜːsən/ James 1736–1796. Scottish writer and literary forger, author of *Fragments of Ancient Poetry collected in the Highlands of Scotland* 1760, followed by the epics *Fingal* 1761 and *Temora* 1763, which he claimed as the work of the 3rd-century bard →Ossian. After his death they were shown to be forgeries.

When challenged by Dr Samuel Johnson, Macpherson failed to produce his originals, and a committee decided 1797 that he had combined fragmentary materials with oral tradition. Nevertheless, the works of 'Ossian' influenced the development of the Romantic movement in Britain and in Europe.

Madison 4th US president James Madison whose proposals at the Constitutional Convention 1787 earned him the title of 'father of the US Constitution'. His second term was marked by the war with Britain 1812-14, known as 'Madison's War', in which Washington was captured and the White House burned.

Macquarie /məˈkwɒri/ Lachlan 1762–1824. Scottish administrator in Australia. He succeeded Admiral →Bligh as governor of New South Wales 1809, raised the demoralized settlement to prosperity, and did much to rehabilitate ex-convicts. In 1821 he returned to Britain in poor health, exhausted by struggles with his opponents. Lachlan River and Macquarie River and Island are named after him.

McQueen /məˈkwiːn/ Steve (Terrence Steven) 1930–1980. US actor, a film star of the 1960s and 1970s, admired for his portrayals of the strong, silent loner, and noted for performing his own stunt work. After television success in the 1950s, he became a film star with *The Magnificent Seven* 1960. His films include *The Great Escape* 1963, *Bullitt* 1968, *Papillon* 1973, and *The Hunter* 1980.

Macready /məˈkriːdi/ William Charles 1793–1873. British actor. He made his debut at Covent Garden, London, 1816. Noted for his roles as Shakespeare's tragic heroes (Macbeth, Lear, and Hamlet), he was partly responsible for persuading the theatre to return to the original texts of Shakespeare and abandon the earlier, bowdlerized versions.

MacWhirter /məkˈwɜːtə/ John 1839–1911. British landscape painter whose works include *June in the Austrian Tyrol, Spindrift* and watercolours.

McWhirter /məkˈwɜːtə/ Norris 1925– . British editor and compiler, with his twin brother, *Ross McWhirter* (1925–1975), of the *Guinness Book of Records* from 1955.

Maderna /maˈdeənə/ Bruno 1920–1973. Italian composer and conductor. He studied with Gian Francesco →Malipiero and Hermann →Scherchen, and collaborated with Luciano →Berio in setting up an electronic studio in Milan. His compositions combine advanced techniques with an elegance of sound, and include a pioneering work for live and prerecorded flute, *Musica su due dimensioni* 1952, numerous concertos, and the aleatoric (involving random choice by the performers) *Aura* for orchestra 1974. *Hyperion* 1965, a 'mobile opera', consists of a number of composed events that may be combined in several ways.

Madison /ˈmædɪsən/ James 1751–1836. 4th president of the USA 1809–17. In 1787 he became a member of the Philadelphia Constitutional Convention and took a leading part in drawing up the US Constitution and the Bill of Rights. He allied himself firmly with Thomas →Jefferson against Alexander →Hamilton in the struggle between the more democratic views of Jefferson and the aristocratic, upper-class sentiments of Hamilton. As secretary of state in Jefferson's government 1801–09, Madison completed the Louisiana Purchase negotiated by James Monroe, whereby France sold an area of about 2,144,000 sq km/828,000 sq mi of land to the USA. During his period of office the War of 1812 with Britain took place.

Madonna /məˈdɒnə/ stage name of Madonna Louise Veronica Ciccone 1958– . US pop singer and actress who presents herself on stage and in videos with an exaggerated sexuality. Her first hit was 'Like a Virgin' 1984; others include 'Material Girl' 1985 and 'Like a Prayer' 1989. Her films include *Desperately Seeking Susan* 1985, *Dick Tracy* 1990, *In Bed with Madonna* 1991, and *A League of Their Own* 1992. Her book *Sex*, a collection of glossy, erotic photographs interspersed with explicit fantasies in the form of short stories, was published 1992, coinciding with the release of the dance album *Erotica*.

Without you, I'm nothing ... without Elvis, you're nothing.

Madonna

Maecenas /maɪˈsiːnəs/ Gaius Cilnius 69–8 BC. Roman patron of the arts who encouraged the work of →Horace and →Virgil.

Maeterlinck /ˈmeɪtəlɪŋk/ Maurice, Count Maeterlinck 1862–1949. Belgian poet and dramatist. His plays include *Pelléas et Mélisande* 1892, *L'Oiseau bleu/The Blue Bird* 1908, and *Le Bourgmestre de Stilmonde/The Burgomaster of Stilemonde* 1918. This last celebrates Belgian resistance in World War I, a subject that led to his exile in the USA 1940. Nobel prize 1911.

Magellan /mə'gelən/ Ferdinand 1480–1521. Portuguese navigator. In 1519 he set sail in the *Victoria* from Seville with the intention of reaching the East Indies by a westerly route. He sailed through the *Magellan Strait* at the tip of South America, crossed an ocean he named the Pacific, and in 1521 reached the Philippines, where he was killed in a battle with the islanders. His companions returned to Seville 1522, completing the voyage under Juan del →Cano.

Magellan was brought up at court and entered the royal service, but later transferred his services to Spain. He and his Malay slave, Enrique de Malacca, are considered the first circumnavigators of the globe, since they had once sailed from the Philippines to Europe.

Magritte /mə'gri:t/ René 1898–1967. Belgian Surrealist painter whose paintings focus on visual paradoxes and everyday objects taken out of context. Recurring motifs include bowler hats, apples, and windows, for example *Golconda* 1953 where men in bowler hats are falling from the sky to a street below.

Magritte joined the other Surrealists in Paris 1927. Returning to Brussels 1930, he painted murals for public buildings, and throughout his life created variations on themes of mystery treated with apparent literalism.

Mahan /mæ'hæn/ Alfred Thayer 1840–1914. US naval officer and military historian, author of *The Influence of Sea Power upon History* 1890–92, in which he propounded a global strategy based on the importance of sea power.

Mahan argued that Britain held a strategic advantage over the central powers and predicted the defeat of the German navy in World War I.

mahatma (Sanskrit 'great soul') title conferred on Mohandas K →Gandhi by his followers as the first great national Indian leader.

Mahdi /ma:di/ (Arabic 'he who is guided aright') in Islam, the title of a coming messiah who will establish a reign of justice on Earth. The title has been assumed by many Muslim leaders, notably the Sudanese sheik Muhammad Ahmed (1848–1885), who headed a revolt 1881 against Egypt and 1885 captured Khartoum.

His great-grandson *Sadiq el Mahdi* (1936–), leader of the Umma party in Sudan, was prime minister 1966–67. He was imprisoned 1969–74 for attempting to overthrow the military regime.

Mahfouz Naguib 1911– . Egyptian novelist and playwright. His novels, which deal with the urban working class, include the semi-autobiographical *Khan al-Kasrain/The Cairo Trilogy* 1956–57. His *Children of Gebelawi* 1959 was banned in Egypt because of its treatment of religious themes. Nobel Prize for Literature 1988.

Mahler /ma:lə/ Alma (born Schindler) 1879–1964. Austrian pianist and composer. She was the daughter of the artist Anton Schindler and abandoned composing when she married the composer Gustav Mahler 1902. After Mahler's death she lived with the architect Walter Gropius; their daughter Manon's death inspired Berg's Violin Concerto. She later married the writer Franz Werfel.

Mahler /ma:lə/ Gustav 1860–1911. Austrian composer and conductor whose work displays a synthesis of Romanticism and new uses of chromatic harmonies and musical forms. He composed 14 symphonies, including three unnumbered (as a student), nine massive repertoire symphonies, the titled *Das Lied von der Erde/Song of the Earth* 1909, and the incomplete *Symphony No. 10*. He also wrote song cycles.

Mahler was born in Bohemia (now Czech Republic); he studied at the Vienna Conservatoire, and conducted in Prague, Leipzig, Budapest, and Hamburg 1891–97. He was director of the Vienna Court Opera from 1897 and conducted the New York Philharmonic from 1910.

To write a symphony is, for me, to construct a world.

Gustav Mahler

Mahmud I /ma:'mu:d/ 1696–1754. Ottoman sultan from 1730. After restoring order to the empire in Istanbul 1730, he suppressed the Janissary rebellion 1731 (the Janissaries were his own bodyguard and standing army) and waged war against Persia 1731–46. He led successful wars against Austria and Russia, concluded by the Treaty of Belgrade 1739. He was a patron of the arts and also carried out reform of the army.

Mahmud II /ma:'mu:d/ 1785–1839. Ottoman sultan from 1808 who attempted to westernize the declining empire, carrying out a series of far-reaching reforms in the civil service and army. The pressure for Greek independence after 1821 led to conflict with Britain, France, and Russia, and he was forced to recognize Greek independence 1830.

In 1826 Mahmud destroyed the Janissaries (the sultan's bodyguard and standing army who revolted against his decision to raise a regular force). Wars against Russia 1807–12 resulted in losses of territory. The Ottoman fleet was destroyed at the Battle of Navarino 1827, and the Ottoman forces suffered defeat in the Russo-Turkish war 1828–29. There was further disorder with the revolt in Egypt of →Mehemet Ali 1831–32, which in turn led to temporary Ottoman-Russian peace. Attempts to control the rebellious provinces failed 1839, resulting in effect in the granting of Egyptian autonomy.

Mahomed /mə'hɒmɪd/ Ismail 1931– . South African lawyer, appointed the country's first non-white judge 1991. As legal adviser to SWAPO, he was the author of Namibia's constitution, which abolished capital punishment. He has defended many anti-apartheid activists in political trials.

Mahomed, born in Pretoria, became a barrister 1957. Classified as Indian under the apartheid system, he was hampered by restrictions on his movements, but went on to become president of Lesotho's Court of Appeal and a member of Swaziland's Appellate Division, and as a member of the Namibian Supreme Court he ruled corporal punishment unconstitutional. He is an eloquent speaker.

Mailer /'meɪlə/ Norman 1923– . US writer and journalist. He gained wide attention with his novel of World War II *The Naked and the Dead* 1948. A commentator on the US social, literary, and political scene, he has run for mayor of New York City.

His other novels include *An American Dream* 1964, *Genius and Lust* 1976, *Ancient Evenings* 1983, *Tough Guys Don't Dance* 1984, and *Harlot's Ghost* 1991. His journalistic work includes *Armies of the Night* 1968 about protest against the Vietnam War, and *The Executioner's Song* 1979 (Pulitzer Prize) about convicted murderer Gary Gilmore. Mailer has also ventured into filmmaking.

Major British prime minister John Major who succeeded Margaret Thatcher 1990 and was re-elected 1992. Features of his premiership include Britain's participation in the Gulf War, a greater commitment to the European Community, replacement of the poll tax with the council tax, worsening unemployment and recession, and the highly criticized management policy of the National Health Service and the coal industry.

Maillart /maɪ'ɑː/ Ella 1903– . Swiss explorer, skier, and Olympic sailor whose six-month journey into Soviet Turkestan was described in *Turkestan Solo* 1934. Her expedition across the Gobi Desert with Peter Fleming is recounted in *Forbidden Journey* 1937.

Maillol /maɪ'ɒl/ Aristide Joseph Bonaventure 1861–1944. French artist who turned to sculpture in the 1890s. His work is mainly devoted to the female nude. It shows the influence of classical Greek art but tends towards simplified rounded forms.

Maillol was influenced by the Nabis, a group of French artists united in their admiration of Paul ➔Gauguin. A typical example of Maillol's work is *Fame* for the Cézanne monument in Aix-en-Provence.

Maimonides /maɪ'mɒnɪdiːz/ Moses (Moses Ben Maimon) 1135–1204. Jewish rabbi and philosopher, born in Córdoba, Spain. Known as one of the greatest Hebrew scholars, he attempted to reconcile faith and reason.

He left Spain 1160 to escape the persecution of the Jews and settled in Fez, and later in Cairo, where he was personal physician to Sultan Saladin. His codification of Jewish law is known as the *Mishneh Torah/Torah Reviewed* 1180; he also formulated the *Thirteen Principles*, which summarize the basic beliefs of Judaism. His philosophical classic *More nevukhim/The Guide to the Perplexed* 1176–91 helped to introduce Aristotelian thought into medieval philosophy.

Maintenon /ˌmæntə'nɒŋ/ Françoise d'Aubigné, Marquise de 1635–1719. Second wife of Louis XIV of France from 1684, and widow of the writer Paul Scarron (1610–1660). She was governess to the children of Mme de Montespan by Louis, and his mistress from 1667. She secretly married the king after the death of Queen Marie Thérèse 1683. Her political influence was considerable and, as a Catholic convert from Protestantism, her religious opinions were zealous.

Maiziere /ˌmez'jeə/ Lothar de 1940– . German conservative politician, leader of the former East German Christian Democratic Union. He became premier after East Germany's first democratic elections in April 1990, until German reunification Oct 1990.

Major /'meɪdʒə/ John 1943– . British Conservative politician, prime minister from Nov 1990. He was foreign secretary 1989 and chancellor of the Exchequer 1989–90. His earlier positive approach to European Community (EC) matters was hindered during 1991 by divisions within the Conservative Party. Despite continuing public dissatisfaction with the poll tax, the National Health Service, and the recession, Major was returned to power in the April 1992 general election. His subsequent handling of a series of political crises called into question his ability to govern the country effectively.

Formerly a banker, he became member of Parliament for Huntingdonshire 1979 and become deputy to Chancellor Nigel Lawson 1987. In 1989 Major was appointed foreign secretary and, after Lawson's resignation, chancellor, within the space of six months. As chancellor he led Britain into the European Exchange Rate Mechanism (ERM) Oct 1990. The following month he became prime minister on winning the Conservative Party leadership election in a contest with Michael Heseltine and Douglas Hurd, after the resignation of Margaret Thatcher. His public statements before the Dec 1991 Maastricht EC summit expressed a mixture of Britain's reluctance and interest in political and economic union. Although victorious in the 1992 general election, he subsequently faced mounting public dissatisfaction regarding his apparent lack of foresight over a range of issues, including the sudden withdrawal of the pound from the European Monetary System (EMS), a drastic pit-closure programme, and past sales of arms to Iraq. His indecisive presidency of the European Community, particularly regarding ratification of the Maastricht Treaty, has also been criticized.

I am my own man.

John Major on succeeding Margaret Thatcher as prime minister Oct 1990

Makarios III /məˈkɑːrɪɒs/ 1913–1977. Cypriot politician, Greek Orthodox archbishop 1950–77. A leader of the Resistance organization EOKA, he was exiled by the British to the Seychelles 1956–57 for supporting armed action to achieve union with Greece (*enosis*). He was president of the republic of Cyprus 1960–77 (briefly deposed by a Greek military coup July–Dec 1974).

Makarova /məˈkɑːrəvə/ Natalia 1940–   . Russian ballerina. She danced with the Kirov Ballet 1959–70, then sought political asylum in the West. Her roles include the title role in *Giselle* and Aurora in *The Sleeping Beauty*.

Malamud /ˈmæləmʌd/ Bernard 1914–1986. US novelist and short-story writer. He first attracted attention with *The Natural* 1952, making a professional baseball player his hero. Later novels, often dealing with the Jewish immigrant tradition, include *The Assistant* 1957, *The Fixer* 1966, *Dubin's Lives* 1979, and *God's Grace* 1982.

Malcolm /ˈmælkəm/ four kings of Scotland, including:

Malcolm III /ˈmælkəm/ called *Canmore c.* 1031–1093. King of Scotland from 1058, the son of Duncan I (murdered by →Macbeth 1040). He fled to England when the throne was usurped by Macbeth, but recovered S Scotland and killed Macbeth in battle 1057. He was killed at Alnwick while invading Northumberland, England.

Malcolm X /ˈmælkəm ˈeks/ assumed name of Malcolm Little 1926–1965. US black nationalist leader. While serving a prison sentence for burglary 1946–53, he joined the Black Muslims sect. On his release he campaigned for black separatism, condoning violence in self-defence, but 1964 modified his views to found the Islamic, socialist Organization of Afro-American Unity, preaching racial solidarity. A year later he was assassinated by Black Muslim opponents while addressing a rally in Harlem, New York City. His *Autobiography of Malcolm X* was published 1964.

If someone puts his hand on you, send him to the cemetery.

Malcolm X *Malcolm X Speaks*

Malebranche /mælˈbrɒnʃ/ Nicolas 1638–1715. French philosopher. His *De la Recherche de la vérité/Search after Truth* 1674–78 was inspired by René →Descartes; he maintained that exact ideas of external objects are obtainable only through God.

Malenkov /ˈmælənkɒf/ Georgi Maximilianovich 1902–1988. Soviet prime minister 1953–55, Stalin's designated successor but abruptly ousted as Communist Party secretary within two weeks of Stalin's death by →Khrushchev, and forced out as prime minister 1955 by →Bulganin.

Malenkov subsequently occupied minor party posts. He was expelled from the Central Committee 1957 and from the Communist Party 1961.

Malevich /ˈmælɪvɪtʃ/ Kasimir 1878–1935. Russian abstract painter. In 1912 he visited Paris and became a Cubist, and 1913 he launched his own abstract movement, *Suprematism*. Later he returned to figurative themes treated in a semi-abstract style.

Malherbe /mæˈleəb/ François de 1555–1628. French poet and grammarian, born in Caen. He became court poet about 1605 under Henry IV and Louis XIII. He advocated reform of language and versification, and established the 12-syllable Alexandrine as the standard form of French verse.

Malik /ˈmælɪk/ Yakob Alexandrovich 1906–1980. Soviet diplomat. He was permanent representative at the United Nations 1948–53 and 1968–76, and it was his walkout from the Security Council in Jan 1950 that allowed the authorization of UN intervention in Korea.

Malinovsky /ˌmælɪˈnɒfski/ Rodion Yakolevich 1898–1967. Russian soldier and politician. In World War II he fought at Stalingrad, commanded in the Ukraine, and led the Soviet advance through the Balkans to capture Budapest 1945. He was minister of defence 1957–67.

Malinowski /ˌmælɪˈnɒfski/ Bronislaw 1884–1942. Polish-born British anthropologist, one of the founders of the theory of functionalism in the social sciences (a view of society as a system made up of a number of interrelated parts, all interacting on the basis of a common value system or consensus about basic values and common goals). His classic study of the peoples of the Trobriand Islands led him to see customs and practices in terms of their function in creating and maintaining social order.

Speaking in terms of evolution, we find that war is not a permanent institution of mankind.

Bronislaw Malinowski speech Sept 1936

Malipiero /ˌmælɪˈpjeərəʊ/ Gian Francesco 1882–1973. Italian composer and editor of →Monteverdi and →Vivaldi. His own works include operas in a Neo-Classical style, based on Shakespeare's *Julius Caesar* 1934–35 and *Antony and Cleopatra* 1936–37.

Mallarmé /ˌmælɑːˈmeɪ/ Stéphane 1842–1898. French poet who founded the Symbolist school with Paul Verlaine. His belief that poetry should be evocative and suggestive was reflected in *L'Après-midi d'un faune/Afternoon of a Faun* 1876, which inspired the composer Debussy.

Later works are *Poésies complètes/Complete Poems* 1887, *Vers et prose/Verse and Prose* 1893, and the prose *Divagations/Digressions* 1897.

Malle /mæl/ Louis 1932– . French film director. After a period as assistant to director Robert Bresson, he directed *Les Amants/The Lovers* 1958, audacious for its time in its explicitness. His subsequent films, made in France and the USA, include *Zazie dans le métro* 1961, *Viva Maria* 1965, *Pretty Baby* 1978, *Atlantic City* 1980, *Au Revoir les enfants* 1988, and *Milou en mai* 1989.

Malory /ˈmæləri/ Thomas 15th century. English author of the prose romance *Le Morte d'Arthur* about 1470. It is a translation from the French, modified by material from other sources, and it deals with the exploits of King Arthur's knights of the Round Table and the quest for the Holy Grail.

Malory's identity is uncertain. He is thought to have been the Warwickshire landowner of that name who was member of Parliament for Warwick 1445 and was charged with rape, theft, and attempted murder 1451 and 1452. If that is so, he must have compiled *Morte d'Arthur* during his 20 years in Newgate prison.

Malpighi /mælˈpiːgi/ Marcello 1628–1694. Italian physiologist who made many anatomical discoveries (still known by his name) in his microscope studies of animal and plant tissues.

Malraux /mælˈrəʊ/ André 1901–1976. French writer. An active antifascist, he gained international renown for his novel *La Condition humaine/Man's Estate* 1933, set during the Nationalist/Communist Revolution in China in the 1920s. *L'Espoir/Days of Hope* 1937 is set in Civil War Spain, where he was a bomber pilot in the International Brigade. In World War II he supported the Gaullist resistance, and was minister of cultural affairs 1960–69.

Malthus /ˈmælθəs/ Thomas Robert 1766–1834. English economist and cleric. His *Essay on the Principle of Population* 1798 (revised 1803) argued for population control, since populations increase in geometric ratio and food supply only in arithmetic ratio, and influenced Charles →Darwin's thinking on natural selection as the driving force of evolution.

Malthus saw war, famine, and disease as necessary checks on population growth. Later editions of his work suggested that 'moral restraint' (delaying marriage, with sexual abstinence before it) could also keep numbers from increasing too quickly, a statement seized on by later birth-control pioneers (the 'neo-Malthusians').

Mamet /ˈmæmɪt/ David 1947– . US playwright. His plays, with their vivid, freewheeling language and sense of ordinary US life, include *American Buffalo* 1977, *Sexual Perversity in Chicago* 1978, and *Glengarry Glen Ross* 1984.

Mamoulian /məˈmuːliən/ Rouben 1898–1987. Armenian stage and film director who lived in the USA from 1923. After several years on Broadway he turned to films, making the first sound version of *Dr Jekyll and Mr Hyde* 1932 and *Queen Christina* 1933. His later work includes *The Mark of Zorro* 1940 and *Silk Stockings* 1957.

Manchu /ˈmæntʃuː/ last ruling dynasty in China, from 1644 until their overthrow 1912; their last emperor was the infant →P'u-i. Originally a nomadic people from Manchuria, they established power through a series of successful invasions from the north, then granted trading rights to the USA and Europeans, which eventually brought strife and the Boxer Rebellion.

Mandela /mænˈdelə/ Nelson (Rolihlahla) 1918– . South African politician and lawyer, president of the African National Congress (ANC) from 1991. As organizer of the then banned ANC, he was imprisoned 1964. In prison he became a symbol of unity for the worldwide anti-apartheid movement. In Feb 1990 he was released, the ban on the ANC having been lifted, and he entered into negotiations with the government about a multiracial future for South Africa. He was married to the South African civil-rights activist Winnie Mandela 1955–92.

Mandela was born near Umbata, in what is today Transkei, the son of a local chief. In a trial of several ANC leaders, he was acquitted of treason 1961, but was once more arrested 1964 and given a life sentence on charges of sabotage and plotting to overthrow the government. In July

1991 he was elected, unopposed, to the presidency of the ANC.

I have cherished the idea of a democratic and free society ... if needs be, it is an ideal for which I am prepared to die.

Nelson Mandela speech Feb 1990

Mandela /mæn'delə/ Winnie (Nomzamo) 1934– . Civil-rights activist in South Africa and wife of Nelson Mandela 1955–92. A leading spokesperson for the African National Congress during her husband's imprisonment 1964–90, she has been jailed for a year and put under house arrest several times. In 1989 she was involved in the abduction of four youths, one of whom, Stompie Seipei, was later murdered. Winnie Mandela was convicted of kidnapping and assault, and given a six-year jail sentence May 1991, with the right to appeal. In April 1992 she and Nelson Mandela separated after 33 years of marriage. In the same year she resigned from her ANC leaderships posts, including her seat on the ANC National Executive Committee Sept 1992.

Mandelbrot /mændəlˌbrɒt/ Benoit B 1924– . Polish-born US scientist who coined the term *fractal geometry* to describe 'self-similar' shape, a motif that repeats indefinitely, each time smaller. The concept is associated with chaos theory.

Mandelshtam /mændlʃtæm/ Osip Emilevich 1891–1938. Russian poet. Son of a Jewish merchant, he was sent to a concentration camp by the communist authorities in the 1930s, and died there. His posthumously published work, with its classic brevity, established his reputation as one of the greatest 20th-century Russian poets.

His wife Nadezhda's memoirs of her life with her husband, *Hope Against Hope*, were published in the West 1970, but not until 1988 in the USSR.

Mandeville /mændɪvɪl/ John. Supposed author of a 14th-century travel manual for pilgrims to the Holy Land, originally written in French and probably the work of Jean d'Outremeuse of Liège. As well as references to real marvels, such as the pyramids, there are tales of headless people with eyes in their shoulders and other such fantastic inventions.

Manet /mæ'neɪ/ Edouard 1832–1883. French painter, active in Paris. Rebelling against the academic tradition, he developed a clear and unaffected Realist style. His subjects were mainly contemporary, such as *Un Bar aux Folies-Bergère/A Bar at the Folies-Bergère* 1882 (Courtauld Art Gallery, London).

Manet, born in Paris, trained under a history painter and was inspired by Goya and Velázquez and also by Courbet. His *Déjeuner sur l'herbe/Picnic on the Grass* 1863 and *Olympia* 1865 (both

Musée d'Orsay, Paris) offended conservative tastes in their matter-of-fact treatment of the nude body. He never exhibited with the Impressionists, although he was associated with them from the 1870s.

Manley /mænli/ Michael (Norman) 1924– . Jamaican politician, leader of the socialist People's National Party from 1969, and prime minister 1972–80 and 1989–92. He resigned the premiership because of ill health March 1992 and was succeeded by P J Patterson. Manley left parliament April 1992. His father, *Norman Manley* (1893–1969), was the founder of the People's National Party and prime minister 1959–62.

Mann /mæn/ Anthony. Stage name of Emil Anton Bundmann 1906–1967. US film director who made a series of violent but intelligent 1950s Westerns starring James Stewart, such as *Winchester '73* 1950. He also directed the epic *El Cid* 1961. His other films include *The Glenn Miller Story* 1954 and *A Dandy in Aspic* 1968.

Mann /mæn/ Heinrich 1871–1950. German novelist who fled to the USA 1937 with his brother Thomas Mann. His books include *Im Schlaraffenland/In the Land of Cockaigne* 1901; *Professor Unrat/The Blue Angel* 1904, depicting the sensual downfall of a schoolmaster; a scathing trilogy dealing with the Kaiser's Germany *Das Kaiserreich/The Empire* 1918–25; and two volumes on the career of Henry IV of France 1935–38.

Mann /mæn/ Horace 1796–1859. US political leader and education reformer. Resigning from the Massachusetts state legislature 1937, he serve as secretary of the state school board 1837–48. In that position he helped raise the level of funding and instruction for public education.

Born in Franklin, Massachusetts, Mann was educated at Brown University and was admitted to the bar 1823. After serving in the US House of Representatives 1848–53, he became president of Antioch College 1853–59. He served in the Massachusetts House of Representatives 1827–33 and Massachusetts Senate 1835–37.

Mann /mæn/ Thomas 1875–1955. German novelist and critic, concerned with the theme of the artist's relation to society. His first novel was *Buddenbrooks* 1901, which, followed by *Der Zauberberg/The Magic Mountain* 1924, led to a Nobel prize 1929. Notable among his works of short fiction is *Der Tod in Venedig/Death in Venice* 1913.

Mann worked in an insurance office in Munich and on the staff of the periodical *Simplicissimus*. His opposition to the Nazi regime forced him to leave Germany and in 1940 he became a US citizen. Among his other works are a biblical tetralogy on the theme of Joseph and his brothers 1933–44, *Dr Faustus* 1947, *Die Bekenntnisse des Hochstaplers Felix Krull/Confessions of Felix Krull* 1954, and a number of short stories, including 'Tonio Kröger' 1903.

Manning English novelist Olivia Manning. Her experiences in Bucharest, Greece and Egypt inspired the Balkan and Levant Trilogies which were adapted for television under the title Fortunes of War.

Mannerheim /ˈmænəheɪm/ Carl Gustav Emil von 1867–1951. Finnish general and politician, leader of the conservative forces in the civil war 1917–18 and regent 1918–19. He commanded the Finnish army 1939–40 and 1941–44, and was president of Finland 1944–46.

After the Russian Revolution 1917, a Red (socialist) militia was formed in Finland with Russian backing, and independence was declared in Dec. The Red forces were opposed by a White (counterrevolutionary) army led by Mannerheim, who in 1918 crushed the socialists with German assistance. In 1944, after leading the defence against Soviet invasion in two wars, he negotiated the peace settlement with the USSR and became president.

Manners family name of dukes of Rutland; seated at Belvoir Castle, Lincolnshire, England.

Mannheim /ˈmænhaɪm/ Karl 1893–1947. Hungarian sociologist who settled in the UK 1933. In *Ideology and Utopia* 1929 he argued that all knowledge, except in mathematics and physics, is ideological, a reflection of class interests and values; that there is therefore no such thing as objective knowledge or absolute truth.

Mannheim distinguished between ruling class ideologies and those of utopian or revolutionary groups, arguing that knowledge is thus created by a continual power struggle between rival groups and ideas. Later works such as *Man and Society* 1940 analysed contemporary mass society in terms of its fragmentation and susceptibility to extremist ideas and totalitarian governments.

Manning /ˈmænɪŋ/ Henry Edward 1808–1892. English priest, one of the leaders of the Oxford Movement. In 1851 he was converted to Roman Catholicism, and in 1865 became archbishop of Westminster. He was created a cardinal 1875.

Manning /ˈmænɪŋ/ Olivia 1911–1980. British novelist. Among her books are the semi-autobiographical series set during World War II. These include *The Great Fortune* 1960, *The Spoilt City* 1962, and *Friends and Heroes* 1965, forming the 'Balkan trilogy', and a later 'Levant trilogy'.

Manoel I /mənˈwel/ 1469–1521. King of Portugal from 1495, when he succeeded his uncle John II (1455–1495). He was known as 'the Fortunate', because his reign was distinguished by the discoveries made by Portuguese navigators and the expansion of the Portuguese empire.

Man Ray /reɪ/ adopted name of Emmanuel Rudnitsky 1890–1977. US photographer, painter, and sculptor, active mainly in France; associated with the Dada movement. His pictures often showed Surrealist images like the photograph *Le Violon d'Ingres* 1924.

Man Ray was born in Philadelphia, but lived mostly in Paris from 1921. He began as a painter and took up photography in 1915, the year he met the Dada artist Duchamp in New York. In 1922 he invented the **rayograph**, a black-and-white image obtained without a camera by placing objects on sensitized photographic paper and exposing them to light; he also used the technique of solarization (partly reversing the tones on a photograph). His photographs include portraits of many artists and writers.

Mansart /mɒnˈsɑː/ Jules Hardouin; see →Hardouin-Mansart, Jules.

Mansell /ˈmænsəl/ Nigel 1954– . English motor-racing driver. Runner-up in the world championship on two occasions, he became world champion 1992 and in the same year announced his retirement from Formula One racing. He won over 30 Grand Prix races – more than any other British driver.

Mansell started his Formula One career with Lotus 1980 and won the European Grand Prix 1985. He drove for the Williams team 1985–88, then 1989–90 for Ferrari, before returning to Williams 1991–92.

Mansfield /ˈmænzfiːld/ Jayne. Stage name of Vera Jayne Palmer 1933–1967. US actress who had a short career as a kind of living parody of Marilyn Monroe in films including *The Girl Can't Help It* 1956 and *Will Success Spoil Rock Hunter?* 1957.

Mansfield /ˈmænsfiːld/ Katherine. Pen name of Kathleen Beauchamp 1888–1923. New Zealand writer who lived most of her life in England. Her delicate artistry emerges not only in her volumes of short stories – such as *In a German Pension* 1911, *Bliss* 1920, and *The Garden Party* 1923 – but also in her *Letters* and *Journal*.

Manzoni Alessandro Manzoni whose great novel Ipromessi sposi/The Betrothed took six years to write. In later life he participated in the movement for Italian unification and helped to establish the Florentine dialect as the standard Italian.

Born near Wellington, New Zealand, she was educated in London, to which she returned after a two-year visit home, where she published her earliest stories. She married the critic John Middleton Murry 1913.

Manson /ˈmænsən/ Patrick 1844–1922. Scottish physician who showed that insects are responsible for the spread of diseases like elephantiasis and malaria.

Manson spent many years in practice in the Far East. On his return to London, he founded the School of Tropical Medicine.

Mantegna /mænˈtenjə/ Andrea c. 1431–1506. Italian Renaissance painter and engraver, active chiefly in Padua and Mantua, where some of his frescoes remain. Paintings such as *The Agony in the Garden* c. 1455 (National Gallery, London) reveal a dramatic linear style, mastery of perspective, and strongly Classical architectural detail.

Mantegna was born in Vicenza. Early works include frescoes for the Eremitani Church in Padua painted during the 1440s (badly damaged). From 1460 he worked for Ludovico Gonzaga in Mantua, producing an outstanding fresco series in the Ducal Palace (1470s) and later *The Triumphs of Caesar* (Hampton Court, near London). He was influenced by the sculptor Donatello and in turn influenced the Venetian painter Giovanni Bellini (his brother-in-law) and the German artist Albrecht Dürer.

Mantle /ˈmæntl/ Mickey (Charles) 1931– . US baseball player. Signed by the New York Yankees, he broke into the major leagues 1951. A powerful switch-hitter (able to bat with either hand), he also excelled as a centre-fielder. In 1956 he won baseball's Triple Crown, leading the American League in batting average, home runs, and runs batted in.

He retired 1969 after 18 years with the Yankees and seven World Series championships.

Manuel II 1889–1932. King of Portugal 1908–10. He ascended the throne on the assassination of his father, Carlos I, but was driven out by a revolution 1910, and lived in England.

Manutius /məˈnjuːʃɪəs/ Aldus 1450–1515. Italian printer, established in Venice (which he made the publishing centre of Europe) from 1490; he introduced italic type and was the first to print books in Greek.

Manzoni /mændˈzəʊni/ Alessandro, Count Manzoni 1785–1873. Italian poet and novelist, author of the historical romance *I promessi sposi/The Betrothed* 1825–27, set in Spanish-occupied Milan during the 17th century. Verdi's *Requiem* commemorates him.

Manzù /mændˈzuː/ Giacomo 1908–1991. Italian sculptor who, from the 1930s, worked mostly in bronze. Although a left-wing agnostic, he received many religious commissions, including the *Door of Death* 1964 for St Peter's basilica, Rome. His figures reveal a belief in the innate dignity of the human form.

Mao Zedong /maʊ dzɪˈdʌŋ/ or *Mao Tse-tung* 1893–1976. Chinese political leader and Marxist theoretician. A founder of the Chinese Communist Party (CCP) 1921, Mao soon emerged as its leader. He organized the Long March from SE to NW China 1934–36 and the war of liberation 1937–49, following which he established a People's Republic and Communist rule in China; he headed the CCP and government until his death. His influence diminished with the failure of his 1958–60 Great Leap Forward, but he emerged dominant again during the 1966–69 Cultural Revolution. Mao adapted communism to Chinese conditions, as set out in the *Little Red Book*.

Mao, son of a peasant farmer in Hunan province, was once library assistant at Beijing University and a headmaster at Changsha. He became chief of CCP propaganda under the Guomindang (Nationalist) leader Sun Yat-sen (Sun Zhong Shan) until dismissed by Sun's successor Chiang Kai-shek (Jiang Jie Shi). In 1931–34 Mao set up a Communist republic at Jiangxi and, together with Zhu De, marshalled the Red Army and organized the Long March to Shaanxi to evade Nationalist suppressive tactics. CCP head from 1935, Mao secured an alliance with the Nationalist forces 1936–45 aimed at repelling the Japanese invaders. At Yen'an, he built up a people's republic 1936–47 and married his third wife →Jiang Qing 1939. Civil war with the Nationalists was renewed from 1946 until 1949 when Mao defeated them at Nanking and established the People's Republic and Communist party rule under his leadership. During the civil war, he successfully employed mobile, rural-based guerrilla tactics.

Mao served as party head until his death Sept 1976 and as state president until 1959. After the damages of the Cultural Revolution, the Great

Helmsman, as he was called, working with his prime minister Zhou Enlai, oversaw a period of reconstruction from 1970 until deteriorating health weakened his political grip in the final years.

Mao's writings and thoughts dominated the functioning of the People's Republic 1949–76. He wrote some 2,300 publications, comprising 3 million words; 740 million copies of his *Quotations* have been printed. He stressed the need for rural rather than urban-based revolutions in Asia, for reducing rural-urban differences, and for perpetual revolution to prevent the emergence of new elites. Mao helped precipitate the Sino-Soviet split 1960 and was a firm advocate of a nonaligned Third World strategy. Since 1978, the leadership of Deng Xiaoping has reinterpreted Maoism, criticized its policy excesses, and commercialized the nation, but many of Mao's ideas remain valued.

Political power grows out of the barrel of a gun.

Mao Zedong 'Problems of War and Strategy'

Map /mæp/ Walter *c.* 1140–*c.* 1209. Welsh cleric and satirist in the service of Henry II as an itinerant justice in England; envoy to Alexander III of Scotland. His *De Nugis Curialium* was a collection of gossip and scandal from royal and ecclesiastical courts.

Mapplethorpe /ˈmeɪpəlθɔːp/ Robert 1946–1989. US art photographer known for his use of racial and homoerotic imagery in chiefly fine platinum prints. He developed a style of polished elegance in his gallery art works, whose often culturally forbidden subject matter caused controversy.

Maradona /ˌmærəˈdɒnə/ Diego 1960– . Argentine footballer who was voted the best player of the 1980s by the world's press. He has won 79 international caps, and has helped his country to two successive World Cup finals. He was South American footballer of the year 1979 and 1980.

He played for Argentinos Juniors and Boca Juniors before leaving South America for Barcelona, Spain, 1982 for a transfer fee of approximately £5 million. He moved to Napoli, Italy, for £6.9 million 1984, and contributed to their first Italian League title. In 1992 he joined Seville, Spain.

Marat /ˈmærɑː/ Jean Paul 1743–1793. French Revolutionary leader and journalist. He was elected to the National Convention 1792, where he carried on a long struggle with the right-wing Girondins, ending in their overthrow May 1793. In July he was murdered by Charlotte →Corday, a member of the Girondins.

Marc /mɑːk/ Franz 1880–1916. German Expressionist painter, associated with Wassily Kandinsky in founding the *Blaue Reiter* movement which explored colours, folk art, and the necessity of painting 'the inner, spiritual side of nature'. Animals played an essential part in Marc's view of the world, and bold semi-abstracts of red and blue horses are characteristic of his work.

Marceau /mɑːˈsəʊ/ Marcel 1923– . French mime artist. He is the creator of the clown-harlequin Bip and mime sequences such as 'Youth, Maturity, Old Age, and Death'.

Marchais /mɑːˈʃeɪ/ Georges 1920– . Leader of the French Communist Party (PCF) from 1972. Under his leadership, the party committed itself to a 'transition to socialism' by democratic means and entered into a union of the left with the Socialist Party (PS). This was severed 1977, and the PCF returned to a more orthodox pro-Moscow line, since when its share of the vote has decreased.

Marchais joined the PCF 1947 and worked his way up through the party organization to become its general secretary. He was a presidential candidate 1981, and sanctioned the PCF's participation in the Mitterrand government 1981–84. He remained leader of the PCF despite a fall in its national vote from 21% 1973 to 10% 1986.

Marchand /mɑːˈʃɒn/ Jean Baptiste 1863–1934. French general and explorer. In 1898, he headed an expedition in Africa from the French Congo, which occupied the town of Fashoda (now Kodok) on the White Nile. The subsequent arrival of British troops under Kitchener resulted in a crisis that nearly led to war between Britain and France.

Marcian /ˈmɑːʃən/ 396–457. Eastern Roman emperor 450–457. He was a general who married Pulcheria, sister of Theodosius II, and became emperor at the latter's death. He convened the Council of Chalcedon (the fourth Ecumenical Council of the Christian Church) 451 and refused to pay tribute to Attila the Hun.

Marciano /ˌmɑːsiˈɑːnəʊ/ Rocky (Rocco Francis Marchegiano) 1923–1969. US boxer, world heavyweight champion 1952–56. He retired after 49 professional fights, the only heavyweight champion to retire undefeated.

Born in Brockton, Massachussetts, he was known as the 'Brockton Blockbuster'. He knocked out 43 of his 49 opponents.

Marciano was killed in a plane crash.

Marconi /mɑːˈkəʊni/ Guglielmo 1874–1937. Italian electrical engineer and pioneer in the invention and development of radio. In 1895 he achieved radio communication over more than a mile, and in England 1896 he conducted successful experiments that led to the formation of the company that became Marconi's Wireless Telegraph Company Ltd. He shared the Nobel Prize for Physics 1909.

After reading about radio waves, he built a device to convert them into electrical signals. He then tried to transmit and receive radio waves over increasing distances. In 1898 he successfully transmitted signals across the English Channel, and in 1901 established communication with St John's, Newfoundland, from Poldhu in Cornwall, and in 1918 with Australia.

Marconi was an Italian delegate to the Versailles peace conference 1919 after World War I.

Marco Polo see →Polo, Marco.

Marcos /ˈmɑːkɒs/ Ferdinand 1917–1989. Filipino right-wing politician, president from 1965 to 1986, when he was forced into exile in Hawaii. He was backed by the USA when in power, but in 1988 US authorities indicted him and his wife Imelda Marcos for racketeering, embezzlement, and defrauding US banks; Marcos was too ill to stand trial.

Marcos was convicted while a law student 1939 of murdering a political opponent of his father, but eventually secured his own acquittal. In World War II he was a guerrilla fighter, survived the Japanese prison camps, and became president 1965. His regime became increasingly repressive, with secret pro-Marcos groups terrorizing and executing his opponents. He was overthrown and exiled 1986 by a popular front led by Corazon →Aquino, widow of a murdered opposition leader. A US grand jury investigating Marcos and his wife alleged that they had embezzled over $100 million from the government of the Philippines, received bribes, and defrauded US banks.

Marcos /ˈmɑːkɒs/ Imelda 1930– . Filipino politician and socialite, wife of Ferdinand Marcos, in exile 1986–91. She was acquitted 1990 of defrauding US banks. Under indictment for misuse of Philippine state funds, she returned to Manila Nov 1991 and was an unsuccessful candidate in the 1992 presidential elections.

After her husband's death 1989, Imelda Marcos stood trial in New York City 1990 in answer to charges of concealing ownership of US property and other goods, purchased with stolen Philippine-government funds. She was acquitted, her lawyer claiming the responsibility had lain solely with her husband.

In 1991, the Philippines' government lifted its ban on Imelda Marcos returning to her homeland in the hope of recouping an estimated $350 million from frozen Marcos accounts in Swiss banks. Simultaneously, they filed 11 charges of tax evasion against her and 18 against her children.

Marcus Aurelius Antoninus /ˈmɑːkəs ɔːˈriːliəs ˌæntəˈnaɪnəs/ AD 121–180. Roman emperor from 161 and Stoic philosopher. Although considered one of the best of the Roman emperors, he persecuted the Christians for political reasons. He wrote the philosophical *Meditations*.

Born in Rome, he was adopted (at the same time as Lucius Aurelius Verus) by his uncle, the emperor Antoninus Pius, whom he succeeded in 161. He conceded an equal share in the rule to Lucius Verus (died 169). Marcus Aurelius spent much of his reign warring against the Germanic tribes and died in Pannonia, where he had gone to drive back the invading Marcomanni.

Waste no more time arguing what a good man should be. Be one.

Marcus Aurelius Antoninus
Meditations 2nd century AD

Marcuse /mɑːˈkuːzə/ Herbert 1898–1979. German political philosopher, in the USA from 1934; his theories combining Marxism and Freudianism influenced radical thought in the 1960s. His books include *One-Dimensional Man* 1964.

Marcuse preached the overthrow of the existing social order by using the system's very tolerance to ensure its defeat; he was not an advocate of violent revolution. A refugee from Hitler's Germany, he became professor at the University of California at San Diego 1965.

Many people are afraid of freedom. They are conditioned to be afraid of it.

Herbert Marcuse in *L'Express* 1968

Margaret /ˈmɑːɡrət/ (Rose) 1930– . Princess of the UK, younger daughter of George VI and sister of Elizabeth II. In 1960 she married Anthony Armstrong-Jones, later created Lord Snowdon, but they were divorced 1978. Their children are *David, Viscount Linley* (1961–) and *Lady Sarah Armstrong-Jones* (1964–).

Margaret /ˈmɑːɡrət/ the Maid of Norway 1282–1290. Queen of Scotland from 1285, the daughter of Eric II, king of Norway, and Princess Margaret of Scotland. When only two years old she became queen of Scotland on the death of her grandfather, Alexander III, but died in the Orkneys on the voyage from Norway to her kingdom.

Her great-uncle Edward I of England arranged her marriage to his son Edward, later Edward II. Edward declared himself overlord of Scotland by virtue of the marriage treaty, and 20 years of civil war and foreign intervention followed.

Margaret of Anjou /ɒnˈʒuː/ 1430–1482. Queen of England from 1445, wife of →Henry VI of England. After the outbreak of the Wars of the Roses 1455, she acted as the leader of the Lancastrians, but was defeated and captured at the battle of Tewkesbury 1471 by Edward IV.

Her one object had been to secure the succession of her son, Edward (born 1453), who was killed at Tewkesbury. After five years' imprisonment Margaret was allowed in 1476 to return to her native France, where she died in poverty.

Margaret, St /ˈmɑːgrət/ 1045–1093. Queen of Scotland, the granddaughter of King Edmund Ironside of England. She went to Scotland after the Norman Conquest, and soon after married Malcolm III. The marriage of her daughter Matilda to Henry I united the Norman and English royal houses.

Through her influence, the Lowlands, until then purely Celtic, became largely anglicized. She was canonized 1251 in recognition of her benefactions to the church.

Margrethe II /mɑːˈgreɪdə/ 1940– . Queen of Denmark from 1972, when she succeeded her father Frederick IX. In 1967, she married the French diplomat Count Henri de Laborde de Monpezat, who took the title Prince Hendrik. Her heir is Crown Prince Frederick (1968–).

Marguerite of Navarre /ˌmɑːgəˈriːt, naˈvɑː, ˌdɒŋguˈleɪm/ also known as *Margaret d'Angoulême* 1492–1549. Queen of Navarre from 1527, French poet, and author of the *Heptaméron* 1558, a collection of stories in imitation of Boccaccio's *Decameron*. The sister of Francis I of France, she was born in Angoulême. Her second husband 1527 was Henri d'Albret, king of Navarre.

Maria Theresa /məˈriːə təˈreɪzə/ 1717–1780. Empress of Austria from 1740, when she succeeded her father, the Holy Roman emperor Charles VI; her claim to the throne was challenged and she became embroiled, first in the War of the Austrian Succession 1740–48, then in the Seven Years' War 1756–63; she remained in possession of Austria but lost Silesia. The rest of her reign was peaceful and, with her son Joseph II, she introduced social reforms.

She married her cousin Francis of Lorraine 1736, and on the death of her father became archduchess of Austria and queen of Hungary and Bohemia. Her claim was challenged by Charles of Bavaria, who was elected emperor 1742, while Frederick of Prussia occupied Silesia. The War of the Austrian Succession followed, in which Austria was allied with Britain, and Prussia with France; when it ended 1748, Maria Theresa retained her heritage, except that Frederick kept Silesia, while her husband had succeeded Charles as emperor 1745. Intent on recovering Silesia, she formed an alliance with France and Russia against Prussia; the Seven Years' War, which resulted, exhausted Europe and left the territorial position as before. After 1763 she pursued a consistently peaceful policy, concentrating on internal reforms; although her methods were despotic, she fostered education, codified the laws, and abolished torture. She also expelled the Jesuits. In these measures she was assisted by her son, Joseph II, who became emperor 1765, and succeeded her in the Habsburg domains.

Marie /məˈriː/ 1875–1938. Queen of Romania. She was the daughter of the duke of Edinburgh, second son of Queen Victoria of England, and married Prince Ferdinand of Romania in 1893 (he was king 1922–27). She wrote a number of literary works, notably *Story of My Life* 1934–35. Her son Carol became king of Romania, and her daughters, Elisabeth and Marie, queens of Greece and Yugoslavia respectively.

Marie Antoinette /məˈriː ˌæntwəˈnet/ 1755–1793. Queen of France from 1774. She was the daughter of Empress Maria Theresa of Austria, and married →Louis XVI of France 1770. Her reputation for extravagance helped provoke the French Revolution of 1789. She was tried for treason Oct 1793 and guillotined.

Marie Antoinette influenced her husband to resist concessions in the early days of the Revolution – for example, →Mirabeau's plan for a constitutional settlement. She instigated the disastrous flight to Varennes, which discredited the monarchy, and welcomed foreign intervention against the Revolution, betraying French war strategy to the Austrians 1792.

Marie de France /də ˈfrɒns/ *c.* 1150–1215. French poet, thought to have been the half-sister of Henry II of England, and abbess of Shaftesbury 1181–1215. She wrote *Lais* (verse tales that dealt with Celtic and Arthurian themes) and *Ysopet*, a collection of fables.

Marie Antoinette French queen Marie Antoinette, whose courage and frankness at her trial for treason became the subject of much literature. Disliked for her love of luxury and her Austrian connections, Marie Antoinette prompted Louis XVI to resist all new ideas and adopt the retrograde policy that was his undoing.

Marie de' Medici /deɪ 'medɪtʃi/ 1573–1642. Queen of France, wife of Henry IV from 1600, and regent (after his murder) for their son Louis XIII. She left the government to her favourites, the Concinis, until Louis XIII seized power and executed them 1617. She was banished, but after she led a revolt 1619, →Richelieu effected her reconciliation with her son. When she attempted to oust him again 1630, she was exiled.

Marie Louise /luːˈiːz/ 1791–1847. Queen consort of Napoleon I from 1810 (after his divorce from Josephine), mother of Napoleon II. She was the daughter of Francis I of Austria (see Emperor →Francis II) and on Napoleon's fall returned with their son to Austria, where she was granted the duchy of Parma 1815.

Mariette /ˌmæriˈet/ Auguste Ferdinand François 1821–1881. French Egyptologist whose discoveries from 1850 included the 'temple' between the paws of the Sphinx. He founded the Egyptian Museum in Cairo.

Marin /mærɪn/ John 1870–1953. US painter of seascapes in watercolour and oil, influenced by Impressionism. He visited Europe 1905–11 and began his paintings of the Maine coast 1914.

Marinetti /ˌmærɪˈneti/ Filippo Tommaso 1876–1944. Italian author who in 1909 published the first manifesto of Futurism, which called for a break with tradition in art, poetry, and the novel, and glorified the machine age.

Marinetti illustrated his theories in *Mafarka le futuriste: Roman africaine/Mafarka the Futurist: African novel* 1909. His best-known work is *Manifesto technico della letteratura futuristica/Technical manifesto of futurist literature* 1912 (translated 1971). He also wrote plays, a volume on theatrical practice 1916, and a volume of poems *Guerra sola igiene del mondo/War the only hygiene of the world* 1915.

We can admire nothing else today but the formidable symphonies of bursting shells and the crazy sculptures modelled by our inspired artillery among the enemy hordes!

Filippo Tommaso Marinetti reporting Italy's invasion of Libya in *L'Intransigent* 1911

Marini /məˈriːni/ Marino 1901–1980. Italian sculptor. Inspired by ancient art, he developed a distinctive horse-and-rider theme and a dancers series, reducing the forms to an elemental simplicity. He also produced fine portraits in bronze.

Marion /mæriən/ Francis c. 1732–1795. American military leader. He waged a successful guerrilla war against the British after the fall of Charleston 1780 during the American Revolution. Establishing his field headquarters in inaccessible areas, he became popularly known as the 'Swamp Fox'. He played a major role in the American victory at Eutaw Springs 1781.

Born in Berkeley County, South Carolina, Marion in the South Carolina Senate after the war.

Mariotte /mærjɒt/ Edme 1620–1684. French physicist and priest known for his recognition in 1676 of Boyle's law about the inverse relationship of volume and pressure in gases, formulated by Irish physicist Robert Boyle 1672. He had earlier, in 1660, discovered the eye's blind spot.

Maritain /ˌmærɪˈtæn/ Jacques 1882–1973. French philosopher. Originally a disciple of Henri →Bergson, as in *La philosophie bergsonienne/Bergsonian Philosophy* 1914, he later became the best-known of the Neo-Thomists, applying the methods of Thomas →Aquinas to contemporary problems, for example *Introduction à la Philosophie/Introduction to Philosophy* 1920.

Marius /meəriəs/ Gaius 155–86 BC. Roman military commander and politician, born near Arpinum. He was elected consul seven times, the first time in 107 BC. He defeated the Cimbri and the Teutons (Germanic tribes attacking Gaul and Italy) 102–101 BC. Marius tried to deprive Sulla of the command in the east against Mithridates and, as a result, civil war broke out 88 BC. Sulla marched on Rome, and Marius fled to Africa, but later Cinna held Rome for Marius and together they created a reign of terror in Rome.

Marivaux /ˌmærɪˈvəu/ Pierre Carlet de Chamblain de 1688–1763. French novelist and dramatist. His sophisticated comedies include *Le Jeu de l'amour et du hasard/The Game of Love and Chance* 1730 and *Les Fausses confidences/False Confidences* 1737; his novel *La Vie de Marianne/The Life of Marianne* 1731–41 has autobiographical elements. Marivaux gave the word *marivaudage* (oversubtle lovers' conversation) to the French language.

He was born and lived for most of his life in Paris, writing for both of the major Paris theatre companies: the Comédie Française and the Comédie Italienne, which specialized in commedia dell'arte.

Mark Antony /mɑːk 'æntəni/ Antonius, Marcus 83–30 BC. Roman politician and soldier. He was tribune and later consul under Julius Caesar, serving under him in Gaul. In 44 BC he tried to secure for Caesar the title of king. After Caesar's assassination, he formed the Second Triumvirate with Octavian (→Augustus) and Lepidus. In 42 he defeated Brutus and Cassius at Philippi. He took Egypt as his share of the empire and formed a liaison with →Cleopatra. In 40 he returned to Rome to marry Octavia, the sister of Augustus. In 32 the Senate declared war on Cleopatra. Antony was defeated by Augustus at the battle of Actium 31 BC. He returned to Egypt and committed suicide.

Markevich /mɑːkˈjevɪtʃ/ Igor 1912–1983. Russian-born composer and conductor who settled in Paris 1927. He composed the ballet *L'Envol* *d'Icare/The Flight of Icarus* 1932, and the cantata *Le Paradis Perdu/Paradise Lost* 1933–35 to words by Milton. After World War II he concentrated on conducting.

Markievicz /mɑːˈkjɪvɪtʃ/ Constance Georgina, Countess Markievicz (born Gore Booth) 1868–1927. Irish nationalist who married the Polish count Markievicz 1900. Her death sentence for taking part in the Easter Rising of 1916 was commuted, and after her release from prison 1917 she was elected to the Westminster Parliament as a Sinn Féin candidate 1918 (technically the first British woman member of Parliament), but did not take her seat.

Markov /ˈmɑːkɒv/ Andrei 1856–1922. Russian mathematician, formulator of the Markov chain, an example of a stochastic (random) process.

Markov /ˈmɑːkɒv/ Georgi 1929–1978. Bulgarian playwright and novelist who fled to the UK 1971; he was assassinated by being jabbed with a poisoned umbrella.

Markova /mɑːˈkəʊvə/ Alicia. Adopted name of Lilian Alicia Marks 1910– . British ballet dancer. Trained by →Pavlova, she was ballerina with →Diaghilev's company 1925–29, was the first resident ballerina of the Vic-Wells Ballet 1933–35, partnered Anton →Dolin in their own Markova-Dolin Company 1935–37, and danced with the Ballets Russes de Monte Carlo 1938–41 and Ballet Theatre, USA, 1941–46. She is associated with the great classical ballets, such as *Giselle*.

Marks /mɑːks/ Simon, 1st Baron of Broughton 1888–1964. English chain-store magnate. His father, Polish immigrant Michael Marks, had started a number of 'penny bazaars' with Yorkshireman Tom Spencer 1887; Simon Marks entered the business 1907 and built up a national chain of Marks and Spencer stores.

Mark, St /mɑːk/ 1st century AD. In the New Testament, Christian apostle and evangelist whose name is given to the second Gospel. It was probably written AD 65–70, and used by the authors of the first and third Gospels. He is the patron saint of Venice, and his emblem is a winged lion; feast day 25 April.

His first name was John, and his mother, Mary, was one of the first Christians in Jerusalem. He was a cousin of Barnabas, and accompanied Barnabas and Paul on their first missionary journey. He was a fellow worker with Paul in Rome, and later became Peter's interpreter after Paul's death. According to tradition he was the founder of the Christian church in Alexandria, and St Jerome says that he died and was buried there.

Marlborough /ˈmɔːlbrə/ John Churchill, 1st Duke of Marlborough 1650–1722. English soldier, created a duke 1702 by Queen Anne. He was granted the Blenheim mansion in Oxfordshire in recognition of his services, which included defeating the French army outside Vienna in the Battle of Blenheim 1704, during the War of the Spanish Succession.

In 1688 he deserted his patron, James II, for William of Orange, but in 1692 fell into disfavour for Jacobite intrigue. He had married Sarah Jennings (1660–1744), confidante of the future Queen Anne, who created him a duke on her accession. He achieved further victories in Belgium at the battles of Ramillies 1706 and Oudenaarde 1708, and in France at Malplaquet 1709. However, the return of the Tories to power and his wife's quarrel with the queen led to his dismissal 1711 and his flight to Holland to avoid charges of corruption. He returned 1714.

Marley /ˈmɑːli/ Bob (Robert Nesta) 1945–1981. Jamaican reggae singer, a Rastafarian whose songs, many of which were topical and political, popularized reggae worldwide in the 1970s. One of his greatest hit songs is 'No Woman No Cry'; his albums include *Natty Dread* 1975 and *Exodus* 1977.

Marlowe /ˈmɑːləʊ/ Christopher 1564–1593. English poet and dramatist. His work includes the blank-verse plays *Tamburlaine the Great c.* 1587, *The Jew of Malta c.* 1589, *Edward II* and *Dr Faustus*, both *c.* 1592, the poem *Hero and Leander* 1598, and a translation of Ovid's *Amores*.

Marlowe was born in Canterbury and educated at Cambridge University, where he is thought to have become a government agent. His life was turbulent, with a brief imprisonment in connection with a man's death in a brawl (of which he was cleared), and a charge of atheism (following statements by the playwright Thomas →Kyd under torture). He was murdered in a Deptford tavern, allegedly in a dispute over the bill, but it may have been a political killing.

Marmontel /ˌmɑːmɒnˈtel/ Jean François 1723–1799. French novelist and dramatist. He wrote tragedies and libretti, and contributed to the *Encyclopédie*. In 1758 he obtained control of the journal *Le Mercure/The Mercury*, in which his *Contes moraux/Moral Studies* 1761 appeared. Other works include *Bélisaire/Belisarius* 1767 and *Les Incas/The Incas* 1777.

Marmontel was appointed historiographer of France 1771, secretary to the Académie 1783, and professor of history at the Lycée 1786, but retired 1792 to write his *Mémoires d'un père/Memoirs of a Father* 1804.

Marot /ˈmærəʊ/ Clément 1496–1544. French poet, known for his translation of the *Psalms* 1539–43. His graceful, witty style became a model for later writers of light verse.

Born at Cahors, he accompanied Francis I to Italy 1524 and was taken prisoner at Pavia; he was soon released, and by 1528 was a salaried member of the royal household. Suspected of heresy, he fled to Turin, where he died.

Marquand /ˈmɑːkwɒnd/ J(ohn) P(hillips) 1893–1960. US writer. Author of a series of stories fea-

Marsalis US virtuoso saxophonist Branford Marsalis, elder brother of trumpeter Wynton Marsalis. He has recorded with jazz greats Miles Davis and Dizzy Gillespie as well as pop stars Sting and Tina Turner. He has also recorded arrangements of classical pieces by French and Russian composers with the English Chamber Orchestra.

turing the Japanese detective Mr Moto, he later made his reputation with gently satirical novels of Boston society, including *The Late George Apley* 1937 and *H M Pulham, Esq* 1941.

Marquet /mɑːˈkeɪ/ Pierre Albert 1876–1947. French painter of landscapes and Parisian scenes, chiefly the river Seine and its bridges. He was associated with Fauvism, a short-lived but influential movement which made bold use of colours, but he soon developed a more conventional, naturalistic style.

Marquette /mɑːˈket/ Jacques 1637–1675. French Jesuit missionary and explorer. He went to Canada 1666, explored the upper lakes of the St Lawrence River, and in 1673 with Louis Jolliet (1645–1700), set out on a voyage down the Mississippi on which they made the first accurate record of its course.

Márquez Gabriel García. See →García Márquez, Colombian novelist.

Marquis /ˈmɑːkwɪs/ Don(ald Robert Perry) 1878–1937. US author. He is chiefly known for his humorous writing, including *Old Soak* 1921, which portrays a hard-drinking comic, and *archy and mehitabel* 1927, verse adventures typewritten by a literary cockroach.

Marryat /ˈmæriət/ Frederick (Captain) 1792–1848. British naval officer and writer. His adventure stories include *Peter Simple* 1834 and *Mr Midshipman Easy* 1836; he also wrote a series of

children's books, including *Children of the New Forest* 1847.

Marsalis /mɑːˈsɑːlɪs/ Branford 1960– . US saxophonist. Born in New Orleans, he was taught by his father Ellis Marsalis, and played alto in Art Blakey's Jazz Messengers 1981, alongside brother Wynton Marsalis. He was tenor/soprano lead saxophonist on Wynton's 1982 world tour, and has since recorded with Miles Davis, Tina Turner, and Dizzy Gillespie. His first solo recording was *Scenes in the City* 1983.

Marsalis /mɑːˈsɑːlɪs/ Wynton 1961– . US trumpet player who has recorded both classical and jazz music. He was a member of Art Blakey's Jazz Messengers 1980–82 and also played with Miles Davis before forming his own quintet. At one time this included his brother Branford Marsalis on saxophone.

Marsh /mɑːʃ/ Ngaio 1899–1982. New Zealand writer of detective fiction. Her first detective novel *A Man Lay Dead* 1934 introduced her protagonist Chief Inspector Roderick Alleyn.

Originally an actress, and later a theatre producer, she went to England 1928 and worked as an interior decorator.

Marsh /mɑːʃ/ Othniel Charles 1831–1899. US palaeontologist. As official palaeontologist for the US Geological Survey from 1882, he identified many previously unknown fossil species and was an early devotee of Charles →Darwin. He wrote *Odontornithes* 1880, *Dinocerata* 1884, and *Dinosaurs of North America* 1896.

Born in Lockport, New York, USA, Marsh was educated at Yale University and in Germany. As first professor of palaeontology in the USA at the Yale faculty, he mounted fossil-hunting expeditions to the West from 1870. He served as president of the American Academy of Sciences 1883–95.

Marsh /mɑːʃ/ Rodney 1947– . Australian cricketer who holds the world record for a wicketkeeper with 355 dismissals in Test cricket. A Western Australian, he originally played for his state as a batsman. He was the first player to reach a Test double of 3,000 runs and 300 dismissals.

Marshall /ˈmɑːʃəl/ Alfred 1842–1924. English economist, professor of economics at Cambridge University 1885–1908. He was a founder of neoclassical economics, and stressed the power of supply and demand to generate equilibrium prices in markets, introducing the concept of elasticity of demand relative to price. His *Principles of Economics* 1890 remains perhaps the chief textbook of neo-classical economics.

Marshall /ˈmɑːʃəl/ George Catlett 1880–1959. US general and diplomat. He was army Chief of Staff in World War II, secretary of state 1947–49, and secretary of defence Sept 1950–Sept 1951. He initiated the *Marshall Plan* 1947 (a programme of US financial aid to Europe) and received the Nobel Peace Prize 1953.

Marshall /mɑːʃl/ John 1755–1835. US politician and jurist. He held office in the US House of Representatives 1799–1800 and was secretary of state 1800–01. As chief justice of the US Supreme Court 1801–35 under President Adams, he established the independence of the Court, the supremacy of federal over state law, and laid down universally accepted interpretations of the US constitution.

Born in Prince William (now Faquier) County, Virginia, Marshall served intermittently in the Continental Army until 1780 and then studied law. As a Federalist, he served in the Virginia state legislature and 1797 became a minister to France.

He defined the role of the federal government in *McCulloch* v *Maryland* 1819, when Marshall wrote the opinion that when federal and state laws conflict, federal law supersedes that of the states, and in *Gibbons* v *Ogden* 1824, when he wrote that a state could not enact laws that give exclusive rights to its waters.

Marshall /mɑːʃəl/ John Ross 1912–1988. New Zealand National Party politician, notable for his negotiations of a free-trade agreement with Australia. He was deputy to K J Holyoake as prime minister and succeeded him Feb–Nov 1972.

Marshall /mɑːʃl/ Thurgood 1908–1993. US jurist and civil-rights leader. As US Supreme Court justice from 1967, he frequently presided over landmark civil rights cases such as *Brown* v *Board of Education* 1954. The first black associate justice, he was a strong voice for civil and individual rights throughout his career.

Born in Baltimore, Maryland, USA, Marshall received a law degree from Howard University 1933. Active in civil rights, he was named director of the National Association for the Advancement of Colored People (NAACP) Legal Defense and Education Fund 1940. He was named to the US Court of Appeals 1961 and served as US solicitor general 1965–67. In 1967 President Johnson appointed him to the US Supreme Court.

Marsilius of Padua /mɑːˈsɪliəs/ 1270–1342. Italian scholar and jurist. Born in Padua, he studied and taught at Paris and in 1324 collaborated with John of Jandun (*c.* 1286–1328) in writing the *Defensor pacis/Defender of the Peace*, a plea for the subordination of the ecclesiastical to the secular power and for the right of the people to choose their own government. He played a part in the establishment of the Roman republic 1328 and was made archbishop of Milan.

Martens /mɑːtəns/ Wilfried 1936– . Prime minister of Belgium 1979–92, member of the Social Christian Party. He was president of the Dutch-speaking CVP 1972–79 and, as prime minister, headed several coalition governments in the period 1979–92 when he was replaced by Jean-Luc Dehaene heading a new coalition.

Martial /mɑːʃəl/ (Marcus Valerius Martialis) AD 41–104. Latin poet and epigrammatist. His poetry, often bawdy, reflects contemporary Roman life. He left over 15 books of miscellaneous verse, mostly elegiac couplets (a hexameter followed by a pentameter).

Born in Bilbilis, Spain, Martial settled in Rome AD 64, and lived by his literary and social gifts. He is renowned for correctness of diction, versification, and form.

My poems are licentious, but my life is pure.

Martial *Epigrams* AD 86

Martin /mɑːtɪn/ (Basil) Kingsley 1897–1969. English journalist who edited the *New Statesman* 1931–60 and made it the voice of controversy on the left.

Martin /mɑːtɪn/ Archer John Porter 1910– . British biochemist who received the 1952 Nobel Prize for Chemistry for work with Richard Synge on paper chromatography in 1944.

Martin /mɑːtɪn/ John 1789–1854. British Romantic painter of grandiose landscapes and ambitious religious subjects, such as *Belshazzar's Feast* (several versions).

Other examples of his work are *The Great Day of His Wrath* and *The Plains of Heaven* 1851–53 (both Tate Gallery, London). Martin often made mezzotints (types of engraving) from his work.

Martin /mɑːtɪn/ Richard 1754–1834. Irish landowner and lawyer known as 'Humanity Martin'. He founded the British Royal Society for Prevention of Cruelty to Animals 1824.

Martin /mɑːtɪn/ Violet Florence 1862–1915. Irish novelist who wrote under the pen name Martin Ross. She collaborated with her cousin Edith Somerville on tales of Anglo-Irish provincial life – for example, *Some Experiences of an Irish RM* 1899.

Martin /mɒːtɪn/ five popes, including:

Martin V 1368–1431. Pope from 1417. A member of the Roman family of Colonna, he was elected during the Council of Constance, and ended the Great Schism between the rival popes of Rome and Avignon.

Martin du Gard /mɑːˈtæn djuː ˈgɑː/ Roger 1881–1958. French novelist who realistically recorded the way of life of the bourgeoisie in the eight-volume *Les Thibault/The World of the Thibaults* 1922–40. Nobel prize 1937.

Martineau /mɑːtɪnəʊ/ Harriet 1802–1876. English journalist, economist, and novelist who wrote popular works on economics, children's stories, and articles in favour of the abolition of slavery.

Martineau /mɑːtɪnəʊ/ James 1805–1900. British Unitarian minister and philosopher. A great orator, he anticipated Anglican modernists in his theology.

Martinez /mɑːˈtiːnes/ Maria Montoya 1890–1980. Pueblo Indian potter who revived the traditional silvery black-on-black ware (made without the wheel) at San Ildefonso Pueblo, New Mexico, USA.

Martínez Ruiz /mɑːˈtiːneθ ruˈiːθ/ José. Real name of ➔Azorín, Spanish author.

Martini /mɑːˈtiːni/ Simone c. 1284–1344. Italian painter, a master of the Sienese school. He was a pupil of Duccio and continued the graceful linear patterns of Sienese art but introduced a fresh element of naturalism. His patrons included the city of Siena, the king of Naples, and the pope. Two of his frescoes are in the Town Hall in Siena: the *Maestà* about 1315 and the horseback warrior *Guidoriccio da Fogliano* (the attribution of the latter is disputed). From 1333 to 1339 Simone worked at Assisi where he decorated the chapel of St Martin with scenes depicting the life of the saint, regarded by many as his masterpiece.

Martins /mɑːtɪnz/ Peter 1946– . Danish-born US dancer, choreographer, and ballet director, principal dancer with the New York City Ballet (NYCB) from 1965, its joint ballet master (with Anthony Tudor) from 1983, and its director from 1990. He trained with August Bournonville and brought that teacher's influence to the NYCB.

Martins trained at the Royal Danish Ballet School, joining the company 1965, and the same year joined the NYCB as a principal. He created roles in, among others, Robbins's *Goldberg Variations* 1971 and Balanchine's *Violin Concerto* and *Duo Concertant* both 1972, and choreographed, for example, *Calcium Night Light* 1978.

Martin, St /mɑːtɪn/ 316–400. Bishop of Tours, France, from about 371, and founder of the first monastery in Gaul. He is usually represented as tearing his cloak to share it with a beggar. His feast day is Martinmas, 11 Nov.

Born in Pannonia, SE Europe, a soldier by profession, Martin was converted to Christianity, left the army, and lived for ten years as a recluse. After being elected bishop of Tours, he worked for the extinction of idolatry and the extension of monasticism in France.

Martinů /mɑːtɪnuː/ Bohuslav (Jan) 1890–1959. Czech composer who studied in Paris. He settled in New York after the Nazi occupation of Czechoslovakia 1939. The quality of his music varies but at its best it is richly expressive and has great vitality. His works include the operas *Julietta* 1937 and *The Greek Passion* 1959, symphonies, and chamber music.

Marvell /mɑːvəl/ Andrew 1621–1678. English metaphysical poet and satirist. His poems include 'To His Coy Mistress' and 'Horatian Ode upon Cromwell's Return from Ireland'. He was committed to the parliamentary cause, and was member of Parliament for Hull from 1659. He devoted his last years mainly to verse satire and prose works attacking repressive aspects of government.

Marvin /mɑːvɪn/ Lee 1924–1987. US film actor who began his career playing violent, often psychotic villains and progressed to playing violent, occasionally psychotic heroes. His work includes *The Big Heat* 1953, *The Killers* 1964, and *Cat Ballou* 1965.

A spectre is haunting Europe – the spectre of communism.

Karl Marx *The Communist Manifesto* 1848

Marx /mɑːks/ Karl (Heinrich) 1818–1883. German philosopher, economist, and social theorist whose account of change through conflict is known as historical, or dialectical, materialism. His *Das Kapital/Capital* 1867–95 is the fundamental text of Marxist economics, and his systematic theses on class struggle, history, and the importance of economic factors in politics have exercised an enormous influence on later thinkers and political activists.

Marx was born in Trier, the son of a lawyer, and studied law and philosophy at Bonn and Berlin. During 1842–43, he edited the *Rheinische Zeitung/Rhineland Newspaper* until its suppression. In 1844 he began his life-long collaboration with Friedrich ➔Engels, with whom he developed the Marxist philosophy, first formulated in their joint works, *Die heilige Familie/The Holy Family* 1844 and *Die deutsche Ideologie/German Ideology* 1846 (which contains the theory demonstrating the material basis of all human activity: 'Life is not determined by consciousness, but consciousness by life'), and Marx's *Misère de la philosophie/Poverty of Philosophy* 1847. Both joined the Communist League, a German refugee organization, and in 1847–48 they prepared its programme, *The Communist Manifesto*. During the 1848 revolution Marx edited the *Neue Rheinische Zeitung/New Rhineland Newspaper*, until he was expelled from Prussia 1849.

He then settled in London, where he wrote *Die Klassenkämpfe in Frankreich/Class Struggles in France* 1849, *Die Achtzehnte Brumaire des Louis Bonaparte/The 18th Brumaire of Louis Bonaparte* 1852, *Zur Kritik der politischen Ökonomie/Critique of Political Economy* 1859, and his monumental work *Das Kapital/Capital*. In 1864 the International Working Men's Association was formed, whose policy Marx, as a member of the general council, largely controlled. Although he showed extraordinary tact in holding together its diverse elements, it collapsed 1872 due to Marx's disputes with the anarchists, including the Russian ➔Bakunin. The second and third volumes of *Das Kapital* were edited from his notes by Engels and published posthumously.

Marx's philosophical work owes much to the writings of ➔Hegel, though he rejected Hegel's idealism.

Marx Brothers Best remembered for their anarchic film comedies of the 1930s, the Marx Brothers first gained success with such Broadway shows as I'll Say She Is 1924. Groucho, known for his wisecracking puns and non sequiturs, also wrote an autobiography, Groucho and Me 1959 and a serious study of the American tax system.

Marx Brothers team of US film comedians: Leonard *Chico* (from the 'chicks' – women – he chased) 1887–1961; Adolph, the silent *Harpo* (from the harp he played) 1888–1964; Julius *Groucho* (from his temper) 1890–1977; Milton *Gummo* (from his gumshoes, or galoshes) 1897–1977, who left the team before films; and Herbert *Zeppo* (born at the time of the first zeppelins) 1901–1979, part of the team until 1935. They made a total of 13 zany films 1929–49 including *Animal Crackers* 1930, *Duck Soup* 1933, *A Night at the Opera* 1935, and *Go West* 1940.

They appeared in musical comedy but made their reputation on Broadway in *Cocoanuts* 1926 (later filmed). In Hollywood they made such films as *Monkey Business* 1931 and *A Day at the Races* 1937. After the team disbanded 1948, Groucho, who carried the comedy line, continued to make films and appeared on his own television quiz show, *You Bet Your Life* 1947–62.

Mary /meəri/ *Queen of Scots* 1542–1587. Queen of Scotland 1542–67. Also known as *Mary Stuart*, she was the daughter of James V. Mary's connection with the English royal line from Henry VII made her a threat to Elizabeth I's hold on the English throne, especially as she represented a champion of the Catholic cause. She was married three times. After her forced abdication she was imprisoned but escaped 1568 to England. Elizabeth I held her prisoner, while the Roman Catholics, who regarded Mary as rightful queen of England, formed many conspiracies to place her on the throne, and for complicity in one of these she was executed.

Mary's mother was the French Mary of Guise. Born in Linlithgow (now in Lothian region, Scotland), Mary was sent to France, where she married the dauphin, later Francis II. After his death she returned to Scotland 1561, which, during her absence, had turned Protestant. She married her cousin, the Earl of →Darnley, 1565, but they soon quarrelled, and Darnley took part in the murder of

Mary's secretary, →Rizzio. In 1567 Darnley was assassinated as the result of a conspiracy formed by the Earl of →Bothwell, possibly with Mary's connivance, and shortly after Bothwell married her. A rebellion followed; defeated at Carberry Hill, Mary abdicated and was imprisoned. She escaped 1568, raised an army, and after its defeat at Langside fled to England, only to be imprisoned again. A plot against Elizabeth I devised by Anthony Babington led to her trial and execution at Fotheringay Castle 1587.

Mary /meəri/ Duchess of Burgundy 1457–1482. Daughter of Charles the Bold. She married Maximilian of Austria 1477, thus bringing the Low Countries into the possession of the Habsburgs and, ultimately, of Spain.

Mary /meəri/ of Guise, or Mary of Lorraine 1515–1560. French wife of James V of Scotland from 1538, and from 1554 regent of Scotland for her daughter →Mary Queen of Scots. A Catholic, she moved from reconciliation with Scottish

Mary Queen of Scots Mary Queen of Scots did not display the political acumen and discretion of her cousin Elizabeth I. The focus of many Catholic plots against Elizabeth, Mary was finally executed for her complicity in the Babington conspiracy.

Protestants to repression, and died during a Protestant rebellion in Edinburgh.

Mary /ˈmeəri/ Queen 1867–1953. Consort of George V of the UK. The daughter of the Duke and Duchess of Teck, the latter a grand-daughter of George II, in 1891 she became engaged to the Duke of Clarence, eldest son of the Prince of Wales (later Edward VII). After his death 1892, she married 1893 his brother George, Duke of York, who succeeded to the throne 1910.

Mary /ˈmeəri/ two queens of England:

Mary I *Bloody Mary* 1516–1558. Queen of England from 1553. She was the eldest daughter of Henry VIII by Catherine of Aragon. When Edward VI died, Mary secured the crown without difficulty in spite of the conspiracy to substitute Lady Jane →Grey. In 1554 Mary married Philip II of Spain, and as a devout Roman Catholic obtained the restoration of papal supremacy and sanctioned the persecution of Protestants. She was succeeded by her half-sister Elizabeth I.

Mary II 1662–1694. Queen of England, Scotland, and Ireland from 1688. She was the Protestant elder daughter of the Catholic →James II, and in 1677 was married to her cousin →William III of Orange. After the 1688 revolution she accepted the crown jointly with William.

During his absences from England she took charge of the government, and showed courage and resource when invasion seemed possible 1690 and 1692.

Mary Magdalene, St /ˌmægdəˈliːni/ 1st century AD. In the New Testament, the woman whom Jesus cured of possession by evil spirits, was present at the Crucifixion and burial, and was the first to meet the risen Jesus. She is often identified with the woman of St Luke's gospel who anointed Jesus' feet, and her symbol is a jar of ointment; feast day 22 July.

Mary of Modena /ˈmɒdɪnə/ 1658–1718. Queen consort of England and Scotland. She was the daughter of the Duke of Modena, Italy, and married James, Duke of York, later James II, 1673. The birth of their son James Francis Edward Stuart was the signal for the revolution of 1688 that overthrew James II. Mary fled to France.

Masaccio /məˈzætʃəʊ/ (Tomaso di Giovanni di Simone Guidi) 1401–1428. Florentine painter, a leader of the early Italian Renaissance. His frescoes in Sta Maria del Carmine, Florence, 1425–28, which he painted with Masolino da Panicale (c. 1384–1447), show a decisive break with Gothic conventions. He was the first painter to apply the scientific laws of perspective, newly discovered by the architect Brunelleschi.

Masaccio's frescoes in the Brancacci Chapel of Sta Maria del Carmine include scenes from the life of St Peter (notably *The Tribute Money*) and a moving account of *Adam and Eve's Expulsion from Paradise*. They have a monumental grandeur,

Mary I Mary I, eldest daughter of Henry VIII, who came to the throne after the deposition of Lady Jane Grey. She repealed the laws establishing Protestantism in England and re-established Catholicism 1555 and began persecuting Protestants. This resulted in the death of about 300 people, including bishops Ridley, Latimer and Cranmer, all burnt at the stake.

without trace of Gothic decorative detail, unlike the work of his colleague and teacher Masolino. Masaccio's figures have solidity and weight and are clearly set in three-dimensional space.

Other works by Masaccio are the *Trinity c.* 1428 (Sta Maria Novella, Florence) and the *Pisa polyptych* (National Gallery, London, Staatliche Museen, Berlin, and Museo di Capodimonte, Naples). Although his career marks a turning point in Italian art, he attracted few imitators (Fra Filippo Lippi's early style followed Masaccio).

Masaryk /ˈmæsərɪk/ Jan (Garrigue) 1886–1948. Czechoslovak politician, son of Tomáš Masaryk. He was foreign minister from 1940, when the Czechoslovak government was exiled in London in World War II. He returned 1945, retaining the post, but as a result of political pressure by the communists committed suicide.

Masaryk /ˈmæsərɪk/ Tomáš (Garrigue) 1850–1937. Czechoslovak nationalist politician. He directed the revolutionary movement against the Austrian Empire, founding with Eduard Beneš and Stefanik the Czechoslovak National Council, and in 1918 was elected first president of the newly formed Czechoslovak Republic. Three times re-elected, he resigned 1935 in favour of Beneš.

After the communist coup 1948, Masaryk was systematically removed from public memory in order to reverse his semi-mythological status as the forger of the Czechoslovak nation.

Mascagni /mæs'kɑːnji/ Pietro 1863–1945. Italian composer of the one-act opera *Cavalleria rusticana/Rustic Chivalry*, first produced in Rome 1890.

Masefield /meɪsfiːld/ John 1878–1967. English poet and novelist. His early years in the navy inspired *Salt Water Ballads* 1902 and several adventure novels; he also wrote children's books, such as *The Box of Delights* 1935, and plays. He was poet laureate from 1930.

The Everlasting Mercy 1911, characterized by its forcefully colloquial language, and *Reynard the Fox* 1919 are long verse narratives. His other works include the novel *Sard Harker* 1924 and the critical work *Badon Parchments* 1947.

Masekela /mæsə'keɪlə/ Hugh 1939– . South African trumpet player, exiled from his homeland since 1960, who has recorded jazz, rock, and *mbaqanga* (township jive). His albums include *Techno-Bush* 1984.

Masire /mæsɪəreɪ/ Quett Ketumile Joni 1925– . President of Botswana from 1980. In 1962, with Seretse →Khama, he founded the Botswana Democratic Party (BDP) and in 1965 was made deputy prime minister. After independence 1966, he became vice president and, on Khama's death 1980, president, continuing a policy of nonalignment.

Masire was a journalist before entering politics, sitting in the Bangwaketse Tribal Council and then the Legislative Council before cofounding the BDP. A centrist, he has helped Botswana become one of the most stable states in Africa.

Maskelyne /mæskəlɪn/ Nevil 1732–1811. English astronomer who accurately measured the distance from the Earth to the Sun by observing a transit of Venus across the Sun's face 1769. In 1774 he measured the mass of the Earth by noting the deflection of a plumb line near Mount Schiehallion in Scotland.

He was the fifth Astronomer Royal 1765–1811. He began publication 1766 of the *Nautical Almanac*, containing tables for navigators.

Mason /meɪsən/ A(lfred) E(dward) W(oodley) 1865–1948. British novelist, author of a tale of cowardice redeemed in the Sudan, *The Four Feathers* 1902, and a series featuring the detective Hanaud of the Sûreté, including *At the Villa Rose* 1910.

Mason /meɪsən/ James 1909–1984. English actor who portrayed romantic villains in British films of the 1940s. After *Odd Man Out* 1947 he worked in the USA, playing intelligent but troubled, vulnerable men, notably in *A Star Is Born* 1954. He returned to Europe 1960, where he made *Lolita* 1962, *Georgy Girl* 1966, and *Cross of Iron* 1977.

Massasoit /mæsə'sɔɪt/ also known as Ousamequin, 'Yellow Feather' *c.* 1590–1661. American chief of the Wampanoag, a people inhabiting the coasts of Massachusetts Bay and Cape Cod. He formed alliances with Plymouth Colony 1621 and Massachusetts Bay Colony 1638. After his death, his son Metacomet, known to the English as 'King →Philip', took over his father's leadership.

Massasoit was born in the area of modern Bristol, Rhode Island.

Masséna /mæseɪ'nɑː/ André 1756–1817. Marshal of France. He served in the French Revolutionary Wars and under the emperor Napoleon was created marshal 1804, duke of Rivoli 1808, and prince of Essling 1809. He was in command in Spain 1810–11 in the Peninsular War and was defeated by British troops under Wellington.

Massenet /mæsə'neɪ/ Jules Emile Frédéric 1842–1912. French composer of opera, ballets, oratorios, and orchestral suites.

His many operas include *Hérodiade* 1881, *Manon* 1884, *Le Cid* 1885, and *Thaïs* 1894; among other works is the orchestral suite *Scènes pittoresques* 1874.

Massey /mæsi/ Vincent 1887–1967. Canadian Liberal Party politician. He was the first Canadian to become governor general of Canada (1952–59).

He helped to establish the Massey Foundation 1918 which funded the building of Massey College and the University of Toronto.

Massey /mæsi/ William Ferguson 1856–1925. New Zealand politician, born in Ireland; prime minister 1912–25. He led the Reform Party, an offshoot of the Conservative Party, and as prime minister before World War I concentrated on controlling militant unions and the newly formed Federation of Labour.

Massine /mæ'siːn/ Léonide 1895–1979. Russian choreographer and dancer with the Ballets Russes. He was a creator of comedy in ballet and also symphonic ballet using concert music.

He succeeded Mikhail →Fokine at the Ballets Russes and continued with the company after Sergei →Diaghilev's death, later working in both the USA and Europe. His works include the first Cubist-inspired ballet, *Parade* 1917, *La Boutique fantasque* 1919, and *The Three-Cornered Hat* 1919.

Massinger /mæsɪndʒə/ Philip 1583–1640. English dramatist, author of *A New Way to Pay Old Debts c.* 1625. He collaborated with John →Fletcher and Thomas →Dekker, and has been credited with a share in writing Shakespeare's *Two Noble Kinsmen* and *Henry VIII*.

Ambition, in a private man a vice,
Is, in a prince, the virtue.

Philip Massinger *The Bashful Lover*

Masson /mæsɒ/ André 1896–1987. French artist and writer, a leader of Surrealism until 1929. His interest in the unconscious mind led him to experiment with 'automatic' drawing – simple pen-and-ink work, and later multitextured accretions of pigment, glue, and sand.

Masson left the Surrealist movement after a quarrel with the writer André Breton. During World War II he moved to the USA, then returned to France and painted landscapes.

Masters /ˈmɑːstəz/ Edgar Lee 1869–1950. US poet. In his book *Spoon River Anthology* 1915, a collection of free-verse epitaphs, the people of a small town tell of their frustrated lives.

Masters /ˈmɑːstəz/ John 1914–1983. British novelist, born in Calcutta, who served in the Indian army 1934–47. He wrote a series of books dealing with the Savage family throughout the period of the Raj – for example, *Nightrunners of Bengal* 1951, *The Deceivers* 1952, and *Bhowani Junction* 1954.

Masterson /ˈmæstəsən, ˈmɑːs-/ Bat (William Barclay) 1853–1921. US marshal and sportswriter. In 1878 he succeeded his murdered brother, Edward, as marshal in Dodge City, Kansas, and gunned down his brother's killers in the famous gunfight at the OK Corral 1881 at Tombstone in Arizona. He moved to New York 1902, where he became a sportswriter for the *Morning Telegraph*.

Born in Iroquois County, Illinois, and raised in Kansas, Masterson worked in his early adult years as a buffalo hunter and scout before becoming a deputy marshal in Dodge City 1876. He briefly served with Wyatt →Earp 1880 before moving to Kansas City.

Mastroianni /mæstrɔɪˈɑːni/ Marcello 1924– . Italian film actor, most popular for his carefully understated roles as an unhappy romantic lover in such films as Antonioni's *La notte/The Night* 1961. He starred in several films with Sophia Loren, including *Una giornata speciale/A Special Day* 1977, and worked with Fellini in *La dolce vita* 1960, *81/2*.

Masur /ˈmæzʊə/ Kurt 1928– . German conductor, music director of the New York Philharmonic from 1990. He was conductor of the Dresden Philharmonic Orchestra 1955–58 and 1967–72, before making his London debut 1973 with the New Philharmonia. He was prominent in the political campaigning that took place prior to German unification.

Mata Hari /ˈmɑːtə ˈhɑːri/ Stage name of Gertrud Margarete Zelle 1876–1917. Dutch courtesan, dancer, and probable spy. In World War I she had affairs with highly placed military and government officials on both sides and told Allied secrets to the Germans. She may have been a double agent, in the pay of both France and Germany. She was shot by the French on espionage charges.

Mather /ˈmeɪθə/ Cotton 1663–1728. American theologian and writer. He was a Puritan minister in Boston, and wrote over 400 works of history, science, annals, and theology, including *Magnalia Christi Americana/The Great Works of Christ in America* 1702, a vast compendium of early New England history and experience. Mather appears to have supported the Salem witch-hunts.

Mather /ˈmæðə/ Increase 1639–1723. American colonial and religious leader. As a defender of the colonial right to self-government, he went to England 1688 to protest revocation of the Massachusetts charter. However, his silence during the Salem witch trials of 1692 lessened his public influence. His eldest son was Cotton →Mather.

Born in Dorchester, Massachusetts, and educated at Harvard University, Mather served as a cleric in England during the Puritan Commonwealth, returning to Massachusetts 1661 where he was named teacher of Boston's Second Church 1664. He was president of Harvard 1685–1701.

Mathewson /ˈmæθjuːsən/ Christy (Christopher) 1880–1925. US baseball player. He was signed by the New York Giants of the National League 1900 and during a 17–year major-league career, he amassed an impressive record of 373 wins and 188 losses. He retired from play 1916, becoming manager of the Cincinnati Reds 1916–18.

Born in Factoryville, Pennsylvania, Mathewson attended Bucknell University.

Mathewson was elected to the Baseball Hall of Fame 1936.

Matilda /məˈtɪldə/ 1102–1167. Claimant to the throne of England. On the death of her father, Henry I, 1135, the barons elected her cousin Stephen to be king. Matilda invaded England 1139, and was crowned by her supporters 1141. Civil war ensued until Stephen was finally recognized as king 1153, with Henry II (Matilda's son) as his successor.

Matilda was recognized during the reign of Henry I as his heir. She married first the Holy Roman emperor Henry V and, after his death, Geoffrey Plantagenet, Count of Anjou (1113–1151).

Matisse /mæˈtiːs/ Henri 1869–1954. French painter, sculptor, illustrator, and designer; one of the most original creative forces in early 20th-century art. His work concentrates on designs that emphasize curvaceous surface patterns, linear arabesques, and brilliant colour. Subjects include odalisques (women of the harem), bathers, and dancers; later works include pure abstracts, as in his collages of coloured paper shapes and the designs 1949–51 for the decoration of a chapel for the Dominican convent in Vence, near Nice.

In 1904 Matisse worked with Signac in the south of France in a Neo-Impressionist style. The following year he was the foremost of the Fauve painters exhibiting at the Salon d'Automne, painting with bold brushstrokes, thick paint, and strong colours. He soon abandoned conventional perspective in his continued experiments with colour, and in 1910 an exhibition of Islamic art further influenced him towards the decorative. He settled in the south of France 1914. His murals of *The Dance* 1932–33 (Barnes Foundation, Merion, Pennsylvania) are characteristic.

Matsudaira /mɑːtsudaɪra/ Tsuneo 1877–1949. Japanese diplomat and politician who became the first chair of the Japanese Diet (parliament) after World War II.

Matsudaira negotiated for Japan at the London Naval Conference of 1930 and acted as imperial household minister 1936–45, advising the emperor, but was unsuccessful in keeping Japan out of a war with the Western powers.

Matsukata /mɑːtsukata/ Masayoshi, Prince 1835–1924. Japanese politician, premier 1891–92 and 1896–98. As minister of finance 1881–91 and 1898–1900, he paved the way for the modernization of the Japanese economy.

Matsuoka /mɑːtsuɔka/ Yosuke 1880–1946. Japanese politician, foreign minister 1940–41. A fervent nationalist, Matsuoka led Japan out of the League of Nations when it condemned Japan for the seizure of Manchuria. As foreign minister, he allied Japan with Germany and Italy. At the end of World War II, he was arrested as a war criminal but died before his trial.

Matsys /mætsaɪs/ (also *Massys* or *Metsys*) Quentin *c.* 1464–1530. Flemish painter, born in Louvain, active in Antwerp. He painted religious subjects such as the *Lamentation* 1511 (Musées Royaux, Antwerp) and portraits set against landscapes or realistic interiors.

His works include the *St Anne Altarpiece* 1509 (Musées Royaux, Brussels) and a portrait of *Erasmus* 1517 (Museo Nazionale, Rome).

Matthau /mæθaʊ/ Walter. Stage name of Walter Matuschanskavasky 1922– . US character actor, impressive in both comedy and dramatic roles. He gained film stardom in the 1960s after his stage success in *The Odd Couple* 1965. His many films include *Kotch* 1971, *Charley Varrick* 1973, and *The Sunshine Boys* 1975.

Matthews /mæθjuːz/ Stanley 1824–1889. US jurist. Appointed by President Garfield as associate justice of the US Supreme Court 1881–99, his most important decision, *Hurtado* v *California* 1888, was an important constitutional definition of due process of law.

Born in Cincinnati, Ohio, USA, Matthews graduated from Kenyon College and studied law in Cincinnati. He served in the Ohio Senate 1855–57 and as a US attorney for the southern district of Ohio 1858–61. After the American Civil War (1861–65), he sat as a judge of the Cincinnati Superior Court and then returned to private practice.

Matthews /mæθjuːz/ Stanley 1915– . English footballer who played for Stoke City, Blackpool, and England. He played nearly 700 Football League games, and won 54 international caps. He was the first Footballer of the Year 1948 (again 1963), the first European Footballer of the Year 1956, and the first footballer to be knighted.

An outstanding right-winger, he had the nickname 'the Wizard of the Dribble' because of his ball control. At the age of 38 he won an FA Cup Winners' medal when Blackpool beat Bolton Wanderers 4–3, Matthews laying on three goals in the last 20 minutes. He continued to play first-division football after the age of 50.

Matthew, St /mæθjuː/ 1st century AD. Christian apostle and evangelist, the traditional author of the first Gospel. He is usually identified with Levi, who was a tax collector in the service of Herod Antipas, and was called by Jesus to be a disciple as he sat by the Lake of Galilee receiving customs dues. His emblem is a man with wings; feast day 21 Sept.

Matthias Corvinus /məˈθaɪəs kɔːˈvaɪnəs/ 1440–1490. King of Hungary from 1458. His aim of uniting Hungary, Austria, and Bohemia involved him in long wars with Holy Roman emperor Frederick III and the kings of Bohemia and Poland, during which he captured Vienna (1485) and made it his capital. His father was János →Hunyadi.

Mattox /mætəks/ Matt 1921– . US jazz dancer and teacher. He pioneered jazz dance in the USA and appeared in many films; for example, *Seven Brides for Seven Brothers* 1954. From 1970 he taught at the Dance Centre, London, and later in Paris.

Mature /məˈtjʊə/ Victor 1915– . US actor, film star of the 1940s and early 1950s. He gave memorable performances in, among others, *My Darling Clementine* 1946, *Kiss of Death* 1947, and *Samson and Delilah* 1949.

Mauchly /mɒxli/ John William 1907–1980. US physicist and engineer who, in 1946, constructed the first general-purpose computer, the ENIAC, in collaboration with John →Eckert. Their company was bought by Remington Rand 1950, and they built the UNIVAC 1 computer 1951 for the US census.

The idea for ENIAC grew out of work carried out by the two during World War II on ways of automating the calculation of artillery firing tables for the US Army.

Maudling /mɔːdlɪŋ/ Reginald 1917–1979. British Conservative politician, chancellor of the Exchequer 1962–64, contender for the party leadership 1965, and home secretary 1970–72. He resigned when referred to during the bankruptcy proceedings of the architect John Poulson, since (as home secretary) he would have been in charge of the Metropolitan Police investigating the case.

Maufe /mɔːf/ Edward 1883–1974. British architect. His works include the Runnymede Memorial and Guildford Cathedral.

Mauger /mɔːgə/ Ivan Gerald 1939– . New Zealand speedway star. He won the world individual title a record six times 1968–79.

Maugham /mɔːm/ (William) Somerset 1874–1965. English writer. His work includes the novels *Of Human Bondage* 1915, *The Moon and Six-*

pence 1919, and *Cakes and Ale* 1930; the short-story collections *The Trembling of a Leaf* 1921 and *Ashenden* 1928; and the plays *Lady Frederick* 1907 and *Our Betters* 1923.

Maugham was born in Paris and studied medicine at St Thomas's, London. During World War I he was a secret agent in Russia; his *Ashenden* spy stories are based on this experience.

Maupassant /ˌməʊpæˈsɒn̩/ Guy de 1850–1893. French author who established a reputation with the short story 'Boule de Suif/Ball of Fat' 1880 and wrote some 300 short stories in all. His novels include *Une Vie/A Woman's Life* 1883 and *Bel-Ami* 1885. He was encouraged as a writer by Gustave →Flaubert.

Mauriac /ˌmɔːriˈæk/ François 1885–1970. French novelist. His novel *Le Baiser au lépreux/A Kiss for the Leper* 1922 describes the conflict of an unhappy marriage. The irreconcilability of Christian practice and human nature is examined in *Fleuve de feu/River of Fire* 1923, *Le Désert de l'amour/The Desert of Love* 1925, and *Thérèse Desqueyroux* 1927. Nobel Prize for Literature 1952.

Let us be wary of ready-made ideas about courage and cowardice: the same burden weighs infinitely more heavily on some shoulders than on others.

François Mauriac *Second Thoughts*

Maurice /ˈmɒrɪs/ (John) Frederick Denison 1805–1872. Anglican cleric from 1834, co-founder with Charles →Kingsley of the Christian Socialist movement. He was deprived of his professorships in English history, literature, and divinity at King's College, London, because his *Theological Essays* 1853 attacked the doctrine of eternal punishment; he became professor of moral philosophy at Cambridge 1866.

Maurois /mɔːˈwɑː/ André. Pen name of Emile Herzog 1885–1967. French novelist and writer whose works include the semi-autobiographical *Bernard Quesnay* 1926 and fictionalized biographies, such as *Ariel* 1923, a life of Shelley.

In World War I he was attached to the British Army, and the essays in *Les Silences du Colonel Bramble* 1918 offer humorously sympathetic observations on the British character.

Mauroy /mɔːˈwɑː/ Pierre 1928– . French socialist politician, prime minister 1981–84. He oversaw the introduction of a radical reflationary programme.

Mauroy worked for the FEN teachers' trade union and served as national secretary for the Young Socialists during the 1950s, rising in the ranks of the Socialist Party in the northeast region. He entered the National Assembly 1973 and was prime minister in the Mitterrand government of

Maury *US naval officer and oceanographer Matthew Maury. He wrote* Navigation *after a voyage around the world 1830 and* The Physical Geography of the Sea *1855.*

1981, but was replaced by Laurent Fabius in July 1984. He was first secretary (leader) of the Socialist Party 1988–1992.

Maury /ˈmɔːri/ Matthew Fontaine 1806–1873. US naval officer, founder of the US Naval Oceanographic Office. His system of recording oceanographic data is still used today.

Maurya dynasty /ˈmaʊriə/ Indian dynasty *c.* 321–*c.* 185 BC, founded by *Chandragupta Maurya* (321–*c.* 279 BC). Under Emperor →Asoka most of India was united for the first time, but after his death in 232 the empire was riven by dynastic disputes.

Mavor /ˈmeɪvə/ O H real name of the Scottish playwright James →Bridie.

Mawson /ˈmɔːsən/ Douglas 1882–1958. Australian explorer who reached the magnetic South Pole on →Shackleton's expedition of 1907–09.

Mawson led Antarctic expeditions 1911–14 and 1929–31. Australia's first permanent Antarctic base was named after him. He was professor of mineralogy at the University of Adelaide 1920–53.

Maxim /ˈmæksɪm/ Hiram Stevens 1840–1916. US-born British inventor of the first automatic machine gun, in 1884.

Maximilian /ˌmæksɪˈmɪliən/ 1832–1867. Emperor of Mexico 1864–67. He accepted that title when the French emperor Napoleon III's troops occupied the country, but encountered resistance from the deposed president Benito →Juárez. In 1866, after the French troops withdrew on the insistence of the USA, Maximilian was captured by Mexican republicans and shot.

Maximilian I /ˌmæksɪˈmɪliən/ 1459–1519. Holy Roman emperor from 1493, the son of Emperor Frederick III. He had acquired the Low Countries through his marriage to Mary of Burgundy 1477.

He married his son Philip I (the Handsome) to the heiress to the Spanish throne, and undertook long wars with Italy and Hungary in attempts to extend Habsburg power. He was the patron of the artist Dürer.

Maxwell /ˈmækswəl/ (Ian) Robert (born Jan Ludvik Hoch) 1923–1991. Czech-born British publishing and newspaper proprietor who owned several UK national newspapers, including the *Daily Mirror*, the Macmillan Publishing Company, and the New York *Daily News*. At the time of his death the Maxwell domain carried debts of some $3.9 billion.

Born into a poor Jewish family in Czechoslovakia, he escaped to Romania 1939 and later to Britain. His father was shot and his mother and other members of his family died in Auschwitz. As a young man, he had a distinguished wartime army career, and was awarded the Military Cross.

He founded two major organizations: the family-owned Liechtenstein-based Maxwell Foundation, which owns 51% of Mirror Group Newspapers; and Maxwell Communication Corporation, 67% owned by the Maxwell family, which has shares in publishing, electronics, and information companies. He was also the publisher of the English edition of *Moscow News* from 1988, and had private interests (not connected with the Maxwell Corporation) in the Hungarian newspapers *Esti Hirlap* and *Magyar Hirlap* (he owned 40% of the latter, from 1989), the German *Berliner Werlag*, and the Israeli *Maariv*.

Maxwell was Labour member of Parliament for Buckingham 1964–70. Acquiring the Mirror Group of newspapers from Reed International 1984, he introduced colour and made it profitable. In 1990 he bought the US book publisher Macmillan and in 1991 the New York *Daily News*, which was on the verge of closure after a bitter labour dispute.

In the UK the national newspapers owned by the Maxwell Foundation 1984–91 were the *Daily Mirror*, *Sunday Mirror*, and *People* (all of which support the Labour party); in 1990 the weekly *European* was launched.

In late 1991 Maxwell, last seen on his yacht off the Canary Islands, was found dead at sea. His sons Kevin and Ian were named as his successors.

When I pass a belt I cannot resist hitting below it.

Robert Maxwell *New York Times* March 1991

Maxwell /ˈmækswəl/ James Clerk 1831–1879. Scottish physicist. His main achievement was in the understanding of electromagnetic waves:

Maxwell's equations bring together electricity, magnetism, and light in one set of relations. He contributed to every branch of physical science – studying gases, optics, and the sensation of colour. His theoretical work in magnetism prepared the way for wireless telegraphy and telephony.

Born in Edinburgh, he was professor of natural philosophy at Aberdeen 1856–60, and then of physics and astronomy at London. In 1871, he became professor of experimental physics at Cambridge. His principal works include *Perception of Colour, Colour Blindness* 1860, *Theory of Heat* 1871, *Electricity and Magnetism* 1873, and *Matter and Motion* 1876. Although thought of as a theoretical physicist, he was an able experimenter; he was ranked by Einstein as second only to Isaac Newton.

May /meɪ/ Thomas Erskine 1815–1886. English constitutional jurist. He was Clerk of the House of Commons from 1871 until 1886, when he was created Baron Farnborough. He wrote a practical *Treatise on the Law, Privileges, Proceedings, and Usage of Parliament* 1844, the authoritative work on parliamentary procedure.

Mayakovsky /ˌmaɪəˈkɒfski/ Vladimir 1893–1930. Russian Futurist poet who combined revolutionary propaganda with efforts to revolutionize poetic technique in his poems '150,000,000' 1920 and 'V I Lenin' 1924. His satiric play *The Bedbug* 1928 was taken in the West as an attack on philistinism in the USSR.

Mayer /ˈmaɪə/ Julius Robert von 1814–1878. German physicist who in 1842 anticipated James →Joule in deriving the mechanical equivalent of heat, and Hermann von →Helmholtz in the principle of conservation of energy.

Mayer /ˈmeɪə/ Louis B(urt). Adopted name of Eliezer Mayer 1885–1957. Russian- born US film producer. Attracted to the entertainment industry, he became a successful theatre-owner in New England and in 1914 began to buy the distribution rights to feature films. Mayer was soon involved in film production, moving to Los Angeles 1918 and becoming one of the founders of Metro-Goldwyn-Mayer (MGM) studios 1924. In charge of production, Mayer instituted the Hollywood 'star' system. He retired from MGM 1951.

Mayer /ˈmeɪə/ Robert 1879–1985. British philanthropist who founded the Robert Mayer Concerts for Children and the Transatlantic Foundation Anglo-American Scholarships.

Maynard Smith /ˈmeɪnɑːd ˈsmɪθ/ John 1920– . British biologist. He applied game theory to animal behaviour and developed the concept of the evolutionary stable strategy (ESS) as a mathematical technique for studying the evolution of behaviour.

His books include *The Theory of Evolution* 1958 and *Evolution and the Theory of Games* 1982.

Mayo /ˈmeɪəʊ/ William James 1861–1939. US surgeon, founder, with his brother Charles Horace

Mayo (1865–1939), of the *Mayo Clinic* for medical treatment 1889 in Rochester, Minnesota.

Specialist – a man who knows more and more about less and less.

William James Mayo

Mays /meɪz/ Willie (Howard Jr) 1931– . US baseball player who played with the New York (later San Francisco) Giants 1951–72 and the New York Mets 1973. He hit 660 career home runs, third best in baseball history, and was also an outstanding fielder and runner. He was the National League's Most Valuable Player 1954 and 1965.

Born in Westfield, Alabama, USA, Mays was elected to the Baseball Hall of Fame 1979.

Mazarin /ˌmæzəˈræŋ/ Jules 1602–1661. French politician who succeeded Richelieu as chief minister of France 1642. His attack on the power of the nobility led to the Fronde (a rebellious movement against him) and his temporary exile, but his diplomacy achieved a successful conclusion to the Thirty Years' War, and, in alliance with Oliver Cromwell during the British protectorate, he gained victory over Spain.

Mazowiecki /ˌmæzorˈjetski/ Tadeusz 1927– . Polish politician, founder member of Solidarity, and Poland's first postwar noncommunist prime minister 1989–90. Forced to introduce unpopular economic reforms, he was knocked out in the first round of the Nov 1990 presidential elections, resigning in favour of his former colleague Lech →Wałesa.

A former member of the Polish parliament 1961–70, he was debarred from re-election by the authorities after investigating the police massacre of Gdańsk strikers. He became legal adviser to Lech Wałesa and, after a period of internment, edited the Solidarity newspaper *Tygodnik Solidarność*. In 1989 he became prime minister after the elections denied the communists their customary majority. A devout Catholic, he is a close friend of Pope John Paul II.

Mazzini /mætˈsiːni/ Giuseppe 1805–1872. Italian nationalist. He was a member of the revolutionary society, the Carbonari, and founded in exile the nationalist movement Giovane Italia (Young Italy) 1832. Returning to Italy on the outbreak of the 1848 revolution, he headed a republican government established in Rome, but was forced into exile again on its overthrow 1849. He acted as a focus for the movement for Italian unity.

Mazzini, born in Genoa, studied law. For his subversive activity with the Carbonari he was imprisoned 1830, then went to France, founding in Marseille the Young Italy movement, followed by an international revolutionary organization, Young Europe, 1834. For many years he lived in exile in France, Switzerland, and the UK, and was condemned to death in his absence by the Sardinian government, but returned to Italy for the revolution of 1848. He conducted the defence of Rome against French forces and, when it failed, he refused to join in the capitulation and returned to London, where he continued to agitate until his death in Geneva, Switzerland.

Mboya /əmˈbɔɪə/ Tom 1930–1969. Kenyan politician, a founder of the Kenya African National Union (KANU), and minister of economic affairs from 1964 until his assassination.

Meade /miːd/ George Gordon 1815–1872. US military leader. During the American Civil War, he commanded the Pennsylvania volunteers at the Peninsular Campaign, Bull Run, and Antietam 1862. He led the Army of the Potomac, and the Union forces at Gettysburg 1863. After the war, he served as military governor of Georgia, Alabama, and Florida 1868–69.

Born in Cadiz, Spain, Meade graduated from West Point military academy 1835. After working on private railroad and surveying projects 1836–42, he returned to the army, serving in the Mexican War 1846–48.

Mead /miːd/ George Herbert 1863–1931. US philosopher and social psychologist who helped to found the philosophy of pragmatism.

He taught at the University of Chicago during its prominence as a centre of social scientific development in the early 20th century, and is regarded as the founder of symbolic interactionism. His work on group interaction had a major influence on sociology, stimulating the development of role theory, phenomenology, and ethnomethodology.

Mead /miːd/ Margaret 1901–1978. US anthropologist who popularized cultural relativity and challenged the conventions of Western society with *Coming of Age in Samoa* 1928 and subsequent works. Her fieldwork has later been criticized. She was a popular speaker on civil liberties, ecological sanity, feminism, and population control.

Meade /miːd/ James Edward 1907– . British Keynesian economist. He shared a Nobel prize in 1977 for his work on trade and capital movements, and published a four-volume *Principles of Political Economy* 1965–76.

Meade /miːd/ Richard 1938– . British equestrian in three-day events. He won three Olympic gold medals 1968 and 1972, and was twice a world champion.

He is associated with horses such as Cornishman, Laureston, and The Poacher, and has won all the sport's major honours.

Mechnikov /metʃnɪkɒf/ Ilya 1845–1916. Russian scientist who discovered the function of white blood cells and phagocytes. After leaving Russia and joining →Pasteur in Paris, he described how these 'scavenger cells' can attack the body itself (autoimmune disease). He shared the Nobel Prize for Medicine 1908 with Paul →Ehrlich.

Medawar /medəwə/ Peter (Brian) 1915–1987. Brazilian-born British immunologist who, with Macfarlane →Burnet, discovered that the body's resistance to grafted tissue is undeveloped in the newborn child, and studied the way it is acquired.

Medawar's work has been vital in understanding the phenomenon of tissue rejection following transplantation. He and Burnet shared the Nobel Prize for Medicine 1960.

Medici /medɪtʃi/ noble family of Florence, the city's rulers from 1434 until they died out 1737. Family members included →Catherine de' Medici, Pope →Leo X, Pope →Clement VII, →Marie de' Medici.

Medici /medɪtʃiː/ Cosimo de' 1389–1464. Italian politician and banker. Regarded as the model for Machiavelli's *The Prince*, he dominated the government of Florence from 1434 and was a patron of the arts. He was succeeded by his inept son *Piero de' Medici* (1416–1469).

Medici /medɪtʃiː/ Cosimo de' 1519–1574. Italian politician, ruler of Florence; duke of Florence from 1537 and 1st grand duke of Tuscany from 1569.

We read that we ought to forgive our enemies; but we do not read that we ought to forgive our friends.

Cosimo de' Medici

Medici /medɪtʃiː/ Ferdinand de' 1549–1609. Italian politician, grand duke of Tuscany from 1587.

Medici /medɪtʃiː/ Giovanni de' 1360–1429. Italian entrepreneur and banker, with political influence in Florence as a supporter of the popular party. He was the father of Cosimo de' Medici.

Medici /medɪtʃiː/ Lorenzo de', *the Magnificent* 1449–1492. Italian politician, ruler of Florence from 1469. He was also a poet and a generous patron of the arts.

Medvedev /mɪd'vjedef/ Vadim 1929– . Soviet communist politician. He was deputy chief of propaganda 1970–78, was in charge of party relations with communist countries 1986–88, and in 1988 was appointed by the Soviet leader Gorbachev to succeed the conservative Ligachev as head of ideology. He adhered to a firm Leninist line.

Mee /miː/ Margaret 1909–1988. English botanical artist. In the 1950s, she went to Brazil, where she accurately and comprehensively painted many plant species of the Amazon basin.

She is thought to have painted more species than any other botanical artist.

Meegeren /meɪɡərən, Dutch 'meɪxərə/ Hans van 1889–1947. Dutch forger; mainly of Vermeer's paintings. His 'Vermeer' *Christ at Emmaus* was bought for Rotterdam's Boymans Museum in 1937. He was discovered when a 'Vermeer' sold to the Nazi leader Goering was traced back to him after World War II. Sentenced to a year's imprisonment, he died two months later.

Mehemet Ali /mɪ'hemɪt 'ɑːli/ 1769–1849. Pasha (governor) of Egypt from 1805, and founder of the dynasty that ruled until 1953. An Albanian in the Ottoman service, he had originally been sent to Egypt to fight the French. As pasha, he established a European-style army and navy, fought his Turkish overlord 1831 and 1839, and conquered Sudan.

Mehta /meɪtə/ Zubin 1936– . Indian conductor who became music director of the New York Philharmonic 1978. He is known for his flamboyant style of conducting and his interpretations of the Romantic composers.

Meier /meɪə/ Richard 1934– . US architect whose white designs spring from the poetic modernism of the →Le Corbusier villas of the 1920s. His abstract style is at its most mature in the Museum für Kunsthandwerk (Museum of Arts and Crafts), Frankfurt, Germany, which was completed 1984.

Earlier schemes are the Bronx Developmental Centre, New York (1970–76), and the Athenaeum–New Harmony, Indiana (1974). He is the architect for the Getty Museum, Los Angeles.

Meiji /meɪdʒiː/ Mutsuhito 1852–1912. Emperor of Japan from 1867, when he took the title *meiji tennō* ('enlightened sovereign'). During his reign (known as the Meiji era) Japan became a world industrial and naval power. He abolished the feudal system and discrimination against the lowest caste, established state schools, and introduced conscription, the Western calendar, and other measures in an attempt to modernize Japan, including a constitution 1889.

The son of Emperor Komei, he took the personal name Mutsuhito when he became crown prince 1860.

Meikle /miːkəl/ Andrew 1719–1811. Scottish millwright who in 1785 designed and built the first practical threshing machine for separating cereal grains from the husks.

Meinhof /maɪnhɔf/ Ulrike 1934–1976. West German urban guerrilla, member of the *Baader–Meinhof gang* in the 1970s (the gang was active against what it perceived as US imperialism).

A left-wing journalist, Meinhof was converted to the use of violence to achieve political change by the imprisoned Andreas Baader. She helped free Baader and they became joint leaders of the urban guerrilla organization the Red Army Faction. As the faction's chief ideologist, Meinhof was arrested in 1972 and, in 1974, sentenced to eight years' imprisonment. She committed suicide in 1976 in the Stammheim high-security prison.

Meir /meɪˈɪə/ Golda 1898–1978. Israeli Labour (*Mapai*) politician. Born in Russia, she emigrated to the USA 1906, and in 1921 went to Palestine. She was foreign minister 1956–66 and prime minister 1969–74. Criticism of the Israelis' lack of preparation for the 1973 Arab-Israeli War led to election losses for Labour and, unable to form a government, she resigned.

Meitner /ˈmaɪtnə/ Lise 1878–1968. Austrian physicist who worked with Otto ➔Hahn and was the first to realize that they had inadvertently achieved the fission of uranium. Driven from Nazi Germany because of her Jewish origin, she later worked in Sweden, where she published the results of their work. She refused to work on the atom bomb.

Melanchthon /məˈlæŋkθən/ Philip. Assumed name of Philip Schwarzerd 1497–1560. German theologian who helped Luther prepare a German translation of the New Testament. In 1521 he issued the first systematic formulation of Protestant theology, reiterated in the Confession of Augsburg (statement of the Protestant faith) 1530.

Melba /ˈmelbə/ Nellie, adopted name of Helen Porter Mitchell 1861–1931. Australian soprano. One of her finest roles was Donizetti's *Lucia*. *Peach melba* (half a peach plus vanilla ice cream and melba sauce, made from sweetened, fresh raspberries) and *melba toast* (crisp, thin toast) are named after her.

Melbourne /ˈmelbən/ William Lamb, 2nd Viscount 1779–1848. British Whig politician. Home secretary 1830–34, he was briefly prime minister in 1834 and again 1835–41. Accused in 1836 of seducing Caroline ➔Norton, he lost the favour of William IV.

Melbourne was married 1805–25 to Lady Caroline Ponsonby (novelist Lady Caroline Lamb, 1785–1828). He was an adviser to the young Queen Victoria.

Méliès /melˈjes/ Georges 1861–1938. French film pioneer. From 1896 to 1912 he made over 1,000 films, mostly fantasies (*Le Voyage dans la Lune/A Trip to the Moon* 1902). He developed trick effects, slow motion, double exposure, and dissolves, and in 1897 built Europe's first film studio at Montreuil.

Beginning his career as a stage magician, Méliès' interest in cinema was sparked by the Lumière brothers' *cinématographe*, premiered 1895. He constructed a camera and founded a production company, Star Film. Méliès failed to develop as a filmmaker and he went bankrupt 1913.

Mellon /ˈmelən/ Andrew William 1855–1937. US financier who donated his art collection to found the National Gallery of Art, Washington DC, in 1937. His son, *Paul Mellon* (1907–   ) was its president 1963–79. He funded Yale University's Center for British Art, New Haven, Connecticut, and donated major works of art to both collections.

Melbourne English Whig politician William Lamb, 2nd Viscount Melbourne, a supporter of Parliamentary reform. He was prime minister when Queen Victoria came to the throne and showed tact and benevolence in guiding her through her early years of rule.

Melville /ˈmelvɪl/ Henry Dundas, Viscount Melville 1742–1811. British Tory politician, born in Edinburgh. He entered Parliament 1774, and as home secretary 1791–94 persecuted the parliamentary reformers. His impeachment for malversation (misconduct) 1806 was the last in English history.

Melville /ˈmelvɪl/ Herman 1819–1891. US writer whose *Moby-Dick* 1851 was inspired by his whaling experiences in the South Seas. These experiences were also the basis for earlier fiction, such as *Typee* 1846 and *Omoo* 1847. *Billy Budd* was completed just before his death and published 1924. Although most of his works were unappreciated during his lifetime, today he is one of the most highly regarded of US authors.

Melville was born in Albany, New York. His family was left destitute when his father became bankrupt and died when Melville was 12. He went to sea as a cabin boy in 1839. His love for the sea was inspired by this and later voyages. He published several volumes of verse, as well as short stories (*The Piazza Tales* 1856). Melville worked in the New York customs office 1866–85, writing no prose from 1857 until *Billy Budd*. A friend of Nathaniel Hawthorne, he explored the dark, troubled side of American experience in novels of unusual form and great philosophical power.

Billy Budd was the basis of an opera by Benjamin Britten 1951, and was made into a film 1962.

Memling /ˈmemlɪŋ, - lɪŋk/ (or **Memlinc**) Hans *c.* 1430–1494. Flemish painter, born near Frankfurt-am-Main, Germany, but active in Bruges. He painted religious subjects and portraits. Some of his works are in the Hospital of St John, Bruges, including the *Adoration of the Magi* 1479.

Memling is said to have been a pupil of van der Weyden, but his style is calmer and softer. His portraits include *Tommaso Portinari and His Wife* (Metropolitan Museum of Art, New York), and he decorated the *Shrine of St Ursula* 1489 (Hospital of St John, Bruges).

Menander /meˈnændə/ *c.* 342–291 BC. Greek comic dramatist, born in Athens. His work was virtually unknown until the discovery 1905 of substantial fragments of four of his plays in Eygptian papyri (many had been used as papier-mâché for Egyptian mummy cases). In 1957 the only complete Menander play, *Dyscholos/The Bad-Tempered Man*, was found.

Mencius /ˈmenʃiəs/ Latinized name of Mengzi *c.* 372–289 BC. Chinese philosopher and moralist, in the tradition of Confucius. Mencius considered human nature innately good, although this goodness required cultivation, and based his conception of morality on this conviction.

Born in Shantung (Shandong) province, he was founder of a Confucian school. After 20 years' unsuccessful search for a ruler to put into practice his enlightened political programme, based on people's innate goodness, he retired. His teachings are preserved as the *Book of Mengzi*.

Mencken /ˈmeŋkən/ H(enry) L(ouis) 1880–1956. US essayist and critic, known as 'the sage of Baltimore'. His unconventionally phrased, satiric contributions to the periodicals *The Smart Set* and *American Mercury* (both of which he edited) aroused controversy.

Injustice is relatively easy to bear; what stings is justice.

H L Mencken *Prejudices*

Mendel /ˈmendl/ Gregor Johann 1822–1884. Austrian biologist, founder of genetics. His experiments with successive generations of peas gave the basis for his theory of particulate inheritance rather than blending, involving dominant and recessive characters. His results, published 1865–69, remained unrecognized until the early 20th century.

Mendel was abbot of the Augustinian abbey at Brünn (now Brno, Czech Republic) from 1868.

Mendeleyev /ˌmendəˈleɪef/ Dmitri Ivanovich 1834–1907. Russian chemist who framed the periodic law in chemistry 1869, which states that the chemical properties of the elements depend on their relative atomic masses. This law is the basis of the periodic table of elements, in which the ele-

ments are arranged by atomic number and organized by their related groups.

For this work, Mendeleyev and Lothar →Meyer (who presented a similar but independent classification of the elements) received the Davy medal in 1882. From his table Mendeleyev predicted the properties of elements then unknown (gallium, scandium, and germanium).

Mendelsohn /ˈmendlsən/ Erich 1887–1953. German Expressionist architect who designed the Einstein Tower, Potsdam, 1919–20. His later work fused Modernist and Expressionist styles; in Britain he built the de la Warr Pavilion 1935–36 in Bexhill-on-Sea, East Sussex. In 1941 he settled in the USA, where he built the Maimonides Hospital, San Francisco, 1946–50.

Mendelssohn (-Bartholdy) /ˈmendlsən bɑːrˈtɒldi/ (Jakob Ludwig) Felix 1809–1847. German composer, also a pianist and conductor. As a child he composed and performed with his own orchestra and as an adult was helpful to →Schumann's career. Among his best-known works are *A Midsummer Night's Dream* 1827; the *Fingal's Cave* overture 1832; and five symphonies, which include the Reformation 1830, the Italian 1833, and the Scottish 1842. He was instrumental in promoting the revival of interest in J S Bach's music.

Mendes /ˈmendɪs/ Chico (Filho Francisco) 1944–1988. Brazilian environmentalist and labour leader. Opposed to the destruction of Brazil's rainforests, he organized itinerant rubber tappers into the Workers' Party (PT) and was assassinated by Darci Alves, a cattle rancher's son. Of 488 similar murders in land conflicts in Brazil 1985–89, his was the first to come to trial.

Born in the NW Amazonian state of Acre, Mendes became an outspoken opponent of the destruction of Brazil's rainforests for cattle ranching purposes, and received death threats from ranchers. (Rubber-tapping is sustainable rainforest use.) Mendes was awarded the UN Global 500 Ecology Prize in 1987.

Mendès-France /ˌmɒndesˈfrɒns/ Pierre 1907–1982. French prime minister and foreign minister 1954–55. He extricated France from the war in Indochina, and prepared the way for Tunisian independence.

Mendoza /menˈdəʊsə/ Antonio de *c.* 1490–1552. First Spanish viceroy of New Spain (Mexico) 1535–51. He attempted to develop agriculture and mining and supported the church in its attempts to convert the Indians. The system he established lasted until the 19th century. He was subsequently viceroy of Peru 1551–52.

Menelik II /ˈmenəlɪk/ 1844–1913. Negus (emperor) of Abyssinia (now Ethiopia) from 1889. He defeated the Italians 1896 at Aduwa and thereby retained the independence of his country.

Menem /ˈmenem/ Carlos (Saul) 1935– . Argentine politician, president from 1989; leader of the

Peronist (Justicialist Party) movement. As president, he introduced sweeping privatization and public spending cuts, released hundreds of political prisoners jailed under the Alfonsín regime, and sent two warships to the Gulf to assist the USA against Iraq in the 1992 Gulf War (the only Latin American country to offer support to the USA). He also improved relations with the UK.

The son of Syrian immigrants to La Rioja province in the 1920s, Menem joined the Justicialist Party while training to be a lawyer. In 1963 he was elected president of the party in La Rioja and in 1983 became governor. In 1989 he defeated the Radical Civic Union Party (UCR) candidate and became president of Argentina. Despite anti-British speeches during the election campaign, President Menem soon declared a wish to resume normal diplomatic relations with the UK and to discuss the future of the Falkland Islands in a spirit of compromise.

Menéndez de Avilés /mə'nendəs deɪ ˌɑː/ Pedro 1519–1574. Spanish colonial administrator in America. Philip II of Spain granted him the right to establish a colony in Florida to counter French presence there. In 1565 he founded St Augustine and destroy the French outpost at Fort Caroline.

Born in Avilés, Spain, he saw service in the navy of Charles V and was named to the vital post of captain general of the Indies fleet 1554. His later attempts to establish colonies in the Chesapeake region were unsuccessful but Menéndez maintained a firm Spanish claim on the Florida peninsula.

Menes /ˈmiːniːz/ c. 3200 BC. Traditionally, the first king of the first dynasty of ancient Egypt. He is said to have founded Memphis and organized worship of the gods.

Mengistu /menˈgɪstuː/ Haile Mariam 1937– . Ethiopian soldier and socialist politician, head of state 1977–91 (president 1987–91). He seized power in a coup and was confronted with severe problems of drought and secessionist uprisings, but survived with help from the USSR and the West until his violent overthrow.

As an officer in the Ethiopian army, Mengistu took part in the overthrow in 1974 of Emperor →Haile Selassie and in 1977 led another coup, becoming head of state. In 1987 civilian rule was formally reintroduced, but with the Marxist-Leninist Workers' Party of Ethiopia the only legally permitted party. In May 1991, two secessionist forces closed in on the capital of Addis Ababa, and Mengistu fled the country.

Mengs /meŋs/ Anton Raffael 1728–1779. German Neo-Classical painter, born in Bohemia. He was court painter in Dresden 1745 and in Madrid 1761; he then worked alternately in Rome and Spain. The ceiling painting *Parnassus* 1761 (Villa Albani, Rome) is an example of his work.

Mengs's father was a painter of miniatures at the Dresden court and encouraged his son to specialize in portraiture. In 1755 he met the art connoisseur Johann Winckelmann (1717–1768), a founder of Neo-Classicism; Mengs adopted his artistic ideals and wrote a treatise on *Beauty in Painting*.

Menninger /ˈmenɪŋə/ Karl Augustus 1893–1990. US psychiatrist, instrumental in reforming public mental-health facilities. With his father, prominent psychiatrist Charles Menninger, he founded the Menninger Clinic in Topeka 1920 and with his brother William, also a psychiatrist, established the Menninger Foundation 1941.

Born in Topeka, Kansas, USA, and educated at the University of Kansas, Menninger received his MD degree from Harvard University 1917. Among his influential books were *The Human Mind* 1930, *Man Against Himself*, and *The Vital Balance* 1963.

Menotti /meˈnɒti/ Gian Carlo 1911– . Italian-born US composer. He was co-librettist with Samuel →Barber for the latter's *Vanessa* and *A Hand of Bridge*, and wrote both music and libretti for operas, including *The Medium* 1946, *The Telephone* 1947, *The Consul* 1950, *Amahl and the Night Visitors* 1951 (the first opera to be written for television), and *The Saint of Bleecker Street* 1954. He has also written orchestral and chamber music.

Menuhin /ˈmenuɪn/ Yehudi 1916– . US-born violinist and conductor. A child prodigy, he achieved great depth of interpretation, and was often accompanied on the piano by his sister **Hephzibah** (1921–1981). He conducted his own chamber orchestra and founded schools in Surrey, England, and Gstaad, Switzerland, for training young musicians.

He made his debut with an orchestra at the age of 11 in New York but moved to London 1959 and became a British subject 1985. He founded the Yehudi Menuhin school in Stoke d'Abernon 1963.

Menzies /ˈmenzɪz/ Robert Gordon 1894–1978. Australian politician, leader of the United Australia (now Liberal) Party and prime minister 1939–41 and 1949–66.

A Melbourne lawyer, he entered politics 1928, was attorney-general in the federal parliament 1934–39, and in 1939 succeeded Joseph Lyons as prime minister and leader of the United Australia Party, resigning 1941 when colleagues were dissatisfied with his leadership of Australia's war effort. In 1949 he became prime minister of a Liberal–Country Party coalition government, and was re-elected 1951, 1954, 1955, 1958, 1961, and 1963; he followed America's lead in committing Australia to the Vietnam War and retired soon after, in 1966. His critics argued that he did not show enough interest in Asia, and supported the USA and white African regimes too uncritically. His defenders argued that he provided stability in domestic policy and national security.

Menzies /ˈmenzɪz/ William Cameron 1896–1957. US art director of films, later a director and producer, who was one of Hollywood's most imaginative and talented designers. He was responsible for the sets of such classics as *Gone With the Wind* (Academy Award for best art direction) 1939 and *Foreign Correspondent* 1940. His films as director include *Things to Come* 1936 and *Invaders from Mars* 1953.

Mercator /mɜːˈkeɪtə/ Gerardus 1512–1594. Latinized form of the name of the Flemish mapmaker Gerhard Kremer. He devised the first modern atlas, showing **Mercators projection** in which the parallels and meridians on maps are drawn uniformly at 90°. It is often used for navigational charts, because compass courses can be drawn as straight lines, but the true area of countries is increasingly distorted the further north or south they are from the equator.

Mercer /ˈmɜːsə/ David 1928–1980. British dramatist. He first became known for his television plays, including *A Suitable Case for Treatment* 1962, filmed as *Morgan*; stage plays include *After Haggerty* 1970.

Merchant /ˈmɜːtʃənt/ Ismail 1936– . Indian film producer, known for his stylish collaborations with James ➔Ivory on films including *Shakespeare Wallah* 1965, *The Europeans* 1979, *Heat and Dust* 1983, *A Room with a View* 1985, *Maurice* 1987, and *Howard's End* 1992.

Merckx /merks/ Eddie 1945– . Belgian cyclist known as 'the Cannibal'. He won the Tour de France a joint record five times 1969–74.

Merckx turned professional 1966 and won his first classic race, the Milan–San Remo, the same year. He went on to win 24 classics as well as the three major tours (of Italy, Spain, and France) a total of 11 times. He was world professional road-race champion three times and in 1971 won a record 54 races in the season. He rode 50 winners in a season four times. He retired in 1977.

Meredith /ˈmerədɪθ/ George 1828–1909. English novelist and poet. He published the first realistic psychological novel *The Ordeal of Richard Feverel* 1859. Later works include *Evan Harrington* 1861, *The Egoist* 1879, *Diana of the Crossways* 1885, and *The Amazing Marriage* 1895. His verse includes *Modern Love* 1862 and *Poems and Lyrics of the Joy of Earth* 1883.

Speech is the small change of silence.

   George Meredith *The Ordeal of Richard Feverel*

Mergenthaler /ˈmɜːɡənˌtɑːlə/ Ottmar 1854–1899. German-born American who invented a typesetting method. He went to the USA in 1872 and developed the first linotype machine (for casting hot-metal type in complete lines) 1876–86.

Mérimée /ˌmerɪˈmeɪ/ Prosper 1803–1870. French author. Among his works are the short novels *Colomba* 1841, *Carmen* 1846, and the *Lettres à une inconnue/Letters to an Unknown Girl* 1873.

Born in Paris, he entered the public service and under Napoleon III was employed on unofficial diplomatic missions.

Merleau-Ponty /meəˌləʊpɒnˈtiː/ Maurice 1908–1961. French philosopher, one of the most significant contributors to phenomenology after Edmund ➔Husserl. He attempted to move beyond the notion of a pure experiencing consciousness, arguing in *The Phenomenology of Perception* 1945 that perception is intertwined with bodily awareness and with language. In his posthumously published work *The Visible and the Invisible* 1964, he argued that our experience is inherently ambiguous and elusive and that the traditional concepts of philosophy are therefore inadequate to grasp it.

Merovingian dynasty /merəˈvɪndʒɪən/ Frankish dynasty, named after its founder, **Merovech** (5th century AD). His descendants ruled France from the time of Clovis (481–511) to 751.

Mersenne /mɑːˈsen/ Marin 1588–1648. French mathematician and philosopher who, from his base in Paris, did much to disseminate throughout Europe the main advances of French science. In mathematics he defined a particular form of prime number, since referred to as a Mersenne prime.

Mesmer /ˈmesmə/ Friedrich Anton 1734–1815. Austrian physician, an early experimenter in hypnosis, which was formerly (and popularly) called *mesmerism* after him.

He claimed to reduce people to trance state by consciously exerted 'animal magnetism', their willpower being entirely subordinated to his. Expelled by the police from Vienna, he created a sensation in Paris in 1778, but was denounced as a charlatan in 1785.

Mesrine /mezˈriːn/ Jacques 1937–1979. French criminal. From a wealthy family, he became a burglar celebrated for his glib tongue, sadism, and bravado, and for his escapes from the police and prison. Towards the end of his life he had links with left-wing guerrillas. He was shot dead by the police.

Messager /ˌmesɑːˈʒeɪ/ André Charles Prosper 1853–1929. French composer and conductor. He studied under ➔Saint-Saëns. Messager composed light operas, such as *La Béarnaise* 1885 and *Véronique* 1898.

Messalina /ˌmesəˈliːnə/ Valeria *c.* AD 22–48. Third wife of the Roman emperor ➔Claudius, whom she dominated. She was notorious for her immorality, forcing a noble to marry her AD 48, although still married to Claudius, who then had her executed.

Messerschmitt /ˈmesəʃmɪt/ Willy 1898–1978. German aeroplane designer whose Me109 was a standard Luftwaffe fighter in World War II, and whose Me-262 (1942) was the first mass-produced jet fighter.

Messiaen /ˌmesjˈɒŋ/ Olivier 1908–1992. French composer and organist. His music is mystical in character, vividly coloured, and incorporates transcriptions of birdsong. Among his works are the *Quartet for the End of Time* 1941, the large-scale *Turangalîla Symphony* 1949, and solo organ and piano pieces.

His theories of melody, harmony, and rhythm, drawing on medieval and oriental music, have inspired contemporary composers such as →Boulez and →Stockhausen.

I doubt that one can find in any music, however inspired, melodies and rhythms that have the sovereign freedom of bird song.

Olivier Messiaen

Messier /ˌmesiˈeɪ/ Charles 1730–1817. French astronomer who discovered 15 comets and in 1781 published a list of 103 star clusters and nebulae. Objects on this list are given M (for Messier) numbers, which astronomers still use today, such as M1 (the Crab nebula) and M31 (the Andromeda galaxy).

Meštrović /meˈʃtrəvɪtʃ/ Ivan 1883–1962. Yugoslav sculptor, a US citizen from 1954. His works include portrait busts of the sculptor Rodin (with whom he is often compared), President Hoover, Pope Pius XI, and many public monuments.

Metacomet Wampanoag leader better known as King →Philip.

Metalious /məˈteɪliəs/ Grace (born Repentigny) 1924–1964. US novelist. She wrote many short stories but made headlines with *Peyton Place* 1956, an exposé of life in a small New England town, which was made into a film 1957 and a long-running television series.

Metastasio /ˌmetəˈstæziəʊ/ Pen name of Pietro Trapassi 1698–1782. Italian poet and the leading librettist of his day, creating 18th-century Italian *opera seria* (serious opera).

Metaxas /ˌmetækˈsæs/ Ioannis 1870–1941. Greek general and politician, born in Ithaca. He restored →George II (1890–1947) as king of Greece, under whom he established a dictatorship as prime minister from 1936, and introduced several necessary economic and military reforms. He led resistance to the Italian invasion of Greece in 1941, refusing to abandon Greece's neutral position.

Methodius, St /meˈθəʊdiəs/ *c.* 825–884. Greek Christian bishop, who with his brother Cyril translated much of the Bible into Slavonic. Feast day 14 Feb. See →Cyril and Methodius.

Metsu /ˈmetsjuː/ Gabriel 1629–1667. Dutch painter, born in Leiden, active in Amsterdam from 1657. His main subjects were genre (domestic) scenes, usually with a few well-dressed figures. He was skilled in depicting rich glossy fabrics.

Metternich /ˈmetənɪk/ Klemens (Wenzel Lothar), Prince von Metternich 1773–1859. Austrian politician, the leading figure in European diplomacy after the fall of Napoleon. As foreign minister 1809–48 (as well as chancellor from 1821), he tried to maintain the balance of power in Europe, supporting monarchy and repressing liberalism.

At the Congress of Vienna 1815, Metternich advocated cooperation by the great powers to suppress democratic movements. The revolution of 1848 forced him to flee to the UK; he returned 1851 as a power behind the scenes.

Meyer /ˈmaɪə/ Alfred 1895–1990. German-born British neuropathologist, in the UK from 1933. His most significant work was on the anatomical aspects of frontal leucotomy, and the nature of the structural abnormalities in the brain associated with temporal lobe epilepsy.

Meyerbeer /ˈmaɪəbeə/ Giacomo. Adopted name of Jakob Liebmann Beer 1791–1864. German composer of spectacular operas, including *Robert le Diable* 1831 and *Les Huguenots* 1836. From 1826 he lived mainly in Paris, returning to Berlin after 1842 as musical director of the Royal Opera.

Let me tell you that I – who am but a humble worm – am sometimes ill for a whole month after a first night.

Giacomo Meyerbeer

Meynell /ˈmenl/ Alice (born Thompson) 1847–1922. British poet. She published *Preludes* 1875 and her collected poems appeared in 1923. She married the author and journalist Wilfrid Meynell (1852–1948).

Miandad /miˈændæd/ Javed 1957– . Pakistani Test cricketer, his country's leading run-maker. He scored a century on his Test debut in 1976 and has since become one of a handful of players to make 100 Test appearances. He has captained his country and helped Pakistan to win the 1992 World Cup. His highest score of 311 was made when he was aged 17.

Micah /ˈmaɪkə/ 8th century BC. In the Old Testament, a Hebrew prophet whose writings denounced the oppressive ruling class of Judah and demanded justice.

Michael /ˈmaɪkəl/ Mikhail Fyodorovich Romanov 1596–1645. Tsar of Russia from 1613. He was elected tsar by a national assembly, at a time of chaos and foreign invasion, and was the first of the Romanov dynasty, which ruled until 1917.

Michael /ˈmaɪkəl/ 1921– . King of Romania 1927–30 and 1940–47. The son of Carol II, he succeeded his grandfather as king 1927 but was displaced when his father returned from exile 1930. In 1940 he was proclaimed king again on his father's abdication, overthrew 1944 the fascist dictatorship of Ion Antonescu (1882–1946), and enabled Romania to share in the victory of the Allies at the end of World War II. He abdicated and left Romania 1947.

On 25 Dec 1990 King Michael, with his wife Anne and daughter Sophia, attempted to return to Romania, but he was expelled early the following day.

Michaux /miːˈʃəʊ/ André 1746–1802. French botanist and explorer. As manager of a royal farm, he was sent by the French government 1782 and 1785 on expeditions to collect plants and select timber for shipbuilding. Together with his son François (1770–1852), he travelled to Carolina, Florida, Georgia, and, in 1792, to Hudson's Bay. On his return to France, he compiled the first guide to the flora of E America. François Michaux wrote the first book on American forest trees 1810–13.

Trifles make perfection, and perfection is no trifle.

Michelangelo Buonarroti

Michelangelo /ˌmaɪkəlˈændʒələʊ ˌbwɒnəˈrɒti/ Buonarroti 1475–1564. Italian sculptor, painter, architect, and poet, active in his native Florence and in Rome. His giant talent dominated the High Renaissance. The marble *David* 1501–04 (Accademia, Florence) set a new standard in nude sculpture. His massive figure style was translated into fresco in the Sistine Chapel 1508–12 and 1536–41 (Vatican). Other works in Rome include the dome of St Peter's basilica.

Born near Florence, he was a student of Ghirlandaio and trained under the patronage of Lorenzo de' Medici. His patrons later included several popes and Medici princes. In 1496 he completed the *Pietà* (St Peter's, Rome), a technically brilliant piece that established his reputation. Also in Rome he began the great tomb of Pope Julius II: *The Slaves* (Louvre, Paris) and *Moses* (S Pietro in Vincoli, Rome) were sculpted for this unfinished project. His grandiose scheme for the Sistine Chapel tells, on the ceiling, the Old Testament story from Genesis to the Deluge, and on the altar wall he later added a vast *Last Judgement*.

From 1516 to 1534 he was again in Florence, where his chief work was the design of the Medici sepulchral chapel in S Lorenzo. Back in Rome he became chief architect of St Peter's in 1547. His friendship with Vittoria Colonna (1492–1547), a noblewoman, inspired many of his sonnets and madrigals.

The devil has a care of his footmen.

Thomas Middleton
A Trick to Catch the Old One 1608

Michelet /miːʃˈleɪ/ Jules 1798–1874. French historian, author of a 17-volume *Histoire de France/History of France* 1833–67, in which he immersed himself in the narrative and stressed the development of France as a nation. He also produced a number of books on nature, including *L'Oiseau/The Bird* 1856 and *La Montagne/The Mountain* 1868.

Michels /ˈmɪklz/ Robert 1876–1936. German social and political theorist. Originally a radical, he became a critic of socialism and Marxism, and in his last years supported Hitler and Mussolini. In *Political Parties* 1911 he propounded the *Iron Law of Oligarchy*, arguing that in any organization or society, even a democracy, there is a tendency towards rule by the few in the interests of the few, and that ideologies such as socialism and communism were merely propaganda to control the masses. He believed that the rise of totalitarian governments – both fascist and communist – in the 1930s confirmed his analysis and proved that the masses were incapable of asserting their own interests.

Michelson /ˈmaɪkəlsən/ Albert Abraham 1852–1931. German-born US physicist. In conjunction with Edward Morley, he performed in 1887 the *Michelson–Morley experiment* to detect the motion of the Earth through the postulated ether (a medium believed to be necessary for the propagation of light). The failure of the experiment indicated the nonexistence of the ether, and led →Einstein to his theory of relativity. Michelson was the first American to be awarded a Nobel prize, in 1907.

He invented the *Michelson interferometer* and made precise measurement of the speed of light. From 1892 he was professor of physics at the University of Chicago.

Michelucci /ˌmiːkeˈluːtʃi/ Giovanni 1891–1990. Italian architect. He produced numerous urban projects which combined a restrained modernism with sensitive contextualism, for example, the Sta Maria Novella Station in Florence 1934–37. He departed from his rationalist principles in the design of the church of San Giovanni 1961 by the Autostrada del Sole near Florence.

Mickiewicz /ˌmɪtskiˈevɪtʃ/ Adam 1798–1855. Polish revolutionary poet, whose *Pan Tadeusz* 1832–34 is Poland's national epic. He died in Constantinople while raising a Polish corps to fight against Russia in the Crimean War.

Middleton /ˈmɪdltən/ Thomas c. 1570–1627. English dramatist. He produced numerous romantic plays, tragedies, and realistic comedies, both alone and in collaboration, including *A Fair Quarrel* and

The Changeling 1622 with Rowley; *The Roaring Girl* with Dekker; and *Women Beware Women* 1621.

His political satire *A Game at Chess* 1624 was concerned with the plots to unite the royal houses of England and Spain, and caused a furore with the authorities.

Mies van der Rohe /ˈmiːs ˌvæn də ˈrəʊə/ Ludwig 1886–1969. German architect who practised in the USA from 1937. He succeeded Walter →Gropius as director of the Bauhaus school of architecture and design 1929–33. He designed the bronze-and-glass Seagram building in New York City 1956–59 and numerous apartment buildings.

He became professor at the Illinois Technical Institute 1938–58, for which he designed new buildings on characteristically functional lines from 1941. He also designed the National Gallery, Berlin 1963–68.

Mifune /mɪfune/ Toshiro 1920– . Japanese actor who appeared in many films directed by Akira →Kurosawa, including *Rashomon* 1950, *Shichinin no samurai/Seven Samurai* 1954, and *Throne of Blood* 1957. He has also appeared in European and American films: *Grand Prix* 1966, *Hell in the Pacific* 1969.

Mihailović /mɪˈhaɪləvɪtʃ/ Draza 1893–1946. Yugoslav soldier, leader of the guerrilla Chetniks of World War II against the German occupation. His feud with Tito's communists led to the withdrawal of Allied support and that of his own exiled government from 1943. He turned for help to the Italians and Germans, and was eventually shot for treason.

Miles /maɪlz/ Bernard (Baron Miles) 1907– . English actor and producer. He appeared on stage as Briggs in *Thunder Rock* 1940 and Iago in *Othello* 1942, and his films include *Great Expectations* 1947. He founded a trust that in 1959 built the City of London's first new theatre for 300 years, the Mermaid.

Milford Haven, Marquess of /ˈmɪlfəd ˈheɪvən/ title given in 1917 to Prince →Louis of Battenberg (1854–1921).

Milhaud /miːˈjəʊ/ Darius 1892–1974. French composer, a member of the group of composers known as Les Six. Among his works are the operas *Christophe Colombe* 1928 and *Bolívar* 1943, and the jazz ballet *La Création du monde* 1923. He lived in both France and the USA.

He collaborated on ballets with Paul →Claudel. In 1940 he went to the USA as professor of music at Mills College, California, and became professor of composition at the National Conservatoire in Paris 1947. Much of his later work – which includes chamber, orchestral, and choral music – is polytonal.

Mill /mɪl/ James 1773–1836. Scottish philosopher and political thinker who developed the theory of utilitarianism, according to which an action is morally right if it has consequences that lead to happiness and wrong if it brings about the reverse.

He is remembered for his political articles, and for the rigorous education he gave his son John Stuart Mill.

Born near Montrose, Mill moved to London 1802. Associated for most of his working life with the East India Company, he wrote a vast *History of British India* 1817–18. He was one of the founders of University College, London, together with his friend and fellow utilitarian Jeremy Bentham.

Mill /mɪl/ John Stuart 1806–1873. English philosopher and economist who wrote *On Liberty* 1859, the classic philosophical defence of liberalism, and *Utilitarianism* 1863, a version of the 'greatest happiness for the greatest number' principle in ethics. His progressive views inspired *On the Subjection of Women* 1869.

He was born in London, the son of James Mill. In 1822 he entered the East India Company, where he remained until retiring in 1858. In 1826, as described in his *Autobiography* 1873, he passed through a mental crisis; he found his father's bleakly intellectual Utilitarianism emotionally unsatisfying and abandoned it for a more human philosophy influenced by Coleridge. In *Utilitarianism*, he states that actions are right if they bring about happiness and wrong if they bring about the reverse of happiness. *On Liberty* moved away from the utilitarian notion that individual liberty was necessary for economic and governmental efficiency and advanced the classical defence of individual freedom as a value in itself and the mark of a mature society; this change can be traced in the later editions of *Principles of Political Economy* 1848. He sat in Parliament as a Radical 1865–68 and introduced a motion for women's suffrage. His philosophical and political writings include *A System of Logic* 1843 and *Considerations on Representative Government* 1861.

Mill Educated by his father, John Stuart Mill was reading Plato and Demosthenes with ease at the age of ten. His Autobiography gives a painful account of the teaching methods that turned him against Utilitarianism.

Millais /ˈmɪleɪ/ John Everett 1829–1896. British painter, a founder member of the Pre-Raphaelite Brotherhood (PRB) in 1848. By the late 1850s he had dropped out of the PRB, and his style became more fluent and less detailed.

One of his PRB works, *Christ in the House of His Parents* 1850 (Tate Gallery, London), caused an outcry on its first showing, since its realistic detail was considered unfitting to the sacred subject.

Later works include sentimental child-studies, such as *The Boyhood of Raleigh* 1870 (Tate Gallery, London) and *Bubbles* 1886 (a poster for Pears soap) and portraits. He was elected president of the Royal Academy in 1896.

Millay /mɪˈleɪ/ Edna St Vincent 1892–1950. US poet who wrote romantic, emotional verse, including *Renascence and Other Poems* 1917 and *The Harp-Weaver and Other Poems* 1923 (Pulitzer Prize 1924).

Miller /ˈmɪlə/ Arthur 1915– . US playwright. His plays deal with family relationships and contemporary American values, and include *Death of a Salesman* 1949 and *The Crucible* 1953, based on the Salem witch trials and reflecting the communist witch-hunts of Senator Joe →McCarthy. He was married 1956–61 to the film star Marilyn Monroe, for whom he wrote the film *The Misfits* 1960.

Among other plays are *All My Sons* 1947, *A View from the Bridge* 1955, and *After the Fall* 1964, based on his relationship with Monroe. He also wrote the television film *Playing for Time* 1980.

Miller /ˈmɪlə/ Glenn 1904–1944. US trombonist and, as bandleader, exponent of the big-band swing sound from 1938. He composed his signature tune 'Moonlight Serenade' (a hit 1939). Miller became leader of the US Army Air Force Band in Europe 1942, made broadcasts to troops throughout the world during World War II, and disappeared without trace on a flight between England and France.

Miller /ˈmɪlə/ Henry 1891–1980. US writer. From 1930 to 1940 he lived a bohemian life in Paris, where he wrote his novels *Tropic of Cancer* 1934 and *Tropic of Capricorn* 1938. They were so outspoken and sexually frank that they were banned in the USA and England until the 1960s.

Miller /ˈmɪlə/ Stanley 1930– . US chemist. In the early 1950s, under laboratory conditions, he tried to imitate the original conditions of the Earth's atmosphere (a mixture of methane, ammonia, and hydrogen), added an electrical discharge, and waited. After a few days he found that amino acids, the ingredients of protein, had been formed.

Miller /ˈmɪlə/ William 1782–1849. US religious leader. Ordained as a Baptist minister 1833, Miller predicted that the Second Advent would occur 1844. Many of his followers sold their property in expectation of the end of the world. Although Miller's movement disbanded soon after, his teachings paved the way for later Adventist sects.

Born in Pittsfield, Massachusetts, and raised in New York, Miller later settled in Vermont. Convinced that the Second Coming of Jesus was imminent, he began to preach about the millennium.

Miller /ˈmɪlə/ William 1801–1880. Welsh crystallographer, developer of the *Miller indices*, a coordinate system of mapping the shapes and surfaces of crystals.

Millet /miˈleɪ/ Jean François 1814–1875. French artist, a leading member of the Barbizon school, who painted scenes of peasant life and landscapes. *The Angelus* 1859 (Musée d'Orsay, Paris) was widely reproduced in his day.

Millett /ˈmɪlɪt/ Kate 1934– . US radical feminist lecturer, writer, and sculptor whose book *Sexual Politics* 1970 was a landmark in feminist thinking. She was a founding member of the *National Organization of Women* (NOW). Later books include *Flying* 1974, *The Prostitution Papers* 1976, *Sita* 1977, and *The Loony Bin Trip* 1991, describing a period of manic depression and drug therapy.

Millikan /ˈmɪlɪkən/ Robert Andrews 1868–1953. US physicist, awarded a Nobel prize 1923 for his determination of the electric charge on an electron 1913.

His experiment, which took five years to perfect, involved observing oil droplets, charged by external radiation, falling under gravity between two horizontal metal plates connected to a high-voltage supply. By varying the voltage, he was able to make the electrostatic field between the plates balance the gravitational field so that some droplets became stationary and floated. If a droplet of weight W is held stationary between plates separated by a distance d and carrying a potential difference V, the charge, e, on the drop is equal to Wd/V.

Millin /ˈmɪlɪn/ Sarah Gertrude (born Liebson) 1889–1968. South African novelist, an opponent of racial discrimination, as seen in, for example, *God's Step-Children* 1924.

Mills /mɪlz/ C Wright 1916–1962. US sociologist whose concern for humanity, ethical values, and individual freedom led him to criticize the US establishment.

Originally in the liberal tradition, Mills later adopted Weberian and even Marxist ideas. He aroused considerable popular interest in sociology with such works as *White Collar* 1951; *The Power Elite* 1956, depicting the USA as ruled by businessmen, military experts, and politicians; and *Listen, Yankee* 1960.

Mills /mɪlz/ John 1908– . English actor who appeared in films such as *In Which We Serve* 1942, *The Rocking Horse Winner* 1949, *The Wrong Box* 1966, and *Oh! What a Lovely War* 1969. He received an Academy Award for *Ryan's Daughter* 1971. He is the father of the actresses Hayley Mills and Juliet Mills.

Mills Brothers /mɪlz/ US vocal group who specialized in close-harmony vocal imitations of instruments, comprising Herbert Mills (1912–), Harry Mills (1913–1982), John Mills (1889–1935), and Donald Mills (1915–   ). Formed 1922, the group first broadcast on radio in 1925, and continued to perform until the 1950s. Their 70 hits include 'Lazy River' 1948 and 'You Always Hurt the One You Love' 1944.

Milne /mɪln/ A(lan) A(lexander) 1882–1956. English writer. His books for children were based on the teddy bear and other toys of his son Christopher Robin (*Winnie-the-Pooh* 1926 and *The House at Pooh Corner* 1928). He also wrote children's verse (*When We Were Very Young* 1924 and *Now We Are Six* 1927) and plays, including an adaptation of Kenneth Grahame's *The Wind in the Willows* as *Toad of Toad Hall* 1929.

Milne was educated at Westminster and Cambridge, where he studied mathematics. At the age of 24 he was assistant editor of *Punch* magazine.

Some critics have seen in the Pooh series a parallel with Milne's rejection of Christianity, in that Pooh and Piglet take comfort by belief in a god, Christopher Robin, who the reader knows to be a thoughtless child who cannot even spell.

Milner /mɪlnə/ Alfred, Viscount Milner 1854– 1925. British colonial administrator. As governor of Cape Colony 1897–1901, he negotiated with →Kruger but did little to prevent the second South African War; and as governor of the Transvaal and Orange River colonies 1902–05 after their annexation, he reorganized their administration. In 1916 he became a member of Lloyd George's war cabinet.

Milosevic /mɪ'lɔʃavɪts/ Slobodan 1941–   . Serbian communist politician, party chief and president of Serbia from 1986; re-elected Dec 1990 in multiparty elections. Milosevic wielded considerable influence over the Serb-dominated Yugoslav federal army during the 1991–92 civil war and has continued to back Serbian militia in Bosnia-Herzegovina 1992, although publicly disclaiming any intention to 'carve up' the newly independent republic.

Milosevic was educated at Belgrade University and rapidly rose through the ranks of the Yugoslavian Communist Party (LCY) in his home republic of Serbia, helped by his close political and business links to Ivan Stambolic, his predecessor as local party leader. He won popular support within Serbia for his assertive nationalist stance, encouraging street demonstrations in favour of the reintegration of Kosovo and Vojvodina autonomous provinces into a 'greater Serbia'. Serbia's formal annexation of Kosovo Sept 1990 gave him a landslide majority in multiparty elections Dec 1990, but in March 1991 there were 30,000-strong riots in Belgrade, calling for his resignation.

Miłosz /ˈmiːwɒʃ/ Czesław 1911–   . Polish writer, born in Lithuania. He became a diplomat before defecting and becoming a US citizen. His poetry in English translation, classical in style, includes *Selected Poems* 1973 and *Bells in Winter* 1978.

His collection of essays *The Captive Mind* 1953 concerns the impact of communism on Polish intellectuals. Among his novels are *The Seizure of Power* 1955, *The Issa Valley* 1981, and *The Land of Ulro* 1984. Nobel Prize for Literature 1980.

Milstein /mɪlstaɪn/ César 1927–   . Argentine-born British molecular biologist who developed monoclonal antibodies, giving immunity against specific diseases. He shared the Nobel Prize for Medicine 1984.

Milstein, who settled in Britain 1961, was engaged on research into the immune system at the Laboratory of Molecular Biology in Cambridge. He and his colleagues devised a means of accessing the immune system for purposes of research, diagnosis, and treatment. They developed monoclonal antibodies (MABs), cloned cells that, when introduced into the body, can be targeted to seek out sites of disease. The full potential of this breakthrough is still being investigated. However, MABs, which can be duplicated in limitless quantities, are already in use to combat disease. Milstein shared the Nobel Prize for Medicine 1984 with two colleagues, Georges Köhler and Niels Jerne.

Milton /mɪltən/ John 1608–1674. English poet whose epic *Paradise Lost* 1667 is one of the landmarks of English literature. Early poems including *Comus* (a masque performed 1634) and *Lycidas* (an elegy 1638) showed Milton's superlative lyric gift. Latin secretary to Oliver Cromwell during the Commonwealth period, he also wrote many pamphlets and prose works, including *Areopagitica* 1644, which opposed press censorship.

Born in London and educated at Christ's College, Cambridge, Milton was a scholarly poet, ambitious to match the classical epics, and with strong theological views. Of polemical temperament, he published prose works on republicanism and church government. His middle years were devoted to the Puritan cause and pamphleteering, including one on divorce (*The Doctrine and Discipline of Divorce* 1643, which was based on his own experience of marital unhappiness) and another (*Areopagitica*) advocating freedom of the press. From 1649 he was (Latin) secretary to the Council of State. His assistants (as his sight failed) included Andrew →Marvell. He married Mary Powell 1643, and their three daughters were later his somewhat unwilling scribes. After Mary's death 1652, the year of his total blindness, he married twice more, his second wife Catherine Woodcock dying in childbirth, while Elizabeth Minshull survived him for over half a century.

Paradise Lost 1667 and the less successful sequel *Paradise Regained* 1671 were written when he was blind and in some political danger (after the restoration of Charles II), as was *Samson Agonistes* 1671, a powerful if untheatrical play.

He is buried in St Giles's, Cripplegate, London.

Milton English epic and lyric poet John Milton, whose Paradise Lost, 12 books in blank verse loosely based on the Biblical narrative of the Fall, was written to 'justify the works of God to men'. He also wrote pamphlets, in favour of divorce and freedom of the press.

Minamoto or *Genji* in Japanese history, an ancient Japanese clan, the members of which were the first ruling shoguns 1192–1219. Their government was based in Kamakura, near present-day Tokyo. After the death of the first shogun, Minamoto Yoritomo (1147–1199), the real power was exercised by the regent for the shogun; throughout the Kamakura period (1192–1333), the regents were of the Hōjō family.

The Minamoto claimed descent from a 9th-century emperor. Minamoto Yoriyoshi (988–1075) was a warlord who built up a power base in the Kanto region when appointed by the court to put down a rebellion there. During the 11th and 12th centuries the Minamoto and the Taira military clan were rivals for power at the court and in the country. The Minamoto emerged victorious in 1185 and Yoritomo received the patent of shogun 1192. Zen teaching and Buddhist sculpture flourished during their shogunate.

Mindszenty /ˈmɪndsenti/ József 1892–1975. Roman Catholic primate of Hungary. He was imprisoned by the communist government 1949, but escaped 1956 to take refuge in the US legation. The pope persuaded him to go into exile in Austria 1971, and he was 'retired' when Hungary's relations with the Vatican improved 1974. His remains were returned to Hungary from Austria and reinterred at Esztergom 1991.

Mingus /ˈmɪŋgəs/ Charles 1922–1979. US jazz bassist and composer. He played with Louis Armstrong, Duke Ellington, and Charlie Parker. His experimentation with atonality and dissonant effects opened the way for the new style of free collective jazz improvisation of the 1960s.

Based on the West Coast until 1951, Mingus took part in the development of cool jazz. Subsequently based in New York, he worked with a number of important musicians and expanded the scope of the bass as a lead instrument. Recordings include *Pithecanthropus Erectus* 1956 and *Mingus at Monterey* 1964.

Minnelli /mɪˈneli/ Liza 1946– . US actress and singer, daughter of Judy →Garland and the director Vincente Minnelli. She achieved stardom in the Broadway musical *Flora, the Red Menace* 1965 and in the film *Cabaret* 1972. Her subsequent films include *New York, New York* 1977 and *Arthur* 1981.

Minnelli /mɪˈneli/ Vincente 1910–1986. US film director who specialized in musicals and occasional melodramas. His best films, such as *Meet Me in St Louis* 1944 and *The Band Wagon* 1953, display a powerful visual flair.

Minto /ˈmɪntəʊ/ Gilbert, 4th Earl of 1845–1914. British colonial administrator who succeeded Curzon as viceroy of India, 1905–10. With John Morley, secretary of state for India, he co-sponsored the Morley Minto reforms of 1909. The reforms increased Indian representation in government at provincial level, but also created separate Muslim and Hindu electorates which, it was believed, helped the British Raj in the policy of divide and rule.

Mintoff /ˈmɪntɒf/ Dom(inic) 1916– . Labour prime minister of Malta 1971–84. He negotiated the removal of British and other foreign military bases 1971–79 and made treaties with Libya.

Minton /ˈmɪntən/ Thomas 1765–1836. English potter. He first worked under the potter Josiah Spode, but in 1789 established himself at Stoke-on-Trent as an engraver of designs (he originated the 'willow pattern') and in the 1790s founded a pottery there, producing high-quality bone china, including tableware.

Minuit /ˈmɪnjuɪt/ Peter *c.* 1580–1638. Dutch colonial administrator in America. As a founder of New Amsterdam on Manhattan Island 1626 and its director general, he negotiated with the local Indians and supervised the construction of Fort Amsterdam. Ousted from his post 1631 by the Dutch Reformed Church, he helped found the Swedish colony of Fort Christina at the modern site of Wilmington, Delaware, 1638.

Born in Prussia, Minuit took part in the colonization activities of the Dutch West India Company in America. He was lost in a hurricane in the West Indies.

Mirabeau /ˈmɪrəbəʊ/ Honoré Gabriel Riqueti, Comte de 1749–1791. French politician, leader of the National Assembly in the French Revolution. He wanted to establish a parliamentary monarchy on the English model. From May 1790 he secretly acted as political adviser to the king.

Mirabeau was from a noble Provençal family. Before the French Revolution he had a stormy career, was three times imprisoned, and spent several years in exile. In 1789 he was elected to the States General. His eloquence won him the leadership of the National Assembly; nevertheless, he was out of sympathy with the majority of the deputies, whom he regarded as mere theoreticians.

Miranda /mɪˈrændə/ Carmen. Stage name of Maria de Carmo Miranda da Cunha 1909–1955. Portuguese dancer and singer who lived in Brazil from childhood. Her Hollywood musicals include *Down Argentine Way* 1940 and *The Gang's All Here* 1943. Her hallmarks were extravagant costumes and headgear adorned with tropical fruits, a staccato singing voice, and fiery temperament.

Mirandola /mɪˈrændələ/ Italian 15th-century philosopher. See →Pico della Mirandola.

Mirman /mɜːmən/ Sophie 1956–   . British entrepreneur, founder of the Sock Shop, launched on the US market in 1987. After the collapse of Sock Shop in 1990, she launched an upmarket children's shop, Trotters.

Miró /mɪˈrəʊ/ Joan 1893–1983. Spanish Surrealist painter, born in Barcelona. In the mid-1920s he developed a distinctive abstract style with amoeba shapes, some linear, some highly coloured, generally floating on a plain background.

During the 1930s his style became more sombre and after World War II he produced larger abstracts. He experimented with sculpture and printmaking and produced ceramic murals (including two in the UNESCO building, Paris, 1958). He also designed stained glass and sets for the ballet director Sergei Diaghilev.

Mirren /mɪrən/ Helen 1946–   . British actress whose stage roles include Shakespearean ones; for example, Lady Macbeth and Isabella in *Measure for Measure*. Her films include *The Long Good Friday* 1981 and *Cal* 1984.

Mirrlees /mɜːliːz/ Hope 1887–1978. British writer whose fantasy novel *Lud-in-the-Mist* 1926 contrasts the supernatural with the real world.

Mishima /mɪʃɪmə/ Yukio 1925–1970. Japanese novelist whose work often deals with sexual desire and perversion, as in *Confessions of a Mask* 1949 and *The Temple of the Golden Pavilion* 1956. He committed hara-kiri (ritual suicide) as a protest against what he saw as the corruption of the nation and the loss of the samurai warrior tradition.

The period of childhood is a stage on which time and space become entangled.

Yukio Mishima *Confessions of a Mask* 1949

Mistinguett /ˌmiːstæŋˈget/ Stage name of Jeanne Bourgeois 1873–1956. French actress and dancer.

A leading music-hall artist in Paris from 1899, she appeared in revues at the Folies-Bergère, Casino de Paris, and Moulin Rouge. She was known for the song 'Mon Homme' and her partnership with Maurice Chevalier.

Mistral /mɪsˈtrɑːl/ Gabriela. Pen name of Lucila Godoy de Alcayaga 1889–1957. Chilean poet who wrote *Sonnets of Death* 1915. She was awarded the Nobel Prize for Literature 1945.

She was consul of Chile in Spain, and represented her country at the League of Nations and the United Nations.

Mitchell /mɪtʃəl/ Arthur 1934–1990. US dancer, director of the Dance Theater of Harlem, which he founded with Karel Shook (1920–   ) in 1968. Mitchell was a principal dancer with the New York City Ballet 1956–68, creating many roles in Balanchine's ballets.

Mitchell /mɪtʃəl/ Joni. Adopted name of Roberta Joan Anderson 1943–   . Canadian singer, songwriter, and guitarist. She began in the 1960s folk style and subsequently incorporated elements of rock and jazz with confessional, sophisticated lyrics. Her albums include *Blue* 1971 and *Hejira* 1976.

Mitchell /mɪtʃəl/ Juliet 1940–   . British psychoanalyst and writer. She came to public notice with an article in *New Left Review* 1966 entitled 'Women: The Longest Revolution,' one of the first attempts to combine socialism and feminism using Marxist theory to explain the reasons behind women's oppression. She published *Women's Estate* 1971 and *Psychoanalysis and Feminism* 1974.

Mitchell /mɪtʃəl/ Margaret 1900–1949. US novelist, born in Atlanta, Georgia, which is the setting for her one book, the bestseller *Gone With the Wind* 1936, a story of the US Civil War. It was filmed starring Vivien Leigh and Clark Gable in 1939.

Mitchell /mɪtʃəl/ Peter 1920–1992. British chemist. He received a Nobel prize in 1978 for work on the conservation of energy by plants during respiration and photosynthesis.

Mitchell /mɪtʃəl/ R(eginald) J(oseph) 1895–1937. British aircraft designer whose Spitfire fighter was a major factor in winning the Battle of Britain during World War II.

Mitchell /mɪtʃəl/ Thomas Livingstone 1792–1855. Scottish-born surveyor and explorer in Australia who led expeditions through New South Wales 1831–32 and 1835–36, Victoria 1836, and Queensland 1846. He established that the Darling River joined the Murray, and helped to open the Maranoa region, Queensland, to pastoralism.

Mitchum /mɪtʃəm/ Robert 1917–   . US film actor, a star for more than 30 years as the big, strong, relaxed modern hero. His films include *Out of the Past* 1947, *The Night of the Hunter* 1955, and *The Friends of Eddie Coyle* 1973.

Mitterrand A socialist, François Mitterrand was committed to economic and social reforms at the beginning of his presidency 1981. Although it proved impossible to carry through these reforms, Mitterrand preserved his position by the skilled political manoeuvring for which he earned the nickname 'the Fox'.

Mitford /ˈmɪtfəd/ Mary Russell 1787–1855. English author, remembered for her sketches in *Our Village* 1824–32 describing Three Mile Cross, near Reading, where she lived.

Mitford sisters /ˈmɪtfəd/ the six daughters of British aristocrat Lord Redesdale, including:
   Nancy (1904–1973), author of the semi-autobiographical *The Pursuit of Love* 1945 and *Love in a Cold Climate* 1949, and editor and part author of *Noblesse Oblige* 1956 elucidating 'U' (upperclass) and 'non-U' behaviour; *Diana* (1910–), who married Oswald →Mosley; *Unity* (1914–1948), who became an admirer of Hitler; *Jessica* (1917–), author of the autobiographical *Hons and Rebels* 1960 and *The American Way of Death* 1963.

Mithridates VI Eupator /ˌmɪθrɪˈdeɪtiːz/ known as *the Great* 132–63 BC. King of Pontus (NE Asia Minor, on the Black Sea) from 120 BC. He massacred 80,000 Romans in overrunning the rest of Asia Minor and went on to invade Greece. He was defeated by →Sulla in the First Mithridatic War 88–84; by →Lucullus in the Second 83–81; and finally by →Pompey in the Third 74–64. He was killed by a soldier at his own order rather than surrender.

Mitre /ˈmɪtreɪ/ Bartólome 1821–1906. Argentine president 1862–68. In 1852 he helped overthrow the dictatorial regime of Juan Manuel de Rosas, and in 1861 helped unify Argentina. Mitre encouraged immigration and favoured growing commercial links with Europe. He is seen as a symbol of national unity.

Mitsotakis /ˌmɪtsəʊˈtɑːkɪs/ Constantine 1918– . Greek politician, leader of the conservative New Democracy Party from 1984, prime minister from April 1990. Minister for economic coordination 1965 (a post he held again 1978–80), he was arrested by the military junta 1967, but escaped from house arrest and lived in exile until 1974. In 1980–81 he was foreign minister.

Mitterrand /ˌmiːtəˈrɒŋ/ François 1916– . French socialist politician, president from 1981. He held ministerial posts in 11 governments 1947–58, and founded the French Socialist Party (PS) 1971. In 1985 he introduced proportional representation, allegedly to weaken the growing opposition from left and right. Since 1982 his administrations have combined economic orthodoxy with social reform.

Mitterrand studied law and politics in Paris. During World War II he was prominent in the Resistance. He entered the National Assembly as a centre-left deputy for Nièvre. Opposed to General de Gaulle's creation of the Fifth Republic 1958, he formed the centre-left anti-Gaullist Federation of the Left in the 1960s. In 1971 he became leader of the new PS. An electoral union with the Communist Party 1972–77 established the PS as the most popular party in France.

Mitterrand was elected president 1981. His programme of reform was hampered by deteriorating economic conditions after 1983. When the socialists lost their majority March 1986, he was compelled to work with a right-wing prime minister, Jacques Chirac, and grew in popularity. He defeated Chirac to secure a second term in the presidential election May 1988.

Mix /mɪks/ Tom (Thomas) 1880–1940. US actor who was the most colourful cowboy star of silent films. At their best, his films, such as *The Range Riders* 1910 and *King Cowboy* 1928, were fast-moving and full of impressive stunts.

Miyake /mɪˈjɑːkeɪ/ Issey 1938– . Japanese fashion designer, active in Paris from 1965. He showed his first collection in New York and Tokyo 1971, and has been showing in Paris since 1973. His 'anti-fashion' looks combined Eastern and Western influences: a variety of textured and patterned fabrics were layered and wrapped round the body to create linear and geometric shapes. His inspired designs have had a considerable influence on the fashion scene.

Miyamoto Musashi *c.* 1584–1645. Japanese samurai, author of a manual on military strategy and sword fighting, *Gorinsho/The Book of Five Rings* 1645, which in English translation 1974 became popular in the USA as a guide to business success.

In Japan, Miyamoto Musashi is popular as the hero of a long historical novel that glamorizes his martial-arts exploits and has been the basis for a series of films and comic books. The historical Miyamoto was a painter as well as a fencer, and spent his life travelling Japan in search of Zen enlightenment.

Mizoguchi /ˌmɪzɒˈgutʃɪ/ Kenji 1898–1956. Japanese film director whose *Ugetsu Monogatari* 1953 confirmed his international reputation. Notable for his sensitive depiction of female psychology, he also directed *Blood and Soul* 1923, *The Poppies* 1935, *Sansho daiyu/Sansho the Bailiff* 1954, and *Street of Shame* 1956.

Mladenov /mlæˈdeɪnɒf/ Petar 1936– . Bulgarian Communist politician, secretary general of the Bulgarian Communist Party from Nov 1989, after the resignation of →Zhivkov, until Feb 1990. He was elected state president in April 1990 but replaced four months later.

Möbius /ˈmɜːbiəs/ August Ferdinand 1790–1868. German mathematician. He discovered the Möbius strip, a structure made by giving a half twist to a flat strip of paper and joining the ends together; it has certain remarkable properties, arising from the fact that it has only one edge and one side. He is considered to be one of the founders of topology, the branch of geometry that deals with those properties of a figure that remain unchanged even when the figure is transformed.

Mobutu /məˈbuːtuː/ Sese Seko Kuku Ngbeandu Wa Za Banga 1930– . Zairean president from 1965. He assumed the presidency in a coup, and created a unitary state under a centralized government. The harshness of some of his policies and charges of corruption have attracted widespread international criticism. In 1991 opposition leaders forced Mobutu to agree formally to give up some of his powers but the president continued to oppose constitutional reform. His decision Jan 1993 to pay his regular army with near worthless banknotes resulted in mutiny and the accidental shooting of the French ambassador by troops loyal to the president, causing French and Belgium governments to intervene and prepare to evacuate civilians.

Modigliani /ˌmɒdɪlˈjaːni/ Amedeo 1884–1920. Italian artist, active in Paris from 1906. He painted and sculpted graceful nudes and portrait studies. His paintings - for example, the portrait of *Jeanne Hebuterne* 1919 (Guggenheim Museum, New York) – have a distinctive elongated, linear style.

Modigliani was born in Livorno. He was encouraged to sculpt by Constantin Brancusi, and his series of strictly simplified heads reflects a shared interest in archaic sculptural styles. He led a dissolute life and died of the combined effects of alcoholism, drug addiction, and tuberculosis.

Mogul emperors N Indian dynasty 1526–1857, established by →Zahir ('Babur'). Muslim descendants of Tamerlane, the 14th-century Mongol leader, the Mogul emperors ruled until the last one was dethroned and exiled by the British 1857; they included →Akbar, →Aurangzeb, and →Shah Jahan.

Mohamad /məˈhæməd/ Mahathir bin 1925– . Prime minister of Malaysia from 1981 and leader of the United Malays' National Organization (UMNO). His 'look east' economic policy emulates Japanese industrialization.

Mahathir bin Mohamad was elected to the House of Representatives 1964 and gained the support of the dominant UMNO's radical youth wing as an advocate of economic help to *bumiputras* (ethnic Malays) and as a proponent of a more Islamic social policy. Mahathir held a number of ministerial posts from 1974 before being appointed prime minister and UMNO leader 1981. He was re-elected 1986, but has alienated sections of UMNO by his authoritarian leadership.

Mohammed /məʊˈhæmɪd/ alternative form of →Muhammad, founder of Islam.

Moholy-Nagy /məʊˈhɔɪ ˈnɒdʒ/ Laszlo 1895–1946. US photographer, born in Hungary. He lived in Germany 1923–29, where he was a member of the Bauhaus school, and fled from the Nazis 1935. Through the publication of his illuminating theories and practical experiments, he had great influence on 20th-century photography and design.

Mohs /məʊz/ Friedrich 1773–1839. German mineralogist who 1812 devised *Mohs' scale* of minerals, classified in order of relative hardness.

Moi Daniel arap 1924– . Kenyan politician, president from 1978. Leader of Kenya African National Union (KANU), he became minister of home affairs 1964, vice president 1967, and succeeded Jomo Kenyatta as president. He enjoys the support of Western governments but has been widely criticized for Kenya's poor human-rights record. From 1988 his rule became increasingly authoritarian and in 1992 he was elected president in the first free elections amid widespread accusations of fraud.

Moissan /mwæˈsʌn/ Henri 1852–1907. French chemist. For his preparation of pure fluorine 1886, Moissan was awarded the 1906 Nobel Prize for Chemistry. He also attempted to create artificial diamonds by rapidly cooling carbon heated to high temperatures. His claims of success were treated with suspicion.

Molière /ˈmɒlieə/ Pen name of Jean Baptiste Poquelin 1622–1673. French satirical playwright from whose work modern French comedy developed. One of the founders of the Illustre Théâtre 1643, he was later its leading actor. In 1655 he wrote his first play, *L'Etourdi*, followed by *Les Précieuses Ridicules* 1659. His satires include *L'Ecole des femmes* 1662, *Le Misanthrope* 1666, *Le Bourgeois Gentilhomme* 1670, and *Le Malade imaginaire* 1673. Other satiric plays include *Tartuffe* 1664

Moltke *Prussian general Count Helmuth von Moltke devised tactical command methods for modern mass armies, and was amongst the first generals to base strategy on the use of railways for rapid accessibility and movement of troops.*

(banned until 1697 for attacking the hypocrisy of the clergy), *Le Médecin malgré lui* 1666, and *Les Femmes savantes* 1672.

Molière's comedies, based on the exposure of hypocrisy and cant, made him vulnerable to many attacks (from which he was protected by Louis XIV) and marked a new departure in the French theatre away from reliance on classical Greek themes.

Molinos /məʊ'liːnɒs/ Miguel de 1640–1697. Spanish mystic and Roman Catholic priest. He settled in Rome and wrote several devotional works in Italian, including the *Guida spirituale/Spiritual Guide* 1675, which aroused the hostility of the Jesuits. In 1687 he was sentenced to life imprisonment. His doctrine is known as quietism.

Molnár /məʊlnɑː/ Ferenc 1878–1952. Hungarian novelist and playwright. His play *Liliom* 1909 is a study of a circus barker (a person who calls out to attract the attention of members of the public), adapted as the musical *Carousel*.

Molotov /mɒlətɒf/ Vyacheslav Mikhailovich. Assumed name of V M Skriabin 1890–1986. Soviet communist politician. He was chair of the Council of People's Commissars (prime minister) 1930–41 and foreign minister 1939–49 and 1953–56. He negotiated the 1939 nonaggression treaty with Germany (the Hitler–Stalin pact), and, after the German invasion 1941, the Soviet partnership with the Allies. His postwar stance prolonged the Cold War and in 1957 he was expelled from the government for Stalinist activities.

Moltke /mɒltkə/ Helmuth Carl Bernhard, Count von 1800–1891. Prussian general. He became

chief of the general staff 1857, and was responsible for the Prussian strategy in the wars with Denmark 1863–64, Austria 1866, and France 1870–71.

Moltke /mɒltkə/ Helmuth Johannes Ludwig von 1848–1916. German general (nephew of Count von Moltke, the Prussian general), chief of the German general staff 1906–14. His use of General Alfred von Schlieffen's (1833–1913) plan for a rapid victory on two fronts failed and he was relieved of command after the defeat at the Marne.

Momoh /məʊməʊ/ Joseph Saidu 1937– . Sierra Leone soldier and politician, president 1985–92. An army officer who became commander 1983, with the rank of major-general, he succeeded Siaka Stevens as president when he retired; Momoh was endorsed by Sierra Leone's one political party, the All-People's Congress. He dissociated himself from the policies of his predecessor, pledging to fight corruption and improve the economy. In April 1992 he fled to neighbouring Guinea after a military takeover.

Monck /mʌŋk/ or **Monk** George, 1st Duke of Albemarle 1608–1669. English soldier. During the Civil War he fought for King Charles I, but after being captured changed sides and took command of the Parliamentary forces in Ireland. Under the Commonwealth he became commander in chief in Scotland, and in 1660 he led his army into England and brought about the restoration of Charles II.

Mond /mɒnd/ Ludwig 1839–1909. German chemist who perfected a process for recovering sulphur during the manufacture of alkali.

Mond moved to England 1862 and became a British subject 1867. In 1873, he helped to found the firm of Brunner, Mond, and Company, which pioneered the British chemical industry. His son *Alfred Mond, 1st Baron Melchett* (1868–1930), was a founder of Imperial Chemical Industries (ICI).

Mondale /mɒndeɪl/ Walter 'Fritz' 1928– . US Democrat politician, unsuccessful presidential candidate 1984. He was a senator 1964–76 from his home state of Minnesota, and vice president to Jimmy Carter 1977–81. After losing the 1984 presidential election to Ronald Reagan, Mondale retired from national politics to resume his law practice.

Mondrian /mɒndriɑːn/ Piet (Pieter Mondriaan) 1872–1944. Dutch painter, a pioneer of abstract art. He lived in Paris 1919–38, then in London, and from 1940 in New York. He was a founder member of the de Stijl movement, believing that all life, work, and leisure should be surrounded by art, and chief exponent of Neo-Plasticism, a rigorous abstract style based on the use of simple geometric forms and pure colours. He typically painted parallel horizontal black lines which intersected vertical ones, creating square and rectangular blocks within the framework, some of which he filled with primary colours, mid-grey, or black, others being left white.

In Paris from 1911 Mondrian was inspired by Cubism. He returned to the Netherlands during World War I, where he used a series of still lifes and landscapes to refine his ideas, ultimately developing a pure abstract style. His aesthetic theories were published in the journal *De Stijl* from 1917, in *Neoplasticism* 1920, and in the essay 'Plastic Art and Pure Plastic Art' 1937. From the New York period his *Broadway Boogie-Woogie* 1942–43 (Museum of Modern Art, New York) reflects a late preoccupation with jazz rhythms.

Monet /mɒneɪ/ Claude 1840–1926. French painter, a pioneer of Impressionism and a lifelong exponent of its ideals; his painting *Impression, Sunrise* 1872 gave the movement its name. In the 1870s he began painting the same subjects at different times of day to explore the effects of light on colour and form; the *Haystacks* and *Rouen Cathedral* series followed in the 1890s, and from 1899 he painted a series of *Water Lilies* in the garden of his house at Giverny, Normandy (now a museum).

Monet was born in Paris. In Le Havre in the 1850s he was encouraged to paint by Boudin, and met Jongkind, whose light and airy seascapes made a lasting impact. From 1862 in Paris he shared a studio with Renoir, Sisley, and others, and they showed their work together at the First Impressionist Exhibition 1874.

Monet's work from the 1860s onwards concentrates on the evanescent effects of light and colour, and from the late 1860s he painted in the classic Impressionist manner, juxtaposing brushstrokes of colour to create an effect of dappled, glowing light. His first series showed the Gare St Lazare in Paris with its puffing steam engines. Views of the water garden in Giverny gradually developed into large, increasingly abstract colour compositions. Between 1900 and 1909 he produced a series of water-lily mural panels for the French state (the Orangerie, Paris).

Moniz /mɒnɪz, Portuguese mʊˈniːʃ/ Antonio Egas 1874–1955. Portuguese neurologist, pioneer of prefrontal leucotomy (surgical separation of white fibres in the prefrontal lobe of the brain) to treat schizophrenia and paranoia; the treatment is today considered questionable. He shared the 1949 Nobel Prize for Medicine.

Monk /mʌŋk/ Thelonious (Sphere) 1917–1982. US jazz pianist and composer who took part in the development of bebop. He had a highly idiosyncratic style, but numbers such as 'Round Midnight' and 'Blue Monk' have become standards.

Monmouth /mʌnməθ/ James Scott, Duke of Monmouth 1649–1685. Claimant to the English crown, the illegitimate son of Charles II and Lucy Walter. After James II's accession 1685, Monmouth landed in England at Lyme Regis, Dorset, claimed the crown, and raised a rebellion, which was crushed at Sedgemoor in Somerset. He was executed with 320 of his accomplices.

When →James II converted to Catholicism, the Whig opposition attempted unsuccessfully to secure Monmouth the succession to the crown by the Exclusion Bill, and having become implicated in a Whig conspiracy, the Rye House Plot 1683, he fled to Holland.

Monnet /mɒneɪ/ Jean 1888–1979. French economist. The originator of Winston Churchill's offer of union between the UK and France 1940, he devised and took charge of the French modernization programme under Charles de Gaulle 1945. In 1950 he produced the 'Shuman Plan' initiating the coordination of European coal and steel production in the European Coal and Steel Community (ECSC), which developed into the Common Market (EC).

Monod /mɒnəʊ/ Jacques 1910–1976. French biochemist who shared the 1965 Nobel Prize for Medicine (with two colleagues) for research in genetics and microbiology.

Monroe /mənˈrəʊ/ James 1758–1831. 5th president of the USA 1817–25, a Democratic Republican. He served in the American Revolution, was minister to France 1794–96, and in 1803 negotiated the Louisiana Purchase whereby the USA purchased some 2,144,000 sq km/828,00 sq mi of American land from France. He was secretary of state 1811–17. His name is associated with the Monroe Doctrine, a declaration that European colonial ambitions in the western hemisphere would be considered to be threats to US peace and security.

Monroe The period of 5th US president James Monroe's presidency was known as the 'era of good feeling' due to its lack of factional quarrels. His most popular acts were the recognition of the Spanish American republics, and the promulgation of the Monroe Doctrine in a message to Congress 1823.

Monroe /mən'rəʊ/ Marilyn. Stage name of Norma Jean Mortenson or Baker 1926–1962. US film actress, the voluptuous blonde sex symbol of the 1950s, who made adroit comedies such as *Gentlemen Prefer Blondes* 1953, *How to Marry a Millionaire* 1953, *The Seven Year Itch* 1955, *Bus Stop* 1956, and *Some Like It Hot* 1959. Her second husband was baseball star Joe di Maggio, and her third was playwright Arthur →Miller, who wrote *The Misfits* 1961 for her, a serious film that became her last. She committed suicide, taking an overdose of sleeping pills.

Monsarrat /mɒnsəræt/ Nicholas 1910–1979. English novelist who served with the navy in the Battle of the Atlantic, the subject of his book *The Cruel Sea* 1951.

Montagu /mɒntəgju:/ Ashley 1905– . British-born US anthropologist. As a critic of theories of racial determinacy, he was a forceful defender of human rights and wrote such important works as *Man's Most Dangerous Myth: The Fallacy of Race* 1942. In 1950 he helped draft the definitive UNESCO 'Statement on Race'.

Born in London, Montagu was educated at the University of London, Columbia University, and the University of Florence. He received his PhD from Columbia under Franz →Boas 1937. He became well known for popularizing social issues, such as 'psychosclerosis', the so-called hardening of the psyche, in *Growing Young* 1981.

Montagu /mɒntəgju:/ Edward Douglas Scott, 3rd Baron Montagu of Beaulieu 1926– . British car enthusiast, founder of the Montagu Motor Museum at Beaulieu, Hampshire, and chair of English Heritage (formerly Historic Buildings and Monuments Commission) 1983–92.

Montagu /mɒntəgju:/ Lady Mary Wortley (born Pierrepont) 1689–1762. British society hostess renowned for her witty and erudite letters. She was well known in literary circles, associating with writers such as Alexander Pope, with whom she later quarrelled. She introduced inoculation against smallpox into Britain.

Montagu-Douglas-Scott family name of the dukes of Buccleuch; seated at Bowhill, Selkirk, Scotland; Boughton House, Northamptonshire, England; and Drumlanrig, Dumfriesshire, Scotland; descended from the Duke of →Monmouth.

Montaigne /mɒn'teɪn/ Michel Eyquem de 1533–1592. French writer, regarded as the creator of the essay form. In 1580 he published the first two volumes of his *Essais*; the third volume appeared in 1588. Montaigne deals with all aspects of life from an urbanely sceptical viewpoint. Through the translation by John Florio in 1603, he influenced Shakespeare and other English writers.

He was born at the Château de Montaigne near Bordeaux, studied law, and in 1554 became a counsellor of the Bordeaux *parlement*. Little is known of his earlier life, except that he regularly visited Paris and the court of Francis II. In 1571 he retired to his estates, relinquishing his magistracy. He toured Germany, Switzerland, and Italy 1580–81, returning upon his election as mayor of Bordeaux, a post he held until 1585.

Montale /mɒn'tɑːle/ Eugenio 1896–1981. Italian poet and writer. His pessimistic poetry, for which he was awarded a Nobel prize in 1975, includes *Ossi di seppia/Cuttlefish bones* 1925 and *Le Occasioni/Occasions* 1939. In 1989 it was revealed that much of his literary journalism, such as his regular column in the *Corriere della Sera* newspaper, was in fact written by an American, Henry Frost.

Montana /ˌmɒntə'nɑː/ Claude 1949– . French fashion designer who promoted the broad-shouldered look. He established his own business and launched his first collection 1977.

Montana /mɒn'tænə/ Joe 1956– . US football player who has appeared in four winning Super Bowls as quarterback for the San Francisco 49ers 1982, 1985, 1989, and 1990, winning the Most Valuable Player award in 1982, 1985, and 1990. He threw a record five touchdown passes in the 1990 Super Bowl.

He graduated from Notre Dame university, where he led his team to the national college championship 1978. He was the leading passer in the National Football Conference 1981, 1984, and 1985. He recovered from a serious back injury in 1986 to become the leading passer in the National Football League 1987, setting league records for touchdowns thrown (31) and consecutive completions (22). In the 1989 Super Bowl, he set a record for passing yardage and the most passes without an interception (33).

Montand /mɒn'tɒn/ Yves 1921–1991. French actor and singer who achieved fame in the thriller *Le Salaire de la peur/The Wages of Fear* 1953 and continued to be popular in French and American films, including *Let's Make Love* 1960 (with Marilyn Monroe), *Le Sauvage/The Savage* 1976, *Jean de Florette* 1986, and *Manon des sources* 1986.

Montcalm /mɒnt'kɑːm/ Louis-Joseph de Montcalm-Gozon, Marquis de 1712–1759. French general, appointed military commander in Canada 1756. He won a succession of victories over the British during the French and Indian War, but was defeated in 1759 by James →Wolfe at Québec, where both he and Wolfe were killed; this battle marked the end of French rule in Canada.

Montespan /ˌmɒntes'pɒn/ Françoise-Athénaïs de Rochechouart, Marquise de Montespan 1641–1707. Mistress of Louis XIV of France from 1667. They had seven children, for whom she engaged as governess the future Madame de →Maintenon, who later supplanted her. She retired to a convent in 1691.

Montesquieu /ˌmɒntes'kjɜː/ Charles Louis de Secondat, baron de la Brède 1689–1755. French philosophical historian, author of the *Lettres* *persanes*/*Persian Letters* 1721. *De l'Esprit des lois*/*The Spirit of the Laws* 1748, a 31-volume philosophical disquisition on politics and sociology as well as legal matters, advocated the separation of powers within government, a doctrine that became the basis of liberal constitutions.

Born near Bordeaux, Montesquieu became adviser to the Bordeaux parliament 1714. After the success of *Lettres persanes*, he adopted a literary career, writing *Considérations sur les causes de la grandeur des Romains et de leur décadence*/*Considerations on the Greatness and Decadence of the Romans* 1734.

Montessori /ˌmɒntɛˈsɔːri/ Maria 1870–1952. Italian educationalist. From her experience with mentally handicapped children, she developed the *Montessori method*, an educational system for all children based on an informal approach, incorporating instructive play and allowing children to develop at their own pace.

We teachers can only help the work going on, as servants wait upon a master.

Maria Montessori *The Absorbent Mind*

Monteux /mɒnˈtɜː/ Pierre 1875–1964. French conductor. Ravel's *Daphnis and Chloe* and Stravinsky's *Rite of Spring* were first performed under his direction. He conducted Sergei →Diaghilev's Ballets Russes 1911–14 and 1917, and the San Francisco Symphony Orchestra 1935–52.

Monteverdi /ˌmɒntɪˈveədi/ Claudio (Giovanni Antonio) 1567–1643. Italian composer. He contributed to the development of the opera with *Orfeo* 1607 and *The Coronation of Poppea* 1642. He also wrote madrigals, motets, and sacred music, notably the *Vespers* 1610.

Montez /mɒntez/ Lola. Stage name of Maria Gilbert 1818–1861. Irish actress and dancer. She appeared on the stage as a Spanish dancer, and in 1847 became the mistress of King Ludwig I of Bavaria, whose policy she dictated for a year. Her liberal sympathies led to her banishment through Jesuit influence in 1848. She died in poverty in the USA.

Montezuma II /ˌmɒntɪˈzuːmə/ 1466–1520. Aztec emperor 1502–20. When the Spanish conquistador Cortés invaded Mexico, Montezuma was imprisoned and killed during the Aztec attack on Cortés's force as it tried to leave Tenochtitlán, the Aztec capital city.

Montfort /mɒntfət/ Simon de Montfort, Earl of Leicester *c.* 1208–1265. English politician and soldier. From 1258 he led the baronial opposition to Henry III's misrule during the second Barons' War and in 1264 defeated and captured the king at Lewes, Sussex. In 1265, as head of government, he summoned the first parliament in which the towns were represented; he was killed at the Battle of Evesham during the last of the Barons' Wars.

Born in Normandy, the son of *Simon de Montfort* (about 1160–1218) who led a crusade against the Albigenses, he arrived in England in 1230, married Henry III's sister, and was granted the earldom of Leicester.

Montgolfier /mɒnˈɡɒlfieɪ/ Joseph Michel 1740–1810 and Étienne Jacques 1745–1799. French brothers whose hot-air balloon was used for the first successful human flight 21 Nov 1783.

They were papermakers of Annonay, near Lyon, where on 5 June 1783 they first sent up a balloon filled with hot air. After further experiments with wood-fuelled paper balloons, they went aloft themselves for 20 minutes above Paris. The Montgolfier experiments greatly stimulated scientific interest in aviation.

Montgomery /mənˈtɡʌməri/ Bernard Law, 1st Viscount Montgomery of Alamein 1887–1976. British field marshal. In World War II he commanded the 8th Army in N Africa in the Second Battle of El Alamein 1942. As commander of British troops in N Europe from 1944, he received the German surrender 1945.

At the start of World War II he commanded part of the British Expeditionary Force in France 1939–40 and took part in the evacuation from Dunkirk. In Aug 1942 he took command of the 8th Army, then barring the German advance on Cairo; the victory of El Alamein in Oct turned the tide in N Africa and was followed by the expulsion of Field Marshal Rommel from Egypt and rapid Allied advance into Tunisia. In Feb 1943 Montgomery's forces came under US general Eisenhower's command, and they took part in the conquest of Tunisia and Sicily and the invasion of Italy. Montgomery was promoted to field marshal in 1944. In 1948 he became permanent military chair of the Commanders-in-Chief Committee for W European defence, and 1951–58 was deputy Supreme Commander Europe. Created 1st Viscount Montgomery of Alamein 1946.

Montgomery commanded the Allied armies during the opening phase of the invasion of France in Jun 1944, and from Aug the British and imperial troops that liberated the Netherlands, overran N Germany, and entered Denmark. At his 21st Army Group headquarters on Lüneberg Heath, he received the German surrender on 3 May 1945. He was in command of the British occupation force in Germany until Feb 1946, when he was appointed chief of the Imperial General Staff.

Montgomery /mənˈtɡʌməri/ Robert (Henry) 1904–1981. US film actor of the 1930s and 1940s. He directed some of his later films, such as *Lady in the Lake* 1947, before turning to television and Republican politics. His other films include *Night Must Fall* 1937 and *Mr and Mrs Smith* 1941.

Montherlant /ˌmɒnteəˈlɒŋ/ Henri Millon de 1896–1972. French author. He was a Nazi sympathizer. His novels, which are marked by an obsession with the physical, include *Aux Fontaines du désir/To the Fountains of Desire* 1927 and *Pitié pour les femmes/Pity for Women* 1936. His most critically acclaimed work is *Le Chaos et la nuit/Chaos and Night* 1963.

Monti /ˈmɒnti/ Eugenio 1928– . Italian bobsleigh driver who won Olympic gold medals in two- and four-crew bobs in 1968, and between 1957 and 1968 won 11 world titles.

His two-person successes were shared with the brakemen Renzo Alvera and Sergio Siorpaes, both Italian. On his retirement in 1968 Monti became manager to the Italian team.

Montrose /mɒnˈtrəʊz/ James Graham, 1st Marquess of Montrose 1612–1650. Scottish soldier, son of the 4th earl of Montrose. He supported the Covenanters against Charles I, but after 1640 changed sides. Defeated in 1645 at Philiphaugh, he escaped to Norway. Returning in 1650 to raise a revolt, he survived shipwreck only to have his weakened forces defeated, and (having been betrayed to the Covenanters) was hanged in Edinburgh.

He either fears his fate too much,
Or his deserts are small,
That puts it not unto the touch
To win or lose it all.

Lord Montrose 'My Dear and Only Love'

Moody /ˈmuːdi/ Dwight Lyman 1837–1899. US evangelist. During the American Civil War 1861–65, he provided medical and moral support to the troops. In the 1870s he became a popular evangelist and founded the Northfield Seminary (now School) for girls 1879 and the Mount Hermon School for boys 1881, both in Massachusetts.

Born in East Northfield, Massachusetts, USA, Moody moved to Boston as a young man and joined the Congregational Church 1856. Later settling in Chicago, he devoted himself to preaching among the poor. In 1889 he founded the Chicago (later Moody) Bible Institute.

Moody Helen Wills married name of US tennis player Helen Newington →Wills.

Moon /muːn/ Sun Myung 1920– . Korean industrialist and founder of the Unification Church (*Moonies*) 1954. From 1973 he launched a major mission in the USA and elsewhere. The church has been criticized for its manipulative methods of recruiting and keeping members. He was convicted of tax fraud in the USA 1982.

Moon has allegedly been associated with extreme right-wing organizations, arms manufacture, and the Korean Central Intelligence Agency.

Moon /muːn/ William 1818–1894. English inventor of the *Moon alphabet* for the blind. Devised in 1847, it uses only nine symbols in different orientations. From 1983 it has been possible to write it with a miniature typewriter.

Moorcock /ˈmʊəkɒk/ Michael 1939– . English writer, associated with the 1960s new wave in science fiction, editor of the magazine *New Worlds* 1964–69. He wrote the Jerry Cornelius novels, collected as *The Cornelius Chronicles* 1977, and *Gloriana* 1978.

Moore /mʊə/ (John) Jeremy 1928– . British major general of the Commando Forces, Royal Marines, 1979–82. He commanded the land forces in the UK's conflict with Argentina over the Falklands 1982.

Moore /mʊə/ Bobby (Robert Frederick) 1941–1993. British footballer. Captain of West Ham United and England, he led them to victory over West Germany in the 1966 World Cup final at Wembley Stadium.

Between 1962 and 1970 he played a then record 108 games for England. He played the last of his 668 Football League games for Fulham against Blackburn Rovers in 1977, after a career spanning 19 years. He later played in Hong Kong before becoming a director of Southend United and in 1984 he became their manager. He later became sports editor of the *Sunday Sport* newspaper.

Moore /mʊə/ Charles 1925– . US architect with an eclectic approach to design. He was an early exponent of Post-Modernism in, for example, his students' housing for Kresge College, University of California at Santa Cruz, 1973–74, and the Piazza d'Italia in New Orleans, 1975–78, which is one of the key monuments of Post-Modernism.

Sea Ranch, California 1964–65, one of his earliest projects, is in the vernacular timber tradition. At Kresge College he created a stage set of streets and fora. The Piazza d'Italia was built for the local Italian community and has a fountain in the shape of Italy.

Moore /mʊə/ Dudley 1935– . English actor, comedian, and musician, formerly teamed with comedian Peter Cook. Moore became a Hollywood star after appearing in '*10*' 1979. His other films, mostly comedies, include *Bedazzled* 1968, *Arthur* 1981, and *Santa Claus* 1985.

Moore /mʊə/ G(eorge) E(dward) 1873–1958. British philosopher. Educated at Trinity College, Cambridge University, he was professor of philosophy at the university 1925–39, and edited the journal *Mind*, to which he contributed 1921–47. His books include *Principia Ethica* 1903, in which he attempted to analyse the moral question 'What is good?', and *Some Main Problems of Philosophy* 1953, but his chief influence was as a teacher.

Moore /mʊə/ George (Augustus) 1852–1933. Irish novelist, born in County Mayo. He studied art in Paris 1870, and published two volumes of poetry there. His first novel, *A Modern Lover* 1883, was sexually frank for its time and banned in some quarters. It was followed by others, including *Esther Waters* 1894.

Moore /mʊə/ Gerald 1899–1987. British pianist, renowned as an accompanist of singers, a role he raised to equal partnership.

Moore /mʊə/ Henry 1898–1986. British sculptor. His subjects include the reclining nude, mother and child groups, the warrior, and interlocking abstract forms. Many of his post-1945 works are in bronze or marble, including monumental semi-abstracts such as *Reclining Figure* 1957–58 (outside the UNESCO building, Paris), and often designed to be placed in landscape settings.

Moore claimed to have learned much from archaic South and Central American sculpture, and this is reflected in his work from the 1920s. By the early 1930s most of his main themes had emerged, and the Surrealists' preoccupation with organic forms in abstract works proved a strong influence; Moore's hollowed wooden shapes strung with wires date from the late 1930s. Abstract work suggesting organic structures recurs after World War II, for example in the interwoven bonelike forms of the *Hill Arches* and the bronze *Sheep Pieces* 1970s, set in fields by his studio in Hertfordshire.

Moore, born in Yorkshire, studied at Leeds and the Royal College of Art, London. As an official war artist during World War II, he made a series of drawings of London's air-raid shelters.

Moore /mʊə/ John 1761–1809. British general, born in Glasgow. In 1808 he commanded the British army sent to Portugal in the Peninsular War. After advancing into Spain he had to retreat to Corunna in the NW, and was killed in the battle fought to cover the embarkation.

He entered the army in 1776, serving in the American and French Revolutionary Wars and against the Irish rebellion of 1798.

Moore /mʊə/ Marianne 1887–1972. US poet. She edited the literary magazine *The Dial* 1925–29, and published several volumes of witty and intellectual verse, including *Observations* 1924, *What are Years* 1941, and *A Marianne Moore Reader* 1961. She also published translations and essays. Her work is noted for its observation of detail. T S Eliot was an admirer of her poetry.

Moore /mʊə/ Roger 1928– . English actor who starred in the television series *The Saint* 1962–70, and assumed the film role of James Bond in 1973 in *Live and Let Die*.

Moore /mʊə/ Thomas 1779–1852. Irish poet, born in Dublin. Among his works are the verse romance *Lalla Rookh* 1817 and the *Irish Melodies* 1807–35. These were set to music by John Stevenson 1807–35 and include 'The Minstrel Boy' and 'The Last Rose of Summer'.

Moore British general John Moore in a portrait by Thomas Lawrence (c. 1800). Moore, who first distinguished himself in the attack on Corsica 1794 during the French Revolutionary War, created the rapidly moving light infantry regiments and a new drill system that contributed to later British successes.

Moorhouse /mʊəhaʊs/ Adrian 1964– . English swimmer who won the 100 metres breaststroke at the 1988 Seoul Olympics.

He has won gold medals at both the Commonwealth Games and the European Championships but was disqualified from first place for an illegal turn during the 1986 world championships.

Moorhouse /mʊəhaʊs/ Geoffrey 1931– . British travel writer, born in Bolton, Lancashire. His books include *The Fearful Void* 1974, and (on cricket) *The Best-Loved Game* 1979.

Morandi /mɒˈrændi/ Giorgio 1890–1964. Italian still-life painter and etcher whose subtle studies of bottles and jars convey a sense of calm and repose.

Moravia /məˈreɪvɪə/ Alberto. Pen name of Alberto Pincherle 1907–1991. Italian novelist. His first successful novel was *Gli indifferenti/The Time of Indifference* 1929, but its criticism of Mussolini's regime led to the government censoring his work until after World War II. Later books include *La romana/Woman of Rome* 1947, *La ciociara/Two Women* 1957, and *La noia/The Empty Canvas* 1961, a study of an artist's obsession with his model.

Moray Earl of Moray another spelling of →Murray, regent of Scotland 1567–70.

Morazán /ˌmɒrəˈsɑːn/ Francisco 1792–1842. Central American politician, born in Honduras. He was elected president of the United Provinces of Central America in 1830. In the face of secessions he attempted to hold the union together by force but was driven out by the Guatemalan dictator Rafael Carrera. Morazán was eventually captured and executed in 1842.

More /mɔː/ (St) Thomas 1478–1535. English politician and author. From 1509 he was favoured by →Henry VIII and employed on foreign embassies. He was a member of the privy council from 1518 and Lord Chancellor from 1529 but resigned over Henry's break with the pope. For refusing to accept the king as head of the church, he was executed. The title of his political book *Utopia* 1516 has come to mean any supposedly perfect society.

Son of a London judge, More studied Greek, Latin, French, theology, and music at Oxford, and law at Lincoln's Inn, London, and was influenced by the humanists John Colet and →Erasmus, who became a friend. In Parliament from 1504, he was made Speaker of the House of Commons in 1523. He was knighted in 1521, and on the fall of Cardinal Wolsey became Lord Chancellor, but resigned in 1532 because he could not agree with the king on his ecclesiastical policy and marriage with Anne Boleyn. In 1534 he refused to take the oath of supremacy to Henry VIII as head of the church, and after a year's imprisonment in the Tower of London he was executed.

Among Thomas More's writings are the Latin *Utopia* 1516, sketching an ideal commonwealth; the English *Dialogue* 1528, a theological argument against the Reformation leader Tyndale; and a *History of Richard III*. He was also a patron of artists, including →Holbein. More was canonized in 1935.

More /mɔː/ Kenneth 1914–1982. British actor, a wholesome film star of the 1950s, cast as leading man in adventure films and light comedies such as *Genevieve* 1953, *Doctor in the House* 1954, and *Northwest Frontier*.

Moreau /mɔːˈrəʊ/ Gustave 1826–1898. French Symbolist painter. His works are atmospheric: biblical, mythological, and literary scenes, richly coloured and detailed; for example, *Salome Dancing Before Herod* 1876.

In the 1890s Moreau taught at the Ecole des Beaux-Arts in Paris, where his pupils included Matisse and Rouault. Much of his work is in the Musée Moreau, Paris.

Moreau /mɔːˈrəʊ/ Jean Victor Marie 1763–1813. French general in the Revolutionary Wars who won a brilliant victory over the Austrians at Hohenlinden 1800; as a republican he intrigued against Napoleon and, when banished, joined the Allies and was killed at the Battle of Dresden.

Moreau /mɔːˈrəʊ/ Jeanne 1928– . French actress who has appeared in international films, often in passionate, intelligent roles. Her work includes *Les Amants/The Lovers* 1958, *Jules et Jim/Jules and Jim* 1961, *Chimes at Midnight* 1966, and *Querelle* 1982.

Moresby /ˈmɔːzbi/ John 1830–1922. British naval explorer and author. He was the first European to visit the harbour in New Guinea, now known as Port Moresby.

Morgagni /mɔːˈɡænji/ Giovanni Battista 1682–1771. Italian anatomist. As professor of anatomy at Padua, Morgagni carried out more than 400 autopsies, and developed the view that disease was not an imbalance of the body's humours but a result of alterations in the organs. His work *On the Seats and Causes of Diseases as Investigated by Anatomy* 1761 formed the basis of pathology.

Morgan /ˈmɔːɡən/ Henry c. 1635–1688. Welsh buccaneer in the Caribbean. He made war against Spain, capturing and sacking Panama 1671. In 1674 he was knighted and appointed lieutenant governor of Jamaica.

Morgan /ˈmɔːɡən/ J(ohn) P(ierpont) 1837–1913. US financier and investment banker whose company (sometimes criticized as 'the money trust') became the most influential private banking house after the Civil War, being instrumental in the formation of many trusts to stifle competition. He set up the US Steel Corporation 1901 and International Harvester 1902.

Morgan /ˈmɔːɡən/ Lewis Henry 1818–1881. US anthropologist who pioneered the study of NE American Indian culture and was adopted by the Iroquois.

Morgan /ˈmɔːɡən/ Thomas Hunt 1866–1945. US geneticist, awarded the 1933 Nobel Prize for Medicine for his pioneering studies in classical genetics. He was the first to work on the fruit fly *Drosophila*, which has since become a major subject of genetic studies. He helped establish that the genes were located on the chromosomes, discovered sex chromosomes, and invented the techniques of genetic mapping.

Morisot /ˌmɒrɪˈsəʊ/ Berthe 1841–1895. French Impressionist painter who specialized in pictures of women and children.

Morland /ˈmɔːlənd/ George 1763–1804. English painter whose picturesque rural subjects were widely reproduced in engravings. He was an admirer of Dutch and Flemish painters of rustic life.

Morley /ˈmɔːli/ Edward 1838–1923. US physicist who collaborated with Albert →Michelson on the *Michelson–Morley experiment* 1887. In 1895 he established precise and accurate measurements of the densities of oxygen and hydrogen.

Morley /ˈmɔːli/ John, 1st Viscount Morley of Blackburn 1838–1923. British Liberal politician and writer. He entered Parliament in 1883, and was secretary for Ireland in 1886 and 1892–95. As secretary for India 1905–10, he prepared the way (with Viceroy Gilbert →Minto) for more representative government.

He was Lord President of the Council 1910–14, but resigned in protest against the declaration of war. He published lives of the philosophers Voltaire and Rousseau and the politicians Burke and Gladstone. He received a peerage in 1908.

Simplicity of character is no hindrance to subtlety of intellect.

John Morley *Life of Gladstone*

Morley /ˈmɔːli/ Malcolm 1931– . British painter, active in New York from 1964. He coined the term *Superrealism* for his work in the 1960s.

Morley /ˈmɔːli/ Robert 1908– . English actor and playwright, active in both Britain and the USA. His film work has been mainly character roles, in such movies as *Marie Antoinette* 1938, *The African Queen* 1952, and *Oscar Wilde* 1960.

Morley /ˈmɔːli/ Thomas 1557–1602. English composer. A student of William →Byrd, he became organist at St Paul's Cathedral, London, and obtained a monopoly on music printing. A composer of the English madrigal school, he also wrote sacred music, songs for Shakespeare's plays, and a musical textbook.

Moro /ˈmɔːrəʊ/ Aldo 1916–1978. Italian Christian Democrat politician. Prime minister 1963–68 and 1974–76, he was expected to become Italy's president, but he was kidnapped and shot by Red Brigade urban guerrillas.

Morricone /ˌmɒrɪˈkəʊni/ Ennio 1928– . Italian composer of film music. His atmospheric scores for 'spaghetti Westerns', notably the Clint →Eastwood movies *A Fistful of Dollars* 1964 and *The Good, the Bad and the Ugly* 1966, created a vogue for lyrical understatement. His highly ritualized, incantatory style pioneered the use of amplified instruments and solo voices, using studio special effects.

Morris /ˈmɒrɪs/ Henry 1889–1961. British educationalist. He inspired and oversaw the introduction of the 'village college' and community school/education, which he saw as regenerating rural life. His ideas were also adopted in urban areas.

Morris emphasized the value of providing single-site centres of continuing education and leisure activity for both adults and children alike. He persuaded Walter →Gropius, together with Maxwell Fry, to design the Village College at Impington, near Cambridge, 1939. He was chief education officer for Cambridgeshire 1922–54.

Morris /ˈmɒrɪs/ Robert 1734–1806. American political leader. A signatory of the Declaration of Independence 1776, he served in the Continental Congress 1775–78. In 1781 he was appointed superintendent of finance and dealt with the economic problems of the new nation. He served as one of Pennsylvania's first US senators 1789–95.

Born in Liverpool, England, Morris emigrated to America 1747, joining a merchant firm in Philadelphia and became a cautious supporter of American independence. He attended the Constitutional Convention 1787.

Morris /ˈmɒrɪs/ Thomas, Jr 1851–1875. British golfer, one of the first great champions. He was known as 'Young Tom' to distinguish him from his father (known as 'Old Tom'). Morris Jr won the British Open four times between 1868 and 1872.

Morris /ˈmɒrɪs/ William 1834–1896. English designer, a founder of the Arts and Crafts movement, socialist, and writer who shared the Pre-Raphaelite painters' fascination with medieval settings. In 1861 he cofounded a firm that designed and produced furniture, carpets, and a wide range of decorative wallpapers, many of which are still produced today. His Kelmscott Press, set up 1890 to print beautifully designed books, influenced printing and book design. The prose romances *A Dream of John Ball* 1888 and *News from Nowhere* 1891 reflect his socialist ideology. He also lectured on socialism.

Morris abandoned his first profession, architecture, to study painting, but had a considerable influence on such architects as William Lethaby and Philip →Webb. As a founder of the Arts and Crafts movement, Morris did much to raise British craft standards. His first book of verse was *The Defence of Guenevere* 1858.

William Morris was born in Walthamstow, London, and educated at Oxford, where he formed a lasting friendship with the Pre-Raphaelite artist Edward →Burne-Jones and influenced by the art critic John Ruskin and the painter and poet Dante →Rossetti.

Morris published several volumes of verse romances, notably *The Life and Death of Jason* 1867 and *The Earthly Paradise* 1868–70; a visit to Iceland 1871 inspired *Sigurd the Volsung* 1876 and general interest in the sagas. He joined the Social Democratic Federation 1883, but left it 1884 because he found it too moderate, and set up the Socialist League. To this period belong the critical and sociological studies *Signs of Change* 1888 and *Hopes and Fears for Art* 1892. and the narrative poem 'The Pilgrims of Hope' 1885.

Have nothing in your houses that you do not know to be useful, or believe to be beautiful.

William Morris *Hopes and Fears for Art*

Morrison /mɒrɪsən/ Herbert Stanley, Baron Morrison of Lambeth 1888–1965. British Labour politician. He was a founder member and later secretary of the London Labour Party 1915–45, and a member of the London County Council 1922–45. He entered Parliament in 1923, and organised the Labour Party's general election victory in 1945. He was twice defeated in the contest for leadership of the party, once to Clement Attlee in 1932, and then to Hugh Gaitskell 1955. A skilful organiser, he lacked the ability to unite the party.

He was minister of transport 1929–31, home secretary 1940–45, Lord President of the Council and leader of the House of Commons 1945–51, and foreign secretary March–Oct 1951.

Morrison /mɒrɪsən/ Toni 1931– . US novelist whose fiction records black life in the South. Her works include *Song of Solomon* 1978, *Tar Baby* 1981, *Beloved* 1987, based on a true story about infanticide in Kentucky, which won the Pulitzer Prize 1988, and *Jazz* 1992.

Morrison /mɒrɪsən/ Van (George Ivan) 1945– . Northern Irish singer and songwriter whose jazz-inflected Celtic soul style was already in evidence on *Astral Weeks* 1968 and has been highly influential. Among other albums are *Tupelo Honey* 1971, *Veedon Fleece* 1974, and *Avalon Sunset* 1989.

Morrissey Stage name of Steven Patrick Morrissey 1959– . English rock singer and lyricist, founder member of the Manchester-based group the →Smiths 1983–87 and subsequently a solo artist. his lyrics reflect on everyday miseries or glumly celebrate the England of his childhood.

Morrissey The lyrics of English singer Morrissey have a melancholy social realism. He has drawn inspiration from English popular culture from music hall to 1960s soap opera. His self-deprecating humour and use of a natural vernacular in songwriting distinguished his work from the outset.

Solo albums include *Viva Hate* 1987 and *Your Arsenal* 1992.

Morse /mɔːs/ Samuel (Finley Breese) 1791–1872. US inventor. In 1835 he produced the first adequate electric telegraph, and in 1843 was granted $30,000 by Congress for an experimental line between Washington DC and Baltimore. With his assistant Alexander Bain (1810–1877) he invented the Morse code.

He was also a respected portrait painter.

Mortensen /mɔːtɪnsən/ Stanley 1921–1991. English footballer. He was centre forward for the Blackpool Football Club 1946–55, and won 25 international caps while playing for the England team.

Mortimer /mɔːtɪmə/ John 1923– . English barrister and writer. His works include the plays *The Dock Brief* 1958 and *A Voyage Round My Father* 1970, the novel *Paradise Postponed* 1985, and the television series *Rumpole of the Bailey*, from 1978, centred on a fictional barrister.

Mortimer /mɔːtɪmə/ Roger de, 8th Baron of Wigmore and 1st Earl of March c. 1287–1330. English politician and adventurer. He opposed Edward II and with Edward's queen, Isabella, led a rebellion against him 1326, bringing about his abdication. From 1327 Mortimer ruled England as the queen's lover, until Edward III had him executed.

A rebel, he was imprisoned by Edward II for two years before making his escape from the Tower of London to France. There he joined with the English queen, Isabella, who was conducting negotiations at the French court, and returned with her to England in 1326. Edward fled when they landed with their followers, and Mortimer secured Edward's deposition by Parliament. In 1328 he was created Earl of March. He was popularly supposed responsible for Edward II's murder, and when the young Edward III had him seized while with the queen at Nottingham Castle, he was hanged, drawn, and quartered at Tyburn, London.

Morton /mɔːtn/ Henry Vollam 1892–1979. English journalist and travel writer, author of the *In Search of* ... series published during the 1950s. His earlier travel books include *The Heart of London* 1925, *In the Steps of the Master* 1934, and *Middle East* 1941.

Morton /mɔːtn/ J(ohn) B(ingham) 1893–1979. British journalist who contributed a humorous column to the *Daily Express* 1924–76 under the pen name *Beachcomber*.

Morton /mɔːtn/ Jelly Roll. Stage name of Ferdinand Joseph La Menthe 1885–1941. US New Orleans-style jazz pianist, singer, and composer. Influenced by Scott Joplin, he was a pioneer in the development of jazz from ragtime to swing by improvising and imposing his own personality on the music. His 1920s band was called the Red Hot Peppers.

Morton /mɔːtn/ William Thomas Green 1819–1868. US dentist who in 1846, with C Thomas Jackson (1805–1880), a chemist and physician, introduced ether as an anaesthetic. They patented the process and successfully publicized it.

Moseley /məʊzli/ Henry Gwyn-Jeffreys 1887–1915. English physicist. From 1913 to 1914 he devised the series of atomic numbers (reflecting the charges of the nuclei of different elements) that led to the revision of the Mendeleyev's periodic table of the elements.

A student of Ernest →Rutherford, Moseley devoted his career to research on the structure of the atom. He concluded that the atomic number is equal to the charge on the nucleus; therefore his periodic table was arranged by atomic number (instead of atomic mass, as presented by Mendeleyev). When the elements are so arranged, problems appearing in the Mendeleyev version are resolved.

Moses /məʊzɪz/ c. 13th century BC. Hebrew lawgiver and judge who led the Israelites out of Egypt to the promised land of Canaan. On Mount Sinai he claimed to have received from Jehovah the oral and written Law, including the *Ten Commandments* engraved on tablets of stone. The first five books of the Old Testament – in Judaism, the *Torah* – are ascribed to him.

According to the Torah, the infant Moses was hidden among the bulrushes on the banks of the Nile when the pharaoh commanded that all newborn male Hebrew children should be destroyed. He was found by a daughter of Pharaoh, who reared him. Eventually he became the leader of the Israelites in their *Exodus* from Egypt and their 40 years' wandering in the wilderness. He died at the age of 120, after having been allowed a glimpse of the Promised Land from Mount Pisgah.

Moses /məʊzɪz/ 'Grandma' (born Anna Mary Robertson) 1860–1961. US painter. She was self-taught, and began full-time painting in about 1927, after many years as a farmer's wife. She painted naive and colourful scenes from rural American life.

Moses /məʊzɪz/ Ed(win Corley) 1955– . US track athlete and 400 metres hurdler. Between 1977 and 1987 he ran 122 races without defeat.

He first broke the world record in 1976, and set a time of 47.02 seconds set in 1983. He was twice Olympic champion and twice world chapion.

Moses /məʊzɪz/ Robert 1888–1981. US public official and urban planner. As parks commissioner for New York State 1924–64 and New York City 1934–60, he oversaw the development of bridges, highways, and public facilities. Serving as New York secretary of state 1927–28, he was the unsuccessful Republican candidate for New York governor 1934.

Born in New Haven, Connecticut, USA, and educated at Yale and Oxford universities, Moses received his PhD from Columbia University 1914. Known as a power broker, he held tremendous power in the USA for more than 40 years.

He was hired by the New York City municipal government and later headed a state redevelopment programme. He served as chair of the Triborough Bridge and Tunnel Authority 1946–68, chair of the New York State Power Authority 1954–63, and president of the 1964–65 New York World's Fair.

Mosley /məʊzli/ Oswald (Ernald) 1896–1980. British politician, founder of the British Union of Fascists (BUF). He was a member of Parliament 1918–31, then led the BUF until his internment 1940–43 during World War II. In 1946 Mosley was denounced when it became known that Italy had funded his prewar efforts to establish fascism in Britain, but in 1948 he resumed fascist propaganda with his Union Movement, the revived BUF.

His first marriage was to a daughter of the Conservative politician Lord Curzon, his second to Diana Freeman-Mitford, one of the →Mitford sisters.

Moss /mɒs/ Stirling 1929– . English racing-car driver. Despite being one of the best-known names in British motor racing, Moss never won the world championship. He was runner-up on four occasions, losing to Juan Manuel →Fangio in 1955, 1956, and 1957, and to fellow Briton Mike Hawthorn (1929–1959) in 1958.

In his early days he drove solely for British manufacturers before moving to the Italian firm Maserati, and then to the German Mercedes team, returning once more to British firms such as Vanwall in 1958 and later to Lotus. A bad accident at Goodwood in 1962 ended his career but he maintained contact with the sport and in recent years has taken part in sports-car races.

Mossadeq /mɒsədek/ Muhammad 1880–1967. Iranian prime minister 1951–53. A dispute arose with the Anglo-Iranian Oil Company when he called for the nationalization of Iran's oil production, and when he failed in his attempt to overthrow the shah, he was arrested by loyalist forces with support from the USA. From 1956 he was under house arrest.

Mössbauer /mɜːsˌbaʊə/ Rudolf 1929– . German physicist who discovered in 1958 that in certain conditions a nucleus can be stimulated to emit very sharply defined beams of gamma rays. This became known as the *Mössbauer effect*. Such a beam was used in 1960 to provide the first laboratory test of →Einstein's general theory of relativity. For his work on gamma rays Mössbauer shared the 1961 Nobel Prize for Physics with Robert →Hofstadter.

Mostel /mɒ'stell/ Zero (Samuel Joel) 1915–1977. US comedian and actor, mainly in the theatre. His films include *Panic in the Streets* 1950, *A Funny Thing Happened on the Way to the Forum* 1966, *The Producers* 1967, and *The Front* 1976.

Mountbatten Admiral Louis Mountbatten, 1942. Great-grandson of Queen Victoria, Mountbatten was supreme allied commander in SE Asia 1943–45.

Motherwell /ˈmʌðəwel/ Robert 1915–1991. US painter associated with the New York school of action painting which emphasized the importance of the physical act of painting. Borrowing from Picasso, Matisse, and the Surrealists, Motherwell's style of Abstract Expressionism retained some suggestion of the figurative. His works include the 'Elegies to the Spanish Republic' 1949–76, a series of over 100 paintings devoted to the Spanish Revolution.

Mott /mɒt/ Nevill Francis 1905– . English physicist who researched the electronic properties of metals, semiconductors, and noncrystalline materials. He shared the Nobel Prize for Physics 1977 with US physicists Philip Anderson (1923–) and John Van Vleck (1899–1980).

Mountbatten /ˈmaʊntˈbætn/ Louis, 1st Earl Mountbatten of Burma 1900–1979. British admiral and administrator. In World War II he became chief of combined operations 1942 and commander in chief in SE Asia 1943. As last viceroy of India 1947 and first governor general of India until 1948, he oversaw that country's transition to independence. He was killed by an Irish Republican Army bomb aboard his yacht in the Republic of Ireland.

Moyse /mwaːz/ Marcel 1889–1984. French flautist. Trained at the Paris Conservatoire, he made many recordings and was an eminent teacher.

Mozart /ˈməʊtsɑːt/ Wolfgang Amadeus 1756–1791. Austrian composer and performer who showed astonishing precocity as a child and was an adult virtuoso. He was trained by his father, *Leopold Mozart* (1719–1787). From an early age

he composed prolifically, his works including 27 piano concertos, 23 string quartets, 35 violin sonatas, and more than 50 symphonies including the E flat K543, G minor K550, and C major K551 ('Jupiter') symphonies, all composed 1788. His operas include *Idomeneo* 1781, *Le Nozze di Figaro/The Marriage of Figaro* 1786, *Don Giovanni* 1787, *Così fan tutte/Thus Do All Women* 1790, and *Die Zauberflöte/The Magic Flute* 1791. Strongly influenced by →Haydn, Mozart's music marks the height of the Classical age in its purity of melody and form.

Mozart's career began when, with his sister, Maria Anna, he was taken on a number of tours 1762–79, visiting Vienna, the Rhineland, Holland, Paris, London, and Italy. Mozart not only gave public recitals, but had already begun to compose. In 1772 he was appointed master of the archbishop of Salzburg's court band. He found the post uncongenial, since he was treated as a servant, and in 1781 he was suddenly dismissed. From then on he lived mostly in Vienna, and married Constanze Weber in 1782. He supported himself as a pianist, composer, and teacher, but his lack of business acumen often resulted in financial difficulties. His *Requiem*, unfinished at his death, was completed by a pupil. Mozart had been in failing health, and died impoverished. His works were catalogued chronologically by the musicologist Ludwig von Köchel (1800–1877) in 1862. The K-number system of identifying Mozart's works, which is still used, is based on this catalogue.

If only the whole world could feel the power of harmony.

Wolfgang Amadeus Mozart, letter 1778

Mubarak /muːˈbɑːræk/ Hosni 1928– . Egyptian politician, president from 1981. Vice president to Anwar Sadat from 1975, Mubarak succeeded him on his assassination. He has continued to pursue Sadat's moderate policies, and has significantly increased the freedom of the press and of political association, while trying to repress the growing Islamic fundamentalist movement.

Mubarak commanded the air force 1972–75 and was responsible for the initial victories in the Egyptian campaign of 1973 against Israel. He led Egypt's opposition to Iraq's 1990 invasion of Kuwait and had an instrumental role in arranging the Middle East peace conference in Nov 1991.

Mugabe /muːˈgɑːbi/ Robert (Gabriel) 1925– . Zimbabwean politician, prime minister from 1980 and president from 1987. He was in detention in Rhodesia for nationalist activities 1964–74, then carried on guerrilla warfare from Mozambique. As leader of ZANU he was in an uneasy alliance with Joshua →Nkomo of ZAPU (Zimbabwe African People's Union) from 1976. The two parties merged 1987.

His failure to anticipate and respond to the 1991–92 drought in southern Africa adversely affected his popularity.

Muggeridge /mʌgərɪdʒ/ Malcolm 1903–1990. English journalist and author. He worked for the *Guardian*, the *Calcutta Statesman*, the London *Evening Standard*, and the *Daily Telegraph* before becoming editor of *Punch* 1953–57.

Muhammad /məˈhæməd/ or *Mohammed*, *Mahomet c.* 570–632. Founder of Islam, born in Mecca on the Arabian peninsula. In about 616 he claimed to be a prophet and that the *Koran* was revealed to him by God (it was later written down by his followers), through the angel Jibra'el. He fled from persecution to the town now known as Medina in 622: the flight, *Hegira*, marks the beginning of the Islamic era.

Originally a shepherd and caravan conductor, Muhammad found leisure for meditation by his marriage with a wealthy widow in 595, and received his first revelation in 610. After some years of secret teaching, in which he taught submission to the will of Allah (Islam), he openly declared himself the prophet of God. The message, originally conveyed to the Arab people, became a universal message, and Muhammad the prophet of humankind. Following persecution from local townspeople, he fled to Medina. After the battle of Badr in 623, he was continuously victorious, entering Mecca as the recognized prophet of Arabia 630. Islam had spread throughout the Arabian peninsula by 632. The succession was troubled.

Muir /mjʊə/ Jean 1933– . British fashion designer who worked for Jaeger 1956–61 and set up her own fashion house 1961. In 1991 she launched a knitwear collection. Her clothes are characterized by soft, classic, tailored shapes in leathers and soft fabrics.

Muir /mjʊə/ John 1838–1914. Scottish-born US conservationist. From 1880 he headed a campaign that led to the establishment of Yosemite National Park. He was named adviser to the National Forestry Commission 1896 and continued to campaign for the preservation of wilderness areas for the rest of his life.

Born in Scotland, Muir emigrated to the USA with his family 1849. After attending the University of Wisconsin, he travelled widely and compiled detailed nature journals of his trips. He moved to California 1868 and later explored Glacier Bay in Alaska and mounted other expeditions to Australia and South America.

Muldoon /mʌlˈduːn/ Robert David 1921–1992. New Zealand National Party politician, prime minister 1975–84, during which time he pursued austere economic policies such as a wage-and-price policy to control inflation.

A chartered accountant, he was minister of finance 1967–72, and in 1974 replaced John Marshall as leader of the National Party, after the lat-

ter had been criticized as insufficiently aggressive in opposition. He became prime minister in 1975; he sought to introduce curbs on trade unions, was a vigorous supporter of the Western alliance, and a proponent of reform of the international monetary system. He was defeated in the general election of 1984 and was succeeded as prime minister by the Labour Party's David Lange. Muldoon announced his retirement from politics 1992.

Muller /mʌlə/ Hermann Joseph 1890–1967. US geneticist who discovered the effect of radiation on genes by his work on fruit flies. He was awarded the Nobel Prize for Medicine 1946.

Müller /mjuːlə/ Johannes Peter 1801–1858. German comparative anatomist whose studies of nerves and sense organs opened a new chapter in physiology by demonstrating the physical nature of sensory perception. His name is associated with a number of discoveries, including the *Müllerian ducts* in the mammalian fetus and the lymph heart in frogs.

Müller /mʊlə/ Paul 1899–1965. Swiss chemist awarded a Nobel prize in 1948 for his discovery 1939 of the first synthetic contact insecticide, DDT.

Mulliken /mʌlɪkən/ Robert Sanderson 1896–1986. US chemist and physicist who received the 1966 Nobel Prize for Chemistry for his development of the molecular orbital theory.

Mulock /mjuːlɒk/ unmarried name of British novelist Dinah →Craik.

Mulready /mʌlredi/ William 1786–1863. Irish painter of rural scenes, active in England. In 1840 he designed the first penny-postage envelope, known as the *Mulready envelope*.

Mulroney /mʌlˈrəʊni/ Brian 1939– . Canadian politician, Progressive Conservative Party leader from 1983, prime minister from 1984. He achieved a landslide in the 1984 election, and won the 1988 election on a platform of free trade with the USA, but with a reduced majority. Opposition within Canada to the Meech Lake agreement, a prerequisite to signing the 1982 Constitution, continued to plague Mulroney in his second term. By 1991 his public-opinion standing had fallen to an unprecedented low level. A revised reform package oct 1992 failed to gain voters' approval. By 1991 his public-opinion standing had fallen to an unprecedented low level and in Feb 1993 he announced his resignation.

Mumford /mʌmfəd/ Lewis 1895–1990. US urban planner and social critic, concerned with the adverse effect of technology on contemporary society.

His books, including *Technics and Civilization* 1934 and *The Culture of Cities* 1938, discussed the rise of cities and proposed the creation of green belts around large conurbations. His view of the importance of an historical perspective in urban planning for the future is reflected in his major work *The City in History* 1961.

Murat *French cavalry commander who distinguished himself in Napoleon's army, Joachim Murat married Bonaparte's sister Maria Annunciata. He was made king of Naples and introduced reforms and encouraged Italian nationalism. After the fall of Napoleon he was captured, court-martialled, and shot.*

Munch /muŋk/ Edvard 1863–1944. Norwegian painter and printmaker. He studied in Paris and Berlin, and his major works date from the period 1892–1908, when he lived mainly in Germany. His paintings often focus on neurotic emotional states. The *Frieze of Life* 1890s, a sequence of highly charged, symbolic paintings, includes some of his most characteristic images, such as *Skriket/The Scream* 1893. He later reused these in etchings, lithographs, and woodcuts.

Munch was influenced by van Gogh and Gauguin but soon developed his own expressive style, reducing his compositions to broad areas of colour with sinuous contours emphasized by heavy brushstrokes, distorting faces and figures. His first show in Berlin 1892 made a great impact on young German artists. In 1908 he suffered a nervous breakdown and returned to Norway. Later works include a series of murals 1910–15 in the assembly halls of Oslo University.

Münchhausen /mun'tʃauzən/ Karl Friedrich, Freiherr (Baron) von 1720–1797. German soldier, born in Hanover. He served with the Russian army against the Turks, and after his retirement in 1760 told exaggerated stories of his adventures. This idiosyncrasy was utilized by the German writer Rudolph Erich Raspe (1737–1794) in his extravagantly fictitious *Adventures of Baron Munchausen* 1785, which he wrote in English while living in London.

Mungo, St another name for St →Kentigern, first bishop of Glasgow.

Munnings /mʌnɪŋz/ Alfred 1878–1959. British painter excelling in racing and hunting scenes. As president of the Royal Academy 1944–49 he was outspoken in his dislike of 'modern art'.

Munro /mən'rəʊ/ Alice 1931– . Canadian author, known for her insightful short stories. Collections of her work include *Dance of the Happy Shades* 1968 and *The Progress of Love* 1987. She has written only one novel, *Lives of Girls and Women* 1971.

Munro /mən'rəʊ/ H(ugh) H(ector) English author who wrote under the pen name →Saki.

Murakami /ˌmuərə'kɑːmi/ Haruki 1949– . Japanese novelist and translator, one of Japan's bestselling writers, influenced by 20th-century US writers and popular culture. His dreamy, gently surrealist novels include *A Wild Sheep Chase* 1982 and *Norwegian Wood* 1987.

Murasaki /ˌmuərə'saki/ Shikibu *c.* 978–*c.* 1015. Japanese writer, a lady at the court. Her masterpiece of fiction, *The Tale of Genji*, is one of the classic works of Japanese literature, and may be the world's first novel.

She was a member of the Fujiwara clan, but her own name is not known; scholars have given her the name Murasaki after a character in the book. It deals with upper-class life in Heian Japan, centring on the affairs of Prince Genji. A portion of her diary and a number of poems also survive.

There are those who do not dislike wrong rumours if they are about the right men.
Murasaki Shikibu,
The Tale of Genji c. 1010

Murat /mjuə'rɑː/ Joachim 1767–1815. King of Naples 1808–1815. An officer in the French army, he was made king by Napoleon, but deserted him in 1813 in the vain hope that Austria and Great Britain would recognize him. In 1815 he attempted unsuccessfully to make himself king of all Italy, but when he landed in Calabria in an attempt to gain the throne he was captured and shot.

Murchison /mɜːtʃɪsən/ Roderick 1792–1871. Scottish geologist responsible for naming the Silurian period (in his book *The Silurian System* 1839). He surveyed Russia 1840–45. In 1855 he became director-general of the UK Geological Survey.

Murdoch /mɜːdɒk/ (Keith) Rupert 1931– . Australian-born US media magnate with worldwide interests. His UK newspapers, generally right-wing, include the *Sun*, the *News of the World*, and *The Times*; in the USA, he has a 50% share of 20th Century Fox, six Metromedia TV stations, and newspaper and magazine publishing companies. He purchased a 50% stake in a Hungarian tabloid, *Reform*, from 1989.

His newspapers (which also include *Today* and the *Sunday Times*) and 50% of Sky Television, the UK's first satellite television service, are controlled by News International, a wholly owned subsidiary of the Australian-based News Corporation. In

Nov 1990 Sky Television and its rival company British Satellite Broadcasting merged to form British Sky Broadcasting (BSkyB). Over 70% of newspapers sold in Australia are controlled by Murdoch.

Murdoch /ˈmɜːdɒk/ Iris 1919– . English novelist, born in Dublin. Her novels combine philosophical speculation with often outrageous situations and tangled human relationships. They include *The Sandcastle* 1957, *The Sea, The Sea* 1978, and *The Message to the Planet* 1989.

A lecturer in philosophy, she became in a fellow of St Anne's College, Oxford University 1948, and published *Sartre, Romantic Rationalist* 1953. Her novel *A Severed Head* 1961 was filmed 1983.

Writing is like getting married. One should never commit oneself until one is amazed at one's luck.

Iris **Murdoch**, *The Black Prince*

Murdock /ˈmɜːdɒk/ William 1754–1839. Scottish inventor, the first to use coal gas for domestic lighting. He illuminated his house and offices using coal gas in 1792, and in 1797 and 1798 he held public demonstrations of his invention.

Murger /mjʊəˈʒeə/ Henri 1822–1861. French writer, born in Paris. In 1848 he published *Scènes de la vie de bohème/Scenes of Bohemian Life* which formed the basis of Puccini's opera *La Bohème*.

Murillo /mjʊəˈrɪləʊ/ Bartolomé Esteban *c.* 1617–1682. Spanish painter, active mainly in Seville. He painted sentimental pictures of the Immaculate Conception; he also specialized in studies of street urchins.

Murillo was born in Seville. Visiting Madrid in the 1640s, he was befriended by the court painter Velázquez. After his return to Seville he received many religious commissions. He founded the academy of painting in Seville 1660 with the help of Herrera the Younger.

Murnau /ˈmʊənaʊ/ F W. Adopted name of Friedrich Wilhelm Plumpe 1889–1931. German silent-film director, known for his expressive images and 'subjective' use of a moving camera in *Der letzte Mamm/The Last Laugh* 1924. Other films include *Nosferatu* 1922 (a version of the Dracula story), *Sunrise* 1927, and *Tabu* 1931.

Murphy /ˈmɜːfi/ Audie 1924–1971. US actor and war hero who starred mainly in low-budget Westerns. His work includes *The Red Badge of Courage* 1951, *The Quiet American* 1958, and *The Unforgiven* 1960.

Murphy /ˈmɜːfi/ Dervla 1931– . Irish writer whose extensive travels have been recorded in books such as *Full Tilt* 1965.

Murphy /ˈmɜːfi/ Eddie 1961– . US film actor and comedian. His first film, *48 Hours* 1982,

introduced the street-wise, cocksure character that has become his speciality. Its great success, and that of his next two films, *Trading Places* 1983 and *Beverly Hills Cop* 1984, made him one of the biggest box-office draws of the 1980s.

Murphy began his career at 15 as a stand-up comedian before becoming a regular on the US television show *Saturday Night Live*. Other films include *Beverley Hills II* 1987, his filmed live show *Eddie Murphy Raw* 1987, *Coming to America* 1988, which he co-wrote, *Harlem Nights* 1989, which he produced and directed, and *Boomerang* 1992.

Murray /ˈmʌri/ family name of the dukes of Atholl; seated at Blair Castle, Perthshire, Scotland.

Murray /ˈmʌri/ (George) Gilbert (Aime) 1866–1957. British scholar. Born in Sydney, Australia, he was taken to England in 1877, and was professor of Greek at Glasgow University 1889–99 and at Oxford 1908–36. Author of *History of Ancient Greek Literature* 1897, he became known for verse translations of the Greek dramatists, such as Euripides, which made the plays more accessible to readers.

Murray /ˈmʌri/ James Augustus Henry 1837–1915. Scottish philologist. He was the first editor of the *Oxford English Dictionary* (originally the *New English Dictionary*) from 1878 until his death; the first volume was published 1884.

He edited more than half the dictionary single-handed, working in a shed (nicknamed the Scriptorium) in his back garden.

Murray /ˈmʌri/ James Stuart, Earl of Murray, or Moray 1531–1570. Regent of Scotland from 1567, an illegitimate son of James V. He was one of the leaders of the Scottish Reformation, and after the deposition of his half-sister →Mary Queen of Scots, he became regent. He was assassinated by one of her supporters.

Murray /ˈmʌri/ Joseph E 1919– . US surgeon whose work in the field of controlling rejection of organ transplants earned him a shared Nobel Prize for Medicine 1990.

Murrow /ˈmʌrəʊ/ Edward R(oscoe) 1908–1965. US broadcast journalist who covered World War II from London for the Columbia Broadcasting System (CBS).

Murry /ˈmʌri/ John Middleton 1889–1957. English writer. He produced studies of Dostoievsky, Keats, Blake, and Shakespeare; poetry; and an autobiographical novel, *Still Life* 1916. In 1913 he married the writer Katherine Mansfield, whose biography he wrote. He was a friend of the writer D H Lawrence.

Musashi /məˈsʌʃɪ/ Miyamato Japanese exponent of the martial arts, whose manual *A Book of Five Rings* on samurai strategy achieved great popularity in the USA when it appeared in translation 1974.

Musashi Miyamoto; see →Miyamoto Musashi, Japanese samurai.

Museveni /muːˈsevəni/ Yoweri Kaguta 1945– . Ugandan general and politician, president from 1986. He led the opposition to Idi Amin's regime 1971–78 and was minister of defence 1979–80 but, unhappy with Milton Obote's autocratic leadership, formed the National Resistance Army (NRA). When Obote was ousted in a coup in 1985, Museveni entered into a brief power-sharing agreement with his successor, Tito Okello, before taking over as president. Museveni leads a broad-based coalition government.

Museveni was educated in Uganda and at the University of Dar es Salaam, Tanzania. He entered the army, eventually rising to the rank of general. Until Amin's removal Museveni led the anti-Amin Front for National Salvation, and subsequently the National Resistance Army (NRA), which helped to remove Obote from power.

Musgrave /ˈmʌzgreɪv/ Thea 1928– . Scottish composer. Her works, in a conservative modern idiom, include concertos for horn, clarinet, and viola; string quartets; and operas, including *Mary, Queen of Scots* 1977.

Musial /ˈmjuːziəl/ Stan(ley Frank). Nicknamed 'Stan the Man'. 1920– . US baseball player. During his playing career of 22 years, he led the National League 6 times in hits, 8 times in doubles, 5 times in triples, and 7 times in batting average. He played his last season 1963 and was hired by the Cardinals as an executive.

Born in Donora, Pennsylvania, USA, Musial was an outstanding high-school athlete and was signed by the St Louis Cardinals 1938 and played as a Cardinal outfielder and first baseman from 1941.

Musial was elected to the Baseball Hall of Fame 1969.

Musil /ˈmuːzɪl/ Robert 1880–1942. Austrian novelist, author of the unfinished *Der Mann ohne Eigenschaften/The Man without Qualities* (three volumes, 1930–43). Its hero shares the author's background of philosophical study and scientific and military training, and is preoccupied with the problems of the self viewed from a mystic but agnostic viewpoint.

The glass I drink from is not large, but at least it is my own.

Alfred de Musset, *La Coupe et les lèvres*

Musset /ˈmjuːseɪ/ Alfred de 1810–1857. French poet and playwright. He achieved success with the volume of poems *Contes d'Espagne et d'Italie/Stories of Spain and Italy* 1829. His *Confession d'un enfant du siècle/Confessions of a Child of the Century* 1835 recounts his broken relationship with George Sand.

Born in Paris, he abandoned the study of law and medicine to join the circle of Victor Hugo. Typical of his work are the verse in *Les Nuits/Nights* 1835–37 and the short plays *Comédies et proverbes/Comedies and Proverbs* 1840.

Mussolini /ˌmʊsəˈliːni/ Benito 1883–1945. Italian dictator 1925–43. As founder of the Fascist Movement 1919 and prime minister from 1922, he became known as *Il Duce* ('the leader'). He invaded Ethiopia 1935–36, intervened in the Spanish Civil War 1936–39 in support of Franco, and conquered Albania 1939. In June 1940 Italy entered World War II supporting Hitler. Forced by military and domestic setbacks to resign 1943, Mussolini established a breakaway government in N Italy 1944–45, but was killed trying to flee the country.

Mussolini was born in the Romagna, the son of a blacksmith, and worked in early life as a teacher and journalist. He became active in the socialist movement, from which he was expelled 1914 for advocating Italian intervention in World War I. In 1919 he founded the Fascist Movement, whose programme combined violent nationalism with demagogic republican and anticapitalist slogans, and launched a campaign of terrorism against the socialists. This movement was backed by many landowners and industrialists and by the heads of the army and police, and in Oct 1922 Mussolini was in power as prime minister at the head of a coalition government. In 1925 he assumed dictatorial powers, and in 1926 all opposition parties were banned. During the years that followed, the political, legal, and education systems were remodelled on Fascist lines.

Mussolini's Blackshirt followers were the forerunners of Hitler's Brownshirts, and his career of conquest drew him into close cooperation with Nazi Germany. Italy and Germany formed the Axis alliance 1936. During World War II, Italian defeats in N Africa and Greece, the Allied invasion of Sicily, and discontent at home destroyed Mussolini's prestige, and in July 1943 he was compelled to resign by his own Fascist Grand Council. He was released from prison by German parachutists in Sept 1943 and set up a 'Republican Fascist' government in N Italy. In April 1945 he and his mistress, Clara Petacci, were captured by partisans at Lake Como while heading for the Swiss border, and shot. Their bodies were taken to Milan and hung upside down in a public square.

Mussorgsky /mʊˈsɔːgski/ Modest Petrovich 1839–1881. Russian composer who was largely self-taught. His opera *Boris Godunov* was completed in 1869, although not produced in St Petersburg until 1874. Some of his works were 'revised' by →Rimsky-Korsakov, and only recently has their harsh original beauty been recognized.

Mussorgsky, born in Karevo, resigned his commission in the army in 1858 to concentrate on music while working as a government clerk. A member of the group of nationalist composers, the Five, he was influenced by both folk music and literature. Among his other works are the incomplete operas *Khovanshchina* and *Sorochintsy Fair*, the orchestral *A Night on the Bald Mountain* 1867, the suite for piano *Pictures at an Exhibition* 1874, and many songs. Mussorgsky died in poverty, from alcoholism.

Mustafa Kemal /ˈmʊstəfə kəˈmɑːl/ Turkish leader who assumed the name of →Atatürk.

Muti /ˈmuːti/ Riccardo 1941– . Italian conductor of the Philharmonia Orchestra, London, 1973–82, the Philadelphia Orchestra from 1981, and artistic director of La Scala, Milan, from 1986. He is known as a purist, devoted to carrying out a composer's intentions to the last detail.

Mutsuhito /ˌmutsuˈhitəʊ/ personal name of the Japanese emperor →Meiji.

Muybridge /ˈmaɪbrɪdʒ/ Eadweard. Adopted name of Edward James Muggeridge 1830–1904. British photographer. He made a series of animal locomotion photographs in the USA in the 1870s and proved that, when a horse trots, there are times when all its feet are off the ground. He also explored motion in birds and humans.

Muzorewa /ˌmuːzəˈreɪwə/ Abel (Tendekayi) 1925– . Zimbabwean politician and Methodist bishop. He was president of the African National Council 1971–85 and prime minister of Rhodesia/Zimbabwe 1979–80. He was detained for a year in 1983–84. He is leader of the minority United Africa National Council.

Muzorewa was educated at Methodist colleges in Rhodesia and Nashville, Tennessee.

Mwinyi /mwiˈʔiːni/ Ali Hassan 1925– . Tanzanian socialist politician, president from 1985, when he succeeded Julius Nyerere. He began a revival of private enterprise and control of state involvement and spending.

Myers /ˈmaɪəz/ F(rederic) W(illiam) H(enry) 1843–1901. English psychic investigator and writer, coiner of the word 'telepathy'. He was a founder and one of the first presidents of the Society for Psychical Research (1900).

If our first clear facts about the unseen world seem small and trivial, should that deter us from the quest? As well might Columbus have sailed home again, with America in the offing, on the ground that it was not worth while to discover a continent which manifested itself only by dead logs.

F W H Myers, *Human Personality*

Myrdal /ˈmɜːdɑːl/ Gunnar 1898–1987. Swedish economist, author of many works on development economics. He shared a Nobel prize in 1974 with F A Hayek.

Myron /ˈmaɪrən/ c. 500–440 BC. Greek sculptor. His *Discobolus/Discus-Thrower* and *Athene and Marsyas*, much admired in his time, are known through Roman copies. They confirm his ancient reputation for brilliant composition and naturalism.

Nabokov /nə'bəʊkɒf/ Vladimir 1899–1977. US writer who left his native Russia 1917 and began writing in English in the 1940s. His most widely known book is *Lolita* 1955, the story of the middle-aged Humbert Humbert's infatuation with a precocious girl of 12. His other books include *Laughter in the Dark* 1938, *The Real Life of Sebastian Knight* 1945, *Pnin* 1957, and his memoirs *Speak, Memory* 1947.

Born in St Petersburg, Nabokov settled in the USA 1940, and became a US citizen 1945. He was professor of Russian literature at Cornell University 1948–59, producing a translation and commentary on Pushkin's *Eugene Onegin* 1963. He was also a lepidopterist (a collector of butterflies and moths), a theme used in his book *Pale Fire* 1962.

Life is a great surprise. I do not see why death should not be an even greater one.

Vladimir Nabokov *Pale Fire* 1962

Nadar /nə'dɑː/ adopted name of Gaspard-Félix Tournachon 1820–1910. French portrait photographer and caricaturist. He took the first aerial photographs (from a balloon 1858) and was the first to take flash photographs (using magnesium bulbs).

Nader /neɪdə/ Ralph 1934– . US lawyer and consumer advocate. Called the 'scourge of corporate morality', he led many major consumer campaigns. His book *Unsafe at Any Speed* 1965 led to US car-safety legislation.

Nadir /neɪdɪə/ Shah (Khan) c. 1880–1933. King of Afghanistan from 1929. Nadir played a key role in the 1919 Afghan War, but was subsequently forced into exile in France. He returned to Kabul in 1929 to seize the throne and embarked on an ambitious modernization programme. This alienated the Muslim clergy and in 1933 he was assassinated by fundamentalists. His successor as king was his son →Zahir Shah.

Nagy /nɒdʒ/ Imre 1895–1958. Hungarian politician, prime minister 1953–55 and 1956. He led the Hungarian revolt against Soviet domination in 1956, for which he was executed.

Nagy, an Austro-Hungarian prisoner of war in Siberia during World War I, became a Soviet citizen after the Russian Revolution, and lived in the USSR 1930–44. In 1953, after Stalin's death, he became prime minister, introducing liberal measures such as encouraging the production of consumer goods, but was dismissed 1955 by hardline Stalinist premier Rákosi. Reappointed Oct 1956 during the Hungarian uprising, he began taking liberalization further than the Soviets wanted; for example, announcing Hungarian withdrawal from the Warsaw Pact. Soviet troops entered Budapest, and Nagy was dismissed Nov 1956. He was captured by the KGB and shot. In 1989 the Hungarian Supreme Court recognized his leadership of a legitimate government and quashed his conviction for treachery.

Nahayan /ˌnɑːhəˈjɑːn/ Sheik Sultan bin Zayed al- 1918– . Emir of Abu Dhabi from 1969, when he deposed his brother, Sheik Shakhbut. He was elected president of the supreme council of the United Arab Emirates 1971. In 1991 he was implicated, through his majority ownership, in the international financial scandals associated with the Bank of Commerce and Credit International.

Before 1969 Sheik Nahayan was governor of the eastern province of Abu Dhabi, one of seven Trucial States in the Persian Gulf and Gulf of Oman, then under British protection. An absolute ruler, he was unanimously re-elected emir 1986 by other UAE sheiks, among whom he enjoys considerable popularity.

Nahum /neɪhəm/ 7th century BC. In the Old Testament, a Hebrew prophet, possibly born in Galilee, who forecast the destruction of Nineveh, the Assyrian capital, by the Medes in 612 BC.

Naipaul /naɪpɔːl/ V(idiadhar) S(urajprasad) 1932– . British writer, born in Trinidad of Hindu parents. His novels include *A House for Mr Biswas* 1961, *The Mimic Men* 1967, *A Bend in the River* 1979, and *Finding the Centre* 1984. His brother **Shiva(dhar) Naipaul** (1940–1985) was also a novelist (*Fireflies* 1970) and journalist.

Naismith /neɪsmɪθ/ James 1861–1939. Canadian-born inventor of basketball. He invented basketball as a game to be played indoors during the winter, while attending the Young Men's Christian Association (YMCA) Training School in Springfield, Massachusetts, USA, 1891. Among his books is *Basketball, Its Origin and Development*, published posthumously 1941.

Born in Almonte, Ontario, Canada, Naismith was educated at McGill University, where he later served as director of physical education. He received an MD degree from the University of Colorado and served on the physical education faculty of the University of Kansas 1898–1937.

Najibullah /ˌnædʒɪˈbʊlə/ Ahmadzai 1947– . Afghan communist politician, state president 1986–92. A member of the Politburo from 1981, he was leader of the People's Democratic Party of Afghanistan (PDPA) from 1986. Although his government initially survived the withdrawal of Soviet troops Feb 1989, continuing pressure from the mujaheddin forces resulted in his eventual overthrow.

A Pathan, Najibullah joined the communist PDPA 1965, allying with its gradualist Parcham (banner) faction, and was twice imprisoned for anti-government political activities during the 1960s and 1970s. After the Soviet invasion Dec 1979, Najibullah became head of the KHAD secret police and entered the PDPA Politburo 1981. He replaced Babrak Karmal as leader of the PDPA, and thus the nation, May 1986. His attempts to broaden the support of the PDPA regime had little success, and his hold on power became imperilled 1989 following the withdrawal of the Soviet military forces. The mujaheddin continued to demand his resignation and resisted any settlement under his regime. In the spring of 1992, he was captured while attempting to flee the country and placed under United Nations protection, pending trial by an Islamic court.

Nakasone /ˌnækəˈsəʊneɪ/ Yasuhiro 1917– . Japanese conservative politician, leader of the Liberal Democratic Party (LDP) and prime minister 1982–87. He stepped up military spending and increased Japanese participation in international affairs, with closer ties to the USA. He was forced to resign his party post May 1989 as a result of having profited from insider trading in the Recruit scandal. After serving a two-year period of atonement, he rejoined the LDP April 1991.

Nakasone was educated at Tokyo University. He held ministerial posts from 1967 and established his own faction within the conservative LDP. In 1982 he was elected president of the LDP and prime minister. He encouraged a less paternalist approach to economic management. Although embarrassed by the conviction of one of his supporters in the 1983 Lockheed corruption scandal, he was re-elected 1986 by a landslide.

Namath /ˈneɪməθ/ Joe (Joseph William) 1943– . US football player. In 1965 he signed with the New York Jets of the newly established American Football League and in 1969 led the team to a historic upset victory over the Baltimore Colts in Super Bowl III. After leaving the Jets 1977, he briefly played with the Los Angeles Rams.

Born in Beaver Falls, Pennsylvania, Namath played quarterback for the University of Alabama, leading his team to victory in the 1965 Orange Bowl. Knee injuries forced his retirement as a player 1978.

He later became a sports broadcaster and actor.

Namatjira /ˌnæməˈtʃɪərə/ Albert 1902–1959. Australian Aboriginal painter of watercolour landscapes of the Australian interior. Acclaimed after an exhibition in Melbourne in 1938, he died destitute.

Namuth /ˈnɑːmuːt/ Hans 1915–1990. German-born US photographer who specialized in portraits and documentary work. He began as a photojournalist in Europe in the 1930s and opened a portrait studio in New York in 1950. His work includes documentation of the Guatemalan Mam Indians (published as *Los Todos Santeros* 1989) and of US artists from the 1950s (published as *Artists 1950–1981*). He also carried out assignments for magazines.

Nanak /ˈnɑːnək/ 1469– c. 1539. Indian guru and founder of Sikhism, a religion based on the unity of God and the equality of all human beings. He was strongly opposed to caste divisions.

At 50, after many years travelling and teaching, he established a new town: Kartarpur, in the Punjab. Here he met his most trusted follower, Lehna. On his death-bed, Guru Nanak announced Lehna as his successor, and gave him the name Guru Angad.

Nana Sahib /ˈnɑːni ˈsɑːb/ popular name for Dandhu Panth 1820–c. 1859. The adopted son of a former peshwa (chief minister) of the Maratha people of central India, he joined the rebels in the Indian Mutiny 1857–58, and was responsible for the massacre at Kanpur when safe conducts given to British civilians were broken and many women and children massacred. After the failure of the mutiny he took refuge in Nepal.

Nancarrow /ˌnænˈkærəʊ/ Conlon 1912– . US composer who settled in Mexico 1940. Using a player-piano as a form of synthesizer, punching the rolls by hand, he experimented with complicated combinations of rhythm and tempo, producing a series of studies that anticipated minimalism and brought him recognition in the 1970s.

Nansen /ˈnænsən/ Fridtjof 1861–1930. Norwegian explorer and scientist. In 1893, he sailed to the Arctic in the *Fram*, which was deliberately allowed to drift north with an iceflow. Nansen, accompanied by F Hjalmar Johansen (1867–1923), continued north on foot and reached 86° 14′ N, the highest latitude then attained. After World War I, Nansen became League of Nations high commissioner for refugees. Nobel Peace Prize 1923.

He made his first voyage to Greenland waters in a sealing ship 1882, and in 1888–89 attempted to cross the Greenland icefield. He was professor of zoology and oceanography at the University of Christiania (now Oslo). Norwegian ambassador in London 1906–08.

The *Nansen passport* issued to stateless persons is named after him.

Napier /neɪpɪə/ Charles James 1782–1853. British general. He conquered Sind in India (now a province of Pakistan) 1841–43 with a very small force and governed it until 1847. He was the first commander to mention men from the ranks in his dispatches.

Napier /neɪpɪə/ John 1550–1617. Scottish mathematician who invented logarithms 1614 and 'Napier's bones', an early mechanical calculating device for multiplication and division.

Napier /neɪpɪə/ Robert Cornelis, 1st Baron Napier of Magdala 1810–1890. British field marshal. Knighted for his services in relieving Lucknow during the Indian Mutiny, he took part in capturing Peking (Beijing) 1860 during the war against China in 1860. He was commander in chief in India 1870–76 and governor of Gibraltar 1876–82.

Napoleon I /nə'pəʊlɪən/ Bonaparte 1769–1821. Emperor of the French 1804–14 and 1814–15. A general from 1796 in the Revolutionary Wars, in 1799 he overthrew the ruling Directory and made himself dictator. From 1803 he conquered most of Europe (the *Napoleonic Wars*) and installed his brothers as puppet kings (see ➔Bonaparte). After the Peninsular War and retreat from Moscow 1812, he was forced to abdicate 1814 and was banished to the island of Elba. In March 1815 he reassumed power but was defeated by British forces at the Battle of Waterloo and exiled to the island of St Helena. His internal administrative reforms and laws are still evident in France.

Napoleon, born in Ajaccio, Corsica, received a commission in the artillery 1785 and first distinguished himself at the siege of Toulon 1793. Having suppressed a royalist uprising in Paris 1795, he was given command against the Austrians in Italy and defeated them at Lodi, Arcole, and Rivoli 1796–97. Egypt, seen as a halfway house to India, was overrun and Syria invaded, but his fleet was destroyed by the British admiral ➔Nelson at the Battle of the Nile. Napoleon returned to France and carried out a coup against the government of the Directory to establish his own dictatorship, nominally as First Consul. The Austrians were again defeated at Marengo 1800 and the coalition against France shattered, a truce being declared 1802. A plebiscite the same year made him consul for life. In 1804 a plebiscite made him emperor.

While retaining and extending the legal and educational reforms of the Jacobins, Napoleon replaced the democratic constitution established by the Revolution with a centralized despotism, and by his concordat with Pius VII conciliated the Catholic church. The *Code Napoléon* remains the basis of French law.

War was renewed by Britain 1803, aided by Austria and Russia from 1805 and Prussia from 1806. Prevented by the British navy from invading Britain, Napoleon drove Austria out of the war by victories at Ulm and Austerlitz 1805, and Prussia by the victory at Jena 1806. Then, after the battles of Eylau and Friedland, he formed an alliance with Russia at Tilsit 1807. Napoleon now forbade entry of British goods to Europe, attempting an economic blockade known as the Continental System, occupied Portugal, and in 1808 placed his brother Joseph on the Spanish throne. Both countries revolted, with British aid, and Austria attempted to re-enter the war but was defeated at Wagram. In 1796 Napoleon had married ➔Josephine de Beauharnais, but in 1809, to assert his equality with the Habsburgs, he divorced her to marry the Austrian emperor's daughter, ➔Marie Louise.

When Russia failed to enforce the Continental System, Napoleon marched on and occupied Moscow, but his army's retreat in the bitter winter of 1812 encouraged Prussia and Austria to declare war again 1813. He was defeated at Leipzig and driven from Germany. Despite his brilliant campaign on French soil, the Allies invaded Paris and compelled him to abdicate April 1814; he was banished to the island of Elba, off the west coast of Italy. In March 1815 he escaped and took power for a hundred days, with the aid of Marshal ➔Ney, but Britain and Prussia led an alliance against him at Waterloo, Belgium, in June. Surrendering to the British, he again abdicated, and was exiled to the island of St Helena, 1,900 km/1,200 mi west of Africa, where he died. His body was brought back 1840 to be interred in the Hôtel des Invalides, Paris.

Napoleon III Napoleon III, emperor of France 1852–70. While exiled in London 1848, he enlisted as a special constable during the Chartist demonstrations. In the same year he returned to France to be elected president of the Second Republic, establishing the Second Empire by coup d'état 1852.

Napoleon II /nə'pəʊliən/ 1811–1832. Title given by the Bonapartists to the son of Napoleon I and →Marie Louise; until 1814 he was known as the king of Rome and after 1818 as the duke of Reichstadt. After his father's abdication 1814 he was taken to the Austrian court, where he spent the rest of his life.

Napoleon III /nə'pəʊliən/ 1808–1873. Emperor of the French 1852–70, known as *Louis-Napoleon*. After two attempted coups (1836 and 1840) he was jailed, then went into exile, returning for the revolution of 1848, when he became president of the Second Republic but soon turned authoritarian. In 1870 he was manoeuvred by the German chancellor Bismarck into war with Prussia; he was forced to surrender at Sedan, NE France, and the empire collapsed.

The son of Louis Bonaparte and Hortense de Beauharnais, brother and step-daughter respectively of Napoleon I, he led two unsuccessful revolts against the French king Louis Philippe, at Strasbourg 1836 and at Boulogne 1840. After the latter he was imprisoned. Escaping in 1846, he lived in London until 1848. He was elected president of the newly established French republic in Dec, and set himself to secure a following by posing as the champion of order and religion against the revolutionary menace. He secured his re-election by a military coup d'état 1851, and a year later was proclaimed emperor. Hoping to strengthen his regime by military triumphs, he joined in the Crimean War 1854–55, waged war with Austria 1859, winning the Battle of Solferino, annexed Savoy and Nice 1860, and attempted unsuccessfully to found a vassal empire in Mexico 1863–67. In so doing he aroused the mistrust of Europe and isolated France.

At home, his regime was discredited by its notorious corruption; republican and socialist opposition grew, in spite of severe repression, and forced Napoleon, after 1860, to make concessions in the direction of parliamentary government. After losing the war with Prussia he withdrew to England, where he died. His son by Empress →Eugénie, *Eugène Louis Jean Joseph Napoleon*, Prince Imperial (1856–79), was killed fighting with the British army against the Zulus in Africa.

Narasimha Rao /ˌnæərə'sɪŋhə 'raʊ/ P(amulaparti) V(enkata) 1921– . Indian politician, prime minister of India from 1991 and Congress (I) leader. He governed the state of Andhra Pradesh as chief minister 1971–73, and served in the Congress (I) cabinets of Indira and Rajiv Gandhi as minister of external affairs 1980–85 and 1988–90 and of human resources 1985–88. He took over the party leadership after the assassination of Rajiv Gandhi. Elected prime minister the following month, he instituted a reform of the economy.

Narayan /nə'raɪən/ Jaya Prakash 1902–1979. Indian politician. A veteran socialist, he was an associate of Vinobha Bham in the Bhoodan movement for rural reforms that took place during the last years of the Raj. He was prominent in the protest movement against Indira Gandhi's emergency regime, 1975–77, and acted as umpire in the Janata leadership contest that followed Indira Gandhi's defeat in 1977.

Nares /neəz/ George Strong 1831–1915. Scottish vice-admiral and explorer who sailed to the Canadian Arctic on an expedition in search of John →Franklin 1852, and again in 1876 when he discovered the Challenger Mountains. During 1872–76 he commanded the Challenger Expedition. His Arctic explorations are recounted in *Voyage to the Polar Seas* 1878.

Narses /nɑːsiːz/ 478–c. 573. Byzantine general. Originally a eunuch slave, he later became an official in the imperial treasury. He was joint commander with the Roman general Belisarius in Italy 538–39, and in 552 destroyed the Ostrogoths at Taginae in the Apennines.

Nash /næʃ/ (Frederic) Ogden 1902–1971. US poet and wit. He published numerous volumes of humorous, quietly satirical light verse, characterized by unorthodox rhymes and puns. They include *I'm a Stranger Here Myself* 1938, *Versus* 1949, and *Bed Riddance* 1970. Most of his poems first appeared in the *New Yorker*, where he held an editorial post and did much to establish the magazine's tone.

Nash /næʃ/ John 1752–1835. English architect. He laid out Regent's Park, London, and its approaches. Between 1813 and 1820 he planned Regent Street (later rebuilt), repaired and enlarged Buckingham Palace (for which he designed Marble Arch), and rebuilt Brighton Pavilion in flamboyant oriental style.

Nash /næʃ/ John Northcote 1893–1977. English illustrator, landscape artist, and engraver. He was the brother of the artist Paul Nash.

With few exceptions our artists have painted 'by the light of nature' ... This immunity from the responsibility of design has become a tradition.

Paul Nash letter to *The Times* 1933

Nash /næʃ/ Paul 1889–1946. English painter, an official war artist in world wars I and II. In the 1930s he was one of a group of artists promoting avant-garde styles in the UK. Two of his works are *Totes Meer/Dead Sea* (Tate Gallery, London) and *The Battle of Britain* (Imperial War Museum, London).

Nash was born in London. In his pictures of World War I, such as *The Menin Road*, in the Imperial War Museum, he created strange patterns out of the scorched landscape of the Western Front. During World War II he was appointed official war artist to the Air Ministry.

Nash /næʃ/ (Richard) 'Beau' 1674–1762. British dandy. As master of ceremonies at Bath from 1705, he made the town a fashionable spa resort, and introduced a polished code of manners into polite society.

Nash /næʃ/ Walter 1882–1968. New Zealand Labour politician. He was born in England, and emigrated to New Zealand 1909. He held ministerial posts 1935–49, was prime minister 1957–60, and leader of the Labour Party until 1963.

Nashe /næʃ/ Thomas 1567–1601. English poet, satirist, and anti-Puritan pamphleteer. Born in Suffolk, he settled in London about 1588, where he was rapidly drawn into the Martin Marprelate controversy (a pamphleteering attack on the clergy of the Church of England by Puritans), and wrote at least three attacks on the Martinists. Among his later works are the satirical *Pierce Pennilesse* 1592 and the religious *Christes Teares over Jerusalem* 1593; his *The Unfortunate Traveller* 1594 is a picaresque narrative mingling literary parody and mock-historical fantasy.

Nasmyth /neɪsmɪθ/ Alexander 1758–1840. Scottish portrait and landscape painter. His portrait of the poet Robert Burns hangs in the Scottish National Gallery.

Nasmyth, born in Edinburgh, concentrated from 1806 on landscapes, usually Classical and Italianate and often featuring buildings. He is regarded as the creator of the Scottish landscape-painting tradition. He was also a set designer and an inventor, experimenting with the application of steam power to ship propulsion.

Nasmyth /neɪsmɪθ/ James 1808–1890. Scottish engineer and machine-tool manufacturer, whose many inventions included the steel hammer in 1839. At his factory near Manchester, he developed the steam hammer for making large steel forgings (the first of which was the propeller shaft for Brunel's steamship *Great Britain*).

Abdel Nasser is no more than a transient phenomenon that will run its course and leave.

Gamal Abdel Nasser 1967

Nasser /næsə/ Gamal Abdel 1918–1970. Egyptian politician, prime minister 1954–56 and from 1956 president of Egypt (the United Arab Republic 1958–71). In 1952 he was the driving power behind the Neguib coup, which ended the monarchy. His nationalization of the Suez Canal 1956 led to an Anglo-French invasion and the Suez Crisis, and his ambitions for an Egyptian-led union of Arab states led to disquiet in the Middle East (and in the West). Nasser was also an early and influential leader of the nonaligned movement.

Nasser entered the army from Cairo Military Academy, and was wounded in the Palestine War of 1948–49. Initially unpopular after the 1952 coup, he took advantage of demands for change by initiating land reform and depoliticizing the army. His position was secured by an unsuccessful assassination attempt 1954 and his handling of the Suez Crisis 1956.

Nast /næst/ Thomas 1840–1902. German-born US illustrator and cartoonist. During the American Civil War, Nast served as a staff artist for *Harper's Weekly* and later drew its editorial cartoons. His vivid caricatures helped bring down New York's Boss Tweed, the corrupt politician, and established the donkey and the elephant as the symbols of Democrats and Republicans, respectively.

Nation /neɪʃn/ Carrie Amelia Moore 1846–1911. US Temperance Movement crusader during the Prohibition 1920–33. Protesting against Kansas state's flagrant disregard for the prohibition law, she marched into illegal saloons with a hatchet, lecturing the patrons on the abuses of alcohol and smashing bottles and bar.

Born in Kentucky, she briefly worked as a teacher in Missouri. After the death of her alcoholic first husband, she became the country's most outspoken prohibitionist. She circulated *Smasher's Mail* as part of her campaign.

Navratilova /ˌnævrætɪˈləʊvə/ Martina 1956– . Czech tennis player who became a naturalized US citizen 1981. The most outstanding woman player of the 1980s, she had 55 Grand Slam victories by 1991, including 18 singles titles. She has won the Wimbledon singles title a record nine times, including six in succession 1982–87.

Navratilova won her first Wimbledon title in 1976 (doubles with Chris Evert). Between 1974 and 1988 she won 52 Grand Slam titles (singles and doubles), second only to Margaret →Court. Her first Grand Slam win was mixed doubles at the 1974 French Championship (with Ivan Molina, Colombia).

Nazarbayev /ˌnæzəˈbaɪev/ Nursultan 1940– . President of Kazakhstan from 1990. In the Soviet period he was prime minister of the republic 1984–89 and leader of the Kazakh Communist Party 1989–91, which established itself as the independent Socialist Party of Kazakhstan (SPK) Sept 1991. He advocates free-market policies, yet enjoys the support of the environmentalist lobby. He joined the Communist Party at 22 and left it after the failed Soviet coup 1991.

N'Dour /ən'dʊə/ Youssou 1959– . Senegalese singer, songwriter, and musician whose fusion of traditional mbalax percussion music with bluesy Arab-style vocals, accompanied by African and electronic instruments, became popular in the West in the 1980s on albums such as *Immigrés* 1984 with the band Le Super Etoile de Dakar.

Neagle /ˈniːgəl/ Anna 1904–1986. English actress, made a star by her producer- director husband Herbert Wilcox (1890–1977), whose films include *Nell Gwyn* 1934, *Victoria the Great* 1937, and *Odette* 1950.

Neale /niːl/ John Mason 1818–1866. Anglican cleric. He translated ancient and medieval hymns, including 'Jerusalem, the Golden'.

Neave /niːv/ Airey (Middleton Sheffield) 1916–1979. British intelligence officer and Conservative member of Parliament 1953–79, a close adviser to Prime Minister Thatcher. During World War II he escaped from Colditz, a German high-security prison camp. As shadow undersecretary of state for Northern Ireland from 1975, he became a target for extremist groups and was assassinated by an Irish terrorist bomb.

Nebuchadnezzar /ˌnebjʊkədˈnezə/ or *Nebuchadrezzar II* king of Babylonia from 60 BC. Shortly before his accession he defeated the Egyptians at Carchemish and brought Palestine and Syria into his empire. Judah revolted, with Egyptian assistance, 596 and 587–586 BC; on both occasions he captured Jerusalem and took many Hebrews into captivity. He largely rebuilt Babylon and constructed the hanging gardens.

Necker Jacques 1732–1804. French politician. As finance minister 1776–81, he attempted reforms, and was dismissed through Queen Marie Antoinette's influence. Recalled 1788, he persuaded Louis XVI to summon the States General (parliament), which earned him the hatred of the court, and in July 1789 he was banished. The outbreak of the French Revolution with the storming of the Bastille forced his reinstatement, but he resigned Sept 1790.

Needham /ˈniːdəm/ Joseph 1900– . British biochemist and sinologist known for his work on the history of Chinese science. He worked first as a biochemist concentrating mainly on problems in embryology. In the 1930s he learned Chinese and began to collect material. The first volume of his *Science and Civilisation in China* was published in 1954 and by 1989 fifteen volumes had appeared.

Nefertiti /ˌnefəˈtiːti/ or *Nofretete* queen of Egypt who ruled *c.* 1372–50 BC; wife of the pharaoh →Ikhnaton.

Nehru /ˈneəruː/ Jawaharlal 1889–1964. Indian nationalist politician, prime minister from 1947. Before the partition (the division of British India into India and Pakistan), he led the socialist wing of the Nationalist Congress Party, and was second in influence only to Mohandas →Gandhi. He was imprisoned nine times by the British 1921–45 for political activities. As prime minister from the creation of the dominion (later republic) of India in Aug 1947, he originated the idea of nonalignment (neutrality towards major powers). His daughter was Prime Minister Indira →Gandhi.

Neizvestny /neɪzˈvestni/ Ernst 1926– . Russian artist and sculptor who argued with Khrushchev in 1962 and eventually left the country 1976. His works include a vast relief in the Moscow Institute of Electronics and the Aswan monument, the tallest sculpture in the world.

Nekrasov /nɪˈkraːsɒf/ Nikolai Alekseevich 1821–1877. Russian poet and publisher. He espoused the cause of the freeing of the serfs and identified himself with the peasants in such poems as 'Who Can Live Happy in Russia?' 1876.

Nelson /ˈnelsən/ Azumah 1958– . Ghanaian featherweight boxer, world champion from 1984 to 1987.

Nelson won the 1978 Commonwealth Games at featherweight, the World Boxing Championship (WBC) featherweight title in 1984, beating Wilfredo Gomez, and in 1988 captured the super-featherweight title by beating Mario Martinez.

Nelson /ˈnelsən/ Horatio, Viscount Nelson 1758–1805. English admiral. He joined the navy in 1770. In the Revolutionary Wars against France he lost the sight in his right eye 1794 and lost his right arm 1797. He became a national hero, and rear admiral, after the victory off Cape St Vincent, Portugal. In 1798 he tracked the French fleet to Aboukir Bay and almost entirely destroyed it in the Battle of the Nile. In 1801 he won a decisive victory over Denmark at the Battle of Copenhagen, and in 1805, after two years of blockading Toulon, another over the Franco-Spanish fleet at the Battle of Trafalgar, near Gibraltar.

Nelson was almost continuously on active service in the Mediterranean 1793–1800, and lingered at Naples for a year, during which he helped to crush a democratic uprising and fell completely under the influence of Lady →Hamilton. In 1800 he returned to England and soon after separated from his wife, Frances Nesbit (1761–1831). He was promoted to vice admiral 1801, and sent to the Baltic to operate against the Danes, nominally as second in command; in fact, it was Nelson who was responsible for the victory of Copenhagen and for negotiating peace with Denmark. On his return to England he was created a viscount.

In 1803 he received the Mediterranean command and for nearly two years blockaded Toulon. When in 1805 his opponent, the French admiral Pierre de Villeneuve (1763–1806), eluded him, Nelson pursued him to the West Indies and back, and on 21 Oct defeated the combined French and Spanish fleets off Cape Trafalgar, 20 of the enemy ships being captured. Nelson himself was mortally wounded. He is buried in St Paul's Cathedral, London.

England expects every man will do his duty.

Horatio Nelson at the Battle of Trafalgar 1805

Nemerov /ˈnemərɒv/ Howard 1920– . US poet, critic, and novelist. He published his poetry collection *Guide to the Ruins* 1950, a short-story collection *A Commodity of Dreams* 1959, and in 1977 his *Collected Poems* won both the National Book Award and the Pulitzer Prize.

Nennius /ˈneniəs/ c. 800. Welsh historian, believed to be the author of a Latin *Historia Britonum*, which contains the earliest reference to King Arthur's wars against the Saxons.

Knowledge is the death of research.

Hermann Nernst

Nernst /ˈneənst/ (Walther) Hermann 1864–1941. German physical chemist. His investigations, for which he won the 1920 Nobel Prize for Chemistry, were concerned with heat changes in chemical reactions. He proposed in 1906 the principle known as the ***Nernst heat theorem*** or the third law of thermodynamics: the law states that chemical changes at the temperature of absolute zero involve no change of entropy (disorder).

Born in Briesen, Prussia, Nernst was professor of chemistry at Göttingen 1905, and Berlin. He suffered under the Nazi regime because two of his daughters married Jews.

Nero /ˈnɪərəʊ/ AD 37–68. Roman emperor from 54. He is said to have murdered his stepfather →Claudius' son Britannicus, his own mother, his wives Octavia and Poppaea, and many others. After the great fire of Rome 64, he persecuted the Christians, who were suspected of causing it. Military revolt followed 68; the Senate condemned Nero to death, and he committed suicide.

Son of Domitius Ahenobarbus and Agrippina, Nero was adopted by Claudius, and succeeded him as emperor in 54. He was a poet and connoisseur of art, and performed publicly as an actor and a singer.

Neruda /neˈruːdə/ Pablo. Pen name of Neftalí Ricardo Reyes y Basualto 1904–1973. Chilean poet and diplomat. His work includes lyrics and the epic poem of the American continent *Canto General* 1950. He was awarded the Nobel Prize for Literature 1971. He served as consul and ambassador to many countries.

After World War II he entered political life in Chile as a communist, and was a senator 1945–48. He went into exile in 1948 but returned in 1952; he later became consul to France 1971–72.

Nerva /ˈnɜːvə/ Marcus Cocceius Nerva AD c. 35–98. Roman emperor. He was proclaimed emperor on Domitian's death AD 96, and introduced state loans for farmers, family allowances, and allotments of land to poor citizens.

Nerval /neəˈvæl/ Gérard de. Pen name of Gérard Labrunie 1808–1855. French writer and poet, precursor of French Symbolism and Surrealism.

His writings include the travelogue *Voyage en Orient* 1851; short stories, including the collection *Les Filles du feu* 1854; poetry; a novel *Aurélia* 1855, containing episodes of visionary psychosis; and drama. He lived a wandering life, and suffered from periodic insanity, finally taking his own life.

Nervi /ˈneəviː/ Pier Luigi 1891–1979. Italian architect who used soft steel mesh within concrete to give it flowing form. For example, the Turin exhibition hall 1949, the UNESCO building in Paris 1952, and the cathedral at New Norcia, near Perth, Australia, 1960.

Nesbit /ˈnezbɪt/ E(dith) 1858–1924. English author of children's books, including *The Story of the Treasure Seekers* 1899 and *The Railway Children* 1906. Her stories often have a humorous magical element, as in *Five Children and It* 1902. *The Treasure Seekers* is the first of several books about the realistically squabbling Bastable children. Nesbit was a Fabian socialist and supported her family by writing.

Your feelings are a beastly nuisance, if once you begin to let yourself think about them.

E Nesbit
The Story of the Treasure Seekers 1899

Neumann /ˈnɔɪmæn/ Balthasar 1687–1753. German Rococo architect and military engineer, whose work includes the bishop's palace in Würzburg.

Neutra /ˈnɔɪtrɑː/ Richard Joseph 1892–1970. Austrian-born architect who became a US citizen 1929. His works, often in impressive landscape settings, include Lovell Health House, Los Angeles (1929), and Mathematics Park, Princeton, New Jersey.

Neville Brothers, the US rhythm-and-blues group, exponents of the New Orleans style, internationally successful from the 1980s. There are four Neville brothers, the eldest of whom has been active from the 1950s in various musical ventures. Albums include *Yellow Moon* 1989.

Aaron Neville (1941–) had hits as a vocalist in the 1960s, for example 'Tell It Like It Is' 1966. Two of the brothers – Art (1938–) and Cyril (1950–) – were in the Meters, a critically acclaimed group formed in the late 1960s, whose albums include *The Wild Tschoupitoulas* 1976. The Neville Brothers line-up comprising all four brothers, plus other musicians, was formed 1978.

Newbolt /ˈnjuːbəʊlt/ Henry John 1862–1938. English poet and naval historian. His works include *The Year of Trafalgar* 1905 and *A Naval History of the War* 1920 on World War I. His *Songs of the Sea* 1904 and *Songs of the Fleet* 1910 were set to music by Charles Villiers Stanford.

Newby /ˈnjuːbi/ (George) Eric 1919– . English travel writer and sailor. His books include *A Short Walk in the Hindu Kush* 1958, *The Big Red Train Ride* 1978, *Slowly Down the Ganges* 1966, and *A Traveller's Life* 1985.

Newcastle /ˈnjuːkɑːsəl/ Thomas Pelham-Holles, Duke of Newcastle 1693–1768. British Whig politician, prime minster 1754–56 and 1757–62. He served as secretary of state for thirty years from 1724, then succeeded his younger brother Henry →Pelham as prime minister 1754. In 1756 he resigned as a result of setbacks in the Seven Years' War, but returned to office 1757 with →Pitt the Elder (1st Earl of Chatham) taking responsibility for the conduct of the war.

Newcomen /ˈnjuːkʌmən/ Thomas 1663–1729. English inventor of an early steam engine. He patented his 'fire engine' 1705, which was used for pumping water from mines until James →Watt invented one with a separate condenser.

Ne Win /ˌneɪ ˈwɪn/ adopted name of Maung Shu Maung 1911– . Myanmar (Burmese) politician, prime minister 1958–60, ruler from 1962 to 1974, president 1984–81, and chair until 1988 of the ruling Burma Socialist Programme Party (BSPP). His domestic 'Burmese Way to Socialism' policy programme brought the economy into serious decline.

Active in the Nationalist movement during the 1930s, Ne Win joined the Allied forces in the war against Japan in 1945 and held senior military posts before becoming prime minister in 1958. After leading a coup in 1962, he ruled the country as chair of the revolutionary council until 1974, when he became state president. Although he stepped down as president 1981, he continued to dominate political affairs, but was forced to resign as BSPP leader 1988 after riots in Rangoon (now Yangon).

Newlands /ˈnjuːləndz/ John Alexander Reina 1838–1898. English chemist who worked as an industrial chemist; he prepared in 1863 the first periodic table of the elements arranged in order of relative atomic masses, and pointed out the 'Law of Octaves' whereby every eighth element has similar properties. He was ridiculed at the time, but five years later Russian chemist Dmitri Mendeleyev published a more developed form of the table, also based on atomic masses, which forms the basis of the one used today (arranged by atomic number).

Newman /ˈnjuːmən/ Barnett 1905–1970. US painter, sculptor, and theorist. His paintings are solid-coloured canvases with a few sparse vertical stripes. They represent a mystical pursuit of simple or elemental art. His sculptures, such as *Broken Obelisk* 1963–67, consist of geometric shapes on top of each other.

Newman /ˈnjuːmən/ John Henry 1801–1890. English Roman Catholic theologian. While still an Anglican, he wrote a series of *Tracts for the Times*,

Newcastle British Whig politician Thomas Pelham-Holles, Duke of Newcastle, in a portrait by William Hoare (c. 1752). Credited with holding the Whig party together despite George III's opposition, the Duke of Newcastle was compelled to give William Pitt the Elder the lead in the House of Commons and direction of foreign affairs.

which gave their name to the Tractarian Movement (subsequently called the Oxford Movement) for the revival of Catholicism. He became a Catholic 1845 and was made a cardinal 1879. In 1864 his autobiography, *Apologia pro vita sua*, was published.

Newman, born in London, was ordained in the Church of England 1824, and in 1827 became vicar of St Mary's, Oxford. There he was influenced by the historian R H Froude and the Anglican priest Keble, and in 1833 published the first of the *Tracts for the Times*. They culminated in *Tract 90* 1841 which found the Thirty-Nine Articles of the Anglican church compatible with Roman Catholicism, and Newman was received into the Roman Catholic Church in 1845. He was rector of Dublin University 1854–58 and published his lectures on education as *The Idea of a University* 1873. His poem *The Dream of Gerontius* appeared in 1866, and *The Grammar of Assent*, an analysis of the nature of belief, in 1870. He wrote the hymn 'Lead, kindly light' 1833.

To attempt to be guided by love alone, would be like attempting to walk in a straight line by steadily gazing on some star. It is too high.

John Henry Newman sermon April 1837

Newman /ˈnjuːmən/ Paul 1925– . US actor and director, Hollywood's leading male star of the 1960s and 1970s. His films include *Somebody Up There Likes Me* 1956, *Cat on a Hot Tin Roof* 1958, *The Hustler* 1961, *Sweet Bird of Youth* 1962, *Hud* 1963, *Cool Hand Luke* 1967, *Butch Cassidy and the Sundance Kid* 1969, *The Sting* 1973, *The Verdict* 1983, *The Color of Money* 1986 (for which he won an Academy Award), and *Mr and Mrs Bridge* 1991.

He directed his wife Joanne Woodward in *Rachel, Rachel* 1968 and other films and was noted as a racing-car driver and for his philanthropic activities. The profits from his Newman's Own specialty foods were donated to charity.

Newton /ˈnjuːtn/ Isaac 1642–1727. English physicist and mathematician who laid the foundations of physics as a modern discipline. He discovered the law of gravity, created calculus, discovered that white light is composed of many colours, and developed the three standard laws of motion still in use today. During 1665–66, he discovered the binomial theorem, and differential and integral calculus, and also began to investigate the phenomenon of gravitation. In 1685, he expounded his universal law of gravitation. His *Philosophiae naturalis principia mathematica*, usually referred to as *Principia*, was published in 1687, with the aid of Edmund →Halley.

Born at Woolsthorpe, Lincolnshire, he was educated at Grantham grammar school and Trinity College, Cambridge, of which he became a Fel-

Newton Portrait of English physicist and mathematician Isaac Newton by Godfrey Kneller (1702). Applying mathematical method to the study of nature, Newton believed that the order he found in the natural world could only have proceeded from a creator God. He was the first scientist to be buried in Westminster Abbey.

low in 1667. He was elected a Fellow of the Royal Society in 1672, and soon afterwards published his *New Theory about Light and Colours. De Motu corporum in gyrum/On the motion of bodies in orbit* was written in 1684. Newton resisted James II's attacks on the liberties of the universities, and sat in the parliaments of 1689 and 1701/1702 as a Whig. Appointed warden of the Royal Mint in 1696, and master in 1699, he carried through a reform of the coinage. He was elected president of the Royal Society in 1703, and was knighted in 1705. Most of the last 30 years of his life were taken up by studies of theology and chronology, and experiments in alchemy. He was buried in Westminster Abbey.

If I have seen farther it is by standing on the shoulders of giants.

Isaac Newton letter to Robert Hooke Feb 1675

Ney /neɪ/ Michael, Duke of Elchingen, Prince of Ney 1769–1815. Marshal of France under →Napoleon I, who commanded the rearguard of the French army during the retreat from Moscow, and for his personal courage was called 'the bravest of the brave'. When Napoleon returned from Elba, Ney was sent to arrest him, but instead deserted to him and fought at Waterloo. He was subsequently shot for treason.

The son of a cooper, he joined the army in 1788, and rose from the ranks. He served throughout the Revolutionary and Napoleonic Wars.

Ngugi wa Thiong'o /əŋˈguːgi wɑː θiˈɒŋgəʊ/ 1938– . Kenyan writer of essays, plays, short stories, and novels. He was imprisoned after the performance of the play *Ngaahika Ndeenda/I Will Marry When I Want* 1977 and lived in exile from 1982. His novels, written in English and Gikuyu, include *The River Between* 1965, *Petals of Blood* 1977, and *Caitaani Mutharaba-ini/Devil on the Cross* 1982, and deal with colonial and post-independence oppression.

Nguyen Van Linh /ˈnuːjən væn ˈlɪn/ 1914– . Vietnamese communist politician, member of the Politburo 1976–81 and from 1985; party leader 1986–91. He began economic liberalization and troop withdrawal from Cambodia and Laos.

Nguyen, born in North Vietnam, joined the anti-colonial Thanh Nien, a forerunner of the current Communist Party of Vietnam (CPV), in Haiphong 1929. He spent much of his subsequent party career in the South as a pragmatic reformer. He was a member of CPV's Politburo and secretariat 1976–81, suffered a temporary setback when party conservatives gained the ascendancy, and re-entered the Politburo in 1985, becoming CPV leader in Dec 1986 and resigning from the post June 1991.

Nichiren /nɪtʃɪren/ 1222–1282. Japanese Buddhist monk, founder of the sect that bears his name. It bases its beliefs on the *Lotus Sūtra*, which Nichiren held to be the only true revelation of the teachings of Buddha, and stresses the need for personal effort to attain enlightenment.

Nicholas /nɪkələs/ two tsars of Russia:

Nicholas I 1796–1855. Tsar of Russia from 1825. His Balkan ambitions led to war with Turkey 1827–29 and the Crimean War 1853–56.

Nicholas II 1868–1918. Tsar of Russia 1894–1917. He was dominated by his wife, Tsarina →Alexandra, who was under the influence of the religious charlatan →Rasputin. His mismanagement of the Russo-Japanese War and of internal affairs led to the revolution of 1905, which he suppressed, although he was forced to grant limited constitutional reforms. He took Russia into World War I in 1914, was forced to abdicate in 1917 after the Russian Revolution and was executed with his family.

Nicholas of Cusa /kjuːzə/ or *Nicolaus Cusanus* 1401–1464. German philosopher, involved in the transition from scholasticism to the philosophy of modern times. He argued that knowledge is learned ignorance (*docta ignorantia*) since God, the ultimate object of knowledge, is above the opposites by which human reason grasps the objects of nature. He also asserted that the universe is boundless and has no circumference, thus breaking with medieval cosmology.

Nicholas, St /nɪkələs/ also known as *Santa Claus* 4th century AD. In the Christian church, patron saint of Russia, children, merchants, sailors, and pawnbrokers; bishop of Myra (now in Turkey). His legendary gifts of dowries to poor girls led to the custom of giving gifts to children on the eve of his feast day, 6 Dec, still retained in some countries, such as the Netherlands; elsewhere the custom has been transferred to Christmas Day. His emblem is three balls.

Nicholson /nɪkəlsən/ Ben 1894–1982. English abstract artist. After early experiments influenced by Cubism and de Stijl (see →Mondrian), Nicholson developed a style of geometrical reliefs, notably a series of white reliefs (from 1933).

Son of poster artist William →Nicholson, he studied at the Slade School of Art, London, as well as in Europe and in California. He was awarded the Order of Merit 1968. He married the sculptor Barbara Hepworth.

Nicholson /nɪkəlsən/ Jack 1937– . US film actor who, in the late 1960s, captured the mood of nonconformist, uncertain young Americans in such films as *Easy Rider* 1969 and *Five Easy Pieces* 1970. He subsequently became a mainstream Hollywood star, appearing in *Chinatown* 1974, *One Flew over the Cuckoo's Nest* (Academy Award) 1975, *The Shining* 1979, *Terms of Endearment* (Academy Award) 1983, and *Batman* 1989.

Nicholson /nɪkəlsən/ John 1822–1857. British general and colonial administrator in India, born in Ireland. He was administrative officer at Bannu in the Punjab 1851–56, and was highly regarded for the justness of his rule. Promoted to brigadier general 1857 on the outbreak of the Indian Mutiny, he defeated resistance in the Punjab, but was killed during the storming of Delhi.

Nicholson /nɪkəlsən/ William 1872–1949. English artist who developed the art of poster design in partnership with his brother-in-law, James Pryde. They were known as 'The Beggarstaff Brothers'. He was the father of Ben Nicholson.

Nicklaus /nɪkləs/ Jack (William) 1940– . US golfer, nicknamed 'the Golden Bear'. He won a record 20 major titles, including 18 professional majors between 1962 and 1986.

Nicklaus played for the US Ryder Cup team six times 1969–81 and was nonplaying captain 1983 and 1987 when the event was played over the course he designed at Muirfield Village, Ohio.

He was voted the 'Golfer of the Century' 1988.

Nicolle /nɪ'kɒl/ Charles 1866–1936. French bacteriologist whose discovery in 1909 that typhus is transmitted by the body louse made the armies of World War I introduce delousing as a compulsory part of the military routine. Nobel Prize for Medicine 1928.

His original observation was that typhus victims, once admitted to hospitals, did not infect the staff; he speculated that transmission must be via the skin or clothes, which were washed as standard procedure for new admissions. The experimental evidence was provided by infecting a healthy monkey using a louse recently fed on an infected chimpanzee.

Nicolson /nɪkəlsən/ Harold 1886–1968. British author and diplomat. His works include biographies (*Lord Carnock* 1930; *Curzon: The Last Phase* 1934; and *King George V* 1952) and studies such as *Monarchy* 1962, as well as *Diaries and Letters* 1930–62. He married Vita →Sackville-West in 1913.

Intellectuals incline to be individualists, or even independents, are not team conscious and tend to regard obedience as a surrender of personality.

Harold Nicolson
in *Observer* Oct 1958

Niebuhr /niːbʊə/ Barthold Georg 1776–1831. German historian. He was Prussian ambassador in Rome 1816–23, and professor of Roman history at Bonn until 1831. His three-volume *History of Rome* 1811–32 critically examined original sources.

Niebuhr /ni:buə/ Karsten 1733–1815. Danish map-maker, surveyor, and traveller, sent by the Danish government to explore the Arabian peninsula 1761–67.

Niebuhr /ni:buə/ Reinhold 1892–1971. US Protestant theologian, a Lutheran minister. His *Moral Man and Immoral Society* 1932 attacked depersonalized modern industrial society but denied the possibility of fulfilling religious and political utopian aspirations, a position that came to be known as Christian Realism. Niebuhr was a pacifist, activist, and socialist but advocated war to stop totalitarianism in the 1940s.

Nielsen /ni:lsən/ Carl (August) 1865–1931. Danish composer. His works show a progressive tonality, as in his opera *Saul and David* 1902 and six symphonies.

He also composed concertos for violin 1911 and clarinet 1928, chamber music, piano works, and songs.

Niemeyer /ni:maɪə/ Oscar 1907– . Brazilian architect, joint designer of the United Nations headquarters in New York and of many buildings in Brasília, capital of Brazil.

Niemöller /ni:mɜ:lə/ Martin 1892–1984. German Christian Protestant pastor. He was imprisoned in a concentration camp 1938–45 for campaigning against Nazism in the German church. He was president of the World Council of Churches 1961–68.

Niepce /njeps/ Joseph Nicéphore 1765–1833. French pioneer of photography. Niepce invented heliography, a precursor of photography that fixed images onto pewter plates coated with pitch and required eight-hour exposures. He produced the world's first photograph from nature 1826 and later collaborated with →Daguerre on the faster daguerreotype process.

The first photograph was a positive image, a view from Niepce's attic bedroom. The image was captured, after an eight-hour exposure, in a camera obscura on a metal plate coated with light-sensitive bitumen. The place has survived and is to be found in the University of Texas.

Nietzsche /ni:tʃə/ Friedrich Wilhelm 1844–1900. German philosopher who rejected the accepted absolute moral values and the 'slave morality' of Christianity. He argued that 'God is dead' and therefore people were free to create their own values. His ideal was the *übermensch*, or 'Superman', who would impose his will on the weak and worthless. Nietzsche claimed that knowledge is never objective but always serves some interest or unconscious purpose.

His insights into the relation between thought and language were a major influence on philosophy. Although claimed as a precursor by Nazism, many of his views are incompatible with totalitarian ideology. He is a profoundly ambivalent thinker whose philosophy can be appropriated for many purposes.

Born in Röcken, Saxony, he attended Bonn and Leipzig universities and was professor of Greek at Basel, Switzerland, 1869–80. He had abandoned theology for philology, and was influenced by the writings of Schopenhauer and the music of Wagner, of whom he became both friend and advocate. Both these attractions passed, however, and ill-health caused his resignation from the university. He spent his later years in northern Italy, in the Engadine, and in southern France. He published *Morgenröte/The Dawn* 1880–81, *Die fröhliche Wissenschaft/The Gay Science* 1881–82, *Also sprach Zarathustra/Thus Spoke Zarathustra* 1883–85, *Jenseits von Gut und Böse/Between Good and Evil* 1885–86, *Zur Genealogie der Moral/Towards a Genealogy of Morals* 1887, and *Ecce Homo* 1888. He suffered a permanent breakdown in 1889 from overwork and loneliness.

Morality is the herd instinct in the individual.

Friedrich Nietzsche
Die fröhliche Wissenschaft 1882

Nightingale /naɪtɪŋgeɪl/ Florence 1820–1910. English nurse, the founder of nursing as a profession. She took a team of nurses to Scutari (now Üsküdar, Turkey) in 1854 and reduced the Crimean War hospital death rate from 42% to 2%. In 1856 she founded the Nightingale School and Home for Nurses in London.

Born in Florence, Italy, she trained in Germany and France. She was the author of the classic *Notes on Nursing*; she was awarded the Order of Merit 1907.

Nijinsky /nɪ'dʒɪnski/ Vaslav 1890–1950. Russian dancer and choreographer. Noted for his powerful but graceful technique, he was a legendary member of →Diaghilev's Ballets Russes, for whom he choreographed Debussy's *Prélude à l'Après-midi d'un faune* 1912 and *Jeux* 1913, and Stravinsky's *The Rite of Spring* 1913.

Nijinsky also took lead roles in ballets such as *Petrushka* 1911. He rejected conventional forms of classical ballet in favour of free expression. His sister was the choreographer **Bronislava Nijinska** (1891–1972).

Nimitz /nɪmɪts/ Chester William 1885–1966. US admiral, commander in chief of the US Pacific fleet. He reconquered the Solomon Islands 1942–43, Gilbert Islands 1943, the Marianas and Marshalls 1944, and signed the Japanese surrender 1945 as the US representative.

Nin /nɪn/ Anaïs 1903–1977. French-born US novelist and diarist. Her extensive and impressionistic diaries, published 1966–76, reflect her interest in dreams, which along with psychoanalysis are recurring themes of her gently erotic novels (such as *House of Incest* 1936 and *A Spy in the House of Love* 1954).

Born in Paris, she started out as a model and dancer, but later took up the study of psycho-analysis. She emigrated to the USA in 1940, becoming a prominent member of Greenwich Village literary society in New York.

Life shrinks or expands in proportion to one's courage.

Anaïs Nin *Diary* June 1941

Nithsdale /nɪθsdeɪl/ William Maxwell, 5th Earl of Nithsdale 1676–1744. English Jacobite leader who was captured at Preston, brought to trial in Westminster Hall, London, and condemned to death 1716. With his wife's assistance he escaped from the Tower of London in women's dress, and fled to Rome.

Niven /nɪvən/ David 1909–1983. Scottish-born US film actor, in Hollywood from the 1930s. His films include *Wuthering Heights* 1939, *Separate Tables* 1958 (Academy Award), *The Guns of Navarone* 1961, and *The Pink Panther* 1964. He published two best-selling volumes of autobiography, *The Moon's a Balloon* 1972 and *Bring on the Empty Horses* 1975.

Nixon /nɪksən/ Richard (Milhous) 1913– . 37th president of the USA 1969–74, a Republican. He attracted attention as a member of the Un-American Activities Committee 1948, and was vice president to Eisenhower 1953–61. As president he was responsible for US withdrawal from Vietnam, and forged new links with China, but at home his culpability in the cover-up of the Watergate scandal and the existence of a 'slush fund' for political machinations during his re-election campaign 1972 led to his resignation 1974 when threatened with impeachment.

Of a Quaker family, Nixon grew up in Whittier, California; he became a lawyer, entered Congress in 1947, and in 1948, as a member of the Un-American Activities Committee, pressed for the investigation of Alger →Hiss, accused of being a spy. Nixon was senator from California from 1951 until elected vice president. He lost the presidential election 1960 to J F Kennedy, partly because televised electoral debates put him at a disadvantage. He did not seek presidential nomination in 1964, but in a 'law and order' campaign defeated Vice-President Humphrey 1968 in one of the most closely contested elections in US history.

In 1969 he formulated the Nixon Doctrine abandoning close involvement with Asian countries, but escalated the war in Cambodia by massive bombing. Re-elected 1972 in a landslide victory over George McGovern, he resigned 1974, the first US president to do so, under threat of impeachment on three counts: obstruction of the administration of justice in the investigation of Watergate; violation of constitutional rights of

Nixon 37th US president Richard Milhous Nixon, the only president ever to resign from office. During his presidency Nixon began the gradual withdrawal of US troops from Vietnam and improved relations with the Eastern bloc. He resigned August 9, 1974 over his involvement in the Watergate scandal.

citizens, for example attempting to use the Internal Revenue Service, Federal Bureau of Investigation, and Central Intelligence Agency as weapons against political opponents; and failure to produce 'papers and things' as ordered by the Judiciary Committee. He was granted a pardon 1974 by President Ford and turned to lecturing and writing.

Nkomo /əŋ'kəuməu/ Joshua 1917– . Zimbabwean politician, vice-president from 1988. As president of ZAPU (Zimbabwe African People's Union) from 1961, he was a leader of the black nationalist movement against the white Rhodesian regime. He was a member of Robert →Mugabe's cabinet 1980–82 and from 1987.

After completing his education in South Africa, Joshua Nkomo became a welfare officer on Rhodesian Railways and later organizing secretary of the Rhodesian African Railway Workers' Union. He entered politics 1950 and rose to become president of ZAPU. He was soon arrested, with other black African politicians, and was in detention during 1963–74. After his release he joined forces with Robert Mugabe as a joint leader of the Patriotic Front 1976, opposing the white-dominated regime of Ian Smith. Nkomo took part in the Lancaster House Conference, which led to Rhodesia's independence as the new state of Zimbabwe, and became a cabinet minister and vice president.

Western culture is not suitable for us without modification.

Joshua Nkomo in *Observer* Feb 1980

Nkrumah /əŋˈkruːmə/ Kwame 1909–1972. Ghanaian nationalist politician, prime minister of the Gold Coast (Ghana's former name) 1952–57 and of newly independent Ghana 1957–60. He became Ghana's first president 1960 but was overthrown in a coup 1966. His policy of 'African socialism' led to links with the communist bloc.

Originally a teacher, he studied later in both Britain and the USA, and on returning to Africa formed the Convention People's Party (CPP) 1949 with the aim of immediate self-government. He was imprisoned in 1950 for incitement of illegal strikes, but was released the same year. As president he established an authoritarian regime and made Ghana a one-party (CPP) state 1964. He then dropped his stance of nonalignment and drew closer to the USSR and other communist countries. Deposed from the presidency while on a visit to Beijing (Peking) 1966, he remained in exile in Guinea, where he was made a co-head of state until his death, but was posthumously 'rehabilitated' 1973.

Nobel /nəʊˈbel/ Alfred Bernhard 1833–1896. Swedish chemist and engineer. He invented dynamite in 1867 and ballistite, a smokeless gunpowder, in 1889. He amassed a large fortune from the manufacture of explosives and the exploitation of the Baku oilfields in Azerbaijan, near the Caspian Sea. He left this fortune in trust for the endowment of five Nobel prizes.

Second to agriculture, humbug is the biggest industry of our age.

Alfred Nobel

Noel-Baker /nəʊəl ˈbeɪkə/ Philip John 1889–1982. British Labour politician. He was involved in drafting the charters of both the League of Nations and the United Nations. He published *The Arms Race* 1958, and was awarded the 1959 Nobel Peace Prize.

Nofretete alternative name for ➔Nefertiti, queen of Egypt.

Noguchi /nəʊˈɡuːtʃi/ Hideyo 1876–1928. Japanese bacteriologist who studied syphilitic diseases, snake venoms, trachoma, and poliomyelitis. He discovered the parasite of yellow fever, a disease from which he died while working in British W Africa.

Nolan /nəʊlən/ Sidney 1917–1992. Australian artist. He created atmospheric paintings of the outback, exploring themes from Australian history such as the life of the outlaw Ned Kelly and the folk heroine Mrs Fraser.

Noland /nəʊlənd/ Kenneth 1924– . US painter, associated with Abstract Expressionism. In the 1950s and early 1960s he painted targets, or concentric circles of colour, in a clean, hard-edged style on unprimed canvas. His work centred on geometry, colour, and symmetry. His later 1960s paintings experimented with the manipulation of colour vision and afterimages, pioneering the field of Op art.

Nolde /nɒldə/ Emil. Adopted name of Emil Hansen 1867–1956. German Expressionist painter. Nolde studied in Paris and Dachau, joined the group of artists known as Die Brücke 1906–07, and visited Polynesia 1913; he then became almost a recluse in NE Germany. Many of his themes were religious.

Nollekens /nɒlɪkənz/ Joseph 1737–1823. English sculptor, specializing in portrait busts and memorials. He worked in Rome 1759–70. On his return to London he enjoyed great success, executing busts of many eminent people: George III, the Prince of Wales (later George IV), the politicians Pitt the Younger and Fox, the actor Garrick, the writer Sterne, and others.

Nono /nəʊnəʊ/ Luigi 1924–1990. Italian composer. His early vocal compositions have something of the spatial character of ➔Gabrieli, for example *Il Canto Sospeso* 1955–56. After the opera *Intolleranza* 1960 his style moved away from serialism to become increasingly expressionistic. His music is frequently polemical in subject matter, and a number of works incorporate tape-recorded elements.

Nordenskjöld /nɔːdnʃəʊld/ Nils Adolf Erik 1832–1901. Swedish explorer. He made voyages to the Arctic with the geologist Torell and in 1878–79 discovered the Northeast Passage. He published the results of his voyages in a series of books, including *Voyage of the Vega round Asia and Europe* 1881.

Norfolk /nɔːfək/ Miles Fitzalan-Howard, 17th Duke of Norfolk 1915– . Earl marshal of England, and premier duke and earl; seated at Arundel Castle, Sussex, England. As earl marshal, he is responsible for the organization of ceremonial on major state occasions.

Noriega /ˌnɒriˈeɪɡə/ Manuel (Antonio Morena) 1940– . Panamanian soldier and politician, effective ruler of Panama from 1982, as head of the National Guard, until deposed by the USA 1989. An informer for the US Central Intelligence Agency, he was known to be involved in drug trafficking as early as 1972. He enjoyed US support until 1987. In the 1989 US invasion of Panama, he was forcibly taken to the USA, tried, and convicted of trafficking in 1992.

Noriega was commissioned in the National Guard 1962, and received US counterintelligence training. He became intelligence chief 1970 and Chief of Staff 1982. He wielded considerable political power behind the scenes, which led to his enlistment by the CIA, and he was seen as an ally against Nicaragua until the Irangate scandal (an arms-for-hostages deal with Iran) limited US covert action there. In the 1984 and 1989 presidential elections, Noriega claimed a fraudulent victory for his candidate. Bribes accepted by Nor-

Nordenskjöld *Swedish polar explorer Nils Nordenskjöld, leader of the expedition which discovered the
Northeast Passage from the Atlantic to the Pacific
along the north coast of Asia 1878–79. He also
explored and mapped the island of Spitsbergen.*

iega for tacitly permitting money laundering and
the transshipment of cocaine are estimated at $15
million, but after 1985 he cooperated with the US
Drug Enforcement Administration. However,
relations between Panama and the USA deteriorated and in Dec 1989 President Bush ordered an
invasion of the country by 24,000 US troops.
Noriega was seized and taken to the USA for trial.
In April 1992 he was given a 40-year prison sentence for drug trafficking and racketeering.

Norman /ˈnɔːmən/ Greg 1955– . Australian
golfer, nicknamed 'the Great White Shark'. After
many wins in his home country, he enjoyed success on the European PGA Tour before joining
the US Tour. He has won the World Match-Play
title three times.

Norman /ˈnɔːmən/ Jessye 1945– . US soprano,
born in Augusta, Georgia. She made her operatic
debut at the Deutsche Opera, Berlin, 1969. She is
acclaimed for her interpretation of *Lieder*, as well
as operatic roles, and for her powerful voice.

Norman /ˈnɔːmən/ Montagu, 1st Baron Norman
1871–1950. British banker. Governor of the Bank
of England 1920–44, he handled German reparations (financial compensation exacted by the
Allies) after World War I, and, by his advocacy of
a return to the gold standard in 1925 and other
policies, was held by many to have contributed to
the economic depression of the 1930s.

Norris /ˈnɒrɪs/ Frank 1870–1902. US novelist. A
naturalist writer, he wrote *McTeague* 1899, about
a brutish San Francisco dentist and the love of

gold. He completed only two parts of his projected trilogy, the *Epic of Wheat: The Octopus* 1901,
dealing with the struggles between wheat farmers,
and *The Pit* 1903, describing the Chicago wheat
exchange.

North /nɔːθ/ Frederick, 8th Lord North
1732–1792. British Tory politician. He entered
Parliament in 1754, became chancellor of the
Exchequer in 1767, and was prime minister in a
government of Tories and 'king's friends' from
1770. His hard line against the American colonies
was supported by George III, but in 1782 he was
forced to resign by the failure of his policy. In
1783 he returned to office in a coalition with
Charles →Fox, and after its defeat retired from
politics.

North /nɔːθ/ Oliver 1943– . US Marine lieutenant colonel. In 1981 he was inducted into the
National Security Council (NSC), where he
supervised the mining of Nicaraguan harbours
1983, an air-force bombing raid on Libya 1986,
and an arms-for-hostages deal with Iran 1985
which, when uncovered 1986 (Irangate), forced
his dismissal and trial.

North was born into a San Antonio, Texas, military family and was a graduate of the US Naval
Academy, Annapolis. He led a counterinsurgency
Marine platoon in the Vietnam War 1968–69,
winning a Silver Star and Purple Heart. After
working as a Marine instructor, as well as participating in a number of overseas secret missions, he
became the NSC deputy director for political military affairs.

After Irangate, North was convicted on felony
charges of obstructing Congress, mutilating government documents, and taking an illegal gratuity;
he was fined $150,000. In Sept 1991, it was
announced that all charges against him were being
dropped on the grounds that, since his evidence
before Congressional committees July 1987 had
been widely televised, it was impossible to give
him a fair trial.

North /nɔːθ/ Thomas 1535–1601. English translator, whose version of →Plutarch's *Lives* 1579
was the source for Shakespeare's Roman plays.

Northcliffe /ˈnɔːθklɪf/ Alfred Charles William
Harmsworth, 1st Viscount Northcliffe
1865–1922. British newspaper proprietor, born in
Dublin. Founding the *Daily Mail* 1896, he revolutionized popular journalism, and with the *Daily
Mirror* 1903 originated the picture paper. In 1908
he also obtained control of *The Times*. His brother **Harold Sidney Harmsworth, 1st Viscount
Rothermere** (1868–1940), was associated with
him in many of his newspapers.

Northrop /ˈnɔːθrəp/ John 1891–1987. US chemist.
In the 1930s he crystallized a number of enzymes,
including pepsin and trypsin, showing conclusively that they were proteins. He shared the 1946
Nobel Prize for Chemistry with Wendell →Stan-
ley and James →Sumner.

Northumberland /nɔːˈθʌmbələnd/ John Dudley, Duke of Northumberland *c.* 1502–1553. English politician, son of the privy councillor Edmund Dudley (beheaded 1510), and chief minister until Edward VI's death 1553. He tried to place his daughter-in-law Lady Jane →Grey on the throne, and was executed on Mary I's accession.

Norton /nɔːtn/ Caroline 1808–1877. British writer, granddaughter of R B →Sheridan. Her works include *Undying One* 1830 and *Voice from the Factories* 1836, attacking child labour.

In 1836 her husband falsely accused Lord Melbourne of seducing her, obtained custody of their children, and tried to obtain the profits from her books. Public reaction to this prompted changes in the laws of infant custody and married women's property rights.

Nostradamus /ˌnɒstrəˈdɑːməs/ Latinized name of Michel de Nôtredame 1503–1566. French physician and astrologer who was consulted by Catherine de' Medici and was physician to Charles IX. His book of prophecies in rhyme, *Centuries* 1555, has had a number of interpretations.

Nott /nɒt/ John 1932– . British Conservative politician, minister for defence 1981–83 during the Falkland Islands conflict with Argentina.

Novak /ˈnəʊvæk/ Kim (Marilyn Pauline) 1933– . US film actress who starred in such films as *Pal Joey* 1957, *Bell, Book and Candle* 1958, *Vertigo* 1958, *Kiss Me Stupid* 1964, and *The Legend of Lyla Clare* 1968.

Novalis /nəʊˈvɑːlɪs/ Pen name of Friedrich Leopold von Hardenberg 1772–1801. Pioneer German Romantic poet who wrote *Hymnen an die Nacht/Hymns to the Night* 1800, prompted by the death of his fiancée Sophie von Kühn. He left two unfinished romances, *Die Lehrlinge zu Sais/The Novices of Sais* and *Heinrich von Ofterdingen*.

Poetry heals the wounds inflicted by reason.

Novalis *Detached Thoughts*

Novello /nəˈveləʊ/ Ivor. Stage name of Ivor Novello Davies 1893–1951. Welsh composer and actor-manager. He wrote popular songs, such as 'Keep the Home Fires Burning', in World War I, and musicals in which he often appeared as the romantic lead, including *Glamorous Night* 1925, *The Dancing Years* 1939, and *Gay's the Word* 1951.

Noverre /nɒˈveə/ Jean-Georges 1727–1810. French choreographer, writer, and ballet reformer. He promoted *ballet d'action* (with a plot) and simple, free movement, and is often considered the creator of modern classical ballet. *Les Petits Riens* 1778 was one of his works.

Noyce Robert Norton 1927–1990. US scientist and inventor, with Jack Kilby, of the integrated circuit (chip), which revolutionized the computer and electronics industries in the 1970s and 1980s. In 1968 he and six colleagues founded Intel Corporation, which became one of the USA's leading semiconductor manufacturers.

Noyes /nɔɪz/ Alfred 1880–1958. English poet who wrote poems about the sea and the anthology favourites 'The Highwayman', 'Barrel Organ', and 'Go down to Kew in lilac-time …'.

Noyes /nɔɪz/ John Humphrey 1811–1886. US religious and communal leader. He formulated the 'doctrine of free love' 1837 and in 1848 founded the Oneida Community in central New York which served as a forum for his social experiments. In 1879 Noyes was forced to move to Canada to avoid legal action against him. The former community, which made silverware and steel traps, became a joint stock company 1881.

Born in Brattleboro, Vermont, Noyes was educated at Dartmouth and the Andover Seminary. While at Yale Divinity School, he announced that he had achieved human perfection and was promptly expelled. An advocate of alternative forms of marriage, he founded a religious society in Putney, Vermont 1836.

Nu /nuː/ U (Thakin) 1907– . Myanmar politician, prime minister of Burma (now Myanmar) for most of the period from 1948 to the military coup of 1962. Exiled from 1966, U Nu returned to the country 1980 and, in 1988, helped found the National League for Democracy opposition movement.

Formerly a teacher, U Nu joined the Dobhama Asiayone ('Our Burma') nationalist organization during the 1930s and was imprisoned by the British authorities at the start of World War II. He was released 1942, following Japan's invasion of Burma, and appointed foreign minister in a puppet government. In 1945 he fought with the British against the Japanese and on independence became Burma's first prime minister. Excepting short breaks during 1956–57 and 1958–60, he remained in this post until General →Ne Win overthrew the parliamentary regime in 1962.

Nuffield /ˈnʌfiːld/ William Richard Morris, Viscount Nuffield 1877–1963. English manufacturer and philanthropist. Starting with a small cycle-repairing business, in 1910 he designed a car that could be produced cheaply, and built up Morris Motors Ltd at Cowley, Oxford.

He endowed Nuffield College, Oxford, 1937 and the Nuffield Foundation 1943.

Nujoma /nuːˈdʒəʊmə/ Sam 1929– . Namibian left-wing politician, president from 1990, founder and leader of SWAPO (the South-West Africa People's Organization) from 1959. He was exiled in 1960 and controlled guerrillas from Angolan bases until the first free elections were held 1989, taking office early the following year.

Nunn /nʌn/ Trevor 1940– . British stage director, linked with the Royal Shakespeare Company
from 1968. He received a Tony award (with John
Caird 1948–) for his production of *Nicholas
Nickleby* 1982 and for the musical *Les Misérables*
1987.

Nureyev /njʊˈreɪef/ Rudolf 1938–1993. Russian
dancer and choreographer. A soloist with the
Kirov Ballet, he defected to the West during a visit
to Paris in 1961. Mainly associated with the Royal
Ballet (London) and as Margot ➜Fonteyn's principal partner, he was one of the most brilliant
dancers of the 1960s and 1970s. Nureyev danced
in such roles as Prince Siegfried in *Swan Lake* and
Armand in *Marguerite and Armand*, which was
created specifically for Fonteyn and Nureyev. He
also danced and acted in films and on television
and choreographed several ballets.

*I dance to please myself. If you try to
please everybody, there is no originality.*
Rudolf Nureyev *St Louis Post Despatch* Jan 1964

Nyerere /njəˈreəri/ Julius (Kambarage) 1922– .
Tanzanian socialist politician, president 1964–85.
He devoted himself from 1954 to the formation of
the Tanganyika African National Union and subsequent campaigning for independence. He
became chief minister 1960, was prime minister of
Tanganyika 1961–62, president of the newly
formed Tanganyika Republic 1962–64, and first
president of Tanzania 1964–85.

He was head of the Organization of African
Unity 1984.

Nyers /njeəʃ/ Rezso 1923– . Hungarian socialist leader. A member of the politburo from 1966
and the architect of Hungary's liberalizing economic reforms in 1968, he was ousted from power
by hardliners 1974. In 1988 he was brought back
into the politburo, and became head of the newly
formed Hungarian Socialist Party in 1989.

In 1940 Nyers joined the Hungarian Social
Democratic Party, which in 1948 was forcibly
merged with the communists. He became secretary of the ruling Hungarian Socialist Worker's
Party's (HSWP) central committee 1962. He was

Nureyev *Russian-born ballet dancer and choreographer Rudolf Nureyev, whose skill and versatility gained
him international acclaim. He revised the choreography
of some ballets to satisfy the demands of his skill, agility, and strength; in 1964 he reworked* Swan Lake, *giving the male dancer the dominant role, following a
precedent set by Nijinsky.*

removed from his HSWP posts in 1974 and his
career remained at a standstill until a new reform
initiative got under way 1988.

Nykvist /niːkvɪst/ Sven 1922– . Swedish director of photography, associated with the director
Ingmar Bergman. He worked frequently in the
USA from the mid-1970s onwards. His films
include *The Virgin Spring* 1960 (for Bergman),
Pretty Baby 1978 (for Louis Malle), and *Fanny
and Alexander* 1982 (for Bergman).

Nyman /naɪmən/ Michael 1944– . British composer whose highly stylized music is characterized
by processes of gradual modification by repetition
of complex musical formulas. His compositions
include scores for the British filmmaker Peter
➜Greenaway; a chamber opera, *The Man Who
Mistook His Wife for a Hat* 1989; and three string
quartets.

Oakley Annie (Phoebe Anne Oakley Mozee) 1860–1926. US sharpshooter, member of Buffalo Bill's Wild West Show (see William →Cody). Even though she was partially paralysed in a train crash 1901, she continued to astound audiences with her ability virtually until her death. Kaiser Wilhelm of Germany had such faith in her talent that he allowed her to shoot a cigarette from his mouth.

Oastler /ˈəʊstlə/ Richard 1789–1861. English social reformer. He opposed child labour and the poor law 1834, which restricted relief, and was largely responsible for securing the Factory Act 1833 and the Ten Hours Act 1847. He was given the nickname of the 'Factory King' for his achievements on behalf of workers.

Oates /əʊts/ Joyce Carol 1938– . US writer. Her novels, often containing surrealism and violence, include *A Garden of Earthly Delights* 1967, *Them* 1969, *Unholy Loves* 1979, *A Bloodsmoor Romance* 1982, and *Because It Is Bitter, and Because It Is My Heart* 1990.

Oates /əʊts/ Laurence Edward Grace 1880–1912. British Antarctic explorer who accompanied Robert Falcon →Scott on his second expedition to the South Pole. On the return journey, suffering from frostbite, he went out alone into the blizzard to die rather than delay the others.

I am just going outside, and may be some time.

Laurence Oates,
last words 16 March 1912

Oates /əʊts/ Titus 1649–1705. English conspirator. A priest, he entered the Jesuit colleges at Valladolid, Spain, and St Omer, France, as a spy 1677–78, and on his return to England announced he had discovered a 'Popish Plot' to murder Charles II and re-establish Catholicism. Although this story was almost entirely false, many innocent Roman Catholics were executed during 1678–80 on Oates's evidence.

In 1685 Oates was flogged, pilloried, and imprisoned for perjury. He was pardoned and granted a pension after the revolution of 1688.

Oberon /ˈəʊbərɒn/ Merle. Stage name of Estelle Merle O'Brien Thompson 1911–1979. Indian-born British actress (but claiming to be Tasmanian) who starred in several films by Alexander Korda (to whom she was briefly married 1939–45), including *The Scarlet Pimpernel* 1935. She played Cathy to Laurence Olivier's Heathcliff in *Wuthering Heights* 1939, and after 1940 worked successfully in the USA.

Obote /əʊˈbəʊti/ (Apollo) Milton 1924– . Ugandan politician who led the independence movement from 1961. He became prime minister 1962 and was president 1966–71 and 1980–85, being overthrown by first Idi →Amin (Dada) and then by Lt-Gen Tito Okello.

Obraztsov /ˌɒbrəstˈsɒf/ Sergei 1901– . Russian puppeteer, head of the Moscow- based State Central Puppet Theatre, the world's largest puppet theatre (with a staff of 300). The repertoire was built up from 1923.

Obrenovich /əˈbrenəvɪtʃ/ Serbian dynasty that ruled 1816–42 and 1859–1903. The dynasty engaged in a feud with the rival house of Karageorgevich, which obtained the throne by the murder of the last Obrenovich 1903.

O'Brien /əʊˈbraɪən/ Margaret (Angela Maxine) 1937– . US child actress, a star of the 1940s. She received a special Academy Award 1944, but her career, which included leading parts in *Lost Angel* 1943, *Meet Me in St Louis* 1944, and *The Secret Garden* 1949, did not survive into adolescence.

O'Brien /əʊˈbraɪən/ Willis H 1886–1962. US film animator and special-effects creator, responsible for one of the cinema's most memorable monsters, the giant ape in *King Kong* 1933.

We ought to have as great a regard for religion as we can, so as to keep it out of as many things as possible.

Sean O'Casey *The Plough and the Stars* 1926

O'Casey /əʊˈkeɪsi/ Sean. Adopted name of John Casey 1884–1964. Irish dramatist. His early plays are tragicomedies, blending realism with symbolism and poetic with vernacular speech: *The Shadow of a Gunman* 1922, *Juno and the Paycock* 1925, and *The Plough and the Stars* 1926. Later plays include *Red Roses for Me* 1946 and *The Drums of Father Ned* 1960.

He also wrote the anti-war drama *The Silver Tassie* 1929, *The Star Turns Red* 1940, *Oak Leaves and Lavender* 1947, and a six-volume autobiography.

Occam /ˈɒkəm/ or **Ockham** William of *c.* 1300–1349. English philosopher and scholastic logician who revived the fundamentals of nominalism. As a Franciscan monk he defended evangelical poverty against Pope John XXII, becoming known as the Invincible Doctor. He was imprisoned in Avignon, France, on charges of heresy 1328 but escaped to Munich, Germany, where he died. The principle of reducing assumptions to the absolute minimum is known as *Occam's razor*.

Ochoa /əʊˈtʃəʊə/ Severo 1905– . Spanish-born US biochemist. He discovered an enzyme able to assemble units of the nucleic acid RNA in 1955, while working at New York University. For his work towards the synthesis of RNA, Ochoa shared the 1959 Nobel Prize for Medicine with Arthur →Kornberg.

Ochs Adolph Simon 1858–1935. US newspaper publisher. In 1896 he gained control of the then-faltering *New York Times* and transformed it into a serious, authoritative publication. Among Ochs's innovations were a yearly index and a weekly book-review section.

Ockham William. English philosopher; see →Occam.

O'Connell /əʊˈkɒnl/ Daniel 1775–1847. Irish politician, called 'the Liberator'. Although ineligible, as a Roman Catholic, to take his seat, he was elected member of Parliament for County Clare 1828 and so forced the government to grant Catholic emancipation. In Parliament he cooperated with the Whigs in the hope of obtaining concessions until 1841, when he launched his campaign for repeal of the union.

In 1823 O'Connell founded the Catholic Association to press Roman Catholic claims. His reserved and vacillating leadership and conservative outlook on social questions alienated his most active supporters, who broke away and formed the nationalist Young Ireland movement.

[Peel's smile is] like the silver plate on a coffin.

Daniel O'Connell referring to Sir Robert Peel

O'Connor /əʊˈkɒnə/ Feargus 1794–1855. Irish parliamentarian, a follower of Daniel →O'Connell. He sat in Parliament 1832–35, and as editor of the *Northern Star* became an influential figure of the radical working-class Chartist movement.

O'Connor /əʊˈkɒnə/ Flannery 1925–1964. US novelist and short-story writer. Her works have a great sense of evil and sin, and often explore the religious sensibility of the Deep South. Her short

O'Connell Calling for complete Roman Catholic emancipation, Irish politician Daniel O'Connell founded the Catholic Association, which agitated for repeal of civil disabilities by mass meetings. He was imprisoned 1844 and fined for seditious conspiracy, but was released 14 weeks later on a writ of error by the House of Lords.

stories include *A Good Man Is Hard to Find* 1955, *Everything That Rises Must Converge* 1965, *The Habit of Being* 1979, and *Flannery O'Connor: Collected Works* 1988.

Her novels are *Wise Blood* 1952 and *The Violent Bear It Away* 1960. Her work exemplifies the post-war revival of the Gothic novel in Southern US fiction.

O'Connor /əʊˈkɒnə/ Sandra Day 1930– . US jurist and the first female associate justice of the US Supreme Court 1981– . Considered a moderate conservative, she dissented in *Texas v. Johnson* 1990, a decision that ruled that the legality of burning the US flag in protest was protected by the First Amendment.

Octavian /ɒkˈteɪviən/ original name of →Augustus, the first Roman emperor.

Odets /əʊˈdets/ Clifford 1906–1963. US playwright, associated with the Group Theatre and the most renowned of the social-protest playwrights of the Depression era. His plays include *Waiting for Lefty* 1935, about a taxi drivers' strike, *Awake and Sing* 1935, *Golden Boy* 1937, and *The Country Girl* 1950.

In the late 1930s he went to Hollywood and became a successful film writer and director, but he continued to write plays.

Odoacer /ˌɒdəʊˈeɪsə/ 433–493. King of Italy from 476, when he deposed Romulus Augustulus, the last Roman emperor. He was a leader of the barbarian mercenaries employed by Rome. He was overthrown and killed by Theodoric the Great, king of the Ostrogoths.

Odoyevsky /ˌɒdəˈjefski/ Vladimir 1804–1869. Russian writer whose works include tales of the supernatural, science fiction, satires, children's stories, and music criticism.

Oersted /ˈɜːsted/ Hans Christian 1777–1851. Danish physicist who founded the science of electromagnetism. In 1820 he discovered the magnetic field associated with an electric current.

O'Faolain /əʊˈfeɪlən/ Sean (John Whelan) 1900–1991. Irish novelist, short-story writer, and biographer. His first novel, *A Nest of Simple Folk* 1933, was followed by an edition of translated Gaelic, *The Silver Branch* 1938. His many biographies include *Daniel O'Connell* 1938 and *De Valera* 1939, about the nationalist whom he had fought beside in the Irish Republican Army.

Offa /ˈɒfə/ died 796. King of Mercia, England, from 757. He conquered Essex, Kent, Sussex, and Surrey; defeated the Welsh and the West Saxons; and established Mercian supremacy over all England south of the river Humber.

Offenbach /ˈɒfənbɑːk/ Jacques 1819–1880. French composer. He wrote light opera, initially for presentation at the *Bouffes parisiens*. Among his works are *Orphée aux enfers/Orpheus in the Underworld* 1858, *La belle Hélène* 1864, and *Les contes d'Hoffmann/The Tales of Hoffmann* 1881.

O'Flaherty /əʊˈflɑːhəti/ Liam 1897–1984. Irish author, best known for his short stories published in volumes such as *Spring Sowing* 1924, *The Tent* 1926, and *Two Lovely Beasts* 1948. His novels, set in County Mayo, include *The Neighbour's Wife* 1923, *The Informer* 1925, and *Land* 1946.

Ogden /ˈɒgdən/ C(harles) K(ay) 1889–1957. English writer and scholar. With I A ➔Richards he developed the simplified form of English known as Basic English, built on a vocabulary of just 850 words. Together they wrote *Foundations of Aesthetics* 1921 and *The Meaning of Meaning* 1923.

The belief that words have a meaning of their own account is a relic of primitive word magic, and it is still a part of the air we breathe in nearly every discussion.

C K Ogden *The Meaning of Meaning* 1923

Ogdon /ˈɒgdən/ John 1937–1989. English pianist, renowned for his interpretation of Chopin, Liszt, and Busoni. In 1962 he took joint first prize with Vladimir Ashkenazy at the Tchaikovsky Piano Competition in Moscow.

For a number of years unable to perform as a result of depression, he recovered to make a successful return to the concert hall shortly before his death.

Oglethorpe /ˈəʊgəlθɔːp/ James Edward 1696–1785. English soldier and colonizer of Georgia.

He served in parliament for 32 years and in 1732 obtained a charter for the colony of Georgia, USA, intended as a refuge for debtors and for European Protestants.

O'Higgins /əʊˈhɪgɪnz/ Bernardo 1778–1842. Chilean revolutionary, known as 'the Liberator of Chile'. He was a leader of the struggle for independence from Spanish rule 1810–17 and head of the first permanent national government 1817–23.

Ohm /əʊm/ Georg Simon 1787–1854. German physicist who studied electricity and discovered the fundamental law that bears his name. The SI unit of electrical resistance is named after him, and the unit of conductance (the reverse of resistance) was formerly called the mho, which is Ohm spelled backwards.

Nobody sees a flower – really – we haven't time – and to see takes time like to have a friend takes time.

Georgia O'Keeffe

Oistrakh /ˈɔɪstrɑːk/ David Fyodorovich 1908–1974. Soviet violinist, celebrated for performances of both standard and contemporary Russian repertoire. Shostakovich wrote both his violin concertos for him. His son *Igor* (1931–   ) is equally renowned as a violinist.

O'Keeffe /əʊˈkiːf/ Georgia 1887–1986. US painter, based mainly in New York and New Mexico, known chiefly for her large, semi-abstract studies of flowers and bones, such as *Black Iris* 1926 (Metropolitan Museum of Art, New York) and the *Pelvis Series* of the 1940s.

Her mature style stressed contours and subtle tonal transitions, which often transformed the subject into a powerful and erotic abstract image. In 1946 she settled in New Mexico, where the desert landscape inspired many of her paintings.

Okeghem /ˈɒkəgem/ Johannes (Jean d') c. 1420–1497. Flemish composer of church music, including masses and motets. He was court composer to Charles VII, Louis XI, and Charles VIII of France.

Okri Ben 1959–   . Nigerian novelist, broadcaster, and journalist whose novel *The Famished Road* won the 1991 Booker Prize. He published his first book *Flowers and Shadows* 1980, and wrote his second, *The Landscapes Within* 1982, while still a student at university in Essex, England.

He worked for the BBC World Service as a broadcaster 1984–85 and was poetry editor of *West Africa* magazine 1980–87. Short story collections include *Incidents at the Shrine* 1987 and *Stars of the New Curfew* 1988. His first book of poems *An African Elegy* 1992 is based on contemporary Africa.

Okubo /əʊˈkuːbəʊ/ Toshimichi 1831–1878. Japanese samurai leader whose opposition to the Tokugawa shogunate made him a leader in the Meiji restoration 1866–88.

Okuma /əʊˈkuːmə/ Shigenobu 1838–1922. Japanese politician and prime minister 1898 and 1914–16. He presided over Japanese pressure for territorial concessions in China, before retiring 1916.

Olaf /ˈəʊləf/ five kings of Norway, including:

Olaf I Tryggvesson 969–1000. King of Norway from 995. He began the conversion of Norway to Christianity and was killed in a sea battle against the Danes and Swedes.

Olaf II Haraldsson 995–1030. King of Norway from 1015. He offended his subjects by his centralizing policy and zeal for Christianity, and was killed in battle by Norwegian rebel chiefs backed by →Canute of Denmark. He was declared the patron saint of Norway 1164.

Olaf V 1903–1991. King of Norway from 1957, when he succeeded his father, Haakon VII.

After the German invasion of Norway 1940 Olav, as crown prince, became a rallying point for his compatriots by holding out against German air raids for two months and later, in exile in England, playing an important part in liaison with resistance movements in Norway as well as building up the Free Norwegian forces in Britain.

Olazabal /ˌəʊləsəˈbæl/ Jose Maria 1966– . Spanish golfer, one of the leading players on the European circuit. After a distinguished amateur career he turned professional 1986. He was a member of the European Ryder Cup teams 1987, 1989, and 1991.

He won the English amateur championship 1984 and the Youths title the following year. He finished second in the European money list in his second year as a professional.

Olbers /ˈɒlbəs/ Heinrich 1758–1840. German astronomer. A medical doctor, Olbers was a keen amateur astronomer and a founder member of the *Celestial Police*, a group of astronomers who attempted to locate a supposed 'missing planet' between Mars and Jupiter.

During his search he discovered two asteroids, Pallas 1802 and Vesta 1807. Also credited to Olbers are a number of comet discoveries, a new method of calculating cometary orbits, and the stating of Olbers' paradox. In 1920 Olbers retired from medicine to devote himself to astronomy.

Olbrich /ˈɒlbrɪʃ/ Joseph Maria 1867–1908. Viennese architect who worked under Otto →Wagner and was opposed to the overornamentation of Art Nouveau. His major buildings, however, remain Art Nouveau in spirit: the Vienna Sezession 1897–98, the Hochzeitsturm 1907, and the Tietz department store in Düsseldorf, Germany.

Oldenbarneveldt /ˌəʊldənˈbɑːnəvelt/ Johan van 1547–1619. Dutch politician, a leading figure in the Netherlands' struggle for independence from Spain, who helped William the Silent negotiate the Union of Utrecht 1579.

As leader of the Republican party he opposed the war policy of stadholder (magistrate) Maurice of Orange and negotiated a 12-year truce with Spain 1609. His support of the Remonstrants (Arminians) in the religious strife against Maurice and the Gomarists (Calvinists) effected his downfall and he was arrested and executed.

Oldenburg /ˈəʊldənbɜːg/ Claes 1929– . US Pop artist, known for 'soft sculptures', gigantic replicas of everyday objects and foods, made of stuffed canvas or vinyl. One characteristic work is *Lipstick* 1969 (Yale University).

Oldenburg /ˈəʊldənbɜːg/ Henry 1615–1677. German official, residing in London from 1652, who founded and edited in 1665 the first-ever scientific periodical *Philosophical Transactions*. He was secretary to the Royal Society 1663–1677 and through his extensive correspondence acted as a clearing house for the science of the day.

Oldfield /ˈəʊldfiːld/ Barney 1878–1946. US racing-car driver. Henry Ford employed him as a driver for his experimental racing car 1902 and in the following year Oldfield set the world land speed record of 60 mph/96.6 kph. In 1910 he reached a speed in excess of 130 mph/209 kph.

Born in Wauseon, Ohio, USA, Oldfield established a reputation as a successful bicycle racer as a youth. A familiar figure at races across the country, he retired from competitive driving 1918 and spent the rest of his career as a consultant to various automobile and tyre makers.

Oldfield /ˈəʊldfiːld/ Bruce 1950– . English fashion designer who set up his own business 1975. His evening wear is worn by the British royal family, film stars, and socialites.

Old Pretender nickname of →James Edward Stuart, the son of James II of England.

Olds /əʊldz/ Ransom Eli 1864–1950. US car manufacturer. In 1895 he produced a gas-powered car and in the following year founded the Olds Motor Vehicle Company. Reorganizing the operation as the Olds Motor Works he produced his popular Oldsmobiles from 1899 in Detroit. He pioneered the assembly-line method of car production that would later be refined by Henry Ford.

Born in Geneva, Ohio, USA, and raised in Michigan, Olds experimented with steam-powered prototype automobiles from 1886. After selling the Olds Motor Works 1904, Olds established the Reo Motor Car Company, serving as its president 1904–24 and chair of the board 1924–36.

Olga, St /ˈɒlgə/ the wife of Igor, the Scandinavian prince of Kiev. Her baptism around 955 was a decisive step in the Christianization of Russia.

Oliphant Scottish writer Margaret Oliphant's best known novels, The Chronicles of Carlingford, *earned her the sobriquet a 'feminist Trollope'. Her astonishing literary output consisted not only of novels, but also several biographies, literary histories, travel books, translations, and tales of the supernatural.*

Oliphant /ˈɒlɪfənt/ Margaret 1828–1897. Scottish writer, author of over 100 novels, biographies, and numerous articles and essays. Her major work is the series *The Chronicles of Carlingford* 1863–66, including *The Perpetual Curate* and *Hester*.

Olivares /ˌɒlɪˈvɑːres/ Count-Duke of (born Gaspar de Guzmán) 1587–1645. Spanish prime minister 1621–43. He overstretched Spain in foreign affairs and unsuccessfully attempted domestic reform. He committed Spain to recapturing the Netherlands and to involvement in the Thirty Years' War 1618–48, and his efforts to centralize power led to revolts in Catalonia and Portugal, which brought about his downfall.

Oliver /ˈɒlɪvə/ Isaac *c.* 1556–1617. English painter of miniatures, originally a Huguenot refugee, who studied under Nicholas →Hilliard. He became a court artist in the reign of James I. His sitters included the poet John Donne.

Olivier /əˈlɪvieɪ/ Laurence (Kerr), Baron Olivier 1907–1989. English actor and director. For many years associated with the Old Vic theatre, he was director of the National Theatre company 1962–73. His stage roles include Henry V, Hamlet, Richard III, and Archie Rice in John Osborne's *The Entertainer*. His acting and direction of filmed versions of Shakespeare's plays received critical acclaim for example, *Henry V* 1944 and *Hamlet* 1948.

Olivier appeared on screen in many films, including *Wuthering Heights* 1939, *Rebecca* 1940, *Sleuth* 1972, *Marathon Man* 1976, and *The Boys from Brazil* 1978. The Olivier Theatre (part of the National Theatre on the South Bank, London) is named after him.

Olmsted /ˈəʊmsted/ Frederick Law 1822–1903. US landscape designer. Appointed superintendent of New York's Central Park 1857, Olmsted and his partner Calvert Vaux directed its design and construction. After the American Civil War 1861–65, he became a sought-after planner of public parks, designing the grounds of the World's Columbian Exposition 1893.

Born in Hartford, Connecticut, Olmsted became interested in scientific farming and founded a successful nursery business 1844. A keen observer of social and economic conditions, he published his travel journals of the South as *Journeys and Explorations in the Cotton Kingdom* 1861.

Olson /ˈəʊlsən/ Charles 1910–1970. US poet, associated with the Black Mountain school of experimental poets and originator of the theory of 'composition by field'. His *Maximus Poems* published in volumes 1953–75 were a striking attempt to extend the American epic poem beyond Ezra Pound's *Cantos* or William Carlos Williams's *Paterson*.

Omar /ˈəʊmɑː/ 581–644. Adviser of the prophet Muhammad. In 634 he succeeded Abu Bakr as caliph (civic and religious leader of Islam), and conquered Syria, Palestine, Egypt, and Persia. He was assassinated by a slave. The Mosque of Omar in Jerusalem is attributed to him.

Omar Khayyám /ˈəʊmɑː kəɪˈjæm/ *c.* 1050–1123. Persian astronomer, mathematician, and poet. In the West, he is chiefly known as a poet through Edward →Fitzgerald's version of *The Rubaiyat of Omar Khayyám* 1859.

Khayyám was born in Nishapur. He founded a school of astronomical research and assisted in reforming the calendar. The result of his observations was the *Jalālī* era, begun 1079. He wrote a study of algebra, which was known in Europe as well as in the East.

What is acting but lying and what is good acting but convincing lying?

Laurence Olivier *Autobiography* 1982

Omayyad dynasty /əʊˈmaɪæd/ Arabian dynasty of the Islamic empire who reigned as caliphs (civic and religious leaders of Islam) 661–750, when they were overthrown by Abbasids. A member of the family, Abd Al-Rahmam, escaped to Spain and in 756 assumed the title of emir of Córdoba. His dynasty, which took the title of caliph in 929, ruled in Córdoba until the early 11th century.

Onassis /əʊˈnæsɪs/ Aristotle (Socrates) 1906–1975. Turkish-born Greek shipowner. In 1932 he started what became the largest independent shipping line and during the 1950s he was one of the first to construct supertankers. In 1968 he married Jacqueline Kennedy, widow of US president John F Kennedy.

O'Neill /əʊˈniːl/ Eugene (Gladstone) 1888–1953. US playwright, the leading dramatist between World Wars I and II. His plays include *Anna Christie* 1922, *Desire under the Elms* 1924, *The Iceman Cometh* 1946, and the posthumously produced autobiographical drama *Long Day's Journey into Night* 1956 (written 1940). He was awarded the Nobel prize for Literature 1936.

O'Neill was born in New York. He had varied experience as gold prospector, sailor, and actor. Other plays include *Beyond the Horizon* 1920, *The Great God Brown* 1925, *Strange Interlude* 1928 (which lasts five hours), *Mourning Becomes Electra* 1931 (a trilogy on the theme of Orestes from Greek mythology, and *A Moon for the Misbegotten* 1947 (written 1943).

O'Neill /əʊˈniːl/ Terence, Baron O'Neill of the Maine 1914–1990. Northern Irish Unionist politician. In the Ulster government he was minister of finance 1956–63, then prime minister 1963–69. He resigned when opposed by his party on measures to extend rights to Roman Catholics, including a universal franchise.

Onsager /ˈɒnsɑːgə/ Lars 1903–1976. Norwegian-born US physical chemist. He worked on the application of the laws of thermodynamics to systems not in equilibrium, and received the 1968 Nobel Prize for Chemistry.

Oort /ɔːt/ Jan Hendrik 1900– . Dutch astronomer. In 1927, he calculated the mass and size of our Galaxy, the Milky Way, and the Sun's distance from its centre, from the observed movements of stars around the Galaxy's centre. In 1950 Oort proposed that comets exist in a vast swarm, now called the *Oort cloud*, at the edge of the solar system.

In 1944 Oort's student Hendrik van de Hulst (1918–) calculated that hydrogen in space would emit radio waves at 21 cm/8.3 in wavelength, and in the 1950s Oort's team mapped the spiral structure of the Milky Way from the radio waves given out by interstellar hydrogen.

Ophuls /ˈɒphʊls/ Max. Adopted name of Max Oppenheimer 1902–1957. German film director, whose style is characterized by a bittersweet tone and intricate camera movement. He worked in Europe and the USA, attracting much critical praise for such films as *Letter from an Unknown Woman* 1948, *La Ronde* 1950, and *Lola Montes* 1955.

Opie /ˈəʊpi/ John 1761–1807. British artist. Born in St Agnes, Cornwall, he was a portrait painter in London from 1780, later painting historical pictures and genre scenes. He became a professor at the Royal Academy 1805 and his lectures were published posthumously 1809.

I mix them with my brains, sir.

John Opie
when asked with what he mixed his colours

Opie /ˈəʊpi/ Peter Mason 1918–1982 and Iona Margaret Balfour 1923– . Husband-and-wife team of folklorists who specialized in the myths and literature of childhood. Their books include the *Oxford Dictionary of Nursery Rhymes* 1951 and *The Lore and Language of Schoolchildren* 1959. In 1987 their collection of children's books was sold to the Bodleian Library, Oxford, for £500,000.

Oppenheimer /ˈɒpənˌhaɪmə/ J(ulius) Robert 1904–1967. US physicist. As director of the Los Alamos Science Laboratory 1943–45, he was in charge of the development of the atom bomb (the Manhattan Project). When later he realized the dangers of radioactivity, he objected to the development of the hydrogen bomb, and was alleged to be a security risk 1953 by the US Atomic Energy Commission (AEC).

Oppenheimer was the son of a German immigrant. Before World War II he worked with the physicist Ernest Rutherford in Cambridge. He was rehabilitated by the AEC 1963 when it granted him the Fermi award for accomplishments in physics.

Oppenheimer US physicist J Robert Oppenheimer led the Manhattan Project, which produced the atom bomb. However, when he opposed the construction of the hydrogen bomb and advocated international control of atomic energy, he was accused of communist sympathies. He wrote several nontechnical books, including Science and the Common Understanding *1954.*

Orange, House of /ˈɒrɪndʒ/ royal family of the Netherlands. The title is derived from the small principality of Orange in S France, held by the family from the 8th century to 1713. They held considerable possessions in the Netherlands, to which, after 1530, was added the German county of Nassau.

From the time of William, Prince of Orange, the family dominated Dutch history, bearing the title of stadholder (magistrate) for the greater part of the 17th and 18th centuries. The son of Stadholder William V became King William I 1815.

Orbison /ˈɔːbɪsən/ Roy 1936–1988. US pop singer and songwriter specializing in slow, dramatic ballads, such as 'Only the Lonely' 1960 and 'Running Scared' 1961. His biggest hit was the jaunty 'Oh, Pretty Woman' 1964.

Born in Texas, Orbison began in the mid-1950s as a rockabilly singer on Sun Records. In the 1970s he turned to country material but made a pop comeback 1988 as a member of the Traveling Wilburys with Bob Dylan, George Harrison (ex-Beatle), Tom Petty (1952–), and Jeff Lynne (1947–).

Orczy /ˈɔːtsi/ Baroness Emmusca 1865–1947. Hungarian-born English novelist who wrote the historical adventure *The Scarlet Pimpernel* 1905. The foppish Sir Percy Blakeney, bold rescuer of victims of the French Revolution, appeared in many sequels.

Orellana /ˌɒrelˈjɑːnə/ Francisco de 1511–1546. Spanish explorer who travelled with Francesco →Pizarro from Guayaquil, on the Pacific coast of South America, to Quito in the Andes. He was the first person known to have navigated the full length of the Amazon from the Napo River to the Atlantic Ocean 1541–43.

Orff /ˈɔːf/ Carl 1895–1982. German composer, an individual stylist whose work is characterized by sharp dissonances and percussion. Among his compositions are the cantata *Carmina Burana* 1937 and the opera *Antigone* 1949.

Orford, 1st Earl of /ˈɔːfəd/ title of the British politician Robert →Walpole.

Organ /ˈɔːgən/ (Harold) Bryan 1935– . English portraitist whose subjects have included Harold Macmillan, Michael Tippett, Elton John, and the Prince and Princess of Wales.

Origen /ˈɒrɪdʒen/ c. 185–c. 254. Christian theologian, born in Alexandria, who produced a fancifully allegorical interpretation of the Bible. He castrated himself to ensure his celibacy.

Orlando /ɔːˈlændəʊ/ Vittorio Emanuele 1860–1952. Italian politician, prime minister 1917–19. He attended the Paris Peace Conference after World War I, but dissatisfaction with his handling of the Adriatic settlement led to his resignation. He initially supported Mussolini but was in retirement 1925–46, when he returned to the assembly and then the senate.

Ormandy /ˈɔːməndi/ Eugene 1899–1985. Hungarian-born US conductor, music director of the Philadelphia Orchestra 1936–80. Originally a violin virtuoso, he championed →Rachmaninov and →Shostakovich.

Ormonde /ˈɔːmənd/ James Butler, Duke of Ormonde 1610–1688. Irish general. He commanded the Royalist troops in Ireland 1641–50 during the Irish rebellion and the English Civil War, and was lord lieutenant 1644–47, 1661–69, and 1677–84. He was created a marquess 1642 and a duke 1661.

Orozco /ɒˈrɒskəʊ/ José Clemente 1883–1949. Mexican painter who painted murals inspired by the Mexican revolution of 1910, such as the series in the Palace of Government, Guadalajara, 1949.

Orpen /ˈɔːpən/ William Newenham Montague 1878–1931. Irish portraitist and genre artist, active mainly in London. He was elected a member of the Royal Academy 1919.

Orr /ˈɔː/ Bobby (Robert) 1948– . Canadian ice-hockey player who played for the Boston Bruins 1967–76 and the Chicago Blackhawks 1976–79 of the National Hockey League. He was voted the best defence every year 1967–75, and was Most Valuable Player 1970–72. He was the first defence to score 100 points in a season, and was leading scorer 1970 and 1975.

Orsini /ɔːˈsiːni/ Felice 1819–1858. Italian political activist, a member of the Carbonari secret revolutionary group, who attempted unsuccessfully to assassinate Napoleon III in Paris Jan 1858. He was subsequently executed, but the Orsini affair awakened Napoleon's interest in Italy and led to a secret alliance with Piedmont at Plombières 1858, directed against Italy.

Ortega Saavedra /ɔːˈteɪgə/ Daniel 1945– . Nicaraguan socialist politician, head of state 1981–90. He was a member of the Sandinista Liberation Front (FSLN), which overthrew the regime of Anastasio Somoza 1979. US-sponsored Contra guerrillas opposed his government from 1982.

A participant in underground activities against the Somoza regime from an early age, Ortega was imprisoned and tortured several times. He became a member of the national directorate of the FSLN and fought in the two-year campaign for the Nicaraguan Revolution. Ortega became a member of the junta of national reconstruction, and its coordinator two years later. The FSLN won the free 1984 elections, but in Feb 1990, Ortega lost the presidency to US- backed Violeta Chamorro.

Ortega y Gasset /ɔːˈteɪgə iː gæˈset/ José 1883–1955. Spanish philosopher and critic. He considered communism and fascism the cause of the downfall of Western civilization. His *Toward a Philosophy of History* 1941 contains philosophical reflections on the state and an interpretation of the meaning of human history.

Orton /ˈɔːtn/ Joe 1933–1967. English dramatist in whose black comedies surreal and violent action takes place in genteel and unlikely settings. Plays include *Entertaining Mr Sloane* 1964, *Loot* 1966, and *What the Butler Saw* 1968. His diaries deal frankly with his personal life. He was murdered by his lover Kenneth Halliwell.

The kind of people who always go on about whether a thing is in good taste invariably have very bad taste.

Joe Orton

Orwell /ˈɔːwel/ George. Pen name of Eric Arthur Blair 1903–1950. English author. His books include the satire *Animal Farm* 1945, which included such sayings as 'All animals are equal, but some are more equal than others', and the prophetic *Nineteen Eighty-Four* 1949, portraying the dangers of excessive state control over the individual. Other works include *Down and Out in Paris and London* 1933.

Born in India and educated in England, he served for five years in the Burmese police force, an experience reflected in the novel *Burmese Days* 1935. Life as a dishwasher and tramp were related in *Down and Out in Paris and London*, and service for the Republican cause in the Spanish Civil War in *Homage to Catalonia* 1938. He also wrote numerous essays.

Doublethink means the power of holding two contradictory beliefs in one's mind simultaneously, and accepting both of them.

George Orwell *Nineteen Eighty-Four*

Osborn /ˈɒzbɔːn/ Henry Fairfield 1857–1935. US palaeontologist. He made his first fossil-hunting expedition to the West 1877. He was staff palaeontologist with the US Geological Survey 1900–24 and president of the American Museum of Natural History 1908–33.

Born in Fairfield, Connecticut, USA, Osborn was educated at Princeton University. Appointed to the Princeton faculty 1881, he was named professor of biology at Columbia 1891. In the same year, he also began to serve as curator of vertebrate palaeontology at the American Museum of Natural History.

Osborne /ˈɒzbɔːn/ Dorothy 1627–1695. English letter-writer. In 1655 she married Sir William Temple (1628–99), to whom she addressed her letters, written 1652–54 and first published 1888.

Osborne /ˈɒzbɔːn/ John (James) 1929– . English dramatist. He became one of the first Angry Young Men (anti-establishment writers of the 1950s) of British theatre with his debut play, *Look Back in Anger* 1956. Other plays include *The Entertainer* 1957, *Luther* 1960, and *Watch It Come Down* 1976.

Oscar /ˈɒskə/ two kings of Sweden and Norway:

Oscar I 1799–1859. King of Sweden and Norway from 1844, when he succeeded his father, Charles XIV. He established freedom of the press, and supported Denmark against Germany 1848.

Oscar II 1829–1907. King of Sweden and Norway 1872–1905, king of Sweden until 1907. He was the younger son of Oscar I, and succeeded his brother Charles XV. He tried hard to prevent the separation of his two kingdoms but relinquished the throne of Norway to Haakon VII 1905.

He was an international arbitrator in Samoa, Venezuela, and the Anglo-American dispute.

Oshima /ˈəʊʃɪmə/ Nagisa 1932– . Japanese film director whose violent and sexually explicit *Ai No Corrida/In the Realm of the Senses* 1977 caused controversy when first released. His other work includes *Death by Hanging* 1968 and *Merry Christmas Mr Lawrence* 1983, which starred the singer David Bowie.

Osman I /ˈɒzmən/ or **Othman I** 1259–1326. Turkish ruler from 1299. He began his career in the service of the Seljuk Turks, but in 1299 he set up a kingdom of his own in Bithynia, NW Asia, and assumed the title of sultan. He conquered a great part of Anatolia, so founding a Turkish empire. His successors were known as 'sons of Osman', from which the term Ottoman Empire is derived.

Ossian /ˈɒsɪən/ (Celtic **Oisin**) legendary Irish hero, invented by the Scottish writer James →Macpherson. He is sometimes represented as the son of →Finn MacCumhaill, about 250, and as having lived to tell the tales of Finn and the Ulster heroes to St Patrick, about 400. The publication 1760 of Macpherson's poems, attributed to Ossian, made Ossian's name familiar throughout Europe.

Ostade /ˈɒstɑːdə/ Adriaen van 1610–1685. Dutch painter and engraver, known for pictures of tavern scenes and village fairs. A native of Haarlem, Ostade may have studied under Frans Hals. His brother, **Isaac van Ostade** (1621–49), excelled in portraying winter landscapes and roadside and farmyard scenes.

Östberg /ˈɜːstbɜːɡ/ Ragnar 1866–1945. Swedish architect who designed the City Hall, Stockholm, Sweden 1911–23.

Ostrovsky /ɒˈstrɒfski/ Alexander Nikolaevich 1823–1886. Russian playwright, founder of the modern Russian theatre. He dealt satirically with the manners of the middle class in numerous plays, for example *A Family Affair* 1850. His fairytale play *The Snow Maiden* 1873 inspired the composers Tchaikovsky and Rimsky-Korsakov.

Ostwald /ˈɒstvælt/ Wilhelm 1853–1932. German chemist who devised the Ostwald process (the oxidation of ammonia over a platinum catalyst to give nitric acid). His work on catalysts laid the foundations of the petrochemical industry. He won the Nobel Prize for Chemistry 1909.

Oswald, St /ˈɒzwəld/ c. 605–642. King of Northumbria from 634, after killing the Welsh king Cadwallon. He became a Christian convert during exile on the Scottish island of Iona. With the help of St Aidan he furthered the spread of Christianity in N England.

Oswald was defeated and killed by King Penda of Mercia. His feast day is 9 Aug.

Othman /ɒθˈmɑːn/ c. 574–656. Third caliph (leader of the Islamic empire) from 644, a son-in-law of the prophet Muhammad. Under his rule the Arabs became a naval power and extended their rule to N Africa and Cyprus, but Othman's personal weaknesses led to his assassination. He was responsible for the compilation of the authoritative version of the Koran, the sacred book of Islam.

Othman I another name for the Turkish sultan →Osman I.

Otho I /ˈəʊθəʊ/ 1815–1867. King of Greece 1832–62. As the 17-year-old son of King Ludwig I of Bavaria, he was selected by the European powers as the first king of independent Greece. He was overthrown by a popular revolt.

Otis /ˈəʊtɪs/ Elisha Graves 1811–1861. US engineer who developed a lift that incorporated a safety device, making it acceptable for passenger use in the first skyscrapers. The device, invented 1852, consisted of vertical ratchets on the sides of the lift shaft into which spring-loaded catches would engage and 'lock' the lift in position in the event of cable failure.

O'Toole /əʊˈtuːl/ Peter 1932– . Irish-born English actor who made his name as *Lawrence of Arabia* 1962, and who then starred in such films as *Becket* 1964 and *The Lion in Winter* 1968. Subsequent appearances were few and poorly received by critics until *The Ruling Class* 1972, *The Stuntman* 1978, and *High Spirits* 1988.

Otto /ˈɒtəʊ/ Nikolaus August 1832–1891. German engineer who in 1876 patented an effective internal-combustion engine.

Otto /ˈɒtəʊ/ four Holy Roman emperors, including:

Otto I 912–973. Holy Roman emperor from 936. He restored the power of the empire, asserted his authority over the pope and the nobles, ended the Magyar menace by his victory at the Lechfeld 955, and refounded the East Mark, or Austria, as a barrier against them.

Otto IV c. 1182–1218. Holy Roman emperor, elected 1198. He engaged in controversy with Pope Innocent III, and was defeated by the pope's ally, Philip of France, at Bouvines 1214.

Otway /ˈɒtweɪ/ Thomas 1652–1685. English dramatist. His plays include the tragedies *Alcibiades* 1675, *Don Carlos* 1676, *The Orphan* 1680, and *Venice Preserv'd* 1682.

Children blessings seem, but torments are;/ When young, our folly, and when old, our fear.

Thomas Otway *Don Carlos* 1676

Oughtred /ˈuːtrɪd/ William 1575–1660. English mathematician, credited as the inventor of the slide rule 1622. His major work *Clavis mathematicae/The Key to Mathematics* 1631 was a survey of the entire body of mathematical knowledge of his day. It introduced the 'x' symbol for multiplication, as well as the abbreviations 'sin' for sine and 'cos' for cosine.

Ouida /ˈwiːdə/ Pen name of Marie Louise de la Ramée 1839–1908. British romantic novelist, author of *Under Two Flags* 1867 and *Moths* 1880.

Ousmane Sembène 1923– . Senegalese writer and film director. His novels, written in French, include *Le Docker noir* 1956, about his experiences as a union leader in Marseille; *Les Bouts de bois/God's Bits of Wood* 1960; *Le Mandat/The Money Order* 1966; and *Xala* 1974, the last two of which he made into films (1968 and 1975).

Ouspensky /uːˈspenski/ Peter 1878–1947. Russian mystic. Originally a scientist, he became a disciple of →Gurdjieff and expanded his ideas in terms of other dimensions of space and time, for example in *Tertium Organum* 1912.

Outram /ˈuːtrəm/ James 1803–1863. British general, born in Derbyshire. He entered the Indian Army 1819, served in the Afghan and Sikh wars, and commanded in the Persian campaign of 1857. On the outbreak of the Indian Mutiny, he cooperated with General Henry Havelock (1795–1857) to raise the siege of Lucknow, and held the city until relieved by Sir Colin Campbell (later Baron Clyde).

Ovid /ˈɒvɪd/ (Publius Ovidius Naso) 43 BC–AD 17. Roman poet whose poetry deals mainly with the themes of love (*Amores* 20 BC, *Ars amatoria/The Art of Love* 1 BC), mythology (*Metamorphoses* AD 2), and exile (*Tristia* AD 9–12).

Born at Sulmo, Ovid studied rhetoric in Rome in preparation for a legal career, but soon turned to literature. In 8 BC he was banished by Emperor Augustus to Tomi, on the Black Sea, where he died. This punishment, supposedly for his immoral *Ars amatoria*, was probably due to some connection with Julia, the profligate daughter of Augustus.

Owen /ˈəʊɪn/ David 1938– . British politician, Labour foreign secretary 1977–79. In 1981 he was one of the founders of the Social Democratic

Party (SDP), and in 1983 became its leader. Opposed to the decision of the majority of the party to merge with the Liberals 1987, Owen stood down, but emerged 1988 as leader of a rump SDP, which was eventually disbanded 1990. In 1992 he was chosen to replace Lord Carrington as EC mediator in the peace talks on Bosnia-Herzegovina. Together with UN mediator Cyrus Vance, he was responsible for devising a peace plan dividing the republic into 10 semi-autonomious provices.

Owen /ˈəʊɪn/ Richard 1804–1892. British anatomist and palaeontologist. He attacked the theory of natural selection and in 1860 published an anonymous and damaging review of Charles →Darwin's work. He was Director of the Natural History Museum, London, 1856–1883 and was responsible for the first public exhibition of dinosaurs.

Owen /ˈəʊɪn/ Robert 1771–1858. British socialist, born in Wales. In 1800 he became manager of a mill at New Lanark, Scotland, where by improving working and housing conditions and providing schools he created a model community. His ideas stimulated the cooperative movement (the pooling of resources for joint economic benefit).

From 1817 Owen proposed that 'villages of cooperation', self-supporting communities run on socialist lines, should be founded; these, he believed, would ultimately replace private ownership. His later attempt to run such a community in the USA failed.

Owen /ˈəʊɪn/ Wilfred 1893–1918. English poet. His verse, owing much to the encouragement of Siegfried →Sassoon, expresses his hatred of war, for example *Anthem for Doomed Youth*, published 1921.

Owens /ˈəʊɪnz/ Jesse (James Cleveland) 1913–1980. US track and field athlete who excelled in the sprints, hurdles, and the long jump. At the 1936 Berlin Olympics he won four gold medals.

The Nazi leader Hitler is said to have stormed out of the stadium at the 1936 Berlin Olympic Games, in disgust at the black man's triumph. Owens held the world long-jump record for 25 years 1935–60. At Ann Arbor, Michigan, on 25 May 1935, he broke six world records in less than an hour.

Oxenstjerna /ˈʊksənˌʃeənə/ Axel Gustafsson, Count Oxenstjerna 1583–1654. Swedish politician, chancellor from 1612. He pursued Gustavus Adolphus's foreign policy, acted as regent for Queen Christina, and conducted the Thirty Years' War to a successful conclusion.

Oxford and Asquith, Earl of /ˈæskwɪθ/ title of British Liberal politician Herbert Henry →Asquith.

Owen British anatomist and palaeontologist, Richard Owen was a pioneer in the scientific identification and classification of species. He reconstructed the newly discovered remains of the archaeopteryx and the New Zealand moa.

Oyono /ˌɔɪəʊˈnəʊ/ Ferdinand 1929– . Cameroon novelist, writing in French. His work describes Cameroon during the colonial era, for example *Une Vie de boy/Houseboy* 1956 and *Le vieux Nègre et la médaille/The Old Man and the Medal* 1956.

Ozal /əʊˈzɑːl/ Turgut 1927–1993. Turkish Islamic right-wing politician, prime minister 1983–89, president from 1989. He has been responsible for improving his country's relations with Greece, but his prime objective has been to strengthen Turkey's alliance with the USA.

Ozal first entered government service, then worked for the World Bank 1971–79. In 1980 he was deputy to Prime Minister Bulent Ulusu under the military regime of Kenan Evren, and, when political pluralism returned 1983, he founded the Islamic, right-of-centre Motherland Party (ANAP) and led it to victory in the elections of that year. In the 1987 general election he retained his majority and Nov 1989 replaced Evren as Turkey's first civilian president for 30 years.

Ozu /ˈəʊzuː/ Yasujiro 1903–1963. Japanese film director who became known in the West only in his last years. *Tokyo Monogatari/Tokyo Story* 1953 illustrates his typical low camera angles and his theme of middle-class family life.

His other major films include *Late Spring* 1949 and *Autumn Afternoon* 1962.

P

Pabst /pɑːpst/ G(eorg) W(ilhelm) 1885–1967. German film director whose films include *Die Büchse der Pandora*/*Pandora's Box* 1928, *Das Tagebuch einer Verlorenen*/*The Diary of a Lost Girl* 1929, both starring Louise →Brooks, the striking antiwar story *Westfront 1918* 1930, and *Die Dreigroschenoper*/*The Threepenny Opera* 1931.

Pachomius, St /pəˈkəʊmiəs/ 292–346. Egyptian Christian, the founder of the first Christian monastery, near Dendera on the river Nile.

Originally for Copts (Egyptian Christians), the monastic movement soon spread to include Greeks.

Pacino /pəˈtʃiːnəʊ/ Al(berto) 1940– . US film actor who played powerful, introverted but violent roles in films such as *The Godfather* 1972, *Serpico* 1973, and *Scarface* 1983. *Dick Tracy* 1990 added comedy to his range of acting styles, and *The Godfather Part III* added subdued style to his virtuoso performances.

Packer /ˈpækə/ Kerry (Francis Bullmore) 1937– . Australian media proprietor. He is chair of Consolidated Press Holdings, which he priva-

Paderewski Ignacy Jan Paderewski, Polish virtuoso pianist, composer, and politician, who was the first Polish prime minister after independence from Russia 1918, and was a lifelong Polish patriot. His last composition, Symphony in B minor, is a musical portrait of the history of Poland.

tized in 1983, a conglomerate founded by his father which produces such magazines as the *Australian Women's Weekly* and the *Bulletin*. CPH also has interests in radio and television stations. In 1977 he created World Series Cricket, which introduced one-day matches and coloured kit to the game.

Paderewski /ˌpædəˈrefski/ Ignacy Jan 1860–1941. Polish pianist, composer, and politician. After his debut in Vienna 1887 he became celebrated in Europe and the USA as an interpreter of the piano music of Chopin. During World War I he helped organize the Polish army in France; in 1919 he became prime minister of the newly independent Poland, which he represented at the Peace Conference, but continuing opposition forced him to resign the same year. He resumed a musical career 1922, was made president of the Polish National Council in Paris 1940, and died in New York.

Paganini /ˌpægəˈniːni/ Niccolò 1782–1840. Italian violinist and composer, a virtuoso soloist from the age of nine. He invented all the virtuoso techniques that have since been included in violin composition. His works for the violin ingeniously exploit the potential of the instrument. His raffish appearance, wild amours, and virtuosity (especially on a single string) fostered a rumour of his being in league with the devil.

Page /peɪdʒ/ Earle (Christmas Grafton) 1880–1961. Australian politician, leader of the Country Party 1920–39 and briefly prime minister in April 1939. He represented Australia in the British war cabinet 1941–42 and was minister of health 1949–55.

Page /peɪdʒ/ Frederick Handley 1885–1962. British aircraft engineer, founder 1909 of one of the earliest aircraft-manufacturing companies and designer of long-range civil aeroplanes and multi-engined bombers in both world wars; for example, the Halifax, flown in World War II.

Pagnol /pænˈjɒl/ Marcel 1895–1974. French film director, producer, author, and playwright whose work includes *Fanny* 1932 and *Manon des sources* 1952. His autobiographical *La Gloire de mon père*/*My Father's Glory* 1957 was filmed 1991. He regarded the cinema as recorded theatre; thus his films, although strong on character and background, fail to exploit the medium fully as an independent art form.

Paige /peɪdʒ/ Satchel (Leroy Robert) 1906–1982. US baseball player. As a pitcher, he established a near-legendary record, leading the Kansas City Monarchs of the Negro National League to the championship 1942. In 1948, with the end of racial segregation in the major leagues, Paige joined the Cleveland Indians. He later played with the St Louis Browns 1951–53.

Born in Mobile, Alabama, USA, Paige began playing professional baseball in the Negro leagues in the 1920s.

He was elected to the Baseball Hall of Fame 1971.

Paine /peɪn/ Thomas 1737–1809. English left-wing political writer, active in the American and French revolutions. His pamphlet *Common Sense* 1776 ignited passions in the American Revolution; others include *The Rights of Man* 1791 and *The Age of Reason* 1793. He advocated republicanism, deism, the abolition of slavery, and the emancipation of women.

Paine, born in Thetford, Norfolk, was a friend of US scientist and politician Benjamin Franklin and went to America 1774, where he published several republican pamphlets and fought for the colonists in the revolution. In 1787 he returned to Britain. *The Rights of Man* is an answer to the conservative theorist Burke's *Reflections on the Revolution in France*. In 1792, Paine was indicted for treason and escaped to France, to represent Calais in the National Convention. Narrowly escaping the guillotine, he regained his seat after the fall of Robespierre. Paine returned to the USA 1802 and died in New York.

Pakula /pəkuːə/ Alan J 1928– . US film director, formerly a producer, whose compelling films include *Klute* 1971, *The Parallax View* 1974, and *All the President's Men* 1976. His later work includes *Sophie's Choice* 1982 and *Presumed Innocent* 1990.

In his role as producer he was involved with *Fear Strikes Out*, *To Kill A Mockingbird* 1962 and *The Stalking Moon* 1969, all directed by Robert Mulligan (1925–   ).

Palamas /pæləməs/ Kostes 1859–1943. Greek poet. He enriched the Greek vernacular by his use of it as a literary language, particularly in his poetry, such as in *Songs of My Fatherland* 1886 and *The Flute of the King* 1910, which expresses his vivid awareness of Greek history.

Palance /pæləns/ Jack. Stage name of Walter Jack Palahnuik 1920–   . US film actor, often cast as a brooding villain: his films include *Shane* 1953, *Contempt* 1963, and *Batman* 1989. In 1992 he received an Academy Award as best supporting actor in *City Slickers* 1991.

Palestrina /pælɪ'striːnə/ Giovanni Pierluigi da 1525–1594. Italian composer of secular and sacred choral music. Apart from motets and madrigals, he also wrote 105 masses, including *Missa Papae Marcelli*.

Paley /peɪli/ Grace 1922–   . US short-story writer and critic. Her stories express Jewish and feminist experience with bitter humour, as in *The Little Disturbances of Man* 1960 and *Later the Same Day* 1985.

Paley /peɪli/ William 1743–1805. English Christian theologian and philosopher. He put forward the argument from design theory, which reasons that the complexity of the universe necessitates a superhuman creator and that the existence of this being (God) can be deduced from a 'design' seen in all living creatures. His views were widely held until challenged by Charles →Darwin. His major treatises include *The Principles of Moral and Political Philosophy* 1785, *A View of the Evidences of Christianity* 1794, and *Natural Theology* 1802.

Palissy /pælɪ'siː/ Bernard 1510–1589. French potter who made richly coloured rustic pieces, such as dishes with realistic modelled fish and reptiles. He was favoured by the queen, Catherine de' Medici but was imprisoned in the Bastille as a Huguenot in 1588, and died there.

Palladio /pə'laːdiəʊ/ Andrea 1518–1580. Italian Renaissance architect noted for his harmonious and balanced classical structures. He designed numerous country houses in and around Vicenza, Italy, making use of Roman classical forms, symmetry, and proportion. The Villa Malcontenta and the Villa Rotonda are examples of houses designed from 1540 for patrician families of the Venetian Republic. He also designed churches in Venice and published his studies of classical form in several illustrated books.

His ideas were revived in England in the early 17th century by Inigo Jones and in the 18th century by Lord Burlington and later by architects in Italy, Holland, Germany, Russia, and the USA. Examples of Neo-Classical architecture influenced by 'Palladian' buildings include Washington's home at Mount Vernon, USA, the palace of Tsarskoe Selo in Russia, and Prior Park, England.

Palme /paːlmə/ (Sven) Olof 1927–1986. Swedish social-democratic politician, prime minister 1969–76 and 1982–86. As prime minister he carried out constitutional reforms, turning the Riksdag into a single-chamber parliament and stripping the monarch of power, and was widely respected for his support of Third World Countries. He was assassinated Feb 1986.

Palme, educated in Sweden and the USA, joined the SAP 1949 and became secretary to the prime minister 1954. He led the SAP youth movement 1955–61. In 1963 he entered government and held several posts before becoming leader of the Social Democratic Labour Party (SAP) 1969. Palme was shot by an unknown assassin in the centre of Stockholm while walking home with his wife after an evening visit to a cinema.

Palmer /ˈpɑːmə/ A(lexander) Mitchell 1872–1936. US public official. He held office in the US House of Representatives 1909–15. A Quaker, he declined an appointment as secretary of war under President Wilson, and served instead as custodian of alien property during World War I. As US attorney general 1919–21, he led the controversial 'Palmer Raids' against alleged political radicals.

Born in Moosehead, Pennsylvania, Palmer was educated at Swarthmore College and was admitted to the bar 1893. After establishing a private legal practice in Stroudsburg, Pennsylvania, he became active in state Democratic politics.

Palmer /ˈpɑːmə/ Arnold (Daniel) 1929– . US golfer who helped to popularize the professional sport in the USA in the 1950s and 1960s. He won the Masters 1958, 1960, 1962, and 1964; the US Open 1960; and the British Open 1961 and 1962.

Born in Pennsylvania, he won the US amateur title 1954, and went on to win all the world major professional trophies except the US PGA Championship. In the 1980s he enjoyed a successful career on the US Seniors Tour.

Palmer /ˈpɑːmə/ Geoffrey Winston Russell 1942– . New Zealand Labour politician, prime minister 1989–90, deputy prime minister and attorney-general 1984–89.

A graduate of Victoria University, Wellington, Palmer was a law lecturer in the USA and New Zealand before entering politics, becoming Labour member for Christchurch in the House of Representatives 1979. He succeeded David →Lange on Lange's resignation as prime minister but resigned himself the following year.

Palmer /ˈpɑːmə/ Samuel 1805–1881. English landscape painter and etcher. He lived in Shoreham, Kent, 1826–35 with a group of artists who were all followers of William Blake and called themselves 'the Ancients'. Palmer's expressive landscape style during that period reflected a strongly spiritual inspiration.

Palmerston /ˈpɑːməstən/ Henry John Temple, 3rd Viscount Palmerston 1784–1865. British politician. Initially a Tory, in Parliament from 1807, he was secretary-at-war 1809–28. He broke with the Tories 1830 and sat in the Whig cabinets of 1830–34, 1835–41, and 1846–51 as foreign secretary. He was prime minister 1855–58 (when he rectified Aberdeen's mismanagement of the Crimean War, suppressed the Indian Mutiny, and carried through the Second Opium War) and 1859–65 (when he almost involved Britain in the American Civil War on the side of the South).

Palmerston succeeded to an Irish peerage 1802. He served under five Tory prime ministers before joining the Whigs. His foreign policy was marked by distrust of France and Russia, against whose designs he backed the independence of Belgium and Turkey. He became home secretary in the coalition government of 1852, and prime minister on its fall, and was responsible for the warship *Alabama* going to the Confederate side in the American Civil War. He was popular with the people and made good use of the press, but his high handed attitude annoyed Queen Victoria and other ministers.

Die, my dear Doctor, that's the last thing I shall do!

Lord Palmerston (last words)

Palumbo /pəˈlʌmbəʊ/ Peter 1935– . British property developer. Appointed chair of the Arts Council 1988, he advocated a close partnership between public and private funding of the arts, and a greater role for the regions. His planned skyscraper by the German architect Ludwig Mies van der Rohe beside he Mansion House, London, was condemned by Prince Charles as 'a giant glass stump'.

Panchen Lama /ˈpɑːntʃən ˈlɑːmə/ 10th incarnation 1935–1989. Tibetan spiritual leader, second in importance to the →Dalai Lama. A protégé of the Chinese since childhood, the present Panchen Lama is not universally recognized. When the Dalai Lama left Tibet 1959, the Panchen Lama was deputed by the Chinese to take over, but was stripped of power 1964 for refusing to denounce the Dalai Lama. He did not appear again in public until 1978.

Pandit /ˈpændɪt/ Vijaya Lakshmi 1900–1990. Indian politician, member of parliament 1964–68. She was involved, with her brother Jawaharlal →Nehru, in the struggle for India's independence and was imprisoned three times by the British. She was the first woman to serve as president of the United Nations General Assembly, 1953–54, and held a number of political and diplomatic posts until her retirement 1968.

Pankhurst /ˈpæŋkhɜːst/ Emmeline (born Goulden) 1858–1928. English suffragette. Founder of the Women's Social and Political Union 1903, she launched the militant suffragette campaign 1905. In 1926 she joined the Conservative Party and was a prospective Parliamentary candidate.

She was supported by her daughters *Christabel Pankhurst* (1880–1958), political leader of the movement, and *Sylvia Pankhurst* (1882–1960). The latter was imprisoned nine times under the 'Cat and Mouse Act', and was a pacifist in World War I.

Panufnik /pəˈnuːfnɪk/ Andrzei 1914–1991. Polish composer and conductor. A pupil of Weingartner, he came to Britain in 1954. His music is based on an intense working out of small motifs.

Paolozzi /paʊˈlɒtsi/ Eduardo 1924– . English sculptor, a major force in the Pop art movement in London in the mid-1950s. He typically uses bronze casts of pieces of machinery to create robotlike structures.

He designed the mural decorations for Tottenham Court Road tube station, London, installed 1983–85.

Papandreou /ˌpæpænˈdreɪuː/ Andreas 1919– . Greek socialist politician, founder of the Pan-Hellenic Socialist Movement (PASOK), and prime minister 1981–89, when he became implicated in the alleged embezzlement and diversion of funds to the Greek government of $200 million from the Bank of Crete, headed by George Koskotas, and as a result lost the election. In Jan 1992 a trial cleared Papandreou of all corruption charges.

Son of a former prime minister, he studied law in Athens and at Harvard. He was director of the Centre for Economic Research in Athens 1961–64, and economic adviser to the Bank of Greece. He was imprisoned April–Dec 1967 for his political activities, after which he founded PASOK. After another spell in overseas universities, he returned to Greece 1974. He was leader of the opposition 1977–81, and became Greece's first socialist prime minister. He was re-elected 1985, but defeated 1989 after damage to his party and himself from the Koskotas affair. After being acquitted Jan 1992, Papandreou's request for a general election was rejected by the government.

Papen /ˈpɑːpən/ Franz von 1879–1969. German right-wing politician. As chancellor 1932, he negotiated the Nazi-Conservative alliance that made Hitler chancellor 1933. He was envoy to Austria 1934–38 and ambassador to Turkey 1939–44. Although acquitted at the Nuremberg trials, he was imprisoned by a German denazification court for three years.

Papineau /ˌpæpɪˈnəʊ/ Louis Joseph 1786–1871. Canadian politician. He led a mission to England to protest against the planned union of Lower Canada (Québec) and Upper Canada (Ontario), and demanded economic reform and an elected provincial legislature. In 1835 he gained the cooperation of William Lyon →Mackenzie in Upper Canada, and in 1837 organized an unsuccessful rebellion of the French against British rule in Lower Canada. He fled the country, but returned 1847 to sit in the United Canadian legislature until 1854.

Papp /pæp/ Joseph 1921–1991. US theatre director, and founder of the New York Shakespeare Festival 1954 held in an open-air theatre in the city's Central Park. He also founded the New York Public Theater 1967, an off-Broadway forum for new talent, which staged the first productions of the musicals *Hair* 1967 and *A Chorus Line*.

Productions directed by Papp include *The Merchant of Venice* and a musical version of *The Two Gentlemen of Verona* (Tony award 1972). Many of Papp's productions achieved great success when transferred to Broadway.

What is accomplished with fire is alchemy, whether in the furnace or the kitchen stove.

Paracelsus

Paracelsus /ˌpærəˈselsəs/ Adopted name of Theophrastus Bombastus von Hohenheim 1493–1541. Swiss physician, alchemist, and scientist. He developed the idea that minerals and chemicals might have medical uses (iatrochemistry). He introduced the use of laudanum (which he named) for pain-killing purposes. Considered by some to be something of a charlatan, his books were also criticized because of their mystical content. However, his rejection of the ancients and insistence on the value of experimentation make him a leading figure in early science.

He lectured in Basel on the need for observational experience rather than traditional lore in medicine: he made a public bonfire of the works of his predecessors Avicenna and Galen. He was the disseminator in Europe of the medieval Islamic alchemists' theory that matter is composed of only three elements: salt, sulphur, and mercury.

Pardo Bazán /ˈpɑːdəʊ bəˈθæn/ Emilia 1852–1921. Spanish writer, author of more than 20 novels, 600 short stories, and many articles. *Los Pazos de Ulloa/The House of Ulloa* 1886 and its sequel *La madre naturaleza/Mother Nature* 1887, set in her native Galicia, describe the decline of the provincial aristocracy.

Paré /pæˈreɪ/ Ambroise 1509–1590. French surgeon who introduced modern principles to the treatment of wounds. As a military surgeon, Paré developed new ways of treating wounds and amputations, which greatly reduced the death rate among the wounded. He abandoned the practice of cauterization (sealing with heat), using balms and soothing lotions instead, and used ligatures to tie off blood vessels.

Paré eventually became chief surgeon to Charles IX. He also made important contributions to dentistry and childbirth, and invented an artificial hand.

Pareto /pəˈreɪtəʊ/ Vilfredo 1848–1923. Italian economist and political philosopher. A vigorous opponent of socialism and liberalism, he justified inequality of income on the grounds of his empirical observation (*Pareto's law*) that income distribution remained constant whatever efforts were made to change it.

Pareto was born in Paris. He produced the first account of society as a self-regulating and interdependent system that operates independently of human attempts at voluntary control. A founder of welfare economics, he put forward a concept of 'optimality', which contends that optimum conditions exist in an economic system if no one can be made better off without at least one other person becoming worse off.

Park Scottish surgeon and explorer Mungo Park whose tracing of the Niger river determined the direction of its flow. His journey's hardships and adventures, including his four months' imprisonment by an Arab chief, were told in Travels in the Interior of Africa *1799 which was a popular success.*

Paris /pærɪs/ Henri d'Orléans, Comte de Paris 1908– . Head of the royal house of France. He served in the Foreign Legion under an assumed name 1939–40, and in 1950, on the repeal of the *loi d'exil* of 1886 banning pretenders to the French throne, returned to live in France.

Paris /pærɪs/ Matthew *c.* 1200–1259. English chronicler. He entered St Albans Abbey 1217, and wrote a valuable history of England up to 1259.

Park /pɑːk/ Merle 1937– . Rhodesian-born English ballerina. She joined the Sadler's Wells Ballet 1954, and by 1959 was a principal soloist with the Royal Ballet. She combined elegance with sympathetic appeal in such roles as Cinderella.

Park /pɑːk/ Mungo 1771–1806. Scottish explorer who traced the course of the Niger river 1795– 97. He disappeared and probably drowned during a second African expedition in 1805–06. He published *Travels in the Interior of Africa* 1799.

Park spent eighteen months in the Niger Basin while tracing the river. Even though he did not achieve his goal of reaching Timbuktu, he proved that it was feasible to travel through the interior of Africa.

Park Chung Hee /pɑːk ˌtʃʊŋ ˈhiː/ 1917–1979. President of South Korea 1963–79. Under his rule South Korea had one of the world's fastest-growing economies, but recession and his increasing authoritarianism led to his assassination 1979.

Parker /pɑːkə/ Bonnie 1911–1943. US criminal; see →Bonnie and Clyde.

Parker /pɑːkə/ Charlie (Charles Christopher 'Bird', 'Yardbird') 1920–1955. US alto saxophonist and jazz composer, associated with the trumpeter Dizzy Gillespie in developing the bebop style. His mastery of improvisation inspired performers on all jazz instruments.

Parker's most important recordings were made in the 1940s, many with a group that included Miles Davis on trumpet. He was also very influential as a live performer.

Parker /pɑːkə/ Dorothy (born Rothschild) 1893–1967. US writer and wit, a leading member of the Algonquin Round Table. She reviewed for the magazines *Vanity Fair* and *The New Yorker*, and wrote wittily ironic verses, collected in several volumes including *Not So Deep As a Well* 1940, and short stories.

Parker /pɑːkə/ Matthew 1504–1575. English cleric. He was converted to Protestantism at Cambridge University. He received high preferment under Henry VIII and Edward VI, and as archbishop of Canterbury from 1559 was largely responsible for the Elizabethan religious settlement (the formal establishment of the Church of England).

Parkes /pɑːks/ Henry 1815–1896. Australian politician, born in the UK. He promoted education and the cause of federation, and suggested the official name 'Commonwealth of Australia'. He was five times premier of New South Wales 1872–91.

Parkes, New South Wales, is named after him.

Inertia rides and riddles me;
That which is called Philosophy.

Dorothy Parker,
Not So Deep as a Well 'The Veteran' 1927

Parkinson /pɑːkɪnsən/ Cecil (Edward) 1931– . British Conservative politician. He was chair of the party 1981–83, and became minister for trade and industry, but resigned Oct 1984 following disclosure of an affair with his secretary. In 1987 he rejoined the cabinet as secretary of state for energy, and in 1989 became transport secretary. He left the cabinet when John Major became prime minister 1990 and later announced his intention to retire from active politics.

Parkinson /pɑːkɪnsən/ Cyril Northcote 1909– . English writer and historian, celebrated for his study of public and business administration, *Parkinson's Law* 1958, which included the dictum: 'Work expands to fill the time available for its completion.'

Parkinson /pɑːkɪnsən/ James 1755–1824. British neurologist who first described Parkinson's disease.

Parkinson /pɑːkɪnsən/ Norman. Adopted name of Ronald William Parkinson Smith 1913–1990.

English fashion and portrait photographer who caught the essential glamour of each decade from the 1930s to the 1980s. Long associated with the magazines *Vogue* and *Queen*, he was best known for his colour work, and from the late 1960s took many official portraits of the royal family.

Parkman /ˈpɑːkmən/ Francis 1823–1893. US historian and traveller who chronicled the European exploration and conquest of North America in such books as *The California and Oregon Trail* 1849 and *La Salle and the Discovery of the Great West* 1879.

Parkman viewed the defeat by England of the French at Québec 1759 (described in his *Montcalm and Wolfe* 1884) as the turning point of North American history, insofar as it swung the balance of power in North America towards the British colonies, which would form the United States of America.

Parmenides /pɑːˈmenɪdiːz/ *c.* 510–450 BC. Greek pre-Socratic philosopher, head of the Eleatic school (so called after Elea in S Italy). Against Heraclitus' doctrine of Becoming, Parmenides advanced the view that nonexistence was impossible, that everything was permanently in a state of being. Despite evidence of the senses to the contrary, motion and change are illusory – in fact, logically impossible – because their existence would imply a contradiction. Parmenides saw speculation and reason as more important than the evidence of the senses.

Parmigianino /ˌpɑːmɪdʒəˈniːnəʊ/ Francesco 1503–1540. Italian painter and etcher, active in Parma and elsewhere. He painted religious subjects and portraits in a Mannerist style, with elongated figures, for example *Madonna of the Long Neck c.* 1535 (Uffizi, Florence).

Parmigianino was the first Italian artist to make original etchings (rather than copies of existing paintings).

These Englishmen despise us because we are Irish, but we must stand up to them. That's the only way to treat an Englishman – stand up to him.

Charles Stewart Parnell letter to his brother

Parnell /ˈpɑːnel/ Charles Stewart 1846–1891. Irish nationalist politician. He supported a policy of obstruction and violence to attain Home Rule, and became the president of the Nationalist Party 1877. In 1879 he approved the Land League (Irish peasants-rights organization), and his attitude led to his imprisonment 1881. His career was ruined 1890 when he was cited as co-respondent in a divorce case.

Parnell, born in County Wicklow, was elected member of Parliament for Meath 1875. He welcomed Gladstone's Home Rule Bill, and contin-

Parnell *Irish politician Charles Parnell, who agitated fiercely for Irish Home Rule. He united nationalists and supported the Land League in an attempt to solidify the Home Rule Confederation. In spite of his great ability, his relationship with Katherine O'Shea (whom he later married) led to his political downfall.*

ued his agitation after its defeat 1886. In 1887 his reputation suffered from an unfounded accusation by *The Times* of complicity in the murder of Lord Frederick ➔Cavendish, chief secretary to the Lord-lieutenant of Ireland. Three years later came the adultery scandal, and for fear of losing the support of Gladstone, Parnell's party deposed him. He died suddenly of rheumatic fever at the age of 45.

Parr /pɑː/ Catherine 1512–1548. Sixth wife of Henry VIII of England. She had already lost two husbands when in 1543 she married Henry VIII. She survived him, and in 1547 married Lord Seymour of Sudeley (1508–1549).

Parry /ˈpæri/ Charles Hubert Hastings 1848–1918. English composer. His works include songs, motets, and the setting of Milton's 'Blest Pair of Sirens' and Blake's 'Jerusalem'.

Parry /ˈpæri/ William Edward 1790–1855. English admiral and Arctic explorer. He made detailed charts during explorations of the Northwest Passage (the sea route between the Atlantic and Pacific oceans) 1819–20, 1821–23, and 1824–25.

He made an attempt to reach the North Pole 1827. The Parry Islands, Northwest Territories, Canada, are named after him.

Parsons /ˈpɑːsənz/ Charles Algernon 1854–1931. English engineer who invented the Parsons steam turbine 1884, a landmark in marine engineering and later universally used in electricity generation to drive an alternator.

Parsons /pɑːsnz/ Louella 1893–1972. US newspaper columnist. Working for the →Hearst syndicate, she moved to Hollywood 1925 and began a gossip column and a popular radio programme 'Hollywood Hotel' 1934. For over 40 years she exerted great influence (some damaging) over the lives of stars and studios. She published her memoirs as *The Gay Illiterate* 1944 and *Tell It to Louella* 1961.

Born in Freeport, Illinois, USA, Parsons began her newspaper career in Dixon, Illinois, soon after high school. In 1914 she moved to Chicago and worked as a reporter for the *Tribune* and *Record-Herald*, where she wrote a regular movie column. Parsons was hired by the *New York Morning Telegraph* 1918 before joining the Hearst syndicate.

Parsons /pɑːsənz/ Talcott 1902–1979. US sociologist who attempted to integrate all the social sciences into a science of human action. He was professor of sociology at Harvard University from 1931 until his death, and author of over 150 books and articles. His theory of structural functionalism dominated US sociology from the 1940s to the 1960s, and as an attempt to explain social order and individual behaviour, it was a major step in establishing sociology as an academic and scientific discipline.

Only in certain types of society can science flourish, and conversely without a continuous and healthy development and application of science such a society cannot function properly.

Talcott Parsons,
The Social System 1951

Parton /pɑːtn/ Dolly 1946– . US country and western singer and songwriter whose combination of cartoonlike sex-symbol looks and intelligent, assertive lyrics made her popular beyond the genre, with hits like 'Jolene' 1974, but deliberate crossover attempts were less successful. She has also appeared in films, beginning with *9 to 5* 1980, and established a theme park Dollywood in Tennessee 1986.

Partridge /pɑːtrɪdʒ/ Eric 1894–1979. New Zealand lexicographer. He studied at Oxford University and settled in England to write a number of dictionaries, including *A Dictionary of Slang and Unconventional English* 1934 and 1970, and *Dictionary of the Underworld, British and American* 1950.

Pascal /pæskæl/ Blaise 1623–1662. French philosopher and mathematician. He contributed to the development of hydraulics, the calculus, and the mathematical theory of probability.

In mathematics, Pascal is known for his work on conic sections and, with Pierre de Fermat, on the probability theory. In physics, Pascal's chief work concerned fluid pressure and hydraulics. *Pascal's principle* states that the pressure everywhere in a fluid is the same, so that pressure applied at one point is transmitted equally to all parts of the container. This is the principle of the hydraulic press and jack.

Pascal's triangle is a triangular array of numbers in which each number is the sum of the pair of numbers above it. Plotted at equal distances along a horizontal axis, the numbers in the rows give the binomial probability distribution with equal probability of success and failure, such as when tossing fair coins.

In 1654 Pascal went into the Jansenist monastery of Port Royal and defended a prominent Jansenist, Antoine Arnauld (1612–1694), against the Jesuits in his *Lettres Provinciales* 1656. His *Pensées* 1670 was part of an unfinished defence of the Christian religion.

Pasmore /pɑːsmɔː/ Victor 1908– . English painter, a member of the Euston Road School (which favoured a subdued, measured style) in the 1930s. He painted landscapes and, from 1947, abstract paintings and constructions, reviving the early ideas of the Constructivists.

Pasolini /pæsəliːni/ Pier Paolo 1922–1975. Italian director, poet, and novelist. His early work is coloured by his experience of life in the poor districts of Rome, where he lived from 1950. From his Marxist viewpoint, he illustrates the decadence and inequality of society, set in a world ravaged by violence and sexuality. Among his films are *Il vangelo secondo Mateo/The Gospel According to St Matthew* 1964, *The Decameron* 1970, *I racconti de Canterbury/The Canterbury Tales* 1972, and the notorious *Salò/Salo – The 120 Days of Sodom* 1975, which included explicit scenes of sexual perversion.

Pasolini's writings (making much use of first Friulan and later Roman dialect) include the novels *Ragazzi di vita/The Ragazzi* 1955 and *Una vita violenta/A Violent Life* 1959, filmed with success as *Accattone!* 1961. He was murdered by a 17-year-old youth.

The heart has its reasons which reason knows nothing of.

Blaise Pascal *Pensées*

Passfield /pɑːsfiːld/ Baron Passfield. Title of the Fabian socialist Sidney →Webb.

Passy /pæsi/ Frédéric 1822–1912. French economist who shared the first Nobel Peace Prize 1901 with Jean-Henri Dunant. He founded the Inter-national League for Permanent Peace 1867, and was cofounder, with the English politician William Cremer (1828–1908), of the Inter-Parliamentary Conferences on Peace and on Arbitration 1889.

Pasternak /ˈpæstənæk/ Boris Leonidovich 1890–1960. Russian poet and novelist. His novel *Dr Zhivago* 1957 was banned in the USSR as a 'hostile act', and was awarded a Nobel prize (which Pasternak declined). *Dr Zhivago* has since been unbanned and Pasternak has been posthumously rehabilitated.

Born in Moscow, he remained in Russia when his father, the artist Leonid Pasternak (1862–1945), emigrated. His volumes of lyric poems include *A Twin Cloud* 1914 and *On Early Trains* 1943, and he translated Shakespeare's tragedies into Russian.

In the field of observation, chance only favours those who have been prepared for it.

Louis Pasteur 1911

Pasteur /pæstɜ:/ Louis 1822–1895. French chemist and microbiologist who discovered that fermentation is caused by microorganisms. He also developed a vaccine for rabies, which led to the foundation of the Institut Pasteur in Paris 1888.

Pasteur saved the French silkworm industry by identifying two microbial diseases that were decimating the worms. He discovered the pathogens responsible for anthrax and chicken cholera, and developed vaccines for these diseases. He inspired his pupil Joseph →Lister's work in antiseptic surgery. *Pasteurization* to make dairy products free from the tuberculosis bacteria is based on his discoveries.

Paston family family of Norfolk, England, whose correspondence and documents (known as the Paston letters) for 1422–1509 throw valuable light on the period.

Patel /pəˈteɪl/ Vallabhbhai Jhaverbhai 1875–1950. Indian political leader. A fervent follower of Mahatma Gandhi and a leader of the Indian National Congress, he held a number of positions in Pandit Jawaharlal Nehru's first government after independence.

Patel participated in the Satyagraha (the name given to the struggle for Indian independence by non-violent, non-cooperative means) at Kaira in 1918. He was a member of the right wing of the Indian National Congress and supported the conservative opposition to the reform of Hindu law as it applied to the lack of rights of Hindu women.

Pater /ˈpeɪtə/ Walter (Horatio) 1839–1894. English critic. A stylist and passionate supporter of 'art for art's sake', he published *Studies in the History of the Renaissance* 1873, *Marius the Epicurean* 1885, *Imaginary Portraits* 1887, and other works.

Paterson /ˈpætəsən/ Banjo (Andrew Barton) 1864–1941. Australian journalist and versifier, author of the popular song 'Waltzing Matilda', adapted from a folk song.

Paterson /ˈpætəsən/ William 1745–1806. Irish-born US Supreme Court justice and political leader. A member of the Constitutional Convention 1787, he was elected one of New Jersey's first US senators 1789. After serving as New Jersey governor 1790–93, Paterson was appointed to the US Supreme Court by President Washington, serving as associate justice 1793–1806. He was noted for his vigorous prosecution of cases under the Sedition Act of 1798.

Born in Ireland, Paterson emigrated to America with his family 1747 and graduated from Princeton University 1763. Admitted to the bar 1769, he served as a member of the provincial congress 1775–76 and as New Jersey attorney general 1776–83.

Pathé /ˈpæθeɪ/ Charles 1863–1957. French film pioneer who began his career selling projectors in 1896 and with the profits formed Pathé Frères with his brothers. In 1901 he embarked on film production and by 1908 had become the world's biggest producer, with branches worldwide. He also developed an early colour process and established a weekly newsreel, *Pathé Journal*. World War I disrupted his enterprises and by 1918 he was gradually forced out of business by foreign competition.

Patinir /ˌpɑːtɪˈnɪə/ (also *Patenier* or *Patinier*) Joachim *c.* 1485–1524. Flemish painter, active in Antwerp, whose inspired landscape backgrounds dominated his religious subjects. He is known to have worked with Quentin Matsys and to have painted landscape backgrounds for other artists' works.

Patmore /ˈpætmɔ:/ Coventry 1823–1896. British poet and critic. He was a librarian at the British Museum 1846–66, and as one of the →Pre-Raphaelite Brotherhood published the sequence of poems *The Angel in the House* 1854–63 and the collection of odes *The Unknown Eros* 1877.

All art constantly aspires towards the condition of music.

Walter Pater *Studies in the History of the Renaissance* 1873

Paton /ˈpeɪtn/ Alan 1903–1988. South African writer. His novel *Cry, the Beloved Country* 1948 focused on racial inequality in South Africa. Later books include the study *Land and People of South Africa* 1956, *The Long View* 1968, and his autobiography *Towards the Mountain* 1980.

Born in Pietermaritzburg, he became a schoolmaster and in 1935 the principal of a reformatory near Johannesburg, which he ran along enlightened lines.

Patou /pæ'tu:/ Jean 1880–1936. French clothes designer who opened a fashion house 1919. He was an overnight success, and his swimsuits and innovative designs became popular in the 1920s. He dominated both the couture and the ready-to-wear sectors of the fashion world until his death, and had a great influence on the designers he employed, many of whom went on to make names for themselves.

Patrick, St /pætrɪk/ 389–c. 461. Patron saint of Ireland. Born in Britain, probably in S Wales, he was carried off by pirates to six years' slavery in Antrim, Ireland, before escaping either to Britain or Gaul – his poor Latin suggests the former – to train as a missionary. He is variously said to have landed again in Ireland 432 or 456, and his work was a vital factor in the spread of Christian influence there. His symbols are snakes and shamrocks; feast day 17 March.

Patrick is credited with founding the diocese of Armagh, of which he was bishop, though this was probably the work of a 'lost apostle' (Palladius or Secundinus). Of his writings only his *Confessio* and an *Epistola* survive.

Patten /pætn/ Chris(topher Francis) 1944– . British Conservative politician, governor of Hong Kong from 1992. He was Conservative Party chair 1990–92, orchestrating the party's campaign for the 1992 general election, in which he lost his parliamentary seat. He accepted the governorship of Hong Kong for the crucial five years prior to its transfer to China.

A former director of the Conservative Party research department, he held junior ministerial posts under Prime Minister Margaret Thatcher, despite his reputation of being to the left of the party, and eventually joined the cabinet. As environment secretary 1989–90, he was responsible for administering the poll tax.

Patterson /pætəsən/ Harry 1929– . English novelist, born in Newcastle. He has written many thrillers under his own name, including *Dillinger* 1983, as well as under the pseudonym Jack Higgins, including *The Eagle Has Landed* 1975.

Patti /pæti/ Adelina 1843–1919. Anglo-Italian soprano renowned for her performances of Lucia in *Lucia di Lammermoor* and Amina in *La sonnambula*. At the age of 62 she was persuaded out of retirement to make a number of gramophone recordings, thus becoming one of the first opera singers to be recorded.

Patton /pætn/ George (Smith) 1885–1945. US general in World War II, known as 'Old Blood and Guts'. He was appointed to command the 2nd Armored Division 1940 and became commanding general of the First Armored Corps 1941. In 1942 he led the Western Task Force that landed at Casablanca, Morocco. After commanding the 7th Army, he led the 3rd Army across France and into Germany, and in 1945 took over the 15th Army.

In war nothing is impossible, provided you use audacity.

George S Patton
War As I Knew It 1947

Paul /pɔ:l/ Elliot Harold 1891–1958. US author. His works include the novel *Indelible* 1922, about two young musicians, and the travel book *The Narrow Street/The Last Time I Saw Paris* 1940.

Paul /pɔ:l/ Les. Adopted name of Lester Polfuss 1915– . US inventor of the solid-body electric guitar in the early 1940s, and a pioneer of recording techniques including overdubbing and electronic echo. The Gibson Les Paul guitar was first marketed 1952 (the first commercial solid-body guitar was made by Leo →Fender). As a guitarist in the late 1940s and 1950s he recorded with the singer Mary Ford (1928–1977).

Paul /pɔ:l/ 1901–1964. King of the Hellenes (Greece) from 1947, when he succeeded his brother George II. He was the son of Constantine I. In 1938 he married Princess Frederika (1917–), daughter of the Duke of Brunswick.

Paul /pɔ:l/ six popes, including:

Paul VI Giovanni Battista Montini 1897–1978. Pope from 1963. His encyclical *Humanae Vitae/Of Human Life* 1968 reaffirmed the church's traditional teaching on birth control, thus following the minority report of the commission originally appointed by Pope John rather than the majority view.

He was born near Brescia, Italy. He spent more than 25 years in the Secretariat of State under Pius XI and Pius XII before becoming archbishop of Milan in 1954. In 1958 he was created a cardinal by Pope John, and in 1963 he succeeded him as pope, taking the name of Paul as a symbol of ecumenical unity.

Paul I /pɔ:l/ 1754–1801. Tsar of Russia from 1796, in succession to his mother Catherine II. Mentally unstable, he pursued an erratic foreign policy and was assassinated.

Pauli /paʊli/ Wolfgang 1900–1958. Austrian physicist who originated the *exclusion principle*: in a given system no two fermions (electrons, protons, neutrons, or other elementary particles of half-integral spin) can be characterized by the same set of quantum numbers. He also predicted the existence of neutrinos. He was awarded a Nobel prize 1945 for his work on atomic structure.

Pauling /pɔ:lɪŋ/ Linus Carl 1901– . US chemist, author of fundamental work on the nature of the chemical bond and on the discovery of the helical structure of many proteins. He also investigated the properties and uses of vitamin C as related to human health. He won the Nobel Prize for Chemistry 1954. An outspoken opponent of nuclear testing, he also received the Nobel Peace Prize in 1962.

Paulinus /pɔːˈlaɪnəs/ died 644. Roman missionary to Britain who joined St →Augustine in Kent 601, converted the Northumbrians 625, and became the first archbishop of York. Excavations 1978 revealed a church he built in Lincoln.

Paul, St /pɔːl/ c. AD 3–c. AD 68. Christian missionary and martyr; in the New Testament, one of the apostles and author of 13 epistles. Originally opposed to Christianity, he took part in the stoning of St Stephen. He is said to have been converted by a vision on the road to Damascus. After his conversion he made great missionary journeys, for example to Philippi and Ephesus, becoming known as the Apostle of the Gentiles (non-Jews). His emblems are a sword and a book; feast day 29 June.

The Jewish form of his name is Saul. He was born in Tarsus (now in Turkey), son of well-to-do Pharisees, and had Roman citizenship. On his return to Jerusalem after his missionary journeys, he was arrested, appealed to Caesar, and (as a citizen) was sent to Rome for trial about 57 or 59. After two years in prison, he may have been released before his final arrest and execution under the emperor Nero.

St Paul's theology was rigorous on such questions as sin and atonement, and his views on the role of women were adopted by the Christian church generally.

Paulus /ˈpaʊlʊs/ Friedrich von 1890–1957. German field marshal in World War II, commander of the forces that besieged Stalingrad (now Volgograd) in the USSR 1942–43; he was captured and gave evidence at the Nuremberg trials before settling in East Germany.

Pausanias /pɔːˈseɪnɪæs/ 2nd century AD. Greek geographer, author of a valuably accurate description of Greece compiled from his own travels, *Description of Greece*, also translated as *Itinerary of Greece*.

Pavarotti /ˌpævəˈrɒti/ Luciano 1935– . Italian tenor whose operatic roles have included Rodolfo in *La Bohème*, Cavaradossi in *Tosca*, the Duke of Mantua in *Rigoletto*, and Nemorino in *L'Elisir d'amore*. He gave his first performance in the title role of *Otello* in Chicago, USA 1991.

Pavlov /ˈpævlɒv/ Ivan Petrovich 1849–1936. Russian physiologist who studied conditioned reflexes in animals. In classical conditioning, described by Pavlov, a new stimulus can evoke an automatic response by being repeatedly associated with a stimulus that naturally provokes a response. For example, the sound of a bell repeatedly associated with food will eventually trigger salivation, even if sounded without the food being provided. His work had a great impact on behavioural theory and learning theory. He received the Nobel Prize for Medicine 1904.

Pavarotti With the luxurious warmth and versatility of his voice, Italian lyric tenor Luciano Pavarotti has done much to popularize opera. His own popularity has grown steadily since his 1963–64 European tour, and he has appeared in several films and has made many recordings.

Pavlov /ˈpævlɒv/ Valentin 1937– . Soviet communist politician, prime minister Jan–Aug 1991. He served in the Finance Ministry, the State Planning Committee (Gosplan), and the State Pricing Committee before becoming minister of finance 1989. In Jan 1991 he replaced Nikolai Ryzhkov as prime minister, with the brief of halting the gathering collapse of the Soviet economy. In Aug 1991 he was a member of the eight-man junta which led the abortive anti-Gorbachev coup. In the midst of the coup, he relinquished his position as premier, citing health reasons. He was arrested when the coup was finally thwarted.

Pavlova /ˈpævləvə/ Anna 1881–1931. Russian dancer. Prima ballerina of the Imperial Ballet from 1906, she left Russia 1913, and went on to become one of the world's most celebrated exponents of classical ballet. With London as her home, she toured extensively with her own company, influencing dancers worldwide with roles such as Mikhail →Fokine's *The Dying Swan* solo 1905.

Paxton /ˈpækstən/ Joseph 1801–1865. English architect, garden superintendent to the Duke of Devonshire from 1826 and designer of the Great Exhibition building 1851 (the Crystal Palace), which was revolutionary in its structural use of glass and iron.

Paxton English architect and horticulturalist Joseph Paxton, knighted for designing the Crystal Palace, a feature of the Great Exhibition of 1851. The Palace was based on his glass and iron conservatory for Chatsworth House where he was garden superintendent for the Duke of Devonshire.

Paz /pɑːs/ (Estenssoro) Victor 1907– . President of Bolivia 1952–56, 1960–64, and 1985–89. He founded and led the Movimiento Nacionalista Revolucionario (MNR) which seized power 1952. His regime extended the vote to Indians, nationalized the country's largest tin mines, embarked on a programme of agrarian reform, and brought inflation under control.

After holding a number of financial posts Paz entered politics in the 1930s and in 1942 founded the MNR. In exile in Argentina during one of Bolivia's many periods of military rule, he returned in 1951 and became president in 1952. He immediately embarked on a programme of political reform, retaining the presidency until 1956 and being re-elected 1960–64 and again in 1985, returning from near-retirement at the age of 77. During his long career he was Bolivian ambassador to London 1956–59 and a professor at London University 1966. Following an indecisive presidential contest 1989, Paz was replaced by Jaime Paz Zamora of the Movement of the Revolutionary Left (MIR). The latter was elected by congress after entering into a power-sharing agreement with former military dictator, Hugo Banzer Suarez.

Paz /pɑːs/ Octavio 1914– . Mexican poet and essayist. His works reflect many influences, including Marxism, surrealism, and Aztec mythology. His long poem *Piedra del sol*/*Sun Stone* 1957 uses contrasting images, centring upon the Aztec Calendar Stone (representing the Aztec

universe), to symbolize the loneliness of individuals and their search for union with others. Nobel Prize for Literature 1990.

Peacock /ˈpiːkɒk/ Thomas Love 1785–1866. English satirical novelist and poet. His works include *Headlong Hall* 1816, *Nightmare Abbey* 1818, *Crotchet Castle* 1831, and *Gryll Grange* 1860.

Peacock worked for the East India Company from 1819 and was instrumental in the development of the earliest gunboats during the 1830s.

Peake /piːk/ Mervyn (Lawrence) 1911–1968. English writer and illustrator, born in China. His novels include the grotesque fantasy trilogy *Titus Groan* 1946, *Gormenghast* 1950, and *Titus Alone* 1959. Among his collections of verse are *The Glassblowers* 1950 and the posthumous *A Book of Nonsense* 1972.

He illustrated most of his own work and produced drawings for an edition of *Treasure Island* 1949, and other works.

Peale /piːl/ Charles Willson 1741–1827. American artist, head of a large family of painters. His portraits of leading figures in the Revolutionary War include the earliest known portrait of George Washington, painted in 1772.

Peale /piːl/ Norman Vincent 1898–. US religious leader. Through his radio programme and book *The Art of Living* 1948, he became one of the best-known religious figures in the USA. His *The Power of Positive Thinking* 1952 became a national bestseller. Peale was elected president of the Reformed Church in America in 1969.

Born in Bowersville, Ohio, USA, Peale was educated at Ohio Wesleyan University and was ordained in the Methodist Episcopal Church in 1922. After serving congregations in Brooklyn 1924–27 and Syracuse 1927–32, he became pastor of the Marble Collegiate Church in New York City.

Pears /pɪəz/ Peter 1910–1986. English tenor. A co-founder with Benjamin →Britten of the Aldeburgh Festival, he was closely associated with the composer's work and sang the title role in *Peter Grimes*.

Pearse /pɪəs/ Patrick Henry 1879–1916. Irish poet prominent in the Gaelic revival, a leader of the Easter Rising 1916. Proclaimed president of the provisional government, he was court-martialled and shot after its suppression.

Pearson /ˈpɪəsən/ Drew 1897–1969. US newspaper correspondent who from 1932 wrote the syndicated column 'Washington Merry-Go-Round'. After his death the column was taken over by newspaper columnist and writer, Jack Anderson (1922–).

Pearson /ˈpɪəsən/ Karl 1857–1936. British statistician who followed Francis →Galton in introducing statistics and probability into genetics and who developed the concept of eugenics (improving the human race by selective breeding). He introduced the term standard deviation into statistics.

Pearson /ˈpɪəsən/ Lester Bowles 1897–1972. Canadian politician, leader of the Liberal Party from 1958, prime minister 1963–68. As foreign minister 1948–57, he represented Canada at the United Nations, playing a key role in settling the →Suez Crisis 1956. Nobel Peace Prize 1957.

Pearson served as president of the General Assembly 1952–53 and helped to create the UN Emergency Force (UNEF) that policed Sinai following the Egypt–Israel war of 1956. As prime minister, he led the way to formulating a national medicare (health insurance) law.

Peary /ˈpɪəri/ Robert Edwin 1856–1920. US polar explorer who, after several unsuccessful attempts, became the first person to reach the North Pole on 6 April 1909. In 1988 an astronomer claimed Peary's measurements were incorrect.

He sailed to Cape Sheridan in the *Roosevelt* with his aide Matthew Henson, and they then made a sledge journey to the Pole.

Peck /pek/ (Eldred) Gregory 1916– . US film actor specializing in strong, upright characters. His films include *Spellbound* 1945, *Duel in the Sun* 1946, *Gentleman's Agreement* 1947, *To Kill a Mockingbird* 1962, for which he won an Academy Award, and (cast against type as a Nazi doctor) *The Boys from Brazil* 1974.

Peckinpah /ˈpekɪnpɑː/ Sam 1925–1985. US film director, often of Westerns, usually associated with slow-motion, blood-spurting violence. His best films, such as *The Wild Bunch* 1969, exhibit a thoughtful, if depressing, view of the world and human nature.

Pedro I 1798–1834. Emperor of Brazil 1822–31. The son of John VI of Portugal, he escaped to Brazil on Napoleon's invasion, and was appointed regent 1821. He proclaimed Brazil independent 1822 and was crowned emperor, but abdicated 1831 and returned to Portugal.

Pedro II 1825–1891. Emperor of Brazil 1831–89. He proved an enlightened ruler, but his antislavery measures alienated the landowners, who compelled him to abdicate.

Peel /piːl/ Robert 1788–1850. British Conservative politician. As home secretary 1822–27 and 1828–30, he founded the modern police force and in 1829 introduced Roman Catholic emancipation. He was prime minister 1834–35 and 1841–46, when his repeal of the Corn Laws caused him and his followers to break with the party.

Peel, born in Lancashire, entered Parliament as a Tory 1809. After the passing of the Reform Bill of 1832, which he had resisted, he reformed the Tories under the name of the Conservative Party, on a basis of accepting necessary changes and seeking middle-class support. He fell from prime ministerial office because his repeal of the Corn

Laws 1846 was opposed by the majority of his party. He and his followers then formed a third party standing between the Liberals and Conservatives; the majority of the Peelites, including Gladstone, subsequently joined the Liberals.

Peele /piːl/ George 1558–1597. English dramatist. He wrote a pastoral, *The Arraignment of Paris* 1584; a fantastic comedy, *The Old Wives' Tale* 1595; and a tragedy, *David and Bethsabe* 1599.

Péguy /peɪˈgiː/ Charles 1873–1914. French Catholic socialist who established a socialist publishing house in Paris. From 1900 he published on political topics *Les Cahiers de la quinzaine/Fortnightly Notebooks* and on poetry, including *Le Mystère de la charité de Jeanne d'Arc/The Mystery of the Charity of Joan of Arc* 1897.

Pei /peɪ/ Ieoh Ming 1917– . Chinese-born US Modernist/high-tech architect, noted for the use of glass walls. His buildings include the Bank of China Tower, Hong Kong, 1987, and the glass pyramid in front of the Louvre, Paris, 1989.

Pei became a US citizen 1948. Other of his works are Dallas City Hall, Texas; East Building, National Gallery of Art, Washington DC, 1978; John F Kennedy Library Complex and the John Hancock Tower, Boston 1979; and the National Airlines terminal at Kennedy Airport, New York.

Peel *British politician Robert Peel, who was prime minister for two separate terms between 1834 and 1846. His wealthy father bought him a Parliamentary seat when he was 21. He established the first modern police force, whose officers were popularly referred to as 'peelers' or 'bobbies'.*

Peirce /pɪəs/ Charles Sanders 1839–1914. US philosopher and logician, founder of pragmatism (which he later called pragmaticism), who argued that genuine conceptual distinctions must be correlated with some differences of practical effect. He wrote extensively on the logic of scientific enquiry, suggesting that truth could be conceived of as the object of an ultimate consensus.

Pelagius /pe'leɪdʒɪəs/ 360–420. British theologian. He taught that each person possesses free will (and hence the possibility of salvation), denying Augustine's doctrines of predestination and original sin. Cleared of heresy by a synod in Jerusalem 415, he was later condemned by the pope and the emperor.

Pelé /peleɪ/ Adopted name of Edson Arantes do Nascimento 1940– . Brazilian soccer player. A prolific goal scorer, he appeared in four World Cup competitions 1958–70 and led Brazil to three championships (1958, 1962, 1970).

He spent most of his playing career with the Brazilian team, Santos, before ending it with the New York Cosmos in the USA.

He wore the No. 10 ten shirt.

Pelham /peləm/ Henry 1696–1754. British Whig politician. He held a succession of offices in Robert Walpole's cabinet 1721–42, and was prime minister 1743–54. His brother Thomas Pelham-Holles, 1st Duke of →Newcastle, succeeded him as prime minister.

Penda /pendə/ c. 577–654. King of Mercia, an Anglo-Saxon kingdom in England, from about 632. He raised Mercia to a powerful kingdom, and defeated and killed two Northumbrian kings, Edwin 632 and →Oswald 641. He was killed in battle by Oswy, king of Northumbria.

Penderecki /ˌpendə'retski/ Krzystof 1933– . Polish composer. His expressionist works, such as the *Threnody for the Victims of Hiroshima* 1961 for strings, employ cluster and percussion effects. He later turned to religious subjects and a more orthodox style, as in the *Magnificat* 1974 and the *Polish Requiem* 1980–83. His opera *The Black Mask* 1986 explored a new vein of surreal humour.

Pendlebury /pendlbəri/ John Devitt Stringfellow 1904–1941. British archaeologist. Working with his wife, he became the world's leading expert on Crete. In World War II he was deputed to prepare guerrilla resistance on the island, was wounded during the German invasion, and shot by his captors.

Penn /pen/ Irving 1917– . US fashion, advertising, portrait, editorial, and fine art photographer. In 1948 he took the first of many journeys to Africa and the Far East, resulting in a series of portrait photographs of local people, avoiding sophisticated technique. He was associated for many years with *Vogue* magazine in the USA.

Penn /pen/ William 1644–1718. English member of the Society of Friends (Quakers), born in London. He joined the Society 1667, and in 1681 obtained a grant of land in America (in settlement of a debt owed by the king to his father) on which he established the colony of Pennsylvania as a refuge for persecuted Quakers.

Let the people think they govern and they will be governed.

William Penn,
Some Fruits of Solitude 1693

Penney /peni/ William 1909–1991. British scientist who worked at Los Alamos, New Mexico, 1944–45, developing the atomic bomb, and directed the tests of Britain's first atomic bomb at the Monte Bello Islands off Western Australia 1952. He developed the advanced gas-cooled nuclear reactor used in some UK power stations.

Penston /penstən/ Michael 1943–1990. British astronomer at the Royal Greenwich Observatory 1965–90. From observations made with the Ultraviolet Explorer Satellite of hot gas circulating around the core of the galaxy NGC 4151, he and his colleagues concluded that a black hole (an object whose gravity is so great that nothing can escape from it) of immense mass lay at the galaxy's centre.

Pepin /pepɪn/ *the Short* c. 714–c. 768. King of the Franks from 751. The son of →Charles Martel, he acted as Mayor of the Palace to the last Merovingian king, Childeric III, deposed him and assumed the royal title himself, founding the →Carolingian dynasty. He was →Charlemagne's father.

Pepusch /peɪpʊʃ/ Johann Christoph 1667–1752. German composer who settled in England about 1700. He contributed to John Gay's ballad operas *The Beggar's Opera* and *Polly*.

Strange to see how a good dinner and feasting reconciles everybody.

Samuel Pepys *Diary* Nov 9 1665

Pepys /piːps/ Samuel 1633–1703. English diarist. His diary 1659–69 was a unique record of both the daily life of the period and the intimate feelings of the man. Written in shorthand, it was not deciphered until 1825. Pepys was imprisoned 1679 in the Tower of London on suspicion of being connected with the Popish Plot (see Titus →Oates).

Pepys was born in London, entered the navy office 1660, and was secretary to the Admiralty 1672–79.

He was reinstated in 1684 but finally deprived of his post after the 1688 Revolution, for suspected disaffection.

Perahia Murray 1947– . US pianist and conductor, the first American to win the Leeds International Piano Competition, in 1972. His affinity for the late classical and early romantic periods is highlighted in his interpretations of Chopin, Schumann, and Mendelssohn. He has recorded all of the Mozart piano concertos with the English Chamber Orchestra, conducting from the keyboard.

Perceval /ˈpɜːsɪvəl/ Spencer 1762–1812. British Tory politician. He became chancellor of the Exchequer 1807 and prime minister 1809. He was shot in the lobby of the House of Commons 1812 by a merchant who blamed government measures for his bankruptcy.

Percy /ˈpɜːsi/ family name of dukes of Northumberland; seated at Alnwick Castle, Northumberland, England.

Percy /ˈpɜːsi/ Henry 'Hotspur' 1364–1403. English soldier, son of the 1st Earl of Northumberland. In repelling a border raid, he defeated the Scots at Homildon Hill in Durham 1402. He was killed at the battle of Shrewsbury while in revolt against Henry IV.

Percy /ˈpɜːsi/ Thomas 1729–1811. English scholar and bishop of Dromore from 1782. He discovered a manuscript collection of songs, ballads, and romances, from which he published a selection as *Reliques of Ancient English Poetry* 1765, which was influential in the Romantic revival.

Perelman /ˈperəlmən/ S(idney) J(oseph) 1904–1979. US humorist. His work was often published in *The New Yorker* magazine, and he wrote film scripts for the Marx Brothers. He shared an Academy Award for the script of *Around the World in 80 Days* 1956.

Peres /ˈperes/ Shimon 1923– . Israeli socialist politician, prime minister 1984–86. Peres was prime minister, then foreign minister, under a power-sharing agreement with the leader of the Consolidation Party (Likud), Yitzhak →Shamir. From 1989 to 1990 he was finance minister in a new Labour–Likud coalition.

Peres emigrated from Poland to Palestine 1934, but was educated in the USA. In 1959 he was elected to the Knesset (Israeli parliament). He was leader of the Labour Party 1977–1992, when he was replaced by Yitzhak Rabin.

Perey /ˈpereɪ/ Marguérite (Catherine) 1909–1975. French nuclear chemist who discovered the radioactive element francium in 1939. Her career, which began as an assistant to Marie Curie 1929, culminated with her appointment as professor of nuclear chemistry at the University of Strasbourg 1949 and director of its Centre for Nuclear Research 1958.

Pérez de Cuéllar /ˈperes də ˈkweɪjɑː/ Javier 1920– Peruvian diplomat, secretary general of the United Nations 1982–91. He raised the standing of the UN by his successful diplomacy in end-

Perahia US virtuoso pianist Murray Perahia specializes in interpretations of small-scale late Classical and early Romantic music for both solo and chamber ensembles. He recorded the Mozart piano concertos with the English Chamber Orchestra, conducting from the keyboard as the composer would have done.

ing the Iran–Iraq War 1988 and securing the independence of Namibia 1989.

A delegate to the first UN General Assembly 1946–47, he subsequently held several ambassadorial posts. He was unable to resolve the Gulf conflict resulting from Iraq's invasion of Kuwait 1990 before combat against Iraq by the UN coalition began Jan 1991, but later in 1991 he negotiated the release of Western hostages held in Beirut.

Pérez Galdós /ˈperes gælˈdɒs/ Benito 1843–1920. Spanish novelist, born in the Canary Islands. His works include the 46 historical novels in the cycle *Episodios nacionales* and the 21-novel cycle *Novelas españolas contemporáneas*, which includes *Doña Perfecta* 1876 and the epic *Fortunata y Jacinta* 1886–87, his masterpiece. In scale he has been compared to the French writer Honoré de Balzac and the English novelist Charles Dickens.

Peri /ˈpeəri/ Jacopo 1561–1633. Italian composer who served the Medici family, the rulers of Florence. His experimental melodic opera *Euridice* 1600 established the opera form and influenced Monteverdi. His first opera, *Dafne* 1597, is now lost.

Pericles /ˈperɪkliːz/ c. 490–429 BC. Athenian politician who dominated the city's affairs from 461 BC (as leader of the democratic party), and under whom Greek culture reached its height. He created a confederation of cities under the leadership of Athens, but the disasters of the Peloponnesian War led to his overthrow 430 BC. Although quickly reinstated, he died soon after.

Perkin /ˈpɜːkɪn/ William Henry 1838–1907. British chemist. In 1856 he discovered the mauve dye that originated the aniline dye industry.

Perkins /ˈpɜːkɪnz/ Anthony 1932–1992. US film actor who played the mother-fixated psychopath Norman Bates in Alfred Hitchcock's *Psycho* 1960 and *Psycho II* 1982. He played shy but subtle roles in *Friendly Persuasion* 1956, *The Trial* 1962, and *The Champagne Murders* 1967. He also appeared on the stage in London and New York.

Perkins /ˈpɜːkɪnz/ Frances 1882–1965. US public official. She became the first female cabinet officer when she served as secretary of labour under F D Roosevelt 1933–45. Under Truman she was a member of the federal civil service commission 1946–53.

Born in Boston, USA, and educated at Mount Holyoke, Perkins worked at Hull House in Chicago before receiving a master's degree in economics from Columbia University 1910. Holding a succession of posts in state regulatory agencies, she became a reformer of labour standards. She served on the State Industrial Board 1923–29 and was appointed New York State's industrial commissioner 1929.

Perls /pɜːlz/ Laura (born Lore Posner) 1906–1990. German-born US psychotherapist who, together with her husband, Fritz, helped develop the gestalt method of psychotherapy. The gestalt treatment relies on a wide range of techniques to treat emotional illness, including some derived from theatre and dance movement. Perls and her husband founded the New York Institute for Gestalt Therapy 1952.

Perón /pəˈrɒn/ (María Estela) Isabel (born Martínez) 1931– . President of Argentina 1974–76, and third wife of Juan Perón. She succeeded him after he died in office, but labour unrest, inflation, and political violence pushed the country to the brink of chaos. Accused of corruption, she was held under house arrest for five years. She went into exile in Spain.

Perón /pəˈrɒn/ Evita (María Eva) (born Duarte) 1919–1952. Argentine populist leader. A successful radio actress, she married Juan →Perón in 1945. When he became president the following year, she became his chief adviser and virtually ran the health and labour ministries, devoting herself to helping the poor, improving education, and achieving women's suffrage. She was politically astute and sought the vice-presidency 1951, but was opposed by the army and withdrew.

Perón /pəˈrɒn/ Juan (Domingo) 1895–1974. Argentine politician, dictator 1946–55 and from 1973 until his death. His populist appeal to the poor was enhanced by the charisma and political work of his second wife Eva (Evita) Perón. After her death in 1952 his popularity waned and he was deposed in a military coup 1955. He returned from exile to the presidency 1973, but died in

office 1974, and was succeeded by his third wife Isabel Perón.

A professional army officer, Perón took part in the right-wing military coup that toppled Argentina's government 1943 and his popularity with the *descamisados* ('shirtless ones') led to his election as president 1946. He instituted social reforms, but encountered economic difficulties.

Perrault /peˈrəʊ/ Charles 1628–1703. French author of the fairy tales *Contes de ma mère l'oye/Mother Goose's Fairy Tales* 1697, which include 'Sleeping Beauty', 'Little Red Riding Hood', 'Blue Beard', 'Puss in Boots', and 'Cinderella'.

Perrin /peˈræn/ Jean 1870–1942. French physicist who produced the crucial evidence that finally established the atomic nature of matter. Assuming the atomic hypothesis, Perrin demonstrated how the phenomenon of Brownian movement (the continuous random movement of particles in a fluid medium as they are subjected to impact from the molecules of the medium) could be used to derive precise values for Avogadro's number (see →Avogadro). He was awarded the 1926 Nobel Prize for Physics.

Perry /ˈperi/ Fred (Frederick John) 1909– . English lawn-tennis player, the last Briton to win the men's singles at Wimbledon 1936. He also won the world table-tennis title 1929. Perry later became a television commentator and a sports goods manufacturer.

Perry /ˈperi/ Matthew Calbraith 1794–1858. US naval officer, commander of the expedition of 1853 that reopened communication between Japan and the outside world after 250 years' isolation. Evident military superiority enabled him to negotiate the Treaty of Kanagawa 1854, giving the USA trading rights with Japan.

Perry /ˈperi/ Oliver Hazard 1785–1819. US naval officer. During the Anglo-American War 1812–14 he played a decisive role in securing American control of Lake Erie. Ordered there in 1813, he was responsible for the decisive victory over the British at the Battle of Put-in-Bay and participated in the Battle of the Thames.

Born in South Kingston, Rhode Island, USA, Perry began his naval career 1799 as a midshipman and saw action in the Tripolitan War. He died of fever while on a cruise to South America.

Perse /pɜːs/ Saint-John. Pen name of Alexis Saint-Léger 1887–1975. French poet and diplomat, a US citizen from 1940. His first book of verse, *Eloges* 1911, reflects the ambience of the West Indies, where he was born and raised. His later works include *Anabase* 1924, an epic poem translated by T S Eliot in 1930. He was awarded a Nobel prize in 1960.

Entering the foreign service in 1914, he was secretary general 1933–40. He then emigrated permanently to the USA, and was deprived of French citizenship by the Vichy government.

Pershing /ˈpɜːʃɪŋ/ John Joseph 1860–1948. US general. He served in the Spanish War 1898, the Philippines 1899–1903, and Mexico 1916–17. He commanded the US Expeditionary Force sent to France 1917–18.

Perugino /ˌperuˈdʒiːnəʊ/ Pietro. Original name of Pietro Vannucci 1446–1523. Italian painter, active chiefly in Perugia. He taught Raphael who absorbed his soft and graceful figure style. Perugino produced paintings for the lower walls of the Sistine Chapel of the Vatican 1481 and in 1500 decorated the Sala del Cambio in Perugia.

Perutz /pəˈruːts/ Max 1914– . Austrian-born British biochemist who shared the 1962 Nobel Prize for Chemistry with John Kendrew for work on the structure of the haemoglobin molecule.

Perutz moved to Britain in 1936 to work with John Bernal (1901–1971) at Cambridge University. After internment in Canada as an alien during World War II he returned to Cambridge and completed his research in 1959.

Pessoa /pəˈsəʊə/ Fernando 1888–1935. Portuguese poet. Born in Lisbon, he was brought up in South Africa and was bilingual in English and Portuguese. His verse is considered to be the finest written in Portuguese this century. He wrote under three assumed names, which he called 'heteronyms' – Alvaro de Campos, Ricardo Reis, and Alberto Caeiro – for each of which he invented a biography.

Pestalozzi /ˌpestəˈlɒtsi/ Johann Heinrich 1746–1827. Swiss educationalist who advocated the French philosopher Jean-Jacques Rousseau's 'natural' principles (of natural development and the power of example), and described his own theories in *Wie Gertrude ihre Kinder lehrt/How Gertrude Teaches her Children* 1801. He stressed the importance of mother and home in a child's education.

International Children's Villages named after Pestalozzi have been established, for example at Sedlescombe, East Sussex, UK.

Pétain /peˈtæn/ Henri Philippe 1856–1951. French general and right-wing politician. His defence of Verdun 1916 during World War I made him a national hero. In World War II he became prime minister June 1940 and signed an armistice with Germany. Removing the seat of government to Vichy, a health resort in central France, he established an authoritarian regime. He was imprisoned after the war.

In 1917 Pétain was created French commander in chief, although he became subordinate to Marshal Foch 1918. He suppressed a rebellion in Morocco 1925–26. As a member of the Higher Council of National Defence he advocated a purely defensive military policy, and was strongly conservative in politics. On the Allied invasion he was taken to Germany, but returned 1945 and was sentenced to death for treason, the sentence being commuted to life imprisonment.

Peter /ˈpiːtə/ Laurence J 1910–1990. Canadian writer and teacher, author (with Raymond Hull) of *The Peter Principle* 1969, in which he outlined the theory that people tend to be promoted into positions for which they are incompetent.

In a hierarchy every employee tends to rise to the level of his incompetence.

Laurence J Peter
The Peter Principle 1969

Peter /ˈpiːtə/ three tsars of Russia:

Peter I *the Great* 1672–1725. Tsar of Russia from 1682 on the death of his brother Tsar Feodor; he assumed control of the government 1689. He attempted to reorganize the country on Western lines; the army was modernized, a fleet was built, the administrative and legal systems were remodelled, education was encouraged, and the church was brought under state control. On the Baltic coast, where he had conquered territory from Sweden, Peter built his new capital, St Petersburg.

After a successful campaign against the Ottoman Empire 1696, he visited Holland and Britain to study Western techniques, and worked in Dutch and English shipyards. In order to secure an outlet to the Baltic, Peter undertook a war with Sweden 1700–21, which resulted in the acquisition of Estonia and parts of Latvia and Finland. A war with Persia 1722–23 added Baku to Russia.

Peter II 1715–1730. Tsar of Russia from 1727. Son of Peter the Great, he had been passed over in favour of Catherine I 1725 but succeeded her 1727. He died of smallpox.

Peter III 1728–1762. Tsar of Russia 1762. Weak-minded son of Peter I's eldest daughter, Anne, he was adopted 1741 by his aunt →Elizabeth, Empress of Russia, and at her command married the future Catherine II 1745. He was deposed in favour of his wife and probably murdered by her lover, Alexius Orlov.

Peter I /ˈpiːtə/ 1844–1921. King of Serbia from 1903. He was the son of Prince Alexander Karageorgevich and was elected king when the last Obrenovich king was murdered 1903. He took part in the retreat of the Serbian army 1915, and in 1918 was proclaimed first king of the Serbs, Croats, and Slovenes (renamed Yugoslavia in 1921).

Peter II /ˈpiːtə/ 1923–1970. King of Yugoslavia 1934–45. He succeeded his father, Alexander I, and assumed the royal power after the overthrow of the regency 1941. He escaped to the UK after the German invasion, and married Princess Alexandra of Greece 1944. He was dethroned 1945 when Marshal Tito came to power and the Soviet-backed federal republic was formed.

Peter Damian, St /ˈpiːtə ˈdeɪmiən/ real name Pietro Damianai 1007–1072. Italian monk who was associated with the initiation of clerical reform by Pope Gregory VII.

Peter Lombard /ˈpiːtə ˈlɒmbɑːd/ 1100–1160. Italian Christian theologian whose *Sententiarum libri quatuor* considerably influenced Catholic doctrine.

Peter, St /ˈpiːtə/ Christian martyr, the author of two epistles in the New Testament and leader of the apostles. He is regarded as the first bishop of Rome, whose mantle the pope inherits. His real name was Simon, but he was nicknamed Kephas ('Peter', from the Greek for 'rock') by Jesus, as being the rock upon which he would build his church. His emblem is two keys; feast day 29 June.

Originally a fisherman of Capernaum, on the Sea of Galilee, Peter may have been a follower of John the Baptist, and was the first to acknowledge Jesus as the Messiah. Tradition has it that he later settled in Rome; he was martyred during the reign of the emperor Nero, perhaps by crucifixion. Bones excavated from under the Basilica of St Peter's in the Vatican 1968 were accepted as those of St Peter by Pope Paul VI.

Peter the Hermit /ˈpiːtə/ 1050–1115. French priest whose eloquent preaching of the First Crusade sent thousands of peasants marching against the Turks, who massacred them in Asia Minor. Peter escaped and accompanied the main body of crusaders to Jerusalem.

Petipa /pəˌtiˈpɑː/ Marius 1818–1910. French choreographer who created some of the most important ballets in the classical repertory. For the Imperial Ballet in Russia he created masterpieces such as *La Bayadère* 1877, *The Sleeping Beauty* 1890, *Swan Lake* 1895 (with Ivanov), and *Raymonda* 1898.

Petit /pəˈtiː/ Alexis 1791–1820. French physicist, co-discoverer of *Dulong and Petit's law*, which states that the specific heat capacity of an element is inversely proportional to its relative atomic mass.

Petőfi /ˈpetɜːfi/ Sándor 1823–1849. Hungarian nationalist poet. He published his first volume of poems 1844. He expressed his revolutionary ideas in the semi-autobiographical poem 'The Apostle', and died fighting the Austrians in the battle of Segesvár.

Petrarch /ˈpetrɑːk/ (Italian *Petrarca*) Francesco 1304–1374. Italian poet, born in Arezzo, a devotee of the Classical tradition. His *Il Canzoniere* is composed of sonnets in praise of his idealized love 'Laura', whom he first saw 1327 (she was a married woman and refused to become his mistress).

From 1337 he often stayed in secluded study at his home at Vaucluse, near Avignon, then the residence of the popes. Petrarch, eager to restore the glories of Rome, wanted to return the papacy there. He was a friend of the poet Giovanni Boccaccio, and supported the political reformer Cola di Rienzi's attempt to establish a republic 1347.

Petrie /ˈpiːtri/ (William Matthew) Flinders 1853–1942. English archaeologist who excavated sites in Egypt (the pyramids at Gîza, the temple at Tanis, the Greek city of Naucratis in the Nile delta, Tell el Amarna, Naquada, Abydos, and Memphis) and Palestine from 1880.

Petrie's work was exacting and systematic, and he developed dating sequences of pottery styles that correlated with dynastic and predynastic events.

Petronius /pəˈtrəʊniəs/ Gaius, known as *Petronius Arbiter*, died *c.* AD 66. Roman author of the licentious romance *Satyricon*. He was a companion of the emperor Nero and supervisor of his pleasures.

Pevsner /ˈpevznə/ Nikolaus 1902–1983. Anglo-German art historian. Born in Leipzig, he fled from the Nazis to England. He became an authority on architecture, especially English. His *Outline of European Architecture* was published 1942 (and numerous other editions). In his series *The Buildings of England* (46 volumes) 1951–74, he built up a first-hand report on every notable building in the country.

Phaedrus /ˈfiːdrəs/ *c.* 15 BC–*c.* AD 50. Roman fable writer, born in Macedonia. He was born a slave and freed by Emperor Augustus. The allusions in his fables (modelled on those of Aesop) caused him to be brought to trial by a minister of Emperor Tiberius. His work was popular in medieval times.

Phalaris /ˈfælərɪs/ 570–554 BC. Tyrant of the Greek colony of Acragas (Agrigento) in Sicily. He is said to have built a hollow bronze bull in which his victims were roasted alive. He was killed in a people's revolt.

The *Letters of Phalaris* attributed to him were proved by the British scholar Richard Bentley to be a forgery of the 2nd century AD.

Phidias /ˈfɪdiæs/ mid-5th century BC. Greek Classical sculptor. He supervised the sculptural programme for the Parthenon (most of it is preserved in the British Museum, London, and known as the *Elgin marbles*). He also executed the colossal statue of Zeus at Olympia, one of the Seven Wonders of the World.

He was a friend of the political leader Pericles, who made him superintendent of public works in Athens.

Philby /ˈfɪlbi/ Harry St John Bridger 1885–1960. British explorer. As chief of the British political mission to central Arabia 1917–18, he was the first European to visit the southern provinces of Najd. He wrote *The Empty Quarter* 1933, and *Forty Years in the Wilderness* 1957.

Philby /ˈfɪlbi/ Kim (Harold) 1912–1988. British intelligence officer from 1940 and Soviet agent from 1933. He was liaison officer in Washington 1949–51, when he was confirmed to be a double agent and asked to resign. Named in 1963 as having warned Guy Burgess and Donald Maclean (similarly double agents) that their activities were known, he fled to the USSR and became a Soviet citizen and general in the KGB. A fourth member of the ring was Anthony Blunt.

Philip /fɪlɪp/ Duke of Edinburgh 1921– . Prince of the UK, husband of Elizabeth II, a grandson of George I of Greece and a great-great- grandson of Queen Victoria. He was born in Corfu, Greece but brought up in England.

He was educated at Gordonstoun and Dartmouth Naval College. During World War II he served in the Mediterranean, taking part in the battle of Matapan, and in the Pacific. A naturalized British subject, taking the surname Mountbatten March 1947, he married Princess Elizabeth in Westminster Abbey 20 Nov 1947, having the previous day received the title Duke of Edinburgh. In 1956 he founded the Duke of Edinburgh's Award Scheme to encourage creative achievement among young people. He was created a prince of the UK 1957, and awarded the Order of Merit 1968.

Philip /fɪlɪp/ 'King'. Name given to Metacomet by the English c. 1639–1676. American chief of the Wampanoag people. During the growing tension over Indian versus settlers' land rights, Philip was arrested and his people were disarmed 1671. Full-scale hostilities culminated in 'King Philip's War' 1675, and Philip was defeated and murdered 1676. Although costly to the English, King Philip's War ended Indian resistance in New England.

Born in Rhode Island, Metacomet was the son of Wampanoag chieftain →Massasoit.In 1662, after the death of his father and elder brother, he assumed power and was called 'King Philip' by the English colonists.

Philip /fɪlɪp/ six kings of France, including:

Philip II (Philip Augustus) 1165–1223. King of France from 1180. As part of his efforts to establish a strong monarchy and evict the English from their French possessions, he waged war in turn against the English kings Henry II, Richard I (with whom he also went on the Third Crusade), and John (against whom he won the decisive battle of Bouvines in Flanders 1214).

Philip IV *the Fair* 1268–1314. King of France from 1285. He engaged in a feud with Pope Boniface VIII and made him a prisoner 1303. Clement V (1264–1314), elected pope through Philip's influence 1305, moved the papal seat to Avignon 1309 and collaborated with Philip to suppress the Templars, a powerful order of knights. Philip allied with the Scots against England and invaded Flanders.

Philip VI 1293–1350. King of France from 1328, first of the house of Valois, elected by the barons on the death of his cousin, Charles IV. His claim was challenged by Edward III of England, who defeated him at Crécy 1346.

Philip II of Macedon /fɪlɪp/ 382–336 BC. King of Macedonia from 359 BC. He seized the throne from his nephew, for whom he was regent, conquered the Greek city states, and formed them into a league whose forces could be united against Persia. He was assassinated while he was planning this expedition, and was succeeded by his son →Alexander the Great.

Philip's tomb was discovered at Vergina, N Greece, in 1978.

Philip /fɪlɪp/ five kings of Spain, including:

Philip I *the Handsome* 1478–1506. King of Castile from 1504, through his marriage 1496 to Joanna the Mad (1479–1555). He was the son of the Holy Roman emperor Maximilian I.

Philip II 1527–1598. King of Spain from 1556. He was born at Valladolid, the son of the Habsburg emperor Charles V, and in 1554 married Queen Mary of England. On his father's abdication 1556 he inherited Spain, the Netherlands, and the Spanish possessions in Italy and the Americas, and in 1580 he annexed Portugal. His intolerance and lack of understanding of the Netherlanders drove them into revolt. Political and religious differences combined to involve him in war with England and, after 1589, with France. The defeat of the Spanish Armada (the fleet sent to invade England in 1588) marked the beginning of the decline of Spanish power.

Philip II Known as 'His Most Catholic Majesty', Philip II of Spain's implacable opposition to Protestantism led him to develop the Inquisition at home and sparked off the Netherlanders' revolt 1581. It also brought him into conflict with England, culminating in the defeat of the Spanish Armada 1588 and the loss of Spanish naval supremacy.

Philip V 1683–1746. King of Spain from 1700. A grandson of Louis XIV of France, he was the first Bourbon king of Spain. He was not recognized by the major European powers until 1713.

Philip Neri, St /nɪəri/ 1515–1595. Italian Roman Catholic priest who organized the Congregation of the Oratory. He built the oratory over the church of St Jerome, Rome, where prayer meetings were held and scenes from the Bible performed with music, originating the musical form oratorio. Feast day 26 May.

Philippa of Hainault /fɪlɪpə/ 1311–1369. Daughter of William III Count of Holland; wife of King Edward III of England, whom she married in York Minster 1328, and by whom she had 12 children (including Edward the Black Prince, Lionel Duke of Clarence, John Duke of Lancaster, Edmund Duke of York, and Thomas Duke of Gloucester). She was admired for her clemency and successfully pleaded for the lives of the six burghers of Calais who surrendered to to save the town from destruction 1347. Queen's College, Oxford, was founded in her honour and established by Royal Charter 1341.

Philip, St /fɪlɪp/ 1st century AD. In the New Testament, one of the 12 apostles. He was an inhabitant of Bethsaida (N Israel), and is said to have worked as a missionary in Anatolia. Feast day 3 May.

Philip the Good /fɪlɪp/ 1396–1467. Duke of Burgundy from 1419. He engaged in the Hundred Years' War as an ally of England until he made peace with the French at the Council of Arras 1435. He made the Netherlands a centre of art and learning.

Phillip /fɪlɪp/ Arthur 1738–1814. British vice admiral, founder and governor of the convict settlement at Sydney, Australia, 1788–1792, and hence founder of New South Wales.

Philips /fɪlɪps/ Anton 1874–1951. Dutch industrialist and founder of an electronics firm. The Philips Bulb and Radio Works 1891 was founded with his brother Gerard, at Eindhoven. Anton served as chair of the company 1921–51, during which time the firm became the largest producer of electrical goods outside the USA.

Phillips /fɪlɪps/ Wendell 1811–1884. US reformer. After attending the World Anti-Slavery Convention in London 1840, he became an outspoken proponent of the abolition of slavery. In addition to abolition he espoused a variety of other social causes, including feminism, prohibition, unionization, and improved treatment of American Indians.

Born in Boston and educated at Harvard University, Phillips was admitted to the bar 1834. Critical of the Mexican War 1846–48 and the conduct of the American Civil War 1861–65 by President Lincoln, Phillips was a reform candidate for governor of Massachusetts 1870.

Philo Judaeus /faɪləʊ dʒuːˈdiːəs/ lived 1st century AD. Jewish philosopher of Alexandria who in AD 40 undertook a mission to Caligula to protest against the emperor's claim to divine honours. In his writings Philo Judaeus attempts to reconcile Judaism with Platonic and Stoic ideas.

He [God] made a world only perceptible to the intellect, and then completed one visible to the external senses, using the first one as a model.

Philo Judaeus
On the Creation of the World

Phiz /fɪz/ pseudonym of Hablot Knight Browne 1815–1882. British artist who illustrated the greater part of the *Pickwick Papers* and other works by Charles Dickens.

Phyfe /faɪf/ Duncan c. 1768–1854. Scottish-born US furniture maker. Establishing his own workshop in New York City 1792, he gained a national reputation. Although derived from earlier English and Greco-Roman designs, the Phyfe style was distinctive in its simplicity of line with elaborate ornamentation and carving. In 1837 he reorganized his firm as Duncan Phyfe and Sons.

Phyfe emigrated to America with his family 1784. He settled in Albany, New York, and learned the cabinetmaker's trade. He remained active until his retirement in 1847.

Piaf /piːæf/ Edith. Stage name of Edith Gassion 1915–1963. French singer and songwriter, a cabaret singer in Paris from the late 1930s. She is remembered for the defiant song 'Je ne regrette rien/I Regret Nothing' and 'La Vie en rose' 1946.

Piaget /piˈæʒeɪ/ Jean 1896–1980. Swiss psychologist distinguished by his studies of child development in relation to thought processes, and concepts of space, time, causality, and objectivity.

Piano /piˈɑːnəʊ/ Renzo 1937– . Italian architect who designed (with Richard →Rogers) the Pompidou Centre, Paris, completed 1977. Among his other buildings are the Kansai Airport, Osaka, Japan and a sports stadium in Bari, Italy, both using new materials and making imaginative use of civil-engineering techniques.

Piazzi /piˈætsi/ Giuseppe 1746–1826. Italian astronomer, director of Palermo Observatory. In 1801 he identified the first asteroid, which he named Ceres.

Picabia /pɪˈkɑːbiə/ Francis 1879–1953. French painter, a Cubist from 1909. On his second visit to New York, 1915–16, he joined with Marcel Duchamp in the Dadaist revolt and later took the movement to Barcelona. He associated with the Surrealists for a time. His work was generally provocative and experimental.

Picasso /pɪˈkæsəʊ/ Pablo 1881–1973. Spanish artist, active chiefly in France, one of the most inventive and prolific talents in 20th-century art. His Blue Period 1901–04 and Rose Period 1905–06 preceded the revolutionary *Les Demoiselles d'Avignon* 1907 (Metropolitan Museum of Art, New York), which paved the way for Cubism. In the early 1920s he was considered a leader of the Surrealist movement. In the 1930s his work included metal sculpture, book illustration, and the mural *Guernica* 1937 (Casón del Buen Retiro, Madrid), a comment on the bombing of civilians in the Spanish Civil War. He continued to paint into his eighties.

Picasso was born in Málaga, son of an art teacher, José Ruiz Blasco, and an Andalusian mother, Maria Picasso López; he stopped using the name Ruiz in 1898. He was a mature artist at the age of 10, and at 16 was holding his first exhibition. In 1900 he made an initial visit to Paris, where he was to settle. From 1946 he lived mainly in the south of France where, in addition to painting, he experimented with ceramics, sculpture, sets for ballet (for example *Parade* in 1917 for Diaghilev), book illustrations (such as Ovid's *Metamorphoses*), and portraits (Stravinsky, Valéry, and others).

Art is a lie that makes us realize the truth.

Pablo Picasso Sept 1958

Piccard /pɪˈkɑː/ Auguste 1884–1962. Swiss scientist. In 1931–32, he and his twin brother, *Jean Félix* (1884–1963), made ascents to 17,000 m/ 55,000 ft in a balloon of his own design, resulting in useful discoveries concerning stratospheric phenomena such as cosmic radiation. He also built and used, with his son *Jacques Ernest* (1922–), bathyscaphs for research under the sea.

Born in Basel, he became professor of physics at the University of Brussels 1922.

Pickett /ˈpɪkɪt/ George Edward 1825–1875. US military leader. At the outbreak of the American Civil War 1861, he joined the Confederate army, rising to the rank of brigadier general 1862. Although he saw action in many battles, he is best remembered for leading the bloody, doomed 'Pickett's Charge' at Gettysburg 1863.

Born in Richmond, Virginia, Pickett graduated from West Point military academy 1846 and was commended for bravery during the Mexican War 1846–48. After service in Texas 1849–55, he was transferred to the Pacific Northwest. After the end of the Civil War 1865 Pickett declined further military appointments and retired to private life.

Pickford /ˈpɪkfəd/ Mary. Stage name of Gladys Mary Smith 1893–1979. Canadian-born US actress. The first star of the silent screen, she was

known as 'America's Sweetheart', and played innocent ingenue roles into her thirties. In 1919 she formed United Artists with Charlie Chaplin, D W Griffith, and her second husband (1920–36) Douglas Fairbanks.

Her films include *Rebecca of Sunnybrook Farm* 1917, *Pollyanna* 1920, *Little Lord Fauntleroy* 1921, and *Coquette* 1929, her first talkie (Academy Award). She was presented a special Academy Award 1976.

Pico della Mirandola /ˈpiːkəʊ ˌdelə mɪˈrændələ/ Count Giovanni 1463–1494. Italian mystic philosopher. Born at Mirandola, of which his father was prince, he studied Hebrew, Chaldean, and Arabic, showing particular interest in the Jewish and theosophical system, the kabbala. His attempt to reconcile the religious base of Christianity, Islam, and the ancient world earned Pope Alexander VI's disapproval.

Pieck /piːk/ Wilhelm 1876–1960. German communist politician. He was a leader of the 1919 Spartacist revolt and a founder of the Socialist Unity Party 1946. He opposed both the Weimar Republic and Nazism. From 1949 he was president of East Germany; the office was abolished on his death.

Pierce /pɪəs/ Franklin 1804–1869. 14th president of the USA, 1852–56. A Democrat, he held office in the US House of Representatives 1833–37, and the US Senate 1837–42. Chosen as a compromise candidate of the Democratic party, he was elected president 1852. Despite his expansionist foreign policy, North–South tensions grew more intense, and Pierce was denied renomination 1856.

Born in Hillsboro, New Hampshire, Pierce was admitted to the bar 1827. He served in the New Hampshire state legislature 1829–33. Returning to New Hampshire from the Senate 1942, he served briefly as US attorney and saw action in the Mexican War 1846–48.

Piercy /ˈpɪəsi/ Marge 1937– . US poet and novelist. Her fiction looks at the fringes of American social life and the world of the liberated woman. Her novels include the utopian *Woman on the Edge of Time* 1979, *Fly Away Home* 1984, and *Summer People* 1989.

Piero della Francesca /piˈeərəʊ ˌdelə frænˈtʃeskə/ c. 1420–1492. Italian painter, active in Arezzo and Urbino; one of the major artists of the 15th century. His work has a solemn stillness and unusually solid figures, luminous colour, and compositional harmony. It includes a fresco series, *The Legend of the True Cross* (S Francesco, Arezzo), begun about 1452. Piero wrote two treatises, one on mathematics, one on the laws of perspective in painting.

Piero di Cosimo /piˈeərəʊ diː ˈkɒzɪməʊ/ c. 1462– 1521. Italian painter, known for his inventive pictures of mythological subjects, often featuring fauns and centaurs. He also painted religious subjects and portraits.

Pietro da Cortona /pi'etrəʊ/ (Pietro Berrettini) 1596–1669. Italian painter and architect, a major influence in the development of Roman High Baroque. His enormous fresco *Allegory of Divine Providence* 1633–39 (Barberini Palace, Rome) glorifies his patron the pope and the Barberini family, and gives a convincing illusion of reality.

Pigalle /piːˈgæl/ Jean Baptiste 1714–1785. French sculptor. In 1744 he made the marble *Mercury* (Louvre, Paris), a lively, naturalistic work. His subjects ranged from the intimate to the formal, and included portraits.

Pigalle studied in Rome 1736–39. In Paris he gained the patronage of Madame de Pompadour, the mistress of Louis XV. His works include *Venus, Love and Friendship* 1758 (Louvre, Paris), a nude statue of *Voltaire* 1776 (Institut de France, Paris), and the grandiose *Tomb of Marechal de Saxe* 1753 (Strasbourg).

Piggott /ˈpɪgət/ Lester 1935– . English jockey. He adopted a unique high riding style and is renowned as a brilliant tactician. A champion jockey 11 times between 1960 and 1982, he has ridden a record nine Epsom Derby winners. Piggott retired from riding 1985 and took up training. In 1987 he was imprisoned for tax evasion. He returned to racing in 1990.

He was associated with such great horses as Nijinsky, Sir Ivor, Roberto, Empery, and The Minstrel. Piggott won all the major races, including the English classics.

At least 60% of horses don't really want to do their best. Winning doesn't mean all that much to them.

Lester Piggott

Pigou /ˈpɪguː/ Arthur Cecil 1877–1959. British economist whose notion of the 'real balance effect' (the 'Pigou effect') contended that employment was stimulated by a fall in prices, because the latter increased liquid wealth and thus demand for goods and services.

Pike /paɪk/ Zebulon Montgomery 1779–1813. US explorer and military leader. In 1806 he was sent to explore the Arkansas River and to contest Spanish presence in the area. After crossing Colorado and failing to reach the summit of the peak later named after him, he was captured by the Spanish, who released him 1807. Promoted to brigadier general, he was killed in action in the War of Anglo-American War 1812–14.

Born in Lamberton, New Jersey, Pike joined the army at age 15 and served in the Department of the West. In 1805 he was sent by the governor of the Louisiana Territory to explore the source of the Mississippi River.

Pilate /ˈpaɪlət/ Pontius early 1st century AD. Roman procurator of Judea AD 26–36. The New Testament Gospels describe his reluctant ordering of Jesus' crucifixion, but there has been considerable debate about his actual role in it; many believe that pressure was put on him by Jewish conservative priests.

Pilate was unsympathetic to the Jews; his actions several times provoked riots, and in AD 36 he was recalled to Rome to account for the brutal suppression of a Samaritan revolt. The Greek historian Eusebius says he committed suicide after Jesus' crucifixion

Another tradition says he became a Christian, and he is regarded as a saint and martyr in the Ethiopian Coptic and Greek Orthodox churches.

Pilcher /ˈpɪltʃə/ Percy 1867–1899. English aviator who was the first Briton to make a successful flight in a heavier-than-air craft, called the *Bat*, 1895. Like Otto →Lilienthal, Pilcher made flights only downhill from gliders, using craft resembling the modern hang glider. Pilcher's next successful aircraft was the *Hawk*, launched 1896 at Eynsford, Kent, by a tow line. He was killed 1899 flying the *Hawk* near Rugby in the Midlands.

Pilsudski /pɪlˈsʊdski/ Józef (Klemens) 1867–1935. Polish nationalist politician, dictator from 1926. Born in Russian Poland, he founded the Polish Socialist Party 1892 and was twice imprisoned for anti-Russian activities. During World War I he commanded a Polish force to fight for Germany but fell under suspicion of intriguing with the Allies and was imprisoned by the Germans 1917–18. When Poland became independent 1919, he was elected chief of state, and led an unsuccessful Polish attack on the USSR 1920. He retired 1923, but in 1926 led a military coup that established his dictatorship until his death.

Pincus /ˈpɪŋkəs/ Gregory Goodwin 1903–1967. US biologist who, together with Min Chueh Chang (1908–) and John Rock (1890–1984), developed the contraceptive pill in the 1950s.

As a result of studying the physiology of reproduction, Pincus conceived the idea of using synthetic hormones to mimic the condition of pregnancy in women. This effectively prevents impregnation.

Pindar /ˈpɪndə(r)/ *c.* 552–442 BC. Greek poet, born near Thebes. He is renowned for his choral lyrics, the 'Pindaric odes', written in honour of the victors of athletic games.

Pindling /ˈpɪndlɪŋ/ Lynden (Oscar) 1930– . Bahamian prime minister 1967–92. After studying law in London, he returned to the island to join the newly formed Progressive Liberal Party and then became the first black prime minister of the Bahamas.

Pinero Arthur Wing 1855–1934. British dramatist. A leading exponent of the 'well-made' play, he enjoyed great contemporary success with his farces, beginning with *The Magistrate* 1885. More substantial social drama followed with *The Second*

Mrs Tanqueray 1893, and comedies including *Trelawny of the 'Wells'* 1898.

Pinkerton /ˈpɪŋkətən/ Allan 1819–1884. US detective, born in Glasgow. In 1852 he founded *Pinkerton's National Detective Agency*, and built up the federal secret service from the espionage system he developed during the US Civil War.

Pink Floyd British psychedelic rock group, formed 1965. The original members were Syd Barrett (1946–), Roger Waters (1944–), Richard Wright (1945–), and Nick Mason (1945–). Their albums include *The Dark Side of the Moon* 1973 and *The Wall* 1979, with its spin-off film starring Bob Geldof.

Pinkham /ˈpɪŋkəm/ Lydia E 1819–1893. US entrepreneur and patent medicine proprietor who claimed she could cure any 'female complaint'.

Pinkham began her manufacturing business in a cellar kitchen where she developed and mixed her own formulae. Although her claims of cures were never substantiated, her mixtures became increasingly popular, as was the Department of Advice she set up with an all-female staff to deal with the huge volume of enquiries the Lydia E Pinkham Medicine Co attracted.

Pinochet (Ugarte) /ˈpiːnəʊʃeɪ uˈɡɑːteɪ/ Augusto 1915– . Military ruler of Chile from 1973, when a coup backed by the US Central Intelligence Agency ousted and killed President Salvador Allende. Pinochet took over the presidency and governed ruthlessly, crushing all opposition. He was voted out of power when general elections were held in Dec 1989 but remains head of the armed forces until 1997.

In 1990 Pinochet's attempt to reassert political influence was firmly censured by President Patricio Aylwin.

Pinter /ˈpɪntə/ Harold 1930– . English dramatist, originally an actor. He specializes in the tragicomedy of the breakdown of communication, broadly in the tradition of the Theatre of the Absurd – for example, *The Birthday Party* 1958 and *The Caretaker* 1960. Later plays include *The Homecoming* 1965, *Old Times* 1971, *Betrayal* 1978, and *Mountain Language* 1988.

One way of looking at speech is to say that it is a constant stratagem to cover nakedness.

Harold Pinter

Pinturicchio /ˌpɪntʊˈrɪkiəʊ/ (or *Pintoricchio*) pseudonym of Bernardino di Betto *c.* 1454–1513. Italian painter, active in Rome, Perugia, and Siena. His chief works are the frescoes in the Borgia Apartments in the Vatican, painted in the 1490s, and in the Piccolomini Library of Siena Cathedral, 1503–08. He is thought to have assist-

Piper English painter and designer John Piper's vivid use of draughtsmanship is best seen in his pictures of bombed buildings of World War II. He designed the stained glass for Coventry Cathedral and also published books on art, architecture, and topography.

ed ➔Perugino in decorating the Sistine Chapel, Rome.

Piozzi /piˈɒtsi/ Hester Lynch (born Salusbury) 1741–1821. Welsh writer. She published *Anecdotes of the late Samuel Johnson* 1786 and their correspondence 1788. Johnson had been a constant visitor to her house in Streatham, London, when she was married to her first husband, Henry Thrale, but after Thrale's death Johnson was alienated by her marriage to the musician Gabriele Mario Piozzi (1740–1809). *Thraliana*, her diaries and notebooks of the years 1766–1809, was published 1942.

Piper /ˈpaɪpə/ John 1903–1992. British painter, printmaker, and designer. His subjects include traditional Romantic views of landscape and architecture. As an official war artist in World War II he depicted damaged buildings. He also designed theatre sets and stained-glass windows for Coventry Cathedral and the Catholic Cathedral, Liverpool.

Pirandello /ˌpɪrənˈdeləʊ/ Luigi 1867–1936. Italian writer. His plays include *La morsa/The Vice* 1912, *Sei personaggi in cerca d'autore/Six Characters in Search of an Author* 1921, and *Enrico IV/Henry IV* 1922. The themes and treatment of his plays anticipated the work of Brecht, O'Neill, Anouilh, and Genet. Nobel Prize 1934.

His novel *Il fu Mattia Pascal/The Late Mattia Pascal* 1904 was highly acclaimed, along with many short stories.

Piranesi /ˌpɪrəˈneɪzi/ Giambattista 1720–1778. Italian architect, most significant for his powerful etchings of Roman antiquities and as a theorist of architecture, advocating imaginative use of Roman models. Only one of his designs was built, Sta Maria del Priorato, Rome.

Piran, St /ˈpɪrən/ *c.* 500 AD. Christian missionary sent to Cornwall by St Patrick. There are remains of his oratory at Perranzabuloe, and he is the patron saint of Cornwall and its nationalist movement; feast day 5 March.

Pirquet Clemens von 1874–1929. Austrian paediatrician and pioneer in the study of allergy.

Pisanello /ˌpiːzəˈneləʊ/ nickname of Antonio Pisano *c.* 1395–1455. Italian artist active in Verona, Venice, Naples, Rome, and elsewhere. His panel paintings reveal a rich International Gothic style. He was also an outstanding portrait medallist. His frescoes in the Palazzo Ducale in Mantua were rediscovered after World War II.

Pisano /piːˈsɑːnəʊ/ Andrea *c.* 1290–1348. Italian sculptor who made the earliest bronze doors for the Baptistery of Florence Cathedral, completed 1336.

Pisistratus /paɪˈsɪstrətəs/ *c.* 605–527 BC. Athenian politician. Although of noble family, he assumed the leadership of the peasant party, and seized power 561 BC. He was twice expelled, but recovered power from 541 BC until his death. Ruling as a dictator under constitutional forms, he was the first to have the Homeric poems written down, and founded Greek drama by introducing the Dionysiac peasant festivals into Athens.

Pissarro /pɪˈsɑːrəʊ/ Camille 1831–1903. French Impressionist painter, born in the West Indies. He went to Paris in 1855, met Jean-Baptist-Camille Corot, then Claude Monet, and became a leading member of the Impressionists. He experimented with various styles, including Pointillism, in the 1880s.

His son *Lucien Pissarro* (1863–1944) worked in the same style for a time.

He lived in the UK from 1890.

Piston /ˈpɪstən/ Walter (Hamor) 1894–1976. US composer and teacher. He wrote a number of textbooks, including *Harmony* 1941 and *Orchestration* 1955. His Neo-Classical works include eight symphonies, a number of concertos, chamber music, the orchestral suite *Three New England Sketches* 1959, and the ballet *The Incredible Flautist* 1938.

Pitman /ˈpɪtmən/ Isaac 1813–1897. English teacher and inventor of Pitman's shorthand. He studied Samuel Taylor's scheme for shorthand writing, and in 1837 published his own system, *Stenographic Soundhand*, fast, accurate, and adapted for use in many languages.

A simplified *Pitman Script*, combining letters and signs, was devised 1971 by Emily D Smith.

His grandson *(Isaac) James Pitman* (1901–85) devised the 44-letter *Initial Teaching Alphabet* in the 1960s to help children to read.

Pitt /pɪt/ William, *the Elder*, 1st Earl of Chatham 1708–1778. British Whig politician, 'the Great Commoner'. As paymaster of the forces 1746–55, he broke with tradition by refusing to enrich himself; he was dismissed for attacking the duke of Newcastle, the prime minister. He served effectively as prime minister in coalition governments 1756–61 (successfully conducting the Seven Years' War) and 1766–68.

Entering Parliament 1735, Pitt led the Patriot faction opposed to the Whig prime minister Robert Walpole and attacked Walpole's successor, Carteret, for his conduct of the War of the Austrian Succession. Recalled by popular demand to form a government on the outbreak of the Seven Years' War 1756, he was forced to form a coalition with Newcastle 1757. A 'year of victories' ensued 1759, and the French were expelled from India and Canada. In 1761 Pitt wished to escalate the war by a declaration of war on Spain, George III disagreed and Pitt resigned, but was again recalled to form an all-party government 1766. He championed the Americans against the king, though rejecting independence, and collapsed during his last speech in the House of Lords – opposing the withdrawal of British troops – and died a month later.

Unlimited power is apt to corrupt the minds of those who possess it.

William Pitt the Elder
House of Lords, 9 Jan 1770

Pitt /pɪt/ William, *the Younger* 1759–1806. British Tory prime minister 1783–1801 and 1804–06. He raised the importance of the House of Commons, clamped down on corruption, carried out fiscal reforms, and effected the union with Ireland. He attempted to keep Britain at peace but underestimated the importance of the French Revolution and became embroiled in wars with France from 1793; he died on hearing of Napoleon's victory at Austerlitz.

Son of William Pitt the Elder, he entered Cambridge University at 14 and Parliament at 22. He was the Whig Shelburne's chancellor of the Exchequer 1782–83, and with the support of the Tories and king's friends became Britain's youngest prime minister 1783. He reorganized the country's finances and negotiated reciprocal tariff reduction with France. In 1793, however, the new French republic declared war and England fared badly. Pitt's policy in Ireland led to the 1798 revolt, and he tried to solve the Irish question by the Act of Union 1800, but George III rejected the Catholic emancipation Pitt had promised as a condition, and Pitt resigned 1801.

Pitt William Pitt the Younger entered Parliament at the age of 22 and two years later became England's youngest prime minister.

On his return to office 1804, he organized an alliance with Austria, Russia, and Sweden against Napoleon, which was shattered at Austerlitz. In declining health, he died on hearing the news, saying: 'Oh, my country! How I leave my country!' He was buried in Westminster Abbey.

Pitt-Rivers /pɪt 'rɪvəz/ Augustus Henry 1827–1900. English archaeologist and general. He made a series of model archaeological excavations on his estate in Wiltshire, England, being among the first to recognize the value of everyday objects as well as art treasures. The *Pitt-Rivers Museum*, Oxford, contains some of his collection.

Pius /paɪəs/ 12 popes, including:

Pius IV 1499–1565. Pope from 1559, of the →Medici family. He reassembled the Council of Trent, which had initiated the Counter-Reformation, and completed its work 1563.

Pius V 1504–1572. Pope from 1566. He excommunicated Elizabeth I of England, and organized the expedition against the Turks that won the victory of Lepanto.

Pius VI (Giovanni Angelo Braschi) 1717–1799. Pope from 1775. He strongly opposed the French Revolution, and died a prisoner in French hands.

Pius VII 1742–1823. Pope from 1800. He concluded a concordat (papal agreement) with France 1801 and took part in Napoleon's coronation, but relations became strained. Napoleon annexed the papal states, and Pius was imprisoned 1809–14. After his return to Rome 1814, he revived the Jesuit order.

Pius IX 1792–1878. Pope from 1846. He never accepted the incorporation of the Papal States and of Rome in the kingdom of Italy. He proclaimed the dogmas of the Immaculate Conception of the Virgin 1854 and papal infallibility 1870; his pontificate was the longest in history.

Pius X (Giuseppe Melchiore Sarto) 1835–1914. Pope from 1903, canonized 1954. He condemned Modernism in a manifesto 1907 (Modernism being a movement in the Church of England which attempts to reconsider Christian beliefs in the light of modern scientific theories and historical methods, without abandoning the essential doctrines).

Pius XI (Achille Ratti) 1857–1939. Pope from 1922. He signed the concordat (papal agreement) with Mussolini 1929.

Pius XII (Eugenio Pacelli) 1876–1958. Pope from 1939. He was conservative in doctrine and politics, and condemned Modernism (see →Pius X). He proclaimed the dogma of the bodily assumption of the Virgin Mary 1950 and in 1951 restated the doctrine (strongly criticized by many) that the life of an infant must not be sacrificed to save a mother in labour. He was criticized for failing to speak out against atrocities committed by the Germans during World War II and has been accused of collusion with the Nazis.

Pizarro /pɪˈzɑːrəʊ/ Francisco *c.* 1475–1541. Spanish conquistador who took part in the expeditions of Vasco Núñez de Balboa and others. He explored the NW coast of South America in 1526–27, and conquered Peru 1531 with 180 followers. The Inca king Atahualpa was seized and murdered. In 1535 Pizarro founded the Peruvian city of Lima. Internal feuding led to Pizarro's assassination.

His half-brother *Gonzalo Pizarro* (*c.* 1505–1548) explored the region east of Quito 1541–42. He made himself governor of Peru 1544, but was defeated and executed.

Plaatje /ˈplɑːtʃi/ Solomon Tshekiso 1876–1932. Pioneer South African black community leader who was the first secretary general and founder of the African National Congress 1912.

Place /pleɪs/ Francis 1771–1854. English Radical. He showed great powers as a political organizer, and made Westminster a centre of pro-labour union Radicalism. He secured the repeal of the anti-union Combination Acts 1824.

Planck /plæŋk/ Max 1858–1947. German physicist who framed the quantum theory 1900. His research into the manner in which heated bodies radiate energy led him to report that energy is emitted only in indivisible amounts, called quanta, the magnitudes of which are proportional to the frequency of the radiation. His discovery ran counter to classical physics and is held to have marked the commencement of the modern science. Nobel Prize for Physics 1918.

Plantagenet /plæntædzənɪt/ English royal house, reigning 1154–1399, whose name comes from the nickname of Geoffrey, Count of Anjou (1113–1151), father of Henry II, who often wore in his hat a sprig of broom, *planta genista*. In the 1450s, Richard, Duke of York, took 'Plantagenet' as a surname to emphasize his superior claim to the throne over Henry VI's.

Plath /plæθ/ Sylvia 1932–1963. US poet and novelist whose powerful, highly personal poems, often expressing a sense of desolation, are distinguished by their intensity and sharp imagery. Her *Collected Poems* 1981 was awarded a Pulitzer Prize. Her autobiographical novel *The Bell Jar* 1961 deals with the events surrounding a young woman's emotional breakdown.

Plath was born in Boston, Massachusetts, attended Smith College and was awarded a Fulbright scholarship to study at Cambridge University, England, where she met the poet Ted Hughes, whom she married 1956; they separated in 1962. She committed suicide while living in London. Collections of her poems include *The Colossus* 1960 and *Ariel* 1965, published after her death.

Platini Michel 1955–   . French footballer who was the inspiration of the French team that won the 1984 European Championship. He was the first to be elected European Footballer of the Year on three successive years 1983–85. After starting his career in France with Nancy and St Etienne, he moved to Italy in 1982 where he played for Juventus. He represented his country on 72 occasions, scoring a record 41 goals and playing in three World Cups. He became manager of the French national team in 1988.

Plato /pleɪtəʊ/ *c.* 428–347 BC. Greek philosopher, pupil of Socrates, teacher of Aristotle, and founder of the Academy school of philosophy. He was the author of philosophical dialogues on such topics as metaphysics, ethics, and politics. Central to his teachings is the notion of Forms, which are located outside the everyday world – timeless, motionless, and absolutely real.

Plato's philosophy has influenced Christianity and European culture, directly and through Augustine, the Florentine Platonists during the Renaissance, and countless others.

Born of a noble family, he entered politics on the aristocratic side, and in philosophy became a follower of Socrates. He travelled widely after Socrates' death, and founded the educational establishment, the Academy, in order to train a new ruling class.

Of his work, some 30 dialogues survive, intended for performance either to his pupils or to the public. The principal figure in these ethical and philosophical debates is Socrates and the early ones employ the Socratic method, in which he asks questions and traps the students into contradicting themselves; for example, *Iron*, on poetry. Other dialogues include the *Symposium*, on love,

Phaedo, on immortality, and *Apology and Crito*, on Socrates' trial and death. It is impossible to say whether Plato's Socrates is a faithful representative of the real man or an articulation of Plato's own thought. Plato's philosophy rejects scientific rationalism (establishing facts through experiment) in favour of arguments, because mind, not matter, is fundamental, and material objects are merely imperfect copies of abstract and eternal 'ideas'. His political philosophy is expounded in two treatises, *The Republic* and *The Laws*, both of which describe ideal states. Platonic love is inspired by a person's best qualities and seeks their development.

Plautus /plɔːtəs/ *c.* 254–184 BC. Roman dramatist, born in Umbria, who settled in Rome and worked in a bakery before achieving success as a dramatist. He wrote at least 56 comedies, freely adapted from Greek originals, of which 20 survive. Shakespeare based *The Comedy of Errors* on his *Menaechmi*.

A man is a wolf rather than a man to another man, when he hasn't yet found out what he's like.

Plautus

Player /pleɪə/ Gary 1935–   . South African golfer who won major championships in three decades and became the youngest winner of the British Open 1959. A match- play specialist, he won the world title five times.

His total of nine 'majors' is the fourth (equal) best of all time. He is renowned for wearing all-black outfits. In the 1980s he was a successful Seniors player.

Playfair /pleɪfeə/ William Henry 1790–1857. Scottish Neo-Classical architect responsible for much of the design of Edinburgh New Town in the early 19th century. His Royal Scottish Academy 1822 and National Gallery of Scotland 1850 in Greek style helped to make Edinburgh the 'Athens of the North'.

Pleasance /plezəns/ Donald 1919–   . English actor, often seen as a sinister outcast; for example, as the tramp in Harold Pinter's *The Caretaker* 1960 which he also played in the film version of 1963, *Will Penny* 1968, and *The Eagle Has Landed* 1976 (as the Nazi Himmler).

Plekhanov /plɪˈxɑːnɒf/ Georgi Valentinovich 1857–1918. Russian Marxist revolutionary and theorist, founder of the Menshevik party. He led the first populist demonstration in St Petersburg, became a Marxist and, with Lenin, edited the newspaper *Iskra* (spark). In 1903 his opposition to Lenin led to the Bolshevik-Menshevik split.

He returned to Russia 1917 but died in Finland.

Plethon /pliːθɒn/ George Gemisthos 1353–1452. Byzantine philosopher who taught for many years at Mistra in Asia Minor. A Platonist, he maintained a resolutely anti-Christian stance and was the inspiration for many of the ideas of the 15th-century Florentine Platonic Academy.

Plimsoll /ˈplɪmsəl/ Samuel 1824–1898. English social reformer, born in Bristol. He sat in Parliament as a Radical 1868–80, and through his efforts the Merchant Shipping Act was passed in 1876, providing for Board of Trade inspection of ships, and the compulsory painting of a *Plimsoll line* to indicate safe loading limits.

Pliny the Elder /ˈplɪni/ (Gaius Plinius Secundus) *c.* AD 23–79. Roman scientist and historian; only his works on astronomy, geography, and natural history survive. He was killed in an eruption of Vesuvius, the volcano near Naples.

Pliny the Younger /ˈplɪni/ (Gaius Plinius Caecilius Secundus) *c.* AD 61–113. Roman administrator, nephew of Pliny the Elder, whose correspondence is of great interest. Among his surviving letters are those describing the eruption of Vesuvius, his uncle's death, and his correspondence with the emperor →Trajan.

Plisetskaya /plɪˈsetskiə/ Maya 1925– . Soviet ballerina and actress. She attended the Moscow Bolshoi Ballet School and succeeded Galina Ulanova as prima ballerina of the Bolshoi Ballet.

Plomer /ˈpluːmə/ William 1903–1973. South African novelist, author of *Turbot Wolfe* 1925, an early criticism of South African attitudes to race. He settled in London in 1929 and wrote two autobiographical volumes.

Plutarch /ˈpluːtɑːk/ *c.* AD 46–120. Greek biographer whose *Parallel Lives* has the life stories of pairs of Greek and Roman soldiers and politicians, followed by comparisons between the two. Thomas North's 1579 translation inspired Shakespeare's Roman plays.

Plutarch was born in Chaeronea. He lectured on philosophy in Rome and was appointed procurator of Greece by Emperor Hadrian.

Pocahontas /ˌpɒkəˈhɒntəs/ *c.* 1595–1617. American Indian princess alleged to have saved the life of John Smith, the English colonist (later president of Virginia 1608–09), when he was captured by her father Powhatan. She married an Englishman, John Rolfe, in 1614 and has many US descendants. She died of smallpox in Gravesend, Kent.

Po Chü-i alternative transliteration of →Bo Zhu Yi, Chinese poet.

Poe /pəʊ/ Edgar Allan 1809–1849. US writer and poet. His short stories are renowned for their horrific atmosphere, as in 'The Fall of the House of Usher' 1839 and 'The Masque of the Red Death' 1842, and for their acute reasoning (ratiocination), as in 'The Gold Bug' 1843 and 'The Murders in the Rue Morgue' 1841 (in which the investigators Legrand and Dupin anticipate Conan Doyle's Sherlock Holmes). His poems include 'The Raven' 1845.

Plimsoll English social reformer Samuel Plimsoll, known as 'the sailors' friend'. Among the evils he fought against were the overloading and undermanning of vessels and the deliberate launching of unseaworthy ships in order to collect insurance after shipwreck.

His novel, *The Narrative of Arthur Gordon Pym of Nantucket* 1838, has attracted critical attention.

Poe, born in Boston, was orphaned 1811 and joined the army 1827 but was court-martialled 1830 for deliberate neglect of duty. He failed to earn a living by writing, became an alcoholic, and in 1847 lost his wife (commemorated in his poem 'Annabel Lee'). His verse, of haunting lyric beauty, influenced the French Symbolists (for example, 'Ulalume' and 'The Bells').

Poincaré /ˈpwæŋkæreɪ/ Jules Henri 1854–1912. French mathematician who developed the theory of differential equations and was a pioneer in relativity theory. He suggested that Isaac Newton's laws for the behaviour of the universe could be the exception rather than the rule. However, the calculation was so complex and time-consuming that he never managed to realize its full implication.

He also published the first paper devoted entirely to topology (the branch of geometry that deals with the unchanged properties of figures).

Science is built up with facts, as a house is with stones. But a collection of facts is no more a science than a heap of stones is a house.

Jules Henri Poincaré,
La Science et l'hypothèse 1902

Polk *As 11th president of the USA, James Polk settled the Oregon Boundary dispute with Britain and successfully conducted the Mexican War, which resulted in the annexation of California. Devoted to the Democratic principles of his predecessors, Thomas Jefferson and Andrew Jackson, Polk set up a revenue tariff and an independent treasury.*

Poincaré /pwæŋkæreɪ/ Raymond Nicolas Landry 1860–1934. French politician, prime minister 1912–13, president 1913–20, and again prime minister 1922–24 (when he ordered the occupation of the Ruhr, Germany) and 1926–29.

Poindexter /pɔɪndekstə/ John Marlan 1936– . US rear admiral and Republican government official. In 1981 he joined the Reagan administration's National Security Council (NSC) and became national security adviser 1985. As a result of the Irangate scandal (an arms-for-hostages deal with Iran), Poindexter was forced to resign 1986, along with his assistant, Oliver North.

Poisson /pwæsn/ Siméon Denis 1781–1840. French applied mathematician. In probability theory he formulated the *Poisson distribution*, which is widely used in probability calculations. He published four treatises and several hundred papers on aspects of physics, including mechanics, heat, electricity and magnetism, elasticity, and astronomy.

Poitier Sidney 1924– . US actor and film director, Hollywood's first black star. His films as an actor include *Something of Value* 1957, *Lilies of the Field* 1963, and *In the Heat of the Night* 1967, and as director *Stir Crazy* 1980.

Polanski /pəˈlænski/ Roman 1933– . Polish film director, born in Paris. His films include *Repulsion* 1965, *Cul de Sac* 1966, *Rosemary's Baby* 1968, *Tess* 1979, and *Frantic* 1988, and *Bitter Moon* 1992.

Pole /pəʊl/ Reginald 1500–1558. English cardinal from 1536 who returned from Rome as papal legate on the accession of Mary I in order to readmit England to the Catholic Church. He succeeded Cranmer as archbishop of Canterbury 1556.

Politian /pɒˈlɪʃən/ (Angelo Poliziano) Pen name of Angelo Ambrogini 1454–1494. Italian poet, playwright, and exponent of humanist ideals. He was tutor to Lorenzo de →Medici's children, and professor at the University of Florence; he wrote commentaries and essays on Classical authors.

Polk /pəʊk/ James Knox 1795–1849. 11th president of the USA 1845–49, a Democrat, born in North Carolina. He allowed Texas admission to the Union, and forced the war on Mexico that resulted in the annexation of California and New Mexico.

Pollaiuolo /pɒˌlaɪuːˈəʊləʊ/ Antonio *c.* 1432–1498 and Piero *c.* 1441–1496. Italian artists, active in Florence. Both brothers were painters, sculptors, goldsmiths, engravers, and designers. Antonio is said to have been the first Renaissance artist to make a serious study of anatomy. The *Martyrdom of St Sebastian* 1475 (National Gallery, London) is considered a joint work.

The brothers also executed two papal monuments in St Peter's basilica, Rome. The major individual works are Piero's set of *Virtues* in Florence and Antonio's engraving *The Battle of the Nude Gods* about 1465. Antonio's work places a strong emphasis on the musculature of the human figure in various activities.

Pollock /pɒlək/ Jackson 1912–1956. US painter, a pioneer of Abstract Expressionism and the foremost exponent of the technique of action painting (emphasizing the physical act of painting), a style he developed around 1946.

In the early 1940s Pollock moved from a vivid Expressionist style, influenced by Mexican muralists such as Siqueiros and by Surrealism, towards a semi-abstract style. The paintings of this period are colourful and vigorous, using jumbled signs or symbols like enigmatic graffiti. He moved on to the more violently expressive abstract style, placing large canvases on the studio floor and dripping or hurling his paint on them. He was soon recognized as the leading Abstract Expressionist and continued to develop his style, producing even larger canvases in the 1950s.

Painting is self-discovery. Every good artist paints what he is.

Jackson Pollock

Polo /pəʊləʊ/ Marco 1254–1324. Venetian traveller and writer. He travelled overland to China 1271–75, and served the emperor Kublai Khan until he returned to Europe by sea 1292–95. He was captured while fighting for Venice against

Genoa, and, while in prison 1296–98, dictated an account of his travels.

After his father (Niccolo) and uncle (Maffeo) returned from a trading journey to China 1260–69, Marco began his own trip overland to China. Once there, he learned Mongolian and served the emperor Kublai Khan, returning nearly 20 years later by sea to his native country. His accounts of his travels remained the primary source of information about the Far East until the 19th century.

I have not told half of what I saw.

Marco Polo last words

Pol Pot /pɒl 'pɒt/ (also known as *Saloth Sar*, *Tol Saut*, and *Pol Porth*) 1925– . Cambodian politician and leader of the Khmer Rouge communist movement that overthrew the government 1975. After widespread atrocities against the civilian population, his regime was deposed by a Vietnamese invasion 1979. Pol Pot continued to help lead the Khmer Rouge until their withdrawal in 1989.

Pol Pot was a member of the anti-French resistance under Ho Chi Minh in the 1940s. In 1975 he proclaimed Democratic Kampuchea with himself as premier. His policies were to evacuate cities and put people to work in the countryside. The Khmer Rouge also carried out a systematic extermination of the Western-influenced educated and middle classes (1–4 million). In 1989 Pol Pot officially resigned from his last position within the Khmer Rouge (although many analysts contend that he has continued to exert firm control over the organization).

Polybius /pəˈlɪbɪəs/ *c.* 201–120 BC. Greek politician and historian. He was involved with the Achaean League against the Romans and, following the defeat of the Macedonians at Pydna in 168 BC, he was taken as a political hostage to Rome. He returned to Greece in 151 and was present at the capture of Carthage by his friend Scipio in 146. His history of Rome in 40 books, covering the years 220–146, has largely disappeared.

Polycarp, St /ˈpɒlɪkɑːp/ *c.* 69–*c.* 155. Christian martyr allegedly converted by St John the Evangelist. As bishop of Smyrna (modern Izmir, Turkey), he carried on a vigorous struggle against various heresies for over 40 years. He was burned alive at a public festival; feast day 26 Jan.

Polykleitos /ˌpɒlɪˈklaɪtɒs/ 5th century BC. Greek sculptor whose *Spear Carrier* 450–440 BC (Roman copies survive) exemplifies the naturalism and harmonious proportions of his work. He created the legendary colossal statue of *Hera* in Argos, in ivory and gold.

Pompadour /ˈpɒmpədʊə/ Jeanne Antoinette Poisson, Marquise de Pompadour 1721–1764. Mistress of →Louis XV of France from 1744, born in Paris. She largely dictated the government's ill-fated policy of reversing France's anti-Austrian policy for an anti-Prussian one. She acted as the patron of the Enlightenment philosophers Voltaire and Diderot.

Pompey /ˈpɒmpi/ *the Great* (Gnaeus Pompeius Magnus) 106–48 BC. Roman soldier and politician, consul 70–60 BC. From 60 BC to 53 BC, he was a member of the First Triumvirate with Julius →Caesar and Marcus Lucius →Crassus, but took the opposite side in the civil war from 49 BC.

Originally a supporter of Lucius Cornelius →Sulla and the aristocratic party, Pompey joined the democrats when he became consul with Crassus in 70 BC. He defeated →Mithridates VI Eupator of Pontus, and annexed Syria and Palestine. He married Caesar's daughter Julia (died 54 BC) in 59 BC. When the Triumvirate broke down after 53 BC, Pompey returned to the aristocratic party. On the outbreak of civil war 49 BC he withdrew to Greece, was defeated by Caesar at Pharsalus 48 BC, and was murdered in Egypt.

Pompidou /ˌpɒmpiˈduː/ Georges 1911–1974. French conservative politician, president 1969–74. He negotiated a settlement with the Algerians 1961 and, as prime minister 1962–68, with the students in the revolt of May 1968.

An adviser on General de Gaulle's staff 1944–46, Pompidou held administrative posts until he became director-general of the French House of Rothschild 1954, and even then continued in close association with de Gaulle, helping to draft the constitution of the Fifth Republic 1958–59. He was elected to the presidency on de Gaulle's resignation.

Ponce de León /ˈpɒnseɪ deɪ leɪˈɒn/ Juan *c.* 1460–1521. Spanish soldier and explorer. He is believed to have sailed with Columbus 1493, and served 1502–04 in Hispaniola. He conquered Puerto Rico 1508, and was made governor 1509. In 1513 he was the first European to reach Florida.

He returned to Spain 1514 to report his 'discovery' of Florida (which he thought was an island), and was given permission by King Ferdinand to colonize it. In the attempt, he received an arrow wound of which he died in Cuba.

Poncelet /ˌpɒnsəˈleɪ/ Jean-Victor 1788–1867. French mathematician and military engineer who advanced projective geometry. His book *Traité des propriétés projectives des figures*, started in 1814 and completed 1822, deals with the properties of plane figures that remain unchanged when projected.

Pontiac /ˈpɒntiæk/ *c.* 1720–1769. North American Indian, chief of the Ottawa from 1755. From 1763 to 1764 he led the 'Conspiracy of Pontiac' in an attempt to stop British encroachment on Indian lands. He succeeded against overwhelming odds, but eventually signed a peace treaty 1766, and was murdered by an Illinois Indian at the instigation of a British trader.

Pontormo /pɒnˈtɔːməʊ/ Jacopo Carucci 1494–1557. Italian painter, active in Florence. He developed a dramatic Mannerist style, with lurid colours.

Pontormo worked in →Andrea del Sarto's workshop from 1512. An early work, *Joseph in Egypt* about 1515 (National Gallery, London), is already Mannerist. His mature style is demonstrated in *The Deposition* about 1525 (Sta Felicità, Florence), an extraordinary composition of interlocked figures, with rosy pinks, lime yellows, and pale apple greens illuminating the scene. The same distinctive colours occur in the series of frescoes he painted 1522–25 for the Certosa monastery outside Florence.

Pop /pɒp/ Iggy. Stage name of James Newell Osterberg 1947– . US rock singer and songwriter, initially known as *Iggy Stooge*, lead singer with a seminal garage band called the Stooges (1967–74), whose self-destructive proto-punk performances became legendary. His solo career began with *The Idiot* 1977 and *Lust for Life* 1977, composed and produced by David Bowie, who also contributed to *Blah, Blah, Blah* 1986.

Pope /pəʊp/ Alexander 1688–1744. English poet and satirist. He established his reputation with the precocious *Pastorals* 1709 and *Essay on Criticism* 1711, which were followed by a parody of the heroic epic *The Rape of the Lock* 1712–14 and 'Eloisa to Abelard' 1717. Other works include a highly Neo-Classical translation of Homer's *Iliad* and *Odyssey* 1715–26.

Pope had a biting wit, which he expressed in the form of heroic couplets. As a Catholic, he was subject to discrimination, and he was embittered by a deformity of the spine. His edition of Shakespeare attracted scholarly ridicule, for which he revenged himself by a satire on scholarly dullness, the *Dunciad* 1728. His philosophy, including *An Essay on Man* 1733–34 and *Moral Essays* 1731–35, was influenced by the politician and philosopher Henry Bolingbroke. His finest mature productions are his *Imitations of the Satires of Horace* 1733–38 and his personal letters. Among his friends were the writers Swift, Arbuthnot, and Gay. His line 'A little learning is a dangerous thing' is often misquoted.

Popov /pɒpɒv/ Alexander 1859–1905. Russian physicist who devised the first aerial, in advance of →Marconi (although he did not use it for radio communication). He also invented a detector for radio waves.

Popper Karl (Raimund) 1902– . Austrian philosopher of science. His theory of falsificationism says that although scientific generalizations cannot be conclusively verified, they can be conclusively falsified by a counterinstance; therefore, science is not certain knowledge but a series of 'conjectures and refutations', approaching, though never reaching, a definitive truth. For Popper, psychoanalysis and Marxism are unfalsifiable and therefore unscientific.

His major work on the philosophy of science is *The Logic of Scientific Discovery* 1935. Other works include *The Poverty of Historicism* 1957 (about the philosophy of social science), *Conjectures and Refutations* 1963, and *Objective Knowledge* 1972.

Born and educated in Vienna, Popper became a naturalized British subject 1945 and was professor of logic and scientific method at the London School of Economics 1949–69. He opposes Wittgenstein's view that philosophical problems are merely pseudoproblems. Popper's view of scientific practice has been criticized by T S →Kuhn and other writers.

Porritt /pɒrɪt/ Jonathon 1950– . British environmental campaigner, director of Friends of the Earth 1984–90. He has stood in both British and European elections as a Green (formerly Ecology) Party candidate.

Porsche /pɔːʃ/ Ferdinand 1875–1951. German car designer. Among his designs were the Volkswagen (German 'people's car', popularly known as the Beetle), first produced in the 1930s, which became an international success in the 1950s–1970s, and Porsche sports cars.

Porson /pɔːsən/ Richard 1759–1808. British Classical scholar, professor of Greek at Cambridge from 1792 and editor of the Greek dramatists Aeschylus and Euripides.

Porter /pɔːtə/ Cole (Albert) 1892–1964. US composer and lyricist, mainly of musical comedies. His witty, sophisticated songs like 'Let's Do It' 1928, 'I Get a Kick Out of You' 1934, and 'Don't Fence Me In' 1944 have been widely recorded and admired. His shows, many of which were made into films, include *The Gay Divorcee* 1932 and *Kiss Me Kate* 1948.

Porter /pɔːtə/ Edwin Stanton 1869–1941. US director, a pioneer of silent films. His 1903 film *The Great Train Robbery* lasted an unprecedented 12 minutes and contained an early use of the close-up. More concerned with the technical than the artistic side of his films, which include *The Teddy Bears* 1907 and *The Final Pardon* 1912, Porter abandoned filmmaking 1916.

Porter /pɔːtə/ Eric 1928– . English actor. His numerous classical roles include title parts in *Uncle Vanya*, *Volpone*, and *King Lear*; on television he played Soames Forsyte in *The Forsyte Saga*.

Porter /pɔːtə/ George 1920– . English chemist. From 1949 he and Ronald Norrish (1897–1978) developed the technique by which flashes of high energy are used to bring about and study extremely fast chemical reactions. He shared the 1967 Nobel Prize for Chemistry with Norrish and German chemist Manfred Eigen.

Porter was director of the Royal Institution 1966–85 and president of the Royal Society 1885–90. In the 1960s he became a familiar figure through his appearances on British television.

Porter /ˈpɔːtə/ Katherine Anne 1890–1980. US writer. She published three volumes of short stories (*Flowing Judas* 1930, *Pale Horse, Pale Rider* 1939, and *The Leaning Tower* 1944); a collection of essays, *The Days Before* 1952; and the allegorical novel *Ship of Fools* 1962 (made into a film 1965). Her *Collected Short Stories* 1965 won a Pulitzer Prize.

Porter /ˈpɔːtə/ Rodney Robert 1917–1985. British biochemist. In 1962 Porter proposed a structure for human immunoglobulin in which the molecule was seen as consisting of four chains. Porter was awarded, with Gerald Edelman, the 1972 Nobel Prize for Medicine.

Portland /ˈpɔːtlənd/ William Bentinck, 1st Earl of Portland 1649–1709. Dutch politician who accompanied William of Orange to England 1688, and was created an earl 1689. He served in William's campaigns.

Portland /ˈpɔːtlənd/ William Henry Cavendish Bentinck, 3rd Duke of Portland 1738–1809. British politician, originally a Whig, who in 1783 became nominal prime minister in the Fox–North coalition government. During the French Revolution he joined the Tories, and was prime minister 1807–09.

Portsmouth /ˈpɔːtsməθ/ Louise de Kéroualle, Duchess of Portsmouth 1649–1734. Mistress of Charles II of Britain, she was a Frenchwoman who came to England as Louis XIV's agent 1670, and was hated by the public.

Potemkin /pəˈtemkɪn/ Grigory Aleksandrovich, Prince Potemkin 1739–1791. Russian politician. He entered the army and attracted the notice of Catherine II, whose friendship he kept throughout his life. He was an active administrator who reformed the army, built the Black Sea Fleet, conquered the Crimea, developed S Russia, and founded the Kherson arsenal 1788 (the first Russian naval base on the Black Sea).

Potter /ˈpɒtə/ Beatrix 1866–1943. English writer and illustrator of children's books, beginning with *Peter Rabbit* 1900 and *The Tailor of Gloucester* 1902, based on her observation of family pets and wildlife around her home from 1905 in the English Lake District.

Other books in the series include *The Tale of Mrs Tiggy Winkle* 1904, *The Tale of Jeremy Fisher* 1906, and a sequel to Peter Rabbit, *The Tale of the Flopsy Bunnies* 1909. She grew up in London but was a self-taught naturalist. Her diaries, written in a secret code, were translated and published 1966. Her Lake District home is now a museum.

Potter /ˈpɒtə/ Dennis (Christopher George) 1935– . English playwright. His television plays *Pennies from Heaven* 1978 (feature film 1981), *Brimstone and Treacle* 1976 (transmitted 1987, feature film 1982), and *The Singing Detective* 1986 all aroused great interest through serious concern about social issues, inventive form, and marked avoidance of euphemism or delicacy.

Educated at New College, Oxford, Potter was a journalist and TV critic before becoming known as a playwright. He stood unsuccessfully as a parliamentary candidate for the Labour Party in 1964 and *Vote, Vote, Vote for Nigel Barton*, his first television drama, was shown in 1965.

Potter /ˈpɒtə/ Paulus 1625–1654. Dutch painter and etcher, active in Delft, The Hague, and Amsterdam; he specialized in rural scenes. His paintings of animals include *The Young Bull* 1647 (Mauritshuis, The Hague).

Potter /ˈpɒtə/ Stephen 1900–1969. British author of humorous studies in how to outwit and outshine others, including *Gamesmanship* 1947, *Lifemanship* 1950, and *One Upmanship* 1952.

Poulenc /ˈpuːlæŋk/ Francis (Jean Marcel) 1899–1963. French composer and pianist. A self-taught composer of witty and irreverent music, he was a member of the group of French composers known as *Les Six*. Among his many works are the operas *Les Mamelles de Tirésias* 1947, and *Dialogues des Carmélites* 1957, and the ballet *Les Biches* 1923.

Poulsen /ˈpəʊlsən/ Valdemar 1869–1942. Danish engineer who in 1900 was the first to demonstrate that sound could be recorded magnetically – originally on a moving steel wire or tape; his device was the forerunner of the tape recorder.

Pound /paʊnd/ (Alfred) Dudley Pickman Rogers 1877–1943. British admiral of the fleet. As First Sea Lord and chief of the British naval staff 1939–43, he was responsible for the effective measures taken against the German submarine U-boats in World War II.

Pound /paʊnd/ Ezra 1885–1972. US poet who lived in London from 1908. His *Personae* and *Exultations* 1909 established the principles of Imagism, asserting the principles of free verse, complex imagery, and poetic impersonality. His largest work was the series of *Cantos* 1925–1969 (intended to number 100), which attempted a massive reappraisal of history.

In Paris 1921–25, he was a friend of the writers Gertrude Stein and Ernest Hemingway. He then settled in Rapallo, Italy. His anti-Semitism and sympathy with the fascist dictator Mussolini led him to broadcast from Italy in World War II, and he was arrested by US troops 1945. Found unfit to stand trial, he was confined in a mental hospital until 1958.

His first completely modern poem was 'Hugh Selwyn Mauberley' 1920. He also wrote versions of Old English, Provençal, Chinese, ancient Egyptian, and other verse.

And even I can remember/A day when the historians left blanks in their writings,/I mean for things they didn't know.

Ezra Pound *Draft of XXX Cantos*

Poussin French painter Nicolas Poussin whose career began under Mannerist influence but who gravitated towards Classical dignity, clarity, and adherence to rules. Working for most of his life in Rome, he produced his greatest paintings in the form of poetic evocations of mythological and Biblical scenes.

Poussin /puːˈsæŋ/ Nicolas 1594–1665. French painter, active chiefly in Rome; court painter to Louis XIII 1640–43. He was one of France's foremost landscape painters in the 17th century. He painted mythological and literary scenes in a strongly Classical style; for example, *Rape of the Sabine Women* about 1636–37 (Metropolitan Museum of Art, New York).

Poussin went to Rome 1624 and studied Roman sculpture in the studio of the Italian Baroque painter and architect →Domenichino. His style reflects painstaking preparation: he made small wax models of the figures in his paintings, experimenting with different compositions and lighting. Colour was subordinate to line.

Powell /paʊəl/ Adam Clayton, Jr 1908–1972. US political leader. A leader of New York's black community, he was elected to the city council 1941. He was appointed to the US Congress 1944, and later became chairman of the House Education and Labor Committee. Following charges of corruption, he was denied his seat in Congress 1967. Re-elected 1968, he won back his seniority by a 1969 decision of the US Supreme Court.

Born in New Haven, Connecticut, USA, and educated at Colgate University, Powell received a doctorate from Shaw University 1938.

Powell /pəʊəl/ Anthony (Dymoke) 1905– . English novelist who wrote the series of 12 volumes *A Dance to the Music of Time* 1951–75 that begins shortly after World War I and chronicles a period of 50 years in the lives of Nicholas Jenkins and his circle of upper-class friends.

Powell /paʊəl/ Cecil Frank 1903–1969. English physicist. From the 1930s he and his team at Bristol University investigated the charged subatomic particles in cosmic radiation by using photographic emulsions carried in weather balloons. This led to his discovery of the pion (pi meson) 1946, a particle whose existence had been predicted by the Japanese physicist Hideki Yukawa 1935. Powell was awarded a Nobel prize in 1950.

Powell /paʊəl/ Colin (Luther) 1937– . US general, chair of the Joint Chiefs of Staff from 1989 and, as such, responsible for the overall administration of the Allied forces in Saudi Arabia during the Gulf War 1991. A Vietnam War veteran, he first worked in government 1972 and was national security adviser 1987–89.

Powell was born in New York, the son of Jamaican immigrants; he joined the army in the 1950s, was sent to Vietnam 1962 and volunteered to return 1968. He worked for Caspar →Weinberger and Frank →Carlucci at the Office of Management and Budget 1972, before being posted to Korea 1973. He returned to Washington as assistant to Carlucci at the Defense Department 1981–83 and as adviser to Weinberger 1983–86 and was promoted to general. After a year in West Germany he was recalled to Washington following the Irangate scandal (an arms-for-hostages deal), first as assistant to Carlucci and then replacing him as national security adviser. In 1989 he was made a four-star general and chair of the Joint Chiefs of Staff.

Powell /paʊəl/ (John) Enoch 1912– . British Conservative politician. He was minister of health 1960–63, and contested the party leadership 1965. In 1968 he made a speech against immigration that led to his dismissal from the shadow cabinet. He resigned from the party 1974, and was Official Unionist Party member for South Down, Northern Ireland 1974–87.

Brought up as a prodigy, he studied Classics at Trinity College, Cambridge, and became a Fellow 1934. He was professor of Greek at the University of Sydney, Australia 1937–39 when he resigned to enter the British army, becoming its youngest brigadier 1944 at the age of 32. At the end of World War II he joined the Conservative Party Research department.

He was an MP for Wolverhampton from 1950 and subsequently a member of the Cabinet. Declining to stand in the Feb 1974 election, he attacked the Heath government and resigned.

Powell /paʊəl/ Michael 1905–1990. English film director and producer. Some of his most memorable films were made in collaboration with Hungarian screenwriter Emeric Pressburger. They produced a succession of ambitious and richly imaginative films, including *A Matter of Life and Death* 1946, *Black Narcissus* 1947, and *The Red Shoes* 1948.

Powell's films range from *The Life and Death of Colonel Blimp* 1943 to the opera movie *The Tales of Hoffman* 1951, but after the partnership with Pressburger was amicably dissolved, Powell went on to make generally less rewarding films. The most distinctive was the voyeuristic horror story of *Peeping Tom* 1960.

Powell /paʊəl/ Lewis Stanley 1907– . US jurist. He was associate justice of the US Supreme Court 1971–87 under President Nixon. A conservative, Powell voted to restrict Fifth Amendment guarantees against self-incrimination and for capital punishment. In *United States* v *Nixon* 1974, he sided with the majority in limiting executive privilege.

Born in Suffolk, Virginia, USA, Powell received his undergraduate and law degrees from Washington and Lee universities and an MA in law from Harvard University.

He practised in Virginia, becoming president of the American Bar Association 1964–65 and president of the American College of Trial Lawyers 1968–69. He retired from the Court 1987 for health reasons.

Powell /paʊəl/ Mike 1963– . US long jumper who in 1991 broke US athlete Bob Beamon's world long-jump record of 8.90 m (which had stood since 1968) with a leap of 8.95 m. At the same time, he dealt Carl Lewis his first long-jump defeat since 1981. Powell also topped the world long-jump rankings in 1990.

Powell /paʊəl/ William 1892–1984. US film actor who co-starred with Myrna Loy in the *Thin Man* series 1934–1947. He also played suave leading roles in *My Man Godfrey* 1936, *Life with Father* 1947, and *Mister Roberts* 1955.

Powys /pəʊɪs/ John Cowper 1872–1963. English novelist. His mystic and erotic books include *Wolf Solent* 1929 and *A Glastonbury Romance* 1933. He was one of three brothers (*Theodore Francis Powys* 1875–1953 and *Llewelyn Powys* 1884–1939), all writers.

Poynter /pɔɪntə/ Edward John 1836–1919. British artist, first head of the Slade School of Fine Art, London, 1871–75, and president of the Royal Academy in succession to John Millais. He produced decorous nudes, mosaic panels for Westminster Palace 1870, and scenes from ancient Greece and Rome.

Pozsgay /pɒʒgaɪ/ Imre 1933– . Hungarian socialist politician, presidential candidate for the Hungarian Socialist Party from 1989. Influential in the democratization of Hungary 1988–89, he was rejected by the electorate in the parliamentary elections of March 1990, coming a poor third in his constituency.

Pozsgay joined the ruling Hungarian Socialist Workers' Party (HSWP) 1950 and was a lecturer in Marxism-Leninism and an ideology chief in Bacs county 1957–70. He was minister of education and culture from 1976 before becoming head of the Patriotic People's Front umbrella organization 1982. Noted for his reformist social-democratic instincts, he was brought into the HSWP

politburo in 1988 as a move towards political pluralism began. Having publicly declared that 'communism does not work', he helped remould the HSWP into the new Hungarian Socialist Party 1989 and was selected as its candidate for the presidency.

Prasad /prəsaɪd/ Rajendra 1884–1963. Indian politician. He was national president of the Indian National Congress several times between 1934 and 1948 and India's first president after independence 1950–62.

Trained as a lawyer, Prasad was a loyal follower of Mahatma Gandhi.

Praxiteles /præk'sɪtəliːz/ mid-4th century BC. Greek sculptor, active in Athens. His *Aphrodite of Knidos* about 350 BC (known through Roman copies) is thought to have initiated the tradition of life-size freestanding female nudes in Greek sculpture.

Premadasa /ˌpreməˈdɑːsə/ Ranasinghe 1924– . Sri Lankan politician, a United National Party member of Parliament from 1960, prime minister from 1978, and president from 1988, having gained popularity through overseeing a major house-building and poverty-alleviation programme. He has sought peace talks with the Tamil Tiger guerrillas.

From a slum background and a member of the dhobi (laundryworkers' caste), Premadasa was elected deputy mayor of Colombo 1955. He served successively as minister of local government from 1968, UNP Chief Whip from 1970, and leader of the House from 1977, before being appointed prime minister. He was elected president Dec 1988. He opposed the 1987 Indo-Sri Lankan peace-keeping agreement aimed at solving the Tamil crisis, and in 1990 secured the withdrawal of the Indian forces.

Preminger /premɪŋgə/ Otto (Ludwig) 1906–1986. Austrian-born US film producer, director, and actor. He directed *Margin for Error* 1942, *Laura* 1944, *The Moon Is Blue* 1953, *The Man with the Golden Arm* 1955, *Anatomy of a Murder* 1959, *Skidoo!* 1968, and *Rosebud* 1974. His films are characterized by an intricate technique of storytelling and a masterly use of the wide screen and the travelling camera.

Prempeh I /prempeɪ/ chief of the Ashanti people in W Africa. He became king 1888, and later opposed British attempts to take over the region. He was deported and in 1900 the Ashanti were defeated. He returned to Kumasi (capital of the Ashanti region, now in Ghana) 1924 as chief of the people.

I don't collect any old reviews, scrapbooks, anything ... in order to be able to work I need to forget what I have done.

Otto Preminger

Prendergast /ˈprendəgɑːst/ Maurice 1859–1924. US painter who created a decorative watercolour style, using small translucent pools of colour, inspired by the Impressionists.

He studied in Paris in the 1890s and was influenced by the Nabis painters Pierre Bonnard and Edouard Vuillard. In 1898 he visited Italy. His *Umbrellas in the Rain, Venice* 1899 (Museum of Fine Arts, Boston) is typical of his work.

Prescott /ˈpreskɒt/ John Leslie 1938– . British Labour Party politician, a member of the shadow cabinet from 1983.

A former merchant sailor and trade-union official, he was member of parliament for Kingston-on-Hull (East) 1970–83 and since 1983 has been member of Parliament for Hull East. In 1975, he became a member of the European Parliament, despite being opposed to Britain's membership of the European Community. A strong parliamentary debater and television performer, he was sometimes critical of his colleagues. In 1988, he unsuccessfully challenged Roy Hattersley for the deputy leadership, and again failed to win the post 1992.

Prescott /ˈpreskət/ William Hickling 1796–1859. US historian, author of *History of the Reign of Ferdinand and Isabella, the Catholic* 1838, *History of the Conquest of Mexico* 1843, and *History of the Conquest of Peru* 1847.

Presley /ˈprezli/ Elvis (Aaron) 1935–1977. US singer and guitarist, the most influential performer of the rock-and-roll era. With his recordings for Sun Records in Memphis, Tennessee, 1954–55 and early hits such as 'Heartbreak Hotel', 'Hound Dog', and 'Love Me Tender', all 1956, he created an individual vocal style, influenced by Southern blues, gospel music, country music, and rhythm and blues. His records continued to sell in their millions into the 1990s.

Presley was born in Tupelo, Mississippi. His first records were regional hits in the South, and he became a nationwide star in 1956, Sun having sold his recording contract to RCA at the instigation of his new manager, the self-styled Colonel Tom Parker (1909–   ), a former carnival huckster. Of the four films Presley made in the 1950s, *Loving You* 1957 and *Jailhouse Rock* 1957 offer glimpses of the electrifying stage performer he then was. After his army service 1958–60, the album *Elvis Is Back* 1960 and some gospel-music recordings made that year were outstanding, but from then on his work deteriorated quickly. By the time of his death, Presley had long been a caricature. His early contribution to rock music was, however, inestimable, and his Memphis home, Graceland, draws large numbers of visitors each year.

Pressburger /ˈpresbɜːgɑ/ Emeric 1902–1988. Hungarian producer, screenwriter, and director known for his partnership with Michael ➔Powell. Forming the production company, the Archers in 1942, Powell and Pressburger collaborated on 14 films between 1942 and 1956, such as *The Red Shoes* 1948.

Prester John /ˈprestə ˈdʒɒn/ legendary Christian prince. During the 12th and 13th centuries, Prester John was believed to be the ruler of a powerful empire in Asia. From the 14th to the 16th century, he was generally believed to be the king of Abyssinia (now Ethiopia) in N E Africa.

Preston /ˈprestən/ Peter (John) 1938– . British newspaper editor and executive. In 1975 he became editor of the moderate left-wing daily *Guardian* and from 1988 he was also its company chair.

Previn /ˈprevɪn/ André (George) 1929– . US conductor and composer, born in Berlin. After a period working as a composer and arranger in the US film industry, he concentrated on conducting. He was principal conductor of the London Symphony Orchestra 1968–79. He was appointed music director of Britain's Royal Philharmonic Orchestra 1985 (a post he relinquished the following year, staying on as principal conductor), and of the Los Angeles Philharmonic in 1986.

Prévost d'Exiles /preˈvəʊ degˈziːl/ Antoine François 1697–1763. French novelist, known as Abbé Prévost, who combined a military career with his life as a monk. His *Manon Lescaut* 1731 inspired operas by Massenet and Puccini.

Price /praɪs/ Leontyne 1927–. US opera singer. She played a leading singing role in Ira Gershwin's revival of his musical *Porgy and Bess* 1952–54. Gaining a national reputation, she made her operatic debut in San Francisco 1957. Price appeared at La Scala in Milan 1959 and became a regular member of the Metropolitan Opera in New York 1961.

Born in Laurel, Mississippi, USA, and educated at Central State College in Ohio, Price was trained as a soprano at the Juilliard School of Music in New York.

Price /praɪs/ Vincent 1911– . US actor, star of such horror films as *House of Wax* 1953, the cult favourite *The Tingler* 1959, and *The Fall of the House of Usher* 1960.

Priestley /ˈpriːstli/ J(ohn) B(oynton) 1894–1984. English novelist and playwright. His first success was a novel about travelling theatre, *The Good Companions* 1929. He followed it with a realist novel about London life, *Angel Pavement* 1930. As a playwright he was often preoccupied with theories of time, as in *An Inspector Calls* 1945.

Priestly had a gift for family comedy, for example, the play *When We Are Married* 1938. He was also known for his wartime broadcasts and literary criticism, such as *Literature and Western Man* 1960. Later novels include *Lost Empires* 1965 and *The Image Men* 1968.

Priestley English chemist and cleric Joseph Priestley, who isolated and identified gases, such as oxygen, hydrogen chloride, ammonia, and sulphur dioxide. A Presbyterian minister and a political radical, his support for the French Revolution made him unpopular in England and Priestley moved to the USA in 1794.

Priestley /ˈpriːstli/ Joseph 1733–1804. English chemist who identified oxygen 1774.

A Unitarian minister, he was elected Fellow of the Royal Society 1766. In 1791 his chapel and house in Birmingham were sacked by a mob because of his support for the French Revolution. In 1794 he emigrated to the USA.

Prigogine /prɪˈɡəʊʒɪn/ Ilya 1917– . Russian-born Belgian chemist who, as a highly original theoretician, has made major contributions to the field of thermodynamics for which work he was awarded the 1977 Nobel Prize for Physics. Earlier theories had considered systems at or about equilibrium. Prigogine began to study 'dissipative' or non-equilibrium structures frequently found in biological and chemical reactions.

Primo de Rivera /ˈpriːməʊ deɪ rɪˈveərə/ Miguel 1870–1930. Spanish soldier and politician, dictator from 1923 as well as premier from 1925. He was captain-general of Catalonia when he led a coup against the ineffective monarchy and became virtual dictator of Spain with the support of Alfonso XIII. He resigned 1930.

Prince /prɪns/ Hal (Harold) 1928– . US director of musicals such as *Cabaret* 1968 and *Follies* 1971 on Broadway in New York, and *Evita* 1978 and *Sweeney Todd* 1980 in London's West End.

Prince /prɪns/ Stage name of Prince Rogers Nelson 1960– . US pop musician who composes, arranges, and produces his own records and often plays all the instruments. His albums, including *1999* 1982 and *Purple Rain* 1984, contain elements of rock, funk, and jazz. His stage shows are energetic and extravagant.

His band, the Revolution, broke up after four years in 1986. His hits include 'Little Red Corvette' from *1999*, 'Kiss' from *Parade* 1986, and 'Sign O' The Times' from the album of the same name 1987. He has also starred in several films, including *Purple Rain* 1984 and *Graffiti Bridge* 1990. His home town of Minneapolis, Minnesota, has become a centre for recording as a result of his success.

Prior /praɪə/ James 1927– . British Conservative politician. He held ministerial posts from 1970. As employment secretary he curbed trade-union activity with the Employment Act 1980, and was Northern Ireland secretary 1981–84. After his resignation 1984 he became chair of the General Electric Company.

Prior /praɪə/ Matthew 1664–1721. British poet and diplomat. He was associated under the Whigs with the negotiation of the treaty of Ryswick 1697 ending the war with France and under the Tories with that of Utrecht 1714 ('Matt's Peace') ending the War of the Spanish Succession, but on the Whigs' return to power he was imprisoned by the government leader Walpole 1715–17. His gift as a poet was for light occasional verses.

Pritchett /ˈprɪtʃɪt/ V(ictor) S(awdon) 1900– . English short-story writer, novelist, and critic, with an often witty and satirical style. His short stories were gathered in *Collected Stories* 1982 and *More Collected Stories* 1983. His critical works include *The Living Novel* 1946 and biographies of the Russian writers Turgenev 1977 and Chekhov 1988.

The profoundly humorous writers are humorous because they are responsive to the hopeless, uncouth concatenations of life.

V S Pritchett
The Living Novel & Later Appreciations

Profumo /prəˈfjuːməʊ/ John (Dennis) 1915– . British Conservative politician, secretary of state for war from 1960 to June 1963, when he resigned on the disclosure of his involvement with Christine Keeler, mistress also of a Soviet naval attaché. In 1982 Profumo became administrator of the social and educational settlement Toynbee Hall in London.

Prokhorov /ˈprɒxərɒf/ Aleksandr 1916– . Russian physicist whose fundamental work on microwaves in 1955 led to the construction of the first practical maser (the microwave equivalent of the laser) by Charles ➔Townes, for which they shared the 1964 Nobel Prize for Physics.

Prokofiev /prə'kɒfief/ Sergey (Sergeyevich) 1891–1953. Soviet composer. His music includes operas such as *The Love for Three Oranges* 1921; ballets for Sergei →Diaghilev, including *Romeo and Juliet* 1935; seven symphonies including the *Classical Symphony* 1916–17; music for films; piano and violin concertos; songs and cantatas (for example, that composed for the 30th anniversary of the October Revolution); and *Peter and the Wolf* 1936.

Prokofiev was essentially a classicist in his use of form, but his extensive and varied output demonstrates great lyricism, humour, and skill. Born near Ekaterinoslav, he studied at St Petersburg under Nikolay Rimsky-Korsakov and achieved fame as a pianist. He left Russia in 1918 and lived for some time in the USA and in Paris, but returned in 1927 and again in 1935.

Propertius /prə'pɜːʃəs/ Sextus *c.* 47–15 BC. Roman elegiac poet, a member of →Maecenas' circle, who wrote of his love for his mistress 'Cynthia'.

From a mere nothing springs a mighty tale.

Sextus Propertius *Elegies*

Prost /prɒst/ Alain 1955– . French motor-racing driver who was world champion 1985, 1986, and 1989, the first French world drivers' champion. At the beginning of 1991 he had won a record 44 Grands Prix from 169 starts.

He raced in Formula One events from 1980 and had his first Grand Prix win 1981 (French GP) driving a Renault. In 1984 he began driving for the McLaren team. He moved to Ferrari in 1990 for two years but was without a drive at the start of the 1992 season. He is known as 'the Professor'.

Proudhon /pruː'dɒn/ Pierre Joseph 1809–1865. French anarchist, born in Besançon. He sat in the Constituent Assembly of 1848, was imprisoned for three years, and had to go into exile in Brussels. He published *Qu'est-ce que la propriété/What is Property?* 1840 and *Philosophie de la misère/Philosophy of Poverty* 1846; the former contains the dictum 'property is theft'.

Proust /pruːst/ Joseph Louis 1754–1826. French chemist. He was the first to state the principle of constant composition of compounds – that compounds consist of the same proportions of elements wherever found.

Proust /pruːst/ Marcel 1871–1922. French novelist and critic. His immense autobiographical work *A la Recherche du temps perdu/Remembrance of Things Past* 1913–27, consisting of a series of novels, is the expression of his childhood memories coaxed from his subconscious; it is also a precise reflection of life in France at the end of the 19th century.

Born at Auteuil, Proust was a delicate, asthmatic child; until he was 35 he moved in the fashionable circles of Parisian society, but after the death of his parents 1904–05 he went into seclusion in a cork-lined room in his Paris apartment, and devoted the rest of his life to writing his masterpiece.

Prout /praʊt/ William 1785–1850. British physician and chemist. In 1815 Prout published his hypothesis that the relative atomic mass of every atom is an exact and integral multiple of the hydrogen atom. The discovery of isotopes (atoms of the same element that have different masses) in the 20th century bore out his idea.

Prud'hon /pruː'dɒn/ Pierre 1758–1823. French Romantic painter. He became drawing instructor and court painter to the emperor Napoleon's wives.

After winning the Prix de Rome 1784, Prud'hon visited Italy but, unlike his contemporary Jacques Louis David, he was unaffected by the Neo-Classical vogue; his style is indebted to the Italian painter Antonio →Correggio.

Prynne /prɪn/ William 1600–1669. English Puritan. He published in 1632 *Histriomastix*, a work attacking stage plays; it contained aspersions on the Queen, Henrietta Maria, for which he was pilloried and lost his ears. In 1637 he was again pilloried and branded for an attack on the bishops. He opposed the execution of Charles I, and actively supported the Restoration.

Przhevalsky /pʃɛ'vælski/ Nikolai Mikhailovitch 1839–1888. Russian explorer and soldier. In 1870 he crossed the Gobi Desert to Beijing and then went on to the upper reaches of the Chang Jiang River. His attempts to penetrate Tibet as far as Lhasa failed on three occasions, but he continued to explore the mountain regions between Tibet and Mongolia, where he made collections of plants and animals, including a wild camel and a wild horse (the species is now known as *Przhevalsky's horse*).

The Kirghiz town of Karakol on the eastern shores of Lake Issyk Kul where he died was renamed Przhevalsky in 1889.

Ptolemy /'tɒləmi/ (Claudius Ptolemaeus) *c.* 100–AD 170. Egyptian astronomer and geographer who worked in Alexandria. His *Almagest* developed the theory that Earth is the centre of the universe, with the Sun, Moon, and stars revolving around it. In 1543 the Polish astronomer →Copernicus proposed an alternative to the *Ptolemaic system*. Ptolemy's *Geography* was a standard source of information until the 16th century.

Ptolemy /'tɒləmi/ dynasty of kings of Macedonian origin who ruled Egypt over a period of 300 years; they included:

Ptolemy I *c.* 367–283 BC. Ruler of Egypt from 323 BC, king from 304. He was one of →Alexander the Great's generals, and possibly his half-brother (and married his lover, →Thaïs). He established the library in Alexandria.

It is more kingly to enrich others than to enjoy wealth oneself.

Ptolemy I

Ptolemy XIII 63–47 BC. Joint ruler of Egypt with his sister-wife Cleopatra; she put him to death.

Puccini /pʊˈtʃiːni/ Giacomo (Antonio Domenico Michele Secondo Maria) 1858–1924. Italian opera composer whose music shows a strong gift for melody and dramatic effect and whose operas combine exotic plots with elements of *verismo* (realism). They include *Manon Lescaut* 1893, *La Bohème* 1896, *Tosca* 1900, *Madame Butterfly* 1904, and the unfinished *Turandot* 1926.

Pudovkin /puːˈdɒfkɪn/ Vsevolod Illationovich 1893–1953. Russian film director whose films include the silent *Mother* 1926, *The End of St Petersburg* 1927, and *Storm over Asia* 1928; and the sound films *Deserter* 1933 and *Suvorov* 1941.

Puget /pjuːˈʒeɪ/ Pierre 1620–1694. French Baroque sculptor who developed a powerful and expressive style. He created a muscular statue of the tyrant *Milo of Croton* 1672–82 (Louvre, Paris) for the garden of the palace of Versailles.

Puget worked in Italy 1640–43 and was influenced by →Michelangelo and →Pietro da Cortona. After 1682 he failed to gain further court patronage because of his stubborn temperament and his severe style.

Pugin /pjuːdʒɪn/ Augustus Welby Northmore 1812–1852. English architect, collaborator with Charles →Barry in the detailed design of the Houses of Parliament. He did much to revive Gothic architecture in England.

P'u-i /puːˈjiː/ (or *Pu-Yi*) Henry 1906–1967. Last emperor of China (as Hsuan Tung) from 1908 until his deposition 1912; he was restored for a week 1917. After his deposition he chose to be called Henry. He was president 1932–34 and emperor 1934–45 of the Japanese puppet state of Manchuko.

Captured by Soviet troops, he was returned to China 1949 and put on trial in the new People's Republic of China 1950. Pardoned by Mao Zedong 1959, he became a worker in a botanical garden in Beijing.

Pulaski /pəˈlæski/ Casimir 1747–1779. Polish patriot and military leader. Hired by Silas →Deane and Benjamin Franklin in their campaign to recruit for the American Revolution 1775–83 he was placed in command of the Continental cavalry 1777. He saw action at Valley Forge 1777–78,

and after a dispute with General Anthony Wayne, was given an independent cavalry command. He died in action in the siege of Savannah.

Born in Padolia, Poland, Pulaski embarked on a military career early in life. He was forced into exile after participating in the unsuccessful Polish defence against the Russian invasion 1770–72.

Pulitzer /ˈpʊlɪtsə/ Joseph 1847–1911. Hungarian-born US newspaper publisher. He acquired *The World* 1883 in New York City and, as a publisher, his format set the style for the modern newspaper. After his death, funds provided in his will established 1912 the school of journalism at Columbia University and the annual Pulitzer Prizes in journalism, literature, and music (from 1917).

Pullman /ˈpʊlmən/ George 1831–1901. US engineer who developed the Pullman railway car. In an attempt to improve the standard of comfort of rail travel, he built his first Pioneer Sleeping Car 1863. He formed the Pullman Palace Car Company 1867 and in 1881 the town of Pullman, Illinois, was built for his workers.

Purcell /ˈpɜːsəl/ Henry 1659–1695. English Baroque composer. His work can be highly expressive, for example, the opera *Dido and Aeneas* 1689 and music for Dryden's *King Arthur* 1691 and for *The Fairy Queen* 1692. He wrote more than 500 works, ranging from secular operas and incidental music for plays to cantatas and church music.

Purcell English Baroque composer and musician Henry Purcell began his career as a boy chorister of the Chapel Royal under Charles II. In the years before his death, he composed some of his greatest church music, such as the Te Deum. He died young and was buried in Westminster Abbey.

Purchas /ˈpɜːtʃɪs/ Samuel 1577–1626. English compiler of travel books, rector of St Martin's Ludgate, 1614–26. His collection *Purchas, his Pilgrimage* 1613, was followed by another in 1619, and in 1625 by *Hakluytus Posthumus or Purchas his Pilgrimes*, based on papers left by the geographer Richard Hakluyt.

Pusey /ˈpjuːzi/ Edward Bouverie 1800–1882. English Church of England priest from 1828. In 1835 he joined J H →Newman in issuing the *Tracts for the Times*. After Newman's conversion to Catholicism, Pusey became leader of the High Church Party or Puseyites, striving until his death to keep them from conversion.

Pushkin /ˈpʊʃkɪn/ Aleksandr 1799–1837. Russian poet and writer. His works include the novel in verse *Eugene Onegin* 1823–31 and the tragic drama *Boris Godunov* 1825. Pushkin's range was wide, and his willingness to experiment freed later Russian writers from many of the archaic conventions of the literature of his time.

Pushkin was born in Moscow. He was exiled 1820 for his political verse and in 1824 was in trouble for his atheistic opinions. He wrote ballads such as *The Gypsies* 1827, and the prose pieces *The Captain's Daughter* 1836 and *The Queen of Spades* 1834. He was mortally wounded in a duel with his brother-in-law.

Puttnam /ˈpʌtnəm/ David (Terence) 1941– . English film producer who played a major role in reviving the British film industry internationally in the 1980s. Films include *Chariots of Fire* 1981, *The Killing Fields* 1984 (both of which won several Academy Awards), and *Memphis Belle* 1990.

Puvis de Chavannes /pjuːˈviːs də ʃæˈvæn/ Pierre Cécile 1824–1898. French Symbolist painter. His major works are vast decorative schemes, mainly on mythological and allegorical subjects, for public buildings such as the Panthéon and Hôtel de Ville in Paris. His work influenced Paul Gauguin. The Boston Public Library, Massachusetts, also has his murals. His *Poor Fisherman* 1881 (Louvre, Paris) was a much admired smaller Symbolist work.

Pyke /paɪk/ Margaret 1893–1966. British birth-control campaigner. In the early 1930s she became secretary of the National Birth Control Association (later the Family Planning Association, FPA), and campaigned vigorously to get local councils to set up family-planning clinics. She became chair of the FPA in 1954.

Pym /pɪm/ Barbara 1913–1980. English novelist, born in Shropshire, whose novels include *Some Tame Gazelle* 1950, *The Sweet Dove Died* 1978, and *A Few Green Leaves* 1980.

Habit is Heaven's own redress:/it takes the place of happiness.

    Aleksandr Pushkin, *Eugene Onegin* 1823–31

Pym /pɪm/ Francis 1922– . British Conservative politician. He was defence secretary 1979–81, and succeeded Lord Carrington as foreign minister 1982, but was dismissed in the post-election reshuffle 1983.

Pym /pɪm/ John 1584–1643. English Parliamentarian, largely responsible for the petition of right 1628. As leader of the Puritan opposition in the Long Parliament from 1640, he moved the impeachment of Charles I's advisers the Earl of Strafford and William Laud, drew up the Grand Remonstrance, and was the chief of five members of Parliament Charles I wanted arrested 1642. The five hid themselves and then emerged triumphant when the king left London.

Pynaker Adam 1622–1673. Dutch landscape painter. It is thought that Pynaker spent some three years in Italy. His landscape style reflects the Italianate influence in the way it combines cloudless skies with the effect of clear, golden light on a foreground of trees and foliage. *Barges on a River* (Hermitage, St Petersburg) is his masterpiece but *Landscape with Sportsmen and Game* (Dulwich Picture Gallery), is a more typical work.

Pynchon /ˈpɪntʃən/ Thomas 1937– . US novelist who created a bizarre, labyrinthine world in his books, the first of which was *V* 1963. *Gravity's Rainbow* 1973 represents a major achievement in 20th-century literature, with its fantastic imagery and esoteric language, drawn from mathematics and science.

His other works include *The Crying of Lot 49* 1966 and *Vineland* 1990.

Pyrrho *c.* 360–*c.* 270 BC. Greek philosopher, founder of Scepticism, who maintained that since certainty was impossible, peace of mind lay in renouncing all claims to knowledge.

One more such victory and we are lost.

Pyrrhus after defeating the Romans at Asculum,
                              279 BC.

Pyrrhus /ˈpɪrəs/ *c.* 318–272 BC. King of Epirus, Greece, from 307, who invaded Italy 280, as an ally of the Tarentines against Rome. He twice defeated the Romans but with such heavy losses that a *Pyrrhic victory* has come to mean a victory not worth winning. He returned to Greece 275 after his defeat at Beneventum, and was killed in a riot in Argos.

Pythagoras /paɪˈθægərəs/ *c.* 580–500 BC. Greek mathematician and philosopher who formulated Pythagoras' theorem.

Much of his work concerned numbers, to which he assigned mystical properties. For example, he classified numbers into triangular ones (1, 3, 6, 10, ...), which can be represented as a triangular array, and square ones (1, 4, 9, 16, ...), which form squares. He also observed that any two adjacent triangular numbers add to a square number (for example, $1 + 3 = 4$; $3 + 6 = 9$; $6 + 10 = 16$; ...).

Pythagoras was the founder of a politically influential religious brotherhood in Croton, S Italy (suppressed in the 5th century). Its tenets included the immortality and transmigration of the soul.

Pythagorus of Rhegium 5th century BC. Greek sculptor. He was born on the island of Samos and settled in Rhegium (Reggio di Calabria), Italy. He made statues of athletes and is said to have surpassed his contemporary Myron in this field.

Pytheas /ˈpɪθiəs/ 4th century BC. Greek navigator from Marseille who explored the coast of W Europe at least as far north as Denmark, sailed around Britain, and reached what he called Thule, the most northern place known (possibly the Shetlands).

Qaboos /əˈbuːs/ bin Saidq 1940– . Sultan of Oman, the 14th descendant of the Albusaid family. Opposed to the conservative views of his father, he overthrew him 1970 in a bloodless coup and assumed the sultanship. Since then he has followed more liberal and expansionist policies, while maintaining his country's position of international nonalignment.

My parliament is the street. I myself talk to my Omanis ... I do not want a parliament of coffee drinkers, who steal my precious time and only talk.

Qaboos bin Saidq 1979

Qaddafi alternative form of →Khaddhafi, Libyan leader.

Qin dynasty /tʃɪn/ Chinese imperial dynasty 221–206 BC. Shi Huangdi was its most renowned emperor. The Great Wall of China was built at this time.

Quant /kwɒnt/ Mary 1934– . British fashion designer who popularized the miniskirt in the UK. Her Chelsea boutique, Bazaar, revolutionized women's clothing and make-up in the 'swinging London' of the 1960s. In the 1970s she extended into cosmetics and textile design.

Quantrill /ˈkwɒntrɪl/ William Clarke 1837–1865. US proslavery outlaw who became leader of an irregular unit on the Confederate side in the American Civil War. Frank and Jesse →James were members of his gang (called Quantrill's Raiders).

Quasimodo /ˌkwɑːzɪˈməʊdəʊ/ Salvatore 1901–1968. Italian poet. His first book *Acque e terre/Waters and Land* appeared 1930. Later books, including *Nuove poesie/New Poetry* 1942 and *Il falso e vero verde/The False and True Green* 1956, reflect a growing preoccupation with the political and social problems of his time. Nobel prize 1959.

Quayle /kweɪl/ Anthony 1913– . English actor and director. From 1948–56 he directed at the Shakespeare Memorial Theatre, and appeared as Falstaff in *Henry IV*, Petruchio in *The Taming of the Shrew*, and played the title role in *Othello*. He played nonclassical parts in *Galileo*, *Sleuth*, and *Old World*.

Quayle /kweɪl/ (J) Dan(forth) 1947– . US Republican politician, vice president 1989-93. A congressman for Indiana 1977–81, he became a senator 1981.

Born into a rich and powerful Indianapolis newspaper-owning family, Quayle was admitted to the Indiana bar 1974, and was elected to the House of Representatives 1976 and to the Senate 1980. When George Bush ran for president 1988, he selected Quayle as his running mate, admiring his conservative views and believing that Quayle could deliver the youth vote. This choice encountered heavy criticism because of Quayle's limited political experience. As Bush's vice president, Dan Quayle attracted criticism for, among other things, his enlistment in the 1960s in the Indiana National Guard, which meant that he was not sent overseas during the Vietnam War.

Queensberry /ˈkwiːnzbəri/ John Sholto Douglas, 8th Marquess of Queensberry 1844–1900. British patron of boxing. In 1867 he formulated the *Queensberry Rules*, which form the basis of today's boxing rules.

He was the father of Lord Alfred →Douglas and it was his misspelled insult to Oscar Wilde that set in motion the events leading to the playwright's imprisonment.

Queneau /keˈnəʊ/ Raymond 1903–1976. French Surrealist poet and humorous novelist. His works include *Zazie dans le Métro/Zazie in the Metro* 1959, a portrayal of a precocious young Parisian woman.

Quennell /kwɪˈnel/ Peter 1905– . British biographer and critic. He edited the journal *History Today* 1951–79, and wrote biographies of Byron 1935, Ruskin 1949, Pope 1968, and Dr Johnson 1972.

Quetelet /ˌketˈleɪ/ Lambert Adolphe Jacques 1796–1874. Belgian statistician. He developed tests for the validity of statistical information, and gathered and analysed statistical data of many kinds. From his work on sociological data came the concept of the 'average person'.

Quevedo y Villegas /keˈveɪdəʊ iː viːˈjeɪgəs/ Francisco Gómez de 1580–1645. Spanish novelist and satirist. His picaresque novel *La vida del buscón/The Life of a Scoundrel* 1626 follows the tradition of the roguish hero who has a series of adventures. *Sueños/Visions* 1627 is a brilliant series of satirical portraits of contemporary society.

Quilter /ˈkwɪltə/ Roger 1877–1953. English composer. He wrote song settings of →Tennyson and →Shakespeare, including 'Now Sleeps the Crimson Petal' 1904 and 'To Daisies' 1906, and the *Children's Overture* 1920.

Quimby /ˈkwɪmbi/ Fred(erick) 1886–1965. US film producer, head of MGM's short films department 1926-56. Among the cartoons produced by this department were the *Tom and Jerry* series and those directed by Tex →Avery.

Quincy /ˈkwɪnsi/ Josiah 1772–1864. US public official. A staunch Federalist, he served in the US House of Representatives 1805–13, opposing the trade policies of the Jefferson administration and the Louisiana Purchase of 1803. As an opponent of US involvement in the Anglo-American War 1812–14, he resigned from Congress and returned to Boston, where he was mayor 1823–28.

Born in Braintree, Massachusetts, Quincy was educated at Harvard University and was admitted to the bar 1793. He served as president of Harvard 1829–45 and wrote a number of historical works before embarking on a political career.

Quine /kwaɪn/ Willard Van Orman 1908– . US philosopher and logician. In *Two Dogmas of Empiricism* 1951 he argued against the analytic/synthetic distinction. In *Word and Object* 1960 he put forward the thesis of radical untranslatability, the view that a sentence can always be regarded as referring to many different things.

Quinn /kwɪn/ Anthony 1915– . Mexican-born US actor, in films from 1935. Famous for the title role in *Zorba the Greek* 1964, he later played variations on this larger-than-life character. Other films include Fellini's *La Strada* 1954.

In Europe an actor is an artist. In Hollywood, if he isn't working, he's a bum.

Anthony Quinn

Quintero /kɪnˈteːəʊ/ Serafin Alvárez and Joaquin Alvárez. Spanish dramatists; see →Alvárez Quintero.

Quintilian /kwɪnˈtɪliən/ (Marcus Fabius Quintilianus) *c.* AD 35–95. Roman rhetorician. He was born at Calgurris, Spain, taught rhetoric in Rome from AD 68, and composed the *Institutio Oratoria/The Education of an Orator*, in which he advocated a simple and sincere style of public speaking.

Quisling /ˈkwɪzlɪŋ/ Vidkun 1887–1945. Norwegian politician. Leader from 1933 of the Norwegian Fascist Party, he aided the Nazi invasion of Norway 1940 by delaying mobilization and urging non-resistance. He was made premier by Hitler 1942, and was arrested and shot as a traitor by the Norwegians 1945. His name became a generic term for a traitor who aids an occupying force.

R

Rabelais /ˈræbəleɪ/ François 1495–1553. French satirist, monk, and physician whose name has become synonymous with bawdy humour. He was educated in the Renaissance humanist tradition and was the author of satirical allegories, including *La Vie inestimable de Gargantua/The Inestimable Life of Gargantua* 1535 and *Faits et dits héroïques du grand Pantagruel/Deeds and Sayings of the Great Pantagruel* 1533, about two giants (father and son).

Rabi /ˈrɑːbi/ Isidor Isaac 1898–1988. Russian-born US physicist who developed techniques to measure accurately the strength of the weak magnetic fields generated when charged elementary particles, such as the electron, spin about their axes. The work won him the 1944 Nobel Prize for Physics.

Rabin /ˈræbiːn/ Yitzhak 1922– . Israeli Labour politician, prime minister 1974–77 and from 1992. Rabin was minister for defence under the conservative Likud coalition government 1984–90. His policy of favouring Palestinian self-government in the occupied territories contributed to the success of the centre-left party in the 1992 elections.

Rabuka Sitiveni 1948– . Fijian soldier and politician, prime minister from 1992. When the 1987 elections in Fiji produced an Indian-dominated government, Rabuka staged two successive coups (the first short-lived). Within months of the second, he stepped down, allowing a civilian government to take over. In May 1992 he was nominated as the new Fijian premier.

Rabuka joined the Fijian army at an early age and was trained at Sandhurst military academy, England. He commanded a unit of the UN peace-keeping force in Lebanon, for which he was awarded the OBE. In May 1987 Rabuka removed the new Indian-dominated Fijian government at gunpoint, but the governor-general regained control within weeks; in Sept he staged a second coup and proclaimed Fiji a republic, withdrawing from the Commonwealth. He gave way to a civilian government Dec 1987 and served as home-affairs minister, but resigned the post 1990. In May 1992 he was nominated prime minister.

Rachel /ræˈʃel/ Stage name of Elizabeth Félix 1821–1858. French tragic actress who excelled in fierce, passionate roles, notably Phaedra in Racine's tragedy *Phèdre*, which she took on tour to Europe, the USA, and Russia.

Rachmaninov /rækˈmænɪnɒf/ Sergei (Vasilevich) 1873–1943. Russian composer, conductor, and pianist. After the 1917 Revolution he went to the USA. His dramatically emotional Romantic music has a strong melodic basis and includes operas, such as *Francesca da Rimini* 1906, three symphonies, four piano concertos, piano pieces, and songs. Among his other works are the *Prelude in C-Sharp Minor* 1882 and *Rhapsody on a Theme of Paganini* 1934 for piano and orchestra.

Racine /ræˈsiːn/ Jean 1639–1699. French dramatist and exponent of the classical tragedy in French drama. His subjects came from Greek mythology and he observed the rules of classical Greek drama. Most of his tragedies have women in the title role, for example *Andromaque* 1667, *Iphigénie* 1674, and *Phèdre* 1677.

An orphan, Racine was educated by Jansenists at Port Royal, but later moved away from an ecclesiastical career to success and patronage at court. His ingratiating flattery won him the suc-

Rafsanjani The president of Iran, Ali Akbar Rafsanjani. He is viewed as the most pragmatic and influential member of Iran's post-Khomeini collective leadership.

cess he craved in 1677 when he was appointed royal historiographer. After the failure of *Phèdre* in the theatre he no longer wrote for the secular stage, but influenced by Madame de →Maintenon wrote two religious dramas, *Esther* 1689 and *Athalie* 1691, which achieved posthumous success.

Radcliffe /ˈrædklɪf/ Ann (born Ward) 1764–1823. English novelist, an exponent of the Gothic novel or 'romance of terror' who wrote, for example, *The Mysteries of Udolpho* 1794.

Radić /ˈrɑːdɪtʃ/ Stjepan 1871–1928. Yugoslav nationalist politician, founder of the Croatian Peasant Party 1904. He led the Croat national movement within the Austro-Hungarian Empire and advocated a federal state with Croatian autonomy. His opposition to Serbian supremacy within Yugoslavia led to his assassination in parliament.

Raeburn /ˈreɪbɜːn/ Henry 1756–1823. Scottish portrait painter, active mainly in Edinburgh. He developed a technique of painting with broad brushstrokes directly on the canvas without preparatory drawing. He was appointed painter to George IV 1823. *The Reverend Robert Walker Skating c.* 1784 (National Gallery, Edinburgh) 1784 is typical.

Raeder /ˈreɪdə/ Erich 1876–1960. German admiral. Chief of Staff in World War I, he became head of the navy 1928, but was dismissed by Hitler in 1943 because of his failure to prevent Allied Arctic convoys from reaching the USSR. Sentenced to life imprisonment at the Nuremberg trials of war criminals, he was released 1955 on grounds of ill health.

Rafelson /ˈreɪfəlsən/ Bob (Robert) 1934– . US film director who gained critical acclaim for his second film, *Five Easy Pieces* 1971. His films include *The King of Marvin Gardens* 1972, *Stay Hungry* 1976, and *The Postman Always Rings Twice* 1981.

Raffles /ˈræfəlz/ Thomas Stamford 1781–1826. British colonial administrator, born in Jamaica. He served in the British East India Company, took part in the capture of Java from the Dutch 1811, and while governor of Sumatra 1818–23 was responsible for the acquisition and founding of Singapore 1819.

Rafsanjani /ˌræfsændʒɑːˈniː/ Hojatoleslam Ali Akbar Hashemi 1934– . Iranian politician and cleric, president from 1989. When his former teacher Ayatollah →Khomeini returned after the revolution of 1979–80, Rafsanjani became the speaker of the Iranian parliament and, after Khomeini's death, state president and effective political leader.

Rafsanjani was born near Kerman, SE Iran, to a family of pistachio farmers. At 14 he went to study Islamic jurisprudence with Khomeini in the to Shi'ites holy city of Qom and qualified as an *alim* (Islamic teacher). During the period

Raglan *English general FitzRoy Somerset, 1st Baron Raglan, took over the command of the British forces in the Crimea 1854. He won the battles of Alma and Inkerman, but was responsible for the ambiguous order that led to the loss of the Light Brigade at Balaclava.*

1964–78, he acquired considerable wealth through his construction business but kept in touch with his exiled mentor and was repeatedly imprisoned for fundamentalist political activity. His attitude became more moderate in the 1980s.

Raft /rɑːft/ George 1895–1980. US film actor, usually cast as a sharp-eyed gangster (as in *Scarface* 1932). His later work included a cameo in *Some Like It Hot* 1959.

Raglan /ˈræglən/ FitzRoy James Henry Somerset, 1st Baron Raglan 1788–1855. English general. He took part in the Peninsular War under Wellington, and lost his right arm at Waterloo. He commanded the British forces in the Crimean War from 1854. The *raglan sleeve*, cut right up to the neckline with no shoulder seam, is named after him.

Don't carry away that arm till I have taken off my ring.

Lord Raglan

Rahere /ˈreɪhɪə/ died 1144. Minstrel and favourite of Henry I of England. In 1123, having recovered from malaria while on a pilgrimage to Rome, he founded St Bartholomew's priory and St Bartholomew's hospital in London.

Raleigh Portrait of English courtier, adventurer, and writer Walter Raleigh by Nicolas Hilliard (c. 1590), National Portrait Gallery, London. His expeditions to find treasure in the Americas were unsuccessful although they introduced the potato and tobacco to Europe. Raleigh soon became a favourite of Elizabeth I, but his haughty, impatient manner brought him many bitter enemies.

Rahman /muːˈdʒiːbʊə/ Sheik Mujibur 1921–1975. Bangladeshi Nationalist politician, president 1975. He was arrested several times for campaigning for the autonomy of East Pakistan. He won the elections 1970 as leader of the Awami League but was again arrested when negotiations with the Pakistan government broke down. After the civil war 1971, he became prime minister of the newly independent Bangladesh. He was presidential dictator Jan–Aug 1975, when he was assassinated.

Rahman /rɑːmən/ Tunku Abdul 1903–1990. Malaysian politician, first prime minister of independent Malaya 1957–63 and of Malaysia 1963–70.

Born at Kuala Keda, the son of the sultan and his sixth wife, a Thai princess, the Tunku studied law in England. After returning to Malaya he founded the Alliance Party 1952. The party was successful in the 1955 elections, and the Tunku became prime minister of Malaya on gaining independence 1957, continuing when Malaya became part of Malaysia 1963. His achievement was to bring together the Malay, Chinese, and Indian peoples within the Alliance Party, but in the 1960s he was accused of showing bias towards Malays. Ethnic riots followed in Kuala Lumpur 1969 and, after many attempts to restore better relations, the Tunku retired 1970. In his later years he voiced criticism of the authoritarian leadership of Mahathir bin Mohamad.

Raikes /reɪks/ Robert 1735–1811. English printer who started the first Sunday school (for religious purposes) in Gloucester 1780 and who stimulated the growth of weekday voluntary 'ragged schools' for poor children.

Raine /reɪn/ Kathleen 1908– . English poet. Her volumes of poetry include *Stone and Flower* 1943 and *The Lost Country* 1971, and reflect both the Northumberland landscape of her upbringing and the religious feeling which led her to the Roman Catholic Church 1944.

Rainier III /reɪnɪeɪ/ 1923– . Prince of Monaco from 1949. He was married to the US film actress Grace Kelly.

Rais /reɪ/ Gilles de 1404–1440. French marshal who fought alongside Joan of Arc. In 1440 he was hanged for the torture and murder of 140 children, but the court proceedings were irregular. He is the historical basis of the Bluebeard character.

Raleigh /rɔːli/ or *Ralegh* Walter *c.* 1552–1618. English adventurer. He made colonizing and exploring voyages to North America 1584–87 and South America 1595, and naval attacks on Spanish ports. His aggressive actions against Spanish interests brought him into conflict with the pacific James I. He was imprisoned for treason 1603–16 and executed on his return from an unsuccessful final expedition to South America.

Raleigh was knighted 1584, and made several attempts 1584–87 to establish a colony in 'Virginia' (now North Carolina, USA). In 1595 he led an expedition to South America (described in his *Discoverie of Guiana* 1596) and distinguished himself in expeditions against Spain in Cádiz 1596 and the Azores 1597. After James I's accession 1603 he was condemned to death on a charge of conspiracy, but was reprieved and imprisoned in the Tower of London, where he wrote his unfinished *History of the World*. Released 1616 to lead a gold-seeking expedition to the Orinoco River in South America, which failed disastrously, he was beheaded on his return under his former sentence.

Ramakrishna /ˌrɑːməˈkrɪʃnə/ 1834–1886. Hindu sage, teacher, and mystic (one dedicated to achieving oneness with or a direct experience of God or some force beyond the normal world). Ramakrishna claimed that mystical experience was the ultimate aim of religions, and that all religions which led to this goal were equally valid.

Ramakrishna's most important follower, Swami Vivekananda (1863–1902), set up the Ramakrishna Society 1887, which now has centres for education, welfare, and religious teaching throughout India and beyond.

Raman /rɑːmən/ Venkata 1888–1970. Indian physicist who in 1928 discovered what became known as the *Raman effect*: the scattering of monochromatic (single-wavelength) light when passed through a transparent substance. Awarded a Nobel prize in 1930, in 1948 he became director of the Raman Research Institute and national research professor of physics.

Rambert /ˈrɒmbeə/ Marie. Adopted name of Cyvia Rambam 1888–1982. British ballet dancer and teacher born in Poland, who became a British citizen 1918. One of the major innovative and influential figures in modern ballet, she was with the Diaghilev ballet 1912–13, opened the Rambert School 1920, and in 1926 founded the *Ballet Rambert* which she directed. It became a modern dance company from 1966 with Norman Morrice as director, and was renamed the Rambert Dance Company 1987.

We want to create an atmosphere in which creation is possible.

Marie Rambert

Rambouillet /ˌrɒmbuːˈjeɪ/ Catherine de Vivonne, Marquise de Rambouillet 1588–1665. French society hostess, whose salon at the Hôtel de Rambouillet in Paris included the philosopher Descartes, and the writers La Rochefoucauld and Madame de Sévigné. The salon was ridiculed by the dramatist Molière in his *Les Précieuses ridicules* 1659.

Ram Das /rɑːm dɑːs/ 1534–1581. Indian religious leader, fourth guru (teacher) of Sikhism 1574–81, who founded the Sikh holy city of Amritsar.

Rameau /ræˈməʊ/ Jean-Philippe 1683–1764. French organist and composer. He wrote *Treatise on Harmony* 1722 and his varied works include keyboard and vocal music and many operas, such as *Castor and Pollux* 1737.

Ramée /rɑːˈmeɪ/ Louise de la. English novelist who wrote under the name →Ouida.

Rameses alternative spelling of →Ramses, name of kings of ancient Egypt.

Ramphal /ˈræmfɑːl/ Shridath Surendranath ('Sonny') 1928– . Guyanese politician. He was minister of foreign affairs and justice 1972–75 and secretary general of the British Commonwealth 1975–90.

Rampling /ˈræmplɪŋ/ Charlotte 1945– . British actress whose films include *Georgy Girl* 1966, *The Damned* 1969, and *The Night Porter/Il Portiere di Notti* 1974.

Ramsay /ˈræmzi/ Allan 1686–1758. Scottish poet, born in Lanarkshire. He published *The Tea-Table Miscellany* 1724–37 and *The Evergreen* 1724, collections of ancient and modern Scottish song, including revivals of the work of such poets as William Dunbar and Robert Henryson. He was the father of painter Allan Ramsay.

Ramsay /ˈræmzi/ Allan 1713–1784. Scottish portrait painter. After studying in Edinburgh and Italy, he established himself as a portraitist in London and became painter to George III in 1760. His portraits include *The Artist's Wife* about 1755 (National Gallery, Edinburgh).

Ramsay /ˈræmzi/ William 1852–1916. Scottish chemist who, with Lord Rayleigh, discovered argon 1894. In 1895 Ramsay produced helium and in 1898, in cooperation with Morris Travers, identified neon, krypton, and xenon. In 1903, with Frederick Soddy, he noted the transmutation of radium into helium, which led to the discovery of the density and relative atomic mass of radium. Nobel prize 1904.

Ramses /ˈræmsiːz/ or *Rameses* 11 kings of ancient Egypt, including:

Ramses III king of Egypt about 1200–1168 BC. He won a naval victory over the Philistines and other Middle Eastern peoples, and asserted his control over Palestine.

Rand /rænd/ Ayn. Adopted name of Alice Rosenbaum 1905–1982. Russian-born US novelist. Her novel *The Fountainhead* 1943 (made into a film 1949), describing an idealistic architect who destroys his project rather than see it altered, displays her persuasive blend of vehement anti-communism and fervent philosophy of individual enterprise.

Rand /rænd/ Sally (Helen Gould Beck) 1904–1979. US exotic dancer. During the 1930s she worked as a dancer in Chicago and developed her trademark nude dance routine to Chopin and Debussy, which featured the coy use of huge ostrich fans. Playing a role in the 1965 burlesque revival on Broadway, she continued to dance until 1978.

Born in Hickory County, Missouri, USA, Rand joined the circus as an acrobat as a teenager. She later moved to Hollywood where she played supporting roles in a number of silent films.

Her appearances at the 1933 Chicago Exposition and at later fairs and expositions across the country made her a popular favourite.

Randolph /ˈrændɒlf/ Asa Philip 1889–1979. US labour and civil rights leader. Devoting himself to the cause of unionization, especially among black Americans, he was named a vice president of the American Federation of Labor and Congress of Industrial Organizations (AFL-CIO) 1957. He was one of the organizers of the 1963 civil rights march on Washington.

Born in Crescent City, Florida, USA, Randolph was educated at the City College of New York and became involved in labour-organizing activities as a student.

He founded the periodical *Messenger* 1917 and after successfully organizing railroad workers, he served as the president of the Brotherhood of Sleeping Car Porters 1925–68.

Ranjit Singh /ˈrændʒɪt ˈsɪŋ/ 1780–1839. Indian maharajah. He succeeded his father as a minor Sikh leader 1792, and created a Sikh army that conquered Kashmir and the Punjab. In alliance with the British, he established himself as 'Lion of the Punjab', ruler of the strongest of the independent Indian states.

Ranjitsinhji /ˌrʌndʒɪt'sɪndʒi/ K S (Ranji) 1872–1933. Indian prince and cricketer who played for Sussex and England. A top batsman, he scored 3,065 runs in 1900, and five double centuries in one season.

Rank /ræŋk/ J(oseph) Arthur 1888–1972. British film magnate. Having entered films in 1933 to promote the Methodist cause, by the mid-1940s he controlled, through the Rank Organization, half the British studios and more than 1,000 cinemas.

The Rank Organization still owns the Odeon chain of cinemas, although film is now a minor part of its activities.

Ranke /ræŋkə/ Leopold von 1795–1886. German historian whose quest for objectivity in history had great impact on the discipline. His attempts to explain 'how it really was' dominated both German and outside historical thought until 1914 and beyond. His *Weltgeschichte/World History* (nine volumes 1881–88) exemplified his ideas.

Ransom /rænsəm/ John Crowe 1888–1974. US poet and critic. He published his romantic but antirhetorical verse in, for example, *Poems About God* 1919, *Chills and Fever* 1924, and *Selected Verse* 1947.

He was born in Tennessee, and was a leader of the Southern literary movement that followed World War I. As a critic and teacher he was a powerful figure in the New Criticism movement, which shaped much literary theory from the 1940s to the 1960s.

Ransome /rænsəm/ Arthur 1884–1967. English journalist (correspondent in Russia for the *Daily News* during World War I and the Revolution) and writer of adventure stories for children, such as *Swallows and Amazons* 1930 and *Peter Duck* 1932.

Ransome /rænsəm/ Robert 1753–1830. English ironfounder and agricultural engineer, whose business earned a worldwide reputation in the 19th and 20th centuries. He introduced factory methods for the production of an improved range of ploughs from 1789. The firm remained at the forefront of advances in agricultural mechanization in connection with steam engines, threshing machines, and lawnmowers.

Rao /raʊ/ P(amulaparti) V(enkata) Narasimha 1921– . Indian politician; see →Narasimha Rao.

Rao /raʊ/ Raja 1909– . Indian writer. He wrote about Indian independence from the perspective of a village in S India in *Kanthapura* 1938 and later, in *The Serpent and the Rope* 1960, about a young cosmopolitan intellectual seeking enlightenment.

Rao was born at Hassan, Karnataka. He studied at Montpellier and the Sorbonne in France. Collections of stories include *The Cow of the Barricades* 1947 and *The Policeman and the Rose* 1978.

Raoult /raːˈuː/ François 1830–1901. French chemist. In 1882, while working at the University of Grenoble, Raoult formulated one of the basic laws of chemistry. *Raoult's law* enables the relative molecular mass of a substance to be determined by noting how much of it is required to depress the freezing point of a solvent by a certain amount.

Raphael Sanzio /ræfeɪəl ˈsænziəʊ/ (Raffaello Sanzio) 1483–1520. Italian painter, one of the greatest of the High Renaissance, active in Perugia, Florence, and Rome (from 1508), where he painted frescoes in the Vatican and for secular patrons. His religious and mythological scenes are harmoniously composed; his portraits enhance the character of his sitters and express dignity. Many of his designs were engraved. Much of his later work was the product of his studio.

Raphael was born in Urbino, the son of Giovanni Santi (died 1494), a court painter. In 1499 he went to Perugia, where he worked with →Perugino, whose graceful style is reflected in Raphael's *Marriage of the Virgin* (Brera, Milan). This work also shows his early concern for harmonious disposition of figures in the pictorial space. In Florence 1504–08 he studied the works of Leonardo da Vinci, Michelangelo, Masaccio, and Fra Bartolommeo. His paintings of this period include the *Ansidei Madonna* (National Gallery, London).

Pope Julius II commissioned him to decorate the papal apartments (the Stanze) in the Vatican. In Raphael's first fresco series there, *The School of Athens* 1509 is a complex but classically composed grouping of Greek philosophers and mathematicians, centred on the figures of Plato and Aristotle. A second series of frescoes, 1511–14, includes the dramatic and richly coloured *Mass of Bolsena*.

Raphael was increasingly flooded with commissions. Within the next few years he produced mythological frescoes in the Villa Farnesina in Rome (1511–12), cartoons for tapestries for the Sistine Chapel, Vatican (Victoria and Albert Museum, London), and the *Sistine Madonna* about 1512 (Gemäldegalerie, Dresden, Germany), and portraits, for example of Baldassare Castiglione about 1515 (Louvre, Paris). One of his pupils was →Giulio Romano.

Rasputin /ræs'pjuːtɪn/ (Russian 'dissolute') Grigory Efimovich 1871–1916. Siberian Eastern Orthodox mystic who acquired influence over the tsarina →Alexandra, wife of →Nicholas II, and was able to make political and ecclesiastical appointments. His abuse of power and notorious debauchery (reputedly including the tsarina) led to his murder by a group of nobles.

Rasputin, the illiterate son of a peasant, began as a wandering 'holy man'. Through the tsarina's faith in his power to ease her son's suffering from haemophilia, he became a favourite at the court, where he instigated wild parties under the slogan 'Sin that you may obtain forgiveness'. A larger-than-life character, he even proved hard to kill: when poison had no effect, his assassins shot him and dumped him in the river Neva.

Rathbone /ˈræθbəʊn/ (Philip St John) Basil 1892–1967. South African-born British character actor, a specialist in villains. He also played Sherlock Holmes (the fictional detective created by Arthur Conan Doyle) in several films. He worked mainly in Hollywood, in such films as *The Adventures of Robin Hood* 1938 and *The Hound of the Baskervilles* 1939.

Rathenau /ˈrɑːtənaʊ/ Walther 1867–1922. German politician. He was a leading industrialist and was appointed economic director during World War I, developing a system of economic planning in combination with capitalism. After the war he founded the Democratic Party, and became foreign minister 1922. The same year he signed the Rapallo Treaty of Friendship with the USSR, cancelling German and Soviet counterclaims for indemnities for World War I, and soon after was assassinated by right-wing fanatics.

Rattigan /ˈrætɪgən/ Terence 1911–1977. English playwright. His play *Ross* 1960 was based on the character of T E Lawrence (Lawrence of Arabia). Rattigan's work ranges from the comedy *French Without Tears* 1936 to the psychological intensity of *The Winslow Boy* 1945. Other plays include *The Browning Version* 1948 and *Separate Tables* 1954.

Rattle /ˈrætl/ Simon 1955– . English conductor. Principal conductor of the Birmingham Symphony Orchestra from 1980, he is renowned for his eclectic range and for interpretations of Mahler and Sibelius.

Ratushinskaya /ˌrætuːˈʃɪnskəjə/ Irina 1954– . Soviet dissident poet. Sentenced 1983 to seven years in a labour camp plus five years in internal exile for criticism of the Soviet regime, she was released 1986. Her strongly Christian work includes *Grey is the Colour of Hope* 1988.

Rau /raʊ/ Johannes 1931– . German socialist politician. The son of a Protestant pastor, Rau became state premier of North Rhine–Westphalia 1978. In Jan 1987 he stood for chancellor of West Germany but was defeated by the incumbent conservative coalition.

Rauschenberg /ˈraʊʃənbɜːg/ Robert 1925– . US Pop artist, a creator of happenings (art in live performance) and incongruous multimedia works such as *Monogram* 1959 (Moderna Museet, Stockholm), a car tyre around the body of a stuffed goat daubed with paint. In the 1960s he returned to painting and used the silk-screen printing process to transfer images to canvas. He also made collages.

Ravel /ˈrævel/ (Joseph) Maurice 1875–1937. French composer. His work is characterized by its sensuousness, unresolved dissonances, and 'tone colour'. Examples are the piano pieces *Pavane pour une infante défunte* 1899 and *Jeux d'eau* 1901,

Ray John Ray's Catalogus Plantarum Angliae/Catalogue of English Plants *1670 was a landmark in the history of botanical classification. His* Wisdom of God Manifested in the Works of Creation *1691 was widely read and appreciated.*

and the ballets *Daphnis et Chloë* 1912 and *Boléro* 1928.

Rawlinson /ˈrɔːlɪnsən/ Henry Creswicke 1810–1895. English orientalist and political agent in Baghdad in the Ottoman Empire from 1844. He deciphered the Babylonian cuneiform and Old Persian scripts of →Darius I's trilingual inscription at Behistun, Persia, continued the excavation work of A H →Layard, and published a *History of Assyria* 1852.

Rawls /ˈrɔːlz/ John 1921– . US philosopher. In *A Theory of Justice* 1971, he revived the concept of the social contract (unofficial agreement between a government and organized labour that in return for control of prices, rents, and so on, workers would refrain from economically disruptive wage demands) and its enforcement by civil disobedience.

Rawsthorne /ˈrɔːsθɔːn/ Alan 1905–1971. British composer. His *Theme and Variations* for two violins 1938 was followed by other tersely energetic works including *Symphonic Studies* 1939, the overture *Street Corner* 1944, *Concerto for Strings* 1950, and a vigorously inventive sonata for violin and piano, 1959.

Ray /reɪ/ John 1627–1705. English naturalist who devised a classification system accounting for nearly 18,000 plant species. It was the first system to divide flowering plants into monocotyledons and dicotyledons, with additional divisions made on the basis of leaf and flower characters and fruit types.

Ray /reɪ/ Nicholas. Adopted name of Raymond Nicholas Kienzle 1911–1979. US film director, critically acclaimed for his socially aware dramas such as *Rebel Without a Cause* 1955. His films include *In a Lonely Place* 1950, *Johnny Guitar* 1954, and *55 Days at Peking* 1963.

Ray /reɪ/ Satyajit 1921–1992. Indian film director, internationally known for his trilogy of life in his native Bengal: *Pather Panchali, Unvanquished,* and *The World of Apu* 1955–59. Later films include *The Music Room* 1963, *Charulata* 1964, *The Chess Players* 1977, and *The Home and the World* 1984.

Rayburn /ˈreɪbɜːn/ Samuel Taliaferro 1882–1961. US political leader. A Democrat, he was elected to the US Congress 1912. He supported President Roosevelt's New Deal programme 1933, and was elected majority leader 1937 and Speaker of the House 1940. With the exception of two terms, he served as Speaker until his death. His tenure in the House 1912–61 was the longest on record.

Born in Roane County, Tennessee, USA, and raised in Texas, Rayburn received a law degree from the University of Texas 1908. He served in the state legislature 1907–12. A leader of the Democratic party, Rayburn chaired the national conventions in 1948, 1952, and 1956.

Rayleigh /ˈreɪli/ John W Strutt, 3rd Baron 1842–1919. British physicist who wrote the standard *Treatise on Sound,* experimented in optics and microscopy, and, with William Ramsay, discovered argon. Nobel prize 1904.

He was professor of experimental physics at Cambridge 1879–84, and was president of the Royal Society 1905–08, when he became chancellor of Cambridge University.

Reade /riːd/ Charles 1814–1884. British novelist and playwright, author of the historical epic, set in the 15th century, *The Cloister and the Hearth* 1861.

Reagan /ˈreɪgən/ Ronald (Wilson) 1911– . 40th president of the USA 1981–89, a Republican. He was governor of California 1966–74, and a former Hollywood actor. Reagan was a hawkish and popular president. He adopted an aggressive policy in Central America, attempting to overthrow the government of Nicaragua, and invading Grenada 1983.

In 1987, Irangate (the sale of arms to Iran, violating US law and a public ban on arms to Iran) was investigated by the Tower Commission; Reagan admitted that USA–Iran negotiations had become an 'arms for hostages deal', but denied knowledge of resultant funds being illegally sent to the Contras in Nicaragua. He increased military spending (sending the national budget deficit to record levels), cut social programmes, introduced deregulation of domestic markets, and cut taxes. His Strategic Defense Initiative, announced 1983, proved controversial owing to the cost and unfeasibility. He was succeeded by George →Bush.

Reagan was born in Tampico, Illinois, the son of a shoe salesman who was bankrupted during the Depression. He became a Hollywood actor 1937 and appeared in 50 films, including *Bedtime for Bonzo* 1951 and *The Killers* 1964. As president of the Screen Actors' Guild 1947–52, he became a conservative, critical of the bureaucratic stifling of free enterprise, and named names before the House Un-American Activities Committee. He joined the Republican Party 1962, and his term as governor of California was marked by battles against students. Having lost the Republican presidential nomination 1968 and 1976 to Nixon and Ford respectively, Reagan won it 1980 and defeated President Carter. He was wounded in an assassination attempt 1981. The invasion of Grenada, following a coup there, generated a revival of national patriotism, and Reagan was re-elected by a landslide 1984. His insistence on militarizing space through the Strategic Defense Initiative, popularly called Star Wars, prevented a disarmament agreement when he met the Soviet leader →Gorbachev 1985 and 1986, but a 4% reduction in nuclear weapons was agreed 1987. In 1986, he ordered the bombing of Tripoli, Libya, in alleged retaliation for the killing of a US soldier in Berlin by a guerrilla group.

Reardon /ˈrɪədn/ Ray 1932– . Welsh snooker player. One of the leading players of the 1970s, he was six times world champion 1970–78.

Réaumur /ˈreɪəʊmjʊər/ René Antoine Ferchault de 1683–1757. French scientist. His work on metallurgy *L'Arte de convertir le fer forge en acier* 1722 described how to convert iron into steel and stimulated the development of the French steel industry. He produced a six-volume work 1734–42 on entomology, *L'Histoire des insectes/History of Insects,* which threw much new light on the social insects. He also contributed to other areas of science.

Récamier /ˌreɪkæmˈjeɪ/ Jeanne Françoise (born Bernard) 1777–1849. French society hostess, born in Lyon. At the age of 15 she married Jacques Récamier (died 1830), an elderly banker, and held a salon of literary and political celebrities.

Red Cloud /ˌred ˈklaʊd/ (Sioux name *Mahpiua Luta*) 1822–1909. American Sioux Indian leader. Paramount chief of the Oglala Sioux from 1860, he was advocate of accommodation with the US government and signed the Fort Laramie Treaty 1869 which gave the Indians a large area in the Black Hills of Dakota. He resisted any involvement in the war which culminated in the Battle of Little Bighorn 1876.

Born in the area of modern Nebraska, Red Cloud led his followers to the Red Cloud Agency in Nebraska after General Custer's last stand at Little Bighorn. From there they were moved to the Pine Ridge Agency in South Dakota 1878; Red Cloud continued to seek compromise with the government.

Redding /ˈrediŋ/ Otis 1941–1967. US soul singer and songwriter. He had a number of hits in the mid-1960s such as 'My Girl' 1965, 'Respect' 1967, and '(Sittin' on the) Dock of the Bay' 1968, released after his death in a plane crash.

Redford /ˈredfəd/ (Charles) Robert 1937– . US actor and film director. His first starring role was in *Barefoot In The Park* 1967, followed by *Butch Cassidy and the Sundance Kid* 1969, and *The Sting* 1973 (both with Paul →Newman).

His other films as an actor include *All the President's Men* 1976 and *Out of Africa* 1985. He directed *Ordinary People* 1980 and *The Milagro Beanfield War* 1988.

Redgrave /ˈredgreɪv/ Michael 1908–1985. British actor. His stage roles included Hamlet and Lear (Shakespeare), Uncle Vanya (Chekhov), and the schoolmaster in Rattigan's *The Browning Version* (filmed 1951). On screen he appeared in *The Lady Vanishes* 1938, *The Importance of Being Earnest* 1952, and *Goodbye Mr Chips* 1959. He was the father of Vanessa and Lynn Redgrave, both actresses.

Redgrave /ˈredgreɪv/ Vanessa 1937– . British actress. She has played Shakespeare's Lady Macbeth and Cleopatra on the stage, and Olga in Chekhov's *Three Sisters* 1990. She won an Academy Award for the title role in the film *Julia* 1976; other films include *Howards End* 1992. She is active in left-wing politics.

I choose my roles carefully so that when my career is finished, I'll have covered all our current history of oppression.

Vanessa Redgrave 1984

Redmond /ˈredmənd/ John Edward 1856–1918. Irish politician, Parnell's successor as leader of the Nationalist Party 1890–1916. The 1910 elections

Récamier Madame de Récamier' whose salon in the Paris of the Napoleonic and Restoration periods was attended by Madame de Staël, Benjamin Constant, and Chateaubriand who read aloud passages from his works.

saw him holding the balance of power in the House of Commons, and he secured the introduction of a Home Rule bill, which was opposed by Protestant Ulster.

Redmond supported the British cause on the outbreak of World War I, and the bill was passed though its operation was suspended until the war's end. The growth of the nationalist party Sinn Féin (the political wing of the Irish Republican Army) and the 1916 Easter Rising ended his hopes and his power.

Redon /rəˈdɒn/ Odilon 1840–1916. French Symbolist painter and graphic artist. He used fantastic symbols and images, sometimes mythological. From the 1890s he painted still lifes and landscapes. His work was much admired by the Surrealists.

Redon initially worked mostly in black and white, producing charcoal drawings and lithographs, but from 1890, in oils and pastels, he used colour in a way that recalled the Impressionists. The head of Orpheus is a recurring motif in his work.

Redouté /rəduːˈteɪ/ Pierre Joseph 1759–1840. French flower painter patronized by Empress Josephine and the Bourbon court. He taught flower drawing at the Museum of Natural History in Paris and produced volumes of delicate, highly detailed flowers, notably *Les Roses* 1817–24.

Reed /riːd/ Carol 1906–1976. British film producer and director, an influential figure in the British film industry of the 1940s. His films include *Odd Man Out* 1947, *The Fallen Idol* and *The Third Man* both 1950, *Our Man in Havana* 1959, and the Academy Award-winning musical *Oliver!* 1968.

The illegitimate son of actor Herbert Beerbohm Tree, who died when Reed was 11, he followed his father onto the stage as an actor before finding work at Ealing studios as a dialogue coach.

Reed /riːd/ Ishmael 1938– . US novelist. His experimental, parodic, satirical novels exploit traditions taken from jazz and voodoo, and include *The Free-Lance Pallbearers* 1967, *Mumbo Jumbo* 1972, and *Reckless Eyeballing* 1986.

Reed /riːd/ John 1887–1920. US journalist and author. As a supporter of the Bolsheviks, Reed published his account of the Russian Revolution in *Ten Days that Shook the World* 1919. Later indicted in the US for sedition, Reed fled to the Soviet Union, where he died in exile.

Reed /riːd/ Lou 1942– . US rock singer, songwriter, and guitarist; former member (1965–70) of the New York avant-garde group *the Velvet Underground*, perhaps the most influential band of the period. His solo work deals largely with urban alienation and angst, and includes the albums *Berlin* 1973, *New York* 1989, and *Magic and Loss* 1991.

Reed /riːd/ Oliver 1938– . British actor, nephew of the director Carol Reed. He appeared in such films as *Women in Love* 1969, *The Devils* 1971, and *Castaway* 1987.

Reed /riːd/ Walter 1851–1902. US physician and medical researcher. His greatest work was carried out 1900–1901 in Cuba, where a yellow-fever epidemic was ravaging US troops. His breakthrough isolation of the aedes mosquito as the sole carrier of yellow fever led to the eradication of the deadly disease.

Born in Belroi, Virginia, Reed received an MD degree from the University of Virginia 1869. He joined the Army Medical Corps 1875, served as an army surgeon in Arizona 1876–89 and Baltimore 1890–93, and was professor at the Army Medical College 1893–1902.

His 1898 research into the causes and transmission of typhoid fever brought about significant control of the disease in army camps.

Rees-Mogg /ˌriːs ˈmɒg/ Lord William 1928– . British journalist, editor of *The Times* 1967–81, chair of the Arts Council 1982–89, and from 1988 chair of the Broadcasting Standards Council.

The arts are to Britain what sunshine is to Spain.

William Rees-Mogg 1985

Reeves /riːvz/ William Pember 1857–1932. New Zealand politician and writer. He was New Zealand minister of education 1891–96, and director of the London School of Economics 1908–19. He wrote poetry and the classic description of New Zealand, *Long White Cloud* 1898.

Regan /ˈriːgən/ Donald 1918– . US Republican political adviser to Ronald →Reagan. He was secretary of the Treasury 1981–85, and chief of White House staff 1985–87, when he was forced to resign because of widespread belief in his complicity in the Irangate scandal (concerning the sale of arms to Iran, violating US law and a public ban on arms to Iran).

Reger /ˈreɪgə/ (Johann Baptist Joseph) Max(imilian) 1873–1916. German composer and pianist. He taught in Munich 1905–07, was professor at the Leipzig Conservatoire from 1907, and was conductor of the Meiningen ducal orchestra 1911–14. His works include organ and piano music, chamber music, and songs.

Rehnquist /ˈrenkwɪst/ William 1924– . Chief justice of the US Supreme Court from 1986. Under his leadership, the court has established a reputation for conservative rulings on such issues as abortion and capital punishment.

Active within the Republican Party, Rehnquist was appointed head of the office of legal counsel by President Nixon in 1969 and controversially defended such measures as pre-trial detention and wiretapping. He became an associate justice of the Supreme Court in 1972.

Rehoboam /ˌriːhəˈbəuəm/ king of Judah about 932–915 BC, son of Solomon. Under his rule the Jewish nation split into the two kingdoms of *Israel* and *Judah*. Ten of the tribes revolted against him and took Jeroboam as their ruler, leaving Rehoboam only the tribes of Judah and Benjamin.

Reich /raɪk/ Steve 1936– . US composer. His Minimalist music consists of simple patterns carefully superimposed and modified to highlight constantly changing melodies and rhythms; examples are *Phase Patterns* for four electronic organs 1970, *Music for Mallet Instruments, Voices, and Organ* 1973, and *Music for Percussion and Keyboards* 1984.

Reich /raɪk/ Wilhelm 1897–1957. Austrian doctor, who emigrated to the USA 1939. He combined Marxism and psychoanalysis to advocate the positive effects of directed sexual energies and sexual freedom. His works include *Die Sexuelle Revolution/The Sexual Revolution* 1936–45 and *Die Funktion des Orgasmus/The Function of the Orgasm* 1948.

Reichstadt, Duke of /ˈraɪkʃtæt/ title of →Napoleon II, son of Napoleon I.

Reichstein /ˈraɪkstaɪn/ Tadeus 1897– . Swiss biochemist who investigated the chemical activity of the adrenal glands. By 1946 Reichstein had identified a large number of steroids secreted by the adrenal cortex, some of which would later be used in the treatment of Addison's disease. Reichstein shared the 1950 Nobel physiology or medicine prize with Edward →Kendall and Philip Hench (1896–1965).

Reid /riːd/ Thomas 1710–1796. Scottish mathematician and philosopher. His *Enquiry into the Human Mind on the Principles of Common Sense* 1764 attempted to counter the sceptical conclusions of Hume. He believed that the existence of the material world and the human soul is self-evident 'by the consent of ages and nations, of the learned and unlearned'.

Reinhardt /ˈraɪnhɑːt/ Django (Jean Baptiste) 1910–1953. Belgian jazz guitarist and composer, who was co-leader, with Stephane Grappelli, of the Quintet de Hot Club de France 1934–39. He had a lyrical acoustic style and individual technique, and influenced many US musicians.

Reinhardt /ˈraɪnhɑːt/ Max 1873–1943. Austrian producer and director, whose Expressionist style was predominant in German theatre and film during the 1920s and 1930s. Directors such as Murnau and Lubitsch and actors such as Dietrich worked with him. He co-directed the US film *A Midsummer Night's Dream* 1935.

In 1920 Reinhardt founded the Salzburg Festival. When the Nazis came to power, he lost his theatres and, after touring Europe as a guest director, went to the USA, where he produced and directed. He founded an acting school and theatre workshop in Hollywood.

Reisz /raɪs/ Karel 1926–   . Czech film director, originally a writer and film critic, who lived in Britain from 1938, and later in the USA. His first feature film, *Saturday Night and Sunday Morning* 1960, was a critical and commercial success. His other films include *Morgan* 1966, *The French Lieutenant's Woman* 1981, and *Sweet Dreams* 1986.

Remarque /rəˈmɑːk/ Erich Maria 1898–1970. German novelist, a soldier in World War I, whose *All Quiet on the Western Front* 1929, one of the first anti-war novels, led to his being deprived of German nationality. He lived in Switzerland 1929–39, and then in the USA.

Rembrandt /ˈrembrænt/ Harmensz van Rijn 1606–1669. Dutch painter and etcher, one of the most prolific and significant artists in Europe of the 17th century. Between 1629 and 1669 he painted some 60 penetrating self-portraits. He also painted religious subjects, and produced about 300 etchings and over 1,000 drawings. His group portraits include *The Anatomy Lesson of Dr Tulp* 1632 (Mauritshuis, The Hague) and *The Night Watch* 1642 (Rijksmuseum, Amsterdam).

After studying in Leiden and for a few months in Amsterdam (with a history painter), Rembrandt began his career 1625 in Leiden, where his work reflected knowledge of →Elsheimer and →Caravaggio, among others. He settled permanently in Amsterdam 1631 and obtained many commissions for portraits from wealthy merchants. The *Self-Portrait with Saskia* (his wife, Saskia van Uylenburgh) about 1634 (Gemäldegalerie, Dresden, Germany) displays their prosperity in warm tones and rich, glittering textiles.

Saskia died 1642, and that year Rembrandt's fortunes began to decline (he eventually became bankrupt 1656). His work became more sombre and had deeper emotional content, and his portraits were increasingly melancholy: for example, *Jan Six* 1654 (Six Collection, Amsterdam). From 1660 onward he lived with Hendrickje Stoffels, but he outlived her, and in 1668 his only surviving child, Titus, died too.

Rembrandt had many pupils, including Gerard Dou and Carel Fabritius.

A picture is finished when the artist achieves his aim.

Rembrandt

Remick /ˈremɪk/ Lee 1935–1991. US film and television actress. Although often typecast as a teasing but obliging flirt, she delivered intelligent and affecting portrayals of an extensive range of characters in her career. Among her best-known films were *The Long Hot Summer* 1958, *Anatomy of a Murder* 1959, and *Sanctuary* 1961. Her best

performances were perhaps in two 1962 films by Blake Edwards, *Experiment in Terror* and *Days of Wine and Roses*; she earned an Oscar nomination for her role in the latter.

Remington /ˈremɪŋtən/ Eliphalet 1793–1861. US inventor, gunsmith, and arms manufacturer and founder (with his father) of the Remington firm. He supplied the US army with rifles in the Mexican War 1846–48, then in 1856 the firm expanded into the manufacture of agricultural implements. His son Philo continued the expansion.

Remington /ˈremɪŋtən/ Frederic 1861–1909. US artist and illustrator best known for his paintings, sculptures, and sketches of scenes of the American West, which he recorded during several trips to the region.

His lively images of cowboys and horses include the sculpture *Off the Range* (Corcoran Gallery of Art, Washington, DC) and the bronze *Bronco Buster* 1895, of which there are over 300 copies.

Remington /ˈremɪŋtən/ Philo 1816–1889. US inventor of the breech-loading rifle that bears his name. He began manufacturing typewriters 1873, using the patent of Christopher →Sholes (1819–1890), and made improvements that resulted five years later in the first machine with a shift key, thus providing lower-case letters as well as capital letters. The Remington rifle and carbine, which had a falling block breech and a tubular magazine, were developed in collaboration with his father **Eliphalet Remington** (1793–1861).

Renault /rəˈnoʊ/ Mary. Pen name of Mary Challans 1905–1983. English historical novelist who specialized in ancient Greece, with a trilogy on the legendary hero Theseus and two novels on →Alexander the Great: *Fire from Heaven* 1970 and *The Persian Boy* 1972.

Rendell /ˈrendl/ Ruth 1930–   . English novelist and short-story writer, author of a detective series featuring Chief Inspector Wexford. Her psychological crime novels explore the minds of people who commit murder, often through obsession or social inadequacy, as in *A Demon in my View* 1976 and *Heartstones* 1987. *Lake of Darkness* 1980 won the Arts Council National Book Award (Genre Fiction) for that year.

René /rəˈneɪ/ France-Albert 1935–   . Seychelles left-wing politician, the country's first prime minister after independence and president from 1977 after a coup. He has followed a non-nuclear policy of nonalignment.

In 1964 René founded the left-wing Seychelles People's United Party, pressing for complete independence. When this was achieved, in 1976, he became prime minister and James Mancham, leader of the Seychelles Democratic Party, became president. René seized the presidency in 1977 and set up a one-party state. He has survived several attempts to remove him.

Reni /ˈreɪni/ Guido 1575–1642. Italian painter, active in Bologna and Rome (about 1600–14), whose work includes the fresco *Phoebus and the Hours Preceded by Aurora* 1613 (Casino Rospigliosi, Rome). His workshop in Bologna produced numerous religious images, including Madonnas.

Rennie /ˈreni/ John 1761–1821. Scottish engineer who built two bridges over the river Thames in London, both later demolished: Waterloo Bridge 1811–17 and London Bridge 1824–34; he also built bridges, canals, dams (Rudyard dam, Staffordshire, 1800), and harbours.

Rennie studied at Edinburgh University and then worked for James →Watt from 1784. He started his own engineering business about 1791. Waterloo Bridge was demolished 1934–36 and replaced 1944; London Bridge was demolished 1968, bought by a US oil company and reassembled at Lake Havana, Arizona.

Renoir /rənˈwɑː/ Jean 1894–1979. French director whose films, characterized by their humanism and naturalistic technique, include *Boudu sauvé des eaux/Boudu Saved from Drowning* 1932, *La grande Illusion* 1937, and *La Règle du jeu/The Rules of the Game* 1939. In 1975 he received an honorary Academy Award for his life's work. He was the son of the painter Pierre-Auguste Renoir.

I've been 40 years discovering that the queen of all colours is black.

Pierre-Auguste Renoir

Renoir /rənˈwɑː/ Pierre-Auguste 1841–1919. French Impressionist painter. He met Monet and Sisley in the early 1860s, and together they formed the nucleus of the Impressionist movement. He developed a lively, colourful painting style with feathery brushwork and painted many voluptuous female nudes, such as *The Bathers* about 1884–87 (Philadelphia Museum of Art, USA). In his later years he turned to sculpture.

Born in Limoges, Renoir trained as a porcelain painter. He joined an academic studio 1861, and the first strong influences on his style were the Rococo artists Boucher and Watteau and the Realist Courbet. In the late 1860s Impressionism made its impact and Renoir began to work outdoors. Painting with Monet, he produced many pictures of people at leisure by the river Seine. From 1879 he made several journeys abroad, to N Africa, the Channel Islands, Italy, and later to Britain, the Netherlands, Spain, and Germany. After his Italian visit of 1881 he moved towards a more Classical structure in his work, notably in *Les Parapluies/Umbrellas* about 1881–84 (National Gallery, London). In 1906 he settled in the south of France. Many of his sculptures are monumental female nudes not unlike those of →Maillol.

Repin /rɪˈpiːn/ Ilya Yefimovich 1844–1930. Russian painter. His work includes dramatic studies, such as *Barge Haulers on the Volga* 1873, and portraits, including those of Tolstoy and Mussorgsky.

Repton /ˈreptən/ Humphrey 1752–1818. English garden designer, who coined the term 'landscape gardening'. He worked for some years in partnership with John →Nash. Repton preferred more formal landscaping than Capability →Brown, and was responsible for the landscaping of some 200 gardens and parks.

Resnais /reˈneɪ/ Alain 1922– . French film director whose work is characterized by the themes of memory and unconventional concepts of time. His films include *Hiroshima, mon amour* 1959, *L'Année dernière à Marienbad/Last Year at Marienbad* 1961, and *Providence* 1977.

Respighi /resˈpiːgi/ Ottorino 1879–1936. Italian composer, a student of →Rimsky-Korsakov, whose works include the symphonic poems *The Fountains of Rome* 1917 and *The Pines of Rome* 1924 (incorporating the recorded song of a nightingale), operas, and chamber music.

Retz /res/ Jean François Paul de Gondi, Cardinal de Retz 1614–1679. French politician. A priest with political ambitions, he stirred up and largely led the insurrection known as the Fronde. After a period of imprisonment and exile he was restored to favour 1662 and created abbot of St Denis.

Reuter /ˈrɔɪtə/ Paul Julius, Baron de 1816–1899. German founder of the international news agency *Reuters*. He began a continental pigeon post 1849, and in 1851 set up a news agency in London. In 1858 he persuaded the press to use his news telegrams, and the service became worldwide. Reuters became a public company 1984.

Revans /ˈrevənz/ Reginald William 1907– . British management expert, originator of the 'action learning' method of management improvement in which, for example, each department of a firm probes the problem-avoiding system of some other department until the circle is completed, with resultant improved productivity.

Revere Paul 1735–1818. American revolutionary, a Boston silversmith, who carried the news of the approach of British troops to Lexington and Concord on the night of 18 April 1775. On the next morning the first shots of the Revolution were fired at Lexington. Longfellow's poem 'The Midnight Ride of Paul Revere' commemorates the event.

Reynaud /reɪˈnəʊ/ Paul 1878–1966. French prime minister in World War II, who succeeded Edouard Daladier in March 1940 but resigned in June after the German breakthrough. He was imprisoned by the Germans until 1945, and again held government offices after the war.

Reynolds /ˈrenldz/ Albert 1933– . Irish politician, prime minister from 1992. He joined Fianna Fáil 1977, and held various government posts including minister for industry and commerce 1987–88 and minister of finance 1989–92. He became prime minister when Charles →Haughey was forced to resign Jan 1992, but his government was defeated on a vote of confidence Nov 1992.

Reynolds /renldz/ Burt 1936– . US film actor in adventure films and comedies. His films include *Deliverance* 1972, *Hustle* 1975, and *City Heat* 1984.

Reynolds /renldz/ Joshua 1723–1792. English portrait painter, active in London from 1752. He became the first president of the Royal Academy 1768. His portraits display a facility for striking and characterful compositions in a consciously grand manner. He often borrowed classical poses, for example *Mrs Siddons as the Tragic Muse* 1784 (San Marino, California, USA).

Reynolds was apprenticed to the portrait painter Thomas Hudson (1701–79). From 1743 he practised in Plymouth and London and 1749–52 completed his studies in Rome and Venice, concentrating on the antique and the High Renaissance masters. After his return to London he became the leading portraitist of his day with pictures such as *Admiral Keppel* 1753–54 (National Maritime Museum, London).

His *Discourses on Art* 1769–91 contain his theories on the aims of academic art.

Reynolds /renldz/ Osborne 1842–1912. British physicist and engineer who studied fluid flow and devised the *Reynolds number*, which relates to turbulence in flowing fluids.

Rhee /riː/ Syngman 1875–1965. Korean right-wing politician. A rebel under Chinese and Japanese rule, he became president of South Korea from 1948 until riots forced him to resign and leave the country 1960.

Rhine /raɪn/ Joseph Banks 1895–1980. US parapsychologist. His work at Duke University, North Carolina, involving controlled laboratory experiments in parapsychology, including telepathy, clairvoyance, precognition, and psychokinesis, described in *Extra-Sensory Perception* 1934, made ESP a common term.

Rhodes /rəʊdz/ Cecil (John) 1853–1902. South African politician, born in the UK, prime minister of Cape Colony 1890–96. Aiming at the formation of a South African federation and the creation of a block of British territory from the Cape to Cairo, he was responsible for the annexation of Bechuanaland (now Botswana) in 1885. He formed the British South Africa Company in 1889, which occupied Mashonaland and Matabeleland, thus forming *Rhodesia* (now Zambia and Zimbabwe).

Rhodes went to Natal in 1870. As head of De Beers Consolidated Mines and Goldfields of South Africa Ltd, he amassed a large fortune. He entered the Cape legislature 1881, and became prime minister 1890, but the discovery of his complicity in the Jameson Raid to support non-

Reynolds Sir Joshua Reynolds, eminent English portrait painter, master of the Grand Manner. The Neo-Classical idealizing principles of art set forth in his Discourses were vehemently disputed by William Blake. Many of his paintings are poorly preserved because of faults in his original materials and techniques.

Boer colonists in Transvaal forced him to resign 1896. Advocating Anglo-Afrikaner cooperation, he was less alive to the rights of black Africans, despite the final 1898 wording of his dictum: 'Equal rights for every civilized man south of the Zambezi.'

The *Rhodes scholarships* were founded at Oxford University, UK, under his will, for students from the Commonwealth, the USA, and Germany.

So little done, so much to do.

Cecil Rhodes last words

Rhodes /rəʊdz/ Wilfred 1877–1973. English cricketer. He took more wickets than anyone else in the game – 4,187 wickets 1898–1930 – and also scored 39,802 first-class runs.

Playing for Yorkshire, Rhodes made a record 763 appearances in the county championship. He took 100 wickets in a season 23 times and completed the 'double' of 1,000 runs and 100 wickets in a season 16 times (both records). He played his 58th and final game for England, against the West Indies 1930, when he was 52 years old, the oldest ever Test cricketer.

Rhodes /rəʊdz/ Zandra 1940– . English fashion designer known for the extravagant fantasy and luxury of her dress creations. She founded her own fashion house 1968.

Rhys /riːs/ Jean 1894–1979. British novelist, born in Dominica. Her works include *Wide Sargasso Sea* 1966, a recreation, set in a Caribbean island, of the life of the mad wife of Rochester from Charlotte Brontë's *Jane Eyre*.

A room is a place where you hide from the wolves outside and that's all any room is.

Jean Rhys *Good Morning, Midnight* 1958

Ribalta /rɪˈbæltə/ Francisco 1565–1628. Spanish painter, active in Valencia from 1599. Around 1615 he developed a dramatic Baroque style using extreme effects of light and shade (recalling Caravaggio), as in *St Bernard Embracing Christ* about 1620–28 (Prado, Madrid).

Ribbentrop /rɪbəntrɒp/ Joachim von 1893–1946. German Nazi politician and diplomat, foreign minister 1938–45, during which time he negotiated the Non-Aggression Pact between Germany and the USSR. He was tried at Nuremberg as a war criminal 1946 and hanged.

Ribbentrop was born in the Rhineland. Awarded the Iron Cross in World War I, he became a wine merchant in 1919. He joined the Nazi party 1932 and acted as Hitler's adviser on foreign affairs; he was German ambassador to Britain 1936–38. A political lightweight, he was useful to Hitler since he posed no threat.

Ribera /rɪˈbɪərə/ José (Jusepe) de 1591–1652. Spanish painter, active in Italy from 1616 under the patronage of the viceroys of Naples. His early work shows the impact of Caravaggio, but his colours gradually lightened. He painted many full-length saints and mythological figures and genre scenes, which he produced without preliminary drawing.

Ricardo /rɪˈkɑːdəʊ/ David 1772–1823. English economist, author of *Principles of Political Economy* 1817. Among his discoveries were the principle of comparative advantage (that countries can benefit by specializing in goods they produce efficiently and trading internationally to buy others), and the law of diminishing returns (that continued increments of capital and labour applied to a given quantity of land will eventually show a declining rate of increase in output).

Ricci /rɪtʃi/ Sebastiano 1659–1734. Venetian painter who worked throughout Italy as well as in Vienna. Between 1712 and 1714 he was in London where he painted *The Resurrection* for the chapel of the Royal Hospital, Chelsea.

Ricci's revival of the Venetian Renaissance school was so successful that many of his paintings were indistinguishable from those of Veronese. Ricci's lighter palette paved the way for Tiepolo. The English Royal Collection has many works by Ricci.

Rice /raɪs/ Elmer 1892–1967. US playwright. His works include *The Adding Machine* 1923 and *Street Scene* 1929, which won a Pulitzer Prize and was made into an opera by Kurt Weill. Many of his plays deal with such economic and political issues as the Depression (*We, the People* 1933) and racism (*American Landscape* 1939).

Rice /raɪs/ Grantland 1880–1954. US sports journalist. Gaining a reputation for vivid sports writing, he worked for the *New York Herald Tribune* 1914–30. After 1930 he wrote the column 'The Sportlight', setting the standard for modern sports journalism. He succeeded Walter →Camp in selecting the annual All-America football team.

Born in Murfreesboro, Tennessee, USA, and educated at Vanderbilt University, Rice joined the staff of the *Nashville News* 1901 and was hired by the *New York Mail* 1911. His autobiography, *The Tumult and the Shouting* was published 1954.

Rice-Davies /raɪs ˈdeɪvɪs/ Mandy (Marilyn) 1944– . English model. She achieved notoriety in 1963 following the revelations of the affair between her friend Christine →Keeler and war minister John →Profumo, and his subsequent resignation.

Rich /rɪtʃ/ Adrienne 1929– . US radical feminist poet, writer, and critic. Her poetry is both subjective and political, concerned with female consciousness, peace, and gay rights. Her works include *On Lies, Secrets and Silence* 1979 and *The Fact of a Doorframe: Poems, 1950–84* 1984.

In the 1960s her poetry was closely involved with the student and antiwar movements in the USA but since then she has concentrated on women's issues. In 1974, when given the National Book Award, she declined to accept it as an individual, but with Alice Walker and Audrey Rich accepted it on behalf of all women.

Richard /rɪtʃəd/ Cliff. Stage name of Harry Roger Webb 1940– . English pop singer. In the late 1950s he was influenced by Elvis Presley, but became a Christian family entertainer, continuing to have hits in the UK through the 1980s. His original backing group was the *Shadows* (1958–68 and later re-formed).

The Shadows had solo instrumental hits in the early 1960s and their lead guitarist, Hank Marvin (1941–), inspired many British rock guitarists.

Richard /rɪtʃəd/ three kings of England:

Richard I *the Lion-Heart* (French *Coeur-de-Lion*) 1157–1199. King of England from 1189, who spent all but six months of his reign abroad. He was the third son of Henry II, against whom he twice rebelled. In the third Crusade 1191–92 he won victories at Cyprus, Acre, and Arsuf (against →Saladin), but failed to recover Jerusalem. While returning overland he was captured by the Duke of Austria, who handed him over to the emperor Henry VI, and he was held prisoner until a large ransom was raised. He then returned briefly to England, where his brother

John I had been ruling in his stead. His later years were spent in warfare in France, where he was killed.

Himself a poet, he became a hero of legends after his death. He was succeeded by John I.

Richard II 1367–1400. King of England from 1377, effectively from 1389, son of Edward the Black Prince. He reigned in conflict with Parliament; they executed some of his associates 1388, and he executed some of the opposing barons 1397, whereupon he made himself absolute. Two years later, forced to abdicate in favour of ➔Henry IV, he was jailed and probably assassinated.

Richard was born in Bordeaux. He succeeded his grandfather Edward III when only ten, the government being in the hands of a council of regency. His fondness for favourites resulted in conflicts with Parliament, and in 1388 the baronial party headed by the Duke of Gloucester had many of his friends executed. Richard recovered control 1389, and ruled moderately until 1397, when he had Gloucester murdered and his other leading opponents executed or banished, and assumed absolute power. In 1399 his cousin Henry Bolingbroke, Duke of Hereford (later Henry IV), returned from exile to lead a revolt; Richard II was deposed by Parliament and imprisoned in Pontefract Castle, where he died mysteriously.

Richard III 1452–1485. King of England from 1483. The son of Richard, Duke of York, he was created duke of Gloucester by his brother Edward IV, and distinguished himself in the Wars of the Roses. On Edward's death 1483 he became protector to his nephew Edward V, and soon secured the crown for himself on the plea that Edward IV's sons were illegitimate. He proved a capable ruler, but the suspicion that he had murdered Edward V and his brother undermined his popularity. In 1485 Henry, Earl of Richmond (later ➔Henry VII), raised a rebellion, and Richard III was defeated and killed at Bosworth.

Scholars now tend to minimize the evidence for his crimes as Tudor propaganda.

Richard of Wallingford /ˈrɪtʃəd, ˈwɒlɪŋfəd/ 1292–1335. English mathematician, abbot of St Albans from 1326. He was a pioneer of trigonometry, and designed measuring instruments.

Richards /ˈrɪtʃədz/ Frank. Pen name of Charles Harold St John Hamilton 1875–1961. English writer for the children's papers *Magnet* and *Gem*, who invented Greyfriars public school and the fat boy Billy Bunter.

Richards /ˈrɪtʃədz/ Gordon 1905–1986. English jockey and trainer who was champion on the flat a record 26 times between 1925 and 1953.

He started riding 1920 and rode 4,870 winners from 21,834 mounts before retiring 1954 and taking up training. He rode the winners of all the classic races but only once won the Epsom Derby (on Pinza 1953). In 1947 he rode a record 269 winners in a season and in 1933 at Nottingham/Chepstow he rode 11 consecutive winners.

Mother always told me my day was coming, but I never realized that I'd end up being the shortest knight of the year.

Gordon Richards on learning of his knighthood
(attrib.)

Richards /ˈrɪtʃədz/ I(vor) A(rmstrong) 1893–1979. English literary critic. He collaborated with C K ➔Ogden and wrote *Principles of Literary Criticism* 1924. In 1939 he went to Harvard University, USA, where he taught detailed attention to the text and had a strong influence on contemporary US literary criticism.

Richards /ˈrɪtʃədz/ Theodore 1868–1928. US chemist. Working at Harvard University, Boston, for much of his career, Richards concentrated on determining as accurately as possible the relative atomic masses of a large number of elements. Nobel prize 1914.

Richards /ˈrɪtʃədz/ Viv (Isaac Vivian Alexander) 1952– . West Indian cricketer, captain of the West Indies team 1986–91. He has played for the Leeward Islands and, in the UK, for Somerset and Glamorgan. A prolific run-scorer, he holds the record for the greatest number of runs made in Test cricket in one calendar year (1,710 runs in 1976). He retired from international cricket after the West Indies tour of England in 1991.

Richardson /ˈrɪtʃədsən/ Dorothy 1873–1957. English novelist whose works were collected under the title *Pilgrimage* 1938. She was the first English novelist to use the 'stream of consciousness' method in *Pointed Roofs* 1915. Virginia ➔Woolf recognized and shared this technique as part of the current effort to express women's perceptions in spite of the resistance of man-made language, and she credited Richardson with having invented 'the psychological sentence of the feminine gender'.

Richardson /ˈrɪtʃədsən/ Henry Handel. Pen name of Ethel Florence Lindesay Richardson 1870–1946. Australian novelist, the first Australian writer to win a reputation abroad. Her works include *The Getting of Wisdom* 1910, based on her schooldays and filmed 1977. She left Australia when only 18.

Richardson was born in Melbourne. In 1888 she went to study piano in Leipzig, Germany, and her first novel, *Maurice Guest* 1908, is based on these years. The trilogy *The Fortunes of Richard Mahony*, published as *Australia Felix* 1917, *The Way Home* 1925, and *Ultima Thule* 1929, traces the career of a gold-rush migrant from the early 1850s to the mid-1870s and draws heavily on the life of her father.

Richelieu French politician and cardinal, Richelieu. As chief minister 1624 he controlled Louis XIII and directed domestic and foreign policy. He founded the Académie Française and was an enlightened patron of the arts.

Richardson /ˈrɪtʃədsən/ Henry Hobson 1838–1886. American architect, distinguished for his revival of Romanesque style. He designed churches, university buildings, homes, railroad stations, and town libraries. He had a stong influence on Louis →Sullivan.

Richardson /ˈrɪtʃədsən/ Owen Willans 1879–1959. British physicist. He studied the emission of electricity from hot bodies, giving the name thermionics to the subject. At Cambridge University, he worked under J J →Thomson in the Cavendish Laboratory. Nobel prize 1928.

Richardson /ˈrɪtʃədsən/ Ralph (David) 1902–1983. English actor. He played many stage parts, including Falstaff (Shakespeare), Peer Gynt (Ibsen), and Cyrano de Bergerac (Rostand). He shared the management of the Old Vic theatre with Laurence Olivier 1944–50. In later years he revealed himself as an accomplished deadpan comic.

Later stage successes include *Home* 1970 and *No Man's Land* 1976. His films include *Things to Come* 1936, *Richard III* 1956, *Our Man in Havana* 1959, *The Wrong Box* 1966, *The Bed Sitting Room* 1969, and *O Lucky Man!* 1973.

Richardson /ˈrɪtʃədsən/ Samuel 1689–1761. English novelist, one of the founders of the modern novel. *Pamela* 1740–41, written in the form of a series of letters and containing much dramatic conversation, was sensationally popular all across Europe, and was followed by *Clarissa* 1747–48 and *Sir Charles Grandison* 1753–54.

Born in Derbyshire, Richardson was brought up in London and apprenticed to a printer. He set up his own business in London 1719, becoming printer to the House of Commons. All his six young children died, followed by his wife 1731, which permanently affected his health.

Richardson /ˈrɪtʃədsən/ Tony 1928–1991. English director and producer. With George Devine he established the English Stage Company 1955 at the Royal Court Theatre, with productions such as *Look Back in Anger* 1956. His films include *Saturday Night and Sunday Morning* 1960, *A Taste of Honey* 1961, *Tom Jones* 1963, and *Joseph Andrews* 1977.

Richelieu /ˈriːʃljɜː/ Armand Jean du Plessis de 1585–1642. French cardinal and politician, chief minister from 1624. He aimed to make the monarchy absolute; he ruthlessly crushed opposition by the nobility and destroyed the political power of the Huguenots, while leaving them religious freedom. Abroad, he sought to establish French supremacy by breaking the power of the Habsburgs; he therefore supported the Swedish king Gustavus Adolphus and the German Protestant princes against Austria and in 1635 brought France into the Thirty Years' War.

Born in Paris of a noble family, he entered the church and was created bishop of Luçon 1606 and a cardinal 1622. Through the influence of →Marie de' Medici he became →Louis XIII's chief minister 1624, a position he retained until his death. His secretary Père →Joseph was the original Grey Eminence.

Nothing is as dangerous for the state as those who would govern kingdoms with maxims found in books.

Cardinal Richelieu
Political Testament 1687

Richler /ˈrɪtʃlə/ Mordecai 1931– . Canadian novelist, born in Montreal. His novels, written in a witty, acerbic style, include *The Apprenticeship of Duddy Kravitz* 1959 and *St Urbain's Horseman* 1971. Later works include *Joshua Then and Now* 1980 and *Home Sweet Home* 1984.

Richter /ˈrɪktə/ Burton 1931– . US particle physicist. In the 1960s he designed the Stanford Positron–Electron Accelerating Ring (SPEAR), a machine designed to collide positrons and electrons at high energies. In 1974 Richter and his team used SPEAR to produce a new subatomic particle, the (ψ) meson. This was the first example of a particle formed from a charmed quark, the quark whose existence had been postulated by Sheldon Glashow ten years earlier. Richter shared the 1976 Nobel Physics Prize with Samuel Ting, who had discovered the particle independently.

Richter /ˈrɪktə/ Charles Francis 1900–1985. US seismologist, deviser of the Richter scale used to measure the strength of the waves from earthquakes.

Richter /ˈrɪʃtə/ Jean Paul (Johann Paul Friedrich) 1763–1825. German author who created a series of comic eccentrics in works such as the romance *Titan* 1800–03 and *Die Flegeljahre/The Awkward Age* 1804–05. He was born in Bavaria.

Richter /ˈrɪxtə/ Sviatoslav (Teofilovich) 1915– . Russian pianist, an outstanding interpreter of Schubert, Schumann, Rachmaninov, and Prokofiev.

Richthofen /ˈrɪʃthəʊfən/ Ferdinand Baron von 1833–1905. German geographer and traveller who carried out extensive studies in China 1867–70 and subsequently explored Java, Thailand, Myanmar (Burma), Japan, and California.

Richthofen /ˈrɪʃthəʊfən/ Manfred, Freiherr von (the 'Red Baron') 1892–1918. German aviator. In World War I he commanded the 11th Chasing Squadron, known as *Richthofen's Flying Circus*, and shot down 80 aircraft before being killed in action.

Rickenbacker /ˈrɪkənbækə/ Edward Vernon 1890–1973. US racing-car driver, aviator, and airline executive. A racing-car driver in his youth, by 1917 he had established a land speed record of 134 mph/216 kph. He purchased Eastern Airlines 1938 leaving briefly to serve as an adviser to the War Department during World War II. Taking on special missions, he ditched his plane in the Pacific Ocean, drifting for 23 days before being rescued.

Born in Columbus, Ohio, USA, Rickenbacker became a racing-car driver in his teenage years. At the outbreak of World War I, he joined the army and was chosen for pilot's training in France. As a member of the 94th Aero Pursuit Squadron, he gained fame as an air ace, downing 26 German aircraft in four months.

Returning to private business after World War I, he founded the Rickenbacker Motor Co 1921, but dissolved it to purchase Eastern Airlines of which he was president to 1959 and chairman of the board to 1963.

Rickey /ˈrɪki/ Branch Wesley 1881–1965. US baseball executive. As president of the Brooklyn Dodgers 1942–50, he made baseball history by signing Jackie Robinson, the first black American to play in the major leagues. As president of the St Louis Cardinals 1917 and manager 1919–25, he pioneered the minor-league system of developing talent.

Born in Stockdale, Ohio, USA, Rickey received a law degree from the University of Michigan 1911. Always active in athletics, he signed as a catcher with the St Louis Browns 1905–06. With the New York Yankees 1907, he then retired as a player. In 1913 he accepted a managerial job with the Browns.

Rickover /ˈrɪkəʊvə/ Hyman George 1900–1986. Russian-born US naval officer. During World War II, he worked on the atomic bomb project, headed the navy's nuclear reactor division, and served on the Atomic Energy Commission. He was responsible for the development of the first nuclear submarine, the *Nautilus*, 1954. After retiring 1982, he became an outspoken critic of the dangers of nuclear research and development.

Rickover emigrated to the US with his family 1906 and graduated from the US Naval Academy 1922. After further studies in engineering, he became a specialist in the electrical division of the Bureau of Ships. He was promoted to the rank of admiral 1973.

Riding (Jackson) /ˈraɪdɪŋ/ Laura 1901–1991. US poet, a member of the Fugitive Group of poets that flourished in the southern USA 1915–28. She went to England in 1926 and worked with the writer Robert Graves. Having published her *Collected Poems* in 1938, she wrote no more verse, but turned to linguistics in order to analyse the expression of 'truth'.

Ridley /ˈrɪdli/ Nicholas c. 1500–1555. English Protestant bishop. He became chaplain to Henry VIII 1541, and bishop of London 1550. He took an active part in the Reformation and supported Lady Jane Grey's claim to the throne. After Mary's accession he was arrested and burned as a heretic.

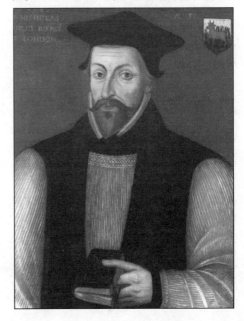

Ridley Portrait of English Protestant bishop and martyr Nicholas Ridley, by an unknown artist (1555). An ardent and outspoken reformer, Ridley had a powerful influence in the church while Edward VI was alive, and helped Archbishop Cranmer compile the English prayer book and the Thirty-nine Articles.

Ridley /ˈrɪdli/ Nicholas 1929– . British Conservative politician, cabinet minister 1983–90. After a period in industry he became active as a 'dry' right-winger in the Conservative Party: a 'Thatcherite' before Margaret →Thatcher had brought the term to public attention. He served under Harold Macmillan, Edward Heath, and Alec Douglas-Home, but did not become a member of the cabinet until 1983. His apparent disdain for public opinion caused his transfer, in 1989, from the politically sensitive Department of the Environment to that of Trade and Industry, and his resignation in July 1990 after criticisms of European colleagues and Germany.

In the autobiographical *'My Style of Government'* 1991 Ridley claimed Thatcher's government was wrongly undermined by Lawson and Howe, who forced her into supporting the European Exchange Rate Mechanism against her better judgement. The memoirs also showed him to be a devoted admirer of Mrs Thatcher.

Rie /riː/ Lucie 1902– . Austrian-born potter who worked in England from the 1930s. Her pottery, exhibited all over the world, is simple and pure in form, showing a debt to Bernard →Leach.

Riefenstahl /ˈriːfənʃtɑːl/ Leni 1902– . German filmmaker. Her film of the Nazi rallies at Nuremberg, *Triumph des Willens/Triumph of the Will* 1934, vividly illustrated Hitler's charismatic appeal but tainted her career. After World War II her work was blacklisted by the Allies until 1952.

Volumes of her still photographs include *The Last of the Nuba* 1973 and *Mein Afrika/My Africa* 1982.

Riel /riˈel/ Louis 1844–1885. French-Canadian rebel, a champion of the Métis (an Indian-French people); he established a provisional government in Winnipeg in an unsuccessful revolt 1869–70 and was hanged for treason after leading a second revolt in Saskatchewan 1885.

Riemann /ˈriːmæn/ Georg Friedrich Bernhard 1826–1866. German mathematician whose system of non-Euclidean geometry, thought at the time to be a mere mathematical curiosity, was used by Einstein to develop his general theory of relativity.

Rienzi /riˈenzi/ Cola di *c.* 1313–1354. Italian political reformer. In 1347, he tried to re-establish the forms of an ancient Roman republic. His second attempt seven years later ended with his assassination.

Riesman /ˈriːsmən/ David 1909– . US sociologist, author of *The Lonely Crowd: A Study of the Changing American Character* 1950. He made a distinction among 'inner-directed', 'tradition-directed', and 'other-directed' societies; the first using individual internal values, the second using established tradition, and the third, other people's expectations, to develop cohesiveness and conformity within a society.

Rietvelt /ˈriːtfelt/ Gerrit Thomas 1888–1964. Dutch architect, an exponent of De Stijl. He designed the Schroeder House at Utrecht 1924; he is also well known for colourful, minimalist chair design.

Rigaud /riːˈgəʊ/ Hyacinthe 1659–1743. French portraitist, court painter to Louis XIV from 1688. His portrait of *Louis XIV* 1701 (Louvre, Paris) is characteristically majestic, with the elegant figure of the king enveloped in ermine and drapery.

Rigg /rɪg/ Diana 1938– . English actress. Her stage roles include Héloïse in *Abelard and Héloïse* 1970, and television roles include Emma Peel in *The Avengers* 1965–67 and Lady Deadlock in *Bleak House* 1985. She became the hostess for *Mystery Theater* on US public television 1989.

Riis Jacob August 1849–1914. Danish- born US journalist, photographer, and reformer. As police reporter for the *New York Evening Sun* 1888–99, he was exposed to the grim realities of urban life, and his photographic exposé of conditions in the New York slums, *How the Other Half Lives* 1890, made the American public aware of the poverty in its own midst.

Riley /ˈraɪli/ Bridget (Louise) 1931– . English Op art painter. In the early 1960s she invented her characteristic style, arranging hard-edged black and white dots or lines in regular patterns that created disturbing effects of scintillating light and movement; *Fission* 1963 (Museum of Modern Art, New York) is an example. She introduced colour in the late 1960s and experimented with silk-screen prints on Perspex.

Riley /ˈraɪli/ James Whitcomb 1849–1916. US poet. His first collection of poems, *The Old Swimmin' Hole*, was published 1883. His later collections include *Rhymes of Childhood* 1890 and *Home Folks* 1900. His use of the Midwestern vernacular and familiar themes earned him the unofficial title 'The Hoosier Poet.'

Born in Greenfield, Indiana, Riley had little formal education and worked at a series of odd jobs before becoming the editor of a local newspaper. In 1877 he began to contribute light verse to the *Indianapolis Journal.*

Rilke /ˈrɪlkə/ Rainer Maria 1875–1926. Austrian writer. His prose works include the semi-autobiographical *Die Aufzeichnungen des Malte Laurids Brigge/Notebook of Malte Laurids Brigge* 1910. His verse is characterized by a form of mystic pantheism that seeks to achieve a state of ecstasy in which existence can be apprehended as a whole.

Rilke was born in Prague. He travelled widely and was for a time the sculptor Rodin's secretary. He died in Switzerland. His poetical works include *Die Sonnette an Orpheus/Sonnets to Orpheus* 1923 and *Duisener Elegien/Duino Elegies* 1923.

Rimbaud /ˈræmˈbəʊ/ (Jean Nicolas) Arthur 1854–1891. French Symbolist poet. His verse was chiefly written before the age of 20, notably *Les*

Illuminations published 1886. From 1871 he lived with →Verlaine.

Although the association ended after Verlaine attempted to shoot him, it was Verlaine's analysis of Rimbaud's work 1884 that first brought him recognition. Rimbaud then travelled widely, working as a trader in North Africa 1880–91.

Rimsky-Korsakov /ˈrɪmski ˈkɔːsəkɒf/ Nikolay Andreyevich 1844–1908. Russian composer. He used Russian folk idiom and rhythms in his Romantic compositions and published a text on orchestration. His operas include *The Maid of Pskov* 1873, *The Snow Maiden* 1882, *Mozart and Salieri* 1898, and *The Golden Cockerel* 1907, a satirical attack on despotism that was banned until 1909.

Other works include the symphonic poem *Sadko* 1867, the programme symphony *Antar* 1869, and the symphonic suite *Scheherazade* 1888. He also completed works by other composers, for example, →Mussorgsky's *Boris Godunov*.

Ringling /ˈrɪŋlɪŋ/ Charles 1863–1926. US circus promoter. With its three rings and large cast, the Ringlings' circus was touted as the 'Greatest Show on Earth,' the byword still most associated with the modern Ringling Brothers and Barnum and Bailey Circus (which the Ringling brothers acquired in 1907).

Born in McGregor, Iowa, Ringling started a vaudeville act in 1882 with his brothers, John, Albert, Otto, and Alfred. The touring act eventually became a small circus and grew more popular after the purchase of an elephant in 1888. With Charles as business manager, the Ringling Brothers Circus toured widely.

Riopelle /ˌriːəʊˈpel/ Jean Paul 1923– . Canadian artist, active in Paris from 1946. In the 1950s he developed an Abstract Expressionist style and produced colourful impasto (with paint applied in a thick mass) paintings and sculptures. His *Encounter* 1956 (Wallraf-Richartz Museum, Cologne, Germany) is a typically rough-textured canvas.

Ripley Robert LeRoy 1893–1949. US cartoonist, creator of the syndicated column 'Believe It or Not!', a highly popular compendium of bizarre facts.

Born in Santa Rosa, California, Ripley began cartooning as a teenager and was hired by the sports department of the *San Francisco Bulletin* 1910. In 1913 he became a sports cartoonist for the *New York Globe* and later began to present sports records in a series called 'Believe It or Not!' Moving from sports to all kinds of oddities and obscure facts, Ripley took his column to the *New York Evening Post* in 1923 and later to national syndication. Through radio and film appearances and continued syndication, Ripley became a national celebrity and master of the bizarre.

Ritter /ˈrɪtə/ Tex (Woodward Maurice) 1905–1974. US singer and actor, popular as a singing cowboy in B-films in the 1930s and 1940s (*Arizona Trail* 1943). He sang the title song to *High Noon* 1952.

Rivera /rɪˈveərə/ Diego 1886–1957. Mexican painter, active in Europe until 1921. He received many public commissions for murals exalting the Mexican revolution. A vast cycle on historical themes (National Palace, Mexico City) was begun 1929. In the 1930s he visited the USA and with Ben Shahn produced murals for the Rockefeller Center, New York (later overpainted because he included a portrait of Lenin). His second wife was the painter Frida →Kahlo.

Rivera /rɪˈveərə/ Primo de. Spanish politician; see →Primo de Rivera.

Rix /rɪks/ Brian 1924– . British actor and manager. He became known for his series of farces at London's Whitehall Theatre, notably *Dry Rot* 1954–58. He made several films for cinema and television, including *A Roof Over My Head* 1977, and promotes charities for the mentally handicapped.

Rizzio /ˈrɪtsiəʊ/ David 1533–1566. Italian adventurer at the court of Mary Queen of Scots. After her marriage to →Darnley, Rizzio's influence over her incited her husband's jealousy, and he was murdered by Darnley and his friends.

Roach /rəʊtʃ/ Hal 1892–1992. US film producer, usually of comedies, who was active from the 1910s to the 1940s. He worked with →Laurel and Hardy, and also produced films for Harold Lloyd and Charley Chase. His work includes *The Music Box* 1932, *Way Out West* 1936, and *Of Mice and Men* 1939.

Robbe-Grillet /rɒb griːˈjeɪ/ Alain 1922– . French writer, the leading theorist of *le nouveau roman* ('the new novel'), for example his own *Les Gommes/The Erasers* 1953, *La Jalousie/Jealousy* 1957, and *Dans le labyrinthe/In the Labyrinth* 1959, which concentrates on the detailed description of physical objects. He also wrote the script for the film *L'Année dernière à Marienbad/Last Year in Marienbad* 1961.

Robbia, della /ˈrɒbiə/ Italian family of sculptors and architects, active in Florence. *Luca della Robbia* (1400–1482) created a number of major works in Florence, notably the marble *cantoria* (singing gallery) in the cathedral 1431–38 (Museo del Duomo), with lively groups of choristers. Luca also developed a characteristic style of glazed terracotta work.

Andrea della Robbia (1435–1525), Luca's nephew and pupil, and Andrea's sons continued the family business, inheriting the formula for the vitreous terracotta glaze. The blue and white medallions of foundling children 1463–66 on the Ospedale degli Innocenti, Florence, are typical. Many later works are more elaborate and highly coloured, such as the frieze 1522 on the façade of the Ospedale del Ceppo, Pistoia.

Robbins Jerome 1918– . US dancer and choreographer, co-director of the New York City Ballet 1969–83 (with George Balanchine). His ballets are internationally renowned and he is considered the greatest US-born ballet choreographer. He also choreographed the musicals *The King and I* 1951, *West Side Story* 1957, and *Fiddler on the Roof* 1964.

First a chorus boy on Broadway, then a soloist with the newly formed American Ballet Theater 1941–46, Robbins was associate director of the New York City Ballet 1949–59. His first ballet, *Fancy Free* 1940, was a great success (and was adapted with Leonard Bernstein into the musical *On the Town* 1944). Other Robbins ballets include *Dancers at a Gathering* 1969, *The Goldberg Variations* 1971, and *Glass Pieces* 1983 (based on W H Auden's poem).

Robert /rɒbət/ two dukes of Normandy:

Robert I *the Devil* Duke of Normandy from 1028. He was the father of William the Conqueror, and is the hero of several romances; he was legendary for his cruelty.

Robert II *c.* 1054–1134. Eldest son of →William I (the Conqueror), succeeding him as duke of Normandy (but not on the English throne) 1087. His brother →William II ascended the English throne, and they warred until 1096, after which Robert took part in the First Crusade. When his other brother →Henry I claimed the English throne 1100, Robert contested the claim and invaded England unsuccessfully 1101. Henry invaded Normandy 1106, and captured Robert, who remained a prisoner in England until his death.

Robert /rɒbət/ three kings of Scotland:

Robert I /bruːs/ *Robert the Bruce* 1274–1329. King of Scotland from 1306, and grandson of Robert de →Bruce. He shared in the national uprising led by William →Wallace, and, after Wallace's execution 1305, rose once more against Edward I of England, and was crowned at Scone 1306. He defeated Edward II at Bannockburn 1314. In 1328 the treaty of Northampton recognized Scotland's independence and Robert as king.

Robert II 1316–1390. King of Scotland from 1371. He was the son of Walter (1293–1326), steward of Scotland, who married Marjory, daughter of Robert I. He was the first king of the house of Stuart.

Robert III *c.* 1340–1406. King of Scotland from 1390, son of Robert II. He was unable to control the nobles, and the government fell largely into the hands of his brother, Robert, Duke of Albany (*c.* 1340–1420).

Roberts /rɒbəts/ Bartholomew 1682–1722. British merchant-navy captain who joined his captors when taken by pirates in 1718. He became the most financially successful of all the sea rovers

until surprised and killed in battle by the British navy.

Roberts /rɒbəts/ David 1796–1864. Scottish painter whose oriental paintings were the result of several trips to the Middle East.

Roberts progressed from interior decorator to scene painter at Drury Lane Theatre, London. From 1831 he travelled around the Mediterranean producing topographical views. Many of these were published in books, including the six-volume *The Holy Land, Syria, Idumea, Arabia, Egypt & Nubia* 1842–49.

Roberts /rɒbəts/ Frederick Sleigh ('Bobs'), 1st Earl Roberts 1832–1914. British field marshal. During the Afghan War of 1878–80 he occupied Kabul, and during the Second South African War 1899–1902 he made possible the annexation of the Transvaal and Orange Free State.

Born in India, Roberts joined the Bengal Artillery in 1851, and served through the Indian Mutiny, receiving the VC, and the Abyssinian campaign of 1867–68. After serving in Afghanistan and making a victorious march to Kandahar, he became commander in chief in India 1885–93 and in Ireland 1895–99. He then received the command in South Africa, where he occupied Bloemfontein and Pretoria.

Roberts /rɒbəts/ Tom (Thomas William) 1856–1931. Australian painter and founder of the *Heidelberg School*, which introduced Impressionism to Australia.

Roberts, born in England, arrived in Australia in 1869, returning to Europe to study 1881–85. He received official commissions, including one to paint the opening of the first Australian federal parliament, but is better known for his scenes of pioneering life.

Robertson /rɒbətsən/ Thomas William 1829–1871. English dramatist. Initially an actor, he had his first success as a dramatist with *David Garrick* 1864, which set a new, realistic trend in English drama of the time; later plays included *Society* 1865 and *Caste* 1867.

Robeson /rəubsən/ Paul 1898–1976. US bass singer and actor. He graduated from Columbia University as a lawyer, but limited opportunities for blacks led him instead to the stage. He appeared in *The Emperor Jones* 1924 and *Showboat* 1928, in which he sang 'Ol' Man River'. He played *Othello* in 1930, and his films include *Sanders of the River* 1935 and *King Solomon's Mines* 1937. An ardent advocate of black rights, he had his passport withdrawn 1950–58 because of his association with left-wing movements. He then left the USA to live in England.

Robespierre /rəubzpjeə/ Maximilien François Marie Isidore de 1758–1794. French politician in the French Revolution. As leader of the Jacobins in the National Convention, he supported the execution of Louis XVI and the overthrow of the right-wing republican Girondins, and in July 1793 was elected to the Committee of Public Safety. A year later he was guillotined; many believe that he was a scapegoat for the Reign of Terror since he ordered only 72 executions personally.

Robespierre, a lawyer, was elected to the National Assembly of 1789–91. His defence of democratic principles made him popular in Paris, while his disinterestedness won him the nickname of 'the Incorruptible'. His zeal for social reform and his attacks on the excesses of the extremists made him enemies on both right and left; a conspiracy was formed against him, and in July 1794 he was overthrown and executed by those who actually perpetrated the Reign of Terror.

Robin Hood /ˌrɒbɪn 'hʊd/ legendary English outlaw and champion of the poor against the rich. He is said to have lived in Sherwood Forest, Nottinghamshire, during the reign of Richard I (1189–99). He feuded with the sheriff of Nottingham, accompanied by Maid Marian and a band of followers known as his 'merry men'. He appears in ballads from the 13th century, but his first datable appearance is in Langland's *Piers Plowman* about 1377.

Robinson /rɒbɪnsən/ Edward G. Stage name of Emanuel Goldenberg 1893–1973. US film actor, born in Romania, who emigrated with his family to the USA 1903. He was noted for his gangster roles, such as *Little Caesar* 1930.

Other films include *Dr Ehrlich's Magic Bullet* 1940, *Double Indemnity* 1944, and *Soylent Green* 1973.

Robinson /rɒbɪnsən/ Edwin Arlington 1869–1935. US poet. His verse, dealing mainly with psychological themes in a narrative style, is collected in volumes such as *The Children of the Night* 1897, which established his reputation. He was awarded three Pulitzer Prizes in poetry: *Collected Poems* 1922, *The Man Who Died Twice* 1925, and *Tristram* 1928.

Robinson /rɒbɪnsən/ Henry Crabb 1775–1867. English writer, whose diaries, journals, and letters are a valuable source of information on his literary friends →Lamb, →Coleridge, →Wordsworth, and →Southey.

Robinson /rɒbɪnsən/ Jackie (Jack Roosevelt) 1919–1972. US baseball player. In 1947 he became the first black American in the major leagues, playing second base for the Brooklyn Dodgers and winning rookie of the year honours. In 1949 he was the National League's batting champion and was voted the league's most valuable player. He had a career batting average of .311.

Born in Cairo, Georgia, USA, Robinson attended the University of California at Los Angeles (UCLA) and joined the Kansas City Monarchs of the Negro National League 1945. He came to the attention of Branch →Rickey and was signed by a Brooklyn Dodgers minor league team. After retirement as a player 1956, Robinson served as the New York governor's special assistant for community affairs 1966–68.

He was elected to the Baseball Hall of Fame 1962.

Robinson /rɒbɪnsən/ Joan (Violet) 1903–1983. British economist who introduced Marxism to Keynesian economic theory. She expanded her analysis in *Economics of Perfect Competition* 1933.

Robinson /rɒbɪnsən/ John Arthur Thomas 1919–1983. British Anglican cleric, bishop of Woolwich 1959–69. A left-wing Modernist, he wrote *Honest to God* 1963, which was interpreted as denying a personal God.

Robinson /rɒbɪnsən/ Mary 1944– . Irish Labour politician, president from 1990. She became a professor of law at 25. A strong supporter of women's rights, she has campaigned for the liberalization of Ireland's laws prohibiting divorce and abortion.

Robinson was born in County Mayo and educated at Trinity College, Dublin, and Harvard University, USA. As a member of the Labour Party, she tried unsuccessfully to enter the Dáil (parliament) in 1990, and then surprisingly won the presidency of her country, defeating the Fianna Fáil frontrunner Brian Lenihan.

Robinson /rɒbɪnsən/ Robert 1886–1975. English chemist, Nobel prizewinner 1947 for his research in organic chemistry on the structure of many natural products, including flower pigments and alkaloids. He formulated the electronic theory now used in organic chemistry.

Robinson The independent candidate Mary Robinson's victory in the 1990 presidential election was seen as a turning point in Irish politics. A Catholic married to a Protestant, she became the first president since 1945 not to have been backed by the dominant Fianna Fáil party.

Robinson /ˈrɒbɪnsən/ Smokey (William) 1940– . US singer, songwriter, and record producer, associated with Motown records from its conception. He was lead singer of the Miracles 1957–72 (hits include 'Shop Around' 1961, 'The Tears of a Clown' 1970) and his solo hits include 'Cruisin'' 1979 and 'Being With You' 1981. His light tenor voice and wordplay characterize his work.

Robinson /ˈrɒbɪnsən/ W(illiam) Heath 1872–1944. English cartoonist and illustrator who made humorous drawings of bizarre machinery for performing simple tasks, such as raising one's hat. A clumsily designed apparatus is often described as a 'Heath Robinson' contraption.

Robinson /ˈrɒbɪnsən/ Sugar Ray. Adopted name of Walker Smith 1920–1989. UK boxer, world welterweight champion 1945–51; he defended his title five times. Defeating Jake LaMotta 1951, he took the middleweight title. He lost the title six times and won it seven times. He retired at the age of 45.

He was involved in the 'Fight of the Century' with Randolph Turpin of the USA 1951, and was narrowly beaten for the light-heavyweight title by Joey Maxim of the USA 1952.

Rob Roy /rɒb ˈrɔɪ/ nickname of Robert MacGregor 1671–1734. Scottish Highland Jacobite outlaw. After losing his estates, he lived by cattle theft and extortion. Captured, he was sentenced to transportation but pardoned 1727. He is a central character in Walter Scott's historical novel *Rob Roy* 1817.

Robsart /ˈrɒbsɑːt/ Amy *c.* 1532–1560. wife of Robert Dudley, the Earl of →Leicester.

Robson /ˈrɒbsən/ Flora 1902–1984. English actress, notable as Queen Elizabeth in the film *Fire Over England* 1931 and Mrs Alving in Ibsen's *Ghosts* 1959.

Rocard /rɒˈkɑː/ Michel 1930– . French socialist politician, prime minister 1988–91. A former radical, he joined the Socialist Party (PS) 1973, emerging as leader of its moderate social-democratic wing. He held ministerial office under President François Mitterrand 1981–85.

Rocard trained at the prestigious Ecole Nationale d'Administration, where he was a classmate of Jacques Chirac. He became leader of the radical Unified Socialist Party (PSU) 1967, standing as its presidential candidate 1969.

Having gone over to the PS, Rocard unsuccessfully challenged Mitterrand for the party's presidential nomination 1981. After serving as minister of planning and regional development 1981–83 and of agriculture 1983–85, he resigned April 1985 in opposition to the government's introduction of proportional representation. In May 1988, however, as part of a strategy termed 'opening to the centre', the popular Rocard was appointed prime minister by Mitterrand. Following his resignation 1991, after his government

only just survived a vote of no confidence, he was viewed as a presidential candidate.

Roche /rəʊʃ/ Stephen 1959– . Irish cyclist. One of the outstanding riders in Europe in the 1980s, he was the first British winner of the Tour de France in 1987 and the first English-speaking winner of the Tour of Italy the same year, as well as the 1987 world professional road-race champion.

Rochester /ˈrɒtʃɪstə/ John Wilmot, 2nd Earl of Rochester 1647–1680. English poet and courtier. He fought gallantly at sea against the Dutch, but chiefly led a debauched life at the court of Charles II. He wrote graceful (but often obscene) lyrics, and his *A Satire against Mankind* 1675 rivals Swift. He was a patron of the poet John Dryden.

Rockefeller /ˈrɒkəfelə/ John D(avison) 1839–1937. US millionaire, founder of Standard Oil 1870 (which achieved control of 90% of US refineries by 1882). He founded the philanthropic *Rockefeller Foundation* 1913, to which his son *John D(avison) Rockefeller Jr* (1874–1960) devoted his life.

The activities of the Standard Oil Trust led to an outcry against monopolies and the passing of the Sherman Anti-Trust Act of 1890. A lawsuit of 1892 prompted the dissolution of the trust, only for it to be refounded in 1899 as a holding company. In 1911, this was also declared illegal by the Supreme Court.

A friendship founded on business is better than a business founded on friendship.

John D Rockefeller

Rockingham /ˈrɒkɪŋəm/ Charles Watson Wentworth, 2nd Marquess of Rockingham 1730–1782. British Whig politician, prime minister 1765–66 and 1782 (when he died in office); he supported the American claim to independence.

Rockne /ˈrɒkni/ Knute Kenneth 1888–1931. Norwegian-born US American football coach. His greatest contribution to football was the extensive use of sophisticated formations and the forward pass. He established an unparalleled lifetime record of 105 wins, 12 losses, and 5 ties – with 5 undefeated, untied seasons.

Rockne emigrated to the USA with his family 1893. As a student at Notre Dame University 1910–14, he was a star football player and became the school's head football coach 1918. Serving in that position until his death, his book *Coaching, the Way of the Winner* was published 1925. His memoirs, *Autobiography*, appeared 1931.

Rockwell /ˈrɒkwel/ Norman 1894–1978. US painter and illustrator who designed magazine covers, mainly for *The Saturday Evening Post*, and cartoons portraying American life.

Roddick /rɒdɪk/ Anita 1943– . British entrepreneur, founder of the Body Shop, which now has branches worldwide. Roddick started with one shop in Brighton, England, 1976, selling only natural toiletries in refillable plastic containers.

Rodgers /rɒdʒəz/ Richard (Charles) 1902–1979. US composer. He collaborated with librettist Lorenz Hart (1895–1943) on songs such as 'Blue Moon' 1934 and musicals such as *On Your Toes* 1936, and with Oscar Hammerstein II (1895–1960) wrote musicals such as *Oklahoma!* 1943, *South Pacific* 1949, *The King and I* 1951, and *The Sound of Music* 1959.

Rodin /rəʊdæn/ Auguste 1840–1917. French sculptor, often considered the greatest of his day. Through his work he freed sculpture from the idealizing conventions of the time by his realistic treatment of the human figure, introducing a new boldness of style and expression. Examples are *Le Penseur/The Thinker* 1880, *Le Baiser/The Kiss* 1886 (marble version in the Louvre, Paris), and *Les Bourgeois de Calais/The Burghers of Calais* 1884–86 (copy in Embankment Gardens, Westminster, London).

Rodin started as a mason, began to study in museums, and in 1875 visited Italy, where he was inspired by the work of Michelangelo. His early statue *Bronze Age* 1877 was criticized for its total naturalism and accuracy. In 1880 he began the monumental bronze *Gates of Hell* for the Ecole des Arts Décoratifs in Paris (inspired by Ghiberti's bronze gates in Florence), a project that occupied him for many years and was unfinished at his death. Many of the figures designed for the gate became independent sculptures. During the 1890s he received two notable commissions, for statues of the writers *Balzac* 1897 (Musée Rodin, Paris) and *Hugo*. He also produced many drawings.

Sculpture is an art of hollows and projections.

Auguste Rodin

Rodney /rɒdni/ George Brydges Rodney, Baron Rodney 1718–1792. British admiral. In 1762 he captured Martinique, St Lucia, and Grenada from the French. In 1780 he relieved Gibraltar by defeating a Spanish squadron off Cape St Vincent. In 1782 he crushed the French fleet under Count de Grasse off Dominica, for which he was raised to the peerage.

Rodnina /rɒd'niːnə/ Irina 1949– . Soviet ice skater. Between 1969 and 1980 she won 23 world, Olympic, and European gold medals in pairs competitions. Her partners were Alexei Ulanov and then Alexsandr Zaitsev.

Roeg /rəʊg/ Nicolas 1928– . English film director and writer, initially a camera operator. His striking visual style is often combined with fractured, disturbing plots, as in *Performance* 1970, *Don't Look Now* 1973, *The Man Who Fell to Earth* 1976, and *The Witches* 1989.

His other films include *Walkabout* 1971, *Bad Timing* 1980, *Castaway* 1986, and *Track 29* 1988.

Roethke /retki/ Theodore 1908–1963. US poet. His father owned a large nursery business, and the greenhouses and plants of his childhood provide the detail and imagery for much of his lyrical, personal, and visionary poetry. Collections include *Open House* 1941, *The Lost Son* 1948, *The Waking* 1953 (Pulitzer Prize), and the posthumous *Collected Poems* 1968.

Rogers /rɒdʒəz/ Carl 1902–1987. US psychologist who developed the client-centred approach to counselling and psychotherapy. This stressed the importance of clients making their own decisions and developing their own potential (self-actualization).

He emphasized the value of genuine interest on the part of a therapist who is also accepting and empathetic. Rogers's views became widely employed.

Rogers /rɒdʒəz/ Ginger. Stage name of Virginia Katherine McMath 1911– . US actress, dancer, and singer. She worked from the 1930s to the 1950s, often starring with Fred Astaire in such films as *Top Hat* 1935 and *Swing Time* 1936. Her later work includes *Bachelor Mother* 1939 and *Kitty Foyle* 1940.

Rogers /rɒdʒəz/ Richard 1933– . British architect. His works include the Centre Pompidou in Paris 1977 (jointly with Renzo Piano) and the Lloyd's building in London 1986.

Rogers /rɒdʒəz/ Roy. Stage name of Leonard Slye 1912– . US actor who moved to the cinema from radio. He was one of the original singing cowboys of the 1930s and 1940s. Confined to B-films for most of his career, he appeared opposite Bob Hope and Jane Russell in *Son of Paleface* 1952. His other films include *The Big Show* 1936 and *My Pal Trigger* 1946.

Rogers /rɒdʒəz/ Will(iam Penn Adair) 1879–1935. US humorist who became a national figure through his syndicated column from 1922; a former cowboy and lariat-twirler, he specialized in aphorisms and homespun philosophy ('Everybody is ignorant, only on different subjects').

Roget /rɒʒeɪ/ Peter Mark 1779–1869. English physician, one of the founders of the University of London, and author of a *Thesaurus of English Words and Phrases* 1852, a text constantly revised and still in print, offering synonyms.

Röhm /rɜːm/ Ernst 1887–1934. German leader of the Nazi Brownshirts, the SA (Sturmabteilung). On the pretext of an intended SA *putsch* (uprising) by the Brownshirts, the Nazis had some hundred of them, including Röhm, killed 29–30 June 1934. The event is known as the Night of the Long Knives.

Rohmer /ˈrəumə/ Eric. Adopted name of Jean-Marie Maurice Schérer 1920– . French film director and writer, formerly a critic and television-documentary director. Part of the French New Wave, his films are often concerned with the psychology of self-deception. They include *Ma Nuit chez Maud/My Night at Maud's* 1969, *Le Genou de Claire/Claire's Knee* 1970, and *Die Marquise von O/The Marquise of O* 1976.

Rohmer /ˈrəumə/ Sax. Pen name of Arthur Sarsfield Ward 1886–1959. English crime writer who created the sinister Chinese character Fu Manchu.

Roh Tae-woo /nəu ˌteɪˈwuː/ 1932– . South Korean right-wing politician and general. He held ministerial office from 1981 under President Chun, and became chair of the ruling Democratic Justice Party 1985. He was elected president 1987, amid allegations of fraud and despite being connected with the massacre of about 2,000 antigovernment demonstrators 1980.

A Korean Military Academy classmate of Chun Doo-hwan, Roh fought in the Korean War and later, during the 1970s, became commander of the 9th Special Forces Brigade and Capital Security Command. Roh retired as a four-star general July 1981 and served as minister for national security, foreign affairs, and, later, home affairs.

Rohwedder /ˈrəuvedə/ Detler 1932–1991. German Social Democrat politician and business executive. In Aug 1990 he became chief executive of Treuhand, the body concerned with the privatization or liquidation of some 8,000 East German businesses. His attempt to force market-oriented solutions on Treuhand was controversial, many preferring a more interventionist stance. He was assassinated the following April.

Roland /ˈrəulənd/ French hero whose real and legendary deeds of valour and chivalry inspired many medieval and later romances, including the 11th-century *Chanson de Roland* and Ariosto's *Orlando Furioso*. A knight of ➔Charlemagne, Roland was killed in 778 with his friend Oliver and the 12 peers of France at Roncesvalles (in the Pyrenees) by Basques. He headed the rearguard during Charlemagne's retreat from his invasion of Spain.

Roland de la Platière /rəuˈlɒŋ də lɑː plætiˈeə/ Jeanne Manon (born Philipon) 1754–1793. French intellectual politician whose salon from 1789 was a focus of democratic discussion. Her ideas were influential after her husband Jean Marie Roland de la Platière (1734–1793) became minister of the interior 1792. As a supporter of the Girondin party, opposed to Robespierre and Danton, she was condemned to the guillotine 1793 without being allowed to speak in her own defence. While in prison she wrote *Mémoires*.

Rolfe /rɒf/ Frederick 1860–1913. English writer who called himself Baron Corvo. A Roman Catholic convert, frustrated in his desire to enter the priesthood, he wrote the novel *Hadrian VII* 1904, in which the character of the title rose from being a poor writer to become pope. In *Desire and Pursuit of the Whole* 1934 he wrote about his homosexual fantasies and friends, earning the poet Auden's description of him as 'a master of vituperation'.

Rolle de Hampole /rəul də ˈhæmpəul/ Richard *c.* 1300–1349. English hermit and author of English and Latin works, including the mystic *Meditation of the Passion*.

Rolling Stones, the British band formed 1962, once notorious as the 'bad boys' of rock. Original members were Mick Jagger (1943–), Keith Richards (1943–), Brian Jones (1942–1969), Bill Wyman (1936–), Charlie Watts (1941–), and the pianist Ian Stewart (1938–1985). A rock-and-roll institution, the Rolling Stones were still performing and recording in the 1990s.

The Stones' earthy sound was based on rhythm and blues, and their rebel image was contrasted with the supposed wholesomeness of the early Beatles. Classic early hits include 'Satisfaction' 1965 and 'Jumpin' Jack Flash' 1968. The albums from *Beggar's Banquet* 1968 to *Exile on Main Street* 1972 have been rated among their best work; others include *Some Girls* 1978 and *Steel Wheels* 1989.

Rollins /ˈrɒlɪnz/ Sonny (Theodore Walter) 1930– . US tenor saxophonist and jazz composer. A leader of the hard-bop school, he is known for the intensity and bravado of his music and for his skilful improvisation.

Rollo /ˈrɒləu/ First duke of Normandy *c.* 860–932. Viking leader. He left Norway about 875 and marauded, sailing up the Seine to Rouen. He besieged Paris 886, and in 912 was baptized and granted the province of Normandy by Charles III of France. He was its duke until his retirement to a monastery 927. He was an ancestor of William the Conqueror.

Rolls /rəulz/ Charles Stewart 1877–1910. British engineer who joined with Henry ➔Royce in 1905 to design and produce cars.

Rolls trained as a mechanical engineer at Cambridge, where he developed a passion for engines of all kinds. After working initially at the railway works in Crewe, he set up a business in 1902 as a motor dealer. Rolls was the first to fly nonstop across the English Channel and back 1910. Before the business could flourish he died in a flying accident.

Romains /rəuˈmæn/ Jules. Pen name of Louis Farigoule 1885–1972. French novelist, playwright, and poet. His plays include the farce *Knock, ou le triomphe de la médecine/Dr Knock* 1923 and *Donogoo* 1930, and his novels include *Mort de quelqu'un/Death of a Nobody* 1911, *Les Copains/The Boys in the Back Room* 1913, and *Les Hommes de bonne volonté/Men of Good Will* (27 volumes) 1932–47.

Romains developed the theory of Unanimism, which states that every group has a communal existence greater than that of the individual, which intensifies the individual's perceptions and emotions.

Romano /rəʊ'mɑːnəʊ/ Giulio. See →Giulio Romano, Italian painter and architect.

Romanov dynasty /rəʊmənɒf/ rulers of Russia from 1613 to the Russian Revolution 1917. Under the Romanovs, Russia developed into an absolutist empire.

The pattern of succession was irregular until 1797. The last tsar, Nicholas II, abdicated March 1917 and was murdered July 1918, together with his family.

Rommel /rɒməl/ Erwin 1891–1944. German field marshal. He served in World War I, and in World War II he played an important part in the invasions of central Europe and France. He was commander of the N African offensive from 1941 (when he was nicknamed 'Desert Fox') until defeated in the Battles of El Alamein.

Rommel was commander in chief for a short time against the Allies in Europe 1944 but (as a sympathizer with the Stauffenberg plot against Hitler) was forced to commit suicide.

The ordinary soldier has a surprisingly good nose for what is true and what is false.

Field Marshal Erwin Rommel

Romney /rʌmni/ George 1734–1802. English portrait painter, active in London from 1762. He became, with Gainsborough and Reynolds, one of the most successful portrait painters of the late 18th century. He painted several portraits of Lady Hamilton, Admiral Nelson's mistress.

Ronsard /rɒn'sɑː/ Pierre de 1524–1585. French poet, leader of the Pléiade group of poets who were inspired by Classical models to improve French verse. Under the patronage of Charles IX, he published original verse in a lightly sensitive style, including odes and love sonnets, such as *Odes* 1550, *Les Amours/Lovers* 1552–53, and the 'Marie' cycle, *Continuation des amours/Lovers Continued* 1555–56.

Röntgen /rʌntgən/ (or *Roentgen*) Wilhelm Konrad 1845–1923. German physicist who discovered X-rays 1895. While investigating the passage of electricity through gases, he noticed the fluorescence of a barium platinocyanide screen. This radiation passed through some substances opaque to light, and affected photographic plates. Developments from this discovery have revolutionized medical diagnosis.

Born at Lennep, he became director of the Physical Institute at Giessen 1879, and at Würzburg 1885, where he conducted his experiments which resulted in the discovery of the rays named after him (now called X-rays), as is the unit of electromagnetic radiation (r). Nobel prize 1901.

Roon /rəʊn/ Albrecht Theodor Emil, Graf von 1803–1879. Prussian field marshal. As war minister from 1859, he reorganized the army and made possible the victories over Austria 1866 and those in the Franco-Prussian War 1870–71.

Rooney /ruːni/ Mickey. Stage name of Joe Yule 1920– . US actor who began his career aged two in his parents' stage act. He played Andy Hardy in the Hardy family series of B-films (1936–46) and starred opposite Judy Garland in several musicals, including *Babes in Arms* 1939.

Roosevelt /rəʊzəvelt/ (Anna) Eleanor 1884–1962. US social worker, lecturer and First Lady; her newspaper column 'My Day' was widely syndicated. She was a delegate to the UN general assembly and chair of the UN commission on human rights 1946–51. She helped to draw up the Declaration of Human Rights at the UN 1945. Within the Democratic Party she formed the left-wing Americans for Democratic Action group 1947. She was married to President Franklin Roosevelt.

Roosevelt /rəʊzəvelt/ Franklin D(elano) 1882–1945. 32nd president of the USA 1933–45, a Democrat. He served as governor of New York 1929–33. Becoming president during the Depression, he launched the *New Deal* economic and social reform programme, which made him popular with the people. After the outbreak of World War II he introduced lend-lease for the supply of war materials and services to the Allies and drew up the Atlantic Charter of solidarity. Once the USA had entered the war 1941, he spent much time in meetings with Allied leaders.

Born in Hyde Park, New York, of a wealthy family, Roosevelt was educated in Europe and at Harvard and Columbia universities, and became a lawyer. In 1910 he was elected to the New York state senate. He held the assistant secretaryship of the navy in Wilson's administrations 1913–21, and did much to increase the efficiency of the navy during World War I. He suffered from polio from 1921 but returned to politics, winning the governorship of New York State in 1929.

When he first became president 1933, Roosevelt inculcated a new spirit of hope by his skilful 'fireside chats' on the radio and his inaugural-address statement: 'The only thing we have to fear is fear itself.' Surrounding himself by a 'Brain Trust' of experts, he immediately launched his reform programme. Banks were reopened, federal credit was restored, the gold standard was abandoned, and the dollar devalued. During the first hundred days of his administration, major legislation to facilitate industrial and agricultural recovery was enacted. In 1935 he introduced the Utilities Act, directed against abuses in the large holding companies, and the Social Security Act, providing for disability and retirement insurance.

The presidential election 1936 was won entirely on the record of the New Deal. During 1935–36 Roosevelt was involved in a conflict over the composition of the Supreme Court, following its nullification of major New Deal measures as unconstitutional. In 1938 he introduced measures for farm relief and the improvement of working conditions.

In his foreign policy, Roosevelt endeavoured to use his influence to restrain Axis aggression, and to establish 'good neighbour' relations with other countries in the Americas. Soon after the outbreak of war, he launched a vast rearmament programme, introduced conscription, and provided for the supply of armaments to the Allies on a 'cash-and-carry' basis. In spite of strong isolationist opposition, he broke a long-standing precedent in running for a third term; he was re-elected 1940. He announced that the USA would become the 'arsenal of democracy'. Roosevelt was eager for US entry into the war on behalf of the Allies. In addition to his revulsion for Hitler, he wanted to establish the USA as a world power, filling the vacuum he expected to be left by the breakup of the British Empire. He was restrained by is olationist forces in Congress, and some argued

Roosevelt Known as 'the poor man's friend' 32nd US president Franklin D Roosevelt led his country through the Depression of the 1930s and World War II. He was elected for an unprecedented fourth term of office 1944.

that he welcomed the Japanese attack on Pearl Harbor.

Public opinion, however, was in favour of staying out of the war, so Roosevelt and the military chiefs deliberately kept back the intelligence reports received from the British and others concerning the imminent Japanese attack on the naval base at Pearl Harbor in Hawaii.

The deaths at Pearl Harbor 7 Dec 1941 incited public opinion, and the USA entered the war. From this point on, Roosevelt concerned himself solely with the conduct of the war. He participated in the Washington 1942 and Casablanca 1943 conferences to plan the Mediterranean assault, and the conferences in Québec, Cairo, and Tehran 1943, and Yalta 1945, at which the final preparations were made for the Allied victory. He was re-elected for a fourth term 1944, but died 1945.

Roosevelt /ˈrəʊzəvelt/ Theodore 1858–1919. 26th president of the USA 1901–09, a Republican. After serving as governor of New York 1898–1900 he became vice president to →McKinley, whom he succeeded as president on McKinley's assassination 1901. He campaigned against the great trusts (associations of enterprises that reduce competition), while carrying on a jingoist foreign policy designed to enforce US supremacy over Latin America.

Roosevelt, born in New York, was elected to the

Roosevelt 26th US president, Theodore Roosevelt. He was the first American to receive the Nobel Peace Prize awarded to him for his efforts in ending the Russo-Japanese war.

state legislature 1881. He was assistant secretary of the Navy 1897–98, and during the Spanish–American War 1898 commanded a volunteer force of 'rough riders'. At age 42, Roosevelt was the youngest man up to then to become president of the USA. In office he became more liberal. He tackled business monopolies, initiated measures for the conservation of national resources, and introduced the Pure Food and Drug Act. He won the Nobel Peace Prize 1906 for his part in ending the Russo-Japanese war. Alienated after his retirement by the conservatism of his successor Taft, Roosevelt formed the Progressive or 'Bull Moose' Party. As their candidate he unsuccessfully ran for the presidency 1912. During World War I he strongly advocated US intervention.

Rosa /ˈrəuzə/ Salvator 1615–1673. Italian painter, etcher, poet, and musician, active in Florence 1640–49 and subsequently in Rome. He created wild, romantic, and sometimes macabre landscapes, seascapes, and battle scenes. He also wrote verse satires.

Born near Naples, Rosa spent much of his youth travelling in S Italy. He first settled in Rome in 1639 and established himself as a landscape painter. In Florence he worked for the ruling Medici family.

Roscellinus /ˌrɒsəˈlaɪnəs/ Johannes c. 1050–c. 1122. Philosopher regarded as the founder of Scholasticism (which sought to integrate biblical teaching with Platonic and Aristotelian philosophy) because of his defence of nominalism (the idea that classes of things are simply names and have no objective reality) against →Anselm.

Roscius Gallus /ˈrɒskiəs ˈgæləs/ Quintus c. 126–62 BC. Roman actor, originally a slave, so

gifted that his name became a byword for a great actor.

Rosebery /ˈrəuzbəri/ Archibald Philip Primrose, 5th Earl of Rosebery 1847–1929. British Liberal politician. He was foreign secretary 1886 and 1892–94, when he succeeded Gladstone as prime minister, but his government survived less than a year. After 1896 his imperialist views gradually placed him further from the mainstream of the Liberal Party.

Rosenberg /ˈrəuzənbɜːg/ Alfred 1893–1946. German politician, born in Tallinn, Estonia. He became the chief Nazi ideologist and was minister for eastern occupied territories 1941–44. He was tried at Nuremberg 1946 as a war criminal and hanged.

Rosenberg /ˈrəuzənbɜːg/ Eugene 1907–1990. Czechoslovak-born architect belonging to the Modern movement, who lived in the UK from 1942. He completed many Modern apartment houses while in Prague in the 1930s. In Britain he specialized in hospital and school design and was in charge of the planning of Warwick University 1965 and the building of St Thomas's Hospital, London, from 1966 onwards.

Rosenberg /ˈrəuzənbɜːg/ Isaac 1890–1918. English poet of the World War I period. Trained as an artist at the Slade school in London, Rosenberg enlisted in the British army 1915. He wrote about the horror of life on the front line, as in 'Break of Day in the Trenches'.

Like that of his contemporary Wilfred Owen, Rosenberg's work is now ranked with the finest World War I poems, although he was largely unpublished during his lifetime. After serving for 20 months in the front line, he was killed on the Somme.

Rosenberg /ˈrəuzənbɜːg/ Julius 1918–53 and Ethel Greenglass 1915–53. US married couple, convicted of being leaders of a nuclear-espionage ring passing information from Ethel's brother via courier to the USSR. The Rosenbergs were executed after much public controversy and demonstration. They were the only Americans executed for espionage during peacetime.

Ross /rɒs/ Betsy 1752–1836. American seamstress remembered as the maker of the first US flag. According to popular legend, she was approached 1776 by family acquaintance George Washington to create an official flag for the new nation. Despite little historical substantiation, it is believed by many that the familiar red and white stripes with white stars on a field of blue was Ross's original concept.

Born in Philadelphia to a devout Quaker family, Ross was born Elizabeth Griscom and married upholsterer John Ross 1773. When he died 1776, she took over his business. Becoming famous after the war, she continued in the upholstery business until her retirement 1827.

includes *Goblin Market and Other Poems* 1862 and expresses unfulfilled spiritual yearning and frustrated love. She was a skilful technician and made use of irregular rhyme and line length.

*Better by far you should forget and smile
Than you should remember and be sad.*

Christina Rossetti `Remember' 1862

Rossetti /rəˈzeti/ Dante Gabriel 1828–1882. British painter and poet, a founding member of the Pre-Raphaelite Brotherhood (PRB) in 1848. As well as romantic medieval scenes, he produced many idealized portraits of women. His verse includes 'The Blessed Damozel' 1850. His sister was the poet Christina Rossetti.

Rossetti, the son of an exiled Italian, formed the PRB with the painters Millais and Hunt but developed a broader style and a personal subject matter, related to his poetry. He was a friend of the critic Ruskin, and of William Morris and his wife Jane, who became Rossetti's lover and the subject of much of his work. His *Poems* 1870 were recovered from the grave of his wife Elizabeth Siddal (1834–62, also a painter, whom he had married in 1860), and were attacked as of 'the fleshly school of poetry'.

Rossi /ˈrɒsi/ Aldo 1931– . Italian architect and theorist. He is strongly influenced by rationalist thought and Neo-Classicism. His main works include the Gallaratese II apartment complex, Milan, 1970; the Modena cemetery, 1973; and the Teatro del Mondo/Floating Theatre, Venice, 1979.

Rossini /rɒˈsiːni/ Gioacchino (Antonio) 1792–1868. Italian composer. His first success was the opera *Tancredi* 1813. In 1816 his 'opera buffa' *Il barbiere di Siviglia/The Barber of Seville* was produced in Rome. During 1815–23 he produced 20 operas, and created (with ➔Donizetti and ➔Bellini) the 19th-century Italian operatic style.

After *Guillaume Tell/William Tell* 1829, Rossini gave up writing opera and his later years were spent in Bologna and Paris. Among the works of this period are the *Stabat Mater* 1842 and the piano music arranged for ballet by ➔Respighi as *La Boutique fantasque/The Fantastic Toyshop* 1919.

Rostand /rɒsˈtɒn/ Edmond 1869–1918. French dramatist, who wrote *Cyrano de Bergerac* 1897 and *L'Aiglon* 1900 (based on the life of Napoleon III), in which Sarah Bernhardt played the leading role.

Rostropovich /ˌrɒstrəˈpəʊvitʃ/ Mstislav 1927– . Russian cellist and conductor, deprived of Soviet citizenship 1978 because of his sympathies with political dissidents. Prokofiev, Shostakovich, Khachaturian, and Britten wrote pieces for him. Since 1977 he has directed the National Symphony Orchestra, Washington DC.

Rossetti British poet and painter Dante Gabriel Rossetti was a central figure in the Pre-Raphaelite movement.

Ross /rɒs/ James Clark 1800–1862. English explorer who discovered the magnetic North Pole 1831. He also went to the Antarctic 1839; Ross Island, Ross Sea, and Ross Dependency are named after him.

He is associated with ➔Parry and his uncle John Ross in Arctic exploration.

Ross /rɒs/ John 1777–1856. Scottish rear admiral and explorer. He served in wars with France and made voyages of Arctic exploration in 1818, 1829–33, and 1850.

Ross /rɒs/ Martin. Pen name of Violet Florence ➔Martin, Irish novelist.

Ross /rɒs/ Ronald 1857–1932. British physician and bacteriologist, born in India. From 1881 to 1899 he served in the Indian medical service, and during 1895–98 identified mosquitoes of the genus *Anopheles* as being responsible for the spread of malaria. Nobel prize 1902.

Rossellini /ˌrɒsəˈliːni/ Roberto 1906–1977. Italian film director. His World War II trilogy, *Roma città aperta/Rome, Open City* 1945, *Paisà/Paisan* 1946, and *Germania anno zero/Germany Year Zero* 1947, reflects his humanism, and is considered a landmark of European cinema.

He and actress Ingrid ➔Bergman formed a creative partnership 1949 which produced *Stromboli* and seven other films over a six-year period, which were neither critical nor box-office successes. Rossellini returned to form with *General della Rovere* 1959, and then went on to make films for television, such as *La Prise de Pouvoir par Louis XIV/The Rise of Louis XIV* 1966.

Rossetti /rəˈzeti/ Christina (Georgina) 1830–1894. English poet, sister of Dante Gabriel Rossetti and a devout High Anglican. Her verse

Roth /rəʊt/ Joseph 1894–1939. Austrian novelist and critic who depicted the decay of the Austrian Empire before 1914 in such novels as *Savoy Hotel* 1924, *Radetsky Marsch/The Radetsky March* 1932, and (after he moved to Paris 1933) *Die hundert Tage/The Hundred Days* 1936. He worked as a journalist during the 1920s in several European capitals. His novels defy easy classification; he stayed aloof from literary groups of his time.

Roth /rɒθ/ Philip 1933– . US novelist whose portrayals of 20th-century Jewish-American life include *Goodbye Columbus* 1959 and *Portnoy's Complaint* 1969. Psychosexual themes are prominent in his work.

Roth's series of semi-autobiographical novels about a writer, Nathan Zuckerman, includes *The Ghost Writer* 1979, *Zuckerman Unbound* 1981, *The Anatomy Lesson* 1984, and *The Counterlife* 1987. *Patrimony* 1991 concerned his father's death.

Rothenstein /rəʊθənstaɪn/ William 1872–1945. British painter, writer, and teacher. His work includes decorations for St Stephen's Hall, Westminster, London, and portrait drawings. He was principal of the Royal College of Art 1920–35, where he encouraged the sculptors Jacob Epstein and Henry Moore, and the painter Paul Nash.

Rothermere /rɒðəmɪə/ Harold Sidney Harmsworth, 1st Viscount 1868–1940. British newspaper proprietor, brother of Lord →Northcliffe.

Rothermere /rɒðəmɪə/ Vere (Harold Esmond Harmsworth), 3rd Viscount 1925– . British newspaper proprietor. As chair of Associated Newspapers (1971–) he controls the right-wing *Daily Mail* (founded by his great-uncle Lord

Rossini Gioacchino Rossini, Italian composer of 36 operas, including The Barber of Seville. Hissed at during its first performance, the opera is now a popular part of the opera repertory, enjoyed for its wit and rich melodies.

→Northcliffe) and *Mail on Sunday* (launched 1982), the London *Evening Standard*, and a string of regional newspapers.

In 1971 Rothermere took control of the family newspapers. He closed the *Daily Sketch* and successfully transformed the *Mail* into a tabloid. In 1977 he closed the London *Evening News* with heavy loss of jobs, but obtained a half-share of the more successful *Evening Standard*, and gained control of the remainder 1985.

Rothko /rɒθkəʊ/ Mark 1903–1970. Russian-born US painter, an Abstract Expressionist and a pioneer of *Colour Field* painting (abstract, dominated by areas of unmodulated, strong colour). Rothko produced several series of paintings in the 1950s and 1960s, including one at Harvard University; one in the Tate Gallery, London; and one for a chapel in Houston, Texas, 1967–69.

Rothschild /rɒθstʃaɪld/ European family active in the financial world for two centuries. *Mayer Anselm* (1744–1812) set up as a moneylender in Frankfurt-am-Main, Germany, and business houses were established throughout Europe by his ten children.

Nathan Mayer (1777–1836) settled in England, and his grandson *Nathaniel* (1840–1915) was created a baron in 1885. *Lionel Walter* (1868–1937) succeeded his father as 2nd Baron Rothschild and was an eminent naturalist. His daughter *Miriam* (1908–) is an entomologist, renowned for her studies of fleas. The 2nd baron's nephew, *Nathaniel* (1910–1990), 3rd Baron Rothschild, was a scientist. During World War II he worked in British military intelligence. He was head of the central policy-review staff in the Cabinet Office (the 'think tank' set up by Edward Heath) 1970–74. Of the French branch, Baron *Eric de Rothschild* (1940–) owns Château Lafite and Baron *Philippe de Rothschild* (1902–) owns Château Mouton-Rothschild, both leading red Bordeaux-producing properties in Pauillac, SW France.

Rouault /ruːˈəʊ/ Georges 1871–1958. French painter, etcher, illustrator, and designer. Early in his career he was associated with the Fauves, who made bold use of vivid colours, but created his own style using heavy, dark colours and bold brushwork. His subjects included sad clowns, prostitutes, and evil lawyers; from about 1940 he painted mainly religious works.

Rouault was born in Paris, the son of a cabinet-maker. He was apprenticed to a stained-glass-maker; later he studied under the Symbolist painter Gustave Moreau and became curator of Moreau's studio. *The Prostitute* 1906 (Musée National d'Art Moderne, Paris) and *The Face of Christ* 1933 (Musée des Beaux-Arts, Ghent, Belgium) represent extremes of Rouault's painting style. He also produced illustrations and designed tapestries, stained glass, and sets for Diaghilev's Ballets Russes, and in 1948 he published a series of etchings, *Miserere*.

Roubiliac /ˌruːbɪˈjæk/ or *Roubillac*, Louis François *c.* 1705–1762. French sculptor, a Huguenot who fled religious persecution to settle in England 1732. He became a leading sculptor of the day, creating a statue of Handel for Vauxhall Gardens 1737 (Victoria and Albert Museum, London).

He also produced lively statues of historic figures, such as Newton, and an outstanding funerary monument, the *Tomb of Lady Elizabeth Nightingale* 1761 (Westminster Abbey, London).

Rouget de Lisle /ruːˈʒeɪ də ˈliːl/ Claude-Joseph 1760–1836. French army officer who composed, while in Strasbourg 1792, the 'Marseillaise', the French national anthem.

Rousseau /ruːˈsəʊ/ Henri 'Le Douanier' 1844–1910. French painter, a self-taught naive artist. His subjects included scenes of the Parisian suburbs and exotic junglescapes, painted with painstaking detail; for example, *Surprised! Tropical Storm with a Tiger* 1891 (National Gallery, London).

Rousseau served in the army for some years, then became a toll collector (hence *Le Douanier*, 'the customs official'), and finally took up full-time painting in 1885. He exhibited at the Salon des Indépendants from 1886 to 1910 and was associated with the group led by Picasso and the poet Apollinaire, but his position was unique. As a naive and pompous person, he was considered ridiculous, yet admired for his inimitable style.

I hate books, for they only teach people to talk about what they do not understand.

Jean-Jacques Rousseau *Emile* 1762

Rousseau /ruːˈsəʊ/ Jean-Jacques 1712–1778. French social philosopher and writer whose *Du Contrat social/Social Contract* 1762, emphasizing the rights of the people over those of the government, was a significant influence on the French Revolution. In the novel *Emile* 1762 he outlined a new theory of education.

Rousseau was born in Geneva, Switzerland. *Discourses on the Origins of Inequality* 1754 made his name: he denounced civilized society and postulated the paradox of the superiority of the 'noble savage'. *Social Contract* stated that a government could be legitimately overthrown if it failed to express the general will of the people. *Emile* was written as an example of how to elicit the unspoiled nature and abilities of children, based on natural development and the power of example.

Rousseau's ideas were condemned by philosophers, the clergy, and the public, and he lived in exile in England for a year, being helped by Scottish philosopher David Hume until they fell out. He was a contributor to the *Encyclopédie* and also wrote operas. *Confessions*, published posthumously 1782, was a frank account of his occasionally immoral life and was a founding work of autobiography.

Rousseau /ruːˈsəʊ/ (Etienne-Pierre) Théodore 1812–1867. French landscape painter of the Barbizon school. Born in Paris, he came under the influence of the British landscape painters Constable and Bonington, sketched from nature in many parts of France, and settled in Barbizon in 1848.

Rowbotham /ˈrəʊbɒtəm/ Sheila 1943– . British socialist, feminist, historian, lecturer, and writer. Her pamphlet *Women's Liberation and the New Politics* 1970 laid down fundamental approaches and demands of the emerging women's movement.

Rowbotham taught in schools and then became involved with the Workers' Educational Association. An active socialist since the early 1960s, she has contributed to several left-wing journals. Her books include *Hidden from History, Women's Consciousness, Man's World* both 1973, *Beyond the Fragments* 1979, and *The Past is Before Us* 1989.

Rowe /rəʊ/ Nicholas 1674–1718. English playwright and poet, whose dramas include *The Fair Penitent* 1702 and *Jane Shore* 1714, in which Mrs Siddons played. He edited Shakespeare, and was poet laureate from 1715.

Rowland /ˈrəʊlənd/ Tiny (Roland W). Adopted name of Roland Fuhrhop 1917– . British entrepreneur, chief executive and managing director of Lonrho, and owner from 1981 of the *Observer* Sunday newspaper.

Born in India, he emigrated to Rhodesia 1947. In 1961 he merged his business interests with the London and Rhodesian Mining and Land Company, now known as Lonrho. After acquiring the *Observer*, he made an unsuccessful bid for the Harrods department store in London.

Rowlandson /ˈrəʊləndsən/ Thomas 1756–1827. English painter and illustrator, a caricaturist of Georgian social life. He published the series of drawings *Tour of Dr Syntax in Search of the Picturesque* 1809 and its two sequels 1812–21.

Rowlandson studied at the Royal Academy schools and in Paris. Impoverished by gambling, he turned from portrait painting to caricature around 1780. Other works include *The Dance of Death* 1815–16 and illustrations for the novelists Smollett, Goldsmith, and Sterne.

Rowley /ˈrəʊli/ William *c.* 1585–*c.* 1642. English actor and dramatist who collaborated with Thomas →Middleton on *The Changeling* 1621 and with Thomas →Dekker and John →Ford on *The Witch of Edmonton* published 1658.

Rowling /ˈrəʊlɪŋ/ Wallace 'Bill' 1927– . New Zealand Labour politician, party leader 1969–75, prime minister 1974–75.

Rowntree /ˈraʊntriː/ Benjamin Seebohm 1871–1954. British entrepreneur and philanthropist. Much of the money he acquired as chair

(1925–41) of the family firm of confectioners, H I Rowntree, he used to fund investigations into social conditions. His writings include *Poverty, A Study of Town Life* 1900. The three **Rowntree Trusts**, which were founded by his father *Joseph Rowntree* (1836–1925) in 1904, fund research into housing, social care, and social policy, support projects relating to social justice, and give grants to pressure groups working in these areas.

Rowntree joined the York-based family business in 1889 after studying at Owens College (later the University of Manchester). The introduction of company pensions (1906), a five-day working week (1919), and an employee profit-sharing scheme (1923) gave him a reputation as an enlightened and paternalistic employer. An associate of David Lloyd George, he was director of the welfare department of the Ministry of Munitions during World War I.

His pioneering study of working-class households in York 1897–98, published as *Poverty, A Study of Town Life*, was a landmark in empirical sociology; it showed that 28% of the population fell below an arbitrary level of minimum income, and 16% experienced 'primary poverty'. Rowntree also wrote on gambling, unemployment, and business organization.

Rowse /raʊs/ A(lfred) L(eslie) 1903– . English popular historian. He published a biography of Shakespeare 1963, and in 1973 controversially identified the 'Dark Lady' of Shakespeare's sonnets as Emilia Lanier, half-Italian daughter of a court musician, with whom the Bard is alleged to have had an affair 1593–95.

Roy /rɔɪ/ Manabendra Nakh 1887–1954. Founder of the Indian Communist Party in exile in Tashkent 1920. Expelled from the Comintern 1929, he returned to India and was imprisoned for five years. A steadfast communist, he finally became disillusioned after World War II and developed his ideas on practical humanism.

Royce /rɔɪs/ (Frederick) Henry 1863–1933. British engineer, who so impressed Charles →Rolls by the car he built for his own personal use 1904 that Rolls-Royce Ltd was formed 1906 to produce automobiles and engines.

Royce /rɔɪs/ Josiah 1855–1916. US idealist philosopher who in *The Conception of God* 1895 and *The Conception of Immortality* 1900 interpreted Christianity in philosophical terms.

Rubbia /rʊbiə/ Carlo 1934– . Italian physicist and, from 1989, director-general of CERN, the European nuclear research organization. In 1983 he led the team that discovered the weakons (W and Z particles), the agents responsible for transferring the weak nuclear force. Rubbia shared the Nobel Prize for Physics with his colleague Simon van der Meer (1925–).

Rubbra /rʌbrə/ Edmund 1901–1986. British composer. He studied under →Holst and was a master of contrapuntal writing, as exemplified in his study *Counterpoint* 1960. His compositions include 11 symphonies, chamber music, and songs.

Rubens /ruːbɪnz/ Peter Paul 1577–1640. Flemish painter, who brought the exuberance of Italian Baroque to N Europe, creating, with an army of assistants, innumerable religious and allegorical paintings for churches and palaces. These show mastery of drama in large compositions, and love of rich colour. He also painted portraits and, in his last years, landscapes.

Rubens entered the Antwerp painters' guild 1598 and went to Italy in 1600, studying artists of the High Renaissance. In 1603 he visited Spain and in Madrid painted many portraits of the Spanish nobility. From 1604 to 1608 he was in Italy again, and in 1609 he settled in Antwerp and was appointed court painter to the archduke Albert and his wife Isabella. His *Raising of the Cross* 1610 and *Descent from the Cross* 1611–14, both in Antwerp Cathedral, show his brilliant painterly style. He went to France 1620, commissioned by the regent Marie de' Medici to produce a cycle of 21 enormous canvases allegorizing her life (Louvre, Paris). In 1628 he again went to Madrid, where he met the painter Velázquez. In 1629–30 he was in London as diplomatic envoy to Charles I, and painted the ceiling of the Banqueting House in Whitehall.

Rubens's portraits range from intimate pictures of his second wife, such as *Hélène Fourment in a Fur Wrap* about 1638 (Kunsthistorisches Museum, Vienna), to dozens of portraits of royalty.

The size of the pictures gives us painters much more courage to represent our ideas adequately and with an appearance of reality.

Peter Paul Rubens 1621

Rubik /ruːbɪk/ Erno 1944– . Hungarian architect who invented the **Rubik cube**, a multi-coloured puzzle that can be manipulated and rearranged in only one correct way, but about 43 trillion wrong ones. Intended to help his students understand three-dimensional design, it became a fad that swept around the world.

Rubinstein /ruːbɪnstaɪn/ Artur 1887–1982. Polish-born US pianist. He studied in Warsaw and Berlin and for 85 of his 95 years appeared with the world's major symphony orchestras, specializing in the music of Mozart, Chopin, Debussy, and the Spanish composers.

Rubinstein /ruːbɪnstaɪn/ Helena 1882–1965. Polish-born cosmetics tycoon, who emigrated to Australia 1902, where she started a cosmetics business. She moved to Europe 1904 and later to the USA, opening salons in London, Paris, and New York.

Rublev /ruːˈblɒf/ (Rublyov) Andrei c. 1360–1430. Russian icon painter. Only one documented work of his survives, the *Holy Trinity* about 1411 (Tretyakov Gallery, Moscow). This shows a basically Byzantine style, but with a gentler expression.

He is known to have worked with →Theophanes the Greek in the Cathedral of the Annunciation in Moscow. In later life Rublev became a monk. The director Tarkovsky made a film of his life 1966.

Rude /ruːd/ François 1784–1855. French Romantic sculptor. He produced the low-relief scene on the Arc de Triomphe, Paris, showing the capped figure of Liberty leading the revolutionaries (1833, known as *The Volunteers of 1792* or *The Marseillaise*).

Rude was a supporter of Napoleon, along with the painter David, and in 1814 both artists went into exile in Brussels for some years. Rude's other works include a bust of *David* 1831 and the monument *Napoleon Awakening to Immortality* 1854 (both in the Louvre, Paris).

Rudolph /ruːdɒlf/ 1858–1889. Crown prince of Austria, the only son of Emperor Franz Joseph. From an early age he showed progressive views that brought him into conflict with his father. He conceived and helped to write a history of the Austro-Hungarian empire. In 1881, he married Princess Stephanie of Belgium, and they had one daughter, Elizabeth. In 1889 he and his mistress, Baroness Marie Vetsera, were found shot in his hunting lodge at Mayerling, near Vienna. The official verdict was suicide, although there were rumours that it was perpetrated by Jesuits, Hungarian nobles, or the baroness's husband.

Rudolph /ruːdɒlf/ two Holy Roman emperors:

Rudolph I 1218–1291. Holy Roman emperor from 1273. Originally count of Habsburg, he was the first Habsburg emperor and expanded his dynasty by investing his sons with the duchies of Austria and Styria.

Rudolph II 1552–1612. Holy Roman emperor from 1576, when he succeeded his father Maximilian II. His policies led to unrest in Hungary and Bohemia, which led to the surrender of Hungary to his brother Matthias 1608 and religious freedom for Bohemia.

Ruisdael /ˈraɪzdɑːl/ or *Ruysdael* Jacob van c. 1628–1682. Dutch landscape painter, active in Amsterdam from about 1655. He painted rural scenes near his native town of Haarlem and in Germany, and excelled in depicting gnarled and weatherbeaten trees. The few figures in his pictures were painted by other artists.

Ruisdael probably worked in Haarlem with his uncle, the landscape painter *Salomon van Ruysdael* (c. 1600–70). Jacob is considered the greatest realist landscape painter in Dutch art. →Hobbema was one of his pupils.

Rumford /ˈrʌmfəd/ Benjamin Thompson, Count Rumford 1753–1814. American-born British physicist. In 1798, impressed by the seemingly inexhaustible amounts of heat generated in the boring of a cannon, he published his theory that heat is a mode of vibratory motion, not a substance.

Rumford spied for the British in the American Revolution, and was forced to flee from America to England 1776. He travelled in Europe, and was created a count of the Holy Roman Empire for services to the elector of Bavaria 1791. He founded the Royal Institute in London 1799.

Runcie /ˈrʌnsi/ Robert (Alexander Kennedy) 1921– . English cleric, archbishop of Canterbury 1980–91, the first to be appointed on the suggestion of the Church Crown Appointments Commission (formed 1977) rather than by political consultation. He favoured ecclesiastical remarriage for the divorced and the eventual introduction of the ordination of women.

Runciman /ˈrʌnsɪmən/ Walter, 1st Viscount 1870–1949. British Liberal politician. He entered Parliament in 1899 and held various ministerial offices between 1908 and 1939. In Aug 1938 he undertook an abortive mission to Czechoslovakia to persuade the Czech government to make concessions to Nazi Germany.

Rundstedt /ˈrʊndstet/ Karl Rudolf Gerd von 1875–1953. German field marshal in World War II. Largely responsible for the German breakthrough in France 1940, he was defeated on the Ukrainian front 1941. As commander in chief in France from 1942, he resisted the Allied invasion 1944 and in Dec launched the temporarily successful Ardennes offensive.

Runge /ˈrʊɡə/ Philipp Otto 1770–1810. German Romantic painter, whose portraits, often of children, have a remarkable clarity and openness. He also illustrated fairy tales by the brothers Grimm.

Runyon /ˈrʌnjən/ (Alfred) Damon 1884–1946. US journalist, primarily a sports reporter, whose short stories in *Guys and Dolls* 1932 deal wryly with the seamier side of New York City life in his own invented jargon.

Rupert /ˈruːpət/ Prince 1619–1682. English Royalist general and admiral, born in Prague, son of the Elector Palatine Frederick V (1596–1632) and James I's daughter Elizabeth. Defeated by Cromwell at Marston Moor and Naseby in the Civil War, he commanded a privateering fleet 1649–52, until routed by Admiral Robert Blake, and, returning after the Restoration, was a distinguished admiral in the Dutch Wars. He founded the Hudson's Bay Company.

Rush /rʌʃ/ Benjamin 1745–1813. American physician and public official. Committed to the cause of the American Revolution 1775–83, he was a signatory of the Declaration of Independence 1776 and was named surgeon general of the Continental army 1777.

Born in Bayberry, Pennsylvania, Rush was educated at the College of New Jersey and received his MD degree from the University of Edinburgh 1768. His involvement in agitation against Washington's leadership led to his resignation. After the war, Rush served on the medical faculty of the University of Pennsylvania 1780–97 and was active in public-health programmes.

From 1797 to his death he was treasurer of the US Mint.

Rushdie /ruʃdi/ (Ahmed) Salman 1947– . British writer, born in India of a Muslim family. His novel *The Satanic Verses* 1988 (the title refers to verses deleted from the Koran) offended many Muslims with alleged blasphemy. In 1989 the Ayatollah Khomeini of Iran called for Rushdie and his publishers to be killed.

Rushdie was born in Bombay and later lived in Pakistan before moving to the UK. His earlier novels in the magic-realist style include *Midnight's Children* 1981, which deals with India from the date of independence and won the Booker Prize, and *Shame* 1983, set in an imaginary parallel of Pakistan. The furore caused by the publication of *The Satanic Verses* led to the withdrawal of British diplomats from Iran. In India and elsewhere, people were killed in demonstrations against the book and Rushdie was forced to go into hiding. *Haroun and the Sea of Stories*, a children's book, was published 1990.

Rusk /rʌsk/ Dean 1909– . US Democrat politician. He was secretary of state to presidents J F Kennedy and L B Johnson 1961–69, and became unpopular through his involvement with the Vietnam War.

During World War II he fought in Burma (now Myanmar) and China and became deputy Chief of Staff of US forces. After the war he served in the Department of State, and as assistant secretary of state for Far Eastern affairs was prominent in Korean War negotiations.

Ruskin /rʌskɪn/ John 1819–1900. English art critic and social critic. He published five volumes of *Modern Painters* 1843–60 and *The Seven Lamps of Architecture* 1849, in which he stated his philosophy of art. His writings hastened the appreciation of painters considered unorthodox at the time, such as J M W →Turner and the Pre-Raphaelite Brotherhood. His later writings were concerned with social and economic problems.

Born in London, the only child of a prosperous wine-merchant, Ruskin was able to travel widely and was educated at Oxford. In 1848 he married Euphemia 'Effie' Chalmers Gray, but six years later the marriage was annulled.

In *The Stones of Venice* 1851–53, he drew moral lessons from architectural history. From 1860 he devoted himself to social and economic problems, in which he adopted an individual and radical outlook exalting the 'craftsman'. He became increasingly isolated in his views. To this period belong a series of lectures and pamphlets (*Unto this Last*

Ruskin English art critic and social theorist John Ruskin. His vision of a planned society with employment for all and support for the old and destitute seemed sensational when first presented in 1860.

1860, *Sesame and Lilies* 1865 on the duties of men and women, *The Crown of Wild Olive* 1866).

Ruskin was Slade professor of art at Oxford 1869–79, and he made a number of social experiments, such as St George's Guild, for the establishment of an industry on socialist lines. His last years were spent at Brantwood, Cumbria.

Ruskin College was founded in Oxford 1899 by an American, Walter Vrooman, to provide education in the social sciences for working people. It is supported by trade unions and other organizations.

Russ /rʌs/ Joanna 1937– . US writer of feminist science fiction, exemplified by the novel *The Female Man* 1975. Her short stories have been collected in *The Zanzibar Cat* 1983.

Russell /rʌsəl/ Bertrand (Arthur William), 3rd Earl Russell 1872–1970. English philosopher and mathematician who contributed to the development of modern mathematical logic and wrote about social issues. His works include *Principia Mathematica* 1910–13 (with A N →Whitehead), in which he attempted to show that mathematics could be reduced to a branch of logic; *The Problems of Philosophy* 1912; and *A History of Western Philosophy* 1946. He was an outspoken liberal pacifist.

The grandson of Prime Minister John Russell, he was educated at Trinity College, Cambridge, where he specialized in mathematics and became a lecturer 1895. Russell's pacifist attitude in World War I lost him the lectureship, and he was

Russell John Russell, British Liberal politician, was created 1st Earl Russell in 1861. As a young MP of aristocratic background, he helped frame the 1832 Reform Bill and championed its passage through Parliament.

imprisoned for six months for an article he wrote in a pacifist journal. His *Introduction to Mathematical Philosophy* 1919 was written in prison. He and his wife ran a progressive school 1927–32. After visits to the USSR and China, he went to the USA 1938 and taught at many universities. In 1940, a US court disqualified him from teaching at City College of New York because of his liberal moral views. He later returned to England and was a fellow of Trinity College. He was a life-long pacifist except during World War II. From 1949 he advocated nuclear disarmament and until 1963 was on the Committee of 100, an offshoot of the Campaign for Nuclear Disarmament.

Among his other works are *Principles of Mathematics* 1903, *Principles of Social Reconstruction* 1917, *Marriage and Morals* 1929, *An Enquiry into Meaning and Truth* 1940, *New Hopes for a Changing World* 1951, and *Autobiography* 1967–69.

Russell /ˈrʌsəl/ Charles Taze 1852–1916. US religious figure, founder of the Jehovah's Witness sect 1872.

Russell /ˈrʌsəl/ Dora Winifred (born Black) 1894–1986. English feminist who married Bertrand →Russell 1921. The 'openness' of their marriage (she subsequently had children by another man) was a matter of controversy. She was a founding member of the National Council for Civil Liberties in 1934.

She was educated at Girton College, Cambridge, of which she became a Fellow. In 1927 the Russells founded the progressive Beacon Hill School in Hampshire. After World War II she actively supported the Campaign for Nuclear Disarmament.

Russell /ˈrʌsəl/ George William 1867–1935. Irish poet and essayist. An ardent nationalist, he helped found the Irish national theatre, and his poetry, published under the pseudonym 'AE', includes *Gods of War* 1915 and reflects his interest in mysticism and theosophy.

Russell /ˈrʌsəl/ Jane 1921– . US actress who was discovered by producer Howard Hughes. Her first film, *The Outlaw* 1943, was not properly released for several years because of censorship problems. Other films include *The Paleface* 1948, *Gentlemen Prefer Blondes* 1953, and *The Revolt of Mamie Stover* 1957.

Russell /ˈrʌsəl/ John 1795–1883. British 'sporting parson', who bred the short-legged, smooth-coated Jack Russell terrier.

Russell /ˈrʌsəl/ John Peter 1858–1931. Australian artist. Having met Tom →Roberts while sailing to England, he became a member of the French Post-Impressionist group.

Russell /ˈrʌsəl/ John, 1st Earl Russell 1792–1878. British Liberal politician, son of the 6th Duke of Bedford. He entered the House of Commons 1813 and supported Catholic emancipation and the Reform Bill. He held cabinet posts 1830–41, became prime minister 1846–52, and was again a cabinet minister until becoming prime minister again 1865–66. He retired after the defeat of his Reform Bill 1866.

As foreign secretary in Aberdeen's coalition 1852 and in Palmerston's second government 1859–65, Russell assisted Italy's struggle for unity, although his indecisive policies on Poland, Denmark, and the American Civil War provoked much criticism. He had a strained relationship with Palmerston.

Russell /ˈrʌsəl/ Ken 1927– . English film director whose work includes *Women in Love* 1969, *The Devils* 1971, and *Gothic* 1986. He has made television documentaries of the lives of the composers Elgar, Delius, and Richard Strauss.

Russell /ˈrʌsəl/ Lord William 1639–1683. British Whig politician. Son of the 1st Duke of Bedford, he was among the founders of the Whig Party, and actively supported attempts in Parliament to exclude the Roman Catholic James II from succeeding to the throne. In 1683 he was accused, on dubious evidence, of complicity in the Rye House Plot to murder Charles II, and was executed.

Russell /ˈrʌsəl/ William Howard 1821–1907. British journalist, born in Ireland. He was the correspondent for *The Times* during the Crimean War, and created a sensation by exposing the mismanagement of the campaign.

Russell of Liverpool /ˈrʌsəl, ˈlɪvəpuːl/ Edward Frederick Langley Russell, 2nd Baron 1895–1981. British barrister. As deputy judge advocate-general, British Army of the Rhine 1946–47 and 1948–51, he was responsible for all war-crime trials in the British Zone of Germany 1946–50. He published *The Scourge of the Swastika* 1954 and *The Trial of Adolf Eichmann* 1962.

Rust /rʊst/ Mathias 1968– . German aviator who, in May 1987, piloted a light plane from Finland to Moscow, landing in Red Square. Found guilty of 'malicious hooliganism', he was imprisoned until 1988, and again in 1991 following a conviction for attempted manslaughter.

His exploit, carefully timed to take place on the USSR's 'national border-guards' day', highlighted serious deficiencies in the Soviet air-defence system and led to the dismissal of the defence minister.

Rust, despite pleading that his actions had been designed to promote world peace, was sentenced to four years' imprisonment by the Soviet authorities. After serving 14 months in a KGB prison in Lefortovo, he was released and sent home as a humanitarian gesture by the Gorbachev administration. In April 1991, he was sentenced to two-and-a-half-years' imprisonment for attempted manslaughter in 1989, when he stabbed a student nurse who spurned his advances.

Ruth /ruːθ/ Babe (George Herman) 1895–1948. US baseball player, regarded by many as the greatest of all time. He played in ten World Series and hit 714 home runs, a record that stood from 1935 to 1974 and led to the nickname 'Sultan of Swat'.

Ruth started playing 1914 as a pitcher-outfielder for the Boston Braves before moving to the Boston Red Sox later that year. He joined the New York Yankees 1920 and became one of the best hitters in the game. He hit 60 home runs in the 1927 season (a record beaten 1961 by Roger Maris). He is still the holder of the record for most bases in a season: 457 in 1921. Yankee Stadium is known as 'the house that Ruth built' because of the money he brought into the club.

Rutherford /rʌðəfəd/ Ernest 1871–1937. New Zealand physicist, a pioneer of modern atomic science. His main research was in the field of radioactivity, and he discovered alpha, beta, and gamma rays. He named the nucleus, and was the first to recognize the nuclear nature of the atom. Nobel prize 1908.

Rutherford /rʌðəfəd/ Margaret 1892–1972. English film and theatre actress who specialized in formidable yet jovially eccentric roles.

She played Agatha Christie's Miss Marple in four films in the early 1960s and won an Academy Award for her role in *The VIPs* 1963.

Rutledge /rʌtlɪdʒ/ Wiley Blount, Jr 1894–1949. US jurist and associate justice of the US Supreme Court 1943–49 under President Roosevelt. He was known as a liberal, often dissenting from conservative Court decisions, such as in *Wolf v Colorado* 1949, which allowed illegally obtained evidence to be used against a defendant in state courts.

Born in Cloverport, Kentucky, USA, Rutledge studied law at the University of Colorado and was admitted to the bar 1922 and taught law at Colorado, Washington, and Iowa universities 1924–39. In 1939 he was appointed judge of the US Court of Appeals for the District of Columbia.

Rutskoi Aleksander 1947– . Russian politician, founder of the reformist Communists for Democracy group, and vice president of the Russian Federation from 1991. During the abortive Aug 1991 coup he led the Russian delegation to rescue Soviet leader Mikhail Gorbachev from his forced confinement in the Crimea.

A former air officer and highly decorated Afghan war veteran, Rutskoi became increasingly critical of the →Yeltsin administration, especially its price liberalization reforms. In 1992 Yeltsin placed Rutskoi in charge of agricultural reform.

Ruysdael Jacob van. See →Ruisdael, Dutch painter.

Ruyter /raɪtə/ Michael Adrianszoon de 1607–1676. Dutch admiral who led his country's fleet in the wars against England. On 1–4 June 1666 he forced the British fleet under Rupert and Albemarle to retire into the Thames, but on 25 July was heavily defeated off the North Foreland, Kent. In 1667 he sailed up the Medway, burning three men-of-war at Chatham, and capturing others.

Ruyter was mortally wounded in an action against the French fleet off Messina and died at Syracuse, Sicily.

Ruzicka /ruːʒɪtʃkə/ Leopold Stephen 1887–1976. Swiss chemist who began research on natural compounds such as musk and civet secretions. In the 1930s he investigated sex hormones, and in 1934 succeeded in extracting the male hormone androsterone from 31,815 litres/7,000 gallons of urine and synthesizing it. Born in Croatia, Ruzicka settled in Switzerland in 1929. Ruzicka shared the 1939 Nobel Chemistry Prize with Butenandt.

Ryan /raɪən/ Robert 1909–1973. US theatre and film actor who was equally impressive in leading and character roles.

His films include *Woman on the Beach* 1947, *The Set-Up* 1949, and *The Wild Bunch* 1969.

Ryder /raɪdə/ Albert Pinkham 1847–1917. US painter who developed one of the most original styles of his time. He painted with broad strokes that tended to simplify form and used yellowish colours that gave his works an eerie, haunted quality. His works are poetic, romantic, and filled with unreality; *Death on a Pale Horse* 1910 (Cleveland Museum of Art) is typical.

Ryle /raɪl/ Gilbert 1900–1976. British philosopher. His *The Concept of Mind* 1949 set out to show that the distinction between an inner and an outer world in philosophy and psychology cannot be sustained. He ridiculed the mind–body dualism of →Descartes as the doctrine of 'the Ghost in the Machine'.

Ryle /raɪl/ Martin 1918–1984. English radioastronomer. At the Mullard Radio Astronomy Observatory, Cambridge, he developed the technique of sky-mapping using 'aperture synthesis', combining smaller dish aerials to give the characteristics of one large one. His work on the distribution of radio sources in the universe brought confirmation of the Big Bang theory. He won, with Antony →Hewish, the Nobel Prize for Physics 1974.

Rysbrack /ˈrɪzbræk/ John Michael 1694–1770. British sculptor, born in Antwerp, then in the Netherlands. He settled in England in 1720 and produced portrait busts and tombs in Westminster Abbey. He also created the equestrian statue of William III in Queen Square, Bristol 1735.

Ryzhkov /rɪˈʒkɒf/ Nikolai Ivanovich 1929– . Soviet communist politician. He held governmental and party posts from 1975 before being brought into the Politburo and serving as prime minister 1985–90 under Gorbachev. A low-profile technocrat, Ryzhkov was the author of unpopular economic reforms.

An engineering graduate from the Urals Polytechnic in Ekaterinburg (formerly Sverdlovsk), Ryzhkov rose to become head of the giant Uralmash engineering conglomerate. A member of the Communist Party from 1959, he became deputy minister for heavy engineering 1975. He then served as first deputy chair of Gosplan (the central planning agency) 1979–82 and Central Committee secretary for economics 1982–85 before becoming prime minister. He was viewed as a more cautious and centralist reformer than Gorbachev. In 1990 he was nearly forced to resign, as a result of the admitted failure of his implementation of the perestroika economic reform programme, and he survived only with the support of Gorbachev. He stepped down as Soviet premier following a serious heart attack in late Dec 1990. In June 1991, he unsuccessfully challenged Boris →Yeltsin for the presidency of the Russian Federation.

S

Saarinen /ˈsɑːrɪnən/ Eero 1910–1961. Finnish-born US architect distinguished for a wide range of innovative modern designs using a variety of creative shapes for buildings. His works include the US embassy, London, the TWA terminal, New York, and Dulles Airport, Washington DC. He collaborated on a number of projects with his father, Eliel Saarinen.

Always design a thing by considering it in its larger context – a chair in a room, a room in a house, a house in an environment, an environment in a city plan.

Eero Saarinen *Time* July 1956

Saarinen /ˈsɑːrɪnən/ Eliel 1873–1950. Finnish architect and town planner, founder of the Finnish Romantic school. In 1923 he emigrated to the USA, where he contributed to US skyscraper design by his work in Chicago, and later turned to functionalism.

Sabah /ˈsɑːbə/ Sheik Jabir al Ahmadal Jabir al-1928– . Emir of Kuwait from 1977. He suspended the national assembly 1986, after mounting parliamentary criticism, ruling in a feudal, paternalistic manner. On the invasion of Kuwait by Iraq 1990 he fled to Saudi Arabia, returning to Kuwait in March 1991.

Sabatier /səˈbætɪeɪ/ Paul 1854–1951. French chemist. He found in 1897 that if a mixture of ethylene and hydrogen was passed over a column of heated nickel, the ethylene changed into ethane. Further work revealed that nickel could be used to catalyse numerous chemical reactions. Sabatier shared the 1912 Nobel Prize for Chemistry with François →Grignard.

Sabatini /ˌsæbəˈtiːni/ Gabriela 1970– . Argentine tennis player who in 1986 became the youngest Wimbledon semifinalist for 99 years. She was ranked number three in the world behind Monica Seles and Steffi Graf in 1991.

Sabin /ˈseɪbɪn/ Albert 1906– . Polish-born US microbiologist whose involvement in the anti-polio campaigns led to the development of a new, highly effective, live vaccine. The earlier vaccine, developed by the physicist Jonas →Salk, was based on heat-killed viruses. Sabin was convinced that a live form would be longer-lasting and more effective, and he succeeded in weakening the virus so that it lost its virulence. The vaccine can be given by mouth.

Sabu /ˈsɑːbuː/ Stage name of Sabu Dastagir 1924–1963. Indian child actor, the hero of *The Thief of Bagdad* 1940. He performed in Britain and the USA until the 1950s. His other films include *Elephant Boy* 1937 and *Black Narcissus* 1947.

Sacher /ˈzæxə/ Paul 1906– . Swiss conductor. In 1926 he founded the Basel Chamber Orchestra, for which he has commissioned a succession of works from contemporary composers including Bartók, Stravinsky, and Britten.

Sacher-Masoch /ˈzæxə ˈmɑːzɒx/ Leopold von 1836–1895. Austrian novelist. His books dealt with the sexual pleasure of having pain inflicted on oneself, hence masochism.

Sachs /zæks/ Hans 1494–1576. German poet and composer who worked as a master shoemaker in Nuremberg. He composed 4,275 *Meisterlieder/Mastersongs*, and figures prominently in →Wagner's opera *Die Meistersinger von Nürnberg*.

Sackville /ˈsækvɪl/ Thomas, 1st Earl of Dorset 1536–1608. English poet, collaborator with Thomas Norton on *Gorboduc* 1561, written in blank verse and one of the earliest English tragedies.

Sackville-West /ˈsækvɪl ˈwest/ Vita (Victoria) 1892–1962. British poet and novelist, wife of Harold →Nicolson from 1913; *Portrait of a Marriage* 1973 by their son Nigel Nicolson described their married life. Her novels include *The Edwardians* 1930 and *All Passion Spent* 1931; she also wrote the pastoral poem *The Land* 1926. The fine gardens around her home at Sissinghurst, Kent, were created by her.

Sadat /səˈdæt/ Anwar 1918–1981. Egyptian politician. Succeeding →Nasser as president 1970, he restored morale by his handling of the Egyptian campaign in the 1973 war against Israel. In 1974 his plan for economic, social, and political reform to transform Egypt was unanimously adopted in a referendum. In 1977 he visited Israel to reconcile the two countries, and shared the Nobel Peace Prize with Israeli prime minister Menachem Begin 1978. He was assassinated by Islamic fundamentalists.

Sade /sɑːd/ Donatien Alphonse François, Comte de, known as the *Marquis de Sade* 1740–1814. French author who was imprisoned for sexual offences and finally committed to an asylum. He wrote plays and novels dealing explicitly with a variety of sexual practices, including sadism.

S'adi /sɑːˈdiː/ or *Saadi*. Pen name of Sheik Moslih Addin *c*. 1184–*c*. 1291. Persian poet, author of *Bustan/Tree-garden* and *Gulistan/Flower-garden*.

Sagan /ˈseɪgən/ Carl 1934– . US physicist and astronomer, renowned for his popular science writings and broadcasts. His books include *Cosmic Connection: an Extraterrestrial Perspective* 1973, *Broca's Brain: Reflections on the Romance of Science* 1979; *Cosmos* 1980, based on his television series of that name; and the science-fiction novel *Contact* 1985.

Sagan became professor of astronomy and space science at Cornell University, New York, in 1970. His research concerned the chemistry and physics of planetary atmospheres, the origin of life on Earth, the probable climatic effects of nuclear war, and the possibility of life on other planets.

Sagan /sæˈgɒn/ Françoise 1935– . French novelist. Her studies of love relationships include *Bonjour Tristesse/Hello Sadness* 1954, *Un Certain Sourire/A Certain Smile* 1956, and *Aimez-vous Brahms?/Do You Like Brahms?* 1959.

Sainte-Beuve /sænt ˈbɜːv/ Charles Augustin 1804–1869. French critic. He contributed to the *Revue des deux mondes/Review of the Two Worlds* from 1831. His articles on French literature appeared as *Causeries du lundi/Monday Chats* 1851–62, and his *Port Royal* 1840–59 is a study of Jansenism, a creed based on the teachings of St →Augustine.

Grown-ups never understand anything for themselves, and it is tiresome for children to be always and forever explaining things to them.

Antoine de Saint-Exupéry
Le Petit Prince 1943

Saint-Exupéry /ˌsænt ekˌsjuːpəˈriː/ Antoine de 1900–1944. French author who wrote the autobiographical *Vol de nuit/Night Flight* 1931 and *Terre des hommes/Wind, Sand, and Stars* 1939. His children's book *Le Petit Prince/The Little Prince* 1943 is also an adult allegory.

Saint-Gaudens /seɪntˈgɔːdnz/ Augustus 1848–1907. Irish-born US sculptor, one of the leading Neo-Classical sculptors of his time. His monuments include the *Admiral Farragut* 1877 in Madison Square Park and the giant nude *Diana* that topped Stanford →White's Madison Square Garden, both in New York City, and the *Adams Memorial* 1891 in Rock Creek Cemetery, Washington DC.

Saint-Just /sænˈʒuːst/ Louis Antoine Léon Florelle de 1767–1794. French revolutionary. A close associate of →Robespierre, he became a member of the Committee of Public Safety 1793, and was guillotined with Robespierre.

Elected to the National Convention in 1792, he was its youngest member at 25 and immediately made his mark by a radical speech condemning King Louis XVI ('one cannot reign without guilt'). His later actions confirm the tone of his book *The Spirit of the Revolution* 1791 in which he showed his distrust of the masses and his advocacy of repression. On his appointment to the Committee of Public Safety he was able to carry out his theories by condemning 'not merely traitors, but the indifferent', including Danton and Lavoisier, although his own death was to follow within weeks.

Saint-Laurent /ˌsæn ləʊˈrɒŋ/ Yves (Henri Donat Mathieu) 1936– . French fashion designer who has had an exceptional influence on fashion in the second half of the 20th century. He began working for Christian →Dior 1955 and succeeded him as designer on Dior's death 1957. He established his own label 1962 and went on to create the first 'power-dressing' looks for men and women: classical, stylish city clothes.

In 1966 Saint Laurent established a chain of boutiques called Rive Gauche selling his ready-to-wear line. By the 1970s he had popularized a style of women's day wear that was inspired by conventionally 'masculine' garments such as blazers, trousers, and shirts. He launched a menswear collection in 1974.

Saint-Pierre /ˌsæmpiˈeə/ Jacques Henri Bernadin de 1737–1814. French author of the sentimental romance *Paul et Virginie* 1789.

Saint-Saëns /sæn ˈsɒns/ (Charles) Camille 1835–1921. French composer, pianist and organist. Among his many lyrical Romantic pieces are concertos, the symphonic poem *Danse macabre* 1875, the opera *Samson et Dalila* 1877, and the orchestral *Carnaval des animaux/Carnival of the Animals* 1886.

Saint-Simon /ˌsænsiˈmɒn/ Claude Henri, Comte de 1760–1825. French socialist who fought in the American Revolution and was imprisoned during the French Revolution. He advocated an atheist society ruled by technicians and industrialists in *Du Système industrielle/The Industrial System* 1821.

Saint-Simon /ˌsænsiˈmɒn/ Louis de Rouvroy, Duc de 1675–1755. French soldier, courtier, and politician whose *Mémoires* 1691–1723 are unrivalled as a description of the French court.

Sakharov /ˈsækərɒv/ Andrei Dmitrievich 1921–1989. Soviet physicist, known both as the 'father of the Soviet H- bomb' and as an outspoken human-rights campaigner. In 1948 he joined Igor Tamm in developing the hydrogen bomb; he later protested against Soviet nuclear tests and was a founder of the Soviet Human Rights Committee, winning the Nobel Peace Prize 1975. In 1980 he was sent to internal exile in Gorky (now Nizhni-Novgorod) for criticizing Soviet action in Afghanistan. At the end of 1986 he was allowed to return to Moscow and resume his place in the Soviet Academy of Sciences.

He was elected to the Congress of the USSR People's Deputies (CUPD) 1989, where he emerged as leader of its radical reform grouping prior to his death later the same year.

Saki /ˈsɑːki/ pen name of H(ugh) H(ector) Munro 1870–1916. Burmese-born British writer of ingeniously witty and bizarre short stories, often with surprise endings. He also wrote two novels, *The Unbearable Bassington* 1912 and *When William Came* 1913.

Śākyamuni /ʃɑːkjəˈmʊni/ the historical →Buddha, called *Shaka* in Japan (because Gautama was of the Śakya clan).

Saladin /ˈsælədɪn/ or *Sala-ud-din* 1138–1193. Born a Kurd, sultan of Egypt from 1175, in succession to the Atabeg of Mosul, on whose behalf he conquered Egypt 1164–74. He subsequently conquered Syria 1174–87 and precipitated the third Crusade by his recovery of Jerusalem from the Christians 1187. Renowned for knightly courtesy, Saladin made peace with Richard I of England 1192.

Salam /səˈlɑːm/ Abdus 1926– . Pakistani physicist. In 1967 he proposed a theory linking the electromagnetic and weak nuclear forces, also arrived at independently by Steven Weinberg. In 1979 he was the first person from his country to receive a Nobel prize, which he shared with Weinberg and Sheldon Glashow.

Abdus Salam became a scientist by accident, when he won a scholarship to Cambridge in 1945 from the Punjab Small Peasants' welfare fund; he had intended to join the Indian civil service. He subsequently worked on the structure of matter at the Cavendish Laboratory.

Salazar /ˌsæləˈzɑː/ Antonio de Oliveira 1889–1970. Portuguese prime minister 1932–68 who exercised a virtual dictatorship. During World War II he maintained Portuguese neutrality but fought long colonial wars in Africa (Angola and Mozambique) that impeded his country's economic development as well as that of the colonies.

A corporative constitution on the Italian model was introduced 1933, and until 1945 Salazar's National Union, founded 1930, remained the only legal party. Salazar was also foreign minister 1936–47.

Salieri /ˌsæliˈeəri/ Antonio 1750–1825. Italian composer. He taught Beethoven, Schubert, and Liszt, and was the musical rival of Mozart, whom it has been suggested, without proof, that he poisoned, at the emperor's court in Vienna, where he held the position of court composer.

Salinas de Gortiari /səˈliːnəs də ˌgɔːtiˈɑːri/ Carlos 1948– . Mexican politician, president from 1988, a member of the dominant Institutional Revolutionary Party (PRI).

Educated in Mexico and the USA, he taught at Harvard and in Mexico before joining the government in 1971 and thereafter held a number of posts, mostly in the economic sphere, including finance minister. He narrowly won the 1988 presidential election, despite allegations of fraud.

Salinger /ˈsælɪndʒə/ J(erome) D(avid) 1919– . US writer, author of the classic novel of mid-20th-century adolescence *The Catcher in the Rye* 1951. He also wrote short stories about a Jewish family named Glass, including *Franny and Zooey* 1961.

Salisbury /ˈsɔːlzbəri/ Robert Cecil, 1st Earl of Salisbury. Title conferred on Robert →Cecil, secretary of state to Elizabeth I of England.

Salisbury /ˈsɔːlzbəri/ Robert Arthur Talbot Gascoyne-Cecil, 3rd Marquess of Salisbury 1830–1903. British Conservative politician. He entered the Commons 1853 and succeeded to his title 1868. As foreign secretary 1878–80, he took part in the Congress of Berlin, and as prime minister 1885–86, 1886–92, and 1895–1902 gave his main attention to foreign policy, remaining also as foreign secretary for most of this time.

No lesson seems to be so deeply inculcated by the experience of life as that you should never trust experts.

3rd Marquess of Salisbury

Salisbury /ˈsɔːlzbəri/ Robert Arthur James Gascoyne-Cecil, 5th Marquess of Salisbury 1893–1972. British Conservative politician. He was Dominions secretary 1940–42 and 1943–45, colonial secretary 1942, Lord Privy Seal 1942–43 and 1951–52, and Lord President of the Council 1952–57.

Salk /sɔːlk/ Jonas Edward 1914– . US physician and microbiologist. In 1954 he developed the original vaccine that led to virtual eradication of paralytic polio in industrialized countries. He was director of the Salk Institute for Biological Studies, University of California, San Diego, 1963–75.

Sallinen /ˈsælɪnen/ Tyko 1879–1955. Finnish Expressionist painter. Inspired by Fauvism on visits to France 1909 and 1914, he created visionary works relating partly to his childhood experiences of religion. He also painted Finnish landscape and peasant life, such as *Washerwoman* 1911 (Ateneum, Helsinki).

Sallust /ˈsæləst/ Gaius Sallustius Crispus 86–c. 34 BC. Roman historian, a supporter of Julius Caesar. He wrote accounts of Catiline's conspiracy and the Jugurthine War in an epigrammatic style.

and moved to New York, where he cofounded the International Composers' Guild. He did much to promote the harp as a concert instrument, and invented many unusual sounds.

Samson /ˈsæmsən/ 11th century BC. In the Old Testament, a hero of Israel. He was renowned for exploits of strength against the Philistines, which ended when his lover Delilah cut off his hair, the source of his strength, as told in the Book of Judges.

Samuel /ˈsæmjuəl/ 11th–10th centuries BC. In the Old Testament, the last of the judges who ruled the ancient Hebrews before their adoption of a monarchy, and the first of the prophets; the two books bearing his name cover the story of Samuel and the reigns of kings Saul and David.

Samuelson /ˈsæmjuəlsən/ Paul 1915– . US economist. He became professor at the Massachusetts Institute of Technology 1940 and was awarded a Nobel prize 1970 for his application of scientific analysis to economic theory. His books include *Economics* 1948, a classic textbook, and *Linear Programming and Economic Analysis* 1958.

Sanctorius /sæŋkˈtɔːriəs/ Sanctorius 1561–1636. Italian physiologist who pioneered the study of metabolism and invented the clinical thermometer and a device for measuring pulse rate.

Sanctorius introduced quantitative methods into medicine. For 30 years he weighed both himself and his food, drink, and waste products. He determined that over half of normal weight loss is due to 'insensible perspiration'.

Sand /sɒnd/ George. Pen name of Amandine Aurore Lucie Dupin 1804–1876. French author whose prolific literary output was often autobiographical. In 1831 she left her husband after nine years of marriage and, while living in Paris as a writer, had love affairs with Alfred de →Musset, →Chopin, and others. Her first novel *Indiana* 1832 was a plea for women's right to independence.

Her other novels include *La mare au diable/The Devil's Pool* 1846 and *La petite Fadette/The Little Fairy* 1848. In 1848 she retired to the château of Nohant, in central France.

Sandburg /ˈsændbɜːg/ Carl August 1878–1967. US poet. He worked as a farm labourer and a bricklayer, and his poetry celebrates ordinary life in the USA, as in *Chicago Poems* 1916, *The People, Yes* 1936, and *Complete Poems* 1951 (Pulitzer prize). In free verse, it is reminiscent of Walt Whitman's poetry. Sandburg also wrote a monumental biography of Abraham Lincoln, *Abraham Lincoln: The Prairie Years* 1926 (two volumes) and *Abraham Lincoln: The War Years* 1939 (four volumes; Pulitzer Prize). *Always the Young Strangers* 1953 is his autobiography.

Sandby /ˈsændbi/ Paul 1725–1809. English painter, often called 'the father of English watercolour'. He specialized in Classical landscapes,

Salonen Finnish conductor, Esa-Pekka Salonen, a champion of contemporary music, notably the Polish composer Lutoslawski.

Salome /səˈləʊmɪ/ 1st century AD. In the New Testament, granddaughter of the king of Judea, Herod the Great. Rewarded for her skill in dancing, she requested the head of John the Baptist from her stepfather →Herod Antipas.

Salomon /ˈsæləmən/ Haym c. 1740–1785. Polish-born American financier. A supporter of American independence, he supplied provisions to the Continental troops during the American Revolution 1861–65. Accused of being a spy by the British 1776, he was briefly arrested and was captured and sentenced to death 1778. After escaping, he raised large public subscriptions for the continuance of the war.

Born in Poland, Salomon travelled extensively throughout Europe before settling permanently in New York 1772 where he became a successful merchant.

Salonen Esa-Pekka 1958– . Finnish conductor and composer. He studied French horn, and made his UK conducting debut in 1983 as a short-notice replacement for Michael Tilson Thomas, leading to further engagements with the London Philharmonia Orchestra. Appointed chief conductor of the Swedish Radio Symphony Orchestra 1985, he became music director of the Los Angeles Philharmonic Orchestra in 1992.

Salonen made the first recording of Lutoslawski's Symphony No. 3 1986. His hard-edged, relentless style has been compared to that of Pierre →Boulez. His compositions include *Horn Music I* 1976 and *Concerto for Saxophone and Orchestra* 1980.

Salzedo /sælˈzeɪdəʊ/ Carlos 1885–1961. French-born harpist and composer. He studied in Paris using both watercolour and gouache, and introduced the technique of aquatint to England.

Sanders /ˈsɑːndəz/ George 1906–1972. Russian-born British actor, usually cast as a smooth-talking cad. Most of his film career was spent in the USA where he starred in such films as *Rebecca* 1940, *The Moon and Sixpence* 1942, and *The Picture of Dorian Gray* 1944.

Sandwich /ˈsænwɪtʃ/ John Montagu, 4th Earl of Sandwich 1718–1792. British politician. He was an inept First Lord of the Admiralty 1771–82 during the American Revolution, and his corrupt practices were blamed for the British navy's inadequacies.

The Sandwich Islands (Hawaii) were named after him, as are sandwiches, which he invented so that he could eat without leaving the gaming table.

Sandys /sændz/ Duncan Edwin Sandys, Baron Duncan-Sandys 1908–1987. British Conservative politician. As minister for Commonwealth relations 1960–64, he negotiated the independence of Malaysia 1963. He was created a life peer in 1974.

Sanger /ˈsæŋə/ Frederick 1918– . English biochemist, the first person to win a Nobel Prize for Chemistry twice: the first in 1958 for determining the structure of insulin, and the second in 1980 for work on the chemical structure of genes.

Sanger worked throughout his life at Cambridge University. His second Nobel prize was shared with two US scientists, Paul Berg and Walter Gilbert, for establishing methods of determining the sequence of nucleotides strung together along strands of DNA.

Sanger /ˈsæŋə/ Margaret Higgins 1883–1966. US health reformer and crusader for birth control. In 1914 she founded the National Birth Control League. She founded and presided over the American Birth Control League 1921–28, the organization that later became the Planned Parenthood Federation of America, and the International Planned Parenthood Federation 1952.

Born in Corning, New York, USA, Sanger received nursing degrees from White Plains Hospital and the Manhattan Eye and Ear Clinic. As a nurse, she saw the deaths and deformity caused by self-induced abortions and became committed to providing health and birth-control education to the poor. In 1917 she was briefly sent to prison for opening a public birth-control clinic in Brooklyn 1916.

Her *Autobiography* appeared 1938.

San Martin /sæn mɑːˈtiːn/ José de 1778–1850. South American revolutionary leader. He served in the Spanish army during the Peninsular War, but after 1812 he devoted himself to the South American struggle for independence, playing a large part in the liberation of Argentina, Chile, and Peru from Spanish rule.

Santa Anna /ˈsæntə ˈænə/ Antonio López de 1795–1876. Mexican revolutionary who became general and dictator of Mexico for most of the years between 1824 and 1855. He led the attack on the Alamo fort in Texas 1836.

A leader in achieving independence from Spain in 1821, he pursued a chequered career of victory and defeat and was in and out of office as president or dictator for the rest of his life.

Santayana /ˌsæntiˈænə/ George 1863–1952. Spanish-born US philosopher and critic. He developed his philosophy based on naturalism and taught that everything has a natural basis.

Born in Madrid, Santayana grew up in Spain and the USA and graduated from Harvard University. He taught at Harvard 1889–1912. His books include *The Life of Reason* 1905–06, *Skepticism and Animal Faith* 1923, *The Realm of Truth* 1937, *Background of My Life* 1945; volumes of poetry; and the best-selling novel *The Last Puritan* 1935.

Those who cannot remember the past are condemned to repeat it.

George Santayana,
The Life of Reason 1905–06

Sant'Elia /sænˈtelia/ Antonio 1888–1916. Italian architect. His drawings convey a Futurist vision of a metropolis with skyscrapers, traffic lanes, and streamlined factories.

Sānusī /səˈnuːsi/ Sidi Muhammad ibn 'Ali as-*c*. 1787–1859. Algerian-born Muslim religious reformer. He preached a return to the puritanism of early Islam and met with much success in Libya, where he founded the sect named after him.

He made Jaghbub his centre.

San Yu /ˌsænˈjuː/ 1919– . Myanmar (Burmese) politician. A member of the Revolutionary Council that came to power 1962, he became president 1981 and was re-elected 1985. He was forced to resign July 1988, along with Ne Win, after riots in Yangon (formerly Rangoon).

Sapir /səˈpɪə/ Edward 1881–1939. German-born US language scholar and anthropologist who initially studied the Germanic languages but later, under the influence of Franz Boas, investigated native American languages. He is noted for the view now known as *linguistic relativity*: that people's ways of thinking are significantly shaped (and even limited) by the language(s) they use. His main work is *Language: An Introduction to the Study of Speech* 1921.

Sappho /ˈsæfəʊ/ *c*. 612–580 BC. Greek lyric poet, friend of the poet →Alcaeus and leader of a female literary coterie at Mytilene (now **Lesvos**, hence lesbianism). Legend says she committed suicide when her love for the boatman Phaon was unrequited. Only fragments of her poems have survived.

Sardou /sɑːˈduː/ Victorien 1831–1908. French dramatist. He wrote plays with roles for Sarah Bernhardt and Henry Irving; for example, *Fédora* 1882, *La Tosca* 1887 (the basis for the opera by Puccini), and *Madame Sans-Gêne* 1893. George Bernard →Shaw coined the expression 'Sardoodledom' to express his disgust with the contrivances of the 'well-made' play – a genre of which Sardou was the leading exponent.

Sarenzen Gene 1902– . US golfer. He won the first of his two US open titles in 1922 at the age of 20 and a couple of months later added the US PGA title, which he retained the following year. He won the British Open in 1932 and the Masters in 1935, when he became the first person to complete a 'set' of major titles.

Sargent /sɑːˈdʒənt/ (Harold) Malcolm (Watts) 1895–1967. British conductor. From 1923 he was professor at the Royal College of Music, was chief conductor of the BBC Symphony Orchestra 1950–57, and continued as conductor in chief of the annual Henry Wood promenade concerts at the Royal Albert Hall.

Sargent /sɑːˈdʒənt/ John Singer 1856–1925. US portrait painter. Born in Florence of American parents, he studied there and in Paris, then settled in London around 1885. He was a fashionable and prolific painter.

Sargent left Paris after a scandal concerning his décolleté portrait *Madame Gautreau* 1884. Later subjects included the actress Ellen Terry, President Theodore Roosevelt, and the writer Robert Louis Stevenson. He also painted watercolour landscapes and murals.

Sargeson /sɑːˈdʒsən/ Frank 1903–1982. New Zealand writer of short stories and novels including *The Hangover* 1967 and *Man of England Now* 1972.

Sargon /sɑːˈɡɒn/ two Mesopotamian kings:

Sargon II died 705 BC. King of Assyria from 722 BC, who assumed the name of his predecessor. To keep conquered peoples from rising against him, he had whole populations moved from their homelands, including the Israelites from Samaria.

Sarney (Costa) /sɑːˈneɪ/ José 1930– . Brazilian politician, member of the centre-left Democratic Movement (PMDB), president 1985–90.

Sarney was elected vice president 1985 and within months, on the death of President Neves, became head of state. Despite earlier involvement with the repressive military regime, he and his party won a convincing victory in the 1986 general election. In Dec 1989, Ferdinando Collor de Mello of the Party for National Reconstruction was elected to succeed Sarney in March 1990.

Sarnoff /sɑːˈnɒf/ David 1891–1971. Russian-born US broadcasting pioneer, head of the Radio Corporation of America (RCA) from 1930. A telegraph operator for Marconi Wireless from 1906, he became commercial manager of the company when it was taken over by RCA 1919. Named RCA president 1930 and board chair 1947, Sarnoff was an early promoter of TV broadcasting during the 1940s and the first to manufacture colour sets and transmit colour programmes in the 1950s.

Saroyan /səˈrɔɪən/ William 1908–1981. US author. He wrote short stories, such as 'The Daring Young Man on the Flying Trapeze' 1934, idealizing the hopes and sentiments of the 'little man'. His plays include *The Time of Your Life* (Pulitzer prize; refused) 1939, about eccentricity; *My Heart's in the Highlands* 1939; and *Talking to You* 1962.

Sarraute /sæˈrəʊt/ Nathalie 1920– . Russian-born French novelist whose books include *Portrait d'un inconnu/Portrait of a Man Unknown* 1948, *Les Fruits d'or/The Golden Fruits* 1964, and *Vous les entendez?/Do You Hear Them?* 1972. An exponent of the *nouveau roman*, Sarraute bypasses plot, character, and style for the half-conscious interaction of minds.

Three o'clock is always too late or too early for anything you want to do.

Jean-Paul Sartre *Nausea*

Sartre /sɑːtrə/ Jean-Paul 1905–1980. French author and philosopher, a leading proponent of existentialism (the concept of an absurd universe where humans have free will). He published his first novel, *La Nausée/Nausea*, 1937, followed by the trilogy *Les Chemins de la Liberté/Roads to Freedom* 1944–45 and many plays, including *Huis Clos/In Camera* 1944. *L'Etre et le néant/Being and Nothingness* 1943, his first major philosophical work, sets out a radical doctrine of human freedom. In the later work *Critique de la raison dialectique/Critique of Dialectical Reason* 1960 he tried to produce a fusion of existentialism and Marxism.

Sartre was born in Paris, and was the long-time companion of the feminist writer Simone de Beauvoir. During World War II he was a prisoner for nine months, and on his return from Germany joined the Resistance. As a founder of existentialism, he edited its journal *Les Temps modernes/Modern Times*, and expressed its tenets in his novels and plays. According to Sartre, people's awareness of their own freedom takes the form of anxiety, and they therefore attempt to flee from this awareness into what he terms *mauvaise foi* ('bad faith'); this is the theory he put forward in *L'Etre et le néant/Being and Nothingness*. In *Crime passionel/Crime of Passion* 1948 he attacked aspects of communism while remaining generally sympathetic. In his later work Sartre became more sensitive to the social constraints on people's actions. He refused the Nobel Prize for Literature 1964 for 'personal reasons', but allegedly changed his mind later, saying he wanted it for the money.

Sassau-Nguesso /ˌsæsaʊŋˈgesəʊ/ Denis 1943– . Congolese socialist politician, president 1979–92. He progressively consolidated his position within the ruling left-wing Congolese Labour Party (PCT), at the same time as improving relations with France and the USA. In 1990, in response to public pressure, he agreed that the PCT should abandon Marxism-Leninism and that a multiparty system should be introduced.

Sassoon /səˈsuːn/ Siegfried 1886–1967. English writer, author of the autobiography *Memoirs of a Foxhunting Man* 1928. His *War Poems* 1919 express the disillusionment of his generation.

Educated at Cambridge, Sassoon enlisted in the army 1915, serving in France and Palestine. He published many volumes of poetry and three volumes of childhood autobiography, *The Old Century and Seven More Years* 1938, *The Weald of Youth* 1942, and *Siegfried's Journey* 1945. He wrote a biography of the novelist George Meredith 1948 and published *Collected Poems* in 1961.

Soldiers are dreamers; when the guns begin
They think of firelit homes, clean beds, and wives.

Siegfried Sassoon 'Dreamers' 1918

Sassoon /səˈsuːn/ Vidal 1929– . British hairdresser patronized by pop stars and models from the early 1950s. He created many new hairstyles, including the Shape 1959, a layered cut tailored to the bone structure – a radical change from the beehive hairstyles of the 1950s. He stopped cutting in 1974.

Satie /sæˈtiː/ Erik (Alfred Leslie) 1866–1925. French composer. His piano pieces, such as *Gymnopédies* 1888, often combine wit and melancholy. His orchestral works include *Parade* 1917, among whose sound effects is a typewriter. He was the mentor of the group of composers known as *Les Six*.

Before I compose a piece, I walk round it several times, accompanied by myself.

Erik Satie

Satō /ˈsɑːtəʊ/ Eisaku 1901–1975. Japanese conservative politician, prime minister 1964–72. He ran against Hayato Ikeda (1899–1965) for the Liberal Democratic Party leadership and succeeded him as prime minister, pledged to a more independent foreign policy. He shared a Nobel Prize for Peace in 1974 for his rejection of nuclear weapons. His brother *Nobosuke Kishi* (1896–1987) was prime minister of Japan 1957–60.

Saul /sɔːl/ in the Old Testament, the first king of Israel. He was anointed by Samuel and warred successfully against the neighbouring Ammonites and Philistines, but fell from God's favour in his battle against the Amalekites. He became jealous and suspicious of David and turned against him and Samuel. After being wounded in battle with the Philistines, in which his three sons died, he committed suicide.

Saunders /ˈsɔːndəz/ Cicely 1918– . English philanthropist, founder of the hospice movement, which aims to provide a caring and comfortable environment in which people with terminal illnesses can die.

She was the medical director of St Christopher's Hospice in Sydenham, S London, 1967–85, and later became its chair. She wrote *Care of the Dying* 1960.

Saunders /ˈsɔːndəz/ Clarence 1881–1953. US retailer who opened the first self-service supermarket, Piggly-Wiggly, in Memphis, Tennessee, 1919.

Saussure /səʊˈsjʊə/ Ferdinand de 1857–1913. Swiss language scholar, a pioneer of modern linguistics and the originator of the concept of structuralism as used in linguistics, anthropology, and literary theory.

He taught at the universities of Paris and Geneva. His early work, on the Indo-European language family, led to a major treatise on its vowel system. He is best known for *Cours de linguistique générale/Course in General Linguistics* 1916, a posthumous work derived mainly from his lecture notes by his students Charles Bally and Albert Séchehaye. Saussurean concepts include: (1) language seen as both a unified and shared social system (*langue*) and as individual and idiosyncratic speech (*parole*); (2) language described in **synchronic** terms (as a system at a particular time) and in **diachronic** terms (as changing through time).

Saussure /də səʊˈsjʊə/ Horace de 1740–1799. Swiss geologist who made the earliest detailed and first-hand study of the Alps. He was a physicist at the University of Geneva. The results of his Alpine survey appeared in his classic work *Voyages des Alpes/Travels in the Alps* 1779–86.

Savage /ˈsævɪdʒ/ Michael Joseph 1872–1940. New Zealand Labour politician. As prime minister 1935–40, he introduced much social-security legislation.

Savery /ˈseɪvəri/ Thomas *c.* 1650–1715. British engineer who invented the steam-driven water pump, precursor of the steam engine, 1696.

The pump used a boiler to raise steam, which was condensed (in a separate condenser) by an external spray of cold water. The partial vacuum created sucked water up a pipe from the mine shaft; steam pressure was then used to force the water away, after which the cycle was repeated. Savery patented his invention 1698.

Savimbi /səvɪmbi/ Jonas 1934– . Angolan soldier and right-wing revolutionary, founder and leader of the National Union for the Total Independence of Angola (UNITA). From 1975 UNITA under Savimbi's leadership tried to overthrow the government. An agreement between the two parties was reached May 1991, but fighting broke out again following elections Sept 1992.

The struggle for independence from Portugal escalated 1961 into a civil war. In 1966 Savimbi founded the right-wing UNITA, which he led against the left-wing People's Movement for the Liberation of Angola (MPLA), led by Agostinho Neto. Neto, with Soviet and Cuban support, became president when independence was achieved 1975, while UNITA, assisted by South Africa, continued its fight. A cease-fire was agreed June 1989, but fighting continued, and the truce was abandoned after two months. A truce was finally signed May 1991. Civil violence between government and UNITA supporters re-erupted Sept 1992 following an election victory for the ruling party, a result which Savimbi disputed.

Savonarola /ˌsævənəˈrəʊlə/ Girolamo 1452–1498. Italian reformer, a Dominican friar and an eloquent preacher. His crusade against political and religious corruption won him popular support, and in 1494 he led a revolt in Florence that expelled the ruling Medici family and established a democratic republic. His denunciations of Pope →Alexander VI led to his excommunication in 1497, and in 1498 he was arrested, tortured, hanged, and burned for heresy.

Sawchuk /ˈsɔːtʃʌk/ Terry (Terrance Gordon) 1929–1970. Canadian ice-hockey player, often considered the greatest goaltender of all time. He played for Detroit, Boston, Toronto, Los Angeles, and New York Rangers 1950–67, and holds the National Hockey League (NHL) record of 103 shut-outs (games in which he did not concede a goal).

Saw Maung 1929– . Myanmar (Burmese) soldier and politician. Appointed head of the armed forces in 1985 by →Ne Win, he led a coup to remove Ne Win's successor, Maung Maung, in 1988 and became leader of a totalitarian 'emergency government', which remained in office despite being defeated in the May 1990 election. In April 1992 he was replaced as chair of the ruling military junta, prime minister, and commander of the armed forces by Than Shwe.

Saxe /sæks/ Maurice, Comte de 1696–1750. Soldier, illegitimate son of the Elector of Saxony, who served under Prince Eugène of Savoy and was created marshal of France in 1743 for his exploits in the War of the Austrian Succession.

Saxe-Coburg-Gotha /sæks ˈkəʊbɜːɡ ˈɡəʊtə/ Saxon duchy. Albert, the Prince Consort of Britain's Queen Victoria, was a son of the 1st Duke, Ernest I (1784–1844), who was succeeded by Albert's elder brother, Ernest II (1818–1893). It remained the name of the British royal house until 1917, when it was changed to Windsor.

Sayers /ˈseɪəz/ Dorothy L(eigh) 1893–1957. English writer of crime novels featuring detective Lord Peter Wimsey and heroine Harriet Vane, including *Strong Poison* 1930, *The Nine Tailors* 1934, and *Gaudy Night* 1935. She also wrote religious plays for radio, and translations of Dante.

Scalia /skəˈliːə/ Antonin 1936– . US jurist and associate justice of the US Supreme Court 1986– . He concurred with the majority in *Texas* v *Johnson* 1989, that ruled constitutional the burning of the US flag in protest. He dissented in *Edwards* v *Aguillard* 1987 when the Court ruled that states may not mandate the teaching of the theory of creationism to counteract the teaching of the theory of evolution.

Born in Trenton, New Jersey, USA, Scalia graduated from Georgetown University and the Harvard University Law School. From 1971 he worked as a lawyer in the executive branch of the federal government, ultimately becoming assistant attorney general 1974, where he advised the Gerald Ford White House in the Watergate scandal. President Reagan appointed Scalia to the Supreme Court 1986.

He later became professor of law at the University of Chicago, where he was known for his support of economic deregulation and judicial restraint.

Scargill /ˈskɑːɡɪl/ Arthur 1938– . British trade-union leader. Elected president of the National Union of Miners (NUM) 1981, he embarked on a collision course with the Conservative government of Margaret Thatcher. The damaging strike of 1984–85 split the miners' movement.

Scargill became a miner on leaving school and was soon a union and political activist, in the Young Communist League 1955–62 and then a member of the Labour Party from 1966 and president of the Yorkshire miners' union 1973–81. He became a fiery and effective orator. During the 1984–85 miners' strike he was criticized for not seeking an early NUM ballot to support the strike decision. In 1990 an independent inquiry, commissioned by the NUM, found him guilty of breach of duty and maintaining double accounts during the strike.

Scarlatti /skɑːˈlætɪ/ (Giuseppe) Domenico 1685–1757. Italian composer, eldest son of Alessandro →Scarlatti, who lived most of his life in Portugal and Spain in the service of the Queen of Spain. He wrote highly original harpsichord sonatas.

Scarlatti /skɑːˈlætɪ/ (Pietro) Alessandro (Gaspare) 1660–1725. Italian Baroque composer, Master of the Chapel at the court of Naples, who developed the opera form. He composed more than 100 operas, including *Tigrane* 1715, as well as church music and oratorios.

early philosophy influenced →Hegel, but his later work criticizes Hegel, arguing that being necessarily precedes thought.

Scherchen /ˈʃeəʃən/ Hermann 1891–1966. German conductor. He collaborated with →Schoenberg, and in 1919 founded the journal *Melos* to promote contemporary music. He moved to Switzerland in 1933, and was active as a conductor and teacher. He wrote two texts, *Handbook of Conducting* and *The Nature of Music*. During the 1950s he founded a music publishing house, Ars Viva Verlag, and an electronic studio at Gravesano.

Schiaparelli /ˌskjæpəˈreli/ Elsa 1896–1973. Italian couturier and knitwear designer. Her innovative fashion ideas included padded shoulders, sophisticated colours ('shocking pink'), and the pioneering use of zips and synthetic fabrics.

Schiaparelli /ˌskjæpəˈreli/ Giovanni (Virginio) 1835–1910. Italian astronomer who discovered the so-called 'Martian canals'. He studied ancient and medieval astronomy, discovered the asteroid 69 (Hesperia) April 1861, observed double stars, and revealed the connection between comets and meteors. In 1877 he was the first to draw attention to the linear markings on Mars, which gave rise to the 'Martian canal' controversy. These markings are now known to be optical effects and not real lines.

Schiele /ˈʃiːlə/ Egon 1890–1918. Austrian Expressionist artist. Originally a landscape painter, he was strongly influenced by Art Nouveau and developed a contorted linear style. His subject matter included portraits and nudes. In 1911 he was arrested for alleged obscenity.

Schiller /ˈʃɪlə/ Johann Christoph Friedrich von 1759–1805. German dramatist, poet, and historian. He wrote *Sturm und Drang* ('storm and stress') verse and plays, including the dramatic trilogy *Wallenstein* 1798–99. Much of his work concerns the aspirations for political freedom and the avoidance of mediocrity.

He was a qualified surgeon, but after the success of the play *Die Räuber/The Robbers* 1781, he devoted himself to literature and completed his tragedies *Die Verschwörung des Fiesko zu Genua/Fiesco, or, the Genoese Conspiracy* and *Kabale und Liebe/Love and Intrigue* 1783. Moving to Weimar in 1787, he wrote his more mature blank-verse drama *Don Carlos* and the hymn 'An die Freude/Ode to Joy', later used by →Beethoven in his ninth symphony. As professor of history at Jena from 1789 he completed a history of the Thirty Years' War and developed a close friendship with →Goethe after early antagonism. His essays on aesthetics include the piece of literary criticism *Über naive und sentimentalische Dichtung/Naive and Sentimental Poetry*. Schiller became the foremost German dramatist with his classic dramas *Wallenstein*, *Maria Stuart* 1800, *Die Jungfrau von Orleans/The Maid of Orleans* 1801, and *Wilhelm Tell/William Tell* 1804.

Sayers English writer Dorothy L Sayers, author of tasteful and stylish mystery stories featuring the detective Lord Peter Wimsey. She earned a reputation as a leading Christian apologist with two successful plays, written for the Canterbury Festival, and her radio drama The Man Born to be King, first broadcast 1941–42.

Scarman /ˈskɑːmən/ Leslie, Lord Scarman 1911– . English judge and legal reformer. A successful barrister, he was a High Court judge 1961–73 and an appeal-court judge 1973–77, prior to becoming a law lord. He gradually shifted from a traditional position to a more reformist one, calling for liberalization of divorce laws 1965 and campaigning for a bill of rights 1974. As chair of the inquiry into the Brixton riots 1981, he proposed positive discrimination in favour of black people. He campaigned for the release of the wrongly convicted Birmingham Six and the Guildford Four.

Scheele /ˈʃeɪlə/ Karl Wilhelm 1742–1786. Swedish chemist and pharmacist. In the book *Experiments on Air and Fire* 1777, he argued that the atmosphere was composed of two gases. One, which supported combustion (oxygen), he called 'fire air', and the other, which inhibited combustion (nitrogen), he called 'vitiated air'. He thus anticipated Joseph →Priestley's discovery of oxygen by two years.

Scheer /ʃeə/ Reinhard 1863–1928. German admiral in World War I, commander of the High Sea Fleet in 1916 at the Battle of Jutland.

Schelling /ˈʃelɪŋ/ Friedrich Wilhelm Joseph 1775–1854. German philosopher who began as a follower of Fichte, but moved away from subjective idealism, which treats the external world as essentially immaterial, toward a 'philosophy of identity' (*Identitätsphilosophie*), in which subject and object are seen as united in the absolute. His

Schinkel /ˈʃɪŋkəl/ Karl Friedrich 1781–1841. Prussian Neo-Classical architect. Major works include the Old Museum, Berlin, 1823–30, the Nikolaikirche in Potsdam 1830–37, and the Roman Bath 1833 in the park of Potsdam.

Schlegel /ˈʃleɪɡəl/ August Wilhelm von 1767–1845. German Romantic author, translator of Shakespeare, whose *Über dramatische Kunst und Literatur/Lectures on Dramatic Art and Literature* 1809–11 broke down the formalism of the old classical criteria of literary composition. Friedrich von Schlegel was his brother.

Schlegel /ˈʃleɪɡəl/ Friedrich von 1772–1829. German critic who (with his brother August) was a founder of the Romantic movement, and a pioneer in the comparative study of languages.

Schlesinger /ˈʃleɪzɪŋə/ Arthur Meier, Jr 1917– . US historian. His first book, *The Age of Jackson*, won a Pulitzer Prize 1945. Becoming active in Democratic politics, he served as a speechwriter in the presidential campaigns of Adlai Stevenson 1956 and John Kennedy 1960.

Born in Columbus, Ohio, USA, the son of a prominent historian, Schlesinger was educated at Harvard University and served as an intelligence officer during World War II. He was presidential assistant for Latin American Affairs 1961–64 and in 1967 became a professor at the City College of New York.

Schlesinger /ˈʃlesɪndʒə/ John 1926– . English film and television director who was responsible for such British films as *Billy Liar* 1963 and *Darling* 1965. His first US film, *Midnight Cowboy* 1969, was a big commercial success and was followed by *Sunday, Bloody Sunday* 1971, *Marathon Man* 1976, and *Yanks* 1979.

Schliemann /ˈʃliːmən/ Heinrich 1822–1890. German archaeologist. He earned a fortune in business, retiring in 1863 to pursue his lifelong ambition to discover a historical basis for Homer's *Iliad*. In 1871 he began excavating at Hissarlik, Turkey, a site which yielded the ruins of nine consecutive cities and was indeed the site of Troy. His later excavations were at Mycenae 1874–76, where he discovered the ruins of the Mycenaean civilization.

Schluter /ˈsluːtə/ Poul Holmskov 1929– . Danish right-wing politician, leader of the Conservative People's Party (KF) from 1974 and prime minister from 1982–1993. Having joined the KF in his youth, he trained as a lawyer and then entered the Danish parliament (Folketing) in 1964. His centre-right coalition survived the 1990 election and was reconstituted, with Liberal support. He resigned in Jan 1993.

Schmidt /ʃmɪt/ Helmut 1918– . German socialist politician, member of the Social Democratic Party (SPD), chancellor of West Germany 1974–83. As chancellor, Schmidt introduced social reforms and continued Willy →Brandt's policy of Ostpolitik (reconciliation with the communist bloc). With the French president Giscard d'Estaing, he instigated annual world and European economic summits. He was a firm supporter of NATO and of the deployment of US nuclear missiles in West Germany during the early 1980s.

Schmidt was elected to the Bundestag (federal parliament) in 1953. He was interior minister 1961–65, defence minister 1969–72, and finance minister 1972–74. He became federal chancellor (prime minister) on Brandt's resignation in 1974. Re-elected 1980, he was defeated in the Bundestag in 1982 following the switch of allegiance by the SPD's coalition allies, the Free Democratic Party. Schmidt retired from federal politics at the general election of 1983, having encountered growing opposition from the SPD's left wing, who opposed his stance on military and economic issues.

Schmidt-Rottluff /ʃmɪt ˈrɒtlʊf/ Karl 1884–1974. German Expressionist painter and printmaker, a founding member of the movement Die Brücke in Dresden 1905, active in Berlin from 1911. Inspired by Vincent van Gogh and Fauvism, he developed a vigorous style of brushwork and a bold palette. He painted portraits and landscapes and produced numerous woodcuts and lithographs.

Schnabel /ˈʃnɑːbəl/ Artur 1882–1951. Austrian pianist, teacher, and composer. He taught music at the Berlin State Academy 1925–30, but settled in the USA in 1939, where he composed symphonies and piano works. He excelled at playing Beethoven and trained many pianists.

Schneider /ˈʃnaɪdə/ Romy. Stage name of Rosemarie Albach-Retty 1938–1982. Austrian film actress who starred in *Boccaccio '70* 1962, *Der Prozess/The Trial* 1963, and *Ludwig* 1972.

Schoenberg /ˈʃɜːnbɜːɡ/ Arnold (Franz Walter) 1874–1951. Austro-Hungarian composer, a US citizen from 1941. After Romantic early works such as *Verklärte Nacht/Transfigured Night* 1899 and the *Gurrelieder/Songs of Gurra* 1900–11, he experimented with atonality (absence of key), producing works such as *Pierrot Lunaire* 1912 for chamber ensemble and voice, before developing the 12-tone system of musical composition. This was further developed by his pupils Alban →Berg and Anton →Webern.

After World War I he wrote several Neo-Classical works for chamber ensembles. He taught at the Berlin State Academy 1925–33. Driven from Germany by the Nazis, he settled in the USA 1933, where he influenced music scoring for films. Later works include the opera *Moses und Aron* 1932–51.

Schopenhauer /ˈʃəʊpənˌhaʊə/ Arthur 1788–1860. German philosopher whose *The World as Will and Idea* 1818 expounded an atheistic and pessimistic world view: an irrational will is considered as the inner principle of the world, producing an ever-

Schreiner South African novelist and feminist Olive Schreiner. In her later work she expressed her passionate views in favour of women's rights, pacifism, and the Boer cause. The Story of an African Farm 1883 was first published in England under the pseudonym Ralph Iron.

frustrated cycle of desire, of which the only escape is aesthetic contemplation or absorption into nothingness.

This theory struck a responsive chord in the philosopher Nietzsche, the composer Wagner, the German novelist Thomas Mann, and the English writer Thomas Hardy.

Schreiner /ˈʃraɪnə/ Olive 1862–1920. South African novelist and supporter of women's rights. Her autobiographical *The Story of an African Farm* 1883 describes life on the South African veld.

Schrödinger /ˈʃrɜːdɪŋə/ Erwin 1887–1961. Austrian physicist who advanced the study of wave mechanics. Born in Vienna, he became senior professor at the Dublin Institute for Advanced Studies 1940. He shared (with Paul Dirac) a Nobel prize 1933.

Schubert /ˈʃuːbət/ Franz (Peter) 1797–1828. Austrian composer. His ten symphonies include the incomplete eighth in B minor (the 'Unfinished') and the 'Great' in C major. He wrote chamber and piano music, including the `Trout Quintet`, and over 600 lieder (songs) combining the Romantic expression of emotion with pure melody. They include the cycles *Die schöne Müllerin/ The Beautiful Maid of the Mill* 1823 and *Die Winterreise/ The Winter Journey* 1827.

Schulz /ʃʊlts/ Charles M(onroe) 1922– . US cartoonist who created the 'Peanuts' strip, syndi-

cated from 1950. His characters Snoopy, Charlie Brown, Lucy, and Linus have been merchandised worldwide and featured in a 1967 musical, *You're a Good Man, Charlie Brown*.

Schumacher /ˈʃuːmækə/ Fritz (Ernst Friedrich) 1911–1977. German economist who believed that the increasing size of institutions, coupled with unchecked economic growth, created a range of social and environmental problems. He argued his case in books like *Small is Beautiful* 1973, and tested it practically through establishing the Intermediate Technology Development Group.

Schuman /ˈʃuːmɒn/ Robert 1886–1963. French politician. He was prime minister 1947–48, and as foreign minister 1948–53 he proposed in May 1950 a common market for coal and steel (the *Schuman Plan*), which was established as the European Coal and Steel Community 1952, the basis of the European Community.

Schumann /ˈʃuːmən/ Clara (Josephine) (born Wieck) 1819–1896. German pianist. She married Robert →Schumann in 1840 (her father had been his piano teacher). During his life and after his death she was devoted to popularizing his work, appearing frequently in European concert halls.

Schumann /ˈʃuːmən/ Robert Alexander 1810–1856. German Romantic composer. His songs and short piano pieces show simplicity combined with an ability to portray mood and emotion. Among his compositions are four symphonies, a violin concerto, a piano concerto, sonatas, and song cycles, such as *Dichterliebe/Poet's Love* 1840. Mendelssohn championed many of his works.

Only when the form grows clear to you, will the spirit become so too.

Robert Alexander Schumann
'Advice for Young Musicians' 1848

Schumpeter Joseph A(lois) 1883–1950. US economist and sociologist. In *Capitalism, Socialism and Democracy* 1942 he contended that Western capitalism, impelled by its very success, was evolving into a form of socialism because firms would become increasingly large and their managements increasingly divorced from ownership, while social trends were undermining the traditional motives for entrepreneurial accumulation of wealth.

Schumpeter was born in Moravia, now the Czech Republic, and migrated to the USA 1932. He was deeply interested in mathematics, and he took part in the founding of the Econometric Society 1930. His writings established him as an authority on economic theory as well as the history of economic thought. Among other standard reference works, he wrote the *History of Economic Analysis* 1954, published posthumously.

Schurz /ʃʊəts, ʃɜːts/ Carl 1829–1906. German-born US editor and political leader. He held office in the US Senate 1869–75 and served as secretary of the interior under President Hayes 1877–81. He was editor of the *New York Evening Post* 1881–83. A harsh critic of government corruption, he was president of the National Civil Service Reform League 1892–901.

Born in Germany, Schurz emigrated to the USA 1852, studied law, and was admitted to the Wisconsin bar 1859. Named US minister to Spain 1861–62, he returned to see action as a staff officer in the American Civil War (1861–65). After working briefly as editor of the *Detroit Post* 1866, he moved to St Louis.

Schuschnigg /ʃʊʃnɪɡ/ Kurt von 1897–1977. Austrian chancellor 1934–38, in succession to →Dollfuss. He tried in vain to prevent Nazi annexation (*Anschluss*) but in Feb 1938 he was forced to accept a Nazi minister of the interior, and a month later Austria was occupied and annexed by Germany. He was imprisoned in Germany until 1945, when he went to the USA; he returned to Austria 1967.

Schütz /ʃʊts/ Heinrich 1585–1672. German composer, musical director to the Elector of Saxony from 1614. His works include *The Seven Last Words* about 1645, *Musicalische Exequien* 1636, and the *Deutsche Magnificat/German Magnificat* 1671.

Schuyler /skaɪlə/ Philip John 1733–1804. American public official. A member of the Continental Congress 1775–77, he was named general in command of the Department of New York at the outbreak of the American Revolution 1775. Replaced in 1777, he returned to the Continental Congress 1778–81. A supporter of the US Constitution, Schuyler became one of New York's first US senators 1789–91 and later served 1797–98.

Born in Albany, New York, Schuyler inherited extensive real estate holdings in the Mohawk Valley. After service in the French and Indian War 1754–63, he was elected to the provincial assembly 1768.

Schwarzenegger Arnold 1947– . Austrian-born US film actor, one of the biggest box-office attractions of the late 1980s and early 1990s. He starred in sword-and-sorcery films such as *Conan the Barbarian* 1982 and later graduated to large-budget action movies such as *Terminator* 1984, *Predator* 1987, and *Terminator II* 1991.

Schwarzenegger began his career as a bodybuilder and won numerous medals including the 1969 Mr Universe competition. He came to the attention of Hollywood in *Pumping Iron* 1977, a documentary about body-building. He was cast in a series of roles which made much of his physique and little of his character, thus overcoming fears over the apparent obstacle of his Austrian accent. The power of his onscreen personality soon enabled him to play a variety of roles, including a comic role in *Twins* 1989. His other films include *Raw Deal* 1986, *Total Recall* 1990, and *Kindergarten Cop* 1991.

Schwarzkopf /ʃwɔːtskɒpf/ (H) Norman (nicknamed 'Stormin' Norman') 1934– . US general who was supreme commander of the Allied forces in the Gulf War 1991. He planned and executed a blitzkrieg campaign, Desert Storm, sustaining remarkably few casualties in the liberation of Kuwait. He was a battalion commander in the Vietnam War and deputy commander of the 1983 US invasion of Grenada.

A graduate of the military academy at West Point, Schwarzkopf obtained a master's degree in guided-missile engineering. He became an infantryman and later a paratrooper, and did two tours of service in Vietnam. Maintaining the 28-member Arab-Western military coalition against Iraq 1991 extended his diplomatic skills, and his success in the Gulf War made him a popular hero in the USA. He retired from the army Aug 1991.

Schwarzkopf /ʃwaːtskɒpf/ Elisabeth 1915– . German soprano, known for her dramatic interpretation of operatic roles, such as Elvira in *Don Giovanni* and the Marschallin in *Der Rosenkavalier*, as well as songs.

Schweitzer /ʃvaɪtsə/ Albert 1875–1965. French Protestant theologian, organist, and missionary surgeon. He founded the hospital at Lambaréné in Gabon in 1913, giving organ recitals to support his work there. He wrote a life of Bach and *Von reimarus zu Wrede/The Quest for the Historical Jesus* 1906 and was awarded the Nobel Peace Prize in 1952 for his teaching of 'reverence for life'.

Schwinger /ʃwɪŋɡə/ Julian 1918– . US quantum physicist. His research concerned the behaviour of charged particles in electrical fields. This work, expressed entirely through mathematics, combines elements from quantum theory and relativity theory. Schwinger shared the Nobel Prize for Physics 1963 with Richard →Feynman and Sin-Itiro Tomonaga (1906–1979).

Described as the 'physicist in knee pants', he entered college in New York at the age of 15, transferred to Columbia University and graduated at 17. At the age of 29 he became Harvard University's youngest full professor.

Schwitters /ʃvɪtəz/ Kurt 1887–1948. German artist, a member of the Dada movement which was founded in a spirit of rebellion and disillusionment during World War I. He moved to Norway in 1937 and to England in 1940. From 1918 he developed a variation on collage, using discarded rubbish such as buttons and bus tickets to create pictures and structures.

He called these art works *Merz*, and produced a magazine of the same name from 1923. Later he created *Merzbau*, extensive constructions of wood and scrap, most of which were destroyed.

Sciascia /ʃæʃə/ Leonardo 1921–1989. Sicilian novelist who used the detective novel to explore the hidden workings of Sicilian life, as in *Il giorno della civetta/Mafia Vendetta* 1961.

Scipio Africanus Major /ˈskɪpiəʊ ˌæfrɪˈkɑːnəs ˈmeɪdʒə/ 237–c. 183 BC. Roman general. He defeated the Carthaginians in Spain 210–206, invaded Africa 204, and defeated Hannibal at Zama 202.

Scipio Africanus Minor /ˈskɪpiəʊ ˌæfrɪˈkɑːnəs ˈmaɪnə/ c. 185–129 BC. Roman general, the adopted grandson of Scipio Africanus Major, also known as *Scipio Aemilianus*. He destroyed Carthage 146, and subdued Spain 134. He was opposed to his brothers-in-law, the Gracchi (see →Gracchus), and his wife is thought to have taken part in his murder.

Scipio Publius Cornelius /ˈskɪpiəʊ/ died 211 BC. Roman general, father of Scipio Africanus Major. Elected consul 218, during the 2nd Punic War, he was defeated by Hannibal at Ticinus and killed by the Carthaginians in Spain.

Scofield /ˈskəʊfiːld/ Paul 1922– . English actor. His wide-ranging roles include the drunken priest in Graham Greene's *The Power and the Glory*, Harry in Harold Pinter's *The Homecoming*, and Salieri in Peter Shaffer's *Amadeus*. He appeared as Sir Thomas More in both stage and film versions of Robert Bolt's *A Man for All Seasons*.

Scorsese /skɔːˈseɪzi/ Martin 1942– . US director, screenwriter, and producer whose films concentrate on complex characterization and the themes of alienation and guilt. Drawing from his Italian-American Catholic background, his work often deals with sin and redemption, such as in his first major film, *Boxcar Bertha* 1972. His influential, passionate, and forceful movies includes *Mean Streets* 1973, *Taxi Driver* 1976, *Raging Bull* 1980, *The Last Temptation of Christ* 1988, *GoodFellas* 1990, and *Cape Fear* 1991.

Scorsese's other major films include *Alice Doesn't Live Here Anymore* 1974 (featuring his only lead female protagonist), the musical *New York New York* 1977, and *The King of Comedy* 1983.

Scott /skɒt/ (George) Gilbert 1811–1878. English architect. As the leading practical architect in the mid-19th-century Gothic revival in England, Scott was responsible for the building or restoration of many public buildings, including the Albert Memorial, the Foreign Office, and St Pancras Station, all in London.

Scott /skɒt/ Douglas 1913–1990. British industrial designer who produced a remarkable variety of classic designs, including the London Transport Routemaster bus, the red double-decker which has been in service since 1968; the Roma wash basin 1961, still being installed in houses and hotels around the world; and the Raeburn cooker. He set up Britain's first professional product-design course and Mexico's first design school.

Scott /skɒt/ George C(ampbell) 1927– . US actor who played mostly tough, authoritarian film roles. His work includes *Dr Strangelove* 1964, *Patton* 1970, *The Hospital* 1971, and *Firestarter* 1984.

Scott /skɒt/ Giles Gilbert 1880–1960. English architect, grandson of George Gilbert Scott. He designed Liverpool Anglican Cathedral, Cambridge University Library, and Waterloo Bridge, London, 1945. He supervised the rebuilding of the House of Commons after World War II.

Scott /skɒt/ Paul (Mark) 1920–1978. English novelist, author of *The Raj Quartet* consisting of *The Jewel in the Crown* 1966, *The Day of the Scorpion* 1968, *The Towers of Silence* 1972, and *A Division of the Spoils* 1975, dealing with the British Raj in India. Other novels include *Staying On* 1977.

Scott /skɒt/ Peter (Markham) 1909–1989. British naturalist, artist, and explorer, founder of the Wildfowl Trust at Slimbridge, Gloucestershire, England, and a founder of the World Wildlife Fund (now World Wide Fund for Nature).

Scott's paintings were usually either portraits or bird studies. He published many books on birds and an autobiography *The Eye of the Wind* 1961. He was the son of Antarctic explorer R F Scott.

Scott /skɒt/ Randolph. Stage name of Randolph Crane 1903–1987. US actor. He began his career in romantic films before becoming one of Hollywood's Western stars in the 1930s. His films include *Roberta* 1934, *Jesse James* 1939, and *Ride the High Country* 1962.

Scott /skɒt/ Ridley 1939– . English director and producer of some of the most visually spectacular and influential films of the 1980s and 1990s, such as *Alien* 1979, *Blade Runner* 1982, and *1492 – The Search for Paradise* 1992. Criticized for sacrificing storyline and character development in favour of ornate sets, Scott replied with *Thelma and Louise* 1991, a carefully wrought story of female bonding and adventure.

Having started as a set designer, Scott graduated to directing episodes of the television series *Z Cars* before leaving the BBC in 1967. He completed his first film *The Duellists* in 1977. Among his other films are *Legend* 1985, *Someone to Watch Over Me* 1987, and *Black Rain* 1989.

Scott /skɒt/ Robert Falcon (known as *Scott of the Antarctic*) 1868–1912. English explorer who commanded two Antarctic expeditions, 1901–04 and 1910–12. On 18 Jan 1912 he reached the South Pole, shortly after Norwegian Roald →Amundsen, but on the return journey he and his companions died in a blizzard only a few miles from their base camp. His journal was recovered and published in 1913.

Born at Devonport, he entered the navy in 1882. With Scott on the final expedition were Wilson, Laurence →Oates, Bowers, and Evans.

Scott /skɒt/ Walter 1771–1832. Scottish novelist and poet. His first works were translations of German ballads, followed by poems such as 'The Lady of the Lake' 1810 and 'Lord of the Isles' 1815. He gained a European reputation for his historical novels such as *Heart of Midlothian* 1818, *Ivanhoe* 1819, and *The Fair Maid of Perth* 1828. His last years were marked by frantic writing to pay off his debts, after the bankruptcy of his publishing company in 1826.

Born in Edinburgh, Scott was lamed for life following an early attack of poliomyelitis, and in 1797 he married Charlotte Charpentier or Carpenter, of French origin. His *Minstrelsy of the Scottish Border* appeared in 1802, and from then he combined the practice of literature with his legal profession. *The Lay of the Last Minstrel* 1805 was an immediate success, and so too were *Marmion* 1808, *The Lady of the Lake* 1810, *Rokeby* 1813, and *Lord of the Isles* 1815. Out of the proceeds he purchased and rebuilt the house of Abbotsford on the Tweed, but Byron had to some extent now captured the lead with a newer style of verse romance, and Scott turned to prose fiction. *Waverley* was issued in 1814, and gave its name to a long series of historical novels, including *Guy Mannering* 1815, *The Antiquary* 1816, *Old Mortality* 1816, *Rob Roy* 1817, *The Heart of Midlothian* 1818, and *The Bride of Lammermoor* 1819. *Ivanhoe* 1819 transferred the scene to England; *Kenilworth* 1821, *Peveril of the Peak* 1823, *The Talisman* 1825, and *The Fair Maid of Perth* 1828 followed.

In 1820 Scott was created a baronet, but in 1826 he was involved in financial ruin through the bankruptcy of Constable, his chief publisher, with whom fell Ballantyne & Co, the firm of printers and publishers in which Scott had been for many years a sleeping partner. Refusing to accept bankruptcy, he set himself to pay off the combined debts of £114,000. *Woodstock* 1826, a life of Napoleon, and *Tales of a Grandfather* 1827–30 are among the chief products of these last painful years. The last outstanding liabilities were cleared after his death on the security of copyrights. Continuous overwork ended in a nervous breakdown. He died at Abbotsford on 21 Sept 1832. His *Journal* was issued in 1890, and his life by J G Lockhart, his son-in-law, in 1837.

Scott /skɒt/ Winfield 1786–1866. US military leader. During the Mexican War 1846–48 he led the capture of Veracruz and Mexico City. An unsuccessful Whig candidate for president 1852, Scott was still head of the army at the outbreak of the American Civil War 1861 but retired from active service in the same year.

Born in Petersburg, Virginia, Scott attended the College of William and Mary and began his military career 1807. As a colonel in the Anglo-American War 1812–14, he won distinction at the battles of Chippewa and Lundy's Lane.

Promoted to brigadier general, he saw action in the Black Hawk War 1832 and Seminole Wars 1835–37. In 1841 he became general in chief of the army.

Scribe /skriːb/ Augustin Eugène 1791–1861. French dramatist. He achieved recognition with *Une Nuit de la garde nationale/Night of the National Guard* 1815, and with numerous assistants produced many plays of technical merit but little profundity, including *Bertrand et Raton/The School for Politicians* 1833.

Scripps /skrɪps/ James Edmund 1835–1906. US newspaper publisher who established the *Detroit Evening News* 1873, and with his younger brother Edward (1854–1926) created the first US national newspaper chain 1880 with the *St Louis Evening Chronicle* and the *Cincinnati Post*.

Born in London, England, Scripps began his newspaper career in Chicago 1857. He later moved to Michigan and became part owner of the *Detroit Daily Advertiser* in the early 1860s. Together with his brother he founded the *Cleveland Press* 1878. He was also active in Republican politics.

Scruton /skruːtn/ Roger (Vernon) 1944– . British philosopher and right-wing social critic, professor of aesthetics at Birkbeck College, London, from 1985. Advocating the political theories of Edmund ➔Burke in such books as *The Meaning of Conservatism* 1980, he influenced the free-market movements in E Europe.

Scudamore /skjuːdəmɔː/ Peter 1958– . British National Hunt jockey who was champion jockey 1982 (shared with John Francome) and from 1986 to 1991 inclusive. In 1988–89 he rode a record 221 winners, and after the 1990–91 season his total of winners stood at a world record 1,374.

He has won over 30% of his races.

Scullin /skʌlɪn/ James Henry 1876–1953. Australian Labor politician. He was leader of the Federal Parliamentary Labor Party 1928–35, and prime minister and minister of industry 1929–31.

Seaborg /siːbɔːg/ Glenn Theodore 1912– . US nuclear chemist. He was awarded a Nobel prize in 1951 for his discoveries of transuranic elements (with atomic numbers greater than that of uranium), and for production of the radio-isotope uranium-233.

Searle /sɜːl/ Ronald 1920– . British cartoonist and illustrator, who created the schoolgirls of St Trinian's in 1941 and has made numerous cartoons of cats. His drawings, made as a Japanese prisoner of war during World War II, established him as a serious artist. His sketches of places and people include *Paris Sketch Book* 1950 and *Rake's Progress* 1955.

Sebastiano del Piombo /sɪˌbæstiˈɑːnəʊ del piˈɒmbəʊ/ *c.* 1485–1547. Italian painter, born in Venice, one of the great painters of the High Renaissance. Sebastiano was a pupil of ➔Giorgione and developed a similar style of painting. In 1511 he moved to Rome, where his friendship with Michelangelo (and rivalry with Raphael) inspired him to his greatest works, such as *The Raising of Lazarus* 1517–19 (National Gallery, London). He also painted powerful portraits.

Sebastian, St /sɪˈbæstiən/ Roman soldier, traditionally a member of Emperor Diocletian's bodyguard until his Christian faith was discovered. He was martyred by being shot with arrows. Feast day 20 Jan.

Secchi /ˈseki/ Pietro Angelo 1818–1878. Italian astronomer and astrophysicist, who classified stellar spectra into four classes based on their colour and spectral characteristics. He was the first to classify solar prominences, huge jets of gas projecting from the Sun's surface.

Seddon /ˈsedn/ Richard John 1845–1906. New Zealand Liberal politician, prime minister 1893–1906.

Seeger /ˈsiːɡə/ Pete 1919– . US folk singer and songwriter of antiwar protest songs, such as 'Where Have All The Flowers Gone?' 1956 and 'If I Had A Hammer' 1949.

Seeger was active in left-wing politics from the late 1930s and was a victim of the witch-hunt of Senator Joe ➔McCarthy in the 1950s. As a member of the vocal group *the Weavers* 1948–58, he popularized songs of diverse ethnic origin and had several hits.

Seferis /səˈfeəris/ George. Assumed name of Georgios Seferiades 1900–1971. Greek poet and diplomat. Ambassador to Lebanon 1953–57 and to the UK 1957–62, when he helped to resolve the Cyprus crisis. He published his first volume of lyrics 1931 and his *Collected Poems* 1950. Nobel prize 1963.

Segar /ˈsiːɡɑː/ Elzie Crisler 1894–1938. US cartoonist, creator of Popeye the sailor 1929. His characters appeared in comic strips and animated films.

Born in Chester, Illinois, Segar worked at odd jobs before being hired as a cartoonist for the *Chicago Herald* and working briefly as a reporter for the *Chicago Evening American*. In 1919 he moved to New York, where he published 'Thimble Theater,' a comic strip featuring the various members of the Oyl family, including Olive and Castor. In 1929 Segar unveiled his most popular character: Popeye, the feisty, squint-eyed sailor. He also created the hamburger-loving Wimpy and the adventurous baby Swee'pea.

Segovia /sɪˈɡəʊviə/ Andrés 1893–1987. Spanish virtuoso guitarist, for whom works were composed by Manuel de ➔Falla, Heitor ➔Villa-Lobos, and others.

Segrè /seˈɡreɪ/ Emilio 1905–1989. Italian physicist settled in the USA, who in 1955 discovered the antiproton, a new form of antimatter. He shared the 1959 Nobel Prize for Physics with

Selden English antiquarian, politician, and jurist James Selden helped to draw up the Petition of Right 1628. Although he did not approve of the execution of Charles I, he spoke out repeatedly against the power of the monarchy and in favour of the rights of Parliament.

Owen Chamberlain. Segrè had earlier discovered the first synthetic element, technetium (atomic number 43), in 1937.

Seifert /ˈsiːfət/ Jaroslav 1901–1986. Czech poet who won state prizes under the communists, but became an original member of the Charter 77 human-rights movement. His works include *Mozart in Prague* 1970 and *Umbrella from Piccadilly* 1978. Nobel prize 1984.

Selden /ˈseldən/ John 1584–1654. English antiquarian and opponent of Charles I's claim to the divine right of kings (the doctrine that the monarch is answerable to God alone), for which he was twice imprisoned. His *Table Talk* 1689 consists of short essays on political and religious questions.

Seles Monica 1973– . Yugoslavian lawn-tennis player who won her first Grand Slam title, the French Open, at the age of 16. She dominated the major events in 1991 but withdrew from Wimbledon and consequently missed the chance to achieve the Grand Slam. In 1991 she became the youngest woman player ever to achieve number-one ranking.

Seleucus I /səˈluːkəs/ Nicator c. 358–280 BC. Macedonian general under Alexander the Great and founder of the *Seleucid Empire*. After Alexander's death 323 BC, Seleucus became governor and then (312 BC) ruler of Babylonia, founding the city of Seleucia on the river Tigris. He conquered Syria and had himself crowned king 306 BC, but his expansionist policies brought him into conflict with the Ptolemies of Egypt, and he was assassinated by Ptolemy Ceraunus. He was succeeded by his son Antiochus I.

Selfridge /'selfrɪdʒ/ Harry Gordon 1857–1947. US entrepreneur who in 1909 founded Selfridges in London, the first large department store in Britain.

The customer is always right.

Harry Gordon Selfridge
(slogan adopted at his shops)

Selkirk /'selkɜːk/ Alexander 1676–1721. Scottish sailor marooned 1704–09 in the Juan Fernández Islands in the S Pacific. His story inspired Daniel Defoe to write *Robinson Crusoe*.

Sellers /'seləz/ Peter 1925–1980. English comedian and film actor. He made his name in the madcap British radio programme *The Goon Show* 1949–60; his films include *The Ladykillers* 1955, *I'm All Right Jack* 1960, *Dr Strangelove* 1964, five *Pink Panther* films 1964–78 (as the bumbling Inspector Clouseau), and *Being There* 1979.

Selous Frederick Courtney 1851–1917. British explorer and writer. His pioneer journey in the present-day Zambia and Zimbabwe area opened up the country to Europeans. He fought in the first Matabele War (1893) and was killed in the E African campaign in World War I.

Selwyn Lloyd /'selwɪn 'lɔɪd/ John, Baron 1904–1978. British Conservative politician. He was foreign secretary 1955–60 and chancellor of the Exchequer 1960–62.

He was responsible for the creation of the National Economic Development Council, but the unpopularity of his policy of wage restraint in an attempt to defeat inflation forced his resignation. He was Speaker of the House of Commons 1971–76.

Selznick /'selznɪk/ David O(liver) 1902–1965. US film producer whose early work includes *King Kong, Dinner at Eight*, and *Little Women* all 1933. His independent company, Selznick International (1935–40), made such lavish films as *Gone With the Wind* 1939, *Rebecca* 1940, and *Duel in the Sun* 1946.

He had under contract Alfred Hitchcock and Ingrid Bergman who together made several films. He launched the careers of director George Cukor and actors Katharine Hepburn, Fred Astaire, Gregory Peck, and Joan Fontaine.

Semenov /sə'mjɒnɒf/ Nikoly 1896–1986. Russian physical chemist who made significant contributions to the study of chemical chain reactions. Working mainly in Leningrad at the Institute for Chemical Physics, in 1956 he became the first Russian to gain the Nobel Prize for Chemistry, which he shared with Cyril →Hinshelwood.

Semiramis /se'mɪrəmɪs/ lived *c.* 800 BC. Assyrian queen, later identified with the chief Assyrian goddess Ishtar.

Semmelweis /'seməlvaɪs/ Ignaz Philipp 1818–1865. Hungarian obstetrician who unsuccessfully pioneered asepsis (better medical hygiene), later popularized by the British surgeon Joseph →Lister.

Semmelweis was an obstetric assistant at the General Hospital in Vienna at a time when 10% of women were dying of puerperal (childbed) fever. He realized that the cause was infectious matter carried on the hands of doctors treating the women after handling corpses in the postmortem room. He introduced aseptic methods (handwashing in chlorinated lime), and mortality fell to almost zero. Semmelweis was dismissed for his efforts, which were not widely adopted at the time.

Semmes /semz/ Raphael 1809–1877. American naval officer. At the outbreak of the American Civil War 1861, he joined the Confederate navy and attacked Union shipping in the Atlantic. He was placed in command of the Confederate cruiser *Alabama* 1862, losing the ship in a battle with the USS *Kearsarge* in the English Channel 1864.

Born in Charles County, Maryland, Semmes studied law and joined the US Navy 1826, rising to the rank of lieutenant 1836. He practised law after seeing action in the Mexican War 1846–48 and becoming a commander 1851. After the end of the Civil War 1865 he returned to practising law.

Senanayake /ˌsenə'naɪəkə/ Don Stephen 1884–1952. First prime minister of independent Sri Lanka (formerly Ceylon) 1947–52.

Senanayake /ˌsenə'naɪəkə/ Dudley 1911–1973. Prime minister of Sri Lanka 1952–53, 1960, and 1965–70; son of Don Senanayake.

Sendak /'sendæk/ Maurice 1928– . US writer and book illustrator, whose children's books with their deliberately arch illustrations include *Where the Wild Things Are* 1963, *In the Night Kitchen* 1970, and *Outside Over There* 1981.

Seneca /'senɪkə/ Lucius Annaeus *c.* 4 BC–65 AD. Roman Stoic playwright, author of essays and nine tragedies. He was tutor to the future emperor Nero but lost favour after the latter's accession to the throne and was ordered to commit suicide. His tragedies were accepted as classical models by 16th-century dramatists.

Live among men as if God beheld you; speak to God as if man were listening.

Seneca *Epistles*

Senefelder /'zeɪnəˌfeldə/ Alois 1771–1834. German engraver, born in Prague. He is thought to have invented lithography.

Senghor /sɒŋ'gɔː/ Léopold (Sédar) 1906– . Senegalese politician and writer, first president of independent Senegal 1960–80. He was Senegalese deputy to the French National Assembly 1946–58, and founder of the Senegalese Progressive Union. He was also a well-known poet and a founder of *négritude*, a black literary and philosophical movement.

Senghor studied at the Sorbonne in Paris 1935–39 (the first West African to complete the *agrégation* there), where he was a strong advocate of pride in his native Africa, developing the literary movement known as *négritude*, celebrating black identity and lamenting the baneful impact of European culture on traditional black culture.

He served in the French army during World War II, and was in a German concentration camp 1940–42; his wartime experience aided him in leading his country, French West Africa, to independence 1956 as Senegal. His works, written in French, include *Songs of the Shade* 1945, *Ethiopiques* 1956, and *On African Socialism* 1961. He was a founder of the journal *Présence Africaine*.

Senna /senə/ Ayrton 1960– . Brazilian motor-racing driver. He had his first Grand Prix win in the 1985 Portuguese Grand Prix, and progressed to the world driver's title in 1988, 1990, and 1991. He had 26 wins in 100 starts, which he improved with a record four consecutive victories at the start of the 1991 season.

He started his Formula One career with Toleman 1984, and went to Lotus 1985–87, before joining McLaren 1988.

Sennacherib /sɪˈnækərɪb/ died 681 BC. King of Assyria from 705 BC. Son of →Sargon II, he rebuilt the city of Nineveh on a grand scale, sacked Babylon 689, and defeated Hezekiah, king of Judah, but failed to take Jerusalem. He was assassinated by his sons, and one of them, Esarhaddon, succeeded him.

Sennett /senɪt/ Mack. Stage name of Michael Sinnott 1880–1960. Canadian-born US film producer, originally an actor, founder of the Keystone production company 1911, responsible for slapstick silent films featuring the Keystone Kops, Fatty Arbuckle, and Charlie Chaplin. He did not make the transition to sound with much enthusiasm and retired 1935. His films include *Tillie's Punctured Romance* 1914, *The Shriek of Araby* 1923, and *The Barber Shop* (sound) 1933.

Sequoya /səˈkwɔɪə/ George Guess 1770–1843. American Indian scholar and leader. After serving with the US army in the Creek War 1813–14, he made a study of his own Cherokee language and created a syllabary which was approved by the Cherokee council 1821. This helped thousands of Indians towards literacy and resulted in the publication of books and newspapers in their own language.

Sequoya went on to write down ancient tribal history. In later life he became political representative of the Western tribes in Washington, negotiating for the Indians when the US government forced resettlement in Indian territory in the 1830s.

A type of giant redwood tree, the sequoia, is named after him, as is a national park in California.

Sergel /seəgəl/ Johan Tobias 1740–1814. German-born Swedish Neo-Classical sculptor, active mainly in Stockholm. His portraits include *Gustaf III* (Royal Palace, Stockholm) and he made terracotta figures such as *Mars and Venus* (National Museum, Stockholm).

Sergius, St /sɜːdʒiəs/ of Radonezh 1314–1392. Patron saint of Russia, who founded the Eastern Orthodox monastery of the Blessed Trinity near Moscow 1334. Mediator among Russian feudal princes, he inspired the victory of Dmitri, Grand Duke of Moscow, over the Tatar khan Mamai at Kulikovo, on the upper Don, 1380.

Serkin /sɜːkɪn/ Rudolf 1903–1991. Austrian-born US pianist and teacher, in the USA from 1939, remembered for the quality and sonority of his energetic interpretations of works by J S Bach and Viennese classics. He founded, with German violinist Adolf Busch, the Marlboro Festival for chamber music in Vermont, and served as its director from 1952 until his death.

Serkin first appeared at the age of 12 with the Vienna Symphony. He played with the New York Philharmonic orchestra in Switzerland 1936. Emigrating to the USA, he joined the piano faculty of the Curtis Institute in Philadelphia, where he taught until 1975, serving as director from 1968 to 1975.

Serlio /seəliəʊ/ Sebastiano 1475–1554. Italian architect and painter, author of *L'Architettura* 1537–51, which set down practical rules for the use of the Classical orders, and was used by architects of the Neo-Classical style throughout Europe.

Serota /səˈrəʊtə/ Nicholas Andrew 1946– . British art-gallery director. He was director of the Whitechapel Art Gallery from 1976 to 1987, when he became director of the Tate Gallery, London.

Serra /serə/ Junipero 1713–1784. Spanish missionary and explorer in America. A Franciscan friar, he pursued a missionary career and served in Quere1taro 1750–58. He was transferred to Baja California with the expulsion of the Jesuits from Mexico 1767 and in 1969 led a missionary expedition to Alta California. He subsequently established several missions throughout the region.

Born in Majorca, Spain, Serra joined the Franciscan order 1730. After receiving a doctorate in theology, he served on the faculty of the University of Palma 1743–49 before travelling to Mexico City 1750.

Servan-Schreiber /seəˈvɒn ʃraɪˈbeə/ Jean Jacques 1924– . French Radical politician, and founder of the magazine *L'Express* 1953. His *Le Défi americain* 1967 maintained that US economic and technological dominance would be challenged only by a united left-wing Europe. He was president of the Radical Party 1971–75 and 1977–79.

Servetus /sɜːˈviːtəs/ Michael (Miguel Serveto) 1511–1553. Spanish Christian Anabaptist theologian and physician. He was a pioneer in the study of the circulation of the blood and found that it circulates to the lungs from the right chamber of the heart. He was burned alive by the church reformer Calvin in Geneva, Switzerland, for publishing attacks on the doctrine of the Trinity.

Service /sɜːvɪs/ Robert William 1874–1938. Canadian author, born in England. He wrote ballads of the Yukon in the days of the Gold Rush, for example 'The Shooting of Dan McGrew' 1907.

Sessions Roger (Huntington) 1896–1985. US composer whose Modernist, dissonant works include *The Black Maskers* incidental music 1923, eight symphonies, and *Concerto for Orchestra* 1971. He was instrumental in increasing the understanding and appreciation of modern music.

Born in Brooklyn, New York, he attended Harvard and Yale, then studied under Ernest Bloch. He became a leading teacher of composition, serving on the faculties of Boston University, Princeton University; the University of California at Berkeley, and the Juilliard School of Music.

Seton /siːtn/ Ernest Thompson (born Ernest Seton Thompson) 1860–1946. Canadian author and naturalist, born in England. He illustrated his own books with drawings of animals. He was the founder of the Woodcraft Folk youth movement, a non-religious alternative to the scouting movement.

Seton /siːtn/ St Elizabeth Ann Bayley 1774–1821. US religious leader and social benefactor. A convert to Roman Catholicism, she founded schools for the poor. Known as 'Mother Seton,' she was proclaimed the first American saint 1975.

Born in New York, USA, Seton was devoted to the service of the poor and established the Society for the Relief of Poor Widows with Small Children 1797. After a trip to Italy and the death of her first husband, she joined the Roman Catholic Church 1805.

In 1809, with her own funds, she established a Catholic elementary school in Baltimore. Soon afterward becoming a nun, she formed the Sisters of St Joseph and founded St Joseph's College for Women 1809.

Seurat /sɜːrɑː/ Georges 1859–1891. French artist. He originated, with Paul Signac, the Neo-Impressionist technique of Pointillism (painting with small dabs rather than long brushstrokes). Examples of his work are *Bathers at Asnières* 1884 (National Gallery, London) and *Sunday on the Island of La Grande Jatte* 1886 (Art Institute of Chicago).

Seurat also departed from Impressionism by evolving a more formal type of composition based on the classical proportions of the golden section, rather than aiming to capture fleeting moments of light and movement.

If, with the experience of art, I have been able to find scientifically the law of practical colour, can I not discover an equally logical, scientific and pictorial system to compose harmoniously the lines of a picture?

Georges Seurat *L'Art moderne* 1891

Severin /sevərɪn/ Tim 1940– . Writer, historian, and traveller who has re-enacted several 'classic' voyages. In 1961 he led a motorcycle team along the Marco Polo route in Asia and four years later canoed the length of the Mississippi. His Brendan Voyage 1977 followed the supposed transatlantic route taken by St Brendan in the 7th century; the Sinbad Voyage took him from Oman to China 1980–81; the Jason Voyage followed the ancient route of the Argonauts in search of the Golden Fleece 1984; the Ulysses Voyage took him from Troy to Ithaca 1985; and a journey on horseback retraced the route to the Middle East taken by the Crusaders 1987–88.

Severus /sɪˈvɪərəs/ Lucius Septimus 146–211. Roman emperor. He held a command on the Danube when in 193 the emperor Pertinax was murdered. Proclaimed emperor by his troops, Severus proved an able administrator. He was born in N Africa, and was the only African to become emperor. He died at York while campaigning in Britain against the Caledonians.

Severus of Antioch /sɪˈvɪərəs, ˈæntɪɒk/ 467–538. Christian bishop, one of the originators of the Monophysite heresy. As patriarch of Antioch (from 512), Severus was the leader of opposition to the Council of Chalcedon 451, an attempt to unite factions of the early church, by insisting that Christ existed in one nature only. He was condemned by the emperor Justin I in 518, and left Antioch for Alexandria, never to return.

Sévigné /ˌseɪviːnˈjeɪ/ Marie de Rabutin-Chantal, Marquise de 1626–1696. French writer. In her letters to her daughter, the Comtesse de Grignan, she paints a vivid picture of contemporary customs and events.

Seward /suːəd/ William Henry 1801–1872. US public official. A leader of the Republican party, he was appointed secretary of state by President Lincoln 1860. Although seriously wounded in the 1865 assassination of Lincoln, Seward continued to serve as secretary of state under President Andrew Johnson to 1868, purchasing Alaska for the USA from Russia for $7.2 million 1867.

Born in Florida, New York, Seward was educated at Union College and was admitted to the bar 1822. A lawyer, he was elected to the New

York state senate 1830 and served as governor 1838–42 and US senator 1849–61.

Sewell /sjuːəl/ Anna 1820–1878. English author whose only published work, *Black Beauty* 1877, tells the life story of a horse. Although now read as a children's book, it was written to encourage sympathetic treatment of horses by adults.

Sex Pistols, the UK punk rock group (1975–78) that became notorious under the guidance of their manager, Malcolm McLaren (1946–). Their first singles, 'Anarchy in the UK' 1976 and 'God Save the Queen' 1977, unbridled attacks on contemporary Britain, made the Pistols into figures the media loved to hate.

The original line-up was Johnny Rotten (real name John Lydon, 1956–), vocals; Steve Jones (1955–), guitar; Glen Matlock (1956–), bass; and Paul Cook (1956–), drums. Their best-known member, Sid Vicious (real name John Ritchie, 1957–1979), joined in 1977. They released one album, *Never Mind the Bollocks, Here's the Sex Pistols* 1977.

Sexton /sekstən/ Anne 1928–1974. US poet. She studied with Robert Lowell and wrote similarly confessional poetry, as in *To Bedlam and Part Way Back* 1960 and *All My Pretty Ones* 1962. She committed suicide, and her *Complete Poems* appeared posthumously 1981.

Seymour /siːmɔː/ family names of the dukes of Somerset (seated at Maiden Bradley, Wiltshire, England), and marquesses of Hertford (seated at Ragley Hall, Warwickshire, England); they first came to prominence through the marriage of Jane Seymour to Henry VIII.

Seymour /siːmɔː/ Jane c. 1509–1537. Third wife of Henry VIII, whom she married in 1536. She died soon after the birth of her son Edward VI.

Seymour /siːmɔː/ Lynn 1939– . Canadian ballerina of rare dramatic talent. She was principal dancer of the Royal Ballet from 1959 and artistic director of the Munich State Opera Ballet 1978–80.

Sforza /sfɔːtsə/ Italian family that ruled the duchy of Milan 1450–99, 1512–15, and 1522–35. Its court was a centre of Renaissance culture and its rulers prominent patrons of the arts.

The family's original name was Attendoli but it took the name Sforza (Italian 'force') in the early 13th century. Francesco Sforza (1401–66) obtained Milan by marriage to a Visconti in 1441; then his son Galeazzo (1444–76) ruled and became a patron of the arts. After his assassination, his brother Ludovico (1451–1508) seized power, made Milan one of the most powerful Italian states, and became a great patron of artists, especially →Leonardo da Vinci. He was ousted by Louis XII of France 1499, restored 1512–15, then ousted again. His son Francesco (1495–1535) was re-established 1522 by Emperor Charles V. Francesco had no male heirs, and Milan passed to Charles 1535.

Shackleton /ʃækəltən/ Ernest 1874–1922. Irish Antarctic explorer. In 1907–09, he commanded an expedition that reached 88° 23' S latitude, located the magnetic South Pole, and climbed Mount Erebus.

He was a member of Scott's Antarctic expedition 1901–04, and also commanded the expedition 1914–16 to cross the Antarctic, when he had to abandon his ship, the *Endurance*, crushed in the ice of the Weddell Sea. He died on board the *Quest* on his fourth expedition 1921–22 to the Antarctic.

Shadwell /ʃædwəl/ Thomas 1642–1692. English dramatist and poet. His plays include *Epsom-Wells* 1672 and *Bury-Fair* 1689. He was involved in a violent feud with the poet →Dryden, whom he attacked in 'The Medal of John Bayes' 1682 and succeeded as poet laureate.

Shaffer /ʃæfə/ Peter 1926– . English playwright. His plays include *Five Finger Exercise* 1958, the historical epic *The Royal Hunt of the Sun* 1964, *Equus* 1973, and *Amadeus* 1979 about the composer Mozart.

Shaftesbury /ʃɑːftsbəri/ Anthony Ashley Cooper, 1st Earl of Shaftesbury 1621–1683. English politician, a supporter of the Restoration of the monarchy. He became Lord Chancellor in 1672, but went into opposition in 1673 and began to organize the Whig Party. He headed the Whigs' demand for the exclusion of the future James II from the succession, secured the passing of the Habeas Corpus Act 1679, then, when accused of treason 1681, fled to Holland.

Shaftesbury /ʃɑːftsbəri/ Anthony Ashley Cooper, 3rd Earl of Shaftesbury 1671–1713. English philosopher, author of *Characteristics of Men, Manners, Opinions, and Times* 1711 and other ethical speculations.

Shaftesbury /ʃɑːftsbəri/ Anthony Ashley Cooper, 7th Earl of Shaftesbury 1801–1885. British Tory politician. He strongly supported the Ten Hours Act of 1847 and other factory legislation, including the 1842 act forbidding the employment of women and children underground in mines. He was also associated with the movement to provide free education for the poor.

Shah Jahan /ʃɑː dʒəˈhɑːn/ 1592–1666. Mogul emperor of India 1628–58. During his reign the Taj Mahal and the Pearl Mosque at Agra were built. From 1658 he was a prisoner of his son Aurangzeb.

Shahn /ʃɑːn/ Ben 1898–1969. Lithuanian-born US artist. Social Realist painter whose work included drawings and paintings on the →Dreyfus case and the Sacco-Vanzetti case in which two Italian anarchists were accused of murders. He painted murals for the Rockefeller Center, New York (with the Mexican artist Diego Rivera), and the Federal Security Building, Washington, 1940–42.

Shaka /ˈʃɑːɡə/ or **Chaka** c. 1787–1828. Zulu chief who formed a Zulu empire in SE Africa. He seized power from his half-brother 1816 and then embarked on a bloody military campaign to unite the Zulu clans. He was assassinated by his two half-brothers.

His efforts to unite the Zulu peoples of Nguni (the area that today forms the South African province of Natal) initiated the period of warfare known as the Mfecane.

*O! it is excellent
To have a lion's strength, but it is
tyrannous
To use it like a giant.*

William Shakespeare *Measure for Measure*

Shakespeare /ˈʃeɪkspɪə/ William 1564–1616. English dramatist and poet. Established in London by 1589 as an actor and a playwright, he was England's unrivalled dramatist until his death, and is considered the greatest English playwright. His plays, written in blank verse, can be broadly divided into lyric plays, including *Romeo and Juliet* and *A Midsummer Night's Dream*; comedies, including *The Comedy of Errors, As You Like It, Much Ado About Nothing*, and *Measure For Measure*; historical plays, such as *Henry VI* (in three parts), *Richard III*, and *Henry IV* (in two parts), which often showed cynical political wisdom; and tragedies, such as *Hamlet, Macbeth*, and *King Lear*. He also wrote numerous sonnets.

Born in Stratford-on-Avon, the son of a wool dealer, he was educated at the grammar school, and in 1582 married Anne Hathaway. They had a daughter, Susanna, in 1583, and twins Hamnet (died 1596) and Judith in 1595. Early plays, written around 1589–93, were the tragedy *Titus Andronicus*; the comedies *The Comedy of Errors, The Taming of the Shrew*, and *The Two Gentlemen of Verona*; the three parts of *Henry VI*; and *Richard III*. About 1593 he came under the patronage of the Earl of →Southampton, to whom he dedicated his long poems *Venus and Adonis* 1593 and *The Rape of Lucrece* 1594; he also wrote for him the comedy *Love's Labour's Lost*, satirizing →Raleigh's circle, and seems to have dedicated to him his sonnets written around 1593–96, in which the mysterious 'Dark Lady' appears.

From 1594 Shakespeare was a member of the Chamberlain's (later the King's) company of players, and had no rival as a dramatist, writing, for example, the lyric plays *Romeo and Juliet, A Midsummer Night's Dream*, and *Richard II* 1594–95, followed by *King John* and *The Merchant of Venice* in 1596. The Falstaff plays of 1597–99 – *Henry IV* (parts I and II), *Henry V*, and *The Merry Wives of Windsor* (said to have been written at the request of Elizabeth I) – brought his fame to its height. He wrote *Julius Caesar* 1599.

The period ended with the lyrically witty *Much Ado about Nothing, As You Like It*, and *Twelfth Night*, about 1598–1601.

With *Hamlet* begins the period of the great tragedies, 1601–08: *Othello, Macbeth, King Lear, Timon of Athens, Antony and Cleopatra*, and *Coriolanus*. This 'darker' period is also reflected in the comedies *Troilus and Cressida, All's Well that Ends Well*, and *Measure for Measure* around 1601–04.

It is thought that Shakespeare was only part author of *Pericles*, which is grouped with the other plays of around 1608–11 – *Cymbeline, The Winter's Tale*, and *The Tempest* -as the mature romance or 'reconciliation' plays of the end of his career. During 1613 it is thought that Shakespeare collaborated with John Fletcher on *Henry VIII* and *Two Noble Kinsmen*. He had already retired to Stratford in about 1610, where he died on 23 April 1616.

For the first 200 years after his death, Shakespeare's plays were frequently performed in cut or revised form (Nahum Tate's *King Lear* was given a happy ending), and it was not until the 19th century, with the critical assessment of Samuel Coleridge and William →Hazlitt, that the original texts were restored.

Shalmaneser /ˌʃælməˈniːzə/ five Assyrian kings including:

Shalmaneser III king of Assyria 859–824 BC who pursued an aggressive policy and brought Babylon and Israel under the domination of Assyria.

Shamir /ʃæˈmɪə/ Yitzhak 1915– . Polish-born Israeli right-wing politician; prime minister 1983–84 and 1986–92; leader of the Likud (Consolidation Party). He was foreign minister under Menachem Begin 1980–83, and again foreign minister in the →Peres unity government 1984–86.

In Oct 1986, he and Peres exchanged positions, Shamir becoming prime minister and Peres taking over as foreign minister. Shamir was re-elected 1989 and formed a new coalition government with Peres; this broke up 1990 and Shamir then formed a government without Labour membership and with religious support. He was a leader of the Stern Gang of guerrillas (1940–48) during the British mandate rule of Palestine.

Shamyl /ʃəˈmɪl/ c. 1797–1871. Caucasian soldier who led the people of Dagestan in a fight for independence from Russia from 1834 until he was captured 1859.

Shankar /ˈʃæŋkɑː/ Ravi 1920– . Indian composer and musician. A virtuoso of the sitar, he has composed film music and founded music schools in Bombay and Los Angeles.

Shankara 799–833. Hindu philosopher who wrote commentaries on some of the major Hindu scriptures, as well as hymns and essays on religious ideas. Shankara was responsible for the final form of the Advaita Vedanta school of Hindu philosophy, which teaches that Brahman, the supreme being, is all that exists in the universe, everything else is illusion. Shankara was fiercely opposed to Buddhism and may have influenced its decline in India.

Shannon /ˈʃænən/ Claude Elwood 1916– . US mathematician whose paper *The Mathematical Theory of Communication* 1948 marks the beginning of the science of information theory. He argued that information data and entropy are analogous, and obtained a quantitative measure of the amount of information in a given message.

He wrote the first effective program for a chess-playing computer.

Shapiro /ʃəˈpɪərəu/ Karl 1913– . US poet whose work includes the striking *V Letter* 1945, written after service in World War II.

Shapley /ˈʃæpli/ Harlow 1885–1972. US astronomer, whose study of globular clusters showed that they were arranged in a halo around the Galaxy, and that the Galaxy was much larger than previously thought. He realized that the Sun was not at the centre of the Galaxy as then assumed, but two-thirds of the way out to the rim.

Sharif /ʃæˈriːf/ Omar. Stage name of Michael Shalhoub 1932– . Egyptian-born actor (of Lebanese parents), who was Egypt's top male star before breaking into international films after his successful appearance in *Lawrence of Arabia* 1962.

His films include *Dr Zhivago* 1965 and *Funny Girl* 1968.

Sharman /ˈʃɑːmən/ Helen 1963– . The first Briton to fly in space, chosen from 13,000 applicants for a 1991 joint UK-Soviet space flight. Sharman, a research chemist by profession, was launched on 18 May 1991 in *Soyuz TM-12* and spent six days with Soviet cosmonauts aboard the *Mir* space station.

Sharp /ʃɑːp/ Cecil (James) 1859–1924. English collector and compiler of folk dance and song. His work ensured that the English folk-music revival became established in school music throughout the English-speaking world.

He travelled the country to record and save from extinction the folk-song tradition, for example *English Folk Song* 1907 (two volumes). In the USA he tracked down survivals of English song in the Appalachian Mountains and elsewhere.

Sharp /ʃɑːp/ Granville 1735–1813. English philanthropist. He was prominent in the anti-slavery movement and in 1772 secured a legal decision 'that as soon as any slave sets foot on English territory he becomes free'.

Sharpey-Schäfer /ˈʃɑːpi ˈʃeɪfə/ Edward Albert 1850–1935. English physiologist and one of the founders of endocrinology. He made important discoveries relating to the hormone adrenaline, and to the pituitary and other endocrine, or ductless, glands.

He also devised a method of artificial respiration, which improved on existing techniques.

Shastri /ˈʃæstri/ Lal Bahadur 1904–1966. Indian politician, prime minister 1964–66. He campaigned for national integration, and secured a declaration of peace with Pakistan at the Tashkent peace conference 1966.

Before independence, he was imprisoned several times for civil disobedience. Because of his small stature, he was known as 'the Sparrow'.

Shaw /ʃɔː/ George Bernard 1856–1950. Irish dramatist. He was also a critic and novelist, and an early member of the socialist Fabian Society. His plays combine comedy with political, philosophical, and polemic aspects, aiming to make an impact on his audience's social conscience as well as their emotions. They include *Arms and the Man* 1894, *Devil's Disciple* 1897, *Man and Superman* 1905, *Pygmalion* 1913, and *St Joan* 1924. Nobel prize 1925.

Born in Dublin, the son of a civil servant, Shaw went to London in 1876, where he became a brilliant debater and supporter of the Fabians, and worked as a music and drama critic. He wrote five unsuccessful novels before his first play, *Widowers' Houses*, was produced 1892. Attacking slum landlords, it allied him with the realistic, political, and polemical movement in the theatre, pointing to people's responsibility to improve themselves and their social environment.

The volume *Plays: Pleasant and Unpleasant* 1898 also included *The Philanderer, Mrs Warren's*

Shaw Drawing of Irish dramatist George Bernard Shaw whose plays merged polemic with humour in order to raise awareness for social reform. A vegetarian and defender of women's rights, Shaw's essays were often published in the form of prefaces to his plays.

Profession, dealing with prostitution and banned until 1902; and *Arms and the Man* about war. *Three Plays for Puritans* 1901 contained *The Devil's Disciple, Caesar and Cleopatra* (a companion piece to Shakespeare's *Antony and Cleopatra*), and *Captain Brassbound's Conversion*, written for the actress Ellen →Terry. *Man and Superman* 1903 expounds his ideas of evolution by following the character of Don Juan into hell for a debate with the devil.

The 'anti-romantic' comedy *Pygmalion*, first performed 1913, was written for the actress Mrs Patrick →Campbell (and later converted to a musical as *My Fair Lady*). Later plays included *Heartbreak House* 1917, *Back to Methuselah* 1921, and the historical *St Joan* 1924.

Altogether Shaw wrote more than 50 plays and became a byword for wit. His theories were further explained in the voluminous prefaces to the plays, and in books such as *The Intelligent Woman's Guide to Socialism and Capitalism* 1928. He was also an unsuccessful advocate of spelling reform and a prolific letter-writer.

Shaw /ʃɔː/ (Richard) Norman 1831–1912. British architect. He was the leader of the trend away from Gothic and Tudor styles back to Georgian lines. His buildings include Swan House, Chelsea, 1876.

Shays /ʃeɪz/ Daniel *c.* 1747–1825. American political agitator. In 1786 he led Shays Rebellion, an armed uprising of impoverished farmers, against the refusal of the state government to offer economic relief. The riot was suppressed 1787 by a Massachusetts militia force, but it drew public attention to the plight of the western farmers and the need for a stronger central government. Shays was pardoned 1788.

Born in W Massachusetts, Shays served in the 5th Massachusetts Regiment during the American Revolution 1775–83, seeing action at the battles of Bunker Hill, Ticonderoga, and Saratoga.

Shchedrin /ʃtʃɪˈdriːn/ N. Pen name of Mikhail Evgrafovich Saltykov 1826–1889. Russian writer whose works include *Fables* 1884–85, in which he depicts misplaced 'good intentions', and the novel *The Golovlevs* 1880. He was a satirist of pessimistic outlook.

He was exiled for seven years for an early story that proved too liberal for the authorities, but later held official posts.

Shearer /ʃɪərə/ (Edith) Norma 1900–1983. Canadian-born US actress who starred in silent films and in talkies such as *Private Lives* 1931, *Romeo and Juliet* 1936, *Marie Antoinette* 1938, and *The Women* 1939. She was married to MGM executive Irving Thalberg and retired after *Her Cardboard Lover* 1942.

Sheeler /ʃiːlə/ Charles 1883–1965. US painter. He is best known for his paintings of factories and urban landscapes, such as *American Landscape* 1930. He was associated with precisionism, a movement that used sharply defined shapes to represent objects. His style was to photograph his subjects before painting them.

Sheeler was born in Philadelphia, USA.

Shelburne /ʃelbən/ William Petty FitzMaurice, 2nd Earl of Shelburne 1737–1805. British Whig politician. He was an opponent of George III's American policy, and as prime minister in 1783, he concluded peace with the United States of America.

He was created Marquess of Lansdowne in 1784.

Shelley /ʃeli/ Mary Wollstonecraft 1797–1851. English writer, the daughter of Mary Wollstonecraft and William Godwin. In 1814 she eloped with the poet Percy Bysshe Shelley, whom she married in 1816. Her novels include *Frankenstein* 1818, *The Last Man* 1826, and *Valperga* 1823.

Shelley /ʃeli/ Percy Bysshe 1792–1822. English lyric poet, a leading figure in the Romantic movement. Expelled from Oxford University for atheism, he fought all his life against religion and for political freedom. This is reflected in his early poems such as *Queen Mab* 1813. He later wrote tragedies including *The Cenci* 1818, lyric dramas such as *Prometheus Unbound* 1820, and lyrical poems such as 'Ode to the West Wind'. He drowned while sailing in Italy.

Born near Horsham, Sussex, he was educated at Eton public school and University College, Oxford, where his collaboration in a pamphlet *The Necessity of Atheism* 1811 caused his expulsion. While living in London he fell in love with 16-year-old Harriet Westbrook, whom he married 1811. He visited Ireland and Wales, writing pamphlets defending vegetarianism and political freedom, and in 1813 published privately *Queen Mab*, a poem with political freedom as its theme. Meanwhile he had become estranged from his wife and in 1814 left England with Mary Wollstonecraft Godwin, whom he married after Harriet drowned herself 1816. *Alastor*, written 1815, was followed by the epic *The Revolt of Islam*, and by 1818 Shelley was living in Italy. Here he produced the tragedy *The Cenci*; the satire on Wordsworth, *Peter Bell the Third* 1819; and the lyric drama *Prometheus Unbound* 1820. Other works of the period are 'Ode to the West Wind' 1819; 'The Cloud' and 'The Skylark', both 1820; 'The Sensitive Plant' and 'The Witch of Atlas'; 'Epipsychidion' and, on the death of the poet Keats, 'Adonais' 1821; the lyric drama *Hellas* 1822; and the prose *Defence of Poetry* 1821. In July 1822 Shelley was drowned while sailing near Viareggio, and his ashes were buried in Rome.

Poets are the unacknowledged legislators of the world.

Percy Bysshe Shelley *Defence of Poetry* 1821

Shenstone /ˈʃenstən/ William 1714–1763. English poet and essayist whose poems include *Poems upon Various Occasions* 1737, the Spenserian *Schoolmistress* 1742, elegies, odes, songs, and ballads.

Shepard /ˈʃepəd/ Alan (Bartlett) 1923– . US astronaut, the fifth person to walk on the Moon. He was the first American in space, as pilot of the suborbital *Mercury-Redstone 3* mission on board the *Freedom 7* capsule May 1961, and commanded the *Apollo 14* lunar landing mission 1971.

Shepard /ˈʃepəd/ E(rnest) H(oward) 1879–1976. British illustrator of books by A A Milne (*Winnie-the-Pooh* 1926) and Kenneth Grahame (*The Wind in the Willows* 1908).

Shepard /ˈʃepəd/ Sam 1943– . US dramatist and actor. His work combines colloquial American dialogue with striking visual imagery, and includes *The Tooth of Crime* 1972 and *Buried Child* 1978, for which he won a Pulitzer prize. *Seduced* 1979 is based on the life of the recluse Howard Hughes. He has acted in a number of films, including *The Right Stuff* 1983, *Fool for Love* 1986, based on his play of the same name, and *Steel Magnolias* 1989.

Sheppard /ˈʃepəd/ Jack 1702–1724. English criminal. Born in Stepney, E London, he was an apprentice carpenter, but turned to theft and became a popular hero by escaping four times from prison. He was finally caught and hanged.

Sheraton /ˈʃerətən/ Thomas *c.* 1751–1806. English designer of elegant inlaid furniture. He was influenced by his predecessors →Hepplewhite and →Chippendale.

He published the *Cabinet-maker's and Upholsterer's Drawing Book* 1791.

Sheridan /ˈʃerɪdən/ Philip Henry 1831–1888. Union general in the American Civil War. Recognizing Sheridan's aggressive spirit, General Ulysses S →Grant gave him command of his cavalry in 1864, and soon after of the Army of the Shenandoah Valley, Virginia. Sheridan laid waste to the valley, cutting off grain supplies to the Confederate armies. In the final stage of the war, Sheridan forced General Robert E →Lee to retreat to Appomattox and surrender.

If it is abuse – why one is sure to hear of it from one damned good-natured friend or other!

Richard Brinsley Sheridan *The Critic*

Sheridan /ˈʃerɪdən/ Richard Brinsley 1751–1816. Irish dramatist and politician, born in Dublin. His social comedies include *The Rivals* 1775, celebrated for the character of Mrs Malaprop, *The School for Scandal* 1777, and *The Critic* 1779. In 1776 he became lessee of the Drury Lane Theatre. He became a member of Parliament in 1780.

He entered Parliament as an adherent of Charles →Fox. A noted orator, he directed the impeachment of the former governor general of India, Warren Hastings, and was treasurer to the Navy 1806–07. His last years were clouded by the burning down of his theatre in 1809, the loss of his parliamentary seat in 1812, and by financial ruin and mental breakdown.

Sherman /ˈʃɜːmən/ Roger 1721–1793. American public official. He was one of the signatories of the Declaration of Independence 1776, the Articles of Confederation 1781, and the US Constitution 1788. A supporter of American independence, he was a member of the Continental Congress 1774–81 and 1783–84. At the Constitutional Convention 1787 he introduced the 'Connecticut Compromise', providing for a bicameral federal legislature. Sherman served in the US House of Representatives 1789–91 and the US Senate 1791–93.

Born in Newton, Massachusetts, Sherman moved to Connecticut 1743. He later studied law and was admitted to the bar 1754. After service in Connecticut's provincial legislature, he became superior court judge 1766–85.

Sherman /ˈʃɜːmən/ William Tecumseh 1820–1891. Union general in the American Civil War. In 1864 he captured and burned Atlanta; continued his march eastward, to the sea, laying Georgia waste; and then drove the Confederates northward. He was US Army chief of staff 1869–83.

Sherman General William Sherman, who led the Union forces in the American Civil War. He has been called the first modern general because he waged an economic campaign against the civilian population of Georgia and the Carolinas, laying waste to the countryside. He is reputed to have said 'War is hell'.

Sherriff /ˈʃerɪf/ R(obert) C(edric) 1896–1975. British dramatist, remembered for his antiheroic war play *Journey's End* 1929. Later plays include *Badger's Green* 1930 and *Home at Seven* 1950.

Sherrington /ˈʃerɪŋtən/ Charles Scott 1857–1952. English neurophysiologist who studied the structure and function of the nervous system. *The Integrative Action of the Nervous System* 1906 formulated the principles of reflex action. Nobel Prize for Medicine (with E D →Adrian) 1932.

Sherwood /ˈʃɜːwʊd/ Robert 1896–1955. US dramatist. His plays include *The Petrified Forest* 1934, *Idiot's Delight* 1936, *Abe Lincoln in Illinois* 1938, and *There Shall Be No Night* 1940. For each of the last three he received a Pulitzer prize.

Shevardnadze /ˈʃevədˈnɑːdzə/ Eduard 1928– . Georgian politician, Soviet foreign minister 1985–91, head of state of Georgia from 1992. A supporter of →Gorbachev, he was first secretary of the Georgian Communist Party from 1972 and an advocate of economic reform. In 1985 he became a member of the Politburo, working for détente and disarmament. In July 1991, he resigned from the Communist Party (CPSU) and, along with other reformers and leading democrats, established the Democratic Reform Movement. In March 1992 he was chosen as chair of Georgia's ruling military council, and in Oct elected speaker of parliament.

On 20 Dec 1990, he dramatically resigned as foreign minister as a measure of protest against what he viewed as the onset of a dictatorship in the USSR, as reactionary forces, particularly within the military, regained the ascendancy. Following the abortive anti-Gorbachev coup Aug 1991 (in which he stood alongside Boris →Yeltsin) and the dissolution of the CPSU, the Democratic Reform Party stood out as a key force in the 'new politics' of Russia and the USSR. Shevardnadze turned down an offer from President Gorbachev to join the post-coup Soviet security council, but subsequently agreed to join Gorbachev's advisory council. In March 1992, following the ousting of Pesident Gamsakhurdia, he was chosen as chair of Georgia's ruling State Council, and in the first parliamentary elections Oct was elected speaker of parliament (equivalent to president), with 90% of the vote.

Shidehara /ˈʃɪdeɪ ˈhɑːrə/ Kijuro 1872–1951. Japanese politician and diplomat, prime minister 1945–46. As foreign minister 1924–27 and 1929–31, he promoted conciliation with China, and economic rather than military expansion. After a brief period as prime minister 1945–46, he became speaker of the Japanese Diet (parliament) 1946–51.

Shi Huangdi /ʃiː ˌhwæŋdiː/ or *Shih Huang Ti* 259–210 BC. Emperor of China who succeeded to the throne of the state of Qin in 246 BC and reunited China as an empire by 228 BC. He burned almost all existing books in 213 BC to destroy ties with the past; rebuilt the Great Wall; and was buried at Xian in a tomb complex guarded by 10,000 life-size terracotta warriors (excavated by archaeologists in the 1980s).

He had so overextended his power that the dynasty and the empire collapsed with the death of his weak successor in 207 BC.

Shilton /ˈʃɪltən/ Peter 1949– . English international footballer, an outstanding goalkeeper, who has set records for the highest number of Football League appearances (over 900) and England caps (125). First capped by England 1970 he retired from international football 1990, after the England–West Germany World Cup semifinal. In 1992 he became manager of Plymouth Argyle.

Shirer /ˈʃaɪrə/ William L(awrence) 1904– . US journalist, author, and historian. A columnist and commentator for the Columbia Broadcasting System (CBS), from 1937–41 he covered the events leading up World War II. He remained with CBS until 1947 and worked for the Mutual Broadcasting System 1947–49. His best-known book is *The Rise and Fall of the Third Reich* 1960.

Born in Chicago, USA, Shirer was educated at Coe College and joined the Paris bureau of the *Chicago Tribune* 1926. Travelling widely throughout Europe, he joined the Paris staff of the *New York Herald Tribune* 1934. Among his other books is *The Nightmare Years: 1930–1940* 1984.

Shockley /ˈʃɒkli/ William 1910–1989. US physicist and amateur geneticist who worked with John Bardeen and Walter Brattain on the invention of the transistor. They were jointly awarded a Nobel prize 1956. During the 1970s Shockley was criticized for his claim that blacks were genetically inferior to whites in terms of intelligence.

He donated his sperm to the bank in S California established by the plastic-lens millionaire Robert Graham for the passing on of the genetic code of geniuses.

Shoemaker /ˈʃuːmeɪkə/ Willie (William Lee) 1931– . US jockey 1949–90. He rode 8,833 winners from 40,351 mounts and his earnings exceeded $123 million. He retired Feb 1990 after finishing fourth on Patchy Groundfog at Santa Anita, California.

He was the leading US jockey ten times. Standing 1.5 m/4 ft 11 in tall, he weighed about 43 kg/95 lb.

Sholes /ˈʃəʊlz/ Christopher Latham 1819–1890. American printer and newspaper editor who, in 1867, invented the first practicable typewriter in association with Carlos Glidden and Samuel Soulé. In 1873, they sold their patents to →Remington & Sons, a firm of gunsmiths in New York, who developed and sold the machine commercially. In 1878 Sholes developed a shift-key mechanism that made it possible to touch-type.

Sholokhov /ˈʃɒləkɒf, Russian ˈʃɒləxəf/ Mikhail Aleksandrovich 1905–1984. Soviet novelist. His *And Quiet Flows the Don* 1926–40 depicts the Don

Cossacks through World War I and the Russian Revolution. Nobel prize 1965.

Shostakovich /ʃɒstəˈkəʊvɪtʃ/ Dmitry (Dmitriyevich) 1906–1975. Soviet composer. His music is tonal, expressive, and sometimes highly dramatic; it was not always to official Soviet taste. He wrote 15 symphonies, chamber music, ballets, and operas, the latter including *Lady Macbeth of Mtsensk* 1934, which was suppressed as 'too divorced from the proletariat', but revived as *Katerina Izmaylova* 1963.

Shovell /ˈʃʌvəl/ Cloudesley *c.* 1650–1707. English admiral who took part, with George Rooke (1650–1709), in the capture of Gibraltar 1704. In 1707 his flagship *Association* was wrecked off the Isles of Scilly and he was strangled for his rings by an islander when he came ashore.

Shrapnel /ˈʃræpnəl/ Henry 1761–1842. British army officer who invented shells containing bullets, to increase the spread of casualties, first used 1804; hence the word *shrapnel* to describe shell fragments.

Shultz /ʃʊlts/ George P 1920– . US Republican politician, economics adviser to President →Reagan 1980–82, and secretary of state 1982–89. Shultz taught as a labour economist at the University of Chicago before serving in the 1968–74 →Nixon administration, including secretary of labor 1969–70 and secretary of the Treasury 1972–74.

As State Department secretary, he was in charge of the formulation of US foreign policy. He was pragmatic and moderate, against the opposition of Defense Secretary Caspar →Weinberger.

Shushkevich /ʃʊʃˈkjevɪtʃ/ Stanislav 1934– . Belarus politician, president from 1991 after the attempted Soviet coup in Moscow. He was elected to parliament as a 'reform communist' 1990 and played a key role in the creation of the Commonwealth of Independent States.

Shushkevich, the son of a poet who died in the gulag, was deputy rector for science at the Lenin State University in Minsk. He entered politics as a result of his concern at the Soviet cover-up of the Chernobyl nuclear disaster 1986.

Shute /ʃuːt/ Nevil. Pen name of Nevil Shute Norway 1899–1960. English novelist. Among his books are *A Town Like Alice* 1949 and *On the Beach* 1957.

He settled in Australia 1950, having previously flown his own plane to Australia 1948–49 to research material for his books. *On the Beach* 1957 was filmed in 1959.

Sibelius /sɪˈbeɪliəs/ Jean (Christian) 1865–1957. Finnish composer. His works include nationalistic symphonic poems such as *En saga* 1893 and *Finlandia* 1900, a violin concerto 1904, and seven symphonies.

He studied the violin and composition at Helsinki and went on to Berlin and Vienna. In 1940 he abruptly ceased composing and spent the rest of his life as a recluse.

Sibley /ˈsɪbli/ Antoinette 1939– . British dancer. Joining the Royal Ballet 1956, she became senior soloist 1960. Her roles included Odette/Odile, Giselle, and the betrayed girl in *The Rake's Progress*.

Sickert /ˈsɪkət/ Walter (Richard) 1860–1942. English artist. His Impressionist cityscapes of London and Venice, portraits, and domestic and music-hall interiors capture subtleties of tone and light, often with a melancholy atmosphere.

Sickert was born in Munich, the son of a Danish painter, and lived in London from 1868. He studied at the Slade School of Art and established friendships with the artists Whistler and Degas. His work inspired the Camden Town Group; examples include *Ennui* about 1913 (Tate Gallery, London).

Go on, don't worry about the bad paintings, like a balloon your good work will carry the bad up with it.

Walter Sickert
advice to pupils 1926

Siddons /ˈsɪdnz/ Sarah 1755–1831. Welsh actress. Her majestic presence made her suited to tragic and heroic roles such as Lady Macbeth, Zara in Congreve's *The Mourning Bride*, and Constance in *King John*.

She toured the provinces with Roger Kemble, her father, until she appeared in London to immediate acclaim in Otway's *Venice Preserv'd* 1774. This led to her appearing with David →Garrick at Drury Lane. She retired 1812.

Sidmouth, Viscount title of Henry →Addington, British Tory prime minister 1801–04.

Sidney /ˈsɪdni/ Philip 1554–1586. English poet and soldier, author of the sonnet sequence *Astrophel and Stella* 1591, *Arcadia* 1590, a prose romance, and *Apologie for Poetrie* 1595, the earliest work of English literary criticism.

Sidney was born in Penshurst, Kent. He entered Parliament 1581, and was knighted 1583. In 1585 he was made governor of Flushing in the Netherlands, and died at Zutphen, fighting the Spanish.

Siegel /ˈsiːgəl/ Don(ald) 1912–1991. US film director of thrillers, Westerns, and police dramas. Two of his low-budget features, the prison film *Riot in Cell Block 11* 1954 and the science-fiction story *Invasion of the Body Snatchers* 1956, were widely recognized for transcending their lack of resources. Siegel moved on to bigger budgets, but retained his taut, acerbic view of life in such films as the Clint Eastwood vehicles *Coogan's Bluff* 1969 and *Dirty Harry* 1971.

Sieyes French Revolutionary leader and cleric Emmanuel-Joseph Sieyes. He first achieved prominence with the publication of a pamphlet on the third estate Qu'est-ce que le tiers-état. Exiled at the restoration of the monarchy, he lived in Belgium for 15 years before returning 1830.

Siemens /ˈsiːmənz/ German industrial empire created by four brothers. The eldest, *Ernst Werner von Siemens* (1812–1892), founded the original electrical firm of Siemens und Halske 1847 and made many advances in telegraphy. *William (Karl Wilhelm)* (1823–1883) moved to England; he perfected the open-hearth production of steel, pioneered the development of the electric locomotive and the laying of transoceanic cables, and improved the electric generator.

Sienkiewicz /ʃeŋkiˈeɪvɪtʃ/ Henryk 1846–1916. Polish author. His books include *Quo Vadis?* 1895, set in Rome at the time of Nero, and the 17th-century historical trilogy *With Fire and Sword, The Deluge,* and *Pan Michael* 1890–93.

Sieyes /siːeɪˈjes/ Emmanuel-Joseph 1748–1836. French cleric and constitutional theorist who led the bourgeois attack on royal and aristocratic privilege in the States General (parliament) 1788–89. Active in the early years of the French Revolution, he later retired from politics, but re-emerged as an organizer of the coup that brought Napoleon I to power in 1799.

Siger of Brabant /ˈsiːgə, brəˈbænt/ 1240–1282. Medieval philosopher, a follower of →Averroës, who taught at the University of Paris, and whose distinguishing between reason and Christian faith led to his works being condemned as heretical 1270. He refused to recant and was imprisoned. He was murdered while in prison.

Sigismund /ˈsɪgɪsmənd/ 1368–1437. Holy Roman emperor from 1411. He convened and presided over the council of Constance 1414–18, where he promised protection to the religious reformer →Huss, but imprisoned him after his condemnation for heresy and acquiesced in his burning. King of Bohemia from 1419, he led the military campaign against the Hussites.

Signac /siːnˈjæk/ Paul 1863–1935. French artist. In 1884 he joined with Georges Seurat in founding the Salon des Artistes Indépendants and developing the technique of Pointillism (using small dabs of colour laid side by side to create an impression of shimmering light when viewed from a distance).

Signac, born in Paris, was inspired by the Impressionist painter Monet. He laid down the theory of Neo-Impressionism in his book *De Delacroix au Néo-Impressionisme* 1899. From the 1890s he developed a stronger and brighter palette. He and Matisse painted together in the south of France 1904–05.

Signorelli /ˌsiːnjəˈreli/ Luca *c.* 1450–1523. Italian painter, active in central Italy. About 1483 he was called to the Vatican to complete frescoes on the walls of the Sistine Chapel.

He produced large frescoes in Orvieto Cathedral, where he devoted a number of scenes to *The Last Judgment* 1499–1504. The style is sculptural and dramatic, reflecting late 15th-century Florentine trends, but Signorelli's work is more imaginative. He settled in Cortona and ran a workshop producing altarpieces.

Sihanouk /ˌsiːəˈnuːk/ Norodom 1922– . Cambodian politician, king 1941–55, prime minister 1955–70, when his government was overthrown by a military coup led by Lon Nol. With Pol Pot's resistance front, he overthrew Lon Nol 1975 and again became prime minister 1975–76, when he was forced to resign by the Khmer Rouge opposition group. He returned from exile Nov 1991 under the auspices of a United Nations-brokered peace settlement to head the Supreme National Council, a new coalition comprising all Cambodia's warring factions, including the Khmer Rouge.

Educated in Vietnam and Paris, he was elected king of Cambodia 1941. He abdicated 1955 in favour of his father, founded the Popular Socialist Community, and governed as prime minister 1955–70.

After he was deposed 1970, Sihanouk established a government in exile in Beijing and formed a joint resistance front with Pol Pot. This movement succeeded in overthrowing Lon Nol in April 1975 and Sihanouk was reappointed head of state, but was forced to resign April 1976 by the communist Khmer Rouge leadership. Based in North Korea, he became the recognized head of the Democratic Kampuchea government in exile 1982, leading a coalition of three groups opposing the Vietnamese-installed government. International peace conferences aimed at negotiating a settlement repeatedly broke down, fighting intensified, and the Khmer Rouge succeeded in taking some important provincial capitals.

A peace agreement was eventually signed in Paris 23 Oct 1991. On his return from exile, Sihanouk called for an international trial of the leaders of the Khmer Rouge on charges of genocide.

Sikorski /sɪˈkɔːski/ Wladyslaw 1881–1943. Polish general and politician; prime minister 1922–23, and 1939–43 of the Polish government in exile in London during World War II. He was killed in an aeroplane crash near Gibraltar in controversial circumstances.

Sikorsky /sɪˈkɔːski/ Igor 1889–1972. Ukrainian-born US engineer who built the first successful helicopter. He emigrated to the USA 1918, where he first constructed multi-engined flying boats. His first helicopter (the VS300) flew 1939 and a commercial version (the R3) went into production 1943.

Silayev /sɪˈlaɪev/ Ivan Stepanovich 1930–   . Prime minister of the USSR Aug–Dec 1991, a founder member of the Democratic Reform Movement (with former foreign minister ➔Shevardnadze). A member of the Communist Party 1959–91 and of its Central Committee 1981–91, Silayev emerged as a reformer in 1990.

An engineer, Silayev worked 1954–74 in the military-industrial complex in Gorky (now Nizhny Novgorod) and then in the central aviation and machine-tools industries, becoming Soviet deputy prime minister 1985. Chosen to become prime minister of the Russian republic by its new radical president Boris Yeltsin, Silayev formulated an ambitious plan of market-centred reform. After the failure of the Aug 1991 anti-Gorbachev coup, he was appointed Soviet prime minister and given charge of the economy.

Sillitoe /ˈsɪlɪtəʊ/ Alan 1928–   . English novelist who wrote *Saturday Night and Sunday Morning* 1958, about a working-class man in Nottingham, Sillitoe's home town. He also wrote *The Loneliness of the Long Distance Runner* 1959, *Life Goes On* 1985, many other novels, and poems, plays, and children's books.

Sills /sɪlz/ Beverly 1929–   . US operatic soprano. She sang with touring companies and joined the New York City Opera in 1955. In 1979 she became director of New York City Opera and retired from the stage 1980.

Silone /sɪˈləʊneɪ/ Ignazio. Pen name of Secondo Tranquilli 1900–1978. Italian novelist. His novel *Fontamara* 1933 deals with the hopes and disillusionment of a peasant village from a socialist viewpoint. His other works include *Una manciata di more/A Handful of Blackberries* 1952.

Sim /sɪm/ Alistair 1900–1976. Scottish comedy actor. Possessed of a marvellously expressive face, he was ideally cast in eccentric roles, as in the title role in *Scrooge* 1951. His other films include *Inspector Hornleigh* 1939, *Green for Danger* 1945, and *The Belles of St Trinians* 1954.

Simenon /ˈsiːmənɒŋ/ Georges 1903–1989. Belgian crime writer. Initially a pulp fiction writer, in 1931 he created Inspector Maigret of the Paris Sûreté who appeared in a series of detective novels.

Simeon Stylites, St /ˈsɪmɪən staɪˈlaɪtiːz/ *c.* 390–459. Syrian Christian ascetic who practised his ideal of self-denial by living for 37 years on a platform on top of a high pillar. Feast day 5 Jan.

Simmons /ˈsɪmənz/ Jean 1929–   . English actress who worked mainly in Hollywood. She starred in the films *Black Narcissus* 1947, *Guys and Dolls* 1955, and *Spartacus* 1960.

Simon /ˈsaɪmən/ (Marvin) Neil 1927–   . US playwright. His stage plays (which were made into films) include the wryly comic *Barefoot in the Park* 1963, *The Odd Couple* 1965, and *The Sunshine Boys* 1972, and the more serious, autobiographical trilogy *Brighton Beach Memoirs* 1983, *Biloxi Blues* 1985, and *Broadway Bound* 1986. He has also written screenplays and co-written musicals.

The musicals include *Sweet Charity* 1966, *Promises, Promises* 1968, and *They're Playing Our Song* 1978.

Simon /siːˈmɒn/ Claude 1913–   . French novelist. Originally an artist, he abandoned 'time structure' in such novels as *La Route de Flandres/The Flanders Road* 1960, *Le Palace* 1962, and *Histoire* 1967. His later novels include *Les Géorgiques* 1981 and *L'Acacia* 1989. Nobel prize 1985.

Simon /ˈsaɪmən/ Herbert 1916–   . US social scientist. He researched decision-making in business corporations, and argued that maximum profit was seldom the chief motive. Nobel Prize for Economics 1978.

Simon /ˈsaɪmən/ John Allsebrook, Viscount Simon 1873–1954. British Liberal politician. He was home secretary 1915–16, but resigned over the issue of conscription. He was foreign secretary 1931–35, home secretary again 1935–37, chancellor of the Exchequer 1937–40, and lord chancellor 1940–45.

Simon /ˈsaɪmən/ Paul 1942–   . US pop singer and songwriter. In a folk-rock duo with Art Garfunkel (1942–   ), he had such hits as 'Mrs Robinson' 1968 and 'Bridge Over Troubled Water' 1970. Simon's solo work includes the critically acclaimed album *Graceland* 1986, for which he drew on Cajun and African music, and *The Rhythm of the Saints* 1990.

Like a bridge over troubled water, I will ease your mind.

Paul Simon
'Bridge over Troubled Water'

Simone Martini. Sienese painter; see ➔Martini, Simone.

Simpson James Simpson, Scottish obstetrician and professor of medicine and midwifery at Edinburgh University where he introduced the use of anaesthetics in childbirth. He also pursued the cause of hospital reform and became physician to Queen Victoria in Scotland 1847.

Simpson /ˈsɪmpsən/ (Cedric) Keith 1907–1985. British forensic scientist, head of department at Guy's Hospital, London, 1962–72. His evidence sent John Haig (the acid bath murderer) and Neville Heath to the gallows. In 1965 he identified the first 'battered baby' murder in England.

Simpson /ˈsɪmpsən/ James Young 1811–1870. Scottish physician, the first to use ether as an anaesthetic in childbirth 1847, and the discoverer, later the same year, of the anaesthetic properties of chloroform, which he tested by experiments on himself.

Simpson /ˈsɪmpsən/ N(orman) F(rederick) 1919– . British dramatist. His plays *A Resounding Tinkle* 1957, *The Hole* 1958, and *One Way Pendulum* 1959 show the logical development of an abnormal situation, and belong to the Theatre of the Absurd. He also wrote a novel, *Harry Bleachbaker* 1976.

Simpson /ˈsɪmpsən/ Wallis Warfield, Duchess of Windsor 1896–1986. US socialite, twice divorced. She married →Edward VIII 1937, who abdicated in order to marry her. He was given the title Duke of Windsor by his brother, George IV, who succeeded him.

Sinan /sɪˈnɑːn/ 1489–1588. Ottoman architect, chief architect from 1538 to Suleiman the Magnificent. Among the hundreds of buildings he designed are the Suleimaniye in Istanbul, a mosque complex, and the Topkapi Saray, palace of the sultan (now a museum).

Sinatra /sɪˈnɑːtrə/ Frank (Francis Albert) 1915– . US singer and film actor. Celebrated for his phrasing and emotion, especially on love ballads, he is particularly associated with the song 'My Way'. His films from 1941 include *From Here to Eternity* 1953 (Academy Award) and *Guys and Dolls* 1955.

In the 1940s he sang such songs as 'Night and Day' and 'You'd Be So Nice to Come Home To' with Harry James's and Tommy Dorsey's bands; many of his later recordings were made with arranger Nelson Riddle (1921–1985). After a slump in his career, he established himself as an actor. His later career includes film, television, and club appearances, and setting up a record company, Reprise, 1960.

Sinclair /ˈsɪŋkleə/ Clive 1940– . British electronics engineer who produced the first widely available pocket calculator, pocket and wristwatch televisions, a series of home computers, and the innovative but commercially disastrous 'C5' personal transport (a low cyclelike three-wheeled vehicle powered by a washing-machine motor).

Sinclair /ˈsɪŋkleə/ Upton 1878–1968. US novelist. His concern for social reforms is reflected in *The Jungle* 1906, an important example of naturalistic writing, which exposed the horrors of the Chicago meat-packing industry and led to a change in food-processing laws; *Boston* 1928; and his Lanny Budd series 1940–53, including *Dragon's Teeth* 1942, which won a Pulitzer prize.

Sinden /ˈsɪndən/ Donald 1923– . English actor. He has a resonant voice and versatility, his roles ranging from Shakespearean tragedies to light comedies such as *There's a Girl in My Soup*, *Present Laughter*, and the television series *Two's Company*.

I am not a management type. I am an inventor. I am awful at managing established businesses.

Clive Sinclair *Observer* June 1985

Sinding /ˈsɪndɪŋ/ Christian (August) 1856–1941. Norwegian composer. His works include four symphonies, piano pieces (including *Rustle of Spring*), and songs. His brothers Otto (1842–1909) and Stephan (1846–1922) were painter and sculptor, respectively.

Singer /ˈsɪŋə/ Isaac Bashevis 1904–1991. Polish-born US novelist and short-story writer, in the USA from 1935. His works, written in Yiddish, often portray traditional Jewish life in Poland and the USA, and the loneliness of old age. They include *The Family Moskat* 1950 and *Gimpel the Fool and Other Stories* 1957. Nobel prize 1978.

Written in an often magical storytelling style, his works combine a deep psychological insight with dramatic and visual impact. Many of his novels were written for serialization in New York Yiddish newspapers. Among his works are *The Slave* 1960, *Shosha* 1978, *Old Love* 1979, *Lost in Amer-*

ica 1981, *The Image and Other Stories* 1985, and *The Death of Methuselah* 1988. He also wrote plays and books for children.

Singer /sɪŋə/ Isaac Merit 1811–1875. US inventor of domestic and industrial sewing machines. Within a few years of opening his first factory 1851, he became the world's largest manufacturer (despite charges of patent infringement by Elias →Howe), and by the late 1860s more than 100,000 Singer sewing machines were in use in the USA alone.

To make his machines available to the widest market, Singer became the first manufacturer to offer attractive hire-purchase terms.

Singh /sɪŋ/ Vishwanath Pratap 1931–   . Indian politician, prime minister 1989–90. As a member of the Congress (I) Party, he held ministerial posts under Indira Gandhi and Rajiv Gandhi, and from 1984 led an anti-corruption drive. When he unearthed an arms-sales scandal 1988, he was ousted from the government and party and formed a broad-based opposition alliance, the *Janata Dal*, which won the Nov 1989 election. Mounting caste and communal conflict split the Janata Dal and forced him out of office Nov 1990.

Singh was born in Allahabad, the son of a local raja. He was minister of commerce 1976–77 and 1983, Uttar Pradesh chief minister 1980–82, minister of finance 1984–86, and of defence 1986–87, when he revealed the embarrassing Bofors scandal. Respected for his probity and sense of principle, Singh emerged as one of the most popular politicians in India.

Singh, Gobind see →Gobind Singh, Sikh guru.

Sirk /sɜːk/ Douglas. Adopted name of Claus Detlef Sierck 1900–1987. German film director of Danish descent, known for such extravagantly lurid Hollywood melodramas as *All that Heaven Allows* 1956 and *Written on the Wind* 1957.

Siskind /sɪskɪnd/ Aaron 1903–1991. US art photographer who began as a documentary photographer and in 1940 made a radical change towards a poetic exploration of forms and planes, inspired by the Abstract Expressionist painters.

Sisley /sɪzli/ Alfred 1839–1899. French Impressionist painter whose landscapes include views of Port-Marly and the river Seine, painted during floods in 1876.

Sisley studied in an academic studio in Paris, where he met Monet and Renoir. They took part in the First Impressionist Exhibition 1874. Unlike most other Impressionists, Sisley developed his style slowly and surely, without obvious changes.

Sisulu /sɪˈsuːluː/ Walter 1912–   . South African civil-rights activist, one of the first full-time secretary generals of the African National Congress (ANC), in 1964, with Nelson Mandela. He was imprisoned following the 1964 Rivonia Trial for opposition to the apartheid system and released, at the age of 77, as a gesture of reform by President

Sitting Bull Sioux Indian chief Sitting Bull, whose Indian name was Tatanka Iyotake, fought a rearguard action against white incursions into Indian lands. After his defeat of Custer at Little Bighorn, he retreated to Canada, surrendered 1881 and was sent to the Standing Rock reservation.

F W →de Klerk 1989. In 1991, when Mandela became ANC president, Sisulu became his deputy.

Sitting Bull *c.* 1834–1890. North American Indian chief who agreed to Sioux resettlement 1868. When the treaty was broken by the USA, he led the Sioux against Lieutenant Colonel →Custer at the Battle of the Little Bighorn 1876.

He was pursued by the US Army and forced to flee to Canada. He was allowed to return 1881, and he toured in the Wild West show of 'Buffalo Bill' →Cody. He settled on a Dakota reservation and was killed during his arrest on suspicion of involvement in Indian agitations.

Sitwell /sɪtwəl/ Edith 1887–1964. English poet whose series of poems *Façade* was performed as recitations to the specially written music of William →Walton from 1923.

Sitwell /sɪtwəl/ Osbert 1892–1969. English poet and author, elder brother of Edith and Sacheverell Sitwell. He wrote art criticism; novels, including *A Place of One's Own* 1941; and a series of five autobiographical volumes 1945–62.

Sitwell /sɪtwəl/ Sacheverell 1897–1988. English poet and art critic. His work includes *Southern Baroque Art* 1924 and *British Architects and Craftsmen* 1945; poetry; and prose miscellanies such as *Of Sacred and Profane Love* 1940 and *Splendour and Miseries* 1943.

Sixtus /ˈsɪkstəs/ five popes, including:

Sixtus IV 1414–1484. Pope from 1471. He built the Sistine Chapel in the Vatican, which is named after him.

Sixtus V 1521–1590. Pope from 1585. He supported the Spanish Armada against Britain and the Catholic League against Henry IV of France.

Skelton /ˈskeltən/ John *c.* 1460–1529. English poet and tutor to the future Henry VIII. His satirical poetry includes the rumbustious *The Tunnyng of Elynor Rummynge* 1516, and political attacks on Wolsey, such as *Colyn Cloute* 1522.

He ruleth all the roste.

John Skelton 'Why come ye nat to Courte'

Skinner /ˈskɪnə/ B(urrhus) F(rederic) 1903–1990. US psychologist, a radical behaviourist who rejected mental concepts, seeing the organism as a 'black box' where internal processes are not significant in predicting behaviour. He studied operant conditioning and maintained that behaviour is shaped and maintained by its consequences.

He invented the 'Skinner box', an enclosed environment in which the process of learned behaviour can be observed. In it, a rat presses a lever, and learns to repeat the behaviour because it is rewarded by food. Skinner also designed a 'baby box', a controlled environment for infants. His own daughter was partially reared in such a box until the age of two.

His radical approach rejected almost all previous psychology; his text *Science and Human Behavior* 1953 contains no references and no bibliography. His other works include *Walden Two* 1948 and *Beyond Freedom and Dignity* 1971.

Skinner's achievement was to create a science of behaviour in its own right. His influential work in the theoretical validation of behavioral conditioning attempted to explain even complex human behavior as a series of conditioned responses to outside stimuli. Skinner opposed the use of punishment, arguing that it did not effectively control behaviour and had unfavourable side effects. However, his vision of a well-ordered, free society, functioning in the absence of punishment, was one that failed to have much appeal. His research and writings had great influence, attracting both converts and critics. He taught at Harvard University from 1947 to 1974, and was active in research until his death.

Skolimowski /ˌskɒlɪˈmɒfski/ Jerzy 1938– . Polish film director, formerly a writer, active in both his own country and other parts of Europe. His films include *Deep End* 1970, *The Shout* 1978, and *Moonlighting* 1982.

Skryabin /skriˈæbin/ or *Scriabin* Alexander (Nikolayevich) 1872–1915. Russian composer and pianist. His powerfully emotional tone poems such as *Prometheus* 1911, and symphonies such as *Divine Poem* 1903, employed unusual scales and harmonies.

Slade /sleɪd/ Felix 1790–1868. English art collector who bequeathed most of his art collection to the British Museum and endowed Slade professorships in fine art at Oxford, Cambridge, and University College, London. The Slade School of Fine Arts, opened 1871, is a branch of the latter.

Slater /ˈsleɪtə/ Samuel 1768–1835. British-born US industrialist, whose knowledge of industrial technology and business acumen as a mill owner and banker made him a central figure in the New England textile industry. At first working for American firms, he established his own manufacturing company 1798.

Born in England, Slater was trained in machinery manufacture and worked as a mechanical supervisor in a textile mill. Emigrating to the USA 1789, he was quickly hired by several American machine manufacturing firms.

In 1791 he supervised the construction of a mill, based on the design of the English model, in Providence, Rhode Island.

Sleep /sliːp/ Wayne 1948– . British dancer who was a principal dancer with the Royal Ballet 1973–83. He formed his own company, Dash, in 1980, and in 1983 adapted his TV *Hot Shoe Show* for the stage, fusing classical, modern, jazz, tap, and disco.

Slidell /slaɪˈdel/ John 1793–1871. American public official and diplomat. He was named minister to Mexico by President Polk 1845–48 and later served in the US Senate from 1853 to the outbreak of the American Civil War 1861, when he resigned and joined the Confederacy. He was captured and imprisoned by the US navy, living in exile in France after his release 1862.

Born in New York and educated at Columbia University, Slidell moved to New Orleans 1819 and was admitted to the bar. He served as district attorney 1829–33 and US congressman 1843–45. Resigning at the outbreak of the Civil War, he was named Confederate representative to France and was taken prisoner on the high seas by the US Navy.

Slim /slɪm/ William Joseph, 1st Viscount 1891–1970. British field marshal in World War II. He commanded the 1st Burma Corps 1942–45, stemming the Japanese invasion of India, and then forcing them out of Burma (now Myanmar). He was governor general of Australia 1953–60.

Sloan /sləʊn/ John 1871–1951. US painter. Encouraged to paint by Robert →Henri, he later helped organize 'The Eight,' a group of realists who were against academic standards. He moved to New York 1904 and helped to organize the avant-garde Armory Show 1913. His paintings of working-class urban life pioneered the field of American realism.

Born in Lock Haven, Pennsylvania, USA, he started as a newspaper illustrator for several

Philadelphia newspapers. He was president of the Society of Independent Artists 1918–44 and taught at the Art Students League 1916–37.

Sloane /sləʊn/ Hans 1660–1753. British physician, born in County Down, Ireland. He settled in London, and in 1721 founded the Chelsea Physic Garden. He was president of the Royal College of Physicians 1719–35, and in 1727 succeeded the physicist Isaac Newton as president of the Royal Society. His library, which he bequeathed to the nation, formed the nucleus of the British Museum.

Sluter /sluːtə/ Claus c. 1380–1406. N European Gothic sculptor, probably of Dutch origin, active in Dijon, France. His work includes the *Well of Moses c.* 1395–1403 (now in the grounds of a hospital in Dijon) and the kneeling mourners, or *gisants*, for the tomb of his patron Philip the Bold, Duke of Burgundy (Dijon Museum and Cleveland Museum, Ohio).

Smart /smɑːt/ Christopher 1722–1771. English poet. In 1756 he was confined to an asylum, where he wrote *A Song to David* and *Jubilate Agno/Rejoice in the Lamb*, the latter appreciated today for its surrealism.

Smeaton /smiːtn/ John 1724–1792. British engineer, recognized as England's first civil engineer. He rebuilt the Eddystone lighthouse in the English Channel 1759, founded the Society of Engineers 1771, and rediscovered high-quality cement, unknown since Roman times.

Smetana /smetənə/ Bedřich 1824–1884. Czech composer whose music has a distinct national character, as in, for example, the operas *The Bartered Bride* 1866 and *Dalibor* 1868, and the symphonic suite *My Country* 1875–80. He conducted the National Theatre of Prague 1866–74.

Smiles /smaɪlz/ Samuel 1812–1904. Scottish writer, author of the popular Victorian didactic work *Self Help* 1859.

Smirke /smɜːk/ Robert 1780–1867. English Classical architect, designer of the British Museum, London (1823–47).

There is no art which one government sooner learns of another than that of draining money from the pockets of the people.

Adam Smith *The Wealth of Nations* 1776

Smith /smɪθ/ Adam 1723–1790. Scottish economist, often regarded as the founder of political economy. His *The Wealth of Nations* 1776 defined national wealth in terms of labour. The cause of wealth is explained by the division of labour – dividing a production process into several repetitive operations, each carried out by different workers. Smith advocated the free working of individual enterprise, and the necessity of 'free trade'.

He was born in Kirkcaldy, and was professor of moral philosophy at Glasgow 1752–63. He published *Theory of Moral Sentiments* 1759.

Smith /smɪθ/ Al (Alfred Emanuel) 1873–1944. US political leader who served four terms as governor of New York but was unsuccessful as a candidate for the presidency. In 1928 he became the first Roman Catholic to receive a presidential nomination. In his lively, yet unsuccessful, campaign against Herbert Hoover he was called 'The Happy Warrior.'

Born in New York, USA, Smith left school in his teens and became involved in local Democratic politics. After serving in the New York state assembly 1905–15 he became New York County sheriff 1915–17. In 1918 he was elected governor of New York. He was defeated for re-election 1920 but was victorious in 1922, 1924, and 1926.

Smith /smɪθ/ Bessie 1894–1937. US jazz and blues singer, born in Chattanooga, Tennessee. Known as the 'Empress of the Blues', she established herself in the 1920s after she was discovered by Columbia Records. She made over 150 recordings accompanied by such greats as Louis Armstrong and Benny Goodman.

Her popularity waned in the Depression, and she died after a car crash when she was refused admission to a whites-only hospital.

Smith /smɪθ/ David 1906–1965. US sculptor and painter, whose work made a lasting impact on sculpture after World War II. He trained as a steel welder in a car factory. His pieces are large openwork metal abstracts.

Smith turned first to painting and then, about 1930, to sculpture. Using welded steel, he created abstract structures influenced by the metal sculptures of Picasso. In the 1940s and 1950s he developed a more linear style. The *Cubi* series of totemlike abstracts, some of them painted, was designed to be placed in the open air.

Smith /smɪθ/ Henry George Wakelyn 1787–1860. British general. He served in the Peninsular War (1808–14) and later fought in South Africa and India. He was governor of Cape Colony 1847–52. The towns of Ladysmith and Harrismith, South Africa, are named after his wife and himself respectively.

Smith /smɪθ/ Ian (Douglas) 1919– . Rhodesian politician. He was a founder of the Rhodesian Front 1962 and prime minister 1964–79. In 1965 he made a unilateral declaration of Rhodesia's independence and, despite United Nations sanctions, maintained his regime with tenacity. In 1979 he was succeeded as prime minister by Bishop Abel Muzorewa, when the country was renamed Zimbabwe. He was suspended from the Zimbabwe parliament April 1987 and resigned in May as head of the white opposition party.

Smith /smɪθ/ John 1580–1631. English colonist. After an adventurous early life he took part in the colonization of Virginia, acting as president of the North American colony 1608–09. He explored New England in 1614, which he named, and published pamphlets on America and an autobiography. His trade with the Indians may have kept the colonists alive in the early years.

During an expedition among the American Indians he was captured, and his life is said to have been saved by the intervention of the chief's daughter ➔Pocahontas.

Smith /smɪθ/ John 1938– . British Labour politician, party leader from 1992. He was secretary of state for trade 1978–79 and from 1979 held various shadow cabinet posts, culminating in shadow chancellor 1978–92.

A trained lawyer, Smith distinguished himself as a public speaker at an early age. He entered parliament 1970 and served in the administrations of Harold Wilson and James Callaghan. He succeeded Neil Kinnock as party leader July 1992.

Smith /smɪθ/ John Maynard. British biologist, see ➔Maynard Smith.

Smith /smɪθ/ Joseph 1805–1844. US founder of the Mormon religious sect.

Born in Vermont, he received his first religious call in 1820, and in 1827 claimed to have been granted the revelation of the *Book of Mormon* (an ancient American prophet), inscribed on gold plates and concealed a thousand years before in a hill near Palmyra, New York State. He founded the Church of Jesus Christ of Latter-day Saints in Fayette, New York, 1830. The Mormons were persecuted for their beliefs and Smith was killed by an angry mob in Illinois.

Smith /smɪθ/ Kate 1909–1986. US singer. She became one of the most beloved entertainers in the USA, especially noted for her rousing renditions of 'God Bless America.'

Born in Greenville, Virginia, USA, Smith made her Broadway debut 1926. After a succession of singing roles, she gained national fame as a radio personality.

Beginning in 1936, she starred in a weekly programme and adopted the popular tune 'When the Moon Comes over the Mountain' as her theme song. She was featured in a popular television show, 'The Kate Smith Hour', 1950–56.

Smith /smɪθ/ Keith Macpherson 1890–1955 and Ross Macpherson 1892–1922. Australian aviators and brothers who made the first England– Australia flight 1919.

Smith /smɪθ/ Maggie (Margaret Natalie) 1934– . English actress, notable for her commanding presence, fluting voice, and throwaway lines. Her films include *The Prime of Miss Jean Brodie* 1969 (Academy Award), *California Suite* 1978, *A Private Function* 1984, and *A Room with a View* 1986.

Smith /smɪθ/ Matthew 1879–1960. English artist, known for his exuberant treatment of nudes, luscious fruits and flowers, and landscapes.

Smith /smɪθ/ Stevie (Florence Margaret) 1902–1971. British poet and novelist. She published her first book *Novel on Yellow Paper* 1936, and her first collection of poems *A Good Time Was Had by All* 1937. She wrote a further eight volumes of eccentrically direct verse including *Not Waving but Drowning* 1957, and two more novels. *Collected Poems* was published 1975.

Smith /smɪθ/ William 1769–1839. British geologist, the founder of stratigraphy. Working as a canal engineer, he observed while supervising excavations that different beds of rock could be identified by their fossils, and so established the basis of stratigraphy. He also produced the first geological maps of England and Wales.

Smithson /smɪθsən/ Alison (1928–) and Peter 1923– . British architects, teachers, and theorists, best known for their development in the 1950s and 1960s of the style known as Brutalism, for example in Hunstanton School, Norfolk, 1954; the Economist Building, London, 1964; and Robin Hood Gardens, London, 1968–72.

Smithson /smɪθsən/ James 1765–1829. British chemist and mineralogist. The *Smithsonian Institution* in Washington DC, USA, was established in 1846 as 'an establishment for the increase and diffusion of knowledge', following his bequest of $100,000 for this purpose.

It includes a museum, art gallery, zoological park, and astrophysical observatory.

Smollett /smɑlɪt/ Tobias George 1721–1771. Scottish novelist who wrote the picaresque novels *Roderick Random* 1748, *Peregrine Pickle* 1751, *Ferdinand Count Fathom* 1753, *Sir Launcelot Greaves* 1760–62, and *Humphrey Clinker* 1771.

Smuts /smʌts/ Jan Christian 1870–1950. South African politician and soldier; prime minister 1919–24 and 1939–48. He supported the Allies in both world wars and was a member of the British imperial war cabinet 1917–18.

During the Second South African War (1899–1902) Smuts commanded the Boer forces in his native Cape Colony. He subsequently worked for reconciliation between the Boers and the British. On the establishment of the Union of South Africa, he became minister of the interior 1910–12 and defence minister 1910–20. During World War I he commanded the South African forces in E Africa 1916–17. He was prime minister 1919–24 and minister of justice 1933–39; on the outbreak of World War II he succeeded General Hertzog as premier. He was made a field marshal in 1941.

Smuts received the Order of Merit in 1947. Although more of an internationalist than his contemporaries, Smuts was a segregationalist, voting in favour of legislation that took away black rights and land ownership.

Smyth /smaɪθ/ Ethel (Mary) 1858–1944. English composer who studied in Leipzig. Her works include *Mass in D* 1893 and operas *The Wreckers* 1906 and *The Boatswain's Mate* 1916. In 1911 she was imprisoned as an advocate of women's suffrage.

Smythson /smaɪðsən/ Robert 1535–1614. English architect who built Elizabethan country houses, including Longleat 1568–75, Wollaton Hall 1580–88, and Hardwick Hall 1590–97. Their castlelike silhouettes, symmetry, and large gridded windows are a uniquely romantic, English version of Classicism.

Snell /snel/ Willebrord 1581–1626. Dutch mathematician and physicist who devised the basic law of refraction, known as *Snell's law*, in 1621. This states that the ratio between the sine of the angle of incidence and the sine of the angle of refraction is constant.

The laws describing the reflection of light were well known in antiquity, but the principles governing the refraction of light were little understood. Snell's law was published by French mathematician ➔Descartes in 1637.

Snow /snəʊ/ C(harles) P(ercy), Baron Snow 1905–1980. English novelist and physicist. He held government scientific posts in World War II and 1964–66. His sequence of novels *Strangers and Brothers* 1940–64 portrayed English life from 1920 onwards. His *Two Cultures* (Cambridge Rede lecture 1959) discussed the absence of communication between literary and scientific intellectuals in the West, and added the phrase 'the two cultures' to the language.

Snowden /snəʊdn/ Philip, 1st Viscount Snowden 1864–1937. British right-wing Labour politician, chancellor of the Exchequer 1924 and 1929–31. He entered the coalition National Government in 1931 as Lord Privy Seal, but resigned in 1932.

Snowdon /snəʊdn/ Anthony Armstrong-Jones, Earl of Snowdon 1930– . English portrait photographer. In 1960 he married Princess Margaret; they were divorced 1978.

Snyders /snaɪdəs/ Frans 1579–1657. Flemish painter of hunting scenes and still lifes. Based in Antwerp, he was a pupil of ➔Brueghel the Younger and later assisted ➔Rubens and worked with ➔Jordaens. In 1608–09 he travelled in Italy. He excelled at painting fur, feathers, and animals fighting.

Soames /səʊmz/ Christopher, Baron Soames 1920–1987. British Conservative politician. He held ministerial posts 1958–64, was vice president of the Commission of the European Communities 1973–77 and governor of (Southern) Rhodesia in the period of its transition to independence as Zimbabwe, Dec 1979–April 1980. He was created a life peer 1978.

Soane /səʊn/ John 1753–1837. English architect whose individual Neo-Classical designs anticipated contemporary taste. He designed his own house in Lincoln's Inn Fields, London, now the *Soane Museum*. Little remains of his extensive work at the Bank of England, London.

Soares /swɑːres/ Mario 1924– . Portuguese socialist politician, president from 1986. Exiled 1970, he returned to Portugal 1974, and, as leader of the Portuguese Socialist Party, was prime minister 1976–78. He resigned as party leader 1980, but in 1986 he was elected Portugal's first socialist president.

Sobchak /səb'tʃæk/ Anatoly 1937– . Soviet centrist politician, mayor of St Petersburg from 1990, cofounder of the Democratic Reform Movement (with former foreign minister ➔Shevardnadze), and member of the Soviet parliament 1989–91. He prominently resisted the abortive anti-Gorbachev coup of Aug 1991.

Sobchak was born in Siberia, studied law at the University of Leningrad and became professor of economic law there 1983. He was elected to parliament in the semi-free poll of March 1989, chaired the congressional commission into the massacre of Georgian nationalists, and became a leading figure in the radical Interregional Group of deputies. He left the Communist Party 1990 after only two years' membership and in May 1991 was elected mayor of Leningrad (renamed St Petersburg later the same year). When tanks advanced on the city during the coup attempt in Aug, Sobchak negotiated an agreement to ensure that they remained outside, and upheld the democratic cause.

Sobers /səʊbəz/ Gary (Garfield St Aubrun) 1936– . West Indian Test cricketer. One of the game's great all-rounders, he scored more than 8,000 Test runs, took over 200 wickets, held more than 100 catches, and holds the record for the highest Test innings, 365 not out.

Sobers started playing first-class cricket in 1952. He played English county cricket with Nottinghamshire and while playing for them against Glamorgan at Swansea in 1968, he established a world record by scoring six 6s in one over. He played for the West Indies 93 times.

Sobieski /sɒb'jeski/ John. Alternative name for ➔John III, king of Poland.

Socrates /sɒkrətiːz/ c. 469–399 BC. Athenian philosopher. He wrote nothing but was immortalized in the dialogues of his pupil Plato. In his desire to combat the scepticism of the sophists, Socrates asserted the possibility of genuine knowledge. In ethics, he put forward the view that the good person never knowingly does wrong. True knowledge emerges through dialogue and systematic questioning and an abandoning of uncritical claims to knowledge.

The effect of Socrates' teaching was disruptive since he opposed tyranny. Accused in 399 on charges of impiety and corruption of youth, he was condemned by the Athenian authorities to die by drinking hemlock.

Soddy /ˈsɒdi/ Frederick 1877–1956. English physical chemist who pioneered research into atomic disintegration and coined the term isotope. He was awarded a Nobel prize 1921 for investigating the origin and nature of isotopes.

His works include *Chemistry of the Radio-Elements* 1912–14, *The Interpretation of the Atom* 1932, and *The Story of Atomic Energy* 1949. After his chemical discoveries, Soddy spent some 40 years developing a theory of 'energy economics', which he called 'Cartesian economics'. He argued for the abolition of debt and compound interest, the nationalization of credit, and a new theory of value based on the quantity of energy contained in a thing, believing that as a scientist he was able to see through the errors of economists.

Söderberg /ˈsøːdəˌbæri/ Hjalmar (Eric Fredrik) 1869–1941. Swedish writer. His work includes the short, melancholy novels *Förvillelser/Aberrations* 1895, *Martin Bircks ungdom/The Youth of Martin Birck* 1901, *Doktor Glas/Dr Glass* 1906, and the play *Gertrud* 1906.

Solander /səʊˈlændə/ Daniel Carl 1736–1772. Swedish botanist. In 1768, as assistant to Joseph →Banks, he accompanied the explorer James Cook on his first voyage to the S Pacific, during which he made extensive collections of plants.

Solander was born in Norrland, Sweden, and studied under the botanist Linnaeus. In 1771 he became secretary and librarian to Banks and in 1773 became keeper of the natural history department of the British Museum. Named after him are a genus of Australian plants and a cape at the entrance to Botany Bay.

Solomon /ˈsɒləmən/ c. 974–c. 937 BC. In the Old Testament, third king of Israel, son of David by Bathsheba. During a peaceful reign, he was famed for his wisdom and his alliances with Egypt and Phoenicia. The much later biblical Proverbs, Ecclesiastes, and Song of Songs are attributed to him. He built the temple in Jerusalem with the aid of heavy taxation and forced labour, resulting in the revolt of N Israel.

The so-called *King Solomon's Mines* at Aqaba, Jordan (copper and iron), are of later date.

Solon /ˈsəʊlɒn/ c. 638–558 BC. Athenian statesman. As one of the chief magistrates about 594 BC, he carried out the revision of the constitution that laid the foundations of Athenian democracy.

Soloviev /ˌsɒləvˈjɒf/ Vladimir Sergeyevich 1853–1900. Russian philosopher and poet whose blending of neo-Platonism and Christian mysticism attempted to link all aspects of human experience in a doctrine of divine wisdom. His theories, expressed in poems and essays, influenced Symbolist writers such as →Blok.

Solti /ˈʃɒlti/ Georg 1912– . Hungarian-born British conductor. He was music director at the Royal Opera House, Covent Garden, London, 1961–71, and became director of the Chicago Symphony Orchestra 1969. He was also principal conductor of the London Philharmonic Orchestra 1979–83.

Solyman I alternative spelling of →Suleiman, Ottoman sultan.

Solzhenitsyn /ˌsɒlʒəˈnɪtsɪn/ Alexander (Isayevich) 1918– . Soviet novelist, a US citizen from 1974. He was in prison and exile 1945–57 for anti-Stalinist comments. Much of his writing is semi-autobiographical and highly critical of the system, including *One Day in the Life of Ivan Denisovich* 1962, which deals with the labour camps under Stalin, and *The Gulag Archipelago* 1973, an exposé of the whole Soviet labour-camp network. This led to his expulsion from the USSR 1974.

He was awarded a Nobel prize in 1970. Other works include *The First Circle* and *Cancer Ward*, both 1968. His autobiography, *The Oak and the Calf*, appeared 1980. He has adopted a Christian position, and his criticism of Western materialism is also stringent.

The salvation of mankind lies only in making everything the concern of all.

Alexander Solzhenitsyn Nobel lecture 1970

Somerset /ˈsʌməset/ Edward Seymour, 1st Duke of Somerset c. 1506–1552. English politician. Created Earl of Hertford after Henry VIII's marriage to his sister Jane, he became Duke of Somerset and protector (regent) for Edward VI in 1547. His attempt to check enclosure (the transfer of land from common to private ownership) offended landowners and his moderation in religion upset the Protestants, and he was beheaded on a fake treason charge in 1552.

Somerville /ˈsʌməvɪl/ Edith Oenone 1861–1949. Irish novelist who wrote stories of Irish life jointly with her cousin, Violet Martin ('Martin Ross'). Their works include *Some Experiences of an Irish RM* 1890.

Somerville /ˈsʌməvɪl/ Mary (born Fairfax) 1780–1872. Scottish scientific writer who produced several widely used textbooks, despite having just one year of formal education. Somerville College, Oxford, is named after her.

Sommeiler /ˈsɒmələɪ/ Germain 1815–1871. French engineer who built the Mont Cenis Tunnel, 12 km/7 mi long, between Switzerland and France. The tunnel was drilled with his invention the pneumatic drill.

Sommerfeld /ˈzɒməfelt/ Arnold 1868–1951. German physicist, who demonstrated that difficulties with Niels →Bohr's model of the atom, in which electrons move around a central nucleus in circular orbits, could be overcome by supposing that electrons adopt elliptical orbits.

Somoza Debayle /səˈmaʊsə/ Anastasio 1925–1980. Nicaraguan soldier and politician, president

1967–72 and 1974–79. The second son of Anastasio Somoza García, he succeeded his brother Luis Somoza Debayle (1922–1967; president 1956–63) as president of Nicaragua in 1967, to head an even more oppressive regime. He was removed by Sandinista guerrillas in 1979, and assassinated in Paraguay 1980.

Somoza García /sə'məʊsə gɑː'siːə/ Anastasio 1896–1956. Nicaraguan soldier and politician, president 1937–47 and 1950–56. A protégé of the USA, who wanted a reliable ally to protect their interests in Central America, he was virtual dictator of Nicaragua from 1937 until his assassination in 1956. He exiled most of his political opponents and amassed a considerable fortune in land and businesses. Members of his family retained control of the country until 1979, when they were overthrown by popular forces.

Sondheim /'sɒndhaɪm/ Stephen (Joshua) 1930– . US composer and lyricist. He wrote the lyrics of Leonard Bernstein's *West Side Story* 1957 and composed witty and sophisticated musicals, including *A Little Night Music* 1973, *Pacific Overtures* 1976, *Sweeney Todd* 1979, *Into the Woods* 1987, and *Sunday in the Park with George* 1989.

Sontag /'sɒntæg/ Susan 1933– . US critic, novelist, and screenwriter. Her novel *The Benefactor* appeared in 1963, and she established herself as a critic with the influential cultural essays of *Against Interpretation* 1966 and *Styles of Radical Will* 1969. More recent studies, showing the influence of French structuralism, are *On Photography* 1976 and the powerful *Illness as Metaphor* 1978 and *Aids and its Metaphors* 1989.

Somerville Scottish scientific writer Mary Somerville. In 1831 she wrote Celestial Mechanism of the Heavens, a popularized English version of Laplace's Celeste Mécanique. Somerville College, Oxford, one of the first women's colleges, is named after her.

Soong Ching-ling /suːn ˌtʃɪŋ'lɪŋ/ 1890–1981. Chinese politician, wife of the Guomindang Nationalist leader →Sun Yat-sen; she remained a prominent figure in Chinese politics after his death, being a vice chair of the People's Republic of China from 1959.

Sophia /sə'faɪə/ Electress of Hanover 1630–1714. Twelfth child of Frederick V, elector palatine of the Rhine and king of Bohemia, and Elizabeth, daughter of James I of England. She married the elector of Hanover in 1658. Widowed in 1698, she was recognized in the succession to the English throne in 1701, and when Queen Anne died without issue in 1714, her son George I founded the Hanoverian dynasty.

Sophocles /'sɒfəkliːz/ 495–406 BC. Greek dramatist who, with Aeschylus and Euripides, is one of the three great tragedians. He modified the form of tragedy by introducing a third actor and developing stage scenery. He wrote some 120 plays, of which seven tragedies survive. These are *Antigone* 441 BC, *Oedipus Tyrannus, Electra, Ajax, Trachiniae, Philoctetes* 409 BC, and *Oedipus at Colonus* 401 BC.

Sophocles lived in Athens when the city was ruled by Pericles, a period of great prosperity. His many friends included the historian Herodotus. In his tragedies, human will plays a greater part than that of the gods, as in the plays of Aeschylus, and his characters are generally heroic. This is perhaps what he meant when he said of Euripides 'He paints men as they are' and of himself 'I paint men as they ought to be'. A large fragment of his satyric play (a tragedy treated in a grotesquely comic fashion) *Ichneutae* also survives.

Sopwith /'sɒpwɪθ/ Thomas Octave Murdoch 1888–1989. English designer of the Sopwith Camel biplane, used in World War I, and joint developer of the Hawker Hurricane fighter plane used in World War II.

From a Northumbrian engineering family, Sopwith gained a pilot's licence 1910 and soon after set a British aerial duration record for a flight of 3 hours 12 minutes. In 1912 he founded the Sopwith Aviation Company, which in 1920 he wound up and reopened as the Hawker Company, after the chief test pilot Harry Hawker. The Hawker Company was responsible for the Hawker Hart bomber, the Hurricane, and eventually the vertical take-off Harrier jump jet.

Sorel /sɒ'rel/ Georges 1847–1922. French philosopher who believed that socialism could only come about through a general strike; his theory of the need for a 'myth' to sway the body of the people was used by fascists.

Sørensen /'sɜːrənsən/ Søren 1868–1939. Danish chemist who in 1909 introduced the concept of using the pH scale as a measure of the acidity of a solution. On Sørensen's scale, still used today, a pH of 7 is neutral; higher numbers represent alkalinity, and lower numbers acidity.

Sōseki /ˈsəʊseki/ Natsume, pen name of Natsume Kinnosuke 1867–1916. Japanese novelist whose works are deep psychological studies of urban intellectual lives. Strongly influenced by English literature, his later works are somewhat reminiscent of Henry James; for example, the unfinished *Meian/Light and Darkness* 1916. Sōseki is regarded as one of Japan's greatest writers.

Sōseki was born in Tokyo and studied English literature there and (1900–03) in the UK. He became well known with his debut novel, *Wagahai wa neko de aru/I Am a Cat* 1905, followed by the humorous *Botchan* 1906, but found a more serious, sensitive style in his many later novels, such as *Sore kara/And Then* 1909. He also studied classical Chinese literature and Zen Buddhism and wrote on literary theory.

Soult /suːlt/ Nicolas Jean de Dieu 1769–1851. Marshal of France. He held commands in Spain in the Peninsular War, where he sacked the port of Santander 1808, and was Chief of Staff at the Battle of Waterloo. He was war minister 1830–40.

Souphanouvong /ˌsuːfænuːˈvɒŋ/ Prince 1912– . Laotian politician, president 1975–86. After an abortive revolt against French rule in 1945, he led the guerrilla organization Pathet Lao, and in 1975 became the first president of the Republic of Laos.

Sousa John Philip 1854–1932. US bandmaster and composer of marches, such as 'The Stars and Stripes Forever!' 1897.

Souter /ˈsuːtə/ David Hackett 1939– . US jurist, appointed as associative justice of the US Supreme Court by President Bush 1990.

Born in Melrose, Massachusetts, Souter graduated from Harvard College, received a Rhodes scholarship to Oxford University, and graduated from the Harvard Law School. After private practice in New Hampshire, Souter served as state assistant and deputy attorney general before being appointed state attorney general 1976.

He became a judge on the state trial court 1978 and was named to the state supreme court 1983. He was appointed by President Bush to the US Court of Appeals for the First Circuit 1990 and to the Supreme Court later in the same year.

Southampton /saʊθˈhæmptən/ Henry Wriothesley, 3rd Earl of Southampton 1573–1624. English courtier, patron of Shakespeare. Shakespeare dedicated *Venus and Adonis* and *The Rape of Lucrece* to him and may have addressed him in the sonnets.

Southerne /ˈsʌðən/ Thomas 1660–1746. English playwright and poet, author of the tragi-comedies *Oroonoko* 1695–96 and *The Fatal Marriage* 1694.

Southey /ˈsaʊði/ Robert 1774–1843. English poet and author, friend of Coleridge and Wordsworth. In 1813 he became poet laureate but is better known for his *Life of Nelson* 1813, and for his letters.

He abandoned his early revolutionary views, and from 1808 contributed regularly to the Tory *Quarterly Review*.

Soutine /suːˈtiːn/ Chaim 1894–1943. Lithuanian-born French Expressionist artist. He painted landscapes and portraits, including many of painters active in Paris in the 1920s and 1930s. He had a distorted style, using thick application of paint (impasto) and brilliant colours.

Soyer /swɑːˈjeɪ/ Alexis Benoît 1809–1858. French chef who worked in England. Soyer was chef at the Reform Club, London, and visited the Crimea to advise on nutrition for the British army. He was a prolific author of books of everyday recipes, such as *Shilling Cookery for the People* 1855.

Soyinka /ʃɔɪˈɪŋkə/ Wole 1934– . Nigerian author who was a political prisoner in Nigeria 1967–69. His works include the play *The Lion and the Jewel* 1963; his prison memoirs *The Man Died* 1972; *Aké, The Years of Childhood* 1982, an autobiography, and *Isara*, a fictionalized memoir 1989. He was the first African to receive the Nobel Prize for Literature, in 1986.

Spaak /spɑːk/ Paul-Henri 1899–1972. Belgian socialist politician. From 1936 to 1966 he held office almost continuously as foreign minister or prime minister. He was an ardent advocate of international peace.

Spacek /ˈspeɪsek/ Sissy (Mary Elizabeth) 1949– . US film actress who starred in *Badlands* 1973 and *Carrie* 1976, in which she played a repressed telekinetic teenager. Other films include *Coal Miner's Daughter* 1979 and *Missing* 1982.

Spallanzani /ˌspælənˈtsɑːni/ Lazzaro 1729–1799. Italian priest and biologist. He disproved the theory that microbes spontaneously generate out of rotten food by showing that they would not grow in flasks of broth that had been boiled for 30 minutes and then sealed.

Spark /spɑːk/ Muriel 1918– . Scottish novelist. She is a Catholic convert, and her enigmatic satires include: *The Ballad of Peckham Rye* 1960, *The Prime of Miss Jean Brodie* 1961, *The Only Problem* 1984, and *Symposium* 1990.

Spartacus /ˈspɑːtəkəs/ Thracian gladiator who in 73 BC led a revolt of gladiators and slaves in Capua, near Naples. He was eventually caught by Roman general →Crassus and crucified.

Spear /spɪə/ Ruskin 1911–1990. British artist whose portraits include Laurence Olivier (as Macbeth), Francis Bacon, and satirical representations of Margaret Thatcher.

Spector /ˈspektə/ Phil 1940– . US record producer, known for the 'wall of sound', created using a large orchestra, distinguishing his work in the early 1960s with vocal groups such as the Crystals and the Ronettes. He withdrew into semi-retirement in 1966 but his influence can still be heard.

Spee /ʃpeɪ/ Maximilian, Count von Spee 1861–1914. German admiral, born in Copenhagen. He went down with his flagship in the 1914 battle of the Falkland Islands, and the *Graf Spee* battleship was named after him.

Speer /ʃpeə/ Albert 1905–1981. German architect and minister in the Nazi government during World War II. Commissioned by Hitler, Speer, like his counterparts in Fascist Italy, chose an overblown Classicism to glorify the state, as, for example, in his plan for the Berlin and Nuremberg Party Congress Grounds 1934.

Speke /spiːk/ John Hanning 1827–1864. British explorer. He joined British traveller Richard →Burton on an African expedition in which they reached Lake Tanganyika 1858; Speke became the first European to see Lake Victoria.

His claim that it was the source of the Nile was disputed by Burton, even after Speke and James →Grant made a second confirming expedition 1860–63. Speke accidentally shot himself, in England, the day before he was due to debate the matter publicly with Burton.

Spence /spens/ Basil 1907–1976. British architect. He was professor of architecture at the Royal Academy, London, 1961–68, and his works include Coventry Cathedral, Sussex University, and the British embassy in Rome.

Spencer /spensə/ Herbert 1820–1903. British philosopher. He wrote *Social Statics* 1851, expounding his *laissez-faire* views on social and political problems, *Principles of Psychology* 1855, and *Education* 1861. In 1862 he began his ten-volume *System of Synthetic Philosophy*, in which he extended Charles →Darwin's theory of evolution to the entire field of human knowledge. The chief of the ten volumes are *First Principles* 1862 and *Principles* of biology, sociology, and ethics. Other works are *The Study of Sociology, Man v. the State, Essays*, and an autobiography.

Spencer /spensə/ Stanley 1891–1959. English painter who was born and lived in Cookham-on-Thames, Berkshire, and recreated the Christian story in a Cookham setting. His detailed, dreamlike compositions had little regard for perspective and used generalized human figures.

Examples are *Christ Carrying the Cross* 1920 and *Resurrection: Cookham* 1924–26 (both Tate Gallery, London) and murals of army life for the oratory of All Souls' at Burghclere in Berkshire.

Spencer-Churchill family name of the dukes of Marlborough, whose seat is Blenheim Palace, Oxfordshire, England.

Spender /spendə/ Stephen (Harold) 1909– . English poet and critic. His earlier poetry has a left-wing political content, as in *Twenty Poems* 1930, *Vienna* 1934, *The Still Centre* 1939, and *Poems of Dedication* 1946. Other works include the verse drama *Trial of a Judge* 1938, the autobiography *World within World* 1951, and translations. His *Journals 1939–83* were published 1985.

Speke On a Royal Geographical Society expedition to equatorial Africa, English explorer John Speke discovered Lakes Tanganyika (with Richard Burton) and Victoria. He later confirmed his theory that Lake Victoria was the source of the Nile 1860. He accidentally shot himself while shooting partridge in Bath.

Educated at University College, Oxford, he founded with Cyril Connolly the magazine *Horizon* (of which he was co-editor 1939–41) and was co-editor of *Encounter* 1953–67. He became professor of English at University College, London, in 1970.

Spengler /ʃpeŋglə/ Oswald 1880–1936. German philosopher whose *Decline of the West* 1918 argued that civilizations go through natural cycles of growth and decay. He was admired by the Nazis.

Spenser /spensə/ Edmund c. 1552–1599. English poet, who has been called the 'poet's poet' because of his rich imagery and command of versification. His major work is the moral allegory *The Faerie Queene*, of which six books survive (three published 1590 and three 1596). Other books include *The Shepheard's Calendar* 1579, *Astrophel* 1586, the love sonnets *Amoretti* and the *Epithalamion* 1595.

Born in London and educated at Cambridge University, in 1580 he became secretary to the Lord Deputy in Ireland and at Kilcolman Castle completed the first three books of *The Faerie Queene*. In 1598 Kilcolman Castle was burned down by rebels, and Spenser with his family narrowly escaped. He died in London, and was buried in Westminster Abbey.

Sperry /ˈspɛri/ Elmer Ambrose 1860–1930. US engineer who developed various devices using gyroscopes, such as gyrostabilizers (for ships and torpedoes) and gyro-controlled autopilots.

The first gyrostabilizers dated from 1912, and during World War I Sperry designed a pilotless aircraft that could carry up to 450 kg/990 lb of explosives a distance of 160 km/100 mi (the first flying bomb) under gyroscopic control. By the mid-1930s *Sperry autopilots* were standard equipment on most large ships.

Spielberg /ˈspiːlbɜːg/ Steven 1947– . US director, writer, and producer of such phenomenal box-office successes as *Jaws* 1975, *Close Encounters of the Third Kind* 1977, *Raiders of the Lost Ark* 1981, and *ET* 1982. Immensely popular, his films usually combine cliff-hanging suspense with heartfelt sentimentality and a childlike sensibility. He also directed *Indiana Jones and the Temple of Doom* 1984, *The Color Purple* 1985, *Empire of the Sun* 1987, *Indiana Jones and the Last Crusade* 1989, and *Hook* 1992.

I wanted the water to mean shark. The horizon to mean shark. I wanted the shark's presence to be felt everywhere.

Steven Spielberg on his film *Jaws*

Spillane /spɪˈleɪn/ Mickey (Frank Morrison) 1918– . US crime novelist who began by writing for pulp magazines and became known for violent and sexually explicit crime novels featuring his 'one-man police force' hero Mike Hammer; for example, *Vengeance is Mine* 1950 and *The Long Wait* 1951.

Spinoza /spɪˈnəʊzə/ Benedict or Baruch 1632–1677. Dutch philosopher who believed in a rationalistic pantheism that owed much to Descartes' mathematical appreciation of the universe. Mind and matter are two modes of an infinite substance that he called God or Nature, good and evil being relative. He was a determinist, believing that human action was motivated by self-preservation.

Ethics 1677 is his main work. *A Treatise on Religious and Political Philosophy* 1670 was the only one of his works published during his life, and was attacked by Christians. He was excommunicated by the Jewish community in Amsterdam on charges of heretical thought and practice 1656. He was a lens-grinder by trade.

Spitz /spɪts/ Mark Andrew 1950– . US swimmer. He won a record seven gold medals at the 1972 Olympic Games, all in world record times.

He won 11 Olympic medals in total (four in 1968) and set 26 world records between 1967 and 1972. After retiring in 1972 he became a movie actor, two of his films elected candidates for 'The Worst of Hollywood'.

Spock /spɒk/ Benjamin McLane 1903– . US paediatrician and writer on child care. His *Common Sense Book of Baby and Child Care* 1946 urged less rigidity in bringing up children than had been advised by previous generations of writers on the subject, but this was misunderstood as advocating permissiveness. He was also active in the peace movement, especially during the Vietnam War.

In his later work he stressed that his common-sense approach had not implied rejecting all discipline, but that his main aim was to give parents the confidence to trust their own judgement rather than rely on books by experts who did not know a particular child.

Spode /spəʊd/ Josiah 1754–1827. English potter. Around 1800, he developed bone porcelain (made from bone ash, china stone, and china clay), which was produced at all English factories in the 19th century. Spode became potter to King George III 1806.

Sprengel Christian Konrad 1750–1816. German botanist. Writing in 1793 he described the phenomenon of dichogamy, the process whereby stigma and anthers on the same flower ripen at different times and so guarantee cross-fertilization.

Spring /sprɪŋ/ Richard 1950– . Irish Labour Party leader from 1982, who entered into coalition with Garret →FitzGerald's Fine Gael 1982 as deputy prime minister (and minister for energy from 1983).

Springsteen /ˈsprɪŋstiːn/ Bruce 1949– . US rock singer, songwriter, and guitarist, born in New Jersey. His music combines melodies in traditional rock idiom and reflective lyrics about working-class life on albums such as *Born to Run* 1975 and *Born in the USA* 1984, maturing into the 1992 albums *Human Touch* and *Lucky Town*.

The River 1980 and the solo acoustic *Nebraska* 1982 reinforced his reputation as a songwriter. His vast stadium concerts with the E Street Band were marked by his ability to overcome the distance between audience and artist, making him one of rock's finest live performers.

Squanto /ˈskwɒntəʊ/ also known as Tisquantum c. 1580–1622. American Pawtuxet Indian ally of the Plymouth colonists. Kidnapped by the English and taken to England 1605, he returned to New England 1619 as a guide for Captain John Slaine. His own tribe having been wiped out by an epidemic, Squanto settled among the Wampanoag people, serving as interpreter for Chief →Massasoit in his dealings with the Pilgrims.

Born in SE New England, Squanto eventually settled in Plymouth on his return from England, living there until his death.

Staël /stɑːl/ Anne Louise Germaine Necker, Madame de 1766–1817. French author, daughter of the financier Jacques →Necker. She wrote semi-autobiographical novels such as *Delphine*

1802 and *Corinne* 1807, and the critical work *De l'Allemagne* 1810, on German literature. She was banished from Paris by Napoleon in 1803 because of her advocacy of political freedom.

Stahl /ʃtɑːl/ Georg Ernst 1660–1734. German chemist who produced a fallacious theory of combustion. He was professor of medicine at Halle, and physician to the king of Prussia. He argued that objects burn because they contain a combustible substance, phlogiston. Substances rich in phlogiston, such as wood, burn almost completely away. Metals, which are low in phlogiston, burn less well. Chemists spent much of the 18th century evaluating Stahl's theories before these were finally proved false by Antoine →Lavoisier.

Stainer /steɪnə/ John 1840–1901. English organist and composer who became organist of St Paul's in 1872. His religious choral works are *The Crucifixion* 1887, an oratorio, and *The Daughter of Jairus* 1878, a cantata.

Stakhanov /stəˈkɑːnɒf/ Aleksei 1906–1977. Soviet miner who exceeded production norms; he gave his name to the *Stakhanovite* movement of the 1930s, when workers were offered incentives to simplify and reorganize work processes in order to increase production.

Stalin /stɑːlɪn/ Joseph. Adopted name (Russian 'steel') of Joseph Vissarionovich Djugashvili 1879–1953. Soviet politician. A member of the October Revolution Committee 1917, Stalin became general secretary of the Communist Party 1922. After →Lenin's death 1924, Stalin sought to create 'socialism in one country' and clashed with →Trotsky, who denied the possibility of socialism inside Russia until revolution had occurred in W Europe. Stalin won this ideological struggle by 1927, and a series of five-year plans was launched to collectivize industry and agriculture from 1928. All opposition was eliminated in the Great Purge 1936–38. During World War II, Stalin intervened in the military direction of the campaigns against Nazi Germany. His role was denounced after his death by Khrushchev and other members of the Soviet regime.

Born in Georgia, the son of a shoemaker, Stalin was educated for the priesthood but was expelled from his seminary for Marxist propaganda. He became a member of the Social Democratic Party 1898, and joined Lenin and the Bolsheviks 1903. He was repeatedly exiled to Siberia 1903–13. He then became a member of the Communist Party's Politburo, and sat on the October Revolution committee. Stalin rapidly consolidated a powerful following (including Molotov); in 1921 he became commissar for nationalities in the Soviet government, responsible for the decree granting equal rights to all peoples of the Russian Empire, and was appointed general secretary of the Communist Party 1922. As dictator in the 1930s, he disposed of all real and imagined enemies. In recent years increasing evidence has been uncovered revealing Stalin's anti-Semitism, for example, the execution of 19 Jewish activists in 1952 for a 'Zionist conspiracy'.

He met Churchill and Roosevelt at Tehran 1943 and at Yalta 1945, and took part in the Potsdam conference. After the war, Stalin maintained an autocratic rule.

The export of revolution is nonsense. Every country makes its own revolution if it wants to, and if it does not there will be no revolution.

Joseph Stalin interview 1936

Stallone /stəˈləʊn/ Sylvester 1946– . US film actor, a bit player who rocketed to fame as the boxer in *Rocky* 1976. Other films include *First Blood* 1982 and the *Rambo* series from 1985.

Standish /stændɪʃ/ Miles *c.* 1584–1656. American colonial military leader. As military adviser to the Pilgrim Fathers, he arrived in New England 1621 and obtained a charter for Plymouth colony from England 1925. Although one of the most influential figures in colonial New England, he is best remembered through American poet Henry Longfellow's *The Courtship of Miles Standish* 1863.

Born in Lancashire, England, Standish began his military career as a mercenary in the Dutch rebellion against the Spanish. Arriving in New England, he negotiated with the Wampanoag people and supervised the Plymouth colonists' military training, and became one of the colony's chief investors 1627.

He later established the nearby town of Duxbury and settled there 1637.

Stanford /stænfəd/ Charles Villiers 1852–1924. British composer and teacher, born in Ireland, a leading figure in the 19th-century renaissance of British music. His many works include operas such as *Shamus O'Brien* 1896, seven symphonies, chamber music, and church music. Among his pupils were Vaughan Williams, Gustav Holst, and Frank Bridge.

Stanford /stænfəd/ Leland 1824–1893. US public official and railroad developer. Elected governor of California 1861, he became president of the Central Pacific Railroad in the same year, and was one of the founders of the Southern Pacific Railroad 1870. He served in the US Senate 1885–93.

Born in Watervliet, New York, Stanford was educated at Cazenovia Seminary and was admitted to the bar 1848. Settling in California 1856, he became a successful merchant in Sacramento.

Stanhope /stænəp/ Hester Lucy 1776–1839. English traveller who left England in 1810 to tour the east Mediterranean with Bedouins and eventually settled there. She adopted local dress and became involved in Middle Eastern politics.

Stanislavsky /ˌstænɪ'slævski/ Konstantin Sergeivich 1863–1938. Russian actor, director, and teacher of acting. He rejected the declamatory style of acting in favour of a more realistic approach, concentrating on the psychological basis for the development of character. The Actors Studio is based on this approach.

Stanislavsky cofounded the Moscow Art Theatre 1898 and directed productions of Chekhov and Gorky. His ideas, which he described in *My Life in Art* 1924 and other works, had considerable influence on acting techniques in Europe and the USA.

Stanley /stænli/ family name of earls of Derby.

Stanley /stænli/ Henry Morton. Adopted name of John Rowlands 1841–1904. Welsh-born US explorer and journalist who made four expeditions to Africa. He and David →Livingstone met at Ujiji 1871 and explored Lake Tanganyika. He traced the course of the river Zaïre (Congo) to the sea 1874–77, established the Congo Free State (Zaire) 1879–84, and charted much of the interior 1887–89.

Stanley worked his passage over to America when he was 18. He fought on both sides in the US Civil War. He worked for the *New York Herald* from 1867, and in 1871 he was sent by the editor James Gordon Bennett (1795–1872) to find the ailing Livingstone, which he did on 10 Nov. From Africa he returned to the UK and was elected to Parliament 1895.

Stanley /stænli/ Wendell 1904–1971. US biochemist who crystallized the tobacco mosaic virus (TMV) in 1935. He demonstrated that, despite its crystalline state, TMV remained infectious. Together with John Northrop and James Sumner, Stanley received the 1946 Nobel Prize for Chemistry.

Stansfield Lisa 1965– . English pop singer whose soulful vocals with slick productions have won her several of the UK record industry's Brit Awards. She had a UK number-one hit with 'All Around the World' 1989. Her albums *Affection* 1989 and *Real Love* 1992 also enjoyed chart success in the UK and the USA.

Stansfield Smith /stænzfiːld 'smɪθ/ Colin 1932– . English architect under whose leadership from 1973 the work of Hampshire County Architects Department has come to represent the best of public English architecture in recent times. The schools built are generally organic modern buildings that relate to their rural context and are planned with a concern for the way people use buildings. Bishopstoke infants' school is housed under a sweeping teepeelike tiled roof; the Queen's Inclosure First School at Cowplain is more high tech.

Stanton /stæntən/ Edwin McMasters 1814–1869. US public official, secretary of war 1862–68. A lawyer and a Democrat, he was appointed US attorney general by President Buchanan 1860 and then secretary of war by Republican president Lincoln 1862.

Born in Steubenville, Ohio, Stanton attended Kenyon College, was admitted to the bar 1836, and gained a reputation as a skilled lawyer. As secretary of war he was an effective, if autocratic administrator. Although retained in office by President A Johnson, Stanton eventually broke with him over Reconstruction policies and was forced to resign 1868. He was named to the US Supreme Court 1869 by President Grant, but died before taking office.

Stanton /stæntən/ Elizabeth Cady 1815–1902. US feminist who, with Susan B →Anthony, founded the National Woman Suffrage Association 1869, the first women's movement in the USA and was its first president. She and Anthony wrote and compiled the *History of Women's Suffrage* 1881–86. Stanton also worked for the abolition of slavery.

She organized the International Council of Women in Washington DC. Her publications include *Degradation of Disenfranchisement* and *Solitude of Self* 1892, and in 1885 and 1898 she published a two-part feminist critique of the Bible: *The Woman's Bible*.

Stanwyck /stænwɪk/ Barbara. Stage name of Ruby Stevens 1907–1990. US film actress, equally at home in comedy or melodrama. Her films include *Stella Dallas* 1937, *Double Indemnity* 1944, and *Executive Suite* 1954.

Stark /stɑːk/ Freya 1893– . English traveller, mountaineer, and writer who for a long time worked in South America. She described her explorations in the Middle East in many books, including *The Valley of the Assassins* 1934, *The Southern Gates of Arabia* 1936, and *A Winter in Arabia* 1940.

The great and almost only comfort about being a woman is that one can always pretend to be more stupid than one is, and no one is surprised.

Freya Stark
The Valley of the Assassins 1934

Stark /ʃtɑːk/ Johannes 1874–1957. German physicist. In 1902 he predicted, correctly, that high-velocity rays of positive ions (canal rays) would demonstrate the Doppler effect, and in 1913 showed that a strong electric field can alter the wavelength of light emitted by atoms (the *Stark effect*). He was awarded the Nobel Prize for Physics 1919.

Starling /stɑːlɪŋ/ Ernest Henry 1866–1927. English physiologist who discovered secretin and coined the word 'hormone'. He formulated *Starling's law*, which states that the force of the heart's contraction is a function of the length of the muscle fibres. He is considered one of the founders of endocrinology.

Staudinger /ʃtaʊdɪŋə/ Hermann 1881–1965. German organic chemist, founder of macromolecular chemistry, who carried out pioneering research into the structure of albumen and cellulose. Nobel prize 1953.

Stauffenberg /ʃtaʊfənbeək/ Claus von 1907–1944. German colonel in World War II who, in a conspiracy to assassinate Hitler, planted a bomb in the dictator's headquarters conference room in the Wolf's Lair at Rastenburg, East Prussia, 20 July 1944. Hitler was merely injured, and Stauffenberg and 200 others were later executed by the Nazi regime.

Stead /sted/ Christina (Ellen) 1902–1983. Australian writer who lived in Europe and the USA 1928–68. Her novels include *The Man Who Loved Children* 1940, *Dark Places of the Heart* 1966 (published as *Cotter's England* in the UK), and *I'm Dying Laughing* 1986.

Steed /stiːd/ Henry Wickham 1871–1956. British journalist. Foreign correspondent for *The Times* in Vienna 1902–13, he was then foreign editor 1914–19 and editor 1919–22.

Steel /stiːl/ David 1938– . British politician, leader of the Liberal Party 1976–88. He entered into a compact with the Labour government 1977–78, and into an alliance with the Social Democratic Party (SDP) 1983. Having supported the Liberal-SDP merger (forming the Social and Liberal Democrats), he resigned the leadership 1988, becoming the Party's foreign affairs spokesman.

Steel was president of the students' union while at Edinburgh University, and less than three years later became an MP.

Steele /stiːl/ Richard 1672–1729. Irish essayist who founded the journal *The Tatler* 1709–11, in which Joseph →Addison collaborated. They continued their joint work in *The Spectator*, also founded by Steele, 1711–12, and *The Guardian* 1713. He also wrote plays, such as *The Conscious Lovers* 1722.

Steen /steɪn/ Jan 1626–1679. Dutch painter. Born in Leiden, he was also active in The Hague, Delft, and Haarlem. He painted humorous everyday scenes, mainly set in taverns or bourgeois households, as well as portraits and landscapes.

Steer /stɪə/ Philip Wilson 1860–1942. British artist, influenced by the French Impressionists, who painted seaside scenes such as *The Beach at Walberswick* 1890 (Tate Gallery, London). He became a leader (with Walter →Sickert) of the English movement and founder member of the New English Art Club.

Stefan /ʃtefæn/ Joseph 1835–1893. Austrian physicist who established one of the basic laws of

Steele *Irish essayist and dramatist Richard Steele. He collaborated with his friend Joseph Addison and their essays aimed to raise moral and Christian standards as well as to amuse. He founded the Tatler journal 1709 and invented the character of Sir Roger de Coverley in* The Spectator.

heat radiation in 1874, since known as the *Stefan–Boltzmann law*. This states that the heat radiated by a hot body is proportional to the fourth power of its absolute temperature.

Steffens /stefənz/ (Joseph) Lincoln 1866–1936. US investigative journalist. Intent on exposing corruption and fraud in high places, he initiated the style known as 'muckraking' while working for *McClure's* magazine. He later covered the Mexican Revolution and befriended the Soviet leader Lenin.

An expert in financial affairs, Steffens was editor of the *New York Commercial Advertiser* 1897–1901 before moving on to *McClure's* (managing editor 1901–06) where he joined forces with writers Ida Tarbell (1857–1944) and Ray Stannard Baker (1870–1946). His *Autobiography* appeared 1931.

Steichen /staɪkən/ Edward 1897–1973. US photographer in both world wars, and also an innovative fashion and portrait photographer.

Steiger /staɪgə/ Rod(ney Stephen) 1925– . US character actor of the Method school (placing importance on the psychological building of a role). His work includes *On the Waterfront* 1954, *In the Heat of the Night* 1967, and the title role in *W C Fields and Me* 1976.

Stein /ʃtaɪn/ Aurel 1862–1943. Hungarian archaeologist and explorer who carried out projects for the Indian government in Chinese Turkestan and Tibet 1900–15.

Stein /staɪn/ Gertrude 1874–1946. US writer who influenced authors Ernest →Hemingway, Sherwood →Anderson, and F Scott →Fitzgerald with her conversational tone, cinematic technique, use of repetition, and absence of punctuation: devices intended to convey immediacy and realism. Her work includes the self-portrait *The Autobiography of Alice B Toklas* 1933.

Steinbeck /staɪnbek/ John (Ernst) 1902–1968. US novelist. His realist novels, such as *In Dubious Battle* 1936, *Of Mice and Men* 1937, and *The Grapes of Wrath* 1939 (Pulitzer prize 1940), portray agricultural life in his native California, where migrant farm labourers from the Oklahoma dust bowl struggled to survive. Nobel prize 1962.

He published *Tortilla Flat* 1935, a humorous study of the paisanos (farmers) of Monterey, California; many of his books deal with the lives of working people. *East of Eden* was filmed with James Dean. His later work includes *Winter of our Discontent* 1961.

To finish is sadness to a writer – a little death. He puts the last word down and it is done. But it isn't really done. The story goes on and leaves the writer behind, for no story is ever done.

John Steinbeck

Steinberg /staɪnbɜːg/ Saul 1914– . Romanian-born US artist best known for cartoons contributed to the *New Yorker* and other magazines. His work portrays a childlike personal world with allusions to the irrational and absurd.

Steinberg was educated at the University of Bucharest and received his doctorate in architecture from the Reggio Politecnico in Milan 1940. Embarking on a career as a painter and cartoonist, he emigrated to the US 1942.

During World War II he served as an American intelligence officer in Italy. He was inducted into the US National Institute of Arts and Letters 1968.

Steinem /staɪnəm/ Gloria 1934– . US journalist and liberal feminist who emerged as a leading figure in the US women's movement in the late 1960s. She was also involved in radical protest campaigns against racism and the Vietnam War. She cofounded the Women's Action Alliance 1970 and *Ms* magazine. In 1983 a collection of her articles was published as *Outrageous Acts and Everyday Rebellions*.

Steiner /ʃtaɪnə/ Max(imilian Raoul) 1888–1971. Austrian composer of accomplished film music, in the USA from 1914.

He wrote scores for, among others, *King Kong* 1933, *Gone With the Wind* 1939, and *Casablanca* 1942.

Steiner /ʃtaɪnə/ Rudolf 1861–1925. Austrian philosopher, originally a theosophist (see →Blavatsky), who developed his own mystic and spiritual teaching, anthroposophy, designed to develop the whole human being. A number of Steiner schools follow a curriculum laid down by him with a strong emphasis on the arts, although the schools also include the possibilities for pupils to take state exams.

Steinmetz /staɪnmets/ Charles 1865–1923. US engineer who formulated the *Steinmetz hysteresis law* in 1891, which describes the dissipation of energy that occurs when a system is subject to an alternating magnetic force.

Stella /stelə/ Frank 1936– . US painter, a pioneer of the hard-edged geometric trend in abstract art that followed Abstract Expressionism. From around 1960 he also experimented with the shape of his canvases.

Stella /stelə/ Joseph 1877–1946. Italian-born US painter. With artist Max →Weber, he was America's leading Futurist. His cubistic and futuristic views of New York City are captured in such paintings as *Brooklyn Bridge* 1919–20 and *New York Interpreted* 1920–22. His works are mostly mechanical and urban scenes, although his later paintings include tropical landscapes.

Born in Naples, Italy, Stella emigrated to the USA 1902 and studied art at the Art Students' League, New York, USA, and the New York School of Art. He exhibited at the Armory Show 1913 and with the Société Anonyme, of which he was a member.

Stendhal /stæn'dæl/ pen name of Marie Henri Beyle 1783–1842. French novelist. His novels *Le Rouge et le noir/The Red and the Black* 1830 and *La Chartreuse de Parme/The Charterhouse of Parma* 1839 were pioneering works in their treatment of disguise and hypocrisy; a review of the latter by fellow novelist →Balzac in 1840 furthered Stendhal's reputation.

Stendhal was born in Grenoble. He served in Napoleon's armies and took part in the ill-fated Russian campaign. Failing in his hopes of becoming a prefect, he lived in Italy from 1814 until suspicion of espionage drove him back to Paris in 1821, where he lived by literary hackwork. From 1830 he was a member of the consular service, spending his leaves in Paris.

Stenmark /steɪnmɑːk/ Ingemar 1956– . Swedish skier who won a record 85 World Cup races 1974–87, including a record 13 in 1979. He won a total of 18 titles, including the overall title three times.

Stephen /stiːvən/ c. 1097–1154. King of England from 1135. A grandson of William I, he was elected king 1135, although he had previously recognized Henry I's daughter →Matilda as heiress to the throne. Matilda landed in England 1139, and civil war disrupted the country until 1153, when

Stephen acknowledged Matilda's son, Henry II, as his own heir.

Stephen /stiːvən/ Leslie 1832–1904. English critic, first editor of the *Dictionary of National Biography* and father of novelist Virginia →Woolf.

Stephen I, St /stiːvən/ 975–1038. King of Hungary from 997, when he succeeded his father. He completed the conversion of Hungary to Christianity and was canonized in 1803.

Stephens /stiːvnz/ Alexander Hamilton 1812–1883. American public official. A leader of the Whig party, he served in the US House of Representatives 1843–59 and was an opponent of the Mexican War 1846–48 and a strong defender of slavery. In 1861 he was chosen as vice president of the Confederacy. Arrested and briefly imprisoned at the end of the American Civil War 1865, he served again as US Congressman 1872–82.

Born in Taliaferro County, Georgia, Stephens was educated at the University of Georgia and was admitted to the bar 1834. He served in the Georgia state legislature 1836–41 and as governor of Georgia 1882–83.

Stephens /stiːvənz/ John Lloyd 1805–1852. US explorer in Central America, with Frederick →Catherwood. He recorded his findings of ruined Mayan cities in his two-volume *Incidents of Travel in Central America, Chiapas and Yucatan* 1841–43.

Stephen, St /stiːvən/ died *c*. AD 35. The first Christian martyr; he was stoned to death. Feast day 26 Dec.

Stephenson /stiːvənsən/ George 1781–1848. English engineer who built the first successful steam locomotive, and who also invented a safety lamp in 1815. He was appointed engineer of the Stockton and Darlington Railway, the world's first public railway, in 1821, and of the Liverpool and Manchester Railway in 1826. In 1829 he won a £500 prize with his locomotive *Rocket*.

Stephenson /stiːvənsən/ Robert 1803–1859. English civil engineer who constructed railway bridges such as the high-level bridge at Newcastle upon Tyne, England, and the Menai and Conway tubular bridges in Wales. He was the son of George Stephenson.

Steptoe /steptəʊ/ Patrick Christopher 1913–1988. English obstetrician who pioneered in vitro fertilization (uniting eggs and sperm in the laboratory). Steptoe, together with biologist Robert Edwards, was the first to succeed in implanting in the womb an egg fertilized outside the body. The first 'test-tube baby' was Louise Brown, born by Caesarean section in 1978.

Stern /ʃtɜːn/ Otto 1888–1969. German physicist. Stern studied with Einstein in Prague and Zürich, where he became a lecturer in 1914. After World War I he demonstrated by means of the ***Stern–Gerlach apparatus*** that elementary particles have wavelike properties as well as the properties of matter that had been demonstrated. He left Germany for the USA in 1933. He was awarded the Nobel Prize for Physics in 1943.

Sternberg /ʃtɜːnbəːg/ Josef von 1894–1969. Austrian film director, in the USA from childhood. He is best remembered for his seven films with Marlene Dietrich, including *The Blue Angel/Der blaue Engel* 1930, *Blonde Venus* 1932, and *The Devil Is a Woman* 1935, all of which are marked by his expressive use of light and shadow.

Sterne /stɜːn/ Laurence 1713–1768. Irish writer, creator of the comic anti-hero Tristram Shandy. *The Life and Opinions of Tristram Shandy, Gent* 1760–67, an eccentrically whimsical and bawdy novel, foreshadowed many of the techniques and devices of 20th-century novelists, including James Joyce. His other works include *A Sentimental Journey through France and Italy* 1768.

Sterne, born in Clonmel, Ireland, took orders in 1737 and became vicar of Sutton-in-the-Forest, Yorkshire, in the next year. In 1741 he married Elizabeth Lumley, producing an unhappy union largely because of his infidelity. He had a sentimental love affair with Eliza Draper, of which the *Letters of Yorick to Eliza* 1775 is a record.

A man should know something of his own country, too, before he goes abroad.

Laurence Sterne
Tristram Shandy 1760–67

Sterne Irish writer Laurence Sterne in a portrait by Joshua Reynolds, National Portrait Gallery, London. He was known mainly for the eccentric humour and bawdy nature of his early writings. Suffering from tuberculosis, Sterne journeyed to the warmer climate of southern France, inspiring his deeply personal Sentimental Journey through France and Italy.

Steuben /stjuːbən/ Friedrich Wilhelm von, Baron 1730–1794. Prussian military leader in the American Revolution 1775–83. After joining George Washington at Valley Forge 1778, he was named inspector general of the Continental army. He later saw action in the South and was present at the victory of Yorktown 1781.

Born in Prussia, Steuben began his military career in the Seven Years' War 1756–63. After leaving active duty 1763, he was a functionary in the court of Hohenzollern-Hechingen 1764–75 and was made a baron. He left Europe to seek employment as an officer in the American Revolution.

Stevens /stiːvənz/ Alfred 1817–1875. English sculptor, painter, and designer. He created the Wellington monument begun 1858 (St Paul's cathedral, London). He was devoted to High Renaissance art, especially to Raphael, and studied in Italy from 1833 to 1842.

Stevens /stiːvənz/ George 1904–1975. US film director who began as a director of photography. He made such films as *Swing Time* 1936 and *Gunga Din* 1939, and his reputation grew steadily, as did the length of his films. His later work included *A Place in the Sun* 1951, *Shane* 1953, and *Giant* 1956.

Stevens /stiːvnz/ John Paul 1920–. US jurist and associate justice of the US Supreme Court from 1975, appointed by President Ford. A moderate whose opinions and dissents were wide ranging, he opined that the death penalty is not by definition cruel and unusual punishment in *Jurek v Texas* 1976, and that the burning of the US flag in protest is unconstitutional in *Texas v Johnson*.

Born in Chicago, Illinois, USA, Stevens graduated from the University of Chicago and Northwestern University Law School and served as clerk to US Supreme Court Justice Wiley Rutledge.

After entering private practice, he also taught at Chicago and Northwestern before being appointed judge of the US Court of Appeals for the Seventh Circuit.

Stevens /stiːvənz/ Siaka Probin 1905–1988. Sierra Leone politician, president 1971–85. He was the leader of the moderate left-wing All People's Congress (APC), from 1978 the country's only legal political party.

Stevens was a police officer, industrial worker, and trade unionist before founding the APC. He became prime minister in 1968 and in 1971, under a revised constitution, became Sierra Leone's first president. He created a one-party state based on the APC, and remained in power until his retirement at the age of 80.

Stevens /stiːvənz/ Wallace 1879–1955. US poet. An insurance company executive, he was not recognized as a major poet until late in life. His volumes of poems include *Harmonium* 1923, *The Man with the Blue Guitar* 1937, and *Transport to Summer* 1947. *The Necessary Angel* 1951 is a collection of essays. An elegant and philosophical poet, he won the Pulitzer Prize 1954 for his *Collected Poems*.

Stevens of Ludgate /stiːvənz, ˈlʌdgeɪt/ David (Robert), Lord 1936– . British financier and newspaper publisher, chair of United Newspapers (provincial newspaper and magazine group based in the north of England) from 1981 and of Express Newspapers from 1985 (the right-wing *Daily* and *Sunday Express*, the tabloid *Daily Star*, and a few provincial papers).

Stevenson /stiːvənsən/ Adlai 1900–1965. US Democrat politician. As governor of Illinois 1949–53 he campaigned vigorously against corruption in public life, and as Democratic candidate for the presidency 1952 and 1956 was twice defeated by Eisenhower. In 1945 he was chief US delegate at the founding conference of the United Nations.

An editor is one who separates the wheat from the chaff and prints the chaff.

Adlai Stevenson
The Stevenson Wit

Stevenson /stiːvənsən/ Robert 1772–1850. Scottish engineer who built many lighthouses, including the Bell Rock lighthouse 1807–11.

Stevenson /stiːvənsən/ Robert Louis 1850–1894. Scottish novelist and poet, author of the adventure novel *Treasure Island* 1883. Later works included the novels *Kidnapped* 1886, *The Master of Ballantrae* 1889, *Dr Jekyll and Mr Hyde* 1886, and the anthology *A Child's Garden of Verses* 1885.

Stevenson was born in Edinburgh. He studied at the university there and qualified as a lawyer, but never practised. Early works include *An Island Voyage* 1878 and *Travels with a Donkey* 1879. In 1879 he met the American Fanny Osbourne in France and followed her to the USA, where they married in 1880. In the same year they returned to Britain, and he subsequently published a volume of stories, *The New Arabian Nights* 1882, and essays; for example, *Virginibus Puerisque* 1881 and *Familiar Studies of Men and Books* 1882. The humorous *The Wrong Box* 1889 and the novels *The Wrecker* 1892 and *The Ebb-tide* 1894 were written in collaboration with his stepson, Lloyd Osbourne (1868–1920). In 1890 he settled at Vailima, in Samoa, where he sought a cure for his tuberculosis.

Stewart /stjuːət/ Jackie (John Young) 1939– . Scottish motor-racing driver. Until surpassed by Alain →Prost (France) 1987, Stewart held the record for the most Formula One Grand Prix wins (27).

His first win was in 1965, and he started in 99 races. With manufacturer Ken Tyrrell, Stewart built up one of the sport's great partnerships. His last race was the 1973 Canadian Grand Prix. He pulled out of the next race (which would have been his 100th) because of the death of his team-mate Francois Cevert.

He is now a motor-racing commentator.

Stewart /stjuːət/ James 1908– . US actor. He made his Broadway debut in 1932 and soon after worked in Hollywood. Speaking with a soft drawl, he specialized in the role of the stubbornly honest, ordinary American in such films as *Mr Smith Goes to Washington* 1939, *The Philadelphia Story* 1940 (Academy Award), *It's a Wonderful Life* 1946, *Harvey* 1950, *The Man from Laramie* 1955, and *The FBI Story* 1959. His films with director Alfred →Hitchcock include *Rope* 1948, *Rear Window* 1954, *The Man Who Knew Too Much* 1956, and *Vertigo* 1958.

Stewart /stjuːət/ Michael, Baron Stewart of Fulham 1906–1990. English Labour politician, member of Parliament 1945–79. He held ministerial office in the governments of Clement Attlee and Harold Wilson, rising to foreign secretary 1968.

Stewart /stjuːət/ Potter 1915–1985. US jurist and appointed associate justice of the US Supreme Court 1958–81 by President Eisenhower. Seen as a moderate, he is known for upholding civil rights for minorities and for opinions on criminal procedure. He dissented in both *Escabedo* v *Illinois* 1964 and in *In re Gault* 1967, which gave juveniles due process rights.

Born in Chicago, Illinois, USA, Stevens graduated from Yale University and Yale Law School and entered private practice in New York City and Cincinnati, Ohio. He was appointed judge of the US Court of Appeals for the Sixth Circuit 1954.

Stieglitz /staɪglɪts/ Alfred 1864–1946. US photographer. After forming the Photo Secession group in 1903, he began the magazine *Camera Work*. Through exhibitions at his gallery '291' in New York he helped to establish photography as an art form. His works include 'Winter, Fifth Avenue' 1893 and 'Steerage' 1907. In 1924 he married the painter Georgia O'Keeffe, who was the model in many of his photographs.

Stilicho /stɪlɪkəʊ/ Flavius AD 359–408. Roman general, of Vandal origin, who campaigned successfully against the Visigoths and Ostrogoths. He virtually ruled the western empire as guardian of Honorius (son of →Theodosius I) but was executed on the orders of Honorius when he was suspected of wanting to make his own son successor to another son of Theodosius in the eastern empire.

Stilwell /stɪlwel/ Joseph Warren ('Vinegar Joe') 1883–1946. US general in World War II. In 1942 he became US military representative in China,

when he commanded the Chinese forces cooperating with the British (with whom he quarrelled) in Burma (now Myanmar); he later commanded all US forces in China, Burma, and India until recalled to the USA 1944 after differences over nationalist policy with the Guomindang (nationalist) leader Chiang Kai-shek. Subsequently he commanded the US 10th Army on the Japanese island of Okinawa.

Stimson /stɪmsən/ Henry Lewis 1867–1950. US politician. He was war secretary in Taft's cabinet 1911–13, Hoover's secretary of state 1929–33, and war secretary 1940–45.

Sting stage name of Gordon Sumner 1951– . English pop singer, songwriter, actor, and bass player. As a member of the trio **the Police** 1977–83, he had UK number-one hits with 'Message in a Bottle' 1979, 'Walking on the Moon' 1979, and 'Every Breath You Take' 1983. In his solo career he has drawn on a variety of musical influences in such albums as the jazz-based *The Dream of Blue Turtles* 1985, the eclectic *Nothing But the Sun* ... 1989, and *Soul Cages* 1991.

Emerging during the punk era, the Police were one of the first white pop groups to use a reggae-based sound. In his solo work, Sting has continued to blend musical sounds from all over the world into a western rock format. His career as an actor has been critically less successful. His films include *Quadrophenia* 1979, *Brimstone and Treacle* 1982, and *Dune* 1984. He has been heavily involved with fund-raising to preserve the Amazon rainforests and the traditional way of life of the indigenous Indians. He has also set up a record label devoted to recording world music called Pangaea.

Stirling /stɜːlɪŋ/ (Archibald) David 1915–1990. English army colonel and creator of the Special Air Service, which became the elite regiment of the British Army from 1942. In 1967 he cofounded the Watchguard organization, based in Guernsey, employing ex-SAS soldiers to provide bodyguards for Middle East rulers and others. He resigned from this organization in 1972.

I think transitional periods are rather exotic, more so than periods which have settled down and become rather fixed in their output.

James Stirling

Stirling /stɜːlɪŋ/ James 1926–1992. British architect, associated with collegiate and museum architecture. His works include the engineering building at Leicester University, and the Clore Gallery (the extension to house the →Turner collection) at the Tate Gallery, London, opened in 1987.

Stirling /stɜːlɪŋ/ James 1791–1865. Scottish naval officer and colonial administrator, the first governor of Western Australia 1828–39. Having explored the west coast of Australia in 1827, he persuaded the government to proclaim Western Australia a British colony (originally under the name of the Swan River Colony), and returned there with the first settlers in 1829.

Stockhausen Karlheinz 1928– . German composer of avant-garde music who has continued to explore new musical sounds and compositional techniques since the 1950s. His major works include *Gesang der Jünglinge* 1956 and *Kontakte* 1960 (electronic music); and *Sirius* 1977.

Since 1977 all his works have been part of *Licht*, a cycle of seven musical ceremonies intended for performance on the evenings of a week. He has completed *Donnerstag* 1980, *Samstag* 1984, *Montag* 1988, and *Dienstag* 1992. Earlier works include *Klavierstücke I–XIV* 1952–85; *Momente* 1961–64, *Mikrophonie I* 1964.

Stockwood /stɒkwʊd/ Arthur Mervyn 1913– . British Anglican cleric. As bishop of Southwark 1959–80, he expressed unorthodox views on homosexuality and in favour of the ordination of women.

Stoker /stəʊkə/ Bram (Abraham) 1847–1912. Irish novelist, actor, theatre manager, and author. His novel *Dracula* 1897 crystallized most aspects of the traditional vampire legend and became the source for all subsequent fiction and films on the subject.

Stoker wrote a number of other stories and novels of fantasy and horror, such as *The Lady of the Shroud* 1909.

A civil servant from 1866 to 1878, he then became business manager to the theatre producer Henry Irving.

Stokes /stəʊks/ George Gabriel 1819–1903. Irish physicist. During the late 1840s, he studied the viscosity (resistance to relative motion) of fluids. This culminated in *Stokes' law*, $F = 6(\epsilon)rv$, which applies to a force acting on a sphere falling through a liquid, where (ϵ) is the liquid's viscosity and r and v are the radius and velocity of the sphere.

Stokowski /stəˈkɒfski/ Leopold 1882–1977. US conductor, born in London. An outstanding experimentalist, he introduced modern music (for example, Mahler's Eighth Symphony) to the USA; appeared in several films; and conducted the music for Walt Disney's animated film *Fantasia* 1940.

Stone /stəʊn/ Harlan Fiske 1872–1946. US jurist. He was associate justice to the US Supreme Court 1925–41 and chief justice 1941–46 under President Roosevelt. During World War II he authored opinions favouring federal war powers and regulation of aliens.

Born in Chesterfield, New Hampshire, USA, Stone graduated from Amherst College and

Columbia University School of Law. He practised in New York City and taught at Columbia, serving as dean of the law school 1910–23. President Coolidge appointed Stone US attorney general 1924 and to the US Supreme Court 1925.

As an associate justice, Stone favoured judicial restraint, the making of decisions on constitutional rather than personal grounds. He dissented from numerous conservative decisions opposing President F D Roosevelt's New Deal legislation. He supported voting rights and use of the Constitution's commerce clause to justify federal legislation regulating interstate commerce.

Stone /stəʊn/ (John) Richard (Nicholas) 1913– . British economist, a statistics expert whose system of 'national income accounting' has been adopted in many countries. Nobel Prize for Economics 1984.

Stone /stəʊn/ Lucy 1818–1893. US feminist orator and editor. Married to the radical Henry Blackwell in 1855, she gained wide publicity when, after a mutual declaration rejecting the legal superiority of the man in marriage, she chose to retain her own surname despite her marriage. The term 'Lucy Stoner' was coined to mean a woman who advocated doing the same.

In the 1860s she helped to establish the American Woman Suffrage Association and founded and edited the Boston *Woman's Journal*, a suffragist paper that was later edited by her daughter Alice Stone Blackwell (1857–1950).

Stone /stəʊn/ Robert 1937– . US novelist and journalist. His *Dog Soldiers* 1974 is a classic novel about the moral destructiveness of the Vietnam War. *A Flag for Sunrise* 1982 similarly explores the political and moral consequences of US intervention in a corrupt South American republic. Among his other works is *Children of Light* 1986.

Stonehouse /stəʊnhaʊs/ John (Thompson) 1925–1988. British Labour Party politician. An active member of the Co-operative Movement, he entered Parliament in 1957 and held junior posts under Harold Wilson before joining his cabinet in 1967. In 1974 he disappeared in Florida in mysterious circumstances, surfacing in Australia, amid suspicions of fraudulent dealings. Extradited to Britain, he was tried and imprisoned for embezzlement. He was released in 1979, but was unable to resume a political career.

Stopes /stəʊps/ Marie (Carmichael) 1880–1958. Scottish birth-control campaigner. With her husband H V Roe (1878–1949), an aircraft manufacturer, she founded a London birth-control clinic 1921. The Well Woman Centre in Marie Stopes House, London, commemorates her work. She wrote plays and verse as well as the best-selling manual *Married Love* 1918.

Stoppard /stɒpɑːd/ Tom 1937– . Czechoslovak-born British playwright whose works use wit and wordplay to explore logical and philosophical ideas. His play *Rosencrantz and Guildenstern are Dead* 1966 was followed by comedies including *The Real Inspector Hound* 1968, *Jumpers* 1972, *Travesties* 1974, *Dirty Linen* 1976, *The Real Thing* 1982, and *Hapgood* 1988. He has also written for radio, television, and the cinema.

Storey /ˈstɔːri/ David Malcolm 1933– . English dramatist and novelist. His plays include *In Celebration* 1969, *Home* 1970, *Early Days* 1980, and *The March on Russia* 1989. Novels include *This Sporting Life* 1960.

Story /ˈstɔːri/ Joseph 1779–1845. US jurist and associate justice of the US Supreme Court 1811–45 under President Madison. He wrote several decisions defining the role of federal courts in admiralty law. The most notable was *United States v Schooner Amistad* 1841, in which the Court ordered black slaves who had seized a slaving ship repatriated to Africa.

Born in Marblehead, Massachusetts, Story was a graduate of Harvard College and practised law in Massachusetts. He served in the Massachusetts legislature 1805–08 and the US House of Representatives 1808–09, before returning to the Massachusetts legislature, of which he became speaker 1811.

Stoss /ʃtəʊs/ Veit. Also known as *Wit Stwosz c.* 1450–1533. German sculptor and painter, active in Nuremberg and Poland. He carved a wooden altarpiece with high relief panels in St Mary's, Kraków, a complicated design with numerous figures that centres on the *Death of the Virgin.*

Stoss was born in Nuremberg and returned there from Poland. The figure of St Roch in Sta Annunziata, Florence, shows his characteristic figure style and sculpted drapery.

Stowe /stəʊ/ Harriet Beecher 1811–1896. US suffragist, abolitionist, and author of the antislavery novel *Uncle Tom's Cabin*, first published serially 1851–52. The inspiration came to her in a vision in 1848, and the book brought immediate success.

Stowe was a daughter of Congregationalist minister Lyman →Beecher and in 1836 married C E Stowe, a professor of theology. Her book was radical in its time and did much to spread antislavery sentiment, but in the 20th century was criticized for sentimentality and racism.

'Do you know who made you?' 'Nobody, as I knows on,' said the child ... 'I 'spect I grow'd.'

Harriet Beecher Stowe
Uncle Tom's Cabin

Strabo /ˈstreɪbəʊ/ *c.* 63 BC–AD 24. Greek geographer and historian who travelled widely to collect first-hand material for his *Geography*.

Strachey /ˈstreɪtʃi/ (Giles) Lytton 1880–1932. English critic and biographer, a member of the Bloomsbury Group of writers and artists. He wrote *Landmarks in French Literature* 1912. The mocking and witty treatment of Cardinal Manning, Florence Nightingale, Thomas Arnold, and General Gordon in *Eminent Victorians* 1918 won him recognition. His biography of *Queen Victoria* 1921 was more affectionate.

Discretion is not the better part of biography.

Lytton Strachey

Stradivari /ˌstrædɪˈvɑːri/ Antonio (Latin form *Stradivarius*) 1644–1737. Italian stringed instrument maker, generally considered the greatest of all violin makers. He was born in Cremona and studied there with Niccolo →Amati. He produced more than 1,100 instruments from his family workshops, over 600 of which survive. The secret of his mastery is said to be in the varnish but is probably a combination of fine proportioning and ageing.

Strafford /ˈstræfəd/ Thomas Wentworth, 1st Earl of Strafford 1593–1641. English politician, originally an opponent of Charles I, but from 1628 on the Royalist side. He ruled despotically as Lord Deputy of Ireland 1632–39, when he returned to England as Charles's chief adviser and received an earldom. He was impeached in 1640 by Parliament, abandoned by Charles as a scapegoat, and beheaded.

Stowe Harriet Beecher Stowe, author of Uncle Tom's Cabin *1851–52. With its vivid depiction of the sufferings of families torn apart by slavery, the novel greatly furthered the abolitionist cause.*

Strand /strænd/ Paul 1890–1976. US photographer who used large-format cameras for his strong, clear, close-up photographs of natural objects.

Strange /streɪndʒ/ Curtis Northrup 1955– . US golfer, professional from 1976. He has won over 20 tournaments, including two 'majors', the 1988 and 1989 US Opens. In 1989 he became the fourth person to win $5 million in a golfing career.

Strange was born in Virginia. He won his first tournament in 1979 (Pensacola Open). He became the first person to win $1 million in a season in 1988.

Strasberg /ˈstræzbɜːɡ/ Lee 1902–1982. US actor and artistic director of the Actors Studio from 1948, who developed Method acting from →Stanislavsky's system; pupils have included Marlon Brando, Paul Newman, Julie Harris, Kim Hunter, Geraldine Page, Al Pacino, and Robert de Niro.

Strassburg /ˈɡɒtfriːd fɒn ˈstrɑːsbʊəɡ/ Gottfried von, lived c. 1210. German poet, author of the unfinished epic *Tristan und Isolde*, which inspired the German composer →Wagner.

Straus /straʊs/ Oscar 1870–1954. Austrian composer, born in Vienna. A pupil of Max Bruch, he was chief conductor and composer at the überbrettl cabaret, becoming a master of light satirical stage pieces. He is remembered for the operetta *The Chocolate Soldier* 1908.

Strauss /straʊs/ Franz-Josef 1915–1988. German conservative politician, leader of the West German Bavarian Christian Social Union (CSU) party 1961–88, premier of Bavaria 1978–88.

Born and educated in Munich, Strauss, after military service 1939–45, joined the CSU and was elected to the *Bundestag* (parliament) in 1949. He held ministerial posts during the 1950s and 1960s and became leader of the CSU 1961. In 1962 he lost his post as minister of defence when he illegally shut down the offices of *Der Spiegel* for a month, after the magazine revealed details of a failed NATO exercise. In the 1970s, Strauss opposed Ostpolitik (the policy of reconciliation with the East). He left the *Bundestag* to become premier of Bavaria in 1978, and was heavily defeated in 1980 as chancellor candidate. From 1982 Strauss sought to force changes in economic and foreign policy of the coalition under Chancellor Kohl.

Strauss /straʊs/ Johann (Baptist) 1825–1899. Austrian conductor and composer, the son of composer Johann Strauss (1804–1849). In 1872 he gave up conducting and wrote operettas, such as *Die Fledermaus* 1874, and numerous waltzes, such as *The Blue Danube* and *Tales from the Vienna Woods*, which gained him the title 'the Waltz King'.

Strauss /straʊs/ Richard (Georg) 1864–1949. German composer and conductor. He followed the German Romantic tradition but had a strongly personal style, characterized by his bold, colourful orchestration. He first wrote tone poems such as *Don Juan* 1889, *Till Eulenspiegel's Merry Pranks* 1895, and *Also sprach Zarathustra* 1896. He then moved on to opera with *Salome* 1905 and *Elektra* 1909, both of which have elements of polytonality. He reverted to a more traditional style with *Der Rosenkavalier* 1911.

Stravinsky /strəˈvɪnski/ Igor 1882–1971. Russian composer, later of French (1934) and US (1945) nationality. He studied under →Rimsky-Korsakov and wrote the music for the Diaghilev ballets *The Firebird* 1910, *Petrushka* 1911, and *The Rite of Spring* 1913 (controversial at the time for their unorthodox rhythms and harmonies). His versatile work ranges from his Neo-Classical ballet *Pulcinella* 1920 to the choral-orchestral *Symphony of Psalms* 1930. He later made use of serial techniques in such works as the *Canticum Sacrum* 1955 and the ballet *Agon* 1953–57.

Work brings inspiration, if inspiration is not discernible at the beginning.

Igor Stravinsky *Chronicles of My Life* 1935

Streep /striːp/ Meryl 1949– . US actress known for her strong character roles. She became a leading star of the 1980s, winning numerous awards. Her films include *The Deer Hunter* 1978, *Kramer vs Kramer* 1979 (Academy Award), *The French Lieutenant's Woman* 1980, *Sophie's Choice* 1982 (Academy Award), *Out of Africa* 1985, *Ironweed* 1988, *A Cry in the Dark* 1989, and the comedy *Death Becomes Her* 1992 .

Street /striːt/ J(abez) C(urry) 1906–1989. US physicist who, with Edward C Stevenson, discovered the muon (an elementary particle) in 1937.

Street /striːt/ Jessie (Mary, born Grey) 1889–1970. Australian feminist, humanist, peace worker, reformer, and writer. She was involved in the suffragette movement in England and later helped to found the Family Planning Association of Australia, and was active in the campaign for equal pay for women. She initiated the movement that resulted in the 1967 referendum which granted citizenship to Australian Aborigines.

Streeton /striːtn/ Arthur 1867–1943. Australian artist, a founder of the Heidelberg School, who pioneered Impressionistic renderings of Australia's landscape.

Streisand /ˈstraɪsænd/ Barbra (Barbara Joan) 1942– . US singer and actress who became a film star in *Funny Girl* 1968. Her subsequent films include *What's Up Doc?* 1972, *The Way We Were* 1973, and *A Star Is Born* 1979. *Yentl* 1983 was her masterwork, which she directed, scripted, composed, and starred in.

Stresemann /ʃtreɪzəmæn/ Gustav 1878–1929. German politician, chancellor in 1923 and foreign minister from 1923 to 1929 of the Weimar Republic. During World War I he was a strong nationalist but his views became more moderate under the Weimar Republic. His achievements included reducing the amount of war reparations paid by Germany after the Treaty of Versailles 1919; negotiating the Locarno Treaties 1925; and Germany's admission to the League of Nations. He shared the 1926 Nobel Peace Prize with Aristide Briand.

Strindberg /strɪndbɜːg/ August 1849–1912. Swedish playwright and novelist. His plays, influential in the development of dramatic technique, are in a variety of styles including historical plays, symbolic dramas (the two-part *Dödsdansen/The Dance of Death* 1901) and 'chamber plays' such as *Spöksonaten/The Ghost [Spook] Sonata* 1907. *Fadren/The Father* 1887 and *Fröken Julie/Miss Julie* 1888 are among his works.

Born in Stockholm, he lived mainly abroad after 1883, having been unsuccessfully prosecuted for blasphemy in 1884 following publication of his short stories *Giftas/Marrying*. His life was stormy and his work has been criticized for its hostile attitude to women, but he is regarded as one of Sweden's greatest writers.

I see the playwright as a lay preacher peddling the ideas of his time in popular form.

August Strindberg preface to *Miss Julie* 1888

Stroessner /stresnə/ Alfredo 1912– . Military leader and president of Paraguay 1954–89. As head of the armed forces from 1951, he seized power in a coup in 1954 sponsored by the right-wing ruling Colorado Party. Accused by his opponents of harsh repression, his regime spent heavily on the military to preserve his authority. Despite criticisms of his government's civil-rights record, he was re-elected seven times and remained in office until ousted in an army-led coup 1989.

Stroheim /ʃtrəʊhaɪm/ Erich von. Assumed name of Erich Oswald Stroheim 1885–1957. Austrian actor and director, in Hollywood from 1914. He was successful as an actor in villainous roles, but his career as a director was wrecked by his extravagance (*Greed* 1923) and he returned to acting in such international films as *La Grande Illusion* 1937 and *Sunset Boulevard* 1950.

Struve /ʃtruːvə/ Friedrich Georg Wilhelm 1793–1864. German-born Russian astronomer, a pioneer in the observation of double stars. The founder and first director (from 1839) of Pulkovo Observatory near St Petersburg, he was succeeded by his son *Otto Wilhelm Struve* (1819–1905).

His great-grandson *Otto Struve* (1897–1963) left the USSR in 1921 for the USA, where he became joint director of the Yerkes and McDonald observatories 1932 and championed the notion that planetary systems were common around stars.

Stuart /stjuːət/ or *Stewart* royal family who inherited the Scottish throne in 1371 and the English throne in 1603.

Stuart /stjuːət/ Gilbert Charles 1755–1828. American artist. A protégé of the American painter Benjamin →West in London 1776–82, he gained fame as one of the foremost portraitists of the time. Returning to the USA, he set up a studio in Philadelphia 1794. Best known for his portraits of George Washington, he produced portraits of various prominent public figures.

Stuart was born in North Kingstown, Rhode Island, and trained by the Scottish painter Cosmo Alexander. As well as living in England, he spent time in Ireland 1787–93, lived in Washington DC 1803–05, and resided in Boston from 1805 until his death.

Stuart /stjuːət/ John McDouall 1815–1866. Scottish-born Australian explorer. He went with Charles →Sturt on his 1844 expedition, and in 1860, after two unsuccessful attempts, crossed the centre of Australia from Adelaide in the southeast to the coast of Arnhem Land. He almost lost his life on the return journey.

Stubbs /stʌbz/ George 1724–1806. English artist, known for paintings of horses. After the publication of his book of engravings *The Anatomy of the Horse* 1766, he was widely commissioned as an animal painter.

Stubbs began his career as a portrait painter and medical illustrator in Liverpool. In 1754 he went to Rome, continuing to study nature and anatomy. Before settling in London in the 1760s he rented a farm and carried out a series of dissections of horses, which resulted in his book of engravings. The dramatic *Lion Attacking a Horse* 1770 (Yale University Art Gallery, New Haven, Connecticut) and the peaceful *Reapers* 1786 (Tate Gallery, London) show the variety of mood in his painting.

Stukeley /stjuːkli/ William 1687–1765. English antiquarian and pioneer archaeologist, who made some of the earliest accurate observations about Stonehenge 1740 and Avebury 1743. He originated the popular (but erroneous) idea that both were built by Druids.

Sturges /stɜːdʒɪz/ Preston. Adopted name of Edmond Biden 1898–1959. US film director and writer who enjoyed great success with a series of comedies in the early 1940s, including *Sullivan's Travels* 1941, *The Palm Beach Story* 1942, and *The Miracle of Morgan's Creek* 1943.

Sturluson /stʊələʊsɒn/ Snorri 1179–1241. Icelandic author of the Old Norse poems called Eddas and the *Heimskringla*, a saga chronicle of Norwegian kings until 1177.

Sturt /stɜːt/ Charles 1795–1869. British explorer and soldier. In 1828 he sailed down the Murrumbidgee River in SE Australia to the estuary of the Murray in circumstances of great hardship, charting the entire river system of the region.

Born in India, he served in the army, and in 1827 discovered with the Australian explorer Hamilton Hume the river Darling. Drawn by his concept of a great inland sea, he set out for the interior in 1844, crossing what is now known as the Sturt Desert, but failing to penetrate the Simpson Desert.

Stuyvesant /staɪvəsənt/ Peter 1610–1672. Dutch colonial leader in America. Appointed director general of New Netherland 1646, he arrived there in 1647. He reorganized the administration of the colony and established a permanent boundary with Connecticut by the Treaty of Hartford 1650. Forced to surrender the colony to the British 1664, Stuyvesant remained there for the rest of his life.

Born in Holland, Stuyvesant first worked as an official of the Dutch West India Company.

Suárez González /swɑːreθ ɡɒn'θɑːleθ/ Adolfo 1933– . Spanish politician, prime minister 1976–81. A friend of King Juan Carlos, he was appointed by the king to guide Spain into democracy after the death of the fascist dictator Franco.

Suárez worked in the National Movement for 18 years, but in 1975 became president of the newly established Unión del Pueblo Español (Spanish People's Union). He took office as prime minister at the request of the king, to speed the reform programme, but suddenly resigned 1981.

Suchocka Hanna 1946– . Polish politician, prime minister from 1992. She was chosen by President →Walesa as a replacement for prime minister Waldemar Pawlak, who was unable to form a viable government.

Formerly a lecturer in law, Suchocka served on the legislation committee of the Polish parliament (*Sejm*), where her abilities brought her to the attention of influential politicians. She was selected as prime minister mainly because her unaligned background won her the support of seven of the eight parties that agreed to join a coalition government.

Suckling /sʌklɪŋ/ John 1609–1642. English poet and dramatist. He was an ardent Royalist who tried to effect Lord →Strafford's escape from the Tower of London. On his failure, he fled to France and may have committed suicide. His chief lyrics appeared in *Fragmenta Aurea* and include 'Why so pale and wan, fond lover?'

Sucre /suːkreɪ/ Antonio José de 1795–1830. South American revolutionary leader. As chief lieutenant of Simón →Bolívar, he won several battles in freeing the colonies of Ecuador and Bolivia from Spanish rule, and in 1826 became president of Bolivia. After a mutiny by the army and invasion by Peru, he resigned in 1828 and was assassinated in 1830 on his way to join Bolívar.

Suetonius /suːɪtəʊnɪəs/ (Gaius Suetonius Tranquillus) *c.* AD 69–140. Roman historian, author of *Lives of the Caesars* (Julius Caesar to Domitian).

Sugar /ʃʊɡə/ Alan 1947– . British entrepreneur, founder in 1968 of the Amstrad electronics company, which holds a strong position in the European consumer electronics and personal-computer market. In 1985 he introduced a complete word-processing system at the price of £399. Subsequent models consolidated his success internationally.

Suger /suːʒeɪ/ *c.* 1081–1151. French historian and politician, regent of France during the Second Crusade. In 1122 he was elected abbot of St Denis, Paris, and was counsellor to, and biographer of, Louis VI and Louis VII. He began the reconstruction of St Denis as the first large-scale Gothic building.

Suharto /suːhɑːtəʊ/ Raden 1921– . Indonesian politician and general. He ousted Sukarno to become president 1967. He ended confrontation with Malaysia, invaded East Timor 1975, and reached a cooperation agreement with Papua New Guinea 1979. His authoritarian rule has met with domestic opposition from the left. He was re-elected 1973, 1978, 1983, and 1988.

Sukarno /suːkɑːnəʊ/ Achmed 1901–1970. Indonesian nationalist, president 1945–67. During World War II he cooperated in the local

Suharto General Suharto, president of Indonesia. He has made the army the country's primary political institution and the power base for his rule. Since the beginning of his fifth period of office 1988, speculation has been rife concerning his possible retirement. Given Suharto's political shrewdness, it is agreed that any succession is likely to be on his terms.

administration set up by the Japanese, replacing Dutch rule. After the war he became the first president of the new Indonesian republic, becoming president-for-life in 1966; he was ousted by →Suharto.

Suleiman /ˌsuːlɪˈmɑːn/ or *Solyman* 1494–1566. Ottoman sultan from 1520, known as *the Magnificent* and *the Lawgiver*. Under his rule, the Ottoman Empire flourished and reached its largest extent. He made conquests in the Balkans, the Mediterranean, Persia, and N Africa, but was defeated at Vienna in 1529 and Valletta (on Malta) in 1565. He was a patron of the arts, a poet, and an administrator.

Suleiman captured Belgrade in 1521, the Mediterranean island of Rhodes in 1522, defeated the Hungarians at Mohács in 1526, and was halted in his advance into Europe only by his failure to take Vienna, capital of the Austro-Hungarian Empire, after a siege Sept–Oct 1529. In 1534 he turned more successfully against Persia, and then in campaigns against the Arab world took almost all of N Africa and the Red Sea port of Aden. Only the Knights of Malta inflicted severe defeat on both his army and fleet when he tried to take Valletta in 1565.

Sulla /ˈsʌlə/ Lucius Cornelius 138–78 BC. Roman general and politician, a leader of the senatorial party. Forcibly suppressing the democrats in 88 BC, he departed for a successful campaign against →Mithridates VI Eupator of Pontus. The democrats seized power in his absence, but on his return Sulla captured Rome and massacred all opponents. The reforms he introduced as dictator, which strengthened the Senate, were backward-looking and short-lived. He retired 79 BC.

Sullivan /ˈsʌlɪvən/ Arthur (Seymour) 1842–1900. English composer who wrote operettas in collaboration with William Gilbert, including *HMS Pinafore* 1878, *The Pirates of Penzance* 1879, and *The Mikado* 1885. Their partnership broke down in 1896. Sullivan also composed serious instrumental, choral, and operatic works – for example, the opera *Ivanhoe* 1890 – which he valued more highly than the operettas.

Other Gilbert and Sullivan operettas include *Patience* (which ridiculed the Aesthetic movement) 1881, *The Yeomen of the Guard* 1888, and *The Gondoliers* 1889.

Sullivan /ˈsʌlɪvən/ Jim 1903–1977. Welsh-born rugby player. A great goal-kicker, he kicked a record 2,867 points in a 25-year Rugby League career covering 928 matches.

He played rugby union for Cardiff before joining Wigan Rugby League Club in 1921. He kicked 193 goals in 1933–34 (a record at the time) and against Flimby and Fothergill in 1925 he kicked 22 goals, still a record.

Sullivan /ˈsʌlɪvən/ John L(awrence) 1858–1918. US boxer. He won the heavyweight championship from Paddy Ryan 1882 and in the following years

Sullivan Arthur Sullivan, English composer whose prolific partnership with W S Gilbert produced 14 comic operas. It was a collaboration that lasted from 1871 to 1896, broken by a three-year interruption caused by a quarrel over invoices at the Savoy Theatre. He also wrote a Te Deum 1872, cantatas, and hymn-tunes such as Onward Christian Soldiers.

toured widely throughout the USA and British Isles. In 1892 he lost his title to James 'Gentleman Jim' Corbett in the first championship bout held according to the Marquis of Queensberry rules.

Born in Boston, Sullivan briefly attended Boston College before beginning a professional boxing career. After his retirement from the ring, Sullivan became a popular vaudevillian and was a saloonkeeper in New York.

Sullivan /ˈsʌlɪvən/ Louis Henry 1856–1924. US architect, a leader of the Chicago school of architects and an early developer of the skyscraper. His skyscrapers include the Wainwright Building, St Louis, 1890 and the Guaranty Building, Buffalo, 1894. He was the teacher of Frank Lloyd →Wright.

Sullivan was influential in the anti-ornament movement.

Form follows function

Louis Henry Sullivan 1895

Sullivan /ˈsʌlɪvən/ Pat(rick) 1887–1933. Australian-born US animator and cartoonist. He wrote and drew a newspaper comic strip called 'Sammie Johnson', turned it into a silent animated film 1916, and created the first cartoon-film hero to achieve world fame, *Felix the Cat* 1920.

Sully /sjuːˈliː/ Maximilien de Béthune, Duc de Sully 1560–1641. French politician, who served with the Protestant Huguenots in the wars of religion, and, as Henry IV's superintendent of finances 1598–1611, aided French recovery.

Sully-Prudhomme /sjuːˈliː pruːˈdɒm/ Armand 1839–1907. French poet who wrote philosophical verse including *Les Solitudes/Solitude* 1869, *La Justice/Justice* 1878, and *Le Bonheur/Happiness* 1888. He was awarded the Nobel Prize for Literature 1901.

Sumner /ˈsʌmnə/ Charles 1811–1874. US political leader. Elected to the US Senate as a FreeSoil Democrat 1852, he was defeated by South Carolina congressman Preston Brooks 1856 for his uncompromising abolitionist views on the issue of slavery. During the American Civil War 1861–65, he was a Republican leader in Congress. A supporter of Radical Reconstruction, he opposed President Grant's renomination 1872.

Born in Boston and educated at Harvard University, Sumner was admitted to the bar 1833. He travelled in Europe before teaching at Harvard, lecturing on abolitionism and pacifism.

Sumner /ˈsʌmnə/ James 1887–1955. US biochemist. In 1926 he succeeded in crystallizing the enzyme urease and demonstrating its protein nature. For this work Sumner shared the 1946 Nobel Prize for Chemistry with John Northrop and Wendell Stanley.

Sunderland /ˈsʌndələnd/ Robert Spencer, 2nd Earl of Sunderland 1640–1702. English politician, a sceptical intriguer who converted to Roman Catholicism to secure his place under James II, and then reverted with the political tide. In 1688 he fled to Holland (disguised as a woman), where he made himself invaluable to the future William III. Now a Whig, he advised the new king to adopt the system, which still prevails, of choosing the government from the dominant party in the Commons.

In the construction of a country it is not the practical workers, but the planners and idealists that are difficult to find.

Sun Yat-sen

Sun Yat-sen /sʌn jætˈsen/ or *Sun Zhong Shan* 1867–1925. Chinese revolutionary leader, founder of the Guomindang (Nationalist party) 1894, and provisional president of the Republic of China 1912 after playing a vital part in deposing the emperor. He was president of a breakaway government from 1921.

Sun Yat-sen was the son of a Christian farmer. After many years in exile he returned to China during the 1911 revolution that overthrew the Manchu dynasty and was provisional president of the republic in 1912. In an effort to bring unity to China, he soon resigned in favour of the military leader Yuan Shih-k'ai. As a result of Yuan's increasingly dictatorial methods, Sun established an independent republic in S China based in Canton 1921. He was criticized for lack of organizational ability, but his 'three people's principles' of nationalism, democracy, and social reform are accepted by both the Nationalists and the Chinese Communists.

Sun Zhong Shan /sʌn ˌdzʌŋˈʃɑːn/ Pinyin transliteration of →Sun Yat-sen.

Suraj-ud-Dowlah /suˈrɑːdʒ ʊd ˈdaʊlə/ 1728–1757. Nawab of Bengal, India. He captured Calcutta from the British 1756 and imprisoned some of the British in the Black Hole of Calcutta (a small room in which a number of them died), but was defeated in 1757 by Robert →Clive, and lost Bengal to the British at the Battle of Plassey. He was killed in his capital, Murshidabad.

Surrey /ˈsʌri/ Henry Howard, Earl of Surrey *c.* 1517–1547. English courtier and poet, executed on a poorly based charge of high treason. With Thomas →Wyatt, he introduced the sonnet to England and was a pioneer of blank verse.

Surtees /ˈsɜːtiːz/ John 1934– . British racing driver and motorcyclist, the only person to win world titles on two and four wheels.

After winning seven world motorcycling titles 1956–60, he turned to motor racing and won the world title in 1964. He later produced his own racing cars.

Surtees /ˈsɜːtiːz/ R(obert) S(mith) 1803–1864. British novelist. He created Jorrocks, a sporting grocer, and in 1838 published *Jorrocks's Jaunts and Jollities*.

Sutcliff /ˈsʌtklɪf/ Rosemary 1920– . British historical novelist who writes for both adults and children. Her books include *The Eagle of the Ninth* 1954, *Tristan and Iseult* 1971, and *The Road to Camlann* 1981.

Sutherland /ˈsʌðələnd/ Donald 1934– . Canadian-born US film actor who usually appears in off-beat roles. He starred in *M.A.S.H.* 1970, and his subsequent films include *Klute* 1971, *Don't Look Now* 1973, and *Revolution* 1986. He is the father of actor Kiefer Sutherland.

Sutherland /ˈsʌðələnd/ Earl Wilbur Jr 1915–1974. US physiologist, discoverer of cyclic AMP, a chemical 'messenger' made by a special enzyme in the wall of living cells. Many hormones operate by means of this messenger. He was awarded the Nobel Prize for Medicine 1971.

Sutherland /ˈsʌðələnd/ Graham (Vivian) 1903– 1980. English painter, graphic artist, and designer, active mainly in France from the late 1940s. He painted portraits, landscapes, and religious subjects.

In the late 1940s Sutherland turned increasingly to characterful portraiture. His portrait of *Winston Churchill* 1954 was disliked by its subject and eventually burned on the instructions of Lady Churchill (studies survive).

His *Christ in Glory* tapestry 1962 is in Coventry Cathedral. Other work includes ceramics and designs for posters, stage costumes, and sets.

Sutherland /ˈsʌðələnd/ Joan 1926– . Australian soprano. She went to England in 1951, where she made her debut the next year in *The Magic Flute*; later roles included *Lucia di Lammermoor*, Donna Anna in *Don Giovanni*, and Desdemona in *Otello*. She retired from the stage in 1990.

Suu Kyi Aung San 1945– . Myanmar (Burmese) politician and human rights campaigner, leader of the National League for Democracy (NLD), the main opposition to the military junta. When the NLD won the 1990 elections, the junta refused to surrender power, and placed Suu Kyi under house arrest. She was awarded the Nobel Peace Prize 1991 in recognition of her 'non-violent struggle for democracy and human rights' in Myanmar. She is the daughter of former Burmese premier →Aung San.

Educated in India and Oxford University from 1960 she later worked at the UN and married Oxford academic Michael Aris, and settled in England. In protest against human rights abuses and the brutal suppression of dissent in Burma she formed, on her return there from England 1988, the NLD opposition movement to campaign for democratic reform.

Suvorov /suˈvɔːrɒv/ Aleksandr Vasilyevich 1729–1800. Russian field marshal, victorious against the Turks 1787–91, the Poles 1794, and the French army in Italy 1798–99 in the Revolutionary Wars.

Suzman /ˈsuzmən/ Helen 1917– . South African politician and human-rights activist. A university lecturer concerned about the inhumanity of the apartheid system, she joined the white opposition to the ruling National Party and became a strong advocate of racial equality, respected by black communities inside and outside South Africa. In 1978 she received the United Nations Human Rights Award. She retired from active politics in 1989.

Suzuki /suˈzuːki/ Zenkō 1911– . Japanese politician. Originally a socialist member of the Diet in 1947, he became a conservative (Liberal Democrat) in 1949, and was prime minister 1980–82.

Svedberg /ˈsvedˌberi/ Theodor 1884–1971. Swedish chemist. In 1924 he constructed the first ultracentrifuge, a machine that allowed the rapid separation of particles by mass. He was awarded the Nobel Prize for Chemistry 1926.

Svevo /ˈsveivəʊ/ Italo. Pen name of Ettore Schmitz 1861–1928. Italian novelist whose books include *As a Man Grows Older* 1898 and *Confessions of Zeno* 1923.

Swan /swɒn/ Joseph Wilson 1828–1914. English inventor of the incandescent-filament electric lamp and of bromide paper for use in developing photographs.

Swanson /ˈswɒnsən/ Gloria. Stage name of Gloria Josephine Mae Svenson 1897–1983. US actress, a star of silent films who influenced American tastes and fashion for more than 20 years. She retired in 1932 but made several major comebacks. Her work includes *Sadie Thompson* 1928, *Queen Kelly* 1928 (unfinished), and *Sunset Boulevard* 1950.

Swedenborg /ˈswiːdnbɔːg/ Emanuel 1688–1772. Swedish theologian and philosopher. He trained as a scientist, but from 1747 concentrated on scriptural study, and in *Divine Love and Wisdom* 1763 concluded that the Last Judgement had taken place in 1757, and that the **New Church**, of which he was the prophet, had now been inaugurated. His writings are the scriptures of the sect popularly known as Swedenborgians, and his works are kept in circulation by the Swedenborg Society, London.

Sweet /swiːt/ Henry 1845–1912. British philologist, author of works on Old and Middle English, who took to England German scientific techniques of language study. He was said to be the original of Professor Higgins in George Bernard Shaw's play *Pygmalion*.

Swift /swɪft/ Jonathan 1667–1745. Irish satirist and Anglican cleric, author of *Gulliver's Travels* 1726, an allegory describing travel to lands inhabited by giants, miniature people, and intelligent horses. Other works include *The Tale of a Tub* 1704, attacking corruption in religion and learning; contributions to the Tory paper *The Examiner*, of which he was editor 1710–11; the satirical *A Modest Proposal* 1729, which suggested that children of the poor should be eaten; and many essays and pamphlets.

Swift, born in Dublin, became secretary to the diplomat William Temple (1628–1699) at Moor Park, Surrey, where his friendship with the child 'Stella' (Hester Johnson 1681–1728) began in 1689. Returning to Ireland, he was ordained in the Church of England 1694, and in 1699 was made a prebendary of St Patrick's, Dublin. In 1710 he became a Tory pamphleteer, and obtained the deanery of St Patrick in 1713. His *Journal to Stella* is a series of letters, 1710–13, in which he described his life in London. 'Stella' remained the love of his life, but 'Vanessa' (Esther Vanhomrigh 1690–1723), a Dublin woman who had fallen in love with him, jealously wrote to her rival in 1723 and so shattered his relationship with both women. From about 1738 his mind began to fail.

Swinburne /ˈswɪnbɜːn/ Algernon Charles 1837–1909. English poet. He attracted attention with the choruses of his Greek-style tragedy *Atalanta in Calydon* 1865, but he and →Rossetti were attacked in 1871 as leaders of 'the fleshly school of poetry', and the revolutionary politics of *Songs before Sunrise* 1871 alienated others.

Swineshead Richard active about 1350. British scientist and leading member of a group of natural scientists associated with Merton College, Oxford, who attempted to analyse and quantify the various forms of motion. Swineshead was known as 'the Calculator'.

Swinton /ˈswɪntən/ Ernest 1868–1951. British soldier and historian. He served in South Africa and in World War I, and was the inventor of the tank in 1916.

Sydenham /ˈsɪdənəm/ Thomas 1624–1689. English physician, the first person to describe measles and to recommend the use of quinine for relieving symptoms of malaria. His original reputation as 'the English Hippocrates' rested upon his belief that careful observation is more useful than speculation. His *Observationes medicae* was published in 1676.

Sydow /ˈsiːdəʊ/ Max (Carl Adolf) von 1929– . Swedish actor associated with the director Ingmar Bergman. He made his US debut as Jesus in *The Greatest Story Ever Told* 1965. His other films include *The Seventh Seal* 1957, *The Exorcist* 1973, and *Hannah and Her Sisters* 1985.

Sykes Percy Molesworth 1867–1945. English explorer, soldier, and administrator who surveyed much of the territory in SW Asia between Baghdad, the Caspian Sea, and the Hindu Kush during World War I (1914–18).

In 1894 he was the first British consul to Kerman (now in Iran) and Persian Baluchistan. Later he raised and commanded the South Persian Rifles. His histories of Persia and Afghanistan were published in 1915 and 1940.

Symington /ˈsɪmɪŋtən/ William 1763–1831. Scottish engineer who built the first successful steamboat. He invented the steam road locomotive in 1787 and a steamboat engine in 1788. His steamboat the *Charlotte Dundas* was completed in 1802.

Symonds /ˈsɪməndz/ John Addington 1840–1893. British critic who spent much of his life in Italy and Switzerland, and campaigned for homosexual rights. He was author of *The Renaissance in Italy* 1875–86. His frank memoirs were finally published in 1984.

Symons /ˈsɪmənz/ Arthur 1865–1945. Welsh critic, follower of Walter →Pater, and friend of the artists Toulouse-Lautrec and Aubrey Beardsley, the poets Stéphane Mallarmé and W B Yeats, and the novelist Joseph Conrad. He introduced T S Eliot to the poetry of Jules Laforgue and wrote *The Symbolist Movement in Literature* 1900.

Synge /sɪŋ/ J(ohn) M(illington) 1871–1909. Irish playwright, a leading figure in the Irish dramatic revival of the early 20th century. His six plays reflect the speech patterns of the Aran Islands and W Ireland. They include *In the Shadow of the Glen* 1903, *Riders to the Sea* 1904, and *The Playboy of the Western World* 1907, which caused riots at the Abbey Theatre, Dublin, when first performed.

Synge /sɪŋ/ Richard 1914– . British biochemist who investigated paper chromatography (a means of separating mixtures). By 1940 techniques of chromatography for separating proteins had been devised. Still lacking were comparable techniques for distinguishing the amino acids that constituted the proteins. By 1944, Synge and his colleague Archer Martin had worked out a procedure, known as ascending chromatography, which filled this gap and won them the 1952 Nobel Prize for Chemistry.

Szent-Györgyi /sent'dʒɜːdʒi/ Albert 1893–1986. Hungarian-born US biochemist who isolated vitamin C and studied the chemistry of muscular activity. He was awarded the Nobel Prize for Medicine 1937.

In 1928 Szent-Györgyi isolated a substance from the adrenal glands that he named hexuronic acid; when he found the same substance in cabbages and oranges, he suspected that he had finally isolated vitamin C.

Discovery consists of seeing what everybody has seen and thinking what nobody has thought.

Albert Szent-Györgyi

Szilard /ˈsɪlɑːd/ Leo 1898–1964. Hungarian-born US physicist who, in 1934, was one of the first scientists to realize that nuclear fission, or atom splitting, could lead to a chain reaction releasing enormous amounts of instantaneous energy. He emigrated to the USA in 1938 and there influenced →Einstein to advise President Roosevelt to begin the nuclear arms programme. After World War II he turned his attention to the newly emerging field of molecular biology.

Szymanowski Karol (Maliej) 1882–1937. Polish composer of orchestral works, operas, piano music, and violin concertos. He was director of the Conservatoire in Warsaw from 1926.

T

Tacitus /ˈtæsɪtəs/ Publius Cornelius *c.* AD 55–*c.* 120. Roman historian. A public orator in Rome, he was consul under Nerva 97–98 and proconsul of Asia 112–113. He wrote histories of the Roman Empire, *Annales* and *Historiae*, covering the years AD 14–68 and 69–97 respectively. He also wrote a *Life of Agricola* 97 (he married Agricola's daughter in 77) and a description of the German tribes, *Germania* 98.

Tafawa Balewa /təˈfɑːwə bəˈleɪwə/ Alhaji Abubakar 1912–1966. Nigerian politician, prime minister from 1957 to 1966, when he was assassinated in a coup d'état.

Tafawa Balewa entered the House of Representatives 1952, was minister of works 1952–54, and minister of transport 1954–57.

Taft /tæft/ Robert Alphonso 1889–1953. US right-wing Republican senator from 1939, and a candidate for the presidential nomination 1940, 1944, 1948, and 1952. He sponsored the Taft–Hartley Labor Act 1947, restricting union power. He was the son of President William Taft.

Taft William Taft, 27th US president and later chief justice, the only person to have headed both the executive and the judicial branches of the US government. As chief justice of the US Supreme Court, Taft improved the efficiency of the judicial machinery by securing the passage of the Judiciary Act 1925.

Taft /tæft/ William Howard 1857–1930. 27th president of the USA 1909–13, a Republican. He was secretary of war 1904–08 in Theodore Roosevelt's administration, but as president his conservatism provoked Roosevelt to stand against him in the 1912 election. Taft served as chief justice of the Supreme Court 1921–30.

Tagliacozzi /ˌtælʤəˈkɒtsi/ Gaspare 1546–1599. Italian surgeon who pioneered plastic surgery. He was the first to repair noses lost in duels or through syphilis. He also repaired ears. His method involved taking flaps of skin from the arm and grafting them into place.

Taglioni /tælˈjəʊni/ Marie 1804–1884. Italian dancer. A ballerina of ethereal style and exceptional lightness, she was the first to use pointe work, or dancing on the toes, as an expressive part of ballet rather than as sheer technique. She created many roles, including the title role in *La Sylphide* 1832, first performed at the Paris Opéra, and choreographed by her father *Filippo* (1771–1871).

Marie's brother *Paolo* (1808–1884) was a choreographer and ballet master at Berlin Court Opera 1856–83, and his daughter *Marie* (1833–1891) danced in Berlin and London, creating many roles in her father's ballets.

Tagore /təˈgɔː/ Rabindranath 1861–1941. Bengali Indian writer, born in Calcutta, who translated into English his own verse *Gitanjali* ('song offerings') 1912 and his verse play *Chitra* 1896. Nobel Prize for Literature 1913.

An ardent nationalist and advocate of social reform, he resigned his knighthood as a gesture of protest against British repression in India.

The butterfly counts not months but moments, and has time enough.

Rabindranath Tagore
Fireflies 1928

Taine /teɪn/ Hippolyte Adolphe 1828–1893. French critic and historian. He analysed literary works as products of period and environment, as in *Histoire de la littérature anglaise*/*History of English Literature* 1863 and *Philosophie de l'art*/*Philosophy of Art* 1865–69.

Takeshita /tæˈkeʃtə/ Noboru 1924– . Japanese right-wing politician. Elected to parliament as a Liberal Democratic Party (LDP) deputy 1958, he became president of the LDP and prime minister Oct 1987. He and members of his administration were shown in the Recruit scandal to have been involved in insider-trading and he resigned April 1989.

Takeshita, son of a *sake* brewer, trained as a kamikaze pilot during World War II. He was a schoolteacher before beginning his political career in the House of Representatives, rising to chief cabinet secretary to Prime Minister Satō 1971–72 and finance minister under Nakasone.

As prime minister he introduced a *furusato* (home-town) project giving 3,200 towns and villages a grant of 100 million yen (£500,000) each. This benefited construction companies, who were among the main backers of Takeshita's LDP faction. The Recruit scandal and the introduction of a tax-reform bill including a consumption tax in 1988 caused popular approval of Takeshita's government to drop dramatically. His profits from Recruit shares were revealed to be almost £900,000, and in atonement his closest aide committed suicide.

Talbot /ˈtɔːlbət/ William Henry Fox 1800–1877. English pioneer of photography. He invented the paper-based calotype process, the first negative/positive method. Talbot made photograms several years before Louis Daguerre's invention was announced.

In 1851 he made instantaneous photographs and in 1852 photo engravings. *The Pencil of Nature* 1844–46 by Talbot was the first book of photographs published.

Taliesin /tælˈjesɪn/ lived *c.* 550. Legendary Welsh poet, a bard at the court of the king of Rheged in Scotland. Taliesin allegedly died at Taliesin (named after him) in Dyfed, Wales.

Talleyrand /ˈtælɪrænd/ Charles Maurice de Talleyrand-Périgord 1754–1838. French politician and diplomat. As bishop of Autun 1789–91 he supported moderate reform during the French Revolution, was excommunicated by the pope, and fled to the USA during the Reign of Terror (persecution of anti-revolutionaries). He returned and became foreign minister under the Directory 1797–99 and under Napoleon 1799–1807. He represented France at the Congress of Vienna 1814–15.

Speech was given to man to disguise his thoughts.

Charles de Talleyrand

Tallis /ˈtælɪs/ Thomas *c.* 1505–1585. English composer in the polyphonic style. He wrote masses, anthems, and other church music.

Among his works are the setting for 40 voices of *Spem in alium non habui* (about 1573) and a collection of 34 motets, *Cantiones sacrae*, 1575 (of which 16 are by Tallis and 18 by Byrd). In 1575 Elizabeth I granted Tallis and Byrd the monopoly for printing music and music paper in England.

Tambo /ˈtæmbəu/ Oliver 1917–1993. South African nationalist politician, in exile 1960–90, president of the African National Congress (ANC) 1977–91. Because of poor health, he was given the honorary post of national chair July 1991, and Nelson →Mandela resumed the ANC presidency.

Tambo was expelled from teacher training for organizing a student protest, and joined the ANC 1944. He set up a law practice with Mandela in Johannesburg 1952. In 1956 Tambo, with other ANC members, was arrested on charges of treason; he was released the following year. When the ANC was banned 1960, he left South Africa to set up an external wing. He became acting ANC president 1967 and president 1977, during Mandela's imprisonment. In Dec 1990 he returned to South Africa.

Tamerlane /ˈtæmələɪn/ or *Tamburlaine* or *Timur i Leng* 1336–1405. Mongol ruler of Samarkand from 1369 who conquered Persia, Azerbaijan, Armenia, and Georgia. He defeated the Golden Horde 1395, sacked Delhi 1398, invaded Syria and Anatolia, and captured the Ottoman sultan in Ankara 1402; he died invading China.

Tanaka /təˈnɑːkə/ Kakuei 1918– . Japanese right-wing politician, leader of the dominant Liberal Democratic Party (LDP) and prime minister 1972–74. In 1976 he was charged with corruption and resigned from the LDP but remained a powerful faction leader.

In the Diet (Japanese parliament) from 1947, Tanaka was minister of finance 1962–65 and of international trade and industry 1971–72, before becoming LDP leader. In 1974 he had to resign the premiership because of allegations of corruption and 1976 he was arrested for accepting bribes from the Lockheed Corporation while premier. He was found guilty 1983, but remained in the Diet as an independent deputy pending appeal. He was also implicated in the 1988–89 Recruit scandal of insider trading.

Taney /ˈtɔːni/ Roger Brooke 1777–1864. US lawyer. He was President Jackson's attorney general 1831, and US secretary of the treasury 1833–35. In 1835 he was appointed as chief justice of the US Supreme Court. In the Dred Scott 1857 he ruled that Congress had no right to ban slavery in the territories, a decision that gravely aggravated sectional tensions.

Born in Calvert County, Maryland, Taney was educated at Dickinson College and became a barrister 1799. He served as a Maryland state senator 1816–21 and state attorney general 1827–31.

Tange /'tæŋgeɪ/ Kenzo 1913– . Japanese architect. His works include the National Gymnasium, Tokyo, for the 1964 Olympics, and the city of Abuja, planned to replace Lagos as the capital of Nigeria.

Tanguy /tɒŋ'giː/ Yves 1900–1955. French Surrealist painter who lived in the USA from 1939. His inventive canvases feature semi-abstract creatures in a barren landscape.

Tanguy was first inspired to paint by de →Chirico's work and in 1925 he joined the Surrealist movement. He soon developed his characteristic style with bizarre, slender forms in a typically Surrealist wasteland.

Tanizaki /ˌtænɪ'zɑːki/ Jun-ichirō 1886–1965. Japanese novelist. His works include a version of →Murasaki's *The Tale of Genji* 1939–41, *The Makioka Sisters* in three volumes 1943–48, and *The Key* 1956.

Tanner /'tænə/ Beatrice Stella. Unmarried name of actress Mrs Patrick →Campbell.

Tarbell /'tɑːbl/ Ida Minerva 1857–1944. US journalist whose exposés of corruption in high places made her one of the most prominent 'muckrakers' in the USA. She was an editor and contributor to *McClure's Magazine* 1894–1906. Her book *The History of the Standard Oil Company* 1904 sparked antitrust reform.

Born in Erie County, Pennsylvania, USA, Tarbell was educated at Allegheny College and the Sorbonne, Paris, France, and became an editor of the *Chautauquan* 1883. Her autobiography, *All in a Day's Work*, appeared 1939. From 1906 to 1915 she worked on the staff of the *American Magazine*.

Tarkington /'tɑːkɪŋtən/ Booth 1869–1946. US novelist. His novels for young people, which include *Penrod* 1914, are classics. He was among the best-selling authors of the early 20th century with works such as *Monsieur Beaucaire* 1900 and novels of the Midwest, including *The Magnificent Ambersons* 1918 (filmed 1941 by Orson Welles).

Tarkovsky /tɑː'kɒfski/ Andrei 1932–1986. Soviet film director whose work is characterized by an epic style combined with intense personal spirituality. His films include *Solaris* 1972, *Mirror* 1975, *Stalker* 1979, and *The Sacrifice* 1986.

Tarquinius Superbus /tɑː'kwɪniəs suː'pɜːbəs/ lived 5th century BC. Last king of Rome 534–510 BC. He abolished certain rights of Romans, and made the city powerful. He was deposed when his son Sextus raped →Lucretia.

Tartini /tɑː'tiːni/ Giuseppe 1692–1770. Italian composer and violinist. In 1728 he founded a school of violin playing in Padua. A leading exponent of violin technique, he composed the *Devil's Trill* sonata, about 1714.

Tasman /'tæzmən/ Abel Janszoon 1603–1659. Dutch navigator. In 1642, he was the first European to see Tasmania. He also made the first European sightings of New Zealand, Tonga, and Fiji.

He called Tasmania Van Diemen's Land in honour of the governor general of the Netherlands Indies; it was subsequently renamed in his honour 1856.

Tasso /'tæsəʊ/ Torquato 1544–1595. Italian poet, author of the romantic epic poem of the First Crusade *Gerusalemme Liberata/Jerusalem Delivered* 1574, followed by the *Gerusalemme Conquistata/Jerusalem Conquered*, written during the period from 1576 when he was mentally unstable.

At first a law student at Padua, he overcame his father's opposition to a literary career by the success of his romantic poem *Rinaldo* 1562, dedicated to Cardinal Luigi d'Este, who took him to Paris. There he met the members of the Pléiade group of poets. Under the patronage of Duke Alfonso d'Este of Ferrara, he wrote his pastoral play *Aminta* 1573.

Tate /teɪt/ Jeffrey 1943– . English conductor. He was appointed principal conductor of the English Chamber Orchestra 1985 and was principal conductor of the Royal Opera House, Covent Garden, London, 1986–91.

Tate qualified as a doctor before turning to a career in music. He worked at Covent Garden 1970–77 and subsequently with Pierre →Boulez in Bayreuth. He has conducted opera in Paris, Geneva, and at the Metropolitan Opera, New York.

Tate /teɪt/ Nahum 1652–1715. Irish poet, born in Dublin. He wrote an adaptation of Shakespeare's *King Lear* with a happy ending. He also produced a version of the psalms and hymns; among his poems is 'While shepherds watched'. He became British poet laureate 1692.

---

*As pants the hart for cooling streams
When heated in the chase.*

Nahum Tate and Nicholas Brady
The Psalms

Tate /teɪt/ Phyllis (Margaret) 1911–1987. British composer. Her works include *Concerto for Saxophone and Strings* 1944, the opera *The Lodger* 1960, based on the story of Jack the Ripper, and *Serenade to Christmas* for soprano, chorus, and orchestra 1972.

Tati /tæ'tiː/ Jacques. Stage name of Jacques Tatischeff 1908–1982. French comic actor, director, and writer. He portrayed Monsieur Hulot, the embodiment of polite opposition to modern mechanization, in a series of films beginning with *Les Vacances de M Hulot/Monsieur Hulot's Holiday* 1953, and including *Mon Oncle/My Uncle* 1959 and *Playtime* 1968.

Tatlin /tætlɪn/ Vladimir 1885–1953. Russian artist, cofounder of the revolutionary art movement *Constructivism*. After encountering Cubism in Paris 1913 he evolved his first Constructivist works, using raw materials such as tin, glass, plaster, and wood to create abstract sculptures that he suspended in the air.

Tatum /teɪtəm/ Art(hur) 1910–1956. US jazz pianist who, in the 1930s, worked mainly as a soloist. Tatum is considered among the most technically brilliant of jazz pianists and his technique and chromatic harmonies influenced many musicians, such as Oscar Peterson (1925–). He improvised with the guitarist Tiny Grimes (1916–) in a trio from 1943.

Tatum /teɪtəm/ Edward Lawrie 1909–1975. US microbiologist. For his work on biochemical genetics, he shared the 1958 Nobel Prize for Medicine with George Beadle and Joshua Lederberg.

Taube /tɔːbi/ Henry 1915– . US chemist who established the basis of inorganic chemistry through his study of the loss or gain of electrons by atoms during chemical reactions.
   Nobel prize 1983.

Taussig /tausɪg/ Helen Brooke 1898–1986. US cardiologist who developed surgery for 'blue' babies. Such babies never fully develop the shunting mechanism in the circulatory system that allows blood to be oxygenated in the lungs before passing to the rest of the body. The babies are born chronically short of oxygen and usually do not survive without surgery.

Tavener /tævənə/ John (Kenneth) 1944– . English composer whose individual and sometimes abrasive works include the dramatic cantata *The Whale* 1968 and the opera *Thérèse* 1979. He has also composed music for the Eastern Orthodox Church.

Taverner /tævənə/ John 1495–1545. English organist and composer. He wrote masses and motets in polyphonic style, showing great contrapuntal skill, but as a Protestant renounced his art. He was imprisoned 1528 for heresy, and, as an agent of Thomas Cromwell, assisted in the dissolution of the monasteries.

A racing tipster who only reached Hitler's level of accuracy would not do well for his clients.

A J P Taylor
The Origins of the Second World War 1961

Taylor /teɪlə/ A(lan) J(ohn) P(ercivale) 1906–1990. English historian and television lecturer. International history lecturer at Oxford University 1953–63, he established himself as an authority on modern British and European history and did much to popularize the subject, giving the first televised history lectures. His books include *The Struggle for Mastery in Europe 1848–1918* 1954, *The Origins of the Second World War* 1961, and *English History 1914–1945* 1965.
   Taylor lectured at Manchester University 1930–38 and was a fellow of Magdalen College, Oxford, 1938–76.

Taylor /teɪlə/ Elizabeth 1932– . English-born US actress whose films include *National Velvet* 1944, *Cat on a Hot Tin Roof* 1958, *Butterfield 8* 1960 (Academy Award), *Cleopatra* 1963, and *Who's Afraid of Virginia Woolf?* 1966 (Academy Award).

Taylor /teɪlə/ Elizabeth (born Coles) 1912–1975. British novelist. Her books include *At Mrs Lippincote's* 1946 and *Angel* 1957.

Taylor /teɪlə/ Frederick Winslow 1856–1915. US engineer and management consultant, the founder of scientific management. His ideas, published in *Principles of Scientific Management* 1911, were based on the breakdown of work to the simplest tasks, the separation of planning from execution of tasks, and the introduction of time-and-motion studies. His methods were clearly expressed in assembly-line factories, but have been criticized for degrading and alienating workers and producing managerial dictatorship.

Taylor /teɪlə/ Zachary 1784–1850. 12th president of the USA 1849–50. A veteran of the War

Taylor English-born US film actress Elizabeth Taylor in Cleopatra 1963, during the making of which her well-publicized relationship with co-star Richard Burton began. Famous as a child star, she became a celebrated beauty who appeared in many romantic films before gaining a reputation as a dramatic actress.

Taylor 12th US president Zachary Taylor. His successful military campaign during the Mexican War ensured his Whig presidential nomination. Although a slave-owner himself, Taylor supported antislavery elements pressing for the admission of California (acquired from Mexico) to the Union as a free state.

of 1812 and a hero of the Mexican War (1846–48), he was nominated for the presidency by the Whigs in 1848 and was elected, but died less than one and a half years into his term. He was succeeded by Vice President Millard Fillmore.

Since I began to compose I have made it my object to be, in my craft, what the most illustrious masters were in theirs, that is to say... an artisan, just as a shoemaker is.

Pyotr Tchaikovsky

Tchaikovsky /tʃaɪˈkɒfski/ Pyotr Il'yich 1840–1893. Russian composer. His strong sense of melody, personal expression, and brilliant orchestration are clear throughout his many Romantic works, which include six symphonies, three piano concertos, a violin concerto, operas (for example, *Eugene Onegin* 1879), ballets (for example, *The Nutcracker* 1892), orchestral fantasies (for example, *Romeo and Juliet* 1870), and chamber and vocal music.

Professor of harmony at Moscow 1865, he later met →Balakirev, becoming involved with the nationalist movement in music. He was the first Russian composer to establish a reputation with Western audiences.

Tebaldi /teˈbældi/ Renata 1922– . Italian dramatic soprano, renowned for the controlled purity of her voice and for her roles in →Puccini operas.

Tebbit /tebɪt/ Norman 1931– . British Conservative politician. He was minister for employment 1981–83, minister for trade and industry 1983–85, chancellor of the Duchy of Lancaster 1985–87, and chair of the party 1985–87. As his relations with Margaret Thatcher cooled, he returned to the back benches 1987.

Tecumseh /tɪˈkʌmsə/ 1768–1813. North American Indian chief of the Shawnee. He attempted to unite the Indian peoples from Canada to Florida against the encroachment of white settlers, but the defeat of his brother **Tenskwatawa**, 'the Prophet', at the battle of Tippecanoe in Nov 1811 by W H Harrison, governor of the Indiana Territory, largely destroyed the confederacy built up by Tecumseh. He was commissioned a brigadier general in the British army during the War of 1812, and died in battle.

Tedder /tedə/ Arthur William, 1st Baron Tedder 1890–1967. UK marshal of the Royal Air Force in World War II. As deputy supreme commander under US general Eisenhower 1943–45, he was largely responsible for the initial success of the 1944 Normandy landings.

He was air officer commanding RAF Middle East 1941–43, where his method of pattern bombing became known as 'Tedder's carpet'.

Teilhard de Chardin /teɪˈɑː də ʃɑːˈdæŋ/ Pierre 1881–1955. French Jesuit theologian, palaeontologist, and philosopher. He developed a creative synthesis of nature and religion, based on his fieldwork and fossil studies. Publication of his *Le Phénomène humain*/*The Phenomenon of Man*, written 1938–40, was delayed (due to his unorthodox views) until after his death by the embargo of his superiors. He saw humanity as being in a constant process of evolution, moving towards a perfect spiritual state.

Born in the Puy-de-Dôme, he entered the Society of Jesus 1899, was ordained 1911, and during World War I was a stretcher bearer, taking his final vows 1918. From 1951 until his death he lived in the USA.

Tej Bahadur /teɪg bəˈhɑːdʊə/ 1621–1675. Indian religious leader, ninth guru (teacher) of Sikhism 1664–75, executed for refusing to renounce his faith.

Te Kanawa Kiri 1944– . New Zealand soprano. Te Kanawa's first major role was the Countess in Mozart's *The Marriage of Figaro* at Covent Garden, London, 1971. Her voice combines the purity and intensity of the upper range with an extended lower range of great richness and resonance. Apart from classical roles, she has also featured popular music in her repertoire, such as the 1984 recording of Leonard Bernstein's *West Side Story*.

Te Kanawa *Drawing on the rich vocal traditions of her native New Zealand, Kiri Te Kanawa brings both dignity and intelligence to her operatic roles. Her voice, a glowing mezzo-soprano graduating to soprano, gives an impression of sustained physical and emotional power.*

Telemann /ˈteɪləmæn/ Georg Philipp 1681–1767. German Baroque composer, organist, and conductor at the Johanneum, Hamburg, from 1721. He was exceedingly prolific, producing 25 operas, 1,800 church cantatas, hundreds of other vocal works, and 600 instrumental works.

Telford /ˈtelfəd/ Thomas 1757–1834. Scottish civil engineer who opened up N Scotland by building roads and waterways. He constructed many aqueducts and canals, including the Caledonian canal 1802–23, and erected the Menai road suspension bridge 1819–26, a type of structure scarcely tried previously in England. In Scotland he constructed over 1,600 km/1,000 mi of road and 1,200 bridges, churches, and harbours.

In 1963 the new town of Telford, Shropshire, 32 km/20 mi NW of Birmingham, was named after him.

Teller /ˈtelə/ Edward 1908– . Hungarian-born US physicist known as the father of the hydrogen bomb, which he worked upon, after taking part in the atom bomb project, at the Los Alamos research centre, New Mexico, 1946–52. He was a key witness against his colleague Robert →Oppenheimer at the security hearings 1954. He was widely believed to be the model for the leading character in Stanley Kubrick's 1964 film *Dr Strangelove*. More recently he has been one of the leading supporters of the Star Wars programme (Strategic Defense Initiative).

Temple /ˈtempəl/ Shirley 1928– . US actress who became the most successful child star of the

1930s. Her films include *Bright Eyes* 1934 (Academy Award), in which she sang 'On the Good Ship Lollipop', *Curly Top* 1935, and *Rebecca of Sunnybrook Farm* 1938. Her film career virtually ended by the time she was 12. As Shirley Temple Black, she became active in the Republican Party and was US chief of protocol 1976–77. She was appointed US ambassador to Czechoslovakia 1989.

Teng Hsiao-ping /ˈteŋ ʃaʊˈpɪŋ/ alternative spelling of →Deng Xiaoping, Chinese politician.

Teniers /ˈteniəz/ family of Flemish painters, active in Antwerp. **David Teniers the Younger** (David II, 1610–1690) became court painter to Archduke Leopold William, governor of the Netherlands, in Brussels. He painted scenes of peasant life.

As curator of the archduke's art collection, David Teniers made many copies of the pictures and a collection of engravings, *Theatrum Pictorium* 1660. His peasant scenes are humorous and full of vitality, inspired by →Brouwer. His father, **David Teniers the Elder** (David I, 1582–1649), painted religious pictures.

Tenniel /ˈtenjəl/ John 1820–1914. English illustrator and cartoonist, known for his illustrations for Lewis Carroll's *Alice's Adventures in Wonderland* 1865 and *Through the Looking-Glass* 1872.

He joined the satirical magazine *Punch* 1850, and for over 50 years was one of its leading cartoonists.

Tennstedt /ˈtenʃtet/ Klaus 1926– . German conductor, musical director of the London Philharmonic Orchestra 1983–87. He excelled at interpreting works by Mozart, Beethoven, Bruckner, and Mahler.

Tennyson /ˈtenɪsən/ Alfred, 1st Baron Tennyson 1809–1892. English poet, poet laureate 1850–92, whose verse has a majestic, musical quality. His works include 'The Lady of Shalott', 'The Lotus Eaters', 'Ulysses', 'Break, Break, Break', 'The Charge of the Light Brigade'; the longer narratives *Locksley Hall* 1832 and *Maud* 1855; the elegy *In Memoriam* 1850; and a long series of poems on the Arthurian legends *The Idylls of the King* 1857–85.

Tennyson was born at Somersby, Lincolnshire. The death of A H Hallam (a close friend during his years at Cambridge) 1833 prompted the elegiac *In Memoriam*, unpublished until 1850, the year in which he succeeded Wordsworth as poet laureate and married Emily Sellwood.

Tenzing Norgay /ˈtensɪŋ/ known as **Sherpa Tenzing** 1914–1986. Nepalese mountaineer. In 1953 he was the first, with Edmund Hillary, to reach the summit of Mount Everest.

He had previously made 19 Himalayan expeditions as a porter. He subsequently became a director of the Himalayan Mountaineering Institute, Darjeeling.

Terborch /təˈbɔːx/ Gerard 1617–1681. Dutch painter of small-scale portraits and genre (everyday) scenes, mainly of soldiers at rest or wealthy families in their homes. He travelled widely in

Europe. *The Peace of Münster* 1648 (National Gallery, London) is an official group portrait.

Terbrugghen /təˈbrʊxən/ Hendrik 1588–1629. Dutch painter, a leader of the *Utrecht school* with Honthorst. He visited Rome around 1604 and was inspired by Caravaggio's work. He painted religious subjects and genre (everyday) scenes.

Terence /ˈterəns/ (Publius Terentius Afer) 190–159 BC. Roman dramatist, born in Carthage and taken as a slave to Rome, where he was freed and came under →Scipio Africanus Minor's patronage. His surviving six comedies (including *The Eunuch* 161 BC) are subtly characterized and based on Greek models.

Teresa /təˈreɪzə/ Mother. Born Agnes Bojaxhiu 1910– . Roman Catholic nun. She was born in Skopje, Albania, and at 18 entered a Calcutta convent and became a teacher. In 1948 she became an Indian citizen and founded the Missionaries of Charity, an order for men and women based in Calcutta that helps abandoned children and the dying. She was awarded the Nobel Peace Prize 1979.

Jesus said love one another. He didn't say love the whole world.

Mother Teresa March 1980

Teresa, St /təˈriːzə/ 1515–1582. Spanish mystic who founded an order of nuns 1562. She was subject to fainting fits, during which she saw visions. She wrote *The Way to Perfection* 1583 and an autobiography, *Life of the Mother Theresa of Jesus*, 1611. In 1622 she was canonized, and in 1970 was made the first female Doctor of the Church. She was born in Avila.

Tereshkova /ˌterɪʃˈkəʊvə/ Valentina Vladimirovna 1937– . Soviet cosmonaut, the first woman to fly in space. In June 1963 she made a three-day flight in *Vostok 6*, orbiting the Earth 48 times.

Terry /ˈteri/ Alfred Howe 1827–1890. US military leader. He served with distinction in the American Civil War 1861–65. After the war he commanded the Department of Dakota and also served in the Department of the South 1869–72. He was George →Custer's commander in the 1876 Sioux War and later negotiated with Sitting Bull, supervising the opening of the Northern Plains.

Terry was born in Hartford, Connecticut, educated at Yale University, and became a barrister 1849. During the Civil War he was colonel of the 2nd Connecticut militia and was promoted to brigadier general 1865.

Terry /ˈteri/ (John) Quinlan 1937– . British Neo-Classical architect. His work includes country houses, for example Merks Hall, Great Dunmow, Essex, 1982, and the larger-scale Richmond, London, riverside project, commissioned 1984.

Terry *British actress Dame Ellen Terry, who played Mamilius in* The Winter's Tale *at the age of eight. She went on to become the leading Shakespearean actress of her time and had roles written for her by both George Bernard Shaw and James Barrie.*

Terry /ˈteri/ Ellen 1847–1928. British actress, leading lady to Henry →Irving from 1878. She excelled in Shakespearean roles, such as Ophelia in *Hamlet*. She was a correspondent of longstanding with the playwright G B Shaw.

Terry-Thomas /ˈtɒməs/ Stage name of Thomas Terry Hoar Stevens 1911–1990. British film comedy actor who portrayed upper-class English fools and cads in such films as *I'm All Right Jack* 1959, *It's a Mad, Mad, Mad, Mad World* 1963, and *How to Murder Your Wife* 1965.

Tertullian /tɜːˈtʌliən/ Quintus Septimius Florens AD 155–222. Carthaginian Father of the Church, the first major Christian writer in Latin; he became a leading exponent of Montanism, a movement that strove to return to the purity of primitive Christianity.

It is certain because it is impossible.

Tertullian *De Carne Christi*

Tesla /ˈteslə/ Nikola 1856–1943. Croatian electrical engineer who emigrated to the USA 1884. He invented fluorescent lighting, the Tesla induction motor, and the Tesla coil, and developed the alternating current (AC) electrical supply system.

Teyte /teɪt/ Maggie 1888–1976. British lyric soprano. She is remembered for her Mozartian roles, such as Cherubino in *The Marriage of Figaro*, and was coached as Mélisande in *Pelléas et Mélisande* by the opera's composer, Debussy.

Thackeray /ˈθækərɪ/ William Makepeace 1811–1863. English novelist and essayist, born in Calcutta, India. He was a regular contributor to *Fraser's Magazine* and *Punch*. *Vanity Fair* 1847–48 was his first novel, followed by *Pendennis* 1848, *Henry Esmond* 1852 (and its sequel *The Virginians* 1857–59), and *The Newcomes* 1853–55, in which Thackeray's tendency to sentimentality is most marked.

Son of an East India Company official, he was educated at Cambridge. He studied law, and then art in Paris, before ultimately settling to journalism in London. Other works include *The Book of Snobs* 1848 and the fairy tale *The Rose and the Ring* 1855.

Thaïs /ˈθeɪɪs/ 4th century BC. Greek courtesan, mistress of →Alexander the Great and later wife of →Ptolemy I, king of Egypt. She allegedly instigated the burning of Persepolis, the capital of the Persian empire.

Thalberg /ˈθɔːlbɜːg/ Irving Grant 1899–1936. US film-production executive. At the age of 20 he was head of production at Universal Pictures, and in 1924 he became production supervisor of the newly formed Metro-Goldwyn-Mayer (MGM). He was responsible for such prestige films as *Ben-Hur* 1926 and *Mutiny on the Bounty* 1935. With Louis B Mayer he built up MGM into one of the biggest Hollywood studios of the 1930s.

Thales /ˈθeɪliːz/ 640–546 BC. Greek philosopher and scientist. He made advances in geometry, predicted an eclipse of the Sun 585 BC, and, as a philosophical materialist, theorized that water was the first principle of all things, that the Earth floated on water, and so proposed an explanation for earthquakes. He lived in Miletus in Asia Minor.

Thant, U /uː ˈθænt/ 1909–1974. Burmese diplomat, secretary general of the United Nations 1962–71. He helped to resolve the US-Soviet crisis over the Soviet installation of missiles in Cuba, and he made the controversial decision to withdraw the UN peacekeeping force from the Egypt–Israel border 1967.

Tharp /ˈθɑːp/ Twyla 1942– . US modern dancer and choreographer who has worked with various companies, including American Ballet Theater. Her works include *Eight Jelly Rolls* 1971, *Deuce Coupe* 1973, and *Push Comes to Shove* 1976.

Thatcher /ˈθætʃə/ Margaret Hilda (born Roberts), Baroness Thatcher of Kesteven 1925– . British Conservative politician, prime minister 1979–90. She was education minister 1970–74 and Conservative Party leader from 1975. In 1982 she sent British troops to recapture the Falkland Islands from Argentina. She confronted trade-union power during the miners' strike 1984–85, sold off majority stakes in many public utilities to the private sector, and reduced the influence of local government through such measures as the abolition of metropolitan councils, the control of expenditure through 'rate-capping', and the introduction of the community charge, or poll tax,

from 1989. In 1990 splits in the cabinet over the issues of Europe and consensus government forced her resignation. An astute Parliamentary tactician, she tolerated little disagreement, either from the opposition or from within her own party.

Margaret Thatcher was born in Grantham, the daughter of a grocer, and studied chemistry at Oxford before becoming a barrister. As minister for education 1970–74 she faced criticism for abolishing free milk for schoolchildren over eight. She was nevertheless an unexpected victor in the 1975 leadership election when she defeated Edward Heath. As prime minister she sharply reduced public spending to bring down inflation, but at the cost of generating a recession: manufacturing output fell by a fifth, and unemployment rose to over three million. Her popularity revived after her sending a naval force to recapture the Falkland Islands 1982.

Her second term of office was marked by the miners' strike 1984–85, which ended in defeat for the miners and indicated a shifted balance of power away from the unions. In Oct 1984 she narrowly avoided an IRA bomb that exploded during the Conservative Party conference.

Her election victory 1987 made her the first prime minister in 160 years to be elected for a third term, but she became increasingly isolated by her autocratic, aloof stance, which allowed little time for cabinet debate. In 1986 defence minister Michael Heseltine resigned after supporting a European-led plan for the rescue of the Westland helicopter company. In 1989 Nigel Lawson resigned as chancellor when she publicly supported her financial adviser Alan Walters against him. The introduction of the poll tax from 1989 was widely unpopular. Finally, Geoffrey Howe resigned as home secretary in Nov 1990 over her public denial of an earlier cabinet consensus over the single European currency.

Thatcher was the most influential peacetime Conservative prime minister of the 20th century. She claimed to have 'rolled back the frontiers of the state' by reducing income- tax rates, selling off council houses, and allowing for greater individual choice in areas such as education. However, such initiatives often resulted paradoxically in greater central government control. She left the opposition Labour Party in disarray, and forced it to a fundamental review of its policies. Her vindictiveness against the left was revealed in her crusade against local councils, which she pursued at the cost of a concern for social equity.

In 1991, after three months of relative quiescence on the back benches, she made it evident that she intended to remain an active voice in domestic and international politics. She was created a life peer 1992. Her first speech in the House of Lords was an attack on the government's policies.

Themistocles /θəˈmɪstəkliːz/ *c.* 525–*c.* 460 BC. Athenian soldier and politician. Largely through his policies in Athens (creating its navy and strengthening its walls), Greece was saved from Persian conquest. He fought with distinction in the Battle of Salamis 480 BC during the Persian War. About 470 he was accused of embezzlement and conspiracy against Athens, and banished by Spartan influence. He fled to Asia, where Artaxerxes, the Persian king, received him with favour.

Theocritus /θiːˈɒkrɪtəs/ *c.* 310–*c.* 250 BC. Greek poet whose *Idylls* became models for later pastoral poetry. Probably born in Syracuse, he spent much of his life in Alexandria.

Theodora /θiːəˈdɔːrə/ 508–548. Byzantine empress from 527. She was originally the mistress of Emperor Justinian before marrying him in 525. She earned a reputation for charity, courage, and championing the rights of women.

The daughter of a bear-keeper, Theodora became an actress and, as mistress and later wife of the emperor, the most influential woman in Europe, since Justinian consulted her on all affairs of state.

Theodorakis /θɪədəˈrɑːkɪs/ Mikis 1925– . Greek composer. He was imprisoned 1967–70 for attempting to overthrow the military regime of Greece.

Theodoric of Freiburg /θiˈɒdərɪk, ˈfraɪbɜːɡ/ *c.* 1250–1310. German scientist and monk. He studied in Paris 1275–77. In his work *De Iride/On the Rainbow* he describes how he used a water-filled sphere to simulate a raindrop, and determined that colours are formed in the raindrops and that light is reflected within the drop and can be reflected again, which explains secondary rainbows.

Theodoric the Great /θiˈɒdərɪk/ *c.* 455–526. King of the Ostrogoths from 474 in succession to his father. He invaded Italy 488, overthrew King Odoacer (whom he murdered) and established his own Ostrogothic kingdom there, with its capital in Ravenna. He had no strong successor, and his kingdom eventually became part of the Byzantine Empire of Justinian.

Theodosius I /θiːəˈdəʊsiəs/ 'the Great' *c.* AD 346–395. Roman emperor AD 388–95. A devout Christian and an adherent of the Nicene creed, he dealt harshly with heretics and in 391 crushed all forms of pagan religion in the empire. He thus founded the orthodox Christian state, acquiring his title. After his reign, the Roman empire was divided into eastern and western halves.

Theodosius II /θiːəˈdəʊsiəs/ 401–450. Byzantine emperor from 408 who defeated the Persians 421 and 441, and from 441 bought off →Attila's Huns with tribute.

Theophanes the Greek 14th century. Byzantine painter active in Russia. He influenced painting in Novgorod, where his frescoes in Our Saviour of the Transfiguration are dated to 1378. He also worked in Moscow with Andrei →Rublev.

Thérèse of Lisieux, St /təˈreɪz, liːˈsjɜː/ 1873–1897. French saint. She was born in Alençon, and entered a Carmelite convent in Lisieux at 15, where her holy life induced her superior to ask her to write her spiritual autobiography. She advocated the 'Little Way of Goodness' in small things in everyday life, and became known as the 'Little Flower of Jesus'. She died of tuberculosis and was canonized 1925.

Theroux /θəˈruː/ Paul (Edward) 1941– . US novelist and travel writer. His works include the novels *Saint Jack* 1973, *The Mosquito Coast* 1981, *Doctor Slaughter* 1984, and *Chicago Loop* 1990, and accounts of his travels by train *The Great Railway Bazaar* 1975, *The Old Patagonian Express* 1979, *Kingdom by the Sea* 1983, and *Riding the Iron Rooster* 1988.

Thesiger /ˈθesɪdʒə/ Wilfred Patrick 1912– . English explorer and writer. His travels and military adventures in Abyssinia, North Africa, and Arabia are recounted in a number of books, including *Arabian Sands* 1959, *Desert, Marsh and Mountain* 1979, and the autobiographical *The Life of My Choice* 1987.

In deserts, however arid, I had never felt homesick for green fields and woods in spring, but now that I was back in England I longed with an ache that was almost physical to be back in Arabia.

Wilfred Thesiger,
Desert, Marsh and Mountain 1979

Thespis /ˈθespɪs/ 6th century BC. Greek poet, born in Attica, said to have introduced the first actor into plays (previously presented by choruses only), hence the word *thespian* for an actor. He was also said to have invented tragedy and to have introduced the wearing of linen masks.

Thibault /tiːˈbəʊ/ Anatole-Franço is. Real name of French writer Anatole →France.

Thiers /tiˈeə/ Louis Adolphe 1797–1877. French politician and historian, first president of the Third Republic 1871–73. He held cabinet posts under Louis Philippe, led the parliamentary opposition to Napoleon III from 1863, and as head of the provisional government 1871 negotiated peace with Prussia and suppressed the briefly autonomous Paris Commune.

His books include *Histoire de la Révolution française/History of the French Revolution* 1823–27.

Thistlewood /ˈθɪsəlwʊd/ Arthur 1770–1820. English Radical. A follower of the pamphleteer Thomas Spence (1750–1814), he was active in the Radical movement and was executed as the chief leader of the Cato Street Conspiracy to murder government ministers.

Thomas /tɒməs/ Clarence 1948– . US Justice of the Supreme Court whose nomination to the Supreme Court 1991 by President Bush caused controversy. He is opposed to the policy of affirmative action, which positively discriminates in favour of minority groups and from which he himself has benefited; and he is thought unlikely to uphold legislation that makes abortion freely available. At the public televised Senate confirmation hearings, Anita Hill, a former colleague, accused Thomas of sexually harassing her ten years earlier. He denied the allegations.

Thomas was born in Georgia in extreme poverty, and was admitted to Yale law school under a quota system. Under President Reagan, he was head of the Equal Employment Opportunities Commission 1982–90 and became a federal appeals-court judge 1990. It was widely believed that his Republican views and opposition to abortion, rather than his legal experience, caused him to be nominated to the Supreme Court the following year, and the nomination was not supported by the National Association for the Advancement of Colored People, which would normally back a black nominee. Thomas was sworn in in Oct 1991 after being confirmed by 52 votes to 48, the narrowest margin for any nominee to the Supreme Court in the 20th century. The Thomas case exposed American concern over sexual harassment at the workplace and led corporate America to fear that an increased number of harassment suits might ensue.

Thomas /tɒməs/ Dylan (Marlais) 1914–1953. Welsh poet. His poems include the celebration of his 30th birthday 'Poem in October' and the evocation of his youth 'Fern Hill' 1946. His 'play for voices' *Under Milk Wood* 1954 describes with humour and compassion a day in the life of the residents of a small Welsh fishing village, Llareggub. The short stories of *Portrait of the Artist as a Young Dog* 1940 are autobiographical.

Born in Swansea, son of the English teacher at the local grammar school where he was educated, he worked as a reporter on the *South Wales Evening Post*, then settled as a journalist in London and published his first volume *Eighteen Poems* 1934.

Thomas /tɒməs/ Edward (Philip) 1878–1917. English poet, born in London of Welsh parents. He met the US poet Robert Frost and began writing poetry under his influence. Some of his poems were published early in 1917 under the pseudonym Edward Eastaway in *An Anthology of New Verse*. *Poems* was published Oct 1917 after his death in World War I, followed by *Last Poems* 1918.

Thomas /tɒməs/ Lowell (Jackson) 1892–1981. US journalist, a radio commentator for the Columbia Broadcasting System (CBS) 1930–76. Travelling to all World War II theatres of combat and to remote areas of the world, he became one of America's best-known journalists. He was the author of *With Lawrence in Arabia* 1924.

Thomas /tɒməs/ Norman Mattoon 1884–1968. US political leader, six times Socialist candidate for president 1928–48. One of the founders of the American Civil Liberties Union 1920, he also served as a director of the League for Industrial Democracy 1922–37. He was a brilliant speaker and published *A Socialist's Faith* 1951.

Born in Marion, Ohio, USA, Thomas graduated from Princeton University 1905 and after study at the Union Theological Seminary was ordained a Presbyterian minister 1911. As pastor of the East Harlem Church he first confronted the problem of urban poverty and joined the Socialist Party 1918, leaving the ministry for political activism two years later.

By 1950, he noted, most of his so-called radical platform had been adopted by the USA, such as Social Security and public-health programmes.

Thomas /tɒməs/ R(onald) S(tuart) 1913– . Welsh poet whose verse, as in *Song at the Year's Turning* 1955, contrasts traditional Welsh values with encroaching 'English' sterility.

Thomas /tɒməs/ Seth 1785–1859. US clock manufacturer. Establishing his own firm 1812 he became enormously successful in the manufacture of affordable shelf clocks. In 1853 the firm was reorganized as the Seth Thomas Clock Company and continued to prosper into the 20th century.

Born in Wolcott, Connecticut, Thomas trained as a carpenter and cabinetmaker. In 1807 he joined a partnership in Plymouth, Connecticut, for the production of clocks. Seth Thomas Clock Company's headquarters were based in Plymouth Hollow, Connecticut, now renamed Thomaston.

Thomas à Kempis /tɒməs ə 'kempɪs/ 1380–1471. German Augustinian monk who lived at the monastery of Zwolle. He took his name from his birthplace Kempen; his real surname was Hammerken. His *De Imitatio Christi/Imitation of Christ* is probably the most widely known devotional work ever written.

Thomas Aquinas medieval philosopher; see →Aquinas, St Thomas.

Thomas, St /tɒməs/ in the New Testament, one of the 12 Apostles, said to have preached in S India, hence the ancient churches there were referred to as the 'Christians of St Thomas'. He is not the author of the Gospel of St Thomas, the Gnostic collection of Jesus' sayings.

Thompson /tɒmpsən/ Daley (Francis Morgan) 1958– . English decathlete who broke the world record four times since winning the Commonwealth Games decathlon title 1978. He has won two more Commonwealth titles (1982, 1986), two Olympic gold medals (1980, 1984), three European medals (silver 1978; gold 1982, 1986), and a world title (1983). He retired in 1992.

Thompson /tɒmpsən/ David 1770–1857. Canadian explorer and surveyor who mapped extensive areas of W Canada, including the Columbia River, for the Hudson's Bay Company 1789–1811.

Thompson /tɒmpsən/ Flora 1877–1948. English novelist whose trilogy *Lark Rise to Candleford* 1945 describes Victorian rural life.

Thompson /tɒmpsən/ Francis 1859–1907. British poet. In *Sister Songs* 1895 and *New Poems* 1897 Thompson, who was a Roman Catholic, expressed a mystic view of life.

Thompson /tɒmpsən/ John Taliaferro 1860–1940. US colonel, inventor of the Thompson submachine-gun.

Thompson /tɒmpsən/ Richard 1949– . English virtuoso guitarist, songwriter, and singer, whose work spans rock, folk, and avant-garde. He was a member of pioneering folk-rock group Fairport Convention 1966–71, contributing to albums like *What We Did on Our Holidays* 1968.

With his wife Linda Thompson he made several albums such as *Shoot Out the Lights* 1982. Later solo work includes *Rumor and Sigh* 1991.

Thomsen /tɒmsən/ Christian (Jürgensen) 1788–1865. Danish archaeologist. He devised the classification of prehistoric cultures into Stone Age, Bronze Age, and Iron Age.

Thomson /tɒmsən/ Elihu 1853–1937. US inventor. He founded, with E J Houston (1847–1914), the Thomson-Houston Electric Company 1882, later merging with the Edison Company to form the General Electric Company. He made advances into the nature of the electric arc and invented the first high-frequency dynamo and transformer.

Thomson /tɒmsən/ George Paget 1892–1975. English physicist whose work on interference phenomena in the scattering of electrons by crystals helped to confirm the wavelike nature of particles. He shared a Nobel prize with C J →Davisson 1937.

He was the son of J J Thomson.

Thomson /tɒmsən/ J(oseph) J(ohn) 1856–1940. English physicist who discovered the electron. He was responsible for organizing the Cavendish atomic research laboratory at Cambridge University. His work inaugurated the electrical theory of the atom, and his elucidation of positive rays and their application to an analysis of neon led to Frederick →Aston's discovery of isotopes. Nobel prize 1906.

Thomson /tɒmsən/ James 1700–1748. Scottish poet whose descriptive blank verse poem *The Seasons* 1726–30 was a forerunner of the Romantic movement. He also wrote the words of 'Rule, Britannia'.

Thomson /tɒmsən/ James 1834–1882. Scottish poet, remembered for his despairing poem 'The City of Dreadful Night' 1874.

Thomson /tɒmsən/ Virgil 1896–1989. US composer and critic. He studied in France with Nadia →Boulanger 1921–22 and returned to Paris 1925–40, mixing with Gertrude Stein and her circle. He is best known for his opera *Four Saints in Three Acts* 1927–33 to a libretto by Stein, and the film scores *The Plow That Broke the Plains* 1936 and *Louisiana Story* 1948. His music is notable for a refined absence of expression, his criticism for trenchant matter-of-factness, both at odds with the prevailing US musical culture.

Thoreau /θɔːrəʊ/ Henry David 1817–1862. US author and naturalist. His work *Walden, or Life in the Woods* 1854 stimulated the back-to-nature movement, and he completed some 30 volumes based on his daily nature walks. His essay 'Civil Disobedience' 1849, prompted by his refusal to pay taxes, advocated peaceful resistance to unjust laws and had a wide impact, even in the 20th century.

Thorndike /θɔːndaɪk/ Edward Lee 1874–1949. US educational psychologist whose experiments in behaviour of cats and dogs in a 'puzzle box' brought him to the conclusion that learning was improved when it achieved a satisfactory result. He extended this theory to human learning and found that students were encouraged by good results, but that being wrong did not teach them to correct their errors.

Thorndike /θɔːndaɪk/ Sybil 1882–1976. British actress for whom G B Shaw wrote *St Joan*. The Thorndike Theatre (1969), Leatherhead, Surrey, England, is named after her.

Thorndike Known for her versatility in a variety of roles, British actress Sybil Thorndike became the leading actress at the Old Vic, London 1914–18. She was made Dame of the British Empire 1931, made 18 films 1921–63, and gave her last stage performance at the age of 87.

Thorpe /θɔːp/ Jeremy 1929– . British Liberal politician, leader of the Liberal Party 1967–76.

Thorpe /θɔːp/ Jim (James Francis) 1888–1953. US athlete. A member of the 1912 US Olympic Team in Stockholm, he won gold medals for the decathlon and pentathlon but was forced to return when he admitted that he had played semiprofessional baseball. He played major-league baseball 1913–19 and was an outstanding player of professional football 1917–29. His Olympic medals were restored to him by the Amateur Athletic Union 1973.

Born in Prague, Oklahoma, Thorpe attended the Carlisle Indian School in Pennsylvania.

He was named All-American in 1911 and 1912 and was posthumously elected to the Football Hall of Fame 1963.

Thorwaldsen /tɔːvælsən/ Bertel 1770–1844. Danish Neo-Classical sculptor. He went to Italy on a scholarship 1796 and stayed in Rome for most of his life, producing portraits, monuments, and religious and mythological works. Much of his work is housed in the Thorwaldsen Museum, Copenhagen.

Thucydides /θjuːˈsɪdɪdiːz/ c. 455–400 BC. Athenian historian who exercised command in the Peloponnesian War with Sparta 424 with so little success that he was banished until 404. In his *History of the Peloponnesian War*, he attempted a scientific impartiality.

Thunders /θʌndəz/ Johnny. Stage name of John Anthony Genzale 1952–1991. US rock guitarist, singer, and songwriter. Lead guitarist with the trash-glam cult band the New York Dolls 1971–75, he fronted his own group, the Heartbreakers, 1975–77. Moving to London 1976, they became part of the burgeoning punk scene. Thunders's subsequent solo work includes the album *So Alone* 1978.

Thünen /tjuːnən/ Johann von 1785–1850. German economist and geographer who believed that the success of a state depends on the wellbeing of its farmers. His book *The Isolated State* 1820, a pioneering study of land use, includes the earliest example of **marginal productivity theory**, a theory that he developed to calculate the natural wage for a farmworker. He has been described as the first modern economist.

Thurber /θɜːbə/ James (Grover) 1894–1961. US humorist. His short stories, written mainly for the *New Yorker* magazine, include 'The Secret Life of Walter Mitty' 1932, and his doodle drawings include fanciful impressions of dogs.

Partially blind from childhood, he became totally blind in the last ten years of his life but continued to work.

Thynne family name of marquesses of Bath; seated at Longleat, Wiltshire, England.

Thyssen /tɪsən/ Fritz 1873–1951. German industrialist who based his business on the Ruhr iron and steel industry. Fearful of the communist threat, Thyssen became an early supporter of Hitler and contributed large amounts of money to his early political campaigns. By 1939 he had broken with the Nazis and fled first to Switzerland and later to Italy, where in 1941 he was sent to a concentration camp. Released 1945, he was ordered to surrender 15% of his property.

Tiberius /taɪˈbɪəriəs/ Claudius Nero 42 BC–AD 37. Roman emperor, the stepson, adopted son, and successor of Augustus from AD 14. A distinguished soldier, he was a conscientious ruler under whom the empire prospered.

It is the part of a good shepherd to shear his flock, not flay it.

Tiberius AD 2

Tieck /tiːk/ Johann Ludwig 1773–1853. German Romantic poet and collector of folk tales, some of which he dramatized, such as 'Puss in Boots'.

Tiepolo /tiˈepələʊ/ Giovanni Battista 1696–1770. Italian painter, born in Venice. He created monumental Rococo decorative schemes in palaces and churches in NE Italy, SW Germany, and Madrid (1762–70). The style is light-hearted, the palette light and warm, and he made great play with illusion.

Tiepolo painted religious and, above all, historical or allegorical pictures: for example, scenes from the life of Cleopatra 1745 (Palazzo Labia, Venice) and from the life of Frederick Barbarossa 1757 (Kaisersaal, Würzburg Palace). His sons were among his many assistants.

Tiffany /tɪfəni/ Louis Comfort 1848–1933. US artist and glassmaker, son of Charles Louis Tiffany, who founded Tiffany and Company, the New York City jewellers. He produced stained-glass windows, iridescent Favrile (from Latin *faber* 'craftsman') glass, and lampshades in the Art Nouveau style. He used glass that contained oxides of iron and other elements to produce rich colours.

Tikhonov /tiːxənɒf/ Nikolai 1905– . Soviet politician. He was a close associate of President Brezhnev, joining the Politburo 1979, and was prime minister (chair of the Council of Ministers) 1980–85. In April 1989 he was removed from the central committee.

Tilden /tɪldən/ Samuel Jones 1814–1886. US politician. A Democrat, he was governor of New York 1874–76, elected on a reform ticket. He received the Democratic presidential nomination 1876, and although he received a plurality of popular votes, the 1877 electoral college awarded the majority of electoral votes to Rutherford B Hayes.

Born in New Lebanon, New York, Tilden was

Tilson Thomas US conductor Michael Tilson Thomas is also a pianist and composer. His concerts for the Berkshire Music Center, Ojai Music Festival, and New York Philharmonic Young People's Concerts established him firmly in the Bernstein and Boulez tradition of innovative programming and positive support of contemporary music.

educated at Yale and New York universities, and became a barrister 1841.

As chair of the New York State Democratic committee 1866–74, he campaigned against the Tammany Hall Organization and its leader, William 'Boss' Tweed.

Tillich /tɪlɪk/ Paul Johannes 1886–1965. Prussian-born US theologian, best remembered for his *Systematic Theology* 1951–63. Fleeing the Nazis, he arrived in the USA 1933 and served as professor of theology at the Union Theological Seminary 1933–55, Harvard University 1955–62, and the University of Chicago 1962–65.

Born in Prussia, Tillich received his PhD from the University of Breslau 1911. Ordained a pastor in the Evangelical Lutheran Church 1912, he served as a chaplain during World War I. Appointed to a professorship at the University of Frankfurt he was removed by the Nazis and fled to the USA.

Tilly /tɪli/ Jan Tserklaes, Count von Tilly 1559–1632. Flemish commander of the army of the Catholic League and imperial forces in the Thirty Years' War. Notorious for his storming of Magdeburg, E Germany, 1631, he was defeated

by the Swedish king Gustavus Adolphus at Breitenfeld and at the river Lech in SW Germany, where he was mortally wounded.

Tilson Thomas Michael 1944– . US conductor and pianist, principal guest conductor for the Boston Symphony 1969–74 and principal conductor for the London Symphony Orchestra from 1988. His career took off in storybook fashion in 1969 when he took over from an unwell William Steinberg in the middle of a Boston Symphony Orchestra concert. Since then he has appeared and recorded orchestras in the USA, the UK, and the Netherlands.

Tilson Thomas's recordings include premieres of works by Steve Reich and Simon Bainbridge, also pieces by George Gershwin, and the complete Charles Ives symphonies. He has also recorded the complete Beethoven symphonies.

Tinbergen /tɪnbɜːgən/ Jan 1903–1988. Dutch economist. He shared a Nobel prize 1969 with Ragnar Frisch for his work on econometrics (the mathematical-statistical expression of economic theory).

Tinbergen /tɪnbɜːgən/ Niko(laas) 1907– . Dutch zoologist. He was one of the founders of ethology, the scientific study of animal behaviour in natural surroundings. Specializing in the study of instinctive behaviour, he shared a Nobel prize with Konrad →Lorenz and Karl von →Frisch 1973. He is the brother of Jan Tinbergen.

Ting /tɪŋ/ Samuel 1936– . US physicist. In 1974 he and his team at the Brookhaven National Laboratory, New York, detected a new subatomic particle, which he named the J particle. It was found to be identical to the (ψ) particle discovered in the same year by Burton →Richter and his team at the Stanford Linear Accelerator Center, California. Ting and Richter shared the Nobel Prize for Physics 1976.

Tintoretto /ˌtɪntəˈretəʊ/ adopted name of Jacopo Robusti 1518–1594. Italian painter, active in Venice. His dramatic religious paintings are spectacularly lit and full of movement, such as his huge canvases of the lives of Christ and the Virgin in the Scuola di San Rocco, Venice, 1564–88.

Tintoretto was so named because his father was a dyer (*tintore*). He was a student of →Titian and admirer of Michelangelo. *Miracle of St Mark Rescuing a Slave* 1548 (Accademia, Venice) marked the start of his successful career. In the Scuola di San Rocco he created a sequence of heroic scenes with bold gesture and foreshortening, and effects of supernatural light. He also painted canvases for the Doge's Palace.

Tiomkin /tjɒmkɪn/ Dimitri 1899–1979. Russian composer who lived in the USA from 1925. From 1930 he wrote Hollywood film scores, including music for *Duel in the Sun* 1946, *The Thing* 1951, and *Rio Bravo* 1959. His score for *High Noon* 1952 won him an Academy Award.

Tippett Michael (Kemp) 1905– . English composer whose works include the operas *The Midsummer Marriage* 1952, *The Knot Garden* 1970, and *New Year* 1989; four symphonies; *Songs for Ariel* 1962; and choral music including *The Mask of Time* 1982.

Tippu Sultan /tɪpuː ˈsɑːɪb/ c. 1750–1799. Sultan of Mysore (now Karnataka) from the death of his father, →Hyder Ali, 1782. He died of wounds when his capital, Seringapatam, was captured by the British. His rocket brigade led Sir William Congreve (1772–1828) to develop the weapon for use in the Napoleonic Wars.

Tirpitz /tɜːpɪts/ Alfred von 1849–1930. German admiral. As secretary for the navy 1897–1916, he created the German navy and planned the World War I U-boat campaign.

Tirso de Molina /tɪəsəʊ deɪ məˈliːnə/ Pen name of Gabriel Téllez 1571–1648. Spanish dramatist and monk who wrote more than 400 plays, of which eight are extant, including comedies, historical and biblical dramas, and a series based on the legend of Don Juan.

Tiselius /tɪˈseɪliəs/ Arne 1902–1971. Swedish chemist who developed a powerful method of chemical analysis known as electrophoresis. He applied his new techniques to the analysis of animal proteins. Nobel prize 1948.

Tissot /tiːˈsəʊ/ James (Joseph Jacques) 1836–1902. French painter who produced detailed portraits of Victorian high society during a ten-year stay in England.

In the 1880s Tissot visited Palestine. His religious works were much admired.

Titian /tɪʃən/ anglicized form of Tiziano Vecellio c. 1487–1576. Italian painter, active in Venice, one of the greatest artists of the High Renaissance. In 1533 he became court painter to Charles V, Holy Roman emperor, whose son Philip II of Spain later became his patron. Titian's work is richly coloured, with inventive composition. He produced a vast number of portraits, religious paintings, and mythological scenes, including *Bacchus and Ariadne* 1520–23, *Venus and Adonis* 1554, and the *Entombment of Christ* 1559.

Titian probably studied with Giovanni →Bellini but also learned much from →Giorgione and seems to have completed some of Giorgione's unfinished works, such as *Noli Me Tangere* (National Gallery, London). His first great painting is the *Assumption of the Virgin* 1518 (Church of the Frari, Venice), typically sublime in mood, with upward-thrusting layers of figures. Three large mythologies painted in the next few years for the d'Estes of Ferrara show yet more brilliant use of colour, and numerous statuesque figures suggest the influence of Classical art. By the 1530s Titian's reputation was widespread.

In the 1540s Titian visited Rome to paint the pope; in Augsburg, Germany, 1548–49 and 1550–51 he painted members of the imperial court. In his later years he produced a series of mythologies for Philip II, notably *The Rape of Europa* 1562 (Isabella Stewart Gardner Museum, Boston, Massachusetts). His handling became increasingly free and his palette sombre, but his work remained full of drama. He made an impact not just on Venetian painting but on art throughout Europe.

It is not bright colours but good drawing that makes figures beautiful.

Titian

Tito /tiːtəʊ/ adopted name of Josip Broz 1892–1980. Yugoslav communist politician, in power from 1945. In World War II he organized the National Liberation Army to carry on guerrilla warfare against the German invasion 1941, and was created marshal 1943. As prime minister 1946–53 and president from 1953, he followed a foreign policy of 'positive neutralism'.

Born in Croatia, Tito served in the Austrian army during World War I, was captured by the Russians, and fought in the Red Army during the civil wars. Returning to Yugoslavia 1923, he became prominent as a communist and during World War II as partisan leader against the Nazis. In 1943 he established a provisional government and gained Allied recognition (previously given to the Chetniks), and with Soviet help proclaimed the federal republic 1945. As prime minister, he settled the Yugoslav minorities question on a federal basis, and in 1953 took the newly created post of president (for life from 1974). In 1948 he was criticized by the USSR and other communist countries for his successful system of decentralized profit-sharing workers' councils, and became a leader of the nonaligned movement.

Titus /taɪtəs/ Flavius Sabinus Vespasianus AD 39–81. Roman emperor from AD 79. Eldest son of →Vespasian, he stormed Jerusalem 70 to end the Jewish revolt in Roman Palestine. He completed the Colosseum, and enjoyed a peaceful reign, except for →Agricola's campaigns in Britain.

Tobin /təʊbɪn/ James 1918– . US Keynesian economist. He was awarded a Nobel prize 1981 for his 'general equilibrium' theory, which states that other criteria than monetary considerations are applied by households and firms when making decisions on consumption and investment.

Tocqueville /tɒk'viːl/ Alexis de 1805–1859. French politician and political scientist, author of the first analytical study of the US constitution, *De la Démocratie en Amérique*/*Democracy in America* 1835, and of a penetrating description of France before the Revolution, *L'Ancien Régime et la Révolution*/*The Old Regime and the Revolution* 1856.

Elected to the Chamber of Deputies 1839, Tocqueville became vice president of the Constituent Assembly and minister of foreign affairs 1849. He retired after Napoleon III's coup 1851.

Democratic institutions generally give men a lofty notion of their country and themselves.

Alexis de Tocqueville
Democracy in America 1835

Todd /tɒd/ Alexander, Baron Todd 1907– . British organic chemist who won a Nobel prize 1957 for his work on the role of nucleic acids in genetics. He also synthesized vitamins B1, B12, and E.

Todd /tɒd/ Ron(ald) 1927– . British trade-union leader. He rose from shop steward to general secretary of Britain's largest trade union, the Transport and General Workers' (TGWU), a post he held 1985–92. Although a Labour Party supporter, he criticized its attitude toward nuclear disarmament.

Todt /təʊt/ Fritz 1891–1942. German engineer who was responsible for building the first autobahns (German motorways) and, in World War II, the Siegfried Line and the Atlantic Wall.

Togare /təʊ'gɑːri/ Stage name of Georg Kulovits 1900–1988. Austrian wild-animal tamer and circus performer. Togare invented the character of the exotic Oriental lion tamer after watching Douglas Fairbanks in the 1923 film *The Thief of Baghdad*. In his circus appearances he displayed a nonchalant disregard for danger.

Togliatti /tɒl'jæti/ Palmiro 1893–1964. Italian politician who was a founding member of the Italian Communist Party 1921 and effectively its leader for almost 40 years from 1926 until his death. In exile 1926–44, he returned after the fall of the Fascist dictator Mussolini to become a member of Badoglio's government and held office until 1946.

Togliatti trained as a lawyer, served in the army, and was wounded during World War I. He was associated with the revolutionary wing of the Italian Socialist Party that left to form the Communist Party 1921. He edited the newspaper *Il Comunista* 1922–24 and became a member of the party's central committee. He was in Moscow when Mussolini outlawed the party, and stayed there to become a leading member of the Comintern, joining the Secretariat 1935. Returning to Italy after Mussolini's downfall, he advocated coalition politics with other leftist and democratic parties, a policy which came to fruition in the elections of 1948 where the communists won 135 seats.

Tōgō /təʊgəʊ/ Heihachirō 1846–1934. Japanese admiral who commanded the fleet at the battle of Tsushima 1905, when Japan defeated the Russians and effectively ended the Russo-Japanese War of 1904–05.

Tōjō /təʊdʒəʊ/ Hideki 1884–1948. Japanese general and premier 1941–44 during World War II. Promoted to Chief of Staff of Japan's Guangdong army in Manchuria 1937, he served as minister for war 1940–41. He was held responsible for defeats in the Pacific 1944 and forced to resign. After Japan's defeat, he was hanged as a war criminal.

Tokugawa /ˌtɒkʊ'gawə/ military family that controlled Japan as shoguns 1603–1867. *Tokugawa Ieyasu* (1542–1616) was the Japanese general and politician who established the Tokugawa shogunate. The Tokugawa were feudal lords who ruled about one-quarter of Japan.

Toland /təʊlənd/ Gregg 1904–1948. US director of film photography who used deep focus to good effect in such films as *Wuthering Heights* 1939, *Citizen Kane* 1941, *The Grapes of Wrath* 1940, and *The Best Years of our Lives* 1946.

Tolkien /tɒlkiːn/ J(ohn) R(onald) R(euel) 1892–1973. English writer who created the fictional world of Middle Earth in *The Hobbit* 1937 and the trilogy *The Lord of the Rings* 1954–55, fantasy novels peopled with hobbits, dwarves, and strange magical creatures. His work developed a cult following in the 1960s and had many imitators. At Oxford University he was professor of Anglo-Saxon 1925–45 and Merton professor of English 1945–59.

Tolstoy Russian novelist Count Leo Tolstoy wrote his greatest novels, War and Peace and Anna Karenina, while living on his estate at Yasnaya Polyana. Between 1857 and 1861 he fostered an interest in educational reforms on two trips to western Europe, establishing a school for peasants on his return to the estate.

Tolstoy /ˈtɒlstɔɪ/ Leo Nikolaievich 1828–1910. Russian novelist who wrote *War and Peace* 1863–69 and *Anna Karenina* 1873–77. From 1880 Tolstoy underwent a profound spiritual crisis and took up various moral positions, including passive resistance to evil, rejection of authority (religious or civil) and private ownership, and a return to basic mystical Christianity. He was excommunicated by the Orthodox Church, and his later works were banned.

Tolstoy was born of noble family at Yasnaya Polyana, near Tula, and fought in the Crimean War. His first published work was *Childhood* 1852, the first part of the trilogy that was completed with *Boyhood* 1854 and *Youth* 1857. *Tales from Sebastopol* was published 1856; later books include *What I Believe* 1883 and *The Kreutzer Sonata* 1889, and the novel *Resurrection* 1900. His desire to give up his property and live as a peasant disrupted his family life, and he finally fled his home and died of pneumonia at the railway station in Astapovo.

Tomasi /təʊˈmɑːsi/ Giuseppe, Prince of Lampedusa. Italian writer; see →Lampedusa.

Tomba Alberto 1964– . Italian skier who became the Olympic and World Cup slalom and giant-slalom champion in 1988. He won the World Cup giant-slalom championships again in 1991. Tomba's gold medal in the giant slalom at the 1992 Albertville Winter Olympics enabled

him to become the first skier to retain his Olympic gold medal.

Tombaugh /ˈtɒmbɔː/ Clyde (William) 1906– . US astronomer who discovered the planet Pluto 1930.

Tombaugh, born in Streator, Illinois, became an assistant at the Lowell Observatory in Flagstaff, Arizona, in 1929, and photographed the sky in search of an undiscovered remote planet as predicted by the observatory's founder, Percival →Lowell. Tombaugh found Pluto on 18 Feb 1930, from plates taken three weeks earlier. He continued his search for new planets across the entire sky; his failure to find any placed strict limits on the possible existence of planets beyond Pluto.

Tone /təʊn/ (Theobald) Wolfe 1763–1798. Irish nationalist, prominent in the revolutionary society of the United Irishmen. In 1798 he accompanied the French invasion of Ireland, was captured and condemned to death, but slit his own throat in prison.

Tönnies /ˈtʌniəs/ Ferdinand 1855–1936. German social theorist and philosopher, one of the founders of the sociological tradition of community studies and urban sociology through his key work, *Gemeinschaft–Gesellschaft* 1887.

Tönnies contrasted the nature of social relationships in traditional societies and small organizations (*Gemeinschaft*, 'community') with those in industrial societies and large organizations (*Gesellschaft*, 'association'). He was pessimistic about the effect of industrialization and urbanization on the social and moral order, seeing them as a threat to traditional society's sense of community.

Tooke /tʊk/ John Horne 1736–1812. British politician who established a Constitutional Society for parliamentary reform 1771. He was elected a member of Parliament 1801.

Toplady /ˈtɒpleɪdɪ/ Augustus Montague 1740–1778. British Anglican priest, the author of the hymn 'Rock of Ages' 1775.

Torquemada /ˌtɔːkɪˈmɑːdə/ Tomás de 1420–1498. Spanish Dominican monk, confessor to Queen Isabella I. In 1483 he revived the Inquisition on her behalf, and at least 2,000 'heretics' were burned; Torquemada also expelled the Jews from Spain 1492, with a resultant decline of the economy.

Torres Luis Vaez de lived in 17th century. Spanish navigator who, in 1605, sailed with an expedition under the command of Pedro Fernandez de Quiros in search of the supposed southland (*Terra Australis Incognito*). His navigation through the strait between New Guinea and Australia earned him the honour of the strait being named after him.

Torres-García /ˈtɒrɪs gɑːˈθiːə/ Joaquim 1874–1949. Uruguayan artist, born in Montevideo. In

Paris from 1926, he was influenced by →Mondrian and others and, after going to Madrid in 1932, by Inca, and Nazca pottery. His mature style is based on a grid pattern derived from the aesthetic proportion of the golden section.

Torricelli /ˌtɒrɪˈtʃeli/ Evangelista 1608–1647. Italian physicist and pupil of →Galileo who devised the mercury barometer.

Tortelier /tɔːˈteliə/ Paul 1924–1990. French cellist whose powerfully intuitive style brought him widespread fame as a soloist from 1947. Romantic in temperament, he specialized in the standard 19th-century repertoire, from Bach's solo suites to Elgar, Walton, and Kodály.

Tortelier came to prominence in 1947 as soloist in Richard Strauss's *Don Quixote* in London under British conductor Thomas Beecham. From 1956 he taught at the Paris Conservatoire, where his pupils included English cellist Jacqueline du Pré.

Torvill and Dean /ˈtɔːvɪl, ˈdiːn/ British ice-dance champions Jayne Torvill (1957–   ) and Christopher Dean (1959–   ), both from Nottingham. They won the world title four times 1981–84 and were the 1984 Olympic champions.

Toscanini /ˌtɒskəˈniːni/ Arturo 1867–1957. Italian conductor. He made La Scala, Milan (where he conducted 1898–1903, 1906–08, and 1921–29), the world's leading opera house. Opposed to the Fascist regime, in 1936 he returned to the USA, where he had conducted at the Metropolitan Opera 1908–15. The NBC Symphony Orchestra was formed for him in 1937. He retired in 1954.

Totila /ˈtɒtɪlə/ died 522. King of the Ostrogoths, who warred with the Byzantine emperor Justinian for Italy, and was killed by General Narses at the battle of Taginae 552 in the Apennines.

Totò /ˈtəʊtəʊ/ Stage name of Antonio de Curtis Gagliardi Ducas Comneno di Bisanzio 1898–1967. Italian comedian who moved to films from the music hall. His films, such as *Totò le Moko* 1949 and *L'Oro di Napoli/Gold of Naples* 1954, made him something of a national institution.

Toulouse-Lautrec /tuːˈluːz ləʊˈtrek/ Henri Marie Raymond de 1864–1901. French artist, associated with the Impressionists. He was active in Paris, where he painted entertainers and prostitutes. From 1891 his lithograph posters were a great success.

Toulouse-Lautrec showed an early gift for drawing, to which he turned increasingly after a riding accident at the age of 15 left him with crippled and stunted legs. In 1882 he began to study art in Paris. He admired Goya's etchings and Degas's work, and in the 1880s he met Gauguin and was inspired by Japanese prints. Lautrec became a familiar figure drawing and painting in the dance halls, theatres, cafés, circuses, and brothels. Many of his finished works have the spontaneous character of sketches. He often painted with thinned-out oils on cardboard.

Tourneur /ˈtɜːnə/ Cyril 1575–1626. English dramatist. Little is known about his life but *The Atheist's Tragedy* 1611 and *The Revenger's Tragedy* 1607 (thought by some scholars to be by →Middleton) are among the most powerful of Jacobean dramas.

Does the silkworm expend her yellow labours
For thee? for thee does she undo herself?

Cyril Tourneur
The Revenger's Tragedy 1607

Toussaint L'Ouverture /ˈtuːsæŋ ˌluːvəˈtjʊə/ Pierre Dominique *c.* 1743–1803. Haitian revolutionary leader, born a slave. He joined the insurrection of 1791 against the French colonizers and was made governor by the revolutionary French government. He expelled the Spanish and British, but when the French emperor Napoleon reimposed slavery he revolted, was captured, and died in prison in France. In 1983 his remains were returned to Haiti.

Tower /ˈtaʊə/ John 1925–1991. US Republican politician, a senator from Texas 1961–83. Despite having been a paid arms-industry consultant, he was selected 1989 by President Bush to serve as defence secretary, but the Senate refused to approve the appointment because of Tower's previous heavy drinking.

Tower, in 1961 the first Republican to be elected senator for Texas, emerged as a military expert in the Senate, becoming chair of the Armed Services Committee in 1981. After his retirement from the Senate in 1983, he acted as a consultant to arms manufacturers and chaired the 1986–87 *Tower Commission*, which investigated aspects of the Irangate arms-for-hostages scandal.

Townes /ˈtaʊnz/ Charles 1915–   . US physicist who in 1953 designed and constructed the first maser. For this work, he shared the 1964 Nobel prize with Soviet physicists Nikolai Basov and Aleksandr Prokhorov.

Townsend /ˈtaʊnzend/ Sue 1946–   . English humorous novelist, author of *The Secret Diary of Adrian Mole, aged 13¾*

Townshend /ˈtaʊnzend/ Charles 1725–1767. British politician, chancellor of the Exchequer 1766–67. The *Townshend Acts*, designed to assert Britain's traditional authority over its colonies, resulted in widespread resistance. Among other things they levied taxes on imports (such as tea, glass, and paper) into the North American colonies. Opposition in the colonies to taxation without representation precipitated the American Revolution.

Townshend /ˈtaʊnzend/ Charles, 2nd Viscount Townshend (known as 'Turnip' Townshend) 1674–1738. English politician and agriculturalist. He was secretary of state under George I 1714–17, when dismissed for opposing the king's foreign policy, and 1721–30, after which he retired to his farm and did valuable work in developing crop rotation and cultivating winter feeds for cattle (hence his nickname).

Townshend did not, in fact, originate the new techniques with which his name has become associated. Turnips, for example, were already being grown in East Anglia, England, as a fodder crop from at least the 1660s, and it is unlikely that he ever adopted the four-course turnips–barley–clover–wheat rotation. This was not taken up until many years after his death. Through the successful development of his agricultural estate at Rainham in W Norfolk, however, Townshend brought a range of improved cultivation practices to wider public notice.

Townshend /ˈtaʊnzend/ Pete 1945– . UK rock musician, founder member of the →Who; his solo albums include *Empty Glass* 1980.

Toynbee /ˈtɔɪnbi/ Arnold 1852–1883. English economic historian who coined the term 'industrial revolution' in his *Lectures on the Industrial Revolution*, published 1884.

Toynbee Hall, an education settlement in the east end of London, was named after him.

Toynbee /ˈtɔɪnbi/ Arnold Joseph 1889–1975. English historian whose *A Study of History* 1934–61 was an attempt to discover the laws governing the rise and fall of civilizations.

He was the nephew of the economic historian Arnold Toynbee.

Tracy /ˈtreɪsi/ Spencer 1900–1967. US actor distinguished for his understated, seemingly effortless, natural performances. His films include *Captains Courageous* 1937 and *Boys' Town* 1938 (for both of which he won Academy Awards), and he starred with Katharine Hepburn in nine films, including *Adam's Rib* 1949 and *Guess Who's Coming to Dinner* 1967, his final appearance.

Tradescant /trəˈdeskənt/ John 1570–1638. English gardener and botanist, who travelled widely in Europe and is thought to have introduced the cos lettuce to England from the Greek island bearing the same name. He was appointed gardener to Charles I and was succeeded by his son, *John Tradescant the Younger* (1608–1662), after his death. The younger Tradescant undertook three plant-collecting trips to Virginia, USA, and the Swedish botanist Carl Linnaeus named the genus *Tradescantia* in his honour.

The Tradescants introduced many new plants to Britain, including the acacia, lilac, and occidental plane. Their collection of plants formed the nucleus of the Ashmolean Museum in Oxford.

Traherne /trəˈhɜːn/ Thomas 1637–1674. English Christian mystic. His moving lyric poetry and his prose *Centuries of Meditations* were unpublished until 1903.

Trajan /ˈtreɪdʒən/ Marcus Ulpius (Trajanus) AD 52–117. Roman emperor and soldier, born in Seville. He was adopted as heir by →Nerva, whom he succeeded AD 98.

He was a just and conscientious ruler, corresponded with Pliny about the Christians, and conquered Dacia (Romania) 101–07 and much of Parthia. *Trajan's Column*, Rome, commemorates his victories.

Traven /ˈtrævən/ B(en). Pen name of Herman Feige 1882–1969. German-born US novelist whose true identity was not revealed until 1979. His books include the bestseller *The Death Ship* 1926 and *The Treasure of the Sierra Madre* 1934, which was made into a film starring Humphrey Bogart in 1948.

Born in a part of Germany now in Poland, he was in turn known as the anarchist Maret Rut, Traven Torsvan, and Hollywood scriptwriter Hal Croves. Between the two world wars he lived in obscurity in Mexico and avoided recognition.

Travers /ˈtrævəz/ Ben(jamin) 1886–1980. British dramatist. He wrote (for actors Tom Walls, Ralph Lynn, and Robertson Hare) the 'Aldwych farces' of the 1920s, so named from the London theatre in which they were played. They include *A Cuckoo in the Nest* 1925 and *Rookery Nook* 1926.

Travers /ˈtrævəz/ Morris William 1872–1961. English chemist who, with William Ramsay, between 1894 and 1908 first identified what were called the inert or noble gases: krypton, xenon, and radon.

Tree /triː/ Herbert Beerbohm 1853–1917. British actor and theatre manager, half-brother of Max →Beerbohm. Noted for his Shakespeare productions, he was founder of the Royal Academy of Dramatic Art (RADA).

Trefusis /trɪˈfjuːsɪs/ Violet 1894–1972. British society hostess and writer. Daughter of Mrs Keppel, who was later the mistress of Edward VII, she had a disastrous marriage to cavalry officer Denys Trefusis and a passionate elopement with the writer Vita →Sackville-West.

Treitschke /ˈtraɪtʃkə/ Heinrich von 1834–1896. German historian. At first a Liberal, he later adopted a Pan-German standpoint. He is known for the *Deutsche Geschichte im 19 Jahrhundert/History of Germany in the 19th Century* 1879–94.

Trenchard /ˈtrentʃəd/ Hugh Montague, 1st Viscount Trenchard 1873–1956. British aviator and police commissioner. He commanded the Royal Flying Corps in World War I 1915–17, and 1918–29 organized the Royal Air Force, becoming its first marshal 1927. As commissioner of the Metropolitan Police, he established the Police College at Hendon and carried out the Trenchard Reforms, which introduced more scientific methods of detection.

Tressell /tresəl/ Robert. Pseudonym of Robert Noonan 1868–1911. English author whose *The Ragged Trousered Philanthropists*, published in an abridged form 1914, gave a detailed account of the poverty of working people's lives.

Treurnicht /trɜːnɪxt/ Andries Petrus 1921–1993. South African Conservative Party politician. A former minister of the Dutch Reformed Church, he was elected to the South African parliament as a National Party member 1971 but left it 1982 to form a new right-wing Conservative Party, opposed to any dilution of the apartheid system.

Trevelyan /trɪˈvɪljən/ George Macaulay 1876–1962. British historian. Regius professor of history at Cambridge 1927–40, he pioneered the study of social history, as in his *English Social History* 1942.

It [education] has produced a vast population able to read but unable to distinguish what is worth reading, an easy prey to sensations and cheap appeals.

George Macaulay Trevelyan
English Social History 1942

Trevelyan /trɪˈvɪljən/ George Otto 1838–1928. British politician and historian, a nephew of the historian Lord Macaulay, whose biography he wrote 1876.

Trevino Lee Buck 1939– . US golfer who won his first major title, the 1968 US Open, as a virtual unknown, and won it again in 1971. He has also won the British Open and US PGA titles twice, and is one of only five players to have won the US Open and British Open in the same year. He has played in six Ryder Cup matches and was non-playing captain in 1985.

Trevithick /trɪˈvɪθɪk/ Richard 1771–1833. British engineer, constructor of a steam road locomotive 1801 and the first steam engine to run on rails 1804.

Trilling /trɪlɪŋ/ Lionel 1905–1975. US author and literary critic. His books of criticism include *The Liberal Imagination* 1950, *Beyond Culture* 1965, and *The Experience of Literature* 1967. He also produced annotated editions of the works of English poets Matthew Arnold and John Keats.

Born in New York, USA, and educated at Columbia University, Trilling joined the Columbia English Department faculty 1932. He received his PhD 1938 and was appointed professor 1948. His novel *The Middle of the Journey* 1947 is based on the character of Whittaker Chambers, who was to be a protagonist of the Alger →Hiss case.

Tristan /trɪstən/ Flora 1803–1844. French socialist writer and activist, author of *Promenades dans Londres/The London Journal* 1840, a vivid record of social conditions, and *L'Union ouvrière/Workers' Union* 1843, an outline of a workers' utopia.

Tristano /trɪˈstɑːnəʊ/ Lennie (Lennard Joseph) 1919–1978. US jazz pianist and composer. An austere musician, he gave an academic foundatión to the school of cool jazz in the 1940s and 1950s, which was at odds with the bebop tradition. He was also active as a teacher.

Three hours a day will produce as much as a man ought to write.

Anthony Trollope
Autobiography 1883

Trollope /trɒləp/ Anthony 1815–1882. English novelist who delineated provincial English middle-class society in a series of novels set in or around the imaginary cathedral city of Barchester. *The Warden* 1855 began the series, which includes *Barchester Towers* 1857, *Doctor Thorne* 1858, and *The Last Chronicle of Barset* 1867. His political novels include *Can You Forgive Her?* 1864, *Phineas Finn* 1867–69, and *The Prime Minister* 1875–76.

Tromp /trɒmp/ Maarten Harpertszoon 1597–1653. Dutch admiral. He twice defeated the occupying Spaniards 1639. He was defeated by English admiral Blake May 1652, but in Nov triumphed over Blake in the Strait of Dover. In Feb– June 1653 he was defeated by Blake and Monk, and was killed off the Dutch coast. His son, *Cornelius Tromp* (1629–1691), also an admiral, fought a battle against the English and French fleets in 1673.

Trotsky /trɒtski/ Leon. Adopted name of Lev Davidovitch Bronstein 1879–1940. Russian revolutionary. He joined the Bolshevik party and took a leading part in the seizure of power 1917 and raising the Red Army that fought the Civil War 1918–20. In the struggle for power that followed →Lenin's death 1924, →Stalin defeated Trotsky, and this and other differences with the Communist Party led to his exile 1929. He settled in Mexico, where he was assassinated with an ice pick at Stalin's instigation. Trotsky believed in world revolution and in permanent revolution, and was an uncompromising, if liberal, idealist.

Trotsky became a Marxist in the 1890s and was imprisoned and exiled for opposition to the tsarist regime. He lived in W Europe from 1902 until the 1905 revolution, when he was again imprisoned but escaped to live in exile until 1917. Although as a young man Trotsky admired Lenin, when he worked with him organizing the revolution of 1917, he objected to Lenin's dictatorial ways. He was second in command until Lenin's death. Trotsky's later works are critical of the Soviet regime; for example, *The Revolution Betrayed* 1937. His greatest work is his magisterial *History of the Russian Revolution* 1932–33. Official Soviet recognition of responsibility for his assassination through the secret service came in 1989.

Truman *Harry S Truman, 33rd US president, who took office after the death of Franklin D Roosevelt in April 1945. It was his decision to drop the atom bomb on Japan ending World War II. To counter Soviet influence and feared expansion in Europe, he encouraged the formation of NATO and devised a policy of economic and military aid (the Truman Doctrine).*

Trudeau /truːˈdəʊ/ Pierre (Elliott) 1919– . Canadian Liberal politician. He was prime minister 1968–79 and 1980–84. In 1980, having won again by a landslide on a platform opposing Qúebec separatism, he helped to defeat the Québec independence movement in a referendum. He repatriated the constitution from Britain 1982, but by 1984 had so lost support that he resigned.

Truffaut /truˈfəʊ/ François 1932–1984. French New Wave film director and actor, formerly a critic. A popular, romantic, and intensely humane filmmaker, he wrote and directed a series of semi-autobiographical films starring Jean-Pierre Léaud, beginning with *Les Quatre Cent Coups/The 400 Blows* 1959. His other films include *Jules et Jim* 1961, *Fahrenheit 451* 1966, *L'Enfant sauvage/The Wild Child* 1970, and *La Nuit américaine/Day for Night* 1973 (Academy Award).

His passion for cinema led to a job as film critic for *Cahiers du Cinema* during the 1950s before embarking on his career as director. His later work includes *The Story of Adèle H* 1975 and *The Last Metro* 1980. He played one of the leading roles in Steven Spielberg's *Close Encounters of the Third Kind* 1977.

Trujillo Molina /truːˈxiːəʊ məʊˈliːnə/ Rafael (Leónidas) 1891–1961. Dictator of the Dominican Republic from 1930. As commander of the Dominican Guard, he seized power and established a ruthless dictatorship. He was assassinated.

Truman /ˈtruːmən/ Harry S 1884–1972. 33rd president of the USA 1945–53, a Democrat. In Jan 1945 he became vice president to F D Roosevelt, and president when Roosevelt died in April that year. He used the atom bomb against Japan, launched the Marshall Plan to restore W Europe's economy, and nurtured the European Community and NATO (including the rearmament of West Germany).

Born in Lamar, Missouri, he ran a clothing store that was bankrupted by the Great Depression. He became a senator 1934, was selected as Roosevelt's last vice president, and in 1948 was elected for a second term in a surprise victory over Thomas Dewey (1902–1971), governor of New York. At home, he had difficulty converting the economy back to peacetime conditions, and failed to prevent witch-hunts on suspected communists such as Alger →Hiss. In Korea, he intervened when the South was invaded, but sacked General →MacArthur when the general's policy threatened to start World War III. Truman's decision not to enter Chinese territory, betrayed by the double agent Kim Philby, led to China's entry into the war.

Trumbull /ˈtrʌmbl/ John 1756–1843. American artist known for his series of historical paintings of war scenes from the American revolution (1775–83), the most famous of which was his depiction of the signing of the Declaration of Independence 1776.

Born in Lebanon, Connecticut, the son of Governor Jonathan Trumbull, he was educated at Harvard University and saw action during the American Revolution. In 1780 he travelled to England to study art with Benjamin →West and was briefly imprisoned for espionage, returning to the USA 1789.

From 1793 to 1804 he undertook diplomatic assignments in England. He later served as president of the American Academy of Fine Arts 1817–36.

Trump /trʌmp/ Donald 1946– . US millionaire property financier who for his headquarters in 1983 built the skyscraper Trump Tower in New York. He owns three casinos in Atlantic City, New Jersey.

The son of a builder, Trump studied finance and in 1974 negotiated his first big property deal, rebuilding the Commodore Hotel, Manhattan, with financial help from the Hyatt Corporation. In addition to Trump Tower on Fifth Avenue, he built nearby Trump Parc and bought the Plaza Hotel in 1983. One of his casinos is named Trump's Castle.

Truth /truːθ/ Sojourner. Adopted name of Isabella Baumfree, later Isabella Van Wagener 1797–1883. US antislavery and women's-suffrage campaigner. Born a slave, she ran away and became involved with religious groups. In 1843 she was 'commanded in a vision' to adopt the name Sojourner Truth. She published an autobiography, *The Narrative of Sojourner Truth*, in 1850.

She worked as a fund-raiser for the North during the American Civil War.

Ts'ao Chan alternative transcription of Chinese novelist →Cao Chan.

Tschiffley /tʃɪfli/ Aimé Felix 1895–1954. Swiss writer and traveller whose 16,000-km/10,000-mi journey on horseback from Buenos Aires to New York was known as 'Tschiffley's Ride', recounted in *Southern Cross to Pole Star* 1933.

Tsiolkovsky /tsɪəl'kɒfski/ Konstantin 1857–1935. Russian scientist. Despite being handicapped by deafness from the age of ten, he developed the theory of space flight, publishing the first practical paper on astronautics 1903, dealing with space travel by rockets using liquid propellants, such as liquid oxygen.

Tsvetayeva /svɪ'taɪəvə/ Marina 1892–1941. Russian poet, born in Moscow, who wrote most of her verse after leaving the USSR 1923. She wrote mythic, romantic, frenetic verse, including *The Demesne of the Swans*. Her *Selected Poems* was translated 1971.

Tubman /tʌbmən/ Harriet Ross 1821–1913. US abolitionist. Born a slave in Maryland, she escaped to Philadelphia (where slavery was outlawed) 1849. She set up the *Underground Railroad*, a secret network of sympathizers, to help slaves escape to the North and Canada. During the American Civil War she spied for the Union army. She spoke against slavery and for women's rights, and founded schools for emancipated slaves after the Civil War.

Tubman /tʌbmən/ William V S 1895–1971. Liberian politician. The descendant of US slaves, he was a lawyer in the USA. After his election to the presidency of Liberia 1944 he concentrated on uniting the various ethnic groups. Re-elected several times, he died in office of natural causes, despite frequent assassination attempts.

Tudjman Franjo 1922– . Croatian nationalist leader and historian, president from 1990. As leader of the centre-right Croatian Democratic Union (HDZ), he led the fight for Croatian independence. During the 1991–92 civil war his troops were hampered by lack of arms and the military superiority of the Serb-dominated federal army, but Croatia's independence was recognized following a successful UN-negotiated cease-fire Jan 1992. Tudjman was re-elected Aug 1992.

During World War II Tudjman joined Tito's partisan force and rose to the rank of major general before leaving the army 1960. He was expelled from the League of Communists of Yugoslavia 1967 for Croatian nationalist writings and imprisoned for separatist activities 1972–74 and 1981–84. In 1990 he was elected president, having campaigned under a nationalist, anti-Serbia banner. He was criticized for his hesitant conduct during the 1991–92 civil war, but although many soldiers had opted by Dec 1991 to fight under the

banner of the better-equipped right-wing extremist faction, Tudjman retained the vocal support of the majority of Croatians. In Jan 1993 he launched a surprise offensive into the disputed region of Krajina, while simultaneously giving his backing to an EC-UN negotiated peace plan for Bosnia-Herzegovina.

Tudor /tjuːdə/ Anthony 1908–1987. English ballet dancer, choreographer, and teacher, who introduced psychological drama into ballet. His first works were for the →Rambert company (for example, *Lilac Garden* 1936); he cofounded the American Ballet Theater 1939 and created several works for it, including *Pillar of Fire* 1942, *Romeo and Juliet* 1943, and *The Tiller in the Fields* 1978.

Tudor dynasty /tjuːdə/ English dynasty 1485–1603, descended from the Welsh Owen Tudor (c. 1400–1461), second husband of Catherine of Valois (widow of Henry V of England). Their son Edmund married Margaret Beaufort (1443–1509), the great-granddaughter of →John of Gaunt, and was the father of Henry VII, who became king by overthrowing Richard III 1485. The dynasty ended with the death of Elizabeth I 1603.

The Tudors were portrayed in a favourable light in Shakespeare's history plays.

Tu Fu /tuː 'fuː/ or *Du Fu* 712–770. Chinese poet of the Tang dynasty, with Li Po one of the two greatest Chinese poets. He wrote about the social injustices of his time, peasant suffering, and war, as in *The Army Carts* on conscription, and *The Beauties*, comparing the emperor's wealth with the lot of the poor.

Tull /tʌl/ Jethro 1674–1741. English agriculturist who about 1701 developed a drill that enabled seeds to be sown mechanically and spaced so that cultivation between rows was possible in the growth period. His chief work, *Horse-Hoeing Husbandry*, was published 1731.

Tunney /tʌni/ Gene 1898–1978. US boxer. As a professional he won the US light-heavyweight title 1922. He began to fight as a heavyweight in 1924 and was the upset winner over heavyweight champion Jack Dempsey 1926. Tunney retained the title against Dempsey in the famous 'Long Count' bout 1927 and retired undefeated 1928.

Born in New York, Tunney attended LaSalle Academy and worked as a steamship clerk 1912–17. As an amateur boxer, he won the US armed-forces championship in Paris, France, 1919.

After his retirement from boxing, he became successful in business and published *A Man Must Fight* 1932 and *Arms for Living* 1941.

Tunnicliffe /tʌnɪklɪf/ C(harles) F(rederick) 1901–1979. English painter of birds, born in Macclesfield, who worked in Anglesey. His many books include *Bird Portraiture* 1945 and *Shorelands Summer Diary* 1952.

Túpac Amarú /tuːpæk əˈmaːruː/ adopted name of José Gabriel Condorcanqui *c.* 1742–1781. Peruvian Indian revolutionary leader, executed for his revolt against Spanish rule 1780; he claimed to be descended from the last chieftain of the Incas.

Turenne /tjʊˈren/ Henri de la Tour d'Auvergne, Vicomte de Turenne 1611–1675. French marshal under Louis XIV, known for his siege technique. He fought for the Protestant alliance during the Thirty Years' War, and on both sides during the wars of the Fronde.

God is always on the side of the big battalions.

Henri, Vicomte de Turenne

Turgenev /tʊəˈɡeɪnjef/ Ivan Sergeievich 1818–1883. Russian writer, notable for poetic realism, pessimism, and skill in characterization. His works include the play *A Month in the Country* 1849, and the novels *A Nest of Gentlefolk* 1858, *Fathers and Sons* 1862, and *Virgin Soil* 1877. His series *A Sportsman's Sketches* 1852 criticized serfdom.

Turgot /tjʊəˈɡəʊ/ Anne Robert Jacques 1727–1781. French finance minister 1774–76, whose reforming economies led to his dismissal by a hostile aristocracy.

Turing /tjʊərɪŋ/ Alan Mathison 1912–1954. English mathematician and logician. In 1936 he described a 'universal computing machine' that could theoretically be programmed to solve any problem capable of solution by a specially designed machine. This concept, now called the *Turing machine*, foreshadowed the digital computer.

Turner /tɜːnə/ Eva 1892–1990. English soprano. She was prima donna of the Carl Rosa Opera Company 1916–24.

Turner /tɜːnə/ Frederick Jackson 1861–1932. US historian, professor at Harvard University 1910–24. He emphasized the significance of the frontier in US historical development, attributing the distinctive character of US society to the influence of changing frontiers over three centuries of westward expansion.

Turner /tɜːnə/ John Napier 1929– . Canadian Liberal politician, prime minister 1984. He was elected to the House of Commons 1962 and served in the cabinet of Pierre Trudeau until resigning 1975. He succeeded Trudeau as party leader and prime minister 1984, but lost the 1984 and 1988 elections. Turner resigned as leader 1989, and returned to his law practice. He was replaced as Liberal Party chief by Herbert Gray in Feb 1990.

Turner /tɜːnə/ Joseph Mallord William 1775–1851. English landscape painter. He travelled widely in Europe, and his landscapes became increasingly Romantic, with the subject often transformed in scale and flooded with brilliant, hazy light. Many later works anticipate Impressionism; for example, *Rain, Steam and Speed* 1844 (National Gallery, London).

A precocious talent, Turner went to the Royal Academy schools in 1789. In 1792 he made the first of several European tours, from which numerous watercolour sketches survive. His early oil paintings show Dutch influence, but by the 1800s he had begun to paint landscapes in the grand manner, reflecting the styles of →Claude Lorrain and Richard →Wilson.

Many of Turner's most dramatic works are set in Europe or at sea; for example, *Shipwreck* 1805, *Snowstorm: Hannibal Crossing the Alps* 1812 (both Tate Gallery, London), and *The Slave Ship* 1839 (Museum of Fine Arts, Boston, Massachusetts).

His use of colour was enhanced by trips to Italy (1819, 1828, 1835, 1840), and his brushwork became increasingly free. Early in his career he was encouraged by the portraitist Thomas Lawrence and others, but he failed to achieve much recognition and became a reclusive figure. Later he was championed by the critic John Ruskin in his book *Modern Painters* 1843.

Turner was also devoted to literary themes and mythologies; for example, *Ulysses Deriding Polyphemus* 1829 (Tate Gallery). In his old age Turner lived as a recluse in Chelsea under an assumed name. He died there, leaving to the nation more than 300 paintings, nearly 20,000 watercolours, and 19,000 drawings. In 1987 the Clore Gallery extension to the Tate Gallery, London, was opened (following the terms of his will) to display the collection of his works he had left to the nation.

Turner /tɜːnə/ Lana (Julia Jean Mildred Frances) 1920– . US actress who appeared in melodramatic films of the 1940s and 1950s such as *Peyton Place* 1957. Her other films include *The Postman Always Rings Twice* 1946, *The Three Musketeers* 1948, and *Imitation of Life* 1959.

Turner /tɜːnə/ Nat 1800–1831. US slave and Baptist preacher. Believing himself divinely appointed, he led 60 slaves in a revolt – the *Southampton Insurrection* of 1831 – in Southampton County, Virginia. Before he and 16 of the others were hanged, at least 55 slave-owners had been killed.

Turner /tɜːnə/ Robert Edward III 'Ted' 1938– . US businessman and sportsman who developed a conglomerate that includes WTBS, a sports and entertainment cable television channel; CNN, a cable television news network; MGM/UA Entertainment Company; the Atlanta Braves baseball team; and the Atlanta Hawks basketball team. He won the America's Cup 1977.

Born in Cincinnati, Ohio, USA, Turner attended Brown University but left 1960 to work for the family-owned billboard advertising company, which he headed after his father's suicide 1963. He was the prime promoter of the Goodwill Games, first held in Moscow 1986. He is married to actress Jane Fonda.

Turner /ˈtɜːnə/ Tina. Adopted name of Annie Mae Bullock 1938– . US rhythm-and-blues singer who recorded 1960–76 with her husband *Ike Turner* (1931–), including *River Deep, Mountain High* 1966, produced by Phil ➔Spector. She achieved success in the 1980s as a solo artist, recording such albums as *Private Dancer* 1984, and as a live performer.

Turpin /ˈtɜːpɪn/ Ben 1874–1940. US comedian, a star of silent films. Cross-eyes were his hallmark, and a taste for parodying his fellow actors. His work includes *The Shriek of Araby* 1923, *A Harem Knight* 1926, and *Broke in China* 1927.

Turpin /ˈtɜːpɪn/ Dick 1706–1739. English highwayman. The son of an innkeeper, he turned to highway robbery, cattle-thieving, and smuggling, and was hanged at York.

His legendary ride from London to York on his mare Black Bess is probably based on one of about 305 km/190 mi from Gad's Hill to York completed in 15 hours in 1676 by highwayman John Nevison (1639–84).

Tussaud /ˈtuːsəʊ/ Madame (Anne Marie Grosholtz) 1761–1850. French wax-modeller. In 1802 she established an exhibition of wax models of celebrities in London. It was destroyed by fire 1925, but reopened 1928.

Turner Lana Turner, US film actress who was known as the 'Sweater Girl' after her appearance in They Won't Forget, *1937. Her later work in such films as* The Postman Always Rings Twice *is considered to show her more serious acting talent.*

Born in Strasbourg, she went to Paris 1766 to live with her wax-modeller uncle, Philippe Curtius, whom she soon surpassed in technique. During the French Revolution they were forced to take death masks of many victims and leaders (some still exist in the Chamber of Horrors).

Tutankhamen /ˌtuːtənˈkɑːmen/ king of Egypt of the 18th dynasty, about 1360–1350 BC. A son of Ikhnaton (also called Amenhotep IV), he was about 11 at his accession. In 1922 his tomb was discovered by the British archaeologists Lord Carnarvon and Howard Carter in the Valley of the Kings at Luxor, almost untouched by tomb robbers. The contents included many works of art and his solid-gold coffin, which are now displayed in a Cairo museum.

Tutin /ˈtjuːtɪn/ Dorothy 1930– . English actress whose roles include most of Shakespeare's leading heroines (among them Portia, Viola, and Juliet) for the Royal Shakespeare Company, and Lady Macbeth for the National Theatre Company.

Tutu /ˈtuːtuː/ Desmond (Mpilo) 1931– . South African priest, Anglican archbishop of Cape Town and general secretary of the South African Council of Churches 1979–84. One of the leading figures in the struggle against apartheid in the Republic of South Africa, he was awarded the 1984 Nobel Prize for Peace.

Twain /tweɪn/ Mark. Pen name of Samuel Langhorne Clemens 1835–1910. US writer. He established his reputation with the comic masterpiece *The Innocents Abroad* 1869 and two classic American novels, in dialect, *The Adventures of Tom Sawyer* 1876 and *The Adventures of Huckleberry Finn* 1885. He also wrote satire, as in *A Connecticut Yankee at King Arthur's Court* 1889.

Born in Florida, Missouri, Twain grew up along the Mississippi River in Hannibal, Missouri, the setting for many of his major works, and was employed as a riverboat pilot before he moved west; taking a job as a journalist, he began to write. The tale 'The Celebrated Jumping Frog of Calaveras County' was his first success. After a trip by boat to Palestine, he wrote *The Innocents Abroad*. As his writing career blossomed, he also became a lecturer very much in demand. By 1870 he married, and a few years later he and his wife settled in Hartford, Connecticut.

Huckleberry Finn is Twain's masterpiece, for its use of the vernacular, vivid characterization and descriptions, and its theme, underlying the humour, of man's inhumanity to man. He also wrote *Roughing It* 1872, *The Gilded Age* 1873, *Old Times on the Mississippi* 1875, *The Prince and the Pauper* 1882, *Life on the Mississippi* 1883, *Pudd'nhead Wilson* 1894, and *Personal Recollections of Joan of Arc* 1896. His later works, such as *The Mysterious Stranger*, unpublished until 1916, are less humorous and more pessimistic. He is recognized as one of America's finest and most characteristic writers.

Tweed /twiːd/ William Marcy ('Boss') 1823–1878. US politician. He held office in the US House of Representatives 1853–55. In various municipal offices, and from 1867 in New York state senate, he controlled government spending and accumulated a fortune estimated at somewhere between $45 million and $200 million. He was convicted of forgery and larceny and sent to jail 1873–75, when he escaped to Spain.

Born in New York City, USA, Tweed worked briefly as a clerk in his father's factory. Becoming involved in municipal politics, he served as an alderman 1852–56 and emerged as the leader of Tammany Hall (a New York City Democratic club, founded 1789). Escaping to Spain via Cuba 1875, his anonymity was subverted by a Thomas Nast cartoon, from which Tweed was recognized and sent back to New York. He died in prison.

Tyler /ˈtaɪlə/ John 1790–1862. 10th president of the USA 1841–45, succeeding Benjamin →Harrison, who died after only a month in office. Tyler's government annexed Texas 1845.

Tyler was the first US vice president to succeed to the presidency. Because he was not in favour of many of the Whig Party's policies, he was constantly at odds with the cabinet and Congress until elections forced the Whigs from power.

Tyler /ˈtaɪlə/ Wat died 1381. English leader of the Peasants' Revolt of 1381. He was probably born in Kent or Essex, and may have served in the French wars. After taking Canterbury he led the peasant army to Blackheath and occupied London. At Mile End King Richard II met the rebels and promised to redress their grievances, which included the imposition of a poll tax. At a further conference at Smithfield, Tyler was murdered.

Tynan /ˈtaɪnən/ Kenneth Peacock 1927–1980. English theatre critic and author, a leading cultural figure of the radical 1960s. He devised the nude revue *Oh Calcutta!* 1969, first staged in New York.

Tyndale /ˈtɪndl/ William 1492–1536. English translator of the Bible. The printing of his New Testament (the basis of the Authorized Version) was begun in Cologne 1525 and, after he had been forced to flee, completed in Worms. He was strangled and burned as a heretic at Vilvorde in Belgium.

Tyndall /ˈtɪndl/ John 1820–1893. Irish physicist who 1869 studied the scattering of light by invisibly small suspended particles. Known as the *Tyndall effect*, it was first observed with colloidal solutions, in which a beam of light is made visible when it is scattered by minute colloidal particles (whereas a pure solvent does not scatter light). Similar scattering of blue wavelengths of sunlight by particles in the atmosphere makes the sky look blue (beyond the atmosphere, the sky is black).

The mind of man may be compared to a musical instrument with a certain range of notes, beyond which in both directions we have an infinitude of silence.

John Tyndall, *Fragments of Science*

Tyson /ˈtaɪsən/ Mike (Michael Gerald) 1966– . US heavyweight boxer, undisputed world champion from Aug 1987 to Feb 1990. He won the World Boxing Council heavyweight title 1986 when he beat Trevor Berbick to become the youngest world heavyweight champion. He beat James 'Bonecrusher' Smith for the World Boxing Association title 1987 and later that year became the first undisputed champion since 1978 when he beat Tony Tucker for the International Boxing Federation title.

He turned professional 1985. Of Tyson's first 25 opponents, 15 were knocked out in the first round. He was undefeated until 1990, when he lost the championship in an upset to James 'Buster' Douglas. He was scheduled to fight again for the championship, but was convicted 1992 of rape and imprisoned for six years.

Tzu-Hsi /ˌtsuːˈʃiː/ alternative transliteration of →Zi Xi, dowager empress of China.

Tyler *10th US president John Tyler was the first vice president succeed to the presidency. His administration was marked by the end of the Second Seminole War in Florida 1842, the Ashburton treaty (which settled a dispute with Britain over the border between Maine and Canada) 1842, and the admittance of Texas and Florida to the Union 1845.*

U

U2 Irish rock group formed 1977 by singer Bono Vox (born Paul Hewson, 1960–), guitarist Dave 'The Edge' Evans (1961–), bassist Adam Clayton (1960–), and drummer Larry Mullen (1961–). The band's albums include *The Unforgettable Fire* 1984, *The Joshua Tree* 1987, and *Achtung Baby* 1992.

Uccello /uːˈtʃeləʊ/ Paolo. Adopted name of Paolo di Dono 1397–1475. Italian painter, active in Florence, one of the first to use perspective. His surviving paintings date from the 1430s onwards. Decorative colour and detail dominate his later pictures. His works include *St George and the Dragon* about 1460 (National Gallery, London).

Uccello is recorded as an apprentice in Lorenzo Ghiberti's workshop in 1407. His fresco *The Deluge* about 1431 (Sta Maria Novella, Florence) shows his concern for pictorial perspective, but in later works this aspect becomes superficial. His three battle scenes painted in the 1450s for the Palazzo Medici, Florence, are now in the Ashmolean Museum, Oxford, the National Gallery, London, and the Louvre, Paris.

Udall /juːdl/ Nicholas 1504–1556. English schoolmaster and playwright. He was the author of *Ralph Roister Doister* about 1553, the first known English comedy.

As long liveth the merry man (they say),
As doth the sorry man, and longer by a
day.

   Nicholas Udall *Ralph Roister Doister* c. 1553

Uelsmann /juːlzmən/ Jerry 1934– . US photographer who produced dreamlike images, created by synthesizing many elements into one with great technical skill.

Uhland /uːlænt/ Johann Ludwig 1787–1862. German poet, author of ballads and lyrics in the Romantic tradition.

Ulam /uːləm/ Stanislaw Marcin 1909–1985. Polish-born US mathematician. He was a member of the Manhattan Project that produced the first atom bomb 1943–45, and from 1946 collaborated with Edward →Teller on the design of the hydrogen bomb, solving the problem of how to ignite the bomb. All previous designs had collapsed.

Ulanova Galina 1910– . Soviet dancer. Prima ballerina of the Bolshoi Theatre Ballet 1944–61, she excelled as Juliet and Giselle and created the principal role of Katerina in Prokofiev's *The Stone Flower*.

Ulbricht /ʊlbrɪkt/ Walter 1893–1973. East German communist politician, in power 1960–71. He lived in exile in the USSR during Hitler's rule 1933–45. A Stalinist, he became first secretary of the Socialist Unity Party in East Germany 1950 and (as chair of the Council of State from 1960) was instrumental in the building of the Berlin Wall 1961. He established East Germany's economy and recognition outside the Eastern European bloc.

Ullmann /ʊlmən/ Liv 1939– . Norwegian actress notable for her work with the Swedish director Ingmar Bergman. Her films include *Persona* 1966, *Pope Joan* 1972 (the title role), and *Autumn Sonata* 1978.

Umar /uːmɑː/ 2nd caliph (head) of Islam, a strong disciplinarian. Under his rule Islam spread to Egypt and Persia. He was assassinated in Medina.

Umayyad alternative spelling of →Omayyad dynasty.

Umberto /ʊmˈbeətəʊ/ two kings of Italy:

Umberto I 1844–1900. King of Italy from 1878, who joined the Triple Alliance 1882 with Germany and Austria-Hungary; his colonial ventures included the defeat at Aduwa, Abyssinia, 1896. He was assassinated by an anarchist.

Umberto II 1904–1983. Last king of Italy 1946. On the abdication of his father, Victor Emmanuel III, he ruled 9 May–13 June 1946, when he had to abdicate since a referendum established a republic. He retired to Portugal.

Unamuno /uːnəˈmuːnəʊ/ Miguel de 1864–1936. Spanish writer of Basque origin, exiled 1924–30 for criticism of the military directorate of →Primo de Rivera. His works include mystic poems and the study *Del sentimiento trágico de la vida/The Tragic Sense of Life* 1913, about the conflict of reason and belief in religion.

Underwood /ʌndəwʊd/ Leon 1890–1975. British artist and sculptor. He travelled to Iceland, the USA, Mexico, and West Africa, devoting several books to masks, wood carvings, and bronzes. His rhythmic figures are powerful symbols of human myth.

Underwood /ˈʌndəwʊd/ Rory 1963– . English rugby union player who made his international debut 1984, and became the first English player to reach 50 international appearances. His 35 tries are also an English record. He helped England to win successive Grand Slams 1991 and 1992.

Undset /ˈʊnset/ Sigrid 1882–1949. Norwegian novelist, author of *Kristin Lavransdatter* 1920–22, a strongly Catholic novel set in the 14th century. She was awarded the Nobel Prize for Literature 1928.

Ungaretti /ˌʊŋɡəˈreti/ Giuseppe 1888–1970. Italian poet who lived in France and Brazil. His lyrics show a cosmopolitan independence from Italian poetic tradition. His poems, such as the *Allegria di naufragi/Joy of Shipwrecks* 1919, are of great simplicity.

Unitas /juˈnaɪtəs/ John Constantine 1933– . US American football player. He was signed by the Baltimore Colts 1956 and as Colt quarterback for 17 seasons, Unitas led the team to 5 NFL championship titles in the years 1958–71. Following his release from the Colts, Unitas played for the San Diego Chargers 1973. He was one of the greatest passers in the history of the game.

Born in Pittsburgh, USA, Unitas was a football star for the University of Louisville. He was drafted by the Pittsburgh Steelers of the National Football League (NFL) 1955 where he played for one season.

He was elected to the Football Hall of Fame 1979.

Uno /ˈʊnɒ/ Sōsuke 1923– . Japanese conservative politician, member of the Liberal Democratic Party (LDP). Having held various cabinet posts since 1976, he was designated prime minister in June 1989 in an attempt to restore the image of the LDP after several scandals. He resigned after only a month in office when his affair with a prostitute became public knowledge.

Unwin /ˈʌnwɪn/ Raymond 1863–1940. English town planner. He put the Garden City ideals of Ebenezer Howard into practice, overseeing Letchworth, Hertfordshire (begun 1903), Hampstead Garden Suburb, outside London (begun 1907), and Wythenshawe, outside Manchester (begun 1927).

Updike /ˈʌpdaɪk/ John (Hoyer) 1932– . US writer. Associated with the *New Yorker* magazine from 1955, he soon established a reputation for polished prose, poetry, and criticism. His novels include *The Poorhouse Fair* 1959, *The Centaur* 1963, *Couples* 1968, *The Witches of Eastwick* 1984, *Roger's Version* 1986, and *S.* 1988, and deal with the tensions and frustrations of contemporary US middle-class life and their effects on love and marriage.

Updike was born in Shillington, Pennsylvania, and graduated from Harvard University. Two characters recur in Updike's novels: the former basketball player 'Rabbit' Angstrom, who matures in the series *Rabbit, Run* 1960, *Rabbit Redux* 1971, *Rabbit is Rich* 1981 (Pulitzer prize), and *Rabbit at Rest* 1990; and the novelist Henry Bech, who appears in *Bech: A Book* 1970 and *Bech is Back* 1982.

Urban /ˈɜːbən/ six popes, including:

Urban II *c.* 1042–1099. Pope 1088–99. He launched the First Crusade at the Council of Clermont in France 1095.

Urey /ˈjʊəri/ Harold Clayton 1893–1981. US chemist. In 1932 he isolated heavy water and discovered deuterium, for which he was awarded the 1934 Nobel Prize for Chemistry.

During World War II he was a member of the Manhattan Project that produced the atomic bomb, but after the war he advocated nuclear disarmament and world government.

Ursula, St /ˈɜːsjʊlə/ 4th century AD. English legendary saint, supposed to have been martyred with 11 virgins (misread as 11,000 in the Middle Ages) by the Huns in the Rhineland.

Usher /ˈʌʃə/ James 1581–1656. Irish priest, archbishop of Armagh from 1625. He was responsible for dating the creation to the year 4004 BC, a figure that was inserted in the margin of the Authorized Version of the Bible until the 19th century.

Ussher alternative spelling of James →Usher.

Ustinov /ˈjuːstɪnɒf/ Peter 1921– . English stage and film actor, writer, and director. He won an Academy Award for *Spartacus* 1960. Other film appearances include *Topkapi* 1964, *Death on the Nile* 1978, and *Evil under the Sun* 1981. He published his autobiography *Dear Me* 1983.

A diplomat these days is nothing but a head-waiter who's allowed to sit down occasionally.

> **Peter Ustinov** *Romanoff and Juliet* 1956

Utagawa /ˌuːtəˈɡɑːwə/ Kuniyoshi. Japanese printmaker; see →Kuniyoshi Utagawa.

Utamaro /ˌuːtəˈmɑːrəʊ/ Kitagawa 1753–1806. Japanese artist of the *ukiyo-e* ('floating world') school, who created muted colour prints of beautiful women, including informal studies of prostitutes.

His style was distinctive: his subject is often seen close up, sometimes from unusual angles or viewpoints, and he made use of bold curvaceous lines and highly decorative textiles.

Uthman alternative spelling of →Othman, third caliph of Islam.

Utrillo /juːˈtrɪləʊ/ Maurice 1883–1955. French artist. He painted townscapes of his native Paris, many depicting Montmartre, often from postcard photographs.

Vail /veɪl/ Alfred Lewis 1807–1859. US communications pioneer. A close associate of Samuel →Morse 1837, he developed an improved design for the telegraph mechanism, beginning production of the new model 1838. With US Congressional funding for a telegraph line between Washington and Baltimore, Vail renewed his working relationship with Morse 1844.

Born in Morristown, New Jersey, USA, Vail was educated at New York University, and worked as a mechanic at his father's iron foundry. His book *The American Electro Magnetic Telegraph* was published 1845, and he retired from business 1849.

Valdemar /ˈvældəmɑː/ alternative spelling of →Waldemar, name of four kings of Denmark.

Valdivia /vælˈdiːviə/ Pedro de *c.* 1497–1554. Spanish explorer who travelled to Venezuela about 1530 and accompanied Francisco →Pizarro on his second expedition to Peru. He then went south into Chile, where he founded the cities of Santiago 1541 and Valdivia 1544. In 1552 he crossed the Andes to explore the Negro River. He was killed by Araucanian Indians.

Valentine, St /ˈvæləntaɪn/ according to tradition a bishop of Terni martyred at Rome, now omitted from the calendar of saints' days as probably nonexistent. His festival was 14 Feb, but the custom of sending 'valentines' to a loved one on that day seems to have arisen because the day accidentally coincided with the Roman mid-February festival of Lupercalia.

Valentino /ˌvælənˈtiːnəʊ/ Rudolph. Adopted name of Rodolfo Alfonso Guglielmi di Valentina d'Antonguolla 1895–1926. Italian-born US film actor and dancer, the archetypal romantic lover of the Hollywood silent era. His screen debut was in 1919, but his first starring role was in *The Four Horsemen of the Apocalypse* 1921. His subsequent films include *The Sheik* 1921 and *Blood and Sand* 1922.

Valentino /ˌvælənˈtiːnəʊ/ trade name of Valentino Garavani 1932– . Italian fashion designer who opened his fashion house in Rome 1959. He opened his first ready-to-wear boutique ten years later, before showing the line in Paris from 1975. He launched his menswear collection 1972. His designs are characterized by simplicity - elegantly tailored suits and coats, usually marked with a V in the seams.

Valera Éamon de. Irish politician; see →de Valera.

Valéry /ˌvæleəˈriː/ Paul 1871–1945. French poet and mathematician. His poetry includes *La Jeune Parque/The Young Fate* 1917 and *Charmes/Enchantments* 1922.

For most of his adult life (from 1894) he would wake before 5 a.m. and immediately write in his journals, which totalled over 26,000 pages by the time he died. He regarded the journals as his most important writing.

God made everything out of the void, but the void shows through.

Paul Valéry
Mauvaises pensées et autres 1941

Valentino US film actor and archetypal 'Latin lover' Rudolph Valentino. He had emigrated from his native Italy to the USA 1913, but did not achieve stardom until his role in The Four Horsemen of the Apocalypse *1921. His death from a perforated ulcer provoked near riots and suicides from distraught female fans.*

Vallandigham /vəˈlændɪgəm/ Clement Laird 1820–1871. US political leader. He served in the US House of Representatives 1858–63. A staunch Democrat, he supported Stephen Douglas for president 1860 and opposed many of President Lincoln's war policies. He was arrested for sedition 1862 and deported to the Confederacy. Returning to Ohio 1864, he remained a strong foe of the radical Republicans until his death.

Born in New Lisbon, Ohio, USA, and educated at Washington and Jefferson College, Vallandigham was admitted to the bar 1842 before entering the state legislature 1845–47.

Vallee Rudy (Hubert Prior) 1901–1986. US singer, actor, and bandleader. Establishing a clean-cut, college-boy image, he became one of the most popular crooners of the 1920s. He formed his band the Connecticut Yankees 1928 and hosted a radio programme with the theme song 'My Time Is Your Time' (recorded 1929). From 1929 he appeared in films and stage musicals.

Vallee started as a saxophone player and toured with local bands throughout his teenage years. On leaving college he became a singer, the first to be called a crooner (indicating a smooth, intimate style), making records like 'The Vagabond Lover' 1929 and 'Brother, Can You Spare a Dime?' 1932. In Hollywood and on Broadway he began as a romantic lead but turned to comedy in the 1940s; his films include *George White's Scandals* 1934, *Palm Beach Story* 1942, and *How to Succeed*

Van Buren The 1836 election was the only one of three elections that 8th US president Martin Van Buren successfully contested. It was largely secured through the influence of his close ally and predecessor, Andrew Jackson. Although he attempted to tackle the financial panic that darkened his term in office by introducing a measure for a treasury independent of private banks, the situation prevented his re-election.

in Business Without Really Trying 1966. His performing career lasted into the 1980s.

Vallejo /vəˈleɪəʊ, vəˈjeɪh/ Mariano Guadelupe 1808–1890. American military leader in colonial California. During the 1830s, he opposed the rule of autocratic governors sent from Mexico City and in 1838 became the military commander of the province. He was briefly imprisoned during the Bear Flag revolt 1849 before becoming a citizen of the state of California, serving as a member of the state senate.

Born in Monterey, California, Vallejo chose a military career early in life. Stationed in Alta California he helped put down an Indian uprising at San Jose1 1829.

Valle-Inclán /ˈvæljeɪ iːnˈklɑːn/ Ramón María de 1866–1936. Spanish author of erotic and symbolist works including *Sonatas* 1902–05 and, set in South America, the novel *Tirano Banderas/The Tyrant* 1926.

Valois /ˈvælˈwɑː/ branch of the Capetian dynasty, originally counts of Valois (see Hugh →Capet) in France, members of which occupied the French throne from Philip VI 1328 to Henry III 1589.

Vámbéry /ˈvɑːmbeəri/ Arminius 1832–1913. Hungarian traveller and writer who crossed the deserts of Central Asia to Khiva and Samarkand dressed as a dervish, a classic journey described in his *Travels and Adventures in Central Asia* 1864.

Van Allen /væn ˈælən/ James (Alfred) 1914– . US physicist whose instruments aboard the first US satellite *Explorer 1* 1958 led to the discovery of the Van Allen belts, two zones of intense radiation around the Earth. He pioneered high-altitude research with rockets after World War II.

Vanbrugh /ˈvænbrə/ John 1664–1726. English Baroque architect and dramatist. He designed Blenheim Palace, Oxfordshire, and Castle Howard, Yorkshire, and wrote the comic dramas *The Relapse* 1696 and *The Provok'd Wife* 1697.

He was imprisoned in France 1688–93 as a political hostage during the war between France and the Grand Alliance (including Britain).

Van Buren /væn ˈbjʊərən/ Martin 1782–1862. Eighth president of the US 1837–41, a Democrat, who had helped establish the Democratic Party. He was secretary of state 1829–31, minister to Britain 1831–33, vice president 1833-37, and president during the Panic of 1837, the worst US economic crisis until that time, caused by land speculation in the West. Refusing to intervene, he advocated the establishment of an independent treasury, one not linked to the federal government, worsening the depression and losing the 1840 election.

Vance /væns/ Cyrus 1917– . US Democratic politician, secretary of state 1977–80. He resigned because he did not support President Carter's abortive mission to rescue the US hostages in Iran. In 1992 he was chosen as UN negotiator in the peace talks on Bosnia-Herzegovina. Together with EC negotiator Lord Owen, he devised the Vance-Owen peace plan for dividing the republic into 10 semi-autonomous provinces

Van Cortlandt /væn ˈkɔːtlənt/ Stephanus 1643–1700. Dutch-American colonial official. A colonel in New York provincial militia, he served on the governor's council and in 1677 became the first native-born mayor of New York. He was a local judge 1677–91 and justice of the provincial supreme court 1691–1700.

Born in New Amsterdam (New York from 1664), Van Cortlandt was the son of a prominent family of Dutch settlers. He was a prosperous merchant and expanded his landholdings after the English conquest of the colony in 1664.

Vancouver /væn'kuːvə/ George c. 1758–1798. British navigator who made extensive exploration of the west coast of North America. He accompanied Capt James →Cook on two voyages, and served in the West Indies. He also surveyed parts of Australia, New Zealand, Tahiti, and Hawaii.

van de Graaff /ˌvæn də ˈgræf/ Robert Jemison 1901–1967. US physicist who from 1929 developed a high-voltage generator, which in its modern form can produce more than a million volts. It consists of a continuous vertical conveyor belt that carries electrostatic charges (resulting from friction) up to a large hollow sphere supported on an insulated stand. The lower end of the belt is earthed, so that charge accumulates on the sphere. The size of the voltage built up in air depends on the radius of the sphere, but can be increased by enclosing the generator in an inert atmosphere, such as nitrogen.

Vandenberg /ˈvændənbɜːg/ Arthur Hendrick 1884–1951. US public official. A Republican, he was appointed to US Senate seat 1928 and remained in that office for the next 23 years. Although initially an isolationist, he supported F D Roosevelt's war policies and was a supporter of the United Nations 1945. He was chair of the Senate Foreign Relations Committee 1946–48.

Born in Grand Rapids, Michigan, USA, Vandenberg briefly attended the University of Michigan Law School. He left to join the staff of the *Grand Rapids Herald*, of which he became editor 1906 and later became active in state politics.

Vanderbilt /ˈvændəbɪlt/ Cornelius 1794–1877. US industrialist who made a fortune of more than $100 million in steamships and (from the age of 70) by financing railways.

Vanderbilt /ˈvændəbɪlt/ William Henry 1821–1885. US financier and railway promoter. Given control of the Staten Island Railroad 1857, he was named vice president of the New York and Harlem Railroad 1864, acquired other railways, and became president of the New York Central Railroad 1877. Vanderbilt was famous for his contemptuous phrase 'The public be damned'.

Born in New Brunswick, New Jersey, USA, son

of financier Cornelius Vanderbilt, he became the head of a railway trust and was strongly opposed to government regulation of the railway industry. He retired in 1883.

Van der Laan /ˌvæn də ˈlɑːn/ Hans 1904–1991. Dutch architect of monasteries. He studied architecture in the 1920s in Delft before entering the Benedictine order, where he was ordained as a priest 1934. His earliest work was a guest wing added to the abbey in Oosterhaut 1938; his most significant work is the monastery in Vaals, 1956–1982. Here the strength and clarity of the masses and spaces evoke an elementary Classicism.

Van der Post /ˌvæn də ˈpəʊst/ Laurens (Jan) 1906– . South African writer whose books, many of them autobiographical, reflect his openness to diverse cultures and his belief in the importance of intuition, individualism, and myth in human experience. A formative influence was his time spent with the San Bushmen of the Kalahari while growing up, and whose disappearing culture he recorded in *The Lost World of the Kalahari* 1958, *The Heart of the Hunter* 1961, and *Testament to the Bushmen* 1984.

His first novel *In a Province* 1934 was an indictment of racism in South Africa; later works include *Flamingo Feather* 1955, *The Hunter and the Whale* 1967, *A Story like the Wind* 1972, and *A Far-off Place* 1974. He wrote about Japanese prisoner-of-war camps in *The Seed and the Sower* 1963.

He was knighted in 1980.

Organized religion is making Christianity political, rather than making politics Christian.

Laurens Van der Post in *Observer* 9 Nov 1986

---

van der Waals /ˌvæn də ˈvɑːls/ Johannes Diderik 1837–1923. Dutch physicist who was awarded a Nobel prize 1910 for his theoretical study of gases. He emphasized the forces of attraction and repulsion between atoms and molecules in describing the behaviour of real gases, as opposed to the ideal gases dealt with in Boyle's law and Charles's law.

Van Devanter /ˌvæn dɪˈvæntə/ Willis 1859–1941. US jurist. He was appointed as US Supreme Court justice 1910–37 by President Taft. Active in Republican politics, he served as assistant US attorney general 1897–1903 and federal circuit judge 1903–10. A staunch conservative, Van Devanter was a bitter opponent of the New Deal until his retirement.

Born in Marion, Indiana, USA, Van Devanter was educated at Asbury University and received a law degree from the University of Cincinnati 1881. Settling in Cheyenne, Wyoming, he served as city attorney 1887–88 and chief justice of the territorial supreme court 1888–90.

van Diemen /væn 'diːmən/ Anthony 1593–1645. Dutch admiral, see →Diemen, Anthony van.

Van Doren /væn 'dɔːrən/ Mark 1894–1972. US poet and writer. He published his first collection, *Spring Thunder*, in 1924. His anthology *Collected Poems* 1939 won a Pulitzer Prize. He was an editor of *The Nation* 1924–28 and published the novels *The Transients* 1935 and *Windless Cabins* 1940.

Born in Hope, Illinois, USA, Van Doren was educated at the University of Illinois and received his PhD 1920 from Columbia University, where he taught English 1920–59. His autobiography appeared in 1958 and his last collection of poems, *Good Morning*, in 1973.

Van Dyck Anthony. Flemish painter, see →Dyck, Anthony Van.

Vane /veɪn/ Henry 1613–1662. English politician. In 1640 elected a member of the Long Parliament, he was prominent in the impeachment of Archbishop →Laud and in 1643–53 was in effect the civilian head of the Parliamentary government. At the Restoration of the monarchy he was executed. ·

Vane /veɪn/ John 1927– . British pharmacologist who discovered the wide role of prostaglandins in the human body, produced in response to illness and stress. He shared the 1982 Nobel Prize for Medicine with Sune Bergström (1916–) and Bengt Samuelson (1934–) of Sweden.

van Eyck Aldo. Dutch architect; see →Eyck, Aldo van.

van Eyck Jan. Flemish painter; see →Eyck, Jan van.

van Gogh Vincent. Dutch painter; see →Gogh, Vincent van.

van Leyden Lucas. Dutch painter; see →Lucas van Leyden.

van Meegeren Hans. Dutch forger; see →Meegeren, Hans van.

Van Rensselaer /væn ˌrensə'lɪə/ Stephen 1764–1839. American public official and soldier. A commander during the Anglo-American War 1812–4 he suffered a serious defeat at Queenstown, Canada. He was a US congressman 1822–29. As president of the New York Canal Commission 1825–39 he oversaw the construction of the Erie Canal.

Born in New York, Van Rensselaer was educated at Harvard University and inherited extensive real estate holdings. He served in the New York state assembly 1789–91, in the state senate 1791–96, and as a major general in the militia.

He founded the Rensselaer Polytechnic Institute 1824.

Vansittart /væn'sɪtət/ Robert Gilbert, 1st Baron Vansittart 1881–1957. British diplomat, noted for his anti-German polemic. He was permanent undersecretary of state for foreign affairs 1930–38

and chief diplomatic adviser to the foreign secretary 1938–41.

van't Hoff /vænt 'hɒf/ Jacobus Henricus 1852–1911. Dutch physical chemist. He explained the 'asymmetric' carbon atom occurring in optically active compounds. His greatest work – the concept of chemical affinity as the maximum work obtainable from a reaction – was shown with measurements of osmotic and gas pressures, and reversible electrical cells. He was the first recipient of the Nobel Prize for Chemistry, in 1901.

Varah /vɑːrə/ Chad 1911– . British priest who founded the Samaritans.

Vardon /vɑːdn/ Harry 1870–1937. British golfer, born in Jersey. He won the British Open a record six times 1896–1914. Vardon was the first UK golfer to win the US Open 1900.

He formed a partnership with James Braid and John Henry Taylor, which became known as 'the Great Triumvirate', and dominated British golf in the years up to World War I.

Varèse /vəˈrez/ Edgard 1885–1965. French composer who settled in New York 1916 where he founded the New Symphony Orchestra 1919 to advance the cause of modern music. His work is experimental and often dissonant, combining electronic sounds with orchestral instruments, and includes *Hyperprism* 1923, *Intégrales* 1931, and *Poème Electronique* 1958.

Vargas /vɑːgəs/ Getúlio 1883–1954. President of Brazil 1930–45 and 1951–54. He overthrew the republic 1930 and in 1937 set up a totalitarian, pro-fascist state known as the *Estado Novo*. Ousted by a military coup 1945, he returned as president 1951 but, amid mounting opposition and political scandal, committed suicide 1954.

Vargas Llosa /vɑːgəs 'jəʊsə/ Mario 1937– . Peruvian novelist, author of *La ciudad y los perros/The Time of the Hero* 1963 and *La guerra del fin del mundo/The War at the End of the World* 1982.

As a writer he belongs to the magic realist school. *La tía Julia y el escribidor/Aunt Julia and the Scriptwriter* 1977 is a humorously autobiographical novel. His other works are *Historia de Mayta/The Real Life of Alejandro Mayta* 1985, an account of an attempted revolution in Peru in 1958, and *The Storyteller* 1990.

In his political career, Vargas Llosa began as a communist and turned to the right; he ran unsuccessfully for the presidency 1990. He has been criticized for being out of touch with Peru's large Quechua Indian community.

Varley /vɑːli/ John 1778–1842. English painter of watercolour landscapes, and friend of the poet and artist William →Blake.

Vasarély /ˌvæzəreɪ'liː/ Victor 1908– . French artist, born in Hungary. In the 1940s he developed his precise geometric compositions, full of visual puzzles and effects of movement, which he created with complex arrangements of hard-edged geometric shapes and subtle variations in colours.

He was active in Paris from 1930, then in the south of France from 1960. He initially worked as a graphic artist, concentrating on black and white.

Vasari /vəˈsɑːri/ Giorgio 1511–1574. Italian art historian, architect, and painter, author of *Lives of the Most Excellent Architects, Painters and Sculptors* 1550 (enlarged and revised 1568), in which he proposed the theory of a Renaissance of the arts beginning with Giotto and culminating with Michelangelo. He designed the Uffizi Palace, Florence.

Vasari was a prolific Mannerist painter. His basic view of art history has remained unchallenged, despite his prejudices and his delight in often ill-founded, libellous anecdotes.

Vasco da Gama /ˈvæskəʊ də ˈgɑːmə/ Portuguese navigator; see →Gama.

Vassar /ˈvæsə/ Matthew 1792–1868. British-born US entrepreneur and educational philanthropist. A proponent of higher education for women, he endowed Vassar Female College in Poughkeepsie, New York, 1861. The school opened 1865 with a full college curriculum and became one of the finest women's educational institutions in the USA.

Born in England, Vassar came to the USA with his family 1796. He worked in his father's brewery in Poughkeepsie before establishing his own firm 1811, and successfully expanded his business interests and real-estate investments.

Vassilou /væˈsiːluː/ Georgios Vassos 1931– . Greek-Cypriot politician and entrepreneur, president of Cyprus from 1988. A self-made millionaire, he entered politics as an independent and in 1988 won the presidency, with Communist Party support. He has since, with United Nations help, tried unsuccessfully to heal the rift between the Greek and Turkish communities.

Vauban /vəʊˈbɒn/ Sébastien le Prestre de 1633–1707. French marshal and military engineer. In Louis XIV's wars he conducted many sieges and rebuilt many of the fortresses on France's east frontier.

Vaughan /vɔːn/ Henry 1622–1695. Welsh poet and physician. He published several volumes of metaphysical religious verse and prose devotions. His mystical outlook on nature influenced later poets, including Wordsworth.

Vaughan /vɔːn/ Sarah (Lois) 1924–1990. US jazz singer whose voice had a range of nearly three octaves. She began by singing bebop with such musicians as Dizzy Gillespie and later moved effortlessly between jazz and romantic ballads. She toured very widely and had several hit singles, including 'Make Yourself Comfortable' 1954, 'Mr Wonderful' 1956, and 'Broken-Hearted Melody' 1959.

Vaughan Williams /vɔːn ˈwɪljəmz/ Ralph 1872–1958. English composer. His style was tonal and often evocative of the English countryside through the use of folk themes. Among his works are the

Vaughan US jazz vocalist Sarah Vaughan, noted for her mastering of such vocal techniques as vibrato, vocal leaps, 'skat' singing, and improvisation. Her vocal control and the beauty of her tone were the hallmarks of her singing, and she made a major vocal contribution to the development of bebop.

orchestral *Fantasia on a Theme by Thomas Tallis* 1910; the opera *Sir John in Love* 1929, featuring the Elizabethan song 'Greensleeves'; and nine symphonies 1909–57.

He studied at Cambridge, the Royal College of Music, with Max →Bruch in Berlin, and Maurice →Ravel in Paris. His choral poems include *Toward the Unknown Region* (Whitman) 1907 and *On Wenlock Edge* (Housman) 1909, *A Sea Symphony* 1910, and *A London Symphony* 1914. Later works include *Sinfonia Antartica* 1953, developed from his film score for *Scott of the Antarctic* 1948, and a Ninth Symphony 1958. He also wrote *A Pastoral Symphony* 1922, sacred music for unaccompanied choir, the ballad opera *Hugh the Drover* 1924, and the operatic morality play *The Pilgrim's Progress* 1951.

Veblen /ˈveblən/ Thorstein (Bunde) 1857–1929. US social critic. His insights on culture and economics were expressed in his books *The Theory of the Leisure Class* 1899 and *The Theory of Business Enterprise* 1904. He was a founder of the New School for Social Research in New York 1919.

Born in Cato, Wisconsin, USA, and raised in Minnesota, Veblen was educated at Carleton College and received his PhD from Yale University 1884. He taught at Chicago, Stanford, and Missouri universities and edited the *Journal of Political Economy* 1892–1905.

Veeck /vek/ William Louis, Jr 1914–1986. US baseball executive and pioneer of new marketing techniques. As owner of St Louis Browns 1951–53 and Chicago White Sox 1959–61, he introduced innovations in the sale of television rights and the drafting of amateurs that later became standard in professional sports.

Born in Chicago, USA, Veeck was the son of the owner of major league baseball's Chicago Cubs, and attended Kenyon College. He became part owner of the Cleveland Indians, and helped guide them to a World Series victory 1948.

Vega /ˈləʊpeɪ də ˈveɪgə/ Lope Felix de (Carpio) 1562–1635. Spanish poet and dramatist, one of the founders of modern Spanish drama. He wrote epics, pastorals, odes, sonnets, novels, and, reputedly, over 1,500 plays (of which 426 are still in existence), mostly tragicomedies. He set out his views on drama in *Arte nuevo de hacer comedias/The New Art of Writing Plays* 1609, while reaffirming the classical form. *Fuenteovejuna* 1614 has been acclaimed as the first proletarian drama.

He was born in Madrid, served with the Armada 1588, and in 1613 took holy orders.

Veidt /faɪt/ Conrad 1893–1943. German film actor, memorable as the sleepwalker in *Das Kabinett des Dr Caligari/The Cabinet of Dr Caligari* 1919 and as the evil caliph in *The Thief of Bagdad* 1940.

Veil /veɪ/ Simone 1927– . French politician. A survivor of Hitler's concentration camps, she was minister of health 1974–79 and framed the French abortion bill. She was president of the European Parliament 1979–81.

Velázquez /vɪˈlæskwɪz/ Diego Rodríguez de Silva y 1599–1660. Spanish painter, born in Seville, the outstanding Spanish artist of the 17th century. In 1623 he became court painter to Philip IV in Madrid, where he produced many portraits of the royal family as well as occasional religious paintings, genre scenes, and other subjects. *Las Meninas/The Ladies-in-Waiting* 1655 (Prado, Madrid) is a complex group portrait that includes a self-portrait, but nevertheless focuses clearly on the doll-like figure of the Infanta Margareta Teresa.

His early work in Seville shows exceptional realism and dignity, delight in capturing a variety of textures, rich use of colour, and contrasts of light and shade. In Madrid he was inspired by works by Titian in the royal collection and by Rubens, whom he met in 1628. He was in Italy 1629–31 and 1648–51; on his second visit he painted *Pope Innocent X* (Doria Gallery, Rome).

Velázquez's work includes an outstanding formal history painting, *The Surrender of Breda* 1634–35 (Prado), studies of the male nude, and a reclining female nude, *The Rokeby Venus* about 1648 (National Gallery, London). Around half of the 100 or so paintings known to be by him are owned by the Prado, Madrid.

Velde, van de /ˌvæn də ˈfeldə/ family of Dutch artists. Both *Willem van de Velde* the Elder (1611–93) and his son *Willem van de Velde* the Younger (1633–1707) painted sea battles for Charles II and James II (having settled in London 1672). Another son *Adriaen van de Velde* (1636–1672) painted landscapes.

Willem the Younger achieved an atmosphere of harmony and dignity in highly detailed views of fighting ships at sea. The National Maritime Museum in Greenwich, London, has a fine collection of his works.

Vendôme /vɒnˈdəʊm/ Louis Joseph, Duc de Vendôme 1654–1712. Marshal of France under Louis XIV, he lost his command after defeat by the British commander Marlborough at Oudenaarde, Belgium, 1708, but achieved successes in the 1710 Spanish campaign during the War of the Spanish Succession.

Veneziano Domenico. Italian painter; see →Domenico Veneziano.

Venizelos /ˌvenɪˈzelɒs/ Eleuthérios 1864–1936. Greek politician born in Crete, leader of the Cretan movement against Turkish rule until the union of the island with Greece in 1905. He later became prime minister of the Greek state on five occasions, 1910–15, 1917–20, 1924, 1928–32, and 1933, before being exiled to France in 1935.

Having led the fight against Turkish rule in Crete, Venizelos became president of the Cretan assembly and declared the union of the island with Greece in 1905. As prime minister of Greece from 1910, he instituted financial, military, and constitutional reforms and took Greece into the Balkan Wars 1912–13. As a result, Greece annexed Macedonia, but attempts by Venizelos to join World War I on the Allied side led to his dismissal by King Constantine. Leading a rebel government in Crete and later in Salonika, he declared war on Bulgaria and Germany and secured the abdication of King Constantine.

As prime minister again from 1917 he attended the Paris Peace Conference in 1919. By provoking a war with Turkey over Anatolia in 1920 he suffered an electoral defeat. On his last return to office in 1933, he was implicated in an uprising by his supporters and fled to France, where he died.

Ventris /ˈventrɪs/ Michael (George Francis) 1922–1956. English archaeologist. Deciphering Minoan Linear B, the language of the tablets found at Knossos and Pylos, he showed that it was a very early form of Greek, thus revising existing views on early Greek history. *Documents in Mycenaean Greek*, written with John Chadwick (1920–), was published shortly after he died.

Venturi /venˈtjʊəri/ Robert 1925– . US architect. He pioneered Post-Modernism through his books *Complexity and Contradiction in Architecture* 1967 (Pulitzer Prize 1991) and *Learning from Las Vegas* 1972. In 1986 he was commissioned to design the extension to the National Gallery, London, opened 1991.

He is famous for his slogan 'Less is a bore', countering German architect Ludwig Mies van der Rohe's 'Less is more'.

Verdi /ˈveədi/ Giuseppe (Fortunino Francesco) 1813–1901. Italian opera composer of the Romantic period, who took his native operatic style to new heights of dramatic expression. In 1842 he wrote the opera *Nabucco*, followed by *Ernani* 1844 and *Rigoletto* 1851. Other works include *Il Trovatore* and *La Traviata* both 1853, *Aïda* 1871, and the masterpieces of his old age, *Otello* 1887 and *Falstaff* 1893. His *Requiem* 1874 commemorates Alessandro →Manzoni.

During the mid-1800s, Verdi became a symbol of Italy's fight for independence from Austria, frequently finding himself in conflict with the Austrian authorities, who felt that his operas encouraged Italian nationalism.

I would be willing to set even a newspaper or a letter, etc., to music, but in the theatre the public will stand for anything except boredom.

Giuseppe Verdi letter to Antonio Somma 1854

Vergil alternative spelling for →Virgil, Roman poet.

Verlaine /veəˈleɪn/ Paul 1844–1896. French lyric poet who was influenced by the poets Baudelaire and →Rimbaud. His volumes of verse include *Poèmes saturniens/Saturnine Poems* 1866, *Fêtes galantes/Amorous Entertainments* 1869, and *Romances sans paroles/Songs without Words* 1874. In 1873 he was imprisoned for attempting to shoot Rimbaud. His later works reflect his attempts to lead a reformed life. He was acknowledged as leader of the Symbolist poets, who used words for their symbolic rather than concrete meaning.

All the rest is mere fine writing.

Paul Verlaine *Jadis et Naguère* 1885

Vermeer /veəˈmɪə/ Jan 1632–1675. Dutch painter, active in Delft. Most of his pictures are genre scenes, with a limpid clarity and distinct air of stillness, and a harmonious palette often focusing on yellow and blue. He frequently depicted solitary women in domestic settings, as in *The Lacemaker* (Louvre, Paris).

Vermeer is thought to have spent his whole life in Delft. There are only 35 paintings ascribed to him. His work fell into obscurity until the mid-to-late 19th century, but he is now ranked as one of the greatest Dutch artists.

In addition to genre scenes, his work comprises one religious painting, a few portraits, and two townscapes, of which the fresh and naturalistic *View of Delft* about 1660 (Mauritshuis, The Hague) triggered the revival of interest in Vermeer. *The Artist's Studio*, about 1665–70 (Kunsthistorisches Museum, Vienna), is one of his most elaborate compositions; the subject appears to be allegorical, but the exact meaning remains a mystery.

Verne /vɜːn/ Jules 1828–1905. French author of tales of adventure that anticipated future scientific developments: *Five Weeks in a Balloon* 1862, *Journey to the Centre of the Earth* 1864, *Twenty Thousand Leagues under the Sea* 1870, and *Around the World in Eighty Days* 1873.

Verney /ˈvɜːni/ Edmund 1590–1642. English courtier, knight-marshal to Charles I from 1626. He sat as a member of both the Short and the Long Parliaments and, though sympathizing with the Parliamentary position, remained true to his allegiance: he died at his post as royal standard bearer at the Battle of Edgehill.

The *Verney papers*, a collection of his memoirs and other personal papers, are a valuable record of this and later periods. His son Ralph (1613–96) supported the Parliamentarians.

Vernier /ˈveənɪeɪ/ Pierre 1580–1637. French mathematician who invented a means of making very precise measurements with what is now called the vernier scale. He was a French government official and in 1631 published *La construction, l'usage, et les propriétez du quadrant nouveau matheématique/The construction, uses and properties of a new mathematical quadrant*, in which he explained his method.

Vernon /ˈvɜːnən/ Edward 1684–1757. English admiral who captured Portobello from the Spanish in the Caribbean 1739, with a loss of only seven men.

Veronese /ˌverəʊˈneɪzi/ Paolo *c.* 1528–1588. Italian painter, born in Verona, active mainly in Venice (from about 1553). He specialized in grand decorative schemes, such as his ceilings in the Doge's Palace in Venice, with *trompe l'oeil* effects and inventive detail. The subjects are religious, mythological, historical, and allegorical.

Titian was a major influence, but Veronese also knew the work of Giulio Romano and Michelangelo. His decorations in the Villa Barbera at Maser near Vicenza show his skill at illusionism and a typically Venetian rich use of colour; they are also characteristically full of inventive fantasy. He took the same approach to religious works, and as a result his *Last Supper* 1573 (Accademia, Venice, renamed *The Feast in the House of Levi*) was the subject of a trial by the Inquisition, since the holy event seems to be almost subordinated by profane details: figures of drunkards, soldiers conversing, dogs, and so on.

Verrocchio /ve'rɒkiəʊ/ Andrea del 1435–1488. Italian painter, sculptor, and goldsmith, born in Florence, where he ran a large workshop and received commissions from the Medici family. The vigorous equestrian statue of *Bartolomeo Colleoni*, begun 1481 (Campo SS Giovanni e Paolo, Venice), was his last work.

Verrocchio was a pupil of ➔Donatello and himself the early teacher of Leonardo da Vinci. In his *Baptism* about 1472 (Uffizi, Florence) Leonardo is said to have painted the kneeling angel shown in profile. Verrocchio's sculptures include a bronze *Christ and St Thomas* 1465 (Orsanmichele, Florence) and *David* 1476 (Bargello, Florence).

Verwoerd /fə'vʊət/ Hendrik (Frensch) 1901–1966. South African right-wing Nationalist Party politician, prime minister 1958–66. As minister of native affairs 1950–58, he was the chief promoter of apartheid legislation (segregation by race). He made the country a republic 1961. He was assassinated 1966.

Vesalius /vɪ'seɪliəs/ Andreas 1514–1564. Belgian physician who revolutionized anatomy. His great innovations were to perform postmortem dissections and to make use of illustrations in teaching anatomy.

The dissections (then illegal) enabled him to discover that ➔Galen's system of medicine was based on fundamental anatomical errors. Vesalius's book *De Humani Corporis Fabrica/On The Structure of the Human Body* 1543, together with the major work of the astronomer Copernicus, published in the same year, marked the dawn of modern science.

Vesey /'viːzi/ Denmark *c.* 1767–1822. American resistance leader. Buying his freedom for $600 in 1800, he became an outspoken and eloquent critic of the institution of slavery. Arrested 1822 on suspicion of fomenting a rebellion among local slaves, he and five other black leaders were hanged despite a lack of evidence against them.

Probably born on the Caribbean island of St Thomas, Vesey was purchased 1781 and taken to Charleston, South Carolina, 1783. He established himself as a carpenter 1800.

Vespasian /ve'speɪʒən/ (Titus Flavius Vespasianus) AD 9–79. Roman emperor from AD 69. He was the son of a moneylender, and had a distinguished military career. He was proclaimed emperor by his soldiers while he was campaigning in Palestine. He reorganized the eastern provinces, and was a capable administrator.

Vespucci /ves'puːtʃi/ Amerigo 1454–1512. Florentine merchant. The Americas were named after him as a result of the widespread circulation of his accounts of his explorations. His accounts of the voyage 1499–1501 indicate that he had been to places he could not possibly have reached (the Pacific Ocean, British Columbia, Antarctica).

Veuster /vɜː'steə/ Joseph de 1840–1889. Belgian missionary, known as Father Damien. He entered the order of the Fathers of the Sacred Heart at Louvain, went to Hawaii, and from 1873 was resident priest in the leper settlement at Molokai. He eventually became infected and died there.

Vian /vaɪən/ Philip 1894–1968. British admiral of the fleet in World War II. In 1940 he was the hero of the *Altmark incident*, and in 1941 commanded the destroyers that chased the *Bismarck*.

Vico /'viːkəʊ/ Giambattista 1668–1744. Italian philosopher, considered the founder of the modern philosophy of history. He argued that we can understand history more adequately than nature, since it is we who have made it. He believed that the study of language, ritual, and myth was a way of understanding earlier societies. His cyclical theory of history (the birth, development, and decline of human societies) was put forward in *New Science* 1725.

Vico postulated that society passes through a cycle of four phases: the divine, or theocratic, when people are governed by their awe of the supernatural; the aristocratic, or 'heroic' (Homer, *Beowulf*); the democratic and individualistic; and chaos, a fall into confusion that startles people back into supernatural reverence. This is expressed in his dictum *verum et factum convertuntur* ('the true and the made are convertible'). His belief that the study of language and rituals was a better way of understanding early societies was a departure from the traditional ways of writing history either as biographies or as preordained God's will. He was born in Naples and was professor of rhetoric there 1698. He became historiographer to the king of Naples 1735.

The certitude of laws is an obscurity of judgement backed only by authority.

Giambattista Vico
The New Science 1725–44

Victor Emmanuel /'vɪktər ɪ'mænjuəl/ three kings of Italy, including:

Victor Emmanuel II 1820–1878. First king of united Italy from 1861. He became king of Sardinia on the abdication of his father Charles Albert 1849. In 1855 he allied Sardinia with France and the UK in the Crimean War. In 1859 in alliance with the French he defeated the Austrians and annexed Lombardy. By 1860 most of Italy had come under his rule, and in 1861 he was proclaimed king of Italy. In 1870 he made Rome his capital.

Victor Emmanuel III 1869–1947. King of Italy from the assassination of his father, Umberto I, 1900. He acquiesced in the Fascist regime of Mussolini from 1922 and, after the dictator's fall 1943, relinquished power to his son Umberto II, who cooperated with the Allies. Victor Emmanuel formally abdicated 1946.

Victoria *This engraving from Winterhalter's The First of May, 1851 shows Queen Victoria and Prince Albert with Prince Arthur and the Duke of Wellington. The picture commemorates the joint birthdays of the infant Prince Arthur and his godfather, the Duke. During Queen Victoria's 63-year reign, the longest in British history, the British Empire grew to enormous size and made Britain the richest country in the world.*

We are not amused.

Queen Victoria
on seeing an imitation of herself

Victoria /vɪkˈtɔːriə/ 1819–1901. Queen of the UK from 1837, when she succeeded her uncle William IV, and empress of India from 1876. In 1840 she married Prince →Albert of Saxe-Coburg and Gotha. Her relations with her prime ministers ranged from the affectionate (Melbourne and Disraeli) to the stormy (Peel, Palmerston, and Gladstone). Her golden jubilee 1887 and diamond jubilee 1897 marked a waning of republican sentiment, which had developed with her withdrawal from public life on Albert's death 1861.

Only child of Edward, duke of Kent, fourth son of George III, she was born 24 May 1819 at Kensington Palace, London. She and Albert had four sons and five daughters. After Albert's death 1861 she lived mainly in retirement. Nevertheless, she kept control of affairs, refusing the Prince of Wales (Edward VII) any active role. From 1848 she regularly visited the Scottish Highlands, where she had a house at Balmoral built to Prince Albert's designs. She died at Osborne House, her home in the Isle of Wight, 22 Jan 1901, and was buried at Windsor.

Vidal /viːˈdæl/ Gore 1925– . US writer and critic. Much of his fiction deals satirically with history and politics and includes the novels *Myra Breckinridge* 1968, *Burr* 1973, and *Empire* 1987, plays and screenplays, including *Suddenly Last Summer* 1958, and essays, such as *Armageddon?* 1987.

Vidocq /viːˈdɒk/ François Eugène 1775–1857. French criminal who became a spy for the Paris police 1809, and rose to become chief of the detective department.

Vidor /viːˈdɔː/ King 1894–1982. US film director who made such epics as *The Big Parade* 1925 and *Duel in the Sun* 1946. He has been praised as a cinematic innovator, and received an honorary Academy Award 1979. His other films include *The Crowd* 1928 and *Guerra e Pace/War and Peace* 1956.

Viète /viˈet/ François 1540–1603. French mathematician who developed algebra and its notation. He was the first mathematician to use letters of the alphabet to denote both known and unknown quantities.

Vigée-Lebrun /ˌviːʒeɪləˈbrɜːn/ Elisabeth 1755–1842. French portrait painter, trained by her father (a painter in pastels) and →Greuze. She became painter to Queen Marie Antoinette in the 1780s (many royal portraits survive).

At the outbreak of the Revolution 1789 she left France and travelled in Europe, staying in St Petersburg, Russia, 1795–1802. She resettled in Paris 1809. She published an account of her travels, *Souvenirs* 1835–37, written in the form of letters.

Vigeland /ˈviːɡələn/ Gustav 1869–1943. Norwegian sculptor. He studied in Oslo and Copenhagen and with →Rodin in Paris 1892. His programme of sculpture in Frogner Park, Oslo, conceived 1900, was never finished. The style is heavy and monumental; the sculpted figures and animals enigmatic.

Vigny /viːnˈjiː/ Alfred, Comte de 1797–1863. French romantic writer whose works include the historical novel *Cinq-Mars* 1826, the play *Chatterton* 1835, and poetry, for example, *Les Destinées/Destinies* 1864.

Vigo Jean. Adopted name of Jean Almereida 1905–1934. French director of intensely lyrical experimental films. He made only two shorts, *A Propos de Nice* 1930 and *Taris Champion de Natation* 1934; and two feature films, *Zéro de conduite/Nothing for Conduct* 1933 and *L'Atalante* 1934.

Villa-Lobos /ˈvɪlə ˈləʊbɒs/ Heitor 1887–1959. Brazilian composer. His style was based on folk tunes collected on travels in his country; for example, in the *Bachianas Brasileiras* 1930–44, he treats them in the manner of Bach. His works range from guitar solos to film scores to opera; he produced 2,000 works, including 12 symphonies.

Villard /vɪˈlɑː, -d/ Henry 1835–1900. German-born US journalist and financier. He covered the American Civil War 1861–65 for the New York *Herald* and *Tribune*. An astute investor, he was president of the Edison General Electric Co. 1890–92 and the *New York Evening Post* 1881–1900.

Born in Germany, Villard emigrated to the USA 1853 and settled in Illinois. He was president of the Oregon and California Railroad 1876, served as president of the Northern Pacific Railroad 1881–84, and was Northern Pacific's chair of the board 1889–93.

Villard /vɪˈlɑː, -d/ Oswald Garrison 1872–1949. US editor and civil rights leader. A founder of the National Association for the Advancement of Colored People (NAACP), he was active in antiwar movements. He was president of the *New York Evening Post* 1900–18 and editor of the magazine *The Nation* 1918–32.

Born in Germany during the European travels of his father Henry →Villard, he was educated at Harvard University and joined the staff of the *Philadelphia Press* 1893. After selling the *Post* 1918 he concentrated on its subsidiary, *The Nation*.

His autobiography, *Fighting Years*, appeared 1939.

Villehardouin /ˌviːlɑːˈdwæn/ Geoffroy de *c.* 1160–1213. French historian, the first to write in the French language. He was born near Troyes, and was a leader of the Fourth Crusade, of which his *Conquest of Constantinople* (about 1209) is an account.

Villiers de l'Isle Adam /viːlˈjeɪ də ˈliːl/ Philippe Auguste Mathias, comte de 1838–1889. French poet, the inaugurator of the Symbolist movement. He wrote the drama *Axel* 1890; *Isis* 1862, a romance of the supernatural; verse; and short stories.

Villon /viːˈɒn/ François 1431–*c.* 1465. French poet who used satiric humour, pathos, and lyric power in works written in the slang of the time. Among the little of his work that survives, *Petit Testament* 1456 and *Grand Testament* 1461 are prominent (the latter includes the 'Ballade des dames du temps jadis/Ballad of the Ladies of Former Times').

He was born in Paris and dropped his surname (Montcorbier or de Logos) to assume that of one of his relatives, a canon, who sent him to study at the Sorbonne, where he graduated 1449 and took his MA 1452. In 1455 he stabbed a priest in a street fight and had to flee the city. Pardoned the next year, he returned to Paris but was soon in flight again after robbing the College of Navarre. He stayed briefly at the court of the duke of Orléans until sentenced to death for an unknown offence, from which he was saved by the amnesty of a public holiday. Theft and public brawling continued to occupy his time, in addition to the production of the *Grand Testament* 1461. A sentence of death in Paris, commuted to ten-year banishment 1463, is the last that is known of his life.

Vincent de Paul, St /ˈvɪnsənt də ˈpɔːl/ *c.* 1580–1660. French Roman Catholic priest and founder of the two charitable orders of Dazarists 1625 and Sisters of Charity 1634. After being ordained 1600, he was captured by Barbary pirates and held as a slave in Tunis until he escaped 1607. He was canonized 1737; feast day 19 July.

Vincent of Beauvais /ˈvɪnsənt, bəʊˈveɪ/ *c.* 1190–1264. French scholar, encyclopedist, and Dominican priest. A chaplain to the court of Louis IX, he is remembered for his *Speculum majus/Great Mirror* 1220–44, a reference work summarizing contemporary knowledge on virtually every subject, including science, natural history, literature, and law. It also contained a history of the world from the creation.

It is noteworthy for its positive attitude to classical literature, which had undergone a period of eclipse in the preceding centuries.

Vinson /ˈvɪnsən/ Frederick Moore 1890–1953. US jurist. He held office in the US House of Representatives 1924–28 and 1930–38 and was appointed chief justice of the US Supreme Court 1946–53 by President Truman. He defended federal intervention in social and economic matters, and dissented in *Youngstown Sheet and Tube Co* v *Sawyer* 1952, revoking presidential nationalization of the steel industry during the Korean War.

Born in Louisa, Kentucky, USA, Vinson received his undergraduate and law degrees from Centre College and became a lawyer active in Democratic politics. He was appointed judge of the US Court of Appeals for the District of Columbia 1939.

He supported civil rights, writing the majority opinion in *Shelly* v *Kraemer* 1948, ruling that state courts may not enforce discrimination by private landlords, and *McLaurin* v *Oklahoma State Regents* 1950, attacking the 'separate but equal' doctrine.

Viollet-le-Duc /ˌviːəˈleɪ lə ˈdjuːk/ Eugène Emmanuel 1814–1849. French architect. Leader of the Gothic revival in France, he also restored medieval buildings.

Virchow Rudolf Ludwig Carl 1821–1902. German pathologist, the founder of cellular pathology. Virchow was the first to describe leukaemia (cancer of the blood). In his book *Die Cellulare Pathologie/Cellular Pathology* 1858, he proposed that disease is not due to sudden invasions or changes, but to slow processes in which normal cells give rise to abnormal ones.

Viren Lasse 1949– . Finnish long- distance runner who won the 5,000 metres and 10,000 metres at the 1972 Munich and 1976 Montréal Olympics, becoming the first Olympic athlete successfully to defend both titles at these distances.

Virgil /ˈvɜːdʒəl/ (Publius Vergilius Maro) 70–19 BC. Roman poet who wrote the *Eclogues* 37 BC, a series of pastoral poems; the *Georgics* 30 BC, four books on the art of farming; and his epic masterpiece, the *Aeneid*.

Virgil, born near Mantua, came of the small farmer class. He was educated in Cremona and Mediolanum (Milan) and studied philosophy and rhetoric in Rome before returning to his farm, where he began the *Eclogues* 43 BC. He wrote the *Georgics* at the suggestion of his patron, Maecenas, to whom he introduced Horace. Virgil devoted the last 11 years of his life to the composition of the *Aeneid*, considered the greatest epic poem in Latin literature and a major influence on later European literature.

We may be masters of our every lot
By bearing it.

Virgil *Aeneid*

Virtanen /ˈvɪətənen/ Artturi Ilmari 1895–1973. Finnish chemist who from 1920 made discoveries in agricultural chemistry. Because green fodder tends to ferment and produce a variety of harmful acids, it cannot be preserved for long. Virtanen prevented the process from starting by acidifying the fodder. In this form it lasted longer and remained nutritious. Nobel Prize for Chemistry 1945.

Visconti /vɪˈskɒnti/ Luchino 1906–1976. Italian film, opera, and theatre director. The film *Ossessione* 1942 pioneered neorealist cinema despite being subject to censorship problems from the fascist government. His later works include *Rocco and His Brothers* 1960, *The Leopard* 1963, *The Damned* 1969, and *Death in Venice* 1971. His powerful social commentary led to clashes with the Italian government and Roman Catholic Church.

Vitruvius /vɪˈtruːvɪəs/ (Marcus Vitruvius Pollio) 1st century BC. Roman architect whose ten-volume interpretation of Roman architecture *De architectura* influenced Leon Battista Alberti and Andrea Palladio.

Vitus, St /ˈvaɪtəs/ Christian saint, perhaps Sicilian, who was martyred in Rome early in the 4th century. Feast day 15 June.

Vivaldi /vɪˈvældi/ Antonio (Lucio) 1678–1741. Italian Baroque composer, violinist, and conductor. He wrote 23 symphonies, 75 sonatas, over 400 concertos, including the *Four Seasons* (about 1725) for violin and orchestra, over 40 operas, and much sacred music. His work was largely neglected until the 1930s.

Vladimir I /ˈvlædɪmɪə/ St 956–1015. Russian saint, prince of Novgorod, and grand duke of Kiev. Converted to Christianity 988, he married Anna, Christian sister of the Byzantine emperor →Basil II, and established the Byzantine rite of Orthodox Christianity as the Russian national faith.

Feast day 15 July.

Vlaminck /vlæˈmæŋk/ Maurice de 1876–1958. French painter who began using brilliant colour as an early member of the *Fauves*, mainly painting landscapes. He later abandoned Fauve colour. He also wrote poetry, novels, and essays.

Initially he was inspired by van →Gogh but by 1908 →Cézanne had become the chief influence. Vlaminck was a multitalented eccentric: his pastimes included playing the violin and farming.

Vogel /ˈfəʊgəl/ Hans-Jochen 1926– . German socialist politician, chair of the Social Democratic Party (SPD) 1987–91. A former leader of the SPD in Bavaria and mayor of Munich, he served in the Brandt and Schmidt West German governments in the 1970s as housing and then justice minister and then, briefly, as mayor of West Berlin.

A centrist, compromise figure, Vogel unsuccessfully contested the 1983 federal election as chancellor candidate for the SPD and in 1987 replaced Brandt as party chair; he left that post 1991 as well as standing down as SPD parliamentary leader later in the year.

Voight /vɔɪt/ Jon 1938– . US film actor who starred with Dustin Hoffman in *Midnight Cowboy* 1969. His subsequent films include *Deliverance* 1972, *Coming Home* 1978, and *Runaway Train* 1985.

Volcker /vəʊlkə/ Paul 1927– . US economist. As chair of the board of governors of the Federal Reserve System 1979–87, he controlled the amount of money in circulation in the USA. He was succeeded by Alan Greenspan.

Volta /vɒltə/ Alessandro 1745–1827. Italian physicist who invented the first electric cell (the voltaic pile), the electrophorus (an early electrostatic generator), and an electroscope.

Born in Como, he was a professor there and at Pavia. The volt is named after him.

Voltaire /vɒl'teə/ Pen name of François-Marie Arouet 1694–1778. French writer who believed in deism (a rational 'religion of nature') and devoted himself to tolerance, justice, and humanity. He was threatened with arrest for *Lettres philosophiques sur les Anglais/Philosophical Letters on the English* 1733 (essays in favour of English ways, thought, and political practice) and had to take refuge. Other writings include *Le Siècle de Louis XIV/The Age of Louis XIV* 1751; *Candide* 1759, a parody on →Leibniz's 'best of all possible worlds'; and *Dictionnaire philosophique* 1764.

Voltaire was born in Paris, the son of a notary, and used his pen name from 1718. He was twice imprisoned in the Bastille and exiled from Paris 1716–26 for libellous political verse. *Oedipe/Oedipus*, his first essay in tragedy, was staged 1718.

Voltaire French writer and philosopher Voltaire's most celebrated story, Candide, *satirized the 'all is for the best in this best of all possible worlds' philosophy. Much of his later work outlined his belief in tolerance and practical ways of righting injustice.*

While in England 1726–29 he dedicated an epic poem on Henry IV, *La Henriade/The Henriade*, to Queen Caroline, and on returning to France published the successful *Histoire de Charles XII/History of Charles XII* 1731, and produced the play *Zaïre* 1732. He took refuge with his mistress, the Marquise de →Châtelet, at Cirey in Champagne, where he wrote the play *Mérope* 1743 and much of *Le Siècle de Louis XIV*. Among his other works are histories of Peter the Great, Louis XV, and India; the satirical tale *Zadig* 1748; *La Pucelle/The Maid* 1755, on Joan of Arc; and the tragedy *Irène* 1778. From 1751 to 1753 he stayed at the court of Frederick II (the Great) of Prussia, who had long been an admirer, but the association ended in deep enmity. From 1754 he established himself near Geneva, and after 1758 at Ferney, just across the French border. His remains were transferred 1791 to the Panthéon in Paris.

von Braun /fɒn 'braʊn/ Wernher 1912–1977. German rocket engineer who developed German military rockets (V1 and V2) during World War II and later worked for the space agency NASA in the USA.

During the 1940s his research team at Peenemünde on the Baltic coast produced the V1 (flying bomb) and supersonic V2 rockets. In the 1950s von Braun was part of the team that produced rockets for US satellites (the first, *Explorer I*, was launched early 1958) and early space flights by astronauts.

von Gesner /fɒn 'gesnə/ Konrad 1516–1565. Swiss naturalist who produced an encyclopedia of the animal world, the *Historia animalium* 1551–58.

Gesner was a victim of the Black Death and could not complete a similar project on plants. He is considered a founder of the science of zoology, but was also an expert in languages and an authority on the Classical writers.

von Karajan Herbert. Austrian conductor. See →Karajan, Herbert von.

Vonnegut Kurt, Jr 1922– . US writer whose work generally has a science-fiction or fantasy element; his novels include *The Sirens of Titan* 1958, *Cat's Cradle* 1963, *Slaughterhouse-Five* 1969, which draws on his World War II experience of the fire-bombing of Dresden, Germany, *Galapagos* 1985, and *Hocus Pocus* 1990.

Von Neumann /vɒn 'njuːmən/ John 1903–1957. Hungarian-born US scientist and mathematician, known for his pioneering work on computer design. He invented his 'rings of operators' (called Von Neumann algebras) in the late 1930s, and also contributed to set theory, games theory, cybernetics (with his theory of self-reproducing automata, called *Von Neumann machines*), and the development of the atomic and hydrogen bombs.

He was born in Budapest and became an assistant professor of physical mathematics at Berlin

University before moving to Princeton, USA, in 1929, where he later became professor of mathematics. In the early 1940s he described a design for a stored-program computer.

Voroshilov /ˌvɒrəˈʃiːlɒf/ Klement Efremovich 1881–1969. Marshal of the USSR. He joined the Bolsheviks 1903 and was arrested many times and exiled, but escaped. He became a Red Army commander in the civil war 1918–20, a member of the central committee 1921, commissar for war 1925, member of the Politburo 1926, and marshal 1935. He was removed as war commissar 1940 after defeats on the Finland front and failing to raise the German siege of Leningrad. He was a member of the committee for defence 1941–44 and president of the Presidium of the USSR 1953–60.

Vorster /ˈfɔːstə/ Balthazar Johannes 1915–1983. South African Nationalist politician, prime minister 1966–78, and president 1978–79. During his term as prime minister some elements of apartheid were allowed to lapse, and attempts were made to improve relations with the outside world. He resigned the presidency because of a financial scandal.

Voysey /ˈvɔɪzi/ Charles Francis Annesley 1857–1941. English architect and designer. He designed country houses which were characteristically asymmetrical with massive buttresses, long sloping roofs, and rough-cast walls. He also designed textiles and wallpaper.

Vranitzky /vræˈnɪtski/ Franz 1937– . Austrian socialist politician, federal chancellor from 1986. A banker, he entered the political arena through the moderate, left-of-centre Socialist Party of Austria (SPÖ), and became minister of finance 1984. He succeeded Fred Sinowatz as federal chancellor 1986, heading an SPÖ-ÖVP (Austrian People's Party) coalition.

Vuillard /vwiːˈɑː/ (Jean) Edouard 1886–1940. French painter and printmaker, a founding member of the Nabis, a group of artists united in their admiration of Paul →Gauguin. Vuillard's work is mainly decorative, with an emphasis on surface pattern reflecting the influence of Japanese prints. With →Bonnard he produced numerous lithographs and paintings of simple domestic interiors, works that are generally categorized as *intimiste*.

Vyshinsky /vɪˈʃɪnski/ Andrei 1883–1954. Soviet politician. As commissar for justice, he acted as prosecutor at Stalin's treason trials 1936–38. He was foreign minister 1949–53 and often represented the USSR at the United Nations.

Wace /weɪs/ Robert *c.* 1100–1175. Anglo-Norman poet and chronicler of early chivalry. His major works, both written in Norman French, were *Roman de Brut* (also known as *Geste des Bretons*) 1155, containing material relating to the Arthurian legend, and *Roman de Rou* (or *Geste des Normanz*) 1160–62, covering the history of Normandy.

He was born in Jersey to a noble family, educated at Paris and Caen in Normandy, and made prebend of Bayeux by the gift of Henry II. *Roman de Brut*, dedicated to Eleanor of Aquitaine, was adapted from Geoffrey of Monmouth's *Historia Regum Britanniae*. *Roman de Rou*, dedicated to Henry II, was a chronicle of the dukes of Normandy.

Waddington /ˈwɒdɪŋtən/ David Charles, Baron Waddington 1929– . British Conservative politician, home secretary 1989–90. He trained as a barrister, and became a member of Parliament 1978. A Conservative whip from 1979, Waddington was a junior minister in the Department of Employment and in the Home Office before becoming chief whip 1987. In 1990 he was made a life peer and became leader of the House of Lords in John Major's government.

Wade (Sarah) Virginia 1945– . English tennis player who won the Wimbledon singles title in the Silver Jubilee year of 1977 after fifteen years of striving. She also won the US Open in 1968 and the 1972 Australian Open. She holds a record number of appearances for the Wightman and Federation Cup teams and her total of eight Grand Slam titles is a post-war British record equalled only by Ann Jones.

Wagner /ˈwægnə/ Honus (John Peter) 1874–1955. US baseball player. He had an impressive lifetime batting average of .329. In addition to his fielding skills, he was a great runner; his career record of 722 stolen bases won him the nickname 'the Flying Dutchman'.

Born in Mansfield, Pennsylvania, USA, Wagner began his professional baseball career 1895 and was signed as a shortstop by the Louisville club of the National League 1897. He was acquired by the Pittsburgh Pirates 1899 and remained there until his retirement 1917.

Wagner was elected to the Baseball Hall of Fame 1936.

Wagner /ˈvɑːgnə/ Otto 1841–1918. Viennese architect. Initially designing in the Art Nouveau style, for example Vienna Stadtbahn 1894–97, he later rejected ornament for rationalism, as in the Post Office Savings Bank, Vienna, 1904–06. He influenced such Viennese architects as Josef Hoffmann, Adolf Loos, and Joseph Olbrich.

Wagner /ˈvɑːgnə/ Richard 1813–1883. German opera composer. He revolutionized the 19th-century conception of opera, envisaging it as a wholly new art form in which musical, poetic, and scenic elements should be unified through such devices as the leitmotif. His operas include *Tannhäuser* 1845, *Lohengrin* 1850, and *Tristan und Isolde* 1865. In 1872 he founded the Festival Theatre in Bayreuth; his masterpiece *Der Ring des Nibelungen/The Ring of the Nibelung*, a sequence of four operas, was first performed there in 1876. His last work, *Parsifal*, was produced in 1882.

Wagner's early career was as director of the Magdeburg Theatre, where he unsuccessfully produced his first opera *Das Liebesverbot/Forbidden Love* 1836. He lived in Paris 1839–42 and conducted the Dresden Opera House 1842–48. He fled Germany to escape arrest for his part in the 1848 revolution, but in 1861 he was allowed to return. He won the favour of Ludwig II of Bavaria 1864 and was thus able to set up the Festival Theatre in Bayreuth. The Bayreuth tradition was continued by his wife Cosima (Liszt's daughter, whom he married after her divorce from Hans von ➔Bülow), by his son *Siegfried Wagner* (1869–1930), a composer of operas such as *Der Bärenhäuter*; and by later descendants.

Wagner /ˈwægnə/ Robert 1910–1991. US politician, mayor of New York City 1954–65. He demolished slum areas, built public housing, and was instrumental in introducing members of ethnic minorities into City Hall.

Wagner /ˈwægnə/ Robert F(erdinand) 1877–1953. US Democratic senator 1927–49, a leading figure in the development of welfare provision in the USA, especially in the New Deal era. He helped draft much new legislation, including the National Industrial Recovery Act 1933, the Social Security Act 1936, and the National Labor Relations Act 1935, known as the Wagner Act.

Wagner-Jauregg /ˈvɑːgnə ˈjaʊrek/ Julius 1857–1940. Austrian neurologist. He received a Nobel prize in 1927 for his work on the use of induced fevers in treating mental illness.

Wain /weɪn/ John (Barrington) 1925– . British poet and novelist. His first novel, *Hurry on Down*

1953, expresses the radical political views of the 'Angry Young Men' of the 1950s. He published several volumes of verse, collected in *Poems 1949–79*, and was professor of poetry at Oxford 1973–80.

Wainwright /weɪnraɪt/ Alfred 1907–1991. English author of guidebooks to the Lake District. His first articles appeared 1955 in a local paper, and he eventually produced over 40 meticulously detailed books, including volumes on the Pennine Way and other areas of N England.

Waite /weɪt/ Morrison Remick 1816–1888. US lawyer and chief justice of the USA from 1874, appointed by President Grant. He presided over constitutional challenges to Reconstruction 1865–77, but is best remembered for his decisions upholding the right of states to regulate public utilities.

Born in Lyme, Connecticut, USA, and educated at Yale University, Waite settled in Ohio, where he was admitted to the bar 1839. After serving in the state legislature 1849–50, he returned to private practise. A staunch Republican, he was named US counsel in the 1871 *Alabama* claims case.

Waite /weɪt/ Terry (Terence Hardy) 1939– . British religious adviser (1980–87) to the then archbishop of Canterbury, Dr Robert →Runcie. As the archbishop's special envoy, Waite disappeared 20 Jan 1987 while engaged in secret negotiations to free European hostages in Beirut, Lebanon. He had been taken hostage by an Islamic group and was released 18 Nov 1991.

His kidnapping followed six conversations he held with the US agent Col Oliver →North, who appeared to be hoping to ransom US hostages through Waite.

Waits /weɪts/ Tom 1949– . US singer, songwriter, and musician with a characteristic gravelly voice. His songs typically deal with urban street life and have jazz-influenced arrangements, as on *Rain Dogs* 1985. He has written music for and acted in several films, including Jim Jarmusch's *Down by Law* 1986.

Wajda /vaɪdə/ Andrzej 1926– . Polish film and theatre director, one of the major figures in postwar European cinema. His films are concerned with the predicament and disillusion of individuals caught up in political events. His works include *Ashes and Diamonds* 1958, *Man of Marble* 1977, *Man of Iron* 1981, *Danton* 1982, and *Korczak* 1990.

Wakefield /weɪkfiːld/ Edward Gibbon 1796–1862. British colonial administrator. He was imprisoned 1826–29 for abducting an heiress, and became manager of the South Australian Association, which founded a colony 1836. He was an agent for the New Zealand Land Company 1839–46, and emigrated there in 1853. His son *Edward Jerningham Wakefield* (1820–1879) wrote *Adventure in New Zealand* 1845.

Waksman /wæksmən/ Selman Abraham 1888–1973. US biochemist, born in Ukraine. He coined the word 'antibiotic' for bacteria-killing chemicals derived from microorganisms. Waksman was awarded a Nobel prize in 1952 for the discovery of streptomycin, an antibiotic used against tuberculosis.

Walcott /wɔːlkət/ Derek 1930– . West Indian poet and playwright. His work fuses Caribbean and European, classical and contemporary elements, and deals with the divisions within colonial society and his own search for cultural identity. His works include the long poem *Omeros* 1990, and his adaptation for the stage of Homer's *The Odyssey* 1992; his *Collected Poems* were published in 1986. He won the Nobel Prize for Literature 1992.

Walcott was born in St Lucia and was educated at the University of the West Indies. He has taught writing at the universities of Columbia, Yale, and Harvard. He contributed greatly to the development of an indigenous West Indian theatre, and for 25 years ran a theatre in Trinidad. Other plays include *Dream on Monkey Mountain* 1970, *O Babylon!* 1978, and *Remembrance* 1980.

Wald /wɔːld/ George 1906– . US biochemist who explored the chemistry of vision. He found that a crucial role was played by the retinal pigment rhodopsin, derived in part from vitamin A. For this he shared the 1967 Nobel Prize for Physiology or Medicine with Ragnar Granit (1900–) and Haldan Hartline (1903–1983).

Wald /wɔːld/ Lillian D 1867–1940. US public health administrator and founder of New York City's Henry Street Settlement House 1895. In 1912 she founded the National Organization for Public Health Nursing and was also active in union and antiwar activities.

Born in Cincinnati, Ohio, USA, Wald graduated from the New York Hospital Training School for Nurses 1891. She later worked as a nurse in some of New York's poorest neighbourhoods, providing medical, nutritional, educational, and social-welfare programmes for children and adults.

Her memoirs, *House on Henry Street*, appeared 1915.

Waldemar /vældəmɑː/ or *Valdemar* four kings of Denmark, including:

Waldemar I *the Great* 1131–1182. King of Denmark from 1157, who defeated rival claimants to the throne and overcame the Wends on the Baltic island of Rügen 1169.

Waldemar II *the Conqueror* 1170–1241. King of Denmark from 1202. He was the second son of Waldemar I and succeeded his brother Canute VI. He gained control of land north of the river Elbe (which he later lost), as well as much of Estonia, and he completed the codification of Danish law.

Waldemar IV 1320–1375. King of Denmark from 1340, responsible for reuniting his country by capturing Skåne (S Sweden) and the island of Gotland 1361. However, the resulting conflict with the Hanseatic League led to defeat by them, and in 1370 he was forced to submit to the Peace of Stralsund.

Walden /ˈwɔːldən/ Brian (Alistair) 1932– . British journalist and, from 1977, television presenter. He was a Labour member of Parliament 1964–77.

Walden was a university lecturer before entering Parliament. Disillusioned with party politics, he cut short his parliamentary career in 1977 and became presenter of the current-affairs TV programme *Weekend World*, with a direct and uninhibited style of interviewing public figures. He also contributes to the *Sunday Times* and *Evening Standard* newspapers.

Waldheim /ˈvældhaɪm/ Kurt 1918– . Austrian politician and diplomat, president from 1986. He was secretary general of the United Nations 1972–81, having been Austria's representative there 1964–68 and 1970–71. He was elected president of Austria despite revelations that during World War II he had been an intelligence officer in an army unit responsible for transporting Jews to death camps. His election therefore led to some diplomatic isolation of Austria, and in 1991 he announced that he would not run for re-election.

Waldheim Former Austrian president Kurt Waldheim. He was elected 1986 despite his wartime service with the Nazi German army in Yugoslavia. He was secretary general of the United Nations 1972–81, responsible for several peacekeeping missions in the Middle East, Asia, and other areas, none of which ended hostilities.

Walesa /væˈwensə/ Lech 1943– . Polish trade-union leader and president of Poland from 1990, founder of Solidarity (Solidarność) in 1980, an organization, independent of the Communist Party, which forced substantial political and economic concessions from the Polish government 1980–81 until being outlawed. He was awarded the Nobel Prize for Peace 1983.

As an electrician at the Lenin shipyard in Gdańsk, Walesa became a trade-union organizer and led a series of strikes that drew wide public support. In Dec 1981 Solidarity was outlawed and Walesa arrested, after the imposition of martial law by the Polish leader Gen Jaruzelski. Walesa, a devout Catholic, was released 1982.

After leading a further series of strikes during 1988, he negotiated an agreement with the Jaruzelski government in April 1989 under the terms of which Solidarity once more became legal and a new, semi-pluralist 'socialist democracy' was established. The coalition government elected Sept 1989 was dominated by Solidarity. Rifts appeared, but Walesa went on to be elected president Dec 1990.

Wales, Prince of /weɪlz/ title conferred on the eldest son of the UK's sovereign. Prince →Charles was invested as 21st prince of Wales at Caernarvon 1969 by his mother, Elizabeth II.

Waley /ˈweɪli/ Arthur 1889–1966. English orientalist who translated from both Japanese and Chinese, including such classics as the Japanese *The Tale of Genji* 1925–33 and *The Pillow-book of Sei Shōnagon* 1928, and the 16th-century Chinese novel *Monkey* 1942. He never visited the Far East.

Walker /ˈwɔːkə/ Alice 1944– . US poet, novelist, critic, and essay writer. She was active in the US civil-rights movement in the 1960s and, as a black woman, wrote about the double burden of racist and sexist oppression that such women bear. Her novel *The Color Purple* 1983 (filmed 1985) won the Pulitzer Prize.

Walker /ˈwɔːkə/ Jimmy (James John) 1881–1946. US public official. In 1925 Walker was elected mayor of New York City and in that position became a popular personality, familiarly known to his constituents as 'Jimmy'. Although Walker made great improvements to the city's infrastructure, he was charged with graft and forced to resign 1932.

Born in New York, USA,, Walker attended St Francis Xavier College and was admitted to the bar 1912. Becoming active in Democratic party politics, he served in the state assembly 1909–15 and the state senate 1915–25, where he became a protégé of Al Smith.

Walker /ˈwɔːkə/ Peter (Edward) 1932– . British Conservative politician, energy secretary 1983–87, secretary of state for Wales 1987–90.

As energy secretary from 1983, he managed the government's response to the national miners' strike 1984–85 that resulted in the capitulation of the National Union of Miners. He retired from active politics 1990.

Walker /wɔːkə/ Sebastian 1942–1991. English publisher. Formerly a sales representative, Walker worked his way up to director of the Chatto and Windus publishing house 1977–79, and founded Walker Books Ltd 1978. Walker Books produce some 300 children's books a year, with an emphasis on high quality, following a broadly antisexist and antiracist line. In 1989, Walker Books won four of the five main children's-book awards.

Walker /wɔːkə/ William 1824–1860. US adventurer who for a short time established himself as president of a republic in NW Mexico, and was briefly president of Nicaragua 1856–57. He was eventually executed and is now regarded as a symbol of US imperialism in Central America.

Wall /wɔːl/ Max. Stage name of Maxwell George Lister 1908–1990. English music-hall comedian who towards the end of his career appeared in starring roles as a serious actor, in John Osborne's *The Entertainer* 1974 and in Samuel Beckett's *Waiting for Godot* 1980. In his solo comedy performances he used to do a funny walk.

Wall was born in London, the son of a Scots comedian, and became a well-known dancer before radio enabled his verbal comedy to reach a wider audience. In the 1950s his career declined dramatically after he left his wife and children.

Wallace /wɒlɪs/ Alfred Russel 1823–1913. English naturalist who collected animal and plant specimens in South America and SE Asia, and independently arrived at a theory of evolution by natural selection similar to that proposed by Charles →Darwin.

Wallace /wɒlɪs/ Edgar 1875–1932. English writer of thrillers. His prolific output includes *The Four Just Men* 1905; a series set in Africa and including *Sanders of the River* 1911; crime novels such as *A King by Night* 1926; and melodramas such as *The Ringer* 1926.

Wallace /wɒlɪs/ George Corley 1919– . US politician who was opposed to integration; he was governor of Alabama 1963–67, 1971–79, and 1983–87. He contested the presidency in 1968 as an independent (the American Independent Party) and in 1972 campaigned for the Democratic nomination but was shot at a rally and became partly paralysed.

Wallace /wɒlɪs/ Henry Agard 1888–1965. US editor and public official. Appointed secretary of the treasury by Franklin Roosevelt 1933 he served as vice president during Roosevelt's third term 1941–45. He later broke with Truman and, after serving as editor of the *New Republic* 1946–47, was the unsuccessful Progressive Party candidate for president 1948.

Born in Adair County, Iowa, USA, Wallace was educated at Iowa State College and in 1910 joined the staff of the family-owned periodical *Wallace's*

Farmer. Although his father was a prominent Republican, the younger Wallace joined the Democratic party 1928.

Wallace /wɒlɪs/ Irving. 1916–1990. US novelist, one of the most popular writers of the 20th century. He wrote 17 works of nonfiction and 16 novels; they include *The Chapman Report* 1960, a novel inspired by the →Kinsey Report, and *The Prize* 1962.

Wallace /wɒlɪs/ Lew(is) 1827–1905. US general and novelist. He served in the Mexican War and the American Civil War and subsequently became governor of New Mexico and minister to Turkey. He was credited with saving Washington DC from capture by Confederate forces and served on the tribunal that tried those accused of conspiring to assassinate Abraham →Lincoln. He wrote several historical novels, including *The Fair God* 1873 and *Ben Hur* 1880 which was filmed twice, in 1926 and 1959.

Wallace /wɒlɪs/ Richard 1818–1890. British art collector. He inherited a valuable art collection from his father, the Marquess of Hertford, which was given in 1897 by his widow to the UK as the *Wallace Collection*, containing many 18th-century French paintings. The collection was opened to the public 1900 and is at Hertford House, London.

Wallace /wɒlɪs/ William 1272–1305. Scottish nationalist who led a revolt against English rule 1297, won a victory at Stirling, and assumed the title 'governor of Scotland'. Edward I defeated him at Falkirk 1298, and Wallace was captured and executed.

Wallenberg /wɒlənbɜːɡ/ Raoul 1912–1947. Swedish business executive who attempted to rescue several thousand Jews from German-occupied Budapest 1944, during World War II. He was taken prisoner by the Soviet army 1945 and was never heard from again.

In Hungary he tried to rescue and support Jews in safe houses, and provided them with false papers to save them from deportation to extermination camps. After the arrival of Soviet troops in Budapest, he reported to the Russian commander Jan 1945 and then disappeared. The Soviet government later claimed that he died of a heart attack July 1947. However, rumours persisted into the 1980s that he was alive and held in a Soviet prison camp. In the 1990s the Russians said that he had died as claimed.

Wallenstein /vælənʃtaɪn/ Albrecht Eusebius Wenzel von 1583–1634. German general who, until his defeat at Lützen 1632, led the Habsburg armies in the Thirty Years' War. He was assassinated.

Waller /wɒlə/ Edmund 1606–1687. English poet who managed to eulogize both Cromwell and Charles II; now mainly remembered for lyrics such as 'Go, lovely rose'.

Walpole Robert Walpole, English politician and first 'prime minister', in a portrait by Godfrey Kneller (c. 1710). Walpole established the forerunner of the present-day cabinet. George II presented him with 10 Downing Street, which was to become the permanent London home of all future prime ministers.

Waller /ˈwɒlə/ Fats (Thomas Wright) 1904–1943. US jazz pianist and composer with a forceful stride piano style. His songs, many of which have become jazz standards, include 'Ain't Misbehavin'' 1929, 'Honeysuckle Rose' 1929, and 'Viper's Drag' 1934.

An exuberant, humorous performer, Waller toured extensively and appeared in several musical films, including *Stormy Weather* 1943. His first recordings were on piano rolls and in the 1920s he recorded pipe-organ solos. In the 1930s he worked with a small group (as Fats Waller and his Rhythm Boys), before leading a big band 1939–42.

Wallis /ˈwɒlɪs/ Barnes (Neville) 1887–1979. British aeronautical engineer who designed the airship R-100, and during World War II perfected the 'bouncing bombs' used by the Royal Air Force Dambusters Squadron to destroy the German Möhne and Eder dams in 1943. He also assisted in the development of the Concorde supersonic airliner and developed the swing-wing aircraft.

Wallis /ˈwɒlɪs/ Hal (Harold Brent) 1899–1986. US film producer with a keen eye for choosing potential box-office successes. He was chief executive in charge of production at Warner Brothers 1933–44, when he left to establish his own company, Hal Wallis Productions.

Born in Chicago, USA, Wallis left school early. After moving to Los Angeles 1922, he joined the staff of the Warner Brothers studios. He was named publicity director 1924 and was promoted to studio manager 1928, distinguishing himself as a shrewd business operator.

Walpole /ˈwɔːlpəʊl/ Horace, 4th Earl of Orford 1717–1797. English novelist, letter writer and politician, the son of Robert Walpole. He was a Whig member of Parliament 1741–67. He converted his house at Strawberry Hill, Twickenham (then a separate town SW of London), into a Gothic castle; his *The Castle of Otranto* 1764 established the genre of the Gothic, or 'romance of terror', novel. More than 4,000 of his letters have been published.

Walpole /ˈwɔːlpəʊl/ Hugh 1884–1941. English novelist, born in New Zealand. His books include *The Cathedral* 1922 and *The Old Ladies* 1924. He also wrote the historical 'Lakeland Saga' of the *Herries Chronicle* 1930–33.

Walpole /ˈwɔːlpəʊl/ Robert, 1st Earl of Orford 1676–1745. British Whig politician, the first 'prime minister' as First Lord of the Treasury and chancellor of the Exchequer 1715–17 and 1721–42. He encouraged trade and tried to avoid foreign disputes (until forced into the War of Jenkins's Ear with Spain 1739).

Opponents thought his foreign policies worked to the advantage of France. He held favour with George I and George II, struggling against Jacobite intrigues, and received an earldom when he eventually retired 1742.

Walpurga, St /væl'pʊəgə/ English abbess who preached Christianity in Germany. *Walpurgis Night*, the night of 1 May (one of her feast days), became associated with witches' sabbaths and other superstitions. Her feast day is 25 Feb.

The world is a comedy to those who think; a tragedy to those that feel.

Horace Walpole letter 1769

Walras /ˈvælrɑː/ Léon 1834–1910. French economist. In his *Éléments d'économie politique pure* 1874–77 he attempted to develop a unified model for general equilibrium theory (a hypothetical situation in which demand equals supply in all markets). He also originated the theory of diminishing marginal utility of a good (the increased value to a person of consuming more of a product).

Walsh /ˈwɔːlʃ/ Raoul 1887–1981. US film director, originally an actor. He made a number of outstanding films, including *The Thief of Bagdad* 1924, *The Roaring Twenties* 1939, and *White Heat* 1949.

Walsingham /ˈwɔːlsɪŋəm/ Francis c. 1530–1590. English politician who, as secretary of state from 1573, both advocated a strong anti-Spanish policy and ran the efficient government spy system that made it work.

Walter /wɔːltə/ Hubert died 1205. Archbishop of Canterbury 1193–1205. As justiciar (chief political and legal officer) 1193–98, he ruled England during Richard I's absence and introduced the offices of coroner and justice of the peace.

Walter /wɔːltə/ John 1739–1812. British newspaper editor, founder of *The Times* (originally the *Daily Universal Register* 1785, but renamed 1788).

Walter /wɔːltə/ Lucy *c.* 1630–1658. Mistress of →Charles II, whom she met while a Royalist refugee in The Hague, Netherlands, 1648; the Duke of →Monmouth was their son.

Walters /wɔːltəz/ Alan (Arthur) 1926–   . British economist and government adviser 1981–89. He became economics adviser to Prime Minister Thatcher, but his publicly stated differences with the policies of her chancellor Nigel →Lawson precipitated, in 1989, Lawson's resignation from the government as well as Walters' own departure.

Walters held the post of economics professor at the London School of Economics 1968–75 and has been professor of political economy at the Johns Hopkins University, Baltimore, from 1976. He was also economics adviser to the World Bank 1976–80.

Walther von der Vogelweide /væltə fɒn deə 'fəʊɡəlvaɪdə/ *c.* 1170–1230. German poet, greatest of the Minnesingers, whose songs dealt mainly with courtly love. Of noble birth, he lived in his youth at the Austrian ducal court in Vienna, adopting a wandering life after the death of his patron in 1198. His lyrics deal mostly with love, but also with religion and politics.

Walton /wɔːltən/ Ernest 1903–   . Irish physicist who, as a young doctoral student at the Cavendish laboratory in Cambridge, England, collaborated with John →Cockcroft on investigating the structure of the atom. In 1932 they succeeded in splitting the atom; for this experiment they shared the 1951 Nobel Prize for Physics.

Walton /wɔːltən/ Izaak 1593–1683. English author of the classic fishing text *Compleat Angler* 1653. He was born in Stafford, and settled in London as an ironmonger. He also wrote short biographies of the poets George Herbert and John Donne and the theologian Richard Hooker.

Walton /wɔːltən/ William (Turner) 1902–1983. English composer. Among his works are *Façade* 1923, a series of instrumental pieces designed to be played in conjunction with the recitation of poems by Edith Sitwell; the oratorio *Belshazzar's Feast* 1931; and *Variations on a Theme by Hindemith* 1963.

He also composed a viola concerto 1929, two symphonies 1935, a violin concerto 1939, and a sonata for violin and pianoforte 1950.

Wanamaker /wɒnəmeɪkə/ John 1838–1922. US retailer who developed the modern department store. He established his own firm, John Wanamaker and Company, 1869. Renting an abandoned railroad depot 1876, he merchandised goods in distinct departments; he publicized his stores through extensive advertising.

Born in Philadelphia, USA, Wanamaker worked as a delivery boy and store clerk, founding the dry-goods firm of Brown and Wanamaker with his brother-in-law 1861.

A staunch Republican, Wanamaker served as postmaster general in the Benjamin Harrison administration 1889–93.

Wang /wæŋ/ An 1920–1990. Chinese-born US engineer, founder of Wang Laboratories 1951, one of the world's largest computer companies in the 1970s. He emigrated to the USA 1945 and three years later invented the computer memory core, the most common device used for storing computer data before the invention of the integrated circuit (chip).

Warbeck /wɔːbek/ Perkin *c.* 1474–1499. Flemish pretender to the English throne. Claiming to be Richard, brother of Edward V, he led a rising against Henry VII in 1497, and was hanged after attempting to escape from the Tower of London.

Warburg /vɑːbʊək/ Otto 1878–1976. German biochemist who in 1923 devised a manometer (pressure gauge) sensitive enough to measure oxygen uptake of respiring tissue. By measuring the rate at which cells absorb oxygen under differing conditions, he was able to show that enzymes called cytochromes enable cells to process oxygen. He was awarded the Nobel Prize for Medicine 1931. Warburg also demonstrated that cancerous cells absorb less oxygen than normal cells.

Ward /wɔːd/ Artemus. Pen name of Charles Farrar Browne 1834–1867. US humorist who achieved great popularity with comic writings such as *Artemus Ward: His Book* 1862 and *Artemus Ward: His Travels* 1865, and with his deadpan lectures. He influenced Mark Twain.

Ward /wɔːd/ Barbara 1914–1981. British economist. She became president of the Institute for Environment and Development 1973.

In 1976 she received a life peerage as Baroness Jackson of Wadsworth. Her books include *Policy for the West* 1951, *The Widening Gap* 1971 and her best-known work, *Only One Earth* (with René Dubois) 1972.

Ward /wɔːd/ Leslie 1851–1922. British caricaturist, known under the pseudonym 'Spy' for his caricatures in *Vanity Fair*.

Ward /wɔːd/ Montgomery 1843–1913. US retailer who pioneered the mass marketing of clothing and personal items through the mails. Serving the needs of farm families in remote rural areas, he constantly expanded his catalogue from its inception in 1872. He moved the firm's headquarters to the Ward Tower in Chicago 1900.

Born in Chatham, New Jersey, USA, Ward left school in his teens to become a travelling representative for several Midwestern dry-goods firms. He retired from the day-to-day operations of the firm in 1886.

Ward /wɔːd/ Mrs Humphry (born Mary Augusta Arnold) 1851–1920. English novelist, born in Australia, who wrote didactic books such as *Robert Elsmere* 1888, a study of religious doubt. She was an opponent of women's emancipation.

Warhol /wɔːhəʊl/ Andy. Adopted name of Andrew Warhola 1928–1987. US Pop artist and filmmaker. He made his name in 1962 with paintings of Campbell's soup cans, Coca-Cola bottles, and film stars. In his New York studio, the Factory, he produced series of garish silk-screen prints. His films include the semidocumentary *Chelsea Girls* 1966 and *Trash* 1970.

Warhol was born in Pittsburgh, where he studied art. In the 1950s he became a leading commercial artist in New York. With the breakthrough of Pop art, his bizarre personality and flair for self-publicity made him a household name. He was a pioneer of multimedia events with the Exploding Plastic Inevitable touring show in 1966 featuring the Velvet Underground (see Lou →Reed). In 1968 he was shot and nearly killed by a radical feminist, Valerie Solanas. In the 1970s and 1980s Warhol was primarily a society portraitist, although his activities included a magazine (*Interview*) and a cable TV show.

His early silk-screen series dealt with car crashes and suicides, Marilyn Monroe, Elvis Presley, and flowers. His films, beginning with *Sleep* 1963 and ending with *Bad* 1977, have a strong documentary or improvisational element. His books include *The Philosophy of Andy Warhol (From A to B and Back Again)* 1975 and *Popism* 1980.

In the future everyone will be famous for 15 minutes.

Andy Warhol, *Exposures* 1979

Warlock /wɔːlɒk/ Peter. Pen name of Philip Heseltine 1894–1930. English composer whose style was influenced by the music of the Elizabethan age and by that of →Delius. His works include the orchestral suite *Capriol* 1926 based on 16th-century dances, and the song cycle *The Curlew* 1920–22. His works of musical theory and criticism were published under his real name.

Warner /wɔːnə/ Deborah 1959– . British theatre director who founded the Kick Theatre company 1980. Discarding period costume and furnished sets, she adopted an uncluttered approach to the classics, including productions of many Shakespeare plays and Sophocles' *Electra*.

Warner /wɔːnə/ Rex 1905–1986. British novelist. His later novels, such as *The Young Caesar* and *Imperial Caesar* 1958–60, are based on Classical themes, but he is better remembered today for his earlier works, such as *The Aerodrome* 1941, which are disturbing parables based on the political situation of the 1930s.

Warren /wɒrən/ Earl 1891–1974. US jurist and chief justice of the US Supreme Court 1953–69. He served as governor of California 1943–53. As chief justice, he presided over a moderately liberal court, taking a stand against racial discrimination and ruling that segregation in schools was unconstitutional. He headed the commission that investigated 1963–64 President Kennedy's assassination.

Warren /wɒrən/ Frank 1952– . British boxing promoter who helped bring world-title fights to commercial television. He set up the London Arena in the Docklands. In 1989 he was seriously wounded in a shotgun attack.

Warren /wɒrən/ Joseph 1741–1775. American colonial physician and revolutionary leader. Opposing British colonial rule in Massachusetts, he sent Paul →Revere and William →Dawes to warn the countryside of the approach of the British 1775. Appointed major general of the Massachusetts militia, he was killed at the Battle of Bunker Hill 1775.

Born in Roxbury, Massachusetts, and educated at Harvard University, Warren established a private medical practice in Boston.

Warren /wɒrən/ Robert Penn 1905–1989. US poet and novelist, the only author to receive a Pulitzer prize for both prose and poetry. His novel *All the King's Men* 1946 was modelled on the career of Huey →Long, and he also won Pulitzer prizes for *Promises* 1968 and *Now and Then: Poems* 1976–78. He was the first official US poet laureate 1986–88.

Warton /wɔːtn/ Joseph 1722–1800. English poet, headmaster of Winchester 1766–93, whose verse and *Essay on the Writings and Genius of Pope* 1756–82 marked an 'anti-Classical' reaction.

Warton /wɔːtn/ Thomas Wain 1728–1790. English critic. He was professor of poetry at Oxford 1757–67 and published the first *History of English Poetry* 1774–81. He was poet laureate from 1785.

Warwick /wɒrɪk/ Richard Neville, Earl of Warwick 1428–1471. English politician, called *the Kingmaker*. During the Wars of the Roses he fought at first on the Yorkist side against the Lancastrians, and was largely responsible for placing Edward IV on the throne. Having quarrelled with him, he restored Henry VI in 1470, but was defeated and killed by Edward at Barnet, Hertfordshire.

Washington /wɒʃɪŋtən/ Booker T(aliaferro) 1856–1915. US educationist, pioneer in higher education for black people in the South. He was the founder and first principal of Tuskegee Institute, Alabama, in 1881, originally a training college for blacks, and now an academic institution. He maintained that economic independence was the way to achieve social equality.

North America 1804–24. In the UK, he was the first person to protest against pollution from industry, and created a nature reserve around his home in Yorkshire.

Watkins /wɒtkɪnz/ Gino (Henry George) 1907–1932. English polar explorer whose expeditions in Labrador and Greenland helped to open up an Arctic air route during the 1930s. He was drowned in a kayak accident while leading an expedition in Greenland.

Watson /wɒtsən/ James Dewey 1928– . US biologist whose research on the molecular structure of DNA and the genetic code, in collaboration with Francis ➔Crick, earned him a shared Nobel prize in 1962. Based on earlier works, they were able to show that DNA formed a double helix of two spiral strands held together by base pairs.

Watson /wɒtsən/ John Broadus 1878–1958. US psychologist, founder of behaviourism. He rejected introspection (observation by an individual of his or her own mental processes) and regarded psychology as the study of observable behaviour, within the scientific tradition.

Watson /wɒtsən/ Tom (Thomas Sturgess) 1949– . US golfer who won the British Open five times (1975, 1977, 1980, 1982, 1983) and by 1990 was ranked third in career earnings in professional golf.

Watson, born in Kansas City, turned professional 1971 and has won more than 30 tournaments on the US Tour, including the Masters and US Open. In 1988 he succeeded Jack ➔Nicklaus as the game's biggest money winner, but was overtaken by Tom Kite 1989.

Watson-Watt /wɒtsən 'wɒt/ Robert Alexander 1892–1973. Scottish physicist who developed a forerunner of radar. During a long career in government service (1915–1952) he proposed in 1935 a method of radiolocation of aircraft – a key factor in the Allied victory over German aircraft in World War II.

It is necessary to be slightly underemployed if you want to do something significant.

James Dewey Watson,
The Eighth Day of Creation

Washington First president of the USA, George Washington. Although he tried to keep himself neutral during the time he was president of the Constitutional Convention, he eventually allied himself with the Federalist Party.

Washington /wɒʃɪŋtən/ George 1732–1799. First president of the USA 1789–97. As a strong opponent of the British government's policy, he sat in the Continental Congresses of 1774 and 1775, and on the outbreak of the War of American Independence was chosen commander in chief. After the war he retired to his Virginia estate, Mount Vernon, but in 1787 he re-entered politics as president of the Constitutional Convention. Although he attempted to draw his ministers from all factions, his aristocratic outlook alienated his secretary of state, Thomas Jefferson, who resigned in 1793, thus creating the two-party system.

Washington took part in campaigns against the French and American Indians 1753–57, and was elected to the Virginia House of Burgesses. He was elected president of the USA 1789 and re-elected 1793, but refused to serve a third term, setting a precedent that was followed until 1940. He scrupulously avoided overstepping the constitutional boundaries of presidential power. In his farewell address 1796, he maintained that the USA should avoid European quarrels and entangling alliances. He is buried at Mount Vernon.

Wassermann /væsəmæn/ August von 1866–1925. German professor of medicine. In 1907 he discovered a diagnostic blood test for syphilis, known as the *Wassermann reaction*.

Waterhouse /wɔːtəhaʊs/ Alfred 1830–1905. English architect. He was a leading exponent of Victorian Neo-Gothic using, typically, multi-coloured tiles and bricks. His works include the Natural History Museum in London 1868.

Waterton /wɔːtətən/ Charles 1783–1865. British naturalist who travelled extensively in South and

Watt /wɒt/ James 1736–1819. Scottish engineer who developed the steam engine. He made Thomas ➔Newcomen's steam engine vastly more efficient by cooling the used steam in a condenser separate from the main cylinder.

Steam engines incorporating governors, sun-and-planet gears, and other devices of his invention were successfully built by him in partnership with Matthew ➔Boulton and were vital to the Industrial Revolution.

Watt *Scottish engineer James Watt, inventor of the modern condensing steam engine. The power unit, the watt, is named after him.*

Watteau /'wɒtəʊ/ Jean-Antoine 1684–1721. French Rococo painter. He developed a new category of genre painting known as the *fête galante*, scenes of a kind of aristocratic pastoral fantasy world. One of these pictures, *The Embarkation for Cythera* 1717 (Louvre, Paris), won him membership in the French Academy.

Watteau was born in Valenciennes. At first inspired by Flemish genre painters, he produced tavern and military scenes. His early years in Paris, from 1702, introduced him to fashionable French paintings and in particular to decorative styles and theatrical design. He was also influenced by →Giorgione and →Rubens.

Watts /wɒts/ Alan (Witson) 1915–1973. British-born US philosopher. Educated in England, Watts was a longtime student of Eastern religions and published *The Spirit of Zen* 1936. He emigrated to the USA 1939, graduated from the Seabury-Weston Theological Seminary, and was ordained in the Episcopal Church 1944. Briefly serving as chaplain at Northwestern University, he moved to California and taught philosophy at the College of the Pacific 1951–57. As a popular lecturer and author, he became a spiritual leader of the 'beat generation' of the 1950s. His books include *The Way of Zen* 1957.

Watts /wɒts/ George Frederick 1817–1904. English painter and sculptor. He painted allegorical, biblical, and classical subjects, investing his work with a solemn morality, such as *Hope* 1886 (Tate Gallery, London). Many of his portraits are in the National Portrait Gallery, London. As a sculptor he executed *Physical Energy* 1904 for Cecil Rhodes's memorial in Cape Town, South Africa; a replica is in Kensington Gardens, London.

Watts /wɒts/ Isaac 1674–1748. English Nonconformist writer of hymns, including 'O God, our help in ages past'.

Watts-Dunton /wɒts 'dʌntən/ (Walter) Theodore 1832–1914. British writer, author of *Aylwin* 1898, a novel of gypsy life, poems and critical work. He was a close friend of the painter Rossetti, the writer Borrow, and the poet Swinburne, who shared his house at Putney for many years.

Waugh /wɔː/ Evelyn (Arthur St John) 1903–1966. English novelist. His social satires include *Decline and Fall* 1928, *Vile Bodies* 1930, and *The Loved One* 1948. A Roman Catholic convert from 1930, he developed a serious concern with religious issues in *Brideshead Revisited* 1945. *The Ordeal of Gilbert Pinfold* 1957 is largely autobiographical.

Wavell /'weɪvəl/ Archibald, 1st Earl 1883–1950. British field marshal in World War II. As commander in chief Middle East, he successfully defended Egypt against Italy July 1939. He was transferred as commander in chief India in July 1941, and was viceroy 1943–47.

Waverley /'weɪvəli/ John Anderson, 1st Viscount Waverley 1882–1958. British administrator. He organized civil defence for World War II, becoming home secretary and minister for home security in 1939 (the nationally distributed *Anderson shelters*, home outdoor air-raid shelters, were named after him). He was chancellor of the Exchequer 1943–45.

Wayne /weɪn/ Anthony ('Mad Anthony') 1745–1796. American Revolutionary War officer and Indian fighter. He secured a treaty 1795 that made possible the settlement of Ohio and Indiana. He built Fort Wayne, Indiana, USA.

Wayne /weɪn/ John ('Duke'). Stage name of Marion Morrison 1907–1979. US actor, the archetypal Western hero: plain-speaking, brave, and solitary. His films include *Stagecoach* 1939, *Red River* 1948, *She Wore a Yellow Ribbon* 1949, *The Searchers* 1956, *Rio Bravo* 1959, *The Man Who Shot Liberty Valance* 1962, and *True Grit* 1969 (Academy Award). He was active in conservative politics.

Wayne also appeared in many war films, such as *The Sands of Iwo Jima* 1945, *In Harm's Way* 1965, and *The Green Berets* 1968. His other films include *The Quiet Man* 1952 and *The High and the Mighty* 1954.

I've played the kind of man I'd like to have been.

John Wayne in *Daily Mail* Jan 1974

Wazyk /'væzɪk/ Adam 1905– . Polish writer who made his name with *Poem for Adults* 1955, a protest against the regime that preceded the fall of the Stalinists in 1956. In 1957 he resigned with others from the Communist Party, disappointed by First Secretary Gomulka's illiberalism. He also wrote novels and plays.

Webb /web/ Aston 1849–1930. English architect. His work in London includes the front of Buckingham Palace, Admiralty Arch, and the main section of the Victoria and Albert Museum.

Webb /web/ (Martha) Beatrice (born Potter) 1858–1943 and Sidney (James), Baron Passfield 1859–1947. English social reformers, writers, and founders of the London School of Economics (LSE) 1895. They were early members of the socialist Fabian Society, and were married in 1892. They argued for social insurance in their minority report (1909) of the Poor Law Commission, and wrote many influential books, including *The History of Trade Unionism* 1894, *English Local Government* 1906–29, and *Soviet Communism* 1935.

Sidney Webb was professor of public administration at the LSE 1912–27. He was a member of the Labour Party executive 1915–25, entered Parliament 1922, and was president of the Board of Trade 1924, dominions secretary 1929–30, and colonial secretary 1929–31. Beatrice wrote *The Co-operative Movement in Great Britain* 1891, *My Apprenticeship* 1926, and *Our Partnership* 1948.

Wayne US film actor John Wayne. He started his film career in 1927, using the name Duke Morrison. Wayne went on to make over 175 films.

Webb /web/ Mary 1882–1927. English novelist. Born in Shropshire, she wrote of country life and characters, for example in *Precious Bane* 1924, which became known through a recommendation by Stanley Baldwin.

Webb /web/ Philip (Speakman) 1831–1915. English architect. He mostly designed private houses, including the Red House, Bexley Heath, Sussex, for William →Morris, and was one of the leading figures, with Richard Norman →Shaw and C F A →Voysey, in the revival of domestic English architecture in the late 19th century.

Other houses include Joldwyns, Surrey 1873; Clouds, East Knoyle, Wiltshire 1880, and Standen, East Grinstead 1891–94.

Webber /webə/ Andrew Lloyd. English composer of musicals: see →Lloyd Webber.

Weber /veɪbə/ Carl Maria Friedrich Ernst von 1786–1826. German composer who established the Romantic school of opera with *Der Freischütz* 1821 and *Euryanthe* 1823. He was kapellmeister (chief conductor) at Breslau 1804–06, Prague 1813–16, and Dresden 1816. He died during a visit to London where he produced his opera *Oberon* 1826, written for the Covent Garden theatre.

Weber /veɪbə/ Ernst Heinrich 1795–1878. German anatomist and physiologist, brother of Wilhelm Weber. He applied hydrodynamics to study blood circulation, and formulated *Weber's law*, relating response to stimulus.

Weber's law (also known as the Weber–Fechner law) states that sensation is proportional to the logarithm of the stimulus. It is the basis of the scales used to measure the loudness of sounds.

Weber /veɪbə/ Max 1864–1920. German sociologist, one of the founders of modern sociology. He emphasized cultural and political factors as key influences on economic development and individual behaviour.

Weber argued for a scientific and value-free approach to research, yet highlighted the importance of meaning and consciousness in understanding social action. His ideas continue to stimulate thought on social stratification, power, organizations, law, and religion.

Key works include *The Protestant Ethic and the Spirit of Capitalism* 1902, *Economy and Society* 1922, *The Methodology of the Social Sciences* 1949, and *The Sociology of Religion* 1920.

Weber /veɪbə/ Max 1881–1961. Russian-born US painter and sculptor. Influenced by Parisian avant-garde painters of the Cubist and Futurist schools, he was a prominent figure in importing these styles to the USA and also created Futuristic sculpture.

Born in Russia, he emigrated to New York 1891, where he studied painting and travelled through Europe 1905–09.

Wedgwood English potter Josiah Wedgwood in a portrait by Joshua Reynolds (1782). Responsible for the development of several new wares, Wedgwood's most famous contribution was the production of unglazed blue jasper ware, which he decorated with Neo-Classical figures.

Weber /ˈveɪbə/ Wilhelm Eduard 1804–1891. German physicist who studied magnetism and electricity, brother of Ernst Weber. Working with Karl Gauss, he made sensitive magnetometers to measure magnetic fields, and instruments to measure direct and alternating currents. He also built an electric telegraph. The SI unit of magnetic flux, the *weber*, is named after him.

Webern /ˈveɪbən/ Anton (Friedrich Wilhelm von) 1883–1945. Austrian composer. He was a pupil of →Schoenberg, whose 12-tone technique he adopted. He wrote works of extreme brevity; for example, the oratorio *Das Augenlicht/The Light of Eyes* 1935, and songs to words by Stefan George and poems of Rilke.

Webster /ˈwebstə/ John c. 1580–1634. English dramatist who ranks after Shakespeare as the greatest tragedian of his time and is the Jacobean whose plays are most frequently performed today. His two great plays *The White Devil* 1608 and *The Duchess of Malfi* 1614 are dark, violent tragedies obsessed with death and decay and infused with poetic brilliance.

Webster /ˈwebstə/ Noah 1758–1843. US lexicographer whose books on grammar and spelling and *American Dictionary of the English Language* 1828 standardized US English.

Weddell /ˈwedl/ James 1787–1834. British Antarctic explorer. In 1823, he reached 75°S latitude and 35°W longitude, in the *Weddell Sea*, which is named after him.

Wedekind /ˈveɪdəkɪnt/ Frank 1864–1918. German dramatist. He was a forerunner of Expressionism with *Frühlings Erwachen/The Awakening of Spring* 1891, and *Der Erdgeist/The Earth Spirit* 1895 and its sequel *Der Marquis von Keith. Die Büchse der Pandora/Pandora's Box* 1904 was the source for Berg's opera *Lulu*.

Wedgwood /ˈwedʒwʊd/ C(icely) V(eronica) 1910– . British historian. An authority on the 17th century, she has published studies of *Cromwell* 1939 and *The Trial of Charles I* 1964.

Created Dame of the British Empire 1968, she was awarded the Order of Merit 1969.

Wedgwood /ˈwedʒwʊd/ Josiah 1730–1795. English pottery manufacturer. He set up business in Staffordshire in the early 1760s to produce his agateware as well as unglazed blue or green stoneware (Jasper) decorated with white Neo-Classical designs, using pigments of his own invention.

Weems /wiːmz/ Mason Locke 1759–1825. American writer and cleric. His biography *The Life and Memorable Actions of George Washington*, published around 1800, contained the first published version of the 'cherry-tree' legend which was responsible for much of the Washington myth. He also wrote lives of Francis Marion 1809 and Benjamin Franklin 1815.

Born in Anne Arundel County, Maryland, USA, Weems studied for the ministry in England and was ordained in the Anglican church 1784. Returning to America, he served as a parish cleric until 1792.

Thereafter he still insisted on being addressed as 'Parson Weems'. After becoming the sales agent of a Philadelphia publisher, Weems settled in Virginia 1795 and became an author.

Wegener /ˈveɪɡənə/ Alfred Lothar 1880–1930. German meteorologist and geophysicist, whose theory of continental drift, expounded in *Origin of Continents and Oceans* 1915, was originally known as Wegener's hypothesis. His ideas can now be explained in terms of plate tectonics, the idea that the Earth's crust consists of a number of plates, all moving with respect to one another.

Wei /weɪ/ Jingsheng 1951– . Chinese pro-democracy activist and essayist, imprisoned from 1979 for attacking the Chinese communist system. He is regarded as one of China's most important political prisoners.

The son of a Communist Party official in Anhui province, Wei joined the Red Guards in the Cultural Revolution 1966. In 1978 he joined the Democracy Movement of reformist dissidents in Beijing and published essays critical of the government in the journal *Explorations*, which he cofounded. In 1979, he was arrested and sentenced to 15 years' imprisonment 'for handing military secrets to foreigners'.

Weil /veɪ/ Simone 1909–1943. French writer who became a practising Catholic after a mystical experience in 1938. Apart from essays, her works (advocating political passivity) were posthumously published, including *Waiting for God* 1951, *The Need for Roots* 1952, and *Notebooks* 1956.

A test of what is real is that it is hard and rough. Joys are found in it, not pleasures. What is pleasant belongs to dreams.

Simone Weil, *Gravity and Grace* 1947

Weill /vaɪl/ Kurt (Julian) 1900–1950. German composer, US citizen from 1943. He wrote chamber and orchestral music and collaborated with Bertolt →Brecht on operas such as *Die Dreigroschenoper/The Threepenny Opera* 1928 and *Aufsteig und Fall der Stadt Mahagonny/The Rise and Fall of the City of Mahagonny* 1930, all attacking social corruption (*Mahagonny* caused a riot at its premiere in Leipzig). He tried to evolve a new form of music theatre, using subjects with a contemporary relevance and the simplest musical means. In 1935 he left Germany for the USA where he wrote a number of successful scores for Broadway, among them the antiwar musical *Johnny Johnson* 1936 (including the often covered 'September Song') and *Street Scene* 1947 based on an Elmer Rice play of the Depression.

Weinberg /waɪnbɜːg/ Steven 1933– . US physicist who in 1967 demonstrated, together with Abdus →Salam, that the weak nuclear force and the electromagnetic force (two of the fundamental forces of nature) are variations of a single underlying force, now called the electroweak force. Weinberg and Salam shared a Nobel prize with Sheldon →Glashow in 1979.

Weinerg and Salam's theory involved the prediction of a new interaction, the neutral current (discovered in 1973), which required the presence of charm.

Weinberger /waɪnbɜːgə/ Caspar (Willard) 1917– . US Republican politician. He served under presidents Nixon and Ford, and was Reagan's defence secretary 1981–87.

Weir /wɪə/ Peter 1938– . Australian film director. His films have an atmospheric quality and often contain a strong spiritual element. They include *Picnic at Hanging Rock* 1975, *Witness* 1985, and *The Mosquito Coast* 1986.

Weiser /waɪzə/ Conrad 1696–1760. American colonial public official in Berks County, Pennsylvania from 1729. Familiar with the language and customs of the local Iroquois Indians, he was frequently used as an official interpreter in government dealings with them. Owing to his efforts, peace conferences were held in Philadelphia in 1731 and 1736.

Born in Germany, Weiser emigrated to America 1710, settling in New York's Hudson Valley. Weiser served as judge of Berks County 1752–60 and as colonel of the militia.

Weismann /vaɪsmən/ August 1834–1914. German biologist. His failing eyesight forced him to turn from microscopy to theoretical work. In 1892 he proposed that changes to the body do not in turn cause an alteration of the genetic material.

This 'central dogma' of biology remains of vital importance to biologists supporting the Darwinian theory of evolution. If the genetic material can be altered only by chance mutation and recombination, then the Lamarckian view that acquired bodily changes can subsequently be inherited becomes obsolete.

Weismuller /waɪsˌmʊlə/ Johnny (Peter John) 1904–1984. US film actor, formerly an Olympic swimmer, who played Tarzan in a long-running series of films for MGM and RKO including *Tarzan the Ape Man* 1932, *Tarzan and His Mate* 1934, and *Tarzan and the Leopard Woman* 1946.

Weizmann /vaɪtsmæn/ Chaim 1874–1952. Zionist leader, the first president of Israel (1948–52), and a chemist. He conducted the negotiations leading up to the Balfour Declaration, by which Britain declared its support for an independent Jewish state.

Born in Russia, he became a naturalized British subject, and as director of the Admiralty laboratories 1916–19 discovered a process for manufacturing acetone, a solvent. He became head of the Hebrew University in Jerusalem, then in 1948 became the first president of the new republic of Israel.

Weizmann Chaim Weizmann, Russian-born Zionist leader and the first president of Israel 1948. He conducted scientific research work for the UK in World War I, discovering an improved method of producing acetone 1916.

Weizsäcker /ˈvaɪtsˌzekə/ Richard, Baron von 1920– . German Christian Democrat politician, president from 1984. He began his career as a lawyer and was also active in the German Protestant church and in Christian Democratic Union party politics. He was elected to the West German Bundestag (parliament) 1969 and served as mayor of West Berlin from 1981, before being elected federal president 1984.

Welch /weltʃ/ (Maurice) Denton 1915–1948. English writer and artist. His works include the novel *In Youth is Pleasure* 1944 and the autobiographical *A Voice Through a Cloud* 1950.

Welch /weltʃ/ Raquel. Stage name of Raquel Tejada 1940– . US actress, a sex symbol of the 1960s in such films as *One Million Years BC* 1966, *Myra Breckinridge* 1970, and *The Three Musketeers* 1973.

Welch /weltʃ/ Robert H W, Jr 1899–1985. US anticommunist crusader and business executive. He founded the extreme right-wing John Birch Society 1958 in memory of the American Baptist missionary. A supporter of the losing Republican presidential candidate Barry Goldwater 1964, Welch later became increasingly venomous in his accusations against supposed communist agents and sympathizers.

Born in Chowan County, North Carolina, USA, Welch was educated at the University of North Carolina and joined the family candy business in Boston 1922. Over the years, he supported conservative political causes and by the 1950s had become an outspoken anticommunist.

He founded the magazine *American Opinion* 1956.

Weldon /ˈweldən/ Fay 1931– . British novelist and dramatist whose work deals with feminist themes, often in an ironic or comic manner. Novels include *The Fat Woman's Joke* 1967, *Female Friends* 1975, *Remember Me* 1976, *Puffball* 1980, *The Life and Loves of a She-Devil* 1984 (made into a film with Meryl Streep 1990), and *The Hearts and Lives of Men* 1987. She has also written plays for the stage, radio, and television.

Welensky /wəˈlenski/ Roy 1907–1991. Rhodesian politician. He was instrumental in the creation of a federation of Northern Rhodesia (now Zambia), Southern Rhodesia (now Zimbabwe), and Nyasaland (now Malawi) in 1953 and was prime minister 1956–63, when the federation was disbanded. His Southern Rhodesian Federal Party was defeated by Ian Smith's Rhodesian Front in 1964. In 1965, following Smith's Rhodesian unilateral declaration of Southern Rhodesian independence from Britain, Welensky left politics.

Welhaven /ˈvelhɑːvən/ Johan Sebastian Cammermeyer 1807–1873. Norwegian poet, professor of philosophy at Christiania (now Oslo) 1839–68. A supporter of the Dano-Norwegian culture, he is considered one of the greatest Norwegian masters of poetic form. His works include the satiric *Norges Dæmring/The Dawn of Norway* 1834.

Welles /welz/ (George) Orson 1915–1985. US actor and film and theatre director, whose first film was *Citizen Kane* 1941, which he produced, directed, and starred in. Using innovative lighting, camera angles and movements, it is a landmark in the history of cinema, yet he subsequently directed very few films in Hollywood. His performances as an actor include the character of Harry Lime in *The Third Man* 1949.

In 1937 he founded the Mercury Theater, New York, with John Houseman, where their repertory productions included a modern-dress version of *Julius Caesar*. Welles's realistic radio broadcast of H G Wells's *The War of the Worlds* 1938 caused panic and fear of Martian invasion in the USA. He directed the films *The Magnificent Ambersons* 1942, *The Lady from Shanghai* 1948 with his wife Rita Hayworth, *Touch of Evil* 1958, and *Chimes at Midnight* 1967, a Shakespeare adaptation.

Welles /welz/ Gideon 1802–1878. US politician, one of the founders of the Republican Party 1854. Welles was appointed secretary of the navy by President Lincoln 1861 and in that position supervised the expansion of the Union naval forces and advocated the development of ironclads (wooden, iron-plated warships). An opponent of President Grant, he joined the Liberal Republicans 1872.

Born in Glastonbury, Connecticut, USA, and educated at Norwich University, Welles served as editor of the *Hartford Times* 1826–36. Originally a Democrat he served in the state legislature 1827–35 and held other state and federal offices before co-founding the Republican Party.

Wellesley family name of dukes of →Wellington; seated at Stratfield Saye, Berkshire, England.

Wellesley /ˈwelzli/ Richard Colley, Marquess of Wellesley 1760–1842. British administrator; brother of the 1st Duke of Wellington. He was governor general of India 1798–1805, and by his victories over the Mahrattas of W India greatly extended the territory under British rule. He was foreign secretary 1809–12, and lord lieutenant of Ireland 1821–28 and 1833–34.

Wellesz /ˈvelɪs/ Egon (Joseph) 1885–1974. Austrian composer and musicologist. He specialized in the history of Byzantine, Renaissance, and modern music. He moved to England 1938 and lectured at Oxford from 1943. His compositions include operas such as *Alkestis* 1924; symphonies, notably the Fifth 1957; ballet music; and a series of string quartets.

Wellington /ˈwelɪŋtən/ Arthur Wellesley, 1st Duke of Wellington 1769–1852. British soldier and Tory politician. As commander in the Peninsular War, he expelled the French from Spain 1814. He defeated Napoleon Bonaparte at Quatre-Bras and Waterloo 1815, and was a member of the Congress of Vienna. As prime minister 1828–30, he was forced to concede Roman Catholic emancipation.

Wellington was born in Ireland, the son of an Irish peer, and sat for a time in the Irish parliament. He was knighted for his army service in India and became a national hero with his victories of 1808–14 in the Peninsular War and as general of the allies against Napoleon. At the Congress of Vienna he opposed the dismemberment of France and supported restoration of the Bourbons. As prime minister he modified the Corn Laws but became unpopular for his opposition to parliamentary reform and his lack of opposition to Catholic emancipation. He was foreign secretary 1834–35 and a member of the cabinet 1841–46. He held the office of commander in chief of the forces at various times from 1827 and for life from 1842. His home was Apsley House in London.

Wells /welz/ H(erbert) G(eorge) 1866–1946. English writer of 'scientific romances' such as *The Time Machine* 1895 and *The War of the Worlds* 1898. His later novels had an anti-establishment, anti-conventional humour remarkable in its day, for example *Kipps* 1905 and *Tono-Bungay* 1909. His many other books include *Outline of History* 1920 and *The Shape of Things to Come* 1933, a number of his prophecies from which have since been fulfilled. He also wrote many short stories.

Wells /welz/ Ida Bell 1862–1931. US journalist and political activist. She joined the staff of *New York Age* 1891 and embarked on extensive lecture tours. She served as secretary of the National Afro-American Council 1898–1902 and as a Chicago probation officer 1913–16.

Born in Holly Springs, Mississippi, USA, Wells was educated in a segregated school and became a teacher in Memphis, Tennessee. Losing her job in 1891 as the result of a suit she had filed against state segregation laws, she began a career of political activism after moving to New York City. She later married and settled in Chicago 1895.

Welty /welti/ Eudora 1909– . US novelist and short-story writer, born in Jackson, Mississippi. Her works reflect life in the American South and are notable for their creation of character and accurate rendition of local dialect. Her novels include *Delta Wedding* 1946, *Losing Battles* 1970, and *The Optimist's Daughter* 1972.

Wenceslas, St /wensəslæs/ 907–929. Duke of Bohemia who attempted to Christianize his people and was murdered by his brother. He is patron saint of the Czech Republic and the 'good King Wenceslas' of a popular carol. Feast day 28 Sept.

Wentworth /wentwəθ/ William Charles 1790–1872. Australian politician and newspaper publisher. In 1855 he was in Britain to steer the New South Wales constitution through Parliament, and campaigned for Australian federalism and self-government. He was the son of D'Arcy Wentworth (*c.* 1762–1827), surgeon of the penal settlement on Norfolk Island.

Werfel /veəfəl/ Franz 1890–1945. Austrian poet, dramatist, and novelist, a leading Expressionist. His works include the poems 'Der Weltfreund der Gerichtstag'/'The Day of Judgment' 1919; the plays *Juarez und Maximilian* 1924 and *Das Reich Gottes in Böhmen/The Kingdom of God in Bohemia* 1930; and the novels *Verdi* 1924 and *Das Lied von Bernadette/The Song of Bernadette* 1941.

Born in Prague, he lived in Germany, Austria, and France, and in 1940 escaped from a French concentration camp to the USA, where he died. In 1929 he married Alma Mahler, daughter of the composer Gustav Mahler.

Wergeland /veəgələn/ Henrik 1808–1845. Norwegian lyric poet. He was a leader of the Norwegian nationalist movement and is known for his epic *Skabelsen, Mennesket, og Messias/Creation, Humanity, and Messiah* 1830.

Werner /veənə/ Abraham Gottlob 1750–1815. German geologist, one of the first to classify minerals systematically. He also developed the later discarded theory of neptunism – that the Earth was initially covered by water, with every mineral in suspension; as the water receded, layers of rocks 'crystallized'.

Werner /veənə/ Alfred 1866–1919. Swiss chemist. He was awarded a Nobel prize in 1913 for his work on valency theory, which gave rise to the concept of coordinate bonds and coordination compounds. He demonstrated that different three-dimensional arrangements of atoms in inorganic compounds gives rise to optical isomerism (the rotation of polarized light in opposite directions by molecules that contain the same atoms but are mirror images of each other).

Wertheimer /veəthaimə/ Max 1880–1943. Czech-born psychologist and founder, with Koffka and Kohler, of gestalt psychology, stating that the brain is not a passive receiver of information, but that it structures all its input in order to make sense of it. While travelling on a train 1910 he saw that a light flashing rapidly from two different positions seemed to be one light in motion. This type of perception became the basis for his gestalt concept.

Wesker /weskə/ Arnold 1932– . English playwright. His socialist beliefs were reflected in the successful trilogy *Chicken Soup with Barley, Roots,* and *I'm Talking About Jerusalem* 1958–60. He established a catchphrase with *Chips with Everything* 1962.

In 1962, Wesker tried unsuccessfully to establish a working-class theatre with trade-union backing. Later plays include *The Merchant* 1978.

Wesley /wesli/ Charles 1707–1788. English Methodist, brother of John →Wesley and one of the original Methodists at Oxford. He became a principal preacher and theologian of the Wesleyan Methodists, and wrote some 6,500 hymns.

West US film and vaudeville actress Mae West who wrote and delivered some of the most often quoted lines in film history. She specialized in glamorous roles, made memorable by her languid and sexy delivery of the dialogue. West also wrote plays, the first of which, Sex 1926, caused such a sensation that the authorities closed it down and imprisoned her for ten days for obscenity

Wesley /wesli/ John 1703–1791. English founder of Methodism. When the pulpits of the Church of England were closed to him and his followers, he took the gospel to the people. For 50 years he rode about the country on horseback, preaching daily, largely in the open air. His sermons became the doctrinal standard of the Wesleyan Methodist Church.

He was born at Epworth, Lincolnshire, where his father was the rector, and went to Oxford University together with his brother Charles, where their circle was nicknamed Methodists because of their religious observances. He was ordained in the Church of England 1728 and returned to his Oxford college 1729 as a tutor. In 1735 he went to Georgia, USA, as a missionary. On his return he experienced 'conversion' 1738, and from being rigidly High Church developed into an ardent Evangelical. His *Journal* gives an intimate picture of the man and his work.

Wesley /wesli/ Samuel 1776–1837. Son of Charles →Wesley. He was an organist and composer of oratorios, church and chamber music.

West /west/ Benjamin 1738–1820. American Neo-Classical painter, active in London from 1763. He enjoyed the patronage of George III for many years and painted historical pictures.

His *Death of General Wolfe* 1770 (National Gallery, Ottawa) began a vogue for painting recent historical events in contemporary costume. He became president of the Royal Academy, London 1792.

West /west/ Mae 1892–1980. US vaudeville, stage, and film actress. She wrote her own dialogue, setting herself up as a provocative sex symbol and the mistress of verbal innuendo. She appeared on Broadway in *Sex* 1926, *Drag* 1927, and *Diamond Lil* 1928, which was the basis of the film (with Cary Grant) *She Done Him Wrong* 1933. Her other films include *I'm No Angel* 1933, *Going to Town* 1934, *My Little Chickadee* 1944 (with W C Fields), *Myra Breckinridge* 1969, and *Sextette* 1977. Both her plays and her films led to legal battles over censorship.

Two of her often quoted lines are 'Come up and see me', and 'Beulah, peel me a grape'. Her autobiography, *Goodness Had Nothing to Do with It*, was published 1959.

West /west/ Nathanael. Pen name of Nathan Weinstein 1904–1940. US black-humour novelist. His surrealist-influenced novels capture the absurdity and extremity of American life and the dark side of the American dream. *The Day of the Locust* 1939 explores the violent fantasies induced by Hollywood, where West had been a screenwriter.

Miss Lonelyhearts 1933 is about a newspaper advice columnist who feels the misfortunes of his correspondents; *A Cool Million* 1934 satirizes the rags-to-riches dream of success.

West /west/ Rebecca. Pen name of Cicely Isabel Fairfield 1892–1983. British journalist and novelist, an active feminist from 1911. *The Meaning of Treason* 1959 deals with the spies Burgess and Maclean. Her novels have political themes and include *The Fountain Overflows* 1956 and *The Birds Fall Down* 1966.

Westinghouse /westɪŋhaʊs/ George 1846–1914. US inventor and founder of the Westinghouse Corporation 1886. He patented a powerful air brake for trains 1869, which allowed trains to run more safely with greater loads at higher speeds. In the 1880s he turned his attention to the generation of electricity. Unlike Thomas →Edison, Westinghouse introduced alternating current (AC) into his power stations.

Westmacott /westməkɒt/ Richard 1775–1856. English Neo-Classical sculptor. He studied under Antonio Canova in Rome and was elected to the Royal Academy, London 1811, becoming a professor there 1827–54. His works include monuments in Westminster Abbey and in St Paul's Cathedral, and the *Achilles* statue in Hyde Park, all in London.

Westmoreland /westmɔːlənd/ William (Childs) 1914– . US military leader who served as commander of US forces in Vietnam 1964–68. He was an aggressive advocate of expanded US military involvement there.

Born in Spartanburg County, South Carolina, USA, Westmoreland was a 1936 graduate of West

Point military academy. He served in various administrative capacities at the Pentagon 1953–58. In Vietnam 1963–68, he ended his active military career as army chief of staff 1968–72.

Weston /ˈwestən/ Edward 1886–1958. US photographer. A founder member of the F64 group, a school of photography advocating sharp definition, he was noted for the technical mastery in his Californian landscapes and nude studies.

Westwood /ˈwestwʊd/ Vivienne 1941– . British fashion designer who first attracted attention in the mid-1970s as co-owner of a shop with the rock-music entrepreneur Malcolm McLaren (1946–), which became a focus for the punk movement in London. Early in the 1980s her Pirate and New Romantics looks gained her international recognition. Westwood's dramatic clothes continue to have a wide influence on the public and other designers.

Weyden /ˈwaɪdə/ Rogier van der c. 1399–1464. Netherlandish painter, official painter to the city of Brussels from 1436. He painted portraits and religious subjects, such as *The Last Judgment* about 1450 (Hôtel-Dieu, Beaune). His refined style had considerable impact on Netherlandish painting.

Little is known of his life, and none of his works has been dated, but he was widely admired in his day and his paintings were sent to Italy, Spain, France, and Germany. His *Deposition* before 1443 (Prado, Madrid) shows the influence of Robert →Campin.

Weygand /vɛɪˈgɒn/ Maxime 1867–1965. French general. In 1940, as French commander in chief, he advised surrender to Germany, and was subsequently high commissioner of N Africa 1940–41. He was a prisoner in Germany 1942–45, and was arrested after his return to France; he was released 1946, and in 1949 the sentence of national infamy was quashed.

Whale /weɪl/ James 1886–1957. English film director. He went to Hollywood to film his stage success *Journey's End* 1930, and then directed four horror films: *Frankenstein* 1931, *The Old Dark House* 1932, *The Invisible Man* 1933, and *Bride of Frankenstein* 1935.

Mrs Ballinger is one of those ladies who pursue Culture in bands, as if it were dangerous to meet it alone.

Edith Wharton *Xingu* 1916

Wharton /ˈwɔːtn/ Edith (born Jones) 1862–1937. US novelist. Her work, known for its subtlety and form and influenced by her friend Henry James, was mostly set in New York society. It includes *The House of Mirth* 1905, which made her

reputation; the grim, uncharacteristic novel of New England *Ethan Frome* 1911; *The Custom of the Country* 1913; and *The Age of Innocence* 1920.

Wheatley /ˈwiːtli/ Dennis (Yates) 1897–1977. British thriller and adventure novelist. His works include a series dealing with black magic and occultism, but he also wrote crime novels in which the reader was invited to play the detective, as in *Murder off Miami* 1936, with real clues such as ticket stubs.

Wheatstone /ˈwiːtstən/ Charles 1802–1875. English physicist and inventor. With William Cooke, he patented a railway telegraph in 1837, and, developing an idea of Samuel Christie, devised the *Wheatstone bridge*, an electrical network for measuring resistance. Originally a musical-instrument maker, he invented the harmonica and the concertina.

Wheeler /ˈwiːlə/ Mortimer 1890–1976. English archaeologist. As director-general of archaeology in India in the 1940s he uncovered the Indus Valley civilization. He helped to popularize archaeology by his television appearances.

Wheeler adhered to the philosophy set down by General Pitt-Rivers (the 'father of archaeology', who established the rules for stratigraphic excavation), despite the sometimes less than scientific methodology pursued by his contemporaries. After a number of spectacular excavations in Britain, Wheeler was appointed director-general of archaeology in India 1944–48. He introduced careful methodology into Indian excavations and trained a number of archaeologists there. He became famous for his discovery of the cities of a new civilization which became known as the Indus Valley civilization. It flourished in the later 3rd millenium. Two major cities were excavated, Mohenjo-daro and Harappa. Wheeler revealed a society which was advanced enough to produce ceremonial and state architecture and a complex water, drainage, and waste-disposal system.

While Wheeler was keeper of the London Museum 1926–44, his digs included Caerleon in Wales 1926–27 and Maiden Castle in Dorset 1934–37.

Whewell /ˈhjuːəl/ William 1794–1866. British physicist and philosopher who coined the term 'scientist' along with such words as 'Eocene' and 'Miocene', 'electrode', 'cathode', and 'anode'. Most of his career was connected with Cambridge University, where he became the Master of Trinity College. His most enduring influence rests on two works of great scholarship, *The History of the Inductive Sciences* 1837 and *The Philosophy of the Inductive Sciences* 1840.

Whipple /ˈwɪpəl/ Fred Lawrence 1906– . US astronomer whose hypothesis in 1949 that the nucleus of a comet is like a dirty snowball was confirmed 1986 by space-probe studies of Halley's comet.

Whipple /ˈwɪpəl/ George 1878–1976. US physiologist whose research interest concerned the formation of haemoglobin in the blood. He showed that anaemic dogs, kept under restricted diets, responded well to a liver regime, and that their haemoglobin quickly regenerated. This work led to a cure for pernicious anaemia. He shared the 1934 Nobel Prize for Medicine with George Minot (1885–1950) and William Murphy (1892–1987).

Whistler /ˈwɪslə/ James Abbott McNeill 1834–1903. US painter and etcher, active in London from 1859. His riverscapes and portraits show subtle composition and colour harmonies: for example, *Arrangement in Grey and Black: Portrait of the Painter's Mother* 1871 (Louvre, Paris).

He settled in Chelsea, London, and painted views of the Thames including *Old Battersea Bridge* (*c.* 1872–75) (Tate Gallery, London). In 1877 the art critic John →Ruskin published an article on his *Nocturne in Black and Gold: The Falling Rocket* (now in Detroit) that led to a libel trial in which Whistler was awarded symbolic damages of a farthing (a quarter of an old penny). Whistler described the trial in his book *The Gentle Art of Making Enemies* 1890.

Whistler was born in Massachusetts. He abandoned a military career and in 1855 went to Paris.

Whistler /ˈwɪslə/ Rex John 1905–1944. English artist. He painted fanciful murals, for example *In Pursuit of Rare Meats* 1926–27 in the Tate Gallery restaurant, London. He also illustrated many books and designed stage sets.

White /waɪt/ Byron Raymond 1917–   . US jurist. He worked to elect John F Kennedy to the presidency 1960 and was appointed by him as associate justice of the Supreme Court 1962–   . He was a moderate conservative, usually dissenting on the rights of criminals, but upholding the right of accused citizens to trial by jury.

Born in Fort Collins, Colorado, USA, White graduated from the University of Colorado 1938. He studied at Oxford University, UK, as a Rhodes scholar 1939 and entered Yale Law School 1940. He graduated from Yale 1946 after service with the US navy in World War II. He served as deputy attorney general 1961–62, before being appointed to the Supreme Court. He served as law clerk 1946–47 to Supreme Court associate justice Fred M Vinson.

He also played professional football, with the Pittsburgh Pirates (now Steelers) 1938 and for the Detroit Lions 1940–41. He was elected to the Football Hall of Fame 1954.

White /waɪt/ Edward Douglass, Jr 1845–1921. US jurist. Elected to the US Senate 1891, President Cleveland nominated him as associative justice to the US Supreme Court 1893 and under President Taft he was nominated as chief justice 1911–21. During his office the Court made important decisions on US economic policy as in *United States* v *E C Knight and Co* 1895 when he joined the majority in weakening the Sherman Antitrust Act by removing manufacture of goods from its purview.

Born in Lafourche Parish, Louisiana, USA, White attended Mount St Mary's College (Maryland), the Jesuit College (New Orleans), and Georgetown University, but left his college studies to serve in the Confederate Army. After the American Civil War 1865 he studied law at the University of Louisiana Law School in New Orleans; he was admitted to the bar 1868. Becoming active in Democratic politics, he was elected to the state senate 1874 and was a justice of the Louisiana supreme court 1878–80.

White /waɪt/ E(lwyn) B(rooks) 1899–1985. US writer, long associated with *The New Yorker* magazine and renowned for his satire, such as *Is Sex Necessary?* 1929 (with the humorist James Thurber).

White also wrote two children's classics, *Stuart Little* 1945 and *Charlotte's Web* 1952.

White /ˈhwaɪt/ Gilbert 1720–1793. English cleric and naturalist, born at Selborne, Hampshire, and author of *Natural History and Antiquities of Selborne* 1789.

White /waɪt/ Patrick (Victor Martindale) 1912–1990. Australian writer who did more than any other to put Australian literature on the international map. His partly allegorical novels explore the lives of early settlers in Australia and often deal with misfits or inarticulate people. They include *The Aunt's Story* 1948, *The Tree of Man* 1955, and *Voss* 1957 (based on the ill-fated 19th-century explorer Leichhardt). Nobel Prize for Literature 1973.

Inspiration descends only in flashes, to clothe circumstances; it is not stored up in a barrel, like salt herrings, to be doled out.

Patrick White, *Voss* 1957

White /waɪt/ Stanford 1853–1906. US architect. One of the most prominent US architects of the 19th century, he specialized in the Renaissance style and designed, among many famous projects, the original Madison Square Garden and the Washington Square Arch, both in New York City. A flamboyant and arrogant personality, he was murdered in the rooftop restaurant of Madison Square Garden by the husband of a former lover.

Born in New York City, USA, he co-founded the architectural firm of McKim, Mead and White 1879.

White /waɪt/ T(erence) H(anbury) 1906–1964. English writer who retold the Arthurian legend in four volumes of *The Once and Future King* 1938–58.

Whitefield /ˈwɪtfiːld/ George 1714–1770. British Methodist evangelist. He was a student at Oxford University and took orders 1738, but was suspended for his unorthodox doctrines and methods. For many years he travelled through Britain and America, and by his preaching contributed greatly to the religious revival. Whitefield's Tabernacle was built for him in Tottenham Court Road, London (1756; bombed 1945 but rebuilt).

Whitehead /ˈwaɪthed/ Alfred North 1861–1947. English philosopher and mathematician. In his 'theory of organism', he attempted a synthesis of metaphysics and science. His works include *Principia Mathematica* 1910–13 (with Bertrand →Russell), *The Concept of Nature* 1920, and *Adventures of Ideas* 1933.

He was professor of applied mathematics at London University 1914–24, and professor of philosophy at Harvard University, USA, 1924–37. Other works include *Principles of Natural Knowledge* 1919, *Science and the Modern World* 1925, and *Process and Reality* 1929.

Whitehead /ˈwaɪthed/ Robert 1823–1905. English engineer who invented the self-propelled torpedo 1866.

He developed the torpedo in Austria and within two years of its invention was manufacturing 4 m/13 ft torpedoes which could carry a 9 kg/20 lb dynamite warhead at a speed of 7 knots, subsequently improved to 29 knots. They were powered by compressed air and had a balancing mechanism and, later, gyroscopic controls.

Whitehouse /ˈwaɪthaʊs/ Mary 1910–   . British media activist. A founder of the National Viewers' and Listeners' Association, she has campaigned to censor radio and television for their treatment of sex and violence.

Whitelaw /ˈwaɪtlɔː/ William, Viscount Whitelaw 1918–   . British Conservative politician. As secretary of state for Northern Ireland he introduced the concept of power sharing. He was chief Conservative whip 1964–70, and leader of the House of Commons 1970–72. He became secretary of state for employment 1973–74, but failed to conciliate the trade unions. He was chair of the Conservative Party 1974 and home secretary 1979–83, when he was made a peer. He resigned 1988.

Whiteman /ˈwaɪtmən/ Paul 1890–1967. US dance-band and swing-orchestra leader specializing in 'symphonic jazz'. He commissioned George Gershwin's *Rhapsody in Blue*, conducting its premiere 1924.

Whitlam /ˈwɪtləm/ Gough (Edward) 1916–   . Australian politician, leader of the Labor Party 1967–78 and prime minister 1972–75. He cultivated closer relations with Asia, attempted redistribution of wealth, and raised loans to increase national ownership of industry and resources.

When the opposition blocked finance bills in the Senate, following a crisis of confidence, Whitlam refused to call a general election, and was dismissed by the governor general (Sir John Kerr). He was defeated in the subsequent general election by Malcolm →Fraser.

Whitman /ˈwɪtmən/ Walt(er) 1819–1892. US poet who published *Leaves of Grass* 1855, which contains the symbolic 'Song of Myself'. It used unconventional free verse (with no rhyme or regular rhythm) and scandalized the public by its frank celebration of sexuality.

Born in Long Island, New York, as a young man Whitman worked as a printer, teacher, and journalist. In 1865 he published *Drum-Taps*, a volume inspired by his work as an army nurse during the Civil War. He also wrote an elegy on Abraham Lincoln, 'When Lilacs Last in the Dooryard Bloom'd'. He preached a particularly American vision of individual freedom and human brotherhood.

Do I contradict myself? Very well then I contradict myself (I am large, I contain multitudes).

Walt Whitman, 'Song of Myself' 1855

Whitney /ˈwɪtni/ Eli 1765–1825. US inventor who in 1794 patented the cotton gin, a device for separating cotton fibre from its seeds. Also a manufacturer of firearms, he created a standardization system that was the precursor of the assembly line.

Whitman US poet Walt Whitman whose poetry broke away from conventional form making him one of the most influential writers of his generation. The main themes in his poetry include the sacredness of the self, the beauty of death, the equality of all people, brotherly love, and the immortality of the soul.

---

*The age is dull and mean. Men creep.
Not walk.*

John Greenleaf Whittier, lines inscribed to Friends under Arrest for Treason against the Slave Power 1856

Whittam Smith /ˈwɪtəm ˈsmɪθ/ Andreas 1937– . British newspaper editor, founder and editor from 1986 of the centrist daily the *Independent* and cofounder 1990 of the *Independent on Sunday*.

Whitten-Brown /ˈwɪtn ˈbraʊn/ Arthur 1886–1948. British aviator. After serving in World War I, he took part in the first nonstop flight across the Atlantic as navigator to Capt John →Alcock 1919.

Whittier /ˈwɪtɪə/ John Greenleaf 1807–1892. US poet who was a powerful opponent of slavery, as shown in the verse *Voices of Freedom* 1846. Among his other works are *Legends of New England in Prose and Verse, Songs of Labor* 1850, and the New England nature poem *Snow-Bound* 1866.

Whittington /ˈwɪtɪŋtən/ Dick (Richard) 14th–15th centuries. English cloth merchant who was mayor of London 1397–98, 1406–07, and 1419–20. According to legend, he came to London as a poor boy with his cat when he heard that the streets were paved with gold and silver. His cat first appears in a play from 1605.

Whittle /ˈwɪtl/ Frank 1907– . British engineer who patented the basic design for the turbojet engine 1930. In the Royal Air Force he worked on jet propulsion 1937–46. In May 1941 the Gloster E 28/39 aircraft first flew with the Whittle jet engine. Both the German (first operational jet planes) and the US jet aircraft were built using his principles.

Who, the /huː/ English rock group, formed 1964, with a hard, aggressive sound, high harmonies, and a propensity for destroying their instruments on stage. Their albums include *Tommy* 1969, *Who's Next* 1971, and *Quadrophenia* 1973.

Originally a mod band, the Who comprised Pete Townshend (1945–), guitar and songwriter; Roger Daltrey (1944–), vocals; John Entwistle (1944–), bass; and Keith Moon (1947–1978), drums.

Whymper /ˈwɪmpə/ Edward 1840–1911. English mountaineer. He made the first ascent of many Alpine peaks, including the Matterhorn 1865, and in the Andes scaled Chimborazo and other mountains.

He wrote *Scrambles amongst the Alps* 1871 and *Zermatt and the Matterhorn* 1897.

Wickham /ˈwɪkəm/ Henry 1846–1928. British planter who founded the rubber plantations of Sri Lanka and Malaysia, and broke the monopoly in rubber production then held by Brazil. He collected rubber seeds from Brazil, where they grew naturally, cultivated them at Kew Gardens, Surrey, and re-exported them to the Far East.

Widmark /ˈwɪdmɑːk/ Richard 1914– . US actor who made his film debut in *Kiss of Death* 1947 as a psychopath. He subsequently appeared in a great variety of *film noir* roles as well as in *The Alamo* 1960, *Madigan* 1968, and *Coma* 1978.

Wieland /ˈviːlænt/ Christoph Martin 1733–1813. German poet and novelist. After attempts at religious poetry, he came under the influence of Voltaire and Rousseau, and wrote novels such as *Die Geschichte des Agathon/The History of Agathon* 1766–67 and the satirical *Die Abderiten* 1774 (translated as *The Republic of Fools* 1861); and tales in verse such as *Musarion oder Die Philosophie der Grazien* 1768, *Oberon* 1780, and others. He translated Shakespeare into German 1762–66.

Wien /viːn/ Wilhelm 1864–1928. German physicist who studied radiation and established the principle, since known as Wien's law, that the wavelength at which the radiation from an idealized radiating body is most intense is inversely proportional to the body's absolute temperature. (That is, the hotter the body, the shorter the wavelength.) For this and other work on radiation, he was awarded the 1911 Nobel Prize for Physics.

Wiene /ˈviːnə/ Robert 1880–1938. German film director of the bizarre Expressionist film *Das Kabinett des Dr Caligari/The Cabinet of Dr Caligari* 1919. He also directed *Orlacs Hände/The Hands of Orlac* 1924, *Der Rosenkavalier* 1926, and *Ultimatum* 1938.

Wiener /ˈwiːnə/ Norbert 1894–1964. US mathematician, credited with the establishment of the science of cybernetics in his book *Cybernetics* 1948. In mathematics, he laid the foundation of the study of stochastic processes (those dependent on random events), particularly Brownian movement (the continuous random movement of par-

Wild English criminal Jonathan Wild, whose notorious career was fictionalized by Henry Fielding in The History of the Life of the Late Mr Jonathan Wild the Great.

ticles in a fluid medium – gas or liquid – as they are subjected to impact from the molecules of the medium).

Wiesel /ˈviːzəl/ Elie 1928– . US academic and human-rights campaigner, born in Romania. He was held in Buchenwald concentration camp during World War II, and has assiduously documented wartime atrocities against the Jews in an effort to alert the world to the dangers of racism and violence. Nobel Peace Prize 1986.

Wiggin /ˈwɪgɪn/ Kate Douglas 1856–1923. US writer, born in Philadelphia. She was a pioneer in the establishment of kindergartens in the USA, and wrote the children's classic *Rebecca of Sunnybrook Farm* 1903 and its sequels.

Wigner /ˈwɪgnə/ Eugene Paul 1902– . Hungarian-born US physicist who introduced the notion of parity into nuclear physics with the consequence that all nuclear processes should be indistinguishable from their mirror images. For this, and other work on nuclear structure, he shared the 1963 Nobel Prize for Physics with Maria →Goeppert-Mayer and Hans Jensen (1906–1973).

Wilander /vɪˈlændə/ Mats 1964– . Swedish lawn-tennis player. He won his first Grand Slam event 1982 when he beat Guillermo Vilas to win the French Open, and had won eight Grand Slam titles by 1990. He played a prominent role in Sweden's rise to the forefront of men's tennis in the 1980s, including Davis Cup successes.

Wilberforce /ˈwɪlbəfɔːs/ Samuel 1805–1873. British Anglican bishop of Oxford 1845–69, and from 1869 of Winchester. He defended Anglican orthodoxy against Tractarianism, the Oxford Movement for the revival of English Roman Catholicism.

Wilberforce /ˈwɪlbəfɔːs/ William 1759–1833. English reformer who was instrumental in abolishing slavery in the British Empire. He entered Parliament 1780; in 1807 his bill for the abolition of the slave trade was passed, and in 1833, largely through his efforts, slavery was abolished throughout the empire.

Wilbur /ˈwɪlbə/ Richard 1921– . US poet whose witty verse is found in several volumes, including *Poems 1943–56* 1957 and *The Mind Reader* 1971.

Wild /waɪld/ Jonathan *c.* 1682–1725. English criminal who organized the thieves of London and ran an office that, for a payment, returned stolen goods to their owners. He was hanged at Tyburn.

Wild was the subject of Henry Fielding's satire *Jonathan Wild the Great* 1743 and the model for Macheath in John Gay's *The Beggar's Opera* 1728.

Wilde /waɪld/ Cornel(ius Louis) 1915–1989. Austrian-born US actor and film director, in the USA from 1932. He starred in *A Song to Remember* 1945, and directed *The Naked Prey* 1966 (in which he also acted) and *No Blade of Grass* 1970.

Wilde /waɪld/ Oscar (Fingal O'Flahertie Wills) 1854–1900. Irish writer. With his flamboyant style and quotable conversation, he dazzled London society and, on his lecture tour 1882, the USA. He published his only novel, *The Picture of Dorian Gray*, 1891, followed by witty plays including *A Woman of No Importance* 1893 and *The Importance of Being Earnest* 1895. In 1895 he was imprisoned for two years for homosexual offences; he died in exile.

Wilde was born in Dublin and studied at Dublin and Oxford, where he became known as a supporter of the Aesthetic movement ('art for art's sake'). He published *Poems* 1881, and also wrote fairy tales and other stories, criticism, and a long, anarchic political essay, 'The Soul of Man Under Socialism' 1891. His elegant social comedies include *Lady Windermere's Fan* 1892 and *An Ideal Husband* 1895. The drama *Salome* 1893, based on the biblical character, was written in French; considered scandalous by the British censor, it was first performed in Paris 1896 with the actress Sarah Bernhardt in the title role.

Among his lovers was Lord Alfred →Douglas, whose father provoked Wilde into a lawsuit that led to his social and financial ruin and imprisonment. The long poem *Ballad of Reading Gaol* 1898 and a letter published as *De Profundis* 1905 were written in jail to explain his side of the relationship. After his release from prison 1897, he lived in France and is buried in Paris.

Wilder /ˈwaɪldə/ Billy 1906– . Austrian-born accomplished US screenwriter and film director, in the USA from 1934. He directed and coscripted *Double Indemnity* 1944, *The Lost Weekend* (Academy Award for best director) 1945, *Sunset Boulevard* 1950, *Some Like It Hot* 1959, and the Academy Award-winning *The Apartment* 1960.

Wilder /ˈwaɪldə/ Thornton (Niven) 1897–1975. US playwright and novelist. He won Pulitzer prizes for the novel *The Bridge of San Luis Rey* 1927, and for the plays *Our Town* 1938 and *The Skin of Our Teeth* 1942. His farce *The Matchmaker* 1954 was filmed 1958. In 1964 it was adapted into the hit stage musical *Hello, Dolly!*, also made into a film.

Wilfrid, St /ˈwɪlfrɪd/ 634–709. Northumbrian-born bishop of York from 665. He defended the cause of the Roman Church at the Synod of Whitby 664 against that of Celtic Christianity. Feast day 12 Oct.

Wilhelm /ˈvɪlhelm/ (English *William*) two emperors of Germany:

Wilhelm I 1797–1888. King of Prussia from 1861 and emperor of Germany from 1871; the son of Friedrich Wilhelm III. He served in the Napoleonic Wars 1814–15 and helped to crush the 1848 revolution. After he succeeded his brother Friedrich Wilhelm IV to the throne of Prussia, his policy was largely dictated by his chancellor →Bismarck, who secured his proclamation as emperor.

Wilhelm II 1859–1941. Emperor of Germany from 1888, the son of Frederick III and Victoria, daughter of Queen Victoria of Britain. In 1890 he forced Chancellor Bismarck to resign and began to direct foreign policy himself, which proved disastrous. He encouraged warlike policies and built up the German navy. In 1914 he first approved Austria's ultimatum to Serbia and then, when he realized war was inevitable, tried in vain to prevent it. In 1918 he fled to Holland, after Germany's defeat and his abdication.

Wilkes /wɪlks/ John 1727–1797. British Radical politician, imprisoned for his political views; member of Parliament 1757–64 and from 1774. He championed parliamentary reform, religious toleration, and US independence.

Wilkes, born in Clerkenwell, London, entered Parliament as a Whig 1757. His attacks on the Tory prime minister Bute in his paper *The North Briton* led to his being outlawed 1764; he fled to France, and on his return 1768 was imprisoned. He was four times elected MP for Middlesex, but the Commons refused to admit him and finally declared his opponent elected. This secured him strong working- and middle-class support, and in 1774 he was allowed to take his seat in Parliament.

Wilkie /wɪlki/ David 1785–1841. Scottish genre and portrait painter, active in London from 1805. His paintings are in the 17th-century Dutch tradition and include *The Letter of Introduction* 1813 (National Gallery of Scotland, Edinburgh).

Wilkins /wɪlkɪnz/ George Hubert 1888–1958. Australian polar explorer, a pioneer in the use of surveys by both aircraft and submarines. He studied engineering, learned to fly 1910, and visited both polar regions. In 1928 he flew from Barrow (Alaska) to Green Harbour (Spitsbergen), and in 1928–29 made an Antarctic flight that proved that Graham Land is an island. He also planned to reach the North Pole by submarine.

Wilkins /wɪlkɪnz/ Maurice Hugh Frederick 1916– . New Zealand-born British scientist. In 1962 he shared the Nobel Prize for Medicine with Francis →Crick and James →Watson for his work on the molecular structure of nucleic acids, particularly DNA, using X-ray diffraction.

Wilkins began his career as a physicist working on luminescence and phosphorescence, radar, and the separation of uranium isotopes, and worked in the USA during World War II on the development of the atomic bomb. After the war he turned his attention from nuclear physics to biophysics, and studied the genetic effects of ultrasonic waves, nucleic acids, and viruses by using ultraviolet light.

Wilkins /wɪlkɪnz/ William 1778–1839. English architect. He pioneered the Greek revival in England with his design for Downing College, Cambridge. Other works include the main block of University College London 1827–28, and the National Gallery, London, 1834–38.

Willard /wɪləd/ Frances Elizabeth Caroline 1839–1898. US educationalist and campaigner. Committed to the cause of the prohibition of alcohol, culminating in the Prohibition 1920–33, she served as president of the Women's Christian Temperance Union 1879–98. She was also elected president of the National Council of Women 1888.

Born in Churchville, New York, USA, and raised in Wisconsin, Willard was educated at the Northwestern Female College in Evanston, Illinois. After a career as a teacher, she was appointed dean of women at Northwestern University 1873.

Willem /wɪləm/ Dutch form of →William.

William /wɪljəm/ four kings of England:

William I *the Conqueror* c. 1027–1087. King of England from 1066. He was the illegitimate son of Duke Robert the Devil and succeeded his father as duke of Normandy 1035. Claiming that his relative King Edward the Confessor had bequeathed him the English throne, William invaded the country 1066, defeating →Harold II at Hastings, Sussex, and was crowned king of England.

He was crowned in Westminster Abbey on Christmas Day 1066. He completed the establishment of feudalism in England, compiling detailed records of land and property in the Domesday Book, and kept he barons firmly under control. He died in Rouen after a fall from his horse and is buried in Caen, France. He was succeeded by his son William II.

William II *Rufus, the Red* c. 1056–1100. King of England from 1087, the third son of William I. He spent most of his reign attempting to capture Normandy from his brother →Robert II, duke of Normandy. His extortion of money led his barons to revolt and caused confrontation with Bishop Anselm. He was killed while hunting in the New Forest, Hampshire, and was succeeded by his brother Henry I.

William III *William of Orange* 1650–1702. King of Great Britain and Ireland from 1688, the son of William II of Orange and Mary, daughter of Charles I. He was offered the English crown by the parliamentary opposition to James II. He invaded England 1688 and in 1689 became joint sovereign with his wife, →Mary II. He spent much of his reign campaigning, first in Ireland, where he defeated James II at the battle of the Boyne 1690, and later against the French in Flanders. He was succeeded by Mary's sister, Anne.

Born in the Netherlands, William was made *stadtholder* (chief magistrate) 1672 to resist the French invasion. He forced Louis XIV to make peace 1678 and then concentrated on building up a European alliance against France. In 1677 he married his cousin Mary, daughter of the future James II. When invited by both Whig and Tory leaders to take the crown from James, he landed with a large force at Torbay, Devon. James fled to

France, and his Scottish and Irish supporters were defeated at the battles of Dunkeld 1689 and the Boyne 1690.

William IV 1765–1837. King of Great Britain and Ireland from 1830, when he succeeded his brother George IV; third son of George III. He was created duke of Clarence 1789, and married Adelaide of Saxe-Meiningen (1792–1849) 1818. During the Reform Bill crisis he secured its passage by agreeing to create new peers to overcome the hostile majority in the House of Lords. He was succeeded by Victoria.

William /wɪljəm/ three kings of the Netherlands:

William I 1772–1844. King of the Netherlands 1815–40. He lived in exile during the French occupation 1795–1813 and fought against the emperor Napoleon at Jena and Wagram. The Austrian Netherlands were added to his kingdom by the Allies 1815, but secured independence (recognized by the major European states 1839) by the revolution of 1830. William's unpopularity led to his abdication 1840.

William II 1792–1849. King of the Netherlands 1840–49, son of William I. He served with the British army in the Peninsular War and at Waterloo. In 1848 he averted revolution by conceding a liberal constitution.

William III 1817–1890. King of the Netherlands 1849–90, the son of William II. In 1862 he abolished slavery in the Dutch East Indies.

William /wɪljəm/ *William the Lion* 1143–1214. King of Scotland from 1165. He was captured by Henry II while invading England 1174, and forced to do homage, but Richard I abandoned the English claim to suzerainty for a money payment 1189. In 1209 William was forced by King John to renounce his claim to Northumberland.

William /wɪljəm/ *the Silent* 1533–1584. Prince of Orange from 1544. Leading a revolt against Spanish rule in the Netherlands from 1573, he briefly succeeded in uniting the Catholic south and Protestant northern provinces, but the former provinces submitted to Spain while the latter formed a federation 1579 which repudiated Spanish suzerainty 1581.

William, brought up at the court of Charles V, was appointed governor of Holland by Philip II of Spain 1559, but joined the revolt of 1572 against Spain's oppressive rule and, as a Protestant from 1573, became the national leader and first stadholder. He was known as 'the Silent' because of his absolute discretion. He was assassinated by a Spanish agent.

William /wɪljəm/ (full name William Arthur Philip Louis) 1982– . Prince of the UK, first child of the Prince and Princess of Wales.

William of Malmesbury /mɑːmzbri/ c. 1080– c. 1143. English historian and monk. He compiled the *Gesta regum/Deeds of the Kings* c.1120–40 and

Historia novella, which together formed a history of England to 1142.

William of Wykeham /wɪkəm/ c. 1323–1404. English politician, bishop of Winchester from 1367, Lord Chancellor 1367–72 and 1389–91, and founder of Winchester College (public school) 1378 and New College, Oxford 1379.

Williams J(ohn) P(eter) R(hys) 1949– . Welsh rugby union player. With 55 appearances for his country, he is Wales's most capped player. He played in three Grand Slam winning teams and twice toured with winning British Lions teams. He played for Bridgend and London Welsh.

Williams /wɪljəmz/ (George) Emlyn 1905–1987. Welsh actor and playwright. His plays, in which he appeared, include *Night Must Fall* 1935 and *The Corn Is Green* 1938. He gave early encouragement to the actor Richard Burton.

Williams /wɪljəmz/ George 1821–1905. Founder of the Young Men's Christian Association (YMCA).

Williams /wɪljəmz/ John (Christopher) 1942– . Australian guitarist, resident in London from 1952. After studying with Segovia, he made his formal debut 1958. His extensive repertoire includes contemporary music and jazz. He was a founder member of the pop group Sky 1979–84.

Williams /wɪljəmz/ Roger c. 1603–1683. American colonist, founder of the Rhode Island colony 1636, based on democracy and complete religious freedom. He tried to maintain good relations with the Indians of the region, although he fought against them in the Pequot War and King Philip's War.

Williams /wɪljəmz/ Shirley 1930– . British (Social Democrat Party) politician. She was Labour minister for prices and consumer protection 1974–76, and education and science 1976–79. She became a founder member of the SDP 1981 and its president 1982. In 1983 she lost her parliamentary seat. She is the daughter of the socialist writer Vera →Brittain.

Williams /wɪljəmz/ Ted (Theodore Samuel) 1918– . US baseball player. Establishing a lifetime batting average of .344, he was six times the American League batting champion and twice won the most valuable player award. In 1947 he became the second player ever to twice win the Triple Crown (leading the league in batting, home runs, and runs batted in for a season).

Born in San Diego, California, USA, Williams was signed by the Boston Red Sox and made his major league debut 1939. Named rookie of the year, he went on to a 19-season career with the Red Sox (interrupted by service in World War II and the Korean War).

Williams retired as a player 1960 and served as manager of the Washington Senators 1969–71 and the Texas Rangers 1972. He was elected to the Baseball Hall of Fame 1966.

poser, pianist, and organist, who settled in Britain 1953. His works include operas such as *Our Man in Havana* 1963, symphonies, and chamber music.

He became Master of the Queen's Music in 1975.

William the Marshall /maːʃəl/ 1st Earl of Pembroke *c.* 1146–1219. English knight, regent of England from 1216. After supporting the dying Henry II against Richard (later Richard I), he went on a crusade to Palestine, was pardoned by Richard, and was granted an earldom 1189. On King John's death he was appointed guardian of the future Henry III, and defeated the French under Louis VIII to enable Henry to gain the throne.

He grew up as a squire in Normandy and became tutor in 1170 to Henry, son of Henry II of England. William's life was a model of chivalric loyalty, serving four successive kings of England.

Willis /wɪlɪs/ Norman (David) 1933– . British trade-union leader. A trade-union official since leaving school, he succeeded Len Murray as the general secretary of the Trades Union Congress (TUC) 1984.

He has presided over the TUC at a time of falling union membership, hostile legislation from the Conservative government, and a major review of the role and policies of the Labour Party.

Willkie /wɪlki/ Wendell Lewis 1892–1944. US politician who was the Republican presidential candidate 1940. After losing to F D Roosevelt, he continued as a leader of the liberal wing of the Republican Party. Becoming committed to the cause of international cooperation, he published *One World* 1942.

Born in Elwood, Indiana, USA, Willkie was educated at Indiana University, and became a barrister 1916. After service in World War I, he became corporate counsel for a private utility and an outspoken opponent of the economic policies of the New Deal, for which reason he was nominated as the 1940 Republican presidential candidate.

Wills /wɪlz/ Bob (James Robert) 1905–1975. US country fiddle player and composer. As leader of the band known from 1934 as Bob Wills and his Texas Playboys, Wills became a pioneer of Western swing and a big influence on US popular music. 'San Antonio Rose' 1938 is his most popular song.

Wills began playing 1920 and went on to do local radio shows, the band being named and renamed after the commercial sponsor's product (for a time they were the Light Crust Doughboys, for example). Their repertory drew on blues, popular ballads, and jazz, as well as country, with much original material.

Wills /wɪlz/ Helen Newington 1905– . US tennis player. She won her first US women's title

Willis British trade union leader and TUC general secretary Norman Willis. As general secretary Willis has, for the most part, aligned himself with the 'new realistics' of the union movement, who are prepared to accept some of the Conservative government's industrial relations legislation.

Williams /wɪljəmz/ Tennessee (Thomas Lanier) 1911–1983. US playwright, born in Mississippi. His work is characterized by fluent dialogue and searching analysis of the psychological deficiencies of his characters. His plays, usually set in the Deep South against a background of decadence and degradation, include *The Glass Menagerie* 1945, *A Streetcar Named Desire* 1947, and *Cat on a Hot Tin Roof* 1955, the last two of which earned Pulitzer Prizes.

Williams /wɪljəmz/ William Carlos 1883–1963. US poet. His spare images and language reflect everyday speech. His epic poem *Paterson* 1946–58 celebrates his home town in New Jersey. *Pictures from Brueghel* 1963 won him, posthumously, a Pulitzer prize. His vast body of prose work includes novels, short stories, and the play *A Dream of Love* 1948. His work had a great impact on younger US poets.

Williams-Ellis /wɪljəmz 'elɪs/ Clough 1883–1978. British architect, designer of the fantasy resort of Portmeirion, N Wales.

Williamson /wɪljəmsən/ Henry 1895–1977. English author whose stories of animal life include *Tarka the Otter* 1927. He described his experiences in restoring an old farm in *The Story of a Norfolk Farm* 1941 and wrote the fictional, 15-volume sequence *Chronicles of Ancient Sunlight*.

Williamson /wɪljəmsən/ Malcolm (Benjamin Graham Christopher) 1931– . Australian com-

1923 and her first Wimbledon championship 1927. In the course of an unparalleled amateur tennis career, he went on to win the US title six more times and Wimbledon seven more times. She won two gold medals in the 1924 Paris Olympics.

Born in Centerville, California, USA, Wills was educated at the University of California. From 1929 to 1937 she played under her married name, Helen Wills Moody.

Wilson /wɪlsən/ Angus (Frank Johnstone) 1913–1991. English novelist, short-story writer, and biographer, whose acidly humorous books include *Anglo-Saxon Attitudes* 1956 and *The Old Men at the Zoo* 1961. In his detailed portrayal of English society he extracted high comedy from its social and moral grotesqueries.

Wilson was first known for his short-story collections *The Wrong Set* 1949 and *Such Darling Dodos* 1950. His other major novels include *Late Call* 1964, *No Laughing Matter* 1967, and *Setting the World on Fire* 1980. He also published critical works on Zola, Dickens, and Kipling.

Wilson /wɪlsən/ Brian 1942– . US pop musician and producer, founder member of the →Beach Boys.

Wilson /wɪlsən/ Charles Thomson Rees 1869–1959. British physicist who in 1911 invented the Wilson cloud chamber, an apparatus for studying subatomic particles. He shared a Nobel prize 1927.

Wilson /wɪlsən/ Colin 1931– . British author of *The Outsider* 1956, and of thrillers, including *Necessary Doubt* 1964. Later works, such as *Mysteries* 1978, are about the occult.

Wilson /wɪlsən/ Edmund 1895–1972. US critic and writer, born in New Jersey. *Axel's Castle* 1931 is a survey of symbolism, and *The Wound and the Bow* 1941 a study of art and neurosis. He also produced the satirical sketches in *Memoirs of Hecate County* 1946.

Wilson /wɪlsən/ Edward O 1929– . US zoologist whose books have stimulated interest in biogeography, the study of the distribution of species, and sociobiology, the evolution of behaviour. His works include *Sociobiology: The New Synthesis* 1975 and *On Human Nature* 1978.

Wilson /wɪlsən/ (James) Harold, Baron Wilson of Rievaulx 1916– . British Labour politician, party leader from 1963, prime minister 1964–70 and 1974–76. His premiership was dominated by the issue of UK admission to membership of the European Community, the social contract (unofficial agreement with the trade unions), and economic difficulties.

Wilson, born in Huddersfield, West Yorkshire, was president of the Board of Trade 1947–51 (when he resigned because of social-service cuts). In 1963 he succeeded Hugh Gaitskell as Labour leader and became prime minister the following

year, increasing his majority 1966. He formed a minority government Feb 1974 and achieved a majority of three Oct 1974. He resigned 1976 and was succeeded by James Callaghan. He was knighted 1976 and made a peer 1983.

Wilson /wɪlsən/ Jumbo (Henry Maitland), 1st Baron Wilson 1881–1964. British field marshal in World War II. He was commander in chief in Egypt 1939, led the unsuccessful Greek campaign of 1941, was commander in chief in the Middle East 1943, and in 1944 was supreme Allied commander in the Mediterranean.

Wilson /wɪlsən/ Richard 1714–1782. British painter whose English and Welsh landscapes are infused with an Italianate atmosphere and recomposed in a Classical manner. His work influenced the development of English landscape painting.

Wilson /wɪlsən/ Teddy (Theodore) 1912–1986. US bandleader and jazz pianist. He toured with Benny Goodman 1935–39 and during that period recorded in small groups with many of the best musicians of the time; some of his 1930s recordings feature the singer Billie Holiday. Wilson led a big band 1939–40 and a sextet 1940–46.

Wilson /wɪlsən/ (Thomas) Woodrow 1856–1924. 28th president of the USA 1913–21, a Democrat. He kept the USA out of World War I until 1917, and in Jan 1918 issued his 'Fourteen Points' as a basis for a just peace settlement. At the peace conference in Paris he secured the inclusion of the League of Nations in individual peace treaties, but

Wilson 28th US president Woodrow Wilson, who took the USA into World War I. He created the basis for a peace settlement and the League of Nations. An idealist, Wilson could not overturn the traditional isolationism of the USA, and he failed to obtain the Senate's acceptance of the treaty that set up the League of Nations.

these were not ratified by Congress, so the USA did not join the League. Nobel Peace Prize 1919.

Wilson, born in Virginia, became president of Princeton University 1902. In 1910 he became governor of New Jersey. Elected president 1912 against Theodore Roosevelt and William Taft, he initiated anti-trust legislation and secured valuable social reforms in his progressive 'New Freedom' programme. He strove to keep the USA neutral during World War I but the German U-boat campaign forced him to declare war 1917. In 1919 he suffered a stroke from which he never fully recovered.

Winchell /wɪntʃəl/ Walter 1897–1972. US journalist, born in New York. He was a columnist for the *New York Mirror* 1929–69, and his bitingly satiric writings were syndicated throughout the USA.

Windsor, House of official name of the British royal family since 1917, adopted in place of Saxe-Coburg-Gotha. Since 1960 those descendants of Elizabeth II not entitled to the prefix HRH (His/Her Royal Highness) have borne the surname Mountbatten-Windsor.

Windsor Duchess of. Title of Wallis Warfield →Simpson.

Windsor Duke of. Title of →Edward VIII.

Wingate /wɪŋgeɪt/ Orde Charles 1903–1944. British soldier. In 1936 he established a reputation for unorthodox tactics in Palestine. In World War II he served in the Middle East, and later led the Chindits, the 3rd Indian Division, in guerrilla operations against the Japanese army in Burma (now Myanmar).

Winterhalter /vɪntəhælta/ Franz Xavier 1805–1873. German portraitist. He became court painter to Grand Duke Leopold at Karlsruhe, then, in 1834, moved to Paris and enjoyed the patronage of European royalty.

Winterson /wɪntəsən/ Jeanette 1959– . English novelist. Her autobiographical first novel *Oranges Are Not the Only Fruit* 1985, humorously describes her upbringing as an Evangelical Pentecostalist in Lancashire, and her subsequent realisation of her homosexuality. Later novels include *The Passion* 1987, *Sexing the Cherry* 1989, and *Written On the Body* 1992.

Winthrop /wɪnθrəp/ John 1588–1649. American colonist and first governor of the Massachusetts Bay Colony. A devout Puritan and one of the founders of the Massachusetts Bay Company 1620 and served as Massachusetts governor or deputy governor until his death. He departed for New England with a large group of settlers 1630. He was a founder of the city of Boston the same year.

Born in England and educated at Cambridge University, Winthrop studied law at Gray's Inn and became a barrister 1628. Deeply conservative, he favoured the prosecution and banishment

of Anne →Hutchinson 1638. His *History of New England from 1630 to 1649* was published 1825.

Wise /waɪz/ Robert 1914– . US film director who began as a film editor. His debut was a horror film, *Curse of the Cat People* 1944; he progressed to such large-scale projects as *The Sound of Music* 1965 and *Star* 1968. His other films include *The Body Snatcher* 1945 and *Star Trek: The Motion Picture* 1979.

Wise /waɪz/ Stephen Samuel 1874–1949. Hungarian-born US religious leader. Ordained as a reform rabbi 1893, he served congregations in New York City 1893–1900 and Portland, Oregon, 1900–07, after which he became rabbi of the Free Synagogue in New York. He was president of the American Jewish Congress 1924–49.

Born in Budapest, Wise emigrated to the USA with his family 1875. Educated at the City College of New York, he received a PhD from Columbia University 1901. An ardent Zionist, he attended the Versailles Peace Conference 1919. His autobiography, *Challenging Years*, appeared 1949.

Wise /waɪz/ Thomas James 1859–1937. British bibliographer. He collected the Ashley Library of first editions, chiefly English poets and dramatists 1890–1930, acquired by the British Museum at his death, and made many forgeries of supposed privately printed first editions of Browning, Tennyson, and Swinburne.

Wiseman /waɪzmən/ Nicholas Patrick Stephen 1802–1865. British Catholic priest who became the first archbishop of Westminster 1850.

Wishart /wɪʃət/ George c. 1513–1546. Scottish Protestant reformer burned for heresy, who probably converted John →Knox.

Wister /wɪstə/ Owen 1860–1938. US novelist who created the genre of the Western. He was born in Philadelphia, a grandson of the British actress Fanny Kemble, and became known for stories of cowboys, including *The Virginian* 1902. He also wrote *Roosevelt: The Story of a Friendship 1880–1919* 1930, about his relationship with US president Theodore Roosevelt.

Witt /wɪt/ Johann de 1625–1672. Dutch politician, grand pensionary of Holland and virtual prime minister from 1653. His skilful diplomacy ended the Dutch Wars of 1652–54 and 1665–67, and in 1668 he formed a triple alliance with England and Sweden against Louis XIV of France. He was murdered by a rioting mob.

Witt /vɪt/ Katarina 1965– . German ice-skater. She was 1984 Olympic champion (representing East Germany) and by 1990 had won four world titles (1984–85, 1987–88) and six consecutive European titles (1983–88).

Wittgenstein /vɪtgənʃtaɪn/ Ludwig 1889–1951. Austrian philosopher. *Tractatus Logico-Philosophicus* 1922 postulated the 'picture theory' of language: that words represent things according to social agreement. He subsequently rejected this idea, and developed the idea that usage was more important than convention.

The picture theory said that it must be possible to break down a sentence into 'atomic propositions' whose elements stand for elements of the real world. After he rejected this idea, his later philosophy developed a quite different, anthropological view of language: words are used according to different rules in a variety of human activities – different 'language games' are played with them. The traditional philosophical problems arise through the assumption that words (like 'exist' in the sentence 'Physical objects do not really exist') carry a fixed meaning with them, independent of context.

He taught at Cambridge University, England, in the 1930s and 1940s. *Philosophical Investigations* 1953 and *On Certainty* 1969 were published posthumously.

During World War I he fought with the Austro-Hungarian army and was subsequently imprisoned in Italy to Aug 1919.

The limits of my language mean the limits of my world.

Ludwig Wittgenstein
Tractatus Logico-Philosophicus 1922

Wodehouse /ˈwʊdhaʊs/ P(elham) G(renville) 1881–1975. English novelist, a US citizen from 1955, whose humorous novels portray the accident-prone world of such characters as the socialite Bertie Wooster and his invaluable and impeccable manservant Jeeves, and Lord Emsworth of Blandings Castle with his prize pig, the Empress of Blandings.

Witt *Johann de Witt, Dutch 17th-century politician from a family traditionally opposed to the House of Orange. After resigning from office 1672 he was killed by a mob of angry Orange partisans.*

From 1906, Wodehouse also collaborated on the lyrics of Broadway musicals by Jerome Kern, Gershwin, and others. He spent most of his life in the USA. Staying in France 1941, during World War II, he was interned by the Germans; he made some humorous broadcasts from Berlin, which were taken amiss in Britain at the time, but he was later exonerated, and was knighted 1975. His work is admired for its style and geniality, and includes *Indiscretions of Archie* 1921, *Uncle Fred in the Springtime* 1939, and *Aunts Aren't Gentlemen* 1974.

Woffington /ˈwɒfɪŋtən/ Peg (Margaret) *c.* 1714–1760. Irish actress who played in Dublin as a child and made her debut at Covent Garden, London, 1740. She acted in many Restoration comedies, often taking male roles, such as Lothario in Rowe's *The Fair Penitent.*

Wöhler /ˈvøːlə/ Friedrich 1800–1882. German chemist, a student of Jöns →Berzelius, who in 1828 was the first person to synthesize an organic compound (urea) from an inorganic compound (ammonium cyanate). He also devised a method 1827 that isolated the metals aluminum, beryllium, yttrium, and titanium. from their ores.

Wolf /vɒlf/ Hugo (Filipp Jakob) 1860–1903. Austrian composer whose songs are in the German *Lieder* tradition. He also composed the opera *Der Corregidor* 1895 and orchestral works, such as *Italian Serenade* 1892.

Wolfe /wʊlf/ Gene 1931– . US writer known for the science-fiction series *The Book of the New Sun* 1980–83, with a Surrealist treatment of stock themes, and for the urban fantasy *Free, Live Free* 1985.

Wolfe /wʊlf/ James 1727–1759. British soldier who served in Canada and commanded a victorious expedition against the French general Montcalm in Québec on the Plains of Abraham, during which both commanders were killed. The British victory established their supremacy over Canada.

Wolfe fought at the battles of Dettingen, Falkirk, and Culloden. With the outbreak of the Seven Years' War (the French and Indian War in North America), he was posted to Canada and played a conspicuous part in the siege of the French stronghold of Louisburg 1758. He was promoted to major-general 1759.

Wolfe /wʊlf/ Thomas 1900–1938. US novelist. He wrote four long and hauntingly powerful autobiographical novels, mostly of the South: *Look Homeward, Angel* 1929, *Of Time and the River* 1935, *The Web and the Rock* 1939, and *You Can't Go Home Again* 1940 (the last two published posthumously).

I don't owe a penny to a single soul – not counting tradesmen, of course.

P G Wodehouse *My Man Jeeves*

Wolsey Cardinal Thomas Wolsey, son of a butcher and chaplain to Henry VII. He was in effectual control of England's foreign policy under Henry VIII until he fell from favour 1529. He founded Christ Church, Oxford, under the name of Cardinal's College.

Wolfe /wʊlf/ Tom. Pen name of Thomas Kennerly, Jr 1931– . US journalist and novelist. In the 1960s he was a founder of the 'New Journalism', which brought fiction's methods to reportage. Wolfe recorded US mores and fashions in pop-style essays in, for example, *The Kandy-Kolored Tangerine-Flake Streamline Baby* 1965. His sharp social eye is applied to the New York of the 1980s in his novel *The Bonfire of the Vanities* 1988.

Wolfe coined the term 'radical chic' in the late 1960s, reporting on a party held by New York socialites for the Black Panthers. His book *The Right Stuff* 1979, describing the US space programme, was later filmed. He has been a contributing editor of the US magazine *Esquire* since 1977.

Wolf-Ferrari /vɒlf feˈrɑːri/ Ermanno 1876–1948. Italian composer whose operas include *Il segreto di Susanna/Susanna's Secret* 1909 and the realistic tragedy *I gioielli di Madonna/The Jewels of the Madonna* 1911.

Wolfit /wʊlfɪt/ Donald 1902–1968. British actor and manager. He formed his own theatre company 1937, and excelled in the Shakespearean roles of Shylock and Lear, and Volpone (in Ben Jonson's play).

Wolfson /wʊlfsən/ Isaac 1897–1991. British store magnate and philanthropist, chair of Great Universal Stores from 1946. He established the Wolfson Foundation 1955 to promote health, education, and youth activities, founded Wolfson College, Cambridge, 1965, and (with the Ford Foundation) endowed Wolfson College, Oxford, 1966.

Wollaston /wʊləstən/ William 1766–1828. British chemist and physicist. He amassed a large fortune through his discovery in 1804 of how to make malleable platinum. He went on to discover the new elements palladium 1804 and rhodium 1805. He also contributed to optics through the invention of a number of ingenious and still useful measuring instruments.

Wollstonecraft /wʊlstənkrɑːft/ Mary 1759–1797. British feminist, member of a group of radical intellectuals called the English Jacobins, whose book *A Vindication of the Rights of Women* 1792 demanded equal educational opportunities for women. She married William Godwin and died giving birth to a daughter, Mary (later Mary →Shelley).

Wolseley /wʊlzli/ Garnet Joseph, 1st Viscount Wolseley 1833–1913. British field marshal who, as commander in chief 1895–1900, began modernizing the army.

Wolsey /wʊlzi/ Thomas *c.* 1475–1530. English cleric and politician. In Henry VIII's service from 1509, he became archbishop of York 1514, cardinal and lord chancellor 1515, and began the dissolution of the monasteries. His reluctance to further Henry's divorce from Catherine of Aragon, partly because of his ambition to be pope, led to his downfall 1529. He was charged with high treason 1530 but died before being tried.

Had I but served God as diligently as I have done the King, He would not have given me over in my grey hairs.

Thomas Wolsey
of his own career and sudden downfall

Wonder /wʌndə/ Stevie. Stage name of Steveland Judkins Morris 1950– . US pop musician, singer, and songwriter, associated with Motown Records. Blind from birth, he had his first hit, 'Fingertips', at the age of 12. Later hits, most of which he composed and sang, and on which he also played several instruments, include 'My Cherie Amour' 1973, 'Master Blaster (Jammin')' 1980, and the album *Innervisions* 1973.

Wood /wʊd/ Grant 1892–1942. US painter based mainly in his native Iowa. Though his work is highly stylized, he struck a note of hard realism in his studies of farmers, such as *American Gothic* 1930 (Art Institute, Chicago).

Wood /wʊd/ Haydn 1882–1959. British composer. A violinist, he wrote a violin concerto among other works, and is known for his songs, which include 'Roses of Picardy', associated with World War I.

Wood /wʊd/ Henry (Joseph) 1869–1944. English conductor, from 1895 until his death, of the London Promenade Concerts, now named after him.

He promoted a national interest in music and encouraged many young composers.

He studied at the Royal Academy of Music and became an organist and operatic conductor. As a composer he is remembered for the *Fantasia on British Sea Songs* 1905, which ends each Promenade season.

Wood /wʊd/ John *c.* 1705–1754. British architect, known as 'Wood of Bath' because of his many works in that city. Like many of his designs, Royal Crescent was executed by his son, also *John Wood* (1728–81).

Wood /wʊd/ Mrs Henry (née Ellen Price) 1814–1887. British novelist, a pioneer of crime fiction, who wrote the melodramatic *East Lynne* 1861.

Wood /wʊd/ Natalie. Stage name of Natasha Gurdin 1938–1981. US film actress who began as a child star. Her films include *Miracle on 34th Street* 1947, *Rebel Without a Cause* 1955, *The Searchers* 1956, and *Bob and Carol and Ted and Alice* 1969.

Woodforde /wʊdfəd/ James 1740–1803. British cleric who held livings in Somerset and Norfolk, and whose diaries 1758–1802 form a record of rural England.

Woodward /wʊdwəd/ Joanne 1930– . US actress, active in film, television, and theatre. She was directed by Paul Newman in the film *Rachel Rachel* 1968, and also starred in *The Three Faces of Eve* 1957, *They Might Be Giants* 1971, and *Harry and Son* 1984. She has appeared with Newman in several films, including *Mr and Mrs Bridge* 1990.

Woodward /wʊdwəd/ Robert 1917–1979. US chemist who worked on synthesizing a large number of complex molecules. These included quinine 1944, cholesterol 1951, chlorophyll 1960, and vitamin B12 1971. Nobel prize 1965.

Woolcott /wʊlkət/ Marion Post 1910–1990. US documentary photographer best known for her work for the Farm Security Administration (with Walker →Evans and Dorothea →Lange), showing the conditions of poor farmers in the late 1930s in Kentucky and the deep South.

Woolf /wʊlf/ Virginia (born Virginia Stephen) 1882–1941. English novelist and critic. Her first novel, *The Voyage Out* 1915, explored the tensions experienced by women who want marriage and a career. In *Mrs Dalloway* 1925 she perfected her 'stream of consciousness' technique. Among her later books are *To the Lighthouse* 1927, *Orlando* 1928, and *The Years* 1937, which considers the importance of economic independence for women.

Woollcott /wʊlkət/ Alexander 1887–1943. US theatre critic and literary figure. He was *The New York Times*'s theatre critic 1914–22, a regular contributor to *The New Yorker* from its inception 1925, and hosted the radio interview programme *Town Crier* 1929–42. He appeared on stage in *The Man Who Came to Dinner* 1939 as a character based on himself. Woollcott was a member of the Algonquin Hotel Round Table of wits in New York City, together with Robert Benchley and Dorothy Parker.

Woollett /wʊlɪt/ William 1735–1785. British engraver. In 1775 he was appointed engraver to George III.

Woolley /wʊli/ (Charles) Leonard 1880–1960. British archaeologist. He excavated at Carchemish in Syria, Tell el Amarna in Egypt, Atchana (the ancient Alalakh) on the Turkish-Syrian border, and Ur in Iraq. He is best remembered for the work on Ur, which he carried out for the British Museum and Pennsylvania University Museum 1922–29. Besides his scholarly excavation reports he published popular accounts of his work –*Ur of the Chaldees* 1929 and *Digging Up the Past* 1930 – which helped to promote archaeology to a non-specialist audience.

Woolman /wʊlmən/ John 1720–1772. American Quaker, born in Ancocas (now Rancocas), New Jersey. He was one of the first antislavery agitators and left an important *Journal*. He supported those who refused to pay a tax levied by Pennsylvania, to conduct the French and Indian War, on the grounds that it was inconsistent with pacifist principles.

Woolworth /wʊlwəθ/ Frank Winfield 1852–1919. US entrepreneur. He opened his first successful 'five and ten cent' store in Lancaster, Pennsylvania, in 1879, and, together with his brother C S Woolworth (1856–1947), built up a chain of similar stores throughout the USA, Canada, the UK, and Europe.

Woosnam Ian 1958– . Welsh golfer who, in 1987, became the first UK player to win the World Match-Play Championship. He has since won many tournaments, including the World Cup 1987, World Match-Play 1990, and US Masters 1991. Woosnam was Europe's leading money-winner in 1987 (as a result of winning the $1 million Sun City Open in South Africa) and again in 1990. He was ranked Number One in the world for 50 weeks in 1991–92.

Wootton /wʊtn/ Barbara Frances Wootton, Baroness Wootton of Abinger 1897–1988. British educationist and economist. She taught at London University, and worked in the fields of politics, media, social welfare, and penal reform. Her books include *Freedom under Planning* 1945 and *Social Science and Social Pathology* 1959. She was given a life peerage 1965.

Wordsworth /wɜːdzwəθ/ Dorothy 1771–1855. English writer. She lived with her brother William Wordsworth as a companion and support from 1795 until his death, and her many journals describing their life at Grasmere in the Lake District and their travels provided inspiration and material for his poetry.

Wordsworth *One of the greatest English poets, William Wordsworth, in a portrait by Benjamin Haydon. Wordsworth turned to nature for his inspiration, in particular to his native Lake District.*

Wordsworth /wɜːdzwəθ/ William 1770–1850. English Romantic poet. In 1797 he moved with his sister Dorothy to Somerset to be near →Coleridge, collaborating with him on *Lyrical Ballads* 1798 (which included 'Tintern Abbey'). From 1799 he lived in the Lake District, and later works include *Poems* 1807 (including 'Intimations of Immortality') and *The Prelude* (written by 1805, published 1850). He was appointed poet laureate in 1843.

Wordsworth was born in Cockermouth, Cumbria, and educated at Cambridge University. In 1791 he returned from a visit to France, having fallen in love with Marie-Anne Vallon, who bore him an illegitimate daughter. In 1802 he married Mary Hutchinson. *The Prelude* was written to form part of the autobiographical work *The Recluse*, never completed.

Worner /vɔːnə/ Manfred 1934– . German politician, NATO secretary-general from 1988. He was elected for the Conservative Christian Democratic Union (CDU) to the West German Bundestag (parliament) 1965 and, as a specialist in strategic affairs, served as defence minister under Chancellor Kohl 1982–88. A proponent of closer European military collaboration, he succeeded the British politician Peter Carrington as secretary general of NATO July 1988.

Worrall /wɒrəl/ Denis John 1935– . South African politician, member of the white opposition to apartheid. A co-leader of the Democratic Party (DP), he was elected to parliament 1989.

Worrall, a former academic and journalist, joined the National Party (NP) and was made

ambassador to London 1984–87. On his return to South Africa he resigned from the NP and in 1988 established the Independent Party (IP), which later merged with other white opposition parties to form the reformist DP, advocating dismantling of the apartheid system and universal adult suffrage.

Wotton /wʊtn/ Henry 1568–1639. English poet and diplomat under James I, provost of Eton public school from 1624. He defined an ambassador as 'an honest man sent to lie abroad for the good of his country'. *Reliquiae Wottonianae* 1651 includes the lyric 'You meaner beauties of the night'.

Wouvermans /waʊvəmæn/ family of Dutch painters, based in Haarlem. The brothers *Philips Wouvermans* (1619–1668), *Pieter Wouvermans* (1623–1682), and *Jan Wouvermans* (1629–1666) specialized in landscapes with horses and riders and in military scenes.

Wrangel /ræŋɡəl, ʀussian ˈvræŋɡɪl/ Ferdinand Petrovich, Baron von 1794–1870. Russian vice admiral and Arctic explorer, after whom Wrangel Island (Ostrov Vrangelya) in the Soviet Arctic is named.

Wrangel /ræŋɡəl, Russian ˈvræŋɡɪl/ Peter Nicolaievich, Baron von 1878–1928. Russian general, born in St Petersburg. He commanded a division of Cossacks in World War I, and in 1920, after succeeding Anton Denikin as commander in chief of the White Army, lost to the Bolsheviks in the Crimea.

Wray /reɪ/ Fay 1907– . US film actress who starred in *King Kong* 1933 after playing the lead in Erich von Stroheim's *The Wedding March* 1928, and starring in *Doctor X* 1932 and *The Most Dangerous Game* 1932.

Wren /ren/ Christopher 1632–1723. English architect, designer of St Paul's Cathedral, London, built 1675–1710; many London churches including St Bride's, Fleet Street, and St Mary-le-Bow, Cheapside; the Royal Exchange; Marlborough House; and the Sheldonian Theatre, Oxford.

Wren studied mathematics, and in 1660 became a professor of astronomy at Oxford University. His opportunity as an architect came after the Great Fire of London 1666. He prepared a plan for rebuilding the city, but it was not adopted. Instead, Wren was commissioned to rebuild 51 City churches and St Paul's Cathedral. The west towers of Westminster Abbey, often attributed to him, were the design of his pupil →Hawksmoor.

Wren /ren/ P(ercival) C(hristopher) 1885–1941. British novelist. Drawing on his experiences in the French and Indian armies, he wrote adventure novels including *Beau Geste* 1924, dealing with the Foreign Legion.

Wright /raɪt/ Frank Lloyd 1869–1959. US architect who rejected Neo-Classicist styles for 'organic architecture', in which buildings reflected their natural surroundings. Among his buildings are his Wisconsin home Taliesin East 1925; Falling Water, near Pittsburgh, Pennsylvania, 1936, a house built straddling a waterfall; and the Guggenheim Museum, New York, 1959.

Wright also designed buildings in Japan from 1915 to 1922, most notably the Imperial Hotel in Tokyo 1922. In 1938 he built his winter home in the Arizona desert, Taliesin West, and established an architectural community there. He always designed the interiors and furnishings for his projects, to create a total environment for his patrons.

The physician can bury his mistakes, but the architect can only advise his clients to plant vines.

Frank Lloyd Wright,
New York Times Magazine 1953

Wright /raɪt/ Joseph 1734–1797. British painter, known as *Wright of Derby* from his birthplace. He painted portraits, landscapes, and scientific experiments. His work is often dramatically lit – by fire, candlelight, or even volcanic explosion.

Several of his subjects are highly original: for example *The Experiment on a Bird in the Air Pump* 1768 (National Gallery, London). His portraits include the reclining figure of *Sir Brooke Boothby* 1781 (Tate Gallery, London).

Wright /raɪt/ Joseph 1855–1930. English philologist. He was professor of comparative philology at Oxford University 1901–25, and recorded English

Wren Sir Christopher Wren began designing buildings as an amateur during his early career as professor of astronomy at Oxford. His various solutions to the rebuilding of London churches, and St Paul's Cathedral, after the Great Fire, demonstrate great ingenuity as well as an enduring aesthetic quality.

local speech in his six-volume *English Dialect Dictionary* 1896–1905.

Wright /raɪt/ Judith 1915– . Australian poet, author of *The Moving Image* 1946 and *Alive* 1972.

Wright /raɪt/ Peter 1917– . British intelligence agent. His book *Spycatcher* 1987, written after his retirement, caused an international stir when the British government tried unsuccessfully to block its publication anywhere in the world because of its damaging revelations about the secret service.

Wright joined MI5 in 1955 and was a consultant to the director-general 1973–76, when he retired. In *Spycatcher* he claimed, among other things, that Roger →Hollis, head of MI5 (1955–65), had been a Soviet double agent; this was later denied by the KGB.

Wright /raɪt/ Richard 1908–1960. US novelist. He was one of the first to depict the condition of black people in 20th-century US society with *Native Son* 1940 and the autobiography *Black Boy* 1945.

Between 1932 and 1944 he was active in the Communist Party. Shortly thereafter he became a permanent expatriate in Paris. His other works include *White Man, Listen!* 1957, originally a series of lectures.

Wright /raɪt/ Sewall 1889–1988. US geneticist and statistician. During the 1920s he helped modernize Charles →Darwin's theory of evolution, using statistics to model the behaviour of populations of genes.

Wright's work on genetic drift centred on a phenomenon occurring in small isolated colonies where the chance disappearance of some types of gene leads to evolution without the influence of natural selection.

Wundt /vʊnt/ Wilhelm Max 1832–1920. German physiologist who regarded psychology as the study of internal experience or consciousness. His main psychological method was introspection; he also studied sensation, perception of space and time, and reaction times.

Wyatt /waɪət/ James 1747–1813. English architect, contemporary of the Adam brothers, who designed in the Neo-Gothic style. His overenthusiastic 'restorations' of medieval cathedrals earned him the nickname 'Wyatt the Destroyer'.

Wyatt /waɪət/ Thomas *c.* 1503–1542. English poet. He was employed on diplomatic missions by Henry VIII, and in 1536 was imprisoned for a time in the Tower of London, suspected of having been the lover of Henry's second wife, Anne Boleyn. In 1541 Wyatt was again imprisoned on charges of treason. With the Earl of Surrey, he pioneered the sonnet in England.

Wyatville /waɪətvɪl/ Jeffrey. Adopted name of Jeffrey Wyatt 1766–1840. English architect who remodelled Windsor Castle, Berkshire. He was a nephew of the architect James Wyatt.

Wycherley /wɪtʃəli/ William 1640–1710. English Restoration playwright. His first comedy *Love in a Wood* won him court favour 1671, and later bawdy works include *The Country Wife* 1675 and *The Plain Dealer* 1676.

Wycliffe /wɪklɪf/ John *c.* 1320–1384. English religious reformer. Allying himself with the party of John of Gaunt, which was opposed to ecclesiastical influence at court, he attacked abuses in the church, maintaining that the Bible rather than the church was the supreme authority. He criticized such fundamental doctrines as priestly absolution, confession, and indulgences, and set disciples to work on translating the Bible into English.

Having studied at Oxford University, he became Master of Balliol College there, and sent out bands of travelling preachers. He was denounced as a heretic, but died peacefully at Lutterworth.

Wyeth /waɪəθ/ Andrew (Newell) 1917– . US painter. His portraits and landscapes, usually in watercolour or tempera, are naturalistic, minutely detailed, and often have a strong sense of the isolation of the countryside: for example, *Christina's World* 1948 (Museum of Modern Art, New York).

Wyler /waɪlə/ William 1902–1981. German-born film director who lived in the USA from 1922. He directed *Wuthering Heights* 1939, *Mrs Miniver* 1942, *Ben-Hur* 1959, and *Funny Girl* 1968, among others.

Wylie lived in 19th century. An Aborigine of the King George Sound tribe who accompanied the explorer →Eyre on his 1840–41 expedition. He was Eyre's sole companion for much of the journey, saving him from probable death.

Wyndham /wɪndəm/ John. Pen name of John Wyndham Parkes Lucas Beynon Harris 1903–1969. English science-fiction writer who wrote *The Day of the Triffids* 1951, *The Chrysalids* 1955, and *The Midwich Cuckoos* 1957. A recurrent theme in his work is people's response to disaster, whether caused by nature, aliens, or human error.

Wynne-Edwards /wɪn'edwədz/ Vera 1906– . English zoologist who argued that animal behaviour is often altruistic and that animals will behave for the good of the group, even if this entails individual sacrifice. Her study *Animal Dispersal in Relation to Social Behaviour* was published 1962.

The theory that animals are genetically programmed to behave for the good of the species has since fallen into disrepute. From this dispute grew a new interpretation of animal behaviour, seen in the work of biologist E O →Wilson.

Wyss Johann David 1743–1818. Swiss author of the children's classic *Swiss Family Robinson* 1812–13.

Xavier, St Francis /ˈzeɪvɪə/ 1506–1552. Spanish Jesuit missionary. He went to the Portuguese colonies in the East Indies, arriving at Goa 1542. He was in Japan 1549–51, establishing a Christian mission that lasted for 100 years. He returned to Goa in 1552, and sailed for China, but died of fever there. He was canonized 1622.

Xenophon /ˈzenəfən/ *c.* 430–354 BC. Greek historian, philosopher, and soldier. He was a disciple of →Socrates (described in Xenophon's *Symposium*). In 401 he joined a Greek mercenary army aiding the Persian prince Cyrus, and on the latter's death took command. His *Anabasis* describes how he led 10,000 Greeks on a 1,600-km/1,000-mile march home across enemy territory. His other works include *Memorabilia* and *Apology*.

> *The most pleasing of all sounds, that of your own praise.*
>
> **Xenophon** *Heiro*

> *I am moved to pity, when I think of the brevity of human life, seeing that of all this host of men not one will be alive in a hundred years' time.*
>
> **Xerxes** on surveying his army

Xerxes /ˈzɜːksiːz/ *c.* 519–465 BC. King of Persia from 485 BC when he succeeded his father Darius and continued the Persian invasion of Greece. In 480, at the head of an army of some 400,000 men and supported by a fleet of 800 ships, he crossed the Hellespont strait (now the Dardanelles) over a bridge of boats. He defeated the Greek fleet at Artemisium and captured and burned Athens, but Themistocles retaliated by annihilating the Persian fleet at Salamis and Xerxes was forced to retreat. He spent his later years working on a grandiose extension of the capital Persepolis and was eventually murdered in a court intrigue.

Yahya Khan /jɑːjə 'kɑːn/ Agha Muhammad 1917–1980. Pakistani president 1969–71. His mishandling of the Bangladesh separatist issue led to civil war, and he was forced to resign.

Yahya Khan fought with the British army in the Middle East during World War II, escaping German capture in Italy. Later, as Pakistan's chief of army general staff, he supported General Ayub Khan's 1958 coup and in 1969 became military ruler. Following defeat by India 1971, he resigned and was under house arrest 1972–75.

Yalow /jæləʊ/ Rosalyn Sussman 1921– . US physicist who developed radioimmunoassay (RIA), a technique for detecting minute quantities of hormones present in the blood. It can be used to discover a range of hormones produced in the hypothalamic region of the brain. She shared the Nobel Prize for Medicine 1977 with Roger Guillemin (1924–) and Andrew Schally (1926–).

Yamagata /jæməˈɡɑːtə/ Aritomo 1838–1922. Japanese soldier, politician, and prime minister 1889–93 and 1898. As war minister 1873 and chief of the imperial general staff 1878, he was largely responsible for the modernization of the military system. He returned as chief of staff during the Russo-Japanese War 1904–05 and remained an influential political figure until he was disgraced in 1921 for having meddled in the marriage arrangements of the crown prince.

Yamamoto /jæməˈməʊtəʊ/ Gombei 1852–1933. Japanese admiral and politician. As prime minister 1913–14, he began Japanese expansion into China and initiated political reforms. He became premier again 1923 but resigned the following year.

Yamamoto /jæməˈməʊtəʊ/ Kansai 1944– . Japanese fashion designer who opened his own house 1971. The presentation of his catwalk shows made him famous, with dramatic clothes in an exciting atmosphere. He blends the powerful and exotic designs of traditional Japanese dress with Western sportswear to create a unique, abstract style.

Yamamoto /jæməˈməʊtəʊ/ Yohji 1943– . Japanese fashion designer who formed his own company 1972 and showed his first collection 1976. He is an uncompromising, nontraditionalist designer who swathes and wraps the body in unstructured, loose, voluminous garments.

Yanayev /jəˈnaɪev/ Gennady 1937– . Soviet communist politician, leader of the failed Aug 1991 anti-Gorbachev coup, after which he was arrested and charged with treason. He was vice president of the USSR 1990–91.

Yanayev rose in the ranks as a traditional, conservative-minded communist bureaucrat to become member of the Politburo and Secretariat, and head of the official Soviet trade-union movement from 1990. In Dec 1990 he was President Gorbachev's surprise choice for vice president. In Aug 1991, however, Yanayev became titular head of the eight-member 'emergency committee' that launched the reactionary coup against Gorbachev.

Yang Shangkun /jæŋ ʃæŋˈkʊn/ 1907– . Chinese communist politician. He held a senior position in the party 1956–66 but was demoted during the Cultural Revolution. He was rehabilitated 1978, elected to the Politburo 1982, and to the position of state president 1988.

The son of a wealthy Sichuan landlord and a veteran of the Long March 1934–35 and the war against Japan 1937–45, Yang rose in the ranks of the Chinese Communist Party (CCP) before being purged for alleged revisionism in the Cultural Revolution. He is viewed as a trusted supporter of Deng Xiaoping.

Yeats /jeɪts/ Jack Butler 1871–1957. Irish painter and illustrator. His vivid scenes of Irish life, for example *Back from the Races* 1925 (Tate Gallery, London), and Celtic mythology reflected a new consciousness of Irish nationalism. He was the brother of the poet W B Yeats.

Yeats /jeɪts/ W(illiam) B(utler) 1865–1939. Irish poet. He was a leader of the Celtic revival and a founder of the Abbey Theatre in Dublin. His early work was romantic and lyrical, as in the poem 'The Lake Isle of Innisfree' and plays *The Countess Cathleen* 1892 and *The Land of Heart's Desire* 1894. His later books of poetry include *The Wild Swans at Coole* 1917 and *The Winding Stair* 1929. He was a senator of the Irish Free State 1922–28. Nobel Prize for Literature 1923.

Yeats was born in Dublin. His early poetry, such as *The Wind Among the Reeds* 1899, is romantically and exotically lyrical, and he drew on Irish legend for his poetic plays, including *Deirdre* 1907, but broke through to a new sharply resilient style with *Responsibilities* 1914. In his personal life there was also a break: the beautiful Maude Gonne, to whom many of his poems had been addressed, refused to marry him, and in 1917 he married Georgie Hyde-Lees, whose work as a medium reinforced his leanings towards mystic symbolism, as in the prose work *A Vision* 1925 and 1937. Among his later volumes of verse are *The Tower* 1928 and *Last Poems and Two Plays* 1939. His other prose works include *Autobiographies* 1926, *Dramatis Personae* 1936, *Letters* 1954, and *Mythologies* 1959.

You can erect a throne of bayonets, but you cannot sit on it for long.

Boris Yeltsin 20 Aug 1991

Yeltsin /ˈjeltsɪn/ Boris Nikolayevich 1931– . Russian politician, president of the Russian Soviet Federative Socialist Republic (RSFSR) 1990–91, and president and prime minister of the newly independent Russian Federation from 1991. He directed the Federation's secession from the USSR and the formation of a new, decentralized confederation, the Commonwealth of Independent States (CIS), with himself as the most powerful leader. He established himself internationally as an advocate of nuclear disarmament and domestically as a proponent of price deregulation and accelerated privatization. Faced with severe economic problems, civil unrest, and threats of a communist backlash, he has consistently requested international aid to bring his country out of recession.

Born in Sverdlovsk (now Ekaterinburg), Yeltsin began his career in the construction industry. He joined the Communist Party of the Soviet Union (CPSU) in 1961 and became district party leader. Brought to Moscow by Mikhail Gorbachev and Nikolai Ryzhkov in 1985, he was appointed secretary for construction and then, in Dec 1985, Moscow party chief. His demotion to the post of first deputy chair of the State Construction Committee Nov 1987 was seen as a blow to Gorbachev's perestroika initiative and a victory for the conservatives grouped around Yegor Ligachev. He was re-elected March 1989 with an 89% share of the vote, defeating an official Communist Party candidate, and was elected to the Supreme Soviet in May 1989. A supporter of the Baltic states in their calls for greater independence, Yeltsin demanded increasingly more radical economic reform. In 1990 he renounced his CPSU membership and was elected president of the RSFSR, the largest republic of the USSR. Advocating greater autonomy for the constituent republics within a federal USSR, Yeltsin prompted the Russian parliament in June 1990 to pass a decree giving the republic's laws precedence over those passed by the Soviet parliament. In April 1991, he was voted emergency powers by congress, enabling him to rule by decree, and two months later was popularly elected president. In the abortive Aug 1991 coup, Yeltsin, as head of a democratic 'opposition state' based at the Russian parliament building, played a decisive role, publicly condemning the usurpers and calling for the reinstatement of President Gorbachev. He was instrumental in the creation of the CIS and combined the offices of Russian president and prime minister to push through an ambitious but unpopular programme of price deregulation and accelerated privatization. As the economic situation deteriorated within Russia, his leadership came under increasing challenge. In Feb 1992 he met US president Bush for a summit in the USA pressing for further sweeping reductions in the superpowers' nuclear arsenals. In April 1992 Yeltsin persuaded 18 of the 20 autonomous republics in the Russian Federation to sign a federative treaty. In Dec 1992, in an attempt to prevent a rumoured hardline communist coup, Yeltsin appointed conservative Viktor Chernomyrdin to replace the radical Yegor Gaidar as prime minister, but bound Chernomyrdin to retain the reformist core of the earlier cabinet. In Jan 1993 Yeltsin signed the START II treaty with US president Bush in Moscow.

Yersin /jeəˈsæŋ/ Alexandre Emile Jean 1863–1943. Swiss bacteriologist who discovered the bubonic plague bacillus in Hong Kong 1894 and prepared a serum against it.

Yesenin /jɪˈseɪnɪn/ Sergei alternative form of →Esenin, Russian poet.

Yevele /ˈjiːvəli/ Henry died 1400. English architect, mason of the naves of Westminster Abbey (begun 1375), Canterbury Cathedral, and Westminster Hall (1394), with its majestic hammerbeam roof.

Yevtushenko /jevtʊˈʃeŋkəʊ/ Yevgeny Aleksandrovich 1933– . Soviet poet, born in Siberia. He aroused controversy with his anti-Stalinist 'Stalin's Heirs' 1956, published with Khrushchev's support, and 'Babi Yar' 1961. His autobiography was published 1963.

Yonge /jʌŋ/ Charlotte M(ary) 1823–1901. English novelist. Her books deal mainly with family life, and are influenced by the High Church philosophy of the Oxford Movement. She published *The Heir of Redclyffe* 1853.

York /jɔːk/ English dynasty founded by Richard, Duke of York (1411–60). He claimed the throne through his descent from Lionel, Duke of Clarence (1338–1368), third son of Edward III, whereas the reigning monarch, Henry VI of the rival house of Lancaster, was descended from the fourth son. The argument was fought out in the Wars of the Roses. York was killed at the Battle of Wakefield 1460, but next year his son became King Edward IV, in turn succeeded by his son Edward V and then by his brother Richard III, with whose death at Bosworth the line ended. The Lancastrian victor in that battle was crowned Henry VII and consolidated his claim by marrying Edward IV's eldest daughter, Elizabeth.

York /jɔːk/ Duke of. Title often borne by younger sons of British sovereigns, for example George V, George VI, and Prince →Andrew from 1986.

York /jɔːk/ Frederick Augustus, duke of York 1763–1827. Second son of George III. He was an unsuccessful commander in the Netherlands 1793–99 and British commander in chief 1798–1809.

The nursery rhyme about the 'grand old duke of York' who marched his troops up the hill and down again commemorates him, as does the Duke of York's column in Waterloo Place, London.

Yoshida /jʊˈʃiːdə/ Shigeru 1878–1967. Japanese politician who served as prime minister of Occupied Japan for most of the postwar 1946–54 period.

Young /jʌŋ/ Arthur 1741–1820. English writer and publicizer of the new farm practices associated with the agricultural revolution. When the Board of Agriculture was established 1792, Young was appointed secretary, and was the guiding force behind the production of a county-by-county survey of British agriculture.

His early works, such as *Farmer's Tour through the East of England* and *A Six Months' Tour through the North of England*, contained extensive comment and observations gathered during the course of a series of journeys around the country. He published the *Farmers' Calendar* 1771, and in 1784 began the *Annals of Agriculture*, which ran

Yonge English novelist Charlotte Yonge, whose works have a high moral tone and convey High Church teachings. Although her historical romances were only moderately popular, some of her novels – romantic chronicles of contemporary life – became bestsellers.

for 45 volumes, and contained contributions from many eminent farmers of the day.

Young /jʌŋ/ Brigham 1801–1877. US Mormon religious leader, born in Vermont. He joined the Mormon Church, or Church of Jesus Christ of Latter-day Saints, 1832, and three years later was appointed an apostle. After a successful recruiting mission in Liverpool, England, he returned to the USA and, as successor of Joseph Smith (who had been murdered), led the Mormon migration to the Great Salt Lake in Utah 1846, founded Salt Lake City, and headed the colony until his death.

Young /jʌŋ/ David Ivor (Baron Young of Graffham) 1932– . British Conservative politician, chair of the Manpower Services Commission (MSC) 1982–84, secretary for employment from 1985, trade and industry secretary 1987–89, when he retired from politics. He was subsequently criticized by a House of Commons select committee over aspects of the privatization of the Rover car company.

Young /jʌŋ/ Edward 1683–1765. English poet and dramatist. A country clergyman for much of his life, he wrote his principal work *Night Thoughts on Life, Death and Immortality* 1742–45 in defence of Christian orthodox thinking. His other works include dramatic tragedies, satires, and a long poem, *Resignation*, published 1726.

By night an atheist half believes in God.

Edward Young
Night Thoughts on Life, Death, and Immortality 1742–45

Young /jʌŋ/ John Watts 1930– . US astronaut. His first flight was on *Gemini 3* 1965. He landed on the Moon with *Apollo 16* 1972, and was commander of the first flight of the space shuttle *Columbia* 1981.

Young /jʌŋ/ Lester (Willis) 1909–1959. US tenor saxophonist and jazz composer. He was a major figure in the development of his instrument for jazz music from the 1930s and was an accompanist for the singer Billie Holiday, who gave him the nickname 'President', later shortened to 'Pres'.

Young /jʌŋ/ Neil 1945– . Canadian rock guitarist, singer, and songwriter, in the USA from 1966. His high, plaintive voice and loud, abrasive guitar make his work instantly recognizable, despite abrupt changes of style throughout his career. *Rust Never Sleeps* 1979 and *Arc Weld* 1991 (both with the group Crazy Horse) are among his best work. His album *Harvest Moon* 1992 reflected a return to the more mellow tones of *Harvest* 1972.

Young was a member of Buffalo Springfield, a hippie folk-rock group, 1966–68, and from 1969 a part-time member of Crosby, Stills, Nash, and Young, primarily a vocal-harmony group. He made his solo debut 1968 as a quirky acoustic folk singer, then in 1969 began working on and off with the rock group Crazy Horse. He has written pastiche rockabilly, tortured confessional songs, country music, political anthems, and more. *Freedom* 1989 marked a return to top form.

Young /jʌŋ/ Thomas 1773–1829. British physicist who revived the wave theory of light and identified the phenomenon of interference in 1801.

A child prodigy, he had mastered most European languages and many of the Eastern tongues by the age of 20. He had also absorbed the physics of Newton and the chemistry of Lavoisier. He further displayed his versatility by publishing an account of the Rosetta stone; the work played a crucial role in the stone's eventual decipherment by Jean François →Champollion.

Younghusband /ˈjʌŋhʌzbənd/ Francis 1863–1942. British soldier and explorer, born in India. He entered the army 1882 and 20 years later accompanied the mission that opened up Tibet. He wrote travel books on India and Central Asia and works on comparative religion.

Young Pretender nickname of →Charles Edward Stuart, claimant to the Scottish and English thrones.

Yourcenar /jʊəsəˈnɑː/ Marguerite. Pen name of Marguerite de Crayencour 1903–1987. French writer, born in Belgium. She first gained recognition as a novelist in France in the 1930s with books such as *La Nouvelle Euridyce/The New Euridyce* 1931. Her evocation of past eras and characters, exemplified in *Les Mémoires d'Hadrien/The Memoirs of Hadrian* 1951, brought her acclaim as a historical novelist. In 1939 she settled in the USA. In 1980 she became the first woman to be elected to the French Academy.

Ypres, 1st Earl of title of Sir John →French, British field marshal.

Yukawa /juːˈkɑːwə/ Hideki 1907–1981. Japanese physicist. In 1935 he discovered the strong nuclear force that binds protons and neutrons together in the atomic nucleus, and predicted the existence of the subatomic particle called the meson. He was awarded the Nobel Prize for Physics 1949.

Z

Zadkine /ˈzædkiːn/ Ossip 1890–1967. French Cubist sculptor, born in Russia, active in Paris from 1909. His art represented the human form in dramatic, semi-abstract terms, as in the monument *To a Destroyed City* 1953 (Rotterdam).

Zahir /zəˈhɪə/ ud-din Muhammad 1483–1530. First Great Mogul of India from 1526, called Babur (Arabic 'lion'). He was the great-grandson of the Mongol conqueror Tamerlane and, at the age of 12, succeeded his father, Omar Sheik Mirza, as ruler of Ferghana (Turkestan). In 1526 he defeated the emperor of Delhi at Panipat in the Punjab, captured Delhi and Agra (the site of the Taj Mahal), and established a dynasty that lasted until 1858.

Zahir Shah /zəˈhɪə ˈʃɑː/ Mohammed 1914– . King of Afghanistan 1933–73. Zahir, educated in Kabul and Paris, served in the government 1932–33 before being crowned king. He was overthrown 1973 by a republican coup and went into exile. He became a symbol of national unity for the Mujaheddin Islamic fundamendalist resistance groups.

In 1991 the Afghan government restored Zahir's citizenship and he prepared to return.

Zamenhof /ˈzæmənhɒf/ Lazarus Ludovik 1859–1917. Polish inventor of the international language Esperanto in 1887.

Zampieri /ˌzæmpiˈeəri/ Domenico. Italian Baroque painter, known as →Domenichino.

Zanzotto /zænˈzɒtəʊ/ Andrea 1921– . Italian poet. A teacher from the Veneto, he has published much verse, including the collection *La beltà/Beauty* 1968, with a strong metaphysical element.

Zapata /səˈpɑːtə/ Emiliano 1879–1919. Mexican Indian revolutionary leader. He led a revolt against dictator Porfirio Díaz (1830–1915) from 1911 under the slogan 'Land and Liberty', to repossess for the indigenous Mexicans the land taken by the Spanish. By 1915 he was driven into retreat, and was assassinated.

Zedekiah /ˌzedɪˈkaɪə/ last king of Judah 597–586 BC. Placed on the throne by Nebuchadnezzar, he rebelled, was forced to witness his sons' execution, then was blinded and sent to Babylon. The witness to these events was the prophet Jeremiah, who describes them in the Old Testament.

Zeeman /ˈzeɪmən/ Pieter 1865–1943. Dutch physicist who discovered 1896 that when light from certain elements, such as sodium or lithium (when heated), is passed through a spectroscope in the presence of a strong magnetic field, the spectrum splits into a number of distinct lines. His discovery, known as the *Zeeman effect*, won him a share of the 1902 Nobel Prize for Physics.

Zeffirelli /ˌzefɪˈreli/ Franco 1923– . Italian theatre, opera and film director, and stage designer, acclaimed for his stylish designs and lavish productions. His films include *La Traviata* 1983, *Otello* 1986, and *Hamlet* 1990.

Zeiss /zaɪs/ Carl 1816–1888. German optician. He opened his first workshop in Jena 1846, and in 1866 joined forces with Ernst Abbe (1840–1905) producing cameras, microscopes, and binoculars.

Zelenka /ˈzelɪŋkə/ Jan Dismas 1679–1745. Bohemian composer who worked at the court of Dresden and became director of church music 1729. His compositions were rediscovered in the 1970s.

Zemeckis Robert 1952– . US film director whose successes with *Back to the Future* 1985 and its sequels (1989 and 1990), and *Who Framed Roger Rabbit* 1988 have made him one of the most profitable and accomplished directors of mainstream Hollywood.

A protégé of Steven Spielberg, Zemeckis directed his first film *I Wanna Hold Your Hand* 1978, and had his first major hit with the adventure story *Romancing the Stone* 1984. *Who Framed Roger Rabbit* made elaborate use of live action and cartoon animation and displayed Zemeckis's immense showmanship. Among his other films is the black comedy *Death Becomes Her* 1992.

Zenger /ˈzeŋə/ John Peter 1697–1746. American colonial printer and newspaper editor. In 1733 he founded the *New York Weekly Journal* through which he publicized his opposition to New York governor William Cosby. In 1734 he was arrested for seditious libel. Acquitted by a jury in 1735, he published *A Brief Narrative of the Case and Trial of John Peter Zenger* 1736 and remained a spokesman for the principle of freedom of the press.

Born in Germany, Zenger emigrated to New York 1710 and was apprenticed to a printer. Establishing his own press 1726, Zenger became active in local political affairs.

Zenobia /zɪˈnəʊbɪə/ queen of Palmyra AD 266–272. She assumed the crown as regent for her sons, after the death of her husband Odaenathus, and in 272 was defeated at Emesa (now Homs) by Aurelian and taken captive to Rome.

Zeno of Citium /ˈziːnəʊ, ˈsɪtɪəm/ c. 335–262 BC. Greek founder of the stoic school of philosophy in Athens, about 300 BC.

To live in accordance with nature is to live in accordance with virtue.

Zeno of Citium

Zeno of Elea /ˈziːnəʊ, ˈelɪə/ c. 490–430 BC. Greek philosopher who pointed out several paradoxes that raised 'modern' problems of space and time. For example, motion is an illusion, since an arrow in flight must occupy a determinate space at each instant, and therefore must be at rest.

Zeppelin /ˈzepəlɪn, German ˈtsepəliːn/ Ferdinand, Count von Zeppelin 1838–1917. German airship pioneer. On retiring from the army 1891, he devoted himself to the study of aeronautics, and his first airship was built and tested 1900. During World War I a number of Zeppelin airships bombed England. They were also used for luxury passenger transport but the construction of hydrogen-filled airships with rigid keels was abandoned after several disasters in the 1920s and 1930s. Zeppelin also helped to pioneer large multi-engine bomber planes.

Zernike /ˈzeənɪkə/ Frits 1888–1966. Dutch physicist who developed the phase-contrast microscope 1935. Earlier microscopes allowed many specimens to be examined only after they had been transformed by heavy staining and other treatment. The phase-contrast microscope allowed living cells to be directly observed by making use of the difference in refractive indices between specimens and medium. He was awarded the Nobel Prize for Physics 1953.

Zhao Ziyang /dʒaʊ ˌdziːˈjæŋ/ 1918– . Chinese politician, prime minister 1980–87 and secretary of the Chinese Communist Party 1987–89. His reforms included self-management and incentives for workers and factories. He lost his secretaryship and other posts after the Tiananmen Square massacre in Beijing June 1989.

Zhao, son of a wealthy landlord from Henan province, joined the Communist Youth League 1932 and worked underground as a CCP official during the liberation war 1937–49. He rose to prominence in the party in Guangdong from 1951. As a supporter of the reforms of Liu Shaoqi, he was dismissed during the 1966–69 Cultural Revolution, paraded through Canton in a dunce's cap, and sent to Inner Mongolia.

He was rehabilitated by Zhou Enlai 1973 and sent to China's largest province, Sichuan, as first party secretary 1975. Here he introduced radical and successful market-oriented rural reforms. Deng Xiaoping had him inducted into the Politburo 1977. After six months as vice premier, Zhao was appointed prime minister 1980 and assumed, in addition, the post of CCP general secretary Jan 1987. His economic reforms were criticized for causing inflation, and his liberal views of the pro-democracy demonstrations that culminated in the student occupation of Tiananmen Square led to his downfall.

Zhelev Zhelyu 1935– . Bulgarian politician, president from 1990. In 1989 he became head of the opposition Democratic Forces coalition. He is a proponent of market-centred economic reform and social peace.

The son of peasants, he became professor of philosophy at Sofia University. He was a member of the Bulgarian Communist Party 1961–65, when he was expelled for his criticisms of Lenin. He was made president of Bulgaria 1990 after the demise of the 'reform communist' regime, and was directly elected to the post 1992.

Zhivkov /ˈʒɪvkɒf/ Todor 1911– . Bulgarian Communist Party leader 1954–89, prime minister 1962–71, president 1971–89. His period in office was one of caution and conservatism. In 1991 he was tried for gross embezzlement.

Zhivkov, a printing worker, joined the BCP 1932 and was active in the resistance 1941–44. After the war, he was elected to the National Assembly and soon promoted into the BCP secretariat and Politburo. As BCP first secretary, Zhivkov became the dominant political figure in Bulgaria after the death of Vulko Chervenkov 1956. Zhivkov was elected to the new post of state president 1971 and lasted until the Eastern bloc upheavals of 1989. In 1990 he was charged with embezzlement during his time in office. His trial, which began Feb 1991, was the first in Europe of an ousted communist leader.

Zhou Enlai /dʒəʊ ˌenˈlaɪ/ or *Chou En-lai* 1898–1976. Chinese politician. Zhou, a member of the Chinese Communist Party (CCP) from the 1920s, was prime minister 1949–76 and foreign minister 1949–58. He was a moderate Maoist and weathered the Cultural Revolution. He played a key role in foreign affairs.

Born into a declining mandarin gentry family near Shanghai, Zhou studied in Japan and Paris, where he became a founder member of the overseas branch of the CCP. He adhered to the Moscow line of urban-based revolution in China, organizing communist cells in Shanghai and an abortive uprising in Nanchang 1927. In 1935 Zhou supported the election of Mao Zedong as CCP leader and remained a loyal ally during the next 40 years. He served as liaison officer 1937–46 between the CCP and Chiang Kai-shek's nationalist Guomindang government. In 1949 he became prime minister, an office he held until his death Jan 1976.

Zhou, a moderator between the opposing camps of Liu Shaoqi and Mao Zedong, restored orderly progress after the Great Leap Forward (1958–60) and the Cultural Revolution (1966–69), and was the architect of the Four Modernizations programme 1975. Abroad, Zhou sought to foster Third World unity at the Bandung Conference 1955, averted an outright border confrontation with the USSR by negotiation with Prime Minister Kosygin 1969, and was the principal advocate of détente with the USA during the early 1970s.

Zhu De /dʒuː ˈdeɪ/ or *Chu Teh* 1886–1976. Chinese Red Army leader from 1931. He devised the tactic of mobile guerrilla warfare and organized the Long March to Shaanxi 1934–36. He was made a marshal 1955.

The son of a wealthy Sichuan landlord, Zhu served in the Chinese Imperial Army before supporting Sun Yat-sen in the 1911 revolution. He studied communism in Germany and Paris 1922–25 and joined the Chinese Communist Party (CCP) on his return, becoming commander in chief of the Red Army. Working closely with Mao Zedong, Zhu organized the Red Army's Jiangxi break-out 1931 and led the 18th Route Army during the liberation war 1937–49. He served as head of state (chair of the Standing Committee of the National People's Congress) 1975–76.

Zhukov /ˈʒuːkɒv/ Georgi Konstantinovich 1896–1974. Marshal of the USSR in World War II and minister of defence 1955–57. As chief of staff from 1941, he defended Moscow 1941, counterattacked at Stalingrad (now Volgograd) 1942, organized the relief of Leningrad (now St Petersburg) 1943, and led the offensive from the Ukraine March 1944 which ended in the fall of Berlin.

Zhukov joined the Bolsheviks and the Red Army 1918 and led a cavalry regiment in the Civil War 1918–20. His army defeated the Japanese forces in Mongolia 1939. At the end of World War II, he headed the Allied delegation that received the German surrender, and subsequently commanded the Soviet occupation forces in Germany. Under the Khrushchev regime he was denounced 1957 for obstructing party work and encouraging a Zhukov cult, but was restored 1965.

Zia ul-Haq /zɪə ʊl ˈhæk/ Mohammad 1924–1988. Pakistani general, in power from 1977 until his death, probably an assassination, in an aircraft explosion. He became army chief of staff 1976, led the military coup against Zulfikar Ali →Bhutto 1977, and became president 1978. Zia introduced a fundamentalist Islamic regime and restricted political activity.

Zia was a career soldier from a middle-class Punjabi Muslim family. As army chief of staff, his opposition to the Soviet invasion of Afghanistan 1979 drew support from the USA, but his refusal to commute the death sentence imposed on Zulfikar Ali Bhutto was widely condemned. He lifted martial law 1985.

Ziegler /ˈtsiːɡlə/ Karl 1898–1973. German organic chemist. In 1963 he shared the Nobel Prize for Chemistry with Giulio Natta of Italy for his work on the chemistry and technology of large polymers. He combined simple molecules of the gas ethylene (ethene) into the long-chain plastic polyethylene (polyethene).

Zinneman /ˈtsɪnəmæn/ Fred(erick) 1907– . Austrian film director, in the USA from 1921, latterly in the UK. His films include *High Noon* 1952, *The Nun's Story* 1959, *The Day of the Jackal* 1973, and *Five Days One Summer* 1982.

Zinoviev /zɪˈnɒvief/ Alexander 1922– . Soviet philosopher whose satire on the USSR, *The Yawning Heights* 1976, led to his exile 1978. *The Reality of Communism* 1984 outlined the argument that communism is the natural consequence of masses of people living under deprived conditions, and thus bound to expand.

Zinoviev /zɪˈnɒvief/ Grigory 1883–1936. Russian communist politician whose name was attached to a forgery, the *Zinoviev letter*, inciting Britain's communists to rise, which helped to topple the Labour government 1924.

A prominent Bolshevik, Zinoviev returned to Russia 1917 with Lenin and played a leading part in the Revolution. He became head of the Communist International 1919. As one of the 'Old Bolsheviks', he was seen by Stalin as a threat. He was accused of complicity in the murder of the Bolshevik leader Sergei Kirov 1934, and shot.

Zi Xi /ˈziː ˈtʃiː/ or *Tz'u-hsi* 1836–1908. Dowager empress of China. She was presented as a concubine to the emperor Hsien-feng. On his death 1861 she became regent for her son T"ung Chih and, when he died 1875, for her nephew Guang Xu (1871–1908).

Zoë /ˈzəʊi/ c. 978–1050. Byzantine empress who ruled from 1028 until 1050. She gained the title by marriage to the heir apparent Romanus III Argyrus, but was reputed to have poisoned him (1034) in order to marry her lover Michael. He died 1041 and Zoë and her sister Theodora were proclaimed joint empresses. Rivalry led to Zoë marrying Constantine IX Monomachus with whom she reigned until her death.

Zoffany /ˈzɒfəni/ Johann 1733–1810. British portrait painter, born in Germany, based in London from about 1761. Under the patronage of George III he painted many portraits of the royal family. He spent several years in Florence (1770s) and India (1780s).

Zog /zɒɡ/ Ahmed Beg Zogu 1895–1961. King of Albania 1928–39. He became prime minister of Albania 1922, president of the republic 1925, and proclaimed himself king 1928. He was driven out by the Italians 1939 and settled in England.

Zola French novelist and leading exponent of naturalism in literature Émile Zola. Zola's reforming zeal led him to defend Alfred Dreyfus, who was wrongly convicted of spying, in his famous letter J'accuse.

Zola /ˈzəʊlə/ Émile Edouard Charles Antoine 1840–1902. French novelist and social reformer. With *La Fortune des Rougon/The Fortune of the Rougons* 1867 he began a series of some 20 naturalistic novels, portraying the fortunes of a French family under the Second Empire. They include *Le Ventre de Paris/The Underbelly of Paris* 1873, *Nana* 1880, and *La Débâcle/The Debacle* 1892. In 1898 he published *J'accuse/I Accuse*, a pamphlet indicting the persecutors of →Dreyfus, for which he was prosecuted for libel but later pardoned.

Born in Paris, Zola was a journalist and clerk until his *Contes à Ninon/Stories for Ninon* 1864 enabled him to devote himself to literature. Some of the titles in *La Fortune des Rougon* series are *La Faute de l'Abbé Mouret/The Simple Priest* 1875, *L'Assommoir/Drunkard* 1878, *Germinal* 1885, and *La Terre/Earth* 1888. Among later novels are the trilogy *Trois Villes/Three Cities* 1894–98, and *Fécondité/Fecundity* 1899.

Zoroaster /ˌzɒrəʊˈæstə/ or *Zarathustra* 6th century BC. Persian prophet and religious teacher, founder of Zoroastrianism. Zoroaster believed that he had seen God, Ahura Mazda, in a vision. His first vision came at the age of 30 and, after initial rejection and violent attack, he converted King Vishtaspa. Subsequently, his teachings spread rapidly, becoming the official religion of the king-

dom. According to tradition, Zoroaster was murdered at the age of 70 while praying at the altar.

Zorrilla y Moral /θʊˈriːljə/ José 1817–1893. Spanish poet and playwright. Born in Valladolid, he based his plays chiefly on national legends, such as the *Don Juan Tenorio* 1844.

Zsigmondy /ˈʃɪgmɒndi/ Richard 1865–1929. Austrian chemist who devised and built an ultra-microscope in 1903. The microscope's illumination was placed at right angles to the axis. (In a conventional microscope the light source is placed parallel to the instrument's axis.) Zsigmondy's arrangement made it possible to observe gold particles with a diameter of 10-millionth of a millimetre. He received the Nobel Prize for Chemistry 1925.

Zurbarán /ˌθʊəbəˈræn/ Francisco de 1598–1664. Spanish painter, based in Seville. He painted religious subjects in a powerful, austere style, often focusing on a single figure in prayer.

Zurbarán used deep contrasts of light and shade to create an intense spirituality in his works and received many commissions from religious orders in Spain and South America. During the 1640s the softer, sweeter style of Murillo displaced Zurbarán's art in public favour in Seville, and in 1658 he moved to Madrid.

Zweig /tsvaɪk/ Arnold 1887–1968. German novelist, playwright, and poet. He is remembered for his realistic novel of a Russian peasant in the German army *Der Streit um den Sergeanten Grischa/The Case of Sergeant Grischa* 1927.

Zweig /tsvaɪk/ Stefan 1881–1942. Austrian writer, author of plays, poems, and many biographies of writers (Balzac, Dickens) and historical figures (Marie Antoinette, Mary Stuart). He and his wife, exiles from the Nazis from 1934, despaired at what they saw as the end of civilization and culture and committed suicide in Brazil.

Zwicky Fritz 1898–1974. Bulgarian-born Swiss astronomer who lived in the USA from 1925. He was professor of physics at the California Institute of Technology (Caltech) from 1927 until his retirement 1968. In 1934, he predicted the existence of neutron stars and, together with Walter Baade, named supernovae. He discovered 18 supernovae in total, and determined that cosmic rays originated in them.

Zwingli /ˈzwɪŋgli, German ˈtsvɪŋli/ Ulrich 1484–1531. Swiss Protestant, born in St Gallen. He was ordained a Roman Catholic priest 1506, but by 1519 was a Reformer and led the Reformation in Switzerland with his insistence on the sole authority of the Scriptures. He was killed in a skirmish at Kappel during a war against the cantons that had not accepted the Reformation.

Zworykin Vladimir Kosma 1889–1982. Russian-born US electronics engineer, in the USA from 1919. He invented a television camera tube and the electron microscope.

INDEX

Index Contents

Index by category

Architects

British writers

Classical writers

Classical composers, musicians and singers

Craft and Design

Dancers and choreographers

Painters and sculptors

Photographers

Popular composers musicians and singers

Writers in English
(not British or American)

POLITICS AND HISTORY

African and Oriental figures

Ancient history figures

Archaeologists

British and Commonwealth figures

Historians

Acton, John Emerich Edward Dalberg-Acton, 1st Baron Acton 1834–1902.
Adams, Henry Brooks 1838–1918.
Âli, Mustafa 1541–1600.
Anna Comnena 1083–after 1148.
Bancroft, George 1800–1891.
Barzun, Jacques Martin 1907–.
Beard, Charles Austin 1874–1948.
Bede c. 673–735.
Braudel, Fernand 1902–1985.
Breuil, Henri 1877–1961.
Bryant, Arthur 1899–1985.
Burckhardt, Jacob 1818–1897.
Burnet, Gilbert 1643–1715.
Carlyle, Thomas 1795–1881.
Christine de Pisan 1364–1430.
Dion Cassius AD 150–235.
Erim, Kenan Tevfig 1929–1990.
Froude, James Anthony 1818–1894.
Gibbon, Edward 1737–1794.
Giraldus Cambrensis, c. 1146–1220.
Guizot, François Pierre Guillaume 1787–1874.
Hallam, Henry 1777–1859.
Herodotus c. 484–424 BC.
Holinshed, Ralph c. 1520–c. 1580.
John of Salisbury c. 1115–1180.
Joinville, Jean, Sire de Joinville 1224–1317.
Josephus, Flavius AD 37–c. 100.
Kinglake, Alexander William 1809–1891.
Kuhn, Thomas S 1922–.
Lang, Andrew 1844–1912.
Livy, Titus Livius 59 BC–AD 17.
Lopes, Fernão c. 1380–1460.
Macaulay, Thomas Babington, Baron Macaulay 1800–1859.
Mahan, Alfred Thayer 1840–1914.
Michelet, Jules 1798–1874.
Mommsen, Theodor 1817–1903.
Montesquieu, Charles Louis de Secondat, baron de la Brède 1689–1755.
Nennius c. 800.
Newbolt, Henry John 1862–1938.
Newman, John Henry 1801–1890.
Niebuhr, Barthold Georg 1776–1831.
Parkinson, Cyril Northcote 1909–.
Parkman, Francis 1823–1893.
Pliny the Elder, (Gaius Plinius Secundus) c. AD 23–79.
Polybius c. 201–120 BC.
Prescott, William Hickling 1796–1859.
Ranke, Leopold von 1795–1886.
Rowse, A(lfred) L(eslie) 1903–.
Sallust, Gaius Sallustius Crispus 86–c. 34 BC.
Schiller, Johann Christoph Friedrich von 1759–1805.
Schlesinger, Arthur Meier, Jr 1917–.
Shirer, William L(awrence) 1904–.
Suetonius, (Gaius Suetonius Tranquillus) c. AD 69–140.
Suger c. 1081–1151.
Tacitus, Publius Cornelius c. AD 55–c. 120.
Taine, Hippolyte Adolphe 1828–1893.
Taylor, A(lan) J(ohn) P(ercivale) 1906–1990.

Thiers, Louis Adolphe 1797–1877.
Thucydides c. 455–400 BC.
Toynbee, Arnold 1852–1883.
Toynbee, Arnold Joseph 1889–1975.
Treitschke, Heinrich von 1834–1896.
Trevelyan, George Macaulay 1876–1962.
Trevelyan, George Otto 1838–1928.
Turner, Frederick Jackson 1861–1932.
Vasari, Giorgio 1511–1574.
Villehardouin, Geoffroy de c. 1160–1213.
Wedgwood, C(icely) V(eronica) 1910–.
William of Malmesbury c. 1080–c. 1143.
Xenophon c. 430–354 BC.

Latin American figures

Alberdi, Juan Bautista 1810–1884.
Alessandri Palma, Arturo 1868–1950.
Alfaro, Eloy 1842–1912.
Allende, Salvador 1908–1973.
Almagro, Deigo de 1475–1538.
Alvarado, Pedro de 1485–1541..
Arbenz Guzmán, Jácobo 1913–1971.
Arevalo Bermejo, Juan José 1904–1990.
Artigas, José Gervasio 1764–1850.
Atahualpa c. 1502–1533.
Balmaceda, José Manuel 1840–1891.
Batista, Fulgencio 1901–1973.
Belaúnde Terry, Fernando 1913–.
Belgrano, Manuel 1770–1820.
Betancourt, Rómulo 1908–1981.
Bolívar, Simón 1783–1830.
Bosch, Juan 1909–.
Boyer, Jean-Pierre 1776–1850.
Burnham, Forbes 1923–1985.
Bustamante, Alexander 1884–1977.
Cárdenas, Lázaro 1895–1970.
Castilla, Ramón 1797–1867.
Castro, Cipriano 1858–1924.
Castro, Fidel 1927–.
Christophe, Henri 1767–1820.
Crespo, Joaquín 1845–1898.
Dessalines, Jean Jacques c. 1758–1806.
Díaz, Porfirio 1830–1915.
Díaz del Castillo, Bernal c. 1495–1584.
Duarte, José Napoleon 1925–1990.
Duvalier, François 1907–1971.
Duvalier, Jean-Claude 1951–.
Falcón, Juan Crisóstomo 1820–1870.
Feijó, Diogo Antônio 1784–1843.
Flores, Juan José 1801–1864.
Francia, José Gaspar Rodríguez de 1766–1840.
Frei, Edwardo 1911–1982.
Gallegos, Rómulo 1884–1969.
Galtieri, Leopoldo 1926–.
Garcilaso de la Vega 1539–1616.
Gómez, Juan Vicente 1864–1935.
Guevara, "Che" Ernesto 1928–1967.
Guzmán Blanco, Antonio 1829–1899.
Hidalgo y Costilla, Miguel 1753–1811.
Huáscar c. 1495–1532.
Iturbide, Agustín de 1783–1824.
Juárez, Benito 1806–1872.
Kubitschek, Juscelino 1902–1976.

Las Casas, Bartolomé de 1474–1566.
López, Carlos Antonio 1790–1862.
López, Francisco Solano 1827–1870.
Martí, José 1853–1895.
Maximilian 1832–1867.
Melgarejo, Mariano c. 1820–1871.
Mendes, Chico 1944–1988.
Mendoza, Antonio de c. 1490–1552.
Mitre, Bartólomé 1821–1906.
Monagas, José Tadeo 1784–1868.
Montezuma II 1466–1520.
Montt, Manuel 1809–1800.
Morazán, Francisco 1792–1842.
Morelos, José María 1765–1815.
Mosquera, Tomás Cipriano de 1798–1878.
Narváez, Pánfilo de c. 1480–1525.
Neruda, Pablo 1904–1973.
Núñez, Rafael 1825–1894.
O'Higgins, Bernardo 1778–1842.
Paz, (Estenssoro) Victor 1907–.
Pedro I 1798–1834.
Pedro II 1825–1891.
Pérez Jiménez, Marcos 1914–.
Perón, Isabel 1931–.
Perón, Evita 1919–1952.
Perón, Juan 1895–1974.
Pizarro, Francisco c. 1475–1541.
Ponce de León, Juan c. 1460–1521.
Prescott, William Hickling 1796–1859.
Rivadavia, Bernardino 1780–1845.
Rivera, José Fructuoso c. 1788–1854.
Rosas, Juan Manuel de 1793–1877.
San Martín, José de 1778–1850.
Santa Anna, Antonio López de 1795–1876.
Santa Cruz, Andrés 1792–1865.
Sarmiento, Domingo Faustino 1811–1888.
Somoza García, Anastasio 1896–1956.
Stroessner, Alfredo 1912–.
Sucre, Antonio José de 1795–1830.
Toussaint L'Ouverture, Pierre Dominique c. 1743–1803.
Trujillo Molina, Rafael 1891–1961.
Túpac Amarú c. 1742–1781.
Urquiza, Justo José de 1801–1870.
Valle, José Cecilio del 1776–1834.
Vargas, Getúlio 1883–1954.
Walker, William 1824–1860.
Zapata, Emiliano 1879–1919.

Leaders of the modern world

Adams, Gerry 1948–.
Alfonsín Foulkes, Raúl Ricardo 1927–.
Alia, Ramiz 1925–.
Andreotti, Giulio 1919–.
Aoun, Michel 1935–.
Aquino, Corazon 1933–.
Arafat, Yassir 1929–.
Arendt, Hannah 1906–1975.
Arias Sanchez, Oscar 1940–.
Aristide, Jean-Bertrand 1953–.
Ashdown, Paddy 1941–.
Assad, Hafez al 1930–.
Babangida, Ibrahim 1941–.
Baker, James, III 1930–.
Baker, Kenneth 1934–.
Barre, Raymond 1924–.
Begin, Menachem 1913–1992.
Ben Ali, Zine el Abidine 1936–.
Ben Bella, Ahmed 1916–.

Medieval history figures

Psychiatrists and psychologists

Zoologists

TECHNOLOGY

Inventors, manufacturers and engineers

SOCIETY

Anthropologists

Aristocracy and royalty

Entrepreneurs, industrialists, and economists

Religious figures

THE NATURAL WORLD

Astronomers and astronauts

Ecologists and environmentalists

Explorers

Geographers, geologists and meterologists